for
CD

The ART
of the PIANO

ALSO BY DAVID DUBAL

Reflections from the Keyboard

Conversations with Menuhin

Remembering Horowitz

The Essential Canon of Classical Music

Evenings with Horowitz

D A V I D   D U B A L

The ART
of the PIANO

Its Performers, Literature, and Recordings

THIRD EDITION

Amadeus Press
Pompton Plains, NJ • Cambridge, UK

Published in 2004 by

Amadeus Press, LLC
512 Newark Pompton Turnpike
Pompton Plains, New Jersey 07444
U.S.A.

Amadeus Press
2 Station Road
Swavesey
Cambridge CB4 5QJ, U.K.

For sales, please contact

NORTH AMERICA
AMADEUS PRESS, LLC
c/o Hal Leonard Corp.
7777 West Bluemound Road
Milwaukee, Wisconsin 53213 U.S.A.
Tel. 800-637-2852
Fax 414-774-3259

UNITED KINGDOM AND EUROPE
AMADEUS PRESS
2 Station Road
Swavesey, Cambridge, CB4 5QJ, U.K.
Tel. 01954-232959
Fax 01954-206040

E-mail: orders@amadeuspress.com
Website: www.amadeuspress.com

Printed in the United States of America

Library of Congress Cataloging-in-Publication Data
Dubal, David.
The art of the piano : its performers, literature, and recordings / by
David Dubal.—[3rd ed.]
p. cm.
Includes index.
Includes discographical references (p.   ).
ISBN 1-57467-088-3 (pbk.)
1. Music—Bio-bibliography. 2. Pianists. 3. Piano—Performance. I. Title.
ML105.D8 2004
786.2—dc22
2003023486
Visit our Web site at www.amadeuspress.com

Title Page: Liszt during his Weimar period, around the time of the
composition of his Sonata in B minor

For my brother,
RICHARD DUBAL,
"a man for all seasons"

Acknowledgments

I am most grateful to John Cerullo of Amadeus Press. He is an enlightened publisher who never failed in his encouragement. Carol Flannery, editorial director, has been indispensable to the book's completion.

Jung Lin worked over and over on a difficult manuscript, often under pressure.

For the inclusion of the valuable compact disc of pianists, I deeply thank Allan Evans. His creation of the label is a boon to pianistic culture.

My thanks are especially due to Gail Siragusa, who labored with dedication on the book. Jodi Brandon was an astute copyeditor. Colleen Coyne was a searching proofreader.

My appreciation goes to the designers of the volume, Michelle Thompson and Clare Cerullo. I would also like to thank Allan Gotthelf, Robert Tonucci and Peter Goodrich.

Contents

Preface to the Third Edition (2004) • xi

Preface to the Second Edition (1995) • xvii

Preface to the First Edition (1989) • xix

PART ONE • 1
THE PIANISTS

PART TWO • 383
THE PIANO LITERATURE
With Lists of Exceptional Recordings

ADDENDUM TO THE PIANO LITERATURE • 643

Selected Bibliography • 685

CD Track Listing • 691

Preface to the Third Edition (2004)

When Eve Goodman, Amadeus Press's former editorial director, asked me to write a third edition of *The Art of the Piano*, I was skeptical. After all, it was already a large book and I had completed a second edition some years back. In second or revised editions one often reads that the author has fixed a few errors, changed certain passages, and done a little updating here and there, and there you have it.

But as I scoured the book closely I realized that many things could be expanded and amplified. For example, after reading the section on Beethoven's piano works I felt that it was too sketchy. Looking at Bach, I saw that there was no discussion of the individual preludes and fugues of The Well-Tempered Clavier. After all, the Bach and the Beethoven sonatas have been called "The Pianists' Bible." Of course, books have been written on Beethoven sonatas and Bach's "48," but my task, at least as I see it, is to hopefully whet the musical palette.

Soon I began improving, adding, and entirely rewriting large stretches of the book; there are more than three hundred new computer files. Dozens more pianists have entered Part One; there are new additions in Chopin, Liszt, Godowsky, Medtner, Chabrier, Smetana, Busoni, and much else. There are many quotes of subtle value that I just had to share with my reader, and are included to highlight aspects of the concert pianist's world. This is the moment to express my debt to the many writers from whom I have borrowed quotations and information; their special insights have enriched my efforts. The poet Marianne Moore once said

of quotations, "I've always felt that if charmed by an author, I think it's a very strange and invalid imagination that doesn't long to share it. Somebody else should read it."

Dozens more composers are new to the addenda of the piano literature section. There is so much for the music lover to hear and for the pianist to study, read, learn, and bring to public exposure. The pianistic world cannot be healthy if its practitioners do not extend their repertoires with unfamiliar, neglected, and new music. My own teacher, Arthur Loesser, wrote, "A few composers of the past have been canonized by general consent, are called 'great' and their works recognized as 'classics.' Their exaltation to sainthood colors all their creations, and we continue to contemplate some of their least thoughts, even their noddlings, with respect. But those who have failed to achieve beatification despite their talent, their craft, and the joy they gave to their contemporaries, are not so fortunate. They too have at times brought forth stirring utterances, happy ideas and ingenious constructions, not always inferior to some of those of the 'great'—but they remain disregarded."

It is now paramount that pianists and teachers go beyond the weary path of the "masterpiece" literature, daily being shorn of its spiritual energy. We cannot continue to rely on such a small segment of well-worn pieces. Pianists are used to spending their lives in a restricted garden, attempting to achieve perfection of execution in their few pieces in which to show themselves off.

As the literature grows larger by the year,

with composers seldom able to give their music adequate presentation, pianistic culture in general is seriously declining, and with so many new ways of getting publications in or out of print, and hearing many important pianists of the past whose art is being saved on an increasing number of valuable compact discs. But the public remains more terrified than ever of new or neglected music, snobbishly looking down on anything but the high classics. Almost a century after the Ives Piano Sonatas were completed, we should find them really quite tame; this music too is capable of bringing a tear to the eye. Nor should every piece have to be loved by the public. Most pianists have lost their educative mission, once so much a part of progressive musicians' thinking. Liszt exclaimed, "First to the living." For Schumann, von Bülow, Anton Rubinstein, Busoni, Bauer, Steuermann, and hosts of others, it was their thrilling obligation to relentlessly promote the new. Rudolph Ganz stated, "I believe it is the absolute duty of all public performers to have upon their concert programs at least one group of compositions of the modern school. The living have as much right to be heard as the dead." In his time Beethoven was harsh stuff, by no means the average musical fare of his contemporaries. He would need disciples in many lands who fought for his ascendancy.

When I began writing this book, I knew of course my topic was vast and the volume necessitated being elective. Naturally one person cannot know the immense range of a subject of three centuries of constant growth. I can hardly claim to know the work of every noteworthy pianist, the almost endless number of recordings, or the enormity of the piano literature. My book, therefore, is simply a personal and grateful statement of my own enthusiasms over the years, and when one looks through the work there are bound to be sins of omission. May I beg my reader's indulgence by quoting Samuel Johnson's preface of his celebrated dictionary: "Many seeming faults are to be imputed rather to the nature of the undertaking, than the negligence of the performer." Down the years of the first two editions I have been asked by pianists and correspondents why or how I could have left out certain pianists or composers. Certainly it was not from prejudice, but more likely I just did not know their playing, either "live" or on records; or they may not as yet have garnered sufficient reputations in making international marks.

In a sense this book is an homage to past distinction and considered achievement. *The Art of the Piano* is not a biographical dictionary but a critical appreciation of the pianist's art. To the young aspiring pianist I have hoped to instill, through the vagueness of words, the lingering presence and essence of pianistic achievements. Like great actors of the past, the pianists of yesteryear have forever vanished from the stage, but in their case, they left more than memories: They left recordings, albeit often of imperfect, clouded sound quality, that proclaim a golden age of pianism and music-making of extraordinary individuality. Young pianists hearing Ignaz Friedman, Moriz Rosenthal, or Alfred Cortot playing, say, Chopin, receive inspiring piano lessons while being linked to a long, glorious, and continuous tradition. This continuity with the past is of vital importance to a flourishing pianistic culture.

I have expanded upon many legendary figures of the past. These musicians were of heroic stature, troubadours of the piano who roamed a world that almost deified the piano for countless numbers, bringing otherwise inaccessible feasts of the piano literature. With today's technology most people cannot quite know what the piano meant in its heyday before World War I. The psychological warmth of its presence in the parlor possessed a complex of profound meanings and the only immediate access to all kinds of music. The instrument's form and profile were literally welded to the psyche; it was the gateway to musical culture in a still primarily Victorian producer—work ethic culture, as contrasted with our world of consumer commercialism. Playing the instrument was a road to self-mastery tied to beauty. In our passive age, the person who actually plays music at home is rare, and therefore we are denied those moments of radiant flashes of beauty and accomplishment created, even if poorly, by oneself. Such moments produced a healing for souls damaged by the turbulence of everyday living.

As home music-making sadly disappeared, mothers no longer played and sang to and taught their children. D. H. Lawrence expresses this unbearable nostalgia in his poem *Piano*:

Softly, in the dusk, a woman is singing to
  me;
Taking me back down the vista of years, till
  I see
A child sitting under the piano, in the boom
  of the tingling strings
And pressing the small, poised feet of a
  mother who smiles as she sings.

In spite of myself the insidious mastery of
  song
Betrays me back, till the heart of me weeps
  to belong
To the old Sunday evenings at home, with
  winter outside
And hymns in the cosy parlour, the tinkling
  piano our guide.

So now it is vain for the singer to burst into
  clamour
With the great black piano appassionato.
  The glamour
Of childish days is upon me, my manhood
  is cast
Down in the flood of remembrance, I weep
  like a child for the past.

The impact of Lawrence's lyric is so strong that we too can weep for evenings such as he described, but have never known. . . .

The Art of the Piano is my remembrance and tribute to the instrument that has sustained me, a magical box where all emotions, all nuances, exist. For me it is important that the names and deeds of these pianists continue to be heralded. We are living in a culturally precarious time. We have seen how quickly many things once thought nourishing and important are vanishing with lightning speed.

Today celebrity status in the arts is rare. There are no longer household names for a poet, pianist, conductor, composer, painter, sculptor, dancer, or architect. The new generation of artists will have to fight fiercely for their careers. We can no longer take for granted the future of our orchestras and other cultural institutions. Musicians themselves will have to save their future by becoming true activists in the cause of the preservation of the arts.

To play the piano as an artist, one must be an individual, a personality in a time where life is not only severely mechanized but minutely organized. To be an artist, one must risk the pain of alienation, of being an outsider. The psychologist Abraham H. Maslow wrote: "Every age but ours has had its model, its ideal. All of these have been given up by our culture; the saint, the hero, the gentleman, the knight, the mystic. Almost all we have left is the well-adjusted man without problems, a very pale and doubtful substitute."

And I add that the ideal of the well-adjusted man is achieved artificially by the spread of a pharmacological culture. Could Beethoven have avoided his pain and loneliness through Prozac, or Rachmaninoff his famous depression? But the pianists of the past were still untamed personalities—witness Liszt, Anton Rubinstein, Teresa Carreño, Busoni, Grainger, and so many more. They were people of bewildering gifts and wide culture. When Paderewski appeared in the smallest town, he was a knight of culture. The lion pianist had arrived! The men were awed, the women agog. Mystery and romance lurked in his noble, gentlemanly gestures. Paderewski, proud patriot, a culture-hero who would become the first premier of his downtrodden Poland, played Chopin and people wept openly.

In the last two decades or so, an unprecedented number of the world's most honored pianists have passed away. This has been a disaster for world pianism. True, these artists lived in a century of medical advancement and often lived long lives. But their presence was life-affirming, and they were truly Romantic personalities. To the public, an Arthur Rubinstein overflowed with humanity. I remember a concert in Rome and how people flocked to the rim of the stage as he moved from one end to the other, shaking hand after hand before his next encore. To touch his hands was touchingly human—the hand being the symbol of humanness. Or to be at Horowitz's last recitals, with audiences beside themselves in awe. This man and his music-making represented something fragile and deep; the audience seemed to be gulping in his essence. Horowitz, often called the "last Romantic," unconsciously symbolized the quest for individuality, aspiration, and tradition. The idea that Romanticism is lost, that there could be a "last Romantic," is a tragic and bleak thought. And so many others have since gone: Arrau, Serkin, Kempff, Cherkassky, Jacob Gimpel, Solomon, Carlo Zecchi, Bolet, Leonard Shure, Ania Dorfmann, Cziffra, Glenn Gould, Lili Kraus, Artur Balsam, Paul Jacobs, William Masselos, Louis Kentner, John Ogdon, Gilels, Michelangeli, Nikita Magaloff, Rudolf Firkusny, Tatiana Nikolayeva, Richter, and so many others; each distinctive, they formed a group of musicians possessing indelible standards and the loftiest ideals of artistry. Most of them taught, passing their heritage from master to pupil—a precious legacy.

Pianists are so deeply affected and influenced by their teachers. In this book, who studied with whom is an essential feature. That Czerny studied with Beethoven, and Liszt studied with Czerny, is no mere fact, but the lifeblood of the art and craft. Asked about Czerny, Liszt exclaimed, "I owe him everything," and Leschetizky, when questioned about his "method," simply remarked, "I teach as my master Czerny did." Although Horowitz was born nine years after Anton Rubinstein's death, Horowitz's eyes would light up at his name. He was proud that his teacher, Felix Blumenfeld, was a favorite pupil of Rubinstein. When pianists talk, they always speak with passion of their lineage and heritage; these connections are the lifeline to greatness.

The romance of the piano continues. The instrument still fascinates, obsesses, and compels the innately gifted. To play well is difficult, but as Spinoza said, "All noble things are as difficult as they are rare." The piano demands a monumental sacrifice of time, but I have never heard a pianist begging for a minimum hourly wage. They will suffer and endure deprivation to find the countless hours for practicing. Their dreams are filled with haunting music, but how well they understand Hans von Bülow's searing words: "I crucify, like a good Christ, the flesh of my fingers, in order to make them obedient, submissive machines to the mind, as a pianist must." Indeed the craft, the technique itself, thrills while the music one plays is eternal. At the end of James Huneker's autobiography *Steeplejack*, the great American critic wrote:

I can't play cards or billiards. I can't read day and night. I take no interest in the chess-board of politics and I am not too pious. What shall I do? Music, always music! There are certain compositions by my beloved Chopin to master for which eternity itself would not be too long. That last page of the Second

Ballade as Anton Rubinstein played it, in apocalyptic thunder-tones! Or the study in double-thirds rippled off by the velvety fingers of de Pachmann! I once more place the notes on the piano-desk, courage! Time is fugacious. How many years have I not played that magic music? Music the flying vision . . . Its image melts in shy misty shadows . . . The cloud, the cloud, the singing, shining cloud . . . over the skies and far away . . . The beckoning cloud.

How else may one speak of music except in terms of poetic imagery? All true pianists are ceaselessly reminded of the title of Gary Graffman's memoirs: *I Really Should Be Practicing.* I end this preface to the third edition with my gratitude to the many people who have read the first two editions and have expressed themselves to me in important ways. The writer Marguerite Yourcenar remarked, "Each book which sees a new edition owes something to the discriminating people who have read it."

David Dubal
New York City
Winter 2004

Preface to the Second Edition (1995)

The Art of the Piano was first published in 1989, near the inception of the compact disc revolution, and in the last six years the long-playing record has literally disappeared from the marketplace, so completely has the CD replaced its predecessor. I have had to listen to a great number of compact discs, and in Part Two I have added dozens of new CDs, also indicating the many LPs that have been transferred to CDs. I have deleted only those LPs that I have finally decided were less valuable or too difficult to obtain. I have kept some of the LPs listed because they represent for me hours of intense listening to performances of superior vintage. The comparative listener and collector must search for these LPs because they no longer are easily available. Some will find a new life on compact disc in the future. But the collector's life is never easy; today there are a staggering number of recordings, in print or not, and finding anything can be a trial. My advice is to get catalogues of the smaller recording companies, such as VAI Audio and Pearl, and order directly.

However, this is also an exciting moment for piano lovers. Extraordinary performances from the past are reappearing on CDs in an unprecedented number. All of Horowitz is accessible; unknown recordings of late 1940s Carnegie Hall concerts, including a hair-raising performance of the Chopin F minor Fantasy, were recently issued by RCA. Everything Rachmaninoff recorded is now preserved on CD. Pearl CDs continue to treat early recordings with respect and care. Its historic reissues are exemplary, and through them we have the complete recordings of Ignaz Friedman and Arthur Friedheim, as well as wonderful collections of Paderewski. Indeed, many Liszt and Leschetizky pupils are now accessible to us, and we are enchanted by the incomparable Vladimir de Pachmann and the breezy elegance of Alfred Grünfeld. With the passing of time, Cortot is more wondrous than ever. Listen to the 1919–26 Victor recordings released by Pearl. The Brahms Wiegenlied and Schubert's Litany in Cortot's transcriptions are breathtaking in their ability to create song on the piano. But Cortot is miraculous throughout, and his CDs in each branch of repertory must not be missed. One's enthusiasm also overflows for new CDs of Benno Moiseiwitsch; his best work, including his stunning Weber-Tausig Invitation to the Dance, used to be available only on difficult-to-locate 78s, and we are indebted to APR for finding it and issuing it on the APR label. I could go on to mention CDs now available that capture the art of Edwin Fischer, Michelangeli, Sviatoslav Richter, Eileen Joyce, Mischa Levitzki, Rosita Renard, Egon Petri, Percy Grainger, Simon Barère, Dinu Lipatti, Moriz Rosenthal, Josef Hofmann, Leopold Godowsky, Raoul Koczalski, Harold Bauer, Marguerite Long, Marcelle Meyer, Myra Hess, Heinrich Neuhaus, Vladimir Sofronitsky, Samuel Feinberg, Raoul Pugno, Harold Samuel, and, of course, a great deal of Artur Schnabel, including the indispensable "complete" Beethoven Sonatas.

As the twentieth century concludes, pianists of the future, through these recordings on CD, will be able to construct a magnificent performing history of the piano throughout the century. Many of the artists have direct links to Chopin, Liszt, Anton Rubinstein, Leschetizky, and Debussy. In listening to these treasures, future pianists will have imperishable standards, including extraordinary techniques, to live by.

In Part One, I have corrected errors and added the death dates to some of the great pianists of the century who have passed away since the book's first edition, the two oldest being Horszowski and Kempff. Horowitz, Arrau, and Rudolf Serkin, each born in 1903, have also passed away. Cziffra and Firkušný died in 1994, Michelangeli in 1995. I have added around seventy new entries, of either historical figures or living pianists. I cannot by any means claim to have included all the pianists of importance. The one new "major" career that has developed in the last few years is that of the Russian Evgeny Kissin. In some entries, such as those for Pogorelich and Perahia, I have added additional thoughts. In others, I have given more information, such as the programs of Anton Rubinstein's seven Historical Recitals. In some cases, quotes from others have been entered into the text.

Preface to the First Edition (1989)

The Art of the Piano consists of two sections. Part One is an assessment of history's best-known concert pianists, ranged in alphabetical order. Part Two is a listing of significant works in the piano literature, solo and concerto, in alphabetical order by composer.

In describing the work of pianists of the prerecording era, my method, for the most important figures, is to use quotes by the best "ears" of the time. For example, it is important to know what Liszt thought of John Field's playing, what Clara Schumann felt about Mendelssohn's, or what Wagner wrote about Liszt at the instrument. We may understand Tausig's style of playing through the writings of the important critic Eduard Hanslick, or that of Rafael Joseffy, Tausig's and Liszt's great pupil, through the penetrating writings of James Huneker.

In the case of pianists who have benefited from the invention of recording or whom I have heard in public performance, I write from my personal fund of knowledge and feeling. In my assessments, I have always kept in mind the words of the ancient sage Marcus Aurelius, who said, "Those who criticize have their own reason to guide them, and their own impulse to prompt them." My qualification, then, for establishing my opinions of these artists is a lifetime of passionate enthusiasm for the piano and its literature. For me the world is divided into two groups: those who love the piano and those who see it as simply another musical instrument. For the first group, nothing is as wondrous as great piano playing.

All criticism begins subjectively, but as one devotes a lifetime of listening to piano playing, there emerges a kind of aesthetic truth, a set of values and standards. The connoisseur will come to hear the uniqueness of a pianist's individual sound, his pianistic resource, his interpretive gifts, his temperamental affinities. No pianist has everything. One learns what is permissible in an interpretation, what is imaginative, what is eccentric, what is routine. It takes many careful comparisons to know, for instance, that nobody has ever played *Paganini* in Schumann's *Carnaval* with the swiftness and the verve of Rachmaninoff in his celebrated recording of nearly six decades ago. In addition, the critic must have practical ability in order to understand what are the outer limits of the nervous system in a technical feat. I could not possibly write a book about singers, flutists, violinists, or conductors. In writing, I draw on my own experience of piano playing, performing, recording, and teaching. Without that practical knowledge, my writing would lack authenticity. This grounding in practical knowledge doesn't mean my judgments do not change or that certain pianists do not confuse me (and such confusion is always interesting). I never judge an artist by one recording or live recital. Just as many pianists undergo vast changes during their careers, so I find my own ears always changing, learning, and finding more to hear in the greatest of all instrumental literatures. The book pretends to no completeness, and doubtless many important names have been left out. Such composers as Grieg, Fauré, Schumann, Chabrier, Balakirev,

Szymanowski, and many more who were good pianists are not included as such, since their playing was seldom made public.

Similarly in Part Two, space does not permit a listing of all the important or interesting works in the piano literature, and many for which I feel enthusiasm are not represented. Indeed, several of my choices, such as the Bridge or Bloch sonatas, could have been changed for others. The major masterpieces of the literature, however, are all here. These are the works that should be in every collection. These are the works that every student, teacher, and lover of the instrument is constantly dealing with.

I have also listed recordings of these works. For over two decades, as music director of WNCN in New York, formerly a twenty-four-hour-a-day classical music station, I was in a unique position to listen to thousands of recorded performances. The phonograph was a great invention, and its impact on music has mainly been for the good. As critic Roland Gelatt said, "A partisan historian could perhaps be forgiven for claiming it as the chief marvel and solace of the century." As a result, however, much that is mediocre and homogenized has entered the marketplace. The beauty of the greatest masterworks has been drowned in a sea of competently conventional and dreary playing.

The most dangerous aspect of recording is that it freezes and mummifies a musical work, imprinting on us one performance, one sound, one tempo. A recording has nothing to do with a live performance. Indeed, the compact disc is so seductive in its distance from reality, from real sound, that, for many, being at a live concert is often not only disappointing but irritating. (Seldom does a pianist care to listen to his own recordings. One reason is that they are always the same; the flow of life is gone. How I have longed to hear details of a pianist's playing that were captivating in live performance but missing from the recording.)

In this way, the masterpieces of music may become stale sooner rather than later. The phonograph has certainly helped wipe out amateur piano playing, and there are fewer in an audience who have the kind of discrimination that alone can give rise to "aesthetic ecstasy." The "gifted listener" is dying out, the listener who can lose all imprinting, who has a whole library of knowledge of a work, who has attempted to play it, who has lived with it, who has the freshness of ear to know when a performance is a revelation.

And yet a great recording can have a universality and an artistic truth which remain passionate and which can change as the listener grows musically. It can seem different and equally valid at dawn or at dusk, like a masterpiece of literature, sculpture, or painting; it begs for many hearings. Each masterpiece demands lifelong study. As the adage goes, "Life is short, art is long." If we deal with a great work of art in a cursory way, it will yield little. It takes time and energy to get to know even fairly well Beethoven's *Diabelli* Variations or Chopin's B minor Sonata. The listener needs to build a relationship with each work, just as the interpreter does. The printed page is merely a blueprint; each player, to the best of his or her ability, tries to present what is in the music, what the composer means. "The written page," Aaron Copland wrote, "is only an approximation; it's only an indication of how close the composer was able to come in transcribing his exact thoughts on paper. Beyond that point the interpreter is on his own." Pablo Casals said, "Sometimes, looking at a score, I say to myself, 'What marvelous music. But I must make it so.' "

No matter how genuine one's intention to fulfill the composer's wishes, the performer cannot bring to a work any more or less than the qualities of his or her own temperament. One cannot manufacture a passionate, lyrical, or pastoral trait if one does not have it. On the other hand, one may be both forthright and elegiac, but not at the same moment. The art of interpretation is an art of sacrifice. This is its first law. Two players may, however, separately bring various traits to a score. For example: Horowitz plays the Rachmaninoff Third Concerto with an unbearable nostalgia—it is a memorial to his own lost Russia. His performance is like a wail of despair. On hearing Rachmaninoff himself in his recording of the score, however, one hears a drastically different content. The atmosphere loses its thickness, the tempi are faster, the composition becomes lithe, pantherlike in its elegance. The *creator* of the work need not play with nostalgia; he does not tell the whole tragic story. Though expressive and Romantic, he holds his emotion in check. His very coolness becomes beguiling. An aristocratic musical mind is at work. The approach is perfectly planned and all the notes are chiseled. Rachmaninoff's extraordinary and subtle rhythmic propulsion does not shock us, as Horowitz's does. Rather, he gives a purely musical reading and the heavy languor evaporates.

There are many fine Rachmaninoff Third Concertos. Byron Janis brings to it a feeling of steely acidity; Victor Merzhanov is fascinatingly dry; and Tamás Vásáry is relaxed and autumnally glowing. No one performance can possibly contain all that these pianists reveal through their separate visions. The composer himself cannot transcend this limitation, cannot give a "definitive" reading. Here lies the endless glory of the performer's art, and here lies also one of the special values of recordings. Through them, you may hear many different performances of a work, over and over, to your heart's content. Creative comparative listening is at your bidding, with a legion of artists ready to play for you.

In Part Two, I have chosen performances on either record or compact disc which show a composition in its most diverse moods, giving us a score's largest range and possibilities. (In the text of the book, the words *disc* and *recording* are used interchangeably.) If listening to music becomes a serious way of spending time, then owning different interpretations of a work will be enlightening and will forever change one's musical life. In fact, without such listening the serious composer and interpreter have little to say.

The
PIANISTS

Musical performance is born in those same sublime
regions from which music itself has descended. Whenever
the music is in danger of becoming earthbound, the
performance must elevate it and help it to regain
its original ethereal quality . . . It is the duty
of the performer to liberate it from the
deadness of the printed page and
bring it to life again.

FERRUCCIO BUSONI
(1866–1924)

The indefatigable pursuit of an unattainable perfection,
even though it consist of nothing more than the
pounding of an old piano, is what alone gives
a meaning to our life on this
unavailing star.

LOGAN PEARSALL SMITH
(l865–1946)

Introduction

GEORGE BERNARD SHAW wrote, "The pianoforte is the most important of all musical instruments; its invention was to music what the invention of the printing press was to poetry." The piano is the most suggestive of all musical instruments, with the power to evoke the illusion of a singer, a French horn, a flute, a cello—indeed, the orchestra itself. Actually, the highest notes on the piano are higher than on any orchestral instrument, as the lowest notes are lower than any in the orchestra. Just as the printing press gave to the whole of humanity the literature of every nation, so the piano became the keyboard instrument of the world. Its growth in popularity as a musical instrument began with the French and American revolutions. The piano would ultimately supplant the aristocratic harpsichord and become a symbol of democracy, self-reliance, and personal expression. From a coal miner's humble dwelling to the president's mansion, a house was not a home without a piano in the parlor.

The piano's perfection and dissemination also coincided with the rise of the middle class and the era of Romanticism, when great pianists were heroes. Thousands emulated these troubadours of the keyboard, and the nine-foot concert grand, with its thousands of parts, became a cultural symbol of the luxuriant materialism of the Industrial Revolution. The piano also became the chief instrument of most of the great composers, from Mozart to Debussy, and was responsible for the enormous song literature of the nineteenth century. Imagine a Schubert, Wolf, Mussorgsky, or Fauré song with a harpsichord accompaniment.

By around 1700, polyphonic and religious music were on the wane. Music's emotional range was expanding and becoming personal and secular; people wanted to be entertained by simpler music with a singable melody, filled with sentiment. Thus there was an increasing need for a keyboard instrument capable of producing vocal expression, pure sentiment, and tonal gradation. The harpsichord could not produce a *piano* and *forte*, and the human emotions, which were bursting in the eighteenth century, needed an instrument to weep human tears and sing a melody. The great Stradivarius violins being made then were not adequate for this because they needed harmony. And so the piano was born out of necessity: an instrument that looked like a harpsichord but in every way was different from the plucked instrument; paradoxically, an instrument capable of producing song. Although there were various attempts to make such an instrument, the person acknowledged as the true inventor of the piano came from the same region of Italy as Stradivarius.

He was Bartolomeo Cristofori (1655–1731), a genius who died unsung. I know of no pianos called the Cristofori. From 1709 to 1726, he laboriously made twenty or so instruments, which differed radically from the plucked mechanism of the harpsichord. He called his hammer instrument *gravicembalo col piano e forte*—a harpsichord with soft and loud. The instrument was immediately recognized as special, and one Scipione Maffei wrote in an

Italian journal in 1711: "The production of greater or less sound depends on the degree of power with which the player presses on the keys, by regulating which, not only the piano and forte are heard, but also the gradation and diversity of power."

However, there was no interest in Italy in the new instruments. The piano's destiny lay in Germany, where Bach's friend the organ builder Gottfried Silbermann, in the 1720s, happened on Maffei's article, translated it into German, along with Maffei's diagram drawings of the mechanism. Silbermann had long wanted to make a keyboard capable of *inflection,* and the Maffei article seemed heaven-sent. He set to work and, by the late 1720s, showed his first instruments to Bach for his approval. But Bach disliked them. The treble, he said, was too weak, and the action seemed hard to play. Silbermann, though, undaunted, continued to improve his pianos.

By the 1740s, Frederick the Great had stocked his palaces with fifteen Silbermann pianos. In 1747, Frederick asked to meet Bach, and so it was that Bach tried the king's new pianos. He was happy with them now, and a testimony from Bach was especially valued. But the still polyphonically minded Bach was not about to embrace the new instrument. He, Couperin, and Scarlatti had been creating a magnificent literature for the harpsichord, which was now at its perfection. Voltaire, upon first hearing the early piano, was revolted. "This newcomer," he piped, "will never dethrone the majestic harpsichord. . . . The pianoforte is an ironmonger's invention compared with the harpsichord." However, the new instrument was becoming liked by the musical public, and it fit the musical mood of the time; *galant* music *sounded* sweeter on the piano.

By the 1760s, piano making had moved from Germany to London and Vienna. During the Seven Years' War, twelve keyboard makers, many of them disciples of Silbermann, immigrated to England from Germany. They were dubbed "the Twelve Apostles." The most successful was Johann Zumpe, who constructed a little square piano that became all the rage. Soon, piano sales were exceeding harpsichord sales.

The two finest pianists during the 1770s were Clementi and Mozart. The latter represented the Viennese school of playing, which was distinguished for its precision, rapidity, and clarity, the sound having more of a ping and a crisp radiance. Clementi played the English pianos, which, with their heavier action and larger sonority, seemed to represent more of the might of the Industrial Revolution. By 1800, harpsichord building had practically ceased. It is no coincidence that the piano grew up during the *Sturm und Drang* movement, and that its improvement coincides with the Napoleonic era. "The Little Corporal" was exiled to Elba in 1815, and during a ruthless Paris winter, many gorgeous harpsichords, which had already been relegated to the basement of the Paris Conservatoire, were used for firewood.

The exhilarating and grandiose spirit of Napoleon had to be translated to the more pacific world of the arts. In literature, Napoleon became Byron, and in music the awesome image of Beethoven appeared—disheveled, inspired, improvising godlike harmonies on his battered piano; deaf, but undeterred. Beethoven was the first great Romantic pianist; he triumphed even over disability. He became the prototype for the Romantic genius and has remained so.

By the time of Beethoven's death, the piano was clearly the favored instrument of the growing middle class. Every family aspired to have one. Only one nonpianist performer, outside the field of opera, was held in awe by the public in those halcyon days of Romanticism—Paganini, the wizard of the violin, whose appeal lay in the supernatural aspects of Romanticism. His art was akin to, say, Mary Shelley's *Frankenstein*. Paganini's demonic quality was soon to become assimilated into the many-sided genius of the greatest pianistic marvel of the time, whose reputation surpassed even Paganini's—Liszt. Liszt symbolized the artist as Romantic hero. The nineteenth century had quelled the Napoleonic spirit into the figure of a magnificent entertainer. In fact, Liszt was often called "the Napoleon of the Piano."

Schiller said, "The gods never come singly," and a flood of piano geniuses came into the world around the same time as Liszt (1811): Chopin, Heller, Hiller, Mendelssohn, Schumann, Alkan, and a host of lesser lights were all born within a five-year period. These first-generation Romantics reached maturity in the early 1830s, precisely at the time when the piano as we know it today became more or less a finished product. The earlier differences between the English and the Viennese pianos were smoothed out in the grand pianos of Bösendorfer, Erard, Pleyel, Broadwood, and others. The instrument, with its cast-iron frame, achieved a range of 7⅓ octaves, utilizing eighty-eight keys. A piano made by Cristofori weighs less than the iron plate alone of the modern piano. In the 1830s, the piano could accomplish the lightning-quick shades of dark and light which the Romantics needed to spend their passion. The piano could sigh or shiver, quiver and swoon, as no instrument had ever done. Aldous Huxley pointed out, "Mozart's melodies may be brilliant, memorable, infectious, but they don't palpitate, don't catch you between wind and water, don't send the listener off into erotic ecstasies." The sound the Romantics wanted was, in Arthur Loesser's words, "a vague, mellow tone-cloud, full of ineffable promise and foreboding, carrying intimations of infinity . . . harboring the mystical suspicion that anything might merge into everything."

The piano became the quintessential Romantic instrument, and the public wanted virtuoso gods who could tame it, sing on it, and show them the stars. As the cult of the individual blossomed during the 1830s and 1840s, pianists far less gifted than Liszt thrived and prospered, many of them achieving personal wealth from the power of music publishing, for performers also composed and their scores sold like wildfire. Piano teaching became a lucrative way of making a living; everyone needed to play the piano. One writer blasphemed that a new trinity had been formed "of which Liszt is the Father, Thalberg the Son, and Dreyschock the Holy Ghost." Frenzied hands flying over the keyboard thrilled people into believing that man could control nature and the machine. Virtuosity became a thing unto itself, and no other instrument could make virtuosity so attractive, so understandable, and so much a force to be emulated.

The pianist Charles Hallé one day found himself playing for the most erudite and revered art critic of the day, John Ruskin. But Ruskin, much to Hallé's disappointment, was overwhelmed by Thalberg's potboiler variations on "Home, Sweet Home." Ruskin explained to Hallé that he did not "care about the art of it . . . but I did care about having a million low notes in perfect cadence and succession of sweetness. I never recognized before so many notes in a given brevity of moment. . . . I have often heard glorious and inventive and noble successions of harmonies, but I never in my life heard variations like that. Also, I had not before been close enough to see your hands, and the invisible velocity was wonderful to me . . . as a human power."

Most of the Romantic pianists of all calibers, like the previous generation of Hummel, Czerny, and Kalkbrenner, were content to promote their own music. How else could it become known? In those early days of concert giving, there were no impresario managements to speak of, and giving a concert was an ordeal. If Chopin, for instance, wanted to give a concert, he booked the hall, took care of the piano, did the publicity, hired singers and other instrumentalists. A concert was more like a variety show. Although Liszt played his first solo recitals in 1839, such events were rare and were generally frowned upon by audiences and critics. The public wanted its money's worth, and the idea of playing alone was thought arrogant. In Chopin's short career, he played only one solo recital. Such an event also needed more educated audiences willing to focus on the music, as well as on the virtuosity of the performer.

It was the magnanimous Liszt who not only established the solo recital but broke the mold of playing only one's own music. From 1834 to 1847, he performed over the length and breadth of Europe, playing the music of the past and introducing the music of his contemporaries. As rapidly as new music was created, Liszt added it to his repertoire. Since program building was now possible with a fully realized piano literature, improvisation—once a staple of the programs of Mozart, Hummel, and Beethoven—was fast disappearing. Liszt, ever the consummate showman, needed to simulate the look of extempore playing without notes, and, with Clara Schumann, began the habit of playing from memory. How could a Romantic tone poet be encumbered by the printed page? One needed to look inspired. Audiences remain in awe of the pianist who can play all those notes by "heart." Liszt's memory playing stuck at once. No other musician must play from memory, but pianists somehow seem incomplete if they have a score with them.

More important, however, was the fact that Liszt established the concept of the "interpretive" musician, and after his retirement, with few exceptions (such as the American Gottschalk in a still backward musical environment), pianists were now expected to perform a wide range of music. From that moment on, the chasm between composer and interpreters grew. After 1850, most pianists still composed, but the great demands of each activity took a toll. Liszt became exclusively a composer; his

rival, Thalberg, having almost no repertoire but that of his own music, retired completely. Liszt also taught, spawning three generations of pianists who concentrated on piano playing above composition.

As piano music became ever more complex and difficult, and the public more educated to good playing, composing and performing could no longer mix. Could Robert Schumann, who desperately wanted to be a concert pianist, have in his short life created such a tremendous output if he had not paralyzed his fourth finger? Absolutely not, and it took his wife almost forty years to incorporate the Schumann literature, work by work, into her repertory. After Liszt retired from performing, Clara Wieck Schumann, younger than Liszt by eight years, became the high priestess of interpretive musicians. Although she composed well, it was her zeal, especially in the German classics dating back to Bach, that made her one of the most influential musicians of her time. For her, the composer stood first, and virtuosity for its own sake had no meaning. Her scrupulous respect for the composer stood in direct opposition to the willful "piano pounders," who, she felt, were influenced by the excesses of Liszt's youthful career.

Clara Schumann was the codifier of the German style of playing, and her influence has been felt down to our time. Hans von Bülow and Theodor Leschetizky (both born in 1830) were next in line as the most potent influences on piano playing. Bülow had studied with Friedrich Wieck, Clara's father, before going to work with Liszt. Bülow hardly bothered to compose, and he espoused Clara Schumann's high German seriousness with passion. Leschetizky, who studied with Liszt's teacher Czerny, may be called the codifier of the Chopin tradition. He set up shop in Vienna, where the pianistic world came to him. With a ravishing tone and high Romanticism, he was the most effective teacher of the nineteenth century. He preferred his students to be Slavic in origin, and from his stable came Essipova, Paderewski, Gabrilowitsch, Friedman, Moiseiwitsch, and hundreds of others. These pianists were primarily poets, dreamers at the keyboard, incomparable stylists, elegant, often wayward and exciting. At the center of their repertoire stood Chopin, a Chopin who could, in weaker moments, degenerate into a "Camille of the Keyboard."

Leschetizky founded an international marketplace of virtuosi. He taught more than two thousand pupils, and the Leschetizky method (though he denied having one) was the golden path to pianistic stardom. Many of his lesser disciples developed the decadent *fin de siècle* style of playing, in which the composer was almost obliterated in an orgy of self-expression. The greatest Leschetizky pupils were primarily colorists and were at their finest in small forms. Anton Rubinstein, also born in 1830, became the roaring father of Russian pianism. He was an artist of unbridled temperament whose blood-and-thunder playing was a revelation to European audiences. No public performer had ever so exposed his soul, and he was capable of extreme sentiment. After Liszt's retirement in 1847, it was Rubinstein, with his animal magnetism, who symbolized to the world the power of which the piano was capable. His programs were marathons; he could give the Chopin Funeral March Sonata as an encore. Anton Rubinstein's name remains sacred in Russia.

America's greatest popularizer of the piano, Louis Moreau Gottschalk (1829–1869), had studied in Paris with Camille Stamaty, who was one of the founders of French piano playing. At the same time, Stamaty was teaching the astounding prodigy Camille Saint-Saëns, who, along with Francis Planté, represented French piano playing to the world. The "*style sévère*" had been developed from the very opening of the Paris Conservatoire. The French espoused perfect neatness of finger-work, *jeu perlé,* which came from Kalkbrenner, Zimmerman,

Marmontel, Alkan, and indeed from Chopin himself. The French tradition is one of elegance, precision, sophistication, and emotional restraint. Saint-Saëns could have been speaking of French pianism when he wrote, "Art is intended to create beauty and character. Feeling only comes after, and art can very well do without it. In fact, it is very much better off when it does."

One might say that the French play on the tops of the keys, the Russians deep into the keys, and the Germans tried to figure out how much pressure should be applied to each key. James Huneker wrote, "I'm seriously studying tone-production, and trying to shake my Parisian staccato touch." Although French piano playing has lost some of its native flavor, the cool stylishness of Gallic playing remains strong.

History's next great pianist was Carl Tausig. Born in 1841, he died at the age of thirty. His teacher, Liszt, quickly helped realize his greatness, and from all accounts he was the most exceptionally equipped pianist of the era, blending the poetry and bravura of the Russian school, the perfection of the French, and the depth and scholarship of the Germans.

The earliest-born pianist to leave a body of recordings was Vladimir de Pachmann (1848–1933), an erratic, sensational miniaturist, born in the fabled musical city of Odessa. But a larger-spirited artist soon emerged to become the most important pianistic figure after Rubinstein's death. Ignacy Jan Paderewski (1860–1941), with Leschetizky's stamp of approval, carried on the tradition of pianist as Romantic hero. He united Byronic and Lisztian traits with an incomparable glamour and fierce patriotism, eventually becoming premier of his beloved Poland. Paderewski was the darling of a new and growing world public; the geographical boundaries of his pianistic career were broad indeed. Paderewski became richer from playing the piano than any other player up to that time.

During the 1860s, a number of formidable and impressive pianists were born, including Arthur Friedheim, Emil von Sauer, Alexander Siloti, Eugene d'Albert, and Moriz Rosenthal, each of whom worked with Liszt. After Paderewski, however, the towering figure of Busoni (1866–1924) looms largest, and though his own music is valuable, it was as a pianist that Busoni was considered supreme. Like Tausig, he seemed to combine the qualities of all schools but with a monumentalism never before realized. Busoni seemed to stun all his colleagues, whether they liked his playing or not. Percy Grainger wrote, "Busoni was a twisted genius making the music sound unlike itself, but grander than itself—more superhuman."

Busoni brought a new intellectual power to piano playing. He played with a symphonic, rhythmic sweep that had never before been heard, and he eliminated any trace of waywardness, mannerism, and sentimentalizing. He aimed for the mystical and the spiritual. Yet, as Egon Petri put it, Busoni seemed to "mold in flesh and blood." He must be considered the greatest pianist since Liszt and Anton Rubinstein.

During the 1870s, the Russian school produced a flood of great pianists inspired by Anton Rubinstein. Each was a superb technician. Godowsky, Rachmaninoff, Lhévinne, and Hofmann would all reside in the United States and enrich its pianistic culture greatly. Godowsky played, taught, and edited music; his playing was a pinnacle of perfection. Hofmann would direct the Curtis Institute of Music, and Lhévinne would teach at the Juilliard School. Rachmaninoff's prestige was vast; when he first toured the United States, in 1909, American piano building was at its peak, with nearly four hundred thousand pianos a year produced by more than 350 makers. Player pianos were popular, and the most celebrated pianists made piano rolls as well as acoustical recordings. Paderewski

recordings, beginning around 1910, did for the popularity of the piano on early records what Caruso did for the voice.

As recording progressed, it changed the way pianists played. Soon they were listening to themselves for the first time. Max Pauer recalled:

When I listened to the first record of my own playing, I heard things which seemed unbelievable to me. Was I, after years of public playing, actually making mistakes that I would be the first to condemn in any one of my own pupils? I could hardly believe my ears, and yet the unrelenting machine showed that in some places I had failed to play both hands exactly together, and had been guilty of other errors no less heinous, because they were trifling. I also learned in listening to my own playing, as reproduced, that I had unconsciously brought out certain nuances, emphasized different voices and employed special accents without the consciousness of having done so.

Recording provided immortality itself. And yet, many pianists were wary of the medium. The Romantic pianist relied on the inspiration of the moment, and the idea of putting down one interpretation forever was widely disliked. Henceforth, music-making would become more cautious. Taking chances wasn't necessarily exciting on a record; it could be downright messy. The grand manner and rhetorical pretension of the era lessened immensely. Because of recordings, pianists were becoming a more "serious" species. They had to learn what sounded good onstage and what sounded good on record. This tremendous battle between live performance and recording has continued through the century. The technological breakthrough of electrical recording came in 1925, and Rachmaninoff was the first to produce an important body of recordings. He not only took recording seriously, but studied the medium closely.

The pianists of the early twentieth century, however, had nonintellectual, gracefully sensuous, charming qualities that were vanishing. Today we call Godowsky, Hofmann, Levitzki, Lhévinne, Rosenthal, Friedman, Sauer, and others the representatives of a golden age of pianism. Charles Rosen wrote: "Today the style of the great pianists of the first quarter of this century and the air of casual elegance cannot be recaptured, and probably we shall never hear it again. Rosenthal, Hofmann, and Rachmaninoff combined technical perfection not only with spontaneity but with the appearance of improvising. Their technical mastery may still be found, but their ease of manner and their sense of high style have been lost forever: They played like gentlemen."

Many important figures born during the 1880s, such as Petri, Schnabel, Backhaus, Edwin Fischer, and Arthur Rubinstein—all German trained—represent the trend away from the idiosyncratic to a larger and well-planned vision of the music they played. Each was a great influence on twentieth-century pianists, and they all took recording seriously, leaving a large recorded legacy. Of this group, only Arthur Rubinstein was eclectic, playing music of all styles. He placed a major emphasis on Chopin, but a Chopin that was respectful, virile, and structured. It took a long time to eradicate the standard melodramatic portrait of Chopin. No longer was Chopin merely an excuse for tortured rubato, altered texts, and the purple passion of de Pachmann and a host of others. In France, Cortot proved that Chopin could retain its glamour as well as its great poetic lyricism.

It must be understood how little music was generally known. Schnabel, in the 1940s, wrote: "During my educational phase in Vienna until 1899, I never heard, in this most musical city on earth, and in the midst of musicians, of the existence of the twenty-seven concertos by Mozart, or Beethoven's Op. 106

or the Diabelli Variations, or Bach's Goldberg Variations, etc."

Rachmaninoff was once told about Schubert's Sonatas, and he was surprised there were any. The spread of a literature takes far longer than one would imagine. When Schnabel completed the first recording on 78s of the thirty-two Sonatas of Beethoven, there were only a few hundred people ready to buy them. Today, hardly a month goes by without half a dozen recordings of Mozart concertos offered to a public that extends to Japan, Korea, and even China. Pianists are now expected to be literal museums of the past and present. They may have to play twenty different concertos a season, as well as several recital programs, flying all over the globe.

Pianists are no longer expected to compose, even during their studies; however, they have had to learn a performing repertoire that has grown enormously since the days of Liszt. It takes never-ending hours of toil to master the complexities of Scriabin, Granados, Debussy, Prokofiev, Bartók, Ives, Messiaen, Boulez, or Stockhausen. The twentieth-century pianist must be eclectic above all else. Arrau, Horowitz, and Serkin—three of the most influential pianists with careers spanning the century—performed huge repertories in their prime, including Scarlatti, Schubert sonatas, and Mozart concertos, which were all virtually new to the public.

Pianists of the Leschetizky atelier were prompted to play only what would be most successful in showing themselves off. When Horowitz played Scarlatti for Rachmaninoff, the latter did not like the music. Twentieth-century "interpreters," though, consider music not in terms of likes and dislikes, but rather in a historical context. One has only to look at the repertoire requirements of a piano competition to understand what awesome demands are made of each aspirant. The twentieth-century pianist must be a scholar. It is an age in which the document rules, the score is sacrosanct, the urtext edition is supreme. Thanks to the medium of recordings, there are now, in every city, critics who grew up listening to all the Mozart Concerti played by various artists. These critics sit in judgment, score in hand, peering at each marking. If the pianist dares overlook a marking or a staccato, he or she becomes a ruthless liar, a defiler of the composer's intention; and of course wrong notes are sins.

In a competition today, an Anton Rubinstein or de Pachmann would be thrown out of the first round. Did Liszt *really* play all the notes in his *Transcendental Etudes*? How many slips of memory did he have? Nobody knew, nobody cared. However, each generation wears a new musical outfit. Yesterday's fashion often seems ridiculous to the present-day sensibility. Today, in fact, younger pianists are beginning to chafe at the often pedantic constraints of recent years. Even at competitions there are signs of a loosening up of the "standardized" performance, and a flight of imagination is not as suspect as before.

One thing is certain: the piano and piano playing are here to stay. More countries produce pianos than ever before—Korea, Brazil, Switzerland, China, Thailand, Australia, Estonia and many others—while Japan has become the world's largest piano producer. The Orient, in its obsession with things Western, has been captivated by the instrument. Asian pianists are filling conservatories and winning competitions. The future of the instrument and its literature are becoming international. Had Beethoven or Liszt ever thought of a Japanese or a Korean pianist?

There are now nearly one million pianos made per year, an incredible number considering that the instrument cannot be mass-produced. The piano has come a long way from the age when Cristofori made his twenty pianos in twenty-five years. And although many think that composers no longer love the piano as they once did, the piano literature of the twentieth century gives abundant proof to the contrary. Indeed, one of the great challenges for the contemporary pianist will be to reveal the wealth of the twentieth century's piano literature to audiences worldwide.

A

LOUIS ADAM
1758–1848—Germany

An early advocate of the piano and one of the father figures of French pianism. He came to Paris from Alsace at the age of sixteen. The first piano to be built in Paris was in 1760, and its first appearance at a concert took place in 1768. Within the next thirty years, the instrument would supplant the harpsichord in popularity. Adam had studied the properties of the piano and became one of the leading pianists in Paris. Soon after the founding of the Paris Conservatoire in 1795, he became one of its first professors.

In 1804 he published his influential *Méthode de Piano du Conservatoire*, which considerably advanced the development of piano technique in Paris as well as an appreciation of the piano's individuality. Adam spoke of the importance of touch, and beauty of sound. In the preface to his *Méthode,* he writes: "The pianoforte is the most frequently used of all the instruments. It is preferred over the harpsichord because it can express sounds as loud or as softly as required and imitate all the subtleties of other instruments, which is quite impossible with the harpsichord."

Adam already anticipated the piano's vast popularity to come during the nineteenth century, and understood the instrument as, in Liszt's words, "a latent orchestra."

Adam composed for the piano, most notably sonatas, nothing of which survives in the repertoire. His son Adolph Adam is the composer of the ballet *Giselle.*

CLARENCE ADLER
1886–1969—United States

A respected pedagogue and pianist who studied with Godowsky and had an influence on many pianists. He taught privately in New York for over half a century.

GUIDO AGOSTI
1901–1989—Italy

A student of Busoni, and one of the best pianistic minds of his country. He made many editions and composed effective transcriptions, including one of scenes from Stravinsky's *Firebird,* very effective and difficult, which has often been performed. Agosti's teaching was widely praised.

PIERRE-LAURENT AIMARD
b. 1957—France

A pupil of Yvonne Loriod at the Paris

Conservatoire. He met Loriod's husband, composer Olivier Messiaen, when he was twelve, and through the couple, became steeped in the composer's artistic credo.

Aimard never neglected the standard literature and his recitals are an admirable combination of the old and new. However it is in contemporary music that he justly rose to fame. His recording of Gyorgi Ligeti's Etudes is a must for the numerous pianists interested in these scores. In them, he extracts every drop of precious music from the array of textural, coordinational, and timbre problems to be found in Ligeti's adventure with the instrument. In his disc of Ligeti's Piano Concerto, he brings luminosity to one of the finest piano concertos of recent years, with all of its complexity ravishingly defined. Naturally Messiaen figures at the core of his musical life, and it is the two-hour cycle of the *Vingt Regards sur l'Enfant-Jésus (Twenty Contemplations of the Infant Jesus Christ)* where Aimard has secured his most ecstatic triumph both publicly and on recordings.

On Aimard's *Vingt Regards* recording on Teldec, he plays these sensuous, multi-layered creations with daring virtuosity, voluptuousness, and an enormous range of dazzling tonal gradations, with a fine ear for subtle pedaling. Ligeti feels he is the leading performer of contemporary music presently. "All of my piano Etudes, Debussy's Etudes, Messiaen's *Vingt Regards,* I have never heard any of these pieces played with such perfection and artistic power."

WEBSTER AITKEN
1908–1981—United States

A pianist of high ability who studied with Sauer and Schnabel. He played and recorded the Schubert Sonatas in the 1930s, when they were still little-known. In 1941, Irving Kolodin called him a "musician's musician, with a quiet but pervasive artistry, an extraordinary persistence in pursuing a plan of a work until it yields all its secrets to him, and a fine technical mastery."

Aitken was a player with strong ideas; there is no conventionality in his work, nor is he concerned with surface beauty. His recording of Beethoven's Sonata, Opus 106, is an intriguing one. Of a live performance of Beethoven's Sonata, Opus 111, Virgil Thomson reported: "Aitken gave a reading not at all traditional . . . if one regretted slightly at moments its relentlessly metallic coloration, one was grateful at all times for the clarity and force of his transcendence and execution."

Aitken championed the "moderns" of his day, programming music of Ives and Carter's Piano Sonata.

WALID AKI
b. 1945—Lebanon

A pupil of the well-known teacher Germaine Mounier and Yvonne Lefébure. He has performed consistently in Europe, with appearances in the United States. On fourteen CDs he has recorded Haydn's complete solo piano works on the Thésis label.

CARLO ALBANESI
1856–1926—Italy

After a great deal of concertizing, he made London his home in 1882, becoming a sought-after teacher. He published a number of compositions, including five Piano Sonatas.

PEDRO ALBÉNIZ

1795–1855—Spain

As a child he studied with his father, the composer Mateo Albéniz. Paris was the Mecca of the Romantic movement, and Albéniz studied with Herz and Kalkbrenner. Rossini was impressed with the young musician, who moved back to Spain in 1829, where he was eventually named maestro de piano for Queen Isabel II. Albéniz composed the usual piano fantasies and variations on opera tunes which fed the appetites for the home consumption of amateurs. These productions are a threadbare relic of a vanished age.

EUGENE D'ALBERT

1864–1932—Scotland

One of the finest musicians of the late nineteenth century. Liszt called him "the astonishing d'Albert" and "the second Tausig." His playing possessed ardor, intellectual power, and Romantic rhetoric in full measure. Beethoven was his specialty, and he made an edition of the Sonatas which is still valuable for its discriminating thoughts on phrasing and fingering.

D'Albert was often audacious in his effects. In 1898 at Leipzig he performed Grieg's *Ballade in the Form of Variations on a Norwegian Folk Song.* The composer heard him and reported: "You should have heard the meandering long fermata on the deep E-flat. I believe he held it for half a minute! But the effect was colossal. And he finished off the old, sorrowful song so slowly, quietly and simply that I was very moved." Around 1900, Arthur Rubinstein heard d'Albert play the Beethoven Fourth Concerto "with a nobility and tenderness," he wrote, which "remained in my mind as the model performance of the work."

After 1910, d'Albert's playing became a jumble of wrong notes, but he continued to be venerated. In a 1913 letter, James Huneker relates: "Heard d'Albert play the other night—audience 2,000 delirious. Such playing, a smear, a blur, 100,000 dropped notes, rotten rhythms, but the whole like something elemental, an earthquake, a tornado, a collision of planets, the sun in a conflagration . . . I stood on my chair to yell with the rest (I was really standing on my head) . . . what a genius at the keyboard."

At a similar concert, Busoni said to some students, "If only you could make such mistakes." Claudio Arrau, who also heard him at this time, felt that "d'Albert's playing was stupendous, his Liszt Sonata heroic." Unfortunately, the records he made give little indication of the qualities that made such a tremendous impression on his contemporaries.

D'Albert played monumental programs. At St. James Hall on 13 June 1898 he gave an epic sonata recital worth noting:

Sonata in A-flat, Op. 110	Beethoven
Sonata in B minor, Op. 58	Chopin
Sonata in A-flat, Op. 39	Weber
Sonata in B minor	Liszt
Sonata in G major, Op. 37	Tchaikovsky

ARTHUR ALEXANDER

1891–1969—New Zealand

He lived in England most of his life and studied with Tobias Matthay, at whose school he later taught. In 1912 he made his debut. Because of excellent musicianship, fine technique, and catholicity of taste, he became one of the best-known pianists and teachers in England. He was a friend of Medtner's and helped considerably in promoting the Russian's work. He also premiered the Second Piano Sonata of Arnold Bax. In 1921 he married the pianist-composer Freda Swain, who wrote a piano concerto for him. The couple appeared often as a well-known two-piano team.

DMITRI ALEXEEV
b. 1947—USSR

A prizewinner in several important competitions, he made his New York recital debut at Carnegie Hall in 1978. He is interested in varied styles of music and plays much Chopin. Alexeev has a big flashy technique and I have heard him in electric performances of several concertos; especially riveting was the Rachmaninoff Paganini *Rhapsody.*

CHARLES VALENTIN ALKAN
1813–1888—France

Studied with Pierre Zimmerman at the Paris Conservatoire. By the age of sixteen, he was advancing toward a successful career as a virtuoso. During the early 1830s he enjoyed the company of the Parisian intellectual and artistic elite and, for a time, lived at the fashionable Square d'Orléans, which was called "a little Athens." There he was especially close to Chopin and George Sand.

But Alkan's reclusive and rather misanthropic tendencies were too strong to contain. Gradually he disappeared from social life and public performance, preferring to be alone, teaching a few wealthy pupils and composing assiduously while immersing himself in Talmudic and Biblical studies. He lived a sad, strange life with few notable events. His ending was tragic—as he reached for his beloved Talmud, which was resting on top of a massive bookcase, the structure toppled over, crushing the emaciated musician to death at seventy-five. While the story may be apocryphal, it suggests that his death was characteristic of his life.

As an ironic requiem piece I would like to reprint the American poet Laurel Speer's poem "Alkan in Black":

Alkan wore black and a stove pipe hat. He
  told
his concierge, "Always say Alkan isn't in."
Liszt said Alkan was the best piano virtuoso
  ever heard. A good review.

Alkan also composed. You don't hear him
  much
anymore because he's too hard. Naturally, he
wrote for himself. Where would the challenge
be in one-step progressions?

Jewish law says the Talmud is a sacred
  book;
nothing must sit higher on a shelf. Alkan
pulled a bookcase over reaching for the
  pesky
relic. He wasn't tall enough and finger-tipped
death to his chest.

This most gifted musician died for Jewish
  lore
and inadequate height? I quarrel with that.

Alkan was a pianist in what the French called *"le style sévére."* It was a precise playing, lucid, sparsely pedaled, and with little tempo rubato. He must have been impressive, as no less than von Bülow and Anton Rubinstein deeply admired him. (Rubinstein's finest concerto, No. 5, is dedicated to Alkan.)

Liszt himself revered him, and once said that he was never nervous playing for anyone but Alkan. Yet, curiously, none of them ever played any of Alkan's work. After years of retirement, Alkan mysteriously emerged in 1874, and for several seasons played annual concerts in Paris which were remarkable for their diversity; yet he offered almost nothing of his own work. Vincent d'Indy heard him at this time, in Beethoven's Sonata Op. 110, and wrote that it "affected me with an enthusiasm such as I have never experienced since."

Alkan's leaving the pianistic arena early in his career may be the main reason for his overwhelming neglect as a composer, which remains an artistic tragedy. Most of the major Romantics were brilliant self-promoters, and in the great rush of the Romantic movement, Alkan's extensive output became buried. The publication in 1847 of his Grand Sonata, Op. 33 (longer than Beethoven's *Hammerklavier*), a work Raymond Lewenthal called "a cosmic event in the composer's development and in the history of piano music," went all but unheralded at the time. Even worse, Alkan was called bizarre and unplayable, and the designation by von Bülow as "the Berlioz of the piano" stuck, as if Alkan had never written dozens of very playable miniatures. In his book *Around Music,* Kaikhosru Sorabji wrote, "Few remarkable and astonishing figures in music have been the subject of such persistent misunderstanding, denigration, and belittlement."

Only Busoni among early twentieth-century pianists was convinced of Alkan's worth, considering him—along with Chopin, Schumann, Liszt, and Brahms—one of the greatest of the post-Beethoven piano composers. Busoni at least attempted to rescue him from oblivion, but with little success. Later, Busoni put the task to his student Egon Petri, who took the challenge seriously and brought out some of Alkan's more important scores.

Not until the 1960s, however, did an important Alkan exploration begin to surface. In the United States, Raymond Lewenthal was deeply gratified by the fine audience response whenever he performed Alkan, and he prepared a long-overdue critical edition. In England, Ronald Smith devoted a prominent place in his programs to Alkan, in addition to writing a biography, *Alkan the Enigma.* John Ogdon, Michael Ponti, and others joined the cause, and a recorded legacy now exists. Ronald Smith has cautioned: "The very diversity and range of his composition has proved a frustrating obstacle to the filing-cabinet minds. Like Beethoven, he seldom if ever repeats himself. . . . These baffling pages, black with marching regiments of notes, become in performance a Pandora's box of demonic power to which only the most fearless player holds the key."

Without knowing something of his output, we lose a vital chapter of nineteenth-century piano music. No serious student of the keyboard can ignore Alkan's amazing writing for the piano, which extended its resources with an extraordinary understanding of the instrument. Alkan was one of the great temperaments of French Romantic art; his vision reminds one of the blazing passions of Géricault, Delacroix, Hugo, and Berlioz.

ILSE VON ALPENHEIM
b. 1927—Austria

Studied at the Salzburg Mozarteum. Her Mozart and Haydn interpretations are admirable, and she has recorded the complete keyboard music of Haydn. Alpenheim was married to the conductor Antal Dorati, whose Piano Concerto and *Variations on a Theme of Bartók* she recorded with insight.

GÉZA ANDA
1921–1976—Hungary

Although Anda played a good Liszt sonata, a congenial Bartók Third Concerto, and a good deal of Schumann and Chopin, his recording of that composer's waltzes is deadly dull. The last years of his life were spent mainly in the preparation and recording of the twenty-five Mozart Concerti. In this magnificent achievement, Anda fulfilled his gifts. For these works he composed his own idiomatic cadenzas and also conducted the orchestra with control and subtlety, achieving a luminous homogeneity of sound. Anda plays with high polish, lovely tone, unforced tempi. All is refined and musical; it is a radiant, sunny, Italianate Mozart. Often he misses the darker strains of Mozart's genius, the undertow of passion, the stabs of pain, the momentary reaching for sublimity. In the slow movements, Anda plays with the taste and poise of a fine musical mind. It was Anda's gorgeous playing, with his widely arched phrasing of the slow movement of the Piano Concerto No. 21, K. 467, that was used so strikingly in the film *Elvira Madigan*.

LUCY ANDERSON
1790–1878—England

It was said she was not a strong technician, but highly musical. She was however able to perform the quite difficult B minor Hummel Concerto at the Philharmonic Society in London in 1819, the first woman pianist to play at the Society. In the following years she appeared with orchestra in London nineteen times, with her last appearance in 1862. Anderson was highly respected, especially as the teacher of the young Queen Victoria and her children. She was an early teacher of Arabella Goddard, the finest English pianist of her day.

RICHARD ANDERSON
1851–1918—Sweden

An eminent pianist, a pupil of Johan van Boom at the Stockholm Conservatory. Anderson performed frequently outside of Sweden, and returned to become an influential member of the Stockholm musical community. He taught at the Royal Conservatory, composed character pieces and a sonata, and taught Wilhelm Stenhammar.

LEIF OVE ANDSNES
b. 1970—Norway

Born in Karmoy, Norway. He studied at the Bergen Conservatory with Jiri Hlinka. Andsnes is becoming one of the leading pianists of the new century, appearing the world over in recital and with all the major orchestras and conductors. From the early 1990s he has been hailed a major talent, and has received prize after prize, including the Gilmore Award in 1997. A freewheeling musician who breathes new life into the Grieg and Liszt concertos, he also champions lesser-known repertoire, and has recorded the Szymanowski *Sinfonia Concertante*, Nielsen piano works, Haydn Sonatas, Janácek piano music, a hale and hardy rendering of the underrated Britten Concerto, Liszt's Second *Mephisto Waltz* and *Valse oubliée* No. 4, and an extra exciting Rachmaninoff Third Concerto. In all of the above one finds a distinctive, warm-hearted musician who plays with the feeling of real enjoyment and with a technique which has no sign of strain in any department.

AGUSTIN ANIEVAS

b. 1934—United States

Studied with Edward Steuermann and Adele Marcus at the Juilliard School. In 1961 he won the Mitropoulos Piano Competition. Though his playing is never profound, Anievas, at his best, has the rare gift of intimacy. Rubato is natural to him and never applied after the fact. His recording of the Chopin Waltzes is ingratiating, and his twenty-four Chopin Etudes show his claim to virtuosity.

CONRAD ANSORGE

1862–1930—Germany

Studied at the Leipzig Conservatory and in the summer of 1885 began studies with Liszt, in the same class as Lamond and Da Motta. He was a highly regarded pianist of his period in the "large" German style of d'Albert, Busoni, and Carreño. He made an American debut in 1887; also pursued teaching, especially in Berlin, and taught Eduard Erdmann and Selim Palmgren. He was past his prime and in ill-health when he made some 78s which were invariably reviewed as heavy-handed, dull, mechanical, and lachrymose. Doubtless Ansorge was miscast in the miniatures I have heard, such as Schumann's Romance in B-flat minor and Schubert's Moment Musical No. 3 in F minor. The pianist also composed, including a Piano concerto and a Sonata, both thickly textured.

ANNIE D'ARCO

1920–1998—France

A pupil of Marguerite Long. She is a typical representative of the slender, lithe, and elegant playing that still survives in French pianism, a style begun by Adam, Zimmerman, and Alkan ten generations ago.

MARTHA ARGERICH

b. 1941—Argentina

Her early studies were with Vincenzo Scaramuzza; later training included working with Friedrich Gulda and Michelangeli. She was the winner in 1957 of the Busoni International Competition in Bolzano and, in 1965, of the Chopin International Competition in Warsaw.

Argerich is one of the most exciting pianists of our time. Onstage her sultry appearance exudes mystery and electricity. In pianistic circles one constantly hears the question: Did you hear Argerich recently? Or: How do you like Argerich's new Schumann or Chopin recording? Do you know her Tchaikovsky concerto with Kondrashin? You can bet every pianist in town will be at an Argerich concert. Audiences are immediately aware of her passionate temperament; they drink in her musical vitality. Argerich has a restless nature and has taken a long time to come to grips with her tremendous talent, raw energy, and animal spirits. Often she has relied on her instinct and primitive strength to propel her through a concert. Although she has considerable musical intelligence, she finds it difficult to meditate on a work's design, its ultimate form. This has caused her to be rather inconsistent, often relying on the heat of the moment. Her inspiration can falter within a wonderful rendition, only to rise again on a surge of impulsive power. Onstage, she carries the day, but defects show up in her recorded output.

Her Liszt Sonata is shapeless, too fast, with the left hand often murky. Her Chopin *Funeral March* Sonata bumps and belches. The Chopin B minor Sonata and the Schumann G minor Sonata rumble, and the slow movements sound artificial. I think she is bored in recording sessions. Even her Prokofiev Third Concerto, for all her hard-edged tone, is not as brilliant as it should be. But these are all earlier recordings. (Even among these, I have a favorite, a fabulous performance of Ravel's *Gaspard de la nuit*. The *Scarbo* movement, darkly hued and fiendish, is charged with a technical abundance that few can achieve.) Argerich also has the vital capacity for growth. Each season she shows increasing discipline and consistency without losing the high tension of white-hot creation. In Carnegie Hall I heard her play the Brahms Sonata Op. 2 in F-sharp minor, a work born of controlled fury—the first movement was steaming, like molten lava, and she uncovered in it a range of colors that I never knew the composition could display. At this same concert she played Prokofiev's own transcriptions from his ballet *Romeo and Juliet*. Her projection was so powerful, her color sense so deft, that there was no reason to long for Prokofiev's lavish orchestration. From the far simpler tone production of her early recordings, she has arrived at a sound that is rich and pliant. Her recordings of the Bach toccatas are well constructed and robust, and Schumann's *Kreisleriana* finds her at her most inspired. Let's hope that Argerich, who has a propensity for canceling concerts, will continue to let audiences all over the world hear her.

In the past decade and a half Argerich has been an exasperating disappointment to her countless admirers who patiently wait for this diva of the piano to perform solo recitals. She well knows that the solo literature should be a concert pianist's chief activity, but for whatever reasons, she has avoided doing so, claiming that it is too lonely being onstage alone. It is astonishing that in her whole career she has thus far only given only one complete Carnegie Hall recital.

Instead when she does not cancel she performs with friends, sometimes with poor results, such as a 2001 recital with Ivry Gitlis, a violinist past his best capacities. Far more pleasurable have been her more frequent concerto appearances with her former husband, Charles Dutoit, conducting. Usually the fare is Chopin's E minor Concerto, Ravel's G major, and the Prokofiev First and Third Concertos in daredevil tempi. In recent years her recorded output has been sparse, but there is a magnificent live performance of the Third Rachmaninoff Concerto from the early 1980s, released in the mid-1990s. It is a magisterial reading; everything is in order, clean and calculated, with an overwhelming technical grasp. In this performance she has achieved her finest concerto performance. Her public remains hungry for her every appearance, and always there are frenzied applause and standing ovations. Martha Argerich is one of the great legends of the piano, and nobody on the concert stage generates such contagious excitement.

CLAUDIO ARRAU
1903–1991—Chile

At the age of sixteen, he won the Liszt Prize, the first of many awards throughout his life. At twenty he made his American debut, playing with the Boston and Chicago symphony orchestras. Then, in 1927, he won the International Pianists' Competition in Geneva; in 1949 he was named "Favorite Son of Mexico"; in 1965 he received the Chevalier de l'Ordre des Arts et des Lettres. And in 1978, the Berlin Philharmonic awarded him its Hans von Bülow Medal. He lived in the United States from 1941 on.

Arrau was born in Chillán, far from the great events that were shaping the century. His gifts were evident at a very early age, and his mother was his first teacher. Soon, however, it became apparent that he needed more advanced instruction and, with the aid of a stipend from the government, he went to Berlin. There he embarked on studies with the most enduring influence of his life—the longtime pupil of Liszt, Martin Krause. Krause nurtured the child, supervised his practicing, read to him, walked with him, taught him other subjects, and took him to concerts, where he heard everything and met everybody. The giants of his youth were Busoni, Carreño, d'Albert; "they were awesome in their scope," he remembered. Krause, conscious of the Lisztian "humanist" climate, taught Arrau a deep humility in his art, and he instilled in his young charge a fierce desire to play in public, a desire which never abated. During those splendid years of guardianship of the young Arrau, Krause accepted not a penny. When his mentor died, Arrau was only sixteen. He was crushed and did not want to work with another teacher, nor did he need to.

During the next decade, Arrau slowly began the process of career building, while constantly adding to his repertoire. When he won the Geneva Prize, Arthur Rubinstein was one of the judges. "It did not take two minutes of his playing," recounts Rubinstein in his memoirs, "before we began nodding to each other, smiling with satisfaction. . . . The competition was like a race between a thoroughbred and some cart horses."

By the 1930s, Arrau was performing worldwide, playing recitals of the complete keyboard works of Bach, Mozart, and Beethoven. In the last half century, he never rested, offering programs beyond the potential and potency of the average performer.

For this artist, pianistic frivolity or mere entertainment was never in order. "Wowing" an audience would have been inconceivable. Arrau thought of Art in the nineteenth-century sense, as sacred, mystical, spiritual. By temperament and education, he was from a vanished era, where Art was not a form of therapy or enjoyment but a way of life. When this gentleman of dignity played, I was taken back to a time when there was less noise and confusion, a time when value was placed on craftsmanship, and even on contemplation.

Arrau had one of the major musical careers of the century. He was not, however, an artist beloved by all listeners. He was a problematic pianist, respected for his musicianly wisdom but often irritating in his conceptions, which could be too ponderous, idiosyncratic in phrasing, or just tedious. His playing could indeed be heavy, and unrelentingly serious. There was always complexity in an Arrau rendering; there were seldom humor, lightness, or sensuousness for their own sake. It was especially interesting that many pianists, particularly those with a Slavic bent, responded poorly to Arrau. Those who see the piano before the music find Arrau, no matter what the repertoire, just too stodgy.

Yet Arrau the pianist was not always the lofty and serious-minded artist we have come to know. His early discs from the late 1920s show a pianist glorying in his technical power, thrilled by his athletic skills and glittering scales, playing with an elegance that he was later to forsake entirely. He plays Balakirev's *Islamey* with a lustful virtuosity, splurging in chordal and sonorous splendor. In Liszt's *Spanish Rhapsody*, he rides the high tide of virtuosity. Also spectacular are his Chopin and Liszt etudes. This was a period of sparkle and panache.

By the mid-1930s, a more dour Arrau emerged, an artist experimenting with the repertoire, finding his way in it, playing huge amounts of Bach and Mozart. But Beethoven was the rudder that set him on his ultimate course. He first played the cycle of Beethoven Sonatas in Mexico City in the 1930s, and ever after made the master of Bonn his main concern. During the 1930s, Arrau emerged as a musical architect, with Fischer and Schnabel affecting him more deeply than any other pianists.

During and after the war years, Arrau's playing became even more austere. There was more angularity in phrasing, more definition, less pedaling for color's sake, and he became more objective in his conceptions. It is often rather bleak playing, such as his Herculean Schubert *Wanderer* Fantasy, selections from Albéniz's *Iberia,* or the dry Chopin Etudes and Scherzos and a wiry Debussy. This period lasted a full twenty years.

In the last quarter century, Arrau's art crystallized. The bleakness of the postwar period had been left behind; there was more optimism in his vision, and the playing had never before been so imbued with lyrical sweep and monumentality of style. His recordings are a marvelous document of his art until around 1982, when such discs as his Schubert Op. 90 Impromptus, Chopin Waltzes and Scherzos, and others sound tired and faded, even plodding at times.

Arrau, like many older artists, returned to Mozart for rejuvenation, but the kind of graciousness Mozart demands was not an innate part of his temperament. His recording of the C minor Sonata is too strenuous, the A minor Rondo too tortured, and the D minor Fantasy, needing simplicity, is too heartrending, full of pedal and torpor. Nor was he a successful player of the concertos. In Mozart there is always a tear beneath the smile, but Arrau reached only for the tear, unconcerned with the benevolence of style.

Arrau committed Chopin to disc *en masse.* His conception of the Polish master is far from the Chopin of the French salon, far from the view of him as a "ladies' composer" (Arrau's words). It took Arrau a long time to come to

Claudio Arrau by David Dubal

terms with Chopin. I cannot pretend to care for all of it, but he developed an authentic Chopin, in which he became, above all, a master of design; here structure is prime, but still sometimes the structure bursts its bounds. It is not a Slavic Chopin, but the essence of the Teutonic type, blended with Arrau's passionate Latin blood. His Chopin during the 1950s was skeletal, but in his later period it was often massive and colorful, possessing many interpretive depths. It is never "light," even in the most insignificant posthumous waltz or "pretty" nocturne. At times, the Arrau Chopin is an amalgam of mistreated or affected rubato and tortured pretension. His old versions of the Impromptus and Scherzos were stylistically uncomfortable, but the newer discs are bloated and structurally piecemeal.

He sees the Nocturnes as important music and attempts to play them as such, but somehow he gives them a transfusion of thick syrup. He emphasizes too many details, and the pauses seem endless—the inflections become harmonically and melodically poky, while the hesitations border on mannerism. These Nocturnes have been stored in the hothouse; all their inherent voluptuousness has become moldy. Arrau would have been most uncomfortable in a Parisian salon listening to the ethereal Pole introduce his amorous "night pieces" to fashionable society. His Chopin is most successful in the Third and Fourth Ballades, the F minor Fantasy, and the *Polonaise-fantaisie,* which has marvelous moments of depth. There are also many creative strokes in the Preludes, side by side with quirky passages.

Arrau's earlier Debussy was transformed in later years. He felt the Preludes are of visionary scope, with a "proximity to death," a phrase he often used. Gone is the much-heralded Gallic clarity of this *"musicien français."* Here, the grace of simplicity rests uneasily in Arrau's music-making; his Debussy seldom has a moment's repose, and he finds in the music a labyrinth of mysterious murmurings.

The composers in whose work Arrau's genius truly blooms and flourishes are Schumann, Beethoven, Liszt, and Brahms. During his last years he also became deeply involved with Schubert, whose music, he felt, posed the most difficult of interpretive problems. His recording of the B-flat Sonata shows many beauties of tone and feeling, yet it strays, lacking directness and charm. His best Schubert disc is a haunting reading of the great C minor posthumous Sonata, with a chilling finale.

For many pianists and audiences, Schumann's large works, so discursive, daring, and thorny, are hard nuts to crack. But Arrau's creativity was perfectly wedded to Schumann's deep Romanticism. The denser the tapestry, the more involved Arrau becomes. His own metric clock fits closely with the seemingly barless music. Free to indulge and experiment, Arrau might actually become playful. Hands occasionally playing purposely slightly out of sync make for an unnerving effect. He brings out inner voices, subtleties of voicing and texture, and, above all, the vernal atmosphere of early German Romanticism. The Fantasy, *Symphonic Etudes, Humoreske, Davidsbündlertänze,* the *Carnaval,* and others are filled with fire, a leaping, soaring spirit, but also with the dark overtones of Schumann's own nightmarish psyche on the brink of mental disaster. Arrau played Schumann with the utmost compassion.

Brahms also fared well with Arrau, whose interpretations of the two Concerti are broadly conceived. They present a properly grand Brahms. In the F minor and F-sharp minor Sonatas and the Scherzo Op. 4, Arrau is more remarkable than in the Variations on a Theme by Paganini or by Handel or in the smaller frame of the Ballades Op. 10.

All pianists should study closely Arrau's Beethoven. He was among the great disseminators of this composer's work, and in the time-honored tradition of von Bülow, d'Albert, and Schnabel, prepared his own edition of the thirty-two Sonatas. His playing offers an abundance of interpretive insight. Here is Arrau the master builder, fired with intellectual curiosity and passion. He sees in Beethoven a mirror of human aspiration, joy, and suffering. This music is Arrau's spiritual home. Playing Beethoven, he is never orthodox; the playing may not set everyone's blood on fire, but it offers a true listening adventure, which grows deeply on a listener.

In the Liszt literature, Arrau can be titanic. For him, Liszt is never small-minded or merely glittering. He finds in Liszt a large landscape—the nature poet, the gypsy, the inventor of an unprecedented technique, a Faustian, a religious ecstatic, and an impressionist.

Arrau's Liszt Sonata has always crowned his repertoire. His live performances of it were usually finer than his recording, which is nevertheless one that should be in any Liszt admirer's library. The twelve *Transcendental*

Etudes, recorded when Arrau was seventy-four, are enormous conceptions carved from the piano's very innards, colorful and bold. Other Arrau landmark Liszt recordings include the Ninth Hungarian Rhapsody, as well as *Les Jeux d'eaux à la Villa d'Este,* a fountain of golden inspiration in which Arrau is at the very height of his art. Also memorable are the trumpeting epic tragedy in his B minor Ballade; the large emotional span of his *Vallée d'Obermann*; and the long, flowering phrasing of the *Bénédiction de Dieu dans la solitude,* where the mystic Liszt is in harmony with Arrau's own penchant for contemplative states.

Arrau's career is an object lesson epitomizing the artist struggling with his daemon, digging deeply into the piano's repertoire, forever searching and studying, and in his ferocious need to express himself musically, finally bringing his art to a world public. It was a relentless, Faustian career. Playing the piano was everything to Claudio Arrau.

LYDIA ARTYIMIW

b. 1954—United States

Her principal teacher was Gary Graffman. She has garnered high prizes at the Leventritt and Leeds competitions. Her recordings show a sensitive, warmhearted pianist who plays with fine craftsmanship.

VLADIMIR ASHKENAZY

b. 1937—USSR

He studied with the renowned teacher Anaida Sumbatyan and, at the age of eighteen, entered the Moscow Conservatory, where he worked under Lev Oborin. Ashkenazy quickly became the pride of the Soviet pianistic world. In 1955 he placed second in the Warsaw Chopin Competition, and the following year saw him triumph in the Brussels Queen Elizabeth Competition. From that moment on, his career prospered. By this time, he had already excited many connoisseurs with his finely grained Chopin F minor Concerto, of chaste and slender proportions. Soon after, his Chopin Etudes filtered to the West, announcing a breathtaking mechanism. His fingers were dauntless, double notes were shaken from the wrist as if by magic, and in the lyric Etude Op. 25, No. 7, he revealed a passionate emotional makeup. In these early recorded specimens, Ashkenazy appeared to be a delectable Slavic miniaturist.

In 1962, Ashkenazy, who should have been beyond the competition circuit, was asked by the powers that be to enter the Tchaikovsky Competition. The already renowned pianist acceded and tied for first place with the British John Ogdon. Shortly thereafter, in 1963, the young virtuoso defected from Mother Russia. At the same time, he left the ranks of important young pianists, moving year by year into higher levels of artistry.

After his defection, Ashkenazy was intent upon musical growth. If he lost some of his Russian taste for musical titillation and quick excitement, he also gained a new knowledge of Classical composers, dedicating himself to the stylistic problems of Mozart, Beethoven, and Schubert. His accounts of the G major and D major Sonatas of Schubert are warm and insightful. In the late 1960s he began to perceive the might of Beethoven's mind, and he produced rich readings of Beethoven sonatas and the Concerti. His concerto performances showed a true instinct for orchestral collaboration. His *Hammerklavier* stands out as the highest achievement of this period.

During these marvelously inspired years of the 1960s, his Chopin took on more color and an emboldened tone. He made recordings of the Ballades and Scherzos, large in style and looking deep into the composer's spirit, while eschewing all mannerism. In such scores as the C-sharp minor Scherzo, the Barcarolle, the B major Nocturne, and the Second Ballade, Ashkenazy produced some of the best Chopin playing put to disc in the 1960s. During this period, he was active in promoting the Brahms Concerti, and produced a library of recordings of Mozart concertos and sonatas, the finest being his A minor Sonata. He also recorded large amounts of Schumann, struggling to understand the German master's stylistic weirdness. He finds his target best in a marvelous reading of the *Symphonic Etudes,* while his other Schumann does not always fare so well, cramped often by a certain dullness. His Ravel *Gaspard de la nuit,* however, is shimmering, and his Liszt etudes are wonderful. In all that he touched there was a deep respect for the composer's wishes, together with a technique that was ravishing. In short, Ashkenazy had cross-pollinated Russian provincialism with cosmopolitanism, a unique mix that made him one of the most exciting and sought-after artists of the time. His career grew to astonishing proportions, and he seemed to be, indeed he was, all over the globe. He continued to play an excellent Prokofiev, and his Rachmaninoff kept expanding in its lyricism. He also added intelligent performances of Scriabin to his repertoire.

Throughout the 1970s and 1980s, Ashkenazy has remained furiously dedicated to his art. Recordings roll off the press—chamber music, Rachmaninoff song accompaniments, the ten Violin Sonatas of Beethoven with Itzhak Perlman, solo works and concertos, the complete Beethoven Sonatas and the complete Chopin works. (How does he have the time to learn so difficult and ungrateful a score as the Chopin Sonata in C minor, Op. 4?) The breadth of his piano recitals remains staggering, from Schubert's *Wanderer* Fantasy to Scriabin's Sixth Sonata, and all of it is played impeccably. But in the last fifteen years

Ashkenazy has lost something—a vitality, an adventurousness with the music. Perhaps even a boredom with the piano is setting in. When he turned to conducting, many felt this was merely to refresh himself, to relax from the rigors of the piano. But no, this restless, intelligent, formidable, and compulsive musical mind has kept at his conducting and is now turning out good readings of the established orchestral repertoire, and each season he grows more skilled in this adopted field.

Recently, some of his orchestral performances have been far more compelling than his piano playing, which sounds tired and tubby—Chopin valses without aroma, mazurkas without the wild wood note, so much seems manufactured. His Beethoven Sonatas are always correct and careful but played with little lust. It is extra homogenized, the favorite Beethoven of the traditional, cautious conservatory student. When a pupil asks the teacher which Opus 2, No. 3 to listen to, the teacher says with confidence, "Hear Ashkenazy's. It is the most normal." And in actuality, the Ashkenazy way is what many audiences want today. High craft, stability, overwhelming professionalism, faithfulness to the text, infallible rhythm, and nothing that disturbs very much—like the clean plastic that pervades our sanitized environment. In this sense, Ashkenazy represents the last decade and a half admirably. He has been at the top of the class, and it is no accident that his career has been so enormously successful. He is stern and serious; one cannot imagine Ashkenazy resorting to the absurdities of some of his colleagues, who are heard on TV commercials and game shows, or in cheap "crossover" albums with "pop" musicians.

Yet Ashkenazy's piano playing seldom sounds inspired, and as there has been a slight change in taste recently, his straightforward objectivity is beginning to sound dull; or is it that we have heard the Ashkenazy "product" too often? He seems to have been playing by formula. At a recent recital, an Ashkenazy fanatic walked out shaking her head, muttering, "It's all there, but where is it?" This opinion is becoming prevalent with many pianists; they are unmoved. Yet they still admire him as one of the most all-encompassing pianistic talents of the present day. Perhaps a rest is due. He seems now to be conducting more than ever. Maybe, with time away from the instrument, a fresh urge to play the piano will bring him into a new chapter in his relationship with the literature he grew up with.

In the last years, Ashkenazy has not received fresh impetus to play the piano publicly; he remains furiously conducting orchestras, and refining very definite orchestral talents. Always a fierce worker, who put many hours daily into piano practice, perhaps he is relieved of what he once called "sweet slavery." However, I am certain that he still refurbishes his vast repertoire and the lure of the piano will bring him back to his pianistic public even if only occasionally.

STEFAN ASKENASE
1896–1985—Poland

A student of Sauer, Askenase achieved a fine reputation in Europe, especially as a Chopin interpreter, and his discs are often poetic and never superficial. The Impromptus and Concerti are especially intriguing.

EMANUEL AX
b. 1949—Poland

He studied at the Juilliard School with Mieczyslaw Münz. In 1973 he won the first Arthur Rubinstein Competition in Tel Aviv.

Ax never shouts, roars, or shows off. His conceptions are clear and direct. He breathes deeply, playing with confidence and spontaneity, unconcerned about hitting a few wrong notes. Style, balance, and good sense always inform his work.

Ax has an affinity with Chopin in all his genres. It's a very healthy, warm, but objective Chopin. The Ax brand never sighs or weeps, and there is never a morbid note. His *Polonaise-fantaisie* is firmly structured. The Nocturne in B major and the E major Scherzo are luscious, the two Concerti full-bodied, if somewhat too slick. The Ballades are rich with color, while his Mazurkas are among the best of his generation, so natural and arresting is his innate sense of rhythm in these dance-poems.

In Mozart he is weaker, not yet having found the key to this elusive music. The Mozart Concerto readings are limited in emotional range, too tasteful and pleasing. Ax generally does not like to disturb; even the forbidding Schoenberg Concerto is somehow Romantically expressive and accessible.

In Beethoven, Ax is comfortable. He has produced fine readings of the *Waldstein* and *Appassionata* Sonatas, charged with Romantic drama. His Liszt is somewhat bland, well padded, and agreeable, with the supercharged flamboyance of this composer missing.

Ax is blessed with an exceptional singing tone, but maintaining this quality often appears to be his prime concern. There needs to be a dash of astringency in his playing. For instance, his plush reading of the Ravel *Valses nobles et sentimentales* could profit by being less Romantic, and his *Scarbo*, which is first-class technically, lacks the devastating sting and drollery of this music. In his desire to wrap everything in a beautiful package, he deprives much music of its true nature. After Liszt heard Henselt, who was renowned for his cantabile playing, he exclaimed, "Ah, I too could have had velvet paws." But Liszt opted instead for a variegated palette of sounds based on the character and needs of the music. Not all music is beautiful, and perhaps this is why Ax has been admirably experimenting with a variety of contemporary music, possibly to relieve his ears of conventional harmony.

The last years have brought Ax to the very pinnacle of his profession, heard worldwide in chamber concerts, solo performances, and concertos; he has added two-piano appearances and recordings with his colleague Yefim Bronfman. A Rachmaninoff CD finds the artists in total sympathy.

Ax is an unyielding workman who has arrived at greater depths of interpretation in the standard literature and performs with relish quite a variety of new music, such as concertos by Ezra Laderman, John Adams, and Penderecki. One usually leaves an Ax concert or hears his recordings with a sense of satisfaction, a feeling born of the artist's balanced and vibrant conceptions.

B

VICTOR BABIN

1908–1972—Russia

He studied with Schnabel and married Vitya Vronsky; they would form a duo-piano team which became famous. Babin composed a great deal, and late in life served as president of the Cleveland Institute of Music.

CARL PHILIPP EMANUEL BACH

1714–1788—Germany

The second son of J. S. Bach was one of the most important musicians of the eighteenth century. His clavichord performances brought tears to the eyes of the historian Dr. Burney. C. P. E. Bach wrote his famous treatise, *The True Art of Playing Keyboard Instruments,* in 1757. At Czerny's first lesson with Beethoven, the boy was told to get a copy immediately. Later in his career, C. P. E. Bach realized that the piano would soon take pride of place over the harpsichord and clavichord. His sonatas were pivotal in defining the sonata form, and Haydn and Mozart deeply appreciated his work.

On the subject of performance, C. P. E. Bach's words remain as valid today as when he wrote them nearly 250 years ago:

Keyboard players whose chief asset is mere technique are clearly at a disadvantage. A performer may have the most agile fingers, be competent at single and double trills, master the art of fingering, read skillfully at sight regardless of key, and transpose extemporaneously without the slightest difficulty; he may play tenths, even twelfths, or runs, cross hands in every conceivable manner, and excel in other related matters; yet he may be something less than a clear, pleasing, or stirring keyboard player. More often than not, one meets technicians, nimble players by profession, who possess all these qualifications and indeed astound us with their prowess without ever touching our sensibilities. They overwhelm our hearing without satisfying it and stun the mind without moving it.

JOHANN CHRISTIAN BACH

1735–1782—Germany

Known as "the English Bach." After J. S. Bach's death in 1750, Johann Christian was brought to Berlin, where his half-brother C. P. E. was court composer to Frederick the Great. Here the young Bach fell in love with the new pianofortes that the king had bought from Gottfried Silbermann. Later, in London, it was J. C. Bach who, on 2 June 1768, for the first time played a group of piano solos at a public concert, probably pieces from his Op. 5 Sonatas. It seems fitting that the piano's debut was given by Bach's youngest son. J. C.

Bach was probably the best pianist of the day in London, and his advocacy of the piano was crucial at that early moment in its history. He was the piano teacher of Queen Charlotte, wife of George III, and he inspired the child Mozart to prefer the piano rather than the harpsichord. Mozart never ceased in his admiration for Johann Christian.

GINA BACHAUER
1913–1976—Greece

Studied at the Athens Conservatory and later in Paris with Cortot, and received a few lessons from Rachmaninoff. From the mid-thirties she toured with success, but was domiciled in Egypt because of the war until 1946, when she settled in London and married the conductor Alec Sherman. From this point she played consistently on the concert stages of the world.

Bachauer brought to the concert hall a contagious excitement. She was a large-scaled, blood-and-thunder Romantic who possessed true bravura in her veins. She loved the meaty virtuoso works—from the Rachmaninoff Third Concerto to Stravinsky's *Petrouchka*—these she played with flair and large swatches of pedal in her quest for color and more color. In classic works she was never austere. Her Beethoven *Waldstein* Sonata in a "live" performance on a compact disc issued by the Gina Bachauer Competition is one of the most riveting *Waldstein*s ever recorded, huge in conception, symphonic in presentation, disciplined, meaty, and technically magnificent. On this disc is a Bach-Tausig Toccata and Fugue in D minor played to the hilt and an intimate *Kinderscenen* of Schumann, along with rare interviews by the pianist. A disc of Brahms Waltzes and the Scriabin Twenty-four Preludes, Op. 11, finds her at her best. Her recording of Ravel's *Garpard de la Nuit*

is played with her usual aplomb, with each composition preceded by Sir John Gielgud's reading of the Aloysius Bertrand poems that inspired Ravel's rapturous triptych. The Gina Bachauer International Competition, held in Salt Lake City, Utah, was founded to perpetuate the memory of a great pianist.

AGATHE BACKER-GRØNDAHL
1847–1907—Norway

Studied in Norway with the renowned Norwegian composer Halfdan Kjerulf and later was a pupil of Theodore Kullak, von Bülow, and finally of Liszt. From all accounts she was an extraordinary pianist. At a London concert, George Bernard Shaw wrote, "A great artist—a serious artist—a beautiful, incomparable unique artist! She morally regenerated us all." Backer-Grøndahl played a large repertoire, and sponsored Grieg's music. Grieg deeply admired her playing and music, and she was soloist in his famous Concerto, with the composer on the podium.

Backer-Grøndahl was the outstanding Scandinavian woman composer of her time, writing songs and piano pieces. Her Etudes de Concert are superbly pianistic, and these works, composed between 1881 and 1903, occupy her Opp. 11, 22, 32, 47, 57, and 58. Her *Fier Skizzer*, Op. 19, Suite in Five Movements, Toccata, Prelude and Grand Menuet, Op. 61 should be revived. All of her music is imaginative with a rich melodic vein. Backer-Grøndahl was influential as a teacher; her son, Fridtjof Backer-Grøndahl (1885–1959), studied with her and was an esteemed pianist with a substantial European career. Agathe Backer-Grøndahl died the same year as Grieg, her last years plagued by deafness.

WILHELM BACKHAUS

1884–1969—Germany

He studied at the Leipzig Conservatory with Alois Reckendorf. In 1899 he took lessons with d'Albert, and in 1905 he won the Rubinstein Prize.

Through seventy performing seasons, Backhaus established himself as one of the century's great German pianists. He was one of the first to record, doing so as early as 1908. Success came to him easily, except in the United States, where he played annually, only to give up trying to establish an American career during the 1920s. American audiences had been conditioned to the stars of Slavic pianism, many of whom had the tendency to place virtuosity and personality before solid musicianship. Backhaus bitterly wrote, "A little show of bravura will turn many of the unthinking auditors into a roaring mob. This is, of course, very distressing to the sincere artist who strives to establish himself by his real worth."

During his almost thirty years' absence from the United States, the American public grew immeasurably in musical sophistication, and the size of the record-buying public grew enormously as well. During that period, Backhaus was given many of the chief assignments in recording the literature, and his readings of the Schumann Fantasy, the Brahms *Paganini* Variations, and history's first set of the Chopin Twenty-four Etudes, peerless in execution, were "musts" in any collection. In 1954, Backhaus returned to Carnegie Hall, where he was at last hailed as one of the greatest of musicians. His all-Beethoven recital was recorded and preserved. Records had made him famous in his absence.

Beethoven was his main musical occupation. For Backhaus, "He transcends them all in dynamic power and his titanic spirit and intensity of thought seem to suggest a god or superman." He recorded the complete sonatas

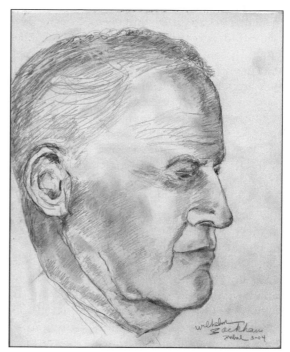

Wilhelm Backhaus by David Dubal

twice, the second set much the same as the first. Backhaus was not an artist to change conception or to grow musically; all was formed early on. Backhaus heard the music simply; subtlety was not his concern, and his emotional range was limited. He was best with a brusque and bumptious Beethoven. In such pages as the arioso of the Sonata Op. 110, one can wince at his insensitivity to the score's suave fluidity and depth of emotion. In general his slow movements are faster than necessary—as though the kind of serious attention they required were beyond him. There is, as well, a definite tendency in such dramatic essays as the Sonatas Opp. 13, 57, and 111 to allow the drama to degenerate into lurid melodrama. Yet Backhaus's Beethoven still retains its great appeal. His playing has a wonderfully muscular animality in which a superb life force is at work. The vitality can be irresistible. Stephen Kovacevich goes so far as to say that

"Backhaus was the only person who ever truly understood Beethoven's *Hammerklavier* Sonata. . . . It's true he may not be faithful to the text in every instance, but the wildness of what he's attempting to do is quite wonderful."

Backhaus also basked in the Brahms repertory, having been one of the earliest advocates of the two concertos. His discs of the smaller pieces exhibit a lovely sound but a curious blandness—the interior pathos is missing.

His Mozart is too earnest; it sounds square and lacks charm. His Schumann, at its best, although dry, was convincing. In Schubert, the dryness became parched, lacking in Viennese charm; it is a heavily made Schubert.

Backhaus was a German who was fond of Chopin. His 1928 recordings of the Twenty-four Etudes are still talked about by pianists. Tamás Vásáry said that he remains "astonished by Backhaus's technical know-how." Backhaus delighted in technical finesse more than in Chopin's puissant poetry. He walks through Chopin's exotic garden but seldom bends to smell the intoxicating blooms.

Backhaus was one of the technical giants of his time; his mechanism was never showy but was solid as rock; his finger dexterity was especially wonderful. He had great faith in scale and arpeggio practice and diligently worked at it his life long. Even at eighty-five, his technical health was impressive. Vladimir Horowitz thought Backhaus "a wonderful pianist . . . I once heard him play the Chopin Etudes and it was remarkable. In the first one in C-major, not a single note fell under the piano. It was fantastic. He heard me play Liszt's *Feux-follets* and came up to me; Horowitz, he said, 'I could never do that.' But he was being nice. He could have if he wanted."

The critic Tim Page writes, "Wilhelm Backhaus holds a place among pianists roughly comparable to that of Everest among mountains. Backhaus had it all—majesty and subtlety, intellectual probity and superhuman technique, presence and grace."

The Andante label has released a magnificent set of four CDs containing a variety of repertoire from his discography, including Beethoven's Fourth and Fifth Concertos, with Landon Ronald conducting (1927–29), the Brahms D minor with Adrian Boult (1932), and the Grieg Concerto with John Barbirolli (1933). Besides several Schubert scores there is Backhaus's own delightful arrangement of Schubert's D major *Marche militaire*, an elegant *Caprice Espagnole* of Moszkowski, the F major Smetana Polka, the "complete" Chopin Etudes, Opus 10, Liszt's Second Rhapsody, Delibes-Dohnányi *Naila Waltzes,* and the 1937 Schumann Fantasy, an object lesson in how to convincingly structure its vast discursive first movement.

KATHERINE BACON
1896–1982—England

Born in Chesterfield, England, Bacon began piano lessons at the age of four. An important talent was detected by the pianist Arthur Newstead, and from age nine she traveled six hundred miles a week to London for lessons with Newstead. From 1913 to 1916 she studied at the Peabody Conservatory in Baltimore. Bacon made her New York debut in 1920, shortly after performing with the New York Philharmonic and other important orchestras. In 1927 she made a deep impression with her seven recitals at Aeolian Hall, in New York, of the complete Beethoven Sonatas. In 1966 she ventured on a Far Eastern tour.

Bacon had a distinguished teaching career and was on the faculty of the Mannes College of Music from 1921 to 1929 and at the Juilliard School from 1940 until 1972. Stanley Waldoff, Saul Braverman, Dubrazka Tomsic, and Jens Nygaard studied with her. Her colleague at Juilliard Joseph Bloch said, "Bacon was a gracious and most natural pianist, convincing in every style. I well remember she was one of the first to champion the Griffes Piano Sonata in the twenties."

PAUL BADURA-SKODA
b. 1927—Austria

At the dawn of the LP era, Badura-Skoda, an elegant young man from Vienna, became involved in studying the Schubert Sonatas and Mozart Concerti. He made many recordings and became one of the most listened-to pianists of his generation. Badura-Skoda is best suited to the German classics, but occasionally leaves this territory. His Ravel disc includes a rather tepid *Gaspard de la nuit*. When playing Chopin, most especially the Twenty-four Etudes, he is temperamentally far from his turf, and the technical material is too hot to handle with comfort.

He has recorded the entire Beethoven Sonata cycle with the courage of a dedicated player, not quite up to every technical challenge, but always with astute intelligence. His Schubert is proficient; at its best it possesses charm and innocence, especially in the *Moments musicaux*. His Schumann gives off some heat, but is mostly too well behaved. His finest work comes in Mozart, which is deft, careful, and balanced, and there is a Haydn sonata disc, played on a fortepiano, that is sparkling and witty, especially in the B minor Sonata. Badura-Skoda's cadenzas to Mozart concertos are invariably pianistic, effective, and imaginative.

ERNÖ BALOGH
1897–1989—Hungary

He studied piano with Bartók and composi-

tion with Kodaly. He won the Liszt Prize and went to Berlin for further study with Leonid Kreutzer. He made a debut in Berlin in 1920 and settled in the United States, where he was heard as soloist, and collaborated with the great soprano Lotte Lehmann, making lieder recordings with her.

ARTUR BALSAM
1906–1994—Poland

One of the distinguished accompanists of the century, a collaborator in the truest sense. Balsam was a musician of rare depth and personal modesty. Onstage he was the companion of many celebrated instrumentalists. Yehudi Menuhin called him "a truly wonderful musician." As a teacher he was admired by many of his younger colleagues, to whom he bequeathed his knowledge. His solo repertoire was immense, and he excelled in sonatas by C. P. E. Bach, Clementi, and Haydn, of which he recorded all fifty-two.

JOSEPH BANOWETZ
b. 1935—United States

He studied in New York with Carl Friedberg and in Vienna with Josef Dichter. Banowetz has had an extensive performing career. He judges international competitions and has written a book, *The Pianist's Guide to Pedaling*. Banowetz has edited much neglected piano music and has recorded a variety of works, from the standard literature to the complete Piano Concertos of Anton Rubinstein and Balakirev's Scherzos and Mazurkas, as well as a fine CD of the music of Scottish composer Ronald Stevenson.

JEAN-JOËL BARBIER

1920–1994—France

A pupil of Louise Terrier and Libussé Novak, both of whom were influenced in their teaching by Blanche Selva. He also studied with Lazare-Lévy. Barbier's specialty was French piano music and his recordings of Chabrier, Satie, and Séverac are beautifully conceived, finely chiseled, and above all picturesque. Barbier's complete Satie on Accord won the Grand Prix du Disque. In 1986 he published a book, *Au piano avec Erik Satie*. He also wrote books of fiction and poetry.

PIERRE BARBIZET

1922–1990—Chile

After studies in Santiago he entered the Paris Conservatoire, taking a first prize in 1944. By his own account he was most influenced by the playing of Arrau, Renard, Nat, Cortot, and Iturbi. He developed into a fine soloist and chamber player. In 1963 he became director of the Marseille Conservatory. Richter in his notebooks and conversations said, "Pierre Barbizet is unquestionably a true musician, his head teeming ideas, his fingers precise." On Erato he recorded the complete Chabrier piano music with understanding and affection.

DANIEL BARENBOIM

b. 1942—Argentina

He has had one of the outstanding musical careers of our time. His piano repertoire is based on the German classics, but he plays the Ravel Concerto and the Bartók Concerti with style. His playing of Liszt's Wagner transcriptions, or the *Rigoletto* paraphrase, is sincere and musicianly, if unexciting, and his reading of the Sonata is beautifully planned, while the *Sonetti del Petrarca* and *Liebestraum* are lyrically ripe. His disc of the Berg Sonata captures the languid neurasthenia so distinctive of turn-of-the-century Vienna. His first set of the Beethoven Sonatas, recorded in his twenties, strives for a dignity, almost a gravity, of utterance. They are played in the German Romantic tradition of the conductors Klemperer and Furtwangler. The slow movements, replete with expressive devices, are somewhat heavy. His more recent set of the Sonatas is more youthful, more vigorous, more dynamic, but often superficial, and his complete recording of Mendelssohn's *Songs without Words* is too often perfunctory. His *Diabelli* Variations, however, shows Barenboim at the top of his form in a splendid and explosive performance. His Schumann *Carnaval* and Brahms *Schumann* Variations are dull, but his Schubert is often golden; especially warm is the B-flat Sonata. For this listener, his piano playing is far more important and absorbing than his conducting. For a time, I thought that the piano's severe exigencies would yield to the very different musculature of conducting, but not so. As a pianist, Barenboim continues to grow and prosper.

In the last decade, Barenboim still gives piano recitals at times, most recently, as of this writing, the complete Beethoven Sonatas at Carnegie Hall, but his work as a famous orchestral and operatic conductor has taken first place in his hectic schedule. His development as a conductor is immense. He was married to the late cellist Jacqueline DuPres. His memoirs have been published.

ALINE VAN BARENTZEN

1897–1981—France

An influential pianist and teacher. She had a varied training with Heinrich Barth, Leschetizky, and Marguerite Long. She was professor of piano at the Paris Conservatoire from 1957 until 1967. Many well-known pianists worked with her, including Jean-Philippe Collard. Barentzen has the distinction of being the first to have recorded Falla's *Nights in the Gardens of Spain,* with Alfredo Casella conducting.

SIMON BARÈRE

1896–1951—Russia

He was born in Odessa, the birthplace of many musicians. Barère died backstage after a heart attack while performing the first movement of the Grieg Concerto at Carnegie Hall with Ormandy and the Philadelphia Orchestra. Glazunov exclaimed, "Barère is an Anton Rubinstein in one hand and a Liszt in the other." He studied with Essipova and Blumenfeld. Barère had one of the sleekest techniques of the twentieth century, casually tossing off the most breathtaking technical feats. When the music was right for him, and when it was difficult enough, he could make the listener's hair stand on end, playing in the grand manner with color and daring. At his worst, he was enamored of his own prowess, crass, or verging on vulgarity. Barère equated tempo with speed itself; he was happy playing fast, but he was never a musical moron—he was born with an unusual nervous system. A true Romantic, he performed according to whim and mood. He played the grandiose side of Liszt marvelously, and his recording of the Sonata is fabulous, as are the *Funérailles, Rhapsodie espagnole,* and *Don Juan* Fantasy, each one tremendous in scope, color, and verve. His recordings of the Scriabin D-sharp minor Etude and the Etude for the Left Hand by Blumenfeld and many smaller works are played with swagger and a luscious sound.

His most celebrated interpretation, one that has become legendary in pianistic circles, is his spine-tingling *Islamey* of Balakirev. And to hear a double-note technique that will raise eyebrows, listen to Barère's Schumann Toccata. The writer Guy Murchie, in his book *The Seven Mysteries of Life,* calculated that "Barère plays Schumann's C major Toccata with its 6,266 consecutive notes in 4.20 at the astonishing average pace of better than twenty-four notes per second, which is slightly faster than the standard speed of movie frames that flash on the screen to create a nonflickering illusion of continuous motion."

DAVID BAR-ILLAN

b. 1930–2003—Israel

He had a large concerto repertoire, never fearing to play the lesser-known score. He played the Robert Starer Concerto, recorded a joyous performance of the Moszkowski E major Concerto, performed the Prokofiev Concerto for Left Hand Alone, and the Tchaikovsky Second. His high-gear virtuosity is often glittering, as in the Liszt *Mephisto Waltz* and B minor Ballade. His tempi are often very fast, his pedaling economical. His Beethoven *Waldstein* Sonata is vital and clipped, his Weber A-flat Sonata delightful throughout. Unfortunately, he has recorded too little, given the quality of his bracing, forthright talent.

Always engrossed in politics, Bar-Illan became editor of the *Jerusalem Post* in the late 1980s, all but leaving his musical career. During Benjamin

Netanyahu's tenure as premier of Israel, the pianist became one of his chief advisors.

KARL HEINRICH BARTH
1847–1923—Germany

He studied with Reinecke and Tausig, and had successful tours as a pianist in Germany and England; later he became an important teacher in Berlin. He taught Arthur Rubinstein without a fee. Rubinstein wrote: "Professor Barth was a formidable personality. . . . I was terrified by him. Nobody before had inspired so much fear in me as this sixty-year-old man. . . . He wanted to improve my sight-reading. At first I was indignant, but now, after all these years, I am able to appreciate, with deep gratitude, how nobly he sacrificed so much of his own free time."

ETHEL BARTLETT
1900–1978—England

A student at the Royal Academy with Tobias Matthay, and later with Artur Schnabel, she made her London debut in 1916. After her marriage to Rae Robertson (1893–1956), also a Matthay student, the couple devoted themselves to the literature of two pianos, having much success as a duo-piano team.

TZIMON BARTO
b. 1964—United States

Barto has a dazzling command of the piano and has performed with great success, mostly in Europe, recording a variety of music, from the Rachmaninoff Third and Bartók Second piano concertos, played in a recklessly flamboyant manner, to the Chopin Preludes and Gershwin's *Rhapsody in Blue*. Barto's playing displays a Romantic temperament that is both fascinating and willful.

BÉLA BARTÓK
1881–1945—Hungary

The greatest Hungarian composer of the twentieth century studied piano with Liszt's pupil István Thomán. Bartók came in second to Wilhelm Backhaus in the 1905 Anton Rubinstein Competition. He was a most original pianist, whose unusual freedom of conception and metrics can be heard on his complete recordings released in Hungary in 1981. Bartók's performances of such pieces as Scarlatti sonatas, the B minor Capriccio of Brahms, and his own music show a totally different kind of artistry from the usual percussive playing that passes for "Bartók." His lavish rubato and his beautiful singing tone, coupled with an elegant virtuoso mechanism, identify him as a pianist from the late-Romantic age, whose interpretations were never bound by the printed page. It is noteworthy that Bartók, as late as the 1930s, played "historical" recitals of the piano literature in Budapest, and that throughout his career he never taught composition, only piano.

When I asked György Sándor, who studied with Bartók for four years, about his playing, the pianist replied: "He was technically a virtuoso on the level of Prokofiev, Dohnányi, Rachmaninoff, and Busoni. And as an interpreter, there are no words to describe the fusion of his world with that of the composers he played. Sequences of notes were turned into richly expressive melodies; harmonies and chords were bursting with tension or brought soothing relief. His rhythms danced with grace or angularity. His Scarlatti, Bach, Mozart, Beethoven, and Debussy were highly personalized and filled with the spirit and pulsating life of the creative instinct."

In the little volume *Conversations with Klemperer* by Peter Heyworth, Klemperer says, "I conducted Bartók's Second Piano Concerto in Vienna with him as soloist. That was a great experience for me. He was a wonderful pianist and musician. The beauty of his tone, the energy and lightness in his playing were unforgettable. It was almost painfully beautiful. He played with great freedom and that was what was so wonderful. He was a strange man—very reserved, very shy, but very sympathetic."

Cecil Gray said, "Béla Bartók was completely inhuman. He hardly existed as a personality, but his impersonality was tremendous—he was the living incarnation and embodiment of the spirit of music. He was pure spirit, in fact, and his frail, intense, and delicate physique gave the impression of something ethereal and disembodied, like a flame burning in oxygen."

Bartók made intriguing editions of Mozart sonatas and the Bach *Well-Tempered Clavier*.

DMITRI BASHKIROV

b. 1931—USSR

He was a student of Alexander Goldenweiser at the Moscow Conservatory. Bashkirov won the Grand Prix at the Marguerite Long Competition in Paris in 1955. He has performed in more than thirty countries. At its best, his playing exhibits a vigorous, intense approach to Schumann, Debussy, Rachmaninoff, and Scriabin. He has recorded a great deal, including Rodion Shchedrin's volatile Piano Sonata and a rhythmically vital Brahms Second Sonata. Since leaving Russia,

Bashkirov has lived in Madrid, where his piano teaching is in heavy demand. He also continues to perform and gives master classes in Europe and America.

EDMUND BATTERSBY

b. 1949—United States

Battersby is a sensitive artist who plays a varied repertoire that includes such pieces as the *Goyescas* of Granados, which he has recorded in a suave and lyrical manner. His disc of Rachmaninoff Preludes and *Etudes-tableaux* avoids the vulgarity which mars so many performances of the Russian master's works. Not to be missed are Battersby's recordings of Schumann and Chopin on early pianos: here the pianist shows his delight and knowledge in the timbres of these instruments. He teaches at Indiana University.

HAROLD BAUER

1873–1951—England

He began musical life as a violinist, but the urge to be a pianist proved irresistible. At the age of twenty he officially changed instruments. By 1900, he was making an American debut with the Brahms D minor Concerto. He obviously did things his way and was always an iconoclast. He wrote: "Because our ancestors were brought up to study the piano a certain way . . . along . . . rigid lines does not mean there are no better, broader, less limited ways of reaching the goals we seek. The only technical study of any kind I have ever done has been that technique which has had an immediate relation to the musical message of the piece I have been studying."

Harold Bauer by David Dubal

in Chopin's Berceuse the pianist refuses to coo and swoon, and in Debussy's *Rêverie* one still hears the lustrous tone that was much remarked upon and compared to Paderewski's.

Bauer gave many premieres, including Debussy's *Children's Corner Suite,* and Ravel dedicated his impressionist miracle, *Ondine,* to him. His many provocative but unscholarly editions of Schumann are now controversial and are seldom used today.

YELENA BECKMAN-SHCHERBINA
1881–1951—Russia

A student of Nikolai Zverev, as were Rachmaninoff and Scriabin. She entered the Moscow Conservatory to study with Paul Pabst. After his death in 1897 she worked with Vassily Safonov and graduated with the coveted Gold Medal. After meeting Scriabin, she began giving performances of his music. In 1913 Debussy was conducting in Moscow, and a meeting spurred her on to acquaint Russian audiences with the French master. She became an advocate of Ravel and Albéniz. A fine chamber player, with Piatigorsky and the violinist Lev Tseytlin she gave the first performance of Ravel's 1913 Piano Trio in Moscow in 1921. She was a pioneer in performing on radio, and in 1940 she became a professor at the Moscow Conservatory. She was not quite a virtuoso, but her playing of smaller works is filled with pleasurable moments and individual turns of phrase. The Meloyda label, vol. II (Russian Piano School), gives us twenty-two tasty treats, such as Arensky's F-sharp Prelude, Rubinstein's A minor *Barcarolle,* the Aliabiev-Liszt *Nightingale,* and best of all, the Scriabin Waltz Op. 38 and a particularly fine Glinka-Balakirev *The Lark.*

Bauer was a Romantic pianist, but with few of the mannerisms of his era. He was always dignified and mellow; grand surges and cavernous sounds were not his style. But he still had the Romantic's notion that the text is not sacred. After a performance of Franck's Prelude, Chorale, and Fugue, a listener showed up backstage telling the pianist, "I am glad to see that you play all the notes in that passage in the bass. So many pianists blur them." Bauer replied, "My dear sir, I didn't play them at all. I purposely leave them out. The passage sounds better that way."

In 1939, while still in fine technical fettle, Bauer recorded some small pieces, as well as one of his specialties, the Brahms F minor Sonata. In it, Bauer shows himself a stalwart and impressive molder of form, kindled by a warm and mature passion. His renderings of sonatas by Scarlatti and of Handel's *Harmonious Blacksmith* are merely pretty; but

LUDWIG VAN BEETHOVEN
1770–1827—Germany

Beethoven spent his first twenty-two years in his birthplace, Bonn, a town of fewer than ten thousand, yet with a rich musical and literary life. Beethoven's father was a minor singer at court, and had an alcohol problem; his mother was sensitive, shy, and quiet. Beethoven's father tried to exploit the boy's talent, hoping to produce a second Mozart. Although Beethoven was a prodigy, his development was too slow to bring in the hoped-for financial results. But his father kept the young boy practicing, "stupendously," as Beethoven later put it, mostly past midnight after his father woke him from a deep sleep. All was not bleak, however, and the boy was fortunate enough to come under the tutelage of an excellent and sensitive musician, Christian Gottlob Neefe, who instructed him in several instruments. The young Beethoven soon joined the court orchestra and was appointed court organist, his first paying job. Equally important, Neefe nurtured him on Bach's *Well-Tempered Clavier,* which he supposedly played from memory by the age of twelve. Only the most cultivated connoisseurs even knew, much less cared for, the "old Bach's" masterpiece. Actually, Beethoven had to learn it from a copy of the manuscript, since *The Well-Tempered Clavier* was not published until 1801.

The first important mention of Beethoven's musical gifts appeared in a magazine of the time: "Louis van Beethoven, a child of eleven, plays the clavier very skillfully, and with power, reads at sight very well, and . . . he plays chiefly *The Well-Tempered Clavier* of Sebastian Bach. . . . Whoever knows this collection of preludes and fugues in all the keys—which might almost be called the non plus ultra of our art—will know what this means. Herr Neefe is now training him in composition. . . . If he goes on as he has begun, he will certainly become a second Mozart."

In the next few years, Beethoven composed a great deal. By 1786, the sixteen-year-old musician was traveling to Vienna, where he played for the thirty-year-old Mozart, whom he revered above all others. Mozart was impressed, telling friends, "Keep your eyes on him; some day he will make a noise in the world."

Beethoven's piano playing attracted considerable attention during his late teen years. Carl Junker, a Bonn musician, tells us, "I have heard the abbé Vogler on the pianoforte by the hour and never failed to wonder at his astonishing execution; but Beethoven, in addition to the execution, has greater clearness and weight of ideas and more expression. In short, he is more for the heart."

But Bonn was too small for Beethoven's talents and, in 1792, he moved to Vienna, where he lived the rest of his life. It was as a pianist that Beethoven gained admittance to the great houses of Vienna's cultured and musically proficient aristocracy. And there had never been a pianist with such power and energy, although many of his compositions seemed wild to his contemporaries. The pianist Johann Tomáschek heard him in Prague in 1798, calling him "the giant among pianoforte players. . . . He played his C major Concerto (No. 1), the Adagio and Rondo grazioso from the Sonata in A, Op. 2, No. 2, and extemporized on a theme from Mozart's *Clemenza di Tito.* His grand style of playing, and especially his bold improvisation, had an extraordinary effect upon me. I felt so shaken that for several days I could not bring myself to touch the piano."

Beethoven lived during the final years of public improvisation. All pianists were expected to be able to improvise, and for the public it was often the most enjoyable part of the concert. His student Ferdinand Ries wrote of his extempore playing that "no artist that I ever heard came at all near the heights which Beethoven attained—the wealth of ideas which forced themselves on him, the caprices to which he surrendered himself, the variety of treatment, the difficulties, were inexhaustible."

But Czerny found that "extraordinary as his extempore playing was, it was less successful in the performance of printed compositions; for, since he never took the time or had the patience to practice anything, his success depended mostly on chance and mood. . . . But when Beethoven was in practice, no one equaled him, not even Hummel, in rapidity of scale passages, trills, leaps, etc."

In extempore playing, he had only two rivals, Hummel and Joseph Wölfl. Beethoven had previously demolished a number of pianists who had come through Vienna. Wölfl, however, several years younger than Beethoven, was a worthy opponent, of whom Beethoven's pupil Ignaz von Seyfried wrote: "Nature had been particularly kind in bestowing upon him a gigantic hand which could span a tenth [obviously a rarity then] as easily as other hands compass an octave, and permitted him to play double-notes . . . with the rapidity of lightning. . . . The combats of the two athletes not infrequently offered an indescribable artistic treat to the numerous and thoroughly select gathering. . . . In his improvisations Beethoven was transported above all earthly things—his spirit had burst all restraining bonds . . . triumphing over transitory terrestrial sufferings."

Wölfl himself was overwhelmed by Beethoven and later dedicated a sonata to him. This meeting took place around 1799, the period of the *Pathétique* Sonata. Beethoven's playing was now becoming distinct from the Classic poise of the Mozart school. During his so-called middle period, he continued to perform; his playing was often sloppy, but possessed a revolutionary and powerful emotionality never before dreamed of in piano playing. Beethoven was already asking Viennese piano makers for sturdier instruments that would withstand his force. He was delighted with a new Erard sent by the firm as a gift in 1803.

Not everyone was impressed with his playing, however. Cherubini called it "rough," and Clementi felt it lacked polish, but admitted "it was always full of spirit."

During the first decade of the nineteenth century, with his hearing deserting him, Beethoven still continued to perform in public. He premiered all of his Piano Concerti, except for No. 5. In 1808 he played the first performance of his Fourth Concerto at a concert that also included first performances of the Fifth and Sixth Symphonies and the Choral Fantasy, as well as movements from his C major Mass and the concert aria "Ah! perfido." (Has there ever been such a concert since?) "He played with astounding cleverness and in the fastest possible tempi," J. F. Reichardt wrote. "The Adagio, a masterly movement of beautifully developed song, he sang on his instrument with a profound melancholy that thrilled me."

During the following years, Beethoven's depression deepened as his hearing loss grew, making his playing often incoherent. In 1815 the celebrated violinist Ludwig Spohr heard him: "Of the former so admired excellence of the virtuoso scarcely anything was left in consequence of his deafness. In forte passages, the poor deaf man hammered in such a way that entire groups of notes were inaudible. . . . I felt moved with the deepest sorrow at such a destiny. . . . Beethoven's almost continual melancholy was no longer a riddle to me now."

Around 1817, the Broadwood piano makers of London had sent Beethoven their newest instrument. It was the most powerful and loudest piano built at the time. Beethoven, in his feeble attempt to hear the sounds in his mind, played on it with a new relish, battering it out of shape. In thanking the Broadwood firm, he wrote, "I shall regard it as an altar upon which I shall place the most beautiful offerings of my spirit to the divine Apollo." Indeed, during this period, he worked on his late sonatas with a new enthusiasm, although he was forever complaining that the piano as

Ludwig van Beethoven by David Dubal

imaginations. The opulent-sounding modern grand is a far more homogenized instrument than perhaps Beethoven would have wanted.

Wilfrid Mellers argues, in *Beethoven and the Voice of God*:

> Nowadays Beethoven's piano music is usually played on large concert grands, and no one feels this needs justification, since the modern piano is regarded as the fulfillment of Beethoven's pianistic aspirations. There is a sense in which it is true that the *Hammerklavier* Sonata encouraged the development of an instrument capable of supporting its level of dynamic intensity; one cannot on the other hand assume that the instrument appropriate to mature Liszt and later nineteenth-century composers is the instrument Beethoven envisaged, and there is some reason to think that the fortepianos of Beethoven's day, however inadequate to the idealities of sound in Beethoven's head, approximate to those idealities more closely than do modern instruments.

an instrument was now inadequate for him. Beethoven had grown completely inward, and his music became an idealization as no other composer's had ever been.

If he was not pleased at being harnessed to the pianos of his day, still one wonders if the "modern" pianos of Bechstein, Steinway, Bösendorfer, Blüthner, and Erard, developed after 1850, would have come closer to his tonal dreams. Today the idea of obsolescence in musical instruments is fast vanishing. The Viennese Classical grand piano was a perfect instrument in itself, quite different from the modern concert grand. It was the diaphanous elasticity of these pianos that had aroused the ears of Haydn, Mozart, Hummel, Czerny, Beethoven, and Schubert. They loved the instruments for their transparency, the crisp and grainy sounds they were capable of achieving. In reality, the sound of the harpsichords of their youth lingered in their sonorous

Listening to or playing Beethoven on a fine fortepiano may well be an ear-opening experience, one that might alter a musician's way of thinking about Beethoven. Mellers tells of hearing Paul Badura-Skoda play the *Moonlight* Sonata on an 1815 Broadwood: "The Presto finale provides, on the Broadwood, the biggest surprise, for it sounds far more tempestuously terrifying than on any modern instrument, even though its dynamic level may be lower." Of a performance of the *Appassionata* Sonata on a Viennese Graf piano, Mellers discloses: "Only after I had heard this recording did I realize how startling to contemporary audiences the work must have been. Moreover, on this instrument it startles us today, as though we were hearing it for the first time: the deep arpeggios are more cavernous, the hammerbeats more minatory, the thickly syncopated chords more shattering, the arpeggios more lacerating, than on a modern grand, the big rich tone of which rounds off the corners, sacrificing bite and edge to volume."

If Mozart was practically lost to the nineteenth century, Beethoven was its chief obsession. Two early advocates, Czerny and Moscheles, mastered his Opus 13, the *Sonate pathétique*, by their tenth year. As interest in personal interpretation in performance grew, Beethoven's music became the backbone of the repertoire. The great interpreters of his Piano Sonatas would be Mendelssohn, Liszt, Clara Schumann, Anton Rubinstein, von Bülow, Sir Charles Hallé, Arabella Godard, d'Albert, Busoni, and, finally, Schnabel, who, in the 1930s, furthered the worldwide dissemination of the Sonatas with his recordings of the complete set. This process of dissemination took roughly one hundred years after Beethoven's death to accomplish. "The essence of Beethoven," writes Louis Kentner, "perhaps the greatest artist ever produced by civilization, lies distilled in the piano sonatas."

The Sonatas, Variations, and Concerti form one of the great creative documents of the ages; their humanity and breadth are perpetual challenges for the creative listener, as well as the player. That Beethoven put at the command of one individual—the pianist—the greatest that music can offer is a blessing that has been appreciated by all serious pianists in every generation since.

ANNA CAROLINE DE BELLEVILLE-OURY
1808–1880—Germany

She studied with Czerny for four years and toured Europe and Russia. Often compared to Clara Wieck, Schumann himself declared, "Belleville is a poetess; Clara is poetry itself."

She settled in London, making a debut there in 1831. She was one of the first to perform Chopin in England. In 1830, Chopin himself reported that "Mlle Belleville played my Variations Op. 2 in Vienna."

Twelve years later, nearing his first trip to London, Chopin sent her a present of the Waltz in F minor, Op. 70, No. 2, published posthumously, and told Belleville: "I would not like it to be made public. What I should like, however, would be to hear you play it, Madame, and to be present where you interpret all the great composers like Mozart, Beethoven and Hummel. Hummel's *Adagio*, which I heard you play at Erard's in Paris some years ago, still rings in my ears . . . few piano performances can make me forget the pleasure of having heard you that evening."

After 1846 she seldom appeared in public but continued to compose nearly two hundred pieces, most of them horribly cloying in sentiment. She wrote a *Bridal Polka*, a *Sunshine Valse*, and dozens of works based on operas, all very lucrative.

FRANZ BENDEL
1833–1874—Czechoslovakia

He studied in Prague probably with Joseph Proksch, and later in Weimar with Liszt. Acclaimed as a superb pianist, he toured extensively. From 1862 he lived in Berlin and taught at Kullak's famed academy. Bendel left over 120 opus numbers, including piano pieces, chamber music, and a piano concerto. Some of the piano music is fascinating, and his *Improvisations*, as he called them, on Wagner, Gounod, Verdi, Brahms, and others are rewarding in their liquid pianism and delightful flow. Bendel's original pieces, such as *Sakontala* and the *Idylle*, are also of real interest, and the *Etude Héroique*,

Op. 27, in B-flat minor, is a treacherous work in sixths of enormous effectiveness.

LUDWIG BERGER

1777–1839—Germany

A pupil of Clementi, Berger was a good pianist and a teacher of renown. His students included Felix and Fanny Mendelssohn, Henselt, and Heinrich Dorn. He composed a large quantity of music; a set of twenty-seven Etudes has exceptional merit. Frederick Marvin has recorded Berger's half-hour Grand Sonata, Op. 7, from 1815, a work exhibiting the *sturm und drang* of the period.

OSCAR BERINGER

1844–1922—England

He studied under Moscheles and Tausig. In 1882 he gave the first English performance of the Brahms Second Piano Concerto, and in 1895 became professor at the Royal Academy of Music in London. Beringer wrote a memoir in 1907, *Fifty Years' Experience of Pianoforte Teaching and Playing*.

CHARLES WILFRID DE BÉRIOT

1833–1914—France

The son of two of the greatest performers of the early nineteenth century, the violinist Charles-Auguste de Bériot and the legendary mezzo-soprano María Malibran. De Bériot was considered a superior pianist, wrote well for the instrument, and taught at the Paris Conservatoire from 1887 to 1903. At the conservatoire his students included Ravel, Ricardo Viñes, Joaquin Maláts, and Granados. Viñes played de Bériot's Second Piano Concerto at his Paris debut.

BORIS BERMAN

b. 1948—USSR

A brilliant pianist born in Moscow. Berman performs frequently and teaches at Yale University. He has a large repertoire but is best known for his Prokofiev interpretations. On Chandos he has recorded the complete sonatas of Prokofofiev and the Concertos Nos. 1, 4, and 5 with Jarvi conducting the Concertgebouw. Worth investigating is his recording of Schnittke's Three Sonatas. Berman has written a book, *Notes from the Pianist's Bench*.

LAZAR BERMAN

b. 1930—USSR

He was a pupil of Goldenweiser and won prizes in several competitions. In 1976, when the craze for Russian performers in the United States was at its peak, Berman, a spiritual descendant of Anton Rubinstein, who created the Russian mystique, made his American debut. Berman had become known through his recordings of the Liszt *Transcendental Etudes*—thrilling performances filled with a highly charged Romanticism. Indeed, never had the *Etudes* been played with such aplomb. Unfortunately, Berman's public performances have been disappointing, often wildly inconsistent; sometimes his playing is just shoddy, at other times he sounds like an automaton. Listening to a Prokofiev Eighth Sonata was an ordeal. But as more recordings were released, I realized that this artist does his best work before the microphones, though he never equaled those early recordings of the *Transcendental Etudes*, Rachmaninoff's complete *Moments musicaux*, or Scriabin's Fantasy. Berman has made records of the Rachmaninoff Third Concerto, Liszt's *Years of Pilgrimage*, and even Clementi's B minor Sonata, which offer playing of musical value, but without that added richness and excitement which were so apparent on the recordings early in his career.

LEONARD BERNSTEIN
1918–1990—United States

The celebrated conductor-composer was also an expert and dynamic pianist in a rather wide repertory. He studied piano with Helen Coates, Heinrich Gebhard, and Isabelle Vengerova. His recording of the Copland Sonata is exhilarating but subtle. His rendering of the Gershwin *Rhapsody in Blue* has an irresistible tang, played with swing, heart, and abandon; and he was born to play the Shostakovich Concerto No. 2. Bernstein also made excellent recordings of Mozart's Fifteenth Concerto and the Ravel concerto.

Bernstein's Symphony No. 2 for Piano and Orchestra, *The Age of Anxiety*, is a remarkable synthesis of jazz and the symphonic form.

MICHEL BÉROFF
b. 1950—France

A pianist of skill and refinement. The French literature suits him best, and his Debussy

performances, especially the Preludes and Etudes, are a pleasure to hear. He has recorded with minute care Messiaen's monumental *Vingt Regards sur l'Enfant Jesus*.

HENRI BERTINI
1798–1876—England

Considered a superb pianist, he began touring at the age of twelve, and later settled in Paris. He is best known for his excellent Piano Studies. On an occasion in 1840, Belleville-Oury and Liszt played a duet of Bertini's.

MARIE BIGOT
1786–1820—Germany

A remarkable pianist whom both Haydn and Beethoven respected. Beethoven was believed to have said to her, "That is not exactly the reading I should have given, but go on. If it is not quite myself, it is something better." She reputedly played the *Appassionata* at sight from the manuscript. After 1809 she settled in Paris, where her salon was musically sophisticated. On Mendelssohn's visit to Paris, the seven-year-old prodigy took a few lessons from her.

MALCOLM BILSON
b. 1935—United States

A pianist and teacher who, in recent years, has become one the best-known advocates of the fortepiano. He has given successful and enlightening classes on the early piano, and his playing of Mozart concertos and sonatas, as well as of some Haydn and Beethoven sonatas, reveals a sensitive musician who is technically adroit, and who is not only a scholar but a passionate performer, with fire and a command of style and form.

MALCOLM BINNS
b. 1936—England

A pupil at London's Royal College. Over the years he has performed under important conductors such as Colin Davis and Pierre Boulez. He has recorded a great deal, including Beethoven's thirty-two Sonatas on period instruments. He has contributed recordings of worthy and lesser-known scores, including the Four Concertos by William Sterndale Bennett, with some stylish playing. Perhaps his finest achievement on disc is the dark and dense *Sonata minacciosa,* Op. 53, No. 2 by Nicolai Medtner.

IDIL BIRET
b. 1941—Turkey

As a child she was encouraged by Nadia Boulanger. At the Paris Conservatoire she worked with Jean Doyen. She graduated at the age of fifteen and continued studies with Cortot and Kempff. From age sixteen she has played worldwide, including tours of Japan and Russia. Biret's discography is well worth serious investigation, including Scriabin's Tenth Sonata, Boulez's Second Sonata, works of Kempff, the Second and Third Sonatas of Miaskovsky, Liszt's important transcriptions of the Nine Symphonies. For Naxos she has recorded the complete piano music of Chopin, some of it lacking poetic style. A valuable record is her *Symphonie Fantastique* of Berlioz

in Liszt's arrangement, which is also fun to hear. As a transcription it is quite literal, but as Charles Rosen says, "Bar by bar, it is also one of the most imaginative conceptions of keyboard writing of the entire nineteenth century." Biret plays it with flair. Also worth locating are her Berg Sonata and a remarkable and very flexible Ravel *Gaspard de la nuit.* Biret is a pianist of piercing intelligence; she commands a big style and technique, and at her best unveils a large-scale formal ability often with a sense of drama and rhetoric.

HANS BISCHOFF
1852–1889—Germany

Studied with Theodor Kullak. He was a pianist, teacher, and scholar of repute. His Bach editions are still used frequently.

MARIE LEOPOLDINE BLAHETKA
1811–1887—Germany

A well-known pianist and a composer who studied with Moscheles and Kalkbrenner. Her *Konzertstück* for Piano and Orchestra, Op. 25, was her best-known composition.

JACQUELINE BLANCARD
b. 1909—France

She studied with Isidor Philipp. Her career has taken her throughout the world. In 1938, she was the first to record the Ravel Left Hand Concerto, with Munch conducting. In 1948, she performed three Mozart concertos for her American debut at Town Hall. Blancard recorded a selection of Debussy etudes in the thirties, and was beguiling in Mozart sonatas; especially fetching is the Sonata No. 17 in B-flat, K. 570.

ÉMILE-ROBERT BLANCHET
1877–1943—Switzerland

An esteemed pupil of Busoni in Weimar and Berlin. Busoni dedicated one of his *An die jugend* to him. His etudes and other larger works have pianistic and musical appeal with many piquant harmonic twists. Nyiregyházi recorded his *Au jardin du vieux serial*. Besides concertizing extensively, he taught at the Lausanne Conservatoire from 1904 to 1917, afterward settling in Paris. Besides his passion for music he exercised his love of mountain-climbing, being the first to climb some of the Alps' most difficult peaks, and wrote books on mountaineering.

JOSEPH BLOCH
b. 1917—United States

A pupil of Rudolph Ganz and Olga Samaroff, he made a New York debut at Town Hall in 1950, and has since had a distinguished career, playing on every continent. Bloch has recorded a variety of music and has given the American premieres of several concertos, such as the Karl Amadeus Hartmann and Albert Roussel. Pierian Recordings has brought out a splendid performance of the Benjamin Lees Concerto. Bloch was an honored member of the Juilliard faculty from 1948 to 1996.

MICHEL BLOCK
1937–2003—Belgium

A student of Beveridge Webster at Juilliard, Block received a special prize at the 1960 Chopin Competition in Warsaw. He is a pianist of considerable interest, with a large repertoire. His recordings include the *Iberia* of Albéniz, and his more recent recordings on Pro Piano, such as the complete *Novelletten* of Schumann, is highly original playing. For many years he taught at Indiana University, teaching such admirable pianists as Thomas Labé.

FANNIE BLOOMFIELD ZEISLER
1863–1927—Austria

Bloomfield Zeisler is one of the least known of the eminent "golden age" pianists. In her time she had an enormous career, and was the leading American woman pianist of her day. She disliked the acoustic recording process and died at the dawn of the electrical era of recording, leaving no examples of her art in either medium. However, she did make piano rolls for the Welte Mignon firm in 1908, 1912, and 1924. These little-known recordings went into oblivion by the early 1930s. Fortunately they have been excellently resurrected in a two-CD set by the Pierian Recording Society. These CDs include many shorter pieces and also present her in the Chopin *Funeral March* Sonata, and Beethoven's Sonata Opus 111. These recordings, even within the limitation of the piano roll process, give us a pianist of large technique and an emotional nature. Bloomfield Zeisler possessed the gift of immediate communication, and the listener cannot escape her powerful grasp. The ear and heart are mesmerized by a passionate musical intelligence. Although small in stature, she was reputed to have a gigantic, supercharged sound. The greatest piano connoisseur of his time, James Huneker first witnessed her in 1885 at her New York debut, writing, "She played Rubinstein's D minor Piano Concerto with such fire and brilliancy that the conductor and orchestra pantingly followed her impetuous lead."

Although born in Bielitz, Austria, her family immigrated to America in her early childhood. She studied in Chicago with Carl Wolfsohn and with the well-known theorist Bernhard Ziehn. A debut took place when she was eleven; the famed pianist Annette Essipova heard her in 1877 and recommended study with her husband, Theodor Leschetizky, in Vienna. As with so many others, Leschetizky's teaching would be the main influence of her life. By age twenty she began creating an international career, and soon was known as "The Sarah Bernhardt of the piano."

Diana Hallman wrote, "She became a widely publicized role model for two generations of young American musicians, many of them female. She was heard with Mahler, Nikisch, Seidl, Strauss, Thomas, Casals, and Kreisler." Her repertoire was large, and sprinkled with such novelties as Chabrier's *Bourrée fantastique*. She often programmed three concertos in Chicago's Orchestra Hall, such as the Mozart C minor, Chopin F minor, and Tchaikovsky B-flat minor Concertos. Her final concert took place in 1925 in Chicago, with the Schumann Concerto and the Chopin F minor.

Op. 17, and a Sonata-Fantasy, Op. 64, are highly romantic. He was the uncle of the pianist-teacher Heinrich Neuhaus and taught him, as well as Simon Barère, Maria Grinberg, and Vladimir Horowitz, who revered his memory.

FELICJA BLUMENTAL
1918–1991—Poland

She studied at the Warsaw Conservatory. During World War II, she went to Brazil, where she continued her career.

Villa-Lobos dedicated his Fifth Concerto to her, and she gave its world premiere. She recorded many albums, notably of neglected works, including concertos by Ries, Clementi, and Albéniz; Szymanowski's *Symphonie concertante*, Op. 60; and many more.

JAKOB BLUMENTHAL
1829–1908—Germany

He studied with Herz at the Paris Conservatoire and earlier with Bocklet in Vienna. After the revolution of 1848, he took refuge in England; he was one of the most popular musicians in London, becoming pianist to Queen Victoria. His piano music and songs were once well known.

FELIX BLUMENFELD
1863–1931—Russia

A student of Anton Rubinstein, Blumenfeld was a brilliant musician. His piano music is eminently playable; a set of Twenty-four Preludes,

HENRYK BOBÍNSKI
1861–1914—Poland

He toured successfully, playing a great deal in Russia. He also composed genre pieces, as well as two Piano Concertos, Opp. 8 and 12.

CARL MARIA VON BOCKLET
1801–1881—Czechoslovakia

A pianist who made a reputation as both performer and teacher. Beethoven had a high regard for him, and he knew Schubert personally; he was the first to bring Schubert's piano music to the public.

MARY LOUISE BOEHM
1928–2003—United States

Boehm worked with Casadesus and Gieseking. She has made recordings of neglected music, including that of Field, Hummel, Kalkbrenner, and Amy Beach, among others. Her recording of Amy Beach's difficult Piano Concerto in C-sharp minor shows her at her finest.

JORGE BOLET
1914–1990—Cuba

He attended the Curtis Institute and studied with David Saperton. In 1937 he won the Naumburg Award. Bolet was a pianist's pianist in the tradition of Godowsky, Hofmann, and Saperton; with Bolet, finesse and purity were the order of the evening. Each note must be in place; no effort was too insignificant. He spun iridescent webs of pianistic gold; cadenzas in colored sprays alighted from the keyboard. His passagework was matched and evenly threaded. His digital skills were prodigious, and he was capable of great tonal refinements. In concert he loved to charm audiences with his wonderful playing of fluff, such as the Weber-Godowsky *Invitation to the Dance.* Fluff it may be, but more dangerous for the pianist than a tightrope act. And how seriously he played these frivolous items. He loved Godowsky, having played for him as a youngster, when he was brought to him by his teacher, Saperton.

A Bolet recital told us that the piano has a luxuriant literature, full of challenge, adventure, amusements, and beauty for those willing to extend themselves without snobbery. Bolet could deliver all-"Ballade" programs — including Grieg's masterpiece, the Ballade in G minor, played with poignancy and playfulness. He played transcriptions of all types, such as Wagner's *Tannhäuser* Overture in Liszt's amazing reduction. Here was the piano in full regalia, appearing to accomplish orchestral miracles.

Bolet was often thought of as a Liszt pianist, and indeed he was at his most exciting with Liszt. His Liszt Sonata was serious and spacious. He was willing to take chances in public: he raged in the *Don Juan* Fantasy; in the *Dante Sonata* his thunder was unequaled; and when he was really in the mood (for Bolet was at times sadly out of the mood), he could truly be infernal. His sonority was suffocating. He played an enormous amount of Liszt, from the Concerti (his recordings are flabby) to the Etudes, the Ballade in B minor, the Twelfth Hungarian Rhapsody, many transcriptions, and the Six *Consolations,* where he delivered the last word in ultra-pianissimos. At times he became so caught up in his tinting that the playing became more prissy than delectable.

He was not at home in the formal gardens of Mozart, Haydn, or Beethoven. He glided through them with a smoothness or a ponderousness that missed all points of tension. He was better equipped for a little Schumann, a little Mendelssohn, and some Chopin, though the last often sounded superficial. His best Chopin playing was the Twenty-four Preludes.

In Brahms he could be clumsy, and in Reger's *Telemann* Variations he was tedious. He was always best when resurrecting some Romantic concerto, such as the Joseph Marx, or the Sgambati Concerto (which he recorded). During his prime, Bolet, on the platform, was the very picture of power, but he never quite managed to break through the barrier of recording. His records are always disappointing to one who has heard him onstage in the heat of battle. In his last several years, a desire to be profound and weighty marred many of these recordings, which as a result lack the stylishness of his earlier years, when his music-making had more happiness, naturalness, and flair. His recordings of the Tchaikovsky First and Rachmaninoff Second concertos are tired and humdrum throughout, and the same may be said of much Liszt playing, especially his recording of the *Transcendental Etudes,* which are earthbound.

JOÃO DOMINGOS BOMTEMPO
1775–1842—Portugal

The first Portuguese pianist of note; in 1833 he headed the Lisbon Conservatory.

ANTHONY DI BONAVENTURA
b. 1930—United States

A student of Isabelle Vengerova at the Curtis Institute. He was a soloist with the New York Philharmonic at the age of thirteen.

He commissioned works from Nono, Ligeti, Ginastera, Persichetti, and others. His recordings of Scarlatti sonatas and Debussy etudes are the products of a refined and sensitive musical mind.

JOHAN VAN BOOM
1807–1872—Netherlands

After piano studies with Hummel and Moscheles, he settled in Stockholm, where his playing was admired. He taught at the Stockholm Conservatory, wrote a piano method, and composed a sonata, as well as chamber works, with his instrument.

LEONTINE BORDES-PÈNE
1858–1924—France

A remarkable pianist who performed a great deal of new French music. Bordes-Pène was the pianist to Eugène Ysaÿe in the premiere of Franck's Violin Sonata, and Franck dedicated to her his *Prelude, Aria, and finale,* which she premiered in May 1888. She was also the dedicatee of d'Indy's *Symphony on a French Mountain Air,* which she introduced in 1886. Stricken with paralysis in 1890, Bordes-Pène moved to Rouen, where she taught.

ALEXANDER BOROVSKY
1889–1968—Latvia

A student of Annette Essipova at the St. Petersburg Conservatory. Borovsky won the gold medal at the conservatory, and in 1910 he placed high at the Rubinstein Competition. In the years to follow he acquired a fine reputation, regularly appearing in public and making many recordings; especially well-known were his pioneering discs of Liszt Rhapsodies. In 1941 Borovsky settled in the United States.

SERGEI BORTKIEWICZ
1877–1952—Russia

A student of Alfred Reisenauer, he played and taught throughout Europe. His etudes and four piano concertos are masterpieces of slick pianism in an idiom laced with Russian Orientalism. His best-known piece is the Etude in B-flat minor, Op. 16, recorded by Rosenthal.

LEONARD BORWICK
1868–1925—England

A pupil of Clara Schumann, Borwick became a well-known pianist, playing throughout Europe, America, and Australia. He was an early advocate of Debussy and Ravel, and he played the entire solo music of Brahms in 1923.

YURI BOUKOFF
b. 1923—Bulgaria

He studied with Yves Nat and Marguerite Long in Paris. Boukoff has had many tours and has recorded the nine Prokofiev Sonatas.

GEORGE BOYLE
1886–1948—Australia

He trained with Busoni. Boyle was considered a fine pianist. His Piano Concerto in D minor deserves to be revived. He composed a body of brilliant piano music, all of which is neglected.

JOHANNES BRAHMS
1833–1897—Germany

The great master from Hamburg was well-grounded from age seven in piano technique by his first teacher, Otto Cossel, and in 1843 he worked with the eminent teacher Eduard Marxsen. Within four years he emerged in public concerts. At age twenty, Brahms had his first encounter with Clara and Robert Schumann, who were at once entranced with his music and piano playing. Schumann exclaimed, "He is a player of genius who can make of the piano an orchestra of lamenting and loudly jubilant voices." Besides his own music Brahms performed a massive literature, including Bach's *Well-Tempered Clavier*, Toccatas, and the Chromatic Fantasy and Fugue, Beethoven's *Eroica* and *Diabelli* Variations, and Schumann's works in quantity, giving the premiere of Schumann's F minor Sonata. He premiered his own D minor and B-flat Concertos. Of the latter, the composer Dame Ethel Smyth noted, "The veins of his forehead stood out, his wonderful bright blue eyes became veiled and he seemed the incarnation of the restrained power in which his work is forged." By the premiere of the B-flat Concerto, Brahms was hardly practicing; the English composer Charles Villiers Stanford wrote: "But never since have I heard a rendering of the concerto, so complete in its outlook or so big in its interpretation. The wrong notes did not really matter, they did not disturb his hearers any more than himself. He took it for granted that the public knew that he had written the right notes, and did not worry himself over such little trifles as hitting the wrong ones."

At home Bach was his constant companion and deepest confidant, *The Well-Tempered Clavier* being always on his piano rack. "With this I rinse my mouth every morning," he said.

He had a fascination with piano technique, and in the Variations on a Theme of Paganini, Op. 35, he produced one of the most subtly difficult works in the literature. He left the first performance of these fiendish "etudes" to Carl Tausig. Ever since, they have been to pianists a touchstone of virtuosity. Later in his career, Brahms completed a volume of technical studies, which are not for performance but are immensely valuable as a key to the demands of his own music and which are seldom used.

ALEXANDER BRAILOWSKY

1896–1976—Russia

Brailowsky had an illustrious career from 1925 to 1965. Born in the Ukrainian capital of Kiev, he attended the Kiev Conservatory from childhood and worked with Vladimir Puchalsky, who would later teach Horowitz.

After graduation and the gold medal from the Kiev Conservatory, there would be further training in Vienna with Theodor Leschetizky, the most eminent teacher of the day. Brailowsky remarked, "The full value of Leschetizky's remarkably liberal teaching came to light only in later years." The war forced Brailowsky to Switzerland, and in Zürich he received some coaching with Busoni. After the war he moved to Paris, where Francis Planté gave the young pianist advice.

In 1919 he made a sensational Paris debut and a career proceeded. Almost from the beginning he was listened to by a large public and made his career in an age of giants such as Cortot, Backhaus, Friedman, Rachmaninoff, Gieseking, Paderewski, Hofmann, Horowitz, and Rubinstein. In 1923 he canceled his season, and returned to a cottage in the French Alps to realize his dream of learning Chopin's 170 compositions.

Late in 1924 he felt ready to undertake the great challenge, and at the Salle Pleyel in three weeks he gave six recitals encompassing the complete works of the Polish master. The timing was perfect and the twenty-eight-year-old pianist would never regret his labors. The series caused a furor; Chopin made Brailowsky famous, and he would repeat the cycle in the capitals of music over thirty times during his career; indeed he would become one of the most popular of all concert pianists. The public excited him; he said, "I am like a race horse in relation to my audience. The awareness of being the center of attraction for a large audience makes me exert myself to the utmost."

I well remember attending a Brailowsky recital at Columbus, Ohio. He presented a gigantic program: Hummel, lots of Chopin, Debussy, Prokofiev, and the Liszt Sonata. The playing was often ungraceful, percussive, tonally restricted, yet the audience of three thousand went wild. They were somehow deeply communicated to, and I've seldom heard such rapturous, instinctive reaction to any performer. For half a century Brailowsky repeated this phenomena the world over. Yes, Brailowsky had onstage an indefinable glamour.

There was no doubt there was definitely a disparity between the musical content of his recitals and recordings as against his wide appeal. Abram Chasins speculated upon this, writing, "This might appear strange in a man who has so little natural ease and affinity for his work, but it accounts for a sincerity, an enthusiasm, and kind of fierce intensity that carries genuine force and vast appeal. Brailowsky works harder at the keyboard than anyone else, but despite his hectic battles he gets through every time . . . It causes me to wonder whether some of his appeal may not derive from the kinship we feel for one who struggles as we all do in some way or other, from the pleasure we get when we witness a final victory over obvious difficulties." Chasins goes much too far in describing Brailowsky's lack of natural ease and affinity for his work. However, let's make it clear that he was a thorough-going professional, with a solid technical equipment which at times possessed brilliance. His interpretations often appear simplified, with little real imagination, lacking the fine frenzy, penetrating mood, and high temperament. I have talked to music lovers whose appreciation of the piano began with Brailowsky and later voted for more subtle interpretations.

In his book *The Great Pianists,* Harold Schonberg gives Brailowsky not even the honor of a sentence to acknowledge him only as one of Leschetizky's legion of pupils. However he cannot easily be dismissed and his recordings keep surfacing and piano lovers still talk of him luminously. BMG issued his two Chopin Concertos from 1949 and 1954. (He made the first recording ever of Chopin's Concerto No. 1 in 1928.) The pianist-critic Harris Goldsmith, speaking of the later readings of the concertos, thinks that "Brailowsky's energetically contoured, sharply etched clarity represents an emerging modernity of outlook that points to such present-day Chopin players as Garrick Ohlsson and Maurizio Pollini." For me, the most attractive Brailowsky is found in the four CDs from his 1928–34 Polydor Berlin Recordings brought out by Danacord. Here we have many examples of vigorous, finely tuned playing, as in Weber's perpetual motion and the Liszt *Gnomenreigen.*

In the Danacord Series he plays the celebrated octave section of the Liszt Sixth Rhapsody with red-blooded octaves and a Twelfth Rhapsody with many fine points. But best of all is the Liszt Concerto No. 1 recorded in 1928. Brailowsky here is loose and rhapsodic; indeed something happened to shake him free of wrong notes and his usual musical inhibition and limited dynamic range. There is rhetorical sweep, and a sound that Leschetizky himself would have applauded.

But let's have the distinguished critic Olin Downes have the last word on the indefinable alchemy Brailowksy possessed in public. This from a New York Carnegie Hall recital of 1925: "Mr. Brailowsky has a sheer instinct for the secrets of the piano. He knows intuitively the colors that the pedal can evoke; he summons a brilliancy in bravura and a liquid beauty of tone in singing passages which, while they have been cultivated, are inborn and can never be merely acquired. . . . He recreates his music with all the freshness of feeling and imagined beauty that it must have had for him when first the eyes fell on the printed page and straying fingers hinted at the wonders it contained."

LOUIS BRASSIN
1840–1884—Germany

An important teacher and pianist. He studied with Moscheles and taught Safonov, Sapellnikov, and Arthur de Greef. He wrote many piano pieces, and his transcription of Wagner's *Magic Fire Music* was often attempted.

RUDOLF BREITHAUPT

1873–1945—Germany

He was the apostle of relaxation in piano playing. A student at the Leipzig Conservatory and at the Stern Conservatory in Berlin, Breithaupt became one of the foremost authorities on piano playing during the early twentieth century. He had been deeply impressed with the playing of Teresa Carreño, who wrote that "the secret of power lies in relaxation; or, I might say power *is* relaxation."

In 1905 he wrote his book *School of Weight and Touch,* which was dedicated to Teresa Carreño and which exercised much influence on the piano teaching of the day. Schnabel called him "a very interesting, original, fascinating man."

ALFRED BRENDEL

b. 1931—Czechoslovakia

He studied with local teachers and in 1949 he received a fourth prize at the Busoni Competition in Bolzano, Italy. During the 1950s he made many recordings, including the first complete set of the Beethoven piano music. For this effort he was given the Grand Prix du Disque. His book, *Musical Thoughts and Afterthoughts*, appeared in 1976. Brendel has played the complete cycle of Beethoven sonatas in many of the world's major capitals, and in 1983 he was the first pianist since Schnabel to play all thirty-two at Carnegie Hall.

These recitals were the best Beethoven playing I have heard from him—intense and often moving; especially good were the earlier sonatas. The world now sees Brendel as one of its supreme Beethoven players. He has recorded the Sonatas twice; while both versions have points of interest, they are different in many respects. In the early set, there is a vital flow and an unself-consciousness that is absent from much of the sonically superior second version. The lightness and lyrical gracefulness of the first edition give way to some unaccountably awkward readings later on. Indeed, this early set contains some of the finest Beethoven ever recorded. The earlier Brendel Beethoven also had a sense of adventure. Nobody has ever played with more charm the marvelous opening of the B-flat Sonata, Op. 22. In it he captures the upward movement exquisitely; the same detail in the later version falls flat. Such points of comparison could be made throughout the Sonatas.

Yet if some naturalness is missing from the second recording, other qualities have deepened. There is more grit in the earlier *Appassionata*, for example, but his growing concern for line over color makes his late Beethoven more cerebral, less brooding. For this listener, his performances of the late sonatas are schoolmasterish—stiff, clipped, and well drilled. He spells out each phrase as if delivering a lecture. I find a kind of heart-chilling smugness in these late sonatas. Of the last five, he is most successful in the Opus 110, where the fugue flows smoothly. His Opus 111 is just too facile, and Opus 101 sounds academic and clumsy. His best readings are the Opus 2, No. 1; Opus 10, No. 2, in a delightful and humorous performance; and a well-thought-out Opus 7, with a beautiful slow movement. His *Moonlight* lacks sensuous appeal, but his *Waldstein* has a wonderful sense of space; his Opus 31, No. 1, has comic appeal.

His Beethoven concertos, as good as they are, achieve little that is new. No. 4 lacks a necessary mystery; No. 5—the *Emperor*—misses dramatic power. But his performances are well structured. I especially like Brendel's playing of some of the variations and small pieces. He is relaxed and takes some rhythmic leeway. But for this listener, his finest Beethoven is his live recording of the *Diabelli* Variations. Here his

Alfred Brendel by David Dubal

fingers and heart are joined in a mighty penetration of Beethoven's seething brain.

Brendel's Mozart is not nearly as interesting as his Beethoven. In the solo sonatas, he sounds airless and charmless. In his many concerto recordings, the playing is academic and much too dry; the magical melodies are square cut and understated. In the Haydn Sonatas, by contrast, Brendel plays with gusto, and he understands Haydn's kind of humor; unfortunately, however, his tone is often ugly.

Only recently has Brendel decided to accommodate Bach to the modern piano, on which his good sense of line brings out the clarity and precision of each voice. How different are his conclusions on the Bach Chromatic Fantasy and Fugue from Edwin Fischer's, with his propulsive Romanticism. (Brendel took some master classes from Fischer.)

It has been said that Brendel has become Schnabel's successor in Schubert, but the two have little in common. Schnabel's Schubert was vocal; Brendel's is far more symphonic, less passionate, and the sound far less beautiful. Brendel's Schubert paints no rustic landscape. It is a large, tight, sometimes militant Schubert. Many "pretty" passages are weeded out, and Brendel, intent on clarifying everything he possibly can, leaves little to suggestiveness.

Brendel's discography is large and filled with performances of Schumann and Brahms, which are all good, but which for me miss the deepest fire and poetry. His Brahms concertos are too straight and bony. His Schumann never reaches the heights. He is too cautious, too serious.

In his youth, Brendel recorded such works as Balakirev's *Islamey* and Stravinsky's *Petrouchka*, and some Chopin. He has been right to disregard this literature. Chopin is not suited to Brendel's temperament, and I cannot imagine him being convincing in a nocturne.

The Romantic composer most suited to Brendel is Liszt, a master he adores and promotes consistently. Brendel is not entirely born for this music because his technique is not quite large enough, not of the high virtuosity of an Argerich or Pollini. It is solid and highly functional, but it lacks, sadly, a real pianistic flexibility. Brendel can play loudly, but he is not a "big" pianist; moreover, he is always on guard against any extreme in his playing. However, he has been striving for the grand sweep and is now trying with all his heart and might to triumphantly "throw off" all restraint. This effort has sometimes been painfully apparent. In his recital of Liszt's *Years of Pilgrimage*, for example, I thought he manufactured an overblown style with an ugliness of tone and a lack of lyric freedom. The whole concert was a torture, full of hand flailing, gesticulating, and facial grimaces, with Brendel making a desperate attempt to release himself from the confines of his highly intellectual frame.

Brendel is commendably trying to merge his intellectual and theoretical bent with a more convincing emotionalization of the music. He wrote, "Feeling is the alpha and the omega of the musician, the point where music comes from and the point to which it has to return." This feeling, the swell of human emotion, has not been fully realized in his art. The analytic has clogged him up, and it is now at odds with his ever more urgent desire to simply let the music speak. It is in Liszt's music that he is making his main attempts at liberation, and his newest recordings give many signs of a great pianist. In his recording of later Liszt, he expresses the true elegiac sorrow of these sketches. In many other pieces, including the Sonata, the Fantasy and Fugue on the Name B-A-C-H, the *Legends*, and the *Bénédiction de Dieu dans la solitude*, there is Liszt playing of some impact.

Brendel is a complicated and important musician, and audiences respond to his playing. He is an artist of the highest motivation, who is deeply committed to the piano and its literature.

After many a season of not attending Alfred Brendel's annual New York recitals, I thought the time had come to hear him again. Of course, Brendel is a musical icon, one of the prime guardians of the Vienesse Classical masters.

Walking to Carnegie Hall, at the corner of Fifty-seventh Street, I stopped for a red light—the traffic noise was horrendous. A woman looked at me and said, "Our spiritual sanctuary is only across the street. Brendel will help us." Indeed, before the pianist appeared, one felt an unusual anticipation throughout the great hall, as expecting some relief and sustenance through a great artist.

In the passage of time, Brendel has aged with a golden glow surrounding his conceptions as an aura. The recital was loveliness personified. Swept away were the jarring moments, the stodgy and cramped passages, the tone too razor sharp. The concert bloomed with a vivacity of touch. He seemed to hold a special affection for the chosen compositions, and I marveled at how pliant his playing was;

he played beyond his instrument, tiny note scratches were meaningless. One palpably felt his attentive enjoyment shining through each piece. There was a confident brio that I had never heard from him.

An all-Mozart first half was rarified. The rather unknown, but important Fantasia in C Minor, K. 396, was rendered with an autumnal, gentle pathos pervading as an undercurrent. Two sonatas from Mozart's nineteenth year, K. 281 in B-flat and K. 282 in E-flat, skipped and sauntered lightly and blithely. One could feel the music promenading before the mind's eye, as Brendel provided provoking accents and touches of delicate jesting. The slow movement of the B-flat sonata, marked "amoroso," was of a rococo tenderness. Brendel's performance reminded me of the corporeal textures and half-tints of a Boucher painting, brought about through subtle pedaling.

After intermission the Viennese feast continued with Schubert's *Drei Klavierstücke*. I could almost feel the cool woods and see the verdant meadows. Again the musical aliveness was so visual that I was hearing the chattering of innocent souls in peasant garb.

Beethoven's Sonata No. 30, Op. 109, is one of the lofty shrines of sonata-variation writing. Brendel's audience appeared visibly moved by the grasp of a formidable interpretive architect, loving more than ever a work of art he has given to the public so many times during his performing life. I will not want to miss Brendel's recitals again.

YEFIM BRONFMAN
b. 1958—USSR

Born in Tashkent, in 1973 he emigrated to Israel, where he studied with Arie Vardi at the Rubin Academy in Tel Aviv. Later, at the Curtis Institute, he worked with Rudolf

Serkin. In 1982, Bronfman made a successful New York debut, and he has since had a worldwide career. He is a pianist of taste and power who is comfortable in many styles from Mozart to Prokofiev. His recording of Bartók's three Concerti won a Grammy Award.

JOHN BROWNING
1932–2003—United States

A student of Rosina Lhévinne at the Juilliard School. A winner of the Leventritt and other competitions, Browning is a perfect example of the eclectic American pianist, involved with many styles, brilliantly equipped both technically and intellectually. Indeed, few equal his level of preparation for a performance. Everything has been passed under the lens of a microscope. Browning knows exactly what he wants to do with every note.

He is gloriously suited to Ravel. Stravinsky called Ravel a Swiss clockmaker, and Browning loves each fine jewel; the Ravelian artifice glitters in his hands. The Left Hand Concerto soars, his *Tombeau de Couperin* is unrivaled, its Toccata golden and perfectly poised, the rhythmic formations breathtaking.

Browning's Prokofiev concertos are deservedly celebrated, and few can equal him in the Third Concerto, which has always been one of his best stage works. He has recorded a very fine Barber Sonata, and his disc of the Barber Concerto with Szell is a collaboration whose quality surpasses the work's actual value. Of other twentieth-century repertoire, there is a remarkable set of twenty-four neo-Romantic preludes by Richard Cumming which are impeccably played. Browning's Chopin Etudes are cold, but in his technical treatment few could match him.

In Schumann, he is rather prosaic. His early recording of the Beethoven *Diabelli* Variations is masterful, a truly epic conception. Lately he has turned to Liszt with a new respect and understanding. His playing of the Sonata is pianistic and coolly patrician. His Rachmaninoff, too, glitters with cold intensity, and his recording of the Second Sonata is calculated to its boiling point. Browning is first and always a superb craftsman, with an unusual fastidiousness, musically and technically, and there is no such thing as a messy Browning concert. Indeed, Browning is always an amazing marksman who considers wrong notes to be practically inadmissible if not sinful.

With Browning's death in January 2003, America lost its most consistent concert pianist. None of his generation performed nearly as many concerts a season. Indeed most of his contemporaries withdrew from the concert stage for various reasons. Ever since Browning won the 1955 Leventritt Competition, and the following season made his New York Philharmonic debut under Mitropoulos, he annually performed in all leading venues.

Samuel Barber wrote his piano concerto for him, which he premiered in 1962 at the opening of Philharmonic Hall (now Avery Fisher Hall) at Lincoln Center. Shortly after, Browning as soloist with George Szell and the Cleveland Orchestra commenced a major tour of the Soviet Union. In 1991 his recording of the Barber Concerto with Slatkin and the St. Louis Symphony won a Grammy Award. His last appearance took place in 2002 at Washington's National Gallery.

Browning's repertoire was enormous and always growing. His last recording was a healthy and bracing helping of Scarlatti sonatas. He could perform Schubert's posthumous A major Sonata with a panoramic flow, not thinking of Schumann's phrase "of a heavenly length." Browning was partial to Mozart concertos and sparkled in them. His Beethoven *Emperor* Concerto lived in a cold olympian region.

Browning was a patrician artist who could

deliver bravura, brilliance, and hard glitter. The overall evenness of his mechanism was extraordinary with a particularly clear, powerful, and penetrating left hand which never failed to chart the composition's harmonic movement. To achieve his high level of consistency he worked endlessly. Of his work method, he stated, "Many people practice with tunnel vision. They work on one little section for days and days—or they whiz through the whole composition quickly. I learn carefully, conscientiously observing every marking, so I don't have to undo bad habits. I then practice in a middle tempo, not too slow, which is the hardest tempo to practice in. When I feel more or less ready, I play the whole piece straight through, three times in the day, no matter what goes wrong. I try to achieve a large arc, which is what you have to do in a performance. You cannot stop and correct yourself when you are onstage."

Browning felt that "especially in America technical standards are going down, not up. This is probably because early training in this country is so often sloppy, appallingly bad. Very little repertoire is learned, and then at seventeen or eighteen they start pushing all of a sudden and by then it's too late to develop an even, clear technique. . . . The high incidence of tendinitis so prevalent today comes from tightness at the keyboard, forcing technique you don't have. It comes from straining."

KATHLEEN BRUCKSHAW
1877–1921—England

She made her debut at age twelve at the Crystal Palace with Anton Rubinstein's Fourth Piano Concerto. She also studied with Stavenhagen in Weimar for three years. After performances with the Berlin Philharmonic, she worked under Busoni. In 1914 she performed Busoni's massive Piano Concerto, with Sir Henry Wood conducting, at Queen's Hall. Bruckshaw composed a great deal of piano music, showing a definite gift for piano writing.

LEONID BRUMBERG
b. 1925—USSR

A student of Heinrich Neuhaus. He is a respected pianist and has recorded Romantic repertoire. He left the Soviet Union in 1981, and teaches at the Vienna Conservatory.

GORDON BRYAN
1895–1957—England

He studied with Oscar Beringer, and had some lessons with Percy Grainger. Bryan held a fine reputation; he performed a great deal in concerts, including chamber music. Bryan gave the first performances of music of Ernest Schelling, Arthur Bliss, and the Constant Lambert Sonata in London, 1929.

RICHARD BÜHLIG
1880–1952—United States

His early studies were in his native Chicago. From 1896 to 1900 he studied with Leschetizky in Vienna and made his official debut in Berlin, where Busoni was impressed. Later he dedicated the third version of his *Fantasia contrappuntistica* to Bühlig. In 1907 he returned to the United States and in the 1920s he made Los Angeles his home, teaching a great deal. Among his pupils were Henry Cowell, Alton

Jones, Earl Wild, and Leon Kirchner. His one commercial disc comes from private performances in 1938 which are preserved on CD on the Dante Label. On it are strangely interesting performances of the Beethoven Sonatas, Op. 106, Op. 109, the B major Prelude and Fugue, Book I of *The Well-Tempered Clavier,* and the Chromatic Fantasy and Fugue. Some of the playing sounds rickety, and rhythmical stability is not a strong point. But there are ideas, a striving for a serious truth, especially in the Sonata Op. 109, where he plays with "the tone that has no tone," as he described to writer Peter Yates. He made a transcription of Bach's *The Art of the Fugue* for solo piano.

HANS VON BÜLOW
1830–1894—Germany

He showed no sign of musical talent or interest until his ninth year. He was found to have an unusually fine ear, and was put under the direction of Friedrich Wieck, who was renowned for his teaching of his daughter Clara (Schumann). He later worked under Plaidy, an effective technique builder. To please his parents, he entered the University of Leipzig in 1848 to pursue a law career. But his attraction to music was too strong, and the newest German compositions fired him with the need to be part of that exciting moment in music history. After Liszt's celebrated first performances of Wagner's *Lohengrin* at Weimar, Bülow left law for good. The decisive influence of his life was knowing and studying with Liszt, who also taught him the rudiments of conducting. He became, with Tausig, the favorite pupil of Liszt's Weimar period (1848–60). Liszt loved him and deeply admired his musical gifts. Liszt said, "He has the most intimate insight into the music, as well as the nobility and perfection of beautiful style."

Liszt, who officially retired from the piano after 1847, gave Bülow the honor of playing the world premiere of his Sonata in B minor in Berlin in 1857. (During that concert Bülow also inaugurated the Bechstein concert grand for public performance.) It was also at that time that Bülow married Liszt's daughter Cosima. Their marriage dissolved in 1869, when she left him for Wagner. Bülow continued to be a passionate Wagnerite, however, and conducted the world premiere of *Tristan und Isolde* at Munich in 1869. He now indefatigably pursued concertizing, becoming the foremost German pianist of his time (Tausig died in 1871).

In 1875 the Chickering piano firm brought him to the United States, in emulation of Anton Rubinstein's 1872 tour for the Steinway piano. He played no fewer than 139 concerts in the New World, and gave the world premiere of Tchaikovsky's B-flat minor Concerto in Boston. (The score is dedicated to von Bülow.) It was an instant success there, and even more so when he performed it under Leopold Damrosch several weeks later in New York.

His career took place during the final stages of development of the piano-building art. Piano makers were in great competition with each other, and these firms did all they could to attract the best artists to their instruments. During Liszt's twelve years of whirlwind touring, he often played on pianos that no first-rate pianist today would deign to touch. But during the second half of the century, with an enormous increase in the public's musical education and the growing importance of musical interpretation, the piano's quality became of paramount concern to a pianist. Bülow was, to the public, the interpretive concert pianist *par excellence*.

In his letters to Carl Bechstein he constantly tells the manufacturer what an artist needs from an instrument. He called Bechstein the "piano pope" but could admonish him on the

Hans von Bülow by David Dubal

quality of his instruments. In 1866 he wrote to him, of a Bechstein, that "I endured tortures at the concert through its inelastic touch and its bad repetition. In short, I had to make superhuman efforts." Bechstein had a preference for softer-sounding instruments, and Bülow says: "You are growing very selfish—in making it sound soft and more pleasing to the audience you allow the individuality of the music and the player to go by the board. I was obliged suddenly to reject the interpretation of years and conform to the mood of the pianoforte action. Having made oneself master of the composition, one is to become the slave of the instrument! Much obliged!"

The last remark sums up the vexation of countless fine pianists during performance. Bülow was delighted with the American Chickerings put at his disposal during his American concerts, and rapturously wrote to his colleague Karl Klindworth: "I notice the most extraordinary transformation in myself. Whereas, before, I frequently played like a pig, I now occasionally play like a god. Chickering's gorgeous pianofortes—undeniably the best in both worlds—have made me into a first-rate pianist. Certainly I practice as I never did before."

Bülow's temperament was viewed as the opposite of Anton Rubinstein's animal magnetism. His interpretations were etched with a cold, scholarly intellect. He was often criticized for a lack of spontaneity and for being too analytic. In 1887 the composer Hugo Wolf wrote a scathing review, "Bülow—as Autopsist." Bülow was famous for his Beethoven and played all of the piano works from memory. But, Wolf objected,

unfortunately, he is on a rather strained footing with Beethoven. . . . Above all, he stands in awe of the living Beethoven. And so to get at him, he simply strikes him dead. . . . The corpse is carefully dissected, the organisms traced in their subtlest ramifications, the intestines examined with the zeal of a haruspex—the course in anatomy is under way. This dissected and sawn-up Beethoven belongs, however, in the conservatory, not in the concert hall. . . . Bülow gives the impression of one who would like to be a painter but can't get beyond anatomy. . . . The only gratifying thing about this Beethoven operation was the skill with which it was performed. Bülow's technical equipment is, indeed, astounding, his infallible knack of wounding or killing at the very first incision is absolutely hair-raising. But to breathe life and soul into the dead body he is utterly wanting in the requisite vaccine. He is merely a skilled surgeon. When Rubinstein and others deal roughly with the living Beethoven from time to time, and, carried away by their enthusiasm, give the mighty man a bloody nose, or do him some other injury, then Bülow is the man to mend the damage. None knows better than he how to patch and glue. This autopsist is forever directing his listeners' attention to liver and kidneys rather than to the pulsating heart.

Yet Bülow was by no means a pedant; his mission was to convey to an audience exactly what he felt the composer wanted to say, and he proceeded to burn the piano literature into the public's consciousness. He was well aware of his intellectuality, which indeed at times made him sound detached or icy. He was also aware that he was viewed as the prototype of the heavy-handed "serious" German school of piano playing. After an all-Liszt recital he wrote, "I played coldly and intellectually. . . . Berlin's chilling atmosphere and the animosity towards me which it engenders have always dried up my inner warmth, so that I invariably played like an advocate of my own 'classical' intelligence." The pianist Edward Dannreuther wrote of Bülow, "All details were thought out and mastered down to the minutest particle; all effects were analyzed and calculated with the utmost subtlety; and yet the whole left an impression of warm spontaneity."

Bülow, even more than Clara Schumann or Liszt, made playing from memory an obligation. (As a conductor, he ordered the orchestral members to perform from memory and standing up.) His impact on American musical taste was as great as Anton Rubinstein's. He astounded the American public on his second tour by playing all of Beethoven's piano music—Sonatas, Variations, and the smaller works—without a note of music. He probably had the largest performing repertoire of his time. He tirelessly promoted the composers he valued. (It was Bülow who invented the celebrated phrase "the three Bs—Bach, Beethoven, and Brahms.") His editions of various composers, including the Beethoven Sonatas, were the most valued of the time. Bülow's practicing always included preludes and fugues from Bach's *Well-Tempered Clavier,* which he called the pianist's "Old Testament," and the Beethoven Sonatas, the "New Testament."

He was the apostle of high seriousness. Eduard Hanslick reported in 1881:

His arrival in a town is enough to quicken the hearts of all who want something more than merely pleasant musical entertainment. One always learns something new. . . . His restless, brilliant mind and his reckless energy flow like a north wind, brisk and refreshing . . . he is a born interpreter, one of the most remarkable I have ever known. . . . Bülow has just made his bow in Vienna. . . . He played the five last great Beethoven sonatas, one after the other, in a single recital. Nothing else. . . . It has only been within the past thirty years that anyone has dared to play one or another of them in public. . . . To play all five at one sitting was considered an impossibility until yesterday. Bülow survived the adventure, and so did the public. Only one who has tried to master these sonatas with his own hands can appreciate Bülow's extraordinary achievement. It is difficult to determine which is more admirable, his memory, his physical stamina, his technique, or the elasticity of his mind. . . . The total impression was fatigue mixed with admiration. If I correctly read the faces of the listeners going home, they said, "Beautiful but never again." Some chose to put it the other way around: "Never again— but beautiful."

Bülow was also an eminent teacher, and the list of his pupils includes Giuseppe Buonamici, José Vianna da Motta, Heinrich Barth, Hermann Goetz, Agathe Backer-Grøndahl, and countless others. To one student he said, "An interpreter should be the opposite of a grave digger. He should bring to light what is hidden and buried." At another lesson he declared: "Piano playing is a difficult art. First we have to learn how to equalize the fingers, and then in polyphonic music to make them unequal again; that being the case, it seems best not to practice the piano at all; and that is the advice I have given to many."

GIUSEPPE BUONAMICI
1846–1914—Italy

A pupil of von Bülow, he was one of the most important Italian pianist-teachers of his time. He made many editions of Beethoven, Schubert, and Schumann.

DAVID BURGE
b. 1930—United States

A pianist with a fine technique who has championed many contemporary scores. He plays with exactitude and the kind of commitment that is necessary for bringing to life difficult contemporary music by Boulez, Dallapiccolo, Berio, and others. Burge has a musical intelligence that finds its way into the most intricate reservoirs of the pieces he plays.

RICHARD BURMEISTER
1860–1944—Germany

Another pupil from Liszt's last years, Burmeister was considered a brilliant executant, and his small compositions received recognition. He had a distinguished teaching career, in Baltimore at the Peabody Conservatory, and at the Scharwenka Conservatory in New York, and later at the Dresden Conservatory. Burmeister added orchestral accompaniments to Chopin's Rondo in E-flat, Op. 16, and re-orchestrated the Second Concerto in F minor,

adding a cadenza in the first movement which Paderewski always utilized.

FERRUCCIO BUSONI
1866–1924—Italy

Throughout the world, a small but educated and potent band of connoisseurs, pianists, critics and music lovers have kept Busoni's name luminous throughout the three quarters of a century since his premature death at fifty-eight. Of the major pianists that have been influenced or deeply affected by his playing and music, one may name Egon Petri, Percy Grainger, Edward Steuermann, Arthur Rubinstein, Gunnar Johansen, Claudio Arrau, Arthur Loesser, John Ogdon, Ernst Levy, Alfred Brendel, Ronald Smith, Ronald Stevenson, and many others. There is no dispute that he was one of the towering pianists in history, ranking in importance with the high immortals of the keyboard such as Chopin, Liszt, Anton Rubinstein, Clara Schumann, Tausig, von Bülow, Schnabel, Paderewski, Hofmann, Rachmaninoff, Richter, Gould, Horowitz, and Arthur Rubinstein, who called him "the awe-inspiring master! . . . with his handsome, pale, Christ-like face, and his diabolical technical prowess, was by far the most interesting pianist . . . a shining example to all musicians for the noble way in which he pursued his career so uncompromisingly, for the high standards he set for his own compositions and for his general culture."

Busoni was one of the last great incarnations of high Romanticism, and his playing projected the feeling that music had no boundaries or limits of expression. As a pianist, Gunnar Johansen recalled, "He outshone all others. In Germany, we didn't speak of Mr. Busoni, we spoke of *Der* Busoni, as if he were a monument. His presence onstage was immense." Arthur Loesser, who first heard him in Berlin in 1911 performing six monumental all-Liszt recitals, called him "unforgettable, shocking even . . . one could never forget his playing." The element of shock, mystery, and awe is documented in most descriptions of his playing. His great pupil Egon Petri thought that in a Busoni performance, "The music became dematerialized; he brought it into another sphere. It had a mystical quality."

Richard Cappel wrote of a 1919 London recital that "[Busoni is] far and away the greatest musical executant now with us; a commanding figure–more, a well-nigh awful one, a maker of music that is tremendous and statuesque; a steely terrible power that regularly cows you as you listen, leaving you almost too humbled to admire."

Percy Grainger wrote: "I cannot recall ever hearing or seeing Busoni play a wrong note. He did not seem to "feel" his way about the keyboard by touching adjacent notes—as most of us do—he smacked the keys right in the middle. . . . I admired him without reservation of any kind and revelled in everything he did pianistically."

The composer Sorabji wrote: "To speak of technical considerations is almost an insult in connection with such a transcendent master, but it may well be asked if any one in Busoni's audiences had ever dreamt that such astonishingly varied qualities of tone could be drawn, coaxed or compelled from one very indifferent piano."

The great critic Cecil Gray wrote, "As a pianist when he is not being deliberately perverse, he is unique and unapproachable. There is no one today who can touch him, and probably there never has been anyone to equal him save Liszt. The degree of his insight into a work at hand is truly astonishing. . . . Every note he invests with a peculiar significance which, one sometimes feels, was not consciously present in the composer's mind, and is certainly not apparent in the printed notes, but which one is sure he would have unhesitatingly endorsed

if he had heard the performance. Busoni, in fact, on occasion seems to achieve an enhancement of the composer's vision, and add to it something of his own without distorting it in any way. This is the summit of interpretive genius."

Busoni's conceptions seemed to possess a revelatory expressive power and a gigantic sweep. Nadia Boulanger considered him "a genius. To say that he played the piano in an extraordinary way is merely to state the blindingly obvious. . . . He played with the air of composing as he played. Busoni's articulation was perfect, and came not only from the astonishing evenness of his technique, but above all from his prodigious sense of rhythm."

It was a rhythm of symphonic proportion yet which was not bound to strict metric playing. It was his ambition to create a musical structure which struck a deep chord in the memory.

Busoni's pedaling was perhaps the most original in the history of the art of piano playing. "The potential effects of the pedals are still unexhausted," he wrote, "because they have remained the slave of a narrow-minded and senseless harmonic theory. The pedal is decried. Senseless irregularities are to blame for this. Let us experiment with sensible irregularities." The composer Otto Luening heard Busoni frequently and attested in his autobiography:

His pedaling was unique and set him apart from any other pianist I have ever heard. He sometimes used two or three pedals at the same time, setting sonority patterns that were somewhat veiled but within which he played with great, bell-like clarity. At times, he would raise or lower a pedal with great rapidity, even on a single note or chord, creating myriad tone colors and strange vibrations. His touch and attacks were always related to the pedaling he was using so that he could transform the piano sounds at will from a vaguely harpsichord resonance to a modern resonating box on which he could simulate singing and orchestral instruments. . . . Busoni avoided strict metrical playing in all performances. He was interested in projecting the form of each piece so that it could be remembered. . . . His performance of the Chopin Ballades went beyond brilliant piano playing. Sometimes he made the instrument sound like an Aeolian harp as described by the poets, or like sound floating from a box of electronic resonators with apparently no relationship to hammered-string sound. Under his hands the piano became both a picture projector and a story teller, and in the Ballades Busoni became a bard.

Not that Busoni was immune from criticism. His pupil Edward Steuermann (commenting in the late 1950s) felt "Busoni's pianism would not be easily understood today, might even be bewildering compared with today's playing (the avoidance of risks, spiritual or stylistic), his bold individualism . . . would appear revolutionary, almost rebellious, and so it was fifty years ago."

Some felt his Beethoven was too violent, for others it was dryly cerebral. Busoni countered with "I built up an ideal of Beethoven which has wrongly been called modern and which is really no more than 'live.' He knew Beethoven's *Pathétique* Sonata sounded revolutionary to ears of 1799, and he wanted to retain that feeling. He wrote: "A greater transformation has not taken place in the history of music, than from the Sonatas of Haydn and Mozart to the *Hammerklavier* Sonata. Beethoven created the modern grand piano through his technique, by making the best use of higher, lower and wider positions on the keyboard, by use of pedals and by the improvement and enrichment of the sound."

Busoni said, "Chopin attracted and repelled me all my life." Chopin was the composer by whom his detractors were most frequently offended, his Chopin being too monumental, lacking in romance, bursting its form with too much muscle. Busoni protested that Chopin had been "prostituted, profaned, vulgarized," had been made into "a typical Balzac novel figure of the 1830s—the pale, interesting, mysterious, elegant stranger in Paris." At a Paris recital after performing the four Chopin Ballades, an elderly gentleman in the audience who had known a few of Chopin's pupils loudly proclaimed, "In the name of Chopin, I protest."

He loved Bach as a nourishing religion, and devoted endless energy to the Leipzig Cantor. As early as his twenty-third year he produced an edition of Bach's Inventions, fascinating and dense in its details of phrasing, fingering, and musical intention. His edition of *The Well Tempered Clavier* bristles with a welter of footnotes, often confusing in their application but brilliantly suggestive. Busoni's editions sought to translate Bach into the terms of the sound of the modern piano.

More than any other pianist of his generation Busoni spread the gospel of Bach's keyboard works. His transcriptions of Bach's music remain his best-known works. Bach-Busoni Chorales, the Chaconne, and various organ works were so well-known that once at a party he was introduced as Mr. Bach-Busoni. The universality of Bachian polyphony was a primary influence on him, and was a basis for his own complex music. His 1910 *Fantasia contrappuntistica*, based on Bach's *The Art of Fugue*, continues to fascinate pianists of intellectual bent and technical endowment.

One of Busoni's goals was to show the public Liszt's importance. Although not a "Liszt pupil," Busoni did more for this composer than most of the army of Liszt's actual students. In 1909, after playing the Liszt Sonata to Liszt's pupil Giovanni Sgambati, Busoni wrote, "He kissed my head and said I quite reminded him of the master, more so than his real pupils." Liszt's life and personality had decidedly influenced Busoni in his own desire to be the complete man and artist, full of altruistic ideals. The two great virtuosos had much in common, and the Italianate Lisztian melody was deeply attractive to Busoni, by temperament, and it lurks in many of his works. Busoni was one of the first to delineate Liszt's historical importance, writing: "I am myself respectfully conscious of the distance which separates me from his greatness. . . . We are all descended from him radically, without excepting Wagner, and we owe to him the lesser things that we can do. Franck, Richard Strauss, Debussy, and the Russians are all branches of this tree."

Busoni's Liszt playing inaugurated a new age in Liszt performance. The six recitals for the Liszt centenary included over seventy works. In his biography of Busoni, Edward J. Dent wrote: "The greater works of Liszt, which minor pianists turn into mere displays for virtuosity because their technique is inadequate for anything beyond that, often sounded strangely easy and simple when they were played by Busoni. The glittering scales and arpeggios became what Liszt intended them to be—a dimly suggested background—while the themes in massive chords or singing melodies stood out clear."

Busoni thought Chopin had become "over-popularised," while Liszt was often ignored. In a letter to his wife Gerda, he says he had been asked to play Chopin's Fantasie Impromptu. He writes, "This well-known piece, a shallow salon study, will never be criticized badly, in the way Liszt's compositions are so frequently criticized." In a letter to Philipp Jarnach, he commented, "How pure and utterly isolated was the figure of Franz Liszt, that cosmopolitan catholic idealist."

Busoni's repertory was immense. In 1898, he performed fourteen concertos with the Berlin Philharmonic in four concerts, which included the Bach D minor, Mozart A major, K. 488, Beethoven G major, Hummel B minor, Beethoven *Emperor*, Weber *Konzertstück*,

Schubert-Liszt *Wanderer* Fantasy, Chopin E minor, Mendelssohn G minor, Schumann A minor, Henselt F minor (the work with which he made his American debut), Rubinstein E flat, Brahms D minor and Liszt A major. In 1913, he gave a series of eight recitals at the Verdi Conservatory in Milan, which he called his Octomeron. "This affair," he wrote, "is a fine demonstration, organized and carried out with the greatest noblesse." The programs were massive. Recital number 1 was devoted to Bach transcriptions and Beethoven's *Waldstein* and Op. 111 Sonatas; number 2 to an all-Beethoven recital; numbers 3 and 4 to Chopin; numbers 5 and 6 to two all-Liszt recitals, one of original works and the other of transcriptions; number 7 to works of Alkan, Schumann, Franck and Brahms; with the final recital of Busoni's own music, including the first performance of the Sonatina Seconda, one of his finest compositions.

As a pianist it was his ambition to add a new work to his performing repertory each season. His consistency was admirable. This list includes a twelve-year period:

Six Paganini-Liszt Etudes–1892 (Boston)
Bach-Busoni Chaconne–1893 (Boston)
Weber Konzertstück–1894 (Hamburg)
Beethoven Sonata Op. 106–1895 (Berlin)
Grieg Piano Concerto–1896 (Copenhagen)
Chopin Twelve Etudes Op. 25–1896 (Berlin)
Weber Sonata in C major–1897 (Berlin)
Chopin Four Ballades (complete)–1899 (London)
Chopin Sonata No. 3 in B minor–1899 (Berlin)
Tchaikovsky Concerto No. 1–1900 (London)
Brahms Variations on a Theme by Paganini–1900 (Berlin)
Liszt Sonata–1900 (Berlin)
Weber Sonata No. 3 in D minor–1901 (Weimar)
Liszt Piano Concerto No. 1–1901 (London)
Alkan, various works–1901, 1902, 1903, 1908 (Berlin)
Saint-Saëns Concerto No. 5–1902 (Hanover)

Chopin Twelve Etudes Op. 10–1902 (Berlin)
Franck Prelude, Chorale, and Fugue–1902 (Berlin)
Schubert Four Impromptus Op. 90–1903 (Berlin)
Liszt Twelve *Transcendental Etudes*–1903 (Berlin)
Beethoven Sonata Op. 110–1903 (Berlin)
Busoni Piano Concerto (Karl Muck conducting)–
    1904 (Berlin)

His expectations of the qualities a great pianist must possess are uncompromising. He wrote: "The pianist must have unusual intelligence and culture, feeling, temperament, imagination, poetry and finally that personal magnetism which sometimes enables the artist to inspire four thousand people, strangers whom chance has brought together, with one and the same feeling. . . . If any of these qualities are missing, the deficiency will be apparent in every phrase he plays."

Busoni hated the recording process of his time. His piano rolls give no indication of his genius. However, he recorded a few pieces at the end of his career. It is sad that this mighty artist left so small a recorded legacy, a taste that only serves to tantalize us. We get but a glimmer of his monumental art and great technical gifts in an abridged version of Liszt's Hungarian Rhapsody No. 13. There are also Bach's Prelude and Fugue in C major and a couple of Chopin works, including humorous touches in two versions of the *Black Key* Etude. But the recording hardly conveys the artistry commented on by the many experts who heard him.

And Busoni was relentless in his quest for perfection, often practicing through the night after performing a brilliant recital. The piano's fascination never left him, and this Faustus of the piano knew that the keyboard relentlessly ate up his relatively limited time on Earth, and everything seemed important to his restless intellect. He wrote to his wife from a grueling concert tour: "I am very nervous, just now, when travelling, and have the continual feeling that time is slipping by me. . . . This makes me bitter sometimes. . . . I take a great deal of trouble to act in the right way, but my life is many-sided. . . . The conflict between what I should like to do, what I could do, and what I must do is very worrying and keeps me in a continual state of tension."

But Busoni, a man of enormous strength and mental stability, typically writes, "But perhaps everything is for the best like this, and who knows if it may not be the means of preserving my energy and even increasing it."

To a friend in 1905, he writes, "What a long road the road to mastery is, even for someone who is very gifted—and often still further for him, because he sets himself bigger problems!" In 1907, he laments to his wife, "It is an effort for me to practise the piano, yet one cannot leave it. It is like an animal whose head always grows again, however much one cuts off." Has there ever been a serious pianist who does not deeply understand these words? As late as 1922, writing to Egon Petri, he says, "One says of contagious diseases that what they gain in propagation, they lose in malignity. Do you find a similar phenomenon with our beloved piano-playing?"

Throughout his career, Busoni dedicated much time to teaching piano. The list of his pupils is formidable and includes Guido Agosti, Beryl Rubinstein, Michael von Zadora, Josef Weiss, Egon Petri, Carlo Zecchi, Maria Carreras, Harriet Cohen, Mana-Zucca, Mieczyslaw Münz, Edward Steuermann, Selim Palmgren, Leo Kestenberg, Rudolf Ganz, Leo Sirota, Émile Blanchet, and many others of virtuoso stature. He taught at Weimar, Vienna, Zurich, Bologna, Boston, Helsingfors, and Berlin. Often he must have been weary from its constant demands, physical and psychological. Writing in 1916 to the great Liszt pupil, the Portuguese pianist José Vianna Da Motta, "I have become most disaffected towards teaching the piano. I find it embarrassing to observe others wandering along the same road (with greater or lesser difficulty) as I continuously travelled and have now finally left behind me; to have to listen to something for 20 minutes, when I have already adjudged it from the first 10 bars—does this strike you as unnatural?"

His twelve dictums for practicing are filled with a Busoni-esque wisdom:

1. Practice the passage with the most difficult fingering; when you have mastered that, play it with the easiest.
2. If a passage offers some particular technical difficulty, go through all similar passages you can remember in other places; in this way you will bring system into the kind of playing in question.
3. Always join technical practice with the study of the interpretation; the difficulty often does not lie in the notes, but in the dynamic shading prescribed.
4. Never be carried away by temperament, for that dissipates strength, and where it occurs there will always be a blemish, like a dirty spot which can never be washed out of a material.
5. Don't set your mind on overcoming the difficulties in pieces which have been unsuccessful because you have previously practiced them badly; it is generally a useless task. But if meanwhile you have quite changed your way of playing, then begin the study of the old piece from the beginning, as if you did not know it.
6. Study everything as if there were nothing more difficult; try to interpret studies for the young from the standpoint of the virtuoso; you will be astonished to find how difficult it is to play a Czerny or Cramer or a Clementi Etude.
7. Bach is the foundation of piano playing, Liszt the summit. The two make Beethoven possible.
8. Take it for granted from the beginning that everything is possible on the piano, even when it seems impossible to you, or really is so.
9. Attend to your technical apparatus so that you are prepared and armed for every possible event; then, when you study a new piece, you can turn all your power to the intellectual content; you will not be held up by the technical problems.
10. Never play carelessly, even when there is nobody listening, or the occasion seems unimportant.
11. Never leave a passage which has been unsuccessful without repeating it; if you cannot do it in the presence of others, then do it subsequently.
12. If possible, allow no day to pass without touching your piano.

C

MICHELE CAMPANELLA

b. 1947—Italy

A strong technician, he has earned a European reputation and has made remarkable recordings of Liszt, Busoni, and others.

MARTIN CANIN

b. 1930—United States

He studied with Rosina Lhévinne at the Juilliard School. He is an expert chamber musician, as well as a solo artist. In 1959, Canin became a member of the piano faculty at the Juilliard School, where his reputation as a teacher flourished.

TERESA CARREÑO

1853–1917—Venezuela

She was one of the most remarkable musicians of her time and a pianist of greatness. Carreño was a prodigy who had a huge success in the United States. As a child in Boston, she played twelve recitals in a season. Gottschalk heard her several times and gave her valuable pianistic advice. Later, she played for Liszt, who was overwhelmed, telling her, "Don't imitate anyone. Keep true to yourself, cultivate your individuality and do not follow blindly in the paths of others." Anton Rubinstein taught her intermittently, calling her "my sunshine," and von Bülow thought she was the most interesting pianist of her generation. She studied also with Chopin's pupil Georges Mathias, and for several years she played in the French *jeu perlé* style. Around 1875, she abandoned piano performance for a few years to pursue a quite successful singing career. She also conducted, and composed many charming salon pieces, as well as a string quartet. In 1892, Eugene d'Albert

Teresa Carreño by David Dubal

65

became her third husband. He was a great influence on her playing, which became deeper and richer. Her repertoire grew in stature, and Beethoven became one of her chief concerns.

She possessed a titanic technique, and few could rival her animal vitality; she was second to none for sheer endurance. She often played Beethoven's Third, Fourth, and Fifth Concerti in a single evening without a shrug. She had a magnificent stage bearing, and her beauty was legendary. "Carreño," wrote James Huneker in his autobiography, "with her exotic coloring, brilliant eyes, and still more brilliant piano-playing, was like a visitor from another star. Her manner of playing for me has always seemed scarlet, as Rubinstein's was golden and Joseffy's silver." Claudio Arrau called her "epical," and decades later he still found her unforgettable: "She was a goddess. She had this unbelievable drive, this power. I don't think I ever heard anyone fill the Berlin Philharmonic, the old hall, with such a sound. And her octaves were *fantastic*. I don't think there's anyone today who can play such octaves. The speed and the power."

Her last recital took place in Havana on 21 March 1917. Unfortunately, she died before electrical recording, and the piano rolls she made, which were disowned by her, give practically no idea that "the Walküre of the piano," as she was often called, was one of the volcanic temperaments in late-nineteenth-century piano playing. Venezuela has commemorated her with a postage stamp in her honor.

MARIA CARRERAS
1872–1966—Italy

Considered a formidable pianist, she was influenced by her teacher Sgambati, the important Liszt disciple; later she had lessons with Busoni. In 1914, for the tenth anniversary of the death of Anton Rubinstein, she was invited to perform in Russia, supposedly at the invitation of the czar. She made an auspicious New York debut in 1923, the important critic W. J. Henderson calling her "a strong and powerful personality."

GABY CASADESUS
1901–1999—France

Born in Marseilles. At the Paris Conservatoire, she studied with Diémer, taking first prize in piano. Very early she played music by Fauré, Ravel, and Florent Schmitt under their guidance. After she married Robert Casadesus, they were heard in duo-piano performances throughout the world. As a soloist her playing was suavely mellow, flexible, and with a special lilt, while her performances of Robert Casadesus's music were infused with a special élan, especially in the Etudes and Fourth Sonata.

Her pupil the American pianist and composer Philip Lasser wrote: "As a pianist, she brought all the sensitivity, subtlety, elegance and power with which she moved in daily life to the music she performed. Blessed with a rich, pure and warm sound, Gaby embodied the unassuming prophet at the piano. . . . The simplicity and modesty of her manner were matched only by her musical wisdom which she tirelessly imparted to her beloved students. When Gaby played, everything of this earth fell away, leaving just the glorious poetry of music."

JEAN CASADESUS
1927–1972—France

The son of Gaby and Robert Casadesus was a pianist of distinction. His recording of Chabrier's *Pièces pittoresques* is a gem.

ROBERT CASADESUS

1899–1972—France

A student of Diémer at the Paris Conservatoire, Casadesus came from a distinguished musical family. To a world public he became the absolute French pianist, his country's finest. Casadesus embodied the qualities of Gallic balance, unforced sound, style, and precision of technique. His sound was crisp, dry, and sparkling, like a vintage champagne. Casadesus was a sophisticated musician, whose pianism was phenomenally supple. His range was wide and his use of the pedals simply astonishing. He composed admirable, pleasurable music, highly crafted and well worth performance. He could play a large-scale work with such concentration that if one were listening well, the performance seemed to be over amazingly soon, he simply presented it all so directly. His rubato in Schumann's *Carnaval* was so subtle that at first it sounded as if he never deviated from the metronome mark, yet it certainly never sounded tight.

His pupil Grant Johannesen said: "He had a commanding ability to guide you through the music and it was so compelling. It's fascinating to consider, too, because his whole approach to music was simple. He was so concentrated that he produced a kind of inner musical excitement. . . . The man shed so much light on *all* the music he played. I can never forget his utter lack of pretension. He caught the spirit of the music and shared it with his audience as something supremely divine."

Casadesus had a large repertoire. His Scarlatti records are beaming, his Bach solid. He played and recorded Beethoven often. It was a cool French-styled Beethoven; the fierce *Sturm und Drang* was not his way. He played an ample amount of Chopin, and the B minor Sonata was architecturally superb. But he was not comfortable in the little pieces, where the deeply personal and darker tones were absent.

His Schumann often had charm, but his style was too fastidious to indulge in the more dissonant side of the German's nature.

Casadesus was one of the superb concerto players. In his hands, the Saint-Saëns Fourth Concerto becomes lordly. His Mozart concertos will always be celebrated, and his own cadenzas are stylish. He could play Liszt's A major Concerto with spirit, and his disc with Szell of Weber's *Konzertstück* will always earn raves, as will his d'Indy *Symphony on a French Mountain Air* and the Franck *Symphonic Variations*.

This charming and civilized artist was at his peak in his interpretations of Ravel and Debussy. His recordings remain indispensable for those who love this literature. Casadesus uses a more economical, less purely sensuous approach to Ravel. His exquisite breeding brings to this music a cool poignancy. His playing may be restrained, but ardor always peeps in. The pianistic finish is high, and the sheer elegance attained in his complete Ravel is irresistible. Never was the adage "less is more" so apt. The music forms a cohesive unity, with phrasing that is sculptured. Casadesus senses Ravel's antique spirit. For example, in the minuet of Ravel's *Sonatine,* he takes us back to the jeweled and graceful eighteenth-century French court.

Casadesus's Debussy is also nearly his very best work. Everywhere he plays with joy, scintillating brightness, and a rhythmic verve. It is a Debussy of taste. He brings to a score like the *Children's Corner Suite* the very springtime of life, each phrase affectionately shaped, and the humor is piquant. I wish he had recorded more Fauré, a composer born for Casadesus's hands. There is no finer Fauré than his recording of three preludes from Op. 103, or the exquisite traceries and refined passion he finds in the Ballade for Piano and Orchestra.

His life was filled with touring, recording, composing, and teaching. He played the two-piano literature with his wife, Gaby, as few such teams ever did—with élan and a rare musicianship.

ALFREDO CASELLA
1883–1947—Italy

One of the important Italian musicians of his generation. He studied with Diémer at the Paris Conservatoire and later taught there. From 1915 on, he taught in Rome at the Santa Cecilia Academy. He made editions of Chopin and Beethoven, and his compositions are often difficult, but stimulating, acerbic, and well worth investigation.

IGNACIO CERVANTES
1847–1905—Cuba

The most illustrious Cuban pianist-composer of the nineteenth century. In 1865 he went to Paris, where he won first prize in piano playing at the Conservatoire. After studies he returned to Havana, where his playing and piano teaching were admired. Around 1875 he began composing his most important work, the thirty-six *Danzas Cubanas*; each of them follow a sixteen plus sixteen bar structure, with descriptive titles, such as La Carcajada (The Hearty Laughter), Gran Señora (Grand Lady), and Amistad (Friendship). The *Danzas Cubanas* are naïve, carefree, classic morsels of Cuban music.

ABRAM CHASINS
1903–1987—United States

As a child he studied with Ernest Hutcheson at the Institute of Musical Art, the precursor of the Juilliard School. By age twenty-three he had been acclaimed for his piano playing but also for the success of his three Chinese pieces. Dazzled by the pianism of Josef Hofmann, the great pianist was impressed by Chasins, but told him that he needed more study. Chasins in his entertaining book *Speaking of Pianists* relates that during a Hofmann lesson "each comment let in a new flood of light."

In 1929, he made his debut in Philadelphia performing the premiere of his first piano concerto. He continued composing; there is a fine set of 24 Preludes. A large-scale piece, *Narrative,* was performed by Arthur Rubinstein and later recorded by his wife, Constance Keene. Chasins's activity as a concert pianist declined when in the 1940s he became music director of New York's classical radio station, WQXR. He taught and gave pianistic advice to a number of pianists.

SHURA CHERKASSKY
1909–1995—Russia

He was born in Odessa but was brought early to the United States. He studied with his mother, Lydia Cherkassky, who had worked with Essipova; as a child, he also studied with Josef Hofmann. Cherkassky's early years were those of a highly visible child prodigy who absorbed a great deal of the Hofmann tradition.

His career had its ups and downs, and it was at a low ebb in this country from the 1940s until around 1975, when finally his appearances in the United States began to rival in success his recitals in London and other European capitals. His concerts have been a revelation for those who have heard him, and a whole generation of young pianists has been inspired by his originality, his unrivaled command of voicing, rubato, and pedaling, and, above all, by his imagination.

Critics have consistently called Cherkassky a throwback to a bygone age, a pianist from the past, a reminder of Hofmann and Godowsky, an eccentric genius with a style closely related to that of the greater pupils of Leschetizky. But this assessment must irritate such an artist, who never thinks of the past or of Hofmann. He is entirely himself, a pianist blessed with a fascinating musicality, a man who works at the piano with a tireless hunger to achieve mastery within each measure. Endless dedication, total guilelessness, and a non-judgmental view of the piano literature permeate his life and his arresting programming. He can play Bernstein's *Touches* better than any young modernist, side by side with Paul Pabst's *Eugene Onegin* paraphrase; the Tchaikovsky or Grieg Sonata receives the same respect as Schumann's *Carnaval* or Liszt's Sonata. He plays Berg's Sonata with perfect understanding, and plays pieces by Mana-Zucca or Chaminade with the same thirst with which he plays *Islamey* or the *Don Juan* Fantasy.

In short, season after season he developed, changed, and grew. Cherkassky is not a throwback, and his conceptions are not imitations of his past master, Hofmann, but vital interpretations in their own right, by a Romantic virtuoso imbued with a love for his instrument and its literature. Recently he decided that his playing was plagued by too many inner voices, which could come off well in concert but sounded cloying on disc. He simply did away with them. They may reappear, but they will always sound different, fresh, and uncalculated.

Cherkassky never remains static. It is impossible for him not to experiment; the stage is part of his life and a tremendous release for him away from his slow-motion practicing, which, he says, people would not believe if they heard it. Cherkassky is always his own best listener, and his stage concentration is formidable. Of course, his interpreta-

Shura Cherkassky by David Dubal

tions are highly personalized, highly colored. He loves to linger and relish the moment. He is an artist who takes enormous chances, and this can throw an audience used to conservative playing into a confused state until it gets used to his mercurial ways. And then again, Cherkassky, Romantic that he is, may not be entirely in the mood to inspire the multitude; or, on occasion, it may take him time to warm to his work. I heard him play a Chopin E minor Concerto as if he were half asleep. It was not until the finale that the pianist was ready to sing, but the wait was worth it, and a movement that had never seemed equal to its companions erupted and swelled magnificently.

At his best, his Chopin playing is fascinating. Here he becomes the Romantic poet of the keyboard. What a seductive, insinuating ring in the A-flat Ballade. His E major Nocturne, Op. 62, is translucent; some of his Chopin preludes are beguiling, the one in F-sharp major played as if upon a cloud. Few pianists can create so hushed an effect. James Methuen-Campbell writes: "The characteristics of his Chopin include a luscious tone, attention to the polyphonic side of the music, marvelously detailed phrasing, and a grasp of the overall shape of a work. It would be impossible to say that he favors fast tempos, because he never follows any rules. He is like a magician at the keyboard, conjuring up near miraculous sounds that the most assiduous listener may hear only once in a lifetime from another pianist."

Cherkassky's Chopin repertoire is huge, and he plays many of the seldom-heard scores, such as the C minor Sonata, Op. 4; the *Là ci darem la mano* Variations for Piano and Orchestra; and the *Allegro de concert, Boléro,* and *Tarantelle.*

A unique Liszt player, he is mainly concerned with surface brilliance and charm. His *Rigoletto* Paraphrase is whipped into a silky froth. But in the Liszt Sonata there is a seriousness, if not a depth, of emotion. It is a rejuvenation of the score in which his imagination soars and his technique is staggering.

One of Cherkassky's chief traits is his elegance, and nowhere is this exhibited more perfectly and joyously than in the large collection of salon pieces and paraphrases he carries in his repertoire. Nobody can touch him in a work like the Strauss-Godowsky *Wine, Women, and Song,* where his fingers weave garlands in counterpoint. He is an exquisite stylist who never lets go of the pulse as he spins out these alluring ten minutes of intricate, sophisticated nostalgia.

Cherkassky often programs Schumann, but these two quirky musicians do not mix well. His *Carnaval* usually sounds spasmodic, even ill-tempered, and the *Symphonic Etudes* are cluttered and nervous. He plays some Schubert, most notably the A major Sonata D. 664, Op. 120, bucolic in mood and with a touching slow movement. Cherkassky is certainly not at home with the Classic masters, and his Beethoven is not thrilling. But one does not go to hear a Cherkassky concert for profundity or solidity. He is instinctive, fragmentary, an improviser and a troubadour, an artist of half-tints, delicate pastels, Romantic vibrations, with a golden if somewhat piercing tone. He is often bubbling with joy, humor, and even shenanigans, and he is also a master of the grand statement, as in the Tchaikovsky Second and the Saint-Saëns Second concertos. Recently, he played the Anton Rubinstein Fourth Concerto, and it sounded better and more coherent than the Hofmann performance on disc. The work had been heard only once in nearly forty years, at the New York Philharmonic concerts (played by Oscar Levant), and one wondered how such a masterpiece of the grand manner could have become neglected. The answer is that the piece is now faded and has been ousted by the Rachmaninoff Concerti. But in the hands of an artist like Cherkassky, it regained all of the pomp that attended its birth, when Anton Rubinstein himself mounted the platform, brought down the house, and claimed his place as the father of Russian pianism. Cherkassky proudly exclaimed, "I am Anton Rubinstein's grandchild." In the last decade of his life, Cherkassky performed works by numerous twentieth-century composers, including Messiaen, Stockhausen, Berio, Berkeley, Ligeti, Morton, Gould, Ives, and Hindemith.

Shura Cherkassky was nearly eighty-five when he died in London. In spite of his advanced age, the musical world was shocked. It had seemed as if Cherkassky would go on for years; Van Cliburn said, "I was sure that he'd be giving a recital on his one-hundredth birthday." There had not been the slightest indication of any diminution of powers; indeed, his technique was perhaps sharper and more accurate, his reflexes more pinpoint, than any other virtuoso who had ever attained that age.

He shone like a beacon in the concert halls of the world, and the poetic imagery effortlessly bursting forth from the keyboard amazed his delighted public. A Cherkassky recital was an event, an adventure; one spoke about it with excitement. It was fun—it could be startling musically!

As the man was a total original, so was his music-making: extroverted, guttural, the tone unforgettable. Listen to his Saint-Saëns–Godowsky *The Swan,* a mix of gold and silver; he heard exactly the sound he craved and those small muscular hands had an unforgettable look on the keyboard. To see this leprechaun of a little man on the concert platform with his inimitable bow was to witness a person totally at ease onstage. Indeed, the stage was Cherkassky's true abode, and the piano was his life. There was never a day that he did not devote himself to it, and he worked at the instrument with a pure passion that defied fatigue.

In speaking of his repertoire, he said: "I love things by Chaminade or *Melody in F* by Rubinstein. They are delicious. They are fruit salads or elegant desserts, and each year I challenge myself with something new and difficult. Sometimes I think I can't do it or I don't understand it, but somehow I persevere. I practice all the time. Nothing stops me from work. I practice at least four hours a day, and if I'm interrupted, which I don't really mind, I start again. It's not so much compulsion as it is a discipline, and in all the world nowhere does discipline count as much as in being a good pianist."

FRÉDÉRIC CHOPIN
1810–1849—Poland

He made his debut in 1818, playing a concerto by Gyrowetz. In 1824 he entered the Warsaw Conservatory; the following year saw the publication of his Rondo in C minor, Op. 1. He premiered his own F minor and E minor Concerti in Warsaw in March and October 1830. Late in that same year, he left Poland forever. He lived and performed in Vienna for eight months and in 1831 arrived in Paris, where he played his F minor Concerto and the *Là ci darem* Variations early in 1832. After 1835, his appearances as a concert pianist were infrequent. In 1837 he entered into his celebrated liaison with the writer George Sand, which ended in 1846. His main source of income was teaching. He gave his last recital in Paris early in 1848, and later that year arrived in Great Britain. He died in Paris in 1849. At his funeral, which was held at the Madeleine, Mozart's *Requiem* was given. He is buried at Père-Lachaise, where, according to legend, there has never been a day when flowers were not placed on his grave.

Chopin spent most of the first twenty years of his life in Warsaw. The Polish capital was rather provincial; still he was able to hear many of the best artists of the time perform there. Italian opera and singing in general had an indelible effect on him, through the performances of such great singers as Angelica Catalani. Long before Liszt heard Paganini, Chopin was learning from his violinistic feats. Hummel, too, played in Warsaw, and his tentative Romanticism and richly ornamented keyboard layout ignited Chopin's precocious genius. Other influences during his adolescence included Spohr's then strangely exotic chromaticism, Field's fragrant Nocturnes, and the mysteriousness of Weber. Of equal importance were the dance forms of his homeland. From the age of eight, Chopin occupied himself with them, haunted by their rhythms, dreaming of an idealized Poland. The last page of music he wrote was a mazurka.

As a pianist, he was left to develop on his own. Warsaw had no piano teachers of importance, and Chopin's instruction was given over to a local violinist, Adalbert Zywny. Awestruck by his pupil's talents, he let Chopin sprout his own unique wings. To his credit, he instilled in him a love for Bach and Mozart, the only masters whom Chopin admired without reservation. There was also the fatherly guidance of his composition teacher Josef Elsner at the Warsaw Conservatory, who understood him and nourished him without too many strictures. When the twenty-one-year-old Chopin arrived in Paris, he was momentarily dazed by the old-fashioned perfection of Kalkbrenner, who tried to convince him to enter upon a three-year course of study with him. Opinions on the matter roared back to him from Warsaw: the pianist Maria Szymanowska screamed, "He is a scoundrel. . . . His real aim is to cramp his genius." Elsner, too, quickly realized that "they have recognized genius in Frédéric and are already frightened that he will outstrip them, so they want to keep their hands on him for three years in order to hold back something of that which nature herself might push forward."

Indeed, Chopin was a new and freer pianist, free from the conventional discipline of stiff bodily action. And his music was entirely new, demanding novel forms of hand coordination. Schumann was the first to understand this, ending his review of the Variations on "Là ci darem la mano," Op. 2, with the now-celebrated line: "Hats off, gentlemen. A genius!" Chopin was well aware of his own originality. At nineteen, he announced to a friend the creation of his Etudes: "I have written a big technical exercise in my own special manner." These would soon be known as his Twenty-four Etudes, Opp. 10 and 25. When first composed, they offered severe stumbling blocks to older players of the day. The German critic Ludwig Rellstab advised, "Those who have distorted fingers may put them right by practicing these studies; but those who have not, should not play them, at least, not without having a surgeon at hand." But the Chopin Etudes have come to rule the world of piano playing, forming an encyclopedic methodology, a summary of Chopin's enlarged vision of piano technique. They provide the equipment for the rest of Chopin's almost invariably difficult music, and give the key to music after Chopin. If only one set of piano etudes were to be preserved, these would be the unanimous choice. They contain all that Clementi, Cramer, Czerny, Berger, Moscheles, Hummel, Steibelt, and others were striving for technically, couched in music of incomparable beauty. They are a challenge for every generation of pianists, and few can feel equally comfortable in all. They are small in form; as each develops a single technical idea, they demand an enormous endurance, while musically they are as exposed as Mozartian writing.

Chopin was one of the most original harmonists in history, creating an exquisite chromatic garden. Gerald Abraham wrote: "Chopin's chromaticism marks a stage of the greatest importance in the evolution of the harmonic language. . . . [He was] the first composer seriously to undermine the solid system of diatonic tonalism created by the Viennese classical masters and the contemporaries in other countries."

As a creator of ornamental *fioritura,* he is without equal in the nineteenth century. Chopin displayed an almost inexhaustible resource in discovering pianistic formations that are uniquely suited to the instrument. To transcribe Chopin or to change the medium in any way destroys the music's evocative power, more than with any other composer. It was born for the piano. Chopin extended the scope of the left hand to such a degree that it constitutes a miracle of imagination. Finally the entire range of the instrument was available for exploration. Just compare a Mozartian Alberti bass or a Field nocturne with a late Chopin nocturne. With Chopin, the impossible was achieved—singing upon the piano. The instrument was suddenly capable of iridescent and shimmering tone, where the pedal counts for all. It was widely noted how Chopin's feet were in constant motion. He was probably the first pianist to consistently use half and quarter pedaling. Never had music been capable of such fluidity, such palpitation, such atmospheric effect.

At an aristocrat's salon Hallé heard the twenty-six-year-old Chopin. He wrote: "That was beyond all words. The few senses I had have quite left me. I could have jumped into the Seine. Everything I hear now seems so insignificant, that I would rather not hear it at all. Chopin! He is no man, he is an angel, a God. (Or what can I say more?) Chopin's compositions played by Chopin! That is a joy never to be surpassed."

Hearing Chopin play the A-flat Etude, Op. 25, No. 1, Schumann imagined "an Aeolian harp that had all the scales, and these were intermingled by the hand of the artist into all sorts of fantastic embellishments. It was rather an undulation brought out more loudly here and there with the pedal, all gorgeously entangled in the harmony."

Chopin's influence, pianistically and harmonically, spans two centuries, from Liszt to Scriabin and Rachmaninoff, to Debussy, Granados, and Szymanowski. His Mazurkas and Polonaises let loose the flood tide of ethnicity in music, which is having an impact even today. This delicate, ethereal being created, in the words of George Sand, "a revolution in the language of music and with only one instrument."

Chopin was consumptive, becoming more frail year by year. He scaled down his playing as a result, developing dozens of gradations of soft sounds. How he envied Liszt his power. Naturally he had a horror of large halls, and late in life he begged his friend, the Irish pianist George Osborne, not to attend a recital he had to give in Scotland. "My playing," he told him, "will be lost in such a large room, and my compositions will be ineffec-tive." Nevertheless, his pupil Georges Mathias attested, "What power! Yes, what power, but it lasted a few bars; and what exaltation and inspiration! The man's whole body vibrated." His technique was flawless, and he always caused great excitement with the evenness of his scales and the careful manipulation of his legato. The pianist-writer Wilhelm von Lenz noticed him "changing his fingers on a key as often as an organ player."

Chopin's close friend Ernest Legouvé, the dramatist and critic who knew his playing well, wrote: "Once at the piano Chopin played until he was exhausted. In the grip of a disease that knows no mercy, dark rings appeared around his eyes, a feverish brightness lit up his face, his lips turned to a vivid red and his breath came in short gasps. He felt, we felt, that something of his life was flowing away with the music; he would not stop and we had not the strength to stop him. The fever which consumed him took possession of us all!"

The chief characteristic of Chopin's playing was his highly personal and wayward use of tempo rubato. He wrote, "The left hand is the conductor; it must not waver or lose ground; do with the right hand what you will and can." (Liszt's description of the much-discussed tempo rubato is more pictorial: "Do you see those trees? The wind plays in the leaves, life unfolds and develops beneath them, but the tree remains.") When Meyerbeer insisted that Chopin played his own Mazurka in ¼ time instead of ¾, Chopin was furious and hotly denied it. Yet when his trusted friend Charles Hallé pointed it out to him, the Pole slyly called the rhythmic aberration a national trait. Berlioz, too, said that Chopin simply could not play in time. In truth, however, the freedom of his playing and his music was not fully understood. The Classicist Ignaz Moscheles, whose playing Chopin called "frightfully Baroque," could not understand Chopin's music until he heard him play it. Moscheles then confessed, "The harsh modulations which strike me disagreeably when I am playing his compositions no longer shock me, because he glides over them in a fairylike way with his delicate fingers."

Chopin's piano music remains the most frequently played in history. He is one of the few universal masters, and has never suffered an eclipse. Almost every note he wrote is in the permanent repertoire. Arthur Rubinstein confirmed: "When the first notes of Chopin sound through the concert hall, there is a happy sign of recognition. All over the world men and women know his music. They love it; they are moved by it. Yet it is not Romantic music in the Byronic sense. It does not tell stories or paint pictures. It is expressive and personal, but still a *pure* art."

Anton Rubinstein called him "the Piano Bard, the Piano Rhapsodist, the Piano Mind, and the Piano Soul," declaring that "whether the spirit of the instrument breathed upon him, I do not know . . . but all possible expressions are found in his compositions, and are all sung by him upon this instrument." The world rightly knows Chopin as "the poet of the piano." Indeed, the instrument's very prestige would be in jeopardy without his contribution.

WINIFRED CHRISTIE
1882–1965—England

She studied with Oscar Beringer at the Royal Academy of Music and later with Harold Bauer. Christie married Emanuel Moór, the inventor of the intriguing Duplex-Coupler piano, a piano with two keyboards. For many years she propagandized this instrument with brilliant performances in America and Europe. She also wrote a group of technical exercises for it.

MARCEL CIAMPI
1891–1980—France

A pupil of Diémer at the Paris Conservatoire. Ciampi stood for much of his career in the forefront of French pianism. He performed extensively both in solo and chamber music; especially notable were his tours with Casals.

Ciampi trained many pianists, including Cécile Ousset and Hephzibah Menuhin. Irving Kolodin in 1940 writes of Ciampi's disc of Debussy's *Feux d'artifice,* saying, "an astonishing bit of piano playing . . . The pianist's formidable tactile sense, the clarity and definition of his finger work are the materials of a completely unusual record." Enesco dedicated his Third Sonata to Ciampi, who also premiered it.

DINO CIANI
1941–1974—Italy

He studied with various teachers in Italy and with Cortot. He was a pianist with expressive power and a technique which encompassed Liszt's *Chasse-neige* and Balakirev's *Islamey.* A great many of his performances have been preserved on CD, including the Weber Sonata No. 2 and Beethoven's *Diabelli* Variations and Debussy Preludes. He was killed in an auto accident, and a piano competition was created in his memory.

ALDO CICCOLINI
b. 1925—Italy

A brilliant pianist who plays internationally and teaches at the Paris Conservatoire. He brings a robust, zestful feeling to his playing, which is colorful but never drenched in pedal. He is never niggling, but shows instead a generosity of spirit. He is at his best in the French piano music of *La Belle Epoque,* standing as Chabrier's leading all-round interpreter. He has done the complete Satie on records, fully expressing the music's whimsy and satire. He has a taste for Saint-Saëns which gives to the five Concerti a streamlined, nonrhetorical sensibility. His Scarlatti is admirable, clear and joyous, but his Debussy is weaker, less focused, and his Albéniz *Iberia* leaves much unstated, achieving a Spanish flavor but without its deeper essence.

WILHELMINE CLAUSS-SZARVADY
1834–1907—Czechoslovakia

She studied in Prague, and from the first, with her tour in 1849, her playing caused a stir. Her great reputation was based mostly on her playing of Bach and Beethoven, although her playing of Chopin was respected.

MUZIO CLEMENTI
1752–1832—Italy

Born four years before Mozart, he was, like Mozart, a child prodigy, playing both the harpsichord and the organ brilliantly. As a child, he studied with teachers in Rome. At the age of nine he became a church organist. By the time he was fourteen, he had composed several church works, and a mass was performed in Rome. His father, a passionate music lover,

was extremely poor and unable to support his son, but a solution was found. At fourteen, Clementi was virtually sold off to a wealthy Englishman, Peter Beckwood, who took him back to his country estate. For the next several years Clementi lived in a carefree atmosphere, with every possible advantage. Best of all, he had the new English Broadwood piano, and he experimented tirelessly on it, developing a far more muscular approach than anyone had attempted, with a new legato style.

At the age of twenty-one, he moved to London, where his playing was quickly appreciated as a great advance over that of J. C. Bach and other early players. From 1770 to 1780, he was keyboard player and conductor at the Italian Opera in London. In 1781, Clementi made his first European tour, during which his playing was recognized at once as entirely new. In Vienna, Clementi encountered Mozart in a grueling pianistic duel played before the emperor at court. The outcome was a draw, but Mozart was irritated and his letters are a rather brutal condemnation of his colleague. He called Clementi a mere mechanic, without a penny's worth of feeling or taste. Mozart was peeved at the Italian's brilliance, calling all Italians charlatans. He hated Clementi's loud, fast octaves, his overall boldness, his passages in thirds (a Clementi specialty), and he warned his sister not to touch Clementi's devilish music for fear of turning stiff. Actually, Mozart sensed in Clementi something wild and frightening. (It must be said that Clementi had nothing but praise for Mozart's singing tone and exquisite style.)

Upon his return to England, Clementi entered the business of making pianofortes. In the end, Clementi's pianos (and view of the piano) triumphed over Mozart's light, flutysounding Viennese pianos, whose tones were too Rococo and reminiscent of the metallic harpsichord for the stronger vibrations of the Romantic style.

In 1802, to promote his pianos, Clementi traveled with his pupil John Field to various European capitals, ending in St. Petersburg, where Clementi pianos made a particularly deep impression. They became revered both in Europe and in America, and Clementi himself grew wealthy. He enjoyed playing the part of a country gentleman who happened to be a genius. He once said, "I'm an old Englishman and a young Italian." He became an English institution, and when he died, in 1832, he received a public funeral and was buried in the cloisters of Westminster Abbey. The tablet reads, "Here lies the Father of the Pianoforte." Indeed, if any one person merits this epitaph, it is Clementi. Not only was he the world's first great pianist, but his sonatas of 1773 may be considered the first music composed for the young instrument's capacity to produce a wide dynamic range through the manipulation of varying pressures.

Not only was Clementi a tireless promoter of the instrument, but he also dramatically improved the art of piano building. He was a music publisher as well, and he brought to the public a stream of new publications, including much of his own music. As a teacher, Clementi helped produce the important pianists of the next generation, including Field and Cramer, and he gave private lessons to a great many wealthy English aristocrats. He eventually charged the enormous sum of one guinea for a forty-minute lesson, and he could fit in a dozen lessons a day in his early years.

In the highly commercial climate of England, Clementi helped to establish respect for the musician and also for the teaching of music, a profession that at the time was deemed neither respectable nor gentlemanly. Haydn and most other musicians were accorded a status little higher than that of servants.

Clementi's enlarged view of piano technique was codified in his 1817 magnum opus, *Gradus ad Parnassum,* a set of one hundred pieces including etudes, slow movements, fugues, and canons. Clementi's pianism was still of the Classical period, but his work in many ways presaged what the piano would eventually be asked to do. Today, the *Gradus* is sadly neglected by teachers, though there is no work to compare with it for building a solid technique.

He also composed sixty-four solo sonatas from 1773 to 1820—the longest career of any sonata composer. Indeed, had Beethoven not lived, Clementi's sonatas would represent a high-water mark in the history of the form. Beethoven was deeply indebted to the Clementi sonatas and kept his volume of them always at hand. Brahms, too, admired Clementi's adventurousness and freedom of form. From the pianistic view, Clementi's etudes formed the foundation for the future of etude writing, culminating in the etudes of Chopin.

Clementi died at eighty, just as the twenty-two-year-old Chopin was putting the finishing touches on his own etudes. It is worth noting that not one of Chopin's own pupils was allowed to touch his etudes until the student had a thorough grounding in Clementi's.

VAN CLIBURN
b. 1934—United States

He began his musical studies with his mother, who in turn had studied with Arthur Friedheim. At eighteen, he arrived in New York to work with the celebrated Mme Lhévinne at Juilliard, where he became her favored pupil. The 1955 Leventritt Award started his career rolling. By the end of 1957, though, it was fading fast. Word of a great new Soviet competition was in the news for 1958. Thinking this could be his break, Mme Lhévinne encouraged him to prepare, and, with classmate Daniel

Pollack, he went to Russia. It was a tense time; the Cold War, a recession at home, and Russia's Sputnik were in the news. Although the Tchaikovsky Competition was designed to show the world the wonderful young artists of Soviet socialism, there just was no escaping the fact that Cliburn was irresistible. This gangling, six-foot-four-inch, curly-haired, homespun southerner drove the Russians to fever pitch with his golden sound and relaxed but grand style. The competition had been reported measure by measure by the *New York Times*, and when Cliburn won the day for America, the country went wild. He returned home a hero of the Cold War, an American who played the piano better than the Russians.

This twenty-four-year-old was given a ticker-tape parade, an unprecedented welcome for a pianist. The Russians consoled themselves with the fact that Cliburn had studied with Rosina Lhévinne, wife of the great Russian master Josef Lhévinne. She knew all the secrets of tonal magic that had emanated from the St. Petersburg and Moscow conservatories. Cliburn was at his best playing music by Russians; he was their spiritual kin. As a result of his victory, he made a recording with the Russian conductor Kiril Kondrashin of the signature piece of the Tchaikovsky Competition—the luscious Concerto No. 1. And what a beautiful reading it remains— sculptural, warm, grandly Romantic. The third movement is played much more slowly than usual, bringing Tchaikovsky's use of a folk song about a blind man to the fore. (If a household had only one classical concerto at that time, it was likely to be Cliburn's Tchaikovsky Concerto No. 1.)

Most of Cliburn's concerto readings from that early period display wonderfully Romantic, plush playing. The best is his Third Rachmaninoff Concerto, followed by the MacDowell D minor, Grieg, Schumann, both of Liszt's, the Prokofiev Third, and the Chopin E minor.

For years after his competition victory, Cliburn played and recorded relentlessly. He has made some good Mozart discs, though his Beethoven may be just too tame, nailed firmly to a conservatory plan. He did make excellent displays of the Prokofiev Sixth Sonata, Rachmaninoff's Second Sonata, Barber's Sonata, a good Liszt Sonata, and much Chopin, such as the pianistically beautiful B minor Sonata, with a feathery scherzo.

But as the years went by, he lacked the time and energy to add to his standard repertoire. He became sloppy; the engaging lyricism and spaciousness were disappearing. The playing got severely predictable, the tempi stodgy, the emotion tepid. He built a piece to a climax only to lose it at its height. There was little doubt Cliburn needed a rest. He must have been weary of being a hero, on the move for twenty years, playing the Tchaikovsky concerto again and again.

And so he quit playing for over a decade, emerging again in 1989 with a dazzling tour of Russia. He also performed with the Philadelphia Orchestra, and his playing was once again proud, vigorous, and poetic. If, however, Cliburn never returns to regular concertizing, he has written one of the most spectacular pages in the history of his instrument, and his accomplishment and his legend will live on. Cliburn has become the most famous American pianist of the century, even a household name.

FRANCE CLIDAT
b. 1932—France

A student of Lazare Lévy, Clidat has great pianistic facility and a rare feeling for Liszt. In her many recordings of this master she is stylish and often grand. Her pedaling is sparse and her fingerwork clean and elegant.

ARNALDO COHEN
b. 1948—Brazil

Born in Rio de Janeiro, he studied with Jacques Klein, and later with Dieter Weber in Vienna. In 1972 he was first-prize winner at the Busoni Competition, which led to engagements in Europe. He has performed with many major orchestras and conductors; in the past few seasons he has made a mark in the United States and his career is gaining impetus. Cohen is a sparkling technician with a large tone; he can toss off the four Scherzos of Chopin with what seems hardly a twitch of the wrist. He frequently is invited to sit on the juries of International Competitions and is a professor of the Royal Academy of Music in London.

HARRIET COHEN
1895–1967—England

A student of Tobias Matthay, she developed into a very individual performer and toured widely. Her Bach playing was highly regarded, and although she had small hands, she was the major exponent of the thick and complicated piano music of Sir Arnold Bax, whose Third Sonata is dedicated to her. She left some fine Bach transcriptions. The Harriet Cohen Medal is given in her memory.

JEAN-PHILIPPE COLLARD
b. 1948—France

He studied at the Paris Conservatoire and has become one of the most successful of present-day French pianists. He has a virtuoso technique and can play with bravura. His recordings of Fauré's piano music are beautifully planned and meticulous. He has a penchant for Rachmaninoff and frequently plays the piano Concerti, especially Nos. 1 and 3. He has recorded No. 3 in a healthy, breezy style.

GEORGE COPELAND
1882–1971—United States

Born in Boston, he studied with local teachers before receiving training from Terasa Carreño and Harold Bauer. He was a staunch supporter of the early-twentieth-century French School. In 1911 while performing in Paris, he was fortunate in meeting Debussy, who worked with him for a period of some months. Richard Aldrich, reviewing a Copeland New York recital, writes most appreciatively of his Debussy performance: "It showed a sympathy with their delicate and poetic qualities and extreme facility in the special technical demands they make on the performer—for there is obviously a "Debussy technique" as there is a technique for others. . . . His interpretation of Chopin had somewhat less of the individual flavor of the music."

ALFRED CORTOT
1877–1962—Switzerland

Alfred Cortot was born in Nyon, Switzerland. The family moved to Paris when Alfred was a child. His first piano lessons were with his sisters, and later he was accepted at the Paris Conservatoire, where he studied with Émile Descombes, a pupil of Chopin, and later with the illustrious Louis Diémer, one of the important French pianists of the second half of the nineteenth century. In 1896, at the age of nineteen, Cortot took the *Premier Prix* in piano at the Conservatoire, and his career was launched as soloist with the famed Colonne and Lamoureux orchestras. Soon after, he was touring Europe performing concertos and solo recitals.

An indefatigable worker, he built up a staggering repertoire and began conducting, as well as becoming a passionate Wagnerian and visiting the Bayreuth Festival as an assistant conductor, soaking up Wagnerian tradition by working with the conductors Felix Mottl and Hans Richter. During these formative years his knowledge of Beethoven deepened through the important pianist Édouard Risler, who helped him veer away from the drier style of current French piano playing.

In Paris in 1902, the twenty-five-year-old conductor gave the first performance of Wagner's *Götterdämmerung* and later *Parsifal*. He also performed the Paris premières of Brahms's *German Requiem*, Liszt's *Saint Elizabeth Oratorio,* and even Beethoven's *Missa Solemnis* which, amazing as it sounds, took eighty-five years to reach Paris from Vienna. Besides this, he championed many contemporary French works both as a conductor and pianist.

Ever restless and musically hungry, he formed a piano trio with Pablo Casals and Jacques Thibaud in 1905, which must rank as one of the finest chamber ensembles in history. Fortunately, their art is captured in several priceless recordings, including Beethoven's "Archduke" Trio, Schubert's B-flat Trio, and the Mendelssohn and Schumann D minor Trios, while Cortot's conducting may be heard in the Brahms Double Concerto, with Casals and Thibaud as soloists.

In spite of these various activities, it was the piano that most attracted his musical spirit. In 1907, Fauré appointed him professor of the pianoforte at the Paris Conservatoire, where he attracted the best students. He remained at the Conservatoire until 1919, when he founded

Alfred Cortot by David Dubal

the École Normale de Musique. Over the years, literally thousands of aspiring pianists came seeking his knowledge at his celebrated master classes. Some had the privilege of studying with him privately, including Gina Bachauer, Dino Ciani, Samson François, Clara Haskil, Magda Tagliaferro, Ruth Slenczynska, Yvonne Léfebure, Vlado Perlemuter, and Dinu Lipatti. He implored his pupils to intimately study the lives of the composers, their letters, and everything possible regarding their music. To Cortot this was a solemn duty. At lessons, he required a written analysis of the music to be played— "a geographical map," as he called it.

Cortot's dedication to his art was tireless. He once warned Lipatti, "If you decide to dedicate your life to this art you must be armed with patience, and be ready for many sacrifices." Cortot's musical advice was often highly detailed. After a public performance by Lipatti of the Liszt Piano Concerto No. 1,

Lipatti wrote home: "At the end of the concert Cortot opened the score and made some interesting remarks. He would have liked bars 22–23, in the third section (Scherzo), played a little more freely, more capriciously. Also in the Scherzo, bars 141–161, he suggested I play a tremolo (similar to the one which precedes the last scale-passage in the Coda) instead of a trill, as only in this way will it sound clearly and powerfully. The same applies to bars 70–72 in the Finale. As to bars 80–85, he suggests I play them in the version given as 'ossia,' not in original form. He also showed me several changes in the score added later by Liszt himself . . . "

Cortot often promoted his favorite pupils, opening many doors for them. Writing to an impressario about Lipatti he says, "It is my duty to bring to your notice a great pianist of the future, and to assure you that this will be to your advantage because I am writing about a real revelation on the horizon of pianists."

Cortot's involvement with the piano led him to prepare some eighty editions of the music of Chopin, Schumann, Liszt, Weber, and others. These are among the most intriguing editions ever made, providing a fund of splendid annotations and ingenious exercises for overcoming technical problems. Cortot was one of the great piano minds, and his writings are sprinkled with his own constant wonder at the masterpieces he played. He also left a treatise on interpretation, as well as two books, the invaluable *La Musique Française de Piano* (1930) and *Aspects de Chopin* (1949).

Cortot made his first American tour in 1918, and during the 1919–20 season in the United States he played forty-nine recitals in less than ninety days, with four separate recital programs. At Carnegie Hall he performed the five Beethoven Concertos, the Schumann Concerto, the Third Rachmaninoff, and the Saint-Saëns Fourth Concerto. During the 1920s and 1930s he made more than 150 recordings, becoming one of the best-selling recording artists of the era. During those busy years, Cortot gave nearly 1,500 recitals in Europe, Russia, and South America, 282 concerts in the United States and 292 in England, all in addition to his editing, conducting, chamber performances, and teaching.

Unfortunately, during World War II he became the high commissioner of the fine arts in the Vichy government and played concerts in Germany. Following the war, Cortot was found guilty of collaboration with the enemy by a French governmental panel, and was suspended from all public musical activity for a period of a year. But as soon as the year was completed, he was once again performing more than one hundred concerts a season. Cortot's health badly declined, becoming ravaged by pain and Parkinson's disease. His farewell performance took place on 10 July 1958, with Casals, but he continued teaching, giving his final master class late in 1961. A comprehensive biography of Cortot's personality and deeds still remains to be written.

There is no division about regarding Cortot as one of the "originals" in the history of interpretation. He was highly unpredictable and relied heavily on inspiration. Much too busy to sit for endless hours practicing, Cortot's memory lapses were terrifying, and his wrong notes could splatter a keyboard. Arthur Rubinstein wrote, "At a concert of Alfred Cortot they would wait with impatience for the moment when his memory would fail." And he was certainly, when out of shape, one of the sloppiest of the great pianists. But Cortot was a genius. There has never been anything like him. His phrasing could curl the toes, bring goose bumps to the flesh, send chills down the spine—and, when he was "in practice," he was a brilliant technician, with an astonishing left hand. The pianist Charles Timbrell interviewed Vlado Perlemuter, a pupil of Cortot's, who said, "He didn't just have one kind of technique. He constantly adapted his technical approach to the music." His pedaling was miraculous. Perlemuter explained, "It's a simple fact that the modern piano is often too harsh without the *una corda* (left) pedal, but too timid with it. So Cortot would often prefer the sound one gets by playing strongly with the *una corda,* if he wanted a sonorous soft sound. It's a sophisticated concept that is not well understood even today." "At my lessons," relates another pupil, Guthrie Luke, "Cortot would often pedal for me, using quarter, half and flutter pedalling."

Once one had heard Cortot's tone, it could never be forgotten. Magda Tagliaferro thought, "His sound was pure enchantment, whether the music was soft or loud." Yvonne Léfebure, who for years was Cortot's chief assistant, wrote, "When you listened to Cortot play, you realised that what he was doing at the piano was not like what other people were doing." In a Cortot performance there could be a new flash of insight, and the audience felt included in a special moment. Through his long career he marveled at the beauty and plasticity of the masterpieces of the piano literature, and, from many accounts, even in old age he transcended a broken body in playing with an often heart-breaking intimacy and poignancy. At his best, everything he touched was heightened with an uncanny elegance. He was so Romantic, truly the most youthfully Romantic of the great pianists. He had an inspired sense of rubato, and one inflection within a phrase can haunt the listener for days. For Cortot, music was aspiration, a reaching for the unknown. He searched for elusive lights and shadows. His playing was the difference between poetry and prose. Magda Tagliaferro declared, "The images that he conjured up were absolutely visionary."

Although musical ideas tumbled from his brain, he was so immersed in the composers he performed that he always communicated the composer's meaning without it ever becoming merely Cortot. He detested distorting the composer's idiom, and his student Thomas Manshardt, in his book *Aspects of Cortot,* related that after playing Franck's *Prelude, Chorale et Fugue* for Cortot, "there was no rage, no outburst; merely a gentle hand on my arm saying very softly, 'you have made one long magnificent error.'" Manshardt says Cortot had a horror of anonymous playing, but hated even more playing with the wrong feeling. In *Mademoiselle, Conversations with Nadia Boulanger,* by Bruno Monsaigeon, the great composition teacher remembers a Cortot performance of the Chopin Preludes: "I went to see him in his dressing-room and declared, 'A lot of people are asking me for my opinion, to describe how you played. I have no idea. All I know is that I've never found the Preludes so beautiful.' He had focused all his light on the Preludes, not the other way around. I had heard the work in all its splendour. My forgetting the interpreter wasn't neglect, on the contrary. It put him very high, because the light of someone who is nothing illuminates nothing."

Cortot's greatest celebrity rests on his Chopin performances. Perhaps Chopin gripped his heart and mind more than any other composer, and his contribution to the worldwide dissemination of the Polish master's works is significant. James Methuen-Campbell wrote that Cortot was an artist who "possessed extreme virtuosity and one of the greatest musical intellects of all time, who managed to combine the two into a perfect blend, and who had a greater affinity with Chopin's music than any other pianist of our age. His discs are for me, and many others, the foundation of Chopin-playing: subtle, melancholic, heroic, deeply communicative and 'full' . . . This playing has a quality that transcends normal music-making—it is as if Cortot is revealing Chopin's soul."

One notes that in 1926 Cortot made history's first complete version of the Preludes, and his Chopin recordings include various versions of the four Ballades, four Impromptus, the fourteen Valses, two Scherzos, six Nocturnes, two Sonatas, the Barcarolle, the Berceuse, Fantasy, and others. There are four versions of the Preludes. Of the 1926 recording, André Gide complains in his diary that he felt Cortot had an "absence of sensuality; in its place, grace and sentimentality." This is true of the 1926 Preludes, but his recording from 1933 displays a deep, almost guttural, sensuality. In Chopin's slower works his glorious sound is heard at its best. A French horn here, a violin there, a momentary harp, cello, or bassoon. As Eric Heidsieck said, "Cortot taught us to be in the habit of thinking of the piano as a 'little orchestra or, at times, maybe a big one.'"

Naturally, Cortot put his hand to Chopin's twenty-seven Etudes, although, when Rachmaninoff was asked his opinion of Cortot's recorded Etudes, the titanic virtuoso made the devastating comment, "too musical." Nevertheless, few pianists are not deeply affected by Cortot's Etudes. I once did a series of radio broadcasts in which I played dozens of performances of Chopin's Etudes to a panel of connoisseurs. In almost every Etude, even with a smudge or technical blur, Cortot's readings were favored. As Philippe Entremont put it, "Even his mistakes were fabulous! Nobody has ever played the Chopin Etudes the way Cortot played them. They are so immense, so gigantic; the nonconformity, the fabulous drive—the poetry of the music was airborne. I am absolutely spellbound by the courage of his playing." In an interview Alfred Brendel said of Cortot, "He is the one pianist who equally satisfies my mind, my senses and my emotions . . . three-dimensional playing . . . "

Cortot's recordings are never less than fascinating. His discography includes a magnificent reading of Weber's A-flat Sonata, a majestic Ravel Left-Hand Concerto with Munch. His Ravel *Jeux d'eau* is luscious, and his disc of the Sonatine glows. Cortot deeply admired Franck, and Cortot's teacher Diémer is the dedicatee and first performer of the Symphonic Variations. Cortot's own recording radiates, and his recording of the Prelude, Chorale and Fugue, as well as the neglected Prelude, Aria and Finale, have never been equaled.

His disc of Mendelssohn's *Variations Sérieuses* is a classic, as is the Saint-Saëns Fourth Concerto, which was one of his specialities. He was said to dislike Chopin's E minor Concerto, but played a ravishing Chopin F minor Concerto. His Debussy Preludes are delicately wrought and sensuous. His recording of smaller works of Liszt are more successful than his seemingly flippant performance of the Liszt Sonata. Of the classic masters there is very little, and although he recorded twice the Beethoven Sonatas, they have not been issued.

Next to Chopin, he most recorded Schumann. Indeed, there are four versions of the Schumann Concerto, three recordings of *Carnaval,* the finest from 1928, as well as *Papillons,* the *Symphonic Etudes, Davidsbündlertänze,* and a *Kreisleriana* of startling poetry and visionary beauty. Cortot's Schumann is chivalric, atmospheric, indeed almost impressionistic at moments, with an ineffable sadness of heart.

Since around 1975, music lovers, tired of the perfection and sameness of countless recorded performances, have been responding ever more to the charm, the soaring imagination, the luminous sound, the bold chance-taking and daring of Cortot's recordings. Each year in my courses at the Juilliard School I take a poll as to the recordings most favored by my pupils in our studies of great pianists. Invariably the choices are Hofmann, Schnabel, Hess, Horowitz, Lipatti, Kapell, Barère, Friedman, Rachmaninoff and, always at or near the top, is Alfred Cortot, whose inspiration to young pianists has a thrilling effect. Recently I played Cortot's recording of Chopin's A-flat Impromptu for a rather bored pianist who had told me he would soon leave the art of music for studies in something more "practical." By the end of the performance the sensitive young pianist was transformed. In a flash his life had changed, and music again lived within him. From that moment, he studied everything that he could hear by Cortot. Indeed, Cortot was an inspired artist, and his recordings remain a testament to a Romantic nature, intoxicated on his own delirious temperament.

JOHANN BAPTIST CRAMER
1771–1858—Germany

His first public performance took place in 1781. Cramer then studied with Clementi for two years. In 1824 he started a music publishing firm. He was a founder of the Royal Philharmonic Society. Besides his well-known etudes, Cramer composed seven concertos, innumerable variations and rondos, and 105 sonatas.

Born in Germany and brought to London as an infant, "Glorious John," as the English called him, was one of the founders of piano playing, and one of the very important performers of Beethoven's generation. He was unusual in his day in that he revered music of the past, playing Bach and Handel whenever he could, and Mozart was his god. Cramer was also a fine improviser and was expected, as were all players of the day, to exhibit this skill at concerts. At thirteen, Cramer made piano history by appearing with his master Clementi in the first public performance of a work for two pianos. By the age of seventeen, he had begun giving regular concerts in England and on the Continent in a career that would last nearly sixty years. His colleague Moscheles described "his thin, well-shaped fingers which are so well suited for legato playing," and called his Mozart "breezes from the sweet south. He sings on the piano . . . he almost transforms a Mozart andante into a vocal piece."

In 1804, Cramer ensured his immortality when he issued the first forty-two of his eighty-four etudes, a landmark in piano technique. Each of these etudes explores a specific mechanistic problem, but they are also interesting as music, and remain to this day worthy of study. Beethoven, who hated most pianists, deeply admired Cramer's playing and his etudes, which he recommended as technical preparation for his own music. He wanted them taught to his nephew and advised Czerny to that effect.

As a pianist and composer, Cramer outlived his time. The wooden pianos of his youth gave way to the huge iron-framed instruments bearing the names Bluthner, Bösendorfer, Bechstein, and Steinway.

In the 1830s, Liszt paid a respectful visit to Cramer, and they played a duet together. Liszt told Moscheles of the visit, roguishly saying, "I was the poisoned mushroom, and I had at my side my antidote of milk." Cramer was considered dry and tame by the younger pianists of the time. He quipped, "Formerly, piano playing was mighty good (*fort bien*). Now it's good and mighty (*bien forte*)." The rich scent of Romanticism was not for Cramer, and he admitted the music was "too strong" for him. Nevertheless, he and his etudes were of vital importance in the development and growth of pianistic virtuosity.

HAROLD CRAXTON
1885–1971—England

A pupil of Tobias Matthay, he had a fine career as accompanist and solo player, and was a distinguished teacher. His editions of Bach and Beethoven are noteworthy.

EVELYNE CROCHET
b. 1934—France

A pupil of Yvonne Lefébure at the Paris Conservatoire, where she took a first prize in 1954. Her early teacher was Rose-Aye Lejour. In Charles Timbrell's book *French Pianism,* Crochet recalls Lejour; she "was a wonderful teacher who made us aware of our responsibilities to the music and really taught us how to 'practice' from A to Z on every single type of problem, musically and technically. Madame Lefébure's teaching was the perfect extension of my work with Lejour. Lefébure taught music through the piano. Each weekly class lasted from one o'clock in the afternoon to eight in the evening with hardly any stop." Crochet also worked with Edwin Fischer and Nadia Boulanger. She made her American debut in the Poulenc Two-Piano Concerto with the composer at the second piano. Her LPs of Fauré are finely spun, with moments of profundity in the late nocturnes. VOX would do well to release these admirable recordings on CD.

Her recent traversal of Bach's *Well-Tempered Clavier* on CD gives articulation to each voice, and her interpretations prove a lifetime of devoted study. Crochet has taught at the New England Conservatory, Rutgers, Brandeis, and Curtis.

SIR CLIFFORD CURZON
1907–1982—England

His early studies were with Matthay in London; later he worked with Schnabel in Berlin for two years and with Landowska in Paris. In 1939 he made his American debut, in New York, with the time-honored, but usually battered, Tchaikovsky First Concerto, which he always played with the greatest respect. During his career, he turned his hand mainly to the great German masters, whose works he clothed with new meanings, adding distinctly to our knowledge of them. His performances of Schumann, Brahms, Schubert and Beethoven always possess breadth of conception, nobility, and passion. Curzon had the quality of universality in his playing, combining an unusual sense of formal design with an expressive simplicity.

Few have had his power to make clear the largest structures of Schubert. Reviewing a 1950 Curzon recital, Virgil Thomson noted this quality: "The Schubert Sonata in D, Op. 53 [D. 850] . . . he walked around in. He did not get lost in it or allow us to forget its plan, but he did take us with him to the windows and show us all its sweet and dreaming views of the Austrian countryside, some of them filled with dancing folk. The terraced dynamics and the abstention from downbeat pulsations . . . kept the rendering impersonal at no loss to expressivity. On the contrary, indeed, the dramatization of it as a form, the scaling of its musical elements gave it evocative power as well as grandeur of proportion. And its enormous variety in the kinds of sound employed, its solid basses, and a dry clarity in the materials of its structural filling prevented monotony from becoming a concomitant of its vastness."

Here is a description of the very ideal in large-scale Schubert playing. It would be equally true of Curzon's recordings of Schumann's Fantasy, Beethoven's *Eroica* Variations, and the Mozart Concerti he so loved. In fact, in his last years Sir Clifford's world was exclusively devoted to Mozart. Each Concerto was refined, warm, playful, dignified, and deeply humane. He never lost the pulse or made a bad sound, and always found an inimitable freshness in these most subtle of all concerti.

He was a great Brahmsian, in the smaller scope as well as in the works of Brahms the giant. To my mind, his recording of the Brahms F minor Sonata is the greatest ever made, and I deeply admire the treasured performances by Bauer, Rubinstein, Kempff, and Arrau. Here Curzon's spirit soars. This diffuse, sprawling score is built up simply and majestically, with an almost unbelievable grasp of form. Never have mind, heart, and fingers so fused: the roll of Curzon's chords is oceanic, not an inflection goes wrong. Of the huge Andante espressivo movement, Curzon wrote, "It is a picture of Romantic love perhaps not excelled in the whole literature of the piano." Curzon paints this picture with a consummate sense of space and atmosphere and overwhelming emotional power.

Curzon is not usually associated with Liszt, but his Liszt record is deeply satisfying, one to which I return often. It includes a finely spun Berceuse, a sadly neglected piece, played with murmuring pedalings. He gives us a sane *Liebestraum*, a beautifully formed *Valse oubliée*, and the *Dance of the Gnomes*, played with ironic humor and with as much care as he lavished on a Schubert impromptu or a Brahms intermezzo. But the high point is a serious but sensuous reading of the great B minor Sonata. In it he achieves a large sonority combined with a deep tenderness, an unflagging rhythm, and an inexorable structural plan.

Curzon was an artist who worked for perfection. I can only imagine what pains he took to arrive at his tremendous achievements.

The poet Stephen Spender wrote: "Clifford Curzon worshipped at a piano-shaped altar. . . . Clifford's soul went into his music. He had the highest standards in everything and, with his beautiful house, garden, pictures, furniture, seemed the best possible product—redeemed and purified by work—of a very high, remote remnant of civilization. Often the great musicians seem like this: they are the orchids of culture, hot-house flowers of the European nineteenth century."

CARL CZERNY
1791–1857—Austria

Czerny started playing the piano at three, was composing at seven, and performed for Beethoven when he was ten years old, playing no less than Mozart's great Concerto No. 25 in C, K. 503, and Beethoven's own recently published *Sonate pathétique*. Beethoven grabbed Czerny as a pupil, instructing him with great diligence and regularity for three years, without compensation. Czerny repaid Beethoven by becoming one of the chief disseminators of his music. By the age of sixteen, Czerny was musically on his own, and flocks of students began coming to him. He was a pianist of the fleet Viennese school of playing, and his performances were considered fluid and brilliant. He never tried to imitate the volatile Beethoven, being a pianist in the neat Hummel tradition. He was extremely nervous about playing in public and did it seldom, but managed to give the Vienna premiere of Beethoven's *Emperor* Concerto in 1811.

As a composer, Czerny was a one-man industry. He could work on five or six pieces at a time, rushing madly from one music stand to another. He produced nearly one thousand opus numbers (some containing more than fifty pieces, such as his Op. 749—*The Art of Finger Dexterity*), all the while maintaining a ten- to twelve-hour teaching day. He wrote in many forms, but his renown rests on his etudes, which have been the pedagogical bread and butter for generations of students.

The Canadian author Robertson Davies wrote: "When I was a child piano lessons involved an intimate acquaintance with the exercises of a friend named Carl Czerny. All of which were intended to be performed at incredible speed. The pupil of those days began with a variety of Czerny, and soon passed on to thick books called *The School of Velocity*, *The School of Finger Dexterity*, and so forth until he approached a work of blood-chilling difficulty called *The Virtuoso Pianist*. I never scaled this awful eminence (I broke down and was flung aside in *Finger Dexterity*) but I heard other students playing it, and such swoops, crashes and wrist-paralyzing convulsions of sound were never heard. The object of learning all this, I was told, was that if, in later life, one broke down in the performance of a concerto one could always fill in with a few spasms of Czerny; the musically ignorant in the audience would never notice the difference, and the musically élite would understand that the pianist was perfectly capable of playing anything."

Czerny has come to mean arduous torture of the fingers and an arid desert musically. H. L. Mencken, in his *Happy Days*, wrote: "For Czerny I never developed an affection, and neither did any other male piano student of my generation. He was admired only by vinegary little girls who wore tight pigtails tied with pink ribbons, and played his infernal scales and arpeggios in a pretentious and offensive manner. As late as 1930, being in Vienna, I visited and desecrated his grave."

Czerny made a fortune not only from his teaching but by accurately gauging the taste of the day. Beethoven and Weber were not the average musical diet. The public wanted tasty opera tunes, well-mannered and polite. Besides his etudes, Czerny concocted no fewer than 304 sets of variations and potpourris, based on eighty-seven operas of the time. These works had a worldwide consumption. As Arthur Loesser says: "His talent was extraordinary. Within the limits of a narrow harmonic scheme, he developed a prodigious understanding of the motion shapes feasible to keyboard-traveling fingers. . . . Rapid, feathery, well-articulated pianistic passagework, chiefly for the right hand, was his best product—just what the light, bouncing, leather-covered little hammer-heads of the Vienna pianos could deliver best . . . always smooth and pretty and rather ear-tickling when played fast."

Czerny was an outstanding teacher. Liszt adored him, modestly professing that "I owe him everything," and dedicated his *Transcendental Etudes* to him. Czerny was Liszt's only piano teacher, instructing him without fee. Theodor Leschetizky, the most famous piano pedagogue of the second half of the nineteenth century, studied with Czerny between ages eleven and fourteen. When he was asked about his own "method," he simply stated that he taught as Czerny did. Leschetizky auditioned for him with Czerny's own Concertino and a set of variations by Herz.

"His manner of teaching," Leschetizky later related, "was somewhat that of an orchestral director. He gave his lessons standing, indicating the different shades of tempo and coloring by gestures. Czerny insisted principally on accuracy, brilliancy, and pianistic effects. I played a great deal of Bach under him, some compositions by Alkan, some by Thalberg, and, above all, those of Beethoven. Czerny taught that Beethoven should be rendered with freedom of delivery and depth of feeling. A pedantic, inelastic interpretation of the master made him wild. He allowed me to play Chopin just as I pleased, and though he appreciated the great Pole, he sometimes said his compositions were sweetish. He understood Mendelssohn. I remember studying the *Songs without Words* almost as soon as they appeared."

Czerny, it seemed, had no personal life. He lived simply, with a house full of cats. Throughout his career, he helped many artists financially, and in his will he bequeathed a large part of his fortune to a school for deaf-mutes.

HALINA CZERNY-STEFANSKA
1922–2000—Poland

The co-winner, with Bella Davidovich, of the

1949 Chopin Competition in Warsaw. She is best known for her Chopin, especially her mazurka playing. A celebrated disc of the Chopin E minor Concerto thought to be by Lipatti has been discovered to be by Czerny-Stefanska. The critic Joachim Kaiser, writing of her Chopin, says, "She puts soul into every up-beat, warmth into every passage, sorrow into every sob."

GYÖRGY CZIFFRA
1921–1994—Hungary

One of the most remarkable piano technicians of all time. His hands were boned and bonded for piano playing and he had breathtaking reflexes. His fingerwork alone was dizzying—tiny hot pearls falling on the proverbial red velvet. Intoxicated by sheer pianistics, he weighted a chord to its smallest ounce, and colored whichever note he wanted us to hear. But Cziffra just would not stop fooling with the score; he was a lapidarian who often made the music rotten with artifice. He was a throwback to a madcap era when such playing was considered a sign of heaven-sent genius, when poetic license and a loose musical morality were often mistaken for freedom. Yet when Cziffra tried to temper himself, or played a repertoire unsuited to his gypsylike temperament, he became earthbound and dull. He was at his best as a rarefied entertainer, and his transcriptions were wonderful. He often blended some trashy playing with delicious and elegant playing. His Liszt was sensational—listen to his set of the Hungarian Rhapsodies—and he could even be serious, as in the Légende–Saint Francis of Paolo Walking on the Waves. He played a great variety of Liszt, from transcriptions (my favorite being the Polonaise from Eugene Onegin) to the Concerti and Totentanz.

Cziffra found Chopin an enigma. His Barcarolle is by turns nervous and too placid. The Polonaises are tawdry, and his recording of the Etudes is a compendium of bad habits and virtuosity for its own sake; nevertheless, he reveals fascinating perspectives on the music.

But enough carping. I don't listen to Cziffra for depth. I simply want to be dazed by one of the great piano trapeze acts. His octaves can only be termed fabulous. When I listen to his transcription in octaves of Rimsky-Korsakov's Flight of the Bumblebee, I ask, what would Alexander Dreyschock or Liszt say? In an age satiated with wonders, such a display is still dazzling, and not only to other pianists.

In the decade following Cziffra's death, I have found more and more pleasures in listening to his discs. His nervous system is perhaps the most amazing in the history of pianism, bringing to the concept of virtuosity a spiritual intensity. What would Liszt himself have said if he heard Cziffra play his Grand Gallop Chromatique or his irradiate performance of the Totentanz for Piano and Orchestra? The English critic Bryce Morrison wrote, "Like Icarus, Cziffra flew dangerously close to the sun; his high-voltage wizardry created an aura and excitement of its own."

But there are musical subtleties everywhere. Listen to his Scarlatti or the Chopin Etudes, which give us a new dimension to these vaunted scores. There are some straight-laced listeners who call his Chopin Etudes a desecration of the Polish master. For me it is courageous, unbounded playing, far from pleasing. But listen to the uncanny playing. You will find new paths to follow.

The virtuoso Cziffra has often astounded. Who else can quite burst a mountainous avalanche of octaves so fearlessly? Listen carefully, compare others in, say, Liszt's Transcendental Etudes. You will find him achieving strange lighting, eerie shadings, lyric delicacies with a twist, and shimmering tones brought by way of ear and pedal combined to create newborn colors. Cziffra could caress his instrument as well as bloody it. He had the true Romantic temperament, a very rare thing. He was a hero of the keyboard, a bewitching artist in the firmament of piano playing, and he will remain a controversial figure.

D

JOSEPH DACHS

1825–1896—Austria

An eminent pianist who taught at the Vienna Conservatory. De Pachmann, Joseph Rubinstein, and Isabelle Vengerova worked with Dachs.

MICHEL DALBERTO

b. 1955—France

A notable pianist who studied at the Paris Conservatoire with Vlado Perlemuter and in Geneva with Magaloff. He was the 1975 winner of the Clara Haskil Competition and went on to win first prize at the 1978 Leeds Competition. Dalberto has distinguished himself in his Schubert recordings, and is equally at home in Brahms, Schumann, and the more poetic works of Liszt.

KATHLEEN DALE

1895–1984—England

She was a student of both Fanny Davies and York Bowen. Dale was a fine accompanist and chamber player. In addition, she wrote a book entitled *Nineteenth Century Piano Music*.

EDWARD DANNREUTHER

1844–1905—Germany

A student of Moscheles, Dannreuther settled in London, giving in 1863 the first performance there of the Chopin F minor Concerto. He taught James Friskin and Harold Samuel. His treatise on *Musical Ornamentation* was the standard work on the subject.

JEANNE-MARIE DARRÉ

1905–1999—France

She studied with Isidor Philipp and Marguerite Long. Darré had a distinguished career as a teacher at the Paris Conservatoire and as a concert pianist. She made her American debut in 1960, and her very smart playing was quickly appreciated. She thrives in objective scores, such as the Ravel G major Concerto, Weber's *Konzertstück*, or any of the Saint-Saëns Concerti, for which she is famous. At her best, she is alert and glittering, possessing a dryness of tone that is characteristic of French pianism in general. At her worst, she sounds curt, even heartless. I heard her in recital with the Twenty-four Chopin Preludes, where she merely prattled without a smattering of involvement. Her Chopin is at its best in the Scherzos, at its worst in the tight-lipped and uncomfortable rubato displayed in the Waltzes.

Her playing at all times manifests an interest in neat, finely grounded pianism; each nut and bolt is squarely placed. Her prime achievement on record is a fascinating portrayal of Liszt's Sonata, which she spins out to 33:20. Darré has placed this complex puzzle under her microscope and dissected its every fragment. She strips the massive work of its usual Faustian rumblings and bombast, giving us the quintessential French Liszt sonata: slim, linear, and controlled from first note to last. It is an abstract Liszt sonata, and the playing is Flaubertian.

season, George Bernard Shaw heard her and wrote, "Miss Fanny Davies was full of speed, lilt, life, and energy. She scampered through a fugue of Bach's with a cleverness and jollity that forced us to condone her utter irreverence."

The Beethoven Fourth Concerto was one of her specialties, and her Schumann playing was respected, deriving, as it did, directly from the great tradition of Mme Schumann herself. She also played the then all but unknown Elizabethan composers. In 1921, Davies was the first ever to give a piano recital in Westminster Abbey. Elgar wrote his Concert Allegro for her.

BELLA DAVIDOVICH
b. 1928—USSR

A student of Igumnov and Flier, she shared first prize with Halina Czerny-Stefanska at the 1949 Chopin Competition in Warsaw. Davidovich had a successful career in the Soviet Union before emigrating to the West, where she has continued to receive acclaim.

Davidovich's pianistic diction is immaculate, each phrase being well tailored and finely calibrated. She has a poetic strain, but elements of rapture, giddiness, or humor are absent. There is a wholesome quality in her work, and her recordings of the four Chopin Ballades, several Beethoven sonatas, and the Saint-Saëns G minor Concerto are satisfying. She has an affinity with Scriabin, and her playing of the Second Sonata finds her at her best.

IVAN DAVIS
b. 1932—United States

He studied with Carlo Zecchi and later with Horowitz for a short time. Davis is best in lighter music. His Gottschalk fairly bubbles. His Grand Scherzo, *Manchega*, and *Tournament Galop* are scintillating, as are such obscurities as Hoffman's *Dixiana*, Mason's *Silver-Spring*, or Bartlett's *Grand Polka de concert*. Here we have a freewheeling pianist who knows how to enjoy the music.

Davis also has an aptitude for Schumann, and his early recording of the *Carnaval* shows the music well fitted to his temperament. He has recorded the *Norma* paraphrase by Liszt with a wide color wheel. In concerto work, his *Rhapsody in Blue* is too jerky, the Liszt Concerti unaccountably ponderous, and his Tchaikovsky B-flat minor just too vulgar.

FANNY DAVIES
1861–1934—England

Davies studied with Reinecke and later with Clara Schumann. She became one of the most celebrated of English pianists. During the 1888

ÉLIE MIRIAM DELABORDE
1839–1913—France

Probably the illegitimate son of Alkan and

considered a formidable pianist. Saint-Saëns dedicated his Third Piano Concerto to him. Olga Samaroff studied with him.

ALICIA DE LARROCHA
b. 1923—Spain

A pupil of Frank Marshall, she made her first public appearance when she was five. At eleven, she made her first orchestral appearance, in a Mozart concerto, with Fernández Arbós conducting. After World War II, she began playing throughout Europe. In 1955 she made her American debut with the Los Angeles Philharmonic. She has received numerous honors, including the Spanish Order of Civil Merit, the Paderewski Medal, and the Harriet Cohen Medal.

De Larrocha takes a rightful place as one of the instrument's greatest players. She is the most comprehensive and important of all Spanish pianists. Born with unusually small hands, she transcended her limitation, overcoming every problem. Yet those small hands were destined for the keyboard; they are sinewy and pliable and the tips are padded. Recordings of her playing at the age of seven reveal more than a prodigy: they show an intense, pure, innocent musicality that expresses Chopin as naturally as a lark sings. She has somehow retained this innocence into maturity. De Larrocha, at her finest, defies analysis. She is a player of pure instinct, guided by an acute musical intelligence. Her formal building is never flabby or spontaneous. She works within a precise time cycle and is never one to capriciously play a score three minutes longer or shorter.

When she performs, the house is packed. With great urgency, this exceedingly small woman, with black fiery eyes and an innocent face, begins a grouping of Scarlatti or Soler sonatas. The playing has a grandly Spanish

Alicia de Larrocha by David Dubal

flourish, the rhythm snaps, the grace and lust of her playing remind us that de Larrocha is blessed with one of the most perfect, kinetic rhythmic senses in the musical world. She performs Spanish music of every era and genre as if each author had composed for her alone.

She must tire of being cast merely as a Spanish specialist. Few pianists have a larger appetite, and this includes hearty portions of the great Schumann literature. She displays her candor, shyness, and range of color in the F-sharp minor *Novellette*. Her *Humoreske* and *Kreisleriana* are full of whimsy. Less forthright, though, are the *Carnaval*, which is a shade cool, and the Fantasy, which is too disjointed.

Her Chopin never whimpers; it is strong, unmannered, and unfettered. A false rubato, an excessive phrase would be anathema to de Larrocha. In Ravel, she is happy; French music in general is one of her chief domains, in which she is crystalline and suave. How she can captivate in a Fauré nocturne or the Poulenc *Suite française*. Or listen to her Mendelssohn *Variations sérieuses* and the neglected Capriccio in A minor, Op. 33—so perfect in their rhythmic symmetry and richness of tone. Mozart is another of her loves, and her best Mozart is gallant and well structured yet also sassy and filled with life. She is happier in the solo works, where she is fully in command, than in the Concerti. She is not always in sympathy with Liszt. Her version of the Sonata seems perfunctory, even dutiful, nor is she suited to such juicy concertos as the Third Rachmaninoff or the Khachaturian. But in Falla's *Nights in the Gardens of Spain* she is magnificent.

She remains the greatest interpreter of Spanish music. The daring and drama of Albéniz's *Iberia,* the poetry and amorous passion of Granados's *Goyescas,* have found in her their ideal interpreter. In these works, her great gift for Spanish national rhythms of all types bursts forth. This music, so often condemned as picture-postcard nationalism, in her hands gains depth and power. She knows that within the scores lies music of mystical and mythic beauty. In her performances of *Iberia* and *Goyescas* there is a spiritualization that brings these works to the heights of epic national poetry.

Her perfectly controlled use of the pedal is an object lesson for all who play these pieces. Her instinct for the right color is unerring. Each line and sonority is woven into a complex tapestry. De Larrocha is not concerned only with producing a singing tone; she also knows when she must produce harshness. Her phrasing, too, is impeccable. She never dreams of throwing a line off kilter for the sake of a meretricious effect.

Her feeling is profound, her conceptions have a cumulative power. Every inflection is felt to the quick, each pause fraught with meaning, even with anxiety. Her *Fête-Dieu à Seville* erupts with pent-up violence. She employs a wide array of weights in voicing her chords; her fingers never fail to bring out whichever tone within a chord she wants highlighted. Liszt said nuance is the pianist's palette, and de Larrocha is a great painter in the Goya manner. One always hears the guitar, the castanets, the click of heels, and love sacred and profane. Through her art, she traces a history of the Spanish heart and landscape. Of all her composers, I think she most deeply and tenderly loves Granados, whether in the late *Danza lente* or the Twelve Spanish Dances; she attains dewy freshness in the early *Valses poéticos,* and plays the arresting, teeming *Goyescas* with more poetry by far than any others who have attempted this composition.

Ernest Newman wrote of Granados's *Goyescas* that "never before has an artist so profoundly entered into and colored the soul of a musician." De Larrocha, in turn, has entered the heart of Granados. Her performance of the great ballade *El Amor y la muerte,* in its fervent but noble melancholy, needs to be heard on a still summer's night, with the waft of lemon trees floating in the air, flooded by a luminous and ghostly moon. De Larrocha's playing has an extraordinary power of evocation.

NIKOLAI DEMIDENKO
b. 1955—Russia

He studied with Bashkirov at the Moscow Conservatory. A prizewinner at international competitions, Demidenko has been a British subject since 1995. He has now appeared with most of the world's leading orchestras, and shines brightly in the Romantic concerto literature. For Hyperion Records he has documented a large and varied corpus. His Wigmore Hall recitals have been favorite events of recent London seasons.

JÖRG DEMUS

b. 1928—Austria

He has had a busy recording career. His records, especially those of the late 1950s and 1960s, sound academic and dim, except for his admirable set of Bach's *Well-Tempered Clavier*. Without trying to imitate the harpsichord, he displays a scholarship, a subtle legato, and a fine use of the pedal. In the fugues, he handles the counterpoint with gentle ease. Schubert is the Classical master whom Demus plays best, with charm and affection, in fact. He is delightful in the G major Sonata. I also value his all-Franck disc, with a well-proportioned Prelude, Fugue, and Variation in the Harold Bauer transcription. Demus plays it with the right amount of Franckian fervor without ever getting sticky.

MISHA DICHTER

b. 1945—China

Studied with Aube Tzerko in Los Angeles, and in New York he received instruction from Rosina Lhévinne at the Juilliard School. In 1966, Dichter won second prize at the third Tchaikovsky Competition in Moscow, where he was the popular favorite.

When he is in the mood, he can be exciting; when not, he is bland indeed. He is capable of keeping interest alive in large scores such as the Brahms D minor Concerto and Schubert's posthumous A major and B-flat major Sonatas. His Beethoven is sturdy and careful, always musicianly. He has made Liszt albums of quality, although his set of the complete Hungarian Rhapsodies shows little inspiration. In Stravinsky's *Petrouchka* he shows the extent of his large and well-padded sound.

He has often been heard in duo-piano performances with his wife, Cipa.

LOUIS DIÉMER

1843–1919—France

He studied at the Paris Conservatoire with Marmontel, whom he succeeded in 1888. He accumulated a long list of pupils, among them Cortot, Robert Casadesus, Yves Nat, and Edouard Risler. Diémer wielded a strong influence on French pianism of his time. Saint-Saëns dedicated his brilliant Fifth Concerto to him, and he gave the premiere of Franck's *Symphonic Variations* in 1886.

THEODOR DÖHLER

1814–1856—Italy

An astounding child prodigy who studied with Czerny. Later he became a sought-after virtuoso. His own music reaches Op. 75, a set of etudes typical of the frippery he touted around Europe, music of immense difficulty with almost no content. The poet Heine called his playing "elegant impotence," but found he had "interesting pallor."

ERNÖ VON DOHNÁNYI

1877–1960—Hungary

He studied with the Liszt pupil István Thomán. Dohnányi may be called the last in the line of virtuoso pianist-composers. In his early career, he was a storming thunderer of a virtuoso, and eventually became one of the most powerful forces in Hungarian music, the virtual czar of piano teaching. Not to have studied with Dohnányi was a distinct disadvantage. Bartók said that it was Dohnányi who revealed to him the greatness of the Liszt Sonata, and Mischa Levitzki worked with him for four years, saying, "I know of no greater teacher." The list of his students is impressive, featuring such names as Géza Anda, György Cziffra, Annie Fischer, Andor Foldes, Edward Kilenyi, Lajos Hernádi, Georg Solti, Imre Ungar, and dozens of other brilliant pianists.

Somehow he always kept up his own playing. Even when he was past eighty, he was a formidable technician, as his recordings attest, and his finger technique was phenomenal. His playing combines nobility and lusty peasantry, yet he also shows a curious turgidity, with rhythmic mixtures which suffer from years of neglect. His *Moonlight* Sonata, recorded when he was eighty, has a first movement that would have been in poor taste in any era. The slow movement is agonized—not the "flower between two abysses" that Liszt once described. But in the finale there are flashes of his primal fire. His playing of Chopin is the old-fashioned and courtly playing of a melancholy improviser. He played his own music marvelously, recording several of his rhapsodies and a few of his valse transcriptions, which are delicious Viennese pastry. The most important of his discs is a masterly rendering of his B minor Concerto and his masterpiece, the Variations on a Nursery Tune for Piano and Orchestra, made with Sir Adrian Boult.

PETER DONOHOE
b. 1953—England

An outstanding pianist in a variety of litera-

ture. He won prizes at the Leeds Competition and the Tchaikovsky Competition in 1982. He studied with Yvonne Loriod in Paris. His recordings of the Liszt Sonata, Busoni Concerto, and Tchaikovsky's Second Concerto are worthy of investigation.

ANTON DOOR
1833–1919—Austria

He was an eminent pianist-teacher who studied with Czerny; years later he taught at the Moscow Conservatory. Tchaikovsky dedicated his captivating *Valse-caprice,* Op. 4, to Door, and Saint-Saëns likewise dedicated his Fourth Piano Concerto to him.

ANIA DORFMANN
1899–1984—Russia

Born in Odessa, she made her debut there at age ten. At thirteen she studied in Paris with Isidor Philipp for a year before having to return to Russia. It seems that Philipp was her only well-known teacher and Dorfman exhibited more traits of the qualities of French pianism than of the Russian school.

The Russian Revolution curtailed her musical development, but in 1920 she was able to return to Paris. A determined careerist, she performed wherever she was asked. By the late twenties she was a popular soloist in England, playing with Sir Henry Wood and Sir Thomas Beecham. In the 1930s her renown spread when she made a series of recordings for British Columbia, including a superb Mendelssohn G minor Concerto with Walter Goehr conducting the London Symphony. This and solo works from that period have been reissued on the Pearl label produced by the pianist and archivist Donald Manildi.

At New York's Town Hall, Dorfmann made a successful American debut in 1936. Toscanini, who seldom used a woman soloist, invited her in 1939 to perform with him at his Beethoven Festival. A later collaboration with the great Italian maestro resulted in their 1945 recording of the Beethoven Concerto No. 1, a recording that had wide circulation. Her later discography includes the Grieg Concerto with Leinsdorf and the complete *Songs without Words* of Mendelssohn. For this listener only a few of these pieces show signs of inspiration in rather parched performances. Perhaps Dorfmann was not the type of artist to be tied to "complete" projects.

Dorfmann won a high place among pianists during the decades of the twenties through the forties. As a woman she was acutely conscious of the extra persistence necessary for a woman to forge a musical career. In his notes to the Pearl release Manildi quotes her from a 1940s interview. Dorfmann said: "Only a great talent that is combined with a terrific, unswerving capacity for work can achieve a successful career. . . . If she is a true artist and her love for music plus her ability to create it is stronger in her than anything else—stronger than the prejudices that make success harder for a woman to win than a man in any field. . . . However if a girl has only moderate talent she should not think of a concert career because there is no need there for an artist of that caliber . . . [but] There is a real place in the world for every degree of musical talent, and we must be wise and patient enough to find it."

In her last years she taught at the Juilliard School, being active almost to the end. Her recordings tell us she had an impressive finger-technique flush with speed and verve. There is a freshness to her best work as well as a stylish quality that permeates the Debussy *La plus que lente,* Strauss-Tausig *Man lebt nur einmal* (We only live once), and Liszt's *Valse-*

Impromptu. There is also an attractive reticence and innate good taste in her delivery of the Beethoven Concerto No. 1 and Mendelssohn Concerto.

Irving Kolodin reviewing the '78 discs wrote, "Dorfmann and Goehr accomplish an extremely congenial reading of this work, one in which there is an abundance of spirit and well-disciplined execution, though no attempt to inflate the score beyond its proper dimension."

BARRY DOUGLAS
b. 1960—Ireland

A native of Belfast. In London he studied at the Royal College of Music. The winner of the 1986 Tchaikovsky Competition, he has attracted a loyal audience. His recordings to my ears sound hard as nails, but in public I have heard some engaging Debussy and Chopin. His Beethoven *Appassionata* I remember as merely ponderous, and I heard a roaring and raw *Hammerklavier* which brought a Carnegie Hall audience to its feet.

GINETTE DOYEN
b. 1921   France

She studied with Lazare-Lévy in Paris and went on to perform internationally. In the 1950s she made several long-playing recordings which have not been transferred to CD. There are moments of poetry in Mendelssohn's *Songs without Words*, which she recorded "complete" for the Westminster label. Of her disc of the Four Chopin Ballades, Harold Schonberg crucifies her, saying, "Doyen's playing is impossibly affected, a model of swooning adolescence."

JEAN DOYEN
1907–1982—France

A pupil in Marguerite Long's class at the Paris Conservatoire, he won a first prize in piano playing in 1922. Doyen was a true champion of French piano music and consistently performed d'Indy, Chabrier, Ravel, and Hahn, among others. One may hear his Fauré on Erato CDs, my main criticism being one of tonal monotony; his Chopin Waltzes are played neatly but with little flair in the brilliant ones. Doyen is a good example of the clipped articulate style of Phillip and Long which has all but disappeared from French pianism. As professor at the Paris Conservatoire from 1940 until 1977 he taught Thérèse Dussaut, Jean-Rodolphe Kars, Françoise Petit, and numerous others.

ALEXANDER DREYSCHOCK
1818–1869—Czechoslovakia

A pupil of Tomáschek, Dreyschock was a prodigy who became one of the kings of the piano. He played almost exclusively his own horrendously difficult music. Reputedly one of the towering technicians of the Romantic age, he specialized in pieces and arrangements for the left hand. He took Chopin's *Revolutionary* Etude in Octaves at an amazing tempo, to the disbelief of his audience. When Johann Baptist Cramer heard him in Paris, he cried, "The man has no left hand! Here are two right hands." He was compared to the titans of the piano. Heine said that he "made a hell of a racket. From Paris, one could hear him in Vienna." He composed a great deal, but not a note remains in the repertoire, although his *Konzertstück* has been recorded by Frank Cooper.

ZBIGNIEW DRZEWIECKI
1890–1971—Poland

A pianist and teacher of distinction and one of the founders and judges of the Chopin Competition in Warsaw. He counted among his students Felicja Blumental, Roger Woodward, Wladyslaw Kedra, Fou Ts'ong, Halina Czerny-Stefanska, Adam Harasiewicz, and Regina Smendzianka.

ALEXANDER DUBUC
1812–1898—Russia

He trained with John Field and was an important figure in early Russian pianism. He taught Alexander Villoing and Nikolai Zverev.

FRANÇOIS-RENÉ DUCHABLE
b. 1952—France

One of the bright lights of contemporary French pianism. In 1964 he entered the Paris Conservatoire, and in 1965 was awarded the first prize in piano playing. In 1968 he took the prize at the Queen Elizabeth Competition and immediately began concertizing on an international scale, appearing in Japan, Israel, Europe, South Africa, and the United States. In 1978 he made appearances with Herbert von Karajan, and he has appeared with the major orchestras of Europe. Arthur Rubinstein admired this young colleague and wrote, "He knows how to use his exceptional gifts to express music and convey intense emotion to his audiences."

Duchable has a wide repertory, but his

Chopin playing has received the most attention. His recording of the Etudes is an exciting excursion into this literature, and his disc of the Second and Third Sonatas reveals an astute sense of form as well as an individual approach to these often-played scores.

LOUISA DULCKEN

1811–1850—Germany

The sister of the violinist Ferdinand David, Dulcken studied with Willy Grund and made her first public appearance in Hamburg at the age of ten. From 1828 she lived in London, becoming a fixture in the pianistic life of England. She was considered an expressive player with a fine technique.

JÓZEF DULEBA

1842–1869—Poland

He studied in his native Poland until 1858 and then worked for two years with Marmontel. He established a fine reputation as a concert pianist, with extensive tours through Europe. He died of wounds received in a duel.

JAN LADISLAV DUSSEK

1760–1812—Czechoslovakia

Dussek was one of the most fascinating figures in the early era of the piano. His fame was widespread, and he was among the first pianists to take advantage of the newly emerging idea of giving concerts in public, to which he brought a showman's flair. Previously, keyboard players had played either with their backs to the public or directly facing them. But Dussek, shrewdly aware of his handsome profile, exhibited it to his audiences. He was dubbed *"Le Beau"* Dussek. His innovation caught on, and from that moment forward, pianists, beautiful or not, have played seated in this manner. Yet Dussek's vanity served a musical purpose. *"Le Beau"* soon discovered that the piano turned to the side with lid raised transmitted a more direct sound to the audience.

It was immediately apparent that his playing was different. Mozart and Clementi cultivated a singing tone, but Dussek seemed truly to "sing" on the instrument. Johann Tomáschek, an excellent pianist, reporting on a Dussek concert in Prague, relates that "after the opening bars, the public uttered one general ah! There was in fact something magical . . . his fingers were like a company of ten singers." Kalkbrenner, a pianist stingy with praise for anyone but himself, said of Dussek that "no other pianist I have ever heard more captivated his audiences." Dussek understood better than any of his contemporaries that the illusion of singing on the piano is dependent on a beautiful legato with judicious pedaling. Few pianists of the day fully understood pedaling, and Dussek was one of the first to notate pedal markings in his music, as well as to mark in his scores novel fingerings which promoted legato. Dussek kept pestering the Broadwood firm to extend the instrument's range from the five-octave compass. Finally, in 1794, he played a six-octave piano for the first time in public. (It would eventually be extended to 7⅓ octaves.)

Dussek was a restless man, and his career included many adventures. The happiest years of his life were spent as friend and teacher to Prince Louis Ferdinand of Prussia (nephew of Frederick the Great). The prince owned thirteen English pianos and was a good composer and pianist. (Beethoven honored him with the dedication of his Third Piano Concerto.) Dussek would even occasionally accompany Louis on military maneuvers. These were the Napoleonic years, and the prince was killed in battle in 1806, at the age of thirty-four. Dussek was grief-stricken, but out of his loss he produced *La Consolation,* Op. 62, and the masterly two-movement sonata *Elégie harmonique sur la mort du Prince Louis Ferdinand* in F-sharp minor, Op. 61, a work of astonishing emotional range and daring. Indeed, upon hearing it one scarcely believes that Dussek could have been born a mere four years after Mozart and died thirteen years earlier than Beethoven, or that he was born half a century before Chopin and Schumann, whose music he sometimes anticipates in an amazing manner.

William S. Newman, in his book *The Sonata Since Beethoven,* writes: "Dussek's best sonatas are regarded here as close to the best of their day, including those of Clementi, Beethoven, Schubert, and Weber—a view that may well surprise all but the relative few who have had the opportunity to explore or re-explore them. . . . Their several innovational styles often go beyond Dussek's environment of high-Classicism and well into that of unequivocal, sometimes fully bloomed, Romanticism."

In his later years, the once-dashing *Le Beau* became obese and alcoholic. He found an influential patron in Talleyrand, who let the pianist eat, drink, and compose. Regardless of his physical state, Dussek showed continual growth in his last works, which culminated in 1812 in the Sonata in F minor, Op. 77, subtitled *L'Invocation*—a work of magnificent depth and power.

Dussek remains the finest Czech-born composer before Smetana, and in several pieces he also anticipates Czech nationalism. Unfortunately, his work has all but disappeared from the living repertoire. He was, however, one of the most important musicians of his era, and the best of his output should be explored by contemporary pianists. He left nearly three hundred works, including twelve Concerti, showing him to be a composer who was deeply aware of the piano's potential.

VICTOR ALPHONSE DUVERNOY
1842–1907—France

A pupil of Marmontel at the Paris Conservatoire. His student pieces were played for several generations.

E

JOSÉ ECHANIZ
1905–1969—Cuba

A pianist and teacher at the Eastman School of Music. He made a number of recordings.

YOURI EGOROV
1954–1988—USSR

Studied with Yakov Zak and emigrated to the West. He made recordings of Chopin Etudes and works by other composers, and had much success with his Schumann playing. His piano technique was well polished, and his conceptions were better planned than those of many of the Russian pianists of his generation.

ILONA EIBENSCHÜTZ
1872–1967—Hungary

A brilliant prodigy who studied with Hans Schmitt at the Vienna Conservatory where she graduated at twelve. Later in Frankfort she worked for four years with Clara Schumann who would introduce her to Brahms. The great composer deeply admired her person and playing, and Eibenschütz championed his later piano pieces. In London, she became a favorite pianist and Shaw was at her debut when she was seventeen, calling her "a wild young woman," and was impressed with "her powers of mechanical execution." Her career burned brightly until her marriage in 1902, when appearances on the concert stage tapered off considerably.

SEVERIN EISENBERGER
1879–1945—Poland

Among his teachers was Leschetizky; from 1914 he taught at the Cracow Conservatory and from 1921 at the Vienna Conservatory. In the early 1930s he immigrated to the United States. Eisenberger's musicianship and highly developed pianism were admired.

JAN EKIER
b. 1913—Poland

A teacher, pianist, and Chopin scholar who has recorded many of Chopin's works in a dry manner.

BRIGITTE ENGERER
b. 1952—Tunis

Her first important teacher was Lucette

Descaves. She made her Paris debut at age ten. For five years she studied at the Moscow Conservatory with Stanislav Neuhaus. Her recordings feature the Romantic repertoire, and the Schumann *Faschingsschwank aus Wein* and Chopin Nocturnes are representative of her rather lean style. From 1994 she has taught piano at the Paris Conservatoire.

PHILIPPE ENTREMONT
b. 1934—France

He studied with Marguerite Long at the Paris Conservatoire. Entremont has long been a favorite with American audiences. Since his late teens he has been building an international career. If a town has a piano, Entremont will get there. Along the way, he has managed to become a fine conductor, holding positions with the Vienna Chamber Orchestra, the New Orleans Philharmonic, and the Denver Symphony. As a pianist, he has an industrious discography; it ranges from luxurious concertos to Clementi and Kuhlau sonatinas, which are a model for young students.

His best playing is contained on his earlier recordings of such concertos as Liszt's Second, Falla's *Nights in the Gardens of Spain,* the Ravel Concerto in G, and Bartók's Second. In later years, he opted for the facile, glamorous gesture, and many discs pall in their artificiality and chunkish pedaling and general puffiness. The Chopin Ballades, for instance, become meandering narratives, and his polonaise playing does no honor to Chopin's patriotism. In these scores, Entremont cannot find "the cannon buried amongst flowers," to borrow a phrase from Schumann. Yet Entremont is a gifted musician, and lately his solo recitals and Mozart concerto readings show a renewed concern for details as well as an intense concentration that had been missing for many seasons.

JULIUS EPSTEIN
1832–1923—Austria

For many years a well-known pianist and teacher at the Vienna Conservatory. His son, Richard Epstein (1869–1919), was an esteemed pianist and editor.

LONNY EPSTEIN
1885–1966—Germany

Studied at the Frankfurt Conservatory and later with Carl Friedberg. For years she taught at the Juilliard School. Although she had a large repertoire, her Mozart playing was especially admired.

EDUARD ERDMANN
1896–1958—Latvia

An important pianist who studied with the Liszt student Conrad Ansorge. His master classes in Cologne from 1925 were filled. Erdmann played music of all periods, gave the premiere of Artur Schnabel's Piano Sonata, toured in Europe, and composed piano works, four Symphonies, and a Piano Concerto. His recordings include his own Foxtrott and a variety of works by Heinz Tiessen, Krenek, Smetana, Brahms, Debussy, and Haydn's F minor Variations, recorded in 1940. All of his work shows a keen musical instinct.

DANIEL ERICOURT
1903–1998—France

A fine pianist who studied at the Paris

Conservatoire. He had an extensive career performing in more than forty countries and appearing with such conductors as Goossens, Celibidache, and Horenstein. As a teen he got to know Debussy, and over the years would record the composer's complete piano works, played with an uncommon sense of line and proportion. These have been transferred to CD on the Ivory Classics label. Ericourt taught in the United States at the Cincinnati Conservatory and the Peabody Conservatory and was for years artist-in-residence at the University of North Carolina at Greensboro. Ericourt's transcription of Ravel's *Pièce en forme de habanera* is recorded by Mieczyslaw Münz on Americus Records.

DOROTHEA ERTMANN

1781–1849—Germany

She was a member of the cultivated Viennese aristocratic elite. Ertmann's playing was a constant delight to Beethoven. His Sonata No. 28, Op. 101, is dedicated to her.

CHRISTOPH ESCHENBACH

b. 1940—Germany

One of the finest German pianists of his generation. Eschenbach is singularly adapted to large forms, and his recordings of the Schubert B-flat Sonata and the Beethoven *Hammerklavier* are spread to the limits of their time scale—the Schubert at 43:30, the Beethoven at 50:00. At times, especially in the central slow movements, Eschenbach becomes somewhat affected and prissy, doting over details. His recording of the Chopin Preludes is technically strong, but is sometimes marred by ridiculous pauses which serve only to detract from the music's urgency. He can play Schumann with purpose, finding nectar in the *Abegg* Variations, while lyricism and drama permeate his performance of the Intermezzi, Op. 4.

The Mozart Concerti rank high for him, and he plays them while conducting from the piano. In recent seasons, Eschenbach has developed into an important conductor.

His finest recorded achievement is Mozart's solo Sonatas and Fantasies. Eschenbach presides over these scores with sparkling dexterity; the slow movements are operatic, and the finales betray a humor that is often missing in these works. Occasionally his tone is too buttery for the idiom, and the rubato too strong; but overall it is significant Mozart playing by a pianist of exceptional musicianship.

VIRGINIA ESKIN

b. 1944—United States

She plays a wide repertoire, but has become best known for her advocacy of women composers of the nineteenth and twentieth centuries. Eskin has recorded such neglected scores as Amy Beach's *Balkan Variations,* Louise Talma's powerful Sonata, and music of Fanny Mendelssohn.

ANNETTE ESSIPOVA

1850–1914—Russia

A pianist of the first rank. She studied with Leschetizky, and was briefly married to him. She played throughout Europe and in America. Essipova helped Paderewski early in his career and premiered several of his compositions, including the Concerto and the now ubiquitous Minuet in G. She returned to Russia, where she was the most capable teacher at the St. Petersburg Conservatory. Her high level of technique and beauty of tone were keenly appreciated in Russian pianism. Her students included Simon Barère, Thomas de Hartmann, Isabelle Vengerova, Lev Pouishnov, Ignace Hilsberg, Sergei Prokofiev, and a host of others. In his memoirs, Paderewski wrote, "She was a charming pianist . . . very feminine. . . . Her playing in many ways was perfect, except when it came to strong, effective pieces—then she was lacking in real force."

MORTON ESTRIN
b. 1923—United States

A pupil of Vera Maurana-Press. He made his New York debut at Town Hall in 1949. Estrin is a strong pianist with excellent technical equipment. He is capable of playing the Scriabin Etudes, Op. 8 and the Rachmaninoff Preludes with brilliance and a modicum of poetry. He has made many recordings and has often performed neglected works such as Joachim Raff's impressive Suite in D minor, Op. 91.

F

EDITH FARNADI
1921–1973—Hungary

Studied at the Franz Liszt Academy in her native Budapest. In 1933 she made her debut, conducting and as soloist in Beethoven's First Concerto. Later she taught at the Academy and performed extensively. She made many discs for Westminster Records, becoming most associated with Liszt's music.

LOUISE FARRENC
1804–1875—France

A distinguished pianist, composer, and the only woman piano faculty member at the Paris Conservatoire for over thirty years. Farrenc supervised the training of her nephew Ernest Reyer, who became one of the most celebrated French composers of the nineteenth century. Farrenc was an admirable pianist who appeared often in public and did not hesitate to perform such recondite works as Beethoven's Sonata, Op. 109. She also performed regularly with her daughter Victorine, her pupil and a superb pianist who died at thirty-three. In 1845 at the age of nineteen at Erard's recital hall, Victorine played Beethoven's problematic Sonata Op. 106, the *Hammerklavier,* a rare event in Paris or anywhere at the time. In 1857 Louise Farrenc took the rather daring step of performing a recital which included Frescobaldi, Couperin, Chambonniéres, and eight other early keyboard composers on the piano. The press thought the music irritating at best, but it awakened in her the desire to, along with her husband, Aristide, begin their seminal critical edition, which would eventually achieve twenty volumes of more than fifty composers with introductory essays by Louise Farrenc. Titled *Le Tréson des Pianistes*, it was daunting editorial work and established a new standard of scholarship in France.

Farrenc's compositions in her time were consistently lauded. When chamber music composition was rather a rarity in the age of Berlioz and Meyerbeer she composed two Quintets, four Trios, and a Nonet, as well as three Symphonies. Her piano music, which Schumann regarded highly, reaches to more than thirty opus numbers, Valses, Nocturnes, Variations, and a great many Etudes; of special interest are the Thirty Etudes, Op. 26, and the Twelve Etudes Brillantes, Op. 41.

With diplomacy and tact Farrenc made her way in the Parisian musical spectrum of her day. In 1850, she wrote to the powerful Auber, director of the Conservatoire, asking for a salary increase and pointing out certain inequities. At the conclusion she states: "I therefore venture to hope, M. le Directeur, that you will agree to fix my honorarium at the same level as these gentlemen, because, setting aside questions of self-interest, if I do not receive the same incentive they do, one might conclude that I have not invested all the zeal, and diligence necessary to fulfill the task which has been entrusted to me."

AMY FAY
1844–1928—United States

Born in Mississippi, she studied in Europe with Tausig and many others before joining Liszt's class. Her letters home were published as *Music-Study in Germany,* which has become a minor classic. It is a volume filled with delightful observations on the sociological situation of a young American student in Germany, drinking in culture and genius. Her views of Liszt are especially revealing. She returned to the United States, where she had a long teaching career.

JOSÉ FEGHALI
b. 1961—Brazil

He gave his first public performance when he was only five years old. In 1976 Feghali studied at London's Royal Academy; later he studied with Maria Curcio. In 1985 he was awarded the gold medal at the seventh Van Cliburn International Competition in Fort Worth. Feghali's technique is well developed and flexible, and his playing is usually colorful.

ALAN FEINBERG
b. 1950—United States

A pianist who has performed in the United States and Europe, often promoting contemporary music. Discs of the Wuorinen Sonata No. 2, Imbrie's Piano Concerto, and piano music of Babbitt and Feldman are topflight. Feinberg is agog with curiosity and brings cool refreshment to our ears in affectionate readings of American virtuoso music. Especially scintillating is his Argo CD of real créme de la créme works, such as Beach's *A Hermit Thrush at Eve, Tyrolean Valse-Fantaisie,* and *Fireflies,* and Gottschalk's virtuosic Potpourri on National Tunes, *L'Union,* as well as *Manchega* and *Souvenir de Porto Rico.* Feinberg has verve, taste, and a big technical command.

SAMUEL FEINBERG
1890–1962—Russia

A formidable figure in Russian pianism. He began piano at age six with A. F. Jensen, and composed his first composition at eleven. Studies proceeded with Alexander Goldenweiser at the Moscow Conservatory, where he graduated in 1911. By the First World War he was already giving performances of Bach's *Well-Tempered Clavier,* the first Russian pianist to perform the cycle in his homeland.

In 1922 he received an appointment to teach piano at the Moscow Conservatory, and had an outstanding career as an educator, also writing articles and two books: *The Destiny of Musical Form* and *Pianism as an Art.*

During the 1920s his performing career was nearly as vast as his growing repertoire. He gave mounds of Schumann, Liszt, Chopin, Debussy, Medtner, the complete Beethoven Sonatas, the 10 Scriabin Sonatas, and the Russian premiere of the Prokofiev Third Concerto. He left a good amount of recordings, of which his Scriabin playing is not to be missed, so improvisationally beguiling, with fluttering pedals purring and limpid. There was nothing in his musical mentality of conventional performance; for example, his *Mephisto Waltz* of Liszt is taken in one gulp. Where is the rhythm? Yet its incisive inner details somehow make for structural pillars. Reckless, languorous, erotic, Feinberg is driven by ecstasy, and the devil takes due notice. Mark Pakman wrote, "He infused every piece with a principal idea and character. . . . Feinberg often accumulated enormous intensity in the very beginning of a musical phrase and then gradually let it subside. His timing was remarkable."

Because of ill-health he stopped performing in 1956, but was recording up to the week of his death. A recent CD on Arbiter presents recordings (1929–1948) and performances of three of his own Bach transcriptions, Beethoven's *Appassionata,* a Scriabin mazurka, Etude Op. 42, No. 3, and especially *Fragilité,* Op. 51, No. 1, with his own Suite Op. 11, four finely tuned lyric miniatures from 1920. His recordings on four CDs of Bach's *Well-Tempered Clavier* may be heard on the label Russian Disc, and although Feinberg admired Glenn Gould's Bach, it is worlds apart. Serious students should closely study these performances. Technically he can perform miracles; musically they are like no other Bach you have heard. It is Bach as a Russian Romantic, and even purists and Baroque authorities may be unwillingly swept away. Sviatoslav Richter wrote, "He played Bach after his own fashion, not like Bach but like late Scriabin. . . . This didn't stop him from having lots of admirers, which is entirely justified, as he was a great musician." Feinberg, speaking of Bach on the piano, said, "We cannot fully imitate harpsichord colors. However, the contemporary piano enables us to make every phrase, every voice expressive by strengthening or weakening the sound. The piano is not a percussion instrument: It is like a chorus of strings."

Feinberg composed a great deal, including effective transcriptions from Bach. Pianists interested in such resurrected Romantic Bach should look at Feinberg's Largo from the Trio Sonata No. 5, BWV 529, and for smoldering fare there is the glorious piano rendering of the Scherzo of Tchaikovsky's Sixth Symphony. In fact the last three Tchaikovsky's symphonies are contained to the piano in Feinberg's elegant arrangements; his ear and mind

translate each piquancy of the original. Doubtless the deepest influence on Feinberg's composing life was Scriabin. The composer himself heard Feinberg's performance of his Fourth Sonata, plying the pianist with compliments. His legacy includes twelve Piano Sonatas composed from the period of the First World War to the end of his life. The early sonatas are Scriabinic in orientation: dark textures, high drama, primarily restless; the five sonatas from the 1920s bring to Scriabin elements of Medtner's rigor and are difficult to read. The later works, perhaps under fear of Soviet scrutiny, become far more diatonically folkish and less impassioned.

VLADIMIR FELTSMAN
b. 1952—USSR

The winner of the Marguerite Long–Jacques Thibaud Competition in Paris in 1971, Feltsman was kept from emigrating from the Soviet Union until 1987, when he came to the United States with great publicity. He played at the White House that year, and then in November he made an auspicious debut at Carnegie Hall. In February of the following year he played the Brahms B-flat Concerto with Zubin Mehta and the New York Philharmonic.

ARMAND FERTÉ
1881–1973—France

A native of Paris, he studied at the Conservatoire with Émile Descombes, and later with Diémer. After making a Paris debut in 1900 he made his mark as pianist, conductor, teacher and as an editor of *The Well-Tempered Clavier,* the thirty-two Beethoven Sonatas and much else.

His students include Pierre Barbizet, Monique de la Bruchollerie, and Joseph Benvenuti.

JACQUES FÉVRIER
1900–1979—France

He worked with Long and Risler and was a pianist especially suited to the French literature. Ravel admired his distinctive playing. Together with the composer, he premiered Poulenc's Concerto for Two Pianos and Orchestra. The recording of it is a delight. Arthur Rubinstein wrote, "Jacques Février is a good pianist and an excellent musician and the best sight-reader I ever met."

JANINA FIALKOWSKA
b. 1951—Canada

She studied in Paris with Yvonne Lefébure and entered the Juilliard School in 1970, working with Sascha Gorodnitzki. In 1974 she was a prizewinner at the first International Arthur Rubinstein Piano Competition. She has appeared as guest artist with many orchestras, including the Concertgebouw in Amsterdam, the Israel Philharmonic, and the Chicago Symphony Orchestra. She is capable of feats of virtuosity in the Rachmaninoff Third Concerto and in Liszt's *Transcendental Etudes,* and she is a persuasive advocate of new music, performing works by Libby Larsen and Sir Andrzej Panufnik.

JOHN FIELD
1782–1837—Ireland

He studied with Clementi and performed in the major capitals of Europe, making a London debut in 1794 and a Paris debut in 1802.

As pianist and the inventor of the nocturne genre, John Field is an important figure in the early history of piano music. He was among the first to create small, self-contained pieces of a subjective nature. During his time, the sonata ruled the thoughts of most composers. Field escaped such formalism in his nocturnes, in which he accompanied his suave Italianate melodies with a freer, more dispersed left hand, with the pedal blending the whole into an illusion of song. With the Field nocturne, intimacy and romance became part of the piano's vocabulary. Around the age of twenty, he settled in St. Petersburg. The musical life of Russia was as yet unformed, and Field established himself as a fashionable teacher despite his dozing through most of the lessons with aristocratic pupils. His eccentricities were the talk of the town. He charged exorbitant fees, and he lived, loved, and drank extravagantly. But his influence on Russian pianism was great. He gave Glinka piano lessons and taught the important pianist-teacher Charles Mayer, who himself had more than seven hundred Russian pupils.

Field's early-Romantic playing possessed a poetic allure. The great violinist Louis Spohr wrote of Field's "dreamy melancholy." Glinka said, "His fingers fell on the keys as large drops of rain that spread themselves like iridescent pearls." In 1832, Liszt heard him in Paris and fell under his spell. He recalled that "Field did not so much play his own nocturnes but dreamed them at the piano. . . . His almost immovable attitude and but slightly expressive face attracted no attention. His eye sought no other eye. His execution flowed clear and limpid. His fingers glided over the keys and the sounds they awoke seemed to follow them like the foaming crest of a wave. It was easy to see that for him his chief auditor was himself. His tranquility was well-nigh somnolent, and the impression he made on his hearers was his least care. No abruptness, no shock, either of gesture or rhythm, ever supervened to interrupt his melodious reverie, whose fondly murmuring melodies, *mezza voce,* spread through the air with the most delicious impressions, the most charming surprises of the heart."

Field's first nocturnes were published in 1814, but were probably composed much earlier. Chopin so perfectly assimilated Field's style that the title *nocturne* has become synonymous with the Polish master, while Field's more naive and gentle night pieces are now seldom played. Yet Busoni felt that to play a Field nocturne well required the highest art. Field was one of the first to divine the potential of the piano's "singing" capacities, and his still-fragrant nocturnes made him one of early Romanticism's most charming advocates.

THOMAS FIELDEN
1883–1974—England

He studied with Rudolf Breithaupt in Berlin and gave recitals in Germany, France, and England. A disciple of the Breithaupt and Matthay methods of piano playing, he wrote *The Science of Pianoforte Technique,* which was published in 1927. In 1953 he became the director of the Rhodesian Academy of Music in Bulawayo, Rhodesia (now Zimbabwe).

KARL FILTSCH
1830–1845—Hungary

The one genius among Chopin students. His sensitivity and perfectly polished mechanism prompted Liszt to say that when Filtsch was to begin touring, he would close up shop. Chopin wept when hearing his own E minor Concerto performed by the young pianist. Tuberculosis claimed Filtsch at the age of

fifteen. Leschetizky, who was the same age, recalled many years later that "Filtsch was a handsome boy . . . a beautiful blond, really too refined and delicate for life's struggle. . . . As a parting gift he gave me an autographed manuscript copy of a Chopin Impromptu . . . saying that he believed I, of all his friends, would best interpret it."

SERGIO FIORENTINO
1927–1998—Italy

Born in Naples, he received his training at the conservatory there. He won several prizes at competitions and performed in Europe establishing a stable career. In the last few years APR Recordings has gathered his discography into nine volumes revealing impressive and insightful playing of Bach, Schumann, Scriabin, Rachmaninoff, Chopin, Prokofiev, and Schubert, as well as Liszt, the composer most frequently associated with his name. Fiorentino's ample display of moods is divided by APR into categories, such as the contemplative Liszt, the virtuoso Liszt, and so forth. From the *Mephisto Waltz* to late pieces, the *Years of Pilgrimage* to the taxing etude called *Ab irato,* one hears the poetry and vitality of a pianist in love with the Lisztian world.

RUDOLF FIRKUŠNÝ
1912–1994—Czechoslovakia

He studied with Vilem Kurz and was the preeminent Czech pianist of the twentieth century.

In a Firkušný performance, one experienced undiluted tonal pleasure. His sound was rich and creamy and he was, above all, musical. Although he gave patrician readings of all the standard concertos, and premiered many works, such as the Howard Hanson concerto and concertos by Martinů and others, Firkušný was at his best when he played alone; then he yielded to his reveries. When he appeared with orchestra, he was weighed down by the orchestral apparatus. His temperament was Romantic, but guided by a precise intellect, and his hands were wonderfully well schooled. Firkušný's stage manner was appealing; he was an aristocrat and had no use for gesticulation.

When Firkušný was totally involved in the music, there would be the rarest of occurrences: the merging of the artist with the instrument. When he wasn't, he became tight-lipped and merely sleek. Firkušný was essentially a lyric bard, who used a wide color spectrum. Especially in later years, he displayed many soft hues. But he had power enough, and his playing would always unroll fluidly and logically in large-scale forms. He was able to make perfect sense of Dussek's half-hour Grand Sonata in F minor, Op. 77 (*L'Invocation*), a piece which would be incoherent in the hands of a merely average player.

Firkušný's Beethoven was well balanced, not a Teutonic Beethoven but Slavic to the core, and his Schubert readings became some of his most esteemed interpretations. His Schubert Sonatas in A minor, D. 784 and D. 845, are both filled with beautiful impressionist tints. Firkušný's recording of the late Schubert Piano Pieces of 1828 is marvelously pliant. His deft rendering of the smaller Brahms pieces alternates between light and dark.

His playing of Mussorgsky's *Pictures at an Exhibition* is among the most impressive of his recordings. He is no casual viewer at a picture gallery, but a moved and observant visitor. Every rest, every line is objectively etched. His Chopin was without affectation, and while an early recording of the Third Sonata was rigid and plain, his Chopin grew more intimate through the years. In whatever he touched,

though, he always retained a reserve which was beguiling.

Throughout his long career, Firkušný promoted Czech music of all periods. He continued to champion Martinů and played that composer's Piano Concerto No. 2. (He also played No. 3, which was dedicated to him.) The primary influence on Firkušný was his study and friendship with the greatest twentieth-century Czech master, Leoš Janáček. Firkušný played the Concertino, the Capriccio for Left Hand and Orchestra, the sonata *In the Mist*, and *On an Overgrown Path*. Every fiber of his being responded to Janáček's unique language. The Dvořák Concerto toured everywhere with Firkušný, who made this score sound even better than it is. He has also recorded Dvořák's Mazurkas and Humoresques, and gives a magical performance of his neglected A major Suite. His bravura is captivating in the pungent polkas of Smetana, whose work he also played often.

ANNIE FISCHER
1914–1995—Hungary

She began her musical life, as so many pianists have, as a child prodigy. By 1925 she was a veteran of the concert stage, and her teacher, Dohnányi, was particularly proud of her. As she grew and developed, her playing was hailed worldwide, and she influenced and inspired the younger generation of Hungarian pianists such as Tamás Vásáry. She disliked recording and felt that it hampered inspiration and the magical aspects of interpretive creation. Fortunately, we have many performances of her art on discs, as well as the complete Beethoven Sonatas, never released in her lifetime but now available on Hungaroton, as well as three compact discs of her Mozart. The Liszt Sonata recorded in 1953 and the

Schubert B-flat Sonata from 1968 display well her majestic and multicolored playing at its most spontaneous.

EDWIN FISCHER
1886–1960—Switzerland

In Berlin, Fischer studied with Martin Krause; later, he taught at the Stern Conservatory for nearly a decade. He played chamber music, conducted, and wrote several books, including one on the Beethoven Sonatas. His master classes were filled with students from all over the world, with Brendel, Barenboim, Badura-Skoda, Demus, and others in attendance.

Fischer, born the year of Liszt's death, was a contemporary of Schnabel and Backhaus, and like theirs his pianism was not characteristic of the arrogant virtuosity of the day. Fischer promoted the great Classical works and played Bach in the original, not in the pumped-up transcriptions that were so popular in his early days. To build a career on such a serious foundation was not easy. Nonetheless, Fischer's burning Classicism attracted Walter, Mengelberg, and Furtwängler, and these conductors constantly engaged him. Later, Fischer conducted his own chamber orchestra in Haydn and Mozart, and performed with the group as soloist in Bach concerti. These lean but passionate presentations were highly influential, and on disc they remain treasures of the recorded art.

Fischer the pianist was monumental, and it was impossible for him to play dully. He retained his nineteenth-century heritage, and although he was a transitional pianist, he sounds very different from a Badura-Skoda or a Brendel, who seem tame and academic by comparison. Listen to Fischer's celebrated recording of Bach's Chromatic Fantasy and Fugue, which is absolutely breathtaking in its white-hot Romanticism. More conservative, but thrilling in detail and regal in contrapuntal mastery, are his recordings of *The Well-Tempered Clavier*. Or hear his Handel Chaconne in G, with its ten degrees of shading, octave doublings, expressive pedaling, which have nothing in common with a modern harpsichordist's reading. I have played this record for scholarly harpsichordists, and they shake their heads in disdain. Fischer, in his Baroque playing, often phrases in Romantic gasps. His Baroque architecture is Venetian in splendor. But what spellbinding conceptions of Bach concertos and preludes and fugues he presents! It is not necessary to call such playing old-fashioned, or even lacking in correctness of style. Fischer's playing may not be to the letter, yet it may be more authentic in spirit than any cold and correct playing steeped in musicology.

He recorded the Schubert Eight Impromptus with the elusive breathing that gives these pieces their dewy freshness. His Mozart was famous, and his readings of the Concerti No. 20 in D minor, No. 22 in E-flat, and No. 25 in C are important recordings, to be studied and relished. His playing of slow movements shows an excruciating sensitivity.

Fischer was an inspiring teacher. Alfred Brendel describes him this way at a master class: "Fischer was electrifying by his mere presence. The playing of timid youths and placid girls would suddenly spring to life when he grasped them by the shoulder. . . . When Fischer outlined the structure of a whole movement the gifted ones among the participants felt they were looking into the very heart of music."

Badura-Skoda was convinced that "Fischer had all the bearings of genius. Everything he did was creative, different, touched by a different source. . . . And yet his massive gifts did not always come through in public. There were moments of agony in his concerts. He was so overly sensitive that he could sabotage his own recitals."

Today there is a growing awareness of

Fischer's immense musical imagination, and his recordings have never been more prized. Numerous young pianists are finding him to be a wellspring of inspiration, hearing in him a fearless interpreter with a musical integrity that shines through every note.

HENRI FISSOT

1843–1896—France

A famed French pianist teacher and a composer of forgotten music. At the Paris Conservatoire he studied with Antoine François Marmontel and taught at that institution from 1887 until his death.

LEON FLEISHER

b. 1928—United States

From childhood he was a student of Artur Schnabel. In 1952, Fleisher was the first American to win the Queen Elizabeth Competition in Brussels. Because of a muscular problem in the right hand, his solo career was ended in 1964. In the intervening years he has conducted a great deal and has appeared in concert in works for the left hand alone. At Baltimore's Peabody Conservatory, he has been an inspiring teacher.

At his peak, Fleisher was the model of clean-cut, intelligent American pianism. His playing offered a fresh, astringent, and at times brash sound, as in Copland's Sonata and Kirchner's First Concerto. Fleisher's motto seemed to be "First there is rhythm," and his rhythmic knife was sharp edged, joyous, and bracing. He used the pedal sparingly, and his technique was on a high virtuoso level. His recordings of the Beethoven Concerti are masterly examples of solidity. He and conductor Szell romp in

the rondos, are tight and precise in ensemble. The slow movements are expressive but not subjective. It is a Beethoven without pretentiousness or metaphysics, the Second Concerto being the best ever recorded. His Brahms was just as successful, and the D minor Concerto has a mighty wallop. He recorded the Brahms *Handel* Variations with an objective frostiness and a ruthless energy that pointed up the work's structural wonders. In the tiny Brahms waltzes, he is entrancing.

Fleisher's playing is so direct that, on first hearing, it may seem somewhat cold. He seems to say, "Here now is the music. It is very good music." His Liszt Sonata is scrubbed clean of cloying sentiments. The Weber *Invitation to the Dance* becomes curiously modern under his hands, no longer the old-fashioned relic from 1819, which had always sounded better in Berlioz's orchestral setting. In Fleisher's rendering of Weber's Fourth Sonata in E minor, he sews together the still Classical form and

Leon Fleisher by David Dubal

the early Romantic material with barely a seam showing. The minuet (one for witches) has a trio which shows off Fleisher's brilliantly controlled fingerwork, and the Andante is conceived with indescribable taste. With such playing, one wonders why this work is not part of the permanent repertoire.

YAKOV FLIER
1912–1978—Russia

Within the Soviet orbit he had a distinguished career as both teacher and performer. He made an American debut with the Rachmaninoff Third Concerto in 1963. Flier possessed a warm virtuosity, and his Chopin playing had heart. The Barcarolle and the E-flat minor Polonaise are very picturesque. Of special merit is a recording of a brilliantly colored Schumann Fantasy. He made a delightful recording of Kabalevsky's Twenty-four Preludes. He is uncomfortable with the style of Mozart's C minor Fantasy, K. 475, which is the case with a great deal of Soviet Mozart playing.

ANDOR FOLDES
1913–1992—Hungary

A student of Dohnányi and the winner of the Liszt Prize in 1933. Foldes is the author of *Keys to the Keyboard*. He made many recordings, some of the best being Bartók's solo music.

SIDNEY FOSTER
1917–1977—United States

He was admitted at age ten to the Curtis Institute of Music, where he studied with Isabelle Vengerova and later with David Saperton. In 1940 Foster was the first winner of the Leventritt Award; his Carnegie Hall debut took place in 1941 with Barbirolli conducting the New York Philharmonic in the First Beethoven Concerto. In 1964 he played sixteen concerts in twenty-two days. Foster performed the premieres of a number of works, such as the Dello Joio Sonatas Nos. 1 and 2.

From 1952 until his death he taught at Indiana University in Bloomington, where his teaching was much admired. Alberto Reyes, who studied with him, wrote, "His sympathetic awareness of the minefield that is the psychological relationship between artist and pupil made the process of studying with him an opportunity for emotional growth as well as musical development."

Foster made only a few recordings including the Sonatinas of Clementi. It was therefore of particular value that the International Piano Archives of Maryland (IPAM) brought out a two-CD set of various live performances at different times. These discs, which include Mendelssohn, Beethoven, and a large array of composers, represent Foster as one of the richly gifted American pianists of his era. Not to be missed are Liszt's *Venezia e Napoli*, many moments of Schumann's *Kreisleriana*, Bartók's Suite, Op. 14, and Palmgren's *May Night*; Mendelssohn's Three Etudes, Op. 104 and Prokofiev's Third Sonatas form highlights of essential recordings of American pianism.

FOU TS'ONG
b. 1934—China

He has won prizes in several competitions, including the Chopin Competition in Warsaw in 1955, where he was also given the special prize for best mazurka playing. He went on to a fine career and is especially well-known in England. He returned to the United States in 1987 with a successful recital at Alice Tully Hall in New York. His recording of Handel's G major Chaconne is an ideal transference of harpsichord music to the piano.

MALCOLM FRAGER
1935–1991—United States

He studied with Carl Friedberg, won the Leventritt Award in 1959, and followed this by winning the 1960 Queen Elizabeth Competition. Frager recorded a superb Prokofiev Second Concerto in the early part of his career. His recording of the twelve MacDowell Virtuoso Studies is a worthy contribution to the performance of American piano music. Moreover, his recordings of Chopin solo pieces and the Weber Piano Concerti are excellent.

AUGUST FRANCKE
1870–1933—Germany

He was a student of Anton Door in Vienna. Francke had a fruitful career as a pianist. In later years he headed the New York College of Music.

SAMSON FRANÇOIS
1924–1970—France

A student of Cortot and Long, François achieved a strong European reputation. He also played in the United States and China.

He was an always intriguing performer who could be erratic and eccentric. His complete recordings of Ravel are among his best work. He composed, and his Piano Concerto was recorded.

CLAUDE FRANK
b. 1925—Germany

A longtime student of Artur Schnabel, Frank came to the United States, where he established a reputation not only as a pianist but also as a valuable teacher. His Beethoven playing—fluid, suave, and often lyrical—is highly prized; he recorded the complete Piano Sonatas.

PETER FRANKL
b. 1935—Hungary

He studied with Lajos Hernádi and Marguerite Long. In 1958 he won the Liszt Prize. Frankl has recorded a great deal, including the complete piano music of Schumann and Debussy. He is sensitive to Schumann's often thickly scored piano writing, and he takes care not to get stuck in mezzo forte when soft playing is required. Frankl's left hand is extremely solid and he often plays with gusto, bringing freshness to such often-played scores as *Carnaval* and *Kinderscenen*.

In Debussy, he opts for a middle road— neither a voluptuous impressionism nor a tightly fitted structure. Frankl's Chopin, such as the Ballades and F minor Fantasy, has shape and is without affectation. In his recordings of the complete Polonaises, he is rather tedious in the famous ones, but he is quite stylish in the unknown and juvenile ones.

NELSON FREIRE

b. 1944—Brazil

Freire studied in Vienna with Bruno Seidlhofer. He is a pianist of impeccable taste in Romantic music. His tempi are often quick, and his technique is sharp and diamondlike. Much admired are his two piano performances with Martha Argerich.

ETELKA FREUND

1879–1977—Hungary

The sister of Robert Freund, she was an outstanding pianist; she studied in Budapest with István Thomán. In Vienna she worked with the pianist Ignaz Brüll and in theory with Brahms's close friend Eusebius Mandyczewski. Although only seventeen, she was a regular guest of Brahms at his home, and as he said, "she played to the engagement of everyone." Later she was a favored pupil of Busoni, who told her brother that "she played the Brahms *Paganini* Variations as I could not at her age." Busoni conducted at her debut in Berlin in 1901, with the Philharmonic in the Beethoven Third Concerto, the Brahms D minor, and his own arrangement and orchestration of Liszt's Spanish Rhapsody. From early in her career she established a lifelong friendship with Bartók. She played superbly until late in life, and her art is alive in works by Bach, Busoni, Brahms, and Bartók on a Pearl CD.

ROBERT FREUND

1852–1936—Hungary

At the Leipzig Conservatory he worked with Moscheles and later with Tausig and attended Liszt's master class. From 1875 until 1921 he lived in Zurich and then returned to Budapest to live. Freund had a fruitful career especially propagating Brahms as well as new music. In 1899 he gave the world premiere of Hans Huber's four-movement Third Concerto in D major, Op. 113. Freund was a man of cultivation; Busoni greatly admired him, writing, "Your opinions have always been a guide to me, and I would ask you to have the patience to carry on following—and criticizing—my progress."

EMIL FREY

1889–1946—Switzerland

He studied with Diémer. In 1910 he won the Rubinstein Prize. Frey taught at the Moscow Conservatory and later in Zurich. He had many successful tours and composed as well.

FANNY FRICKENHAUS

1849–1913—England

A well-known British pianist of her era, she introduced the Piano Concerto of Hermann Goetz to London and gave many other first performances.

CARL FRIEDBERG

1872–1955—Germany

In 1887 he played for Clara Schumann, who soon after became his teacher. Later, Brahms worked with him on most of his piano music.

He made his orchestral debut in 1892, under Mahler. Friedberg had a distinguished career in chamber music and as a soloist, and was an inspiring teacher. In 1953 he recorded several works, including the *Symphonic Etudes* of Schumann.

ARTHUR FRIEDHEIM
1859–1932—Russia

Born in St. Petersburg, Friedheim remains one of the legendary masters of his instrument. In piano lore he is one of the finest and most important stars in the Liszt galaxy, considered to be an uncontested giant of the keyboard—living in an age of pianistic genius. His generation produced Paderewski, Scharwenka, Busoni, Essipova, Joseffy, Carreño, d'Albert, Rosenthal, Sauer, and Siloti, each of these virtuosi born within a few years of each other. Vladimir de Pachmann himself exclaimed, "Friedheim is the God of all pianists" and many others were moved to that opinion. Friedheim's playing gave a sense of the comprehensive; a critic from 1912 wrote: "With Paderewski, one is charmed by his magnetism, poetic conceptions and tone color, Rosenthal excels with his transcendental technique and bravura, Busoni with his musicianship and versatility, while Pachmann captures his auditors by his magic tone production. But Friedheim seems to possess a combination of all these qualities that crown him as being the most satisfying from the artistic and musician's standpoint."

At age nine he made his debut in the Russian emperor's glittering capital, St. Petersburg, with John Field's E-flat major Concerto, a work then still popular in Russia. Friedheim wrote, "My performance of the familiar concerto was greeted with considerable enthusiasm, but I can remember no particular emotion, either of timidity or elation, on that great evening."

After studying with Anton Rubinstein's pupil Carl Stiecke, Friedheim became Rubinstein's pupil when he was fourteen years old. By the time he was sixteen, Rubinstein's wayward temperament had become confusing to Friedheim: "His advice and criticism had begun to vary from day to day. He would say that I was going to be a successful pianist, then he could advise me to give all my time to composition." While continuing to work with Rubinstein he furthered his education in the faculty of philosophy at St. Petersburg University. At eighteen he decided to play for Liszt at Weimar. But impressing Liszt was not easy; Friedheim relates, "He found my playing chaotic." This was in 1878. By 1880, he once again encountered Liszt. This time Liszt was interested: "I played a piano concerto I had written, and Liszt, at a second piano, played the accompaniment at sight. . . . I was so excited, that I could not hide my emotion. From this joyous day in 1880 until the black moment of his death more than six years later, I was to be away from him only when I was out on concert tours."

In Friedheim's fascinating volume, *Life and Liszt,* he says: "I learned much from Rubinstein during the four years I was his pupil, but I was to learn far more from Franz Liszt, whose daring virtuosity had sounded the depths of music, both past and present, and who was now reaching out into the unknown. . . . When I stood with exalted spirits in the presence of that august and legendary figure, Franz Liszt, my greatest hour had struck."

Friedheim was now part of a Liszt entourage of extraordinary disciples, such as Rosenthal, Sauer, Krause, Lamond, Siloti, Tomán, Weingartner, Reisenauer, Stavenhagen, and a trainload of lesser lights. It was a virtual pianist's paradise, each on the move with Liszt's yearly stays in Rome, Budapest, and Weimar. Friedheim wrote, "So stimulating to high aspiration and endeavour was the atmosphere, so great was the desire to excel, not only before the master but before one another, that we accomplished incredible things. All our playing was done, practically without exception, from memory. And, if Liszt suggested that one of us play a certain composition at the next lesson, the possibility of not having it ready never occurred to us."

For Friedheim, these were the years of wine and roses. He lived a life of enchantment. Liszt had cast a magical spell over him, and to be in his presence meant life to him. The progress and the horrors of the oncoming twentieth century seemed far away in the Rome of 1885, or in the beautiful Thuringian principality of Weimar.

After Liszt's death, Friedheim was in demand and played throughout Europe. In 1891 he made an American tour. At his orchestral debut, at the Metropolitan Opera, he performed Beethoven's *Emperor* Concerto and Liszt's Second Concerto with Theodore Thomas conducting. He had been asked to play the Tchaikovsky Piano Concerto No. 1 at the inaugural concert of Carnegie Hall that year, but the pianist hated the piece and refused. However, he had the distinction of being the first major artist to perform at Carnegie's recital hall (now Weill Hall). He gave three recitals, which were appended with an apology stating, "The management of the Arthur Friedheim recitals respectfully request the indulgence of the audience for the inconvenience caused by the noises incidental to the completion of the main hall of this building, it being a matter entirely beyond our control."

One wonders how many hammer blows competed with Friedheim's *Hammerklavier,* or one asks why these three recitals were scheduled in the afternoon and not in the evenings. The following programs are worth noting as Herculean, and characteristic of the massive program building of the Liszt school.

Friday afternoon, 10 April 1891, at 2:30
Wagner-Friedheim: "Vorspiel" from *Die Meistersinger von Nürnberg*
Beethoven: Sonata in D major, Op. 10, No. 3
Beethoven: Sonata in C major, Op. 53 (*Waldstein*)
Chopin: Selected Preludes and Etudes
Chopin: Sonata in B-flat minor, Op. 35
Liszt: Phantasie on Mozart's *Don Juan*

Tuesday afternoon, 14 April 1891, at 2:30
All-Liszt program:
Sonata in B minor
Harmonies poétiques et Religieuses, No. 3, *Bénédiction de dieu dans la solitude*
Hungarian Rhapsody No. 9 (*Pester Karneval*)
Legendes No. 1 *St. François d'assise, [la prédication aux oiseaux]*
Legendes No. 2 *St. François de Paule marchant sur les flots*
Aprés une lecture de Dante (Dante-Fantasia quasi Sonata)
Six etudes d'exécution transcendante d'après Paganini

Friday afternoon, 17 April 1891, at 2:30
Wagner-Friedheim: "Wotan's Zorn," "Abschied von Brünhilde" from *Die Walküre*
Beethoven: Sonata in B-flat major, Op. 106 (*Hammerklavier*)
Chopin: Nocturne in C minor, Op. 48, No. 1
Chopin: Ballade in F minor, Op. 52
Chopin: *Polonaise-fantaisie*, Op. 61
Balakirev: *Islamey, Oriental fantasie*
Liszt: *Mephisto Waltz,* No. 1
Liszt: Fantasie on Bellini's *La Sonnambula*

The brilliant American critic James Huneker, who in 1911 was to publish a biography of Liszt, was apparently not an admirer in 1891. It should be understood how radical and controversial most of Liszt's works were before the twentieth century. Huneker would write: "Friedheim gave us the wonderful—I say 'wonderful' advisedly—B minor Sonata of Liszt. I had never been a Lisztian, but I date my conversion from that time. The potentialities of the piano became living, sounding realities. It was a performance of power, fullness, symmetry and grandeur, of which I shall cherish the memory forever and a day."

Friedheim lived in England from 1897 to 1908. In London, he completed his opera *Die Tanzerin,* which was well-received in Germany. In Manchester he was head of the piano department of the Royal Northern College of Music and the Guildhall School in London. In 1910, he moved his family to New York, where engagements quickly followed in Canada, Mexico, and the United States. (He performed at the White House for the Tafts.)

The war years were difficult and concerts rare. As war hysteria deepened in the United States, his German name made concerts impossible to book. As he said, "Who could have guessed at the reign of terror and hatred that was to be loosed on earth? . . . I might write a great deal about the things that happened to me because of my name." For a time his career was in a shambles, and he took employment as a movie hall pianist.

After 1920 he performed less, preferring to compose, making piano rolls for the Aeolian Duo-Art Company, making his well-known edition of the Chopin Etudes, and teaching privately, including Rildia Bee O'Brien, Van Cliburn's mother, who never ceased to admire Friedheim, the man and teacher. His edition of the Chopin Etudes was widely used. All of his recordings are worth listening to; many of the earliest acoustics, such as Weber's Perpetual Motion, find him hampered to miniatures. In 1998 Nimbus issued a splendid disc of piano rolls from 1916 to 1926. Liszt Rhapsodies Nos. 2, 9, and 10; two Paganini-Liszt Etudes, No. 1 and *La Campanella*; the two Legendes; a rousing *The Banjo* of Gottschalk; and *Papillons* by his friend Rosenthal make a CD which gives us some of the splendour that this

pianist had in the fullness of his glory days. In his memoir he writes: "One learns to stem the flood of one's too-extravagant visions, even to find peace when renunciation is required. . . . I have walked in the path of the makers of music and dreamed their dreams. It all seems so clear now. And I am content."

IGNAZ FRIEDMAN
1882–1948—Poland

Friedman was born in Podgorze, a small town near Cracow, where his father taught him. Like many great performers, the boy was a prodigy and by the age of eight he had often played in public. In Cracow he had been given a rigorous training with Flora Grzwinska, a well-known piano teacher of the time. When he was eighteen, he left for Leipzig to study with the renowned theorist Hugo Riemann. After a year at Leipzig, Vienna beckoned. He wanted to work with the musicologist Guido Adler and especially with Theodor Leschetizky, the most celebrated piano pedagogue of the era, the teacher of Paderewski, Gabrilowitsch, Schnabel, Moiseiwitsch, Horszowski, and many more of the stars of the time. In fact, it appeared necessary to have Leschetizky's stamp of approval and Vienna was overrun by pianists flocking to the Hapsburg capital for Leschetizky's "method." Whether or not he had a method was a vital topic among his disciples. Leschetizky himself said, "I merely teach as Czerny, my teacher, taught me." Friedman was immediately impressed with Leschetizky who, in the beginning, discouraged the young Pole. However, Friedman was to become one of his favourites during the four years he worked with him. And no wonder—as Friedman had all the necessary ingredients that Leschetizky most prized: an all-encompassing technique, beauty of tone, poetic feeling, a sense of solid structure, and a big sound capable of great projection in large halls.

After his Vienna debut in 1904 playing the Liszt E-flat, Tchaikovsky B-flat minor, and the (then-seldom-heard) Brahms D minor Concertos, he was launched on a career of chamber, solo, and concerto playing that would take him to the four corners of the world, from Egypt to Iceland, from South and Central America and Mexico to Asia.

Of a New York recital the famed critic Deems Taylor wrote: "This stubby, grey man has a piano technique so utterly complete that his piano playing does not even seem effortless. He sits at the piano, exerting himself just about as much as would appear seemly in a good average player, and out of the instrument come sounds as it seems impossible for any pair of human hands to evoke—glittering scales that approach, flash by and disappear with the speed of lightning and yet are so cleanly fingered that every note is clear and round; runs in sixths, trills in thirds, chords that flare like trumpets, arpeggios that are like a caress, and never for a moment technique for its own sake."

Like so many pianists of the so-called "Golden Age of the Piano," Friedman was busy as a composer and editor of music. His more than one hundred piano pieces are polished in craft and detail and offer the enterprising pianist entrancing vignettes such as the Gártner-Friedman Waltzes, masterful and nostalgic. Included also are Friedman's *Estampes* and the charming *Elle danse,* dedicated to and danced by Pavlova. The Friedman corpus of piano music was recorded by Gunnar Johansen.

For ambitious pianists looking for virtuoso works, his paraphrases of Strauss waltzes are not only formidable but are among the finest such pieces. Friedman's *Paganini* Variations based on the Twenty-Fourth Caprice may not rank with those of Brahms, but the score is imaginative and full of pianistic surprises.

Friedman's editions of Chopin and Liszt are invaluable, although the Russian pianist-teacher Heinrich Neuhaus hated some of the fingerings in his Chopin editions. He wrote in his *The Art of Piano Playing:* "I cannot understand how such a gifted and forceful pianist as Friedman with his tremendous experience both as a performer and as a teacher could perpetrate such nonsense. But as a matter of fact in his edition of Chopin such nonsense abounds!"

If indeed there are some strange fingerings in Friedman's editions they also contain many subtleties of phrasing, pedaling, and other details. In fact, when Debussy was preparing his "complete" Chopin edition, Friedman's editions were assiduously studied by the French master.

In 1940 he was invited to tour Australia and left France just before the Germans entered. At a concert in the summer of 1943 he felt a cramping of his left hand during a grueling all-Chopin recital which included the B-flat minor Sonata, the B minor Sonata, the Twenty-four Preludes as well as a bouquet of mazurkas, polonaises, and etudes. The following day his hand was numb, and Friedman, an inveterate concertizer, was never to perform in public again.

Ignaz Friedman played close to three thousand concerts. Immensely creative in his interpretations, he constantly experimented with rubato, accents, phrasing, pauses, half- and quarter-pedal effects, and the like. His playing could be extremely elastic or at times quite tight. Occasionally the virtuoso would get the better of him, and his playing on disc of Chopin's A-flat Polonaise is rather flashy, if not vulgar. The A-flat Ballade is far too precious and the *Butterfly* and *Black Key* Etudes are disappointing. The less than six hours of his playing captured on electrical recording represent only a fraction of a large performing repertoire.

The Grieg Concerto, recorded in 1928

with Phillipe Gaubert conducting an unidentified orchestra, finds both conductor and pianist thoroughly unhappy with whatever were the conditions under which it was recorded. Friedman is definitely out of sorts. Unfortunately there is no other recording of his hundreds of concerto appearances with such eminent conductors as Walter, Nikisch, van Beinum, Szell, Sargent, Mengelberg, Damrosch, and many others. However, there is still enough to realize that Friedman at his best produced recordings that are marvels of the Romantic spirit. The late Danish pianist Gunnar Johansen first heard Friedman in Copenhagen during the First World War when Friedman was living, composing, and teaching in the Danish capital. Johansen later told this writer that "it was colossal—now, years later when I hear his recordings, I understand why. He had an individuality like nobody else— nobody plays like Friedman."

One may listen to his Chopin etude in Thirds which makes that of other pianists pale. Josef Lhévinne's equals his technically, but Friedman's is more relaxed, more Romantically autumnal, with a breathing rubato. Or listen to the Revolutionary etude. Nobody has ever approached it for originality and daring. His left and right hands are in two different spheres. The performance is barless and follows laws that only Friedman could follow. Perhaps Friedman's performance would be frowned upon by teachers as a bad example for modern virtuosi. It is unique playing, however, and comparing it to, say, Pollini's "modern" performance—grim, abstract, and literal—is to hear the two extremes of Romantic and modern interpretation.

Another Chopin etude, Op. 10, No. 7, is a *tour de force*. It is astonishing to think that he simply walked into a recording studio on a winter's day in 1930 and dashed it off in an age before editing. Friedman also recorded one of the miracles of Chopin interpretation in the Nocturne in E flat, Op. 55, No. 2, one of the composer's greatest nocturnes. Here we have on disc the very acme of Chopinesque lyricism, a lyricism that transcends all fashion. In Friedman's hands, not an inflection is out of place. There is not a nervous motion to mar the complex linear design, not a patch of purple passion to crush the delicate sentiment. It is the quintessential performance of a Chopin nocturne: Romantic sentiment at its most refined and restrained, with a perpetually singing tone, which alone can ravish the ear and heart.

Today pianists study and treasure Friedman's recorded output and none of it has been more discussed and admired than the thirty-odd minutes of Chopin mazurkas that he recorded six and a half decades ago. These mazurka recordings are now legendary in the annals of piano playing. Friedman's conceptions reveal the powerful authenticity of a man imbued with the essence of this dance form. Yet they have nothing even remotely in common with other mazurka playing. The pianist David Bar-Illan said: "The greater the interpretation, the more impossible to figure it out. A good example is Friedman's recording of the Chopin Mazurkas. I don't understand what he is doing. On purpose I try to imitate them—not to play like him, of course, but to understand what he does. And yet what he does with them remains an enigma."

They seem to have a rhythmic life of their own. He pronounced the bass notes as never before. They are rude, fragrant, earthy, lusty, and filled with coquetry.

Another facet of Friedman's art must be savored: his recording of a group of Mendelssohn's *Songs without Words*. In them, the very spirit of Mendelssohn is kindled, warmed in a radiant light. They melt the heart. In his Mendelssohn performances we find the springtime of life, a sense that all will come in its time and its place. The playing enchants us in the sheer confidence of his phrasing, the lack of anxiety, the clarity of his many touches, the living staccato and smoothness of legato, the loveliness of the tone. Although these nine pieces take less than half an hour, this playing alone would rank Friedman as one of the great Romantic pianists.

Friedman's programs were unusually varied and monumental in scope, scattered through with various novelties, usually of fearsome technical demands, and very different in outline from today's programs.

Budapest, 1908
Chopin: Sonata No. 3 in B minor, Op. 58
Brahms: *Paganini* Variations
Schumann: *Carnaval,* Op. 9
Suk: Menuet
Friedman: *Valse noble*
Liszt: Liebesträume
Henselt-Godowsky: *Were I a Bird* Etude
Schulz-Evler: *On the Beautiful Blue Danube*

Berlin, 1908
Chopin: Sonata No. 3 in B minor, Op. 58
Novak: Sonata *Eroica,* Op. 24
Brahms: *Paganini* Variations, Op. 35, Books 1 & 2
Liszt: *Don Juan* Fantasy

Crakow, 1910
Bach-Busoni: Chaconne
Tchaikovsky: Sonata in G major
Chopin: Nocturne and Valse in A-flat major
Chopin: Scherzo in C-sharp minor
Chopin: Polonaise in E-flat minor
Brzezinsky: Prelude and Fugue in C major
Friedman: Tabalière à musique
Albéniz: Triana
Debussy: La Soirée dans Grenade
Liszt: *Hexaméron*

Stockholm, 1911
Boccherini-Friedman: Pastoral
Anonymous-Friedman: *The Judgement of Paris*
Beethoven: Sonata in C minor, Op. 111
Schumann: *Carnaval,* Op. 9
Chopin: Nocturne, Op. 62, No. 1

Chopin: Ballade in G minor, Op. 23
Chopin: 2 Mazurkas
Chopin: Valse in A-flat major
Chopin: 4 Etudes
Scriabin: *Poem*
Debussy: La Soirée dans Grenade
Liszt: *Funérailles*
Liszt: *Mephisto Waltz*

Besides a legion of encores, his programs offered small pieces by Szymanowski, Paderewski, Novak, Rubinstein, Scriabin, Renner, Ravel, Glazunov, Suk, Pabst, Godowsky, Hummel, Field, Weber, Mendelssohn, Mozart, Tajcevic, Poldini, Dohnányi, and Niemann. All-Chopin and all-Liszt programs were frequently presented.

JAMES FRISKIN
1886–1967—Scotland

A student of Dannreuther, he settled in the United States in 1914. He was one of the original faculty members of the Juilliard School and taught there until his death. Friskin was a fine scholar who was best known for his precise Bach playing and excellent editions. He composed several chamber works. With the pianist Irwin Freundlich, he wrote the useful book *Music for the Piano*.

ADOLFO FUMAGALLI
1828–1856—Italy

He studied at the Milan Conservatory, made a debut in 1848, and had a brief but brilliant career. The best known of his many salon pieces is *Les Clochettes,* Op. 21. He had three brothers who achieved reputations as pianists.

G

OSSIP GABRILOWITSCH

1878–1936 Russia

He studied with Anton Rubinstein at the St. Petersburg Conservatory and worked for two years with Leschetizky. In 1918 he was appointed conductor of the Detroit Symphony, building it into an exemplary ensemble. Gabrilowitsch was one of the most popular pianists of his time. His tone sang, and his legato was smoothness itself. Anton Rubinstein had said of him as a child, "Of course he must become a musician, for he will become great among the great." Much later, Olin Downes wrote, "Always the listener was fascinated, absorbed. Always he was responding, as he listened, to beauty, feeling, and a divine union of imagination and form. . . . He could have no imitators, and no rivals."

Arthur Rubinstein, in his memoirs, writes: "During Gabrilowitsch's seraphic playing of Romantic music one felt one saw a halo over his head. His devotion and integrity to the works performed were such that you felt as if you were sitting at a service in church. Everything sounded right with his pleasant tone and fine pedaling. All the right dynamics were there. I left the hall feeling that one couldn't play better, that everything was perfect, and yet I was not happy. The one thing worth living for, the inspiration was not there."

It is regrettable that so little of his pianistic art was recorded, either acoustically or electrically. He was also a wonderful chamber musician, and a beautiful performance of the Schumann Quintet with the legendary Flonzaley Quartet was recorded. With his friend Harold Bauer, he often appeared in two-piano recitals. Together they made a recording of the Arensky Waltz that is of an exquisite elegance; it is playing that has never been equaled for its lilt, perfect style, and sense of movement. Of his solo playing one may hear 1920s vintage performances of such delectable trifles as Arensky's *Prés de la mer,* Grainger's *Shepherd's Hey,* the Glazunov Gavotte, Moszkowski's *In Autumn,* and his own Melody in E minor.

Gabrilowitsch occasionally gave cycles of piano concertos. His last Carnegie Hall venture, during the 1934–35 season, presented sixteen concertos in five evenings. In 1915 he gave a series of historical recitals consisting of eighty-five works. His father-in-law was Mark Twain. His wife, Clara Clemens, wrote a biography of him.

RUDOLPH GANZ

1877–1972—Switzerland

Ganz grew up in Zurich, where he studied with his aunt, whom Ganz said, "belonged to the guild of old-fashioned piano teachers whose principal preoccupation seemed to be to watch the legendary penny remain on the flat top of the hand during five-finger exercises. If the penny slipped, a large pencil came mercilessly down upon my knuckles."

In 1891, the fourteen-year-old boy heard Brahms in Zurich perform in his piano quintet, and was overwhelmed by the composer's "passionate onslaught upon eighty-eight piano strings." From 1893 to 1896 he studied at the Lausanne Conservatory, and was becoming known as a brilliant all-round musician who seemed to sight-read anything. Once at the last minute, he traveled to Vevey to accompany the celebrated violinist Leopold Auer. Soon after he gave the first performance ever in Switzerland of Rachmaninoff's C-sharp minor Prelude. In 1896 he moved to Strasbourg for more instruction at the Conservatory. There he composed and worked on his organ playing, becoming friendly with Albert Schweitzer. The next step in his education was Berlin, where he worked intensely for a year with Busoni. Ganz remembered, "Busoni opened vistas for me in Beethoven, and from him was born in me my interest in contemporary music . . . Among the moderns, Busoni is the greatest technician of all." Later in 1910 in appreciation of his former pupil, Busoni dedicated to Ganz his first sonatina.

In December 1899 the twenty-two-year-old pianist made an impressive debut with the Berlin Philharmonic, performing Chopin's E minor Concerto, the Fifth Beethoven Concerto, and Liszt's Hungarian Fantasy. Within a few months he conducted the Berlin Philharmonic in the premiere of his E major Symphony. Florenz Ziegfeld, the founder of Chicago's famed musical college, heard Ganz in Berlin in 1900 and invited him to Chicago as a member of the faculty. Ganz succeeded Arthur Friedheim in the piano department and spent five pleasant and productive years in Chicago.

By this time Ganz had become a musician with a mission and brought out first performances of new music. In 1903, as soloist with the Chicago Orchestra, under Theodore Thomas, he gave d'Indy *Symphonie on a French Mountain Air* its first performance in Chicago. Thomas wrote him, saying, "You

have shown that it is possible to play with warmth and moderation simultaneously."

In a Chicago recital in 1905 Ganz became the first pianist in America to perform Ravel's work. When Ravel completed *Gaspard de la nuit* in 1908, the composer "as an expression of gratitude" dedicated the third of the cycle, *Scarbo,* to Ganz.

Leaving Chicago in 1905, the pianist moved his family to New York, where Ganz for the next sixteen years pursued a high-powered international pianistic career. In February 1906, he made his New York debut with Felix Weingartner in the Liszt First Concerto. Weingartner exclaimed, "Ganz stands today unequaled among the younger piano virtuosos." Within days of his orchestral debut he gave a solo recital at Mendelssohn Hall. Richard Aldrich, discussing his reading of Liszt's *Dante Sonata,* wrote, "Mr. Ganz played it with tremendous sweep and sonority and an endurance that knew no limit." The many piano rolls he made for the Welte and Duo Arte companies include music of Debussy, Chopin, Granados, MacDowell's Eroica Sonata, and Korngold's Sonata Op. 2. They reveal a sturdy rhythm, fine organization, and an abundant facility. When some Welte piano rolls were released as LPs in the 1960s, Ganz showed enormous pleasure over them, writing, "One can hear me play without any kind of apology on my part." He continued to promote contemporary compositions and many composers dedicated their compositions to him. In 1914 he gave the first performance in London of the Chicago composer John Alden Carpenter's Piano Sonata. In Jeanne Colette Collester's book, *Rudolph Ganz - A Musical Pioneer,* she quotes him, saying "I believe it is the absolute duty of all public performers to have upon their concert programs at least one group of compositions of the modern school. The living have as much right to be heard as the dead." In 1917 Charles Griffes dedicated to him *The White Peacock.* He would continue bringing forth new music to the public as conductor of the St. Louis Symphony, a post which he held from 1921 to 1927.

In 1928 he resumed his teaching at the Chicago musical college and became president of the institution, a post he held from 1938 to 1954. The pianist Joseph Bloch studied with him from 1935 to 1939 and wrote: "His studio on the ninth floor was like a Cathedral with its icons. . . . The lessons were almost always revelations. He could sight-read anything, and with his huge hands could demonstrate anything. . . . Above all I remember his kindness. For us to hop on the stage in the tenth-floor recital hall and to try out our pieces was a scary experience, and many performances were frankly terrible, but he was always encouraging, never destructive."

In 1941 he performed the world premiere of his Piano Concerto in E-flat, Op. 32, which contains some dazzling writing. Frederick Stock conducted. Ganz remained active for the next thirty years. In July 1971, to celebrate the fiftieth anniversary of his appointment as conductor of the St. Louis Symphony, his brilliant former pupil, the late pianist Sheldon Shkolnik, was soloist in the Ganz Piano Concerto with Leonard Slatkin conducting the St. Louis Symphony.

ANDREI GAVRILOV
b. 1955—USSR

Won the Tchaikovsky Competition in 1974. Later he left for the West. Gavrilov has a wonderful physical mechanism, but in public he can get carried away, often banging and playing too fast, and, in such concertos as the Rachmaninoff Second, he does his best to vulgarize the score. On recordings, he is less ferocious and gives nicely turned out performances of Scriabin preludes and careful readings of Bach.

The great Sviatoslav Richter, in his *Notebooks and Conversations,* writes of Gavrilov's recording of the First Concerto of Prokofiev and the Ravel Left Hand Concerto with Simon Rattle conducting: "Gavrilov plays (I) in a virtuosic manner, (II) with power (sometimes too much), (III) quickly (again sometimes too quickly, and as a result not always clearly), (IV) loudly (as a result the tone is not always attractive), (V) with imagination (not always justified) and (VI) with a real sense of artistry (a little studied) and in a convincing manner. He likes to bring his imagination into play, which often results in empty effects. All in all, a dazzling personality and in many respects close to mine. These recordings bowled me over completely."

Gavrilov is at his top notch in the Philips compilation *Great Pianists of the Twentieth Century,* in music of Grieg, Bach, Handel, Scriabin, and Mozart, but for me he strikes gold in Schumann's *Papillons,* Tchaikovsky's winsome Theme and Variations, Op. 19, No. 6, and a rip-roaring *Islamey* of Balakirev calculated to thrill.

HEINRICH GEBHARD
1878–1963—Germany

As a child, he came to the United States. Later, in Vienna, he studied with Leschetizky for four years. He frequently performed, and wrote a volume, *The Art of Pedaling.* His many students included Leonard Bernstein.

BRUNO-LEONARDO GELBER
b. 1941—Argentina

A gifted pianist who worked with Marguerite Long, among others. From the start of his career he showed a propensity for the German Classics. His Berlin debut presented him in the Brahms D minor Concerto, which he also recorded. His early recordings of Beethoven's Third and Fifth Concertos are full of character and Schumann's *Carnaval* and *Symphonic Etudes* have a fine formal underpinning. Gelber is never coarse; his career never developed the force which had been predicted by connoisseurs.

ABBÉ JOSEPH GELINEK
1757–1825—Czechoslovakia

Mozart was struck by Gelinek's powers of improvisation. In Vienna he became a well-known piano teacher of the aristocracy. His variations, fantasies, and rondos were ready-made for easy consumption; not a note remains.

CECILE STAUB GENHART
1898–1983—Switzerland

A student of Busoni and Emil Frey. In 1924, Genhart joined the piano faculty of the Eastman School of Music, where she spent her entire career, becoming the most sought-after piano teacher of that institution. She introduced the Brahms Second Concerto to Rochester.

ANTON GERKE
1814–1870—Poland

He played and taught at St. Petersburg.

Composed various genre pieces for piano, including *Ten Characteristic Pieces,* Op. 14.

REINE GIANOLI
1915–1979—France

A pupil of Cortot, who has a place in French pianism. He recorded a variety of works including the complete piano music of Schumann, a formidable deed, besides stable performances of Debussy's Preludes and Bach's *English* Suites on LP for Westminster.

WALTER GIESEKING
1895–1956—France

He came from a cultivated family and played piano from an early age, but he was virtually self-taught until 1914, when, at the age of nineteen, he embarked on a course of systematic training. It was his good fortune to become associated with the unusual and experimental pedagogue Karl Leimer, with whom he worked until 1917. Leimer insisted on a visualization method which, when mastered, surpassed countless hours of physical drudgery at the instrument. Later, Leimer wrote of Gieseking: "He does not impress [pieces] upon his memory . . . by playing them over on the piano, but by visualizing them through silent reading. By further development of this idea, one acquires the ability even to prepare the technical execution through visualization, so that, without studying at the instrument itself, the piece can be perfectly performed and this in a most astonishingly short time."

Of course, this process was enhanced by Gieseking's innate genius and musical memory, among the greatest in history. He certainly spent fewer hours at the instrument than most pianists did. He was also a remarkable sight reader, probably of the caliber of Liszt, Saint-Saëns, and Bizet. Stories about his wondrous musical facility are plentiful. He dared to play a premiere of a difficult piano concerto with only days of preparation—from memory! Gieseking also composed with immense ease a fair amount of music, which has had no currency in the repertoire.

Gieseking's hearing was among the most sensitive of any musician's, and he was able to hear overtones that the average ear missed. One of the supreme wizards of the pedal, he seemed to have placed his ear next to the pedals themselves, creating effects that defy description, and his playing was perhaps the most ethereal of all time. Chopin would have adored him.

Gieseking's reflexes were split-second, and he achieved the illusion of a perfect and creamy legato more by calculated artful pedaling than through finger binding. After a chord, Gieseking's fingers were instantly detached rather than remaining bound to the piano. Such lifting off frees the vibratory power of the instrument. Few understood the piano's secrets as he did. His sound flowed through and out of the piano. Gieseking must never have known that the piano is officially called a percussion instrument.

There are many who would name Gieseking the twentieth century's greatest pianistic colorist. His dynamics included the subtlest pianissimos ever heard from a piano—as Huneker said of Chopin, "as ghostly as a lunar rainbow." He was a painter of music, and harmony was his color. He phrased with a unique pliancy coupled to a rhythmic awareness and a sense of forward motion. Nobody had ever brought to piano playing, especially in Debussy, such a feeling of inspiration, a sense of evanescent sound hovering in midair, vulnerable to the slightest breeze. Gieseking reveled in illustrating the elegant titles of Debussy's works, the mythological picturings—the fireworks displays, the scents and rhythms of Spain, the nymphs, the rains, the clanging of bells, the dancers, the desolation of snow, the shuddering west wind, and the child's own secret world; it was tone painting as never before effected or thought possible on the piano. If Debussy wanted the piano to sound hammerless, it was Gieseking who complied best. It's a pity that the French composer never heard his music painted by this artist.

Gieseking was also a great interpreter of Ravel, and his recordings of this French master are flooded with light. It is a Ravel of tremulous liquidity, although in many pieces lacking a needed focus and bite. It was Gieseking who put the seal on Ravel's pianistic fame, and his *Gaspard de la nuit* is a landmark recording. Gieseking's performance of the exotic repertoire of Debussy and Ravel is a major chapter in the history of world pianism. In his finest efforts, it was a kind of playing that had never before been imagined. With these composers, especially with Debussy, a symbiosis took place, a divination of the style. In the very spontaneity of Gieseking's approach, he overlooked many details of the composer's intentions. If one cares for a more solid and etched Debussy, then Gieseking will fail.

Though he produced fine interpretations of other composers and would never have thought himself an "impressionist" specialist, in no other branch of the literature would he experience the sense of comfort and identification he felt with Debussy. It was as though with Debussy he were on a heavenly journey, while with other composers he was earthbound. Earlier in his career he had played much Chopin, but soon relinquished him. He was attracted to Grieg and left on disc many of that composer's *Lyric Pieces,* which he played as precursors of impressionism or, as Debussy saw Grieg, "bonbons wrapped in snow." His Schumann is good work, often gentle, and his *Kinderscenen* a delight. In Schubert, he had an easygoing, graceful manner, and he enjoyed playing Mendelssohn's *Songs without Words.*

Gieseking concentrated on Beethoven a great deal, and his recording of the Fourth Concerto is pretty Beethoven playing. He recorded as many as twenty-three of the Beethoven Sonatas, and many of the slow movements are suavely lyrical. But much of the music is without grit and organizational power. His Beethoven is too refined; it lacks the lion's roar.

As for earlier composers, Gieseking is uninspiring in Bach and Handel, and his recordings of the complete piano music of Mozart are too rosy in hue. He was trained, basically, in the late-Romantic school, where Mozart was often heard essentially as a pretty pattern maker, a Rococo powdered doll. Gieseking's own natural elegance can certainly be heard, and in several of the Mozart Concerti he is more satisfying by far than in the solo music.

He was better suited to the idiom of the late Brahms miniatures. His recordings of them, made in 1953, show Gieseking entering a new phase of growth. He bathes the cerebral, gray-bearded Brahms in a warm, golden glow, with tenderness, freedom of metrics, and a plangent tone. In his hands, the music quivers with ineffable sadness for the youth Brahms never had. The composer himself called these last pieces "the cradle songs of my old age"; each was sent off to Clara Schumann with the advice that even one listener was too many. Gieseking captures this intimate and solitary mood, and he sounds the tone of deep nostalgia in the pieces that recall Vienna. Gieseking was a great explorer of sentiment; he died too young at the age of sixty-one.

EMIL GILELS
1916–1985—USSR

Born in Odessa, he studied with Berthe Ringold and later with Heinrich Neuhaus at the Moscow Conservatory. In 1938 he was the victor at the Queen Elizabeth Competition in Brussels. In 1944, Gilels premiered Prokofiev's Eighth Sonata, which was dedicated to him. In 1951 he became a professor at the Moscow Conservatory. In 1953 he made his first appearances in England; and in 1955, Gilels opened the "culture curtain" with a highly publicized tour of the United States, which had been for many years without contact with Soviet performers. American audiences cherished him from the moment he made his debut in the Tchaikovsky First Concerto, shortly after he recorded it with Reiner. Gilels liked playing in the United States, especially for New York audiences at Carnegie Hall, and he made nearly twenty American tours.

Gilels was born for the stage. He walked to the piano with supreme confidence, with a pride, it seemed, in the great tradition of Russian pianism. Just watching him was fascinating. With his Tartar features, eyes three-quarters closed, the shock of red hair of which he was always conscious, the ecstatic glances toward the heavens, hands lifted high, he was the very picture of the great virtuoso. And indeed he was a virtuoso, with enormous technique and a glorious sonority—a sound that stayed in the ear long after the concert had ended.

Gilels was a great public performer, and audiences knew something wonderful was happening. He was a galvanic concerto player, and he stormed the keyboard as few could; no orchestra could drown him out, and when he was inspired he could turn out the most reckless performances. Listen to the mad, animal excitement in his live recording of the Tchaikovsky Second Concerto with the Leningrad Philharmonic. Gilels had a primal urge to play the piano. At times he played it as though he were giving the instrument a bear hug. It was part of his attraction.

In his twenties and thirties, and even into his forties, Gilels displayed a streak of wildness. Scores were swallowed raw, and he could be quite helter-skelter, as well as a furious banger.

His teacher Neuhaus said of the teenage Gilels that "he was very fond of playing very fast and very loud, and it was only beyond these prominent (though, it is true, captivating) qualities that one could make out the shape of the wonderful artist and virtuoso to be, the Gilels as we know him. I think that I did not point out in vain that the hardest, purely pianistic, task is to play very long, very loud and very fast. The true spontaneous virtuoso instinctively throws himself into this difficulty at an early age, and overcomes it successfully. It requires daring, persistence, temperament, passion, energy, and quick thinking."

In fact, all of these are prime Gilels qualities, which made him one of the few pianists who could play at his best in the largest auditoriums.

As he grew and matured, Gilels went far beyond mere excitement in his music-making. He developed control and the ability to use color. He retained his elemental qualities, but developed into a deeper artist. Many of his interpretations were brooding, strange, and enigmatic, especially in live performance, where they sometimes grew formless, and often his pedaling was irritatingly blurred. He was not always successful, but he was always experimenting. And when it worked, he played divinely. I remember a Chopin Third Sonata with the great Largo movement of such meditative and dreamy introspection that time was suspended. His Brahms had a pensive flavor, and in later years it became more flexible and beautifully voiced, but also suggestive—his disc of the Brahms Ballades exudes an almost grotesque atmosphere in places.

Gilels played Beethoven more and more as the years passed. His set of the five Concerti with Szell is fluid and plastic. Far more interesting are his interpretations of the Sonatas. The playing is always in high relief, with a great deal of color, and Gilels elaborately orchestrates each work. His time cycle is long and often leisurely; his tone is especially large; and as sheer piano playing, the performances are always beautifully made and finely finished. In the late

sonatas he is long-winded, yet fascinating, and many of the early ones seem sluggish, lacking forward motion. Quite frequently his presentations sound overpedaled and thick. In essence his Beethoven is not Germanic, but has been transformed into a Byronic Beethoven—or perhaps even "Pushkinian" would be apt.

Gilels had an enormous repertoire, and the world was blessed by the dozens of recordings he made. Of the Classic composers, he recorded a Carl Philipp Emanuel Bach sonata with its expressively "pathetic" slow movement; a sparkling Clementi C major Sonata; a group of brilliant and fetching Scarlatti sonatas; a joyful Haydn Concerto in D major. His disc of Schubert's *Moments musicaux* is memorable, his Chopin strong-willed. Schumann was one of his best composers, especially in Gilels's later period. He played Liszt with splendor, including the Sonata. His Grieg *Lyric Pieces* had a special charm. He cared for Medtner and championed him. He could be devastating in Stravinsky's *Petrouchka,* and equally so in Tchaikovsky's Sonata in C-sharp minor, a student piece that he charged with energy and played as if it were important.

He gave an aristocratic Third Rachmaninoff Concerto, and his recording with André Cluytens is technically ravishing and musically restrained. I remember when Gilels paid a visit to the Juilliard School and a student asked him how long it took him to learn the "Rock Third." He replied, "I began work on it at age fifteen. I am still working at it."

Gilels had one of the greatest careers of any Soviet musician, and his life's work will not be forgotten.

JACOB GIMPEL
1906–1989—Poland

Born in Lwow, where his early studies were

with his father. Later he attended the Lwow Conservatory, graduating at fifteen. Further work took place in Vienna with Edward Steuermann and in theory with Alban Berg. His Vienna debut at age seventeen was a success and concerts followed. In Amsterdam at age twenty he made his orchestral debut with Monteux conducting him in the Rachmaninoff Second Concerto.

He developed into a superb chamber musician and was often heard in concert with his celebrated brother, the violinist Bronislaw Gimpel. From 1935 to 1937 he made a major world tour with the violinist Bronislaw Huberman.

In 1939, Gimpel established himself in Los Angeles, his base for the rest of his life. To supplement his income he made numerous pianistic appearances in the soundtracks of movies such as *Gaslight, Possessed, Letter From an Unknown Woman,* and others. The highlight of this activity was the delightful piano fantasy he composed on Strauss's Blue Danube Waltz for the Tom and Jerry cartoon *Johann Mouse,* which won the Academy Award. Steuermann, unaware that his former pupil had composed and recorded the segment for the film, seeing it at a movie theatre, exclaimed, "That must be Gimpel! It sounds like a whole orchestra."

During the 1950s Gimpel resumed his European tours, while his American career grew slowly. In Los Angeles he had become a renowned teacher and his master classes were great occasions. The writer Henry Miller often attended, calling them "one of the greatest inspirations in recent years. . . . It opened up all sorts of new directions to me. . . . *Interpretation* . . . concerning everything in life that word is one of the biggest words I know. . . . I learn a little more about the art of interpretation every time I go to his master class."

Gimpel recorded early and later in his career. His son, the writer Peter Gimpel, felt: "The earlier style was more clipped, dry and understated, yet somehow still fascinating. It was not until the late forties that he began deliberately to explore the "world beneath," with broader tempi and rubati, and more imaginative use of pedal and tonal color. This was a natural development rather than a transformation, since from his youth, his pianistic idol was Friedman."

His recordings from the mid-seventies are the most accessible today. On the Genesis label can be found the Schumann Fantasy in a penetrating, highly detailed reading but projecting its thorny form with a rare directness. The Cambria label's four CDs of Chopin from concerts at the Ambassador Auditorium in Los Angeles are discs of importance. The B-flat minor and B minor Sonatas, Barcarolle, Fantasy in F minor, and the Twenty-four Preludes display playing of a committed artist deeply in touch with the glowing poetry and noble passion of these works and equipped with large technical resources.

Like other pianists of his generation, Gimpel added to the transcription literature in a stunning 1942 *Concert Paraphrase of "The Song of the Soldiers of the Sea,"* actually a melody from an 1868 Offenbach operatta. This captivating piece is now published in an edition by Marc-André Hamelin which he has recorded for the Hyperion label.

GREGORY GINZBURG
1903–1961—Russia

He was an elegant Romantic stylist. Connoisseurs should seek out some of Ginzburg's records. At his best, he was one of the most delightful voices of Russian lyric pianism. His playing of such pieces as Liszt's *Rigoletto* paraphrase and *Faust* Waltz had a lightness of spirit, combining gallantry with a special sweetness of tone.

ARABELLA GODDARD

1836–1922—England

The most famous English pianist of the 1860s and 1870s and a performer of extraordinary technical command. Shaw felt "nothing seemed to give her any trouble." As a child, she studied with Kalkbrenner, followed by Thalberg and then her future husband, the critic J. W. Davison.

Goddard was the first pianist to perform Beethoven's *Hammerklavier* in London, which she did at the age of seventeen, and the fact that she played everything from memory was often remarked. In 1857 and 1858, again in London, she performed Beethoven's last five sonatas. In 1872 she was the soloist at the inauguration of Royal Albert Hall, playing the *Emperor* Concerto of Beethoven.

Goddard was one of the first pianists to achieve a world career. In 1872 she left for a three-year tour, playing in Australia, New Zealand, India, China, and throughout America.

LEOPOLD GODOWSKY

1870–1938—Poland

By the age of three, Godowsky was already finding his way around the piano. In 1879 he made his debut in his hometown of Vilna. He denied ever having had a proper teacher. In 1884 he made an American tour, staying for two years. From 1886 to 1890, he toured Europe and spent time in both London and Paris, where he gained the valuable friendship of Saint-Saëns. In 1900 his debut in Berlin proved sensational, and he was called "*ein Hexenmeister der Technik*"; from that date, his pianism was heralded as incomparable. Hofmann and Rachmaninoff, two of the great technicians of history, were awed by his unprecedented digital independence. Arthur Rubinstein gasped, "It would take me five hundred years to get that kind of mechanism."

From 1909 to 1912, he gave master classes in Vienna, then went to live in the United States, where his reputation further flourished. In 1930, after recording extensively in London, he suffered a stroke which paralyzed him. Godowsky never again played in public. He had always been unhappy away from the instrument, never tiring of practicing, testing, and experimenting at the keyboard.

Godowsky was widely sought as a teacher and instructed many fine talents, including Heinrich Neuhaus, who in turn became one of history's great teachers. Neuhaus reminisced:

Godowsky, my incomparable teacher and one of the great virtuoso pianists of the post-Rubinstein era, once told us in class that he never practiced scales. Yet he played them with a brilliance, evenness, speed and beauty of tone which I believe I have never heard excelled. It was a delight to watch those small hands that seemed chiselled out of marble and were incredibly beautiful (as a good thoroughbred racehorse is beautiful, or the body of a magnificent athlete) and see with what simplicity, lightness, ease, logic and, I would say, wisdom, they performed their super-acrobatic task. The main impression was that everything is terribly simple, natural, beautiful and completely effortless. But turn your gaze from his hands to his face, and you see the incredible concentration: Eyes with lids covered, the shape of the eyebrows, the forehead, reflect thought, enormous concentration—and nothing else! Then you see immediately what this apparent lightness, this ease, costs; what enormous spiritual energy is required to create it. This is where real technique comes from!

Yet it was often acknowledged that onstage

Godowsky was paralyzed by inhibition; only rarely did he have the power to move a large public. He seemed happiest when playing for a group of his friends and peers. Then he was the essence of subtlety. Perhaps the explanation can be found in his statement that "the deep things of our art are little understood by general students of the piano. The great artist is an aristocrat, a monarch; his work can only appeal to the few. They alone can understand." He simply had no faith in the ability of the large public to understand the musical and technical subtleties of his mind. "The piano is a marvel," he wrote "perhaps the greatest instrument we have. It is so intimate, yet so impersonal." The instrument fascinated and tormented him, and for a select few he unlocked the secret labyrinths of his own compositions. His fifty-three arrangements based on twenty-six of Chopin's Etudes "are absolutely transcendental in their difficulty," as Neuhaus wrote, "and incomparable for musical humor and inventiveness." James Huneker observed:

> He belongs to the Joseffy-de Pachmann, not to the Rubinstein-Hofmann, group. I once called him the superman of piano-playing.... He is an apparition. A Chopin doubled by a contrapuntalist . . . The spirit of the German cantor and the Polish tone-poet in curious conjunction. He is a miracle-worker. . . . Dramatic passion, flame, and fury are not present; they would be intruders on his map of music. The piano tone is always legitimate, never forced. . . . His ten digits are ten independent voices recreating the ancient polyphonic art of the Flemings. He is like a Brahma at the piano. Before his serene and all-embracing vision every school appears and disappears in the void. The beauty of his touch and tone are only matched by the delicate adjustment of his phrasing to the larger curve of the composition. Nothing musical is foreign to him. He is a pianist for pianists,

and I am glad to say that the majority of them gladly recognize this fact.

There are few excellent pianists who have not at least toyed with the demon at the heart of a difficult Godowsky composition, but few remain with the work, and only a fraction of those ever achieve concert pitch with it. Although highly pianistic, the music, because of its dense polyphony, is difficult to hold in the hand or memory. It shatters, splinters, and crumbles. Perhaps only an audience of pianists who themselves have experienced the grueling tortures required can appreciate the undertaking. It humbles the proudest technician, and so Godowsky's music receives few adequate performances. Earl Wild, a true Godowskian, has confessed: "Many of Godowsky's transcriptions are so difficult and complex that they may easily become an obsession. They plague you! . . . Because of their great physical demands, I find that I never have the total abandon that I wish for. They are even harder than they sound."

Godowsky was aware that he was leading piano music into uncharted technical terrain. In the preface to his Chopin Etude transfigurations, he indicated that "owing to innumerable contrapuntal devices, which frequently compass almost the whole range of the keyboard, the fingering and pedaling are often of a revolutionary character, particularly in the twenty-two Etudes for the left hand alone." Perhaps the ideal that Godowsky desired, the dissolving of hand into sound, was possible only in his most inspired moments alone with the instrument he so passionately believed in.

He pursued an almost philosophical elegance. For many, the Godowskian mold with its serpentine harmonics is too ornate, even decadent. His detractors consider his Chopin etude arrangements, in particular, the impieties of a fevered brain committing sacrilege on masterpieces. He could not, it seemed, help tampering with music. The simplest melody, such as Saint-Saëns's *The Swan,* was bedecked with frills and infused with a tinge of irony. Godowsky's ghostly and lavender harmonies, *Art Nouveau* patterns, and high nostalgia are now understood properly as a continuation of the Romantic's quest for individuality, a desire for color and compound texture. His works contain a figurational phantasmagoria, which only Godowsky's inner ear heard in all its coloration; they need from an interpreter a luxuriant aroma and a voluptuous rubato, with a radical use of pedaling. Many of his pianistic concoctions opened a new realm of piano technique, although it remains a closed book for all but Olympian pianists.

Godowsky's recordings generally are rather disappointing; nor did he, unfortunately, put to record any of his own significant works. He was as aloof in front of the recording machine as he was onstage. His playing sounds detached, but highly organized; there is never a hint of sentimentality. His Beethoven Sonata Opus 81a is businesslike and glib, the magnificence of his technical command apparent in the finale. The Schumann *Carnaval* is somewhat thin; it lacks comeliness, yet has a winsome style all its own. The Chopin B-flat minor Sonata is slightly stilted, yet fascinating in the Funeral March and Finale. He was a great believer in the Grieg Ballade and told Arthur Rubinstein to learn it. His recording of it exhibits coolness and technical finesse. Miniatures, such as the hackneyed *Rustle of Spring* by Sinding, sound plastic and pristine, with all semblance of their popularity vanished.

Godowsky was a master of tightening a composition, giving the auditor its inherent purity. Sentiment remains, but all slithering and cooing disappear. One grows slowly to Godowsky's Puritanism. It took me time to understand his way with the ten Chopin Nocturnes he recorded, purged of color, standing straight, rhythmically tight, bathed in a fine mist. I thought, where has the night gone, where is the mystery, the voluptuous plenitude, the girl with the midnight moon glow? In short, where is the indispensable nocturne? Unlike Rilke, who wrote, "I love the night, and I love the darkness, everything grows from it," Godowsky, it seems, gives us the poise of its sections in an almost toneless but fine threading. He eschews all luxury; there is nothing of Novalis's phrase "consecrated to night." Indeed it seems that Godowsky is consecrated to pedantry. But the change comes gradually for those with patience, and in time, his white light becomes the dawn. Godowsky, sick and ailing when recording these works, was actually creating a new chapter in the history of Chopin Nocturne performance. The pianist must have heard countless horrid nocturne readings. His ears must have been clogged by heated sentimentality, indiscriminate rhythms, bloated self-indulgence, operatic singing tone. He looked at them deeply, and his respect for their original genius gave him the key; and after giving Godowsky the due he deserves, we hear his Chopin Nocturnes with nothing of the usual agitated nightmares but pieces poised and spectral, piercing and intelligent, yet retaining Huneker's phrase, "with harmonies as ghostly as a lunar rainbow." In his complete discography, on Appian Recordings, there are other gems that one may treasure: his Liszt's *Leggierezza,* the Dohnányi Concert Etude in F minor, Henselt's *Wiegenlied,* Op. 45, Rubinstein's Melody and Romance, and above all his own free transcription of Schubert's *Morgengrüss.*

Godowsky was a man of deeply felt sensitivity. Always aware of the precariousness of the moment in performance, he understood the terror and the desire for perfection. In a world of flittering changes, some almost imperceptible, but deeply magnified on the concert stage, Godowsky wrote, "The performer's physical world and mental state, his prevailing mood, the entourage, the weather, seasonal changes—each and all affect his susceptibility. And the more sensitive and sensitized the artist, the more responsive he is, the more he vibrates and throbs in unison with the known and unknown influences and unfathomable forces, the greater, deeper and finer is his art." Godowsky was well aware of the retarding demons that Goethe told Eckermann to be watchful of.

The First World War drove him to desperation "to an extent which almost passes human endurance. It has shaken my belief in man's sanity—it has shattered completely my faith in present day civilization and culture." But he continued to work passionately; he told a friend: "I should have a place where I could retire and hide from the world—where I could meditate and think, where I could be lonely in loneliness. . . . I feel that I am just on the threshold of my creative possibilities—merely commencing to express that which burdens my soul. Every day lost in inactivity is a still-born child of my muse—a wasted opportunity, an irrecoverable loss of unrecorded impressions."

A stroke in 1930 impaired his last years. Public performance was denied him, and composition was difficult. It was a cruel destiny for a man who loved the piano as the chief essence of his life.

Godowsky will always remain a special and intriguing figure in the history of world pianism.

ALEXANDER GOLDENWEISER

1875–1961—Russia

He studied with Siloti at the Moscow Conservatory and premiered several Scriabin pieces, including the B minor Fantasy, Op. 28, in 1908. He remained dedicated to Scriabin's music. He made many recordings, all very Romantic in conception. He was considered a great teacher. Lazar Berman, Samuel Feinberg, Oxana Yablonskaya, and Tatiana Wikolayeva were among his students.

ROBERT GOLDSAND

1911–1991—Austria

He studied in Vienna, making a debut at the age of ten. Soon after he worked with Moriz Rosenthal, who indelibly influenced his style and developed his technique. Goldsand settled in the United States and was before the public for sixty seasons. He was attracted to Chopin and in 1949 he gave recitals for the centenary of the composer's death. His recording of the complete Etudes reveals his superb technique, each piece conveyed with sobriety rather than with poetic impulse. Goldsand's repertoire was extensive and catholic in its selection. He played the established masters with seriousness and reverence, which was applied equally to Hindemith or the concoctions of Godowsky or Schulz-Evler. The pianist and critic Harris Goldsmith studied with him, saying, "He had a debonair technical ease. I recall with astonishment how at a lesson he demonstrated the legato he desired for the right hand of the difficult coda of Chopin's Fourth Ballade, but did so with his left hand." For many years Goldsand taught at the Manhattan School of Music.

STEFANO GOLINELLI

1818–1891—Italy

Had a distinguished career as player and composer. His two hundred opus numbers are exclusively for piano, and include three

Sonatas, Twenty-four Preludes, Op. 23, and Twelve Etudes, Op. 15.

RICHARD GOODE
b. 1943—United States

A student of Nadia Reisenberg and later of Rudolf Serkin. Goode won the Clara Haskil Competition in Geneva in 1973. He is a brilliantly equipped pianist with a fresh and rich musical mind and the sharpest musical sense. He is also a finely attuned chamber player. Goode is interested in a variety of music but does best with the Classical masters. His recordings of the Mozart Seventeenth and Twenty-third Concerti are of the first rank. Goode's Beethoven shows a musical thinker who sees the score as a whole. His Beethoven burns brightly, and the sound is full, limpid, and natural. In Schumann, Goode finds a touching intimacy, which is beautifully portrayed in the *Humoreske*, Op. 20.

He has found the time to dip into some contemporary music. Goode is sympathetic to George Perle's work and has recorded his Ballade.

KATHARINE GOODSON
1872–1958—England

Studied at the Royal Academy of Music with Oscar Beringer and in Vienna with Leschetizky. She had a fine reputation and was especially popular with British audiences. She played mostly the standard repertory, although she ventured to perform novelties like the Delius Concerto and the Concerto by her husband, Arthur Hinton.

STEWART GORDON
b. 1930—United States

A well-known pianist. He has organized festivals and was the major force in creating the William Kapell Competition. For many years he has taught keyboard studies at the University of Southern California. I quote from the dedication of his book *Etudes for Piano Teachers*:

> "To today's new Davidites—
> that is,
> to those who love the piano,
> who love teaching the piano,
> and who will fight to see that the wonderful tradition of piano playing and teaching will live on in our society."

ALEXANDER GORIA
1823–1860—France

He studied with Zimmerman at the Paris Conservatoire. He performed and composed extensively, including his Etudes, Opp. 15, 23, 39, and 43.

SASCHA GORODNITZKI
1905–1986—Russia

He came to the United States as a child, studying with Edwin Hughes and Josef Lhévinne. In 1930 he won the Schubert Memorial Prize. His recordings of the Brahms *Paganini* Variations and the Chopin Etudes show a "big" technician. He was a celebrated teacher at the Juilliard School, and many of his students won prizes in the international competition circuit.

LOUIS MOREAU GOTTSCHALK

1829–1869—United States

He began playing piano at the age of three. His French-Creole mother took him to Paris in 1842, where he worked with Hallé and then with Stamaty, both pupils of Kalkbrenner. He had been denied even an audition at the Paris Conservatoire by Zimmerman, who, with typical French condescension, exclaimed that "America was a land of steam engines . . . the country of railroads but not musicians." (Ironically, Gottschalk's *Bamboula* would, in several years, be an entrance piece for a conservatoire competition at which Gottschalk served as a judge.) By the time he was fifteen, everyone was impressed by him, including Kalkbrenner and Thalberg, and Berlioz became a supporter. He wrote: "Gottschalk is one of the very small number who possess all the different elements of a consummate pianist—all the faculties which surround him with an irresistible prestige, and give him a sovereign power. . . . There is an exquisite grace in his manner of phrasing sweet melodies and scattering the light passages on the top of the keyboard. The boldness, brilliance, and originality of his playing, at once, dazzle and astonish."

In 1845 he made a Paris debut and was soon making the rounds of the fashionable salons, where Chopin heard him and was pleased with the boy's playing of his E minor Concerto. The then-thirty-five-year-old Pole was reputed to have told Gottschalk that he would be a "king among pianists."

His early success as a composer was equal to his acclaim as a pianist. At sixteen, he composed *Bamboula,* based on a Negro melody he had heard as a child in New Orleans. The music of the blacks made an indelible impression on him. Other compositions from his teen years were *La Savane* and *Le Bananier.* These

Louis Moreau Gottschalk by David Dubal

and other pieces were instant hits throughout Europe. Their exotic beat proved irresistible.

The next stage of his career was a spectacular eighteen-month tour in 1851–52 through Spain, where his music took on a Spanish cast in works like *La Jota aragonesa, Minuit á Séville,* and the marvelous concert etude *Manchega.* His Spanish sojourn was capped with a decoration by the queen of Spain. But the sweet smell of American dollars wafted across the ocean, and the luxury-loving Gottschalk came home to America in 1853, at the age of twenty-four. His native land was still in the infancy of music appreciation, and Gottschalk, sanctioned with Europe's highest credentials, took the United States by storm. He was big box office and rivaled even Jenny Lind, the "Swedish Nightingale," who had only recently stolen America's heart. P. T. Barnum had brought her to the United States, and now he wanted the languid, exotic

Gottschalk, who refused his offer.

Like Chopin, Liszt, Mendelssohn, Herz, and Thalberg, Gottschalk, with his slim and pale good looks, embodied the Romantic ideal of the time. His seemingly carefree temperamental personality had great appeal, and women went wild over him. He was often found in the most compromising circumstances; a scandal with a teenage girl in San Francisco received national coverage and sent him packing to South America.

Gottschalk was a great showman, full of ennui and disdain as he entered the stage, slowly peeling off his white gloves. Richard Hoffman, in his book, *Some Musical Recollections of Fifty Years*, wrote: "I have often seen him arrive at a concert in no mood for playing, and declare that he would not appear; that an excuse might be made, but that he would not play . . . but a little coaxing and a final *push* would drive him onto the stage, and after a few moments the fire would kindle and he would play with all the brilliancy which was so peculiarly his own."

And play he did: Gottschalk performed ninety times in seven seasons in New York alone. Those were the days when multiple-piano events were fashionable. (Sometimes eight pianos would grace a stage in Czerny's Fantasy on *William Tell*, or another blockbuster.) On one occasion in New York, Gottschalk and Thalberg contrived a two-piano extravaganza on themes from the hit opera of the day, *Il Trovatore*. Hoffman reported that "a remarkable double trill which Thalberg played in the middle of the piano, while Gottschalk was playing all over the keyboard in the 'Anvil Chorus,' produced the most prodigious volume of tone I have ever heard from the piano."

Gottschalk played throughout the United States, even touring during the Civil War. He often traveled with two Chickering grands—his "Mastodons," as he called them—and no town was too small to be blessed with a performance. He seemed to want to get to know his own country, and his return home had inspired him to compose such extraordinary pieces as *The Banjo* and *Tournament Galop*. Gottschalk's diaries, later published as *Notes of a Pianist,* are a fascinating contribution to Americana of the Civil War period. He performed his *L'Union,* a major virtuoso piece, at a memorial service for Lincoln soon after the assassination.

After a while, though, Gottschalk's need for a more exotic landscape than Victorian America drove him to the West Indies, where he remained for long periods. He wandered throughout the Caribbean, living an almost wild existence, "giving a concert wherever I found a piano, sleeping wherever the night overtook me," as he noted in his diary. During his "Antillean" phase, he alternated between great bursts of inspiration and "madly squandered" times. In one of the most Romantic passages from his diaries, we find Gottschalk "living overlooking an extinct volcano. Perched upon the edge of the crater, on the very top of the mountain, my cabin overlooked the whole country. The rock on which it was built hung over a precipice whose depths were concealed by cacti, convolvuluses and bamboos. . . . Every evening I moved my piano out upon the terrace, and there, in view of the most beautiful scenery in the world, which was bathed by the serene and limpid atmosphere of the tropics, I played, for myself alone. . . . It was there that I composed *La Marche des Gibaros,*" the subtitle of one of Gottschalk's masterpieces, *Souvenir de Porto Rico*. And it was in Santiago, Cuba, that Gottschalk composed one of the most popular piano pieces in history—*The Last Hope*. It had "a melancholy character with which was connected a touching episode of my journey to Santiago, Cuba"—Gottschalk was describing an ill-fated romance—"that seemed to me to unite the conditions requisite for popularity."

For several generations, every well-bred

young lady played *The Last Hope* together with Gottschalk's other best-known title, *The Dying Poet*. Gottschalk had a perfect understanding of the Victorian female piano public's demand for sentimental salon music. Gottschalk scholar Robert Offergeld calls it "his *style pianola*. This genre was also a calculated response to American taste, which liked sad titles, *vox angelica* melodies, pathetic barbershop harmonies, thrilling tremolos, sweepy harp effects, and lots of runs on cue." As Arthur Loesser put it, "By the rarefied monastic standards of latter-day highbrows, *The Last Hope* ranks as trash. However, if there is value in something because it has given satisfaction to a great many people for a long time, then *The Last Hope* must count as an important piece of music."

Gottschalk was a pianist of the Herz/Thalberg type, content to play his own music. Although he had been taught the classical composers by Stamaty, he gave in to the clamor for his own worst music, as well as the best of it. George P. Upton, in his *Musical Memories,* wrote: "How well I remember the last time I saw him! . . . He played for me in his dreamy way the so-called *Moonlight* Sonata of Beethoven . . . and some Mendelssohn *Songs without Words.* . . . I remember asking him why he didn't play that class of music in his concerts. He replied: 'Because the dear public does not want to hear me play it. People would rather hear my *Banjo,* or *Ojos criollos,* or *Last Hope.* Besides there are plenty of pianists who can play that music as well or better than I can, but none of them can play my music half so well as I can. And what difference will it make a thousand years hence, anyway.'"

William Mason, as knowledgeable in music as anyone in America at that time, testified in his *Memories of a Musical Life*: "I knew Gottschalk well, and was fascinated by his playing, which was full of brilliancy and bravura. His strong, rhythmic accent, his vigor and dash, were exciting and always aroused enthusiasm. He was the perfection of his school, and his effects had the effervescence and sparkle of champagne. He was far from being an interpreter. . . . On one occasion, after hearing me play Schumann, he said, 'Mason, I do not understand why you spend so much of your time over music like that; it is stiff and labored, lacks melody, spontaneity and naiveté. It will eventually vitiate your musical taste and bring you into an abnormal state.'"

But by the end of Gottschalk's career a higher level of musical taste was dawning in the United States. Anton Rubinstein's cross-country marathon of the classics would come in 1872. As music appreciation developed in America with a Germanic seriousness, Gottschalk's music disappeared. He was considered too lightweight and flighty, and his worst music drowned out the best. Recently, America has been discovering its past, and the best of Gottschalk is returning to the repertoire.

This troubadour of the piano spent his last years roaming South America, where he won the greatest acclaim. Gottschalk's life of only forty years reads like a biographical romance. Mystery and legend always surrounded him, and even his death was dramatic. He had just completed a new piece, entitled *Morte.* While playing it during a concert in Rio de Janeiro, he fell unconscious at the piano, and died several days later.

Amy Fay, an American piano student studying in Germany, hearing of Gottschalk's death, wrote home, "What a way to die! . . . For the infatuation that I and 999,999 other American girls once felt for him, still lingers in my breast!" He was America's first great concert pianist and the instrument's chief popularizer during the 1850s and 1860s, when piano building in the United States was becoming a major industry. His music glorifies the piano with a dashing boldness, especially in the upper register, and the majority of his compositions require a virtuoso equipment. His is the fresh, scintillating, and brash art of a time when America itself was the most optimistic of places. In his music, one can hear circus bands, Sunday horse races, Caribbean tunes, hints of an emerging ragtime, sassiness, unabashed sentimentality, and good humor. Gottschalk's music should be considered a treasure of the Romantic literature, and the most important pianistic output by an American of the mid-nineteenth century.

GLENN GOULD
1932–1982—Canada

He studied with his mother until he was ten. At three, he was at the piano; at five, composing. In 1938 he heard Josef Hofmann at his last recital in Toronto, which made a deep impression on the six-year-old prodigy. At ten, he entered the Royal Conservatory in Toronto. There he studied piano with Alberto Guerrero (1886–1959), a Chilean-born pianist, who was to have a major impact on Gould. He studied with Guerrero until 1952, although he had graduated from the conservatory in 1946, at age fourteen, the youngest graduate ever.

Gould's debut took place, not as a pianist, but as an organist, in 1945. In 1946, playing the Beethoven Fourth Concerto, he made his debut as piano soloist with orchestra. In 1947 he made his recital debut, and in 1950, CBC broadcast a recital throughout Canada.

It was in 1955 that he made his U.S. debut at the Phillips Gallery in Washington, D.C., giving a typical Gould program, with works by Gibbons, Sweelinck, five three-part inventions by Bach and the G major Partita, Beethoven's Sonata Opus 109, the Webern Variations Opus 27, and the Berg Sonata. Paul Hume, Washington's best-known critic of the time, wrote, "Glenn Gould is a pianist with rare gifts for the world. It must not long delay hearing and according him the honor and

audience he deserves. We know of no pianist anything like him of any age."

On 11 January 1955, Gould repeated his success at New York's Town Hall; the very next day, Columbia signed him to a recording contract. The young pianist chose Bach's *Goldberg* Variations. It caused an instant sensation. There was, after all, something new under the sun. Nobody had ever played Bach this way. Composed by the Leipzig cantor for an insomniac, the *Goldberg* Variations became in Gould's hands an eye-opening, ear-crackling, high-voltage experience—young, fresh, and brash. No amount of conservative criticism or musicological hairsplitting about playing Bach on the wrong instrument could quash the appeal of this recording. It put Gould on the musical map; fame came to him immediately and effortlessly, not through competitions or years of concert giving, but through the singular power of recording.

His life became a marathon of concerts, beginning with his first big American tour in 1956. His American orchestral debut took place with the Detroit Symphony, and the following year he made his New York Philharmonic debut with Bernstein in the Beethoven Second Concerto. At his Berlin Philharmonic debut with von Karajan, he played the Beethoven Third. In 1957 he performed for two weeks in the Soviet Union, the first North American to play in Russia during the Cold War. His totally un-Slavic playing created a furor. Gouldomania sprouted everywhere, and the Russians have never stopped loving him.

During the next few years, Gould's playing, recordings, and madcap personality were everywhere. How he played and what he said caused controversy and delight. George Szell said, "That nut is a genius." However, he was unhappy; he grew to dread the live performances, which he saw as a narcissistic arena, a symbol of competitiveness, almost a blood sport. "At live concerts," he said, "I feel demeaned, like a vaudevillian." More and more he thought music should be a private experience. He felt he was forced to exaggerate dynamics in overly large concert halls. He found that he became too concerned with audience reactions, and worse, he could not repeat and correct what had not been good. He could not be the kind of artist he needed to be. He felt like Chopin, who wrote that he could not "let myself become a machine and give concerts everywhere, grinding out the most insipid works devoid of any worth as long as it paid off." So, quietly, on 28 March 1964, at a recital in Orchestra Hall, Chicago, the not yet thirty-two-year-old Canadian commanding the highest fees retired from the concert stage, never to return. For eight years of his short life he had toured the world, making a sensation everywhere while hating the experience fiercely. Henceforth, he was to give his audiences their "dollars' worth," as he put it, in the kind of performances that he wanted, with the control that only a record could supply. Even years after his retirement, many people were bothered by what they considered his act of disdain for the public. It seemed selfish and arrogant—after all, how could you take the word *concert* away from the word *pianist*? Many of his fans were as eager for his return to the stage as Beatles fanatics were for their heroes'.

Meanwhile, a whole new generation of pianists grew up never hearing this legend in public. It didn't matter, though, because Gould was always present. He had become, through his seclusion and cleverness, a supreme manipulator of the media. He was the subject of a flood of articles. In fact, he became more famous than ever; everybody, including those who never went to a concert in their lives, knew the name Glenn Gould: "Oh, yes, the man who quit playing for people," or "the man who wears his overcoat in the heat." He became a folk legend, flaunting his phobias to the world. The rule that a pianist needed to

Glenn Gould by David Dubal

play in public to sell records did not apply to Gould, who remained a best-seller.

Actually, Gould was the last in line of those artists depicted by Vasari, the biographer of Renaissance painters, when he wrote, "Love for his art makes an artist solitary and meditative . . . he who takes up the study of art should flee the company of men." But Gould was by no means a Michelangelo, who suffered agonies in seclusion; nor was he a Garbo, who wanted to be left alone to no purpose. Gould wanted to have his cake and eat it, too. As he needed to control his performances, he needed to control his life, for there was a great deal to accomplish. But he needed people, too—on his terms. He spent an enormous amount of time, late at night, on phone calls all over the world. This writer spoke to him on occasion, and in those calls his contrapuntal mind let loose with an avalanche of concepts, stories (recounted in various accents), current events, and music criticism. He reveled in his verbal prowess. His voice was marvelously agreeable. He was probably the finest telephone conversationalist in the history of that instrument.

He died 4 October 1982, only a week beyond his fiftieth birthday. It had been a long time since the death of a classical musician had produced such worldwide sorrow. With the news of his death, at WNCN I programmed his recordings throughout the day. Calls and letters of grief kept pouring in. His death was felt by many as a personal loss. The playwright Tina Howe wrote to me: "I write my plays to Glenn Gould, I cook the kids' spaghetti dinners to Glenn Gould, I pay the bills to Glenn Gould. . . . What flattens me out about Gould is his style. It's so maniacal yet elegant. He's a true ecstatic like Proust, Nijinsky, or van Gogh."

For many others, he came to symbolize that rare person—someone who does exactly as he pleases. If he dared to say he hated Mozart, so be it! His irreverence was a tonic, and one got the feeling that he could have done anything, that if he had lived double his years, he would have become an Albert Schweitzer, a Dalai Lama, or the premier of Canada; or perhaps, if his beloved technology had moved fast enough, he would have come out of retirement to play on a distant planet, introducing Bach to the cosmos. Gould was a great Romantic personality, and Gould the artist was in the Romantic tradition. People bought Gould's ideas on Bach as they did Rachmaninoff's on Chopin or Horowitz's on Rachmaninoff. There was not a servile bone in his interpretive body. Had they heard him, the composers he played would have congratulated themselves on the flexibility of their idioms. Actually, Gould himself was an idiom, quite unrelated to conventional music-making. Edward Said, an English professor at Columbia University, wrote, "Gould playing Bach seems like a species of formal knowledge of an enigmatic subject matter."

He was adamant in believing that if you could not add anything new to a well-worn masterpiece, you shouldn't play or record it. No musician so practiced what he preached. If he could have, Gould would have let his public in on the orgiastic fun of editing records by issuing Glenn Gould kits containing all of his "takes," so that each listener could make his own Gould performance.

Of course, Gould will always be best known for his Bach playing, and he would not mind a bit. Bach on the piano had become a nightmare of boring, academic pattern making, full of plushly pedaled, un-Baroque sonorities. Even with the onslaught of new Bachian musicology, which preferred Bach on the harpsichord, Gould's Bach continued to prosper. He was actually rethinking the Bach keyboard literature. It was a process that went far beyond quibbling about the correct instrument. Indeed, the timbre of the piano under Gould's hands became new and unexpected; each voice was a living organism; each ornament was felt with a new density. In short, it was the most creative, magical, and revolutionary playing of any literature. His Bach is re-creative genius of the highest order, and it transcends the question of likes or dislikes.

Gould was also the great contrapuntal pianist in history, with a hearing apparatus almost exclusively polyphonic and with the human voice always at the source of his inspiration. Even his celebrated humming was part of the texture—the chorus. Teachers have forever stopped their students from indulging in this natural outburst of guttural participation. It is not good playing manners, it is not in good taste; but good taste was of no interest to Gould. There was not a conventional thread in anything Gould ever played. His Bach did not stem from any Romantic notion à la Schweitzer, or from Landowska's heady and white-hot Bach, or from the many modern harpsichordists who washed Bach dry in supposedly correct performances devoid of passion.

Gould's Bach is sparse, abstract, yet mysterious. It is never pretty, certainly not sensuous. It is a northern Bach, piercing the listener like the cold. Nor is Gould's a friendly Bach. He is not the pianist to come home and relax to or be soothed by. Gould, with his quicksilver reflexes, is too astonishing for repose. He is after the revealing accent, the hidden hymn in the tenor voice. Gould surely understood Bacon's dictum, "There is no excellent beauty that hath not some strangeness in the proportion," and Bach never wrote a fugue according to the rule book. Gould's vision of the *French* and *English* Suites, the Partitas, the Toccatas, the Two- and Three-Part Inventions, and, above all, *The Well-Tempered Clavier* has brought us closer to Bach's divine art. A year before he died, he rerecorded the *Goldberg* Variations. He had realized that his spirit as a man and his breadth as a musician had changed and grown since his first effort. Here, in the later recording, is a *Goldberg* infused with humanity, and the Aria has a terrible, withdrawn pain that is unforgettable.

If Gould's Bach is famous, then his Mozart is infamous. He disliked Mozart, yet spent much time on him, recording all the Piano Sonatas and the Fantasies. Why? It is a Mozart that many rant and rage over. Gould is laughing at us, putting us on, some say. Or is he merely crazy? This is surely not our idea of dear, sweet Mozart: the Alberti basses sassing the melodies, slow movements without depth; no operatic *scenas,* and all played with a perennial nonlegato touch, and everything too fast. Certainly this is a new sonorous imagery for Mozart. I can't pretend to love it. But I can prefer it to a Romanticized, sugary, or frilly Mozart. It is dashing and perverse and often sarcastic—a Mozart heard by a contrapuntist. Young students hearing it before others may become confused for life. But Gould had fun, I'm sure. He was truly irreverent here.

His Beethoven is another matter, and he recorded plenty of it—eighteen of the sonatas, the Bagatelles, Opp. 33 and 126, three sets of variations, and the five Concerti, the *Emperor* with Stokowski being the best-known. There is no Beethoven quite like it—quixotic, too fast or too slow, sometimes petulant. Gould knows Beethoven is a great master, but the heroic aesthetic of Beethoven bothered him. He couldn't abide the overt emotionalism of some Beethoven interpreters. He wasn't interested in finding the metaphysical meaning in the slow movement of Opus 111. Gould was best in the biting, humorous works, such as the F major Sonata, Op. 10, No. 2, with a finale amazing in its speed and dexterity. Mostly, Gould is beating his chest. But it is a fascinating Beethoven. He points up structures that have become blurred. His tempi let us hear new possibilities in the Beethoven kaleidoscope. His timbres are clearer, the big orchestral sonorities are gone from his economically pedaled Beethoven.

In 1960, Gould recorded ten intermezzi of Brahms. This is his most Romantic, wayward playing, quite different from the Two Rhapsodies and the Opus 10 Ballades that formed his penultimate recording, released shortly after his death. That is a stringent, serious Brahms, with many weird moments. Also available is the legendary Gould-Bernstein collaboration in a live performance of the D minor Concerto. Bernstein had made a public apology before the concert for the very slow tempo that Gould felt was correct. Today the interpretation sounds regal and original. (Many performances of the German classics are getting slower and slower, pretending to a misguided profundity.)

Gould was greatly attracted to music from before Bach, and his recording of Byrd and Gibbons is among his most satisfying projects. Byrd is the greatest of all masters of Elizabethan music, and Gould calls him "the patron saint of keyboard writing." But a pianist must choose this virginal music carefully. This Gould does in the Pavan and Galliards, among others, giving performances that are captivating in the ornaments, and those supremely disciplined fingers—guided by a piercing intelligence—bring the music to life on the piano with great success.

Never was Haydn so sparkling, so clever, as in Gould's hands. The Haydn C major *English* Sonata and the famous E-flat are filled with laughter. How I wish he had played more Scarlatti than the three sonatas he recorded. (Gould called Scarlatti sonatas "popcorn.") There is also a marvelous reading of C. P. E. Bach's *Württemberg* Sonata No. 1.

Hilarity and wisecracking are part of Gould's personality and playing. His own composition, *So You Want to Write a Fugue,* tells us a great deal about this aspect of the man. His friend John McGreevy wrote, "All of those who caught a glimpse of this extraordinary phenomenon witnessed one of the most remarkable human performances of our time."

Gould couldn't resist the unusual. In his recording of Liszt's transcription of the Beethoven Fifth Symphony, Gould is nothing less than sensational, with his individualized sonority and sweep. Not to be outdone by Liszt, Gould himself was an epic transcriber, and his own piano transcriptions of Wagner's *Die Meistersinger* Prelude, *Dawn, Siegfried's Rhine Journey, Götterdämmerung,* and even the *Siegfried Idyll,* which he loved dearly, will amaze the listener. These are not mere piano reductions, but transcriptions that leave every detail intact.

Two other Romantic scores should not be overlooked. Gould considered Bizet's *Variations chromatiques* a masterpiece; it was once orchestrated by Felix Weingartner, but has never received the attention it deserves. Gould plays it with consummate musicianship, if in a rather dry and straightforward way, well suited to the score. On the same disc is his tribute to his grandmother's first cousin Edvard Grieg. This performance of Grieg's only Piano Sonata, Op. 7, is unusual

in every detail, and Gould takes about six more minutes than usual to present his view of Romantic melancholy. More memorable is Gould's last recording, of early piano pieces by Strauss and the Sonata in B minor from Strauss's sixteenth year. The music of Strauss was one of Gould's greatest loves. He recorded the *Ophelia* lieder with Elisabeth Schwarzkopf in 1968. He romped through Strauss's *Burleske* for Piano and Orchestra in the performance that I heard with Louis Lane conducting the Cleveland Orchestra, though he never recorded it. In the Sonata for Piano, he saw a potential that nobody had guessed at. Gould transforms this student work into a breathtaking and momentous piece with his awesome originality, timing, and ability to voice.

One of the very largest segments of Gould's recorded legacy was his contribution in twentieth-century music. He recorded the Berg Sonata, the Křenek Sonata No. 3, the three Sonatas by Hindemith, the Prokofiev Seventh Sonata, an album of Sibelius, Scriabin's Third and Fifth Sonatas, and two Canadians— Hétu's Variations and Morawetz's Fantasy— as well as Schoenberg chamber works, songs, the Piano Concerto, and the complete solo piano music. Of this mass of work, I would rank the Berg Sonata, the Křenek Third Sonata, the Scriabin Third Sonata, and the Schoenberg as high achievements. Gould's recordings of the Hindemith Sonatas are far too fussy, while his reading of the Prokofiev Seventh is not especially successful, except in the third movement, "Precipitato," where Gould's power of calculation makes for high tension. The Scriabin Third, however, while not suited to Gould's idiom, finds him better able to contain the material. He keeps his attention on the placement of the figurations, highlighting the design of the work while stripping it of its lushness. Far better suited to Gould's analytic power is the music of Schoenberg. In the Concerto and the solo pieces Gould is very individualistic—his use of the pedal is taut and his phrasing intricate. The precision and projection of polyphony are stupendous, especially in the Suite for Piano (1924).

Gould never regretted his retirement for a minute. While his colleagues jetted over the entire planet, he lived in his splendid isolation, working on a myriad of projects. He made the musical scores for the films *Slaughterhouse Five, The Terminal Man,* and *The Wars.* He made films, and he wrote continuously, in prose as individual as his playing, producing articles, interviews, and liner notes. This work is collected in *The Glenn Gould Reader.* But most important are his more than ninety recordings of hundreds of scores: priceless examples of the recorded art. Gould's records stir me, rile me; they make me think, smile, and scowl, and he can move me in a way no other pianist can. It takes only one earful to know that it is a performance patented and sealed by Glenn Gould. He loved making records, and he knew that with his splicing tools, he could give his audience exactly what *he* wanted. (His second *Goldberg* Variations took a year of editing.) Indeed, Glenn Gould added more to the prestige of the medium than any other recording artist in history.

In the two decades following Gould's death he has become more than a pianist; he has entered the status of culture-hero. Indeed, Canada's own national artistic hero has become a folk legend. Since his death, book after book has been published, as well as films, in a quest to analyze his personality and art. In Canada there is even a Glenn Gould magazine. For the twentieth anniversary of his death Sony Classical has issued the 1955 and 1981 versions of the *Goldberg,* or should I say Gouldberg Variations, with a third disc of a 1982 interview with critic Tim Page, along with twelve minutes of studio outtakes from the 1955 *Goldberg* Variations recording session. The 1981 version was released in the new digital process of the day, but is now heard in an analogue soundscape which is, I feel, closer to Gould's sound, although some listeners will take time to get used to the new imprint. To compare each variation from both performances is a compelling listening experience.

Gould once wrote, "The purpose of art is not the release of a momentary ejection of adrenaline but rather the gradual, lifelong construction of a state of wonder and serenity." Nothing exemplifies Gould's artistic being better than his second recording of the *Goldberg* Variations. This composition was so staggeringly important to him, and to his idea of the Baroque age, that with his immense integrity, he had to return to it with greater humility, producing his last testament and a spiritual synthesis. Gould's highly audible humming gives the recording a ghostly, haunting atmosphere.

HANS GRAF
1928–1994—Austria

A gifted pianist and a teacher at Vienna's Der Hochschule für Musik. Graf judged many international competitions.

GARY GRAFFMAN
b. 1928—United States

He studied with Isabelle Vengerova at the Curtis Institute, and later with Serkin and Horowitz.

Graffman has a fine musical mind and is a superb craftsman. In a Graffman performance one knows where the music is going. His technique is brilliantly substantial in all departments. His discs of the Beethoven

Appassionata, Waldstein, and Opus 111 have a stark drama. The finest of his excursions into the Classical literature is a taut conception of Schubert's great posthumous Sonata in C minor. His Schumann playing falls short of the quality of fantasy, for which his tone is too hard. In Rachmaninoff, Graffman is adroit and slick, and his Chopin recording is devoid of charm. But his Tchaikovsky First Concerto with Szell is crystal clear, and his Prokofiev Third Concerto is one of the best on records. Here and in his Prokofiev Second and Third Sonatas, Graffman's steely sound and tight-fisted rhythmic sense find an outlet. There is a powerhouse performance of the American composer Benjamin Lee's Fourth Sonata.

It seems to me that Graffman's prime motivation was to sound good, presenting the music with high gloss. He converted the grand manner into a modern American style, in which directness and effect took precedence over eloquence and originality of vision—a type of playing that was most prevalent in the 1940s and 1950s. From the late 1970s muscle damage in his right hand has prevented him from performance. In 1981 he published his autobiography, *I Really Should Be Practicing,* and in 1986 he assumed the position of director of the Curtis Institute of Music. Graffman continues to perform music for left hand, building a considerable repertoire. In 1985 he gave the American premiere of the Korngold Concerto, and in 1993 the world premiere of Ned Rorem's Piano Concerto No. 4 for Left Hand at Carnegie Hall.

PERCY GRAINGER
1882–1961—Australia

The most important Australian-born pianist of his age. Grainger studied in Melbourne with Louis Pabst, and in Frankfurt with James Kwast. He later received valuable advice from Busoni.

He was a collector of folk songs and a dedicated champion of new music. He played many premieres, including the Cyril Scott Sonata, Op. 66, and Nathaniel Dett's *In the Bottoms* Suite, with its famous Juba Dance, which he recorded three times. He was also an early proponent of Debussy, Albéniz, and Ravel. Grieg was enthralled with Grainger, and thought him to be the best interpreter of his works. For the Norwegian, Grainger's playing was "like the sun breaking through the clouds." Grainger played Grieg's Concerto with an unforgettable pungency and brio. His ingenious edition of the Concerto should be consulted by all those studying the score.

Regarding Grainger's playing, Grieg wrote: "As a pianist I do not know to which of the very greatest I should liken him. But all comparison is futile when greatness is the question. He is himself. Possibly I am partial to him because he has actually realized *my* ideals of piano playing. If I had his technique, my conception of the nature of piano playing would have been exactly the same. Like a god his playing lifts us high above suffering and struggles. I had to reach the age of sixty-four to hear Norwegian piano music interpreted with so much understanding and genius. His playing of Norwegian folk dances breaks new ground for me and Norway."

Grainger's most productive days as a virtuoso were roughly from 1900 until the First World War. He played far and wide through the British Isles, Norway, Denmark, South Africa, New Zealand, and Australia. At his New York debut early in 1915, performing to a capacity house at Aeolian Hall with Caruso and other luminaries attending, he programmed the Bach-Busoni Organ Prelude and Fugue in D major, the Brahms Variations and Fugue on a Theme of Handel, a few of his own pieces, as well as Chopin, Ravel, and Albéniz. The critics went wild and were charmed by the variety of his program.

The doyen of New York critics, James Huneker, called him "the Siegfried of the piano," and the powerful Henry T. Finck exclaimed, "In less than half an hour, he convinced his critical audience that he belongs in the same rank as Paderewski and Kreisler. . . . The audience was stunned, bewildered, delighted." The critic Olin Downes once told Grainger, "Your virtuosity utterly amazes me. I have only once before heard a performance of Balakirev's *Islamey* that I could place beside yours, and that was one by Busoni."

Yet, as a pianist, he was extremely insecure and was overtly nervous if he found out a good pianist was in the audience. He claimed: "Real piano players are egged on to do their best when their fellow craftsmen go to hear them, so we are told. But I (knowing myself to be a sham) always play my worst if a piano player is in the hall. My heart sinks into my boots."

As late as 1949, he writes: "I don't have the ability to get good performances of the music I believe in—whether it is my own music or that of other composers. In spite of my long career before the public, I have never learnt the art of showmanship, or the technique of pleasing; curiously enough, I do have the gift of FAME—audiences want to go to hear or see me and all sorts of misguided conductors and musical societies are silly enough to let me try my hand in their forces. But always with the same result. Mutual disappointment, ineffectuality, disgust."

Audiences came in droves to hear Grainger. He was decidedly unique, and even as an old man, his piano playing found a wellspring of youth. His robust playing might be described as "of the great outdoors," so rich and verdant, and as unpredictable as the weather. He often shocked with percussive effects, dissonances, which were smoothed over by others, all of which was interlaced with a ringing, bell-like sound. Grainger played with an overwhelming vitality and an earthy virility. His ruggedness surprised many on first hearing.

In his own music he shines; he is inimitable and unapproachable. The keyboard sizzles and spurts; the punch of his playing, its rhythmic motor vibrates in the auditor. Nobody else has played his *Mock Morris, Molly on the Shore, Spoon River, Handel in the Strand,* or the perennial *Country Gardens* with such rollicking goodwill. Grainger's greatest pianistic asset was his rhythmic dynamism. He once wrote: "Pianists—with their alarming lack of rhythmic neatness, their inability to follow a conductor's beat, their inability to listen while they play—are more in need of some kind of musical teamwork (to offset their all too soloistic study activities) than almost any other class of musicians."

During Grainger's heyday, musical leeway and rhythmic slag were often the rule, and he was a fierce exponent of metronome practice, which he imposed on his students.

However, his discography well shows the spontaneity of his art. He recorded a good deal and was the first pianist to record Chopin's Sonata No. 3 using the electrical process in 1925. John Bird, Grainger's biographer, writes: "This performance has stood the test of time and is the recording to which connoisseurs always turn when Grainger's greatness as a pianist is being discussed. It is played with a ferocity and wild abandon that is at times frightening."

Of the same performance, Wilfred Mellers says: "Percy makes a few cuts and allows himself a sprinkle of wrong notes, but plays with a furious intensity that proves as revelatory of Chopin's wild Polish heart as it is of Grainger's own heroic ferocity. Having heard this, one can have no doubt that Grainger was among the supreme pianists of any time, even without the charisma added, in live performances, or by his extravagant good looks."

The four large solo works he recorded are the *Funeral March* Sonata of Chopin, Schumann's G minor Sonata and *Symphonic Etudes,* and the Brahms F minor Sonata; much in these performances is unorthodox, some is baffling, yet each winning in its way.

Grainger, the man and artist, was a complex being. For those who knew him, his energy was almost alarming. He was an avid sportsman and appears to be one of the first to take jogging seriously, running and walking constantly. His personality would have baffled a team of Freuds, Alders, and Jungs. He was a seething cauldron of conflicts. In 1928 he married Ella Viola Ström after a performance at the Hollywood Bowl before 20,000 people.

ARTHUR DE GREEF
1862–1940—Belgium

He studied with Brassin at the Brussels Conservatoire. Later, he went to study with Liszt. His recordings of the *Hungarian Fantasy* and the Liszt Concerto No. 1, which he studied with the master, are important documents that have fortunately made their way onto LP. He was always a popular favorite in London. In 1889, Shaw heard him and wrote: "Mr. de Greef is a true Belgian, spirited, brilliant, neat, confident, clever, and intensely happy in the consciousness of being all that. His execution is extremely ambidextrous; and he has a prodigious musical gift, besides having a fair share of sense and taste. Grieg prized his playing, collaborating with him in his A minor Concerto."

HÉLÈN GRIMAUD
b. 1969—France

One of the better-known French pianists of her generation, she came to prominence at age fifteen with an effective recording of Rachmaninoff *Etude-tableaux* and the Second Sonata. At the Marseille Conservatory she studied with Pierre Barbizet and at the Paris Conservatoire with Jacques Rouvier. Grimaud is at her best in Schumann, and Brahms. Her playing is fulsome, at times undisciplined, rustling topsy-turvy, and at her best persuasive and communicative; she always captivates her audience. The Brahms Second Sonata and *Kreisleriana* on Denon are intricately layered and well-proportioned playing.

MARIA GRINBERG
1908–1979—Russia

Her teachers were Igumnov and Blumenfeld. Grinberg was a pianist of considerable but well-tempered power, and she was blessed with a Romantic temperament. She was rather versatile, being at ease in the Franck *Symphonic Variations* or the snappy Shostakovich First Concerto. Her Brahms was warm, her Ravel Toccata golden, the *Symphonic Etudes* of Schumann filled with elegiac sorrow. But her best was given to Beethoven. Grinberg recorded all thirty-two Sonatas in a Romantic, earthy style—a Beethoven that is impulsive and technically strong, full of light and dark and the swell of the heart.

COR DE GROOT
1914–1993—Netherlands

He had a thriving career, performing extensively until an arm problem curtailed his public appearances. He taught at the Hague Conservatory and has composed a piano sonatina, several works for piano and orchestra, including Variations-Imaginaires for piano, left hand, and orchestra. De Groot's recordings are clean, nimble, and crisp. Some listeners found him boring. The collection of Ravel, Schumann, and Beethoven issued by Appian find a pianist of distinction and emotional reticence.

STEVEN DE GROOTE
1953–1989—South Africa

Studied with various teachers, including Horszowski. In 1977 he took first prize at the Van Cliburn Competition. His recordings of the Reger and Korngold concertos are effective.

ALFRED GRÜNFELD
1852–1924—Czechoslovakia

A pupil of the Prague Conservatory, he later studied with Theodor Kullak in Berlin. He concertized with the highest acclaim in Europe and also toured in the United States. Grünfeld settled in Vienna, becoming a favorite in the imperial city. The Emperor Franz Joseph was a great admirer and appointed him pianist to the court. Eduard Hanslick wrote, "He is a musician beyond criticism . . . and the greatest favorite with all musical people." His facile, elegant playing of his own deft Strauss transcriptions were once fashionable and made him a popular favorite; many pianists and amateurs created "easy" effects with them and they are fun to play. One may hear his transcription of Strauss's *Voices of Spring* recorded by Ania Dorfmann on Pearl Records, and on VAI is preserved Grünfeld's 1913 performance of the piece, as well as his *Soiree de Vienne* from 1910, both deliciously suave renderings displaying a smoothly brilliant technical mechanism. It should be noted that Grünfeld had

a large repertoire, and his programs included works such as Schumann's *Symphonic Etudes* and Grieg's *Ballade in the Form of Variations on a Norwegian Folk Song*.

FRIEDRICH GULDA
1930–2000—Austria

An excellent pianist who played Mozart, Beethoven, Debussy, and Ravel with affection and insight. Gulda was an accomplished player of jazz. He composed many deft and clever piano pieces. He was best known in Europe, where he also taught.

YOURA GULLER
1895–1981—France

Born in Paris, she had a prodigy career from age five. Guller studied at the Conservatoire with Isadore Philipp, winning first prize in piano at age twelve. Unfortunately, she made few recordings, considering her high reputation, and ill-health plagued her. She made a New York debut in 1973, having achieved legendary status. One may hear her very personal Beethoven Sonatas, Opp. 110 and 111, as well as stylish mazurkas and nocturnes, on the Dante label. *The Art of Youra Guller* was issued on Nimbus.

HORACIO GUTIÉRREZ
b. 1948—Cuba

Studied at the Juilliard School. He came in second at the Tchaikovsky Competition in 1970. Since his debut in New York in 1972,

Gutiérrez has had a worldwide career. He is a pianist capable of virtuoso exploits in the Third Rachmaninoff Concerto. His Liszt is dazzling but never just for show. He can play Haydn's *English* Sonata in C major with many shades of tone without losing its Classical complexion.

H

MONIQUE HAAS
1909–1987—France

She studied with Lazare Lévy and acquired a fine European reputation. Her excellent Debussy and Ravel recordings reveal her fastidious mind and very solid equipment. Sviatoslav Richter, reporting on a 1978 Haas performance of Mozart's Concerto No. 21, K. 467 reviews her, the piano, and critics: "Hass played superbly, but in the second movement the repeated chords in the left hand were a little too powerful, and the papers criticized her for this. I don't think she can be held responsible: the fault is entirely due to the Steinway and its ill-balanced registers. A difficult situation. The critics, once again, understood nothing."

Haas taught at the Paris Conservatoire from 1967 to 1970.

ERNST HABERBIER
1813–1869—Germany

Considered a splendid pianist, Haberbier in his compositions had a method of dividing the most intricate passages between the two hands, thus attaining great speed. His audiences were always delighted with his talent. Haberbier died during a recital. His Etudes Opus 53 are his best and most enjoyable pieces.

INGRID HAEBLER
b. 1926—Austria

She is an artist who plays with polish and taste. Her Mozart is especially admired for these qualities. Her playing has refinement and gentility, as well as a very special tone quality. Haebler has made many recordings of merit.

ELSIE HALL
1879–1976—South Africa

She had an enormously long career. Brahms admired her playing. She championed Medtner, whom she knew in Berlin. Hall had a spirited musical personality with a good technique, even past ninety. George Bernard Shaw heard her in 1889, when she was ten years old, and issued an important admonition for parents of prodigies: "Miss Elsie Hall is an infant phenomenon of the latest fashion, that is, a twelve-year-old pianist [sic]. She played . . . with all the vigor and enjoyment of her age, and as dexterously as you please, being a hardy, wiry girl, with great readiness and swiftness of execution, and unbounded alacrity of spirit. At the same time, there is not the slightest artistic excuse for exploiting her cleverness at concerts; I hope we may not hear of her again in public until she is of an age at which she may fairly be asked to earn her living for herself."

SIR CHARLES HALLÉ

1829–1895—Germany

One of the most venerable figures of nineteenth-century music. Arriving in Paris in 1836 from Hagen, Westphalia, Hallé, like Chopin before him, fell under the spell of Kalkbrenner's pianism. Successful lessons commenced with Charles Osborne, a pupil of Kalkbrenner. Soon his modesty, charm, and musicianship brought him entrée to the highest Parisian cultural circles. Friendships with Berlioz, Heller, Heine, and Chopin deeply inspired him. After the 1848 revolution he went to London, and in August of that year he took "in hand" the musical life of Manchester, where he founded the Hallé Orchestra, building it single-handedly into one of the best professional orchestras of the second half of the nineteenth century. Hallé's music-making as a conductor never stilled his piano playing, and for half a century he performed as soloist a piano concerto at many of his orchestral concerts. He introduced the Grieg Concerto, the Brahms Second, the Dvořák G minor, and the Tchaikovsky Second—each a virtuoso work demanding huge resources of power.

An indefatigable advocate of Beethoven, he even convinced Chopin, no admirer of Beethoven, in a private performance at his request of Beethoven's E-flat Sonata, Op. 31, No. 3. In Hallé's autobiography he writes, "After the finale he said that it was the first time he had liked it, that it had always appeared to him very vulgar. I felt flattered, but was much struck by the oddity of the remark." In 1843, the great pianist Moscheles, who had been struggling with Chopin's style, wrote, "The pianist Hallé, who has been in London for a short while, plays a lot of Chopin, and he plays it well to boot. He has just come from Paris and has definitely brought the true tradition of these nocturnes and mazurkas with him." In 1848 Hallé gave a performance of the *Emperor* Concerto at Covent Garden in London. In 1861 he was probably the first pianist ever to play the complete cycle of Beethoven's thirty-two Sonatas in eight recitals. This he repeated in London several times in the next decades, as well as in Manchester. The last night of his life he was practicing Beethoven's Third Concerto. His playing was described by an unknown critic as "technically adroit, somewhat dry, and without the ability to truly let himself go. His musicianship, however, was impeccable."

But George Bernard Shaw thought: "Nobody who has heard him play . . . has ever accepted the notion that his playing is "icy and mechanical." . . . Is there any audience in the world that would come to hear Anton Rubinstein play a Beethoven Sonata for the twentieth time? Yet Hallé . . . is always sure of his audience. . . . The secret is that he gives you as little as possible of Hallé and as much as possible of Beethoven, of whom people do not easily tire."

Stephen Heller wrote to Hallé: "You have remained my ideal of a pianist, for you never exaggerate. . . . You are never emphatic . . . bombastic, whimpering, affected; for you neither wish to make rocks weep, nor to tame wild beasts, nor to move mountains; you have *true* sentiment, and that is everything."

One suspects many music lovers would have liked to have been in Hallé's apartment in 1839 when Heller brought as his guest an unknown Wagner, poverty stricken in Paris. Heller improvised and Hallé played Schumann's then-still-new *Carnaval* of 1834. The three musicians excitedly wrote a little note of thanks to the composer in Leipzig, which Clara Schumann showed Hallé forty years later.

In 1888 Hallé was knighted. In 1893 he established the Royal Manchester College of Music, to which he was principal and professor of piano. His achievements were vast and he literally made the industrial capital of

Manchester a city indelibly proud of its musical life. When Hallé died, the city mourned with tens of thousands lining the streets. The critic Michael Kennedy wrote in 1972, "As a truly broadminded pioneer and educator, Hallé remains unequaled, in my submission, in the history of British musical life."

MARK HAMBOURG
1879–1960—Russia

A formidable virtuoso who studied with his father Mikhail Hambourg. Paderewski, having heard him, helped to subsidize the youngster to study with Leschetizky in Vienna. Hambourg later wrote, "It was from that great teacher, Leschetizsky, that I learned most everything, not only pertaining to piano playing, but in regard to every aspect of how to live." Leschetizky told him, "You play more like Anton Rubinstein than any pianist I have ever heard." Schnabel was impressed with his octaves, saying they were of "flesh and blood." Hambourg's discs show him to be an artist of temperament, very romantic, and inquisitive. There is available an Arbitor CD devoted to the Hambourg legacy, which includes the Chopin Andante Spianato, which Allan Evans says, "represents a lost art of cantilena playing, which Hambourg learned in the nineteenth century: It sounds as though one is being drawn into a dream-state." The CD contains a highly organized Beethoven Sonata Op. 26, which Evans thinks, "attests to the monumentality of Anton Rubinstein's influence, a rare example of pre-Schnabelian playing." Of special interest is a 1923 recording of Clara Schumann's distinguished pupil Leonard Borwick's transcription of Debussy's *Prelude à l'après-midi d'un faune*, which Hambourg premiered, and which shows his pianistic fluidity.

MICHAEL HAMBOURG
b. 1919—England

She studied with her father, Mark Hambourg, and with Katherine Goodson; in composition with Ralph Vaughan Williams. She did a great deal of performing in a piano duo with her father. She had an extensive career collaborating with Paul Robeson, Richard Tauber, and others, as well as solo performances and teaching.

LEONID HAMBRO
b. 1922—United States

A pianist with a prodigious memory and sight-reading ability. He brings to his interpretations a freshness and fluid technique. He plays Gershwin marvelously and was one of the first to record Griffes. For many years Hambro was the staff pianist for the New York Philharmonic.

MARC-ANDRÉ HAMELIN
b. 1961—Canada

Hamelin has attained high stature among the pianists of his generation, exhibiting in public and on disc an enormous musical curiosity and a hunger to perform peaks of the neglected piano literature which deserve important recognition. Hamelin by no means has disdained the traditional repertory, and although he fights for his own kind of programming, he well knows that Schumann and Chopin cannot be deprived. A recent Philadelphia program consisted of the Haydn C major Sonata, Schumann's *Fantasiestücke*, Op. 12, his own twelve-minute composition completed in 2001, *Con intimissimo sentimento,* a seven-movement affair, much of it enmeshed in softness. The neglected *tour de force* was Alkan's 1857 *Symphonie* for solo piano. It is a blazing score inhabiting a strange and unknown region of Romanticism. Hamelin brings to this a captivating drollery and a sizzling technique. Hamelin has been devoted to Alkan promotion and no pianist should avoid his discs of the Concerto for Solo Piano, the fabulous set of variations, *Le Festin d'Esope,* the *Trois Grand Etudes,* Op. 76, the Sonatine, Op. 61, and the Grande Sonata, Op. 33 and more. In vain one may search the scores for a sloppy moment. The excellence of his Alkan should invite numerous pianists to take a long look at this composer's fascinating soundscapes.

Hamelin's discography abounds in magnificent pianistic dramas. To William Bolcom's *Twelve New Etudes,* he brings verve and humor, while his disc of Sorabji's Sonata No. 1 is of spectacular pianism. Faultless in preparation, execution, and character is the CD of Leo Ornstein's music, a long-needed perusal of this long-lived composer. There is Busoni's *Carmen,* Sonatina, and an impeccable if a bit static reading of Busoni's monumental Concerto.

Do find his recording of the great Ives *Concord* Sonata and the mountainous Reger, Bach Variations, Op. 81, and the Telemann set, Op. 134. And don't miss the hair-raising disc of Rzewski's *The People United Will Never Be Defeated,* of rocking impact. His recorded output includes all ten Sonatas of Scriabin; the pianist states, "Although the text has been scrupulously observed, I feel the fantasy element is especially well reproduced." For this listener, the harmonic structure is clear, but the performances are without the smoldering mystical impressionism that is Scriabin's soul. Medtner is another Russian whom he happily believes to be a master, and he has achieved a mighty task in recording the "complete" fourteen Sonatas. After a long session recording

Medtner's dense sonata *Minacciosa,* he wrote: "I was more exhausted at the end of that day than I care to remember, but at the same time felt very good about what I achieved. The feeling that I am going to contribute a legacy which will help people better appreciate unknown repertoire is always in the back of my mind. It is a wonderful pursuit."

Other major works that he has put to disc are Villa-Lobos's *Rudepoêma;* Rachmaninoff's Second Sonata; Schumann's Fantasy, G minor Sonata, and *Symphonic Etudes*; and Chopin's Second Sonata. There are also great swatches of Percy Grainger, six Sonatas of Sophie Eckhardt-Gramatte, the Canadian composer, small pieces of Georgi Catoire, and a banquet of pieces by Moszkowski, Josef Hofmann, Massenet, Thalberg's Fantasy on Donizetti's *Don Pasquale,* and Jacob Gimpel's perilous Concert Paraphrase of *The Song of the Soldiers of the Sea* (The Marines' Hymn).

His work in the Godowsky gardens is a high watermark—from *Alt Wien* to the punishing *Passacaglia* and most of all the staggering three-CD set on Hyperion of the fifty-three Chopin-Godowsky Studies, twenty-two of these for left hand alone. Although a few pianists have attempted to scale this Everest of technique, nobody has ever presented these pieces with the ease necessary to completely affirm Godowsky's transformations into the wild blue yonder. Hamelin fully pays homage to the digital wonders of Godowsky. In these shrines of piano technique Hamelin is a wonder worker, such suppleness of every hidden muscle of the hand, arm, shoulder, back, and lower spine working in tandem with the pedals. Robert Rimm, in his book *Hamelin and the Eight,* writes: "In Hamelin's playing, the pedals are operated with such guile and transparency that the fierce technical challenges generally remain hidden. . . . Mirroring Godowsky's own abilities and seriousness of intent, Hamelin has achieved sovereign control of the left hand; his layered performances of

Godowsky's left-hand etudes may even spark the illusion of three hands at work."

Although he is best known through his recorded output, each season Hamelin's public career expands. There remains a disparity as yet between his live appearances and the discs. In public I feel that he must broaden his tone in large halls; the sound is somewhat dull and gray, and at times there is an uncomfortable squeamishness in his interpretations.

His apparent technical ease is actually disconcerting. As one listener complained to me at an all-Liszt recital, "This is Liszt? But he makes it sound too easy. This is not Lisztian," and in fact there is a strange blandness, a lack of danger, even a tameness in such blasts as Liszt's "Norma" Paraphrase; the thrill and frenzy which send chills down the spine barely peep out. But it must be understood that Hamelin is an Apollonian rather than a Dionysian spirit. The critic Alex Ross remarked that he "has the mien of a lab technician engaged in unholy experiments." But it is the "unholy" which I miss. Hamelin looks well-adjusted, content, and his bespectacled business look hardly fits some of the magical and vertiginous daring inherent in the music he plays brilliantly. Onstage he does not possess the big personality which sends one off the edge. He looks pleasant, and lusterless, the essential electricity of the great performer-virtuosos, those who makes one's heart beat in some secret recess of the soul, is denied to him. This may be an extra-musical matter, yet many admirable talents have succumbed to oblivion for not having that divine stage spark of Busoni, Paderewski, Cortot, Hess, Horowitz, Rubinstein, Argerich, Richter, Michelangeli, or Rachmaninoff, of whom the English pianist Cyril Smith wrote, "Such was the power of his personality that I have seen members of the audience cower down in their seats as his glance passed over them." It is ever that mysterious alchemy which will not be explained and has no common law whatever.

Arthur Rubinstein once said: "I believe very strongly it's not just what the audience hears, it's what emanates from the artist. That is what makes them come to concerts." Until that miraculous moment when Hamelin onstage exudes a supercharged appeal, connoisseurs of the piano and its more esoteric literature must be content to have at hand his unique discography, so full of gold and glory.

TONG-IL HAN
b. 1941—Korea

A student of Rosina Lhévinne at the Juilliard School. Han won the first prize at the twenty-fourth Leventritt Competition. His many recordings show a pianist with a highly developed technique and a penchant for large-scale works such as the Brahms Sonata Op. 5 and the Schubert A major Sonata, D. 959, in which Han displays a fine sense of form.

CHARLES LOUIS HANON
1820–1900—France

A pianist and teacher whose "Hanon exercises" are used to this day in every country in the world. These are a program of five-finger exercises in both hands which help to build finger equalization.

ADAM HARASIEWICZ
b. 1932—Poland

For six years a student of Zbigniew Drzewiecki, he went on to win the 1955

Chopin Competition over an extraordinary field of contestants—Ashkenazy came in second. Harasiewicz has since recorded the complete Chopin. His is a structured Chopin with never a note out of place, but it lacks variety of tonal gradation.

CLEMENT HARRIS
1871–1897—England

Considered one of Clara Schumann's finest pupils, he was admired for his interpretations of Romantic music. Harris composed various piano works. An adventurous streak brought him to battle on the side of the Greeks against the Turks, where he was killed.

FRITZ HARTVIGSON
1841–1919—Denmark

He studied with von Bülow and had a performing career with a sizable concerto repertoire. He taught at the Royal Academy of Music in London.

CLARA HASKIL
1895–1960—Rumania

She studied with Dohnányi and Cortot and attended some master classes of Busoni. She was a distinctive artist in every sense. Her playing had a deep musicality and a vital intelligence. Her phrasing was always original, and in her work the listener sensed a maturity of feeling. Her metrical command infused the merest ornament with grace. Her flexibility was subtlety itself. Haskil scrutinized carefully all that she touched.

Mozart was her joy of joys, and she played it with the freshness of morning dew. Depending on the work, a slightly suppressed inner passion might appear. Her Schumann was played in the intimate vein, and her recording of the Schubert B-flat Sonata has a hushed majesty. In a minor-key Scarlatti sonata, Haskil managed a peculiar mystery and pensiveness. In the small amount of Chopin she played, she was serious but poetic. Her Chopin F minor Concerto was simply ravishing, the work being one of her specialties. Haskil's art has a timeless quality. It is a pity that she did not record far more than she did. A piano competition in her memory is held in Geneva.

JOHANN HÄSSLER
1747–1822—Germany

Early in his career he had a keyboard contest with Mozart, which he lost. In 1792 he moved to St. Petersburg, becoming one of the dominant musicians in Russia until his death. He repudiated all of the early music that he wrote in Germany, and he began his Op. 1 in Russia. Hässler performed in concert often, and he was a strong advocate of the early piano. He left an effective Sonata-Fantasy, Op. 4 (1795), and twenty-four etudes in the form of valses. His *Grande Gigue* should be revived.

WALTER HAUTZIG
b. 1921—Austria

After studying in Vienna at the State Academy

of Music, he came to the United States in 1939 and attended the Curtis Institute, from which he graduated in 1943. That same year he made his New York debut at Town Hall. Hautzig has played throughout Europe, Latin America, and the Far East. His interpretations show a tasteful, careful approach to the Classical repertoire, as well as a deeply satisfying musicality.

ERIC HEIDSIECK

b. 1936—France

He studied with Cortot and Kempff. Heidsieck has made a fine career as a pianist, including appearances in the Orient. He teaches at the Conservatoire of Lyon, and he is best known in the French repertoire, although he has played complete cycles of the Beethoven Sonatas, as well as Bach and Handel. He has recorded a great deal, especially French music, including deeply felt readings of the Twenty-four Preludes of Michel Merlet (b. 1939).

CLAUDE HELFFER

b. 1922—France

Paris-born Helffer worked with Robert Casadesus. Highly skilled technically, he performs all that he touches with an astute musical mind. His Debussy is finely made and he is one of France's most searching propagandists of twentieth century literature. For Harmonia Mundi he has recorded the complete piano music of Schoenberg, and for Astrée Auvidis the three sonatas of Boulez.

STEPHEN HELLER

1813–1888—Hungary

Heller was born in Pesth and received training from Anton Halm in Vienna. Settling in Paris he was in the circle of Berlioz, Chopin, Alkan, and Charles Hallé. A fine pianist, "there was a singular modesty and reticence in his playing," wrote Hallé, "an indication of expression and nuance, as if he felt shy of telling all the secrets of his heart."

Unfortunately his music, outside of a few teaching pieces, such as *L'avalanche*, is no longer heard. Heller was a Romantic who renounced virtuosity for its own sake (indeed, one may call him anti-virtuosic). He is basically a miniaturist, whose subtlety of style and manner would be swallowed up in large concert halls, while the virtual disappearance of home-music-making accounts for his demise. How unfortunate as "Heller's music is ageless," wrote Maurice Hinson, "Freedom from sentimentality, impeccable workmanship, and refinement and simplicity of outlook go to the making of a miniaturist whose sole object was to perpetuate beauty." In his day, Heller's etudes and preludes were well-known. His Op. 154 offers twenty-one etudes composed in preparation for the execution of Chopin's works. His many dances vibrate, as in the seven *Tarantellas*. H. E. Krehbiel wrote, "His waltzes are dances to be felt and brooded over. The eighteen *Blumen, Frucht und Dornenstücke*, Op. 82 (Flower, Fruit and Thorn Pieces), are proclamations of moods— dreamy, fantastic, aerial, perverse, like those which possessed the creatures of Jean Paul Richter's fancy."

Heller finds a kinship to Robert Schumann, who wrote glowingly of Heller. Of large-scale works there are sonatas of engrossing detail, Opus 9, Opus 65, Opus 69, *Fantasy-Sonata on Mendelssohn's Song "Tis thus decreed,"*

Opus 88, and Opus 143. His finest set of variations are the clever twenty-two *Variations on a Theme of Beethoven,* Op. 130, and *Variations on Schumann's "Warum,"* Op. 142. There are abundant transcriptions on opera themes and songs which are effective and take their historical place among the superior types of this genre. After studying Heller, one clearly hears that he had a definite influence on French music, perhaps most of all in the patrician work of Fauré. As his opus numbers climbed, reaching 150, he continued to expand artistically, and although his music gained in subtlety and formal experimatation, it continued to roam the forests and streams. He is buried close to Chopin at Paris's Père Lachaise cemetery.

ADOLPH VON HENSELT
1814–1889—Germany

Henselt lived a long life but did relatively little to fulfill the wonderful talents he possessed. Pianistically, his prestige never wavered, and though he gave only three recitals during the last thirty-three years of his life, he nevertheless became a legend.

Schumann was the first to write of Henselt's pianistic glory, raving about his "equally developed hands of iron—his strength and endurance" and his "softness, grace, and singing quality." Henselt had a luscious tone, and Liszt was overwhelmed by his "velvet paws." In London, the piano scholar Alfred Hipkins felt "Chopin never had a finer interpreter" and was amazed that "a German played Chopin so well." Von Lenz thought his Chopin playing was "touched by the wand of Oberon."

Realizing that modern piano sonority depended upon widespread chords and arpeggios, he became a fanatic at achieving legato by stretching his hands. Mendelssohn said that Henselt spent all day stretching his fingers over arpeggios. He accomplished with his finger legato what Chopin, Liszt, and Thalberg did with the pedal.

Henselt's music was played throughout the century. Anton Rubinstein included some of his etudes in his historical recitals (though he thought the left-hand extensions bordered on the freakish), and nearly everyone was fascinated by his Piano Concerto in F minor: Liszt loved it, Clara Schumann premiered it, and Busoni made his American debut with it. Other performers of the work included von Bülow, Sauer, Klindworth, Friedheim, de Pachmann, Gottschalk, and Scriabin. Sadly, it fell into oblivion.

In 1889, James Huneker mused: "I refuse to give up my belief in the Henselt Etudes. . . . No, he must not go, for who may replace him? . . . his gentle, elegiac nature, his chivalry . . . his nights are moon-lit, his nightingales sing . . . what charming etudes are in Op. 2 and Op. 5. What a wealth of technical figures, what an imperative legato is demanded . . . and then, above all else—touch, euphony."

But it appears that Henselt is lost to us. Huneker's ravings were about the last cries for Henselt. He was a poet who fell short of genius. Still, his piano layouts are masterful beyond question, and any student interested in building left-hand technique could utilize them with great profit. These pieces influenced the left-hand figurations of Rachmaninoff and Scriabin. His most famous etude, *Were I a Bird,* is a delight in double notes and was once played by everyone. Rachmaninoff's recording is a masterly tribute.

LAJOS HERNÁDI
b. 1906–1961—Hungary

He studied with Dohnányi and Schnabel.

Hernádi composed cadenzas to Mozart concertos and taught at the Liszt Academy in Budapest.

HENRI HERZ
1803–1888—Austria

As a pupil at the Paris Conservatoire he studied with Louis Pradher. In 1818 he won first prize at the conservatoire, the contest piece being Dussek's Twelfth Concerto.

By the age of twenty, the good-looking Herz was the darling of the popular Parisian salons and was becoming the most popular pianist in Paris, even usurping Kalkbrenner's place. Herz was a clever musician, well aware of the ever-increasing popularity of the piano, and accurate in gauging the generally low musical taste of the pleasure-loving Parisian public. It wanted pieces that were easy but brilliant, preferably inoffensive pianistic embroideries based on the opera tune *à la mode*. His ability to create delightful tinklings at the keyboard made him the world's best-selling composer in the 1830s. Herz's pieces were on the piano in the parlor probably more than those of any other composer of the nineteenth century. The idealistic Schumann condemned him as a philistine, but Herz's music must be heard as a barometer of the public's taste, and one need not disdain such lighter music as his better sets of variations.

Herz was not content with only giving concerts and enjoying commercial success. He invented a ridiculous instrument of torture, which he named the "dactylion," and although one could not cross fingers under or over while using it, it was so designed to perfect "five-finger exercises" and thus to make the fingers a mechanism capable of supreme evenness. (This machine was probably conceived in response to Kalkbrenner, who had developed his own device. These and other artificial means of acquiring finger independence were in vogue throughout the century.) Herz also became a piano maker, and a good one. And in Paris he opened a hall bearing his name.

Always full of daring and energy, one day in 1845 he set out for America without one concert booked in advance. He stayed until 1851, having success everywhere he went, playing his own music exclusively. P. T. Barnum saw dollars in Herz and wanted to sign him up, but Herz seemed to do splendidly on his own, playing throughout America, Mexico, and the West Indies. He even managed to establish a piano depot in California for the Herz piano, and began importing them to America. After retiring to Paris, he published a witty book titled *Mes Voyages en Amérique*. In fact, after Leopold de Meyer's visit, Herz was the next most important European piano virtuoso to play in America. He lived a long life, made lots of money and played lots of concerts, published reams of music, had many students, and never worried much about his place in pianistic history. Herz's music will never have a revival, but he must be seen as one of the most successful popularizers of the piano.

DAME MYRA HESS
1890–1965—England

When Myra Hess was born, London's musical life was thriving as never before. Just before her birth, the indomitable Clara Schumann had made annual tours in Britain, where she was idolized. It was a great age of pianists. Liszt himself had died only four years before her birth, and Anton Rubinstein died only four years after.

In 1902, at the age of twelve, she won a medal and a scholarship to the Guildhall School. However, she was not a typical prodigy

Dame Myra Hess by David Dubal

was brought up on Bach. . . . As a student I often played for three hours at a stretch, going through most of the 48 Preludes and Fugues." Invariably throughout her career she began her day with *The Well-Tempered Clavier.*

Hess adored and admired Matthay. Even after his death forty years later, Hess remarked, "He is always beside me when I play." In the 1920s, with Hess's increasing fame, some of which was due to her American concertizing, there began an American migration of students traveling to London to receive Matthay's teaching. The prestige of a single pupil often swells the ranks of the teacher's studio.

Hess made her official debut on 14 November 1907, at the Queens Hall. For the concert, she raised the money not only to rent the hall, but to hire the New Symphony orchestra under its young conductor Thomas Beecham, who was also making his first appearance at the Queens Hall. Hess performed the Saint-Saëns Fourth Concerto and the Beethoven Fourth Concerto. The reviews were mixed, with one critic declaring, "Miss Hess plays as a poet writes." Two months later she made a solo debut at London's Aeolian Hall; on the program, she played selections from Brahms's Op. 117 and Op. 119. One critic condemned her hard-edged tone, which "hurt more in the intermezzi of Brahms, for in them she was rather inclined to exaggerate every feature both of tone and tempo." And thus notice was first taken of Brahms, a composer she would continue to champion throughout her career.

Hess understood, as few have, that the making of a major career takes infinite patience, time, struggle, never-ending work, and strength both physical and emotional. Her musical career was her life and she chided her friend Irene Scharrer for her marriage and children. Hess never let up; season after season she crossed the oceans and continents to attend to her work. The smallest American town would be graced by her presence. She was one

and unlike many gifted children, she was spared any exploitation. Years later she said, "I was a very slow worker. I'm glad I didn't have to begin the life of an artist when I was a child. That is tragic. At twenty they are saying she is not such a good artist as she was at ten."

Hess was thirteen when she met Irene Scharrer, three years older and a talented pianist, who at the time had made her debut with the Leipzig Gewandhaus Orchestra. Scharrer encouraged Hess to audition for her own teacher, the venerable Tobias Matthay at the Royal Academy of Music. It was immediately apparent to Matthay that a rare talent was given to him to develop. Of those early lessons she wrote, "I had a startling awakening to all the beauties of the music of which I had not even dreamed. . . . Till then, I had just played, now I began to think." Matthay deepened Bach's impact on her. She later said, "One should begin to study Bach at an early age. I of the few women whose performing career equaled in success those of the male stars of her era. Her programs were serious; she never thought of playing down to the audience, no matter how provincial. As a fierce proponent of playing Bach's original keyboard music, she often opened a recital with three Preludes and Fugues.

Reviewing a 1925 New York recital, Olin Downes reported: "An incident probably without prescient in the concert annals of this city occurred at the end of the recital—Miss Hess had played an encore . . . when someone in the hall called out 'Bach.' The name was taken up by many others in different parts of the auditorium until 'Bach' could be heard from every part of the house. . . . There are few more promising signs of the times, musically speaking, than the manner in which Bach is constantly gaining in the esteem of the public."

By World War II, Hess was one of the major pianists; by war's end, she became to the public more than a pianist—she was a heroine. From 1939 until the war's end, a time when musical life was severely curtailed in London, she helped organize, played in, and was the major force behind the National Gallery afternoon concerts. She was indefatigable in her own participation and performed more than 160 works, including the complete cycle of the Mozart Concerti. And always she played as only she could play it, her own arrangement, her own "prayer" as she called it—the Bach-Hess *Jesu, Joy of Man's Desiring.*

After the war, her interpretive gifts reached their full power. She dropped the repertoire that did not entirely suit her. (A look at her early discography reveals unexpected selections by MacDowell, Ravel, Falla, Field, Palmgren, Granados, Griffes, and others not now associated with her tastes.) However, many of these performances are idiomatic and worth exploring, such as her Chopin F-sharp major Nocturne, the John Field Fourth Nocturne,

Granados's *The Maiden and the Nightingale,* and in 1942 she recorded the important and expressive piano sonata in three movements, by Howard Ferguson, in a strikingly passionate performance.

Though she was physically small, her presence onstage was imposing. The public felt her eyes blaze with intensity. Hess had a gift for seriousness.

Howard Ferguson wrote: "When she seated herself at the keyboard her apparent serenity was so marked that few people could believe what an abyss of nervous uncertainty it had. Yet in spite of the agonies she suffered before every concert, the moment she stepped on the platform she made the audience feel that they were her friends and that the only thing that mattered was the music they were going to enjoy together."

After her recitals, one came away with that rare feeling that so few can inspire, that perhaps the human race was worthwhile if a Myra Hess existed.

She had a highly developed technique quite capable of attending to the vicious awkwardness of the Brahms Concerti and F minor Sonata, all specialties of hers, and she had plenty of rousing power. Hess had long been an exponent of the Brahms D minor Concerto, but had avoided the B-flat Concerto, fearing that her small hands would not do justice to its massive chordal requirements. She wrote to Sir Adrian Boult, saying, "I think the time has come for us to do the Brahms B-flat, and if we don't do it soon, I shall be too old." Boult acknowledged her need, and with him conducting in October 1938 she played her "first" Brahms B-flat. Many feel the "live" recorded performance she made with Bruno Walter conducting the New York Philharmonic in 1951 is one of the greatest presentations of this score.

The American pianist Ronald Rogers describes a 1956 performance of the Brahms Third Sonata in F minor, Op. 5, at the University of Michigan: "She was like a colossus sitting at the keyboard. Her enormous arm weight, learned from Matthay, enforced the powerful wave of sound which rose up from the instrument, engulfing the audience. It was an awesome power, but totally controlled. I shall never forget that opening movement, with its burning passion, its ungainly pianism. The whole monumental work submitted to her will."In the last seasons of her active musical career, audiences learned to expect a Hess program to include one or more of Beethoven's final three sonatas. In these compositions, she possessed a wholeness of spirit in which technique and mind blended into one. Hess looked for a "truth" in her performance, and perhaps for this reason she intensely disliked making records. The recording studio was too cold for her, and she felt herself helpless without her audience. Certainly her art on disc gives us a good deal, and there are many wonderful things on her recordings, such as enlightened moments of her Schumann *Carnaval, Symphonic Etudes,* and her beautifully projected Schumann Concerto, where she is a master architect perceiving new depths in the score. Her Beethoven Sonata Op. 110 is fervent, but for me her greatest recording—one of the glories of Beethoven performance—is her incomparable playing of the Sonata Op. 109, where she probes the very heart of this poem of humanity. At her least, Hess always lends dignity to her playing; at her best, her readings possess grandeur and dignity. This dignity is her chief trait. It is a "classical" trait, yet with the right amount of sensuousness of sound, which gives to her finest recordings a vision of contemplative spiritual ecstasy.

Hess's friend, the pianist Denise Lassimonne, described a Hess practice session, exemplifying Dame Myra's search for her musical truth. Lassimonne was "all agog to hear how she practiced, so I sat down quietly on the other side of the music-room door with one ear glued to the keyhole. For a long time nothing happened, not a sound. Then there came the soft, soft playing over of a phrase. Again, silence, until a few more quiet notes were experimented with. Once more silence. After a couple of hours of this, she emerged (I had rushed away just in time) and, with a look of complete satisfaction, said, 'I have had the most wonderful practice.'"

BARBARA HESSE-BUKOWSKA
b. 1930—Poland

She studied at the Warsaw Conservatory with Margherita Trombini-Kazuro, and won second prize at the Chopin Competition in 1949. She has been especially applauded for her Chopin interpretations.

KATHERINE RUTH HEYMAN
1879–1944—United States

A pianist who played a great deal of American music in Europe, and in America was a staunch believer in Scriabin when his work was seldom heard in the United States. Of a 1934 recital, Paul Rosenfeld wrote, "Miss Heyman again disclosed the fineness of Scriabin's art and the depth of the experience transmitted by it."

FERDINAND HILLER
1811–1885—Germany

An important pianist-composer; a student of Hummel, at the age of ten he played a Mozart concerto in public. Hiller lived in Paris from

1828 to 1835, and gave (in 1828) the first performance of Beethoven's *Emperor* Concerto in France. He was a scholarly pianist, admired by Mendelssohn, Schumann, and Chopin. He composed many worthy piano pieces, including twenty-four etudes, and his Piano Concerto in F-sharp minor was once a staple of the repertoire up to around 1870.

MAURICE HINSON
b. 1930—United States

He has played widely both in recital and lecture-recital formats, invariably offering imaginative programming. He has written considerably on the piano literature. His *A Guide to the Pianist's Repertoire* and *Music for Piano and Orchestra* are valuable source books. His many splendid editions have found wide favor.

ALFRED HIPKINS
1826–1903—England

A pianist who was also a piano technician with the famed piano firm of Broadwood. He tuned Chopin's piano when the composer was in London in 1848, later writing a book on how Chopin played. Hipkins also had a career as a lecture-recitalist.

IAN HOBSON
b. 1952—England

A native of Wolverhampton, at seventeen he was the youngest recipient of the recital diploma in the history of the Royal Academy of Music. A prize winner at the Cliburn Competition, his career burgeoned in 1981 when he took first prize at the Leeds Competition. For Arabesque Records he has recorded the complete Sonatas of Hummel, Rachmaninoff's Etude-tableaux, as well as the transcriptions and a dozen Chopin-Godowsky etudes. He has a fondness for ornate transcriptions such as the Strauss-Rosenthal *Carnaval de Vienne,* and has several times given the Beethoven Sonatas complete. In the last decade he has added conducting appearances to his schedule, and has often conducted from the keyboard Mozart Concertos.

Hobson's technical equipment is always in smooth order. His musical temperament is emotionally cool, and gobs of color is not a priority. In Rachmaninoff one hears every fragment of the dense padding, without thumping or any vagaries of style. The Hummel Sonatas suit his taste for decorative late Classicism. Hobson is a professor at the University of Illinois.

LUDWIG HOFFMAN
b. 1925—Germany

Has a fine reputation as a concert pianist, recording artist, teacher, and as a judge at international competitions.

RICHARD HOFFMAN
1831–1909—England

A student of Moscheles, he settled in the United States when he was sixteen and made a prominent career. Hoffman concertized frequently, and was the first to play the Chopin E minor

Concerto in New York. He wrote an autobiography, *Some Musical Recollections of Fifty Years,* and composed a large quantity of piano music, some of it excellent. *In Memoriam to L. M. G.* (Louis Moreau Gottschalk), *Dixiana,* and the Impromptu in C minor are gems.

JOSEF HOFMANN
1876–1957—Poland

Beneath a rather blandly cool exterior, Josef Hofmann, whom Rachmaninoff and many others considered the greatest pianist of their time, was a complex person, seething with many undercurrents, and of a paradoxical nature. Hofmann came to maturity with the new century, the first years of which, until the war, were the glorious twilight of a golden age of art. It was also the peak of world piano production; a house was not a home without its piano in the parlor. Hofmann, who had been in the public eye since his fabled prodigy days, was, after Paderewski, the biggest pianistic box-office attraction in the world.

In some ways Hofmann represented new twentieth-century trends. For many pianists, a composer's musical score had become merely a springboard for waywardness. For his time Hofmann took a no-nonsense approach to the composers' markings and intent. He wrote, "I venture to prove to anyone who will play for me—if he be at all worth listening to—that he does not play more than is written (as he may think), but, in fact, a good deal less than the printed page reveals." To some his playing appeared cold and unemotional. What audiences of the era had not yet realized in Hofmann's playing was its unerring rhythmic command. It was a new kind of symphonic rhythm that seemed brash and mechanical. Here was a new modern school of playing, and Hofmann, as well as Rachmaninoff and

Busoni, was accused of lack of feeling. It is interesting that the leading piano connoisseur of the day, James Huneker, felt little empathy for these three giants.

Hofmann, the person, was indeed of the new century. He could hardly look more different than his disheveled master, Anton Rubinstein, whose lion mane symbolized the "long haired musician" invented by Liszt himself. Hofmann was a "modern" young man, and his short hair, neat and businesslike dress, and clean-cut look were frequently noted with approval by journalists; nor was there anything flamboyant about his behavior onstage or off. He shook hands heartily, proudly showing off the bulging muscles of his small hands. An avid sportsman, he was a tireless hiker and mountain climber, a good swimmer and rower, a yachtsman, an excellent billiard player and a fine tennis competitor. (Imagine a Chopin, Liszt, or Anton Rubinstein on a tennis court.) Above all, Hofmann was a gifted inventor with eventually more than sixty patents to his credit, from piano mechanism improvements to shock absorbers. Supposedly, the idea for the windshield wiper came from him, inspired by watching the movement of his metronome. By 1904 he had built from scratch his own elaborate automobile and drove throughout Europe with his friend, the pianist Constantin von Sternberg.

Like most performers of the era, he also composed, but in this respect the twentieth century eluded him. His best compositions are mostly salon miniatures, well-crafted and melodically distinctive but of little originality. Around 1910 he was asked, "What contemporary composers write good piano music?" He replied, "Speaking very generally, there seems to be not very much good music for the piano just at present. By far the best comes from Russia." Was Hofmann ignorant or did he consider "negligible" the recent productions of Debussy, Ravel, Albéniz, Granados, Reger, Cyril Scott, Szymanowski, Busoni, and others?

To his wife he said, "Modern music spoils the old for one, and yet gives nothing to replace the joy afforded by the old school. No melody, nothing which touches the heart."

Josef Hofmann was born in Podgorze, Poland, near Cracow. His father, Casimir, was a remarkable musician, a composer of ballets and operas, a good pianist, and a fine conductor. Mrs. Hofmann, the sturdy underpinning of the family, for a time flourished as a singer at the Cracow Opera. Josef had his first lessons at three and a half from his talented five-year-old sister Wanda. Casimir's own sister was soon responsible for the boy's lessons, and his progress was so swift that the busy Casimir began teaching his son himself. Hofmann was forever grateful to his father as a teacher and a mentor.

He later wrote: "I was fortunate in having a father who realized my musical possibilities and from the very beginning was intensely interested in my career, not merely as a father, but as an artist guiding and piloting every day of my life. . . . I am sure that my father was the author of a great deal of the success that I have enjoyed."

At six, the boy made his debut at a charity concert. He was more than a sensation, and words were hard to find to describe the miraculous skills of the boy wonder. Of course comparisons with Mozart would follow the boy for years, and his early music seemed charming and promising. Casimir was flooded by requests for the child to appear in public, and, although the family sadly needed the revenue, he refused the engagements, letting Josef appear only occasionally for charity affairs.

Anton Rubinstein, the most celebrated of all performing pianists, who loathed prodigies and their parents alike, was astonished when he heard Hofmann at seven, calling him, "a musical phenomenon," telling the influential impresario Hermann Wolff, "This prodigy I believe in, hear him." Wolff, who had orga-nized Rubinstein's "Historical Recitals" in the capitals of Europe, had to prevail upon Casimir to let him manage Josef's career.

But Casimir knew the boy was not yet ready for the stress of such a step, and emphatically refused his persistent offers. Instead, he worked his son harder than ever, building an invincible technique, giving the boy a severe regime of scales, which were to become among the fastest and most even scales of any pianist. He once said: "A well-played scale is a truly beautiful thing, but few people play them well because they do not practice them enough. Scales are among the most difficult things in piano playing and how the student who aspires to rise above mediocrity can hope to succeed without a thorough and far-reaching drill in all kinds of scales, I do not know. I do know, however, that I was drilled unrelentingly in them, and that I have been grateful for this all my life."

Finally, when Joseph was nine, Wolff had his way, and Hofmann began a long European tour; wherever he appeared it was concluded that this natural and unconceited child was the foremost prodigy of the age. During his concerts, he played a varied repertoire, including his own music, and exhibited his gift for improvisation with members of the audience providing themes for him to embroider.

For his debut with the Berlin Philharmonic, Wolff teamed him up with the great pianist-conductor Hans von Bulow, Rubinstein's closest rival as a pianist and one of the finest conductors of the period. At a rehearsal of the Beethoven First Concerto, the boy told Bülow that the cellos were not playing a certain passage correctly. Bülow, a Beethoven specialist, was palpably annoyed as the naïve Josef reproduced on the piano the passage correctly. Bülow succumbed, in embarrassment, to his orchestra, although the concert proved to be a sensation.

Hofmann's hearing was so acute and his absolute pitch so perfect that his feats of ear astounded everyone. In later years he found the rarefication of his absolute pitch "to be a nuisance." He said: "Nor do I believe that the so-called acute sense of hearing, or highly developed sense of absolute pitch, has very much to do with one's real musical ability. The physical hearing is nothing; the spiritual hearing—if one may say so—is what really counts."

Following the child's triumphant procession through Europe, Wolff arranged for an American tour, which was inaugurated with a flourish on 29 November 1887 at New York's Metropolitan Opera House, backed up by a 100-member orchestra. The dimple-chinned boy was quaintly dressed in a striped sailor shirt, knee-breeches, and stockings and, as *The New York Times* reported, "looked, if anything, younger than he is." The program, besides three orchestral works, consisted of the Beethoven Concerto No. 1, Variations by Rameau, Hofmann's own Berceuse, a Chopin group, and Weber's Polacca in Liszt's arrangement for piano and orchestra.

The revered critic of *The New York Times*, W. J. Henderson, wrote:

> The audience was plainly surprised at his appearance, and a general exclamation resulted. . . . He was in looks a bright, healthy, strong, normal boy, with sturdy legs and arms. . . . When he concluded the Beethoven Concerto, a thunder of applause swept through the opera house. Many people leaped to their feet. Men shouted "Bravo!" and women waved their handkerchiefs. Pianists of repute were moved almost to tears. Some wiped the moisture from their eyes. The child had astonished the assembly. He was a marvel. . . . Josef Hofmann played, not only like an artist, but like a master. The tenderness of sentiment, the poetic insight into the meaning, the symmetrical conception of the movement as a whole, and the ability to make the music not only arouse the intelligence but move the heart of the hearer, displayed by this child, were simply wonderful. And these things cannot be taught. . . . Suffice it to say, for the present, that Josef Hofmann, as a musical phenomenon, is worthy of the sensation which he has created. More than that, he is an artist and we can listen to his music without taking into consideration the fact that he is a child.

Shortly after the concert, Josef was taken to meet Thomas Edison and recorded several cylinders on Edison's new recording machine. These first musical recordings in history are unfortunately lost.

Josef blithely went on to play forty lucrative concerts, with another forty scheduled, when the rather new Society for the Prevention of Cruelty to Children used the boy as a test case for cruel treatment. As with most things institutionalized, the individual concerned rarely matters, and the youngster was prevented from playing further concerts in the United States. Hofmann always insisted that he had been having a grand time, and experienced no strain whatever.

Playing to people had become as natural for him as a bird singing. Thrust from the stage and downcast, Josef and his parents prepared to return to Berlin, when Alfred Corning Clark, a New York businessman, emerged as from a movie script, offering Casimir $50,000 on the condition that Josef would not appear in public again until he was eighteen and that Casimir devote himself exclusively to the boy's education. At home, Casimir taught his son until he could offer him no more. Josef had been studying theory and composition with Urban, and was given to the elegant pianist-composer Moritz Moszkowski for piano instruction. Josef worked well under Moszkowski, who helped build his repertoire, especially in Schumann and Chopin. He adored the boy, dedicating to him his sparkling E major Concerto. Hofmann, in turn, played, with incomparable verve, several of Moszkowski's delightful pieces throughout his career. After nearly two years, Moszkowski confessed to Casimir, "The boy knows so much more and plays so much better than I do, I don't know how to teach him."

Fortunately, the great Anton Rubinstein was living in Dresden. Rubinstein in 1862 had founded the St. Petersburg Conservatory, but had never taught privately. Rubinstein heard Hofmann, now sixteen, and gladly accepted him. For two years Hofmann travelled weekly from Berlin to the Hôtel de l'Europe, where Rubinstein stayed while in Dresden. The mighty pianist never played during a lesson, but uncannily awakened Josef's musical curiosity, intellect, and daring. Hofmann wrote:

> His manner of teaching was such that it would have made any other teacher appear to me like a schoolmaster. . . . Rubinstein would always ask me the same question: "Well, what is new in the world?" and I would reply, "I know nothing new, that's why I came to learn something new—from you." He would follow every note of my playing with his eyes riveted on the printed pages. A pedant he certainly was, a stickler for the letter—incredibly so, especially when one considered the liberties he took when he played the same works! Once I called his attention modestly to this seeming paradox, and he answered, "When you are as old as I am now, you may do as I do—if you can." Once I asked him for the fingering of a rather complex passage. "Play it with your nose," he replied, "but make it sound well." He meant help yourself! The Lord helps those who help themselves!

Hofmann, now eighteen, could now begin concertizing again. One day, during the intermission of a Rubinstein concert in Berlin, Rubinstein bluntly told his pupil to prepare his Fourth Piano Concerto in D minor, which Hofmann had not been allowed to play.

Rubinstein wanted it learned in two days, as he was to conduct in Hamburg three days hence. Hofmann vigorously protested that this was not possible, whereupon Rubinstein took his hand, saying, "My boy, for us there are no difficulties." Nor would Rubinstein coach him on it. "It is not necessary," he said. "We understand each other!" The concert was a great success, with Rubinstein embracing his pupil onstage. Hofmann said, "I was not in the seventh, but in the eighth heaven!"

The Hamburg concert took place on 14 March 1894. Afterwards Hofmann casually asked Rubinstein when he would play for him again. His master's answer was a shock, "Never!" Hofmann wrote, "In my despair I asked him why not? 'My dear boy,' Rubinstein replied, 'I have told you all I know about legitimate piano-playing and music-making—and if you don't know know it yet, why, go to the devil!'" The youngster understood that he was now to become his own person. The two never met again. Eight months later, on 19 November 1894, Rubinstein died of heart failure. Hofmann wrote, "The world appeared suddenly entirely empty to me; my grief made me realize how my heart had worshipped not only the artist in him but also the man."

Two days after the news of Rubinstein's death, Hofmann played at Cheltenham, England. He remembered in the Chopin Sonata No. 2, "as I struck the first notes of the Funeral March the whole audience rose from their seats, as if commanded, and remained standing with lowered heads during the whole piece—in honor of the great departed."

For the next twenty years Hofmann ceaselessly played in Europe, America, and Russia, where he was considered Rubinstein's successor. His tours throughout Russia were legendary. In 1913 he played, within as many days, twenty-one recitals in St. Petersburg alone in the vast Salle Noblesse, which seated 3,200, playing 255 compositions before 68,000 people. Such statistics give a good idea of the hunger for piano playing at a time when world piano production was at its zenith. With the coming of the war and the 1917 Revolution, Hofmann never again played in Russia.

In 1905 he married Marie Eustis, a socialite from New Orleans, eleven years his senior. Her father had been the American ambassador to France during the Grover Cleveland administration. Marie had studied piano with the eminent Liszt pupil Giovanni Sgambati. During their first years together she travelled everywhere with him, often under difficult conditions. In her diary she described the Hofmann mania in Russia. "The Hofmannistes," she wrote, "were surrounding our sleigh, they cried 'Down with America, he belongs to us!' I hope I won't be murdered by some jealous girl. They are all crazy enough to do anything." She wrote, at a concert, "I was nearly crushed in my front seat by people trying to get nearer him. One girl grabbed another by the throat and choked her because she touched Josef's shoulder."

In the United States his position was unassailable. Edward Bok, the Philadelphia millionaire and publisher, asked Hofmann to contribute a "Piano Questions" column for the *Ladies Home Journal,* which the pianist conscientiously answered from 1901 until 1914, and which was a popular feature of the magazine.

In 1924 Mary Curtis Bok established the Curtis Institute of Music, where Hofmann taught a few gifted pianists, one of them Shura Cherkassky. In 1927 Hofmann became the school's director, proving to be a fine educator and administrator, bringing to the faculty a group of distinguished musicians, including Efrem Zimbalist, Fritz Reiner, Marcella Sembrich, and Leopold Auer. However, his directorship cut into his concertizing, and when he returned to England in 1933 after many years absence, the audiences were small.

For years, Hofmann's marriage had been in decline. Hofmann's eye for a pretty girl had repeatedly brought him trouble at home. Once, he had been named as defendant in a lawsuit regarding a married woman, which caused much embarrassment. With the arrivals of their three children, Marie opted to stay home with them, while Hofmann strenuously objected, wanting her with him on tour. After an indiscretion, he wrote to her in self-defense: "There is no doubt that I am different from other people, but how else could this be? First, I was born a different animal from others; second, I was brought up differently than others; and third, I've lived a different life than others. Why wonder then and accuse me of certain lacks, when I have so many other qualities which average people do not possess? One cannot be perfect in every respect. One quality usually develops at the expense of another."

By 1927 he had fallen in love with a music student thirty years his junior, and after twenty-two years of marriage, Marie divorced him.

As Hofmann grew older, the always-stoic pianist became taciturn and moody, turning to alcohol to erase his unhappiness. As a performer he was always moody, and like many Romantic pianists never played twice the same. But as the years rolled on, the drinking took its toll and his performances had a dangerous unpredictability.

In the 1930s he still possessed most of his superlative musical and technical powers. The highlight of that decade was his Golden Jubilee Concert of 1937, held at the Metropolitan Opera House, fifty years and a day since his American debut. It was the concert that capped off the career of the sixty-one-year-old pianist, and mirrored Hofmann's unprecedented place in American musical life. The president of the United States, Franklin Roosevelt, who could not attend, wrote, "My regret is the keener because I first heard you play when you were a boy and I was a boy; few, therefore, have followed your career for a longer period, and none with a deeper sense of appreciation than I." Hofmann donated the proceeds of the Jubilee Concert to the Musicians Emergency Fund; and the Musicians Committee for the concert was made up of 140 musicians, many of still-legendary status. Godowsky, Iturbi, Rachmaninoff, Paderewski, Rosenthal, Horowitz, Szigeti, Heifetz, Hess, Martinelli, Stokowski, Toscanini, Lehmann, Salzedo, Farrar, Bampton, Elman, Flagstad, Barbirolli, and Lhévinne, to name some at random, were at the gala event. It was truly a golden age of performers.

In 1938 Hofmann resigned his position at the Curtis Institute, though continuing to perform. His last Carnegie Hall recital took place on 20 January 1946. The concert was a hardship, and Hofmann, aged seventy, retired, an exhausted man. He had been tied to the piano almost from infancy, and music unfortunately had lost the vital freshness necessary for a musician's staying-power. He withdrew from the world to his workshop of inventions, dying at the age of eighty-one in Los Angeles.

During the last years of Hofmann's career the performance of music changed radically. Hofmann's kind of Romantic playing was rapidly disappearing. Instead of a performer's individuality being prized, it had almost become suspect. Instead of a mysterious alchemy where the performer "divined" a score, shedding new insight on it, performers became "respectful" to the composer, in much more conservative, simplified playing, telling the story supposedly exactly as the composers wanted it. This was indeed opposite to what Mahler once said: "What is best in the music is not to be found in the notes."

Hofmann, who had begun his career labeled a "modernist," was now brutally criticized by some critics. The Chopin scholar Arthur Hedley hated the Golden Jubilee recording, " . . . insane prestissimos, the wild fluctuations of rhythm (otherwise known as rubato)—in a word the depths have been reached." B. J. Haggin thought Hofmann's performances "are contrived for their own effect of shock and excitement by their unexpectedness, their exhibition of daring willfulness and perversity."

In his memoirs, *My Many Years,* Arthur Rubinstein wrote: "His chief interest lay in dynamics, in a slowly prepared crescendo ending in a volcanic outburst at the climax, and he felt great satisfaction in frightening the audience by using the violent contrast of a pianissimo followed by a sudden fortissimo smash. . . . And yet, he was a pianist of great stature, because, a musical personality emerged at every concert which I cannot lightly dismiss."

It is Rubinstein's last sentence that tells the story. For years his playing so overwhelmed me that I discounted what bothered me, the blather and sheer striving for effect. At times he could not contain a diabolical desire to shock. In the concert hall, the inspiration of the moment, the onward surge, are what carries the day. But on recordings those shattering torrents can become, upon repeated hearings, nightmarish and perverse.

Yet when Hofmann was at his best, he had a kinetic power that defied description. Although he considered himself small compared with Anton Rubinstein, he too had that elemental power which, when unleashed, could be bloodcurdling.

It is sad that Hofmann, one of the greatest of all pianists, left so little on disc. The best of all his pre-electronic records are the acoustical records of 1923. These included his favorite encore numbers—the Wagner-Brassin Magic Fire Music, the Beethoven-Rubinstein Turkish March, and the Gluck-Brahms Gavotte, among others.

For my ears, his Beethoven *Waldstein* Sonata is cut to shreds, rather nasty-sounding and unidiomatic. His selections from Schumann's *Kreisleriana* are without suggestiveness or true passion. Actually, Hofmann is never warm, though he can charm with his many-hued tone. Of the concerto readings that have survived, some from live broadcasts, the finest is the Anton Rubinstein Fourth Concerto, with Reiner, a glorious unrolling of the grand manner. Also, his recording of the Chopin F minor Concerto gives us peerless virtuoso playing of pristine classic proportion, blessed with a slow movement of luminous beauty. Much less important are readings of the Beethoven Fourth and the Chopin E minor Concerti, which have their special insights, but sound restricted and naked.

Chopin was the composer he played most, and there is nothing in his recordings of Chopin's solo music that does not excite, from the exquisite filigree of the D-flat and B major Nocturnes to the glamour of his Minute Waltz. His Chopin-Liszt *Maiden's Wish* is the most ethereal ever recorded. The first movement of the Chopin B minor Sonata finds him at his most aristocratic, the second subject spun of fine silk, and his recordings of the *Andante Spianato and Grand Polonaise* are endlessly fascinating and of coruscating brilliance, with pedaling that floats in the breeze. Like all geniuses, he had only *his* rules, and to imitate Hofmann's style would be to court disaster. He could play with twenty distint touches, often with a kind of portamento where others play legato, creating a pointillistic effect which is hypnotic. Hofmann was always the craftsman; he once wrote, "Technique is a chest of tools from which the skilled artisan draws what he needs at the right time for the right purpose."

When I listen to his records, I close my eyes and the array of colors elicited by his playing never fails to startle. He had a range of sonority from bright yellow and bronze to pure black, reds, and purple. His climaxes, when they work right, are thrilling. His playing of the D-flat section of the F minor Ballade by Chopin is an ever-widening vista; it seems to grow beyond the music, and the coda of that work is a feat of playing that defies normal

pianistic comprehension. His live performance on record of the G minor Ballade is a blending of courage, color, and abandon. For Harold Schonberg, Hofmann was "perfection plus." He dismissed the Hofmann dissenters as "old-maid critics." But few piano teachers would today sanction their pupils to find his G minor Ballade a tasteful presentation. Indeed, it is far from the field of academe. Yet I have played it to the young generation at Juilliard, pianists bored by the constraints of homogenization, who went wild after hearing it. Most of these twenty-year-old pianists had no idea that such playing could exist, and in public, too. Unanimously, they regretted that styles today are so conservative, that such playing seems impossible for them. But his magnetism was irresistible, and soon my students were asking me for more Hofmann.

Hofmann was never the typical sentimentalist of his time. Indeed, he could be glacial, and almost straitlaced. Hofmann used rubato, certainly, but it was structureal in intent. His rhythm is uniquely imperial, and he was unequalled in fusing sections of a composition. A totally new framework happened with one tiny metronome mark. His spontaneity was deeply calculated. And there is nothing like his chordal playing. Listen to the E-flat minor and A major Polonaises of Chopin or the invincible grasp of chordal mass in the Rachmaninoff G minor Prelude. Or stir your blood with his *Spanish Caprice* by Moszkowski, with the cool elegance of its middle section, the machine-like perfection of the repeated notes, the coda tossed off with dynamite in his fingers, with a disconcerting nonchalance. Of this recording, the pianist Frank Cooper exults, "It is hair-raising, nearly frightening, to hear a piece played like this and to guess at the conceptual power behind so sybaritic a performance."

When listening to Hofmann, at least for those that love him, we are shocked by his colossal daring, his impish humor, his sense of irony. His individuality was fortified by one of the massive technical equipments of all time. His fingers were steel; his trills leapt out of the music, passagework of an ethereal evenness, and those chilling chords. When in the mood, he was poetic and sensuous, demonic, and sometimes maddeningly cantankerous, while the unforgettable sound can only be called "Hoffmannesque." There is no doubt that he was one of the most thrilling pianists in history.

The American painter Paul Hollister, Jr., heard Hofmann frequently, and wrote, "The music seemed to be coming out of the piano all by itself. The organization, control, and calligraphy of what those hands did was almost as beautiful to watch as the sound of the music was to hear. It was like watching felines and their cubs at play. The structure of the music was in Hofmann's small but infinite hands, and the composer's code was in his mind. He had ears that heard architecture."

WILLIAM HOLMES

1812–1885—England

He was among the first students at the new Royal Academy of Music in London. He was esteemed as a pianist and was the teacher of J. W. Davison and Sterndale Bennett. In 1876 he performed his own Piano Concerto in A major in London.

HELEN HOPEKIRK

1856–1945—Scotland

She studied with Leschetizky. Hopekirk espoused the music of MacDowell after she settled in the United States, and was a composer as well.

VLADIMIR HOROWITZ

1903–1989—Russia

He studied with Sergei Tarnowsky and with Felix Blumenfeld, Anton Rubinstein's pupil. At seventeen, he made his debut in a recital at Kharkov, thus commencing one of the most remarkable careers in twentieth-century music. During Horowitz's Russian years, he gave innumerable concerts. After the Revolution, he played eleven programs in Leningrad without repeating a composition. In 1925, Horowitz left Russia and played with overwhelming success in Berlin, Hamburg, and Paris, where he packed the Paris Opera in five recitals. The American impresario Arthur Judson heard him there and signed him for a U.S. concert tour. Horowitz made a spectacular American debut on 12 January 1928 in the Tchaikovsky Concerto No. 1; Beecham, who was also making his debut that night, conducted. Annual concert tours took place to the greatest acclaim until 1936, and then he did not play publicly until 1939. During the war years, however, he maintained a fierce schedule, which included raising money for the war effort.

In 1953, following a Carnegie Hall recital, he retired from the concert stage until 9 May 1965, when he made one of the great comebacks in the history of the performing arts. It was international news, and the anticipation of hearing Horowitz created unparalleled excitement. Music lovers waited for hours to get seats. The recital fulfilled everyone's expectations, and fortunately the event was recorded.

During the next fifteen years, Horowitz made sporadic appearances throughout the United States, and in 1978, to mark the fiftieth anniversary of his American debut, he performed the Rachmaninoff Third Concerto with Ormandy and the New York Philharmonic. It was his first concerto appearance in a quarter century. During the 1980s, Horowitz extended his concertizing to Europe and, for the third time, played at the White House. But it appeared that his playing was deteriorating, and performances in New York and Tokyo were alarmingly off form. Once again, however, he struggled to revive himself, and in 1986 he began playing with a vengeance, making a triumphant return to Russia after more than six decades.

It was felt that Horowitz the artist had reached a new peak, and a worldwide television audience heard the octogenarian maestro playing from Moscow. He returned to Berlin, Hamburg, London, and Paris, where he was received as a cultural hero. After two grueling months on the road, he recouped his honor with a successful return to Japan. Wherever he performed, the world stood at attention. He was featured on the cover of *Time* magazine and received the Presidential Medal of Freedom, as well as decorations from the Soviet, Italian, and French governments.

In 1987 he recorded the Mozart Concerto No. 23, his first studio recording of a concerto since 1951, and played again in the major capitals of Europe, in June giving his first Vienna recital in fifty-three years. Horowitz's audiences sensed that this was music-making of a rarefied nature, poetic and singing, with phrasing of a unique individuality.

Horowitz had come to grips with the inevitable slowing down of his marvelous nervous system. A battle had always raged between his own virtuosity and the desire to be the most sincere of interpreters. For him there were always three stages in his performance: first, the complete mastery of the text; followed by the art of interpretation; and finally, with all of its perils, the act of recreation. The world very often claimed victory for the great virtuoso, pronouncing him the greatest of them all. But in his final years, like a sublime but faded singer or an aging athlete, he gave up what

he could no longer do—play like a lion—and the mighty roar, the floods of fortissimos were withdrawn. He concentrated on new colors, colors such as Monet had realized through his near-blindness, a palette of incandescent pastels that even Horowitz had not dreamed of. In the mid-1980s, he began playing—indeed became all but obsessed with—that most youthful master, Mozart, whose music he performed with indescribable nuance and relaxed beauty. It was a Mozart of Italian vintage, bathed in sunlight, fetching and flirtatious. Only the aged Horowitz could give such a young Mozart to the world.

From the moment Horowitz made his American debut in 1928, audiences went wild for him. Not since the early years of Paderewski had there been such a splash. Olin Downes reported in the *New York Times,* "A mob is a mob, blood is blood; the call of the wild is heard, whether it is a savage beating a drum or a young Russian, mad with excitement and physical speed and powers, pounding on a keyboard." News of Horowitz's successes in the capitals of Europe had traveled quickly, and Carnegie Hall was jammed with the most celebrated virtuosi of the "golden age," many of whom trembled as they went home to reassess their own technical equipment. One of them grumbled, "Our careers will never again be the same."

Horowitz was never dethroned; in fact, he became the yardstick of pianistic prowess. To this day, no review can be more exciting for a young pianist than one calling him or her "another Horowitz"—as if such a complex and towering musician could ever be duplicated. Pianists, of course, may not find congenial all that Horowitz played, but, like him or not, every pianist in the world must come to terms with him. He was the outstanding figure in the pianistic world for more than a half century, as Heifetz was for violinists. I once asked the Polish violinist Wanda Wilkomirska if she thought there was such a thing as a

Vladimir Horowitz by David Dubal

"best violinist." She retorted, "There can be no best anything." But then she looked troubled and added, "I'm sorry. There is a best. It's Horowitz. He is better than anyone, any violinist, any singer, any pianist. Oh, but he is also not human."

When Horowitz burst on the scene, he was in danger of misusing his great powers of virtuosity. Two forces had a salutary influence during those early years: Toscanini, who shaped his intellectual respect for the composer's intent, and Rachmaninoff, who, with his almost cerebral approach to Romantic music, deemed mere showing off to be sinful. To exercise restraint when you know you can raise more excitement than anyone else takes an iron will. With his technical and temperamental gifts, Horowitz could have been the gallery player *par excellence*. And he was a born showstopper. But an artist who engages in acrobatics soon finds himself having to top each effort. Slowly and painfully, Horowitz came to understand André Gide's words: "Any good execution must be an explanation of the piece. But the pianist, like the actor, strives for the effect. And the effect is generally achieved at the expense of the text. The player is well aware that the less I understand, the more I shall be impressed."

Whatever sins he might have committed in the concert hall, Horowitz took recording seriously, compiling the most listened to, and studied, discography in the history of the art. Many of his recordings were pioneering efforts, and his great prestige and authority led many pianists to follow suit. Works that had been neglected began showing up on programs: Haydn's E-flat and F major Sonatas; Czerny's *La Ricordanza*; Clementi's F-sharp minor Sonata; Liszt's *Funérailles*; several Scarlatti sonatas; Kabalevsky's Third Sonata; Prokofiev's Seventh Sonata; Scriabin's Fifth, Ninth, and Tenth Sonatas; Schumann's *Humoreske*; Barber's Sonata; Rachmaninoff's Second Sonata—Horowitz's phenomenal success with these pieces was a powerful stimulus for other pianists to learn them.

The Horowitz discography reveals how little he recorded the warhorses of the literature. He had an abhorrence of the hackneyed. A trademark of his program building in public and on disc was the delicate balance of timings, key relationships, and idioms. He selected his repertoire with great care, playing no work that he had not lived with for a long time.

Scarlatti is the only composer born in the seventeenth century that Horowitz recorded. He made an album of twelve of these priceless binary gems, with another dozen scattered throughout other discs. His interpretations are a lesson in the transference of harpsichord music to the Steinway grand. He employed a large set of dynamics, and used the pedal ingeniously, in washes and dots and dashes. Horowitz packed these works with drama. One hears intrigue, gossip, the clatter of

Madrid cobblestone, the pomp of court, the fetching fandango rhythms, all etched with a remarkable finger precision and spacing of notes. It is a living, breathing Scarlatti, which, once heard, can never be forgotten.

He refused to play Bach in the original in public, believing that modern halls are too big for effective performance. I also suspect that, since he grew up during the decline of Russian Romanticism, "pure" Bach was not really much to his taste. But his recordings of some Bach-Busoni chorales are played to perfection, as is an especially coloristic performance of the large C major Organ Toccata in Busoni's wonderful transcription, which he played as the opening piece of his 1965 Carnegie Hall comeback.

Of Classical composers born during the eighteenth century, Horowitz recorded two Haydn sonatas, four Clementi sonatas and a rondo movement, five sonatas of Mozart, and five of Beethoven, as well as the *Emperor* Concerto and the C minor Variations. He also recorded a set of variations by Czerny and Schubert's posthumous B-flat Sonata.

The capriciousness of Haydn fit Horowitz well. His recording of the Sonata in E-flat is pianistically the finest ever made. Years later, he recorded the smaller Sonata in F major, playing the slow movement with a lavish expressiveness.

His Clementi sonata album from the early 1950s is vintage Horowitz and remains the most effective all-around recorded example of any Clementi sonatas. He understood Clementi historically yet played with stylistic freedom. The finales of the Sonatas in F minor and F-sharp minor brought out the latent passion in Clementi, and his recording of the large-scale Sonata in C major in the late 1970s pulls out all stops, while still remaining within the idiom.

Next in line chronologically is Mozart. Horowitz's 1947 recording of the celebrated Sonata in F, K. 332, is Italianate and operatic in style—a highly inflected and Romanticized Mozart, with a finale that reveals the composer in his most unbuttoned mood. Not as successful is the rather heavy interpretation of the A major Sonata, K. 331, from a live concert in the 1960s; even the concluding Rondo *alla turca* misses the right kind of clangor. The Sonatas in C major, K. 330, and in B-flat, K. 333, are his latest recordings of Mozart, infused with a bewitching flexibility and tonal beauty. His renderings of the Rondo in D and the great B minor Adagio are incomparable. His recording with Giulini of the Mozart A major Concerto, K. 488 has nothing in common with other performances of that work. Humor, bite, a brisk slow movement, and evenness of fingerwork are apparent along with a full-bodied freshness. It will hardly be to everyone's taste, especially the highly inflated second movement.

In 1944, Horowitz recorded Czerny's Variations on *La Ricordanza*. Czerny had turned the naive charm of Rode's aria into a *tour de force* of early Romantic piano music, and Horowitz displayed devastating control and a ravishing sense of style.

Horowitz's nineteenth-century repertoire included only one excursion into Schubert's sonata literature, the B-flat Sonata, written when the composer was dying. It is a controversial Schubert, without much depth, yet one that has a curious impact. The Horowitz Schubert Impromptus of the 1970s are oddly erratic. The E-flat and A-flat are tight instead of expansive, while the G-flat is pumped up into an overblown pool of sound. The Impromptu in B-flat major (recorded in 1986), on the other hand, is played with a beautiful limpidity. His interpretation of the Schubert-Liszt *Soirée de Vienne* No. 6 is all cream puff, and the Schubert-Tausig-Horowitz *Marche militaire* is filled with humor and his characteristic sonority.

Although Horowitz played Beethoven's Sonata in A major, Op. 101, in public, he was not a lover of late Beethoven and found only the early and middle periods congenial. The slow movement of the Opus 10, No. 3, as the pathos of a Greek tragedy, with a sound only Horowitz could achieve. The *Pathétique,* Op. 13, is large-scale and ripe. The *Waldstein* and *Appassionata,* while self-conscious, have a definite power and glitter, as does the *Moonlight* Sonata's finale. His C minor Variations are tightly packed, and the *Emperor* Concerto, with Reiner, is lean but heroically cast.

The first Romantic that Horowitz took to heart is Mendelssohn. His account of several *Songs without Words,* including the *Spring Song,* was delightful and pithy; the *Variations sérieuses* were seething and impregnable technically. In 1981 he returned to Mendelssohn, recording the *Scherzo a capriccio* to rousing effect.

At times there was a clash of personalities between Chopin and Horowitz. At its worst, the pianist's phrasing sounded unnatural; sometimes it was touched with hysteria. He delved deeply in the Chopin repertoire, and his earlier Chopin recordings, such as several etudes and the Fourth Scherzo, are simple and refined. Later, however, his Chopin playing became often shredded and nervous—a public Chopin for gargantuan halls. The bubbling A-flat Impromptu was dour in Horowitz's hands, and the nocturnes he recorded are heavily made up and filled with a dense, musky atmosphere. Still, the famous F-sharp major Nocturne, Op. 15, No. 2, is fascinating in its languor, and the E minor, Op. 72, is overtly dramatic, even Lisztian in its gestures. In the F minor Nocturne, Op. 55, No. 1, Horowitz whimpers and drools, and the celebrated E-flat major Op. 9, No. 2, lacks simplicity in both expression and shape. Yet these nocturnes are filled with a passionate eroticism that can only be termed Horowitzian.

In both of his recordings of the *Funeral March* Sonata, Horowitz revealed a Byronic Chopin, full of burning frustration, willfulness, and bombast. Like a vampire, he extracted every drop of blood from the score, and violence suffuses its thick and murky atmosphere.

In other large Chopin scores, there is an irritable quality, as if he could not tame the Pole. In the B minor Scherzo, he was most successful, properly gnarling his way to the heated coda. But Horowitz found the G minor Ballade an inexhaustible problem. The great work fascinated yet evaded him. Each of his four recordings is different and shows Horowitz fighting to make it his own. Yet each recording reveals startling pianistic creativity, a sense of sonority and tone color that is never less than fully projected and often unique. In the mighty triple fortissimo entrance to the coda on his 1940s 78 version of the Ballade, transferred to LP, there is a thunderclap unequaled for sheer drama in any performance of that Ballade ever recorded. His rendering of the Barcarolle makes me queasy: the waters are troubled, the crooning and warblings are uncomfortable. His early recording of the F minor Ballade is rather plodding and heavy, but his large-scale performance from the 1980s is very convincing, with many original moments.

In the area of the polonaise and mazurka, Horowitz often attained greatness. He had a real flair for the pomp of the polonaise, and his readings of the A major *Military,* the A-flat Opus 53, the A-flat *Polonaise-fantaisie,* and, most of all, the nerve-racking F-sharp minor were enthralling. He was surely one of the great mazurka players, impish and nostalgic, employing a pungent rubato. It is the Chopin genre he loved best and found most conducive, and his playing was without ostentation.

Other memorable Horowitz Chopin performances include a regal *Andante spianato and Grande Polonaise,* Op. 22, and the a Rondo Opus 16 which finds the pianist at his most infectious. There are also two performances of the famed *Revolutionary* Etude. The first one, from 1964, is staggering. It opens with the very "crack of creation," in Huneker's words. Here is the unique Horowitzian spirit with all of its controlled fury: the glistening chords with their gleaming tops; the swirling propulsive left hand, as wondrous as any could possibly be; all of the notes perfectly welded together, with the depth of nuance and that extra drive and cutting edge that only Horowitz could attain. All the while the artist's heart was alive to Chopin's despairing rage. The later Horowitz performance on disc is more casual, is lighter in weight and less colorful, and is more concerned with purely pianistic aspects, resulting in a far less powerful psychological imprint.

In Schumann, Horowitz's creative imagination was fired. Here he found a kindred spirit, childlike but complex: thorny, caressing, fragmented, and full of trickery and whimsy. In no other composer did Horowitz so lay bare his heart. I think he loved Schumann more than any other German master.

His earlier recordings of Schumann—the Toccata, *Traumeswirren, Presto passionato,* and *Arabeske*—all have vitality, but are somewhat superficial. Later, his Schumann became darker. The second recording of the Toccata is far more spacious. The great Fantasy, Op. 17, is deep and tonally glorious; the first recording of the *Kreisleriana,* from the late 1960s, is an unforgettable experience. While Horowitz's rubato could be contorted in his Chopin performances, in Schumann its application was an instinctive drive. Sparks flew; it was a canvas of convulsion. In the 1986 recording, we hear a mellow, almost hallucinatory *Kreisleriana.* For me, the neglected *Humoreske* finds Horowitz at his best, in a performance that at last realizes the potential of this glorious masterpiece. Though he first learned it in the 1930s, Horowitz brought it to public life only in the late 1970s. In Alfred de Vigny's phrase, "A fine life is a thought conceived in youth and realized in maturity." Horowitz's

disc of the Sonata in F minor must rank high in his Schumann contribution; it is so throbbing, fiery, and tender. And the *Kinderscenen* was never far from his fingers, although the children occasionally sounded rather fiendish. He often used *Träumerei* as one of his encores. One wit has said that he put too much trauma in the *Träumerei.* This was true at times, but, as stated, Horowitz seldom played a piece the same way twice.

Horowitz never played much Brahms, and played none at all in his last forty years. He said he was not on good terms with him. However, Brahms's two concertos figured in his performing repertoire, and the 1940 disc of the Second, with his father-in-law, Toscanini, is one of the five commercial discs of concertos that he gave us. It is a bitter, muscular, and taut performance, perhaps the most unidiomatic Brahms Concerto No. 2 ever recorded; one either loves it for its raw passion, or one hates it. There is also a charming recording of the A-flat Waltz and a convincing B-flat minor Intermezzo.

For the general public, Horowitz was possibly most identified with Liszt. His Liszt was often accused of being narcissistic. This stereotype—of two great virtuosi outdoing each other—is put to rest by pianist John Browning, who writes, "I think Liszt is misunderstood in the same way that Vladimir Horowitz has been misunderstood by many people. In Horowitz's playing they hear the speed, they hear the glitter, but they don't hear the ten voices working at once, all separately, and they don't hear the incredible way Horowitz can unify a work that really has no structural unity. They don't listen to the beauty of the colors, so they hear the wrong things."

Horowitz always chose his Liszt carefully. Although the Liszt Sonata was prized by d'Albert, Busoni, Friedheim, Rachmaninoff, and Hofmann, it did not really enter the world repertoire until Horowitz's 1932 recording, which retains its importance and far exceeds the value of his torturous remake of the late 1970s, so full of exaggeration and grandiloquence. The Horowitz comprehension of the grief-stricken *Funérailles* has never been equaled. The range of nuance, the subtlety of his timing, the massiveness of his left-hand octaves have made this work Horowitz's own. My heart quakes when I listen to it. A pianist told me that he had always felt his own octaves so sluggish in this piece that out of curiosity he timed his and Horowitz's and found his own quite a bit faster. Horowitz's neurodynamic system cannot be clocked.

Other great Liszt performances include the piquant *Valse oubliée* No. 1, the *Sonetto 104 del Petrarca*, and *Au bord d'une source*; all have a special fragrance that only Horowitz could evoke. *Vallée d'Obermann*, with his own discreet touching up of the text, is a ripe expression of Horowitz's Byronic Romanticism. A recording of the D-flat *Consolation* captures the Horowitz sound wonderfully, but the temperature is too torrid for the piece's lyricism. His rendering of the *Mephisto Waltz*, with some Busoni additions, as well as his own retouching, is a Liszt with devilish humor. He was also in top form in his monumental performance of the B minor *Ballade*.

There were also Horowitz's own versions of four of the Hungarian Rhapsodies. Each was a reworking of the original, although No. 6 contained only a bit of touching up for added effectiveness. In this, the Horowitz octaves were unbelievable. His view of No. 2 was delicious—very spicy and irresistible; No. 15, the *Ràkóczy March*, was greatly improved by Horowitz, while No. 19 was deliberate and serious. In these performances, which Liszt surely would have sanctioned, Horowitz displayed probably the most astounding muscular sonority in history. In Paganini's time, he too would have been accused of being in league with the devil. No matter the extent of this "virtuosity," however, it was his control, his very coolness, that was exciting. One heard everything clearly. His rhythmic sense seemed so right, and his reflexes were peerless. Horowitz's use of the pedals was ingeniously calculated and often quite sparse: scales were partly pedaled, climaxes possessed extra vibration, and all sorts of finesses were wrought with the *una corda* pedal. It was in Liszt that the sonorous imagery of his playing found all of its variegated splendor. The Horowitz touch defies description. It is a sound that only a piano can make, and that only Horowitz could summon out of it.

Horowitz was at his most stupendous in his performances of the Russian literature. The Tchaikovsky First Concerto, which he played at his American debut, found him kicking the turf like a stallion at the gate. The two early-1940s recordings with Toscanini are immortal: steely, edgy, with the reins tightly held. Nobody who listens can remain unaffected by his strength and raw nerve. A 1952 pirated recording with Szell and the New York Philharmonic at Carnegie Hall, taped in live performance, is totally different—wild and far less controlled, but soaring. Horowitz is having his way, rampaging through the work with fearlessness that has never been approached in this most popular of all concertos. Horowitz's 1940 recording of Tchaikovsky's *Dumka* also should not be missed.

Perhaps the most controversial of his recordings is the Mussorgsky *Pictures at an Exhibition*, which Horowitz substantially amplified to bring out what he felt Mussorgsky really wanted to say pianistically. Purists persist in hating it, and some have sarcastically commented that Horowitz put graffiti on the score. But this pianism is awesome in its impact, and is so perfectly Horowitzian in manner that it must be judged as an extraordinary oddity, a pure melding of intention and realization. He recorded it twice—in the studio and live in concert—and

I find the latter most thrilling.

From the very beginning of his career, Horowitz felt a bond with Rachmaninoff. The two developed a close friendship, and Rachmaninoff was dazzled by the younger artist's playing of the Third Piano Concerto, saying, "Horowitz swallowed it whole." Once, in an extremely uncharacteristic gesture, the composer mounted the platform to embrace Horowitz after a performance of the treacherous work. Horowitz loved this concerto dearly, recording it three times. The 1930 version, conducted by Albert Coates, was severely truncated to fit onto nine 78 sides. Horowitz himself discounted the performance, available now on an LP transfer, but it is fine playing, unaffected and far less turbulent than his other recordings. The 1951 recording with Reiner is the pianist's most characteristic performance—demonic, searing, technically incomparable—with fewer, far more judicious cuts. By 1978, in the uncut, live, in-concert performance with Ormandy, Horowitz's Rachmaninoff Third had become marked by excess and self-absorbed melancholy.

In Horowitz's recordings of various solo pieces by Rachmaninoff, he concentrated on the epic side of the music far more than the composer himself ever did in performance. In the climax of the *Etude-tableau* in E-flat minor, for instance, Horowitz lifts one from one's seat. In the Etude in C major, his freedom of phrasing is exquisite, as is the shimmering light in the G-sharp minor Prelude. Horowitz's playing always evokes an orchestral instrumentation, but unlike many pianists who play orchestrally, he never left his audience longing for the actual orchestra, so completely did he understand the instrument and its plangent sonority. Listen to Horowitz's version of the Second Sonata, in which, with Rachmaninoff's permission, he worked out his own edition of the finale from the composer's two versions. The whole endeavor is a *tour de force* of piano coloration inspired by orchestral sound.

If Horowitz related well to Rachmaninoff's music and pianism, he was even closer spiritually to the mercurial and mystic impressionism of Alexander Scriabin, to whom Horowitz was taken to play as a child. If I had to choose my own favorite segment of the Horowitz art, it would be his Scriabin. Horowitz knew exactly how to bring to life that composer's flickering, flamelike spirit, its vertiginous, supercharged nervosity and quivering eroticism. Even on record his interpretation of Scriabin is ever changing: one of his versions of the D-sharp minor Etude is convulsive, while another, from his late performance in Moscow, almost purrs before the demon sets in.

The early etudes, Opus 2, No. 1, and Opus 8, No. 11, are filled with yearning, while later ones from Opus 42, especially No. 5, capture Scriabin's desire for breathlessness. The bouquet of sixteen Preludes is an indispensable disc for Scriabin lovers. Horowitz's recordings of the Sonatas Nos. 3, 5, 9, and 10 are the zenith of all Scriabin playing. These performances possess a devastating truth. The Sonata No. 3 is declamatory and spasmodic. One can see a blinding light in the trills of the Tenth Sonata. A diabolical sensuality is sparked in the Fifth Sonata, Scriabin's offshoot of the *Poem of Ecstasy,* while one can almost smell the sulfurousness of the Ninth Sonata, of which the 1953 recording is three minuets faster and more satanic than the 1965 performance. Horowitz drew from these scores every molecule of their meaning, and his very passion exhausts the listener. Other great Scriabin performances are the two wonderful *Poems* of Opus 69, played with capriciousness, and the extraordinary work entitled *Vers la flamme,* to which he brought an explosive, pent-up energy, a purification by fire.

It must be said that Horowitz gave to us on record only a small fraction of his repertoire. Horowitz admirers would eat their hearts out if they knew how much he never recorded that he could reel off in the most offhanded manner, including scores of Rachmaninoff and loads of Medtner, a composer he loved and whose music he played with panache. Indeed, his Medtner repertoire was large, and he played to me, from memory, long stretches from the Concerti, Sonatas, and *Fairy Tales*. If you mentioned the Grieg Ballade, or *Islamey* or *Scarbo,* or the two Liszt Concerti or the Chopin F minor, he had played them. If you mentioned Moscheles or Kalkbrenner, an etude sparked from his fingers. If you told him you loved his recording of the Kabalevsky Sonata No. 3, he played you a series of Kabalevsky preludes and then the wonderful Second Sonata, of which he gave the American premiere, as he did of Barber's *Excursions*. If you discussed his transcriptions, he could play you others equally breathtaking from Rimsky-Korsakov operas, which he never performed publicly or recorded. He also had an incomparable ability to sight-read, and when he was in the mood his improvisations were delights. For several years I was privileged to be a constant visitor to his beautiful home, and I almost always left surprised in one way or another, either by an unexpected performance or by a dazzling piece of pianistic wisdom.

Throughout his career, Horowitz gave us indelible performances that expanded our awareness of many works in the piano repertoire, always revealing new avenues of color and detail. His recordings are precious documents of the art of piano playing. Horowitz has shown us more completely than anyone else the glory of this instrument in all its range and sonority.

Posthumously, some important releases to his discography have come to light. I will list a few of the finest performances from these CDs. From 1945-1950, for his own purpose and study, he recorded many of his Carnegie Hall recitals. The RCA releases are blistering with all the expected contagion and white-hot energy of his live recitals. Cast in bronze is Bach's great C minor Toccata, BWV 911, the only presentation of "original" Bach by Horowitz. Among the eleven works on the disc, there is the most unpusillanimous performance ever recorded of Chopin's F minor *Fantaisie*. Not for the tame, it is epic, giving the audience a restless, chilling interpretation. I'm certain the newspaper reviews were awful, and perhaps one day I will look them up to see if I am right. The release is on RCA. Another Victor CD from those years is exclusively twentieth-century repertoire, offering sybaritic playing of three Debussy Etudes and the Intermezzo and Valse Lente from Prokofiev's *Cinderella* in the composer's own transcriptions rendered by the pianist in ironic fashion. Horowitz has a special Prokofiev sound, a mixture of steel and silver. Two Poulenc entertainments, Intermezzo No. 2 and the first Novelette, have a Parisian chic. Horowitz admired the music of Kabalevsky, and his recording of the Third Sonata is well-known. However, in 1947 he gave the New York premiere of the Second Sonata, Op. 45, a twenty-two minute, three-movement creation of dark hue and turbulent action; in it the pianist achieves a synergistic totality. The disc includes eight of Kabalevsky's Twenty-Four Preludes, Op. 38, a fund of ethno-Russian folk material that became a showcase for a variety of touches and leaping exploits. He is equally comfortable in three of the four Excursions of Samuel Barber, each arresting within an American dialect.

I once asked Horowitz if he ever performed Balakirev's *Islamey*, a legendary work of high-wire virtuosity. He replied, "For one season only," and Mrs. Horowitz added that she thought the piece "trashy." However, during one of his Carnegie Hall ventures of the 1940s, he did record it. It has unfortunately not yet been issued, probably because several measures are not intact. I have heard it, and all who admire *Islamey* are missing pianistic splendor. In it Horowitz's range of dynamics, tactile control, and structural bearing are invincible.

Another formidable collection has been preserved on Sony Classical which contains rejected material from various Columbia sessions of the late sixties and early seventies. It happens to be vintage Horowitz, a major harvest of Clementi, Scarlatti, and the only piece he ever recorded by Medtner, a multilayered account of the *Fairy Tale* in A Major, Op. 51, No. 3. The disc contains readings of late Scriabin Poems, Op. 69, Nos. 1 and 2, and the giddy Etude Op. 65, No. 3. Not to be missed is his brooding and anguished playing of the slow Chopin Etude in E-flat minor, Op. 10, No. 6. For the critic Henry T. Finck, "The Etude seems as it were in a sort of double minor, much sadder than ordinary minor," and this is what Horowitz captures.

In recent years broadcast performances of the Tchaikovsky First Piano Concerto have appeared on CD. The wildly propulsive 1953 Silver Jubilee performance with Szell and the New York Philharmonic, of which I wrote in the book, is available on Movimento Musica and Palexa. Another CD, from a live performance from 1948 with Bruno Walter, whom Horowitz admired, and the New York Philharmonic, is spectacular. For all of its visceral bravura, it possesses a precious warmth lacking in his other Tchaikovsky Concerto readings. From 1949 there is a far inferior accounting of the score with William Steinberg conducting a stodgy Hollywood Bowl Orchestra, which can be heard on the Stradivarius label.

Along with the Tchaikovsky, the Rachmaninoff Third Concerto was central to Horowitz's career. Each of his commercial discs is famous, though the 1978 Golden Jubilee with Ormandy is much below par. For a mellow and technically impressive performance, the nationally televised Rachmaninoff Third with Mehta and the New York Philharmonic can be seen and heard on VCR and DVD.

At Carnegie Hall in 1940, Barbirolli and the New York Philharmonic collaborated with Horowitz for the Third Concerto, with Rachmaninoff himself in the audience. Olin Downes, the eminent critic of *The New York Times,* wrote that he was "a most fortunate composer to hear this masterly work of his given so incomparable a reading." One year later the exact forces again gathered at Carnegie Hall in a performance that survives from a broadcast and was issued on APR. Michael Glover writes, "Horowitz and Barbirolli produce a performance which must rank as the fastest ever, yet the instinctive poise of Horowitz's phrasing, the implausible perfection of his articulation, the feverish command of the large-scale chordal writing of the cadenza and the slow movement's central climax make this a fabulous account which stands apart from—in many ways above—all others, including those of Horowitz himself." One gasps at the combination of sheer cat-like elegance and leonine pouncing power. In certain passages Horowitz achieves the outer limits of what the human nervous system must be capable of.

In May of 2003, RCA brought forth a two-record set of a Carnegie Hall recital of November 1975 that had lain dormant for nearly thirty years. Although we find nothing that he had not previously recorded, it is a magnificent contribution to his recorded legacy. The longest offering is Schumann's sublime F minor Sonata (Concerto Without Orchestra), Op. 14, superior and more spontaneous than the 1976 recording based on various live performances. It will come to rank as one of the greatest Schumann performances in the recorded canon. Other highlights from the recital are Rachmaninoff's G Major Prelude, Op. 32, No. 5, dipped in creamy tones and hypnotic in its flexibility. The passionate night heat of the *Etude Tableau* in E-flat minor,

Sunday Afternoon, May 9, 1965, at 3:30 o'clock

THE CARNEGIE HALL CORPORATION

presents

Vladimir Horowitz

Pianist

Bach-Busoni	Organ Toccata in C major
	Prelude
	Intermezzo: Adagio
	Fugue
Schumann	Fantasy in C major, Op. 17
	Fantastic and with passion
	Moderato, energetic throughout
	Lento sostenuto sempre dolce

"Through all the tones that vibrate about Earth's mingled dream, one whispered tone is sounding for ears attent to hear."

FRIEDRICH SCHLEGEL

INTERMISSION

*Scriabin	Sonata No. 9 in One Movement, Op. 68
	Poem in F sharp major, Op. 32
Chopin	Mazurka in C sharp minor, Op. 30, No. 4
	Etude in F major, Op. 10
	Ballade in G minor, Op. 23, No. 1

---

*In memory of the composer on the 50th anniversary of his death, April 27th, 1915.

COLUMBIA RECORDS   STEINWAY PIANO   RCA VICTOR RECORDS

Net Proceeds for the Program Fund of The Carnegie Hall Corporation.

The program for Horowitz's historic comeback recital after his twelve-year retirement from the concert stage. Courtesy of Carnegie Hall Archives.

Op. 39, No. 5, is music born for the pianist's smoldering and voluptuous temperament. Liszt's *Valse Oubliée,* No. 1, is a web of amorous nostalgia and *Au Bord d'une Source* sprays glistening droplets of water. The Chopin A-minor Waltz and B-minor Scherzo find him out of sorts. He perks up in two of his favorite encores, Debussy's *Serenade for a Doll* and Schumann's *Träumerei,* continuing with an extremely ethereal *Etincelles* by Moszkowski. The last of the encores, Rachmaninoff's *Etude Tableau* in D Major, Op. 39, No. 9, is stupendous. Here he lives at the edge of a precipice, splattering a few chords for extra intensity. At age seventy-two the great virtuoso still retained his élan vitale.

As time passes, the Horowitz recordings will be cherished more than ever. His standards of technical magnificence and artistic amplitude will be thrilled to by pianists not yet born. The piano, now nearly three hundred years old, has made an unequaled contribution to music, and its glory is personified by Vladimir Horowitz.

MIECZYSLAW HORSZOWSKI
1892–1993—Poland

A child prodigy, he was called "the Mozart of his age." Early on, he went to Leschetizky and developed into one of the century's respected musicians. He settled in the United States in 1940, teaching at the Curtis Institute. Horszowski had one of the longest performing careers in history. His great gift for chamber music perhaps made the public less aware of his continuous solo career, and an artist of his stature should have been far more recorded than he was.

He spent a lifetime exploring the Classical literature and Bach. His recording of *The Well-Tempered Clavier,* Book I, offers beauti-fully plastic examples of polyphonic playing, and the preludes are restrained and subtle.

Horszowski found in Beethoven scope for never-ending development. In 1954 he gave New York audiences all of the solo output of that master. Though he did not always have a perfect technique, no detail escaped his searching mind.

Mozart was a composer on whom he thrived. Horszowski sensed the essence of the Salzburg master. His Mozart is always glowing, suave, and lighthearted. In Chopin, Horszowski gave his Slavic temperament full sway. It is an affectionate yet serious Chopin, in which the rhythm is forceful but the poetry apparent. His records of the E minor Concerto and the Four Impromptus have a flavor of the past that stems not from old-fashioned playing but from the kind of individual and personalized playing that Chopin so seldom receives today.

With Horszowski's death at age 101, the last remaining link to his great teacher Theodor Leschetizky was severed; he outlived his teacher by nearly eighty years. In the last decade of Horszowski's life, his career took on undreamed-of dimensions for an artist of such advanced age. He played almost up to his death. His audiences were awestruck by his musicianship and poetic musicality. Always notable was a singing tone of purest beauty, the true hallmark of Leschetizky's teaching, possessed also by Friedman, Paderewski, Schnabel, Gabrilowitsch, and others who worked with him. In his last years Horszowski made several recordings which admirably convey his special and intimate sound. A performance of the Chopin D-flat Nocturne is one of the finest examples of nocturne playing ever put on disc. Exceptional also are his Bach English Suite No. 5, Beethoven Sonata Op. 2, No. 2, and Debussy *Children's Corner.*

In 1901, fourteen years before Leschetizky's own death, Angele Potocka, his sister-in-law, wrote a long-forgotten book, *Leschetizky, an Intimate Study.* In it she said of the eight-year-old prodigy who had been studying with Leschetizky:

At present he is a wunderkind of high order. Miecio Horszowski's playing and compositions have already excited the most favorable criticism. . . . It is wonderful to see the chubby hands do so easily what his older companions must work hard to attain, but still more wonderful to note the matured conception and finished performance. . . . Paderewski had expressed a desire to hear the wonderful child. With characteristic gentle confidence, so far removed from conceit, Miecio sat down to the piano and played a number of pieces, some of them original compositions, preluding like a small virtuoso, and taking by storm the heart of the older artist, who caught him in his arms and hailed him as "one destined to shine among the great ones of our glorious Poland."

If any person can be called a miracle of nature, Horszowski deserves the title. In the last luminous years of his career, audiences wanted to grasp this compact being and hold him close for dear life! He appeared to be artistically touched by an angel, the epitome of musical fulfillment, for nearly a century of enchanted music-making.

STEPHEN HOUGH
b. 1961—England

After winning the first Terence Judd Award in 1982, he made a successful Wigmore Hall debut. In 1983 his career was launched with victory in New York's Naumburg Competition. In the years following, Hough has been playing continually. He is a sensitive and stable pianist of high technical attainments. His work is always clean and straightforward, but he is capable of rousing an audience to fever pitch, as in the Saint-Saëns Fifth Concerto. His recorded repertoire is filled with unusual items such as music by York Bowen.

LESLIE HOWARD
b. 1948—Australia

A pianist who has issued excellent recordings of neglected or forgotten sonatas by Gade, Sibelius, Glazunov, Anton Rubinstein, and others. Howard has a fine technique and possesses a feeling for the time-scale of a composition. He lets the music flow comfortably, giving the listener a well-balanced, smoothly proportioned sense of the score. This well-bred player's heart lives in the Romantic repertoire; his playing, however, has no excesses, desperate passion, never a tinge of the neurotic. He plays without great tensions or strain and, in the neglected literature he undertakes, makes good cases for the works he explores. After hearing his Anton Rubinstein sonatas I feel refreshed.

Howard has received well-deserved accolades for the "complete" piano music of his compatriot Percy Grainger. They are usually very suave presentations; nothing comes out sounding awkward or murky.

But his penchant for "completeness" has been achieved by the most astonishing recording project, indeed the largest ever undertaken by a solo instrumentalist: the complete piano music of Franz Liszt. It is a staggering accomplishment, and hail to Hyperion Recordings for their adventuresomeness, and obvious belief in their choice of artist.

When thinking of the sheer bulk of music, one wants to laugh or cry in amazement at a feat which took only fourteen years. I say "only," because it actually seems like a small period of time for the scope of the deed. I shudder to think of just the learning of all those fiendish cadenzas that Liszt loved to spray throughout his music to dazzle his auditors and terrify his executants.

How did such a gargantuan project proceed? Did the pianist awake one morning knowing that day he would begin work on the *Bagatelle Without Tonality* or the Dante Sonata? Was there a method in his madness, or was there a madness in his method? What a book he could write, telling us of how the project began and germinated, of the thousands of highs and lows he must have had on this musical-psychological journey as he worked to conquer this Mount Everest of the piano literature.

Certainly Howard has the zeal of a missionary. He wants the world to know the uniqueness of Liszt's work. This artist well knows that even Liszt's slightest or flawed pieces have moments to savor and delight in. I know that Howard's seriousness of purpose led him to try and test many times over in public performance much of this music before committing it to CD. Yes, laurels have come his way; the Queen of England has given him a grand reception at Buckingham Palace; the city of Budapest has given him a bronze cast of Liszt's hand, and one must not forget that the feat entitles him the honor of entry to the *Guinness Book of World Records,* which may annoy or amuse the pianist.

As a document it is invaluable, as the student may easily study this ungainly body of work. The series includes many world premiere performances, some works prepared by Howard from unpublished manuscripts, and there are compositions unheard since Liszt's lifetime. I am sure that, because of Howard, in the future many pianists will come to study works that they have never known.

Of course Liszt's music begs for many approaches. It is a paradise of pianism, and for sheer splendour nobody possesses Liszt's unrivaled genius for the sound of the instrument, and his emotional range is endless. One must

not get too used to any specific performance, and to hear the same pianist over and again has always been palling and boring for me. Although Howard is not one of the burning temperaments playing the piano, he is never less than musicianly, a scrupulous player; every dot and dash is correct, no rest or tie is missed. In many pieces, as in the *Grand Galop Chromatique*, he is a shade too serious. He cannot encompass Liszt's largeness. But Howard always makes sense, pulling together many problematic passages. What will his next goal be? I am sure he has something grand in mind.

JEAN HUBEAU
1917–1992—France

A celebrated figure in French pianism. A pupil at the Paris Conservatoire, and a composer of a piano concert and chamber music, he was a sought-after teacher.

EDWIN HUGHES
1884–1965—United States

Hughes studied with Joseffy and Leschetizky. He played concerts, made editions of various classics, and was a popular concert artist until World War I.

NICOLAS JOSEF HÜLLMANDEL
1756–1823—Germany

A pupil of C. P. E. Bach, Hüllmandel was considered one of the best pianists of the time. In 1778, Mozart wrote his father that he considered Hüllmandel's piano sonatas to be "very fine." He wrote more than thirty sonatas as well as an early treatise on piano playing.

JOHANN NEPOMUK HUMMEL

1778–1837—Hungary

As a student of Mozart, Hummel lived in his home for two years and made his debut in 1787 at a concert given by the master. The following year the young prodigy was playing through Germany, Bohemia, and Denmark. Soon after, he appeared in Edinburgh and in London, where he worked with Clementi and appeared in a concert with Cramer. By 1800, Hummel was considered one of the great musicians of his age. Hummel's studies with the two main keyboard masters of the high Classical era, Mozart and Clementi, were of great value to him. From Mozart he learned an assured and tasteful Classicism and the lightness of the Viennese school of playing, and from Clementi he gained a foothold into a more sonorous type of playing. Hummel's pianism was especially elegant and note perfect, his pride being his pearl-like scales.

For a time in the early 1800s, he was considered Beethoven's rival. In the art of improvisation, he seemed to be as dazzling as Beethoven, who thought Hummel's playing was monotonous. However, Czerny, who idolized Beethoven, had some lessons with Hummel and admitted that his playing was phenomenal.

Hummel had a superb sense of piano sonority, and his compositions extended the piano's scope considerably, especially in the intricate ornamentation in his slow move-

ments, in which he would weave a fantastic tapestry of Romantic passagework. A particularly good example is the slow movement of his Sonata Opus 106. He was a great influence on the young Romantics. Mendelssohn, Schumann, Chopin, and Liszt all revered him, and Chopin was held spellbound by his playing in Warsaw in 1826. In Hummel's A minor Piano Concerto, one quickly detects this older master's influence on the Chopin E minor Concerto, composed in 1830. Liszt, as a youth, often played Hummel's difficult B minor Concerto, and the young Schumann was overwhelmed by Hummel's Sonata in F-sharp minor, Op. 81, which he called "epic and titanic," and he set out to conquer the piece. (He wanted to study with Hummel, but he could not afford his fee.) Indeed, the composition, published in 1819, served as a harbinger of Romanticism, as did his D minor Piano Septet, which made a great impression when introduced in Vienna about the same time.

In 1828, Hummel published an instruction book which was to be a pianistic bible for generations. He called it *A Complete Theoretical and Practical Course of Instruction on the Art of Playing the Pianoforte*. It was Hummel's attempt to codify modern piano playing in such areas as fingering and ornaments. It included more than two thousand examples. The harpsichordist Ralph Kirkpatrick wrote, "I built up my own keyboard technique very largely on the exercises of Hummel's piano method which contains an admirably organized series designed to take care of nearly everything that the ten fingers need be expected to negotiate." Hummel's Twenty-four Etudes, Op. 125, from 1828, are also a superb summation of his pianistic technique.

Hummel continued to play publicly until around 1830, when he appeared in Paris to a rather cool reception. His immaculately clean-cut style, with very sparse pedal, now seemed dry; a larger, more colorful playing was taking its place. He lived in Weimar during his last years, and it is pleasant to know that the old Goethe often heard him play and was inspired by his improvisations.

BRUCE HUNGERFORD
1922–1977—Australia

He was a student of Ernest Hutcheson and Carl Friedberg. Hungerford was a man of wide interests and unswerving idealism. His death at the very apogee of his musical powers deprived us of the fulfillment of his ambition to record the thirty-two Sonatas of Beethoven. The twenty that he completed are statements of high-minded musicianship, wedded to an immense technical foundation and an extraordinary rhythmical framework. Each Sonata was treated as a universe in itself. He also did some of his best playing within the Schubert canon, and he left a glorious performance of the posthumous A major Sonata, terrifically strong and animated. His record of Brahms exposes many levels of dynamic gradation, and the A major Intermezzo, Op. 118, No. 2, is unusually beautiful in its fineness of voicing. He also made one Chopin recording, containing a powerful Sonata in B minor—firm and vigorous, large-scaled and deeply thoughtful, an intellectual Chopin B minor.

FRANZ HÜNTEN
1793–1878—Germany

He studied with Pradère at the Paris Conservatoire. He later played and taught, and composed salon works, many of which were feeble, though they had a vogue and Hünten grew rich from them.

ERNEST HUTCHESON
1871–1951—Australia

Hutcheson was a child prodigy who went for training at Leipzig, studying there with Reinecke. He made a New York debut in 1915, and became a faculty member at Juilliard, eventually becoming president of the school. He wrote a valuable book, *The Literature of the Piano*, and taught a legion of first-class players.

I

KONSTANTIN IGUMNOV

1873–1948—Russia

A student of Nikolai Zverev, Paul Pabst, and Siloti. Igumnov was an excellent musician and a pianist of sensibility, as well as one of the great teachers at the Moscow Conservatory for nearly half a century. Along with fellow teachers Goldenweiser and Neuhaus, Igumnov molded modern Russian pianism. Lev Oborin, Davidovich, Grinberg, Yakov Flier, and many others enjoyed his instruction.

EUGENE ISTOMIN

1925–2003—United States

He was a student of Serkin and won the Leventritt Award. He toured as a soloist and as a member of the famed Istomin-Stern-Rose trio. From his earliest mature appearances, he was reckoned a pianist of importance. In the last decade his solo career suffered, but there were signs of revitalization.

His early recordings of the First Tchaikovsky and Second Rachmaninoff concertos are steely and exciting investigations of these scores; when he performs them, I forget that they form the core of the most hackneyed concerto literature. His performance of the Brahms B-flat Concerto is huge in formation, reminding me of a great suspension bridge. Istomin feels sympathetic to Schubert's music, and there is a well-constructed D major Sonata on record. An early set of the Chopin Nocturnes finds him stiff and in the wrong climate.

JOSÉ ITURBI

1895–1980—Spain

Iturbi worked for a time with the legendary Joaquin Maláts. Early in life, he had extraordinary success wherever he went, quickly becoming one of the most beloved pianists of his time. In the late 1930s and 1940s, Iturbi acted and performed in Hollywood films, which added immeasurably to his fame. He also conducted a great deal. He played the Romantics best, with Chopin occupying a large part of his repertoire. His 1940s recordings show a charming player with a good structural sense.

In 1952 he was still in form when William Kapell called him "a wonderful pianist. The evenest playing I know."

Later on, Iturbi's work as an interpreter suffered, becoming shallow and less technically adroit. It was noted that his popularity as a movie celebrity hurt his reputation as a serious artist. Whatever the cause, Iturbi as a musician fell below his earlier standards. His sister, Amparo Iturbi (1899–1969), was a fine concert artist who played more atmospherically than her brother.

CHRISTIAN IVALDI

b. 1938—France

Studied early with Lucette Descaves and later with Aline van Barentzen. Ivaldi is one of France's best-known accompanists; he has recorded a variety of music and teaches at the Paris Conservatoire.

J

PAUL JACOBS
1930–1983—United States

He studied with Ernest Hutcheson and Beveridge Webster. Jacobs was staff pianist to the New York Philharmonic. He was a formidable musician, and a pianist with a thoroughly competent equipment. His objective but probing style became a strong influence on many younger pianists. Jacobs was a meticulous performer and never feared to take the unknown road. His readings are cool and refreshing, his Debussy Preludes and Etudes a model of clarity.

In his last years, he fortunately put to disc a tremendous variety of repertoire—Busoni, Messiaen, Stravinsky, Schoenberg, Virgil Thomson, and a splendid version of the Elliott Carter *Night Fantasies*.

ALFRED JAËLL
1832–1882—Italy

Alfred Jaëll studied with Moscheles, and later he traveled almost incessantly, giving concerts in America from 1852 to 1854. He was called "*le pianiste voyageur*" and was usually considered a player of taste and elegance. Von Bülow heard him at Basel in 1866, and reported to the piano builder Carl Bechstein, "Jaëll played a horrible concerto by Hiller very well indeed, then some Chopin, Rheinberger, etc., coarsely and in the worst taste." He gave early performances of new scores such as the Raff Piano Concerto and wrote nocturnes, valses, and other drawing room pieces.

MARIE JAËLL
1846–1925—France

Marie Jaëll, née Trautmann, was the wife of Alfred. She was an important and formidable pianist and teacher, and she was also a writer of books on the psycho-physiological aspects of piano playing. Her piano method, *La Touche* (1899), received considerable attention when it was published.

Jaëll had been a pupil of Herz and Moscheles, and she was given first prize in piano playing at the Paris Conservatoire at the age of sixteen. Later she studied composition with Saint-Saëns, who dedicated his First Piano Concerto and *Etude en forme de valse* to her. After Liszt's death, Saint-Saëns exclaimed, "There is only one person in the world who can play Liszt—Marie Jaëll."

Liszt, who dedicated his *Third Mephisto Waltz* to her, said, "She has the brain of a philosopher and the fingers of an artist." When she was in Weimar in 1883, she played the *Third Mephisto Waltz* to Liszt, who kept asking her to repeat long passages over and over again. To her utter surprise, the following day Liszt appeared with the work completely rewritten, and complimented her by saying, "It was your playing of it yesterday that showed me how it ought to be." Years later, she noted in her diary: "This evening I played the *Third Mephisto Waltz,* which seemed prodigiously intense and frenzied. . . . If only I had been able to play it like this to Liszt! What joy he would have had in hearing this music which is his and mine."

In 1893, Jaëll performed Beethoven's thirty-two Sonatas in six concerts at the Salle Pleyel. She was a distinguished and much sought-after teacher. One of her pupils was Albert Schweitzer, who studied with her in the late 1890s. In his autobiography, *Out of My Life and Thought,* he attempted to explain Jaëll's theory:

> Through thoughtfully differentiated movements of the fingers and of the hand, one can attain both differentiation of sonority and sensitivity to phrasing to achieve an ever more conscious and ever closer relationship with the keys. The finger must cultivate to the utmost its sensitivity to touch. With the perfecting of their sensitivity the player will become at the same time more responsive both to tone color and to color in general. . . . Under Marie Jaëll's guidance I completely transformed my hand. I owe it to her that by well-directed, time-saving practice I became increasingly master of my fingers to the great benefit of my organ playing.

Jaëll also composed; her works include a C minor Piano Concerto and numerous solo pieces.

JENÖ JANDÓ
b. 1952—Hungary

A graduate of the Liszt Academy, where he studied with Kadosa. Jandó is a fine player with a virtuoso technique. He is especially attracted to Liszt, and I well remember a recital of the twelve *Transcendental Etudes.*

BYRON JANIS
b. 1928—United States

In his twenties and thirties, Janis shone brightly in world pianism. His art made a great stir. To the public, he was Horowitz's heir apparent, having studied for several years with the Russian-born master. Indeed, Janis had something of the Horowitz mystique, some of the Horowitz tension, and some of the poetry, too, and he did some exciting, even breathtaking work; his Rachmaninoff First and Third Concerti and his Liszt *Totentanz* and two Concerti sizzle with electricity. His pianism is sleek and chrome-plated, the tempi never slack; his best solo playing, such as in the works of Liszt and Chopin, live in sunlight, brilliant, cool, and clear. His pedaling is careful and conventional, with never a smudge to mar the surface clarity. Because of an ongoing battle with arthritis, his public appearances in the last four decades have been infrequent.

NATALIA JANOTHA
1856–1932—Poland

She studied with Clara Schumann and won many honors as a pianist. She also composed piano pieces, including *Mountain Scenes,* which was dedicated to Mme Schumann. Paderewski dedicated to her his three Polish Dances, Op. 5.

KEITH JARRETT
b. 1946—United States

A wide-ranging musician who plays the classic composers with zest and focus. It does not take long to hear in Jarrett's Bach Preludes and Fugues or Shostakovich Preludes and Fugues a mind full of profundity and whimsy. Jarrett's recordings of Mozart, Bach's *Goldberg* Variations on harpsichord, and Lou Harrison's extraordinary Piano Concerto are worth concentrated listening.

As solo pianist and improviser, he can hold breathless a packed auditorium the size of the Metropolitan Opera House at Lincoln Center, as he sits, stands, gyrates, and unfolds a synthesis of styles, as the composer Adam Berenson says, "with a unique and unprecedented ecstasy."

Jarrett wrote, "The music is dancing more than I am. I have to keep up with it by not having an anchor, so the music can take me somewhere."

GRANT JOHANNESEN
b. 1921—United States

He was a student of Robert Casadesus. Later, he became president of the Cleveland Institute for several years. When Johannesen steps forward, the audience can count on a performance of the most distinguished bearing. He is an artist of uncommon curiosity, and he has delved deeply into virtually unknown literatures. He excels in French repertory, and the essential Johannesen blooms in his deep and affectionate playing of Fauré, where he lets the exquisite music unfold with leisure, but always with point. He knows every inch of its rich fabric, knows its nobility, but knows too when

Fauré becomes fruity, and when that happens he can dissipate a stale sentiment or erase the effect of a trite modulation. In Poulenc, Chabrier, Roussel, and Dukas, Johannesen plays with sophistication and irony and, in the case of Poulenc, he extracts just the right amount of tongue-in-cheek sentimentality.

Johannesen is good in Schumann as well; especially lovely is his *Fantasiestücke*, Op. 12. He also plays Grieg, and his rendering of the Norwegian master's *Ballade in the Form of Variations* is poignant. In Johannesen's Mozart and Bach, there is a tenseness and more of an academic feel, and his Chopin never glitters or boils. But when playing Castro tangos or Copland's Piano Variations, he finds himself totally at ease. Johannesen's unobtrusive patrician readings need sophisticated audiences.

GUNNAR JOHANSEN
1906–1991—Denmark

He studied with Victor Schiøler and in Berlin with Frederic Lamond. His main influence was his work with Egon Petri. He toured Europe and came to the United States, where he taught and was artist in residence at the University of Wisconsin. He composed throughout his career.

Johansen was a large-spirited musician with a questing nature. He performed in public the complete piano music of Beethoven, Mozart, Bach, Schubert, and Chopin. He recorded the whole of Bach's keyboard music in playing that is highly personalized and not convincing to everyone. But it throbs with life and a wealth of detail; especially appealing are the dance movements.

Johansen was dedicated to Liszt. In the past quarter century, he recorded more than fifty albums of Liszt's music. Here we encounter stylistically brilliant playing, often refreshingly reckless, sometimes not fully formed, but with a fervent quality which endears these performances to many Lisztians. It is the playing of an artist who never got over the initial thrill of hearing Liszt's music, and his freshness is engaging. From Liszt, it was only a step toward Busoni. We may imagine those early lessons Johansen had with Petri, the Italian master's greatest piano student. Here was kindled Johansen's love for the dense and difficult music of Busoni, all of which he recorded. After Petri's death, Johansen became Busoni's most impressive all-around exponent. Late in his life Johansen recorded all of the music by Ignaz Friedman on his own label, Artist Direct.

ALBERTO JONÁS
1868–1943—Spain

Jonás studied at the Madrid Conservatory and later with Arthur de Greef at the Brussels Conservatoire. He was a fine pianist and a well-known pedagogue. His *Master School of Modern Piano Playing and Virtuosity*, in seven volumes, is an important anthology featuring excerpts from one thousand examples of the literature, as well as original exercises by Friedheim, Friedman, Goodson, Godowsky, Busoni, and others.

MARYLA JONAS
1911–1959—Poland

As a young prodigy, Jonas studied with Sauer and Turczynski, with advice received from Paderewski. She had a successful career until World War II, when, because of the Nazis, she had to escape to South America. She finally came to the United States, where she made her debut in New York in 1946. Jonas was one of the first pianists to be heard on the newly invented long-playing record. She was not a technical giant, but played with a profound sensitivity. Her recording of Chopin mazurkas displays a ravishing tone, much elongated rubato, and more imagination than we are usually accustomed to in these scores. Pearl has devoted a CD to a selection of her work.

MARTIN JONES
b. 1940—England

Jones has made a reputation as a pianist and a teacher. His recordings of Busoni, Szymanowski, and Mendelssohn reveal refined musicianship, taste, and a good mechanism.

RAFAEL JOSEFFY
1852–1915—Hungary

He worked with Moscheles and Tausig, and then with Liszt. Joseffy's success as a pianist was immediate. In 1879 he left Europe to live in New York, where he was well received. His editions of the complete works of Chopin were widely used, and although his fingerings are unorthodox, they are often ingenious. Joseffy also composed some brilliant etudes and transcriptions, but his most enduring work is an extraordinary volume of exercises, *School of Advanced Playing* (1902).

Joseffy left no recordings, but he was supposed to have been one of the color geniuses of the piano. James Huneker called him "that fixed star in the pianistic firmament, one who refuses to descend to earth and please the groundlings. . . . Rafael Joseffy . . . is for me the most satisfying of all the pianists. Never any excess of emotional display; never silly sentimentalizings, but a lofty, detached style, impeccable technique, tone as beautiful as starlight—yes, Joseffy is the enchanter who wins me with his disdainful spells. . . . His Chopin was as Chopin would have had it given in 1840. And there were refinements of tone-color undreamed of even by Chopin."

The critic Richard Aldrich reports from a 1905 Carnegie Hall performance of the Chopin E minor Concerto: "It does not deeply move, but it entrances with its exquisite perfection, its cool, pure sentiment, its lucidity, symmetry and delicate efflorescence. There are exquisite tints and half tints in his tone, changing and delicate colors. Everything is perfectly controlled, perfectly proportioned and of ultimate refinement. . . . Of passion of power or deep emotional quality there was little."

TEDD JOSELSON
b. 1951—Belgium

A student of Adele Marcus at the Juilliard School, Joselson also studied with Rudolf Serkin and Sir Clifford Curzon. In 1967 he made his debut in Kansas City. In 1992 he gave his two-thousandth concert, in Munich. He plays a large repertoire, from Mozart to Barber, Scriabin, and Prokofiev. His Mozart renditions, especially of the concertos, possess a genial quality.

GENEVIÈVE JOY
b. 1919—France

Joy studied with Yves Nat. She has played many contemporary French scores, including the premiere of her husband Henri Dutilleux's Piano Sonata.

EILEEN JOYCE
1912–1991—Tasmania

A student of Max Pauer, Tobias Matthay, and Artur Schnabel. From the late 1930s through the 1950s, Joyce was frequently heard and admired in England and on the Continent. She tickled audiences by changing gowns between selections or concertos. Her recordings show her to be musically balanced, emotionally reticent, and endowed with a pliable finger technique that in sheer evenness was the envy of many pianists. Her discs of the Schubert E-flat Impromptu, Grieg's *Brooklet*, Fauré's F minor Impromptu, and many other works give pleasure in the purity of her manipulation of the keyboard.

K

ILONA KABOS
1892–1973—Hungary

She studied at Budapest's Royal Academy, where she later taught. In the late 1930s, she moved to London. With Louis Kentner, Kabos played works for two pianos, but she was also a noted soloist. Her best recordings are sympathetic interpretations of Bartók. She taught Peter Frankl, Jeffrey Siegel, Inger Wilkstrom, and others. Late in her career she taught at the Juilliard School.

JOSEPH KALICHSTEIN
b. 1946—Israel

Kalichstein is an admirable pianist, and a teacher at the Juilliard School. He won the Leventritt Competition in 1968, and has forged a successful career ever since, in both chamber and solo music. He has recorded Bartók, Prokofiev, Chopin, Schumann, and Brahms, all of it with depth. His Brahms has special appeal. A Kalichstein concert is always pleasurable; one feels that the artist is totally involved with his music and is himself enjoying every moment.

FRIEDRICH KALKBRENNER
1785–1849—Germany

In 1798 he entered the Paris Conservatoire, where, after four years' work with Louis Adam, he won first prize in piano playing. Kalkbrenner made a Berlin debut in 1805. From 1814 until 1823, he lived, played, and taught in London. Afterward, he made Paris his headquarters.

Kalkbrenner was one of the founders and popularizers of French piano playing. He was famous for his *jeu perlé*, an evenness of scales and arpeggios and elegance in passagework, much favored by generations of French pianists.

From 1824 until around 1830, when the young group of Romantic pianists poured into Paris, Kalkbrenner was considered one of the leading pianists of Europe. He was a transitional player who assimilated some of the new Romantic feeling, but whose playing retained a more Classical precision. Charles Hallé, who worked with him, found in Kalkbrenner's playing "a clearness, a directness, and a neatness that are astonishing." One observer called his execution "as polished as a billiard ball." It was playing of a deft perfection, and Kalkbrenner's evenness in fingerwork was ear tickling.

When Chopin arrived in Paris, he quickly encountered Kalkbrenner and was very impressed: "If Paganini is perfection, Kalkbrenner is his equal, but in quite another style. . . . He is the only one whose shoelaces I am not fit to untie." He raved about Kalkbrenner's enchanting touch, his calm, and his "incomparable evenness." In another letter, he describes Kalkbrenner as "superior to all the pianists I have ever heard," but admits that nobody "can stand him as a man." Kalkbrenner in turn told the young Pole that he needed to study with him for three years to become a finished pianist. Chopin was more than tempted, but bowed out gracefully, explaining to Kalkbrenner "that I know how much I still have to learn but I don't want simply to imitate . . . and three years is too long." Kalkbrenner regretted this decision and told Chopin he had "not a perfect mechanism" and "after I die, there will be no representative of the great school of piano playing left." Chopin consoled him by dedicating his E minor Concerto to him. Other pianists flocked to Paris to study with him, however, among them Camille Stamaty, Marie Pleyel, George Osborne, Thalberg, and many more.

In Paris, Kalkbrenner's music was all the rage. He was expert at making music of tinsel and glitter designed for the musically superficial but piano-crazed public of the day. It provides a deluge of diminished-seventh arpeggiation, lickety-split passagework, and well-rounded *bel canto* tunes, as well as extensive octave passages. Kalkbrenner was proud of his untiring octaves. "Why has God given us wrists," he asked a student, "if not to play octaves with?"

After his death, Kalkbrenner's music disappeared from the repertoire. It was jeered for its almost hedonistic superficiality and became a symbol of philistinism. Liszt refused to listen when a pupil brought in Kalkbrenner's *Sonate pour la main gauche principale*, Op. 42. Many sources indicate that the man was obnoxious and pompous, a true know-it-all, which certainly prejudiced some against playing his music. But after 1850, as pianists became increasingly occupied with the interpretation of masterpieces, even the better Kalkbrenner pieces were considered stale and old-fashioned, although his best-known work, the twenty-minute *Effusio musica*, Op. 68, has been recorded by Mary Louise Boehm.

Basing his opinion on the *Grande sonate brillante*, Op. 177, William Newman feels that "Kalkbrenner's piano music has been deplored undeservedly." The main problem is "the cantilena themes are too similar to each other to have independent character and to serve as landmarks. . . . In short and at best, one is hypnotized mildly without being drawn, driven, or, in fact, moved." But the pianist surely can have a great time in the score, rippling the keyboard, relishing the pretty packaging.

Kalkbrenner also produced four concerti. They attest to a superficial mentality, with a touch of Weber and Hummel. Reviewing a Kalkbrenner concerto, Robert Schumann deplored its "manufactured pathos and affected profundity." Yet Kalkbrenner's Concerto No. 1 in D minor, Op. 61, is graceful and handsomely fitted for the hand. There is a kind of elegance to it, almost a dandyism. Nor would a teacher be remiss in looking at the Kalkbrenner Etudes, which are very resourceful pieces. Even Schumann had to admit that Kalkbrenner was "one of the most skilled and masterly piano composers for finger and hand."

LILIAN KALLIR
b. 1931—Austria

She made a New York debut at the age of seventeen with Dimitri Mitropoulos conducting the New York Philharmonic; later she married

Claude Frank, and has often appeared with him in concert. She is a fine soloist and a respected teacher. Her recording of the Mozart Concerto No. 17, K. 453, shows her at her best.

WILLIAM KAPELL
1922–1953—United States

He studied with Olga Samaroff, won the Naumburg Prize at nineteen, and soon after he made a New York debut. Kapell sprang to prominence early. By the age of twenty, he ranked as a mature artist of the first order, with a rare passion that stood out like a beacon among pianists of his generation. He was killed at the age of thirty-one in an air crash near San Francisco, after a grueling concert tour of Australia. His early death continues to be mourned by the many concertgoers who were privileged to follow his artistic growth. His recordings are cherished as the finest examples of the modern unmannered style of piano playing—pure, passionate, large and clear in structure, and with a unique Romantic intensity. Leon Fleisher felt "without question Willy was the greatest pianistic talent this country ever produced. His raw talent was awesome. He had little time on this earth, but few used it like he did. He started out with the big success pieces, like the Khachaturian, Rachmaninoff, and Prokofiev concertos, but at the end he was coming around to Schubert's posthumous sonatas."

Kapell also had a great interest in the music of his time; even on his early programs he made room for contemporary composers like Prokofiev, Fuleihan, Persichetti, Copland, and many others. Such an undertaking was especially hazardous for a young career builder at that time. As Virgil Thomson wrote in an obituary: "Few artists have ever battled so manfully with management or so unhesitatingly sassed the press. He was afraid of nobody, because his heart was pure. . . . Kapell had become a grown man and a mature artist, a master. He could play great music with authority; his readings of it were at once sound and individual. He had a piano technique of the first class, a powerful mind, a consecration and a working ability such as are granted to few, and the highest aspirations toward artistic achievement."

Indeed, if there was a place called perfection, and if it could be possessed by force, temperament, and an indefatigable energy, then Kapell would relentlessly pursue it. Several months before his death, he wrote to the pianist Shirley Rhoads: "I think greatness in art is something you *come upon,* after only yearning and pain, and a deep sense of being in a dark tunnel. Greatness in art is not something you *tell yourself* you have. It is the oasis, the greatness, the vision, or whatever you want to call it, after traveling the vast desert of lonely and parched feelings. After this, the oasis. And the older a musician gets who has once seen this oasis, the more he wants to live there all the time, so the more frequent are his attainments of greatness and vision."

Kapell was an American eclectic, fascinated by all styles, and as he grew, his repertoire incorporated the suites of Bach, the sonatas and concertos of Mozart and Beethoven, the most sublime Chopin, and the bleak, industrial cityscape of Copland's Variations. Kapell was a master of the miniature, as well, and could titillate the hearer in the Prelude No. 5 in D of Shostakovich, or penetrate to the very core of an intermezzo by Brahms. His *Evocation* by Albéniz is among the best of Spanish playing, slow-burning and sultry, as is his Falla *Nights in the Gardens of Spain.*

Kapell played Liszt with greatness. The *Mephisto Waltz* he recorded when he was twenty-two, with its atmosphere of erotic tension, is still unrivaled. His highly controlled Eleventh Rhapsody is also the best ever recorded. His Beethoven Second Concerto is a pearl. It is youthful and sharply contoured, with a ringing cadenza and a slow movement that is perfectly shaped.

He was also a master of the Russian school, and his Mussorgsky *Pictures at an Exhibition* was rightly admired. His Rachmaninoff Third Concerto blazed with intensity, and his recording of the Second Concerto is deeply lyrical. His recording of the Rachmaninoff *Rhapsody on a Theme of Paganini* remains my favorite; I even prefer it to that of Rachmaninoff himself. Kapell's performance has a modernity to it. It crackles and is technically astounding. His most famous recording will always be the Khachaturian Concerto with Koussevitzky and the Boston Symphony. What sumptuousness, bravura, and rhythmic drive!

Kapell was an important Chopin player, virile and large-scaled. No American-born pianist had ever entered quite so deeply into the spirit of Chopin's Mazurkas. His recordings of this literature should be studied by performers interested in mazurkas without fancy rubato but which reach deeply into the heart while clearly retaining the dance element. Kapell also left a recording of Chopin's great Third Sonata, Op. 58; it is magnificent and symphonic in scope—the playing of a great architect, perfect in its proportion. Overall, it is the greatest recording ever made of the sonata.

Aaron Copland dedicated his huge Piano Fantasy to Kapell's memory. The composer wrote of Kapell:

His questioning and demanding spirit gave off sparks of a youthfulness that never left him. . . . The search for artistic growth, the ideal of maturity was a central and continuing preoccupation with him. . . . What qualities were particularly his? There were brilliance and drama in his playing, songfulness and excitement; on the platform he had the fire and abandon that alone can arouse audiences to fever pitch. He knew his power, and I have no doubt was sometimes frightened by it. . . . No wonder he was unusually nervous before stepping on the platform. Like every basically romantic artist, he never could predict what was about to happen. . . . Characteristically, when playing onstage, Willy often turned his head from the auditorium, the better to forget us, I imagine. Nevertheless, even when most lost within himself, he instinctively projected his playing into the hall, for he was indubitably the performer. I cannot conceive of his ever having given a dull performance.

In a letter to the pianist Shirley Rhoads, written in the year of his death, Kapell writes:

A craftsman is not an artist, but an artist wants always to be a craftsman. . . . If you ever develop enough finger velocity and strength to play the B minor Scherzo (Chopin) with the passion it demands, you will find that what you are doing is not a technical thing. . . . And he that can play a work like the B minor Scherzo easily can't play it at all! I have not, to this day, enough technique to play it evenly, but I have enough to play it with my insides. And while I am still a little out of strength with my silly hands, I realize that I have attained enough strength to give the work my feeling for it. What else can I do? And what care I for the glib fellow who can "toss it off" —This raging storm! That's what I try to do. Sometimes my fingers work, sometimes not— The hell with them! I want to sing anyway. And my heart seldom doesn't work.

YOHEVED KAPLINSKY
b. 1947—Israel

Born in Tel Aviv, Kaplinsky's early study at the Tel Aviv Academy was with Ilona Vincze.

At the Juilliard School she worked with Irwin Fruendlich and later studied with Dorothy Taubman. Kaplinsky was a prizewinner at the Bach International Competition and went on to appear in solo, chamber, and concerto venues. In the last years her teaching has been especially valued, being on the Peabody Conservatory faculty from 1989 to 1997 and at the Juilliard School since 1993. Kaplinsky's master classes and lectures are filled with aspiring young pianists. She has been on the jury of many competitions, including the Cliburn, Cleveland, and Leeds.

JULIAN VON KARÓLYI
1914–1993—Hungary

A pupil in his native Budapest with Dohnányi, he also worked with Josef Pembaur and took master classes with Cortot. Perhaps he was at his best in Chopin. Karólyi's records, in which there are many disparities and flaws, are worth finding. Hardly a contemplative artist, his general impulsiveness often gives off an aura of anxiety, by no means always unattractive or inappropriate. At his worst there is a palpable repulsiveness often found in his work. For example, the Chopin Barcarolle is a bedlam, musically pell-mell, not to mention pure slop here and there. No gondolier crooning, and never a moment of hushed stillness. Often in Chopin his tempi are too fast; not born to a natural rubato, he can be rhythmically a mess while unnatural accents may bump and grind, but he does not indulge in that unbearable bugaboo of so many poor Chopin players, those dreaded ritards that the composer has not asked for. If Wagner absurdly called Chopin a right-hand composer, Karólyi denies the assertion and is far more aware of Chopin's grainy left hand, which is often ignored in pianists pursuing only a singing tone in the right hand. Karólyi also possesses some strong ideas, and when he is in form there are streaks of poetry and he can touch a heroic gesture. Nor is he sentimental, and the music is not drenched with perpetual pedal. Not least this pianist has a remarkable technique. Of Chopin he has recorded much: the Four Ballades, Four Impromptus, the Third Sonata, both Concertos, Twenty-Four Preludes, *Andante spianato and Grand polonaise,* and more. There is a live performance of the F minor Concerto from a 1950 Berlin performance, where he exhibits a blistering technique, operatic fiortura, and much shapely phrasing. In the last movement there is an almost alarming sense of danger in his technical daring.

JULIUS KATCHEN
1926–1969—United States

He studied with David Saperton. Although he died at forty-three, Katchen had been recording since he was nineteen and left a large legacy on disc, from Chopin and Balakirev to Beethoven, Gershwin, Rorem, Ravel, Prokofiev, and Bartók. One of his last recordings is a magisterial conception of Beethoven's final sonata, Opus 111. Katchen will be remembered best, however, as his generation's preeminent interpreter of the piano music of Brahms. Brahms has been said to be a composer whom pianists should play to the public only in their ripe maturity. But the master of austerity and cerebral beauty became in Katchen's hands youthful and fiery. Katchen's Brahms is approachable and even friendly. He somehow glows with a brighter palette.

In the smaller pieces, he is not as secure as in the mighty works. Several of the intermezzi are affected, even a bit prissy, but the Brahms

Handel Variations are played with grit, and the Sonata in F-sharp minor, Op. 2, bursts with abundance and a Lisztian bravura. Katchen has all the virtuosity necessary for the hurdles of the Brahms *Paganini* Variations, and his Ballades, Op. 10, are mysterious, darkly lit, and filled with forest murmurs. In the Ballade in B minor, the goblins appear to be drenched in moonlight.

PETER KATIN
b. 1930—England

Made his debut in 1948. Since that time, he has played in Europe, the United States, and Canada. His recorded output is quite large, ranging from such concertos as the Khachaturian to the complete Preludes of Rachmaninoff and the complete Nocturnes of Chopin. His work is reserved, and musically, his technique equal to the demands of even the Third Rachmaninoff Concerto. Katin premiered and recorded the Grand Fantasy and Toccata by Gerald Finzi.

CYPRIEN KATSARIS
b. 1951—France

He began studying at the age of four. In 1969 he completed his studies at the Paris Conservatoire with a first prize in piano playing; he won prizes at the Queen Elizabeth Competition and the Tchaikovsky Competition. He has brilliantly recorded the Beethoven Nine Symphonies in Liszt's transcriptions, as well as a large discography of Chopin, Mozart, Grieg, and Mendelssohn. For a splendid account of the Chopin Ballades and Scherzos he won the Grand Prix du Disque. Katsaris always concocts interesting programs, and plays with a masterful technique and an unrestrained joy.

MINDRU KATZ
1925–1978—Rumania

Katz had an extreme refinement of tone with many gradations. His technique was strong, and his interpretations from Bach to Fauré are always illuminating. He emigrated to Israel, where he was highly respected as a teacher. He had studied in Rumania with Florica Musicescu, Lipatti's teacher.

HARRY KAUFMAN
1894–1961—United States

He studied with Stojowski in New York and with Josef Hofmann. He was a respected teacher at Philadelphia's Curtis Institute. A much sought-after accompanist, he also performed in chamber music and solo recitals. After hearing a recital by Kaufman, historian Will Durant wrote: "I spent six years writing one book, but you must have spent forty years making it possible for your powers of nerve, muscle, memory and technique to give us last evening's feast. I feel that you gave us forty years of your life and asked nothing in return . . . for such a performance must exhaust body and soul for weeks."

CONSTANCE KEENE
b. 1923—United States

A student of Abram Chasins and a winner of

the Naumburg Award, Keene has played hundreds of solo recitals and appeared with such orchestras as the Boston Symphony, Berlin Philharmonic, and Philadelphia. She has had a long career as a teacher and is on the faculty of the Manhattan School of Music. Her recordings offer an interesting variety of repertoire. She is a tireless worker, and in recent years she has brought out recordings of the complete Hummel Sonatas, Weber's Four Sonatas, and MacDowell's Four Sonatas.

WILHELM KEMPFF
1895–1991—Germany

Wilhelm Kempff by David Dubal

He studied with Barth, held various teaching posts, composed many works, and slowly built his reputation as one of the world's finest musicians and the doyen of German pianists, with a major international reputation.

Kempff's recordings are the marvelous products of a civilized, gentlemanly mind. He had a clear sense of organization, and I always feel warmed by his artistic generosity, keen intelligence, musical dignity, and gentleness.

His Schubert playing is lovely and full of whimsy. He imparts that unique Schubertian amiability which makes for joy. He recorded all the Sonatas and various other pieces. His reading of the final Sonata in B-flat is angelic. Only in the *Wanderer* Fantasy does Kempff's playing lumber.

Kempff is often radiant in Brahms; his E-flat minor Scherzo and F minor Sonata are all heart, and the smaller pieces can be jewels in his hands. In Schumann, Kempff is even more successful. It is a compassionate, sympathetic Schumann. The darker recesses of the composer's soul are closed to scrutiny; instead, Kempff's Schumann is filled with fragrance and the apple-cheeked youth of early German Romanticism, all optimism and fancy. He is

best in the *Davidsbündlertänze, Kinderscenen,* and a flickering *Papillons,* less successful in the *Symphonic Etudes* and *Kreisleriana.*

While Kempff is not known as a Chopinist, he played a variety of Chopin's music, including the F minor Concerto, with a velvety sound. He was not a blazing virtuoso, but his innate lyricism and sense of style are in harmony with the music of the Polish master. But ultimately, this idiom is not natural for him, nor is Liszt, though here, too, Kempff can be satisfying. He has a wonderful sense of poise in Liszt and produces a feeling of calm. Even in the bombast of Liszt's *Légende—Saint Francis Walking on the Waves*—the German pianist finds peace. He gets through Liszt's pyrotechnics by using good sense and slower tempi.

Kempff, who was also an organist, gave much time to Bach. His own Bach transcriptions were sensitive and beautifully tailored to the piano. In his recordings of the original works, such as the Preludes and Fugues and the *Goldberg* Variations, he offers a smoothly polished surface, a fine legato, and a rare qualification for counterpoint. But his Bach is somewhat stagnant and slow moving, without pith.

Ultimately, Kempff's greatest value for this listener is in his Beethoven—not the usual bugle-calling, heavy-handed Germanic Beethoven, but a Beethoven of grace, fullness, and air. It is a lighter-weight Beethoven—not monumental, but intimate and gracious. Kempff is not after huge rumblings, yet is able to produce large effects without forcing the sound. In fact, I suspect that the power of the contemporary keyboard at full throttle repelled him a bit; extremes of sonority were not often heard in his playing. In Beethoven, Kempff's technique, although not virtuosic, somehow fits the music perfectly, and he exhibits the whole range of Beethovenian mechanism with perfect ease, everything as clear as a mountain stream. His interpretations are infused with imagination, depth of feeling, color, and suggestive power. Kempff had a faultless ear, and his phrasing is shapely and subtle.

For me, the highlights of Kempff's Beethoven come in Op. 2, No. 2; Op. 2, No. 3; Op. 10, No. 2; Op. 14, No. 1; Op. 27, No. 1; Opp. 53, 54, 57, 90, 101, 109, and 110; as well as in the Piano Concerto No. 4.

of Beethoven. Kentner was never one to stay on the well-worn path, and he premiered the Bartók Second Concerto, Rawsthorne's First Concerto, and Tippett's Concerto. He was a musician of profound learning and knew every corner of Beethoven's world. In the slow movements especially, he achieved a warm depth of tone and expression.

Kentner's admiration for Liszt sustained itself throughout his career. He played all genres of this complex composer and was an advocate of the more enigmatic later works. In Kentner's penetrating Liszt playing, there is never a tinge of triteness, no mere titillation, no speedy sprints. His discs of the often abused and much maligned Hungarian Rhapsodies are young and fresh and underscore the gypsy element in them. With his exceptionally powerful hands, Kentner could produce a big sound. His reflexes were not comparable to those of the greatest virtuosi, nor was his finger articulation pure; but Kentner knew marvelously well how to exploit his resources, and he was capable of mustering plenty of excitement as he scurried across the keyboard in Liszt's *Transcendental Etudes* or produced grandiloquent drama in the B minor Ballade. He also made delightful recordings of the fascinating Balakirev Sonata in B-flat minor and the multicolored Liapunov Twelve *Transcendental Etudes*, which the composer aptly dedicated to Liszt's memory.

LOUIS KENTNER

1905–1987—Hungary

He studied piano with Arnold Székely and composition with Kodály. In the 1930s he settled in London. He made his American debut in 1956 with seven recitals at Town Hall, at which he played the complete Sonatas

JOHANN KESSLER

1800–1872—Austria

He was an esteemed pianist-composer. Chopin dedicated the German edition of his Twenty-four Preludes to him, and Liszt played some of his etudes, which occupy his Opp. 20 and 51, pieces that have real technical value.

EDWARD KILENYI
1910–2000—United States

Although born in the United States, Kilenyi studied with Dohnányi in Budapest. Before he was thirty he was given some plush recording assignments, such as the Schumann Symphonic Etudes and the Twenty-Four Chopin Etudes, Fourteen Waltzes, and *Funeral March* Sonata. Later in his career he concentrated on teaching; his presence and contribution at Florida State University's music school were appreciated by his many students. After the Second War he brought Dohnányi to teach at the University. In the late thirties Kilenyi recorded three excerpts from Dohnányi's *Ruralia Hungarica* Suite, which are interpreted with vigor. As a fitting memorial, Appian has issued on two CDs many of his *Pathé* recordings of 1937–39 containing the Chopin Etudes Opus 10, the Sonata Opus 35, Liszt's *Mephisto Waltz,* and Totentanz for Piano and Orchestra, among other items. Kilenyi lacked any high degree of imagination and showed scant traces of originality, but at times could generate some raw excitement and dash, such as in Liszt's *La Campanella.* His technique was solidly efficient and occasionally brilliant; in his playing he could alternate ponderous pages with an earnestness which is somehow attractive and which cannot be labeled merely prosaic.

JOHN KIRKPATRICK
1905–1990—United States

He studied piano with Isidor Philipp and composition with Nadia Boulanger. Kirkpatrick was a scholar and editor of seventeenth- and eighteenth-century music. He was the pianist who premiered, in 1938, the Ives *Concord, Mass.*

Sonata. His recording of this formidable work is a landmark in the recording of American music.

EVGENY KISSIN
b. 1971—USSR

The most exciting pianist on the international pianistic scene within recent memory. The announcement of a Kissin concert guarantees a sold-out house. He began studies at age six at the Gnessin School of Music for Gifted Children in Moscow with Anna Pavlovna Kantor, the only teacher he has ever had, who is still with him for every concert, tidying up details. There is obviously a rare alliance of sympathy between them.

By age twelve, Kissin's name had resounded through Russia, and at that tender age he recorded the two Chopin Concerti with extraordinary finesse and poetry. During the next few years he added immeasurably to his repertoire, and it is reputed that his powers of concentration, learning ability, and memory are phenomenal. Through his teen years he continued to appear before the public and was heard often in Japan.

In 1988, Herbert von Karajan honored the pianist by inviting him to play Tchaikovsky's First Concerto at the Berlin Philharmonic's New Year's Eve Gala. Unfortunately, the recording of the event is a rather dull affair in the slow tempos that von Karajan preferred in this warhorse. After great expectation, Kissin made his American debut with Zubin Mehta and the New York Philharmonic in September 1990, giving an exquisite performance of the Chopin E minor Concerto, followed several days later by the F minor Concerto. Soon after, he made his Carnegie Hall debut to rapturous applause, performing among other things Schumann's *Symphonic Etudes,* Prokofiev's Sixth Sonata, and Liszt's *Spanish Rhapsody*. Not for years had New York been so excited by a debut. The recording made at the recital is a very special document of highly polished virtuoso pianism, although the sheer contagion of the event will always be missing from the recording. Kissin's personal appearance shows an elevated seriousness, and his total control and command of every note display an unswerving attention span. He seems almost to demand that his audience listen carefully.

In 1993, Kissin traveled the world with an all-Chopin program. Here was a Chopin large in scale, firm, calm, flowing, and without affectation, excessive rubato, or rhythmic eccentricity. The program was composed of three nocturnes, the B minor Sonata, the F minor Fantasy, seven mazurkas, and the F-sharp minor Polonaise. In each style his playing possessed a mature ripeness, a sound of lyrical loveliness, and a youthful ardor.

Kissin has an acute acoustical sense and is a master of performing in large halls. He is capable of massive power, as in the Third Rachmaninoff Concerto, where he literally swamps an orchestra in the manner of a Gilels. His Liszt playing is shapely and rigorously organized. As yet, he displays little of Lisztian eroticism or anything like the mighty inner tensions in Horowitz's Liszt. Kissin's Liszt is tender without being cloying, as in *Ricordanza* and the *Liebestraüme*. In the *Spanish Rhapsody* and Twelfth Rhapsody he cunningly brings out the compositions' latent orchestral coloring. His *Feux follets* is a dream performance, actually surpassing Richter, and in the F minor *Transcendental Etude* Kissin ravages the keyboard but without the pounding that the piece is accustomed to. In his renditions of Schubert-Liszt Songs, the melodies are vocally sculpted, and the octaves of the *Erlkönig* are awesome, both in sonority and in laser accuracy. He seems somewhat aloof in Schubert's *Wanderer Fantasy*, but he possesses a rare grasp of the difficult structure of the A minor Sonata,

Op. 143. Kissin's Schumann, the *Abegg Variations*, *Arabeske, Symphonic Etudes,* and *Fantasy* shine with poesy, though much of his Schumann still lies on the surface. He has yet to come to terms with the wayward form of the *Fantasy*. It is in such works as Shostakovich's caustically witty First Concerto and Prokofiev's Third Concerto that he is comfortably at home, and he persuasively portrays the stinging vehemence and bittersweet tenderness of Prokofiev's epic Sixth Sonata. Of the Brahms that I have heard, the Seven Pieces, Op. 116, fall short of the mark and show minimal integration with the later style of the great German master.

Kissin in his early twenties has achieved a level of triumphant success reserved for few performers. Let us hope that neither the wear and tear of jet travel, endless expectations, and constant appearances before a ravenous public nor the tedious business aspects of a great career will damage him physically or psychically. A major and indelible career is not made from a few sensational seasons. There is yet a vast piano literature to be responsible to. Time will tell if an even deeper, richer, and more varied emotional nature will reveal itself.

In the past seasons Kissin has more than proved his staying power on the concert stage. He is as thoroughgoing a professional as ever there was and with a musical consistency and technical security that is remarkable. If, in his early thirties, he has not yet shown a more varied approach to the music he plays, one must be pleased to listen to pianism of sunlit and spectacular splendors, of a tone lustrous and succulent. Kissin is a true Romantic of a generalized nature. By this I mean his playing of Chopin, Schumann, and Liszt, his best composers, are not special different idioms for him; he merely hears them as romantic and appealing, after which he applies to each of them all of his lavish ripeness. Of course, he is well aware of the difference between great music and lesser, but what matters to him, I feel, is to achieve a poetic and shimmering surface fused with his ability to create spaciousness within the structure. No matter how brilliant Kissin's playing, everything is highly arched. His work gives deep and honest pleasure. One seldom leaves a Kissin concert disappointed, although his recordings occasionally ring flat.

His hands appear sculpted to encompass any extreme. Lytton Strachey said of Sarah Bernhardt that as an actor she had "a mastery over her medium of so overwhelming a kind as to become an obsession." And so it is of Kissin; his preparation is relentless and ruthless, his seriousness of purpose begging perfection. And no resource is lacking in his technical and tonal plenitude. His concerts are amazing in their cleanliness; nary a scratched note mars the picture; and his chordal playing are sonorous marvels.

Of his latest records, Frank's Prelude, Choral and Fugue is musky, darkly lit, and organ-toned; his Brahms *Paganini* Variations are so well-oiled and lazily played that one forgets the fear and technical distress that confronts many pianists facing this work's secret pitfalls. In the Mussorgsky *Pictures at an Exhibition* he booms with a golden glow and fat resonance, if not with the terrors of hell. His Chopin Twenty-four Preludes are a bit puffy, with few interesting phrases to dwell upon; all goes by with a steady caution. Where are the nervous junctures, the craven ravages of the Twenty-fourth Prelude, marked "appassionato" with its blood-curdling final Ds in the bowels of the instrument? Kissin is no hellion!

In his earlier years there used to occur in his live concerts impulsive, tiny glistening moments of rapture; one never knew when they would happen. They were gasps, as if he were overwhelmed by the intoxicating beauty; for a measure or two, he became suffocated, and from close up one saw his complexion heighten, the flush of color perfectly matching the gulp of pure passion. At such moments one palpably felt his audience transfixed. At this point he performs all with a magnificent normalcy, and he is the standard of our age. No pianist could possibly contain all, and Kissin may not be endowed with a growing imagination or the deepest emotional nature. I doubt if he will ever convey the erotic, the ironic, the racy or bawdy, the weird, or overt gaiety, a kind of whispered toneless sound, a disembodied tonal asceticism bringing us into another sphere. His projections are vital and hedonistic; the inner pulse is never heard, nor are tragic elements. Kissin's earthy delivery precludes hallucinations, or the freezing night winds of the soul.

But again, I am selfish, for this artist creates a luscious and lyric, vibrant and luxurious art. Such gorgeousness is far beyond the capability, musically and technically, of the homogenized lackluster majority.

And Kissin is no stingy pianist. He knows his public is in love, and when encores are dispersed, his dictum is not "less is more"; instead, as the ravenous cheering continues, he plys us with another delectable selection. He once told me of a recital in Bologna where he was particularly inspired, and "the audience kept applauding. They just wouldn't stop. Soon I was playing the sixth, seventh, and the eighth encore. I was by then so inspired that I played thirteen encores. Everybody was in total rapture. Finally the firemen protested at 12:30, because the gorgeous Teatro Comunale was a municipal building and it had to close."

Kissin is not only generous, but wonderfully strong physically, and I am certain he could have carried the morning hours, and at feast's end most everyone would have remained there wide-eyed in a state of enchantment.

ANATOLE KITAIN
1903–1980—Russia

He studied in Russia with Blumenfeld,

and pursued a concert career with success, performing throughout the Soviet Union.

Through the auspices of various people and organizations, he was able to leave the Soviet Union. From 1936 to 1939 he made a number of recordings for Columbia, which are available on CD through APR and which give us a dazzling picture of a pianist of the first order. There is Liszt's *Vallée d'Obermann* and *Feux-follets,* sixteen Brahms waltzes, Chopin's E-flat Rondo, Op. 16, and the Strauss-Godowsky *Metamorphosis on Fledermaus,* among others.

Around 1940 he immigrated to the United States, and he lived in Mexico for around a decade, returning to New York, where in 1963 he gave his last New York appearance. He spent a great deal of time teaching. His pupil Frederick Berenstein wrote, "He was a challenging and demanding teacher, but ultimately very rewarding."

CLOTILDE KLEEBERG

1866–1909—France

A product of the Paris Conservatoire, she was a successful concert artist whose playing was described as unaffected and vigorous. She was one of the first to revive the old French clavecinist composers.

JACQUES KLEIN

1930–1982—Brazil

He studied with William Kapell. In 1953 he won the Geneva Competition, subsequently performing as well as teaching in his native country.

AUGUST KLENGEL

1782–1852—Germany

Studied piano with Milchmayer, an inventor of a piano which supposedly could produce fifty different types of sound. His performances of Bach were praised. In emulation of Bach he composed his Canons and Fugues for piano. In 1829 Chopin wrote from Prague: "Klengel is, of all my pianistic acquaintances, the one who pleases me most. He played me his fugues for two hours. One might say that they form a sequel to Bach's: there are forty-eight of them, and as many canons. . . . He plays quite nicely but (*entre nous*) it might be better."

WALTER KLIEN

1928–1991—Austria

Klien studied at the Vienna Academy and for a time with Michelangeli. He was a pianist who concentrated on the German-based repertoire. He recorded the complete Brahms piano music with intelligent artistry, and his Mozart was often charming.

KARL KLINDWORTH

1830–1916—Germany

In the early 1850s he studied with Liszt, who considered Klindworth, along with von Bülow and Tausig, to be the finest of his students from his Weimar period (1848–60). Liszt asked Klindworth to play his new B minor Sonata privately for Wagner. Later, Klindworth transcribed Wagner's *Ring* and

Tristan und Isolde for piano. These arrangements are, in their way, the work of an amazing talent. His original compositions are difficult; the *Polonaise-fantaisie* may be especially interesting to pianists looking for a novelty. Klindworth made an edition of Chopin's works, which can be consulted with profit. In 1868 he became a professor at the Moscow Conservatory, and from 1882 he resided in Berlin, where he was considered one of the best teachers of his time.

ZOLTÁN KOCSIS
b. 1952—Hungary

He studied with Pál Kadosa, he won prizes in several competitions, and he began touring in his early twenties. Kocsis is a composer as well as a performer, and he has made transcriptions of Wagner, some of which he has recorded. He is a pianist of great vitality and a steel-like technical command, with an especially rare feeling for Bartók and Liszt. He plays the most demanding repertoire, from Bach's *Art of the Fugue* to the Rachmaninoff Third Concerto.

RAOUL KOCZALSKI
1885–1948—Poland

A famous child prodigy, who supposedly appeared in public more than a thousand times before he was twelve. His only teacher was the renowned Chopin pupil Karol Mikuli, teacher of Michalowski and Rosenthal. Thus Koczalski proudly held a direct link to Chopin, whose music was his specialty, and Koczalski recorded a great deal of it. His performances are infused with a sense of inti-

macy, a Romantic melancholy, a distinctive feeling for their design, and a refined technical mechanism.

Pearl recordings issued CDs of a group of Koczalski's Chopin recordings. Most noteworthy are his amber-colored F minor Ballade, a splendid E minor Concerto, and several etudes, including the famed Etude in Thirds, which is remarkable. James Methuen-Campbell wrote, "It seems that the variety Koczalski could bring to Chopin in respect of tone, touch, and poetry was virtually limitless." Arthur Rubinstein was particularly mean-spirited when writing of him in his memoirs: "Raoul Koczalski, an ex-child prodigy who was covered with medals when he was six, some of them hanging on his bottom; he lived in Germany and developed into a very bad pianist."

In addition to composing more than seventy works, Koczalski wrote a book on Chopin.

LOUIS KÖHLER
1820–1886—Germany

Hermann Goetz and Alfred Reisenauer were among the many students of this honored pianist and teacher, who wrote numerous pedagogical works for piano.

ANTOINE DE KONTSKI
1817–1899—Poland

He studied with John Field. "His wonderful execution," wrote Ernst Pauer, "created everywhere a sensation." He was a salon pianist and turned out hundreds of drawing-room pieces, including the once-popular *The Awakening of the Lion.* He had a long career, beginning a two-year world tour at the age of eighty.

STEPHEN KOVACEVICH
b. 1940—United States

A student of Myra Hess. Beethoven has been Kovacevich's abiding interest. His readings are serious in tone, and he takes great care in setting up the building blocks in a large musical structure. His technique is solid, and he has an incisive rhythmic sense. In such epics as the Diabelli Variations, his monochromatic delivery and crisp tone give the music an unusual solemnity. He is not frightened of explosive sforzandos, and his crescendi are tightly drawn. He is especially excellent in the Sonata Opus 101, where he brings out the exultant joy in the fugue.

Kovacevich has also issued fine Bartók and Brahms performances, and his one recording of Chopin is largely convincing.

VLADIMIR KRAINEV
b. 1944—USSR

In Moscow he trained at the Central Music School with Anaida Sumbatian, the teacher of Ashkenazy. Later he studied at the Moscow Conservatory with Heinrich Neuhaus. From age nineteen he performed brilliantly at international competitions; he won the silver medal at Leeds in 1965, was the victor in the Vianna da Motta Competition at Lisbon, and in 1970, he shared first prize with John Lill in the Tchaikovsky Competition. The next years were busy with performing in the Soviet Union and Europe. Krainev is a dynamic player, and a brilliant concerto collaborator with such major conductors as Boulez, Rozhdestvensky, and Leinsdorf.

Kreinev's playing of Liszt and Prokofiev is especially appealing, investing a large technique and rhythmic stability in combination with poetic fervor. For the last decade he has taught in Germany.

LILI KRAUS
1905–1986—Hungary

She studied at the Royal Academy in Budapest, and later with Steuermann and Schnabel. Kraus was captured and interned by the Japanese during World War II and had no access to a piano for more than three years. She made her American debut in 1949.

As early as the 1930s, Kraus made dozens of records. Her appearances always summoned a devoted audience. Onstage she was the *grande dame* who had come to reveal the message of the masters. During the LP era she recorded many of the works she most revered, including the complete Mozart Concerti, many solo sonatas, and a good deal of the Schubert repertoire, as well as some Bartók. She is heard to advantage in a nicely lyrical Schumann Concerto, the Beethoven Third Concerto, and a rather petite and engaging performance of Weber's *Konzertstück*. In the Mozart literature, Kraus was more comfortable in the *galant* sonatas than in the profound A minor and C minor Sonatas. Her recorded cycle of the Concerti shows stylistic authority, cadenzas of her own composition, and graciousness in the slow movements. But the overall impression is of plainness. In these recordings, the orchestral collaboration held her back; there is no symbiosis between orchestra and soloist. With Schubert, her structural planning of the big sonatas fails to integrate the composer's disparate elements, nor are the notes always played easily. In the B-flat Sonata she sounds sodden, and the A minor Sonata, D. 845, is inflated, while her impromptus are rhythmically and tonally flat. These works flowed more easily from her in the concert hall than in the recording studio.

MARTIN KRAUSE

1853–1918—Germany

A student of Reinecke at the Leipzig Conservatory. In 1882 he met Liszt and worked with him. Krause was a good pianist and a teacher capable of inspiring the many gifted students who came to him, including Edwin Fischer and Arrau. Krause reveled in the grand tradition of Liszt and imparted to the young Arrau an awe for his art.

LEONID KREUTZER

1884–1953—Russia

He studied with Essipova and, from 1908, was based in Berlin. Later, he made an edition of the works of Chopin. During the 1930s, Kreutzer was a respected teacher in Japan, where he was an influence on that country's immersion in Western pianistic culture.

ANTON KUERTI

b. 1932—Austria

He studied with Arthur Loesser in Cleveland, as well as with Rudolf Serkin at the Curtis Institute. In 1957 he won the Leventritt Competition.

Kuerti is a driven artist. His playing often displays compulsiveness and a fierce, lean power, even anger. I have heard him play the entire set of Scriabin's formidable Twelve Etudes, Op. 8, in tempi so fast that I thought a crack-up must be imminent. It was roller-coaster playing, but Kuerti sat there perfectly calm—only the audience was frenzied. One never feels at ease at a Kuerti recital, but the excitement he inspires is born of the involvement of an artist seized by the moment.

On recording, Kuerti is less frenetic. He has filtered out the extraneous elements that make for his high-risk live performances. The records are still highly charged but in a more crystallized, more cerebral way. Of his many recordings, one can mention his Alban Berg Sonata, where every phrase is played *morbidezza,* yet clearly structured. He delivers the Scriabin Sixth Sonata as though it were a mystical message. His Schumann F minor Sonata is filled with characteristic Schumannian storm and stress, and his Liszt Sonata is icy but of exceptional interest, played with chordal pomp and glittering preciseness.

Throughout his career, Kuerti has been partial to Mendelssohn, whom he loves to play lightly and fast. He refreshes warhorses like the *Rondo capriccioso,* and he makes the finale of the F-sharp minor Fantasy crackle and pop. But his finest achievement is certainly his stark and original reading of the thirty-two Beethoven Sonatas. One may dislike his raspy conceptions, as I often do, but he plays Beethoven with a raw conviction that is compelling.

VALERI KULESHOV

b. 1962—USSR

In Moscow he worked with Bashkirov and Petrov. He was the co-winner of the 1987

Busoni Competition. A skillful musician, he likes to perform as encores Horowitz's *Carmen Variations* and the like. One of his best efforts on disc is the Vivaldi-Stradal D minor Organ Concerto.

THEODOR KULLAK
1818–1882—Germany

He was a student of Czerny, and a child prodigy who developed into an outstanding pianist and an effective composer. Kullak was one of the most successful and influential teachers of the nineteenth century. Moszkowski, Scharwenka, and Hans Bischoff studied with him, as did his son, the pianist Franz Kullak. His most famous pedagogical work is *School of Octaves,* which was once used by teachers everywhere.

VILÉM KURZ
1872–1945—Czechoslovakia

He made his debut in 1890, and performed extensively. Kurz became the foremost piano teacher in Czechoslovakia. Rudolf Firkušný studied with him for years.

RADOSLAV KVAPIL
b. 1934—Czechoslovakia

Studied in Brno and later with Heinrich Neuhaus in Moscow. He is a sympathetic pianist with a large repertoire, chiefly known for his interpretations of Czech music, which include recordings of the complete piano works of Dvořák.

JAMES KWAST
1852–1927—Netherlands

He studied with Reinecke, Kullak, and Brassin. Kwast settled in Frankfurt, where he became a noted teacher. Carl Friedberg and Percy Grainger were among his many pupils. So was Frieda Hodapp-Kwast (1880–1949), his second wife, who "was the most prodigious talent amongst women pianists I have ever encountered," said Grainger; "her renderings were always deeply expressive and human."

RENA KYRIAKOU
1916–1994—Greece

Born on the island of Crete, she was a composer prodigy and, at six, at her first recital in Athens, she played a group of her own works. Sent to Vienna she worked with Paul Weingarten and in Paris with Isador Philipp, in whose class she achieved the conservatory's "premier prix de Paris." Kyriakou went on to play throughout Europe, often with major conductors such as Sargent, Mitropoulos, Groves, and Solti. She was soloist in her Piano Concerto with the Suisse Romande Orchestra, and her recordings of the complete Mendelssohn piano music on Vox won her many admirers, as well as the complete piano music of Chabrier. Her pianism is of the school of Philipp, fleet-fingered, clearheaded, little rubato, sparse of pedaling, and of a low emotional temperature.

L

KATIA LABÈQUE
b. 1953—France

MARIELLE LABÈQUE
b. 1956—France

Katia and Marielle Labèque are sisters. Both of them studied at the Paris Conservatoire with Pommier, and together they have developed a worldwide reputation as a piano duo. The Labèques play with dashing spirit, occasional foot stomping, and high showmanship. They do not disdain lighter music and give rousing renderings, for instance, of Scott Joplin's rags. Their discography includes the twenty-one Hungarian Dances by Brahms and concertos by Bartók, Stravinsky, and Poulenc.

FERNANDO LAIRES
b. 1925—Portugal

He studied with Isidor Philipp and James Friskin, and he has performed widely. Laires taught at the Peabody Conservatory in Baltimore, and is now on the faculty of the Eastman School. Laires's wife, Nelita True, is a highly regarded pianist and teacher.

JERZY LALEWICZ
1875–1951—Poland

At St. Petersburg he studied piano with Essipova and composition with Liadov and Rimsky-Korsakov. In 1900, Lalewicz won the prestigious Rubinstein Competition, and thereafter he began touring. He held several teaching positions at the Odessa and Cracow conservatories, and he taught in Vienna from 1912 to 1919. In 1921, he immigrated to Buenos Aires, where he became an Argentine citizen. He taught Pia Sebastiani, Mieczyslaw Münz, Zygmunt Dygat, Leo Podolsky, and Josef Rosenstock.

ALEXANDER LAMBERT
1862–1929—Poland

He was a student of Julius Epstein in Vienna, and later of Liszt. Lambert settled in the United States, where he performed, and taught Mana-Zucca, whose charming *Valse brillante* is dedicated to him. Vera Brodsky and Beryl Rubinstein also worked with him.

FREDERIC LAMOND
1868–1948—Scotland

A final link to Liszt, the greatest inspirational

force in the history of piano playing; with Lamond's death in February 1948, followed by that of Portuguese pianist Jose Vienna Da-Matta in June of that year, the last of Liszt's pupils passed into history. After studying with von Bülow, it was Arthur Friedheim who introduced the seventeen-year-old Lamond to the Abbé Liszt in Weimar.

Lamond relates in his memoirs that Liszt "read the letter of introduction, turned to me with his commanding yet kindly eyes and said, 'You play among other things the Fugue from Op. 106,' here he hummed the theme, which sounded from his lips like the growl of a lion, and said, giving me a friendly slap on the shoulder, 'Tomorrow you play the Fugue from Op. 106—' and the interview was at an end. I rushed from the room in an indescribable state of mind."

In his long career Lamond lived in Germany for long periods, leaving when the Nazis came to power. He loved Beethoven above all else and produced an edition of the Sonatas. He left a fair amount of recordings; many of them exhibit his serious nature, also a sense of elegance, beautiful singing tone, and a smoothly efficient technique. He also composed piano and chamber music.

WANDA LANDOWSKA
1877–1959—Poland

Landowska studied piano with Michalowski, but early in the century she turned to the harpsichord. Although there had been several attempts, as early as Moscheles, to revive the harpsichord in Baroque music, it was not until Landowska's arrival, with her keen personality and dazzling playing, that the musical world again took serious notice of the instrument and its rightful role in performing the works of the period. Peter Yates wrote of her early

recording of Bach's *Goldberg* Variations that it "was an event as decisive for the future, and the recovery of the past of music, as the first performance of Stravinsky's *Rite of Spring* or the conception of the twelve-tone method." Later, she recorded Bach's *Well-Tempered Clavier,* her "last will and testament," as she called it, and one of the most gigantic interpretive feats ever put on records.

She was born in the Romantic era, and her performances burn with power and with an exciting virtuosity. Onstage, Landowska was magnetic. Her concerts were consecrations from Bach, and her extraordinary face seemed illuminated by his wisdom. She once told a colleague, "You play Bach your way, I'll play him his way." Landowska never abandoned the piano, however, and her recordings of Mozart concertos and sonatas are Romantic and entirely individual.

LANG LANG
b. 1982—China

Extravagantly hyped by more than a dozen publicists worldwide working for his celebrity, Lang is the newest sensation to the world of serious piano playing. He studied at the Central Music Conservatory in Beijing, then at the Curtis Institute in Philadelphia with Gary Graffman.

His success has been overwhelming. Audiences respond to his sizzling technical apparatus and are even more thrilled by what is called "showmanship," which is blatantly exhibited onstage and within the compositions attempted. Some irritated critics have labeled him the Liberace of classical piano playing. Libby knew his public, and apparently so does Lang as he gesticulates his way to the bank through extroverted body language and dreamy stares to the heavens.

Although young pianists are livid that Lang Lang is their new representative in the art, most predict he is here to stay. Indeed, radio commercials and the print media say, "The future of classical music has arrived. His name is Lang Lang." If this be true, I would be depressed and in need of pharmalogical help. Hopefully, in the future Lang will be embarrassed by such arrogant and preposterous claims. From the beginning of his career, there has been too much the taint of commerce around him. Great music has been too much "crossed over," and art always rebels when mixed with impurities. Let us hope that this undoubtedly gifted young man drops the circus frippery and gets as deep into his art as might be possible for him.

At a Carnegie Hall recital, *The New York Times* critic Anthony Tommasini wrote, "For all its color, flair and energy, his playing was often incoherent, self-indulgent and slambang crass." Early in the recital, he wrote, "Mr. Lang was already up to his attention-grabbing tricks. Coyly prolonging the upbeat, milking the tune (*Abegg Variations* of Schumann) emotively, making everything cute. Then came a series of calculated effects; passages would disappear for no particular reason into some hazy mist of pianissimos as Mr. Lang, in a trademark mannerism, tilted his head back and looked to the heavens." Tommasini called his C major Haydn Sonata, "Some tinkle-tinkle imitation of a Haydn sonata." The critic said he stayed for one encore: Schumann's *Träumerei*, saying, "It was not easy to hear that wistfully beautiful melody so yanked around." He ended his devastating review with "I didn't want to be a party pooper, let alone impede the future of classical music."

Unless Lang gets "burnout," he is likely to continue to perform and titillate a largely musically uneducated public, performing ad nauseum the same few concerts which will fulfill a crowd that merely attends to be in the company of a media star. Kitsch art and celebrity performers are the spirit of the day. Lang may be Thurday night's fare in Rachmaninoff's Second Concerto, with audiences devoting the rest of their week to rappers and hiphoppers, who glory in calling themselves artists, a word they clearly adore.

In his early recording, Lang showed much promise and many dignified and musical moments, such as in the Brahms late piano works of Opus 118. On that recording he plays Balakirev's *Islamey*, in which he brings a folksy mood, the caravan passing through the mountains in the thin air. It's very evocative, and the whirling thrusts of his octaves hit their mark. It is a beautifully framed, sagacious *Islamey*, not a phrase fabricated, with all the animal instincts in touch.

But since his debut recording, small degenerations have crept forward, and he has been blunted by the curse of over-ripeness. Must everything be laden with deep expressiveness? Must Rachmaninoff's Third weep in every misguided, corpulent ritard? Speed is intoxicating, and Mendelssohn reveled in it, but Lang, with his extraordinary nervous system, must put the break on, for Mendelssohn's G minor Concerto's sake.

It will be up to Lang if he does not succumb to the marketing mentality. It is difficult to please over and again a hungry public. Lang has a hard road ahead of him. Can he merge his very real musical gifts and performing charisma with the interpreter's main mission, that of being a servant to great music?

ADELINA DE LARA
1872–1961—England

A student of Clara Schumann who became well known as a Schumann player. She made recordings and also composed.

RUTH LAREDO
b. 1937—United States

She was a student of Serkin at the Curtis Institute. Laredo has molded a fine career, and her numerous recordings include the ten Scriabin Sonatas (which she has played in cycle in New York), garnished with smaller pieces, and seven albums offering the complete solo output of Rachmaninoff.

Laredo was nurtured on the Germanic literature, but by learning a great deal of Russian music later on, she entered the world of a quite different kind of pianism, which has extended her musical outlook, musicianship, and technique.

JACOB LATEINER
b. 1928—Cuba

He studied with Isabelle Vengerova at the Curtis Institute, and later studied composition with Arnold Schoenberg. He made his debut in 1945, with Ormandy and the Philadelphia Orchestra. His best-known recording is of Beethoven's Sonata Op. 111. He has taught at Juilliard for more than three decades.

SIEGMUND LEBERT
1822–1884—Germany

He was a student of Johann Tomáschek and Dionys Weber. Lebert played in public frequently and was a founder of the Stuttgart Conservatory. He published many instructive methods and studies.

FÉLIX LE COUPPEY
1811–1887—France

A student at the Paris Conservatoire. Le Couppey was a renowned pianist and teacher. He received the Legion of Honor, and his educational works, such as the *Ecole du mécanisme du piano*, were once popular.

YVONNE LEFÉBURE
1898–1986—France

She studied with Cortot and performed throughout Europe, where she was considered one of the foremost French pianists of her time. Lefébure gave numerous master classes and frequently appeared in London, in Germany, and at the Casals Prades Festival. In 1948 she played in the United States. A highly regarded teacher, she numbered among her pupils Imogen Cooper, Evelyne Crochet, and Janina Fialkowska.

ETHEL LEGINSKA
1890–1970—England

Her real name was Ethel Liggins, but it was believed that a Slavic name would be better for her career. At age ten she went to Frankfurt to study with James Kwast, staying there for four years. Then she spent three years in Vienna working under Leschetizky. In 1907 she made her London debut, and from that time on she toured, composed, taught, and organized a women's symphony in Chicago. She composed the first of her four operas, *Gale,* in 1935, the premiere of which she conducted at the Chicago

City Opera. Her playing was always fiercely note perfect. In 1939 she settled in Los Angeles, where she continued to perform and teach.

HENRI LEMOINE
1786–1854—France

He achieved a fine reputation after studies at the Paris Conservatoire, performing, composing, and teaching. He wrote a pedagogic work on the development of technique, titled *Méthode pratique pour le piano,* which was respected in the 1820s.

THEODOR LESCHETIZKY
1830–1915—Poland

He became the most famous piano teacher of the late nineteenth century, with an unrivaled list of students who came to Vienna from the world over. Not to have had Leschetizky's stamp of approval was almost a stigma. The longest surviving of his pupils was Horszowski, who studied with him as a child. In 1884, Paderewski, already twenty-four, went to him. He later wrote: "He fulfilled my heart's desire. I had learned how to work. Yes, I repeat to you, how to *work,* and this is of the utmost importance. . . . Leschetizky, the lodestar of my early years, the greatest teacher of his generation. I do not know of anyone who approaches him now or then. There is absolutely none who can compare with him. He was in that respect a giant—all those I know at the present moment are pygmies, measured by his standards."

Certainly one of his standards was the quality of tone, which he insisted be beautiful and singing. Paderewski was renowned for his sultry, sensuous tone; yet when one listens to the recordings of any of Leschetizky's pupils, whether Moiseiwitsch, Friedman, Hambourg, or Schnabel, one hears in each an unforgettable sound. Leschetizky himself had it and was, as a pianist, a virtuoso, who studied with Czerny. His last appearance as a pianist took place in 1887, in Vienna, with Beethoven's *Emperor* Concerto.

Although half the piano students in the world heralded his "method," Leschetizky emphatically and repeatedly denied having one. He said: "One pupil needs this, another that; the hand of each differs; the brain of each differs. There can be no rule. I am a doctor to whom my pupils come as patients to be cured of their musical ailments, and the remedy must vary in each case."

Leschetizky's motto was "no art without life, no life without art."

THEODORE LETTVIN
1926–2003—United States

A student of Rudolf Serkin. He won prizes at several competitions, including first prize in the Naumburg. Lettvin is a pianist with a broad spectrum and a particularly fluid technique.

RAY LEV
1912–1968—Russia

Her family came to the United States in 1913. Studies in New York were followed by three years with Matthay in London, where she made a debut in 1932. A lucid performer, everything was airtight and technically solid.

OSCAR LEVANT

1906–1972—United States

As a child he studied in Pittsburgh, and later in New York with Sigismund Stojowski, and years later he studied composition with Schoenberg.

For years Levant was a radio personality, an actor in thirteen films, often with his piano as a costar, and late in life a frequent guest on talk shows. He wrote three droll volumes of autobiography: *A Smattering of Ignorance, Memoirs of an Amnesiac, The Unimportance of Being Oscar.* Levant was a complex man and musician. As the poet Paul Valéry said, "No man is the same as the sum of his appearances." Levant perpetrated to the media a helpless neurotic, of mordant wit and tortured mien. He composed for Broadway and wrote some "hit" popular songs, some of real quality, such as "Blame It on My Youth." Unfortunately the shadow of his friend Gershwin closed that vein of creativity. There are a dozen or so serious compositions, including a Sonatina from 1932 which was recorded by Levant and by Joseph Smith, who calls the Andantino movement "a transparent and tender meditation on blues material." In 1942 after composition studies with Schoenberg, he premiered his own Piano Concerto. Virgil Thomson thought, "His music, like his mind, is tough and real and animated by a ferocious integrity. . . . Its off moments are like the Sunday afternoon of a pugilist, all dressed up and no place to go." Levant characteristically felt his music to be inconsequential and when his orchestral score *Caprice* was conducted by Sir Thomas Beecham, he wrote in the program note that he "professes not to like it and sees no reason why Sir Thomas or anyone else should want to play it." Levant's composing career ended.

However, Levant's pianistic life flourished; best known for his Gershwin interpretations, his recording of the *Rhapsody in Blue* in 1946 with Ormandy became one of the best-selling classical recordings of the 78 era. His Second Rhapsody and *I Got Rhythm*, Variations for Piano and Orchestra with Morton Gould conducting, and the Concerto in F with André Kostelanetz, as well as the three solo Preludes, are all essential Gershwin recordings, played without a stain of cloying mannerism, fully savoring Gershwin's uniquely tangy lyricism. But Gershwin's compositions are by no means the whole of Levant's discography. He recorded much repertoire for Columbia, a great deal not transferred to CD. There are a dozen or so pieces of Chopin, an equal number of Debussy, and works of Liszt, Rachmaninoff, Shostakovich, Ravel, Poulenc, Mompou, Jelobinsky, Falla, and his own transcriptions of Khachaturian's *Sabre Dance* and *Lullaby* from the Gayne ballet available on Pearl. He recorded his own Piano Concerto with Wallenstein, Honegger's Concertino with Reiner, the Grieg Concerto with Efrem Kurtz, the Khachaturian Concerto, and Anton Rubinstein's Fourth Concerto with Mitropoulos and the First Tchaikovsky with Ormandy. The tally of famous conductors is noteworthy. All performances are first-rate technically, with episodes of routine playing, but some, like Anton Rubinstein's Fourth, with some flair, driving force, and occasional moments of bravura.

Unfortunately Levant, a tortured artist, was beset by extreme stage panic, and his public concert career ended in 1958 with a performance of Gershwin's Concerto at the Hollywood Bowl with an audience of twenty thousand. The pianist, only fifty-two, would live for another fourteen years. He had become hopelessly addicted to tranquilizers and other narcotics. In the last weeks of his life he was heard at home playing the Andantino of Schubert's Sonata in A major, D. 959, a work Schubert had composed on his deathbed.

MISCHA LEVITZKI
1898–1941—Russia

A student of Michalowski, Stojowski, and Dohnányi. He had an international career, playing in Asia and Australia. Levitzki was a favorite with American audiences. He played a fairly small repertoire in a cool-headed, rather detached, yet Romantic style. He was at his best in miniatures. His playing is meticulous; one feels in listening to his recordings that he was groping for a more modern approach to the Romantic literature. He was a transitional pianist who remained a Romantic stylist. His rubato is always fascinating; listen to his very slow reading of the Gluck-Sgambati "Melody" from *Orfeo* (one minute longer than Rachmaninoff's version), or his Chopin A-flat Ballade. Levitzki was always a curt but dashing Liszt player. The Sixth Hungarian Rhapsody shows some of the great octave playing of his time, and he was the first to record on 78s the Liszt E-flat Concerto. He recorded a few of his own delightful waltzes—bits of nostalgia tossed off by the pianist with a tongue-in-cheek casualness.

ERNST LEVY
1895–1981—Switzerland

Studied with Petri and Pugno. Levy was an unusual and powerful pianist. His recordings of late Beethoven are grandly conceived, and his recording of the Liszt Sonata and *Bénédiction de Dieu dans la solitude* is major Liszt playing. In the Sonata, Levy throws all caution to the wind. There is a mocking spirit. It is nervous, lugubrious, recitativo playing—the very essence of the Faustian Liszt. His performance is an exhausting experience, but in the end, Liszt, Levy, and the listener find purification. His *Bénédiction* stands alone in its monumentality and its probing of the secret recesses of Lisztian Romanticism. Levy also conducted and played organ, and composed prolifically. Marsten CD's have issued his highly unusual and moving Beethoven, the Sonatas Opus 101 and Opus 106, particularly immense in scope.

LAZARE LÉVY
1882–1964—Belgium

A student at the Paris Conservatoire with Diémer. He was a brilliant executant, and a teacher who helped produce such students as France Clidat, Lélia Gousseau, Monique Haas, Jean Hubeau, and Yvonne Loriod. He also composed interesting piano works.

RAYMOND LEWENTHAL
1926–1988—United States

He studied with Olga Samaroff at the Juilliard School. Lewenthal was one of that rare breed who are endowed with endless curiosity, forever on the lookout for golden nuggets of the piano's past glories. He was most productive in making many aware of music that tells us about the nineteenth century, its taste and values.

Of all the hibernating composers who interested Lewenthal, it was Charles Alkan who came first. Lewenthal devoted two recordings to this French master, and the playing is as varied as the composer's mercurial moods. There are the amazing and astringent *Sonatine,* the Barcarolle, played upon a mirrored lake, the breakneck virtuosity of the *Quasi Faust,* and the masterful and humorous *Aesop* Variations, plus a whole drawerful of other Alkanian drolleries. Of Lewenthal's other recordings, his performance of the treacherous and thrilling *Norma* paraphrase by Liszt is magnificent, and he revived that weird collection of pieces titled by Liszt the *Hexaméron.*

Lewenthal also gave an admirable account of the important Henselt Concerto, as well as works by Thalberg and Scharwenka. In his last years he virtually disappeared from concert life.

VLADIMIR LEYETCHKISS
b. 1940—USSR

A student of Heinrich Neuhaus at the Moscow Conservatory, Leyetchkiss immigrated to the United States in 1974 and is on the faculty of De Paul University in Chicago. Leyetchkiss has a big technique and plays with zest and freedom of expression. His recordings include Beethoven's *Diabelli* Variations and Tchaikovsky's piano music, played with some style, as well as full-blown performances of Scriabin Etudes. He has composed many piano transcriptions, the best known being a solo version of Stravinsky's *Rite of Spring.*

JOSEF LHÉVINNE
1874–1944—Russia

He was taken early to the Moscow Conservatory to study with Safonov. At fifteen, he had the honor of playing the *Emperor* Concerto with Anton Rubinstein conducting. He was awarded the coveted Gold Medal at the Moscow Conservatory in 1892. In 1895 he won the Anton Rubinstein prize, the most important piano competition of the time. In 1898, Rosina Bessie won the Gold Medal at the conservatory, and soon after, Josef married her. Later they formed a two-piano team, which was one of the finest of the time. Lhévinne continued to pursue his solo career, and made his U.S. debut in 1906, using the Anton Rubinstein Concerto No. 5 as his vehicle. After hardships in Germany during World War I, the Lhévinnes came to America, where they were associated with the Juilliard School. Soon he became one of the most distinguished teachers of the era. He wrote a handbook called *Basic Principles in Pianoforte Playing* and continued to play concerts in the United States and Europe, although he played less than any of his colleagues with a similarly important reputation.

Lhévinne developed and matured in the competitive hothouse atmosphere of the Moscow Conservatory, where his octaves were the talk of the school. The main influence there was the overwhelming artistry of Anton Rubinstein, who heard the boy play, at the age of fourteen, Beethoven's *Eroica* Variations and several Chopin etudes. The great master "jumped to his feet," Lhévinne reported after his performance of the *Ocean* Etude, "kissed me, and wrung my hand. 'You are a big, big boy. Work hard and you will be a great man.' That was the first great moment of my life."

Lhévinne's approach to the piano was, first and always, pianistic: correctness of note and steadiness of rhythm foremost. The sheer control of the pianistic aspects of his art was chilling to his colleagues. His hands, like those of Rachmaninoff, were enormous. He could stretch from middle C to A—thirteen notes. His finger control was so great that Safonov entered him in a telegraph operators' competition, which Lhévinne won easily.

For the Rubinstein Competition, he played the Beethoven *Hammerklavier,* which Rubinstein called "the Ninth Symphony of the piano." Shortly after, in Berlin, the outstanding pianist-teacher James Kwast wrote of his Beethoven that "Lhévinne played with such perfection that it seemed to me I was hearing it from none other than Tausig, who had gone to the grave at an early age."

In his biography of Josef and Rosina Lhévinne, Robert K. Wallace wrote: "As Tausig stood to Liszt, so did Lhévinne to Rubinstein. Josef admired Rubinstein above all other musicians, but did not completely follow his grand manner of interpretation. Lhévinne's temperament led in the direction of purity and perfection, and his playing, even when he was twenty, showed it."

Especially in his early years, however, Lhévinne was a characteristic Russian pianist with temperament to spare, and capable of igniting a spark into a flame.

During the 1920s, when the Soviets allowed none of their artists to go to the West, Lhévinne became one of the treasured links to the Russian grand manner of piano playing. After one of Lhévinne's concerts, the *New York Times* critic Olin Downes worried that "the Russian school of piano playing is vanishing. . . . If its traditions completely disappear the grand interpretive art of the pianist will weaken in favor of something neater and more puny." As Lhévinne matured, his small repertoire became ever more refined. There were some who felt his playing was calculated and cold or even exquisitely dull. Indeed, Josef himself felt Rosina was a warmer, more Romantic pianist.

By the 1930s, his style was confirmed. A typical program would include the Schumann Toccata, Beethoven's *Waldstein,* the Brahms *Paganini* Variations, Chopin's Fourth Ballade, several etudes, and Balakirev's *Islamey.* At his annual Carnegie Hall recitals every pianist worth his salt listened attentively. The recitals were object lessons in high pianism. Indeed, not one of his army of gifted students had anything like Lhévinne's technical equipment.

J. W. Henderson of the *New York Sun* wrote in 1930: "In his youth he was a virtuoso and a magnificent stormer of the keyboard. He thundered his proclamations and sometimes stunned his hearers by sheer power and irresistible technique. This is not the Lhévinne of today. He is now a ripe and mellowed master who has found all the secrets of tone and who sheds the rays of a refulgent beauty through every composition he plays. . . . He sees laterally across the whole breadth of every composition and perpendicularly down into its depths. He makes the plans of his readings with brains and imagination."

Lhévinne was inherently musical, aristocratic, and possessed of poise and balance. His famous recording of Schumann's Toccata shows off his double-note mechanism, but without the frenzy of Barère's reading, which comes close to being a stunt. Lhévinne's recording of the Chopin Etude in Thirds, Op. 25, No. 6, reaches the heights of double-note technique. James Methuen-Campbell says it "silences any criticism. The opening tempo is extremely fast, and all the right-hand entries have an icy precision. . . . Lhévinne's bell-like clarity has never been surpassed on disc." Lhévinne's Chopin etudes, those that he played in public, were always the wonder of the pianistic world. His rhythmic gift was unleashed in his great recording of the *Winter Wind* Etude, Op. 25, No. 11, while the *Octave* Etude, Op. 25, No. 10, is unrivaled. Other pianists can only bow before such herculean octaves, and the almost savage reserves of energy—like a panther ready to spring. When Lhévinne plays the luscious middle section in B major, unlike so many pianists who drool, he controls the structure and phrases with simplicity, knowing well that the general tumult of the composition must not be lost to sentimentality. The sheer power in this and in the *Winter Wind* Etude produces shivers. Lhévinne's great finger technique can be heard in his recording of the Chopin Prelude No. 16 in B-flat minor, which once again, with its control and delicacy of articulation, allied to a left hand that boils in agitation, remains, after more than half a century, the supreme playing of this treacherous work.

Lhévinne's octaves were legendary; they rank with those of Liszt and Tausig, Rosenthal, Levitzki, Rachmaninoff, and Horowitz. His octaves had a life of their own. On disc, they still live brightly in his reading of Chopin's A-flat Polonaise, which was one of his specialties. Another of Lhévinne's great pieces was the Schulz-Evler *On the Beautiful Blue Danube,* based on the celebrated Strauss waltz. Audiences refused to leave without hearing it. Lhévinne plays it without a drop of kitsch. Actually, he re-creates it as seriously as a Beethoven score. It is the playing of an unsentimental Classicist, and its tightness and rhythmic purity are cumulative; when he finally lets the listener breathe, one feels a sigh of relief. Even with all the advances in recording technology, this performance remains as vital today as it was in 1928.

My favorite of Lhévinne's recordings, which would be enough to immortalize him, is the starry Schumann-Liszt *Spring Night.* Here, musical mystery, the awe of youthful, romantic love, and the highest technical polish unite in an indescribable manner.

Lhévinne's attitude was an essentially modern one in that he lets the music speak for itself. He certainly had less creative imagination than Godowsky, Cortot, Hofmann, Rachmaninoff, Friedman, or Horowitz. Virgil Thomson wrote that "he made no effort to charm or to seduce or to preach or to impress. He played as if he were expounding to a graduate seminar: "This is the music, and this is the way to play it." . . . His concept of piano music is an impersonal one. It is norm-centered; it is for all musical men. Any intrusion of the executant's private soul would limit its appeal, diminish its authority. . . . If he seems to some a little distant, let us remind ourselves that remoteness is, after all, inevitable to those who inhabit Olympus."

Although Lhévinne made too few record-ings, they showed not merely an astonishing virtuoso, but one of history's greatest masters of the instrument.

ROSINA LHÉVINNE
1880–1976—Russia

A student of Safonov at the Moscow Conservatory. She married Josef Lhévinne after graduation and proceeded to teach and to perform in a two-piano team with him. Her recordings of the Mozart Twenty-first Concerto and Chopin E minor Concerto, made in her eighties, testify to her tasteful, intimate Romanticism. Her passagework is beautifully even, and there is style in her phrasing.

In the 1950s, Mme Lhévinne replaced the late Olga Samaroff as the most famous piano teacher at the Juilliard School. Students flocked to her studio, where she was the stan-dard-bearer of the golden days of Imperial Russian Romanticism. Her students won countless competitions in her name, the most famous to do so being Van Cliburn, the first winner of the international Tchaikovsky Competition. John Browning, Martin Canin, Daniel Pollack, Misha Dichter, Garrick Ohlsson, Tong-il Han, and Jeaneane Dowis are just a few of her students, many of whom hold posts at universities throughout the world.

JOHN LILL
b. 1944—England

He studied at London's Royal College of Music and won several competitions, including a joint first prize with Vladimir Krainev in the 1970 Tchaikovsky Competition. Lill has recorded and performed in cycle the thirty-two Beethoven Sonatas.

ARTHUR MOREIRA LIMA
b. 1940—Brazil

He studied in Paris with Long and Doyen, also for several years at the Moscow Conservatory. In 1965 he came in second to Martha Argerich at the Chopin Competition in Warsaw. Lima is best known for his engrossing and poetic Chopin interpretations.

DINU LIPATTI
1917–1950—Rumania

He had a superb musical education. After early lessons from his parents, he studied at the Bucharest Conservatory from 1928 to 1932 with the respected piano teacher Florica Musicescu. Later he studied with Alfred Cortot, and with Dukas and Boulanger in composition. For conducting, he worked with Charles Munch. Georges Enesco was his godfather, and Lipatti constantly learned from him.

In the 1930s, he played in Germany and Italy. During the war, he was domiciled in Geneva, where he taught at the conservatoire. After the war, he became established as one of the most gifted pianists of his time. He played in England each year from 1946 to 1950. Tours of Australia and America had to be canceled because of illness—lymphogranulomatosis, which claimed his life at thirty-three. Still, Lipatti managed to record a small but treasured discography. He was also an estimable composer; his works include a Sonatina for the Left Hand and Concertino in the Classic Style, both of which he recorded, and three nocturnes and a Fantasy for Piano Trio. All exhibit a delicate craftsmanship.

There seemed to be an aura surrounding Lipatti. Those who heard him were deeply stirred by his art. Poulenc called him "an artist of divine spirituality." There was a sweetness in his touch and an angelic temperament in his playing. He was a Raphael of the piano, poetic and youthful. There was never a trace of vanity in his style; for him music was a sacred responsibility, and he took the most minute pains in learning and digesting the piano literature. His record company gave him *carte blanche* as to what he would record, but he judged himself mercilessly and asked for three, four, and five years, depending on the work to be prepared. This responsibility to music was understood by all who knew him. He had never played Beethoven in public, considering himself not yet ready for the privilege, until finally, with Artur Schnabel's encouragement, near the end of his life he summoned the courage to give the public the *Waldstein* Sonata.

His recording producer, Walter Legge, wrote of him:

I do not believe that there has been, or will be, a pianist like Dinu Lipatti. It is not a matter of comparisons of quality, it is a matter of difference in kind. Hard as he worked and thought on purely technical problems of touch, sonority and pedaling, he was not a "virtuoso" in the word's modern and debased sense—but certainly in its Seventeenth Century application "a connoisseur." . . . He was a musician, a musician who used the pianoforte as a means of communication and expression. . . . The softness of his sound came through strength. He had enormous and powerful hands—the "little" finger as long as its neighbors—and the shoulders of a wrestler, quite disproportionate to his frail build. As he played, each finger had a life and personality of its own, independent of its neighbors, of his wrists and arms. Each finger seemed prehensile and the ten of them, when he played contrapuntal music, looked like a fantastic ballet danced by ten elephants' trunks each obeying the order of its own mahout. This visual impression of each finger having its own life is evident in the sound of his playing. Every note he played had a life of its own.

Lipatti was a lyric-Romantic pianist but with a cool and patrician sense of Classicism, and an extraordinary technique which was totally at the service of the musical essence. His left hand was peculiarly strong, and his superb rhythmic sense was apparent in every facet of his playing, no matter how Romantic the composition. His color sense was equally refined, and his pedaling was clean and artful, with legato playing as smooth as possible. He took a hackneyed score, such as the Grieg Concerto, and revived the pristine beauty. His Schumann Concerto breathes tenderness and chaste nobility.

Lipatti's finger control was perfect, as was his taste. His Bach B-flat Partita is gentle, precise but flexible, and moderate in tempo. His Mozart A minor Sonata is lofty; his Schubert G-flat Impromptu is an inspired song, simple and straightforward. His disc of the Hess transcription of *Jesu, Joy of Man's Desiring* is the work of a blessed musician, as is the heartfelt yet firm projection of the Kempff transcription of the Siciliano from a Bach flute sonata. The *Alborada del gracioso* of Ravel sparkles, and the Liszt *Sonetto 104 del Petrarca* is controlled but burning with passion. There is a 1943 radio broadcast of Enesco's Third Sonata. It is a complex work of Rumanian folk elements bound to an impressionist palette. The special care in its rendering, the subtle nuance, the fleeting colors, the flexible phrasing and transparent textures provide one of the great examples of piano playing on records.

Chopin was inevitable at Lipatti's concerts. His Chopin Sonata No. 3 in B minor will always be studied and discussed by pianists who seriously love this masterpiece. Lipatti's purity and sensitivity make for one of the great Chopin sonatas on disc. It is a refined, serious Chopin, always reserved, magnificently disciplined, yet with imagination and an inner fervor. One hears these traits also in his exquisite playing of the D-flat Nocturne, and his incomparable artistry in the C-sharp minor Mazurka, Op. 50, No. 3. For the highest refreshment, I constantly come back to Lipatti's recording of the Barcarolle, perhaps the greatest recording of it ever made. There is not a flaw in the filigree; the balance is impeccable. Lipatti left a disc of the fourteen Chopin Waltzes, which many regard as the finest Chopin Waltzes on record, though I find them a shade cool, lacking a vibrant spirit. There is also the poignant live performance of thirteen of the waltzes on Lipatti's last and most celebrated album, a two-record set of his final recital, at the Besançon Festival, 16 September 1950. The artist's strength was at its lowest ebb, the pain excruciating. Though his doctors begged him not to play, he had promised, and for him a promise was not to be ignored. Pumped with cortisone, he proceeded to play a demanding program, completing all but the final E minor Waltz before his strength gave out. Lipatti lingered on for several months, passing away near Geneva on 2 December 1950.

Nadia Boulanger felt "Lipatti was an angel on earth. . . . Noble, profound, gay, right up to his death; he knew very well that there was a time-limit, a limit without remission. . . . He was one of the greatest pianists ever, the very image of a complete musician."

SEYMOUR LIPKIN
b. 1927—United States

A student of Serkin and Horszowski. Lipkin

is an exceptional musician who is active as pianist and teacher. His playing of the classics is never rigid, and he is happy in such contemporary scores as George Perle's Serenade. He teaches at the Curtis Institute and the Juilliard School. In the last seasons, he has performed in New York the complete Beethoven Sonatas and Schubert Sonatas. His recordings of the Beethoven Sonatas are a tribute to his penetrating musicianship and excellent pianism.

EUGENE LIST
1918–1985—United States

A pupil of Olga Samaroff at the Juilliard School, List was a respected pianist in a variety of music. He was helpful in bringing several Gottschalk scores back to public and recorded performance. He made his debut in the Shostakovich Piano Concerto No. 1 in 1934, and in 1942 gave the world premiere of the Chávez Piano Concerto. At the Yalta Conference at the end of world War II, List, then an army sergeant, was brought in by Truman to perform Chopin for Stalin and Churchill. Stalin was pleased, and drank a toast to List. In his book *Mr. Truman's War*, Robert J. Moskin notes, "Proudly, Truman wrote Bess, 'our boy was good.' Later, in the bonhomous spirit of the evening, Truman himself went to the piano and played Paderewski's Minuet in G, to the fascination of the stellar array of guests."

FRANZ LISZT
1811–1886—Hungary

His earliest teacher was his father, Adam Liszt, a good amateur pianist, who worked as a steward at the Esterházy Palace.

In 1820 the nine-year-old prodigy made his debut in Oedenburg playing a concerto by Ferdinand Ries. Soon after, funds were raised for the boy to study in Vienna with the city's best-known teacher, Beethoven's pupil Carl Czerny. In composition, he worked with Salieri. Both masters taught the young and poor Hungarian without a fee. Czerny was astounded by Liszt's native gifts, but was appalled by his lack of discipline. It was Czerny who laid the foundation for the revolutionary pianism that would soon burst upon the European musical world. Czerny was the dedicatee of Liszt's early etudes of 1826, which would eventually become the Twelve *Transcendental* Etudes of his mature years. But Liszt was to profit from Czerny's instruction for only eighteen months before his father became impatient to show off his son's worth and began a terrible exploitation of the young boy. Unlike Chopin and Mendelssohn, who were delicately nurtured at home, Liszt was now continuously on the move. He had even completed an opera, *Don Sanche,* which was performed at the Paris Opera late in 1825.

There was never any time for a formal education, and his life was a series of unprecedented successes. In London, he created a sensation and played before George IV; critics quickly understood his gifts. One writer felt that, at fourteen, Liszt "yields the palm to Hummel alone."

During these early years, when all of society petted him, Liszt—as no other pianist had done before him—learned how to play for and to the public. A large middle class was forming. Halls were being built for entertainment, and Liszt was now the youngest and best of a group of wandering "gypsies" who played, usually, less than the best music.

In 1827 his father died while they were on tour. Already the teenager was dismayed by his life, and now, without an aggressive father, and with an ever-increasing religious bent, the young virtuoso renounced that life and retired from the stage, instead teaching to support himself and his mother. "I would rather be anything in the world," he wrote at this time, "than a musician in the pay of great folk, patronized and paid for by them, like a conjuror or a clever dog." His virtual disappearance caused wonder, and there were even press reports of his death. Soon, however, he was romantically involved with one of his students, a sixteen-year-old aristocrat. Upon discovering their friendship, her father dashed any hopes that Liszt, a mere musician, might keep seeing her. He was completely devastated, and withdrew into religious books and hashish, seldom touching his piano. Some of the strongest traits of his personality were emerging: a love-hate relationship with performing, a deeply mystical attraction to religion, and a hatred for the lowly social level of musicians. His ennui was broken by the fighting on the streets of Paris during the political unrest in 1830.

His latent creativity was stirred, and he felt the urge to compose and play. He was deeply stimulated by three men of genius who were to make an everlasting mark on him. The first was Berlioz, with whom he had a budding friendship and whose epoch-making *Symphonie fantastique* he was soon to hear and to transcribe for the piano. The second was Frédéric Chopin, newly arrived in Paris. The Slavic genius's Etudes and the poetry and delicacy of his playing shocked Liszt into a new awareness of the piano and its technical possibilities. But the third influence—Paganini—was the catalyst that sent Liszt back to the keyboard, with the goal of becoming "the Paganini of the piano." The infernal Italian violinist made his Paris debut in 1831, creating a public furor. "What a man, what a violin, what an artist!" wrote Liszt. "Heavens! What sufferings, what misery, what tortures in those four strings." With these concerts by Paganini, the only performer he could learn from, Liszt came to life, and the modern pianist was born.

Paganini became the spiritual father of piano playing. Liszt began transcribing Paganini's Caprices for the piano; he had to uncover the secrets of virtuosity. For two years, he worked with an unremitting savagery, reading Goethe's *Faust* with Berlioz, coming under the influence of the religious scion Lamennais, and practicing as no other pianist ever had. He wrote: "My mind and fingers have been working like two lost spirits—Homer, the Bible, Plato, Locke, Byron, Hugo, Lamartine, Chateaubriand, Beethoven, Bach, Hummel, Mozart, Weber are all around me. I study them, meditate upon them, devour them with fury. Besides this, I practice four to five hours of exercises, thirds, sixths, octaves, tremolos, repetitions of notes, cadenzas, scales, etc. Ah! provided I don't go mad you will find an artist in me! Yes an artist such as you desire, *such as is required nowadays.*"

When he reappeared, he would have a concert career more triumphant than even Paganini's. Indeed, Liszt may be called the father of the modern career, and the most idolized performer ever to play the piano. He virtually opened the concert corridor of Europe, playing more extensively than any other pianist of the first half of the nineteenth century.

During his "years of splendor," Liszt, with his special caravan, sixty suits of clothing, 360 cravats (one for each day of the year), and his shoulder-length hair, created the Romantic image of the pianist-hero—eyes heaven-sent, nostrils dilated, and held in the throes of inspiration. He was not above theatrics and, like Paganini, he had to be seen as well as heard. The dramatist Ernest Legouvé described Liszt "constantly tossing back his long hair. . . . With lips quivering, he swept the auditorium with the glance of a smiling master." A born showman, he began the finale of Weber's *Konzertstück* so fast that, unable to maintain the tempo, he conveniently fainted away. One writer saw "Liszt's countenance assume that agony of expression, mingled with radiant smiles of joy, which I never saw in any other human face except in the paintings of our Saviour by some early masters." Soon Liszt realized that to share the concert platform with other musicians was unthinkable—and so he invented the solo recital, even coining the term.

In 1839 he took the big step and played history's first solo public concerts, in Milan. The piano's solo function was finally proclaimed, and Liszt proudly said, *Le concert c'est moi* ("the concert is myself"). The piano had come a long way since the variety-show type of concert in which Johann Christian Bach first played a piano solo in public in 1768.

The young Charles Hallé heard him in Paris in 1836, writing, "I went home with a feeling of thorough dejection. Such marvels of executive skill and power I could never have imagined. Liszt was all sunshine and dazzling splendor, subjugating his hearers with a power that none could withstand." He was a giant, and Rubinstein spoke the truth when, at the time when his own triumphs were greatest, he said that "In comparison with Liszt, all other pianists were children. . . . "

As he went from city to city, Europe was gripped by "Lisztomania." After Liszt wrote a rave notice of a Chopin concert, the Pole sarcastically muttered, "Ah, he is giving me a kingdom within his empire." And he was the "emperor" of the piano. Handsome beyond measure, he was likened to Dante, Napoleon, and Byron. If "Paganini had the evil eye," declared Sacheverell Sitwell, then "Liszt had the glamorous eye." Wilfrid Mellers states, "The impact of Liszt on Europe is, indeed, something for which there is no musical parallel. Only in Byron do we find the same combination of aristocratic elegance with Revolutionary force, of fearless sincerity with histrionic virtuosity." To the youth of Europe, Liszt symbolized democratic freedom. Stories quickly circulated regarding his pride and

daring in his espousal of equality. When the dreaded Czar Nicholas I asked Liszt, "What are your politics?" the pianist answered, "I have none, sire, unless I have two hundred thousand bayonets accompanying me."

Liszt also elevated the piano to a new position of power and intimacy. He wrote: "You see, my piano is for me what his frigate is to a sailor, or his horse to an Arab—more indeed: It is my very self, my mother tongue, my life. . . . I confide to it all my dreams, my joys and sorrows. Its strings tremble under my emotion, its yielding keys resound to all my moods."

By the age of thirty-six, however, Liszt the performer was exhausted; he left the concert stage forever, although he would live to seventy-five. He now concentrated his great energies on composition and on making Weimar, where he was appointed court composer, the leading musical center of Germany, reviving the glory that it had had under Schiller and Goethe. Liszt now championed the newest in music, and from Berlioz to Wagner, Weimar promoted what was to be called "the music of the future."

From this period until his death, Liszt taught a torrent of pupils who came from everywhere to seek advice and learn from him the secrets of pianistic truth. Even before his departure from public playing, however, he had managed to have an unprecedented educative influence. His repertoire was the largest ever assembled by one artist. If Paganini and the majority of pianists played only their own music, Liszt played everyone's music, and he did this from Lisbon to St. Petersburg, from Edinburgh to Constantinople, with a zeal that defied description. He assimilated Czerny's Viennese light pianism, and at the same time his respect for Beethoven, with his orchestral coloring, was everlasting. It was Liszt who first brought many of the Beethoven Sonatas to the recital stage. His early travels brought him in touch with all that Clementi, Cramer, and Hummel were doing. He incorporated the singing style of Field and the operatic virtuosity of Weber.

Liszt transcribed Schubert songs, as well as Beethoven's symphonies, and often played them before the public heard the originals. He brought Chopin's music out of the narrow confines of the Parisian salon, as Chopin himself could not do, and he proclaimed his friend to the world. Liszt grappled with the Romantic polyphony of the newest Schumann and played all that was new of the "Romantic" school. Not one of Liszt's exact generation—including Chopin, Hiller, Heller, Alkan, Henselt, Herz, and Thalberg—played such an abundance of new music, while only Mendelssohn dug as deeply into the past.

It had become a commonplace in nineteenth-century criticism to call Liszt the greatest pianist who ever lived, yet the best ears of the time continually attest anew to his supremacy. His own greatest student, Carl Tausig, declared, "No mortal can vie with Liszt; he dwells upon a solitary height." Anton Rubinstein was convinced "we are all children compared with Liszt." Oscar Beringer conceded, "Words cannot describe him as a pianist—he was incomparable and unapproachable." Moriz Rosenthal said, "He played as no one before him, and as no one probably will ever again." Heine wrote, "The piano vanishes and the music is revealed. Liszt played quite alone, or rather accompanied only by his genius . . . the pianist of genius, whose playing often appears to me as the melodious agony of a spectral world."

Hans Christian Andersen marveled: "It did not seem to be the strings of a piano that were sounding. No, every tone was like an echoing drop of water. Anyone who admires the technique of art must bow before Liszt; he that is charmed with the genial, the divine gift, bows still lower. . . . The divine soul flashed from his eyes, from every feature; he grew handsome— handsome as life and inspiration can make one. . . . The instrument appears to be changed into a whole orchestra. This is accomplished by ten fingers, which possess a power of execution that might be termed superhuman."

When Liszt played privately to George Eliot, the novelist realized that "for the first time in my life I beheld real inspiration—for the first time I heard the true tones of the piano." The Russian critic Stassov admitted, "We had never heard anything like it before, never been confronted by such passionate, demonic genius," while the Russian composer Serov exclaimed, "How far the reality surpassed my expectations." For Siloti, Liszt's playing produced "music such as no one could form any idea of without hearing it."

Schumann observed: "But what is most difficult is, precisely, to talk about his art. It is no longer pianoforte playing of this kind or that; instead, it is generally the outward expression of a daring character whom Fortune has permitted to dominate and to triumph not with dangerous implements, but with the peaceful means of art. No matter how many important artists have passed before us in the last years; no matter how many artists equaling Liszt in many respects we ourselves possess, not one can match him in point of energy and boldness."

The critic Rellstab suggested, "It is not *what* Liszt plays, but *how* he plays it." Indeed, whatever music he touched seemed transformed. In a letter to Hiller, Chopin wrote, "Liszt is at this moment playing my Etudes and he transports me out of my proper senses—I should like to steal from him his way of playing my Etudes." In his diary, Moscheles recorded that "Liszt played three of my studies. . . . By his talent he has completely metamorphosed these pieces; they have become more his studies than mine." Berlioz hailed Liszt's "*sensibilité divinatiore*" and called him "the Pianist of the Future." The French master confessed to having found Beethoven's Sonata Opus 106, the *Hammerklavier,* an enigma until Liszt unraveled it for him. Actually, Liszt had learned the mighty work by his tenth year. He recalled that at that time he played the *Hammerklavier* "*fort mal, sans doute, mais avec passion*" ("very badly, no doubt, but with passion"). Of Liszt's own work, Berlioz wrote, "Unfortunately one cannot hope to hear music of this kind often. Liszt created it for himself—and no one else in the world could flatter himself that he could approach being able to perform it."

In 1866 the thirty-one-year-old Saint-Saëns had not yet heard Liszt, who had been retired from the stage for nearly twenty years. Saint-Saëns wrote: "I already considered him to be a genius and had formed in advance an almost impossible conception of his pianism. Imagine my astonishment when I realized that he far exceeded even this expectation. The dreams of my youthful fancy were but prose beside the Dionysiac poetry evoked by his supernatural fingers. . . . Never again shall we see or hear anything like it."

Concerning a performance of Bach's Prelude and Fugue in C-sharp minor, Wagner acknowledged: "I knew, of course, very well what was to be expected of Liszt at the piano, but what I heard when he played this piece I had not anticipated, although I had studied Bach thoroughly. This experience showed me how slight is the value of study as compared with revelation."

Debussy, who had heard the very old Liszt play *Au bord d'une source,* spoke of his use of the pedal as "a sort of breathing apparatus." He had entirely changed piano playing, musically, mentally, and physically. The merely curved fingers, quiet body, light arms and shoulders had virtually no applicability to Liszt's music or playing. The pedagogue Rudolf Breithaupt observed: "What chiefly distinguished Liszt's technique was the absolute freedom of the arms. The secret lay in the unconstrained swinging movements of the arm from the raised shoulder, the bringing out of the tone through the impact of the full elastic mass

on the keys, a thorough command and use of the freely rolling arm, the springing hand, the springing finger. He played by weight—by a swinging and a hurling of weight from a loosened shoulder that had nothing in common with what is known as finger manipulation. It was by a direct transfer of strength from back and shoulders to fingers."

Arthur Friedheim closely observed his teacher and mentor, writing: "All through life Liszt sensed the spiritual, could see and hear things and sounds beyond ordinary ken. He had the intuition, the mystic power to penetrate beyond the empyrean. . . . Surely some occult factor is the only real key to Liszt's character, his art, and the manner in which he affected his audiences."

He had transformed the piano's possibilities with his *Paganini Etudes,* his operatic transcriptions, and his monumental Twelve *Transcendental Etudes,* called by his first biographer, Lina Ramann, "an unparalleled, gigantic work of spiritual technique." Saint-Saëns considered Liszt's influence on the piano so enormous that he knew nothing comparable to it except the revolution in the mechanism of the French language brought about by Victor Hugo. There is no body of piano music so infallibly grateful and malleable for the hand. Liszt seems to gear his pianistic thinking to a universal hand. His music has a built-in playability no matter how difficult it may be.

He brought melody and accompaniment in the same hand to new heights of inventiveness. He divided between the hands colorful and daring chromatic passages. He laid out melodies in the most ringing registers, simulating the cello or French horn. He magnificently used the thumb as a melodic finger, instead of only as a fulcrum. He created worlds of tremolos, vibratos through pedaling. The simple trill was transformed into a stream of transparent light waves. His dense chordal masses were used for unprecedented dark coloring. He elevated octave technique to new heights, ranging in chromatic and diatonic scales, in broken chords, arpeggios, and "blind" interlocking octaves. These "Lisztian" octaves are volcanoes of molten lava. He composes climaxes with the power of a tidal wave. He was almost inexhaustible in the creation of bejeweled cadenzas, sprays of sound; Liszt made these cadenzas into a structural device. In his music, they form a preparation for the next material, or they act as transitional moments before the new action takes place—a sumptuous sounded fermata, so to speak. Liszt was inimitable in imitating effects of orchestral timbre. He saw clearly the piano's latent coloristic and suggestive possibilities, and he called his efforts the "orchestration of the pianoforte."

Aaron Copland wrote:

The sonority chosen instinctively for its sheer beauty of sound . . . is partly the invention of Liszt. No other composer before him understood better how to manipulate tones so as to produce the most satisfying sound texture ranging from the comparative simplicity of a beautifully spaced accompanimental figure to the massive fall of a tumbling cascade of shimmering chords. . . . The profusion of his works and their variety of attack are without parallel in piano literature. He quite literally transforms the piano, bringing out, not only its own inherent qualities, but its evocative nature as well. The piano as orchestra, the piano as harp (*Un Sospiro*), the piano as cimbalom (Hungarian Rhapsody No. 11), the piano as organ, as brass choir, even the percussive piano as we know it (*Totentanz*) may be traced to Liszt's incomparable handling of the instrument. These pieces were born in the piano; they could never have been written at a table.

In all probability, Liszt was the best sight reader ever to play the piano. The various accounts border on the incredible. When Grieg heard him sight-read his then manuscript Concerto, the Norwegian rejoiced, "He was literally over the whole keyboard at once, without missing a note. And how he did play, with grandeur, beauty, genius, unique comprehension. I think I laughed, laughed like an idiot." Ferdinand Hiller told Mendelssohn: "I have just seen a miracle! I was with Liszt at Erard's and showed him the manuscript of my concerto. He played it at sight—it is hardly legible—and with the utmost perfection. It simply can't be played any better than he played it. It was miraculous."

As a teacher, Liszt's influence has been incalculable. He gave no private lessons but used the plan of the master class with electric effect; here all could play for each other while benefiting from the master's wisdom. Technical matters were never mentioned. Practicing was "your own business." From the world over, students burst upon little Weimar (where the din of practice was so prevalent that a city ordinance demanded in those pre–air conditioning days that windows be shut). There has never before or since been such a pianists' paradise. From von Bülow and Tausig to Friedheim, Rosenthal, Siloti, d'Albert, pianists of every nation nurtured themselves on him. Liszt never ceased helping his pupils, and instilled in them the courage to demand their due as artists. He never charged a fee for the countless classes. His motto was "*Génie oblige.*"

His American student William Mason recalled, "He gradually got me worked up to such a pitch of enthusiasm that I put all the grit that was in me into my playing." Amy Fay, from Mississippi, "felt that with a touch of his wand he could transform us all . . . you feel so free with him, and he develops the very spirit of music in you." The pianist Alfred Reisenauer said, "Never have I met a man in any position whom I have not thought would have proved the inferior of Franz Liszt. . . . Liszt's personality can only be expressed by one word, 'colossal.' "

The nineteenth century craved idols, and Liszt gave Europe a bewildering variety of images to worship: the adorable child prodigy; later, the irresistible Don Juan (still later to be disguised as an abbé); and, for much of his long career, the epitome of flaming Romanticism, the very personification of pianistic virtuosity. Even in old age (half saint, half Mephisto, looking for all the world like an aged Apache chieftain), his magnetism never failed to enthrall. The Grand Duke Carl Alexander of Weimar said that "Liszt was what a prince ought to be." Yet no mere prince ever ruled a dominion so wide as the Kingdom of the Keyboard—a realm in which Liszt's sovereignty was unchallenged through seven decades.

Busoni wrote, many years after Liszt's death, that "we are all descended from him radically. I am myself respectfully conscious of the distance which separates me from his greatness. . . . His aims are ascent, ennoblement, and liberation. Only one who is exalted strives to ascend; only one who is noble strives for nobility; only a master of freedom can bestow freedom. He has become the symbol of the pianoforte, which he lifted to a princely position in order that it might be worthy of himself."

HENRY LITOLFF
1818–1891—England

A student of Moscheles, whom Litolff revered. He is scarcely known today, but during the nineteenth century his name loomed large, as a pianist, composer, and publisher who was the first to issue inexpensive editions of the classics of the piano literature. His operas and concert overtures were highly touted by the press and public, and his career as a pianist

brought him success throughout Europe. He was often dubbed "the English Liszt." Liszt admired Litolff's compositions, piano playing, and the man. Liszt's E-flat Concerto is dedicated to Litolff. The two musicians met for the last time in Brussels in 1886, after thirty years' separation.

Both men wept and embraced each other. "How we have changed," remarked Litolff with melancholy. And Liszt, while smiling, exclaimed, "You are right, we are both more beautiful than ever."

Of his large output for piano, only the *Spinnlied*, Op. 81, and the Etude *Les Octaves* outlived the composer for a generation. His major contribution to the art, however, is the series of four concertos which he called *Concerto Symphoniques*. Each present the grand gesture, with pages of originality and splendid touches. Litolff was praised by Berlioz, speaking of his science, ardor, and inspiration as well as exaggeration. Berlioz thought his pianistic ability "belongs to the race of the great pianists, and his nervous, powerful but always rhythmically clear virtuoso playing possesses those same qualities as I have indicated in the composer." The Third Concerto (National Hollandaise), Op. 45, uses Dutch folk tunes. In the nineteenth century Alfred Jaëll performed it in Boston, as did Fannie Bloomfield Zeisler. Michael Ponti has recorded No. 3; the Fourth Concerto, Op. 102, has been recorded by Gerald Robbins. It is the light-winged *Scherzo* from No. 4 which is the best-known movement in the Litolff corpus, and, since its composition in 1851, it has often appeared separately at orchestral programs. Litolff himself gave the premiere in 1854, and played it privately for Liszt, who spoke of the "living" manner of his electric performance.

The Scherzo movement was first recorded by Irene Scharrer, and since then Curzon and others have rippled off its Scherzando sunshine on recordings.

DAVID LIVELY

b. 1953—United States

In Paris he worked with the eminent teacher Jules Gentil at the École Normale for several years. He is a fine musician with a large technique; his best-known recording is Fauré's thirteen nocturnes on Etcetera.

ARTHUR LOESSER

1894–1969—United States

He studied with Sigismund Stojowski and made his debut in Berlin in 1913. Subsequently, Loesser performed throughout the world. In 1926 he settled in Cleveland and became the head of the piano department at the Cleveland Institute of Music. Later he was music critic of the *Cleveland Press*. His book, *Men, Women, and Pianos,* published in 1954, is a social history of the piano and has become a classic.

Loesser was a pianist of immense gifts. He was my own teacher and one of the best musical minds I have ever encountered. Loesser was never the pedant. He would say: "The music is not there on the paper. It's not in those black spots. I can't go along with people who believe they are supposed to be music typists. They are the Fundamentalists. They think they must speak only when Scripture speaks and be silent when Scripture is silent. It's all a misapplication of the Scientific Method, translated to music."

Loesser played all the Classical masters with the kind of aristocratic poise that one can only be born with. His Scarlatti, Clementi, and Haydn were bright and alive with wit. His Mozart was absolutely marvelous in its sense of humor. In Schubert's B-flat Impromptu, Loesser strutted and preened. In Bach's *French* Suites, he was incomparable and ingratiating.

Actually, at a recital of the complete French Suites, he told the audience to forget that Bach wrote the B minor Mass and not to mind one bit if they found their feet tapping to Bach's rhythmic infectiousness. Loesser knew how to dance each Baroque dance and could show a student exactly how a sarabande, gigue, gavotte, or allemande really should go. Bach was his great love, and *The Well-Tempered Clavier* was sacred. His recordings of the forty-eight Preludes and Fugues should have a place of honor in any collection of great Bach playing. He felt:

> Playing Bach's music on a modern piano, an instrument unknown and perhaps unimagined by him, is thus to subject it to a translation. It is possible however, as Bible readers will testify, for translations to be exalting and inspiring. In making this translation my aim is to avoid a futile literalness, or the making of a lifeless archeological restoration; but rather to realize as many living values of the music as is possible, by the use of means other than those available to the composer, notably those of flexible shadings and accents. Moreover I shall attempt to express the relationship of the preludes to their corresponding Fugues through mutual assimilation of their respective moods and movements, rather than through their contrast. I have no authority for this beyond my own *Notion* of fitness.

He had a rare understanding of Schumann, and there is a 1937 recording of the Brahms F-sharp minor Sonata, Op. 2, which is full of Romantic ardor. He played Chopin with classic style, and a spirit of gallantry saturates his recording of the neglected *Variations brillantes,* Op. 12. In James Methuen-Campbell's words, he played Chopin's B major Nocturne, Op. 9, No. 3 "with a melancholy and exquisite pathos."

His last major appearance was in New

York's Town Hall in 1967, when he played a sumptuous program of forgotten gems. The hall was packed, and Loesser played such works as the E major Moszkowski Waltz and Busoni's Second Sonatina with a gusto and prodigious technique that brought the audience to its feet. Fortunately, this recital was recorded for posterity and was transferred to CD with other performances in a two-CD set issued on the Marston label.

KATHLEEN LONG
1896–1968—England

Studied at the Royal College of Music. She played both solo and in chamber works. Her performances of Fauré were admired. She wrote a book, *Nineteenth Century Piano Music*.

MARGUERITE LONG
1874–1966—France

A pupil of Marmontel *fils* at the Paris Conservatoire. She gave her first concert at the age of eleven and her last at seventy-five. She had an enormous career, both as an interpreter, especially of the French literature, and as a teacher of dozens of fine talents, such as Jeanne-Marie Darré, Bernard Ringeissen, Peter Frankl, Ludwig Hoffman, and Philippe Entremont, to name only a few. She knew Debussy, Fauré, and Ravel, and studied their compositions with them. Ravel dedicated to her his G major Concerto, which she premiered with the composer conducting. Her books *At the Piano with Debussy*, *At the Piano with Fauré*, and *At the Piano with Ravel* are especially informative. Her playing was distinguished by clarity, taste, and excellent technique.

ALESSANDRO LONGO
1864–1945—Italy

He studied at the Naples Conservatory, where he later taught. Longo was a concert pianist who composed some interesting piano pieces. His "complete" edition of Domenico Scarlatti's sonatas, for the publisher Ricordi, was a milestone in the resurrection and rediscovery of the great Italian keyboard master. The edition is a Romantic musician's conception of how Scarlatti should sound on the piano, replete with a wide dynamic spectrum.

YVONNE LORIOD
b. 1924—France

A student of Lévy and Ciampi at the Paris Conservatoire. She married Olivier Messiaen and has been closely associated with his music, which she plays with virtuosity and understanding.

ROBERT LORTAT
1885–1938—France

Lortat was a pupil of Diémer at the Paris Conservatoire, and was awarded first prize in piano in 1901. A Paris debut occurred in 1910 and Lortat began extensive concertizing. In 1913, both in Paris and London he performed the "complete" Chopin works, possibly the first to accomplish this feat. He was an early champion of Fauré, performing his solo piano works in four recitals. In 1916 he made a small tour of the United States.

He was the most supercharged rambunctious French Chopin player of his era. Nothing is relaxed or casual. He could make a jumble of a prelude and lapse into some tasteless moments in the Waltzes but there is a fresh, creative imagination going on; he can be pulverizing in the first movement of the *Funeral March* Sonata. He is a driven player, fond of high speeds; above all it is an urgent Chopin. The bulk of his Chopin recordings may be studied on the Dante label, and some listeners will find him to be a fascinating and a disconcerting pianist.

LOUIS LORTIE
b. 1959—Canada

In 1984 he won first prize at the Busoni Competition. Lortie is a stylish pianist who plays with impeccable polish. His interpretations are tasteful, cool, and musicianly. His disc of the Chopin Etudes is finely honed and patrician. In 1992 Lortie was named an officer of the Order of Canada.

JEROME LOWENTHAL
b. 1932—United States

At thirteen he made a debut with the Philadelphia Orchestra. He studied with Alfred Cortot and William Kapell, and at the Juilliard School with Edward Steuermann. A particularly astute performance is his recording of the six-movement Rorem Piano Concerto. His CD of Tchaikovsky's Second and Third Concertos is handsomely played. He has been on the faculty of the Juilliard School for years.

JEAN-MARC LUISADA
b. 1958—France

Early studies with Marcel Ciampi followed at the Paris Conservatoire with Dominique Merlet, in whose class he was awarded a first prize. He further studied with Paul Badura-Skoda and Nikita Magaloff before winning the 1983 Dino Ciani Competition in Warsaw. Luisada's playing is generally colorful and regulated; especially good are his Schumann and Grieg Concerto.

RADU LUPU
b. 1945—Rumania

After an early debut, he was sent to the Moscow Conservatory, where he studied with the great teacher Heinrich Neuhaus. Lupu won first prize at the Van Cliburn Competition in 1966, and in 1969 he was the victor at the Leeds Competition.

Over the past years Lupu's career has been thriving both in concert and as a recording artist. He is a profoundly thoughtful artist and, at his best, possesses a deep insight into Beethoven. His technical apparatus is particularly fine, and one is seldom conscious of hands moving on a piano. It is in Schubert that Lupu finds scope for his best work, and in the Sonatas and shorter pieces we have playing of true stature. In the past decades he has become one of the world's most respected concert artists, filling halls wherever he performs.

DAME MOURA LYMPANY

b. 1916—England

She studied at the Royal Academy with Tobias Matthay and later with Mathilde Verne, making her debut in the Mendelssohn G minor Concerto at the age of twelve. Her career was extensive during the 1940s and 1950s. She let many seasons lapse without playing in New York; then, in November 1981, she returned to Carnegie Hall to find a still large following.

Her performances of Haydn's E minor Sonata and Schumann's *Symphonic Etudes* reminded me of the playing of Eileen Joyce, another Matthay student—it is smooth and on the surface, with little structural development. But the second half of the recital was more suited to her talents as an objective lyricist. Here Lympany was charming in such water pieces as Debussy's *Reflets dans l'eau* and Ravel's *Ondine*. Her technique was facile and fluid, the playing slightly sweet while not extending to huge fortissimos.

In her memoirs, the writer Margaret Anderson wrote: "One of the landmarks in my musical life has been the discovery of Lympany's 'completely beautiful' playing. I knew at once, as she began Debussy's *Clair de lune*, that no one had ever played it so exactly in the right mood for me, the right breathing. Nearly all of Lympany's conceptions are marked by a rare responsiveness to great lyrical music."

M

GEOFFREY DOUGLAS MADGE

b. 1941—Australia

Madge, a native of Adelaide, began piano lessons at the age of eight. In 1963, he settled in Holland, where he has taught at the Hague Conservatory.

Among his numerous recordings are the Xenakis Piano Concerto, the epic *Opus clavicembalisticum* by Sorabji, the daunting complete solo piano music of Busoni issued by Philips on six CDs, the Dimitri Mitropoulos Piano Sonata, and the immense Sonata by Godowsky. Madge has not fully digested all of their mechanical difficulties, although the pianist certainly has facility. His Godowsky and Busoni are rather dry and too careful to portray this multilayered music in all of its potential.

NIKITA MAGALOFF

1912–1993—Russia

A pupil of Philipp at the Paris Conservatoire. Magaloff composed piano pieces, including a toccata, dedicated to Horowitz. He had a distinguished career as soloist and chamber musician. His most renowned playing is in the Chopin literature, which he recorded complete. His readings are small in scale but distinguished in manner. Students from around the world came to Geneva, where he taught at the conservatoire. He was often a judge at international piano competitions. The American pianist Gustavo Romero wrote, "The breadth and depth of Magaloff's artistry and his healthy and altruistic musicianship were a keen source of inspiration to me. He was also a dedicated mentor of many musicians."

GUY MAIER

1892–1956—United States

He studied at the New England Conservatory, then with Schnabel in Berlin. He was often heard with Lee Pattison in two-piano works. He edited many works and taught in California.

JOAQUIN MALÁTS

1872–1912—Spain

He studied with Pujol in his native Barcelona and developed into the finest Spanish pianist of his time, much admired by all who heard his impeccable technique. Maláts also composed, and his lightweight Serenade was once played frequently. It is a pity that this stimulating pianist, who was an inspiration to the composer Albéniz, did not live long enough to make many recordings. He played the Spanish premieres of all twelve pieces of Albéniz's *Iberia*. The composer wrote to Maláts in 1907: "Since I was fortunate enough to hear you play my *Iberia*, I can truly say that I compose only for you. I have just completed, under the spell of your artistry, the third book of *Iberia*. . . . I think that in these pieces, I have taken the Spanish idiom and pianistic technique to their extremes, and I hasten to add, I hold you responsible for it . . . so brace yourself."

WITOLD MALCUZYNSKI
1914–1977—Poland

He was a student of Turczynski at the Warsaw Conservatory. Later, he received coaching from Paderewski. Malcuzynski left a great many recordings. He played Debussy well and Franck's Prelude, Chorale, and Fugue with a feverish attitude. However, he will be most remembered as a Chopin player who was immersed in a nostalgic and idiosyncratic style. He could be original and eccentric within the same piece; spontaneous and prosaic passages abound in his nevertheless fascinating playing. He had a fine career and was very effective as a stage personality. Invariably, the audience reacted favorably to whatever Malcuzynski did.

YEVGENY MALININ
b. 1930—USSR

A pianist who worked under Stanislav Neuhaus.

He has toured throughout Russia and eastern Europe, recorded Scriabin and Beethoven, and was one of the teachers of Ivo Pogorelich.

ALAN MANDEL
b. 1935—United States

A student of Leonard Shure and, at the Juilliard School, of Rosina Lhévinne. Mandel is a dedicated exponent of contemporary music. He recorded all of the Ives piano music, William Albright's *Sonata in Rag,* and music by Elie Siegmeister, all of which is played in a forthright style. He also recorded forty pieces by Gottschalk and the sonatas by MacDowell.

ADELE MARCUS
1905–1995—United States

Studied with Josef Lhévinne and with Schnabel in Berlin, both major influences on her pianistic and musical thought. Marcus won the Naumburg Award and performed frequently throughout her long career, as well as giving master classes. As a teacher at the Juilliard School she attracted many important talents, including Byron Janis, Agustin Anievas, Tedd Joselson, Santiago Rodriguez, Horacio Gutiérrez, Thomas Schumacher, and many others. Jeffrey Biegel, who studied with her for years, wrote: "Marcus influenced me in countless ways. She would say, 'Never do anything to the music, let the music do something to you.' She would quote from the Talmud, 'see it, not just look, hear it, not just listen, if you want to understand the invisible, you must study carefully the visible.'"

IRÉN MARIK

1905–1986—Hungary

In Budapest she studied for two years with Bartok. After working extensively on his music, Bartok exclaimed, "You understand it. Now let's work on Beethoven."

Before World War II Marik frequently performed in England and Germany. She defected to the United States while on a tour. She taught at Sweet Briar College, formed a piano duo with John Ranck, and recorded for Zodiac Records. Marik is a pianist of fine sensibility, a large technique, and a penetrating sound.

ANTOINE-FRANÇOIS MARMONTEL

1816–1898—France

A student of Pierre Zimmerman at the Paris Conservatoire. In 1848, when Zimmerman retired, Marmontel became professor at that institution (a post Alkan desperately wanted). Marmontel became one of France's most respected piano teachers, and he taught an army of pianists. Bizet, Diémer, Théodore Dubois, Debussy, Planté, and Théodore Lack are but a few who achieved renown. He taught at the Conservatoire until 1887 and he was given the Legion of Honor for his service to French art. He wrote many instructive compositions, as well as a book, *Pianistes célèbres*. His son, Antonin Marmontel (1850–1907), taught at the Paris Conservatoire from 1901 until his death, teaching in the women's division. The classes at the Conservatoire were either male or female until 1916. Marmontel taught Magda Tagliaferro and Marguerite Long. Both of them would also be on the faculty of the Paris Conservatoire.

OZAN MARSH

1920–1991—United States

He studied with Sauer and Petri, developing into a special pianist who performed throughout the world. He was at his best in Romantic music, and his playing of the Liszt Concerto No. 1 and the Rachmaninoff Second Sonata displayed grand conceptions, with broad strokes of color. His recording of the important Kabalevsky Second Concerto is an impressive achievement.

FRANK MARSHALL

1883–1959—Spain

He was a student of Granados and a propagandist for his music and Falla's. A fine player whose only recording is accompanying the soprano Conchita Supervia. Marshall taught at the Granados Academy, where he was the only teacher of de Larrocha.

JOÃO CARLOS MARTINS

b. 1940—Brazil

At the age of nine, he won a piano competition in São Paulo. His main teacher was a pupil of Martin Krause, Josef Kliass, with whom he studied until he was nineteen. Early contacts with Tagliaferro and Cortot also had inspired the boy. Bach was his earliest love, and at twelve, he performed the fifteen Two-Part Inventions in public. By the time he was eighteen he was playing the complete *Well-Tempered Clavier*. In 1962, Martins made his New York debut, and soon after, he committed *The Well-Tempered Clavier* to disc, to unusual critical enthusiasm. This was a Bach of enchanting originality and breathtaking technical daring. It was a youthful, joyous Bach, carefree as a lark, but disciplined to pinpoint control. Glenn Gould had closed shop on his concert career in 1964, and it appeared that the new man of the hour would be the young Brazilian virtuoso, poised and prepared, on the brink of a great international career.

But fate said NO! And year after year he has lived in various degrees of painful physical suffering, despair, and soul searching, often leaving his piano for long stretches. From a soccer injury to his arm he disappeared from 1970 to 1975. Through desperation, he would every so often emerge onto the stage like a wounded lion. Somehow he was never quite forgotten, but his life has been plagued by continuous physical battles. In the mid-nineties, while working on his monumental project of recording all of Bach's Concertos and solo works on twenty-two CDs for Concord Concerto Records, he was mugged in Sofia, Bulgaria, and suffered a brain hematoma. Somehow he survived, and after revolutionary treatment he completed his Bachian task. However, as time passed his right hand lost the ability to play. Still, he is persevering and in 2002 Labor Records issued a disc of Martins in repertoire for the left hand, including the Six Etudes for left hand of Saint-Saëns and Ravel's Piano Concerto.

Martins's contribution to his art is his iconoclastic and controversial Bach playing. Like his gigantic country of Brazil, Martins's playing at its best displays mighty contrasts and eruptions, glorious landscapes, and vast resources. It seems to me that the piano playing of Martins reflects the temperamental quirkiness of his nation. From listening to him, it is fair to say that he has been enraptured, intoxicated, and hypnotized by the immortal Leipzig Cantor. It is certainly playing that has captivated some, and irritated its share of listeners. But there is always a passionate spirit, honesty, and a sheer animality. It is lusty and teeming with life. The pianist is obviously not interested in Baroque conventions or in sounding like a harpsichord. His playing is virtuosic, grandiose, and sensual, and he presents his own type of scholarship. Some squeamish listeners may say he is self-indulgent. One wonders, would Bach be alarmed at the sometime extremities of his approach or would the mightiest contrapuntist and greatest of all dance composers be delighted with the superb elasticity of his own creations? Pianistically, Martins delights in his technical apparatus, in his astonishing range and finger control, elongated breath, and grand manner. Witness many a movement such as the mighty Toccata of the E minor Partita. Listen carefully to Martins, for he plays on many levels of consciousness; in the most profound fugues of *The Well-Tempered Clavier,* he finds a heightened religious exaltation.

GIUSEPPE MARTUCCI
1856–1909—Italy

A pupil of Beniamino Cesi, he toured Europe as a first-rank pianist, also becoming a good conductor. Martucci headed the Bologna Conservatory and later the Naples Conservatory. His B-flat minor Concerto was admired by Anton Rubinstein, who conducted it with Cesi at the piano; d'Albert also played it, with the Berlin Philharmonic. Martucci wrote some of the best piano music by an Italian during an era when Italian opera was at its peak. A recording of his piano concerto was made by Horszowski with Toscanini.

FREDERICK MARVIN

b. 1923—United States

A student of Rudolf Serkin. Marvin is also a musicologist. His recordings of Liszt, especially the B minor Ballade and the *Grand Concert Solo,* are large in scale. He recorded several Dussek sonatas in almost symphonic conceptions. He is best known for his scholarship in the music of Soler and has discovered and edited many Soler sonatas. His recordings of that composer's work, especially the unusual Fandango, are distinguished.

WILLIAM MASON

1829–1908—United States

After early pianistic success in America, he went to Europe to work with Moscheles and later with Franz Liszt at Weimar. In 1855 he returned to the United States, where for the next half century he was the leading piano teacher in New York. His brother was cofounder of the piano firm Mason and Hamlin. Mason composed some effective piano music, and his work *Touch and Technic* was long used by piano teachers. He wrote a valuable autobiography, *Memories of a Musical Life.*

The composer Daniel Gregory Mason, nephew of William, once said that his uncle's playing was "an unforgettable musical experience. His rich and at the same time discriminating sensuous feeling voiced itself in the most exquisite piano touch I have ever heard." He wrote a good amount of piano music, mostly faded remnants of a bygone day. There are also some virtuosic pieces that are pretty and pianistically tricky, such as *Silver Spring,* Op. 6, often performed by Steven Mayer.

WILLIAM MASSELOS

1920–1992—United States

Carl Friedberg was his teacher, and he made his New York debut in 1943. A Masselos program was one of variety, but he became known for his chivalry toward new music, devoting a great deal of time to the hard-to-sell wares of an unappreciated branch of the literature. Although his commitment to Scarlatti, Brahms, and Schumann was intense, I suspect his chief delight remained music of his own century—from Griffes and Copland to Ben Weber and Chávez. It was Masselos who gave the belated world premiere, in 1949, of the great Ives First Sonata. His recording is famous, but to have heard him play it in public was truly an experience of elemental fury. He emblazoned its bars in the audience's ears. During the playing, I thought Masselos might burst a blood vessel. Afterward, he was drained. The audience roared, and nobody squawked that the Ives was "ugly." Everyone in the audience became a convert!

GEORGES MATHIAS

1826–1910—France

He studied with Chopin from 1840, and is—along with Karl Mikuli—the most important student of the Polish master. He taught at the Paris Conservatoire for thirty years, and Raoul Pugno, Carreño, Moriz Rosenthal, Alberto Williams, Isidor Philipp, and Ernest Schelling studied with him.

He composed a great deal of piano music and two Concerti. James Methuen-Campbell wrote, "Mathias himself played in a manner which showed that his priorities were in the realm of delicate and sensitive nuances, such as had characterized Chopin's playing. Mathias forms a link between Chopin himself and the modern French school."

Academy. A pianist held in high regard, he was best in the music of Mozart and Beethoven. He wrote a book on Beethoven.

TOBIAS MATTHAY
1858–1945—England

He studied with Sterndale Bennett and taught at the Royal Academy from 1880; later, he opened his own school. Matthay was a well-equipped pianist and composed many genre pieces, but his great fame was won through his work as a pedagogue. His books on piano playing, its theory and application, were considered by many to be gospel. He was undoubtedly the most celebrated teacher of his time in England. The list of his pupils is extensive and impressive; it includes York Bowen, Harold Craxton, Harriet Cohen, Eileen Joyce, Irene Scharrer, and Dame Myra Hess.

Marian McKenna, in her biography of Hess, wrote: "Mr. Matthay was more than a teacher of the piano—he was an idealist and practical moralist, as much interested in shaping his pupils' character as in developing innate musicality. Music he conceived of as a great spiritual art, elevating and enriching life with beautiful thoughts, sounds, feelings and experiences. . . . His ideas about keyboard technique and a psychological approach to the study of the piano—something quite new for that time—proved just what was needed to unlock the rich potential in a pupil like Myra Hess."

DENIS MATTHEWS
1929–1989—England

A student of Harold Craxton at the Royal

CHARLES MAYER
1799–1862—Germany

He studied with John Field and taught hundreds of students while living in Russia. Mayer played frequently and composed prolifically, mostly for the piano. I have recorded his *Valse-étude* in D-flat, Op. 83, an amalgam of Weber and Schumann written with pianistic acumen.

JOHN MCCABE
b. 1939—England

An excellent pianist whose complete Haydn discs are well-known. His own piano music has merit and he has recorded some of it, including his Fantasy on a Theme of Liszt.

NICOLAI MEDTNER
1880–1951—Russia

A pianist of authority and complete technical equipment. Medtner studied at the Moscow Conservatory with Vassily Safonov, who was proud of his protégé. When he graduated in 1900 with the coveted Gold Medal, Safonov remarked that it should have been a Diamond Medal. Soon after he was a prizewinner of the Anton Rubinstein competition, and in Moscow he was soloist in the Tchaikovsky First Concerto with Nikisch directing. Tours of Germany brought him much praise and his performances of Beethoven were especially noted with pleasure.

Beethoven would, for him, become a new means of musical nourishment. In later years, he recorded the Fourth Concerto and the Sonata *Appassionata*. In 1909, he took a professorship at the Moscow Conservatory. After the 1917 Revolution he left Russia, always feeling displaced away. His recordings of his own music are valuable and place him in the ranks of the great pianist-composers. Rachmaninoff wrote, "Both as musician and as a man, he is one of those rare persons who inspire more admiration the closer you get to them."

ANNA MEHLIG
1846–1928—Germany

A dynamic pianist, she was a pupil of Liszt and played in Europe, England, and America. Of her career in America, Liszt said, "Mlle Mehlig has blossomed so well and borne fruit." She was soloist with the Boston Symphony Orchestra and with the Theodore Thomas Orchestra in Chicago.

HENRIK MELCER
1869–1928—Poland

A student of Leschetizky. Melcer had a career as a pianist and teacher at Helsinki and Vienna, and became director of the Warsaw Conservatory in 1922. He composed a great deal of music in many forms. His early First Piano Concerto, recorded by Michael Ponti, is a smashing Romantic showpiece of undeniable effectiveness, expertise, and bravura, with a grand gesture thrown in every sixteen bars.

FANNY MENDELSSOHN
1805–1847—Germany

Felix Mendelssohn's sister Fanny, whom he adored, was a gifted musician who suddenly died at the age of forty-one. When told of her death, Mendelssohn collapsed; he died six months later, at the age of thirty-eight. Few artists have ever packed more into such a short life.

Fanny Hensel, née Mendelssohn, was considered a superb pianist. Felix often told people that she was a better pianist than he was. When Fanny, the eldest of the four Mendelssohn children, was born, her mother proclaimed, "Her fingers look ideal for Bach Fugues." Indeed, by the age of thirteen, she had already committed to memory Book I of *The Well-Tempered Clavier*. Unfortunately, her career was terribly stunted by the ingrained prejudices of her time as well as by her slightly precious family, who considered public appearances beneath the dignity of an upper-class woman. This was in spite of her friendship with Clara Schumann, Jenny Lind, and other women musicians whom she knew well. Aaron Cohen, in his *International Encyclopedia of Women Composers*, quotes her grandfather Moses Mendelssohn as saying, "Moderate learning becomes a lady, but not scholarship. A girl who has read her eyes red deserves to be laughed at."

Although Fanny Mendelssohn-Hensel cannot be called a professional pianist in the strict sense, she was considered one of the finest pianists in Berlin, and was heard semi-publicly almost weekly in the Mendelssohn family's famous Sunday concerts, playing Bach, Handel, Mozart, and Beethoven. Her one "official" public performance took place in 1837, when she played Felix's G minor Concerto. The English critic Henry Chorley described her playing as "more feminine than her brother's, but having a strong family resemblance in its fire, clarity and accomplishment." Her many piano works and the superb Piano Trio show a refined and fastidious talent. The German pianist Sontraud Speidel has championed Fanny Hensel's work.

FELIX MENDELSSOHN
1809–1847—Germany

Mendelssohn, after Mozart, was the most astounding child prodigy in the history of the art, but, unlike Mozart, Mendelssohn was not exploited. Indeed, few have ever been raised in such an atmosphere of wealth, culture, and love, saturated with an affirmation of the humanities and the arts (Mendelssohn's grandfather was the renowned philosopher Moses Mendelssohn).

His early compositions are unique in music. By the age of sixteen, he had written the Octet, and by seventeen, the miraculous Overture to *A Midsummer Night's Dream*. Mendelssohn seemed to be blessed with everything. He was handsome and charming, an excellent dancer and billiards player, an expert horseman, a superb watercolorist, an incomparable letter writer, and a musical genius. He became one of the best conductors of his generation, and one of the greatest pianists of the age. The theorist Heinrich Dorn thought him the greatest of his era. His improvisations were miraculous. His playing was poised and crisp, and his technique was absolutely impeccable.

His first teacher was Clementi's pupil Ludwig Berger, who gave him a severely Classical background. Zelter, the boy's composition teacher, wrote in 1823, "I take his marvelous piano playing for granted." At fourteen, Mendelssohn took some "finishing" lessons from Moscheles. The older man, considered at that time the best pianist in Europe, was stunned by the boy's precocity. Moscheles

noted in his diary that he "gave these lessons without losing sight for a single moment of the fact that I was sitting next to a master, not a pupil."

All doors were opened to him, and at the age of twelve he was the invited guest of Goethe himself, who was deeply affected by the unaffected youngster. In a letter to his parents, Mendelssohn blithely writes, "Every morning I get a kiss from the author of *Faust* and *Werther*. Just fancy that! In the afternoon I played for him for about two hours, partly Bach fugues and partly improvisations."

The powerful critic Ludwig Rellstab was at one of Goethe's gatherings and left an account of Mendelssohn's playing of the overture to *Figaro*: "He began to play it with a lightness, sureness, roundness and clarity such as I have never heard since. At the same time he reproduced the orchestral effects so excellently, so transparently, and by little touches in the instrumentation produced so cunningly the illusion of accompanying voices, that the effect was utterly enchanting and I might almost say that it gave me more pleasure than any orchestral performance ever did."

Mendelssohn's repertoire was large. He played a great deal of Beethoven; one of his specialties was the Fourth Concerto. His interpretation of Weber's *Konzertstück* was considered the ideal. He played Bach and Handel as well as Mozart; especially wonderful was his performance of the Salzburg master's Concerto No. 20 in D minor. Of his playing, the important pianist Ferdinand Hiller attested: "He possessed great skill, certainly power and rapidity of execution—all, in fact, that a virtuoso could desire; but these qualities were forgotten while he was playing, and one almost overlooked even those more spiritual gifts which we call fire, invention, soul, etc. When he sat down to the instrument, music streamed from him with all the fullness of his inborn genius. He was a centaur, and his horse was the piano. What he played, how he played, and that he was the player—were all equally riveting, and it was impossible to separate the execution, the music, and the executant."

In an age when the piano was becoming the most popular domestic instrument, with an ever-growing audience wanting to be entertained, Mendelssohn was uncompromising. He refused to play any potboilers. It is well known that it was Mendelssohn who resurrected Bach's almost-forgotten *Saint Matthew Passion,* and he was also a great proselytizer for *The Well-Tempered Clavier* and Bach's keyboard concerti. In 1831, when Mendelssohn premiered his dazzling G minor Concerto at Munich, he complained in a letter that "even the best pianists had no idea that Mozart and Haydn had composed for the piano; they had just the faintest notion of Beethoven. . . . I gave a long sermon to the leading pianist and reproached her for having contributed nothing towards the knowledge and appreciation of the works of the great masters and for having just followed the popular trend."

Clara Wieck Schumann perhaps knew his playing better than anyone else did. She wrote: "The recollections of Mendelssohn's playing are among the most delightful things in my artistic life. It was to me a shining ideal, full of genius and life. . . . He would sometimes take very quick tempi, but never to the prejudice of the music. . . . He often told me he hardly ever practiced and yet he surpassed everyone."

Mendelssohn was the most famous musician of his age; it was his type of Romanticism that the public loved best and most easily understood. His art is picturesque, generally nonsubjective, and seldom disturbing, as was the art of Schumann or Liszt. In his forty-eight *Lieder ohne Worte* (Songs without Words), Mendelssohn hit upon just the right kind of well-tailored, mild-mannered Romanticism, beautifully calculated for the needs of the Victorian drawing room, where the scores were always on the piano. Mendelssohn was a master of the staccato touch and the scherzando mood. He is irresistible in such airy works as the *Spinning Song, Rondo capriccioso,* Scherzo in E minor, and many others that were born out of Weber's *Momento capriccioso.* Mendelssohn created for the instrument a vision of a happy, sun-drenched world, full of goodwill and magical spells—his piano traveled on gossamer wings.

SOPHIE MENTER
1846–1918—Germany

From all accounts she was one of the great pianists of her time. Menter studied with Tausig and then with Liszt. She had a tremendous career and was perhaps Liszt's greatest female student. He was devoted to her and entranced with her prowess, calling her "a pianist of exceptional virtuosity . . . an incomparable pianist . . . a pianist of the highest rank," and later saying she was "my only legitimate daughter as a pianist." Writing to Olga von Meyendorff in 1881, Liszt reports: "I spent only one day in Rome for Sophie Menter's concert. She played the whole program enclosed herewith superbly, so as to compare favorably with the three or four most famous male pianists. Her *bravura* is absolutely faultless; the rhythm and color are masterfully accented and blended."

Ernst Pauer praised her "nobility of feeling, tenderness and warmth of expression. Her technical execution baffles description." Liszt dedicated to her his transcription of Saint-Saëns's *Dance macabre.* In 1907, James M. Tracey wrote, "No pianist ever had that peculiar asset, 'personal magnetism' to a greater degree." From 1883 to 1887 she taught at the St. Petersburg Conservatory.

HEPHZIBAH MENUHIN
1920–1981—United States

The sister of the great violinist Yehudi Menuhin studied with Marcel Ciampi in Paris, collaborated with her brother, and appeared as soloist worldwide. Yehudi Menuhin said, "Hephzibah had absolutely unbelievable command of the piano. She hated exaggeration, there was a kind of sobriety in her playing, it had to be discovered by a sophisticated public, that realized that kind of playing." Another Menuhin sister, Yalta (b. 1921), was also a pupil of Ciampi and performed to acclaim, as was his son Jeremy (b. 1951).

VICTOR MERZHANOV
b. 1919—USSR

A winner of prizes in piano competitions in the Soviet Union and later a teacher at the Moscow Conservatory. He is greatly respected in the Soviet musical world. Merzhanov has played in Canada and South America, and has judged at the Queen Elizabeth Competition and Busoni Competition. His recording of the Scriabin Fifth Sonata is idiomatically morbid; his Rachmaninoff Third Concerto is dazzling and brittle; and his Brahms *Paganini* Variations has long been admired. For a deeper Merzhanov, listen to his discs of the Grieg Ballade and Mussorgsky's *Pictures at an Exhibition.*

YOLANDA MÉRÖ
1887–1963—Hungary

She studied with her father and then with a pupil of Liszt, Augusta Rennebaum. In 1910 she made her first tour of the United States, with great success. From that time on, her career centered in the United States, and her many recordings reveal a fiery artist with a very efficient technical equipment.

FRANK MERRICK
1886–1981—England

He worked with Leschetizky, performed, playing a great deal of John Field's music, and was a respected teacher in London. He wrote a little volume, *Practicing the Piano.* He also composed and recorded.

NOEL MEWTON-WOOD
1922–1953—Australia

Mewton-Wood moved to London at the age of fourteen, and made a debut at sixteen. Very early his prodigious gifts made a splash, and for a decade and a half he was one of the leading lights of British musical life. A tireless worker, he amassed an enormous repertoire encompassing the mainstream, the rarely played (such as the Weber Sonatas and Busoni Concerto), and the contemporary. Many composers, including Britten, Bliss, Tippett, and Lambert, entrusted him with their music. Mewton-Wood gave the world premiere of Hindemith's *Ludus Tonalis*; Hindemith said, "If you want to hear my music played as it should be, you must hear it played by Mewton-Wood." He was at his best in works of daunting complexity such as Busoni's *Fantasia contrappuntistica* and his bravura shone in his recordings of Tchaikovsky's Concerto, and Concert Fantasy. One remains enthralled with the first two Weber Sonatas reissued on Pearl, and his reading of the Stravinsky Concerto for Piano and Winds is particularly fine. There is also a Chopin F minor Concerto of forceful drama and poetry. The pianist Karl Lutchmayer wrote, "His total technical command coupled to a fierce intellect (which, almost paradoxically, allowed him an exhilarating spontaneity in performance). Perhaps most striking was his range of dynamics, as remarked upon by Sir Henry Wood: 'His *pianissimo* is as beautiful as his *fortissimo* and he reminds me of all the greatest pianists of the past.' Beautiful certainly, but this was the beauty of granite which, never descending into the merely pretty, allowed him an intense clarity in polyphony, and he was not afraid of clangor when the music required it. His early death at so young an age robbed the world of a truly galvanic artist."

LEOPOLD DE MEYER

1816–1883—Austria

A student of Czerny, he had an amazing career. De Meyer was one of the first piano publicists, calling himself "the Lion Pianist." He roamed far and wide, playing in Constantinople in 1843, four years before Liszt arrived there. He was also the first important pianist to play in America, arriving in 1845, before either Herz or Thalberg. He played about sixty concerts, going as far as St. Louis. His publicity stunts and showmanship, as well as his highly demonstrative, muscular playing, electrified audiences. He played exclusively his own music, which, upon reading, reveals a poverty of creativity. In his journal, George Templeton Strong considered de Meyer to be "the most explosive musical bombshell ever to erupt upon the American scene" (at least in 1845).

MARCELLE MEYER

1897–1958—France

A pupil at the Paris Conservatoire who studied with Cortot and Ricardo Viñes. Francis Poulenc, also a student of Viñes, wrote in his memoirs, *My Friends and Myself,* "The great pianist Marcelle Meyer, who was [Viñes's] most brilliant pupil, told me after a performance of *Petrouchka*: 'It was not as difficult as all that, thanks to Viñes!'" Poulenc dedicated his Cinq Impromptus to her. Meyer was responsible for premiering many works, especially of Les Six. She made a delightful recording with Milhaud of his *Scaramouche* Suite for two pianos.

ALEKSANDER MICHALOWSKI

1851–1938—Poland

He studied with Moscheles, Reinecke, and Mikuli. Michalowski played with a beautifully molded, masterful technique and a rich tone. His Chopin playing had a sentimental elegance. He was the teacher of Antoinette Szumowska and Wanda Landowska, and he composed some salon pieces, which are charming and technically inventive.

ARTURO BENEDETTI MICHELANGELI

1920–1995—Italy

Michelangeli has been thought by many to be the greatest Italian pianist to have been born in the twentieth century. In 1939 he won the International Piano Competition at Geneva, but World War II interrupted his work. After his discharge from military duty, Michelangeli quickly scored spectacular European successes, and he made his American debut with the New York Philharmonic in 1948. From the start of his public career, however, he was a quirky concertizer, prone to lightning-quick cancellations. Michelangeli's performing career was characterized by fits and starts. For many music lovers, he became a fascinating enigma. He was one of the few who could create a ticket stampede by the mere announcement of a recital. The question was: would he show up? But if he did appear, it took only a few bars to establish that this would be an unusual musical experience.

At his best, Michelangeli was one of the most refined players in history. His secrets were in coolness and restraint. His realizations of Classical masters possessed an uncanny purity. He delivered Clementi, Haydn, Mozart, Galuppi, and Scarlatti with the greatest delectability—all smooth, dainty, and rhythmically alert. They were worked at in great detail, and the pianistic finish was crystalline. He was a great colorist, too, as in his celebrated performance of Ravel's *Gaspard de la nuit,* which set new standards of technical finesse for that score. The piano became limp to Michelangeli's touch, issuing rare tonal treasures. His finger control achieved a glorious evenness, inhabiting a sphere quite above mere excellence. His performances were a merging of mechanism with music; his pedaling was the result of deep thought and the most sensitive ear.

When he played, Michelangeli seemed to be watching the proceedings with detachment. He was in his element with music that speaks objectively or that is stylistically elegant. As a programmer, he was always refreshingly unhackneyed. If the work at hand was popular, his sympathy for it ran lower. For example,

his Schumann *Carnaval* is finicky, but the *Faschingsschwank aus Wien* by the same composer is prankish and intoxicating in its brashness. I would have thought Michelangeli to be estranged from the more luscious atmosphere of Rachmaninoff's earlier concerti. His recording of the Rachmaninoff Fourth Concerto is Classical, almost prudish. The laconic Ravel G major Concerto Michelangeli played with an immaculacy which has never quite been approached, and the slow movement, with its chain of trills, is hypnotic musically.

In Beethoven, he was best when confronting the earlier works. The formal blocks of the E-flat Sonata, Op. 7, or the First Concerto are sculptured. But the Opus 111, the final sonata, seems contrived. The first movement is fine—it, too, has a solid structure—but Michelangeli did not have a feeling for the variations. He did feel, and in his own individualized way, the sensuous world of Debussy, as though he were swimming in cool water.

He seemed insecure in Chopin and reacted moodily to him. There are moments of great beauty in his Chopin performances, and the shape of his phrasing is always thoughtful. But the organic element in large works is lacking, and the interpretation of the B-flat minor Scherzo droops in the trio, while the luscious long-limbed melody of the Scherzo intimidates him. Even less successful is Michelangeli's performance of the G minor Ballade, which is a flight of oppressive eccentricity. His mazurkas are very disappointing, too. The rubato is strained, by turns inhibited and outlandish. In some, he accentuates the dance element disproportionately.

Some scores, such as the Bach-Busoni Chaconne and the Brahms *Paganini* Variations, brought forth a demonic side of Michelangeli's nature. In these, he released tension with a cold and calculated fury, and he formed his crescendi to perfection. His Bach-Busoni

Chaconne is the standard by which all others are measured. His building of the edifice becomes inexorable. Here Bach counts for little: it is Michelangeli paying homage to Busoni, his great compatriot. A parallel may be made with his famous version of the Brahms *Paganini* Variations. Brahms becomes merely the medium through which the two Italians commune, Paganini conveying to Michelangeli his dark and rarefied secrets of technique. When I listen to this performance, there is the ghostlike feeling that the piano is playing of its own accord. Such playing has an element of mystery. For Michelangeli, music was a rite to be performed, an exorcism.

Michelangeli gave far less to recording than his admirers would like. He was a perfectionist and did not easily authorize release of his recordings. No wonder that the pirated pressings of his live performances are quickly grabbed up by collectors who relish his highly original imprint. The albums should read, "This playing can only be by Arturo Benedetti Michelangeli."

KARL MIKULI
1819–1897—Poland

Had a distinguished career as pianist and teacher. He became a student of Chopin in 1844, and later made an edition of his master's works, which is still used.

SEBASTIAN BACH MILLS
1838–1898—England

Studied with Cipriani Potter and Sterndale Bennett, also with Moscheles and Liszt. He had a successful career and first played in New York in 1860. His playing was widely recognized in the United States, where he eventually made his home. In 1866 he was the pianist at the first concert at Steinway Hall in New York.

JOSÉ MIRÓ
1815–1879—Spain

The outstanding Spanish pianist of the Romantic era. Born in Cádiz, Miró studied with Eugenio Gómez in Seville. At age thirteen he moved to Paris to work with Kalkbrenner, then at the height of his celebrity as a pianist and teacher. In Paris Miró would come into close contact with Herz, Berlini, Chopin, and Döhler. By the middle of 1830, he was touring France, England, and Holland. His basic repertoire consisted of a discreet amount of the classics and Thalberg, Kalkbrenner, Döhler, Herz, and others of the virtuoso school of the day. From a review of a Madrid recital in 1842, the critic wrote of "the clarity and brilliance of his execution; the fierceness and energy he showed in the loud passages; the delicateness in the *cantabiles*; the execution . . . blended with all the fire of genius in order to amaze the spectators, who, astonished and surprised on hearing such marvelous sounds, didn't dare even to breathe so as not to miss a single note."

After great success in Portugal, Miró performed in Boston, New York, Philadelphia, and Havana, Cuba, where he taught for several years. In 1856 he took the professorship at Madrid's Conservatory, writing a piano method which became a part of the conservatory's curriculum. Like most pianists of his generation he composed grand fantasies on opera themes, such as *Norma* and *Semiramide*.

BENNO MOISEIWITSCH

1890–1963—Russia

Born in Odessa, he became a pupil of Leschetizky. When Moiseiwitsch touched his piano, the listener knew that here was a "tone poet." Rachmaninoff loved Moiseiwitsch's golden interpretations of his own music. Moiseiwitsch was primarily a lyricist, and his singing tone with its plasticity of line and colorful palette was the flowering of Leschetizky's ideal. Above all, he was relaxed, and his magnificently supple mechanism flowed with ease. He could discover delightful inner voices, and his sense of rubato was delicious.

Early in his career, like many Romantics of his day, he made "improvements" on the composers, but he later dropped most of these transgressions. His later LPs are suffused with a radiant light, and he paints lovely strokes in soft pastels. Moiseiwitsch said his favorite composer was Schumann, and his playing sang in *Carnaval* and the *Scenes of Childhood*. His best-known performances were in the Chopin repertoire, where his natural elegance and glistening virtuosity were equally at home in the Preludes, Ballades, or Waltzes. In his later years, some of the sheen of his technique disappeared and the swiftness of finger velocity slowed somewhat. His best work is contained in his many 78 discs, some of which are now on CD—for instance, the Weber *Invitation to the Dance,* dressed in Tausig's ingenious arrangement, is piano playing of vivacity, high style, and melting tone.

GERALD MOORE

1899–1987—England

He developed into one of the finest accompanists of the century, collaborating with many of the best singers of his time, such as Schwarzkopf and, later, Fischer-Dieskau. His many recordings show a deep understanding of singing and Romantic lieder literature. He wrote several books, the best known of which is *The Unashamed Accompanist.*

IVAN MORAVEC

b. 1930—Czechoslovakia

He studied with Ilona Kurz and with Michelangeli. He made a career in Europe and gave his U.S. debut in 1964. Since the 1960s, he has produced a wealth of recordings. Moravec is the finest Czech Chopin interpreter of his generation. His is a polished, aristocratic playing, harnessed to a technique of tremendous depth. His many virtues include the ability to sustain a singing line with a velvet tone and to play a pure but vibrant pianissimo. He also has the smoothest legato, and his pedaling is a marvel—he always produces exactly the sound he wants. Moravec has an abundance of temperament, and he can rise to fever pitch in the rapturous codas of the four Chopin Ballades. Not all his playing is to my taste, though. Some of the Chopin preludes bog down, becoming turgid, and Moravec—who revels in slow lyricism—may, in some nocturnes, sound too slow; the perfume becomes too heavy. In public performance he tends to fidget with phrases and loses the continuity of shape.

His Beethoven is played with plasticity. His recording of the *Pastoral* Sonata, Op. 28, is rejuvenating, a breath of sweet country air. I also admire his spacious Franck Prelude, Chorale, and Fugue; a Debussy drenched in sunlight; a Ravel *Sonatine* of exquisite grace; a warmhearted Mozart Sonata in B-flat, K. 570; and a hushed rendering of Janáček's beautiful cycle *In the Mist.*

IGNAZ MOSCHELES
1794–1870—Czechoslovakia

He studied from the age of seven with Dionys Weber in Prague; at fourteen he went to Vienna for extensive study. After 1815 he performed with great success throughout Western Europe. In 1826 he made his home in London, where he taught and played. He became one of the finest teachers of his time, commanding fees twice what Clementi had received. He taught a legion of famous musicians, including Mendelssohn, Thalberg, Louis Brassin, Sir George Henschel, Richard Hoffman, Rafael Joseffy, Sydney Smith, Max Vogrich, and many others. He left a penetrating autobiography and his music fills 142 opus numbers. In 1841 he translated Schindler's *Life of Beethoven* into English.

It is unlikely that any serious reader about music has missed the name of Moscheles. Through much of the nineteenth century, he was everywhere and he knew everyone. He was at the deathbed of Weber in 1826; he was at the sickbed of Beethoven even while preparing the piano score of *Fidelio*; he performed in private the first all-piano concerts in London in the 1830s. In Paris, he played duets with Chopin before Louis Philippe. When the revolutionary "double escapement" piano action by Sébastien Erard was ready, the piano firm first went to Moscheles for approval. When Mendelssohn founded the Leipzig Conservatory, he begged Moscheles to head the piano department. Later, Moscheles became director of the conservatory and helped make the institution the most influential German school of music during the nineteenth century.

In 1831, Moscheles took the first train in England to play a concert at Manchester. "Words," he wrote in his diary, "cannot describe the impression made on me by this steam excursion . . . and the transports I felt

Ignaz Moscheles by David Dubal

with an invention that seemed to me little short of magic." With that trip was inaugurated the modern international concert career.

Moscheles represents the zenith of the Hummel school of refined virtuosity, and had also absorbed the depth, sonority, and brilliance of Clementi and Cramer. Once when Rossini complimented him on his playing, Moscheles responded, "Whatever I am, I owe to the old master Clementi." With Kalkbrenner, Moscheles was the most famous and most respected pianist in Europe around 1820. In his youth he was called "the Prince of Pianists." He was well aware of the improvements that had given new power and flexibility to the piano, bringing it out of the drawing room into larger halls. His fame was assured when, with perfect timing, he stormed the Congress of Vienna (1815) and won princely ovations for his Variations on the *Alexander March*. The young Moscheles knew that audiences were clamoring to hear and see what their now favorite instrument could do. Moscheles could supply "bravura" with the best of them. His *Alexander* Variations were attempted by all who aspired to dazzle at the piano.

But Moscheles was a musician of lofty aims and soon tired of only pleasing the public. He wanted to educate them and play the best music, including older music, which was seldom performed. He even introduced Scarlatti on the harpsichord.

During a Scottish tour, Moscheles makes an interesting appearance in the journal of Sir Walter Scott in January 1828: "Mr. and Mrs. Moscheles were here at breakfast. She is a very pretty little Jewess; he one of the greatest performers on the pianoforte of the day." Two days later, after Moscheles's concert, Scott, who considered himself extremely unmusical, wrote:

> I liked Mr. Moscheles's playing better than I could have expected, considering my own bad ear. But perhaps I flatter myself, and think I understood it better than I did. Perhaps I have not done myself justice, and know more of music than I thought I did. But it seems to me that his variations have a more decided style of originality than those I have commonly heard. . . . Mr. Moscheles gives lessons at two guineas by the hour, and he has actually found scholars in this poor country. . . . I observe his mode of fingering is very peculiar, as he seems to me to employ the fingers of the same hand in playing the melody and managing the bass at the same time, which is surely most uncommon.

As a composer, he fulfilled himself with such admirable works as the Twenty-four Etudes, Op. 70, of 1826; the 1820 G minor Concerto, which was popular for decades; and the *Sonate mélancolique* of 1821. By 1830, with the coming to maturity of the Romantics, Moscheles's influence paled. In their youth, Schumann, Liszt, Henselt, and Chopin were all inspired by Moscheles. The older Moscheles, however, was baffled by the execution and novel figurations of these young Romantics. He was correct when in his later years he saw himself as the link between the old and modern schools of piano playing. His fine pupil Edward Dannreuther wrote, "Moscheles was distinguished by a crisp and incisive touch, clear and precise phrasing, and pronounced preference for minute accentuation. He played octaves with stiff wrists and was chary in the use of the pedals." Of course, a creative use of pedaling was one of the hallmarks of the new piano style. But Moscheles complained that "all effects now, it seems, must be produced by the feet—what is the use of people having hands?"

Grieg, who studied with him at the conservatory, wrote, "He could and did play beautifully. Specially fine were his renderings of Beethoven, whom he adored."

His Etudes were once widely used. Von Bülow considered them an important stepping stone to the playing of the Chopin Etudes, and Chopin himself always used them in his own teaching. Each of the Moscheles Etudes possesses a genuine poetic impulse, which leads directly to the Chopin Etudes. Moscheles proselytized for the best in music. In a period when mere keyboard banging was often heard, he stood as a force for moderation and good taste.

MORITZ MOSZKOWSKI
1854–1925—Germany

He studied with Kullak and proceeded to play in public beginning in 1873. He was admired for his finished, graceful playing and for his compositions, which are great audience pleasers. The best of his salon music is of the highest caliber. He had a wonderful gift for composing music that seems molded to the hand. He was a delightful melodist, and his work can sparkle with humor. Virtuosi such as Rachmaninoff, Hofmann (who studied with him), Lhévinne, Horowitz, and Bolet always found a place for him in their repertoires.

In Paris during his last years, Moszkowski was ill and beset by poverty. A concert in Carnegie Hall on 22 December 1921 was arranged for his benefit. It was a veritable treasure-house of the Golden Age of Pianism. Harold Bauer, Ossip Gabrilowitsch, Fannie Bloomfield Zeisier, Yolanda Mérö, Alexander Lambert, Rudolph Ganz, Percy Grainger, Josef Lhévinne, Ernest Schelling, Ignaz Friedman, Germaine Schnitzer, and Sigismund Stojowski all took part in a multi-piano spectacle. Among the works on the program was Schumann's *Carnaval,* with each pianist playing one section. The concert was a great success and was repeated in Philadelphia.

JOSÉ VIANNA DA MOTTA
1868–1948—Portugal

The last surviving pupil of Liszt and Portugal's most celebrated pianist. After his Lisbon debut at thirteen he went to Berlin and worked with Xaver Scharwenka. In 1885 he attended Liszt's Weimar master classes. After Liszt's death he worked with von Bülow. The next years were busy, concertizing in Russia, Europe, South America, and the United States. During World War I he became director of the Geneva Conservatory. After 1919 he returned to Portugal for the rest of his life. Busoni and Da Motta admired each other, and collaborated; one of Da Motta's best recordings is of Busoni's Fourth Elegy. Da Motta's career was many-sided and he made contributions as an editor of Liszt's music, a propagator

of neglected composers, especially Alkan. Da Motta the pianist was prodigious in the solo literature as well as in chamber ensemble, and he collaborated with Ysaye, Sarasate, and other notables. In 1927 he was the first pianist ever to perform the complete Beethoven Sonatas in cycle in Lisbon for the centenary of the composer's death. Da Motta composed in many forms, and his piano music is charming; he recorded Three Pieces from Opus 9, especially succulent is the rubato evidenced in the *Vals caprichosa,* Op. 9, No. 3. Unfortunately he made few recordings; the most important was Liszt's *Totentanz* for Piano and Orchestra when he was seventy-seven years old in 1945. His entire recorded output has been assembled by Dante Recordings. Da Motta had a great influence on Portuguese pianistic culture. His fine pupil Sequeira Costa founded the Vianna Da Motta International Piano Competition in Lisbon.

GERMAINE MOUNIER
b. 1920—France

One of her chief teachers was Magda Tagliaferro. She performed throughout Europe and Asia and was a teacher at the Paris Conservatoire from 1975 to 1987. Mounier has judged many international competitions.

WOLFGANG AMADEUS MOZART
1756–1791—Austria

The most famous and amazing child prodigy in music history. His father, Leopold, a well-known musician, author of a notable violin method, and a good composer, gave Wolfgang and his sister Maria Anna lessons in their early childhood. Both showed unusual talent, but more energy was spent on the boy, who was already composing little pieces at the age of five, as well as playing the harpsichord at sight. Mozart's infallible ear and prodigious memory were put to good use as he was exhibited on tour throughout Europe. It was an exhausting childhood. His first tour kept him away from his native Salzburg for three years. Indeed, Mozart spent nearly fourteen years of his short life on the road. The best that can be said of those years is that Mozart was kept in constant touch with the musical life of his time, and he absorbed and transformed all that came his way. Although piano playing was in its early stages, Mozart probably began changing from the harpsichord to the pianoforte in 1763, when he met J. C. Bach, the best pianist in London. Mozart was influenced by his music and playing, and when he was eleven, he transcribed sonata movements by J. C. Bach and several other composers into his first four piano concerti, K. 37, 39, 40, and 41. Mozart called them "*pasticci*" and performed them frequently.

By the age of seventeen, he preferred the piano to the harpsichord, and his Concerto No. 5 in D major, K. 175, was the finest Classical piano concerto thus far composed by anyone. This 1773 creation was to be a vehicle for his own constantly improving playing, and significantly, in an age when public performance was in its infancy, he scored it for one of his largest orchestras, using oboes, trumpets, horns, and timpani.

During the next years, he came in touch with one of the best piano makers of the day, Johann Andreas Stein, whose innovations were used by all the Viennese piano builders. A good indication of the aesthetic climate of the time can be found in a remark Stein made to Mozart, who wanted to try out a new church organ Stein had completed. The builder was "much amazed." "What? A man like you, such a great fortepianist, wants to play an instrument on which no tenderness, no expression, no *piano* and *forte* can take place, but which always goes the same?" This, of course, could also have been said about the harpsichord, which was, by 1780, losing ground to the piano.

In 1781, Mozart left a dreaded court post in Salzburg and moved to Vienna, which he called "Clavier Land." Although he had hoped for an imperial court position, he came to depend on the piano as his main source of a livelihood—teaching, and arranging subscription concerts around his own newly composed piano concerti. From 1782 to 1786, Mozart wrote no fewer than fifteen piano concerti, and from one concert he could earn nearly enough to cover his rent for a year. For each concert, Mozart paid a small fee for the hall rental, sold the subscriptions himself, engaged copyists, and hired and rehearsed the orchestra (the Vienna Philharmonic was not yet in existence). He also had to select the program, conduct the concert, and work with the solo singers. The concerts could take place only during Lent, when public concerts were permitted though the theaters were closed for plays and opera by law. Mozart's audiences were amazing in their splendor—everyone of importance in the imperial capital would arrive for his newest concerto: royalty, ambassadors, government officials, socialites, and every prominent musician, including, of course, Mozart's enemy at court, Salieri.

Mozart had recently been in a grueling piano contest with Clementi, before the Emperor Joseph II, and everyone was discussing the relative merits of the two artists. It may have been at one of these concerts that the emperor asked the eminent composer Karl Ditters von Dittersdorf if he preferred Clementi's playing to Mozart's. The composer humbly replied that "Clementi's playing is art alone. Mozart's is art and taste." Mozart, never the most generous colleague, condemned Clementi's music in a letter to his father: "As compositions, they are worthless. They contain no remarkable or striking passages except those in sixths and octaves. And I implore my sister not to practice these passages too much, so that she may not spoil her quiet, even touch and that her hand may not lose its natural lightness, flexibility and smooth rapidity."

Of his own playing, Mozart wrote: "Herr Stein sees and hears that I am more of a player than Beecke—that without making grimaces of any kind I play so expressively that, according to his own confession, no one shows off his pianoforte as well as I. That I always remain strictly in time surprises everyone. They cannot understand that the left hand should not in the least be concerned in a *tempo rubato*. When they play, the left hand always follows."

Mozart's dictum was "It should flow like oil." But his legato playing was probably not as smooth as Clementi's, and Beethoven told Czerny that Mozart still played in a clipped style. Very likely, during the 1770s and 1780s, legato was still the exception, and a detached "harpsichord" style was prevalent, especially on the pedaling systems of pianos of the period. To have a recording of Mozart's playing would answer so many questions of style, tempo, legato, ornamentation. Often, in the Concerti, Mozart only sketched what he wanted to supply in the notation of the slow movements. And how thrilled pianists would be to hear Mozart improvising the cadenzas in the Concerti, although in some, Mozart did write out cadenzas. But, as Tovey points out, "it is doubtful whether he would have regarded any of his written cadenzas to first movements as adequately representing his way of extemporizing."

At any rate, there is no indication that Mozart was displeased with the sonorous qualities of the Viennese five-octave pianos available to him and for which his piano writing was so deftly created. In the past decade or so there have been many performances of Mozart on fortepianos of his time, and they are becoming more prevalent. There is no doubt that the Piano Concerti can sound wonderful when played on a fortepiano. The voluptuous, palpitating, iron-framed piano often sounds slick when blended with Mozart's orchestra. Today's halls, however, are much larger than those of Mozart's day, and the contemporary piano will continue to be used in the Mozart Concerti, which remain the most important body of music for soloist and orchestra.

In the realm of the piano concerto, Mozart has no rival. In the nineteenth century, when played at all, he was usually treated as a frilly, Rococo doll and performed in a mechanical style which passed for Classical "good taste." By 1920, things had changed considerably, and Mozart was heard in all of his depth, passion, humor, and humanity. Artists of the caliber of Busoni, Fischer, Tovey, and Schnabel began exposing large segments of his piano music in concert. By the LP era, pianists had become all but obsessed with this luminous literature. Seldom does a month pass without a slew of Mozart releases by pianists of all persuasions. The Piano Concerti constitute one of the most miraculous chapters in the history of music and, in the context of Mozart's total work, a miracle among miracles.

Alfred Einstein wrote: "Mozart possessed a sensitiveness to sound that has remained altogether unique and was never again to be attained, and above all an entirely different sphere of emotion, at once sensuous and non-sensuous, hovering between grace and melancholy, indeed often changing color with a lightning-like abruptness."

MIECZYSLAW MÜNZ
1900–1976—Poland

Born in Krakow he was a pupil of Jerzy Lalewicz. In Berlin Münz entered the charmed circle of Busoni, and made a debut in that city performing with no less than the Liszt Concerto No. 1, the Franck Symphonic Variations, and the Brahms Concerto No. 1. After settling in the United Sates he embarked on a distinguished teaching career, combined with performing. At various times he taught at the Cincinnati Conservatory, The Curtis Institute in Philadelphia, Baltimore's Peabody Conservatory, New York's Juilliard School, and later in his career he gave classes at Gedai University in Tokyo. His impressive list of students includes Walter Hautzig, Ann Schein, Allan Feinberg, and Emanuel Ax, who worked with him for four years, saying, "He was a great stickler for good piano playing and he made me work very hard and very carefully." From 1920 on, and continuing for twenty years, he performed extensively, and was soloist with Mengelberg, de Sabato, Koussevitsky, and other headline conductors. Unfortunately little exists on recording except an Americus CD, which brings to us a sophisticated musicianship, a high-bred pianism with a formidable evenness in passagework. The reading of Dohnányi's Coppelia Waltz is delightful in its feathery fingerwork and elegant style. Included on the disc is an austere, reserved D minor Mozart Concerto. In mid-life, Munz had a hand ailment which prohibited performance in public.

OLLI MUSTONEN
b. 1967—Finland

In Helsinki he studied piano with Ralf Gothóni and Eero Heinonen and composition with Einojuhani Rautavaara. Mustonen possesses a well-developed technique, and is fiercely independent in his conceptions. His Shostakovich has irony, his Prokofiev brilliance, and his Beethoven is highly original and not to everyone's taste.

N

ISTVÁN NÁDAS
1922–1998—Hungary

A student of Béla Bartók, he also studied composition with Zoltán Kodály. A great pianist, especially in works that exhibit a monumental style. He played many times over and in various cities the complete Beethoven sonatas and Bach's *Well-Tempered Clavier.*

Nádas had a questing musical mind and an original way with whatever he touched. There is a feeling of the austere in his conceptions, and a tone of deep nobility infuses his best work.

Nádas most easily accommodates the German Classic tradition. The Beethoven Piano Concerti, the Brahms B-flat Concerto, the Beethoven *Hammerklavier,* and the *Goldberg* Variations are favorites of his. His recording of Schubert's *Wanderer* Fantasy is grand in scope, and his performances of Schubert's A major Sonata, Opus posthumous, and the Schumann Fantasy are remarkable in their synthetic power.

HIROKO NAKAMURA
b. 1944—Japan

A renowned Japanese pianist, at the Juilliard School in New York she worked with Rosina Lhévinne. In 1965, at the Seventh International Chopin Competition at Warsaw she placed fourth, with Argerich, Moreira-Lima, and Marta Sosinska preceding her. Her career prospered in Japan, and Nakamura became the guiding force of the Hamamatsu International Piano Competition.

ALEXEI NASEDKIN
b. 1942—USSR

He worked with Heinrich Neuhaus and won several prizes in competitions. Perhaps he is best known for his exceptionally lyrical Schubert playing. He has recorded some little-played Tchaikovsky, and in such pieces as *Rêverie,* Op. 8, and the *Valse-caprice,* Op. 4, he plays with a fine sense of rubato, grace, and tonal variety.

YVES NAT
1890–1956—France

One of the most distinguished French pianists of the first half of the twentieth century. His earlier studies were in his native town of Béziers, where he made his first public appearance at age seven. Supposedly, by eleven he knew the Forty-eight Preludes and Fugues of Bach from memory. Soon Nat was encouraged by Saint-Saëns and Fauré and in 1907 he studied at the Paris Conservatoire in Diémer's celebrated class. Although he was plagued by nerves, a major career emerged. In 1911 he performed in America. The pianist said,

"Touring is very difficult; you wear your arms down to stumps. You walk on your knees."

Nat made his first recording in 1929 which included one of his own works, *Pour un petit moujik*. Schumann was one of his favorite masters, and he recorded his *Kinderscenen* Concerto and the *Faschingsschwank aus Wein*. In 1943 he recorded the Franck *Symphonic Variations*; this ended his career on recordings until 1952.

From 1933 he left the concert stage, accepting a post as professor of piano at the Paris Conservatoire, where he continued teaching until his death. Many distinguished pianists worked with him: Jörg Demus, Jean-Bernard Pommier, Pierre Sancan, and Yuri Boukoff are only a few. Most of them considered him an inspiring teacher although he had no interest in the traditional mechanics of playing. He said, "Play with ten thousand fingers, with the whole body."

In 1953, after a twenty-year hiatus, he triumphantly returned to the concert stage at the Théâtre des Champs-Élysées. It was a major public event. From 1950 he began to again record; stimulated by the long-playing recording he worked prodigiously, becoming the first French pianist to record Beethoven's thirty-two Sonatas. He felt, "Beethoven's music is so human, so sanctifying, music that loves you." Among these discs are many treasurable moments which may be heard on eight CDs on EMI. It was a heady period and from 1952 to 1956 he recorded a multitude of music besides Beethoven, especially a great deal of Brahms.

Charles Timbrell in his book, *French Pianism*, writes: "That he remained a virtuoso and first-class musician to the end is clear from his recording of Brahms's *Variations and Fugue on a Theme by Handel*, one of the most striking versions ever made. He meets the work head-on, and brings to it all the requisite color, fire, intellectual rigor, musical continuity, and dexterity."

Nat composed throughout his career. There are a Sonatina for Piano, Preludes, and a Piano Concerto of more than half an hour, a work beautifully designed in its orchestral writing and its deftly skilled pianism. He was soloist at the premiere in 1954, which terminated his public career.

CHARLES NEATE
1784–1877—England

He studied with John Field, played at Covent Garden at his debut in 1800, and was a founder of the Philharmonic Society of London in 1813. He was one of the first in England to appreciate the extent of Beethoven's genius, and traveled to Vienna, where he became friends with the great composer. Later, Neate introduced Beethoven's Concerti Nos. 1 and 5 to English audiences.

HEINRICH NEUHAUS
1888–1964—Russia

Heinrich Neuhaus studied with Blumenfeld and Michalowski in Russia and with Godowsky in Vienna. He taught at the Kiev Conservatory and later at the Moscow Conservatory. He was the cousin of Szymanowski and the nephew of Blumenfeld.

Neuhaus became one of the most famous teachers of the century; his classes at the Moscow Conservatory were crowded with students hoping to gain inspiration. He taught some of the outstanding pianists of Russia, including Gilels and Richter, both of whom greatly acknowledged their debt to him. His warmth and great teaching instincts are evidenced in his book, *The Art of Piano Playing*.

Neuhaus recorded exquisite and intimate

performances of Chopin mazurkas; a conservative but pure reading of the Chopin E minor Concerto, a specialty of his; and the Scriabin Concerto, which is the quintessence of that composer's early music and is played by Neuhaus with perfection of style.

STANISLAV NEUHAUS
1927–1980—USSR

He studied with his father and was a hardier pianist than Heinrich, capable of full-bodied playing but lacking a restrained, delicate sensibility. His recordings of Scriabin, such as the Fourth Sonata, bring out the glittering aspects of the Russian's piano writing. In Chopin, Stanislav Neuhaus achieved a special urgency in the F minor Ballade and *Polonaise-fantaisie*. James Methuen-Campbell wrote, "He had the gadfly sensitivity of an Argerich, and was ideal in the more rhapsodic works, such as the Barcarolle."

EDMUND NEUPERT
1842–1888—Norway

A student of Kullak. From all accounts, he was a marvelous virtuoso. Grieg entrusted him with the premiere of his A minor Concerto in Copenhagen. He left a considerable amount of attractive piano music.

ELLY NEY
1882–1968—Germany

She had a long and notable career, and was giving all-Beethoven recitals only weeks before her death. Like many others, Vienna and Leschetizky attracted her and in Vienna she had lessons with Emil von Sauer as well.

Ney firmly established a European reputation, also touring the United Sates in the early 1920s. Her staples were the German classics, though she occasionally brought Chopin to the stage, and in London performed the Tchaikovsky Concerto, a work that I doubt she cared much for, judging from what appears to be a rather lugubrious temperament. There is an early recording of the Strauss *Burleske* conducted by Willem van Hoogstraten (once, her husband); she gives a less than lighthearted performance, only coming to the quick when a Brahmsian thickness is required. Technically she was ill-prepared for this rendition. Another recording of the earlier 1930s with Hoogstraten is of the very difficult Fifteenth Mozart Concerto, K. 450. Here she is more in her element, but a review by Irving Kolodin says, "Ney plays with firmness and precision but also with a hard tonal quality." Pearl's issuing of her Brahms B-flat Concerto with the Berlin Philharmonic under Max Fiedler from 1939 does the artist far more credit. It's big in conception, but with stretches that lumber along; it's a cerebral Brahms ruminating on deep thoughts, with moments of imagination that a listener will not forget. The same recording offers an ultra-serious *Wanderer* Fantasy of Schubert, with a definite quality that makes it memorable.

In 1955 at Wigmore Hall the writer Alan Vicat heard her in an all-Beethoven program and wrote: "An apparently frail old lady in a long dark dress and matching bolero appeared on the platform and seated herself at the piano, but—at the opening of the Beethoven *Pathétique*—this impression of frailty proved to be completely erroneous! After this she presented Op. 111, the *Appassionata,* and Op. 110 Sonata—she added the Scherzo from Op. 31, No. 3 and the Rondo á capriccio as encores; a memorable and incredible program for a woman her age."

LEONID NIKOLAEV

1878–1942—Russia

He was a student of Safonov, a fine pianist and an honored teacher. Among his pupils at the St. Petersburg Conservatory were Shostakovich, Maria Yudina, Vladimir Sofronitsky, and Nadia Reisenberg, who wrote, "Almost everything I know about the physical side of piano-playing I owe to Nikolaev's extremely detailed schooling. He gave me that which has served me in all the years since."

TATIANA NIKOLAYEVA

1924–1993—USSR

A pupil of Goldenweiser at the Moscow Conservatory, she had a major career in the Soviet Union. Nikolayeva played many premieres, including the Twenty-four Preludes and Fugues of Shostakovich, which are dedicated to her and which she recorded brilliantly. She died in San Francisco while playing a concert devoted to these works.

JOAQUÍN NIN

1879–1949—Cuba

An influential pianist, teacher, and composer. In 1902 in Paris he studied with Moszkowski. Nin performed extensively throughout Europe and South America, often promoting old Spanish music. Arthur Rubinstein in his memoirs notes his "beautiful head of hair. . . . When I asked him about his program for his forthcoming recitals he said, 'I'm playing composers of the pre-Bach period, as well as some Spanish music by Padre Soler and Albéniz.' I

exclaimed joyfully, 'Iberia.' His face took on a disapproving expression. 'Mateo Albéniz.' I had to admit shamefully that I never heard of his namesake." As an editor, Nin compiled in two volumes *33 Piano Sonatas by Old Spanish Composers*, which was published in 1925.

The composer Nin should not be neglected. His work is pianistic, Spanish in idiom, with flamenco guitar effects and rhetorical flourishes. Especially important is *Mensaje á Debussy* (1929), which he called "a symphonic sketch"; a long, stylized *Tempo di Habanera* is a masterful work which should be explored. Nicholas Unwin has recorded Nin on the Centaur label.

JOAQUÍN NIN-CULMELL

1908–2004—Germany

The son of Joaquín Nin, he studied with his father and with Dukas and Falla. Nin-Culmell is a brilliant pianist and a composer whose best-known works are his Tonadas, 48 small pieces cast in a colorful Spanish idiom characterizing dances and folk material of various areas of Spain.

BARBARA NISSMAN

b. 1945—United States

A pianist of remarkable qualities, which include a large technique, color, stamina, and high-relief projection of Romantic concertos which she has performed with Muti, Slatkin, Skrowaczewski, and others worldwide. She has recorded the complete piano music of Ginastera in a rhapsodic style. Ginastera's last work, Third Piano Sonata, is dedicated to her.

In 1989 Nissman became the first pianist

to perform the ten Piano Sonatas of Prokofiev in recital, in New York and London. The Ginastera and Prokofiev recordings can be heard on Pierion CDs; Nissman has a large repertoire which include the Liszt Sonata, Beethoven's *Waldstein* Sonata, Schumann's Fantasy, the Brahms Second Concerto, Scriabin's Fifth Sonata, all works in which her passionate temperament finds full scope. Her recent book *Bartók and the Piano: A Performer's View*, includes her CD of her playing Bartók, and offers many insights.

MINORU NOJIMA

b. 1946—Japan

One of the best-known Japanese pianists of his generation. In 1969 he took the second prize at the Van Cliburn Competition. Nojima has a fantastic facility and musters up a good deal of fire in his performances.

GUIOMAR NOVAES

1896–1979—Brazil

She had piano lessons from Luigi Chiafarelli until she was fourteen, when she went to Paris. Soon after, she entered a competition for foreign students to attend the Paris Conservatoire. She beat out more than two hundred applicants with her playing of Schumann's *Carnaval* and the Chopin A-flat Ballade, among other pieces. The jury included no less than Fauré, Debussy, Moszkowski, and Isidor Philipp, and all were unanimously agreed that Novaes had a musicality of rare beauty. She proceeded to study with Philipp, who gently guided her persuasive individuality. At the age of twenty, in 1916, she arrived in New York and took the town by storm. After her fourth New York recital, she was heralded as "one of the seven wonders of the musical world." W. J. Henderson of the *New York Sun* wrote, "In the range of tonal beauties and immense vitality, only Paderewski or Hofmann could have equaled her." The inimitable phrasemaker James Huneker, with poetic and geographical license, pronounced her "the Paderewska of the Pampas." Another New York critic, the eminent Henry T. Finck, compared her to the great singers of the time. "Her tone," he wrote, "has the limpid purity and beauty that the world adores in voices like Patti's or Sembrich's or Caruso's; in runs these tones are like strings of perfect pearls."

Novaes's playing was first and always personalized. She delighted in details, leaving one wondering why others never saw or savored them. Novaes, although trained at the end of a self-indulgent era, was in her way a quite scrupulous musician. Even at capricious moments, she had that marvelous and indispensable trait of a great interpreter—the power to convince. She possessed a fabulous pianistic flexibility; her art was a compendium of the best Romantic characteristics. The terms *eccentric* or *idiosyncratic* never applied to her. The term *a natural* did. She was meant for piano playing; her hands belonged on the keyboard. Her playing, at its best, was as effortless as a bird in flight. She once said, "Piano playing for some is drudgery, for me it is the greatest joy," but she was also a pianist of unusual discipline. The pianist Allen Tanner told me that he overheard her, even after sixty-five years of playing the *Waldstein* of Beethoven, practicing it slowly and scrupulously with the metronome ruthlessly beating.

Novaes was not a monumental musician, and she never played works not suited to her elastic temperament. She was divine in the Chopin F minor Concerto, Schumann's A minor, and Beethoven's Fourth. She played a large body of Schumann, and her *Carnaval* is fragrant with youth and ardor. Her recording of *Papillons* is another of the highlights of her Schumann playing. In little pieces like *The Prophet Bird,* she could make her listeners shiver. Her sense of nuance was very keen. In Beethoven she was stricter and more conventional, but she could "storm" in the first movement of Opus 111, and her readings of the *Moonlight* and *Les Adieux* were warm, though forgettable. She played very fine Debussy Preludes—not a French Debussy, but one that sounded rather Slavic somehow.

In whatever she touched there was a feeling of intimacy, and it was Chopin she touched most. A Novaes recital without Chopin would not have been tolerated by her large public. She was grand and original in the *Funeral March* Sonata. Her renderings of the Third Scherzo, the Second Impromptu, and the Fourth Ballade were alluring. In the Fourth Ballade, there seemed to be little planning for so large a composition, but her ravishing rubato carries the day. For this admirer, her Chopin B minor Sonata was heavenly; such imagination, poetry, velvety tone, command of nuance, and subtlety of rhythm are seldom encountered. Her recording of this is surely one of the best efforts in a recorded output that is dreadfully uneven. In later life, she made a series of records that are not always characteristic of her playing. Sometimes she is rough-edged and sloppy, as in the Chopin Etudes, and the Preludes are merely dull, as are many nocturnes. She was not for the commercial world; she chose only what suited her best for public demonstration.

Still, she worked hard in her later years, and there are many discs to admire, from her Chopin mazurkas and Debussy preludes to her Mendelssohn recording of a dozen or so *Songs without Words.* Isidor Philipp had told her these last pieces were unduly neglected. Listen to her loving and tender playing of the beautiful *Duetto,* the daintiness of the usually simpering *Spring Song,* the warmth and passion of *May Breezes*; hear her as she trips the light fantastic in the *Spinning Song.*

But records could never yield the totality of Novaes's art; her spontaneous and instinctive music-making needed the immediacy of an audience. Her last New York recital, in 1967 at Avery Fisher Hall, was packed. An aristocratic-looking woman, with a nonchalant dignity, she was doing her job, as she had since childhood. The program contained her old standbys—the *Waldstein* of Beethoven, the *Funeral March* Sonata of Chopin. But what I will never forget was her last encore, the very long and ridiculously awful musically—but wondrously effective technically—Fantasy on the Brazilian National Hymn by Gottschalk. She was spellbinding in her bravura. When in the mood, the great Brazilian virtuosa could project the grand manner with a fascinating flair which brought the entire house, screaming, to its feet.

JAN NOVOTNÝ
b. 1935—Czechoslovakia

He studied in Prague and teaches at the Prague Conservatory. Novotný has played in Europe, South America, and the Far East. His recordings of Smetana are lively and technically solid.

JOSEF NOWAKOWSKI
1800–1865—Poland

A pianist who studied at the Warsaw Conservatory with Josef Elsner, Chopin's composition teacher. Nowakowski performed a great deal in Europe, taught at the Warsaw Conservatory, and wrote a much used piano method. Works such as a Grand Polonaise, Op. 11, are Polish in spirit. His Twelve Grand Etudes are dedicated to Chopin.

ERVIN NYIREGYHÁZI

1903–1987—Hungary

Nyiregyházi was a child prodigy who studied with Dohnányi and Lamond. He had a considerable career until the middle 1920s. During the next decades, he lived and drank, and he married at least nine times. He seldom touched a piano until 1973, when his playing—touted as the great link to the Romantic era—caused an uproar wherever he was heard. Nyiregyházi was heatedly discussed, made several records with a few remarkable moments, and dropped out of sight again, into the oblivion he obviously preferred. There is little doubt that when he was not being musically eccentric, his talent was compelling in sound and intensity.

O

LEV OBORIN
1907–1974—Russia

He studied with Igumnov at the Moscow Conservatory. Oborin was the first winner of the Chopin Competition in Warsaw in 1927. He gave the premiere of the Khachaturian Concerto, which was dedicated to him. He was the teacher of Ashkenazy at the Moscow Conservatory. His performances were square and solid.

JOHN O'CONOR
b. 1947—Ireland

In 1973 he won the International Beethoven Competition in Vienna, and soon after took first prize at the Bösendorfer Competition. He has recorded extensively, including nine discs of Beethoven's piano music, which brought him worldwide notice. His Beethoven is deeply felt. O'Conor's recordings of John Field's Four Sonatas and Nocturnes have a delicate early Romantic charm. O'Conor is a familiar figure on television and radio in Ireland and has helped establish the GPA Dublin International Competition.

JOHN OGDON
1937–1989—England

After studies at the Royal Manchester College of Music, he worked with Denis Matthews and Egon Petri. In 1962 he tied with Ashkenazy at the International Tchaikovsky Competition in Moscow. Ogdon also composed, and recorded his own piano concerto—a splashy, eclectic piece of virtuosity.

Ogdon was a formidable talent of great power; he could play with elephantine strength. He was attracted by works that demanded endurance. He could toss off a program that included the twelve Liszt *Transcendental Etudes,* followed by smaller pieces and concluding with the Liszt Sonata. His propensity for the grandiose led him to such compositions as Ronald Stevenson's eighty-minute *Passacaglia on D S C H* and Messiaen's two-hour-long *Vingt Regards sur l'Enfant Jésus,* or the Alkan Sonata and the colossal Busoni Concerto.

At his best, Ogdon played in a lusty manner, though his stage playing was generally more representative of his powers than his recordings, which tended to be a bit raggedy. He consistently sought out important scores, such as the concertos of Cyril Scott, Michael Tippett, Peter Mennin, and Malcolm Williamson. His disc of Nielsen's piano music, especially the great Piano Suite dedicated to Schnabel, has an austere beauty.

His wife, the pianist Brenda Lucas, wrote a biography of Ogdon, entitled *Virtuoso*, which details his tragic life.

ADÉLE AUS DER OHE
1864–1937—Germany

A student of Kullak and Liszt. She pursued a successful concert career and also composed. She played the Tchaikovsky Piano Concerto No. 1 at the Carnegie Hall inaugural concerts in 1891, with Tchaikovsky conducting. The composer loved her performance; however, she refused to accept any applause for herself.

GARRICK OHLSSON
b. 1948—United States

A brilliant and exuberant pianist. He studied with Sascha Gorodnitzki and Rosina Lhévinne at the Juilliard School. In 1966 he won the Busoni Competition, and soon after, he took the first prize at the Montreal International Competition. In 1970 he became the first American to win the Chopin Competition. Ohlsson is thus assumed to be a prime Chopinist and, in fact, his Chopin discs are worth hearing, especially a spacious and free-wheeling E minor Concerto. In the nocturnes we find a pretty Chopin, slightly dandified. His recordings of the Polonaises are strong but without any internal passion. In Liszt's *Funérailles* and *Mephisto Waltz* Ohlsson displays a large style, with little feeling of urgency. In the Brahms Concerti, especially the D minor, he is convincing and at ease. His Brahms *Paganini* Variations is played with evident pleasure and a fine-tuned tech-

nique. There is a Rachmaninoff transcription album which shows him at his best—exuberant and technically light and airy in such difficult pieces as the Scherzo from Mendelssohn's *A Midsummer Night's Dream*. Recently, he gave a fabulous performance of the Busoni Concerto, a blockbuster of a score, built for the extreme punishment a modern piano is required to withstand. He also had brilliant success in performing all of Chopin's works in six recitals at New York's Lincoln Center.

URSULA OPPENS
b. 1944—United States

She studied with Rosina Lhévinne at Juilliard. Since winning the Busoni Competition in 1969, Oppens has toured in America and Europe, becoming best known for deft reading of contemporary scores. She gave the premiere of Rzewski's effective and huge set of variations, *The People United Will Never Be Defeated*.

NICOLAS ORLOV
1892–1964—Russia

He studied with Igumnov at the Moscow Conservatory and had a large European career. His best playing was in the Romantics.

RAFAEL OROZCO
b. 1946—Spain

He studied with José Cubiles in Madrid, and later received some lessons from Alexis Weissenberg. Orozco was the victor at the 1966 Leeds Competition. His recording of the

Chopin Preludes is expressive and technically excellent. His Third Rachmaninoff Concerto shows a genuine identification with the idiom.

CRISTINA ORTIZ
b. 1950—Brazil

Studied in Paris with Magda Tagliaferro, and later with Rudolf Serkin. In 1969 she was the winner of the Van Cliburn Competition, and has since appeared throughout the world. She plays with sparkle and graciousness.

GEORGE A. OSBORNE
1806–1893—Ireland

In Paris he studied with Kalkbrenner and became a good friend of Chopin. Osborne held his own as a virtuoso in the glittering Paris of the 1830s. In 1843 he moved to London, where he became a fixture of the city's musical life. His well-written drawing-room pieces were popular. The best known of them is *La Pluie des perles,* Op. 61.

CÉCILE OUSSET
b. 1936—France

She studied with Marcel Ciampi and won various prizes before embarking on a concert career. Ousset's recordings show a remarkable finger technique. Her Chopin has some graceful playing mixed with glibness. She is best in such scores as Saint-Saëns's *Allegro appassionato,* where her inherent dryness and nimbleness are heard to advantage.

P

LOUIS PABST

1846–1903—Germany

The brother of Paul Pabst, Louis Pabst had an important career as a teacher and founded the Melbourne Academy of Music in Australia, where he taught the young Percy Grainger. In Russia, he was the teacher of Tina Lerner, Sergei Liapunov, Alexander Goldenweiser, and many others.

PAUL PABST

1854–1897—Germany

Paul Pabst was by all accounts a brilliant pianist, a pupil of Liszt, and the teacher of Konstantin Igumnov at the Moscow Conservatory. He wrote beautifully for the instrument, and his transcriptions especially are admirable. A very elaborate one on Tchaikovsky's opera *Eugene Onegin* has always attracted some pianists with the requisite virtuosity to do justice to it. Cherkassky performed it with thrilling virtuosity. Maurice Hinson writes of the Piano Concerto in E-flat, Op. 82, "a sizzling piano part (especially in the finale) gobbles up the keyboard. Every range of the instrument is brought into play, and a rip-roaring good time (à la Russe) is had by all."

VLADIMIR DE PACHMANN

1848–1933—Russia

He was mostly self-taught until he went to Vienna, at eighteen, to study with Joseph Dachs. Soon after, in 1869, he made a debut in his native Odessa, and continued to perform until he heard Carl Tausig, whose playing drove him into seclusion, where he worked with untiring fortitude. He emerged again in 1882 and developed a huge career. De Pachmann was among the half dozen most famous pianists at the turn of the century. He was born one year before Chopin died, and he was the earliest-born pianist to have his fame substantially enhanced by a large number of recordings. His career was almost as successful in the United States as it was in Europe.

At his peak, from the 1880s until around 1905, de Pachmann was an elegant stylist, skimming over the keys, light as air. In Chopin, he played with an ethereal pianissimo, which he felt represented what Chopin's playing would have been like. James Huneker wrote: "It was all miniature, without passion or pathos or the grand manner, but in its genre his playing was perfection, the polished perfection of an intricately carved ornament. . . . De Pachmann played certain sides of Chopin incomparably, capriciously, even perversely. . . . If in the mood, a recital by him was something unforgettable."

Later, Huneker dubbed him the "Pianissimist"

and also the "Chopinzee." De Pachmann had a perverse streak which often prevailed, and as the years went by, his recitals became a combination of eccentric and bizarre rhythmic aberrations, moments of inspiration, and all sorts of public antics, which audiences loved but which did him harm among his colleagues.

On 18 February 1906, Charles Griffes, the American composer studying in Germany, heard de Pachmann and wrote: "Some of the things he played absolutely perfectly, according to my taste, and then others I didn't like a bit. . . . When he first came out and sat down, he talked first of all to the piano a while and made all sorts of motions to the effect that the stool didn't suit him. Then he got up and went off, and some men came on and pretended to do something to the stool, and he finally began. It is too disgusting and unartistic, but the audience is still more disgusting. They behave themselves as if in a circus, and the more ridiculous de Pachmann is the more they like it."

The writer Arthur Symons had long been intoxicated with de Pachmann's playing, the pianist being the inspiration for Symons's story "Christian Trevalga." In a letter to a friend, Symons described a 1918 de Pachmann recital: "He began in a most uneasy manner—then seemed to say, 'I won't play the piano.' Put his hands in his pockets and goes back into the artist's room. He returns—plays Mozart divinely—Chopin as he always did. In one word: absolute perfection of this man of an abnormal and inhuman genius."

Sir Landon Ronald said to Rachmaninoff, who had somehow never heard him, "You ought to hear him once, because he is different from anyone else in the world." But the stern Rachmaninoff was by no means amused by de Pachmann's clownish persona. The connoisseur must sift through his recordings, but the search is fascinating, for de Pachmann had a flair, a devilish humor—as in his own ending for Chopin's celebrated *Butterfly* Etude—but there was also a deeply poetic nature, a rarefied talent.

De Pachmann had the kind of mercurial temperament that has been largely eradicated in present-day piano playing. He took chances, and often they are musically miscalculated. Nevertheless, he was a fabulous craftsman, capable of playing the Chopin-Godowsky etude paraphrases. Although his best playing came before the birth of recording, his recorded output shows a finely tuned pianist who in public at times could lose his artistic equipoise.

The pianist George Copeland wrote: "De Pachmann played Chopin more beautifully than anybody ever played anything. . . . I have always felt it was the greatest piano-playing I have ever listened to, because his tone quality and the iridescence of his tone, is beyond anything I have ever heard."

IGNACY JAN PADEREWSKI
1860–1941—Poland

In his youth, he taught at the Warsaw Conservatory, but played very little in public. In his twenty-fourth year, he decided to become a concert pianist, and he went to work with the famous Leschetizky, who tried to discourage him because, although he was a good pianist, Paderewski lacked repertoire and a virtuoso technique. But nothing could dissuade him from his goal, and he toiled relentlessly at the piano. He made his debut in Vienna three years after his first lesson with Leschetizky, appearing at a concert with the famous soprano Pauline Lucca—and he was a sensation. From that moment forward, Paderewski was to become the most fabled pianist of his epoch, one of the greatest performing artists ever, as well as the biggest box-office attraction in the history of the piano. To this day, no pianist has played live before more people than Paderewski.

From his first appearances in America in 1891, he was idolized, lovingly called "Paderooski." If the town had a piano, Paderewski, traveling in his private railroad car, would get there. As Liszt had broadened the concert life of Europe, it was "Paddy" who opened the doors to the large American public wanting "culture." Year after year people traveled for hundreds of miles to hear him. His arrival in even a small town sparked celebrations, mayors' speeches, brass bands in renditions of his Minuet in G. He played tirelessly and constantly, his huge programs often lasting up to three hours. Once, in a very small town, he played with a painful finger injury. Asked why he didn't cancel, Paderewski bluntly answered, "I may never come this way again. I couldn't disappoint them."

Paderewski's looks greatly contributed to his aura. In Australia, the young violinist Daisy Kennedy wrote, "This is the most poetic looking pianist I am ever likely to see." He possessed a Swinburnian beauty, with a halo of abundant auburn hair which crowned a presence that is exquisitely captured in Sir Edward Burne-Jones's silverpoint drawing of the pianist. He was the poet-pianist incarnate, the personification of the Pre-Raphaelite image of beauty. Never had there been a more glorious stage presence. He bewitched his audiences with his golden sound and his languorous rubato.

In the 1890s, he was accused of piano pounding, and his fortissimos were considered shattering and often ugly. "It is not his fault," said Henry T. Finck, the important New York critic, "but the fault of his instrument. No piano has ever been built, or ever will be built, which can be converted into the instrument Paderewski demands." During his early period, Paderewski produced, in Finck's words, "tidal waves of sound, cyclonic climaxes." Because of his popularity during those years, he was forced to play in auditoriums far larger than those in which his colleagues were accustomed to performing. During his best years, from 1890

Ignacy Jan Paderewski by David Dubal

through 1905, Paderewski possessed a seminal strength which he did not always channel. This, along with an inordinate desire to please the public, produced the banging effects. Most often, however, his playing was lauded.

Perhaps this period was best summed up by the critic Richard Aldrich: "He touched the deepest and tenderest feelings and tugged irresistibly at the heart-strings of a whole people. He seemed to speak a new language in music; he raised its poetry, its magic, its mystery, its romantic eloquence, to a higher power than his listeners had known. There was a beauty of line as well as of color and atmosphere, a poignance of phrase, a quality of tone, a lyrical accent such, so it seemed, as to make of his playing something never till then quite divined."

By 1910, the endless rounds of touring made piano playing a burden for Paderewski, but he had formed and become dependent on a regal lifestyle, and only through performing was it possible for him to maintain it. During the early 1900s, though, he began to fulfill himself through composition, and he spent long periods of time on a Piano Sonata in E-flat minor, a massive opera, *Manru,* and a Mahler-sized Symphony in B minor, as well as other works, including a fine set of Variations and Fugue, Op. 23. But composing, too, was not enough for such a temperament, and he needed one great outlet to fulfill his destiny of Artist as Romantic Hero. From his earliest years, Paderewski had been a passionate patriot. He yearned for a free Poland. His Romantic patriotism was further inflamed by the failure of the Western European nations to understand Poland's plight. He had become a symbol to the throngs of Poles flocking to his concerts throughout the United States, and soon Paderewski perfected his oratory in ardent patriotic speeches. When the Great War broke out, Paderewski helped organize an army of twenty-two thousand Poles, who were trained in Canada and who would fight with the Allies. He spent his entire personal fortune on the Polish cause and became the very spirit of his oppressed homeland. He achieved an extraordinary degree of world prestige. He was greeted with awe wherever he went. Wilson, Clemenceau, and Lloyd George admired his diplomatic powers. It was Paderewski who signed for his nation in the Versailles Conference, and his influence there was great in the organizing of a free Poland. After the war, he triumphantly became the first premier of Poland.

The strain of post–World War I politics became too brutal for him, however, and after an assassination attempt, he stepped down from office. He was now more than a musician: he was a world leader, a spiritual force, and no man ever played his part with greater nobility.

Paderewski returned to the piano after years of neglect. The piano had always been a monumental struggle for him. His mechanism was not a natural one, and he worked pitiably to achieve what he wanted. His playing was long past its glory; far greater techni-

cians, among them Hofmann, Rachmaninoff, Friedman, Backhaus, and Godowsky, were at their peak, and soon the young Horowitz would be competing for his market. But the crowds kept coming. Paderewski remained, in the words of Marguerite Long, "the sovereign of the piano . . . everything in his makeup, as in his art, was noble and grand." He played through the 1920s and 1930s; in 1936 he acted and played in a film, *Moonlight Sonata,* which presented the first successful recording of the piano's sound on the screen.

Old and frail, Paderewski was still playing the piano when again catastrophe befell his nation in 1939. Everything he earned was poured into helping Poland during World War II, until his death in 1941. The funeral at St. Patrick's Cathedral was attended by thousands. President Roosevelt ordered special burial at Arlington National Cemetery.

Paderewski the pianist lived in an age when individuality was prized; it was also musically an era of self-indulgence, when the performer was king. Most audiences were more concerned with personality than with great music. Lighter pieces by the great composers were often preferable to the difficult-to-digest works. It was easy for an artist simply to stop listening to himself when the majority in the audience wanted the shallow, cheap thrill and charm at any cost. At his worst, Paderewski was almost as self-indulgent as de Pachmann, and his colleagues were often scathing in their comments. "Paderewski," a fellow pianist muttered, "did everything well except play the piano."

After 1910, his art painfully declined; he became stylistically artificial and insular. His interpretations were often marred by mannerisms, and by one in particular—not playing the hands together. However, many still heard the poetry that was always somewhere apparent. Pearl Records has issued five volumes of his recorded art. (He began recording in 1911, at the age of fifty-one, and was to the early days of piano performance on record what

Caruso was to the vocal world.) Listening now to the many recordings he made, one can hear his subtle musicality in many melting phrases of sheer beauty, in small pieces by Schumann, for instance, such as *Warum?* and *Des Abends.* He was not the technical weakling his detractors liked to believe. One has only to listen to his Liszt F minor Concert Etude to hear his deft fingerwork. And there is always a quality of heroism in his Chopin. The *Revolutionary* Etude was more to him than a turbulent "study" for the left hand; it meant faith in humanity. Paderewski had been called "the heart of Poland," and this quality comes through clearly on the ancient recording.

KUN WOO PAIK
b. 1946—Korea

Paik worked with Rosina Lhévinne at the Juilliard School and with Ilona Kabos in London. Paik is a gifted pianist with a brilliant technique which can be heard on his many discs. He has recorded the Ravel Piano Concerti, the complete Piano Concerti of Prokofiev, and the two Rachmaninoff Piano Sonatas. However, Paik's most interesting recording is a Liszt album on which one can hear a riveting performance of Liszt's Fantasia and Fugue on the Name B-A-C-H, a brilliant *Mephisto Waltz,* and an extraordinarily distended *Bénédiction de Dieu dans la solitude,* filled with huge pauses and an impressive command of silence.

SELIM PALMGREN
1878–1951—Finland

A gifted pianist who studied with Henrik

Melcer, Conrad Ansorge, and Busoni. Palmgren toured extensively, often performing some of his own music, which includes five Piano Concertos; No. 2, *The River,* was the most widely recognized. He is at his best in short piano pieces, distinguished often by refined writing. His best-known short piece is the impressionist *May Night.*

MARIA THERESA PARADIS
1759–1824—Austria

She was blind from childhood. Paradis was an early pianist who attained considerable success. Mozart composed his B-flat Concerto, K. 456, for her, and she was heard in France and England. She composed a great deal.

JON KIMURA PARKER
b. 1962—Canada

At the age of five, he appeared with the Vancouver Youth Orchestra, and in 1984 he was the winner of the Leeds International Competition. Parker has sustained a busy career since that victory. He is most impressive in such blockbuster concertos as the Rachmaninoff Third and Prokofiev Third, which he plays with powerful technique and a huge sound.

LEE PATTISON
1890–1966—United States

He studied with Schnabel, played and taught,

and was best known for his duo-piano work with Guy Maier. John Browning studied with him.

ERNST PAUER

1826–1905—Austria

An important pianist who studied with Mozart's son, Franz Xaver Mozart (1791–1844). He made a reputation in London, where he taught at the Royal Academy of Music. He gave some of the first historical recitals and arranged a great many Classical symphonies for four hands. A. J. Hipkins wrote, "As a pianist, his style was distinguished by breadth and nobility of tone, and by a sentiment in which seriousness of thought was blended with profound respect for the intention of the composer."

MAX PAUER

1866–1945—England

He studied with his father and developed into a fine artist, making many editions of the music of Schumann and Beethoven.

JOSEF PEMBAUR

1875–1950—Germany

A pupil of Alfred Reisenauer. A well-known pianist, he established a career on the concert stage and in the teaching studio. He taught for two decades at the Leipzig Conservatory. One of his best-known students was Julian von Károlyi.

LEONARD PENNARIO

b. 1924—United States

He studied with Guy Maier and with Isabelle Vengerova, making his New York debut in 1943. Miklós Rózsa dedicated his Piano Concerto to him; Pennario premiered it in 1967 and then recorded it. He has also played chamber music with Heifetz.

Pennario has been making records steadily since nearly the inception of the LP, and they have sold well. His repertoire is large and leans mostly to the Romantics, and he is rather colorful when exposed to the Khachaturian Concerto or other "juicy" Romantic staples. Pennario is musicianly, with a razor-sharp technique, but perhaps he is basically a remarkable sight reader—able to devour a new score whole but unable to sustain his involvement with it. Often, a Pennario performance sounds as if he is just slightly bored—always extremely competent, yet musically held in check. There is something essentially glib in his work; he adds little of himself to the music. Still, when the music really suits him, especially in lighter fare like Saint-Saëns's *Etude in the Form of a Waltz*, Litolff's Scherzo, or Gottschalk, he can smile and have a jolly good time. He is especially well suited to the Gottschalk idiom. His performance of that remarkable piece of Civil War rhetoric, *L'Union*, Op. 48, dedicated to General McClellan, is played with dash and humor, as Pennario tosses off bushels of octaves with the greatest aplomb.

ERNST PERABO

1845–1920—Germany

At the Leipzig Conservatory he studied with Moscheles. Later, he had a sizable career as a pianist and teacher in the United States, settling in Boston. He taught Amy Cheney (later to be known as the composer Mrs. H. H. A. Beach).

MURRAY PERAHIA
b. 1947—United States

He studied with Jeannette Haien and Mieczyslaw Horszowski. In 1972 he won the Leeds Competition; in 1975 he was the first recipient of the Avery Fisher Award. He toured Japan for the first time in 1977. His career has blossomed into one of the largest and most important of his generation.

Among the pianists of his time, Perahia seems to be the most universally admired. His concerts invariably receive rave reviews, and his lyrical playing has been thought to resemble Dinu Lipatti's. His phrasing flows, bends easily, and flowers with a natural impulse. His work is never marred by idiosyncrasies. Indeed, his art is best fulfilled in a more intimate setting. Perahia has a subtle ear, and each sonority is pure; his pedaling is always clean and yet full. He displays a childlike quality in the *Papillons* of Schumann; a depth of understanding in the *Fantasiestücke*, Op. 12; an elegiac beauty of expression in the *Symphonic Etudes*. His later disc of the Schumann Fantasy finds him a bit constrained in the wilderness of the first two movements, but in the finale he unrolls layers of tonal beauty with acute concentration and vocal plasticity.

Perahia is essentially a "vocal" artist, and it is no wonder that he has a strong affinity with Schubert. He plays the lyric Impromptus wonderfully, but is not at home in the dramatic thunder of the *Wanderer* Fantasy.

Chopin is one of the highlights of Perahia's repertoire. His early recording of the B-flat minor and B minor Sonatas is beautifully wrought, though still tentative stylistically. It is not really an intimate Chopin, nor does he capture the grandeur of these compositions. He hits his stride in the Preludes—the ideal Chopin for his poetic nature. In this recording, Perahia's technical mechanism is more refined than ever, perfectly honed. His later recorded Chopin, especially the Barcarolle, has a beautiful finish. James Methuen-Campbell, in his book, *Chopin Playing*, writes, "Perahia is a near-perfect Chopin player. . . . His grasp of the vital place of counterpoint in Chopin's style also helps to give his playing a depth of understanding that many others lack."

Perahia's best-selling albums have been his luminous readings of the complete Mozart Concerti. Here his singing tone, vocal phrasing, true feeling for chamber music, as well as his command of spacious form, find their ideal outlet. Perahia is never afraid to play Mozart with depth of tone and warmth. His Mozart has a sense of satisfaction and well-being, though it lacks any of the Mozartian operatic flavor.

In Beethoven, his finest playing is in the earlier sonatas, such as the Opus 7 in E-flat, Opus 10, No. 3 in D major, and Opus 22 in B-flat. Here everything is balanced and vibrant. His slow movement of Opus 7 is riveting—music built out of silence. With Perahia, each rest is as important as each note, and his pathos in the slow movement of the Opus 10, No. 3, can move an audience to tears. In later sonatas, as in Opus 81a and Opus 110, he is somewhat reticent, although there are signs in his live performances that Perahia is beginning to project a larger picture of many works that he has previously recorded.

Mendelssohn is another composer whom Perahia finds congenial. He puts on a delightful, zestful performance of the G minor Concerto, and his recording of Mendelssohn's little-known and impressive Sonata Opus 6 is played with weight and character. The recording also contains a dynamic and highly charged *Variations sérieuses,* a suave Prelude

Murray Perahia by David Dubal

and Fugue in E minor, and a surprisingly earthbound *Rondo capriccioso.*

Perahia has not explored much modern repertoire. But his Bartók disc is unusual and nonpercussive, and his playing of the *Improvisations,* Op. 20, is soulful.

In the last half-dozen years, Perahia's playing has undergone changes. He has modified his lyrical touch, opting for a larger, more coloristic sound that projects far and wide. In his solo recitals, he attempts to play far beyond his power. An all-Mozart recital at Carnegie Hall was completely surprising, being a rather brutish affair. And his desire to play Rachmaninoff's *Etudes-tableaux* or Liszt's *Spanish Rhapsody* and *Mephisto Waltz* in a power-packed manner may come from the influence of Horowitz, for whom Perahia frequently played from 1986 until the Russian master's death. There is little doubt that Horowitz stimulated the smaller-scaled pianist to expand his repertoire. Perahia's

technique has benefited from this extension of means, and he has indeed learned to play louder, with an increased brilliance in chord playing and finger mechanism. However, his sound is neither rounder nor larger. So far, he is miscast in the role of the grand virtuoso, which seems to have blunted his sensitivity.

At another Carnegie Hall recital, I was surprised at the sheer lack of subtlety in Beethoven's Sonata Opus 2, No. 2, with its great Rondo Finale, played without air or charm. Meanwhile, a huge portion of Chopin was gulped down, disorganized, hard-hearted, and plain as an egg, with a Berceuse which could hardly lull a babe and was tonally boring, though the codas of the F major and F minor Ballades were played with a technical command I had never heard in Perahia's work.

Perahia might have been bored with being the world's great Mozartian and felt it was time to sink his teeth into the guts of the instrument. Let us hope he will come out of his slam-bang battle and will combine his "objective," sensitive, and delightfully felt Classicism into a larger, more riveting, and individual style in the works of heavyweight pianistic composers.

VLADO PERLEMUTER
1904–2002—Lithuania

He studied at the Paris Conservatoire and with Cortot. He had a long career in Europe and continued to record the Romantic and impressionist repertoire. His performances of Ravel have been appreciated, and within the Chopin literature, many consider him a master. His interpretations have directness coupled with originality in phrasing. Unfortunately, he was never a big technician, and his late recordings, such as the Chopin Preludes and Etudes, show a slowed-down technique which hampers the execution of his musical intentions.

JOHN PERRY
b. 1935—United States

A student of Cecile Genhart. A prizewinner in several international competitions, Perry has performed extensively, and has achieved renown as a teacher at various institutions.

SERGIO PERTICAROLI
b. 1930—Italy

A well-known Italian pianist who studied at the Santa Cecilia Academy and who is still associated with that institution. He has performed consistently, is a sought-after teacher of his instrument, and judges many piano competitions.

EGON PETRI
1881–1962—Germany

He studied with Teresa Carreño as a child. In composition, he worked with Draeseke. His main influence was Busoni, with whom he was associated until Busoni's death. Petri made his debut in 1902. In 1905 he taught in Manchester at the Royal College of Music; thereafter he held various teaching positions.

In 1932, Petri made his American debut; he was revered in this country, teaching at Cornell University and at Mills College in California. Like Busoni, Petri did not cultivate charm or sensuous beauty in his playing. His approach was clearheaded, black upon white, and always monumental. He played the large-scale works most happily, and he had an immense musical authority, which disregarded snobbery. When Liszt's transcriptions were being frowned upon, Petri played them and was dazzling. Like Busoni, he had the greatest faith in Liszt's music. He was capable of the most fabulous deeds of technical daring in the *Transcendental Etudes,* which he programmed in cycle.

Petri was never afraid of the esoteric, and was an even greater champion of the gargantuan piano music of Alkan than Busoni had been. Of course, Petri played Busoni as an article of faith. The solo music and the Concerto were made for him, and his performances of the *Fantasia contrappuntistica* always caused excitement, displaying intellectual and musical powers of a high order. His recording is excellent.

Beethoven was the jewel in the crown of his repertoire; his mighty approach to music was naturally suited to this master. His Beethoven is carved in stone with fierce determination. His interpretations of the Sonata Opus 90, of the *Hammerklavier,* and of Opus 111 are stark tone paintings. He was inhibited and less successful in the songful late Sonatas Opus 109 and Opus 110.

In 1923, Petri visited the Soviet Union, the first Western musician to play there after the Revolution. During his first tour, he played thirty-one times in forty days. His playing had a real impact. Soviet audiences had never heard such a graphic rendering of materials; his forceful intellectuality was simply outside their tradition of Romantic emotive playing. Wise teachers such as Heinrich Neuhaus were deeply impressed. Even in old age, Petri's technique remained superlative. One of his last recordings was a performance of Busoni's piano reduction of Liszt's *Mephisto Waltz* in the orchestral version. Liszt, Busoni, and Petri—the three were perfectly in accord, confident that the piano could do anything.

NIKOLAI PETROV

b. 1943—USSR

He studied at the Central Music School of the Moscow Conservatory with Tatyana Kestner. In 1961 he entered the Conservatory in the class of Yakov Zak, at nineteen he took second prize in the 1962 Van Cliburn Competition, and in 1964 he placed second at the Queen Elizabeth Competition, losing to his compatriot Evgeny Moguilevsky. Petrov has had an extensive career performing in fifty countries, with a repertoire of forty concertos and many individual solo recital programs at his fingertips. He has premiered many works of Soviet composers, including Khachaturian's Concerto-Rhapsody, and Rodion Schehedrin stated that "Petrov's hands are made for my piano music." A grand exponent of Liszt, he takes their difficulties and makes them sound simple, which is a special quality of good Liszt performance. He has recorded the first version of Liszt's *Paganini* Etudes which are indeed transcendental; each strand is clear as crystal cold water. One of his specialties is the Brahms *Paganini* Variations, which sounds like child's play for him. Petrov has said, "The public is as a rule extremely conservative. That is why I consider one of the most vital tasks to help extend the boundaries of the public's idea of a specific composer's creative life. . . . I dream of introducing on the concert stage many overlooked or neglected composers."

ISIDOR PHILIPP

1863–1958—Hungary

He was brought to Paris at the age of three and studied with Georges Mathias at the conservatoire, where he won first prize in piano playing in 1883. He received much good counsel from Stephen Heller and was influenced by him. In 1890 he played in London for the first time. But he became more interested in teaching and in the mechanics of piano playing, and in 1903 he accepted a professorship of the piano at the Paris Conservatoire. In the next half century, Philipp became one of the most important piano teachers in history. His list of students includes such luminaries as Ania Dorfmann, Jeanne-Marie Darré, Nikita Magaloff, Beveridge Webster, and Guiomar Novaes. Philipp's technical exercises for the piano have true originality, and his own piano music contains charming pages.

He supplies words of wisdom in the preface of his *Exercises for Independence of Fingers*: "Practice slowly, with a very supple arm, and strong finger action, depressing each to the bottom with a full, and even tone."

MARIA JOÃO PIRES

b. 1944—Portugal

The distinguished Portuguese pianist was trained at the Lisbon Conservatory, later going to Munich to study with Karl Engel. Pires won several prizes, including first prize at the 1970 Beethoven Competition in Brussels. She is a much-sought-after performer, especially in Europe. Her Schumann playing is quite flexible, bordering dangerously on affectation in such works as the *Arabeske*. Her Chopin Preludes are calmer, though her technique is not large enough to encompass the heaviest demands of several, such as the B-flat minor or the formidable hurdles of the Twenty-fourth

Prelude. But she possesses strong ideas in her Chopin playing.

It is in Mozart that she is most comfortable. It is a smallish Mozart, often of exquisite taste, always technically well groomed and unpretentious. Her concerto performances are tidy, with slow movements that sing. Her conception of the turbulent D minor Concerto, however, is curiously pallid. In the piano sonatas, she is generally excellent, and she has recorded the entire cycle.

JOHANN PISCHNA
1826–1896—Czechoslovakia

He studied in Prague and taught there as well as in Russia. His technical studies are still used in the training of many young players.

JOHANN PETER PIXIS
1788–1874—Germany

Studied with his father. Pixis came to Paris in 1825, obtaining success as a performer, teacher, and composer. He wrote voluminously and had a definite melodic gift. Pixis composed the third piece in the *Hexaméron,* a collaborative composition titled by Liszt, with contributions by Czerny, Thalberg, Chopin, Herz, and Liszt. In later years he resided in Baden-Baden, and his fame extended throughout Europe. He befriended the young Chopin, who wrote in 1831, "Pixis shows me the greatest respect, partly because of my playing and partly because he is jealous about his girl who has kinder looks for me than for him." Chopin honored Pixis with the dedication of

his grand Fantasy on Polish Airs for Piano and Orchestra, Op. 13.

LOUIS PLAIDY
1820–1874—Germany

He began as a violinist and changed, in 1831, to the piano, becoming one of the best-known teachers of his time. Sir Arthur Sullivan, who knew him in Leipzig, wrote: "This popularity arose from his remarkable gift (for it was a gift) of imparting technical power. Were a pupil ever so deficient in execution, under Plaidy's care his faults would disappear, his fingers grow strong, his touch become smooth, singing and equal, and slovenliness be replaced by neatness."

In 1843 he was asked by Mendelssohn to teach at the newly formed Leipzig Conservatory. His technical studies are still occasionally used today.

FRANCIS PLANTÉ
1839–1934—France

He studied with Marmontel and developed into one of the most formidable French pianists. He played in public at the age of seven and continued into his nineties, with a style that was spontaneous and fresh. He was among the first to popularize Mozart and Schumann in France. In 1928 he made a group of recordings, which made him one of the earliest-born pianists to put his art on disc. When Planté was eighty-one, Arthur Rubinstein heard him play "the [Chopin] Tarantelle with a perfect control of his fingers and with the élan of a young man."

MIKHAIL PLETNEV
b. 1957—USSR

A many-sided musician, and a concert pianist of the first order, with a refined and comprehensive technique. Pletnev is equally adept in a Moszkowski Etude, the delights of Tchaikovsky's *Seasons,* or the grand, hammer-and-tongs style of the Second Piano Concerto of the Russian master, a composer Pletnev revels in, and whom he has transcribed in excerpts from *Sleeping Beauty* and the *Nutcracker,* encasing them in fetching pianistic garments. Pletnev is also a conductor of enormous gifts.

As a composer he has written a *Triptych* for Orchestra, a viola concerto, a Capricciosa for Piano and Orchestra, and much else. However, the world's interest in him centers upon his pianism. At thirteen he entered Moscow's Central Music School, and then the Moscow Conservatory. In 1978 he was the first-prize winner of the Tchaikovsky International Competition and proceeded to build a career. It was not until 2000 that he made his Carnegie Hall debut, and a stunning CD was made of the event on Deutsche Grammophon. Highlights are glistening readings of Chopin's Four Scherzi and a multicolored *Islamey.* Of Beethoven, the pianist writes: "I see how many ideas there are, how many 'intonations' cry out to be presented in the right way. There's an enormous amount of quantity of tiny details. All these elements should be audible in my performance, but without disturbing the overall design. It's almost impossible, but I still try to achieve it."

MARIA FÉLICITÉ PLEYEL
(née MOKE)
1811–1875—France

She studied with Moscheles, Herz, and Kalkbrenner, and later with Thalberg. She had a splendid career and was deeply admired by Chopin and also by Liszt, who dedicated his *Norma* paraphrase to her. Chopin dedicated his Nocturnes Opus 9 to her. Berlioz fell in love with her, but she married the piano builder Camille Pleyel. The critic Fétis thought her the most perfect of any pianist. From 1848 until 1872, she was the best-known teacher at the Brussels Conservatoire.

IVO POGORELICH
b. 1958—*Yugoslavia*

He studied at the Moscow Conservatory with Yevgeny Malinen, in 1978 won first prize at the Casagrande Competition in Terni, Italy, and took first prize at the Montreal Competition in 1980. But it was his highly publicized loss at the 1980 Chopin Competition which put him into the spotlight. His controversial playing and presence aroused commotion and dissent among the adjudicators, with Martha Argerich walking out of the jury when Pogorelich didn't get into the finals. Through the power of controversy and his own knack for publicity, Pogorelich became the best-known competition contestant since Van Cliburn won the first Tchaikovsky Competition the year Pogorelich was born. In this case, his loss was his victory and the actual winner went into oblivion. Ever since, competitions as a means of bringing forward outstanding talent have suffered a loss of prestige. These events will continue, but their validity is questioned, most of all by the young pianists who no longer see them as their way to fame and fortune. One may say that since Pogorelich, it has been a post-competition world for pianists, although in 1994 he sponsored the Ivo Pogorelich Competition which was never repeated.

As he often said, the chief influence on his

musical development was Alicia Kezeradze, a teacher and pianist of uncommon ability. Pogorelich began working with her as a teenager and subsequently married her. Since her death in 1996, Pogorelich's flourishing career has severely declined, and he has canceled concerts constantly.

Pogorelich at his best is a fascinating musician. His discography is not large and he never records until the work is ripe for immortality. His Bach Suites are unconventional, and he is not frightened to let loose on the contemporary piano with all its colors released. His Beethoven is intriguing and maddening. It is often grim in seriousness. The slow movements are very slow, the air stagnant. Blandness is forbidden. It is not a friendly Beethoven. In the second movement of the Sonata in E minor, Op. 90, he reveals his fine gift for the manipulation of time. Here there is no usual resorting to twitches and tugs in the many repetitions of the theme. The Opus 22 Sonata in B-flat is unlivable, dry, thudding, and the Sonata Opus 111 is a parched desert with its sublime second movement beyond his power of fulfillment as yet.

Chopin looms large in his repertoire; sensuous color is lacking in the Twenty-four Preludes; each bar is measured to the results wanted. The *Funeral March* Sonata is straightlaced; the trio section of the March finds no angels singing in these Elysian Fields. The Third Sonata in B minor is edgy, spiky, nothing tender here, and Chopin would probably be stunned or at least not amused by Pogorelich's massive torrent. He can bang a piano mercilessly and without depth. He is not comfortable with the Pole; either he is riddled with exaggeration or pedantry. His best Chopin is in the Prelude in C-sharp minor, Op. 45, the F-sharp minor Polonaise, and the E-flat Nocturne, Op. 55, No. 2.

Schumann's interior is still a closed book to him. His *Symphonic Etudes* are strangely academic, while the Toccata, marvelously articulated, is yet pedestrian in tone and distant, without an ounce of humor, an ingredient Pogorelich conceptions eschew. His Ravel is fabulous, the *Valses nobles et sentimentales* diamond-edged, pointillistic, and perfectly spaced. In the *Gaspard de la Nuit* the high craft and perversity of Ravel's piano writing challenges him. *Ondine* is well planned; in *Le Gibet* one feels the sun beating down; the tragedy is real. And in *Scarbo,* the finale of the score, Pogorelich is stupendous, painting a startling pyrotechnical portrait of the infamous Scarbo—preening, ironic, a dangerous scamp, even a necromancer. This is Pogorelich's greatest achievement on disc, and in concert performance, never fails to thrill.

Prokofiev seems to be his favorite Russian; he plays the Sixth Sonata better in a public setting than on recording, which is slightly dry. I heard his Prokofiev Third Sonata in recital and he realized aspects of the score that others have overlooked. Of other Russians there is a fine Scriabin Sonata No. 2, and Mussorgsky's *Pictures at an Exhibition* is a conception stillborn, but he is dazzling in Rachmaninoff's Sonata No. 2, and is sizzling in Balakiriev's *Islamey.* Pogorelich performs with a high level of technical security and consistency, one of the essential marks of a great performer. I heard him three times in the Liszt Sonata, a Faustian, deadly drama in his hands. The story was always told the same way: with a conception and realization which never failed. Every sound was etched in stone, each performance tuned to the exact second. Obviously, he has fought a hard battle to achieve what he is after, and no simple whim will be let in to mar the whole.

One is delighted by the vitality of his playing, as well as by the varied audience and critical reactions. At intermission, instead of no response, there are fierce complaints as well as raves. Yes, he can rile the listener, it's not pleasant playing, but many feel that here is important playing, that his way is new and not a rehash of a thousand insipid interpretations one has heard over and again.

DANIEL POLLACK

b. 1935—United States

Pollack studied in his native Los Angeles with Ethel Leginska and later at Juilliard in Rosina Lhévinne's class, which boasted such talents as John Browning and Van Cliburn. Pollack made an acclaimed New York debut in 1957, and the following year took a prize at the first Tchaikovsky Competition, which his classmate Cliburn won. Pollack has performed worldwide; he is frequently an adjudicator at international competitions and for many years has been professor of piano at the University of Southern California in Los Angeles. Among the most successful works in his repertoire are the *Carnaval* of Schumann, Liszt's *Funérailles*, the Chopin Third Sonata, and the Barber Sonata. His recent recording on Naxos of Barber's piano music finds him in form.

FRANCESCO POLLINI

1763–1846—Austria

He studied with Mozart and developed into a pianist with an excellent technique. In 1809 he became professor of piano playing at the Milan Conservatory. He produced a great deal of piano music and is credited with being the first piano composer to notate his music using three staves. This procedure is found in his 1820 *Trentadue esercizi in forma di toccata*. In his preface, the composer explains: "I propose to offer a simple melody more or less plain, and of varied character, combined with accompaniments of varied rhythms, from which it can be clearly distinguished by a particular expression and touch in the cantilena in contrast to the accompaniment."

MAURIZIO POLLINI

b. 1942—Italy

He studied at the Milan Conservatory. In Warsaw in 1960, at the age of eighteen, he walked off with the first prize at the International Chopin Competition; the jury included Magda Tagliaferro, Heinrich Neuhaus, Nadia Boulanger, and Arthur Rubinstein. "Pollini," said Rubinstein, "showed a complete supremacy over the others." Later he worked with Michelangeli.

Pollini is the most important Italian pianist of the generation after World War II. Shortly after the Chopin Competition, he recorded a poetic Chopin E minor Concerto, which remains some of his finest Chopin playing, and which gave promise of even finer achievements. He withdrew from public performance for several years, however, and the Pollini who has since emerged is a very different artist from the one heard in the Chopin concerto. He developed into a ferociously abstract and hard-boiled player, with the most comprehensive technical equipment of our time, and a ravenous musical mind which can encompass all styles, from Bach to Nono. Indeed, for the younger generation of pianists, he is already a cult figure with an enormous influence. One may hear the obvious aspects of his style being imitated at competitions throughout the world, albeit without Pollini's aristocratic intellectual gifts. The modern pianist's ideal is not the leonine, heaven-storming artist stemming from Anton Rubinstein; not the expressive, intellectual, and snobbish player of the Schnabel school; nor the poet-virtuoso exemplified by Rubinstein and Horowitz. Today's ideal is Pollini—the cool and impassive striver for elemental perfection. He is the "state of the art" pianist. His playing is as sleek and elegant as a stainless-steel skyscraper.

Yet in music that screams for a personal

touch, such as Chopin's Preludes and Etudes, the Brahms Concerti, Schubert Sonatas, and all of Schumann, his unblemished playing sounds antiseptic and driven, with structures so tight that the concert room becomes airless. There is no pause for a moment of impulse. Pollini is never Italianate and, above all, never smiles. He seems to lack a vital imagination; everything sounds like a single conception—one style for all. However, his sense of architecture is great. In fact, there is no pianist today with finer organizational powers than Pollini. He can make Schubert sonatas, which wilt in the hands of many pianists, successful on a structural level, or realize the grandeur of the hypnotic Paderewski or Schumann's F-sharp minor Sonata without losing an audience's attention.

Pollini's programs are always intriguing and never pander to popularity He offers severe chunks of music or one-composer programs. A constant and tireless learner, he has added to his public agenda an evening with Book I of Bach's *Well-Tempered Clavier*, which he performs flawlessly. For this listener, the humanity was missing, but surely the plasticity of the counterpoint and the purebred pianism were more than enough for satisfaction. After countless Pollini recitals, I no longer expect to be moved, but remain astonished by his intellect and coldly compulsive passion. Season after season, one hears relentless performances—his fingers are like laser beams. His playing presents no color, no sexuality, no brooding. I like best his prickly Debussy, his mordant Bartók, his Schoenberg, Webern, and an astounding Boulez Second Sonata, which can even bring down the house.

Pollini's audiences are among the best in the world. They realize that he is a great musician and that he sounds the note of authenticity. Pollini onstage is a lesson in high concentration. He is seated very low, and it seems that rays of energy emanate from his brow as he presents a Beethoven *Hammerklavier*

of awesome dimensions, with an unequaled unraveling of the fugue. A great part of the satisfaction at a Pollini concert comes from his unbelievable technical security, reminiscent of that of the best high-tech CD recordings edited to a hair. Modern audiences are used to this in their listening and find a profound and pure satisfaction in him. One never hears the comment "I like him better on recordings," which is heard so frequently regarding other artists. He can toss off an entire set of Chopin etudes without a scratch, while mere mortal pianists can only dream of the depth of his technical skill in Debussy's Twelve Etudes or in Stravinsky's *Petrouchka*.

JEAN BERNARD POMMIER
b. 1944—France

A pupil of Ives, Nat, and Pierre Sancan at the Paris Conservatoire, where his talents shone brightly. Pommier has performed worldwide, and has also been heard as a conductor. His complete Mozart Sonatas on Virgin Classics are full of wit and the slow movements sing.

MICHAEL PONTI
b. 1937—Germany

Ponti studied in Washington, D. C. Early on, he won prizes in several competitions, and in 1964 he took the first prize in Bolzano at the Busoni Competition. In 1970 he began a series of recordings of lesser-known composers, which earned him a reputation. His New York debut in 1972 included an encore sheet, from which encores were to be selected by audience request.

Ponti has prodigious strength; he must be a compulsive practicer. How else does one gulp down such meaty chunks of repertoire—so many unknown concertos, etudes, fugitive pieces, as well as the complete piano music of Tchaikovsky and Scriabin, albums of Rachmaninoff, Thalberg, Henselt, Moscheles, Scharwenka, and Alkan, and a truckload of piano transcriptions from Grainger to Pabst? I hope he had fun learning them. I know I find pleasure in listening to this harvest of goodies that had been stacked away and forgotten, and this valuable music sheds light on the history of piano writing in the nineteenth century.

Ponti's performances are technically equal to the greatest demands, but he is dreadfully uneven. He does not always use his enormous strength and technique with wisdom, and musically he can be anxious and slipshod. Then, too, there is a nagging tendency to bang his instrument, resulting in ugly and brittle sound. His Scriabin Sonatas, for instance, were too quickly learned; they needed more time for maturation. Scriabin's essential nervosity becomes merely breathless in Ponti's rendering, which is nearly always too fast and flurried. This is a problem with many Ponti performances. In the course of extended listening, one will find that many works have a stylistic sameness in his hands. In his attempt to approximate a certain type of Romantic performance style of the past, he forgets to be himself. This is not always the case, and, surprisingly, in standard repertoire he comes out best. His *Petrouchka* or Brahms *Paganini* Variations, his Chopin Etudes, and his Liszt are well-balanced and idiomatic. In recent years, he has also played much chamber music, which has helped harness his solo playing, giving it more point and discipline. Overall, Ponti plays with freshness and phenomenal bravura, and with a rare, often infectious enthusiasm for his work.

VIKTORIA POSTNIKOVA
b. 1944—USSR

She worked with Yakov Flier at the Moscow Conservatory and was a prizewinner at the 1970 Tchaikovsky International Competition. Postnikova is a fascinating but uneven pianist. She has recorded the five Prokofiev Concertos, the three Concertos of Tchaikovsky, the Brahms First Piano Concerto, and the colossal Busoni Piano Concerto. Postnikova has also recorded solo piano music of Tchaikovsky and Janáček, displaying a refreshing wildness and daring, alternating with moments of turgidity and overpedaling.

CIPRIANI POTTER
1792–1871—England

He studied in London with his father and for five years with Beethoven's early rival Joseph Wölfl. He later befriended Beethoven, who thought he had a talent for composition. Potter was a fine performer who gave the English premieres of Beethoven's Piano Concerti Nos. 3 and 4. In addition, he composed twenty-nine opus numbers, including two Sonatas, two Toccatas, and two sets of studies. In 1855, Wagner conducted one of Potter's works in London.

LEV POUISHNOV
1891–1958—Russia

A student of Essipova, he won the Rubinstein Prize at the St. Petersburg Conservatory in 1910. Pouishnov concertized and taught piano in Tiflis for several years. After the Russian Revolution, he lived in England, and he toured both in Europe and in the United States. His specialty was Chopin, and much to the surprise of his colleagues, Pouishnov advertised himself as "the greatest Chopin player in the world."

LOUIS PRADHER
1781–1843—France

Pradher was a father figure of early French pianism. It was in 1798 that the Paris Conservatoire began concentrating on piano teaching more than harpsichord instruction. Pradher studied with one of the first professors of the piano, Hélène de Montgeroult, who had received some tutoring from Dussek. From 1800 until 1828, Pradher himself taught piano at the conservatoire, his prize pupil being Henri Herz. Pradher composed many piano works, including a concerto.

MENAHEM PRESSLER
b. 1928—United States

A fine pianist with a dependable facility. His recording of the Shostakovich Preludes is characteristic of his best playing. He teaches at Indiana University and was a member of the well-known Beaux Arts Trio.

ANDRÉ PREVIN
b. 1929—Germany

Previn, the brilliant conductor and composer, is a pianist of quality, ranging from jazz to Mozart concerti, which he conducts from the piano. His performances of Gershwin's Concerto in F have flair and bounce.

SERGEI PROKOFIEV
1891–1953—Russia

Prokofiev's contribution to the literature of the piano is of immense value. His Third Piano Concerto undoubtedly is the most-often-performed twentieth-century concerto, and his own recording of the work reveals Prokofiev as a brilliant performer, with strength, individual sound, and a virtuoso technique. The most characteristic aspect of his playing is a vibrant rhythmic sense. In public, he played only his own music—music which, of course, makes great demands on any pianist. Prokofiev's early training was at the St. Petersburg Conservatory, where he studied with the great teacher Annette Essipova, which means that Prokofiev was well-grounded in the Leschetizky manner. For his graduation, his program included his own First Piano Concerto and Liszt's transcription of Wagner's *Tannhäuser* Overture.

JOSEF PROKSCH
1794–1864—Czechoslovakia

A blind pianist who composed, played concerts, and founded a piano academy, which survived into the 1930s, in Prague. Smetana studied piano with him.

DIONYS PRUCKNER
1834–1896—Germany

A student of Liszt, he was a well-known pianist, teacher, and editor.

ÉMILE PRUDENT

1817–1863—France

He worked at the Paris Conservatoire with Zimmerman, winning first prize in piano playing. He became one of the most popular French pianists of the day—a brilliant and pleasing player of mainly his own works, which include many operatic fantasies, etudes, and a B-flat Concerto, premiered by Prudent in London in 1848.

RAOUL PUGNO

1852–1914—France

He worked with the Chopin pupil Georges Mathias and developed into a pianist of world stature. Pugno was one of the first major exponents of Mozart in France, and his elegant style in this composer was much extolled. He played Chopin with a fleet-fingered virtuosity, and his interpretations are preserved on early recordings. He was the first to play Grieg's Concerto not only in France but also in St. Petersburg.

Pugno was a prolific composer in various forms. For piano, he composed a sonata and a set of four pieces, *Les Nuits*.

JUAN PUJOL

1835–1898—Spain

The father of the Spanish school of piano playing and the most famous Catalán piano teacher. His pupils were Ricardo Viñes, Enrique Granados, and Joaquin Maláts. The Catalán tradition is distinguished by an overall sense of improvisation and color, yet with a stress on clarity as well.

Q

ANNE QUEFFÉLEC
b. 1948—France

In 1965 she received a first prize in piano at the Paris Conservatoire in the class of Lélia Gousseau. Later in Vienna she had some lessons with Alfred Brendel. She won first prize at the Munich Competition in 1968 and the Leeds Competition in 1970. She has recorded a great deal on many labels. Her complete Ravel is excellent on Virgin Classics, and a CD of thirteen Scarlatti Sonatas on Erato is vibrant.

R

SERGEI RACHMANINOFF
1873–1943—Russia

After early training, at the age of ten he went to study with Zverev. Later, at the Moscow Conservatory, he worked with his brilliant cousin Alexander Siloti. As a teenager, he played for Anton Rubinstein, whose own playing left an ineradicable impression on him. Although Rachmaninoff was one of the most brilliant pianistic talents at the conservatory, his introverted nature turned more toward composition, and he achieved early fame with the success of his Prelude in C sharp minor, Op. 3, No. 2, a work whose very popularity later plagued the composer. He called the piece the "It" Prelude, since after each concert the audience would chant "Play it." By 1905 he had written much exceptional music, including the glorious Second Piano Concerto, composed after several years of extreme depression. During the first decade of the century, he was also utilizing his conducting skills and became a noted operatic conductor. In 1909 he began his first tour of the United States, for which he wrote his Third Concerto—a work of monumental technical difficulty, which Rachmaninoff said was composed for elephants. He dedicated it to Josef Hofmann, but the great pianist never essayed it publicly. Rachmaninoff premiered it in New York with Walter Damrosch and performed it later in the season with Mahler holding the baton.

In 1915 his classmate Scriabin died, and Rachmaninoff learned some of his music to play in charity concerts for the benefit of his widow and children. It was the first time since his youth that he had played another's works in public. Besides the Scriabin Concerto, he performed an all-Scriabin program that included the Fifth Sonata. Constructing the recital program, Rachmaninoff found it needed another ten minutes and consulted the pianist Alexander Goldenweiser, who advised him to look at the complicated Fantasy in B minor, Op. 28, which Goldenweiser had premiered and was fond of, but which Rachmaninoff had never heard. He liked the score, read through it, and learned it. The concert was three days later, and Goldenweiser would write, "His power of engraving in his memory the whole fabric of a musical work, and playing it with pianistic finish, was truly astounding."

Not until the 1917 Revolution, however, could Rachmaninoff be called a concert pianist. Even with the sudden loss of the property that had supported his family, he refused the lucrative conducting positions that had been offered to him in Boston and Cincinnati and made a decision unprecedented for a man of forty-five. He set about learning a repertoire expansive enough for an international pianistic career, and never slackened from then until months before his death. Rachmaninoff continued to compose, but music now flowed slowly. Outside of Imperial Russia, he felt like a stranger. Western music had taken paths foreign to his nature and conditioning, and the few new works he composed were seldom greeted with bravos. But as a performer, he had become for many the cynosure of the world of the keyboard. His fingers seemed to burn the very keys, so intense was his playing.

At first, several critics were uncomfortable with his powerfully analytic mind. He lacked the casual and wayward sentiment of many of his Russian-trained colleagues. Even Prokofiev had rejected Rachmaninoff's reading of the Scriabin Fifth Sonata, missing the languor with which Scriabin had instilled it. "Behind every composition," Rachmaninoff wrote, "is the architectural plan of the composer. The student should endeavor, first of all, to discover this plan, and then he should build in the manner in which the composer would have had him build." For Rachmaninoff, the musical syntax had to be precise and clear, everything building toward a specific "point," as he called it, of climax. It was his main job as an interpreter to make that "point" clear to his audience. If he missed it, he considered the performance a failure, and he was known to be disconsolate after such concerts. In one season of seventy concerts, he could recall only two that he considered well played.

Rachmaninoff filed and polished every note. He worked untiringly; this greatest pianist-composer of the twentieth century slaved with relentless patience at a daily regimen of scales, arpeggios, octaves, and trills. Spontaneity was not for him. His recordings, unlike those of many of his colleagues, represent his true wishes. He recorded everything over and over until he got the results he needed; for example, his celebrated rendition of his own devilishly difficult transcription of Mendelssohn's *Midsummer Night's Dream* Scherzo was repeated forty-nine times (editing was not then possible). His concerts were jammed, and no pianist could afford not to hear him. The New York critic W. J. Henderson applauded a 1930 performance of Chopin's Second Sonata:

For one listener, this interpretation of the B-flat minor Sonata—in which even the

Funeral March was played differently— closed itself with the magisterial quod erat demonstrandum which left no ground for argument. The logic of the thing was impervious; the plan was invulnerable; the proclamation was imperial. There was nothing left for us but to thank our stars that we had lived when Rachmaninoff did and heard him, out of the divine light of his genius, re-create a masterpiece. It was a day of genius understanding genius. One does not often get the opportunity to be present when such forces are at work. But one thing must not be forgotten: There was no iconoclast engaged; Chopin was still Chopin.

That year Rachmaninoff also recorded the Sonata, and after nearly six decades it remains a towering interpretation of that composition. In whatever work he attempted, no matter how individual his statement, Rachmaninoff's way seemed the right one. Richard Baily, in an article, "Remembering Rachmaninoff," suggests, "It was like being in the presence of God himself. . . . Liszt's *Dante Sonata* was sublime in its sweep and emotional power. At the conclusion, I knew that Liszt was the greatest composer for the piano, and this was his finest composition." In his memoirs, Arthur Rubinstein writes:

Rachmaninoff was a pianist after my heart. He was superlative when he played his own music. A performance of his concertos could make you believe that they were the greatest masterpieces ever written, while when played by other pianists, even at their best, they became clearly what they were: brilliantly written pieces with their Oriental languor which have retained a great hold on the public. But when he played the music of other composers, he impressed me by the novelty and the originality of his conceptions. When he played a Schumann or a Chopin, even if it was contrary to my own feelings, he could convince me by the sheer impact of his personality. He was the most fascinating pianist of them all since Busoni. He had the secret of the golden, living tone which came from the heart, which is inimitable. In my strong opinion, he was a greater pianist than a composer. I fall, I have to admit, under the charm of his compositions when I hear them but return home with a slight distaste for their too brazenly expressed sweetness.

Rachmaninoff's piano works, however, have become increasingly popular with audiences and pianists alike. They present formidable muscular problems and are often dense in number of notes per measure, forming a tapestry of unusual effects and counterpoints. He loved the bells of Moscow, and he exploited the bass of his piano with rousing clangor.

Listening to Rachmaninoff in his own works, solo or concerti, is axiomatic for pianists learning them. Heinrich Neuhaus was once asked by a student for advice on a Rachmaninoff concerto, whereupon he ordered him to listen to Rachmaninoff's recording. In playing his own music Rachmaninoff was sublime, aristocratic, and fragrant, with an iron rhythm and the incomparable long line bathed in moonlight, limpid and pure. His recordings of his music fulfill the axiom "less is more."

Listening to Rachmaninoff's enchanting recorded legacy, one realizes his kind of playing has little to do with the ideals of the present day. His playing, for all its formal logic, tonal gradation, and exquisite sound, makes literalists uncomfortable. The rubati at first seem out of character. His immense individuality in such works as Schubert's A-flat Impromptu or Chopin's C-sharp minor Scherzo sounds unidiomatic in a literal age, where caution is the watchword. Besides the Chopin *Funeral March* Sonata, Rachmaninoff's only other performance of a large-scale solo work on disc is his legendary *Carnaval* of Schumann, which is a marvel of control, chiseled phrasing, and infallible chordal technique. He was greatest in the large forms, and it is a pity that his Beethoven Op. 10, No. 3; Op. 31, No. 2; Opp. 57, 109, and 111; and the C major Concerto were never recorded. His repertoire was packed with Liszt, including what Shura Cherkassky calls "the mightiest of all Liszt Sonatas." He played mazurkas, waltzes, Scherzos, polonaises, the Fantasy in F minor, the Rondo Opus 16, the Tarantelle, and the B minor Sonata of Chopin. His recitals were spiced with Borodin, Rubinstein, Dohnányi, Scarlatti, Mendelssohn, Medtner, Moszkowski, Balakirev's *Islamey,* and even Godowsky's *Künstlerleben* and the *Alceste* Caprice of Saint-Saëns. He liked Grieg, admired the Concerto and the Ballade, and his recording of the Grieg C minor Violin Sonata with Kreisler is one of the great discs of ensemble playing.

John Browning feels that "both Rachmaninoff and Kreisler had that thing which nobody has anymore—a type of elegance that seems to have died out. There's a certain kind of humanity in the performance that can bring tears to the eye. It happens very quickly—it can happen in a single phrase."

Harold Schonberg wrote: "When he played a Liszt transcription of a Schubert song, one immediately realized how unimaginative . . . most singers were. Only the very greatest vocal artists—a Lotte Lehmann or an Elisabeth Schumann—could shape a phrase with equal finesse and authority."

Rachmaninoff was an unforgettable stage personality. Tall as a tree, his hair very close-cropped, he seemed to have the worries of the world etched upon his stony face. He never smiled onstage. Stravinsky called him "a six-and-a-half-foot scowl," but, in fact, his face was expressionless during performance. Francis Robinson recalled: "The fall-out at a Rachmaninoff concert was high. . . . The shattering effect began almost with his first appearance, the austere frame which looked to be as long as his instrument and as gaunt, the angular gait unlike anything that has moved before or since, the withdrawn expression as remote as an icon before centuries of candle smoke."

Rachmaninoff performed almost until his death, from cancer, on 28 March 1943. His last appearances as soloist with orchestra took place at Orchestra Hall in Chicago on 11 and 12 February. Hans Lange conducted him in the Beethoven Piano Concerto No. 1 and in Rachmaninoff's own *Rhapsody on a Theme of Paganini*. On 17 February 1943, in Knoxville, Tennessee, the Russian master performed the final solo recital of his fabled career. This was the program:

Bach	*English* Suite
Schumann	*Papillons*, Op. 2
Chopin	Sonata in B-flat minor

INTERMISSION

Rachmaninoff	Two *Etudes-tableaux*, Op. 39
	B minor
	A minor
Chopin	Two Etudes
	E major, Op. 10, No. 3
	E minor, Op. 25, No. 5
Wagner-Brassin	*Magic Fire Music*
Wagner-Liszt	*Spinning Song*
Liszt	Two Etudes
	D-flat major
	Dance of the Gnomes

Rachmaninoff's place in the history of the instrument must rank near the very top. He is the spiritual son of Anton Rubinstein, and, along with Hofmann, he was the supreme artist of the early-twentieth-century Russian school of piano playing.

JOSEF RAIEFF
1906–2002—Russia

Born in Kharkov, early in his life he came to Chicago, where he graduated from the American Conservatory in that city. Later, in New York, he worked with Alexander Siloti and Josef Lhévinne, and in Berlin with Schnabel. Until the early 1950s Raieff performed extensively with much acclaim. At the Juilliard School he was a distinguished faculty member for fifty-six years; with his recent death the tradition begun by the Lhévinnes and Siloti at the Juilliard School pass into history. He taught dozens of excellent pianists, including Louis Nagel, Daniel Blumenthal, and Wim Statius Muller, whose sixty *Antillean* dances for piano are a delightful contribution to the literature.

DEZSÖ RÁNKI
b. 1954—Hungary

He worked under Pál Kadosa and has toured worldwide since winning several competitions. He stands as one of the most acclaimed pianists in central Europe. His repertoire is large, as is his musical intelligence. He plays with a fresh spirit, as well as an accurate and brilliant technique. His playing of Chopin is still superficial, but his Bartók is vital and sensitive.

JEAN HENRI RAVINA
1818–1906—France

A good pianist, and the composer of many light and effective piano pieces. He published four-hand arrangements of Beethoven's nine symphonies. In 1861 he received the Legion of Honor. As a child, the prodigy Josef Hofmann often played his *Etude de style,* and it was recorded by Arthur Loesser.

WILLY REHBERG
1863–1937—Switzerland

A noted pianist who studied with Robert Freund. He published many instructive editions of the classics. Walter Rehberg (1900–1957), his son, was an excellent pianist who studied with his father and with d'Albert and who performed widely, often presenting the works of the German masters in cycles.

ALEXANDER REINAGLE
1756–1809—England

The first American pianist of importance, Reinagle was born in the same year as Mozart and died the same year as Haydn. He came to Philadelphia in 1786 and established himself as a performer-impresario. He was also the foremost teacher in the city; George Washington's niece studied piano with him. His piano music is gracious and in the style of the Classical era.

CARL REINECKE
1824–1910—Germany

Reinecke was a powerful figure in European music as a composer, conductor, pianist, and teacher. As a child, he studied with his father, Johann Peter, a respected theorist and teacher. The piano shared the stage with the violin through his teen years, but at eighteen, he began touring as a pianist. From 1846 to 1848, he was court pianist in Copenhagen to Christian VIII. During this period, he began a conducting career, which then propelled him to the leadership of the Leipzig Gewandhaus Orchestra, from 1860 to 1895. He also taught piano at the Leipzig Conservatory and became director of that institution, where he upheld the standards of his idol Mendelssohn. He was a conservative musician and, as a composer, he lived long past his day. Born at a time when Beethoven was writing his last quartets, in his later years he inhabited a world of music that was baffling to him. Debussy, Scriabin, Stravinsky, and Schoenberg were beyond his comprehension. Even in his heyday, if one considered oneself a "modern musician," then the advice was to avoid Leipzig.

As a pianist, Reinecke stemmed from Moscheles. Quiet hands and curved fingers sufficed for playing the music he respected. Yet an amazing number of important pianists worked with him and admired him, including Joseffy, Michalowski, Albéniz, Max Vogrich, Martin Krause, Julie Rivé-King, Robert Teichmüller, Fanny Davies, Karl Heinrich Barth, and Ernest Hutcheson, who thought Reinecke's playing was elegant and in the best taste and who noted that he was the best accompanist he had ever heard. The Swiss-born pianist Rudolph Ganz called his Mozart playing "delightful."

As a composer, he wrote clearly, with expert craft. His work is harmonically conventional but not scholastic; his musical impulse is warm and genuine. He left much piano music, including four Concerti; No. 1 in F-sharp minor, Op. 72, was often played by the composer with special success. He also left admirable cadenzas to Mozart concerti.

ALFRED REISENAUER
1863–1907—Norway

A superb pianist who toured relentlessly. He studied with Liszt, and with Louis Köhler. Sergei Bortkiewicz and many others were products of his teaching.

NADIA REISENBERG
1904–1983—Lithuania

She studied with Leonid Nikolaev at the St. Petersburg Conservatory and came to the United States in 1922. Reisenberg was a musicianly pianist who recorded several neglected works, including the Tchaikovsky Sonata and the Paderewski *Polish Fantasy,* as well as many repertory pieces. She had a long and fruitful career as a teacher at the Mannes College of Music, the Juilliard School, and the Rubin Academy in Jerusalem. To honor her, a Nadia Reisenberg archive was established at the International Piano Archives, which are housed at the University of Maryland. Her two CDs of Haydn's Sonatas on Ivory Classics reveal her finely tuned classicism. Her Westminster LPs of six Haydn Sonatas and smaller pieces have been transferred to two CDs and issued on the Ivory Classics label. These performances are a joy in their neat fingerwork and beautifully refined slow movements.

FRANZ REISENSTEIN
1911–1968—Germany

A well-trained pianist with a large repertoire, he studied piano with Solomon and composition with Hindemith. He taught a great deal and composed many substantial piano works.

ROSITA RENARD
1894–1949—Chile

She studied in Berlin with Martin Krause, who was also the teacher of Arrau and of Edwin Fischer. Renard made a big impression as a pianist but retired to teach, emerging at Carnegie Hall only several months before her death; her recital was recorded. Her Chopin Etudes were remarkable for their agility and their distinctive ideas.

ALFONSO RENDANO
1853–1931—Italy

He was a student of Thalberg in Naples and later at the Leipzig Conservatory. He made his debut at the Gewandhaus with success, soon traveling Europe as a pianist. In Naples he became professor of piano at the conservatory. Rendano wrote a great deal of music; his opera *Consuelo,* based on George Sand's novel, premiered in 1902.

THOMAS RICHNER
b. 1911—United States

Best known as a Mozart interpreter. He has written a book on the Mozart sonatas, and his recordings reveal a Mozart that is mellow and flowing.

SVIATOSLAV RICHTER
1915–1997—Russia

He came from a musical family, gave a debut in 1934 at the age of eighteen, and in 1937 went to the Moscow Conservatory to work with Heinrich Neuhaus. In 1949 he was awarded the Stalin Prize, and has since received almost every honor that a Soviet artist could garner.

By the mid-1950s, some of his records had

surfaced in the West, and piano connoisseurs were agog with admiration. Emil Gilels, whose resounding success in the United States whetted the appetite for other Russian performers, uttered the tantalizing phrase "wait till you hear Richter." The great impresario Sol Hurok took the cue, billing Richter "the Pianist of the Century," but could not get him to the West until five years after Gilels had first appeared. At last, in October 1960, Richter embarked on a great tour of the United States, both in solo recitals and with orchestras galore. Erich Leinsdorf was his first conductor, and nothing less than the mighty Brahms Second Concerto was played. Everywhere his success was overwhelming.

Of the twelve weeks during which he rampaged the American continent, his seven Carnegie Hall recitals were the high-water mark. The hall was overflowing, and there was an unequaled excitement from the pianistic community. The late Lonny Epstein of Juilliard raved to me that she had never heard Debussy the way she dreamed it until she heard Richter. The *New York Times* critic Harold Schonberg reported, "Certainly it was the most unparalleled triumph that this writer ever observed." And what a range of repertoire Richter fed his public. I was at each event and was staggered by the glory of his garden. From Haydn and Beethoven, to Debussy and Ravel, Chopin and Schumann, Scriabin, Liszt, Szymanowski, Prokofiev, and more, he played it all with an intensity and purpose never to be forgotten. Richter seemed to be an apparition. The "iron curtain" had risen, and for a lingering moment music appeared to bring us to peace and unity. A Richter concert produces such feelings of idealism; his motto seems to be "Above all, Art." He possesses a granite-like, almost authoritarian stage presence, best observed by the psychologist Allen Wheelis in his little book *How People Change*:

> Sviatoslav Richter strides out on the stage.
> His face is grim; there is anger in the set of his jaw, but not at the audience. This is a passion altogether his own, a force with which he protects what he is about to do. If it had words, it would say, "What I attempt is important and I go about it with utmost seriousness. I intend to create beauty and meaning, and everything everywhere threatens this endeavor: The coughs, the latecomers, the chatting women in the third row, and always those dangers within, distraction, confusion, loss of memory, weakness of hand, all are enemies of my endeavor. I call up this passion to oppose them, to protect my purpose." Now he begins to play, and the anger I see in his bearing I hear in the voice of Beethoven. It knows nothing of meanness or spite; it is the passion of the doer who will not let his work be swept aside. It hurts no one, it asserts life, it is the force that generates form.

This is Richter at his very finest. But there is another Richter: a great experimenter, sometimes inspired, other times doing weird things with pedaling and tempi. One never knows what to expect from this most mercurial, intellectual, exasperating, and profound of all Soviet pianists. When in form, he has one of the most all-encompassing techniques in the history of twentieth-century piano playing. He can be note perfect in one piece, murky, turgid, and splattering notes in the next; sometimes he can be academic to the point of pedantry, or withdrawn and introverted. His complete Bach *Well-Tempered Clavier* shows him a master of contrapuntal control, but he plays with a variety of uncalled-for Romantic nuance, which negates the strength of the music. At times his Chopin is Teutonic, and his Schumann sounds Slavic. Yet whatever he does, it is never arbitrary, never merely likable or homogeneous, nor is the result ever simple. Richter is a far-reaching and inquisitive musical intelligence. He does not seem to have a "style," nor is he searching for one.

He has recorded extensively, and, for the

291

avid listener, Richter provides one of the most interesting of all discographies. I never tire of his Schumann Fantasy, G minor Sonata, or *Humoreske.* I am awestruck by his live performance from Sofia, Bulgaria, of the *Pictures at an Exhibition.* His Beethoven Sonatas Opp. 13 and 26, as well as the *Tempest* and *Appassionata,* are piercing. In Schubert, especially in recent years, Richter has attempted some of his most visionary interpretations. Tempi are so slow in the B-flat Sonata that the listener must breathe silently to follow its movement. Richter's lyricism is never flaccid; while the motion never quite breaks its inexorable course, the rhythmic power so seldom brought properly to the fore in Schubert is ever present. His playing of the *Wanderer* Fantasy is justly famous, and his recording of the posthumous C minor Sonata is majestic—the finale, a winter's journey. Or listen to his pulsating four-movement A minor Sonata (D. 845). And in the *Unfinished* C major Sonata, Richter's first movement seems boundless in scope.

In Liszt, Richter can be a refined miniaturist in the fearful *Feux follets* or *Valse oubliée,* or a Merlin in the concertos and the Sonata. His Scriabin Fifth was a landmark performance of the piece, and his recording of the Sixth Sonata is by far the most intriguing view of that elusive score ever recorded, while his Scriabin Etudes are subdued but a wonder of technical control and variety of nuance. In the Russian repertoire, don't miss his definitive performance of the Tchaikovsky G major Sonata, with a grasp of design and chordal playing that makes this lumbering work sound important. What amazing hands—they seem to be made of marble; his fifth finger is fearsome in its physical strength. Some of his Rachmaninoff is imperial, and many of the Preludes are among the best recorded, as is his First Rachmaninoff Concerto. Richter has always been happy in Prokofiev, especially in the expansiveness of the sonatas, which he has done so much to cham-

pion. Prokofiev dedicated No. 9 to Richter, who makes quite a case for its quality.

Neuhaus, Richter's teacher, once wrote:

When I listen to Richter, very often my hand begins spontaneously to conduct. The rhythmic element in his playing is so strong, the rhythm so logical, so organized, strict and free and is so much the result of his total conception of the work he is performing, that it is impossible to resist the temptation to take part in it by gesture . . . strictness, coordination, discipline, harmony, sureness and mastery. This is the real freedom! With a performer such as Richter, two or three departures from strict rhythm are more effective, more expressive, more meaningful than hundreds of "rhythmic liberties" in a pianist in whom the feeling of harmony, this total concept, is absent.

With Richter's death in Moscow, a great era ended in Russian piano playing. His death caused many heads to bow, and I remember how my answering machine was crowded with messages. "Richter is dead, he gave me so much" was characteristic. He was a restless, ironic man, a solitary wanderer. He was the iron man of the piano and he could shatter and batter an instrument if in the mood. His was a far-reaching and inquisitive musical intelligence. He refused to fit into any mold, does not have a "style," nor was he searching for one. His style was the piano literature itself, and his repertoire was amazing in its breadth, leaving a galaxy of recordings from both studio and the live event. Richter's epitaph might well read "Here was a man madly intoxicated by the piano and its music."

In his last seasons, he neglected large cities, performing in out-of-the-way places, a lamp on the piano, playing from the score, so as not to waste even a moment given over to memorization. He was driven and hungry to play all that he desired. It had only to be whispered that Sviatoslav Richter would be giving a recital, and in a flash pilgrims flocked to hear his benedictions to music.

HANS RICHTER-HAASER
1912–1980—Germany

A pianist of value who made his debut in 1928. He had an international career, and was prized for his master classes. He was best known as a Beethoven player and made several fine recordings of that composer's work.

ROBERT RIEFLING
b. 1911—Norway

He worked with Kempff and took master classes with Edwin Fischer as well. In 1925 he made a debut in Oslo, and he has since played around the world. He is a sensitive artist in a variety of music, from Bach's *Well-Tempered Clavier* and Beethoven Sonatas to important recordings of the beautiful and austere music of his compatriot Fartein Valen.

FERDINAND RIES
1784–1838—Germany

With Czerny, Ries was Beethoven's most important pupil, working with the master from 1801 to 1805. Beethoven cared deeply for him and helped realize Ries's substantial gifts. He was a deft pianist, whose playing was more akin to Hummel's elegance than to the ruggedness of Beethoven's style. Ries is a delightful composer, who contributed more

than fifty sonatas and many chamber and occasional pieces. His Third Concerto in C-sharp minor is admirable. In 1813 he went to London, where he became renowned, and did a great deal to propagate Beethoven's music.

BRUNO RIGUTTO
b. 1945—France

A pupil of Lucette Descaves at the Paris Conservatoire and also of Samson François. He has had a distinguished career as pianist and teacher. In 1983 he was appointed to the faculty of the Paris Conservatoire.

BERNARD RINGEISSEN
b. 1934—France

He studied with Long and Février. In 1951 he took first prize in piano playing at the Paris Conservatoire, and in 1954 won first prize at the Geneva Competition. He has played extensively, judged competitions, and recorded Alkan, Rachmaninoff, and others, with a very facile technique.

ÉDOUARD RISLER
1873–1929—Germany

He was an extraordinary pianist with high powers of emotive projection. In 1889, as a student of Diémer, he won first prize at the Paris Conservatoire. After studies in Paris, he worked with Klindworth, Stavenhagen, and d'Albert, and became an exponent of Beethoven, giving the entire sonata cycle in

London in 1906. He was also, perhaps, the first pianist to essay the complete oeuvre of Chopin in public, although Brailowsky gave himself credit for that feat. Risler presented the premiere, in 1901, of the monumental hour-long Dukas Sonata, as well as Dukas's Variations, Interlude, and finale on a Theme of Rameau, in 1903. Chabrier dedicated to him the *Bourrée fantasque,* which Robert Casadesus called "the first truly modern French piano composition."

In his memoirs, Arthur Rubinstein wrote of Risler's Beethoven: "To this day, I have never heard anybody play these sonatas as beautifully and movingly as Risler. He played them naturally, just as they spoke to him, revealing the highly romantic nature of these masterpieces. . . . The adagio of the *Hammerklavier,* the 'absence' in the *Les Adieux* Sonata, and the D minor, Op. 31, No. 2, made me cry when played by Risler."

THÉODORE RITTER

1841–1886—France

A student of Liszt. His playing was suave and agile, as were the drawing-room pieces he turned out, such as *Les Courriers,* which became his favored composition.

JULIE RIVÉ-KING

1857–1937—United States

A student of Reinecke in Leipzig, she also studied briefly with Liszt before she returned home, becoming one of the busiest concert artists in the United States. She gave more than four thousand concerts during her career.

SANTIAGO RODRIGUEZ

b. 1952—Cuba

The winner of several competitions and various prizes, Rodriguez was awarded the silver medal at the Van Cliburn International Piano Competition in 1981. He is a powerful pianist, at his finest in the Romantic repertoire, and his disc of the Brahms *Paganini* Variations finds him in top form. He has recorded the Surinach Concertino and Castelnuovo-Tedesco's G major Piano Concerto for the Elan label.

PASCAL ROGÉ

b. 1951—France

A pianist of quality who plays French music with style. He studied at the Paris Conservatoire, where he won a first prize. He also worked with Julius Katchen and, in 1971, was awarded a first prize at the Long-Thibaud Competition. He has made many worthwhile recordings.

MARIE-AIMÉE ROGER-MICLOS

1860–1950—France

A noteworthy pianist who studied at the Paris Conservatoire with Louise Aglaé-Massart, who taught there from 1874 to 1887 (in 1908 her student Marie-Jeanne Riss-Arbeau was the first French pianist to play in public the complete works of Chopin in eight recitals in Paris). Roger-Miclos also studied with Henri Herz, and Charles Timbrell notes that she was the only Herz student to make recordings. Timbrell writes, "Roger-Miclos was not only a fine technician but also an unusually interesting musician. . . . She was an active champion of modern composers and of such virtuosic works as Falla's *Fantasia baética,* Tchaikovsky's First Concerto, and Anton Rubinstein's Fourth."

GUSTAVO ROMERO
b. 1965—United States

Born in San Diego, he was a much heralded child prodigy. A graduate of the Juilliard School, where he studied with Herbert Stessin, and later with Nikita Magaloff in Geneva. In 1989 Romero took the first prize in the Clara Haskil competition and has since appeared in Europe, Africa, Asia, and America. He is a pianist of rare attributes, able to rivet the listener's highest attention in Bach's Overture in B minor or bring an audience to their feet in a torrid performance of the Third Rachmaninoff Concerto. His recordings of Mompou's complete *Cançiones y danzas* on the Koch Label impress in clarity and spirit. He has recorded the five Beethoven Concertos in zestful, youthful readings, as well as a dozen Scarlatti Sonatas, each finely delineated.

JEROME ROSE
b. 1937—United States

A pupil of Adolph Baller, Leonard Shure, and Rudolf Serkin, Rose took first prize at the Busoni Competition in 1961. He has had a rewarding career, both in the recording studio and in the concert hall, and has performed worldwide under leading conductors. His repertoire has concentrated on the Romantic literature as well as later Beethoven and Schumann. He is perhaps best known for his Liszt recordings, of which his Liszt *Transcendental Etudes* is a fine achievement. Rose is a vigorous organizer of music festivals. The latest is the International Keyboard Institute & Festival at the Mannes College of Music, where he is on the faculty.

HENRI ROSELLEN
1811–1876—France

A pupil of Zimmerman at the Paris Conservatoire, he achieved popularity as player, teacher, and a composer of easily digestible etudes and miniatures.

CHARLES ROSEN
b. 1927—United States

As a child, he worked with Moriz Rosenthal and Hedwig Kanner-Rosenthal. Rosen graduated from Princeton University in 1947 and received a Ph.D. in literature. He made a New York debut in 1951. He has written several books, the most important being *The Classical Style: Haydn, Mozart, Beethoven.* Rosen held the Charles Eliot Norton Chair of Poetics at Harvard in 1980–81.

I have long listened with great interest to Rosen's playing, especially to his earlier records, which have a coldly passionate climate. Rosen always has a strong point of view. He once stated that "a performance is more than a voluptuous noise or an historical echo from the past." His early record of the Beethoven *Hammerklavier* Sonata has a

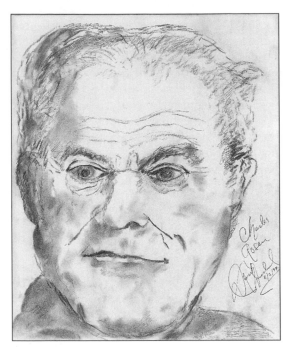

Charles Rosen by David Dubal

Etudes relieves Debussy's music of much of its shimmer, concentrating on their rhythmic boldness. As an interpreter of the modern repertory, Rosen is a musician of importance and courage, who has delivered some of the most durable interpretations of our time, giving life to many recondite works by Boulez, Stravinsky, Schoenberg, Carter, and Bartók. In his playing of Stravinsky's *Movements* or Bartók's *Improvisations,* one is made aware of every cell, every silence. His latest triumph is his disc of Carter's *Night Fantasies,* which finds in Rosen a penetrating advocate.

His live performances lately have been disappointing. There is a general feeling of awkwardness, boorishness, and tight patchiness. Instead of his usual highly organized playing, the music has been given in gulps and chunks, the dynamic range stinted, the sound quite shrill. But Rosen is ever a surprising artist, and his recent Schumann recordings of many major works are vintage, filled with persuasive lyrical moments and countless measures of imagination. This new Schumann is a distinct improvement on his earlier recordings, in which he was definitely inhibited by the composer's discursive expansiveness.

compelling hardness, a quality of bleakness, that fits this mountainous work. It is a performance with a headlong drive in the fugue and a lonely vastness in the first and slow movements. His more recent Beethoven sonatas are not so eventful; they are stiff, arbitrary, and lacking in rhythmic intensity. The poet Stephen Spender heard him in a recital of late Beethoven sonatas and wrote, "Rosen plays with ice-cold precision, cutting up the phrases as though with a knife. At the same time in interpreting the music he communicates a kind of intellectual passion."

Rosen has done some of his best work in Liszt. In the *Don Juan* Fantasy, he confronts the terror buried within its pyrotechnics. And he has made Bach a large part of his musical existence. His *Goldberg* Variations are superbly focused; even more so is *The Art of the Fugue,* which he makes convincing on the contemporary piano. Rosen's recording of the Debussy

MORIZ ROSENTHAL
1862–1946—Poland

He studied with Karl Mikuli, Chopin's pupil, followed by work with Joseffy and, finally, with Liszt for several years. He went to the University of Vienna, where he studied philosophy, and graduated in 1884. That was the beginning of a dazzling career in music. His playing was considered by many to be the ultimate in technical prodigiousness.

From the moment in 1884 when he stepped onstage at Vienna's Bösendorfersaal, his displays of technical daring caused wonder. The composer Hugo Wolf reported, "Rosenthal, in Liszt's appallingly difficult *Don Juan* Fantasy, brought off feats of pianistic athleticism designed to make a moderately accomplished pianist's hair stand on end. The audience was quite beside itself at this labor of Hercules." In 1886, Wolf, comparing him with d'Albert, felt that "the playing of the two virtuosos, in relationship of one to the other, was rather like a brilliant rocket and a glowing coal fire. Rosenthal's playing ignites, d'Albert's warms. The one inspires to deeds, the other to contemplation." Rosenthal, he said, "stormed over the keys like a roaring flood. He played godlessly (godlike sounds too commonplace), and demonstrated beyond the shadow of a doubt that the devil is the supreme authority in art. . . . When he finished, I had the feeling of having escaped from a frightful deadly peril."

And Eduard Hanslick, the most powerful critic in Europe, gulped, "I have almost forgotten what it is to be astonished, but I found young Rosenthal's achievements indeed astonishing." There were also a few quibbles, and the matter of "the unlovely violence with which the keys were pounded in fortissimo passages . . . details characteristic of all the youngsters of the Liszt-Tausig school." But James Huneker, the foremost keyboard connoisseur in America, exclaimed that

the world of Pianism has never matched Rosenthal for speed, power, endurance; he plays his instrument magnificently, overwhelmingly. He is the Napoleon, the conqueror among virtuosi. His tone is very sonorous, his touch singing, and he commands the entire range of nuance from the rippling *fioritura* of the Chopin Barcarolle, to the cannonlike thunderings of the A-flat Polonaise. His octaves and chords baffle all critical experience and appraisement. As others play presto in single notes, so he dashes off double-notes, thirds, sixths and octaves. His *Don Juan* Fantasy, part

Liszt, part Mozart, is entirely Rosenthalian in performance. . . . He is the epitome of the orchestra and in a tonal duel with the orchestra he has never been worsted. . . . His touch is crystal-like in its clearness, therefore his tone lacks the sensuousness of Paderewski and de Pachmann.

Unfortunately, Rosenthal did not record until after his sixtieth year. By that time, a great deal of the brilliance and power had been replaced by poetry and grace, a style of spontaneous elegance, though still mixed with impetuosity. He recorded about forty titles on 78s, and they are among history's great piano discs. There has never been a Chopin Etude Op. 10, No. 1 with more technical finesse, and as a Chopin mazurka stylist, Rosenthal ranks with Friedman. Paderewski thought nobody compared with Rosenthal in playing these exotic dance poems. His Chopin playing became more and more rarefied and concerned with the softest colorations. Rosenthal wrote, "My teachers, Mikuli and Joseffy, delighted my ear with their almost infinite dynamic range from *piano* to *pianissimo,* and *pianissimo.*" He also said that his thirst for big orchestral effects was quenched by the "old thunderer" Liszt.

He recorded several of his own pieces, and in these his playing was unapproachable. Listen not to the piano-roll version but to the 78 recording, transferred to LP, of his *Carnaval de Vienne,* based on Johann Strauss tunes. It has an improvisatory ease and aristocratic savoir faire that seem to have disappeared from music-making forever. Such an impression is confirmed in his earlier disc of the Chopin-Liszt *My Joys*—playing of ethereal loveliness.

Rosenthal was captured on record in only one concerto, the Chopin E minor, recorded in Berlin in 1931. Its presentation is disappointing; the playing sounds somewhat stale and stilted. Of other large-scale works, we have only the Chopin B minor Sonata, made in 1939, but by that time his fabulous motor system had begun to crumble; though flashes of lyricism are apparent, his technique was no longer up to the taxing demands of the work. It is a shame that most listeners since that time have known Rosenthal's playing by this performance, which was totally unrepresentative of his former glory. He was one of the master virtuosi born in the decade of the 1860s. The great conductor Hans Richter once introduced Rosenthal as "the king of pianists," and many would have bowed to that decree.

JACQUES ROUVIER
b. 1947—France

A native of Marseille. His teacher at the celebrated Paris Conservatoire was Aline van Barentzen. For two years he studied with Vlado Perlemuter and later with Pierre Sancan. After winning the Marguerite Long–Jacques Thibaud Competition in 1971 his performing career has brought him to concert halls in many countries. His outstanding readings of Ravel's complete piano music on Calliope are absorbing and fruitful listening, as are his twelve Debussy Etudes, each well conceived if at times lacking in virtuoso brilliance. Rouvier became professor of the piano at the Paris Conservatoire in 1979.

ANTON RUBINSTEIN
1830–1894—Russia

After Liszt, Anton Rubinstein was the most written about and idolized pianist of the nineteenth century. Rubinstein had a powerful mystique, and, seated at his huge iron-framed piano, he was a virtuoso god, singing magically and pouring out emotional floods in the grand manner. With his smoldering temperament, Kalmuck features, and black, disheveled leonine mane, Rubinstein was the very symbol of the piano's power and pride. With Liszt's retirement from the concert stage, Rubinstein reigned supreme over the pianistic kingdom in an age that produced virtuosi of legendary status.

The countless words written of his playing echo one another in their praise. One listener reported: "The impression was so overwhelming, my nerves were so wrought up that I felt stifled. I glanced at my neighbor—she had left the room weeping. We all had a feeling of involuntary terror as if in the presence of some elementary power of nature."

Even as late as 1919, James Huneker could write: "With the death of Rubinstein, no artist of his emotional caliber has appeared on the scene, nor is there likely to be one. . . . He was volcanic. He was as torrid as midday in the tropics. . . . The plangency of his tone, fingers of velvet, fingers of bronze, the sweep, audacity and tenderness of his many styles—ah! There was but one Anton Rubinstein."

The great pianist Arthur Friedheim likened Rubinstein's playing to the Old Testament, gloriously eloquent with the splendors of the world, and Rafael Joseffy said of Rubinstein's touch that it was not that of a pianist but the mellow tones of a French horn. The amorous Leschetizky, teacher of Paderewski, would bribe Rubinstein by saying, "Only play for me, and you may have all my wives and all my sweethearts."

His was probably the most tempestuous temperament that anyone ever brought to a piano. He was also immensely erratic, and he said that he often missed enough notes in one recital to make up yet another. A performer of such temperament needed ten times the technique of an average pianist, for he took daring chances. Later in his career, he suffered drastically "the tortures of the Inquisition," as he called them, because of constant anxiety, stage

Anton Rubinstein by David Dubal

nervousness, and fear of memory loss. A true Romantic virtuoso, he relied on inspiration.

Rubinstein's playing deeply affected the players of his time, and he was the spiritual father of many of the great pianists of the early twentieth century. Paderewski, Rachmaninoff, Lhévinne, Scriabin, and so many others never got over his impact at the piano. Hofmann, his greatest pupil, thought of himself as small by comparison. Rachmaninoff said: "I stored up wonderful memories with which no others in my experience can compare. It was not so much his magnificent technique that held one spellbound, as the profound, spiritually refined musicianship, which spoke from every note and every bar he played, and singled him out as the most original, the unequaled pianist of the world. . . . One of Rubinstein's greatest secrets was his use of the pedal. 'The pedal is the soul of the piano,' said Rubinstein. 'No pianist should ever forget this.'"

As a teacher, Rubinstein asked his students to "will" to dream the sound they wanted and needed. He said, "You think the piano is one instrument! It's a hundred instruments." One of his students wrote: "Rubinstein's sense of touch was almost as keenly developed as that of a blind man. He loved to caress things with his hands. Where others smelled a rose, he touched its soft petals with his fingertips, much as he caressed a piano when drawing forth the witching sweetness of a Chopin nocturne."

He wrote an autobiography, but later summed up his life in six words: "I have lived, loved, and played"—and play he did, from the czar's palace to the mining town of Central City, Colorado. By 1872, America was ripe for a truly great interpreter. Under the auspices of Steinway and Sons, Rubinstein made a monumental tour of the United States, a marathon of incalculable importance in America's musical coming of age. Giving 215 packed concerts within the incredible space of 239 days, Rubinstein literally stunned the American public into an awareness of the piano literature. With his primeval force and elemental freshness, he gave programs of tremendous magnitude (on which his courtesy Variations on "Yankee Doodle" was the only lowbrow fare), and "how 'Ruby' played" became the topic of the day.

Rubinstein was a man of strong opinions: for example, "The human race does not deserve the finale of Beethoven's Sonata Op. 111." He was an unusually brusque man who smiled seldom, but he was amazingly generous. In 1862 he founded the St. Petersburg Conservatory, and during his career he donated well over 300,000 rubles to charitable causes. But it was by his conservatory that he said he wished to be remembered.

As a composer, there were those who thought his name would be enshrined among the immortals. Along with Brahms, he was regarded as one of the most important composers in the anti-Wagner camp. Even his appearance augured well for him—he was the very reincarnation of his supreme god, Beethoven. Some felt he must be the offspring of the great master, and Liszt dubbed him "Van II." Von Bülow gave him the appellation "the Michelangelo of Music." But the time has long since passed when Josef Hofmann stormed and swept the keyboard in his master's D minor Concerto, the only semisurvivor in a vast and proud output. The Fourth Concerto was regularly played, until the Rachmaninoff concertos ousted it; it still has great vitality and melodic appeal. Paderewski heard Rubinstein play it: "It was really overwhelming—impossible to describe. . . . The whole of the first movement is a masterpiece. It is just as if it had been born, like Minerva, from the brain of Jupiter." Now that the boarding-school piano is locked forever, no longer do young girls coo over the Melody in F, swoon to the Romance in E-flat, or dream of the exotic while exhibiting themselves in the *Kamenoi-Ostrow*. Nor do conductors give to their audiences the once-popular *Ocean* Symphony. Rubinstein was a gifted melodist, but unfortunately he said nothing new. His own diatonic harmony would be buried under the spices of Russian nationalism. He is a tragic figure; his music is denied us, and what frustration for those of us who yearn to hear the Rubinstein force at work.

It was in the spring of 1885, under the auspices of the greatest impresario of the time, Hermann Wolff, that Anton Rubinstein conceived the idea of codifying the interpreter's role in a series of seven historical recitals publicly proclaiming the immense territories of the piano literature. These concerts were intended to survey keyboard music from the sixteenth century to Rubinstein's own time, excluding Brahms. This series, given in the major capitals of Europe, was among the important educative ventures of the nineteenth century. Rubinstein, who had become in the last years extremely sloppy pianistically, practiced within this immense repertoire for endless hours for nearly six months before the event. It was his plan to play the series in the evening, for which Wolff charged the highest fees ever recorded at that time, while in the mornings he played the recital for the cities' students and teachers for free. By the fall of that year, he inaugurated the historical recitals in Berlin, giving that city seventeen recitals. Rubinstein casually reported, "Morning and evening concerts were crowded. It was really a great undertaking." The programs bear reprinting; they are gigantic, some of them taking up to three hours without the profuse encores.

RECITAL I

Byrd	*The Carman's Whistle*
Bull	*The King's Hunting Jig*
Couperin	*La Ténébreuse*
	La Favorite
	La Fleurie
	Le Bavolet Flottant
	La Bandoline
	Le Réveil-matin
Rameau	*Le Rappel des oiseaux*
	La Poule
	Gavott et Variations
D. Scarlatti	Fugue in G minor (Cat's Fugue)
	Sonata in A major
J. S. Bach	Chromatic Fantasia and Fugue
	B-flat Gigue from Partita No. 1
	Sarabande and Gavotte in G minor from *English* Suite No. 3
	Preludes and Fugues in C minor and D major
	Preludes in E-flat minor, E-flat major, and B-flat minor from *The Well-Tempered Clavier*
Handel	Air et Variations (*The Harmonious Blacksmith*) from the Suite in E major
	Fugue from the Suite in E minor
	Sarabande and Passacaille from the Suite in G major

C. P. E. Bach	Gigue from the Suite in A major	
	Aria con variazioni in D minor	
	Rondo in B minor	
	La Xénophone	
	Sibylle	
	Les Langueurs Tendres	
	La Complaisante	
Haydn	Variations in F minor	
Mozart	Fantasy in C minor, K. 475	
	Gigue in G major, K. 574	
	Rondo in A minor, K. 511	
	Rondo *alla turca* from the Sonata in A major, K. 331	

RECITAL II

Beethoven	8 Sonatas:
	Op. 27, No. 2, *Moonlight*
	Op. 31, No. 2, *Tempest*
	Op. 53, *Waldstein*
	Op. 57, *Appassionata*
	Op. 90
	Op. 101
	Op. 109
	Op. 111

RECITAL III

Schubert	Fantasia in C major, *Wanderer*
	Six Moments musicaux
	Minuet in B minor from the G major Sonata
	Impromptu in C minor
	Impromptu in E-flat major
Weber	Sonata No. 2 in A-flat major
	Momento capriccioso
	Invitation to the Dance
	Polacca brillante
Mendelssohn	*Variations serieuses*, Op. 54
	Caprice in E minor, Op. 16, No. 2
	11 *Songs without Words*
	Scherzo a capriccio in F-sharp minor

RECITAL IV

Schumann	Fantasia in C major, Op. 17

Kreisleriana, Op. 16
Symphonic Etudes, Op. 13
Sonata in F-sharp minor, Op. 11
Des Abends, In der Nacht, Traumeswirren, Warum? from *Fantasiestücke*, Op. 12
The Prophet-Bird, Op. 82, No. 7
Romanze in D minor, Op. 32, No. 3
Carnaval, Op. 9

RECITAL V

Clementi	Sonata in B-flat major
Field	3 Nocturnes in E-flat major, A major, B-flat major
Moscheles	4 *Etudes caractéristiques*, Op. 95
Henselt	*Poème d'amour*, Op. 3
	Berceuse
	Liebeslied, Op. 5, No. 11
	La Fontaine, Op. 6, No. 1
	Schmerz im Glück, Op. 6, No. 2
	Were I a Bird, Op. 2, No. 6
Liszt	Etude de concert, No. 3 in D-flat
	Valse-caprice
	Consolations in D major and D-flat major
	Au bord d'une source
	Hungarian Rhapsodies, Nos. 6 and 12
	Soirées musicales (after Rossini)
	La Gita in gondola
	La regata Veneziana
	La serertata
	La Danza
Schubert-Liszt	*Auf dem Wasser zu singen*
	Ständchen von Shakespeare
	Soirée de Vienne in A major
Meyerbeer-Liszt	*Réminiscences de Robert le diable*

RECITAL VI

Chopin	Fantasy in F minor
	Six Preludes

Four Mazurkas
Four Ballades
Impromptus, Nos. 2 and 3
Nocturnes in D-flat major,
   G major, C minor
Barcarolle
Three Waltzes in Op. 42; Op. 69,
No. 1; Op. 34, No. 2
Scherzo No. 1
Sonata No. 2 (*Funeral March*)
Berceuse
Polonaises in F-sharp minor,
   C minor, A-flat major

RECITAL VII

Chopin	Eleven Etudes
Glinka	Tarantella
	Barcarolle
	Souvenir de Mazurka
Balakirev	Scherzo in B-flat minor
	Mazurka in A major
	Islamey
Tchaikovsky	*Chant sans paroles*, Op. 2, No. 3
	Valse-Scherzo
	Romance, Op. 5
	Scherzo à la russe, Op. 1, No. 1
César Cui	Quasi-Scherzo, Op. 22, No. 4
	Polonaise in C Major, Op. 22, No. 1
Rimsky-Korsakov	Etude, Novelette, Valse
Liadov	Etude in A-flat, Intermezzo in D major
A. Rubinstein	Sonata in F major, Op. 41
	Theme and Variations from the C minor Sonata, Op. 20
	Scherzo from the A minor Sonata, Op. 100
N. Rubinstein	*Feuillet d'album*
	Valse in A-flat major, Op. 16

Anton Rubinstein's career ended only a few years before the advent of the phonograph. It was rumored that he had made a few early recorded tests; if so, they were never heard,

never found. In any case, it would have been ludicrous to attempt to contain his titanic art within the confines of a primitive technology. Rubinstein unheard remains a legend that still resounds in the annals of the performing arts.

ARTHUR RUBINSTEIN
1887–1982—Poland

After leaving Poland, Arthur Rubinstein studied in Berlin with Karl Heinrich Barth. The first volume of his autobiography, *My Young Years* (1973), tells his remarkable story through his twentieth year. The second volume, *My Many Years* (1980), chronicles his adventures through the next seven decades of his life.

Rubinstein's career was one of the longest chapters in the history of piano playing. He played his final Carnegie Hall recital on 15 March 1976. It was a moving occasion. Afterward, he spoke briefly to the standing audience, who were unaware that this would be his last recital in the great hall where he had experienced so many personal triumphs. But Rubinstein knew he would never return. In June he would play for the last time in London's Wigmore Hall. On both occasions he played Schumann's *Carnaval,* performing with more passion and technical aplomb than I had ever heard from him in this work.

Several days after the recital, I told him so, and the great pianist smiled. He exclaimed: "I am now blind, I can't read my beloved Proust and Joyce, nor can I look at beautiful women.... I am bored and so I am practicing, and I have been practicing the hardest spots in *Carnaval,* which I've neglected for years."

And, he asked, "How did you like my *Paganini*?" Indeed, he had never played it with such speed and verve. Rubinstein continued, "I don't want the public or the critics to say that I am a doddering old man who should not be onstage."

In fact, it had been a recital of startling color and freshness, the embodiment of youth itself. He was certainly the most beloved pianist of his era. He said that he lived unconditionally, and so he played. And just as the man was approachable, so was his music-making. Everyone wanted to hear Rubinstein—and he seemed to be everywhere. If you were in Paris, Rubinstein was playing there; a week later, if you were in Rome, he was there too. When the Rubinstein poster with its familiar line drawing appeared, everyone was glad that he was back in their town. Rubinstein was an exception among pianists—he loved his almost daily touring, the hotels, the bustle and grand whirl, which never tired him. Read the memoirs: he remembered every meal that was delicious, every performance he heard, and every person who was amusing. As Hans Christian Andersen said of Liszt, "Happy man! who can thus travel throughout his whole life, always to see people in their spiritual Sunday dress—yea, even in the wedding garment of inspiration."

When music lovers discuss Arthur Rubinstein's playing, they never speak of him as a virtuoso or a colorist, a scholar or a specialist. He was simply the pianist *par excellence*. There was a wholeness in his playing which defied analysis and which ennobled whatever he played. After Rubinstein had performed, an audience looked fulfilled, musically well fed. He offered his feast with a unique gusto, and even a spray of wrong notes never marred the experience. Someone once said he preferred Rubinstein's wrong notes to many another's right ones. Of course, his occasional sloppiness never came from inattentiveness or technical weakness. For Rubinstein, the moment counted, and he could be seized with inspiration. A Rubinstein concert had the quality of complete authenticity. He had the grand passion for the piano and a blessed temperament. His playing was bracing, invigo-rating, without any hint of sentimentality or of morbidity. No emotion was ever faked. Nor did he ever play down to an audience. His musical nature was sane and balanced; he was the interpreter of normalcy. If one cares for self-absorbed or idiosyncratic playing, for cerebral or extreme playing, then one must look elsewhere. His art had no dark side. He could never have been the object of a cult.

Rubinstein had a wonderful legato, an amazing ear, his sonorities were clear; he had an unfailing steadiness in rhythm, colossal chord playing, and, of course, a golden glorious sound—the quintessentially singing tone. He also played with perfect relaxation. I do not know if it came naturally or was learned through his many years of experience, but he was never tense or cramped. He never hit the keys, never pounded the piano. He utilized weight through his arms and shoulders. When

Arthur Rubinstein by David Dubal

he wanted a mighty sonority in chordal masses, he rose marvelously from the bench and then he swooped down upon the instrument with the grace of an eagle. Rubinstein played, it seemed, from a great pelvic thrust. And how he understood the halls' acoustics; hearing him pedal and envelop a hall in his sound was pure magic. Pianists wouldn't miss a Rubinstein concert: his excursions into the piano literature were worth a hundred lessons.

Rubinstein, a Polish Jew, was disciplined with long study in Germany and was later nurtured in France. He was a cosmopolitan—a citizen of the world, an artist for all people. An amazing range of styles was ingrained in him. He played Debussy and Ravel when their music was hot off the press. Impressionism, from the first, was natural to him, as was most French music. Rubinstein's sense of balance and superb pedaling make his *Valses nobles et sentimentales* one of the most completely beautiful examples of Ravel on disc. He knew best what suited him in Chabrier, Fauré, Poulenc, Falla, Prokofiev, Villa-Lobos, and so many others. His recordings of the Franck Prelude, Chorale, and Fugue are technically magnificent and musically majestic. Franck's religious Romanticism can be easily tarnished with melodrama. Rubinstein, with his impeccable taste, is never cloying.

His 1960 disc of Grieg's *Lyric Pieces* and the *Ballade in the Form of Variations* is fragrantly cool and brisk as a clear mountain stream. He triumphed in the Spanish repertoire and was adored in Spain. He went there, in 1916, for four recitals; he stayed to give 120. Inevitably, somebody would yell during encore time for the Navarra of Albéniz, or his hypnotic rendering of Falla's *Ritual Dance of Fire*. The same triumphs were recounted in South America. In Brazil he discovered the then-unknown Villa-Lobos and played him with sparkling vigor, introducing him to the rest of the world. He was also a close friend of Szymanowski, and he interpreted many of his compatriot's works for the first time. One of his early loves was Scriabin, whose music he eventually deleted from his repertoire, but not before giving the London premiere of the Fifth Sonata. He never deserted Brahms, and one could always hear him in rhapsodies, intermezzi, or the Sonata in F minor, rich and bronzed. His disc of Brahms solo music has never been surpassed for impeccable taste and veiled passion. His Brahms is never tainted by pedantry, nor were his Brahms concertos bloated. The D minor Concerto with Fritz Reiner is nobility itself.

I do not think he really loved Liszt, but he could play the *Valse impromptu* marvelously, seeming to glide across the ballroom floor, and the *Mephisto Waltz, Funéralilles,* and *Valse oubliée* No. 1 have assured style. In performance the Sonata was virile, but the recording is not a success. The Liszt work he played in public with pomp and swing was the Twelfth Rhapsody, and his Liszt Concerto No. 1 contains fine work.

His solo repertoire of the Classic masters was skimpy. He did not play in public the sonatas of Mozart; but the soulful A minor Rondo, K. 511, was his favored solo Mozart work. (He loved several of the concertos and performed them with ease and simplicity.) Bach also was never played, except for the Bach-Busoni Chaconne, and the sonatas of Haydn did not seem to exist for him, although he played the poignant Variations in F minor admirably. He loved Schubert, and in several Impromptus he sang beautifully. In his later years he regularly performed Schubert's final Sonata in B-flat, though on disc it sounds wooden. Nor does the *Wanderer* Fantasy recording show him at his best.

Rubinstein chose his Beethoven carefully, but the five concertos were always on his agenda. His favorite was No. 4, which he first played with Arthur Nikisch conducting. In the concerti, he offered a cultured Beethoven, unpretentious and, especially in the slow movements, perhaps too Romantic for some tastes. Of the sonatas, he gave prominence to the concert favorites. His *Waldstein* was magnificent, and the *Appassionata,* to which he was faithful for three-quarters of a century, was resonant. He never failed to play it with élan and magnanimity. He could give fine readings of Op. 90, the *Pathétique,* the *Moonlight,* and *Les Adieux,* but this listener was most delighted with his performance of Op. 31, No. 3, which was pregnant with life, humor, and energy.

Schumann became, for Rubinstein, the ultimate Romantic. As he aged, his Schumann projected greater purity, and his late recording of the Fantasy captures a rare serenity; it is a milestone in his recording career. The *Fantasiestücke* were always played magically and with the most rounded tone imaginable. They evoke the atmosphere of the springtime of Romanticism. His playing of *In der Nacht* is glorious.

Of course, the names of Chopin and Rubinstein will be forever linked. Yet early in his career Rubinstein's Chopin playing was often considered unpoetic, if not cold. The "Camille of the Keyboard" view of Chopin was deeply entrenched, but Rubinstein felt Chopin's virile, Classical traits strongly. The pianist wanted to desalonify him, to leave behind the often sickly, sentimental readings then prevailing and give Chopin the status and stature he deserved. This was a Chopin new on the musical map, a Chopin that was full-bodied and unneurotic. And it was Rubinstein's perception of the Polish master that changed the attitude of twentieth-century pianists.

For many, Rubinstein's Chopin *is* Chopin. And what a public repertoire he possessed: the two sonatas, four scherzos, four ballades, four impromptus, the Fantasy in F minor, the Berceuse, six nocturnes, six polonaises, the Barcarolle, the Tarantelle, five waltzes, most of the twenty-four preludes, and sixteen etudes—all of which he could play at the drop of a hat—not to mention the complete mazurkas, preludes, and waltzes, which he recorded. The etudes were never recorded because he felt he could not do justice to all of them. The least successful of his Chopin recordings are the Preludes, which are too careful, and consequently lifeless, and the majority of the mazurkas, especially the last of the three sets he made, are academically played and literally stripped of their pungency. But one could write volumes about his best Chopin records. The Barcarolle, for example, is exquisitely paced, the phrasing arched, his breathing natural, his taste and simplicity utterly affecting. Rubinstein transforms even the rarely played Bolero, Op. 19, into something of a masterpiece; it becomes gallant, even regal, in his hands.

Rubinstein was at home in the chivalric style of the polonaises, and they are among the finest of his Chopin recordings. In these national tableaux Rubinstein was incapable of stopping the action to present a pleasing purple passage, and yet every page is infused with his specific and spacious style. Nobody who has heard him play the Polonaise in A-flat, Op. 53, will ever forget his verve and confidence. Rubinstein thrived in the Second and Third Scherzos, which were among his warhorses. Nobody played the Second Scherzo with more splendid spirit; the atmosphere in the concert hall was charged, the coda usually spattered with wrong notes, but the effect was exhilarating.

In the domain of the Romantic piano concerto, Rubinstein was king. Season after season he gave royal readings of the two Brahms concertos and the two Chopin concertos, the Schumann A minor, the Grieg and the Tchaikovsky, the Saint-Saëns Second, the Rachmaninoff Concerto No. 2 and *Rhapsody on a Theme of Paganini,* the Liszt E-flat, the Falla *Nights in the Gardens of Spain.* He never tired of them. No performer in history extracted more juice from these time-honored scores.

Rubinstein's discography is a storehouse of treasures, though by no means the equal of his live performances, which had an irrepressible flow. In the studio, his inspiration was impeded by his fear of blemishes. This fight for cleanliness blunted him; he could not always come out of himself. His best recordings certainly testify to his greatness, yet future generations listening to them will never quite know his glory and the full majesty of his stage bearing and playing. Stravinsky wrote his *Three Scenes from Petrouchka* for Rubinstein, and nobody else has ever played it with such color and *joie de vivre,* even as he missed chunks of chords, yet it was never recorded, probably because he could never feel abandoned enough in a studio to make it come alive. Audiences were essential to Rubinstein; he sensed them to a startling degree, compelled them to participate in the event, and they heightened his art.

More than he loved music, more than he loved the piano—he loved life. He once said, "I am lucky to be a pianist. A splendid instrument, the piano, just the right size so that you cannot take it with you. . . . Instead of practicing I can read. A fortunate fellow, am I not?" For half a century, Arthur Rubinstein was the piano's most dashing cavalier, his joyous bravura proclaiming the grand manner. To an adoring public, he was an inspirational force, an expression of the very best in our civilization. There will never be another like him.

Rubinstein's RCA discography was made available in 1999 by BMG on eighty-two CDs. These discs mirror his active repertoire of his last forty years. In sum, Rubinstein's recordings are in more homes in more countries than any pianist's in history.

As an international "star" with more than one hundred concerts per season, he was in demand in the concerto literature and recital format. However, this gregarious artist loved chamber music and gave the world a number of treasured performances with collaborators such as Szeryng, Heifetz, Feuermann, Piatigorsky (who supposedly was asked who had the most beautiful cello sound, to which he replied, "Rubinstein"), Kochanski, Fournier, the Paganini Quartet, and the Guarneri Quartet.

Rubinstein was soloist with almost every renowned conductor of the late nineteenth century onwards, from Nikisch to Toscanini, Monteux, Klemperer, Stokowski, Walter, Rodzinski, Szell, and Bernstein, to name a few. Unfortunately contractual exclusivity kept the conductors list to a minimum on recording.

Early in his career Rubinstein performed Scriabin's Fifth Sonata and *Vers la Flamme,* Ravel's *Ondine,* and a smattering of things by Busoni, Bartók, Medtner, and the complete *Iberia* of Albéniz, but these were gradually dropped. Unfortunately the three magnificent works composed for and dedicated to him—Falla's *Fantasia baética,* Villa Lobos's *Rudepoêma,* and the *Three Scenes from Petrouchka* of Stravinsky—were never put to record. He once said, "I adore making records, it thrills me. I have a feeling of perpetuation." Indeed, the stupendous achievement of Rubinstein's recorded legacy brings us perpetually closer to an incomparable music-maker. Rubinstein once summed up his existence: "I'm passionately involved with life; I love its change, its color, its movement. To be alive, to be able to speak, to see, to walk . . . it's all a miracle. I have adopted the technique of living from miracle to miracle."

I include a listing of the works for piano and orchestra, and large solo works.

CONCERTOS

Beethoven Five Concertos No. 1, with Krips,
  Leinsdorf, Barenboim
No. 2, with Krips, Leinsdorf, Barenboim
No. 3, with Toscanini, Krips, Leinsdorf, Barenboim
No. 4, with Beecham, Krips, Leinsdorf, Barenboim
No. 5, with Krips, Leinsdorf, Barenboim
Brahms Concerto No. 1, with Reiner, Leinsdorf,
  Mehta
No. 2, with Coates, Munch, Krips, Ormandy
Chopin Fantasy on Polish Airs, with Ormandy

Two Concertos, No. 1, with Barbirolli,
    Wallenstein, Skrowaczewski
No. 2, with Barbirolli, Stemberg, Wallenstein,
    Ormandy
Falla *Nights in the Gardens of Spain,* with
    Golschmann, Jorda, Ormandy
Franck *Symphonic Variations,* with Wallenstein
Grieg Piano Concerto, with Ormandy, Doráti, two
    with Wallenstein
Liszt Piano Concerto No. 1, with Dorati
Mozart Five Piano Concertos, No. 17, with
    Wallenstein
No. 20, with Wallenstein
No. 21, with Wallenstein
No. 23, with Barbirolli, Golschmann, Wallenstein
No. 24, with Krips
Rachmaninoff Piano Concerto No. 2, with
    Golschmann, Reiner, Ormandy
Rhapsody on a Theme of Paganini, with Susskind,
    Reiner
Saint-Saëns Piano Concerto No. 2, with Gaubert,
    Wallenstein, Ormandy
Schumann Piano Concerto, with Steinberg, Krips,
    Giulini
Szymanowski *Symphonie Concertante,* with
    Wallenstein
Tchaikovsky Piano Concerto No. 1, with
    Barbirolli, Mitropoulos, Leinsdorf

SOLO PIANO MUSIC

Bach-Busoni Toccata, Adagio and Fugue, BWV 564
Chaconne (from the D minor Violin Partita), BWV
    1004
Beethoven Sonata in C major, Op. 2, No. 3
Sonata in C minor, Op. 13, "Pathétique"
Sonata in C-sharp minor, Op. 27, No. 2,
    "Moonlight"
Sonata in E-flat major, Op. 31, No. 3
Sonata in C major, Op. 53, "Waldstein"
Sonata in F minor, Op. 57, "Appassionata"
Sonata in E-flat major, Op. 81a, "Les Adieux"
Brahms Piano Sonata No. 3 in F minor, Op. 5
Three Rhapsodies
Four Ballades
Thirteen pieces, from Op. 76, 116, 117, 118, 119

Chopin *Andante spianato and Grande polonaise,*
    Op. 22
Four Ballades
Barcarolle
Berceuse
Four Etudes
Trois Nouvelles Etudes
Fantasy
Four Impromptus
Fifty-one Mazurkas
Nineteen Nocturnes
Seven Polonaises
Twenty-four Preludes
Four Scherzos
Sonata No. 2
Sonata No. 3
Fourteen Waltzes
Debussy Five Preludes
"Image," Book I
Nos. 2 and 3 from *Estampes* and four other small
    pieces
Franck Prelude, Chorale, and Fugue
Grieg Ballade in the Form of Variations on a
    Norwegian Folk Song, Op. 24
Eleven Lyric Pieces
Haydn Andante and Variation in F minor
Liszt *Funérailles*
Mephisto Waltz No. 1
Sonata
Two Hungarian Rhapsodies and four small works
Mendelssohn *Spinning Song,* Op. 67, No. 4, from
    Songs without Words
Milhaud Ipancma Nos. 5, 9, 11 from *Saudades do
    Brasil*
Sumaré
Larenjeiras
Mompou *Cançion y dansa* No. 1
Cançion y dansa No. 6
Mozart Rondo in A minor, K. 511
Poulenc Three Movement Perpétuels
Ravel *Valse nobles et sentementales* and two small
    pieces
Schubert Impromptus No. 3 and 4, D. 899
Wanderer Fantasie, D. 766
Sonata in B-flat major, Op. Posth., D 960

Schumann *Arabesque*
Carnaval
Etudes Symphoniques
Fantasiestücke
Kreisleriana
Two Novellettes and five small pieces

Rubinstein's discography also includes a bouquet of smaller works; the most important performances are of Villa-Lobos's *Próle do bébé*; five mazurkas of Szymanowski; Anton Rubinstein's *Valse-caprice;* Granados's *Maiden and the Nightingale*; four pieces by Falla, including the *Ritual Fire Dance;* Albéniz's *Navarra, Evocación, Triana*; and Fauré's Nocturne in A-flat major.

Weimar of Liszt, who perfected his talent and was a powerful advocate of his gifts as a pianist. Rubinstein (no relation to Anton) was considered a dashing performer. He caught "Wagner fever" and worked with Wagner at Bayreuth. Liszt called him "an out-and-out Wagnerian of the best kind." Rubinstein composed a Fantasy on Tristan and Isolde; especially fine is his transcription of the Siegfried-Idyll, which, "is as successful as possible on the piano," in Liszt's words. (One wonders what Liszt would have thought of Glenn Gould's transcription.) Rubinstein stirred bad blood in Brahms and others, bringing him notoriety. He committed suicide in Switzerland.

BERYL RUBINSTEIN
1898–1952—United States

A pupil of Alexander Lambert, Busoni, and Da Motta. He had a splendid academic career at the Cleveland Institute of Music and became its director. He was a composer of sparkling idiomatic piano works, wrote an outline for teachers called *Piano Pedagogy,* and often played in concert.

His Sonatina in C-sharp minor, dedicated to Olga Samaroff and composed in 1930, is an entertaining three movements of superb accomplishment and should be performed. The 1935 Piano Concerto Hinson calls "one of the strongest American Concertos . . . a beautifully crafted work."

JOSEPH RUBINSTEIN
1847–1884—Russia

A pupil of Joseph Dachs in Vienna and in

NIKOLAI RUBINSTEIN
1835–1881—Russia

The younger brother of the great Anton Rubinstein, he studied with Alexander Villoing and then with Theodor Kullak. He was the founder of the Moscow Conservatory and the teacher of Sauer, Sergei Taneyev, Tchaikovsky, and Siloti. He composed some attractive trifles. His cool, classical, chiseled playing was the opposite of Anton's passionate intensity, yet he was deeply admired by his brother.

FRANZ RUMMEL
1853–1901—England

He studied with Louis Brassin at the Brussels Conservatoire, making his debut at Antwerp in the Henselt Concerto. He had long-standing success as a teacher at the Stern Conservatory and as a performer in many tours, including some in America.

WALTER RUMMEL

1887–1953—Germany

The son of Franz Rummel, he worked with Godowsky and then began touring. He was a friend and early advocate of Debussy. Rummel is best known for his Bach transcriptions, but he also composed original works of quality. He can be heard on the Danté label in some highly personal playing of Chopin and Liszt made between 1928 and 1943.

S

VASSILY SAFONOV
1852–1918—Russia

A very influential figure in Russian musical life. As a pianist, he had early success with his brilliant and finished technique. He was a teacher of renown, counting among his students Pressman, Medtner, Alexander Goedicke, Leonid Nikolaev, Scriabin, and Rosina and Josef Lhévinne. They all worked with him at the Moscow Conservatory, of which he also became director. Safonov was also a conductor of special qualities, who dispensed with the use of a baton. He was a champion of Russian music and did much for Tchaikovsky's cause.

CAMILLE SAINT-SAËNS
1835–1921—France

He studied with Stamaty and was trained in the precision school of playing exemplified by Zimmerman, Kalkbrenner, and Alkan.

Saint-Saëns was possibly the most astonishing prodigy in music after Mozart and Mendelssohn. He was playing Mozart and Beethoven by the age of five and made his debut at ten in Beethoven's Third Concerto.

Saint-Saëns played in public throughout his long and illustrious career; composing for the piano came as naturally to him as did other branches of composition. "I produce music," he said, "as apples are produced from an apple tree." His philosophy was that music should please and satisfy. Emotion of a deep nature was alien to him, and it is unfair to ask more of him than he intended for his art.

Marcel Proust heard him in a Mozart Concerto and wrote:

> In Saint-Saëns's playing there were no *pianissimos* where you feel you'll faint if they go on any longer . . . no broken chords sending instantaneous shivers down your back, none of those *fortissimos* which leave you bruised from head to foot. . . . But his playing was regal . . . every mannerism, over-emphatic or vulgar, spontaneous or cultivated, is eschewed, and carriage and gestures are so stripped of all pomp and formality that only simplicity remains. . . . To this purity and transparency Saint-Saëns's playing has attained. One does not see Mozart's Concerto through a stained glass window or behind footlights, but as if through an air interposed between us and our table, between us and our friend—so pure, that we do not even notice it.

He played the piano brightly, with a liking for very brisk tempi. Arthur Rubinstein, who often played the Saint-Saëns Second Concerto, heard him play the Chopin E major Scherzo, Saint-Saëns's favorite Chopin piece: "Too fast for my taste, but technically perfect." Isidor Philipp, who heard him often, thought, "It is impossible to play the piano with more strength and certainty, more spirit or rhythm, or naturalness. His interpretations are pure marvels of pianistic sculpture."

He kept his piano technique in good shape. In 1920, at age eighty-five, he reported to Fauré: "You cannot imagine how hard I have been practicing your *Valse-caprice* in D-flat, but I have never got it off well enough to put it in my repertoire because I have never been able to practice it consistently enough. When I'm ninety, I shall perhaps be quite sure of it."

In 1915, Saint-Saëns made an edition of Mozart's piano music which was often used. His own solo music, based on the pianism of Liszt, comprises some of the very best lighter pieces in the French repertoire. Liszt wrote to Olga von Meyendorff in 1877:

> I know no one among contemporary artists who, all things considered, is his equal in talent, knowledge, and variety of skills— except for Rubinstein. However, the latter does not have the advantage of being an organist, in which capacity Saint-Saëns is not merely in the first rank but incomparable, as is Sebastian Bach as a master in counterpoint. You don't care much for the organ—the "Pope among instruments"—however, were you to hear Saint-Saëns play an organ worthy of his extraordinary virtuosity, I am convinced that you would be moved and amazed. No orchestra is capable of creating a similar impression; it is the individual in communion with music rising from earth to heaven.

His Toccata, *Allegro appassionato, Etude in the Form of a Waltz,* and many others are scintillating, and his five piano concerti, vulgar as they are in many pages, display a glittering pianism and an alluring feeling for the instrument. One of the finest of the concertos is No. 2, which, Sigismund Stojowski quips, "begins like Bach and ends like Offenbach." Perhaps a finer work is the more refined Fourth Concerto in C minor.

PNINA SALZMAN
b. 1922—Israel

She made her debut at the age of eight and studied with Cortot and later with Magda Tagliaferro at the Paris Conservatoire. She has had a distinguished performing career, is one of Israel's most respected pianist-teachers, and is the head of the piano department at the Rubin Academy in Tel Aviv.

OLGA SAMAROFF
1880–1948—United States

Her real name was Lucy Hickenlooper, but her manager was convinced that she needed a Slavic-sounding name to make a career. She became one of the most remarkable American musicians of the first half of the twentieth century. After native studies in Texas, she was the first American woman to be admitted to the Paris Conservatoire, where her piano teacher was Elie Delaborde, Alkan's illegitimate son, who at first condemned her for being American. Soon her playing changed her master's prejudice. Moving to Berlin in 1898 she met the city's musical giants, and Mahler took a special interest in her. In 1905 she made her New York debut at Carnegie Hall with a disappointing review from the *Times* critic Richard Aldrich, who reported, "Her delivery seldom has much plastic or expressive power. Liszt's Concerto requires at least brilliancy and dash and a certain sentiment in the mellifluous *cantabile*; but Mme. Samaroff's style is too dry to achieve much of either." Samaroff easily withstood these harsh sentences and in the next years forged a brilliant career, while marrying the conductor Leopold Stokowski, whose career she helped enormously.

By the early 1920s she was heard in New York

and other cities in performances of the complete Beethoven Sonatas. She began recording in 1921, and her readings show a very sensitive artist. Many of her discs can be heard on the Opal CD label. Especially excellent is *The White Peacock* of Griffes, Schumann's *Aufschwung,* with a lustrous tone, much rubato, and a thoroughly musical respiration. Her technical brilliance is gleaned in the Paganini-Liszt *La Campanella,* the Wagner-Hutcheson *Ride of the Valkyries,* where she gallops spiritedly, some impressive Chopin playing, and, prominently, her own transcription of Bach's G minor Organ Fugue.

Teaching began occupying Samaroff's restless nature, and she taught extensively at the Philadelphia Conservatory and as a member of the Juilliard faculty in 1924, where she worked the rest of her life, becoming one of the world's most celebrated teachers of the piano. She was a constant propagandist for great music, and her "Layman's music courses," lasting from 1928 to 1948, were well attended. In 1927–28 she took a stint as music critic for the *New York Evening Post.* Arm problems had curtailed her public playing but she wrote four books, of which her memoirs are most important. Among her roster of pupils were Roselyn Tureck, Eugene List, Claudette Sorel, Solveig Lunde, Joseph Batista, William Kapell, and Alexis Weissenberg, who said of Samaroff: "She was a brilliant woman who taught me in a marvelous way. She was one of the few teachers I have ever met whose pupils all played differently, and that you cannot say about many famous teachers. Individuality was something she respected. She had great insight into the personality of her students, and she let people develop their own way."

Her goal, Claudette Sorel wrote, "was to develop independent musicians capable of standing 'undaunted' on their own, through the most exasperating circumstances." Writing to William Kapell, she advises: "The prime requisite for becoming a *master* in *anything* is to master one's own soul! The human being who allows himself to be in a constant inner turmoil over trivial day by day things in life will never get to the plane of *thinking* and *feeling* necessary to adequate functioning in the *highest* regions of art!"

HAROLD SAMUEL
1879–1937—England

He studied first with Mathilde Verne and later with Edward Dannreuther. At his London debut in 1898, he played Bach's *Goldberg* Variations, which at that time were practically unknown. His solo career, however, was at a standstill until 1919, when he played an all-Bach program in London. He soon found a ready audience for large amounts of Bach's keyboard works in their original form. Few pianists played any Bach in public outside of organ arrangements. Samuel often gave, on consecutive days, five or six all-Bach recitals in which he never repeated a work. He was reputedly able to play any Bach work from memory at any given moment.

In the 1920s he recorded a small segment of Bach: the B-flat Partita, the *English* Suite in A minor, the Chromatic Fantasy and Fugue, the Fantasia in C minor, and four preludes and fugues from *The Well-Tempered Clavier.* These discs display an impressive technique, swift and pliable, with interpretations that are very intelligible. Denis Hall wrote: "How modern the approach is to the music, the clarity of texture; the sense of rhythm, phrasing and rubato, the beautifully judged tempi and his highly individual use of dynamics. Samuel looked upon the clavichord's dynamic capabilities as an inherent part of the music, and it was therefore natural to transfer the interpretive qualities of the older instrument to the concert grand."

His Bach playing on the piano is stylistically less Romantic than that of Schnabel, Edwin

Fischer, or Landowska, who chided Samuel for not playing on the harpsichord (Samuel told her, "But Mme Landowska, I don't like the harpsichord"). It is very interesting and immensely profitable to compare the Samuel, Schnabel, Landowska, and Fischer recordings of the Chromatic Fantasy and Fugue.

Samuel was not a Bach specialist, however; he played a large repertoire, from the Elizabethan composers to Ravel, and his Brahms playing was also respected. Howard Ferguson's fine Piano Sonata of 1940 is dedicated to his memory.

PIERRE SANCAN

b. 1916—France

Studied with Yves Nat at the Paris Conservatoire and has taught there. He is considered one of France's finest piano teachers. Sancan has played in public and has also composed.

SAMUEL SANDERS

1940–1999—United States

He studied at the Juilliard School with Irwin Freundlich, later with Martin Canin. Very early in his career, he chose to be an accompanist. In this broad field, he has collaborated with many fine artists. Sanders was a subtle but rich accompanist whose musicianship was a boon to those he worked with. His repertoire was extensive, and he recorded dozens of albums.

GYÖRGY SÁNDOR

b. 1912—Hungary

He studied with Bartók in Budapest and toured Europe extensively, settling in the United States just before World War II. In 1946, Sándor premiered the Bartók Third Concerto with Ormandy, and he has, on occasion, played all three Bartók concertos in one evening. Sándor has made many transcriptions, including Dukas's *Sorcerer's Apprentice* and the chaconne from the Bartók solo violin sonata. His book, *On Piano Playing,* was published in 1981.

JESÚS MARÍA SANROMÁ

1902–1984—Puerto Rico

The most eminent Puerto Rican pianist. A government grant provided funds for him to study in the United States. In New York he studied with Antoinetta Szumowska; in Paris he worked with Cortot and in Berlin with Schnabel. By his early twenties he played concerts in the United States and Europe. A relationship with Koussevitsky brought him the post of staff pianist with the Boston Symphony for twenty years. He was active in contemporary music, giving the American premiere of Stravinsky's *Capriccio* for Piano and Orchestra and recording Ernest Toch's Piano Concerto; he also presented the world premiere of the Vernon Duke, Walter Piston, and Ferde Grofé piano concertos, the latter dedicated to the pianist. He made admirable recordings of Paderewski's Piano Concerto, MacDowell's D minor Concerto, and solo discs of Krenek's Little Suite, Op. 13a and Schoenberg's Six Little Piano Pieces, Op. 19. For years Sanromá was an active force in Puerto Rican musical education and in 1960 he was named head of the piano department of the newly opened conservatory. In Puerto Rico he was duly honored with several awards. Seldom did he play a recital without performing several of Juan Morel Campos's (1857–1896) charming Puerto Rican dances, and he premiered the Parsi Piano Sonata. Sanromá performed in more than 3,000 concerts. His recordings are lively and show a flexible and secure technique with a pleasing sound. Pearl Recordings has resurrected some of his discography on compact disc.

VASSILY SAPELLNIKOV
1868–1941—Russia

He studied with Brassin and Sophie Menter at the St. Petersburg Conservatory, achieving a great reputation as a virtuoso. His specialty was the First Tchaikovsky Concerto. In a letter, Tchaikovsky wrote, "My great consolation is the pianist Sapellnikov, Menter's pupil. . . . My soul gets a rest with him." Shaw first heard him in 1890, in the London premiere of the Tchaikovsky Second Concerto: "It left me without any notion of Sapellnikov's rank as a player: he is, of course, swift and powerful with his fingers, but six bars of a Mozart sonata would have told me more about his artistic gift than twenty whole concertos of the Tchaikovsky sort." Shaw later wrote of his rendering of the Chopin A-flat Polonaise that the octave section "comes from his puissant hands like an avalanche." His few discs, including the Tchaikovsky concerto, show a wonderful left hand, as well as a simple and direct view of the music.

DAVID SAPERTON
1889–1970—United States

He studied in the United States with August Spanuth. In Europe, he attended Busoni's master classes.

Saperton made his New York debut in 1905 with the Chopin E minor Concerto. In 1915 he met Leopold Godowsky, who became the paramount influence in his life, and also became his father-in-law. Saperton devoted a lot of time to conquering Godowsky's Chopin paraphrases, some of which he recorded in masterly fashion.

Saperton was a major technician, and his influence as a teacher has been important. He taught at the Curtis Institute from its early years, and his students included Abbey Simon, Jorge Bolet, Shura Cherkassky, Julius Katchen, Sidney Foster, and many others. His devotion to keyboard mastery and Romantic playing lives on in Bolet, Simon, and Cherkassky, who are descendants, through Saperton, of Leopold Godowsky. These pianists represent, as Harold Schonberg put it, "a philosophy where the piano itself was the be-all and the end-all, less a musical instrument than a way of life."

In listening to Saperton, one is refreshed by the constant flow of musical ideas that today would be eschewed by many conservatory teachers and pupils as excessively mannered.

EMIL VON SAUER
1862–1942—Germany

A student of Nikolai Rubinstein and one of the most successful pianists of the generation of Paderewski, Rosenthal, Friedheim, d'Albert, Carreño, and Busoni. Sauer also worked with Liszt, and we possess a wonderful disc of Liszt's two concerti, recorded when Sauer was seventy-seven, with another Liszt pupil, Felix Weingartner, conducting. It is the only collaboration on record of two Liszt students, and it shows Sauer still capable of excellent playing. His interpretations are slow but beautifully contoured and give us a clue as to how Liszt himself may have played them—unhurried, and grand in elevation.

Sauer, even in his prime, was never simply a bravura pianist, but one who played with great style and elegance and with a beautifully even technique. Sauer was a combination of poet and virtuoso, and he played light music

Emil von Sauer by David Dubal

incomparably. His Chopin discs show a graciousness, but also elements of depth, as in the B minor Sonata.

Sauer was a delightful composer with many smaller works to his credit—Strauss transcriptions, as well as two piano sonatas and two concerti. He was universally considered a great teacher, and he left his mark on artists as diverse as Webster Aitken, Stefan Askenase, Maryla Jonas, Alexander Brailowsky, Ignace Hilsberg, and Elly Ney. Sauer made many editions, the most used being those of Liszt and Brahms.

PIETRO SCARPINI
1911–1997—Italy

An eminent Italian pianist; a pupil of Casella.

He made his debut in Rome in 1937 in Mozart's Concerto in E-flat, K. 271. Scarpini gave a number of first performances in Italy, including the Rachmaninoff *Rhapsody on a Theme of Paganini* in 1937, the world premiere of Dallapiccola's *Sonatina Canonica* dedicated to the pianist in 1943, the first performance in Italy of Prokofiev's Sonata No. 7 in 1946, of the Schoenberg Concerto in 1949, and the complete solo piano music of Schoenberg at the Santa Cecilia Academy in Rome in 1952. Scarpini's repertoire included the Busoni Concerto, which he performed with the Cleveland Orchestra, with Szell conducting, in New York and Cleveland in 1966. One may hear him on an Arbitor CD of the Beethoven Op. 111 and Fourth Concerto with Furtwängler, in performances marked by seriousness and depth of soul. He digs deeply, bringing to light some of the more profound layers of the music. After a performance of the Op. 111, Luigi Dallapiccola wrote, "You had surpassed yourself—inspiration, technique, imagination." After 1970, the pianist was seldom heard in the public arena.

IRENE SCHARRER
1888–1971—England

As a child she elicited praise for her Chopin Etudes from de Pachmann, and gave a command performance before Edward VII. She was a brilliant exponent of the teaching of Tobias Matthay, and was his pupil at the Royal Academy of Music from age twelve; the two remained close until Matthay's death in 1945. At the Royal Academy a friendship bloomed with Myra Hess, and Matthay encouraged and coached them in the two-pianos literature, which culminated in extensive concertizing. Eventually Arnold Bax wrote *Moy*

Mell for the duo. Scharrer's solo career also blossomed, and by 1909 she was recording as well. Much to Myra Hess's chagrin, Scharrer married in her late twenties, having two children. Still she was busy and ventured to New York for concerts after the First World War, and remained a great favorite. At the Promenade concerts in the early thirties she revived the Scherzo movement from Litolff's Concerto No. 4, Op. 102; the recording on Columbia with her mentor, Sir Henry Wood, leading the London Symphony Orchestra became a "best-seller." The work is perfect for her lively, fleet-fingered passagework, and although it has been recorded by Curzon, Lympany, and others, her reading remains the lightest and brightest.

She was a splendid Chopin player, nothing deep; her innate high spirits shy away from any Slavic melancholia. The legendary difficulties of the Etude in Thirds, Op. 25, No. 6, has no peril for her. The other eight Chopin etudes she recorded are suave, nimble-fingered, aristocratic, straightforward, and neat. It was no wonder that Matthay gloried in her playing, as she represented the essence of his school of teaching: brilliant, alert, but relaxed. Nearly eighty minutes of her output are available on Pearl Recordings, including the Litolff. After World War II she was heard infrequently. Her last appearance took place in 1958 with Myra Hess performing the Two-Piano Sonata of Mozart in a concert to commemorate the centenary of Matthay's birth. Unfortunately no recordings of them together exist.

XAVIER SCHARWENKA
1850–1924—Poland

One of the most distinguished and brilliant personalities in the annals of pianism, Scharwenka was an estimable composer and an educator, founding the Scharwenka Conservatory in Berlin in 1891 and in New York City in 1898. As a pianist he cut a swaggering figure across the musical world of the last quarter of the nineteenth century into the twentieth. Although today there is a Scharwenka Society in Lübeck, Germany, the Polish-born pianist and composer has been fairly forgotten. Scharwenka was mostly self-taught until the family moved to Berlin in 1865. There he entered Theodor Kullak's famous Piano Academy to study with Kullak himself. The fifteen-year-old Pole thrived in the heady atmosphere at the academy with fellow pupils Han Bischoff, Jean-Louis Nicodé, Alfred Grünfeld, and Moritz Moszkowski. After two years with Kullak, he made his Berlin Orchestral debut with Mendelssohn's Second Piano Concerto in D minor. The following year an eighteen-year-old Scharwenka joined the faculty of Kullak's Academy.

The young pianist, like most musicians of his time, composed. It was in 1869 that Scharwenka sealed his fate as a composer, publishing a set of Five Polish National Dances, Op. 3, No. 1, in E-flat minor, that instantly became so popular in drawing rooms that Scharwenka feared its renown would destroy his destiny as a composer. He called it "that fatal Polish Romp," and like Rachmaninoff, with his Prelude in C-sharp minor, Op. 3, No. 2 and Sinding with *Rustle of Spring*, the composer sold them for a flat fee, thus depriving himself of future royalties. By Scharwenka's first American tour in 1890, it was estimated that in the United States alone, he could have earned over ninety thousand dollars from its sale. Today these "fatal" minutes of music are all but erased from our musical consciousness. (In a recent concert which included the Polish Dance, the audience was asked if they knew the work. None had heard it.)

Scharwenka developed into a dashing and charming man. During the years he was teaching for Kullak, an American girl from Mississippi named Amy Fay was in Berlin studying with Kullak. Fay regularly wrote home to relate her adventures as a piano student, and sent pen portraits of various musicians; the most important was Liszt. Later she assembled them into a delightful book, *Music Study in Germany*. In it she describes her affection for Scharwenka, possibly under the spell of his recently published Polish Dance. She writes:

> Scharwenka is very handsome. He is a Pole, and is very proud of his nationality. And, indeed, there is something interesting and romantic about being a Pole. The very name conjures up thoughts of revolution, conspiracies, bloody executions, masked balls, and of course, grace, wit and beauty! Scharwenka certainly sustains the traditions of his race as far as the latter qualifications are concerned. I never talked with him, so I don't know what sort of mind he has, but I find myself looking at him and saying to myself, with a certain degree of satisfaction, "He is a Pole." . . . Scharwenka has a clear olive complexion, oval face, hazel eyes (I think) and a mane of brown silky hair, which he wears long, and which falls about his head in a most picturesque and attractive fashion. . . . He plays beautifully and composes after Chopin's manner.

During the 1870s Scharwenka solidified his pianistic career. His First Piano Concerto in B-flat minor, a work much praised by Liszt, received its premiere in 1877. He premiered his four piano concertos, which served as repertory works, into the early 1900s. No. 1 is an exciting concerto, teeming with excellent material, falling just short of the melodic magic necessary for its survival. The working out of the material is brilliant, and the last pages glitter. In 1880 the thirty-year-old virtuoso performed it in Vienna under the redoubtable Hans Richter. Vienna's leading critic, Eduard Hanslick, called Scharwenka "a totally outstanding pianist, dazzling but without charlatanry. The force of his octave playing, the easy, sure flight of his passage work, the lucid delicacy of his ornaments, and the melodic flow of his chained trills, can hardly be bettered by anyone else."

After opening his own conservatory in Berlin, Scharwenka organized a chamber series at the Singakademie; sometime later he conducted a group of orchestral concerts which included such novelties as Liszt's *Dante* Symphony and Berlin's first complete hearing of the Berlioz *Requiem,* with Crown Prince Wilhelm in the audience, who showered Scharwenka with praise.

Always restless, it was time to conquer America, and late in the 1890s, arriving only weeks before Paderewski's first American tour, he caused a sensation. In January 1891, under the baton of the celebrated Anton Seidl, Scharwenka performed his own Piano Concerto No. 1 and Beethoven's *Emperor* to a packed house at the Metropolitan Opera House. From there he went on to play at the White House and continued across the continent with ever-mounting acclaim, always pleasing the crowds with the inevitable *Polish Dance.* For the next two decades he performed extensively in the United States and Canada. One of the highlights of his American concerts occurred in 1910 when a desperately ill Gustav Mahler conducted him in a performance of his fourth Concerto in Carnegie Hall. The year before, Mahler had conducted Rachmaninoff in the Russian's Third Concerto, and both Scharwenka and Rachmaninoff were deeply impressed by Mahler's incontestable greatness as a conductor.

Days after his concert with Mahler he gave a solo recital in Mendelssohn Hall. The recital was typical of his programming, which included some Chopin, including one of his specialties, the F minor Fantasie; Liszt's

Ricordanza and *Mephisto Waltz;* Beethoven's *Appassionata;* and a group of his own work, including the Theme and Variations, Op. 48, a serious score of a dark quality, utilizing a variety of technical means, including plenty of octaves. (The sixteen-year-old Claudio Arrau performed it in Berlin in 1919.) A not-terribly-excited New York critic reported of this 1910 recital that "Mr. Scharwenka's playing is musicianly, sincere and has the high intelligence of a master of his instrument . . . and yet it can be brilliant and dashing, as it was in Liszt's diabolically clever Mephistophelian Waltz."

With the onset of World War I, Scharwenka was prevented from returning to America. After the war, Scharwenka, who had been inundated with a plethora of honors, continued to compose, but his musical idiom at the time of his death seemed dated. (He died in the same year as Puccini, Busoni, and Fauré.)

In the third edition of *Grove's Dictionary of Music,* H. V. Hamilton wrote: "As a pianist Xaver Scharwenka was renowned above all his other qualifications for the beautiful quality of his tone. If he was a specialist as interpreter of one composer rather than another, it was Chopin . . . but of the other great masters his readings were always grand and musicianly, while to hear him play a waltz of Strauss was as dance-inspiring as the magic bells of Papageno."

Earl Wild made a magnificent recording of the Piano Concerto No. 1 in the late 1960s for RCA. The pianist Seta Tanyel has recorded three CDs of Scharwenka's solo piano music on Collins Classics, including the Sonatas, Opp. 6 and 36. Indeed Scharwenka is a composer that one may spend some delightful hours with. His music is outgoing, melodious, crisp, and finely crafted, altogether the manifestation of a man and artist who was comfortable with himself and the world.

ANN SCHEIN
b. 1939—United States

At fourteen she began studying with Mieczyslaw Münz at the Peabody Conservatory in Baltimore. When only seventeen she performed the Rachmaninoff Third Concerto in Mexico City. After a Carnegie Hall debut she received coaching from Myra Hess and Arthur Rubinstein. In 1980 she gave six all-Chopin recitals at Lincoln Center's Alice Tully Hall. Early in her career she recorded for the Kapp label, which brought her to the attention of the record-buying public. Her latest recordings of Schumann on Ivory Classics are tonally vibrant performances of the *Humoreske* and *Davidsbündlertänze,* with a rare understanding of Schumann's introspective and manic moods. For many years Schein taught at the Peabody Conservatory.

ERNEST SCHELLING
1876–1939—United States

He studied with Georges Mathias at the Paris Conservatoire from 1882 to 1885. As a prodigy, he was much discussed, but was plagued by poor health. He later studied for three years with Paderewski. As a pianist Schelling achieved a fine reputation and his music, now forgotten, was often performed. There is a gorgeous reading by Paderewski of his *Nocturne à Ragaze.* On it one can hear why Paderewski hypnotized audiences—his tone is enchanting, with a delicacy in the passagework. Schelling's finest work is a set of variations, *Impressions from an Artist's Life for Piano and Orchestra,* each variation being a portrait of a friend.

ANDRAS SCHIFF

b. 1953—Hungary

He studied with Pál Kadosa at the Liszt Academy in Budapest. Later, in England, he worked with George Malcolm, who was a major influence on his general musicianship. He entered several competitions, but usually placed no higher than third or fourth. His reputation slowly grew, however, and he received widespread notice. In 1978 he made his Carnegie Hall debut, and ever since his career has been of international scope.

Schiff is a refined player, uninterested in mere effect. His playing at times breathes a rarefied atmosphere that may or may not suit the idiom he is attempting. His Bach playing is unusual and tonally often ravishing; he can languish in Bach dances, yet he has such an unfailing sense of structure that all turns out well. He is one of a growing group of pianists who refuse to give Bach away to the harpsichordists. His performance on disc of the *Goldberg* Variations is lyrically conceived and seems to move quickly, even with all repeats. Schiff's piano tone is never anything but agreeable, often too much so. When he is carried away with himself, his tone sounds too sweet, like a soft marshmallow. When he pulls in the reins, he plays with poise, as in many Schubert pieces, when he feels very comfortable. His Mozart is tasteful, limpid, and beautifully played, and again his very individual approach can be hypnotic. Schiff is a Romantic by nature, and it is good to hear his lyricism flow deeply in Mozart. He is not always good in dramatic statements; the wild floods of Beethoven are not suited to his gentle but high-strung temperament.

His Chopin playing can be both interesting and irritating. I heard a performance of the Preludes that was devoid of life. The pianist was playing as if the keyboard were made of eggshells. His best Chopin, however, is without affectation.

Schiff is not especially attracted to the showpiece repertoire, and his playing of the Tchaikovsky concerto, while distinctive in conception, remains a patchwork in performance. Lately, he has been doing splendid work in Dohnányi's *Nursery Tune* Variations, which allow his appealing sense of humor to be displayed. The twentieth-century composer he most esteems is Bartók, whose music he plays with sensitivity and a requisite boldness.

There is little doubt that Schiff is one of the most individual pianists of the present day and that he has the rare ability to express his own point of view in every phrase.

ALOYS SCHMITT

1788–1866—Germany

An important pianist of the 1820s. His teaching was held in high regard, and he taught Ferdinand Hiller. He composed in many forms, and his etudes were often used.

E. ROBERT SCHMITZ

1889–1949—France

Born in Paris, he studied at the city's famed conservatoire with Louis Diemér, taking a first prize in piano. Subsequently he traveled widely, but his career was interrupted by the Great War in 1914, in which he served for thirty-eight months on active duty, suffering two wounds.

In 1919 he made a U.S. debut which was well received, and he made piano rolls for the Aeolian Duo-Art Company. In 1922 in New York he made a roll of his own admirable arrangement of Debussy's *Prélude à l'aprés-midi d'une Faune*, which may be heard on a Nimbus CD.

Schmitz knew Debussy, who coached him in many of his compositions. His book, *The Piano*

Works of Claude Dubussy, contains many insights. Virgil Thomson wrote: "Schmitz knew what every one of these (works) is about, what it should say, how to make it speak. He also knew, from long experience as a teacher all the pitfalls. He knew how faulty fingering or pedaling can make any work of Debussy lose precision."

Schmitz taught a great deal in North America and made numerous and detailed editions, including the Virgil Thomson Etudes. He was highly acclaimed for his interpretations of the French "moderns" and as late as 1946 gave the premiere of Henri Barraud's Piano Concerto.

ARTUR SCHNABEL
1882–1951—Poland

More than a century since his birth and over five decades since his death, Schnabel's music-making remains deeply relevant to music lovers and musicians. "Schnabel represented in piano playing," said Glenn Gould, "something that was quite extraordinary, a way of looking almost directly at the music and bypassing the instrument." This procedure was revolutionary, and has made Schnabel one of the most potent interpretive forces of the century.

When Schnabel was growing up as a student of Leschetizky, the piano literature was mostly restricted to a specific branch of marketable Romantic music, which was beginning to be sold worldwide. Dozens of pianists were now performing in remote parts of the world, where audiences wanted to hear hackneyed Chopin pieces or Liszt's Rhapsodies. Very little Mozart, Haydn, Beethoven, or Bach was known at all.

Schnabel made his debut at the age of sixteen in Vienna's Bösendorfer Hall, playing the usual fare of the day. The program included pieces by Anton Rubinstein, Eduard Schütt, Moszkowski, and Leschetizky. But Leschetizky was certain that his serious young charge was not the usual marketplace concert aspirant. "You will never be a pianist," he said cryptically. "You are a musician." At that moment in history, the distinction was perhaps more evident than ever. Instead of stuffing him only with the standard virtuoso literature, Leschetizky introduced him to some all-but-unknown Schubert sonatas.

Schnabel started his career at the height of the craze for virtuosity; Clara Schumann, von Bülow, and Rubinstein had all died in the 1890s, and taste was running at a particularly low level. To make matters worse, the musically underdeveloped areas on the concert circuit, such as Spain, Portugal, Italy, Latin America, and Australia, had atrocious audiences, who were often noisy and rude. Schnabel, however, had become convinced that his road was to play the great German classics, and his programs were unflinching in their demands, with no encores included. The road was often rough, but he persevered. He wrote to his wife, the lieder singer Therese Behr: "Some audiences in Spanish cities were so disappointed with my programs that I felt I was cheating them. Sometimes on the platform during my performance, I felt how unfair it was towards the audience—like in Seville while I was playing Beethoven's *Diabelli* Variations. I thought: 'Now, *this* is really unfair! I am the only person here who is enjoying this, and I get the money; they pay and have to suffer.'"

The turning point of his career came in 1927, with the Beethoven centennial, when for the first time he played his Beethoven sonata cycle in London. By 1928, for the Schubert centenary, he made deep inroads into the Schubert literature, and he performed more and more frequently the neglected Mozart literature, especially the concerti. In 1931 he was asked to make the first recordings of the complete Beethoven sonatas. The project was finished in 1935. This achievement set the stamp on his celebrity. He became "the heavyweight title holder," as he put it. "As far as the public was concerned," Harold Schonberg noted, "Schnabel was the man who invented Beethoven." Indeed, his authority was such that the whole intellectual community understood Schnabel's Beethoven investigations as something profoundly important.

The literary critic C. Day Lewis, for example, wrote: "When the critic has studied an author, lived with him in spirit over a long space of time, become saturated with him, an affinity may grow up between them so that some of the original power of the master is transmitted to the disciple. Like a great virtuoso, like Schnabel with Beethoven, the critic through his deep understanding may magnify the glory of his master: interpretation becomes an act of creation."

Schnabel once proposed, "It is unfortunate that the popularity of music is chiefly determined by the activities of the "stars," but it would be much better if we were to see the musician through music, rather than music through the musician." He never tired in his search for his ideal. Near the end of his career, he told his son after a recital that "for the first time I succeeded today in playing the last line of Beethoven's Sonata Op. 90 so that *I* found it convincing."

Schnabel dissected a score with both his head and his heart, "Music and musical art," he wrote, "are mysterious, inevitable, tangible and producible realities, cosmically related and individually fashioned; impersonal, personal and super-personal." His record producer Edward Crankshaw described Schnabel's questing nature:

> He had to find out, to discover . . . removing with infinite application layer on layer of opacity, so that his performance of, say, the *Diabelli* Variations in his last years was like looking at the sun without dark glasses. . . . His trills (listen to the recording of the Variations of Beethoven's Opus 111) were not mechanical devices: They were variations of feelings, and always the same variation in the same place. He had a dozen quite dis-

tinct trills and could achieve through these more urgency and variety of expression than most musicians could achieve through the light and shade of a complete movement. His pauses were organic. Through them the music breathed. . . . When he played the arietta of Op. 111, time stood still.

The suggestion still lingers that Schnabel was a cerebral, cold pianist—a scholar and a pedant. On the contrary, he had more in common with his fellow Leschetizky students than with later Beethoven players like Brendel, Pollini, Bishop-Kovacevich, Anton Kuerti, Ashkenazy, or Glenn Gould, who pointed out that "Schnabel had certain trademarks, one of which was the tendency to use these extraordinary rushes in rather complicated stretti-like places. He would take the stretto, and, instead of simply coloring it harmonically, he would actually provide an acceleration almost automatically. It was very graphic, very gripping, but also very theatrical."

In a 1944 review of a Schnabel recital, Virgil Thomson contended: "There is too large a modicum of late nineteenth-century Romanticism in Mr. Schnabel's own personality to make his Beethoven—who was, after all, a child of the late eighteenth—wholly convincing to musicians of the mid-twentieth. No one wishes to deny the Romantic elements in Beethoven. But I do think that they are another kind of Romanticism from Schnabel's, which seems to be based on the Wagnerian theories of expressivity."

Schnabel was indeed a full-blown nineteenth-century Romantic, with a tone as pellucid and haunting as Friedman's or Paderewski's. What he did was to wipe away a great deal of emotional and literary nonsense concerning Beethoven. He played without what he called "inside dynamics," which "were used as substitutes for genuine expression."

As he aged, Schnabel's tempi grew faster in the fast movements and slower in the slow ones. Some of this tendency came, no doubt, from the trauma of the recording process of his time, were he was confined to four minutes a side. In those years, Schnabel, I feel, was still insecure with the rather new "recording audience," and he over-emphasized or underlined many things that more experienced listeners hear easily and naturally.

Despite his apparent disregard for the mechanical side of playing, it must not be thought, as has often been charged, that Schnabel had small technical means or that what he did have was faulty. That is absurd, and Schnabel—a child prodigy—was brilliantly equipped by Leschetizky. There is no doubt that he became lazy in technical matters. He let some basic aspects of his craft slip here and there, and he could splatter a performance with wrong notes. But as Eugene Istomin said, "After all, what do a few botched bars matter on the ascent to Olympus." Schnabel was a busy man, a teacher in the master-class tradition, and a highly serious composer of atonal music, which he himself refused to champion in performance. Certainly practicing bored him. In his many records, I hear at times a kind of futility, even of torture, an artist of magnitude attempting to escape the exigencies of manual technique, of the hands themselves. Schnabel was, however, a very natural pianist, with a magnificent and inborn facility, and of course the most searching test of technique in its deepest sense is the musician's ability to sustain interest, structure, and breath in a long slow movement. In the slow movements of Op. 106 and indeed of many Beethoven sonatas, as well as several of Schubert's sonatas, Schnabel reached the loftiest regions manifested by hands upon a keyboard. Indeed, he was a genius at holding the listener's attention span in long structures. In fact, he helped make better audiences and better listeners.

Although he wore an inconspicuous suit and played without ostentation, Schnabel's concerts became cultural status symbols. Not to attend almost amounted to philistinism. His students adored him and aped his programming. Schnabel had said, "I play only works that I consider better than they can be performed. It is a never-ending task, for they are so total and universal." Those works meant, to Schnabel, the Germans, and an unhealthy snobbery ensued, as many of his student disciples pursued very little else, vying to cram as many Schubert sonatas as possible into a program. As critic Harris Goldsmith puts it, Chopin's Barcarolle and B minor Sonata are also "better than they can be played."

It is interesting to note that when the compact disc came on the market, people instantly asked, "When will Schnabel come out on CD?" It appears that in an era increasingly preoccupied with standardized virtuosity, Schnabel's flaming heart, even his insistence many times on being less than perfect, has become a measure of artistic conscience. As Bruno Walter marveled in his autobiography: "It is one of the encouraging symptoms of contemporary musical life that a pianist of so serious a bent, of so progressive an engrossment in his work, and of so strict an artistic morality, can continue to be eminently successful throughout a long career."

KARL ULRICH SCHNABEL
1909–2001—Germany

The son of Artur Schnabel, Karl studied with Leonid Kreutzer and had a long and distinguished career as a performer, a writer, and a teacher at New York's Manhattan School of Music.

GERMAINE SCHNITZER
1888–1982—France

Born in Paris, she studied with Raoul Pugno, and won a first prize in piano playing in 1902.

A year in Vienna followed, studying with Sauer. After a Berlin debut in 1904 her career made headway as she visited various European cities. The eighteen-year-old made her New York debut in 1906 at Mendelssohn Hall, where she played the Toccata of Saint-Saëns, Schumann's *Carnaval*, Chopin's Ballade No. 3, and the *Bénédiction de Dieu dans la solitude* by Liszt. The *Times* critic Richard Aldrich heard "a fine equipment of technical dexterity and brilliancy . . . and she can control it to a fine-spun delicacy."

Her career continued to flourish through the 1920s.

JOHANN SAMUEL SCHRÖTER
1750–1788—Poland

An important early pianist who made a sensation when his playing was first heard in London. He was among the first musicians to devote themselves to the piano instead of the harpsichord. The celebrated historian Dr. Burney wrote, "He became one of the neatest and most expressive players of his time. It was graceful and in good taste, but so chaste as sometimes to seem deficient in fire and invention."

ANDRÉ-MICHEL SCHUB
b. 1953—France

He was born in France but has lived in the United States since infancy. He studied with Jascha Zayde, as well as Rudolf Serkin. In 1974, Schub made a New York debut. He won the Van Cliburn Competition in 1981.

JULIUS SCHULHOFF
1825–1898—Czechoslovakia

He studied with Johann Tomáschek in Prague and appeared with success in the various capitals of Europe. He was still of the school that promoted playing one's own music, and he never developed a large public repertoire.

Leschetizky, as a young pianist, was deeply influenced by Schulhoff's ravishing tone, which became his ideal. Hearing him for the first time in 1846, Leschetizky wrote:

> He began a composition of his, *Le Chant du berger*. Under his hands, the piano seemed like another instrument . . . not a note escaped me. I began to foresee a new style of playing. That melody standing out in bold relief, that wonderful sonority —all this must be due to a new and entirely different touch. And that cantabile, a legato such as I had not dreamed possible on the piano, a human voice rising above the sustaining harmonies! . . . Schulhoff's playing was a revelation to me. From that day I tried to find that touch. . . . I kept that beautiful sound well in my mind, and it made the driest work interesting.

At that time, Leschetizky had not yet heard Chopin, Liszt, Rubinstein, Clara Schumann, Henselt, or Thalberg, all greater pianists who had brought tone production to the forefront. Leschetizky's revelation, however, is important as a barometer of the warmer, more colorful playing that was being newly demanded, rather than the drier, less pedaled piano playing still prevalent in Vienna at that time.

ADOLF SCHULZ-EVLER

1852–1905—Poland

He was a pianist who studied with Tausig. The author of many compositions, Schulz-Evler survives in the annals of pianism only through his ingenious concert arabesques on themes of *On the Beautiful Blue Danube* by Johann Strauss, Jr. This elaborate network of pianistic machinations has been brilliantly recorded by Josef Lhévinne as well as, more recently, by Shura Cherkassky, Stanley Waldoff, and Jorge Bolet, among others.

CLARA SCHUMANN

(née WIECK)

1819–1896—Germany

She studied exclusively with her father, Friedrich Wieck, whose one object in life was to produce a major pianist in his daughter. In this he succeeded completely, for Clara Wieck became the most influential woman musician of the nineteenth century, and doubtless the greatest woman pianist of the age. Few women have had a more complicated life—she was a good daughter, a dedicated wife to Robert Schumann, a successful and devoted mother, and a glowing friend to Brahms for forty-five years, as well as a teacher of far-reaching influence and a worthy composer. But, as Joan Chissell writes in her monograph on Clara Schumann: "First and foremost, she was a concert pianist. Music-making was the great motivating force of her life, a mission from which any deviation, whatever the counter-claims of a warm and vulnerable human heart, was a betrayal. Nothing less than such a belief could have carried her through travails so arduous, and personal tribulation at times so bitter."

Indeed, Clara Schumann had one of the central careers of nineteenth-century pianism. It was through her valiant efforts that the great interpretive era dawned. Her performing career and the magnitude of her repertoire were equaled by no man: thirteen hundred printed programs have been preserved. She played in public from the age of seven until 1888; only crippling arthritis stopped her restless career. Her hardest times were the sixteen years of marriage to Schumann, when she single-handedly raised eight children, bitterly resenting the curtailment of her concert life. At his death in 1856, she was only thirty-seven. Faced with the pressing need to support her family, she resumed her career, and with a vengeance. Many a physically strong man has bowed under the pressures of touring, but Mme Schumann could give up to five concerts in four towns within a week. And her programs were uncompromising. She was a great educator, and she is among the creators of the modern recital format. Her father, with his eye to the cash box, gave Clara music by Hünten, Kalkbrenner, and Herz, as well as other potboilers, to play as a child. But Clara quickly outgrew such fare, and Friedrich Wieck was hardly pleased when his own student, Robert Schumann (nine years older than Clara), began inundating the impressionable teenager with Bach, Beethoven, Chopin, and, worst of all, his own "weird" music.

Soon, however, she would exclaim, "I will yield to popular demands only in so far as they do not betray my own convictions." Clara was a champion of the new Romanticism of Mendelssohn (she played the wonderful *Capriccio brillant* with the composer conducting in 1835) and Henselt (she loved his Etudes, and she premiered the F minor

Clara Schumann by David Dubal

of piano playing on his conscience." Liszt retorted, "If you want to hear Schumann's music played as it should be, don't listen to Clara." Of course, Clara playing Robert's music became a tradition, and it was through her immense persistence that this great branch of repertory made its impact. Clara Schumann was an institution in England, and her performances of Schumann were sacred writ. Onstage she always wore black, and she was dubbed "the professional widow." Paderewski, in his early London appearances, collided with her on Schumann. In his delightful memoirs, he rejoined:

> The *Times* critic did not agree with my playing of Schumann, of course, because he belonged to Madame Clara Schumann's congregation. So my playing of Schumann displeased him very much. It was revolutionary for him, he was accustomed to that modest and very restrained Schumann-playing as performed by that very old lady! It was a tradition, and I was destroying, or disturbing, that tradition. I played it exactly as Schumann wanted it played—I mean not as to perfection, but as to the dynamics of the composition. When it was *fortissimo,* I played it *fortissimo,* which Madame Schumann, poor lady, could not produce. Therefore, in all these works, which were played in public by her, and which had established a certain tradition, I surprised the audience, and audiences do not like surprises.

Concerto). At the age of twelve, she publicly performed Chopin's *Là ci darem la mano* Variations, Op. 2, and she added Chopin's new pieces to her repertoire literally as they were printed. Robert thought Chopin's playing was incomparable, "but Clara," he wrote, "is a greater virtuoso, and gives almost more meaning to his compositions than Chopin himself." However, she was repelled by Liszt's grand manner and unbridled temperament, although he dedicated his famous *Paganini Etudes* to her. She played some of his transcriptions of Schubert songs, but later abhorred all that she felt he stood for, including his son-in-law Wagner's "music of the future"; she thought *Tristan* the most repugnant music she had ever heard in her life.

Sad to say, she even suppressed Liszt's name from the dedication of Schumann's great Fantasy in her edition of her husband's works. She once said that Liszt had "the decline

But this was in 1890, and Mme Schumann had made her last London appearances in 1888, when she was racked by pain in her wrists and fingers. Nor had Paderewski heard her in her prime, as she was born forty-one years before he was. There had, however, grown up around her school of playing a kind of genteel Victorianism, which must have had little appeal to the vigorous virtuoso of the Leschetizky school.

A much more balanced view of Clara

Schumann comes in a review by the great critic Eduard Hanslick. Clara played six concerts in Vienna early in 1856, containing Beethoven's *Emperor* Concerto, the Thirty-two Variations in C minor, the Sonatas, Op. 31, No. 2, Opp. 81a and 101, and the *Hammerklavier,* besides works of Schumann, Mendelssohn, Weber, Chopin, Henselt, and the young Brahms, including the C major Sonata, Op. 1. Hanslick, reporting on her second concert, maintains:

> As a young girl, she already stood above the insipid trifles of virtuosity and was one of the first to preach the gospel of the austere German masters. . . . Her penetrating understanding of every kind of music . . . is such that she can treat the whole range of technique as a matter completely dominated and utterly at her disposition. In one or another aspect of virtuosity, she may be surpassed by other players, but no other pianist stands quite as she does at the radial point of these different technical directions, focusing their respective virtues on the pure harmony of beauty. Although mere correctness is hardly her objective, it forms the essential basis on which she builds. To give a clear expression to each work in its characteristic musical style and, within this style, to its purely musical proportions and distinctions, is ever her main task.

Sir George Grove felt her place as a pianist was "indubitably in the very first rank; indeed she may perhaps be considered to stand higher than any of her contemporaries, if not as regards the possession of natural or acquired gifts, yet in the use she made of them." Bernard Shaw, upon first hearing her, "recognized, before she had finished the first phrase of Schubert's C minor Impromptu, what a nobly beautiful and poetic player she was. An artist of that sort is the Holy Grail of the critic's quest."

Clara Schumann brought to the concert stage an unprecedented seriousness. She did not consider herself only a performer, but an *interpreter* whose role was to shed light upon music of considered quality. As fine music began to be valued above mere displays of virtuosity, Clara Schumann's interpretations became yardsticks of musical integrity.

THOMAS SCHUMACHER
b. 1937—United States

Schumacher is a distinguished pianist and teacher who studied with Robert Goldsand, Adele Marcus, and Beveridge Webster. For many years he was professor of piano at the University of Maryland, and now teaches at the Eastman School of Music. Schumacher's career has taken him throughout the world, and he is in demand for his revealing master classes. He was soloist with the New York Philharmonic in the world premiere of David Diamond's Piano Concerto. For the Elan label he has recorded Scriabin's Fifth and Ninth Sonatas and the Prokofiev Sonatas Nos. 5, 6, and 9, which are model performances of these Russian masterworks.

LUDWIG SCHUNKE
1810–1834—Germany

A student of Kalkbrenner. By the age of ten, he could play concertos by Hummel and Mozart. He performed his own concerto in London in 1826, with Weber conducting. Later he developed a friendship with Schumann and they lived together. They were, in Schumann's words, "indispensable to each other," and he wrote of their friendship that they were "living out a novel the likes of which may never before have been put into a book." Schumann dedicated to him his great Toccata, which Schunke played magnificently.

Schunke died of tuberculosis before reaching the age of twenty-four. Some of his piano pieces have been recorded, and they display a considerable talent for piano writing.

EDUARD SCHÜTT
1856–1933—Russia

He studied with Reinecke and Leschetizky, was soloist in his own piano concerto, frequently performed, and edited Schumann's piano music. Schütt composed salon music of charm and pianistic finesse.

MIKLOŠ SCHWALB
1903–1981—Hungary

A student of Dohnányi. He made his debut in Budapest in 1920. He later moved to the United States, taught at the New England Conservatory in Boston, and made recordings.

LUDVIG SCHYTTE
1848–1909—Denmark

An admirable pianist who studied with Edmund Neupert. Then, in Weimar, he worked with Liszt. Afterward, he resided in Vienna, where he played, composed, and taught. Schytte's works are beautifully crafted, lightweight music. He composed a piano concerto, Op. 28.

ALEXANDER SCRIABIN
1872–1915—Russia

He studied with Nikolai Zverev and later at the Moscow Conservatory with Safonov. He and Josef Lhévinne were at the conservatory at the same time, and the frail Scriabin once strained his right hand practicing Liszt's *Don Juan* Fantasy and Balakirev's *Islamey* in an attempt to compete with the strength of Lhévinne's virtuosity. It was around this time that he wrote his famous Nocturne for the Left Hand Alone. In 1892 he received the Gold Medal from the conservatory and began concertizing. From 1898 to 1904, he taught at the Moscow Conservatory. In 1906 he made an American debut.

Scriabin was a fascinating and strange man, high-strung and excessive. He thought his art would help bring about a new world order. As composer and pianist, he became totally absorbed in his own work. Arthur Rubinstein, who greatly admired Scriabin's music, reported that when, as a young man, he met the composer, Scriabin asked him, "Who is your favorite composer?" "When I answered without hesitation, 'Brahms,' he banged his fist on the table. 'What, what?' he screamed. 'How can you like this terrible composer and me at the same time?' " Pianists inclined to Classicism or mental balance may have interpretive problems in Scriabin's rarefied world. With its erotic impulse, it is the kind of music which can become addictive. It is also the most original piano music composed in Russia during the first decade and a half of the century.

His compositions of the 1890s had been inspired by the purity and refinement of Chopin. Later Scriabin added both a diabolical quality reminiscent of Liszt, but far more esoteric, and the hyperchromaticism of Wagner's *Tristan*. In his later music, he began using harmonic convolutions built upon fourths, which he termed "the mystery chord." Scriabin was a pianistic genius of a high order, and his work is a musical paradise, filled with the most inventive layouts—treacherous left-hand-writing; novel widespread figuration; imaginative trill effects. He said he wanted his music to express the unheard tones between the keys, an effect calling for creative use of the pedals. This late music is the embodiment of ecstatic and trance-like states.

Although he deigned to play only his own music, Scriabin performed far and wide, and his playing was always controversial. He must have been a pianist of exceptional ardor—Alfred Swan described him as "all nerve and a holy flame." The writer Alexander Pasternak added:

> His playing was unique. . . . It could not be imitated by producing similar tone, or power of softness, for he had a special and entirely different relationship with the instrument, which was his own unrepeatable secret. As soon as I heard the first sounds on the piano, I immediately had the impression that his fingers were producing the sound without touching the keys. His enemies used to say it was not real piano playing, but a twittering of birds or a mewing of kittens. His spiritual lightness was reflected in his playing: in his gait, his movements, his gesticulations, the way he jerked his head up when he spoke. Scriabin's nervous playing was one of his characteristics.

This nervosity of execution is apparent even in the few piano rolls he made, which have been issued on LP. He plays his D-sharp minor Etude, Op. 8, No. 12, in the heat of conflict; his wrists are rotary machines. It's arrhythmical, vertiginous, uniquely ecstatic, and faster than anyone else's. His spiritual descendants are Horowitz and Sofronitsky, and he passed on his tradition by instructing Goldenweiser, Elena Beckman-Scherbina, Konstantin Igumnov, Samuel Feinberg, and others, who continued to play and teach his music even after the Russian Revolution, when his orgiastic, supersensuous, and harmonic adventurousness was considered decadent.

GYÖRGY SEBÖK
1922–1999—Hungary

He studied and taught in Budapest, and settled in the United States. Sebök has recorded, and was a well-known teacher at Indiana University.

HANS SEELING
1828–1862—Czechoslovakia

A very successful concert pianist who composed many character pieces for the piano which were popular, such as the Op. 10 Concert Etudes; *Memories of an Artist*, Op. 13; the Barcarolle; and the *Lorelei*, Op. 2.

ISIDOR SEISS
1840–1905—Germany

A pupil of Friedrich Wieck, he went on to become a successful pianist, a teacher at the Cologne Conservatory, and the composer of many excellent piano pieces.

PHYLLIS SELLICK
b. 1911—England

Early training took place at the Royal Academy of Music in London. Later she worked with Isidor Philipp. Her career was extensive, including teaching and solo playing as well as two piano recitals with her husband Cyril Smith. In 1938 she gave the premiere of Michael Tippett's Piano Sonata No. 1.

BLANCHE SELVA
1884–1942—France

A student at the Paris Conservatoire, she made a debut at thirteen, and at twenty she performed the entire keyboard output of J. S. Bach in seventeen recitals. She was a remarkable musician, who taught at the Schola Cantorum in Paris and at the Prague and Strasbourg conservatories. She was also a brilliant scholar who wrote several books, perhaps the most important being *La Sonate*, published in 1913.

As a pianist, Selva dedicated herself to bringing to the public many works of the modern French school. She premiered and promoted Albéniz's *Iberia*. D'Indy dedicated to Selva his important Sonata, Op. 63, which she premiered in 1908, and Roussel dedicated his fine Suite for Piano, Op. 14, to her.

PETER SERKIN
b. 1947—United States

The son of Rudolf Serkin. He began studying at the Curtis Institute of Music at the age of eleven. His teachers were his father, Horszowski, and Lee Luvisi.

The young Serkin appeared in concert early, and in his teens he toured the United States; in 1959 he made a New York debut. At sixteen, he was performing in public such monumental works as the Bach *Goldberg* Variations. I heard them at that time and was pleased with his wonderful feeling for them. Every note was in place, and while he played with seriousness of purpose, he also displayed charm. His early disc of the *Goldberg* without repeats is very congenial and well designed. Nonetheless, a much later recording made in Freiburg, Germany, repeats included, puts the earlier version in the shade. His later conception is that of a mature artist playing from his brain and his heart, while the earlier one is that of a greatly gifted student toying with the daemon of this testament to Baroque variation form.

From the first there appeared in Peter Serkin's work a very special gentleness. This quality is displayed in a pristine manner in a 1967 disc of Schumann's *Waldscenen*, in which the famous *Prophet Bird* is played with exquisite care and tonal plasticity. On that same album is Serkin's delicately shaped and ethereal view of Schubert's seldom played early E-flat Sonata, D. 568. Serkin's openness and purity of feeling here are utterly captivating; he gives us Schubert's music at its most vulnerable.

Serkin has always warmed to Schubert and has a real connection to his music. It is surely a less weighty and "serious" Schubert than his father's. The only Peter Serkin Schubert playing that has left me cold is a recording of Schubert dances played on a fortepiano that are too dry and cheerless.

He has made several curious Chopin discs; they are uneven and not instantly appealing. Certainly the waltz readings are unconvincing in tempo and in use of rubato. The Barcarolle hardly sails in smooth waters, but perhaps it should be rockier than we are accustomed to. The nocturnes provoke Serkin; though he gorges himself on the slowness of the F-sharp minor Nocturne, Op. 48, No. 2, his conception of the D-flat trio of that nocturne is the most convincing I have heard. His most fascinating Chopin performance is the *Polonaise-fantaisie*, which in its deep ominousness recalls Liszt's description of the work as pathological. In his Chopin, Peter Serkin never strives for lushness of sound, nor has he ever been interested in crashing sonority.

Beethoven is of importance to this deep-thinking artist. He plays many sonatas, but there is an odd cast to his Beethoven; his readings of the *Diabelli* Variations are stark, awkward, constipated, and even maddening. The performance feels like an eternity rather than fifty-five minutes.

Peter Serkin's Mozart is more memorable in concertos than in the solo works. In such pieces as the D minor Fantasy he gets bogged down in too much pedaling and profundity, and his D major Rondo doesn't bubble as it ought. But even his Mozart concertos have not grown on me, though they are unconventional, and his piano sound is distinctive.

No American has been such an advocate for Messiaen's superstructures as Peter Serkin. He is exalted in this music, which stirs in him something deep and suggestive. His three-record set of *Vingt Regards sur l'Enfant Jésus* is certainly a great feat. The usual tendency in this music is to be muddy and smear the textures, or to provide a false ecstasy; Serkin's piercing musical intelligence avoids both of these pitfalls. He lets no rest go unnoticed; he feels purely. It is clean playing of the utmost honesty.

Few others perform the modern literature with such care. How different is his sparse Bartók Concerto No. 1 from his father's more vivid reading. The younger Serkin is ideally suited to the meditative nobility of Bartók's Third Concerto. In his beautifully stated performance of the Schoenberg Concerto, his prime concern is for perfect ensemble playing and control of shape. He has championed works by Stefan Wolfe, such as the Passacaglia, *Form IV,* and Pastorale, and solo pieces by Peter Lieberson: the Bagatelles, and the large-scale Piano Concerto with Ozawa conducting.

Serkin was a founding member of the chamber group Tashi, in which he participated in performances of works by Takemitsu, Berio, and others.

RUDOLF SERKIN
1903–1991—Austria

Studied piano in Vienna with Richard Robert and composition with Joseph Marx and Arnold Schoenberg. Serkin made his debut at the age of twelve, and at seventeen he appeared in recitals with the violinist Adolf Busch. In 1939 he became a member of the faculty of the Curtis Institute, later becoming its president. He had been head of the annual summer festival at Marlboro, Vermont.

Serkin was one of the leading figures in the performing of music in our time. As a teacher at Curtis and as the guiding light at the Marlboro School of Music, he inspired countless musicians to strive for the highest levels of artistic achievement. No other pianist today has so faithful a flock. As a performer and a teacher Serkin remained a fierce idealist who saw human grandeur in the greatest music. He has been a musical conscience to many piano students and concertgoers.

On the concert stage, Serkin appeared slightly desperate. He had an inner drive that was almost frightening. The playing gripped him, taking its toll in panting, sweat, and facial writings; simply put, Serkin spilled out his guts. He was forever looking within the score for a definitive version, his *vision.* But the music never seems quite conquered; it is always on the brink of something uncontrollable. This is what made a Serkin performance so draining. I have seen audiences hushed and totally exhausted as they left the hall. When Serkin was on, there was an exaltation that was like a blazing light. The performances took on an aesthetic truth.

Serkin knew well the musical results that his lofty conceptions could bear, but he was inconsistent in bringing them to fruition. He was a purging spirit, and when he was not achieving his ends, things could turn from bad to banging. His austerity turned ponderous, dry, and stilted, the bleakness of his sound turned brittle. He strove for a profound simplicity, and the effort could turn crude and thumpy, while his curiously untapered phrase endings gave much of his work its peculiar angularity and tautness. There was always stress in a Serkin performance; it underlay all of his playing, from the slenderest of Mozart concerto readings to the Brahms B-flat Concerto. His style was unmistakable. Clearly, this master was not interested in being a colorist; he never luxuriated in either sound or conception. He was not a musical voluptuary, like his contemporary Vladimir Horowitz, but a worker in pen and black ink: a maker of large, lean, expressive forms. When listening to Serkin, I am often reminded of the lithographs of Albrecht Dürer.

An appreciation of Serkin's art does not come easily, especially for Slavic-trained pianists. The trappings are not pretty, and his monochrome palette and ascetic musicality became more extreme in his late years, especially in his recordings.

It has often been said that Serkin was not a natural pianist. Indeed, he did royal battle at the instrument. His physical playing was unorthodox, and he was a pianist made and not born to the keyboard. He seemed to will his hands not to fail him. Yet Serkin had an admirable technique and performed the Chopin etudes publicly, though this music was more an emotional relaxation for him than an affinity.

Serkin's art was at its apex in Beethoven, whose anger and violence he captured. There is no *Pathétique* that matches his in intensity, and no other *Moonlight* Sonata has such Beethovenian wrath in the finale. His *Appassionata* is ruthless in its logic, with a finale that is scorching. He could whip chords into a scathing sound that was entirely Serkinian. Recently I was listening to his recording of the Beethoven Sonata Op. 101. Scalpel in hand, he grotesquely dissects its strange march movement. At first, I was revolted by its ugliness, but soon my mind was won over to his way. How well Serkin understands these cerebral but nerve-racking pages. His Beethoven playing has always been a mainstay for serious collectors, and with his powerful rhythmic sense, he is as successful in the concertos as in the sonatas. The finale of the C major Concerto has a joyous motoric power; his recording of the Fourth Concerto with Toscanini has given untold pleasure; his *Emperor* Concerto is might itself, and his *Diabelli* Variations possess a spectrum of drama that has no equal.

Rudolf Serkin by David Dubal

332

Serkin naturally finds himself at home with Brahms, and his discs of the two concertos are vast in scope. Among my great musical memories are Serkin's performances of these concertos with Szell and the Cleveland Orchestra. They were titanic in the second movement of the B-flat Concerto, the movement Brahms called "a tiny, tiny wisp of a scherzo," while in the first movement of the D minor Concerto, one was reminded that Sir Donald Francis Tovey called the opening the mightiest utterance since the Beethoven Ninth Symphony. Serkin's recording of the Brahms *Handel* Variations is a fine example of his ability to create a cumulative effect. Unlike most, who jauntily charge out with the theme in high relief, Serkin begins almost unpromisingly, if not tentatively, as if to say, let's see how pregnant with variational possibilities this slight tune really is.

I have always found Serkin's Schubert a shade less successful than his Brahms and Beethoven. He achieved a mammoth structure in the great B-flat Sonata; however, his playing sounds too stubborn, too raw, lacking a delicate charm and flow. His greatest achievement in Schubert remains his performance of the posthumous A major Sonata, D. 959, where grandeur and grace are perfectly matcd.

In Mozart, Serkin's superior organization made for important readings of the concerti. They are always solid and serious. His discs of the concertos with Alexander Schneider are justly celebrated. Other outstanding Serkin performances of Mozart are the Rondo in A minor and the Sonata in C minor, which are deeply serious in tone.

Serkin recorded a surprisingly broad repertory of concerti, ranging from the Bartók No. 1, the Prokofiev No. 4, the Reger F minor, in a powerful performance (he championed Reger and publicly performed and recorded his Variations on a Theme by Bach), and the Strauss *Burleske* (a favorite

version of mine), to the bold recordings of the two Mendelssohn concerti. No. 1 in G minor is fresh and glittering, gleefully bursting its seams. Even at eighty-five Serkin continued to play in public, with a somewhat impaired technique but with the same uncompromising commitment and fierce intensity.

JEAN-PAUL SEVILLA
b. 1934—Algeria

A student of Marcel Ciampi, who won the 1959 Geneva Competition. His career has taken him to Asia, South America, and the United States. Since 1970 he has taught at the University of Ottawa; he judges competitions and often gives master classes. An extremely solid pianist, Sevilla is best heard in Roussell's *Sonatine* and Suite, which he has recorded.

GIOVANNI SGAMBATI
1841–1914—Italy

An Italian pianist of great talent. His brilliant performances helped considerably to raise the taste of Italian audiences unused to hearing instrumental music, especially the German classics; he also introduced them to many new compositions by Liszt, Brahms, and Saint-Saëns. As a child, he studied with Amerigo Barberi. In 1860 he settled in Rome, where he played Beethoven, Schumann, and Chopin, as well as Bach and Handel. He gave the Roman premiere of the *Emperor* Concerto. During that period, he studied with Liszt in Rome, and Liszt admired him greatly. He traveled widely, conducting as well as playing. In 1882 he introduced his own piano concerto to England. While in London, he performed privately for Queen Victoria. In 1903 he went to Russia. Sgambati was honored in his homeland and was a founder of the Liceo Musicale, where he taught piano. His music is of a uniformly fine quality. He had a rare facility for writing for his instrument, and some of his work, especially the two piano quintets, deserves to be revived. Rachmaninoff, Levitzki, and Earl Wild have made recordings of his lovely transcription of the "Melody" from Gluck's *Orfeo*; Bolet recorded the Sgambati Concerto in G minor.

DIMITRIS SGOUROS

b. 1969—Greece

He began playing at seven years old. The next year he made a debut. Ever since, this phenomenon has played publicly, showing a tremendous technique in the most stunning virtuoso music. He was performing a splendid Chopin E minor at the age of twelve, and at thirteen he was heard with Rostropovich at Carnegie Hall in the Rachmaninoff Third Concerto, playing it to the hilt with a real flair for the score. He has an assured stage presence and plays with a strength that seems to belie his slight physique.

ARTHUR SHATTUCK

1881–1951—United States

He studied with Leschetizky for a long period, from 1895 to 1902, noting that Leschetizky "on some days would be harsh, critical, exacting;

at other times indifferent." Shattuck toured throughout the world, playing in many far-flung places. He was the first to tour Iceland, and played throughout Egypt. For several months he practiced on his grand piano at an oasis deep in the Sahara. "For a pianist with a vivid imagination," he said, "and a real desire to work, it is an ideal place to study." Shattuck came back to the United States during World War I, and performed successfully for many years.

FRANK SHERIDAN

1898–1962—United States

A student of Harold Bauer, Sheridan was an excellent pianist with a solid technique. His recording of Schumann's *Carnaval* is characteristic of his playing: conservative but poetic. He was a well-known teacher at the Mannes College of Music in New York. It was habitual for him to make students learn the Chopin Etudes, followed by the Liszt *Transcendental Etudes.*

RUSSELL SHERMAN

b. 1930—United States

Sherman is a pianist of perception, beautiful tone, and sympathy in a varied repertoire. His Chopin Twenty-four Preludes are poetic; his Beethoven complete concertos and various sonatas are grand and often profoundly moving in the slow movements. His best-known discs are of Liszt's *Transcendental Etudes,* which he has treated in a thoroughly musical manner.

Sherman studied with Edward Steuermann from the age of eleven. He made his New

York debut at Town Hall in 1945. For some years he disappeared from the concert stage, but since the mid-1970s he has recorded and concertized extensively. For many years he was the chairman of the piano department at the New England Conservatory in Boston.

WILLIAM SHERWOOD
1854–1911—United States

After studies in New York, he traveled to Weimar for finishing lessons with Liszt. In 1876 he returned to America to become one of the distinguished pianists and teachers of his time.

LEONARD SHURE
1910–1995—United States

In Berlin, Shure studied with Schnabel, the most important influence of his musical life. He returned to the United States, where he had a long career as a teacher in Boston, Cleveland, and elsewhere. His interpretations of Beethoven and Schubert are remarkable for their depth of thought and structural coherence. His record producer at Audiofon, Julian H. Kreeger, wrote: "For me, Leonard Shure was the prime exponent of the Schnabel tradition. He had a monumental conception of each work that he performed and he projected them with immense power, originality and utter conviction on a grand scale—perhaps more so than anyone whom I had the privilege of hearing, and he had a consummate technique that made it possible for him to fully articulate his bold, large-scale conceptions."

He taught many fine pianists, including Jerome Rose and Gilbert Kalish.

JEFFREY SIEGEL
b. 1942—United States

He studied in Chicago with Ganz, in New York with Rosina Lhévinne and Ilona Kabos. He has recorded the music of Gershwin with flair and technical abundance, as well as the marvelous Sonata by Henri Dutilleux, in which Siegel is an expert craftsman. At a recent recital, Siegel premiered a very difficult Liszt paraphrase on *Ernani,* which he discovered.

MARTIN SIEVEKING
1867–1950—Netherlands

Sieveking had a fine reputation as a performer and teacher. His early studies were with Leschetizky. He was well-known for his method of weight relaxation. His hand was extremely large, and he played with power and brilliance.

BÉLA SIKI
b. 1923—Hungary

A pupil of Dohnányi and Leo Weiner at the Liszt Academy. In 1947 he won the Geneva Competition and began touring, eventually performing with such conductors as Barbirolli and Ansermet. He has a considerable discography revealing good fingers and discerning musicianship. As a teacher he has been influential. In 1981 Schirmer Books issued his *Piano*

Repertoire: A Guide to Interpretation and Performance. He teaches at the University of Washington at Seattle.

ALEXANDER SILOTI
1863–1945—Russia

He studied with Zverev and Nikolai Rubinstein, later with Liszt. His little volume, *My Memories of Liszt,* is valuable for its many insights into Liszt's personality, playing, teaching, and humanity.

Siloti was a brilliant musician, a dedicated teacher of Rachmaninoff, who was his cousin (and who dedicated his First Piano Concerto and the Preludes Op. 23 to him), as well as of Igumnov and Goldenweiser in Russia, and later a whole generation of young pianists who studied with him at Juilliard.

Siloti made many editions and transcriptions which show a rare perception of the piano. His editions must be looked at with care, as he takes many liberties with the text. He was a true late Romantic, and the composers' intentions were seldom enough for him. Siloti never recorded, but his editions many give one a clue to his performances.

In his early years, he was one of the most influential musicians in St. Petersburg. He was a brilliant fixture of its varied musical life, both as a pianist and as a conductor. Mark W. Grant, in his introduction to Siloti's *My Memories of Liszt,* wrote: "In turn-of-the century Russia it was Siloti who was a more famous pianist, and perhaps a more highly regarded one, than Rachmaninoff; whereas Rachmaninoff was considered precise and over-perfect, Siloti's playing was said to have more charm and sentimentality. This distinction would align Siloti in style with such players as Paderewski, de Pachmann, et al.; Rachmaninoff more with the later Hofmann and Lhévinne."

Siloti's student Bernardo Segall has said of his playing that "it was the Romantic sense of adventure, very Lisztian . . . he played from the heart—direct, with great simplicity and nobility and a beautiful singing tone."

ABBEY SIMON
b. 1922—United States

He studied with David Saperton at the Curtis Institute. In 1941 he won the Naumburg Competition, and he has received the Elizabeth Sprague Coolidge Medal and the Harriet Cohen Medal. His concert tours have taken him all over the world. He has been on the faculty of the Juilliard School since 1977. Chopin is the mainstay of his large repertoire, and he has been recording the complete works. All of his Chopin is pianistic, with just a hint of the Romantic influence of Saperton, his teacher. His disc of the Etudes is the product of a smooth, well-lubricated mechanism. He is straightforward and always musicianly in his somewhat small-scaled but adroit playing. His Chopin can have a few suggestive ideas, and his polished virtuosity is always pleasant. Simon is capable of blinding speed and precision and has an unusually strong left hand. His Rachmaninoff Concerti recordings have an idiomatic ring, and no difficulty seems beyond him. He misses the quality of lushness in the Third Concerto, but is better in the leaner Nos. 1 and 4. His Ravel playing is convincing, the delivery assured. He is commanding in Liszt's *Don Juan* Fantasy, and his Strauss-Godowsky *Die Fledermaus* claims respect. Tonally, he offers little luster, but he plays with taste, if not with the soaring imagination of the greatest artists. I once told him I thought that the finale of his Chopin Second Sonata was admirable. He remarked, "Only a feeble imitation of the Rachmaninoff performance."

LEO SIROTA

1885–1965—Russia

Born in Kiev. A pupil at the St. Petersburg Conservatory before he worked with Busoni. In 1910 he was soloist in Busoni's massive Piano Concerto in Vienna, with the composer conducting. Sirota was a much honored and respected pianist, as well as a teacher in Vienna. Some of his Chopin playing, now on Arbitor, is detailed and beautifully molded.

RUTH SLENCZYNSKA

b. 1925—United States

She studied with various teachers and had a career as a child prodigy, during which she was terribly exploited. Her autobiography, *Forbidden Childhood*, tells her story. After a retirement, she again appeared in concert with good result. She made numerous albums; the playing is secure, with a musician's mind always at attention. She taught at the University of Southern Illinois and continues to perform publicly. Many of her recordings are now on Ivory Classics.

JOSEF SLIVINSKI

1865–1930—Poland

A famous pianist in his day, he studied with Leschetizky. He played in Europe and America, taught in Riga and Warsaw, and was often compared to Paderewski. He was not always a dependable artist; he could begin a concert only to decide he did not like what was coming out and would close the piano and depart well before completing the program. When he was in form, however, it was said he melted an audience with his "soulful" playing.

ALEXANDER SLOBODYANIK

b. 1942—USSR

Ukranian-born Slobodyanik studied with Heinrich Neuhaus at the Moscow Conservatory. A prize winner at the Tchaikovsky Competition, he made an auspicious New York recital in 1968; there followed appearances with major orchestras under Bernstein, Jarvi, Rostropovich, and others. He presents a cool virtuosity, well exhibited in his recordings of the Chopin Etudes. There is also a particularly fine sixth Prokofiev Sonata. He now lives in the United States, and in the past several seasons, little has been heard from him.

REGINA SMENDZIANKA

b. 1924—Poland

She studied with Drzewiecki, developing into an important teacher and pianist. Her recording of her compatriot Grazyna Bacewicz's Sonata No. 2 shows formidable playing, as does the set of the same composer's ten etudes, which receive impeccable readings by her.

JAN SMETERLIN

1892–1967—Poland

A pupil of Godowsky. In his heyday, roughly from 1920 to 1950, Smeterlin was a presence on the world's pianistic scene, being especially well-received in America and England. A friend of Szymanowski, he gave loyal service to his compatriot's music. Best known for his Brahms and Chopin playing, he recorded little, but when he did, such as in the "complete" Chopin Nocturnes, there is felt an intense delicacy. A late all-Chopin disc is unsatisfactory. There is a novel recording issued by VAI of an abridged version of the Schulz-Evler transcription of *The Beautiful Blue Danube* made in 1929, differing completely from Josef Lhévinne's celebrated, stunning, and steely band master approach. Smeterlin, instead, is insinuating and poetic in conception.

LEO SMIT
1921–1999—United States

He was a student of Vengerova. Smit has been identified with contemporary music, especially the music of Aaron Copland, whose piano works he has recorded superlatively. These performances are vivid, beautifully proportioned, and poetic in such scores as the *Four Piano Blues,* which were premiered by Smit. Copland has said, "Smit's brilliant and perceptive performances of my piano works are absolutely outstanding." Although he has done great service for many contemporary scores, and was himself a composer, Smit also played the Classical and Romantic literature with imagination. He had a beautiful sound and an excellent technical equipment.

CYRIL SMITH
1909–1974—England

Considered a remarkable pianist. Smith studied at the Royal College of Music in London with Herbert Fryer. From around 1928 he was in demand as a soloist. He taught at the Royal College from 1934 and often performed with his wife, Phyllis Sellick, as a two-piano team. On a tour in the Soviet Union in 1956 he suffered a stroke. His left hand was unable to play, but with Sellick he performed music for three hands, written for them by Vaughan Williams, Sir Lennox Berkeley, and others.

JOSEPH SMITH
b. 1948—United States

He studied with two remarkable pianists, Seymour Bernstein and Olegna Fuschi. Smith made his New York debut in 1974. His recordings reveal a sensitive musician with a keen ear for structure and detail. A recent "live" performance of MacDowell's "Keltic" Sonata shed new light on the score. Smith's editions of rare piano music are exemplary, and his articles in the magazine *Piano Today* are eagerly read.

RONALD SMITH
b. 1922—England

Studied at the Royal Academy. He made his London debut in 1942. In 1951 he won the Geneva International Competition. In 1954 he recorded Bach's Triple Concerto with Edwin Fischer and Denis Matthews. A wide-ranging musician, Smith plays the standard repertoire, but he has consistently wandered down the byways of the piano literature, playing worthy music by Balakirev and much by Busoni and Alkan. His Alkan discs have been very well received. He is sarcastic and lean in the *Sonatine,* Romantic and raging in the Grana Sonata. Nobody interested in Alkan can afford not to hear Smith's vital investigations of this fascinating, madcap literature.

SYDNEY SMITH
1839–1889—England

A student at the Leipzig Conservatory with Moscheles. He returned to London, where he was much appreciated. As a composer, Smith gave the English piano-playing public dozens of pieces well crafted for the hands. His operatic potpourris and E minor Tarantelle afforded much enjoyment. He had a talent for composing music that achieves the maximum in brilliance with a minimum of difficulty. His works are heirlooms from a Victorian parlor. Neely Bruce recorded his *La Reine des fées—Galop de concert,* three minutes of high-riding pianistic high-jinks.

CARLOS SOBRINO

1861–1927—Spain

A student of the Madrid Conservatory. Later he worked with Anton Rubinstein. Sobrino played frequently in Europe, both as soloist in concertos and in recital, sometimes teaming up with the violinists Sarasate and Ysaÿe.

VLADIMIR SOFRONITSKY

1901–1961—Russia

He studied with Nicolaiev at the St. Petersburg Conservatory. Sofronitsky became a legend in Russia and was one of the signal forces in Soviet pianism. His recitals were highlights of the Moscow musical season and took on cult status. He lived a turbulently Romantic existence and played the piano with a lyrical passion possessed by few. He traveled little, playing in Paris but not America. His many recordings, however, made their impact in the West, and Scriabin is most especially linked with his name. Indeed, Sofronitsky was a profoundly great interpreter of the Russian master. When he was in the mood, a merging of the pianist with Scriabin took place. He seemed born to Scriabin's sensibility, suggestiveness, and vertiginous qualities. In some

of his interpretations, one feels he is about to faint away. Especially vaporous are his luscious, barless presentations of the Fourth and Fifth Sonatas; there is intense heat in the Tenth Sonata, and acid irony in the *Satanic Poem* and Ninth Sonata.

Sofronitsky was essentially an improviser, waiting for inspiration to lift him to the heights. His tone was round, limpid, and penetrating. His conceptions are often languid, and his original musicality is marked by an individual use of rubato. One feels his music-making in half-tints, and he had a metric freedom which produced dreamlike glidings. His readings of such later Scriabin pieces as *Guirlandes, Flames sombres,* and the *Poème-nocturne* are the "liquifications" Scriabin said he wanted, music dripping between the keys. His pedaling is ravishing; for Sofronitsky, the pedal *was* the piano.

Sofronitsky also played mounds of Chopin, Schumann, Rachmaninoff, and other Romantics. He could be both inspired and uneven in the same composition. His Schumann Fantasy and *Carnaval* have beautiful and perfunctory measures side by side. There is one wonderful Chopin mazurka for every three bored ones. In the Classical literature he was less successful. His discs of Schubert's Sonata in B-flat and Beethoven's Sonata Op. 111 are emotional and erratic. Sofronitsky was a true Russian Romantic, and his entirely un-Classical complexion lacked balance. He loved to make records at live concerts, where the audience could stimulate him. When the daemon struck, as in a Rachmaninoff *Etude-tableau,* or when he sulked in a slow and morbid Scriabin prelude, he was a unique and highly charged artist with a rarefied temperament. He had a big technique, though his equipment was by no means as comprehensive as that of Richter, Gilels, or Ashkenazy, and he often needed a dose of good, clean practicing, but there is always something intriguing in a Sofronitsky performance.

GRIGORY SOKOLOV

b. 1950—USSR

Studied with Leah Zelikhman and Moisey Khalfin in Leningrad. At the age of sixteen, Sokolov won first prize at the 1966 Tchaikovsky Competition. He is a pianist of verve, formidable virtuosity, and earsplitting tone, whose recordings include a full-bodied performance of the *Hammerklavier* Sonata, the Chopin Preludes and Second Sonata, and Bach's *Art of the Fugue*. Sokolov also made an electric reading of Saint-Saëns's Second Piano Concerto and gave his first performance in the United States in 1969.

SOLOMON

1902–1988—England

Known to the world only by his first name. He studied with Mathilde Verne and was a prodigy who made his debut with the Tchaikovsky First Concerto at the age of eight. During his career, Solomon gave the premieres of several works, including the Bliss Piano Concerto in 1939. He became one of the best known and loved of British pianists. In 1956 he suffered a massive stroke. The damage proved permanent, and we were denied his revelatory art for the more than three decades that remained of his life. Fortunately, Solomon left many recordings, which prove him to be one of the great British pianists of the century, ranking with Myra Hess and Clifford Curzon.

Solomon, like most English pianists, was eclectic in his musical attractions, with a predilection for the Austro-Germanic literature. Here he is a magnificent interpreter, combining brain power with a splendid equipment of virtuoso caliber and a civilized musicality, which puts balance foremost but allows for plenty of color and excitement, too.

His Beethoven, Schubert, Brahms, and Schumann readings at times reach incomparable levels of musical awareness. He seemed to love these composers especially and equally. Many English pianists have never had Chopin in their blood, and perhaps Solomon was not born to him either, but he approached the Pole with a rare respect, playing him with a gorgeous tone and in the finest taste. It is a Chopin without frills or trumped-up virtuosity. Solomon's Waltzes, Fantasy in F minor, and Fourth Ballade have breeding and control. His Chopin is warmhearted and honest, without any superficiality of style. Solomon occasionally played Liszt, but this was not really his cup of tea, although we can hear his large technique in resounding performances of the *Hungarian Fantasy* and the Fifteenth Rhapsody.

In all that Solomon played, there was an even-tempered well-being and a hearty, throbbing spirit. When necessary, he could roar, and his chords are packed with solidity. His art had a full-blooded richness denied to most English pianists. His rhythmic sense was keen but flexible. He played with an unusual firmness, and his phrasing was fresh and forthright. With his sovereign mastery of the keyboard, he could sustain a "hush" of pure suspense in a slow movement, telling of intense and significant emotion. He could induce the most familiar music to pierce the heart anew; indeed, he seemed naturally to shed new light on whatever he played.

The pianist Gerald Moore felt that "Solomon breathed such a magical freshness into his playing that the listener might almost be persuaded the inspired artist was hearing and revelling in the music for the first time. . . . Interpretation at his level . . . is fundamentally the same art as composition. He not only played—he created music."

Beethoven was one of Solomon's chief interests. It is a Beethoven of expansiveness and joy. He could be tender and humorous, but brilliantly exciting as well; in the *Waldstein* and *Appassionata,* for instance, he can be scalding. But there is never in his Beethoven a trace of mock heroics or metaphysics. It is an earthy Beethoven, full of the world.

Solomon was a majestic Brahms player, titanic in the Second Concerto, intimate in the intermezzi. His disc of the *Handel* Variations is one of the great recordings of a Brahms composition, and Schubert's A minor Sonata D. 784 (Op. 143) is grandly conceived, containing a deep sadness throughout. Solomon is a master of the large canvas, and the sweep of his emotion is never adulterated by petty detail. He was perhaps the century's greatest British exponent of Schumann; this composer touched Solomon's nature deeply. His recording of the *Carnaval,* for example, is peerless. The score swings and dances; there are glossy gowns, the movement rustles. With Solomon playing, *Carnaval* is far more than a string of vignettes; it is a whole and brilliantly living form. The pianist brings the auditor as a spectator to an evening's merriment—indeed, to an orgiastic *Carnaval.* Solomon whispers to the listener Schumann's many intrigues. One hears the music always as music, but Schumann the man—the multifaceted personality of this tragic figure—is revealed by Solomon, himself one of the glorious and tragic pianists of the century.

YONTY SOLOMON

b. 1937—South Africa

After early studies, he worked with Myra Hess. He has performed much, playing many offbeat works, including some by Sorabji, who lifted his "ban" on performances of his works for Solomon.

HILDE SOMER

1930–1980—Austria

She studied with Serkin and Arrau. Somer had a large musical appetite and played a great deal of new music. Some of her finest moments came in the neglected Latin American repertoire. She is at her best in Juan José Castro's exceptional *Sonatina española,* whose finale is a rondo based on Weber's celebrated Perpetuum Mobile in the right hand, while the left is occupied with other material. Somer also helped popularize Ginastera, who composed his Second Concerto for her. She had previously recorded the Sonata and First Concerto. Somer had the right, refreshingly harsh, rugged sound for Chávez's *Poligonos,* a powerful, angular work which the composer called "a piece of piano playing music." She played the 1968 Antonio Tauriello Piano Concerto and made a good recording of the theatrical John Corigliano Piano Concerto.

She also made a disc of Czerny's Sonata in A-flat, as well as two albums of Scriabin's music, where she is rather heavy-handed. At Lincoln Center's Alice Tully Hall, she once gave a "light works" recital of Scriabin's music, using colored lights to highlight its psychedelic aspects.

CLAUDETTE SOREL

1932–1999—France

She studied with Samaroff. Sorel had high-speed fingers and a good musical mind. Her playing had an airy lightness in such pieces as Raff's *La Fileuse,* which she recorded. She was attracted to Rachmaninoff and has recorded his Second Sonata and the three 1887–88 nocturnes. She has edited the work of other Russians, including the attractive Twelve Etudes, Op. 74, by Arensky.

GONZALO SORIANO
1916–1972—Spain

He studied at the Madrid Conservatory; later he toured throughout Europe and the Far East. Soriano had a special way with Spanish music. His playing had a restrained elegance, an intimately hued tone. He convincingly used fascinating and almost imperceptible fluctuations of tempo in such Granados Spanish dances as the *Andaluza, Zarabanda, Jota,* and *Asturiana.* It was an inborn rhythmic knack. Soriano was once asked how one succeeds in Spanish music. He simply replied, "It's a question of accent, as with a foreign language."

AUGUSTE SPANUTH
1857–1920—Germany

A well-known pianist and teacher, Spanuth made his debut in Frankfurt in 1874 and performed and taught in Germany. From 1886 until 1906 his career kept him in the United States, where his finest pupil was David Saperton. He returned to Germany in 1906 to teach at the famed Stern Conservatory. Spanuth composed, and made several editions of Liszt's music.

CAMILLE STAMATY
1811–1870—Italy

He was brought early to Paris but did not have a piano until he was fourteen. He studied with Kalkbrenner, developing into a superb pianist of the Kalkbrenner school, very polished and elegant. Kalkbrenner felt Stamaty was his best student, calling him his musical son. Like all of Kalkbrenner's pupils, Stamaty used the Kalkbrenner hand machine for the development of even playing, using his master's *Méthode pour apprendre le piano à l'aide du guidemains.* Stamaty insisted that his own students use the guide, and since he was the prime piano teacher of two of the great prodigies of history, Gottschalk and Saint-Saëns, one can well believe that there may have been something valuable in Kalkbrenner's invention. Both of these young artists found Stamaty an inspiring teacher.

Stamaty had also spent some time in Leipzig, coming under the spell of Mendelssohn, who prodded him to introduce to Paris the Classical works of Bach, Mozart, and Beethoven, which he did.

As a composer, he produced some marvelous etudes, two piano sonatas, and a concerto, as well as twelve transcriptions, *Souvenir du Conservatoire.* Schumann reviewed some of his work with praise. In 1862 he was made Chevalier of the Legion of Honor.

BERNHARD STAVENHAGEN
1862–1914—Germany

One of Liszt's last and favorite pupils. The master admired his piano playing as well as his billiard playing. His career was very successful. Writing in 1889, Shaw felt his fortissimo was "serious and formidable," not like Paderewski's, which was "violent and elate." He also thought he performed Chopin "like a thousand blacksmiths," finding that many works were played frivolously because they were technically easy to him. He composed as well. The 1894 Piano Concerto in B minor has been given a memorable recording by Roland Keller. It is one of the best post-Lisztian concertos, with an engaging piano part and a well-formed structure. Hinson calls it "an impassioned transposition of the spirit of the Liszt Symphonic Poem to the concerto format," a work of "sustained beauty and inspiration."

DANIEL STEIBELT
1765–1823—Germany

An early piano virtuoso whose reputation was so great that he was considered Beethoven's rival.

Steibelt was a colorful personality. The critic W. J. Henderson wrote: "He was arrogant, vain, affected, and even dishonest; yet his abilities were so great that he was welcomed everywhere. . . . He was a dazzling performer, but it is beyond doubt that he was deficient in the deeper and subtler power of art."

Steibelt, however, was important in the early days of the piano as an efficient promoter of the new instrument, especially of the English pianofortes with their foot pedals, which he utilized far more than the average player. Steibelt is credited with the invention of tremolo passages, which he used to excess. He composed fifty etudes; Nos. 3 and 8 have more than a hint of Mendelssohn. He was heard from London to St. Petersburg performing his eight concerti. The Third Concerto contained the *Storm Rondo,* a celebrated piece of the time; his Eighth Concerto has a choral finale. He also wrote more than eighty Sonatas, many for violin and piano, and 117 Rondos, as well as sonatinas which have a Classical grace.

PAUL ŠTĚPÁN
b. 1925—Czechoslovakia

A well-regarded pianist who plays an abundance of Czech music, some of which he has recorded.

CONSTANTIN VON STERNBERG
1852–1924—Russia

An influential figure of his time. He studied at the Leipzig Conservatory with Moscheles and Reinecke, later with Kullak and Liszt. He toured a great deal, finally settling in Philadelphia. He composed some brilliant etudes and taught George Antheil.

EDWARD STEUERMANN
1892–1964—Poland

An illuminating pianist and teacher of wide influence, and a composer and a musician of deep and humane thought, apparent in his writings. After early studies in his hometown of Sambor, he commuted to Lemberg regularly from 1904 to study with the well-known pianist and teacher Vilém Kurz. When he was eighteen in 1910 Kurz suggested he work with Busoni, whom he respected. It was in Basel that Steuermann encountered Busoni, at a master class, playing for the master the Liszt Sonata. Busoni was impressed and Steuermann more so, moving to Berlin for further study. Somewhat later, after seeing Steuermann's compositions, Busoni recommended the young artist to study composition with Schoenberg, who saw him three times weekly from early 1912. The war years were difficult, and managing a career equally so at that time. It took many seasons and giving many piano lessons to establish himself. During these years he absorbed a copious repertoire but was never happy about his pianistic attainments. Despite very appreciable successes, he wrote, "I am afraid that the most extreme efforts will be of no avail to make a virtuoso consistently successful." In 1936 he traveled to the new world for the rest of his life, settling in New York. He made an auspicious Hollywood Bowl debut with Klemperer, but engagements were not forthcoming.

In 1944, after endless rehearsals, Steuermann performed the premiere of the Schoenberg Piano Concerto with Stokowski conducting the NBC symphony, broadcast nationwide, with Schoenberg listening in Los Angeles. Life in America was financially difficult, and Steuermann leaned heavily on teaching. It was not until 1951 that he joined the faculty of Juilliard. He wrote:

> I believe that the relationship between music teacher and music pupil is something more than "teaching," a profession, a skill, an art. It is the very emanation of the musical culture at present, quite apart from the question of whether the pupil "learns" more or less, whether he is or will be better or will achieve more than the teacher. It is part of the musical life of a community or a nation, more important than the enjoyment of concerts, radios, and music halls, because it embraces the very essence of music, which is hope and development. . . . We have to believe that art is unlimited, art is for me a way to send out feelers subconsciously, in a most differentiated way, for the most hidden and secret desires of our souls.

It is a pity that an artist of his integrity should have recorded so little. There are the complete piano works of Schoenberg, and a disc of Busoni, including the Seven Elegies and Toccata, which are just a shade puny. However, there are tapes from Juilliard recitals. Allan Evans tells me of an uninhibited Beethoven *Diabelli*. The conductor René Leibowitz had heard Steuermann's *Diabelli* in 1948, calling it one of the high points of his musical experience and seeing Schnabel in the audience with tears in his eyes. The philosopher Theodor Adorno took some piano lessons from Steuermann from 1925 and marveled at some of his "wild eruptions," feeling that Schumann was perhaps the music that came closest to his own nature: "It is impossible to describe how, under his hands, the deep crevasses in this music were opened up, to be illuminated by the consoling light of empathy." The pianist Russell Sherman studied with him intensely and thought that in Chopin "he wanted to show how incredibly advanced, harmonically/melodically, Chopin was and that this was rarely brought out by other pianists." Sherman also felt that "Schumann was in a certain sense to him the closest to his own quality of soul, his own generosity and his own feeling of the terminal anguish and sadness of the music."

Steuermann's music lies dormant, although he said, "Composing is not a hobby of mine, but the most serious thing in my artistic personality." Some years ago the American pianist Bruce Brubaker recorded his 1925–26 Piano Sonata. In two movements it probes an atonal canvas of eighteen minutes, exploring expressionistic moods. Also for piano there are the *Four* Klavierstücke (dedicated to Webern, who dedicated to Steuermann his famous Piano Variations), a fine and cohesive cycle. His latest piano work is the 1952 Suite, Prelude, Melody, Misterioso, Chorale, March. Hinson feels, "This work could only have been written by a first-rate pianist." Steuermann made some perceptive editions, and it is especially worth trying to find his editions of Brahms's piano music that he made for Universal Editions around 1930.

SIGISMUND STOJOWSKI
1870–1946—Poland

A pianist and composer who studied with Diémer at the Paris Conservatoire. Later he worked with Paderewski, who said, "You are an improviser, with results good or bad attendant on caprice." In 1926, Paderewski recorded, with engaging style, Stojowski's *Chant d'amour* and *By the Brookside*. Stojowski settled in New York, where he achieved success as a pianist and was the teacher of Oscar Levant and Arthur Loesser.

In his *Memoirs of an Amnesiac*, Oscar Levant remembers his debt to his teacher: "A good deal of what I know of music and also what I feel about it owes its origin to Sigismund Stojowski, who is not only a brilliant pedagogue but a warmly sympathetic human being. The several years I spent studying piano in New York with him remain among the most profitable and worth remembering in my life."

Stojowski was also a prolific composer, who wrote a Rhapsodie Symphonique for Piano and Orchestra, which Paderewski performed often, and Two Concertos, Opp. 3 and 32, both of which are strong in melody, beautifully scored, and grateful to play, showing the influence of the piano writing of Saint-Saëns.

AUGUST STRADAL
1860–1930—Czechoslovakia

He worked with Anton Door at the Vienna Conservatory before coming to study with Liszt, whose music he interpreted with bravura and color. He wrote music and authored several books.

SOULIMA STRAVINSKY
1910–1995—Switzerland

The son of the great composer, Soulima Stravinsky studied in Paris with Philipp. He made an American debut in 1948. He was often heard in his father's music.

EVELYN SUART
1881–1950—India

An English pianist who spent her early years in India. Suart studied with Pugno in Paris and with Leschetizky in Vienna. Her concert tours took her all over Europe. She was a champion of the new, and at age nineteen she introduced Rachmaninoff's First Piano Concerto in its original version to England. She also performed the piano music of Debussy, Ravel, Balfour Gardiner, Cyril Scott, and other British composers.

JEFFREY SWANN
b. 1951—United States

A pianist of high quality and great appeal who worked with Beveridge Webster at the Juilliard School. He was a gold medalist at the 1972 Queen Elizabeth International Competition.

Swann's discography includes an album of Busoni's piano music and the complete *Années de pèlerinage* of Liszt as well as a compact disc of Liszt's virtuoso piano pieces, among them the four *Mephisto Waltzes,* all played with virtuosity and an understanding of these sardonic works.

ROBERTO SZIDON

b. 1941—Brazil

Szidon is heard to advantage in Heitor Villa-Lobos's music, especially the *Rudepoêma*, which Villa-Lobos composed for Arthur Rubinstein. He recorded the complete Scriabin Sonatas, although these recordings are too harsh in sound and too tense; they do display a remarkable mental command structurally.

WLADYSLAW SZPILMAN

1911–2000—Poland

At the Warsaw Conservatory he studied with Michalowski, and in Berlin with Leonid Kreutzer and Schnabel. Returning to Warsaw in 1933 he began establishing himself as a composer and pianist with the violinist Bronislaw Gimpel. In 1963 he founded the Warsaw piano quartet, which performed until 1986. During the war as a Jew in Warsaw, he managed to escape deportation to Treblinka. His autobiography documents his perilous fight for survival, which was made into a movie by Polanski, *The Pianist*. A CD of his playing may be heard on Sony and documents a pianist of light touch, radiant tone, accomplished technique, and a poetic temperament. The disc includes his own 1940 concertino for piano and orchestra, composed under the extreme stress of Warsaw's nightmare. There are fine readings of Schumann, Albéniz, Rachmaninoff, and two recordings of the Chopin

Nocturne in C-sharp minor, Opus Posthumous, which he was playing at the studios of the Polish Radio, where he was music director, when a bomb hit the premises. In 1945, returning to his post at the Polish Radio, he began with the Chopin at the point when the bomb interrupted him.

ANTOINETTE SZUMOWSKA

1868–1938—Poland

From 1890 to 1895, she studied with Paderewski in Paris. Earlier, she was at the Warsaw Conservatory with Michalowski. In the United States, she performed solo and chamber music as the pianist in the Adamowski Trio.

MARIA SZYMANOWSKA

1790–1832—Poland

Celebrated in her time, Szymanowska studied with John Field in Moscow. She was called "the feminine Field," and her nocturnes show some resemblance to his characteristic B-flat Nocturne, with its early-Romantic feeling, which Chopin knew well. Goethe was infatuated with her and rated her playing even above Hummel's, calling her "an incredible player." Schumann thought well of her twelve etudes, and she also composed a set of twenty-four mazurkas.

T

GABRIEL TACCHINO

b. 1934—France

His playing is buoyant and well planned. His career has taken him to the Far East, as well as throughout Europe. His recordings of Poulenc and Saint-Saëns are delightful. He studied at the Paris Conservatoire and took away prizes from the Busoni Competition and the Long-Thibaud Competition.

MAGDA TAGLIAFERRO

1890–1987—Brazil

Tagliaferro had one of the longest careers ever, continuing to play well into her nineties. In 1983, in Carnegie Hall, she astounded listeners with her fresh, captivating playing, filled with curves and color and wrought with an amazingly loose wrist and flying fingerwork. She studied with Cortot, whose memory she revered. She knew Fauré well, and her style in his music is slim, persuasive, and elegant. She remained a tiller of the Fauré garden, and her style of playing him is slim and elegant.

She left many recordings; Villa-Lobos dedicated to her his 1929 *Momoprecoce* for Piano and Orchestra. There is a CD, transferred from the original 78s, of Reynaldo Hahn's Piano Concerto of 1930, with Hahn conducting. The sophisticated chic of the score is very Parisian. Tagliaferro remained faithful to Hahn's music, often programming his Sonatina.

GINO TAGLIAPIETRA

1887–1954—Italy

In Vienna he studied with Julius Epstein and in Berlin Busoni influenced his style. Besides concertizing he was on the faculty of the Liceo at Venice. Tagliapietra was an attractive composer, writing small pieces as well as a 1929 Concertino for Piano and Orchestra, still entrenched in a late Romantic idiom.

YUJI TAKAHASHI

b. 1938—Japan

A pianist of tremendous skill, especially in twentieth-century music, including brilliant performances of Messiaen and of Iannis Xenakis, with whom he studied composition. Xenakis's *Herma* was dedicated to him, and he premiered it. He has also composed a good deal. His composition *Maeander* (1973) was written for his sister, Aki Takahashi (b. 1944), also a brilliant concert pianist, who studied with Ray Lev.

Takahashi once wrote, "A musician serves people by filtering their collective imagination through his technical knowledge and bringing it back to them as a musical form."

SERGEI TARNOWSKY
1883–1976—Russia

He began lessons at age five, and at eight he studied with Henryk Bobínski. At the St. Petersburg Conservatory, he worked with Annette Essipova. He made a debut with the Berlin Philharmonic in the Arensky Fantasy and concertos by Tchaikovsky and Rachmaninoff. Among his pupils at the Kiev Conservatory was Vladimir Horowitz, whom he taught from the age of eleven to sixteen; Vladimir Yampolsky and Alexander Uninsky also studied with him. Coming to the United States in 1930, he taught for twenty years at De Paul University in Chicago. Later, in Los Angeles, he taught Horacio Gutiérrez. A few years before his death in Los Angeles, he recorded for Genesis Records fourteen piano pieces by Russian composers.

ROBERT TAUB
b. 1960—United States

Has played and recorded a considerable repertoire, including much contemporary music, as well as the Scriabin Sonatas for Harmonia Mundi. For Vox Classics he recorded the complete Beethoven Sonatas, and wrote a book, *Playing the Beethoven Sonatas*. He was artist-in-residence at Princeton's Institute for Advanced Study.

CARL TAUSIG
1841–1871—Poland

This short-lived favorite pupil of Liszt was by all accounts the most perfect and highly polished pianist of his time. Many felt that in certain branches of technique he outshone his beloved master, who said of Tausig, "Men such as he are so rare that one does not know where to come across them." At his death, von Bülow eulogized, "Here is the whole history of piano playing from the beginning to this day."

Tausig prided himself on playing all representative works for the piano from memory. His programs were serious and stupendous, and in the short years of his concertizing he did a great deal to celebrate the best in music. This is a characteristic program from 1870, when such a dose of piano music was still new and the institution of the piano recital was still young:

Beethoven Sonata Op. 53, *Waldstein*
Bach Bourrée
Mendelssohn *Presto scherzando*
Chopin Barcarolle Op. 60
Chopin Two Mazurkas
Weber-Tausig *Invitation to the Dance*
Schumann *Kreisleriana*
Schubert-Liszt Serenade
Liszt Hungarian Rhapsody No. 6

He once showed Wilhelm von Lenz how he could play "forever" the octaves in the Chopin Polonaise in A-flat. In refusing to show strain, he was akin to Thalberg, but, unlike his great predecessor, who idealized only the singing touch, Tausig was master of a whole range of touches—from the crystalline to the dramatic. Amy Fay wrote, "I never expect to hear such piano playing again. . . . He was absolutely infallible." Wagner wrote, "His furious piano playing made me tremble."

Not everyone loved his playing, though. In 1862, when Tausig was only twenty-one, Eduard Hanslick reviewed a Vienna recital: "What must one think of the ear of an artist who does not hear the howling metallic rattling of the abused chords or is not disturbed by it? And what a choking, squeezing, and strangling of tones you get when he finally sets loose his whole pack of hounds!"

Hanslick reminded his readers that "Tausig again stuck to his trying practice of presenting himself alone the whole evening, admitting neither singing nor accompanying instruments."

Notwithstanding Hanslick, Tausig was to be the most idolized German pianist of that decade, a great interpreter first and foremost. He taught some important pianists in his short life, and opened a piano conservatory in Berlin. Karl Barth, Oscar Beringer, Joseffy, and many others came to study with him. But it seems his teaching could be as violent as some of his playing. Amy Fay declared: "His idea of teaching is to utter such cries of encouragement as 'Terrible, shocking, dreadful, Oh God, Oh God!' He would then push the pupil aside violently, play the passage himself, and tell the pupil to do it just so."

Tausig lives on as a composer of some fabulous piano transcriptions and paraphrases in the Lisztian manner, the most celebrated being his arrangement of Bach's Toccata and Fugue in D minor and an exceedingly clever adaptation of Weber's *Invitation to the Dance*, a real lesson in transforming its "Classical" pianism into a more "textured" style. His Fantasy on themes from Moniuszko's opera *Halka* was once well-known and has been recorded by Michael Ponti, and his Strauss paraphrase, *One Only Lives Once*, is immortalized in Rachmaninoff's 1927 recording.

His few original works, such as the two Concert Etudes, Op. 1, and the ballade *The Ghost Ship*, are genuinely wonderful pages of German Romanticism. The Ballade is fearsome, heavily octaved, and eerily pictorial. Tausig's monument to piano pedagogy is his set of Daily Exercises, which are superb builders of finger dexterity.

Tausig set standards for the achievement of pure virtuosity, not for its own sake but as a means of penetrating to the core the masterpieces of the piano literature—an idea that he helped to spread. He remains a legend in piano lore.

FRANKLIN TAYLOR
1843–1919—England

A student of Clara Schumann, Taylor became an influential teacher, made many editions, and was by all accounts a fine pianist.

IGNACE TEDESCO
1817–1882—Czechoslovakia

A student of Tomáschek, he pursued a fruitful career as a concert pianist and composer of salon music.

ROBERT TEICHMÜLLER
1863–1939—Germany

His chief teacher was Reinecke at the Leipzig Conservatory, where he later taught. He achieved a fine reputation as a performer and edited several volumes of the classics.

PART I

MOZART'S IL DON GIOVANNI.

Terzetto..." Ah taci ingiusto core,"

Miss RAINFORTH, Mr. WEISS, and Mr. BALFE.

CANTATA—Wind of the Winter Night, whence comest thou?

Mr. H. RUSSELL.

Words by Charles Mackay, Esq.

"Wind of the winter night, whence comest thou?
And whither, oh whither, art wandering now?

Sad, sad is thy voice, on this desolate moor,
And mournful, oh mournful, thy howl at my door."

BALFE'S ARIA,

" La speranza.".........Madame BALFE.

NEW FANTASIA, PIANOFORTE,

On Airs from Lucrezia Borgia (first time of performance)....Mr. THALBERG.

BISHOP'S SONG,

" Peace inviting.".......Miss RAINFORTH.

ROSSINI'S IL CONTE UGOLINO,

Aria, " Già il momento.".................Mr. WEISS.

" Già il momento s'appressava
Che a lor pane si ricava,
Ma ognun d'essi dubitar.
Chè di quella torre infame,
Ch'ora ha il titol della fame,
L'uscio udirono inchiodar."

Andante, Pianoforte, in D flat, Op. 32, followed by a **Grand Studio,**
Mr. THALBERG.

This two-page program of a Thalberg concert in London in 1842 is typical of the early Romantic period, before the solo piano recital became entrenched in musical life.

Right: *An autograph from Thalberg's second American tour.*

PART II.

BALFE'S FALSTAFF.

Duo, " Voi siete un uom di spirito."......Mr. WEISS and Mr. BALFE.

Fantasia, Corno,....Mr. MAYER.

BENEDICT'S BALLAD,
" The Sleeper,"...........Miss RAINFORTH.

Hush! from all voice, save of Music, forbear,
   Speak in low murmurs, tread lightly the ground ;
Let her sleep on, while her long auburn hair
   Waves o'er her shoulder in tresses unbound.
Lo ! her lips open, as if in a prayer ;
   Mark how the shadow hath passed from her brow :
Ah ! what a smile of contentment was there ;
   Surely she wanders in fairy land now.

She is at home with her sisters at play,
   In the hall meadow, around the yew tree ;
O, in all revel of Christmas or May,
   None was so airy, so lively as she.
Lo ! she's joining their laughter again,
   Mocking the linnet aloft on the bough ;
All is forgotten, bereavement and pain ;
   Surely she wanders in fairy land now.

Now she smiles brighter—a voice at her heart
   Whispers the vows that she answered of old ;
How hath she yearned, since she saw it depart,
   Once again, waking, that face to behold !
Ah ! 'tis in vain ; for the drear ocean wave
   Hides her belov'd in its chambers below.
Call her not back to remember a grave !
   Hush ! let her meet him in fairy land now !

Grand Fantasia, Pianforte, on the Minuet and Serenade in Don Giovanni, *(by desire)* ....Mr. THALBERG.

Ballad, " The Ivy green,"....Mr. RUSSELL.
Written by Charles Dickens, Esq.

Oh ! a dainty plant is the Ivy green,
That creepeth o'er ruins old.

LOVER'S BALLAD,
" When first I o'er the mountain trod,"......Madame BALFE.

When first I over the mountain trod,
How fresh the flowers, how green the sod !
The breeze seem'd whisp'ring soft delight,
And the fountains sparkled like diamonds bright.

But now I wander o'er the mountain lone,
The flowers are drooping, their fragrance gone ;
The breeze of morn like a wail appears,
And the dripping fountain seems weeping tears.

And are ye changed, oh, ye lovely hills ?
Less sparkling are ye, bright mountain rills ?
Does the fragrant bloom from the flowers depart ?
No ! there's nothing chang'd but *this breaking heart.*

Pianoforte.

New Grand Capriccio on the 1st Finale and Introduction to Semiramide........Mr. THALBERG.

S. Thalberg

Boston, April 6th 1857

SIGISMOND THALBERG

1812–1871—Switzerland

He studied with some of the most famous piano practitioners of the era: Hummel, Moscheles, Pixis, and Kalkbrenner. Thalberg made a debut in Vienna in 1830. By 1834 he was appointed court pianist to the emperor of Austria. His tours took him through Germany, Belgium, Holland, Russia, Spain, and England. In 1855 he gave concerts in Brazil, and in 1857 his concerts in the United States caused a sensation. He composed two operas, a piano concerto, nocturnes, etudes, valses, a sonata, and *L'Art du chant appliqué au piano*, Op. 70. He was best-known for his sixty fantasies and variations on various operas.

Thalberg was one of the great stars in the Romantic firmament. He was aristocratic and handsome, his manners were perfect, his dress impeccable. He was the illegitimate son of a baroness and a count: even this blemish had an aura of romance. Everywhere he was the darling of the public. Indeed, Thalberg was the only pianist capable of threatening Franz Liszt's supremacy throughout Europe.

Unfortunately, Thalberg's celebrity now rests on his rivalry with Liszt. During the 1830s, the question of who was the mightier pianist was taken quite seriously by Romantic-minded and claque-ridden Paris. Finally, a contest of pianistic daring was devised, in which the two titans of the keyboard tested their prowess and played their choicest commodities. All of Parisian high society came to applaud for either the demonic Liszt or the gentlemanly Thalberg. The poet Heine reported, "Everywhere in the room were pale faces, palpitating breasts, and emotional breathing." But neither Thalberg nor Liszt could manage to win the day. The eccentric Princess Belgiojoso, who arranged the pianistic duel, decided for history when she gasped, "Thalberg is the best pianist in the world; Liszt is the only one." Later, Liszt said of Thalberg's singing tone that "Thalberg could play the violin on the piano." (In fact, Thalberg studied singing for five years.)

The twenty-year-old Chopin heard him in 1830 and wrote to a friend: "Thalberg plays famously but he is not my man; he is younger than I, popular with the ladies, writes potpourris on themes from Masaniello, produces *piano* with the pedal instead of with the hand, takes tenths as easily as I do octaves, and wears diamond shirt-studs."

Thalberg possessed one of the most perfect mechanisms of his era. It was a point of honor with him never to show the slightest exertion during a performance. He was indefatigable in his striving for perfection and could practice through the night on one measure. A story circulated that an Englishman, having followed him from concert to concert for several years in the hope of hearing Thalberg play just one wrong note, finally blew his brains out in despair of ever hearing the long-awaited clinker.

Like Chopin and Liszt, Thalberg was of the new school of multitextured pianism. In his music, especially his many operatic fantasies, he employed a compositional technique that, to the simpler ears of his time, sounded as if there were three hands playing. It was accomplished by highlighting his melody with clever use of the thumbs, surrounded by arpeggiated figures of various kinds. With the use of the sustaining pedal, he could keep both hands free, while the melody was singing out in bold relief. (He had probably learned much from the technique of the harpist Elias Parish-Alvars, 1808–1849.) Thalberg's arpeggio technique was so smooth and rounded that he was nicknamed "Old Arpeggio." In the early years of the development of virtuosity, it was not unheard of for some awed member of the audience to stand on his chair trying to see where Thalberg's third hand came from. As James Huneker wrote: "He knew his public and tickled the ears of the groundlings with his fantasias and variations on popular operatic airs. The prayer from Rossini's "Moses in Egypt" was a favorite, and as played by the greatest singer on the keyboard—Thalberg had the mellowest touch among his contemporaries—and with his lyric thumb he intoned the melody."

In his heyday, Thalberg's music was played everywhere there was a piano to be played. Two of his supreme potboilers, the Variations on "Home, Sweet Home," Op. 72, and the Variations on "The Last Rose of Summer," Op. 73, were popular around the world. These have been recorded by Michael Ponti and show off Thalberg's superb talent for pianistic effect. He wrote a Piano Concerto in F minor, Op. 5, reminiscent of Hummel, Weber, and Rossini, all within a latticework of finely grounded pianism. The score was too derivative and trite to survive, yet an aroma of the period surrounds it. Of greater importance is the large C minor Sonata, Op. 56, a showy work with Classical intent, containing moments of nobility.

His most ingenious use of the piano, however, is in his operatic fantasies and paraphrases, which were cherished in a time of unashamed virtuosity. Clara Schumann in her younger years played several of these concoctions, as did Anton Rubinstein and the young César Franck, and Brahms too performed them. Actually, the calculation of effects in a Thalberg paraphrase amounts to a kind of genius. Indeed, Mendelssohn, who used Thalberg's three-handed effect in his E minor Prelude, wrote, "A Fantasia by him is a piling up of the choicest, finest effects and an astounding climax of difficulties and elegances. Everything is so thought-out, refined, with such sureness and knowledge and in such good taste." Among Thalberg's characteristic fantasies are the Rossini *Moses*, Op. 33, which rode a wave of popularity for decades; the Fantasy on Rossini's *Barber of Seville*,

Op. 63; the Fantasy on Donizetti's *Don Pasquale,* Op. 67; and the Meyerbeer *Les Huguenots* Fantasy, Op. 20. Each one is fanciful and creative in its use of themes from the opera. The music makes no pretension, though, to anything more than the tinsel it is. It is an elegant and idealized pianism, magnificently notated.

Daniel L. Hitchcock expresses something of Thalberg's intent: "Whatever else it may be, Thalberg's music is three-dimensional—existing within and without. Melody is the nucleus—whether great arcs of sound, undulations of harmony, or sparks of note fragments. Only a portion comes from the instrument, the rest hovers about it, or passes through as though coming from a great distance."

Unfortunately, Thalberg's harmonic imagination was far weaker than his purely pianistic invention; and in an age of growing chromaticism, his harmonic simplicity wedded to a complex pianistic fabric began to sound pale. Through his three-handed formations, however, Thalberg gave piano scoring another dimension—one which Liszt favorably utilized as part of his orchestrally conceived style, and which is part of the texture of the keyboard music of Franck, Fauré, Granados, and many others.

JEAN-YVES THIBAUDET
b. 1961—France

He studied at the Paris Conservatoire with Lucette Descaves and Aldo Ciccolini. In New York, Thibaudet distinguished himself by winning the 1981 Young Concert Artists Auditions, and he has performed and recorded ever since then. In 1992 he performed the complete piano music of Ravel in New York. Thibaudet has a virtuoso technique and plays with dashing brilliance.

ISTVÁN THOMÁN
1862–1940—Hungary

One of the foremost piano teachers of his time in Hungary, Thomán taught Dohnányi and Bartók, and was deeply respected by them. Thomán was himself a pupil of Liszt from 1881 to 1885.

IGNACE TIEGERMAN
1893–1968—Poland

A prodigy who studied with Leschetizky for four years and with Friedman in Vienna and Berlin. Friedman said "he was the greatest talent he ever worked with"—no small encomium from one of history's mightiest players. A Vienna recital from 1922 offers a typical program: the Schumann F-sharp minor Sonata, Debussy's *Reflets dans l'eau, Poissons d'or,* Ravel's *Ondine,* Granados's *Fandango,* and the Liszt Sonata. But shyness, political tensions, and ill health were against the career that many predicted for him. He ended up in Cairo, Egypt, where this Polish-Jew opened a conservatory, taught, and successfully performed on various occasions. In doing research on Friedman, the piano archeologist Allan Evans found bits of Tiegerman's recordings and began a longtime search to resurrect some of his legacy for Arbitor CDs in a CD titled *The Lost Legend of Cairo.* Evans ranks Tiegerman in eminence with Friedman, and, listening to the jewels contained on these two CDs, one may agree with him—his performance of Chopin's B minor Sonata is monumental, technically on a Himalayan peak. The poetry in the F minor Ballade and Barcarolle is never precious, but rounded, firmly structured, with billows of sound. Digital problems do not exist; the F-sharp minor Prelude is encased in plush purple velvet with the rumbling agitation intact. The two Field nocturnes on the disc are idyllic, and the three Brahms pieces are ambrosia. Never is there a rushed moment; nothing is overheated or sugarcoated, like Friedman at his best—all is there to savor. The CD also offers the Saint-Saëns Fifth Concerto, "The Egyptian," with that exotic, corny, slow movement; even with poor recorded sound Tiegerman's tone is luminous. Evans in his fortitude has put Tiegerman where he belongs: in the great panorama of pianists.

VERA TIMANOFF
1855–1942—Russia

A student of Anton Rubinstein and Tausig as well as Liszt, who called her "an artist of rare talent." She made a few piano rolls, and lived and taught at St. Petersburg.

PEDRO TINTORER
1814–1891—Spain

Born at Palma de Mallorca, Tintorer studied in Madrid and in 1832 went to the Madrid Conservatory to work with Pedro Albéniz, one of the founders of Spanish pianism. Two years later he was taking lessons from Pierre Zimmerman and possibly received some coaching from Liszt in Paris. Tintorer composed a great deal of piano music, as well as pedagogic methods. Linton E. Powell says of his salon piece *Flor de España:* "Here we find a work in the 'grand manner,' with even a Rossini *crescendo* thrown in . . . Effective right-hand figurations . . . and a syncopated right-hand melody recalling Chopin's Waltz in A-flat major Op. 42."

MARIA TIPO
b. 1930—Italy

Presently one of the best-known Italian pianists, she shows a special feeling for the music of Clementi and an astonishing affinity for the music of Scarlatti, which she has abundantly recorded. Tipo's Scarlatti delights in its technical finesse as well as its vibrant sense of rhythm.

JAMES TOCCO
b. 1944—United States

He has had a successful career as a concert pianist and teacher. His concerto and solo repertory is large, and Tocco has recorded the Griffes piano music, the four MacDowell Sonatas, and an album of the solo piano music of Bernstein. He premiered John Corigliano's *Etude Fantasy*. His playing is brilliant and musicianly.

JOHANN TOMÁSCHEK
1774–1850—Czechoslovakia

A fine musician; a pianist, composer, and teacher of importance. He left 110 opus numbers, and he was one of the first composers of his time to write expressive short pieces. His *Eclogues,* Opp. 35, 39, 47, 51, 53, 66, and 83, and *Dithyrambs,* Opp. 52 and 65, were esteemed by Schubert and Schumann. Julius Schulhoff, Ignace Tedesco, and Alexander Dreyschock were among his many students. He also taught the critic Eduard Hanslick.

DUBRAVKA TOMSIC
b. 1940—Yugoslavia

After studies in her native Dubrovnik, Tomsic studied at the Juilliard School, being a prize pupil of Katherine Bacon. Later she had some lessons with Arthur Rubinstein. Tomsic has had a world career and has taught at the Ljubljana Conservatory. Her recordings of Beethoven Concerti and Sonatas prove her to be richly musical with a solid technique. She has been on the jury of several important international competitions.

ALEXANDER TORADZE
b. 1953—USSR

Born in Tbilisi, Georgia, Toradze trained in Moscow with Yakov Zak. In 1977 he won a prize at the Van Cliburn Competition. In 1983 he immigrated to the United States. Toradze is a lusty player, with plenty of original ideas and a style of playing that capitalizes on extremes of louds and softs. He is never afraid of making a grand gesture, and audiences respond often rapturously to his guttural playing, characterized by heat and terrific velocity. He has often been heard in the five Prokofiev Concerti. Toradze has been an inspiring teacher at Indiana University.

SIR DONALD FRANCIS TOVEY
1875–1940—Scotland

A musical scholar, writer on music, composer, and extraordinary pianist. The great violinist Joachim helped promote his talents. He said, "I have discussed music with Schumann and Brahms, but not with that young Tovey. He knows too much." Tovey's *Essays in Musical Analysis* have been staple reading for musicians. He composed Classical, austere music; a large Piano Concerto in A major has been totally neglected.

James Friskin wrote: "Like all the compositions of this amazing musician, this employs a classical musical vocabulary and technique. The Concerto is a work of great dignity, beauty and power with a command of resource that actually challenges comparison with its great models. The idiom, of course, belongs to a bygone day."

As a pianist, Tovey had a huge repertoire, and his programs were uncompromising. He was a great teacher also. Myra Hess in her prime once asked him if she could play for him. "I shall never forget the inspiration of those two hours," she wrote.

In his book, *Reflections,* Pablo Casals says of Tovey: "Besides being probably the greatest musicologist of our time—I have never known anyone with his knowledge of music—Tovey was a wonderful composer. He was also a superlative pianist, in some ways the best I ever heard. The fact is I regard Tovey as one of the greatest musicians of our time."

DAVID TUDOR
b. 1926—United States

A brilliant exponent of avant-garde music, as well as a composer who utilizes electronic music. He has premiered many works, including Sylvano Bussotti's *Five Piano Pieces for David Tudor,* Cage's *Concert for Piano and Orchestra,* Stockhausen's *Kontakte,* and the American premiere of the Boulez Piano Sonata No. 2.

JOSEF TURCZYNSKI
1884–1953—Poland

A student of Essipova in St. Petersburg and of Busoni in Vienna. In 1915 he taught at the Kiev Conservatory; he returned to Poland after the Revolution. At the Warsaw Conservatory, his fame spread as a teacher and as a fine interpreter of Chopin. His students included Ryszard Bakst, Malcuzynski, Czerny-Stefanska, and others of high caliber. Turczynski was one of the editors of the now-established "Paderewski edition" of the complete works of Chopin, begun in 1941 and completed by 1949.

ROSALYN TURECK
1914–2003—United States

In Chicago she studied with Sophia Brilliant Levin and Jan Chiapusso, and later at Juilliard with Olga Samaroff. At the age of twenty-one, she made a Carnegie Hall debut in the Brahms B-flat Concerto. She held four honorary doctoral degrees and was visiting professor at numerous universities. There is a Tureck Archive at the Library of the Performing Arts at Lincoln Center.

Although Tureck's fame is now exclusively tied to Bach playing, she performed other repertoire in addition to premiering a number of modern compositions. Tureck presented her first all-Bach recital in 1937, and her appetite for the Leipzig master never abated. In fact,

Rosalyn Tureck by David Dubal

mellow interpretive maturity and a passionate investigation of the music's emotions. She is always involved, but there is also the feeling of great knowledge. "I do what Bach tells me," she has said. "I never tell the music what to do."

Tureck was proficient on the clavichord, fortepiano, and harpsichord as well, and often taught other instrumentalists, including guitarists, her way with Bach. She was, however, primarily a pianist and believed that Bach can be played convincingly on the contemporary piano. But she stated emphatically that

> I do not play the piano as a nineteenth century instrument or with current pianistic style and technique. Mine is a new piano technique, built from the established art of historical performance practices plus the structural requirements of Bach's music. The piano is capable of immeasurable tonal and stylistic approaches. It is not limited to or by the Romantic style of the nineteenth century or the percussive style of the twentieth. Given the combination of the knowledge of the scholar, the aesthetic sensitivity of the conscientious artist, and a technique emerging from eighteenth-century principles of music and performance, the piano is a valid and profoundly successful medium for the performance of Bach's keyboard music.

Students interested in her approach may consult her three volumes, *An Introduction to the Performance of Bach*.

One of Tureck's programs consisted of the *Goldberg* Variations, played first on piano and then on the harpsichord (repeats included). An interesting comparison is between her older version of the *Goldberg* Variations on piano and her more recent disc on the harpsichord. The changes are many and suggest the long gestation period Tureck went through to arrive at her final conception. There are many who love her old discs of *The Well-Tempered Clavier* from the 1960s. Indeed, nobody interested in that great work should forgo listening to them.

each year her researches brought her new light on Bach's music. Tureck's public has always been a dedicated group, and a Tureck Bach convocation sometimes has the look of a cult. It is certainly worship on a high level, and Tureck was an artist with a big personality. One did not leave unmoved. Every page she attempted had its own fascination, its own sense of timing. She had marvelous finger independence that colored each voice; each contrapuntal unit is delicately attenuated. Yet she was never idiosyncratic. Her Bach was the product of great erudition and toil. Her perfect legato, variety of touches, and rhythmic flexibility came from a saturation of scholarship. Nothing in her art happened quickly. When she played the Chromatic Fantasy and Fugue, one was certain that she had "studied the twenty-two extant manuscripts that circulated in the eighteenth century, as well as sixty editions." She worked for twelve years before bringing her performance to the public. Her recording of it is a magnificent blending of

On July 17, 2003, I hosted and programmed a tribute for Rosalyn Tureck at the International Keyboard Institute and Festival at the Mannes College of Music in New York City. Tureck was terminally ill, but sent a message to the audience before the concert.

RONALD TURINI
b. 1933—Canada

He took prizes in several competitions, including tying Pollini for second prize at the 1958 Geneva International Piano Competition. He later studied with Horowitz for a time. Turini has toured the United States, as well as the Soviet Union. He plays with a refined craftsmanship.

AUBE TZERKO
1908–1995—Canada

A pupil of Schnabel; an excellent pianist and a renowned teacher.

U

MITSUKO UCHIDA
b. 1948—Japan

She studied in Japan, and in Europe with Askenase and Kempff, later winning prizes at the Leeds and the Chopin competitions. She is a fastidious musician with a well-developed technique. Her Mozart playing is pliable, the phrasing well-defined and always with vocal intent. She is at her finest in the slow movements of the sonatas and in such scores as the A minor Rondo. Her Chopin, too, has many points of interest. She plays Schoenberg with insight, and her Debussy Etudes are stunning realizations.

IMRE UNGAR
1909–1972—Hungary

A brilliant pianist who worked with Dohnányi.

At the second Chopin Competition at Warsaw in 1932 he scored the same amount of points for first place as Alexander Uninsky. It must have been an excruciatingly tense moment when the victor was decided by a toss of a coin—Ungar lost! Although blind, he pursued a successful concert career, performing an extensive repertoire.

ALEXANDER UNINSKY
1910–1972—Russia

The 1932 winner of the Chopin Competition. He studied at the Kiev Conservatory with Sergei Tarnowsky, and at the Paris Conservatoire with Lazare Lévy. Uninsky was a less emotional pianist than many Russians. His playing was finished, but dry. His best recording is a precise and finely spun reading of the Chopin Etudes.

V

MADELEINE DE VALMALÉTE
1899–1999—France

A pupil of Isadore Philipp whose career blossomed in the 1920s. In 1930 she made the first recording of Ravel's *Le Tombeau de Couperin*. Charles Timbrell calls it "outstanding, clean and alacritous in the outer movements and stylishly upbeat and transparent in the dances." Her playing of the Toccata from Le Tombeau is an inseparable marriage of form and matter. It is the French school of piano playing at its zenith. It is no wonder that Saint-Saëns was impressed.

TAMÁS VÁSÁRY
b. 1933—Hungary

He studied with József Gát and Lajos Hernádi, and as a child, he received advice from Dohnányi. He also studied composition with Kodály. After the Hungarian uprising in 1956, Vásáry settled in London, where he added conducting to his career. He has made a distinguished series of piano recordings, essentially of the Romantic literature.

Vásáry is a poet-pianist, a dreamy bard. For him, music must first be beautiful. It must also be Romantic and emotional. In Vásáry at his peak, we have a luscious colorist replete with an exceptionally wide dynamic range, an artist capable of ravishing lighting effects. His pedaling is plush and creamy, the technique well oiled and balanced.

Chopin is never far from his field. His multicolored imagination depicts this artful literature with all kinds of felicitous lingerings. He can also become overrefined; Vásáry can suspend a note for so long that one wonders if the phrase will continue. In his quest for a free improvised art, he occasionally gets caught up in detail and hovers dangerously at the brink of arrhythmic action, where formlessness lurks. In recent years, however, this happens much less.

Vásáry plays a great deal of Liszt. In the Sonata, the *Legends,* the *Years of Pilgrimage,* and the *Don Juan* Fantasy, he appeals not to the virtuoso Liszt but to Liszt the colorful tone poet. He has recorded all of Rachmaninoff's concerti, and they are warm readings filled with a ripe, unsentimental nostalgia. His Debussy is well formed, clean, and without mannerism. In Schubert, he is fragrant and affectionate. His performance of Schubert's G major Sonata-Fantasy, D. 894, is luxuriant in its evergreen lyricism. Vásáry's searching spirit always looks at the music from his own highly individual point of view. His various Brahms pieces are among the most vital of his recorded output, and his several Mozart concertos find a flexible interpreter.

ISABELLE VENGEROVA
1877–1956—Lithuania

She studied with Essipova; also with Joseph

Dachs, as well as with Leschetizky for an extended period. Vengerova taught at the St. Petersburg Conservatory. In 1921 she came to the United States, where she taught in New York, as well as at the Curtis Institute in Philadelphia from 1924. She was the teacher of Samuel Barber, Leonard Bernstein, Jacob Lateiner, Leo Smit, Sidney Foster, Ignace Hilsberg, Leonard Pennario, Lilian Kallir, and Gary Graffman, who discussed her at length in his autobiography, *I Really Should Be Practicing*. "Vengerova," he wrote, "was really only interested in the piano and how to coax the largest range of beautiful, subtle, dazzling, dramatic, velvety and singing sonorities from that intractable black beast." In short, she exemplified all of the qualities of the Russian school of pianism with which she grew up. Many of her detractors called her intimidating, impatient, tyrannical, and even sadistic, but her forceful personality inspired many others. Bernstein called her his "beloved tyranna," saying, "The Vengerova influence abides in my playing (when I play well), and I am ever in her debt." The composer Samuel Barber also worked with her and never failed in his appreciation, saying he learned more from her about melody than from his composition studies.

In his memoir *Perfect Pitch*, her nephew Nicolas Slonimsky wrote: "Her students could be sure that she would not leave off until every minuscule detail, every nuance, every action of the loud and soft pedal was brought to perfection. . . . Aunt Isabelle imposed merciless discipline on her students, no matter how talented. Because of that, or in spite of that, the "Vengerova stamp" became a mark of distinction."

ILANA VERED
b. 1943—Israel

She studied in Paris with Perlemuter and Darré, and in New York with Rosina Lhévinne. Vered is a stylish virtuoso with great technical flair. Her recordings of the twenty-four Chopin etudes show a remarkable dexterity, as does her disc of Moszkowski's virtuoso etudes.

MATHILDE VERNE
1865–1936—England

A pupil of Franklin Taylor, she then studied for six years with Clara Schumann. She took part in the concert life of London and opened a school for piano. Her sister Adela Verne (1872–1952) was an acclaimed concert pianist.

VLADIMIR VIARDO
b. 1949—USSR

He received piano studies in Moscow, and was the winner of the 1973 Van Cliburn Competition. In Russia he has had a formidable career, and is respected as a teacher and virtuoso. In 1988 he returned to the United States in a series of triumphant appearances, crowned by a Carnegie Hall performance of the Rachmaninoff Third Concerto with the Dallas Symphony.

ALEXANDER VILLOING
1804–1878—Russia

A student of Dubuc and the only teacher of Anton Rubinstein. His *Practical School of Piano Playing* was used for years in Russia.

RICARDO VIÑES

1875–1943—Spain

He studied with Pujol and later at the Paris Conservatoire. He became one of the most persuasive interpreters of the Spanish and French modern schools. His playing of Falla, Debussy, Ravel, de Séverac, Poulenc, and so many others brought him great distinction. Falla's *Nights in the Gardens of Spain* is dedicated to him. Poulenc studied piano with him and wrote, "I owe him everything; no one taught the pedal, that essential factor in modern music, better than Viñes. He could play clearly within a flood of pedal work, which seems paradoxical. And what a mastery of staccato touch!"

ELISO VIRSALADZE

b. 1942—USSR

Studied with her grandmother, Anastasia Virsaladze, at the Tbilisi Conservatory. From 1955 at the Moscow Conservatory she worked with Yakov Zak. She has concentrated mostly on Mozart, Schumann, Liszt, and Chopin. Virsaladze has a flexible command of the piano, and plays with fire and tenderness. Sviatoslav Richter wrote of a 1993 recital, "Can one imagine a more beautiful Schumann than the one offered to us this evening by Eliso Virsaladze? Not since Neuhaus have I heard Schumann like it."

PANTCHO VLADIGEROV

1899–1978—Bulgaria

The most distinguished Bulgarian composer and pianist, and the early teacher of Alexis Weissenberg. An international piano competition held in Sofia is named for him.

MAX VOGRICH

1852–1916—Austria

A student of Reinecke and Moscheles at the Leipzig Conservatory. He lived, taught, and performed in Australia, London, and New York. He composed a piano concerto and edited Schumann and others. His *Staccato-Caprice* makes a brilliantly effective encore.

ARCADI VOLODOS

b. 1972—USSR

A native of St. Petersburg. Studies in voice and conducting took first place in his early years. Not until 1987, at the unusually late age of fifteen, did he decide to concentrate on the piano as his major musical activity. In Moscow at the conservatory he worked with Galina Egiazarova. Jacques Rouvier taught him in Paris and in Madrid he received lessons from Dimitri Bashkirov. It would be in only nine years, in 1996, that Volodos would make a New York debut, and a recording debut for Sony Classical.

Few pianists in the last years have so captured the public's applause, and he has appeared throughout the world with the most eminent conductors, to ever mounting acclaim and valediction from the press. His recording producer, Thomas Frost, calls him "a neo-romantic in the best sense of the word: he engenders in his audience a wide range of emotional responses, from serenity to rousing excitement, without ever loosening the reins of a guiding intellect." Indeed, it seems Volodos can be heard thinking. He knows every ounce of the key-bed, the exact weighting of each chord. As a colorist he loves soft pastel coloration in his Schubert, and even in Schumann's *Kreisleriana,* which made me nervous in its prissiness, although admiring the fact that each arched lavishly pedaled phrase was doubtless his way with the visionary score. But it was off-center, dispassionate, and tricksy. His recording of the Rachmaninoff Third Concerto with Levine has fine movements, but also contains ponderous, fat sounds where leanness would be preferred, with a more smoldering temperament. It's a "gilding the lily" Rachmaninoff, which the great composer-pianist may have disdained. There is a Schubert disc with no less than the verdant G major Sonata, D. 894; here he is slow-moving and stagnant, and it is of a "heavenly length" that mortifies the average pianist and listener not withstanding many beautiful colors. The piece's first movement especially seems to dissolve into space. The disc offers a delightful novelty in an 1815 E major Sonata (unfinished), D. 157, which once again draws out the pianist's luminous sound and many touches.

His debut recording offers tantalizing repertoire, two luscious transcriptions by Volodos himself of Rachmaninoff songs and three Schubert-Liszt songs, played with the highest polish and idiomatic identification. The former singer is thrilled with highly charged melodic lines. The CD includes more transcriptions: the Prokofiev pieces from *Cinderella* are dry and teasing, and two Samuel Feinberg arrangements, the *Largo* from the Trio Sonata No. 5 breathes serenity, while the *Scherzo* from the *Pathétique* Symphony of Tchaikovsky is incomparable virtuoso pianism. And Volodos has nerve, arranging Mozart's famous *Turkish March* from the A major Sonata, K. 331. He must have had a good time making it, with a naughty glint in his eye. And he dauntlessly gives us two of Horowitz's own blistering creations: the 1968 version of his *Carmen* variations and the spine-tickling Second Rhapsody of Liszt. Does he compare here with Horowitz himself? Yes, is the answer, with even more

insouciance than the earlier Russian master's recordings, if without the subtle difference of Horowitz's unique rhythmic knife cutting each note to the quick. The Horowitzian temperament is more daemonic; Volodos is really an angelic character and for that reason makes only elegant facsimiles. But in their buttery and brilliant pianism one can only take one's hat off to him. And when Volodos gives his audiences his various Horowitz transcriptions the concert hall resounds like a sports stadium, with the kind of delirium given to grand-slam hitters. One other transcription should be noted: that *Flight of the Bumblebee* in the raucous interlocking octave version by the legendary György Cziffra. I think in this case Volodos is neck and neck with the great Cziffra.

JAN VOŘIŠEK
1791–1825—Czechoslovakia

He studied with Tomáschek, played concerts, and composed some good piano sonatas.

RALPH VOTAPEK
b. 1939—United States

He studied with Robert Goldsand and Rosina Lhévinne in New York. Votapek established himself as a musician of note in his early twenties by winning two piano competitions: the Naumburg Competition in 1959 and the first Van Cliburn Competition three years later, in 1962. Votapek has performed in concert throughout the world, including South America, where he has gone on fifteen tours. Votapek is artist-in-residence at Michigan State University. A recent recording of Granados is well-crafted playing.

VITYA VRONSKY

1909–1992—Russia

She studied with Schnabel. Vronsky married Victor Babin, and thereafter she and her husband achieved renown in the Vronsky and Babin piano duo.

ANDRÉ WATTS

b. 1946—Germany

He studied in Philadelphia, and at the age of ten played a Haydn concerto at a Philadelphia Orchestra children's concert. In 1963 he made an overnight sensation appearing on national television in the Liszt E-flat Concerto, with Leonard Bernstein conducting. Bernstein was so impressed with the youth's pianistic finesse that he predicted "gianthood" for Watts. Immediately afterward, they recorded the Liszt concerto. In 1967, Watts made a world tour for the U.S. State Department. During this time he continued studies with Leon Fleisher. In 1973 he played in the Soviet Union. At the age of twenty-six, he was given an honorary doctorate by Yale University, the youngest person ever to receive that honor from Yale.

Watts never had to build his career through the drain of competitions. In his case, one TV exposure began the road to stardom, and Watts has never stopped since. He is a rugged professional with a deeply ingrained technique, which is very secure onstage. He is an especially fine concerto player, and the Liszt E-flat Concerto that he recorded as a youngster of sixteen is engaging and natural in its lyricism, unforced in its virtuosity. His scales are smooth and the tops of his octaves glistening. It is all singularly elegant. From that period, there are also a delightful Haydn Sonata in E-flat, a fleet Paganini-Liszt Etude in E-flat, and a nicely balanced and restrained C minor Nocturne of Chopin, Op. 48, No. 1.

André Watts by David Dubal

But as Watts developed, the elegance disappeared, and a harder, more lustful tone appeared. His conceptions became stolid. He recorded a Rachmaninoff Third Concerto, a respectable Schubert album, a journeyman's Liszt Sonata, and an electric Liszt *Totentanz*. His Gershwin album lacks style, with a lumbering *Rhapsody in Blue* in the solo version. His Chopin Sonata in B-flat minor and F minor Concerto display nothing more than competence; the heated drama of the sonata is missing, and the concerto is perfunctory.

After those discs, Watts literally disappeared from the recording studio for years. His public career thrived, and he continued to have great success with audiences, but the artist in him did not seem to grow. His recitals had more than a hint of vulgarity, with banging and other meretricious effects. He seemed convinced that these pieces, played more idiomatically, would not move an audience. He lost all semblance of his naturalness.

Just when I was about to drop Watts from my concertgoing, though, I did a double take on listening to his disc "André Watts Live in Tokyo," where he is gallant in two Scarlatti sonatas, once again elegant in the Haydn Sonata No. 48 in C major, and quite childlike in Debussy's *Children's Corner Suite*. Not one to give up on any pianist of talent, I went to several more Watts recitals at Avery Fisher Hall, only to be disappointed again. Gershwin, Chopin, Liszt, all writhed in bloated playing. Where was the Watts of Tokyo? When two Liszt records were released, I gave a listen and found a high level of Liszt playing, this new version of the Sonata being better by far than his early one. And even finer is the album containing a good selection of the "later" Liszt, played with genuine affection, dash, tenderness, and simplicity.

Watts may now be past the phase when he played down to his audience. These latest records show an honest musicality and reveal that Watts may yet grow to the "gianthood" predicted for him by Leonard Bernstein.

DANIEL WAYENBERG
b. 1929—France

In Paris he coached with Marguerite Long for many years. In 1949 he took a second at the Long-Thibaud Competition. In New York he made his debut in 1953 with Metropoulos

conducting the New York Philharmonic. Wayenberg performs a large repertoire with elan and is a brilliant concerto performer.

CARL MARIA VON WEBER
1786–1826—Germany

He studied for a short time with Michael Haydn, the great composer's brother, and later with the gifted musician Abbé Vogler. Weber the pianist, however, may be said to have been self-taught. He was one of the best conductors of the time and was the creator of German Romantic opera. He also had a pleasing singing voice until his vocal cords were partially destroyed when he took a glass of nitric acid that he had thought was wine. He had a literary bent, writing well-turned criticism, and he could draw well. In many ways he was the model for Schumann, but unlike that unhappy master, who injured his hand in his feverish attempts to achieve pianistic virtuosity, Weber was a concert pianist, one of the most original of the first quarter of the nineteenth century.

Weber's career in Germany was a revelation for the budding young Romantics. He was distinguished-looking, worldly, had a Byronic limp, and died of consumption at only forty, days after conducting his last opera, *Oberon*, in London. His life was the stuff of which legends are made. Philipp Spitta wrote of the youthful Weber: "His life had been that of a wandering minstrel or troubadour. Roving restlessly from place to place, winning all hearts by his sweet, insinuating, lively melodies, his eccentricities making him an imposing figure to the young of both sexes, and an annoyance to the old, exciting the attention of everybody, and then suddenly disappearing, his person uniting in the most seductive manner aristocratic bearing and tone with indolent dissipation; his moods alternating between uproarious spirits and deep depression—in all ways he resembled a figure from some romantic poem."

Although Weber never studied with a major pianist, he prided himself on a thorough knowledge of all aspects of technique. He thought the school of Viennese pianists headed by Hummel was superficial, dry, and correct. Weber wanted the piano to have a music that spoke of mystery and poetry, of forest glens and chivalry, as he had achieved in his operas.

Weber's hands were enormous, possibly spanning a twelfth. He wrote some of the most complicated piano music of the early 1800s, with difficult left-hand figurations and choral layouts of abnormally large stretches. His music calls for finger independence in new ways, such as having one hand play staccato and legato within a single passage. An excellent guitarist, he invented wonderful strumming effects for the piano. His music dashingly takes the most adventurous leaps until Liszt.

As a pianist, he performed in public primarily his own music, but privately he played Beethoven sonatas for his pupil Julius Benedict "with a fire and precision and a thorough entering into the spirit of the composer, which would have given the mighty Ludwig the best proof of Weber's reverence and admiration for his genius." This was in 1821, and Weber had already written his own four piano sonatas, the two concerti, and the *Konzertstück,* which became one of the warhorses of nineteenth-century virtuosi. John Warrack, in his biography of Weber, states the unique importance of the score: "The *Konzertstück* is a keystone work of Romantic piano writing, crowning the bridge that leads from Dussek, Hummel, Kalkbrenner, Prince Louis Ferdinand and their contemporaries into the mid-nineteenth-century and Mendelssohn, Schumann, Chopin and Liszt, while its influence was consciously acknowledged as late as 1929 by one of Weber's greatest modern admirers, Stravinsky, in his Capriccio."

When Liszt first heard Weber's music, he was beside himself with glee. Mendelssohn was mesmerized, and Chopin, who criticized almost everybody's work, sighed, "An angel passes through the sky," when his student Georges Mathias played Weber's A-flat Sonata for him. Brahms and Tchaikovsky were so fascinated with the celebrated Rondo from the C major Sonata, known as the Perpetuum Mobile, that for fun they were both impelled to transfer the right hand to the left hand.

It was in 1819 that Weber launched the dance form of the century—the waltz. His immortal *Invitation to the Dance* linked all the popular elements of Romanticism in piano writing of a poetic virtuosity. The *Invitation* was the most-played piano work for decades after its composition.

Today Weber is seldom found on recital programs, nor are his two piano concertos and *Konzertstück* often heard in orchestral programs. Yet his music has a fresh piquancy and an endearing innocence. He was the richest genius among the transitional composers born in the early stage of Romanticism, and some of his music will always exert a special magic.

BEVERIDGE WEBSTER
1908–1999—United States

His father taught him in his native Pittsburgh, and in Paris he studied with Isidor Philipp at the Paris Conservatoire, and later with Artur Schnabel.

Webster had an important career as a soloist with major orchestras, an adjudicator of international competitions, and for more than three decades an eminent teacher at the Juilliard School, where he taught Paul Jacobs, Michel Block, and Jeffrey Swann.

He recorded a great deal: outstanding readings of works ranging from the

Hammerklavier Sonata of Beethoven, and Weber and Schubert sonatas, to Copland's Variations, Rachmaninoff's *Etudes-tableaux,* Ravel's *Gaspard de la nuit,* and Elliott Carter's Sonata, in which Webster's performance is packed with intellectual control and hard, raw technical command. He also had one of the most impressive of concerto repertoires and investigated every idiom in his seemingly insatiable delight in the literature.

Webster was a spontaneous performer who could be spotless in one piece and quite messy in the next, but when inspiration struck and all elements happened to blend, he was a deeply moving artist. I vividly recall a Town Hall recital, which ranks high in my recital experiences, where he played the most ravishing Schubert Sonata-Fantasy, Schumann's *Waldscenen,* Liszt's *Dante Sonata,* and other works, with unforgettable impact, precision, and tonal balance.

Webster's sight-reading prowess was legendary: once when looking at a terribly complex score just sent to him, Edward Steuermann said to his pupil, David Porter, "What I do with a piece like this, is to take it down the hall to Beveridge Webster. If *he* can't read it at sight, then I know it is unplayable."

ALEXIS WEISSENBERG
b. 1929—Bulgaria

He played a concert at the age of eight, while studying with Bulgaria's most famous musician, Pantcho Vladigerov. In 1946 he graduated from the Juilliard School, where he worked under Olga Samaroff. Weissenberg, in 1947, won the Leventritt Competition and made his American debut with the New York Philharmonic, with Szell conducting. For nearly ten years Weissenberg was busy with concertizing. In 1956 he left the concert stage for nearly a decade to study. He reappeared after this hiatus with great success, bringing the public a larger and rejuvenated solo repertoire, which includes Bach to Bartók and Stravinsky, with a considerable amount of Chopin, Debussy, Scarlatti, and a great deal of Schumann, as well as a big concerto repertoire, containing the Bartók Second; the two Chopin, Brahms, Tchaikovsky; the five Beethoven; the Prokofiev Third; the Ravel D major; and the Rachmaninoff Third.

Onstage, Weissenberg is a presence of unusual magnetism. An air of high seriousness mingles with tension. Weissenberg is there to do battle with a dragon—he must vanquish the piano. He plays with extreme economy of movement; a smile never passes across his lips. His programs are invariably challenges for himself and the audience. Weissenberg must impose his will on the score. It is not Schumann's *Carnaval* but "his" *Carnaval.* I do not mean that Weissenberg has no respect for the composer; quite the contrary. But he has stated publicly that as an interpreter it is his responsibility to pass the masters through the filter of his own sensibility, a contemporary sensibility. Certainly the stamp of Weissenberg's personality is indelibly imprinted on his interpretations. One quickly recognizes a Weissenberg performance once one is familiar with his art.

Weissenberg is also a controversial artist. Some find his playing repellent, while others are visibly moved and deeply shaken by his work. I have never been less than fascinated by his self-confident performances, which are always deeply thought out to the last detail. Weissenberg's playing has not changed one note since his return to the stage more than twenty seasons back. He knows what he wants and ferociously goes after it. But it is always a battle. Each season he plays one hundred concerts, and seldom fewer than four in New York. In one concert he may hit his mark, while three others can be lacking almost everything he desires. This pattern of hit-or-miss has become more pronounced in the last years, and he seems once again to be feeling a weariness with the stage. For the Bulgarian-born virtuoso, public performance seems to be a life-and-death struggle, an act of love-hate.

While both fans and detractors agree that Weissenberg has a fabulous mechanism, this does not mean he doesn't miss notes. The listener who wants pretty playing and melting emotions need not attend his work. Phenomenal facility or not, Weissenberg would assuredly have been laughed off the stage in 1900. Once Arthur Rubinstein's Chopin was thought unfeeling and Rachmaninoff and Hofmann icy, and doubtless Chopin would be amazed at Weissenberg's granitic reading of his Third Sonata, but we must learn to listen to a re-creative artist in the context of his era. So today too one may consider Weissenberg's Chopin Nocturnes, if not brutal, at least unpoetic. Yet after several hearings they emerge as not insensitive or abrupt, but rather quite musical on his terms.

Weissenberg is never interpretively irresponsible. He dusts off accumulations of literary affectation in the nocturnes. His is not a languishing Chopin. He analyzes his Chopin and finds quite a bit of psychological disturbance, even violence. Actually, Weissenberg too is a Romantic, a present-day Romanticist, more blaring, more cruel than those of the nineteenth century. In his art there seems to be a sadomasochistic streak. When all is going well, however, he can fuse his relentless personality into Schumann's *Symphonic Etudes* (the five posthumous variations always included) and find in the score all that was latent in Schumann's personality, but that comes to the fore with electrical shock in Weissenberg's staggering conception—by far my favorite of his Schumann performances.

A characteristic Weissenberg program presented us with three large-scale works, beginning with Haydn's E-flat Sonata; if Weissenberg had played it on Haydn's own wooden piano, he would have demolished the instrument. Ah! if Haydn could have been sitting next to me—how I would have liked to see his face. (I don't want to give the impression that Weissenberg is devoid of all repose or color, or that he cannot play softly, and he certainly can play slowly.) For the next piece, Weissenberg launched into the Liszt Sonata, which in his hands is ruthless, steely, and elemental, with an almost gruesome power, so much so that he makes me realize how twentieth-century, in an emotional sense, this score can be. After intermission, the pianist offered the seldom-played thirty-five-minute Rachmaninoff First Sonata. Blocks of sound roared from his piano; it was pandemonium. He played as loud as anyone in the history of the piano. The contemplation of sonority is a complex issue. But those chords were not merely banged, or percussive either. Most important, this fairly

Alexis Weissenberg by David Dubal

problematic composition was compelling in Weissenberg's hands because of his belief in his own playing.

He is not an endearing artist, but he burns with an intense flame. And I often leave the hall shaken up in one way or another. Outside of giving master classes during the last years, Weissenberg, because of illness, has seldom been heard on the concert stage.

ERNST WENZEL
1808–1880—Germany

A student of Friedrich Wieck. He was friends with Mendelssohn and Schumann and was a well-liked pianist and the teacher, at the Leipzig Conservatory, of Grieg, Sir George Henschel, and Ernst Perabo.

FRIEDRICH WIECK
1785–1873—Germany

The father of Clara Wieck Schumann and her only teacher. He was a superb musician and influenced all who studied with him. Robert Schumann learned much from him, and was deeply pained by the rift between them over his love for Clara. Clara Wieck was ever grateful to her father for his remarkable teaching and devotion during her formative years. Mendelssohn knew his value and tried to secure him as a teacher at his newly founded Leipzig Conservatory in 1844. Among his many pupils were Wenzel and von Bülow, in addition to Alwin Wieck, his son (1821–1885), and another daughter, Marie Wieck (1832–1916), whose final public appearance at the age of eighty-three was, ironically, in Schumann's Piano Concerto.

ALEKSANDER WIELHORSKI
1889–1952—Poland

A Polish pianist who made many successful tours of Europe and England. He settled in Warsaw and combined his pianistic activities with teaching at the Warsaw Conservatory. His Impromptu No. 2 and Quasi-Waltz became well-known piano pieces.

JOSEF WIENIAWSKI
1837–1912—Poland

A well-known pianist and brother of the great violinist Henri Wieniawski. He studied with Zimmerman and Marmontel, and later with Liszt. He composed salon works and was a professor at the Moscow Conservatory.

EARL WILD
b. 1915—United States

Wild studied with Paul Doguereau and Egon Petri. In 1939 he became the first pianist ever to give a recital on American television. He is also a composer, and his transcriptions of Gershwin and Rachmaninoff songs show his special understanding of the piano. Wild has premiered many new works, including the Paul Creston Concerto, and his tours have taken him throughout the world. He has had a distinguished recording career and has recorded over two hundred solo works, as well as such concertos as the MacDowell Second, the Menotti, the Scharwenka, and the Paderewski. In 1986, for the centennial of Liszt's death, he played three Liszt recitals in Chicago, New York, and other cities.

He made his reputation slowly. He was born at a time when Americans trusted only artists who were European born and bred. He won no competition, and he began his career during the Great Depression. He joined NBC as a staff pianist, survived there for eight years, and participated when needed as a member of the NBC Symphony under Toscanini. Later, in 1942, the great conductor asked Wild to perform with him in Gershwin's *Rhapsody in Blue*. In fact, he was the first American soloist to perform with Toscanini. For a long time Wild was typecast as a Gershwin performer because of the sassy verve in his performances of the *Rhapsody* and Concerto in F. Later, Wild composed a Grand Fantasy on *Porgy and Bess*.

Wild has one of the world's great piano mechanisms. He is a tireless worker who thinks constantly about the difficulties at hand. Few understand the instrument as well as he. He has delighted in uncovering exciting works that lay coated with dust, and the public responds with enthusiasm to his clever programming. He has even given all-transcription programs to a packed Carnegie Hall. Wild is an elegant stylist, tossing off the most difficult works as a magician shakes his rabbit out of a hat. He is lavish in his use of rubato. A witty man, he once told me that his performance of the Chopin Ballade in G minor one evening had had enough rubato to last for two years. (I remember thinking how ghastly the performance had been.) But he is a true stage personality, and he seldom plays the same way twice. He likes the danger and thrill of performance, and at times he can border on kitsch. On the other hand, he can also pull the reins in and play like a drill sergeant.

He has added immeasurably to our enjoyment of neglected composers like Balakirev, Godowsky, Medtner, d'Albert, and many others. His Brahms *Paganini* Variations sizzle, and he rejoices in Liszt. It is not a deep Liszt, and a goodly dose of vulgarity appears here and there. But his passagework has a kind of glossiness that only he achieves. That sound alone gives his playing a unique glow. His best Liszt record is called "The Daemonic Liszt," and in it he plays the *Faust* Waltz rhapsodically and the *Valse infernale* wickedly.

I don't much like most of his Chopin, which is either trite or wimpy. What he does with Liszt cannot be done with a purist like Chopin. He glories, however, in Rachmaninoff, in which he is first-rate in the preludes and concerti, all played with gusto and a beguiling tone. He plays the French composers, too, although his Franck, Ravel, and Fauré are not memorable. The Wild that I find irresistible can be heard in such works as Thalberg's Fantasies on Donizetti's *Don Pasquale* and Rossini's *Semiramide*, where Wild amplifies and "improves" the score, as pianists did unashamedly in an earlier era. He delights in the delicious chromatic scales; he is dazzling in the frippery of the passagework. In these and other works, such as the Herz Variations on "Non piu mesta" from Rossini's *La Cenerentola*, Wild gracefully jumps all the hurdles. He plays with aplomb and a twinkle in his eye, with light heart and hand. He has a simple athletic enjoyment in what hands can do at such high levels of discipline.

Wild is a superb Godowsky player. In a piece like the *Symphonic Metamorphosis on Themes from Johann Strauss's "Künstlerleben,"* he knows exactly how to voice those ghostly, sickly harmonies and how to untangle the excruciating labyrinth of notes into a luminous glorification of the piano. For Godowsky enthusiasts, this is the purest, most classically played Godowsky.

Wild is a true virtuoso of the old school, happy as can be when giving his transcription "fests," unconcerned about the pedant's frown and truly enjoying his wonderful, unabashed Romanticism and his ability to galvanize audiences. His own piano pieces are extremely effective; best known are his Virtuoso Etudes on Gershwin's Songs, and his own recording of them is peerless.

DAVID WILDE
b. 1935—England

A pianist of repute, he has made recordings and written on music. He is best known for his Liszt playing.

ALBERTO WILLIAMS
1862–1952—Argentina

The foremost Argentinian pianist and composer of his day. He studied piano at the Paris Conservatoire with Georges Mathias and composition with César Franck. In Buenos Aires he opened a music school and was popular as a pianist; his Chopin playing was particularly admired. Williams composed very well for the piano, and his pieces include a *Sonata Argentina*.

AUGUST WINDING
1835–1899—Denmark

He studied with Reinecke and Dreyschock, making his debut in Copenhagen at twenty-one. He went on to a fine career as a pianist and composer. His cadenzas to Mozart concertos are still used.

PAUL WITTGENSTEIN
1887–1961—Austria

He worked under Leschetizky and pursued his career as concert pianist until he lost his right arm fighting on the Russian front in World War I. He vowed to continue playing and learned the existing left-hand literature; also, he commissioned many concertos for left hand alone. The best of these are Prokofiev's Piano Concerto No. 4, Britten's *Diversions,* and the great Ravel Concerto for the Left Hand, which Wittgenstein premiered in Vienna on 27 November 1931.

EDWARD WOLFF
1816–1880—Poland

He studied in Warsaw at the conservatory. His composition teacher was Joseph Elsner, who also taught Chopin. He made his debut as a pianist in Vienna. In 1835 he moved to Paris, where he resided for the rest of his career. He had many students, including Chabrier. He was a prolific composer and transcriber. With de Beriot he published 32 Duets for Violin and Piano; he wrote a Piano Concerto, Op. 39; and he left over three hundred works for solo piano, including five sets of Etudes, Opp. 20, 50, 90, 100, and 189.

JOSEPH WÖLFL
1772–1812—Austria

In addition to being one of Europe's leading pianists, Wölfl was a rival of Beethoven, whom he tied in a contest of improvisations.

Wölfl composed voluminously, including seven concerti, twenty-four sets of variations, and fifty-eight solo sonatas. Some of this output contains very good music. His C minor Sonata, Op. 25, is bold in outline, wide in emotional range, and quite skillfully bound together.

He lived in an age interested in exploring

new avenues in piano technique, and Wölfl, who had a large hand, was in the forefront of this development. His once famed Sonata Op. 41, from 1808, is subtitled *Non plus ultra*; its variation finale is still technically mean. (Dussek was soon to write a sonata, *Plus ultra.*) Every important pianist of Wölfl's generation, such as Cramer, Berger, and Steibelt, was spinning out sets of etudes, and Wölfl's was called *Practical School for the Pianoforte,* consisting of fifty exercises.

HERMANN WOLLENHAUPT

1829–1863—Germany

He studied with Julius Knorr and Moritz Hauptmann. Wollenhaupt immigrated to New York in 1845, and there he established himself not only as a brilliant performer and teacher but also as a composer of one hundred well-bred salon pieces.

ROGER WOODWARD

b. 1943—Australia

Woodward studied with Drzewiecki in Warsaw for six years. He has made a recording of some of Chopin's works, but he is especially noted for his exemplary readings of twentieth-century music. Among his best known recordings are the Shostakovich Preludes and Fugues.

FRIEDRICH WÜHRER

1900–1975—Austria

He was a highly acclaimed pianist who was especially known for his fine artistry in the Austro-Germanic repertory. Wührer was a student at the Vienna Conservatory, and later he became a teacher there. His many recordings offer some interpretive insights. Among them, the Schubert Sonatas have special value.

Y

OXANA YABLONSKAYA

b. 1941—USSR

She studied with Anaida Sumbatyan and at the Moscow Conservatory with Goldenweiser. She made her American debut at Carnegie Hall in 1977 and now teaches at Juilliard. She is an excellent technician, and her interpretations are grand in character.

MARIA YUDINA

1899–1970—Russia

After studying with Nikolaev at the St. Petersburg Conservatory, Yudina, who was a fascinating and eccentric personality, went on to become a legendary figure in Russian musical circles. She made numerous recordings, and her concerts were nearly always packed.

Yudina played a large repertoire, and she had the courage to program some of the moderns, such as Hindemith, Bartók, and Křenek, for whose Piano Concerto No. 2 she gave the Russian premiere.

Shostakovich thought that Yudina "played Liszt like no one else," but he felt differently about her rendering of his own Sonata No. 2 in E minor. As he wrote in his memoirs, "I think Yudina plays my sonata badly. The tempos are all off and there's a free, shall we say, approach to the text. But perhaps I'm wrong, I haven't heard the recording in a while."

She was a rebellious personality, sometimes perverse in her interpretations. Richter wrote, "I remember a performance of the Second Chopin Nocturne that was so heroic that it no longer sounded like a piano but a trumpet."

Z

CHRISTIAN ZACHARIAS

b. 1950—Germany

Among other teachers he studied in Paris with Perlemuter. Zacharias is publicly a consistent artist with a smooth and large technical mechanism. He is fond of Scarlatti and plays him frequently, with great audience response. His Mozart playing is never frilly, and his disc of the A major Concerto, K. 488 has a pettiness to it. I last heard him in Fort Worth, Texas, in exquisite playing of Schumann's *Kinderscenen.*

MICHAEL VON ZADORA

1882–1946—United States

Zadora was a student of Leschetizky and subsequently of Busoni, whose music he often played. His recording of Busoni's Sonatina No. 6, *Super Carmen,* is the work of a virtuoso.

YAKOV ZAK

1913–1976—Russia

He studied at the Moscow Conservatory with Heinrich Neuhaus, and later he became a professor there. Zak was an objective player, but somewhat dry. His recording of Kabalevsky's Third Sonata is typical of his playing. He taught

many first-rate artists; among his students were Youri Egorov and Alexander Toradze.

JUANA ZAYAS

b. 1940—Cuba

After studying the piano in Paris, Zayas settled in the United States. She has appeared in concert here as well as in Europe. Her discs of the Chopin Etudes and Preludes have earned praise.

CARLO ZECCHI

1903–1984—Italy

He studied in Rome, then with Busoni. He was a pianist of impeccable technique, with a fine sense of tonal values. He played Scarlatti with finesse, and Chopin with style and a beguiling elasticity of phrasing. Zecchi was also a famed conductor and teacher. He died during the 1984 Busoni Competition, where he was to be a judge.

IGOR ZHUKOV

b. 1936—USSR

He was a student of Heinrich Neuhaus. He traveled to Paris, where he won a prize at the

Long-Thibaud Competition in 1957. Since that time, he has had a busy career in the Soviet Union, where he has recorded prolifically. His Scriabin is special; he brings out the composer's mysticism in elongated and elastic performances.

GÉZA ZICHY
1849–1924—Hungary

A member of the Hungarian nobility, Count Zichy lost his right arm in a hunting accident when he was seventeen, but continued his pianistic training, eventually studying with Liszt. Liszt admired the man, the musician, as well as the poetry he wrote. Liszt said, "He belongs to the not numerous category of the best aristocrats. . . . He is an astonishing artist of the left hand." He created a furor; in Paris, the playwright Victorien Sardou heard him and wrote, "He has but one arm and plays with four hands," and Ernst Pauer felt, "He reached so wonderful a degree of facility and technical perfection that his performances were received with bewildered astonishment and phrenetic acclamations." His compositions and arrangements for left hand which formed the bulk of his repertoire have not survived.

KRYSTIAN ZIMERMAN
b. 1956—Poland

He began lessons at five with his father, and then proceeded to train under Andrzej Jasinski, a relatively unknown teacher-pianist who was Zimerman's only other piano instructor. In 1975 the eighteen-year-old student won the Chopin Competition in Warsaw.

From that moment forward, Zimerman has played throughout the world.

His work possesses a fresh lyricism. His Chopin has a rare finesse; he presents a light-hearted quality in such works as the Waltzes and plays the mazurkas with some style and without exaggeration. He has a fine sense of form, with a vital feeling for plastic beauty. His repertoire is fairly eclectic, and he plays Brahms with rich color, Szymanowski with tremulous and exquisite contour, Mozart and Schubert with a pristine elegance. He has a tendency in his sheer gracefulness to overlook a certain pithiness in weighty music, such as the Brahms F minor Sonata, and in a work like Liszt's A major Concerto he skims over its theatricality to become absorbed mostly in its poetic issues.

At present, he is experimenting with his conceptions, and many of them are in flux; at times he distorts as he aims for an ever freer expression. However, Zimerman is one of the finest young pianists of his generation. His playing may lack fierce passion, but this emotional restraint combined with a highly Romantic and sensitive nature, as well as one of the most elastic techniques on the concert stage, makes for luminous sound and piano playing of great appeal.

PIERRE ZIMMERMAN
1785–1853—France

He studied the piano at the Paris Conservatoire from 1798, working with Boieldieu. In 1800 he took first prize in piano playing, beating out even Kalkbrenner, who placed second. In 1820, after much teaching experience, he became a full professor of the piano at the conservatoire, holding this post until 1848.

Zimmerman became one of the leading piano teachers of his time, with many eminent students to his credit. His best-known pupils were Alkan, Prudent, Marmontel, Ravina, Alexander Goria, Josef Wieniawski, and César Franck. He received the Legion of Honor and composed dozens of works.

AGNES ZIMMERMANN

1847–1925—Germany

She was brought early to London, where she studied at the Royal Academy of Music with Cipriani Potter and then with Ernst Pauer. Subsequently becoming a well-known pianist, she was happiest with the Classical composers. In 1872 she gave the first performance in England of Beethoven's interesting transcription for piano of his great Violin Concerto. She wrote a piano sonata, Op. 22.

NIKOLAI ZVEREV

1832–1893—Russia

He studied with Dubuc and with Henselt, later becoming a prominent teacher in Moscow. He had one of the great piano classes in history, and as a molder of young talent he must have had special gifts. Indeed, he was considered a perfectionist as well as a demanding teacher. He trained many of his pupils through their formative teen years and then sent them on to the Moscow Conservatory for further study. These pupils included Igumnov, Scriabin, Rachmaninoff, Siloti, Goldenweiser, Pressman, Maximov, and many others who rose to distinction.

The
PIANO
LITERATURE

with Lists of
Exceptional Recordings

I love to see two truths at the same time. Every good
comparison gives the mind this advantage.

JOSEPH JOUBERT
(1754–1824)

Introduction

Part Two presents a brief discussion of each composition. I often include the date of the work when available, and occasionally give timings of a work's duration when I think it necessary. When I say a concerto is thirty minutes long, I mean that this is the average timing of the work. Naturally there will be considerable deviation in this respect. One performance of the Liszt Sonata may be only twenty-six minutes while another may run to as long as thirty-three.

After each composition, I have listed various recordings which represent the widest diversity of interpretation. If, for example, listeners were to hear each of my selections for the Brahms Second Piano Concerto, they would form a great knowledge of the work's potential and interpretive possibilities. Through such "comparative listening" one becomes open-minded and always curious as to the next performance. In these selections I do not rank the performances. They are different, but always represent professional craftsmanship. Naturally the sonics of the recordings vary greatly.

Even when not listed in my text, I would try to have any recordings by Cortot, Gieseking, Casadesus, Rachmaninoff, Rosenthal, Backhaus, Lhévinne, Godowsky, Hess, Barère, Friedman, Moiseiwitsch, Edwin Fischer, Hofmann, Kapell, Lipatti, Rubinstein, Rudolf Serkin, Schnabel, Arrau, Gould, Michelangeli, Gilels, de Larrocha, and Horowitz. All of these artists possessed unique musical personalities, and interpretive gifts of a high order. Present-day pianists should take it for granted to be thoroughly familiar with their respective styles. Jorge Bolet says, "I wish that every young pianist would really study—I don't mean just listen, but really study, the performances of Rachmaninoff, Horowitz, Moiseiwitsch, Hofmann, and Friedman and really analyze what made their performances so great."

My selections include mono (although I do not indicate if they are mono) as well as stereo LPS and CDS. If the score is an LP, the abbreviation LP is used. I have not used record numbers (catalogue numbers), which would needlessly clutter the text. Today many recordings are being transferred to CD or have been remastered digitally. Some are reissued on cheaper labels, and many selections are also available on cassettes.

Although a majority of the recordings listed are easily available, my concern is not what is temporarily available. This is a discography. Some labels (such as Dover or Remington) are now defunct, some labels are foreign, and many albums are out of print, temporarily or forever. Nonetheless, the world of the record collector is an exciting one. Never before have there been so many stores in major cities where one can locate gems that one has been yearning to have. Recently I found an old Westminster recording of Busoni's *Fantasia contrappuntistica* played by the great Egon Petri, which had been on my mind for some time. Record collectors, it seems, are now more numerous than book collectors. George Steiner points out:

Habits of the bibliophile—of the library cormorant, as Coleridge called him—have shifted to the collector of records and performances. The furtive manias, the condescensions of expertness, the hunter's zeal which bore once on first editions, colophons, the in-octavo of a remaindered text, are common now among music lovers. There is a science and market in old pressings, in out-of-stock albums, in worn 78s, as there have been in used books. Catalogues of recordings and rare tapes are becoming as exegetic as bibliographies.

There is a vast pianistic legacy ready to be listened to. Recording has given the performer immortality. What would we not give to hear Mozart, Beethoven, Chopin, and Liszt play! At least future generations will not have to guess how Cortot, Richter, Horowitz, or Gould played.

Since the second edition of *The Art of the Piano*, the world has changed forever. With the vast influence of the Internet, everything is now somehow available, and one may purchase, or download, music once extremely difficult to find from all eras. There is a healthy trade in LPs and I have decided not to prune many of the albums from the discography that were once, it seemed, too difficult to obtain. A little exploration on the Internet will most likely or eventually prove fruitful. Many people still prefer LPs above CDs.

In the last several years small firms such as Allan Evans's Arbitor Recordings have given us many rare historical offerings. He has developed a process that he calls "sonic depth technology," a way of reaching into parts of the walls that expose the sound. Larger companies like RCA (BMG) have issued "complete" recordings of William Kapell and the nearly ninety CDs in the RCA Rubinstein discography. Philips's Great Pianists of the Twentieth Century is a welcome boon to collectors, offering 200 CDs that incorporate many labels contributing to the project.

Others such as Appian and Marston continue to release treasures. Nimbus has mined the piano roll heritage in its *Grand Piano* series. VAI does valuable work in CDs and in films. There is a growing interest in films of important pianists, and there are successful festivals of these films such as those on Glenn Gould, Horowitz, and Richter and anthologies such as *The Art of Piano*, and my own video on VHS and DVD, the *Golden Age of the Piano* from Philips Classics.

A

ISAAC ALBÉNIZ
1860–1909—Spain

He composed 250 piano pieces, mostly of slight value. The composer disowned his early music. After 1890, he came into contact with Debussy, Fauré, and Dukas and forged a sophisticated impressionist art, which culminated in his crowning glory, *Iberia* (twelve pieces, 1906-09). Here Albéniz paints an idealized Spain, mostly set in Andalucia. The pieces are of immense technical difficulty, rich in textural fabric, intricate in voicing, and awkward in hand placement. One day, Manuel de Falla and Ricardo Viñes came upon Albéniz wandering the streets in despair. He told them, "Last night I came near to burning the manuscripts of *Iberia*, for I saw that what I had written was unplayable." Fortunately, some have mastered the cruel tasks and have revealed Albéniz's synthesis of Spanish moods and dances.

The Complete Piano Music:
BASELGA: BIS

Iberia, Book I

Evocación: Marked "Allegretto expressivo." Albéniz uses seven flats for most of its notation. It is technically the simplest of the *Iberia*, asking for tonal discrimination in its slow-burning lyric intensity. In form it is the Spanish dance known as the *fandanguillo*.

El Puerto: A depiction of the harbor of Santa Maria teeming with life. The rhythms are derived from such Andalusian dances as the polo, the seguiría gitana, and the bulerías. Albéniz asks the performer to play "tres brusque," to play "toujours joyeux," and "tres langoureux."

Fête-Dieu à Seville ("Corpus Christi Day in Seville"): A superb use of the piano, asking for excellent staccato and chord technique. Albéniz describes, with joy and pathos, a processional on this religious occasion. In nine minutes, Albéniz's sense of smoldering Spanish drama and repressed violence produces an overwhelming effect.

Iberia, Book II

Rondeña: A lighter work but difficult to make coherent in its contrasting rhythms. It is also difficult to extrapolate the melodies from the web of texture. James Gibb writes: "The middle section of this piece shows specially subtle choice of harmony and skill in placing notes which suggest a vocal line with guitar accompaniment: Although the voice part is played in the middle register of the piano, it sounds as if the singer is straining in the upper range of his voice. Here the art of mimicry is transcended and we have a truly creative and individual contribution to piano writing."

Almería: A Spanish port town. In the composition we find the tarantas, which is a dance

Isaac Albéniz by David Dubal

explained that in *El Albancín* "one redis-covers the fragrance of the blossom-filled nights of Spain . . . the tone of a muted guitar which sings its sorrow to the night, sings with sudden awakenings and nervous starts." Albéniz attempts to make the performer aware of the great tonal variety he desires with dif-ferent markings, ranging from piano to pp, ppp, pppp, and ppppp.

El Polo: Andalusian song and dance. A sobbing chant persists throughout the piece, embedded in a tone of melancholy, bitterness, and irony.

Lavapiés: Working-class quarter of Madrid. A formidable work of virtuosity and rhythmic verve. Albéniz exploits the dance called the chulos. The lean, brittle chords have a dashing glitter.

Iberia, Book IV

Málaga: A difficult malaguena; hard-edged, full of vitality with a peculiarly Spanish sadness and fatality, which in the hands of an unsym-pathetic executant can become monotonous.

Jerez: The famous wine city, the home of sherry. Along with *Almería* and *Fête-Dieu à Seville*, the longest work of *Iberia*. Here Albéniz reaches the very essence of what he aspired to in his music. Debussy wrote that, without actually using folk themes, "it is as if he had imbibed them, had so absorbed them that they passed into his art without it being possible to draw the line of demarcation."

Eritaña: A tavern on the outskirts of Seville. Debussy stated that a "flowing tide of humanity bursts into laughter, accompanied by tambou-rines. Never has music achieved such differen-tiated, such colorful impressions, and the eyes close as though blinded by these pictures all too vivid in hue."

native to that city, as well as aspects of the jota. *Almería* is somewhat less demanding technically than *Rondeña*. It asks the inter-preter to play with a lavish color wheel and with imaginative freedom. The middle section touches the depths of the soul of *Andalucía*. *Almería* is perhaps the loveliest music Albéniz wrote.

Triana: The most famous piece of the cycle. The name is taken from a Seville suburb. *Triana* is a sparkling virtuoso piece with the beguiling rhythm of the pasodoble. The gypsy element is apparent throughout.

Iberia, Book III

El Albaicín: The gypsy quarter of Granada. Albéniz marks the score "Allegro assai," ma melancolico. Debussy admired the score. He

Iberia:

ARRAU (Book I): Great Pianists of the
    Twentieth Century
AYBAR: Connoisseur Society (LP)
BLOCK: Connoisseur Society (LP)
CICCOLINI: Seraphim (LP)
DE LARROCHA: London
REQUEJO: Claves
URIBE: Orion (LP)

Navarra

Twenty-six measures were left unfinished at
Albéniz's death. They were completed by de
Séverac. *Navarra* is a pendant to the *Iberia*
cycle, sharing its intense nationalism. Gibb
writes, "The extremes of Spanish masculine
pride and grandiloquence, almost toppling
into self-parody, are presented with Lisztian
brilliance and spaciousness."

DE LARROCHA: London
RUBINSTEIN: RCA

Cantos de España;
La Vega; Azulejos

Other Albéniz compositions that are known
are the five pieces that comprise the suite
Cantos de España, Op. 232. With its
Moorish prelude, description of *Córdoba*,
and brilliant Seguidillas, the suite evokes
an enchanted Spain. Even more popular is
the Tango from the *España* suite of 1890,
Op. 165. Of greater importance, but virtually unknown, are the very long (fourteen
minutes) *La Vega* and *Azulejos* ("Colored
Tiles"), which was completed by Granados
after Albéniz's death.

DE LARROCHA: EMI
JONES: Nimbus

CHARLES VALENTIN ALKAN
1813–1888—France

Alkan left some of the most inspired piano
music of nineteenth-century France, and is
finally coming to be appreciated as a visionary
Romantic. His works have been feared by
pianists because of their extreme difficulty and
the physical strength necessary to play them.
But in fact he created many smaller works
which cover a wide range of emotions and
technical skill.

Shorter Pieces

Alkan's "miniatures" include the haunting *La
Chanson de la folle au bord de la mer* ("Song
of the Mad Woman on the Seashore"), No. 8
of his Twenty-five Preludes; the magical *Petit
Conte*; the piquant Barcarolle, Op. 65, No. 6;
Les Soupirs, a sensuous piece of impressionism;
and *Le Tambour bat aux champs*, Op. 50, No.
2 ("The Drum Beats in the Fields"), which is,
in Raymond Lewenthal's words, "one of the
bitterest, most vehement and sarcastic com-
mentaries on the folly of war that has ever
been written." The composer Bernard van
Dieren thinks it possesses "a depth of imagery,
an incandescence of statement, and a universality of meaning which remind one of the
intense lines of Poe or Blake."

SMITH (25 short pieces): Arabesque

Sonatine, Op. 61

Surely the most grueling sonatine in the literature. Composed in 1861, it is in four movements, totaling eighteen minutes. There is
nothing else like it from its era. The writing
is lean, the sarcasm is devastating. Kaikhosru

Sorabji calls it "vehement, droll, gargoylelike, childlike and naive in turn . . . almost as if Berlioz had written a Beethoven sonata."

Sonatine and short works:
LEWENTHAL: CBS (LP)
RINGEISSEN: Harmonia Mundi
SMITH: Arabesque; EMI

Grande Sonate, Op. 33

Composed in 1847, this is a problematic and fascinating score, running to forty-five minutes. It is subtitled *Les Quatre Ages*; each movement depicts a man at a different state of life—twenty, thirty, forty, and fifty years old. Only the second movement, titled *Quasi-Faust*, is in sonata form. Raymond Lewenthal plays only that movement in his recording. However, Ronald Smith has spent years exploring this weird and magnificent work, and his recording is a compelling document. In *Quasi-Faust* in particular, Alkan hurls all caution to the wind. Joseph Bloch writes of the Sonata that "as a conception it is astounding and without parallel in the Romantic piano literature." Lewenthal observes that in this work "Alkan deals with the hopes, triumphs, joys, and sorrows of a human being." He finds it "the most difficult piano sonata since Beethoven's *Hammerklavier,* and the strangest one before the Ives sonatas."

The composer went to extreme lengths to tell his would-be interpreters his intentions, and the score is strewn with adjectives and phrases such as "palpitant," "amoureuse-ment," "avec désespoir," "satanique-ment," "avec délices," "avec bonheur," "déchirant," and many more.

HAMELIN: Hyperion
LEWENTHAL: RCA
REACH: Vogue
SMITH: Arabesque; EMI

Twelve Etudes in All the Minor Keys, Op. 39

In 1847, Alkan composed Twelve Etudes in the Major Keys, Op. 35. Hans von Bülow reviewed them enthusiastically, calling Alkan "the Berlioz of the piano." The Op. 35 are of interest musically and technically, yet they remain etudes in size and intention. In the decade to follow, Alkan was practically silent. In 1857, however, his most monumental work appeared—the Twelve Etudes in the Minor Keys, Op. 39, which grew to absurd proportions, "rather like Frankenstein's monster," as Ronald Smith says. The Twelve Etudes span 277 pages of uncompromising, obsessive madness and a technical hardship never before seen in a work for the piano.

No. 1, *Comme le vent* ("Like the Wind"), is marked "Prestissimamente." Smith calls it "a kind of nightmare tarantella which falls roughly into sonata form."

No. 2, *En rythme molossique,* is a harsh work in 6/4 meter. To play it demands the strength of an Olympic weight lifter. The ending, with its repeated low Ds, is a study in monotony.

No. 3, *Scherzo diabolico,* is the shortest of these pieces. It includes very difficult finger-work with a mighty chordal trio of Byronic, blood-curdling melodrama.

Alkan's *Symphony for Solo Piano* occupies Nos. 4, 5, 6, and 7 of the Op. 39. Here the composer indulges his love for orchestral sonorities and creates a cogent work of pure musical effect. The first movement, in C minor, is concise and dignified. The second movement, *Marche funèbre,* conjures up an immense procession. Lewenthal suggests, "Think of soft-playing military band instruments through this wonderful trio, and bear in mind the first movement of Berlioz's *Symphonie funèbre et triomphale* throughout all of this movement." The third movement is, ironically, a menuet, of the least genteel quality. Cross-rhythms and irregular phrase groups (a characteristic of Alkan's style) are jaggedly flung against a lyrical trio. The fourth movement is, for Lewenthal, "like a wild ride in hell." This half-hour composition will amaze the listener with its anticipatory glances toward Bruckner, Brahms, Mahler, Nielsen, and others.

In Etudes Nos. 8, 9, and 10, titled *Concerto for Solo Piano,* Alkan evokes both soloist and orchestra; the work is gargantuan—121 pages in length. The first movement alone is 1,341 measures in seventy-two pages of a classical concerto form, which takes about thirty-five minutes of playing time. Alkan is ingenious in raising the voice of his soloist above the roar of a great orchestral body. The movement is surely one of the splendid pieces of architectural planning. Smith speaks of "the far-flung tonal strategy that holds the vast construction together." He also notes "an uncanny anticipation of the arctic world of Sibelius's Fourth Symphony."

The slow movement, an Adagio in C-sharp minor, contains some beautiful writing, as well as what Smith calls "a grimly realistic episode over which the spirit of Mahler seems to preside." The finale is marked "Allegretto alla barbaresca," a rondo in F-sharp minor. Bloch writes, "Its harmonic clashes, its barbaric rhythmic drive, its strange cross-rhythms give an almost Bartókian effect. And it is one of the real virtuoso pieces—a closing number guaranteed to have any audience sitting on the edge of its seats."

No. 11 is an Ouverture in B minor of tremendous scope—the longest of any of the etudes except the first movement of the Concerto. Bloch thinks it "perhaps the weakest member of Opus 39," but this recondite study becomes adventurous in Ronald Smith's heroic performance. He absolutely exults in Alkan's work.

No. 12 is a ten-minute set of variations, *Le Festin d'Esope,* which in Bloch's estimation "belongs among the important Variation-works of the piano literature. Its neglect by pianists is inexplicable."

Wilfred Mellers speaks of "the necromantic quality of Alkan's pianism." The score is fraught with tension, wry humor, and mocking fury, producing a cumulative effect of startling power.

Twelve Etudes Op. 39:
RINGEISSEN: Marco Polo
SMITH: Arabesque

Selected Etudes Op. 39:
LEWENTHAL (Symphony for Solo Piano & Le Festin d'Esope): High Performance
PETRI (four selections): Pearl
PONTI (Nos. 1–7, 12): Candide (LP)

Symphony for Solo Piano:
HAMELIN: Hyperion
SALMAN: Titanic

Concerto for Solo Piano:
HAMELIN: Music and Arts

B

JOHANN SEBASTIAN BACH
1685-1750—Germany

In selecting the piano literature for Part Two of this book, I have not included works of pre-piano composers, except in the case of Bach and Scarlatti, simply because pianists seldom perform or record on the piano such keyboard works as those of the Elizabethan masters (although Bull's Walsingham Variations and numerous other works can be made to sound splendid on the contemporary piano). The same is true of the enormous wealth of Baroque composers such as Froberger, Kuhnau, Telemann, or the extraordinary French keyboard literature, headed by the luminous François Couperin and the magisterial Rameau.

Even Bach, once indispensable to the pianist's world, is now shared by the harpsichordists who swear that the great Leipzig cantor can only be heard properly on his own instruments. Claudio Arrau said, "Any shades of crescendo and diminuendo and other inflections which can only be achieved on a modern piano hinder Bach's meaning. These qualities of the piano creep into Bach whether you like it or not." Indeed Arrau's Bach is certainly heavily inflected with the piano's characteristics. Some pianists, in an attempt at a kind of compromise, learn Bach without pedal. Each pianist, however, has had to come to grips with the Bachian idiom in his or her own manner, and Bach's elasticity has no boundary.

Pianists will certainly not give up Bach; for the fingers and mind there is nothing more nourishing. Casals and Stravinsky began their day with the "48" and as Schumann said, "Let no day pass without studying the Preludes and Fugues."

Today we find beauty in instruments once thought outmoded or even extinct. The nineteenth century saw everything in light of industrial progress, and the sensibility of the age thought the harpsichord and clavichord insufficient instruments. They were certain that Bach would automatically have saluted the modern Steinway as the true instrument to project his tonal dreams. This attitude was summed up by the pianist Edwin Hughes, a Leschetizky pupil, when he wrote: "On account of the limitations of the harpsichord, Bach doubtless did what any other good musician had to do in playing it or composing for it; in his mind's ear he imagined the nuances that he was unable to reproduce on its keyboard, just as in playing the clavichord he doubtless let his fancy expand indefinitely the tiny-toned dynamic range of that charming instrument."

On the harpsichord or the piano, the music of Bach remains one of the incomparable glories in the history of human culture. There have been few musicians who have not learned from him. His spirit lived on in Beethoven, Schumann, Chopin, Mendelssohn, Brahms, Schoenberg, and countless examples. James Huneker wrote, "With my prying nose I dipped into all composers, and found that the houses they erected were stable in the exact proportion that Bach used in the foundation."

Chromatic Fantasia and Fugue in D minor

The Chromatic Fantasy is one of Bach's most often performed larger works. Its emotional content remains "Romantic" for each generation.

BARÈRE: Enterprise
BRENDEL: Philips
BÜHLIG: Dante
HEWITT: Hyperion
SCHIFF: Hungaroton
SCHNABEL: Perennial Records
TURECK: VAI
WEISSENBERG: Angel

Concerto in the Italian Style (Italian Concerto)

Composed for the double manual harpsichord; the slow movement's expressive singing works well on the modern piano.

GOULD: Sony
KATZ: Cembal d'Amour
SCHNABEL: Perennial Records (LP)
Y. TAKAHASHI: Denon

The Six English Suites, Six French Suites, and Six Partitas

These suites represent the most sophisticated use of Baroque dance forms. Bach gave his students the *French* and *English* Suites to learn after they had mastered the Two- and Three-Part Inventions. The Partitas are the most complex of Bach's keyboard suites and the most frequently performed in the concert halls of the world. The *French* Suites are the least complex because they lack the first-movement preludes of the Partitas and the *English* Suites.

English and French Suites (complete):
GOULD: Sony
MARTINS: Labor

English Suites:
ARGERICH (No. 2): DG
POGORELICH (Nos. 2 & 3): DG

Partitas:
GOULD: SONY
LIPATTI (No. 1): Angel
MARTINS: Labor
SCHIFF: London
WEISSENBERG (No.4): Great Pianists of the 20th Century

Aria with Thirty Variations (The Goldberg Variations)

The peak of Baroque variation writing, this work is titanic in scope. John Gillespie calls it "the crowning achievement of the Baroque keyboard." Charles Rosen asserts: "The elegance of the *Goldberg* Variations is its glory: It is the most worldly of Bach's achievements, with the *Italian Concerto.* . . . Except for the *Saint Matthew Passion,* in no other work is the depth of Bach's spirit so easily accessible, and its significance so tangible."

Nonetheless, its enormous length and contrapuntal mastery keep the score from the hands of tyros.

GOULD (early and late): (1955) Sony Classical; (1981) Sony Classical
KEMPFF: DG
MARTINS: Labor
P. SERKIN: Pro Arte
TIPO: Angel

The Fifteen Two-Part and Fifteen Three-Part Inventions

These compositions in two and three voices are masterpieces of contrapuntal perfection.

The fifteen Three-Part Inventions are quite difficult, and they thoroughly lay the foundation for the study of *The Well-Tempered Clavier*.

GOULD: CBS
NIKOLAYEVA: Harmonia Mundi
SCHIFF: London

The Well-Tempered Clavier

Book I (1722), BWV 846–869 Twenty-four Preludes and Fugues, Book II BWV 870–893 Twenty-four Preludes and Fugues (1738–42)

Bach's "48" Preludes and Fugues of *The Well-Tempered Clavier* were called, by von Bülow, the pianist's old testament (the sonatas of Beethoven being the new testament). Arthur Loesser sees "its vast range through all phases of feeling, from a brisk delight in muscular playfulness through harrowing depths of personal introspection up to heights of grandeur unsurpassed in music." The '48' as they have become universally known is one of the great feats of the human intellect." Ernest Hutcheson calls it "a treasury of musical scholarship, giving final definition to instrumental counterpoint."

I think Bach, who wrote for the glory of God, would not be angry with Sacheverell Sitwell when the writer said "there has been demonstration of the universal truth by Fugue, and it may be that more wisdom is found in that than in the religions and religious books of all the world together."

Book I
Prelude and Fugue No. 1 in C major

Landowska wrote, "What was Bach's intention in leading us to his monumental *Well-Tempered Clavier* through a gate of such dreamlike atmosphere as we find in the first prelude? Those immortal broken chords of radiantly white harmonies have been possibly attempted by more players than any other piece by Bach."

The Fugue in four voices, Landowska says, "is an apotheosis of the key of C major. In every Prelude and Fugue that follows, one always feels the same will to plunge into each tonality, major or minor, thus glorifying the victory of equal temperament."

Prelude and Fugue No. 2 in C minor

When played well with dabs of pedal, this prelude gives the impression of a string orchestra. It is a proud piece of asymmetrical architecture; Busoni sees its "flickering flames." It demands evenness in both hands. David Schulenberg wrote, "It surely ought to be played with fire and not as an anticipation of twentieth-century (or even nineteenth-century) machinery." João Carlos Martins feels "the heart stands still at the entrance of the cadenza-type passage work" near the end.

The Fugue is masterful with its five episodes, composed with three voices without stretto. Landowska points out, "The last two episodes combine the rhythm of the subject with fragments of the first counter subject."

Prelude and Fugue No. 3 in C-sharp major

"This prelude," Cecil Gray wrote, "is one of these sweetly fluting pastoral movements of which Bach alone possesses the secret; for sheer sunny gaiety such as this there is no composer to approach him, except possibly Haydn." In No. 3, Bach prefers the seven sharps to the five flats of D-flat major. Thus there is no Prelude and Fugue in D-flat.

The Fugue is in three voices. There are six episodes; each inversion is of unhampered skill. The Fugue needs rhythmic control and vitality, with complete independence for the double-note passages.

Prelude and Fugue No. 4 in C-sharp minor

Wagner called Liszt's playing of this a revelation. It's a supreme masterpiece and one of the longest of the Preludes and Fugues. Schulenberg says, "The underlying rhythm seems to be that of a Siciliano, that is, a slow gigue. But the convolutions of the melodic line obscure any dance character." Landowska calls it "an eloquent avowal of Bach's love for Couperin and French music." It is an aria yet the texture is polyphonic.

The five-voice Fugue is amazing in that, from the shortest Fugue subject of the "48" of four notes, Bach creates a Gothic cathedral. The grandeur is almost unbearable if properly played.

Prelude and Fugue No. 5 in D major

The Prelude will always be a test for even finger technique. Here is freshness personified; Hutcheson says, "It bubbles along like a cheerful brook."

The Fugue in four voices is an overture in the French style, of Lully or Rameau; its brightness shouts the D major tonality.

Prelude and Fugue No. 6 in D minor

The Prelude possesses a restless, tragic undercurrent with its basso continuo and a wondrous chromatic cadenza at the end.

The Fugue in three voices has a trill tacked

to its subject giving a stately but slightly anxious curve. The strettos and inversions are ingenious.

Prelude and Fugue No. 7 in E-flat major

The Prelude is monumental and the only one to more than double the size of the Fugue in length and density. One is gripped by a feeling of the eternal in this piece. Schulenberg goes so far as to call it the greatest Prelude in Book I.

The three-voice Fugue, in the words of Gray, "mocks at and makes fun of the prelude."

Prelude and Fugue No. 8 in E-flat minor

"Passion" music with recitatives, of an eloquence reserved for Bach only. Implicit is the religious and tragic spirit. The Fugue in three voices maintains the profound pitch in a work of equal complexity to the Prelude. Gray says, "It is in the combination of this deep, transcendent emotion with the non plus ultra of inspired craftsmanship that this fugue is well-nigh supreme."

Prelude and Fugue No. 9 in E major

The Prelude, rather a French pastoral, reminds me of a Watteau painting in its airy bucolic mood. It's a true clavichord piece, and one imagines Bach at night lulling to sleep one of his newborn, all sweet gentility in its slightly lilting 12/8 metre.

The three-voice Fugue with its tiny subject is ambiguous as to its ending, a brilliant and yet strange little work. Martins says, "The fugue, with its pungent little subject jabbing and poking is always peeping out and always so unexpectedly."

Prelude and Fugue No. 10 in E minor

The Prelude is one of Bach's lyrical chants. Here is a divine flute melody. The second half needs fine finger control.

The Fugue is the only one of the "48" that is only in two voices, passionate and pungent in its broken chordal procession.

Prelude and Fugue No. 11 in F major

Hutcheson finds the Prelude "debonair, the writing of the invention type"; it's a dialogue between the hands with striking trills. Gray calls it "a ballet of atoms and molecules," and of the Sunlight Fugue in three voices, he says, "Such a fugue as this has the same seeming simplicity as a flower, and the same bewildering complexity when submitted to the scrutiny and analysis of the microscope."

Prelude and Fugue No. 12 in F minor

Landowska calls the Prelude "a kind of allemande in lute style." It's in four voices, richly harmonic with a feeling of haunting melancholy.

The Fugue in four voices has three countersubjects and is an introverted, but intense, work.

Prelude and Fugue No. 13 in F-sharp major

The Prelude is of the two-part invention variety, full of interesting syncopation.

The Fugue, in three voices lacks a stretto;

the countersubject, which Landowska calls "of infinite tenderness," waits until the twelfth measure to appear.

Prelude and Fugue No. 14 in F-sharp minor

The Prelude is an aria flowing restlessly in a dialogue of the hands. One hears perhaps an organ, flutes, and continuo.

The four-voice Fugue is severe and laden with sorrow, with few fugal devices used.

Prelude and Fugue No. 15 in G major

An exhilarating two-part invention, bright of light, needing strong independent fingers. Martins says, "The fugue in three voices possesses, it seems, every structural element that a fugue is capable of as well as being a kind of virtuoso dance in three voices."

Prelude and Fugue No. 16 in G minor

An inspired aria; the glory of this sad Prelude is long-sustained trills asking perfection of articulation.

A perfect embroidery, the Fugue, with its four voices, is a noble and pensive lament—a tour de force of Fugue creation, with two of the most amazing strettos of Book I. To achieve tonal discrimination and balance of voices asks for deft control from the executant.

Prelude and Fugue No. 17 in A-flat major

The Prelude is crisp and incisive, with a joy in living.

The four-voice Fugue has no strettos or inversions and, for Bach, little intellectual effort.

Prelude and Fugue No. 18 in G-sharp minor

The Prelude is rather gentle in arioso style with the quality of innocence.

The Fugue is in four voices, of which Tovey thinks, "With all its apparent simplicity and squareness this is one of the profoundest of the forty-eight."

Prelude and Fugue No. 19 in A major

The Prelude is a three-part invention of perfect organization, with Bach, as usual, wearing his learning lightly in its spirited measures.

The three-voice Fugue displays dazzling counterpoint using three subjects. Schulenberg is convinced that "the Prelude and Fugue in A major is among the high points of the *Well-Tempered Clavier I,* though rarely recognized as such. Perhaps it seems too cheerful or the subject of the fugue is too eccentric to be taken seriously."

Prelude and Fugue No. 20 in A minor

The Prelude has been called colorless and somewhat academic, the fugue dry. This Prelude and Fugue is often an enigma to executants.

The four-voice Fugue is treacherous to memorize, and it is one of the longest of the species, congested in its contrapuntal contraptions. There are fourteen strettos, direct or in inversion or combined.

Prelude and Fugue No. 21 in B-flat major

This short Prelude is an example of Bach's most idiomatic keyboard writing; the division of passagework between the hands sparkles like diamonds.

The Fugue is in three voices, and its long subject has the complement of two countersubjects.

Prelude and Fugue No. 22 in B-flat minor

A sublime Bachian prayer, the Prelude seldom fails to affect in a good performance.

The Fugue, along with the C-sharp minor, is the only fugue in five voices. It is an apotheosis of fugue writing, beyond the understanding of compositional device and analysis.

Its expressive world is a glorification of Bach's all-encompassing knowledge and human compassion.

Prelude and Fugue No. 23 in B major

The brief Prelude has a seemingly artless simplicity.

The Fugue in four voices is short, peaceful, and easy to love.

Prelude and Fugue No. 24 in B minor

The key of B minor reminds us that this tonality is special to Bach in his vocabulary of profundity.

The Fugue in four voices is sorrowful with no point of return. Bach actually gives it a tempo marking, largo. In it is the sound of eternity. Gray says, "It might have been written today or be written tomorrow." Wagner put its chromatic secrets in *Tristan,* and Schoenberg felt its powerful light.

Book II
Prelude and Fugue No. 1 in
C major

The Prelude is masterful; Hutcheson calls it "dispersed counterpoint in four parts, a continuous melody threading its way effortlessly from voice to voice." The years between both books had brought Bach to ever increasing ways and means of bringing his material through the hands, one may say Bach's majesty of the hands.

The Fugue is in three voices. Martins thinks he hears trumpets, and Landowska calls the subject "a glorification of the mordant."

Prelude and Fugue No. 2 in
C minor

A fine Prelude in the form of two voices divided into two parts; a true harpsichord piece.

The Fugue is in four voices with all sorts of inversion, augmentation, and strettos.

Prelude and Fugue No. 3 in
C-sharp major

The Prelude has a fugato in its midst and is made from five-part chords. Landowska thinks it "a dreamy prelude." Hutcheson asserts, "In the three-part fugue we find a little model of easy scholarship. Note especially that the exposition is written in stretto—a quite unusual procedure—with the third voice

entering in inversion." Martins is sure that Bach is having lots of fun.

Prelude and Fugue No. 4 in
C-sharp minor

A sophisticated Prelude in the French style, replete with ornaments *à la* Couperin. Martins hears it as a lament in three voices. There is an anxious feeling, as if attempting to reach peace through its chromatic second subject."

The three-voice Fugue unrolls in serious triplets.

Prelude and Fugue No. 5 in
D major

The Prelude reminds Landowska of the theme of the Christmas oratorio and of the allegro from the overture to the Partita No. 3 in D major.

The opening is a fanfare crying out for trumpets and high festivities. Schulenberg ranks it as "one of the most magnificent pieces in *The Well-Tempered Clavier II.*" The Prelude is immense, larger than the four-voice Fugue which, in Gray's words, "is one of the greatest marvels of workmanship, not merely in the forty-eight, but in all the music of Bach, and even in all music whatsoever. From first bar to last the entire structure evolves from the subject."

Prelude and Fugue No. 6 in
D minor

An intense Prelude, opening with a startling mordent in the left hand which truly defines the idea of a mordant as "to bite." One hears the double manual harpsichord billowing in turbulence.

The three-voice Fugue is rather gloomy in its understated gravity.

Prelude and Fugue No. 7 in E-flat major

A picturesque, sweet, and wholesome Prelude.

The Fugue is a marvel in four voices, noble but warm. Landowska points out, "In the magnificent episode from the forty-third to the fifty-eighth measures the voices converse with humor. Fugue No. 7 concludes in overwhelming joy."

Prelude and Fugue No. 8 in D-sharp minor

Landowska calls this Prelude "a cantilena veiled with melancholy." It is in two sections marked with repeats.

The Fugue also has a special sadness. For Martins the four-voice Fugue "sounds deeply in D-sharp minor, whereas in Book I the fugue sounds totally in E-flat minor. Bach must have known this was no trick of the ear." The countersubject to the Fugue is of exceptional contrast.

Prelude and Fugue No. 9 in E major

Very flowing, even capricious. Hutcheson goes far in calling this "the crowning glory of the forty-eight," but it surely does breathe a noble lyricism.

The four-voice Fugue is for an imagined a cappela chorus with astonishing strettos.

Prelude and Fugue No. 10 in E minor

Another Prelude of the two-part invention type in binary form. Musically it's rather serene. Landowska states, "Though only in two voices, the writing is rich and complex."

The Fugue subject for this three-voice work is one of the longest in *The Well-Tempered Clavier.* The subject is regal; although there are no strettos, there are fine episodes, with the Fugue ending on a Picardy third.

Prelude and Fugue No. 11 in F major

An outstanding Prelude, composed in four and five voices.

The Fugue is penetrating and unusual; one feels it to be suited to the organ. The three-voice Fugue is a hymn bursting with life. In Gray's words: "There is no regular countersubject, no strettos, diminutions, augmentations, inversions, or any other kind of learned device in this fugue. It is as if Bach had deliberately set out to show that it was perfectly possible to write a good fugue and yet to dispense with every element and every procedure deemed necessary by pundits and pedants."

Prelude and Fugue No. 12 in F minor

An often played and poignant Prelude in two parts with a double bar.

The three-voice Fugue presents no contrapuntal devices. Tovey says, "It shows it is possible for a fugue to enjoy life without stretti, double counterpoints, inversions, etc."

Prelude and Fugue No. 13 in F-sharp major

A long and fluid Prelude which needs a firm rhythmic flow, with effective dotted rhythms *á la française.* The Fugue subject possesses a measured trill and the countersubject has the feel of a gavotte.

Prelude and Fugue No. 14 in F-sharp minor

Gray thinks, "With this prelude and fugue, we find ourselves in the presence of one of the loftiest peaks in the whole Himalayan range of the forty-eight." The Prelude is impassioned and of great lyric and emotional appeal. As Landowska states, "When Bach writes of sorrow, it never crushes us, perhaps because there is no brace of bitterness. This music, even if it describes rebellion or anguish, fortifies us." Hugo Riemann calls it "a prelude of wondrous beauty—an outpouring of the inmost soul, fresh with youth, overflowing with love." It is forty-two bars of miraculous melodic flow.

In the three-voice Fugue we find three subjects of varied character. The stern Fugue stands in portentous contrast to the Prelude, a microcosm of humanity on a keyboard.

Prelude and Fugue No. 15 in G major

A very airy Prelude in binary form, which is usually played too fast; it is simple in structure and instantly engages the ear. The Fugue in three voices sounds for Martins "like country peasants playing a bagpipe." For Landowska it is possibly à Courante al'Italienne.

Prelude and Fugue No. 16 in G minor

Schulenberg finds both the Prelude and Fugue to be forbidding, with a complex polyphony in the Fugue. Hutcheson thinks the Prelude suggests a Handelian overture. Martins hears the Prelude as funereal, with the Fugue portraying the power of destiny. The work is monumental in design; the composer himself gives us the tempo marking—"largo."

The Fugue is worked out in four voices with bleak, insistent intensity.

Prelude and Fugue No. 17 in A-flat major

A Prelude of considerable length and of instrumental luminosity, written in two parts. The Fugue in four voices has a subject which appears fifteen times. For Landowska, "in each appearance we experience a new happiness."

Prelude and Fugue No. 18 in G-sharp minor

A musical unity is present in the mood of both the Prelude and Fugue. The Prelude is of a haunting poetry.

The Fugue in three voices is considered by some analysts to be a double fugue (a fugue with two subjects). The second one is highly chromatic in nature; Martins calls it a "fugato song." Landowska counts eleven episodes that enrich the glowing life of the Fugue.

Prelude and Fugue No. 19 in A major

Hutcheson is convinced that this is "one of the less important pieces of Book II, agreeable in mood but seldom played." It's in the form of a three-part invention and pastoral in tone.

The Fugue in three voices needs perfect physical control at every point and is especially tricky to put to memory.

Prelude and Fugue No. 20 in A minor

A strange but intriguing work, also a very difficult work to memorize, very chromatic and rather compulsive.

The three-voice Fugue of only twenty-eight measures is a miracle of compression, powerful and grand.

Prelude and Fugue No. 21 in B-flat major

The heavenly Prelude is far longer than the Fugue.

Hutcheson says, "The fugue (in three voices) is unique in that the theme begins on the supertonic, quite contrary to Bach's almost invariable practice." But Bach ever surprises in his digressions.

Prelude and Fugue No. 22 in B-flat minor

A supreme masterwork and one of the great works of the late Baroque era. The Prelude of elegiac sorrow is magnificently developed polyphonically.

The four-part Fugue is an encyclopedia of fugal writing. One learns from the Fugue that the form is mystical mathematics. The somber Fugue in four voices is a monument of strettos and inversion ending on a Picardy third.

Prelude and Fugue No. 23 in B major

The Prelude is serene and of crystal beauty. The four-voice Fugue is comparatively simple in design and of good nature.

Prelude and Fugue No. 24 in B minor

After ninety-four pieces, *The Well-Tempered Clavier* ends not with a granite or a marble monument but with an unpretentious charming little Prelude in two equal voices.

The Fugue in three voices is rather gay and carefree. Martins says, "When I play the last bars, there is a sigh that can't be described.

How is it that this artist could take only twelve tones and manipulate them as if they were the endless stars of the galaxy?" The fugue ends with pure simplicity and human kindness.

S. FIENBERG: Russian Disc
E. FISCHER: EMI
GOULD: CBS
MARTINS: Labor
RICHTER: JVC/Melodiya
SCHIFF: London

MILY BALAKIREV
1837–1910—Russia

Islamey—Oriental Fantasy

Balakirev, a fine pianist, could never quite master the hardships of his own *Islamey*. Liszt was reputed to have sight-read it. It remains one of the wonderful works of Russian virtuoso pianism. The Rubinstein brothers, von Bülow, and Tausig played it frequently, and Ravel greatly admired it; his *Scarbo* stems directly from its pianism. Balakirev wrote a quantity of appealing, beautifully scored piano music, the finest being his neglected and unconventional Piano Sonata in B-flat minor recorded by Earl Wild on Ivory Classics.

Islamey:
ARRAU: Philips: Great Pianists of the Twentieth Century
BARÈRE: APR
BRONFMAN: Sony Classics
CIANI: Dynamic
GAVRILOV: EMI Classics
OGDEN: Philips: Great Pianists of the Twentieth Century

SAMUEL BARBER
1910–1981—United States

Sonata in E-flat minor, Op. 26 (1949)

Barber's major achievement for the piano and the most popular American sonata since its composition. The work is in four compact movements, concluding with a brilliantly jaunty fugue. Other pieces for solo piano are his *Four Excursions, Ballade, Souvenirs,* and the nocturne *Homage to John Field.* Barber also composed a fine Piano Concerto, for John Browning, who played it with success everywhere.

> *Sonata:*
> BROWNING: MusicMasters
> CLIBURN: RCA
> HOROWITZ: RCA
> OHLSSON: Arabesque

BÉLA BARTÓK
1881–1945—Hungary

Bartók's contribution to the piano literature brought to the instrument an entirely new personality and sonorous language. The music contains asymmetrical phrase groups, irregular meters, keyless modal melodies, wonderful tonal clashes, the drone bass, and block chordal accompaniments, much of it inspired by Magyar folk music. It sounds new, yet its roots are ancient. Bartók was a pianist of great originality, as may be heard on his complete recordings issued by Hungaroton on six CDs.

Fourteen Bagatelles, Op. 6 (1908)

One of the finest sets of piano music of its decade. Unlike much of Bartók, these are not folk-inspired; each piece is ingenious in its application of sonority. When Busoni first heard them he exclaimed, "At last something new."

> ANDERSZEWSKI: Miami Piano Festival
> HAGOPIAN: Etcetera
> LOWENTHAL: Pro Piano
> SILVERMAN: Orion (LP)

Three Etudes, Op. 18 (1918)

Extraordinary music, and technically hazardous. All three total only eight minutes. In No. 2, Bartók has assimilated Debussy's and Ravel's impressionism into his own style.

> GABOS: Hungaroton
> P. JACOBS: Nonesuch
> ROSEN: Epic (LP)

Improvisations, Op. 20 (1920)

A subtly connected set of eight pieces based on Hungarian peasant songs.

> GABOS: Hungaroton
> KOCSIS: Philips
> NISSMAN: Pierian
> PERAHIA: CBS
> SONG: Pro Piano

Sonata for Piano (1926)

One of the most frequently performed of Bartók's solo piano works; in three movements. It is angular, dissonant, and powerful.

ARGERICH: Exclusive
CIANI: Dynamic
KALICHSTEIN: Vanguard
KOCSIS: Denon
KOVACEVICH: Philips (LP)

Out of Doors Suite (1926)

A tremendously effective cycle of five pieces, very difficult to play: *With Drums and Pipes, Barcarolla, Musettes, Night's Music,* and *The Chase.*

HELFFER: Musique d'Abord
PERAHIA: CBS

Mikrokosmos, Six Volumes—153 Progressive Pieces (1926–37)

A precious folk treasury for the young. Bartók carves out the pianist's gradual growth through pieces which progressively present an ever-widening awareness of compositional devices and pianistic problems.

BARTÓK (thirty-one selections): Sony
    Masterworks
MASSELOS: MHS (LP)
RÁNKI: Telefunken
SANDOR: Sony Classics

Fifteen Hungarian Peasant Songs

This is a cycle characteristic of Bartók's folk settings.

KOCSIS: Denon
RICHTER: CBS/Melodiya (LP)
SCHIFF: Denon

Piano Concerto No. 1 (1926)

Bartók's three piano concerti are classics of the twentieth-century concerto repertoire. No. 1 utilizes a large percussion battery and needs an excellent conductor.

POLLINI, Abbado/Chicago Symphony: DG
P. SERKIN, Ozawa/Chicago Symphony: RCA

Piano Concerto No. 2 (1932)

The Second Concerto is a technical tour de force, with a splashy and dissonant orchestral part. The most dashing of the three concerti.

ASHKENAZY, Solti/London Philharmonic:
    London
POLLINI, Abbado/Chicago Symphony: DG
WEISSENBERG, Ormandy/Philadelphia: RCA

Béla Bartok by David Dubal

Piano Concerto No. 3 (1945)

The Third Concerto is the least taxing technically, the least complex orchestrally, and the easiest to grasp on first hearing. The slow movement, Adagio religioso, is an unearthly chant.

> ANDA, Fricsay/Berlin Symphony: DG
> ASHKENAZY, Solti/Chicago Symphony: London
> KATCHEN, Kertesz/London Symphony: London
> RÁNKI, Ferencsik/Hungarian State: Hungaroton
> SANDOR: Vox

LUDWIG VAN BEETHOVEN

1770–1827—Germany

The Thirty-two Piano Sonatas

Beethoven's piano sonatas form one of the great contributions to the musical art. Each is a landmark in the history of the form. Beethoven, the perfectly polished craftsman, was the first musical artist who consciously sought for originality with each sonata daringly different from each other. "The essence of Beethoven," wrote the pianist Louis Kentner, "perhaps the greatest artist ever produced by civilization, lies in the piano sonatas."

Aaron Copland best summed up Beethoven's greatness:

> Beethoven brought three startling innovations to music: first, he altered our very conception of the art by emphasizing the psychological element implicit

in the language of sounds. Secondly, his own stormy and explosive temperament was, in part, responsible for a dramatization of the whole art of music. . . . Both of these elements—the psychological orientation and the instinct for drama—are inextricably linked in my mind with his third and possibly most original achievement, the creation of musical form dynamically conceived on a scale never before attempted and of an inevitability that is irresistible.

> ARRAU: Philips
> ASHKENAZY: London
> BACKHAUS: London
> BARENBOIM: DG
> BRENDEL: Philips
> BRENDEL: Vox
> A. FISCHER (Complete Sonatas): Hungaraton
> FRANK: Music and Arts
> GOODE: Nonesuch
> GULDA: Amadeo
> HOBSON: Zephyr
> KEMPFF: DG
> LIPKIN: Newport Classics
> NAT: EMI
> O'CONOR: Telarc
> ROBERTS: NIMBUS
> SCHNABEL: EMI
> TAUB: Vox

Sonata No. 1 in F minor, Op. 2, No. 1 (1795) 18 minutes

From the beginning we hear the later Beethoven in the early. The pianist Eugene d'Albert declared that in the Op. 2, No. 1, he already heard the *Appassionata* in the first movement. Beethoven, fervent son of the democratic ascendancy, vents an almost modern sense of frustration and intensity. In the first movement the upward motive seethes with biting restlessness. The adagio slow movement is an incomplete sonata form in F major, based on the third movement of his Piano Quartet Wo 036, composed at fifteen. Its suavity resembles Johann Stamitz, C. P. E. Bach, and J. C. Bach more than Mozart or Haydn. The minuetto, tinged with nobility and cross accents, has little in common with a danceable minuet by, say, Boccherini. The prestissimo finale is a sonata form in which is announced that the world of music will soon change under Beethoven—or, as Wilhelm Kempff asserts, "The world now knows that here was a musician born to unleash and conquer demoniacal forces."

GOULD: Odyssey
GRINBERG: Melodiya
KOCSIS: Philips
NAOUMOFF: Thésis
PERAHIA: Sony Classical

Sonata No. 2 in A major, Op. 2, No. 2 (1795) 25 minutes

A work of great complexity and length, demanding a well-developed, flexible technique. The A major sonata shows its vast fund of humor, of many shades of jesting, playful and ferociously boisterous. The cellular terse opening of the first movement seems so slight that one wonders how Beethoven would proceed. But as the pianist Ernest Hutcheson wrote, "Nothing is more typical of his genius than this unique power to make much of little, to build from tiny units, musical structure of immense proportions, coherence, and grandeur."

The Largo Appassionata tells us that in writing a largo, Beethoven truly means a slower tempo than adagio. The piano writing is inventive, yet gives the effect of other instruments; indeed, this is a prime characteristic of Beethoven's piano music. In the slow movement the staccato basses sound like cello pizzicati.

In Op. 2, No. 2, Beethoven substitutes the traditional minuet movement of the "sonata idea" for his own invention, the scherzo (in Italian, a joke). Here his unbuttoned rollicking high spirits take flight. In the highly detailed Finale, Rondo Grazioso, Beethoven gives us an exquisitely ornamented movement which was said to be a favorite of the composer's. The long pedal effects create a misty atmosphere, especially on early pianos. The work ends in an affably gentle manner.

GILELS: DG
HORSZOWSKI: Nonesuch
PERAHIA: Sony Classical
ROBERTS: Nimbus
SHEHORI: Cembal d'Amour

Sonata No. 3 in C major, Op. 2, No. 3 (1795) 25 minutes

Beethoven frequently performed it early in his career. A splendid virtuosic verve is paramount in the first movement's Allegro con brio. Alfred Brendel says, "With all its pianistic brilliance, this is a very orchestral piece. I think the modern piano can reproduce its orchestral color better than the pianos of Beethoven's time." The second movement, an adagio in E major, is far from the "home key" and is a bold color change. A penetrating hymn-like melody begins a heavenly movement, showing how Romantic early Beethoven can be. In the E minor middle section there are graceful hand crossings while Beethoven converses with angels in this rather "operatic" page.

The third movement is a fast-paced scherzo (allegro), graceful but with a hint of the ominous. Mendelssohn must have loved its Finale, an extended Rondo allegro assai. The third subject in F major becomes, in Kempff's words, "a musical offering" to the creator of all things. The C major sonata is packed with technical pitfalls and it is apparent that

Beethoven wanted to write a C major sonata that outshines Clementi, or Dussek's, in the same key.

BAR-ILLAN: Audiofon
GELBER: Denon
GOULD: CBS
KEMPFF: Philips: Great Pianists of the
  Twentieth Century
MICHELANGELI: EMI
OHLSSON: Arabesque
RICHTER: Praga
RUBINSTEIN: RCA

Sonata No. 4 in E-flat major, Op. 7 (1796) 30 minutes

After his trio of debut sonatas, Beethoven was supremely confident of his ability in large tonal spaces. Proudly he called the sonata a grosse sonata, the longest of the early sonatas, or of any eighteenth-century sonata. Indeed, except for the sonata Op. 106, it is Beethoven's longest sonata. Czerny tells us that it was created in a passionate state of mind, for Beethoven was at the time infatuated by the Countess Babette von Keglevics, to whom it was dedicated.

The first movement, Allegro molto e con brio, is technically demanding and is often taken too slowly. The slow movement in C major, marked "Largo con gran espressione," is magnificent. But, as Brendel points out, it needs a degree of silence that the audience of a large hall rarely permits. "It is a striking fact," wrote Kempff, "that Beethoven spoke in a more personal manner and revealed his innermost secrets more fully in the piano sonata slow movements than in the violin sonatas or even in most of the symphonies." With its double-dotted rhythm, Mellers finds "the heroic note of the old Baroque world, while imbuing it with Beethovenian expressiveness so that it becomes a humanistic hymn."

After the stately nobility of the slow movement, the third movement allegro comes as a breath of fresh air. Not a minuet, it is also not a typical scherzo. The trio in E-flat minor offers a threatening moment. The rondo finale, poco allegretto e grazioso, exhibits a fetching episode which Beethoven imbues with ornamental elaboration. The coda is an unexpected page formed from the accompaniment of the second subject and wistfully dissolves to a lyrical ending. John Gillespie calls the rondo "a landmark in perfection for this form. It has seldom been equaled, never surpassed."

BENZ: Thorofon
GRINBERG: Melodiya
HUNGERFORD: Vanguard
MICHELANGELI: DG
PERAHIA: Sony
SHERMAN: Sine Qua Non

Sonata No. 5 in C minor, Op. 10, No. 1 (1796–98) 14 minutes

Louis Kentner thinks this sonata is "a remarkably good 'key' to Beethoven's style, a gate through which the student may enter this world better than through any other." The sonata for the first time presents a three-movement format. The Allegro molto e con brio demands intensity of expression and pinpoint rhythm. Its tenseness is alleviated by a Gluck-like second subject. Of the middle movement Kempff wrote that "had nothing of Beethoven's come down to us except the adagio molto, it would have sufficed to assure him a place among the immortals." In Eric Blom's analysis, "The slow movement has the first and second subjects and the coda of a sonata, but no working-out section." The finale, a short headlong prestissimo, is artfully composed in sonata form with coda. Only Beethoven could compose a movement on material which at first glance seems unpromising but which in fact contains protean energy.

GILELS: DG
GOULD: Odyssey
HUNGERFORD: Vanguard
KOVACEVICH: Philips: Great Pianists of the
    Twentieth Century
LIPKIN: Newport Classics
NIKOLAYEVA: Melodiya

Sonata No. 6 in F major, Op. 10, No. 2 (1796–1798) 15 minutes

In three concise movements; the first movement bubbles in merriment, teaming with small units bursting with developmental potential. The exposition ends on CGC, in downward octaves.

Beethoven now ignores all the material of his frothy exposition to build his development section on this skimpy motive of three notes, interrupting it with a long episode of triplets in broken octaves. Returning to the three-note motive, he moves headlong through various keys and finds himself in a hopeless but humorous dilemma; instead of ending his development section in the correct key of F major, he ends on A, the dominant of D major. After a fermata, time to think, so to speak, Beethoven blithely produces a delicious stroke of structural imagination, beginning his recapitulation in the wrong key of D major. With humorous desperation he works his way to the proper key to begin his true recapitulation.

The middle movement, marked "Allegretto," opens with an insinuating unison in the tonic minor. The trio with its warm chords proceeds to passages of early Beethovenian pathos, in Tovey's words.

The Finale opens in mock fugal style, being cast as a monothematic sonata form. It needs

lightness, fluent fingers, and strong broken octaves for its presto tempo.

ARRAU: Philips
GILELS: DG
GOULD: Odyssey
HOBSON: ZEPHYR
HORSZOWSKI: Thesis
KAMENÍKOVÁ: Supraphon
LORTIE: Chandos

Sonata No. 7 in D major, Op. 10, No. 3 (1796–1798) 25 minutes

A frequently performed sonata in four tightly argued and shapely movements, asking for a variety of technical accomplishments. The first movement, presto, is high-spirited and leaves one unprepared for the largo e mesto, in D minor, a movement which Brendel considers "one of the greatest slow movements Beethoven ever wrote." This poem of grief sounds the fatalistic note of a Greek drama which Tovey asserts, "is not only Beethoven's first essay in tragedy, but is by far the most tragic piece of music that had ever been written up to that time."

As if embarrassed by such an outcry, the composer brings us back to the late eighteenth century, with an old-fashioned courtly minuet. The Rondo marked "allegro" is full of sunny humor. In describing the concept of humor in music, the writer Arthur Koestler wrote, "A concert audience may occasionally smile, but will hardly ever laugh; which goes to show that the emotions evoked by musical humor are of a subtler kind than those of the verbal and visual variety."

FISCHER: EMI
HOROWITZ: RCA
IGUMOV: Dante
PAPERNO: Cedille

Sonata No. 8 in C minor, Op. 13, "Grand Sonata Pathétique" (1798–99) 17 minutes

The best known of the early sonatas. The first movement begins with an introduction marked "grave." With this page, Beethoven stands at the threshold of nineteenth-century Romantic emotionalism. The slow movement, adagio cantabile, is an exquisite love song; the second episode, in Eric Blom's words, "beginning in A-flat minor, is like a duet between a mezzo-soprano and a baritone." The Rondo finale must be played with a penetrating sadness instead of the almost-jaunty presentation it usually gets. Claudio Arrau thought it "full of anxiety, a tremendous anxiety infuses it."

BACKHAUS: Philips: Great Pianists of the
    Twentieth Century
BARENBOIM: DG
CLIBURN: RCA
GOULD: Sony Classical
HOROWITZ: CBS
KAMENÍKOVÁ: Supraphon
L. BERMAN: Sony Classical
LUPU: London
MORAVEC: VAI
PERAHIA: Sony Classical
R. SERKIN: Sony Classical
RUBINSTEIN: RCA

Sonata No. 9 in E major, Op. 14, No. 1 (1798–1799) 14 minutes

Beethoven retreats from the tempestuous world of the Sonata *Pathétique* to a comparatively intimate sonata in three movements. The first movement is pure string quartet writing for the piano, and it should be noted that Beethoven transcribed this sonata for quartet, proudly noting, "I know as an absolute certainty that my arrangement would be difficult to rival." Of the second movement allegretto Kempff feels, "Brahms must have loved it for its veiled ambiguity of mood, which is a pearl of great price." For his finale we have a good-natured allegro comodo with all sorts of subtle variants.

BACHAUER: Mercury
FOLDES: AURC
GOULD: Sony Classical
GRINBERG: Melodiya
RICHTER: CBS
SEEMANN: Orfeo
TAUB: Vox

The Death of Beethoven by David Dubal

Sonata No. 10 in G major, Op. 14, No. 2 (1798–99) 14 minutes

In three movements, the first a charming pastel of vernal beauty with a spring storm in the development section. The first subject is unforgettable in its limpid grace. The andante movement is a precious march-like theme which Schumann must have admired and for which Beethoven writes three variations and a coda. Here is Beethoven's first set of variations in the piano sonatas. The finale, allegro assai, is curiously marked "scherzo" and is, in fact, a Rondo full of delightful play.

GOULD: Odyssey
HORSZOWSKI: Arbitor
MERZHANOV: Melodiya (LP)
RICHTER: Melodiya
GILELS: DG

Sonata No. 11 in B-flat major, Op. 22 (1800–01) 25 minutes

Calling it a grand solo sonata, Beethoven was well pleased with this work and asked his publisher for ten ducats for his second piano concerto and twenty for this sonata.

Its course is untroubled and extraverted; Denis Matthews thinks the Op. 22 a work of consolidation rather than adventure, gathering strength from convention. The Allegro con brio opens with a theme soaring skyward. The adagio con molto espressione is, in Mellers's words, "an operatic aria in sonata form." The minuetto is of perfect grace and lilt. The rondo, marked "allegretto," is languid with gallant sighs for an already vanished day; in its midst fugato passages bring some confusion to the decorum, but the sonata ends in gladness fulfilled to the brim.

CICCOLINI: Nuova Era
HAMBOURG: Arbitor
MICHELANGELI: Music and Arts
O'CONOR: Telarc

OPPENS: Music and Arts
PERAHIA: Sony Classical
R. SERKIN: Sony Classical

Sonata No. 12 in A-flat major, Op. 26 (1800–1801) 25 minutes

An unconventional work in four movements which contains no sonata-allegro movement, but which is so chemically organized that there is an inevitability and unity from within.

The first movement is a theme with five leisurely variations. Chopin, usually not sympathetic to Beethoven, performed the first movement. Certainly Mozart preceded Beethoven in the elegant variations of the first movement of his A major Sonata, K. 331, but there is no Mozart here. Maurizio Pollini feels that in Beethoven's early sonatas "he created a new way of writing for the piano, totally different from that of Mozart or Haydn." The Scherzo movement, allegro molto, is playful, with a lyric trio. The major surprise of the sonata is the third movement, *Marcia Funebre*, subtitled *sulla morte d'un eroe* (Funeral March on the Death of a Hero). The movement was inspired by a funeral march by Ferdinando Paër (1771–1839), in his forgotten opera, *Achilles*. Beethoven attended the premiere with the composer, and when listening to the somber strains of Paër's music, Beethoven turned to the composer, saying, "How beautiful! How interesting! I shall have to compose that." The piece is full of fanfare and drum rolls.

The finale, marked "allegro," is a flowing, highly organized rondo, technically speaking; the pianist James Frisken calls it "an excellent study in rotation technique."

BRENDEL: Vox
LAMOND: BPS
GILELS: DG
RICHTER: RCA
ROBERTS: Nimbus
R. SERKIN: Arkadia

Sonata No. 13 in E-Flat major, Op. 27, No. 1, "Sonata quasi una Fantasia" (1800–01)

15 minutes

A masterpiece which has been somewhat slighted because of the popularity of its sister sonata, Op. 27, No. 2—the so-called Moonlight Sonata. In both of these works, Beethoven breaks new formal ground; here and in the Op. 27, No. 2, he felt compelled to add the subheading Sonata quasi una Fantasia. It is a four-movement structure with much "interlocking and interacting," as Brendel puts it.

The first movement is highly unusual in that the tempo is slow, with an insertion of a quick section which is part dance, part drama. The following movement is a storm-filled Allegro molto e vivace in C minor, in the form of a scherzo, which sets the stage for one of those eloquent Adagios which can only be called Beethovenian. The finale is glorious; the ending presents the Adagio movement's theme again, but, as Wilhelm Kempff exclaims, "not rising from twilight depths but on a higher and brighter level, a song of thanksgiving such as only Beethoven could create."

BILSON (fortepiano): Nonesuch
CHERKASSKY: Nimbus
GILELS: DG
LIPKIN: Newport Classics
POLLINI: DG
ROSEN: Nonesuch
WATTS: Seraphim

Sonata No. 14 in C-sharp minor, Op. 27, No. 2, "Sonata quasi una Fantasia"—"Moonlight" (1801) 15 minutes

One of the most popular of the sonatas. Its evocative title was bestowed to all generations by Ludwig Rellstab, the Berlin poet and critic, who saw in the first movement, Andante sostenuto, the moon over Lake Lucerne. Doubtless Rellstab did see moonlight, and many others have seen and felt much else in this yearning lamentation which was something entirely new in music. Its structure shows subtle references to sonata allegro form. Tovey calls it "continuous melody on an enormous scale with elements of development and recapitulation." Kempff says that it is "the first precursor of impressionism, we see with our ears, hear with our eyes. A pale light glimmers above the whispered pianissimo triplets, from whose dark depths the grief laden melody ascends." In placing the slow movement first, Beethoven achieves a psychological shock.

The second movement is an allegretto, which Liszt called "a flower between two abysses." The trio is rustic. It is a perfect resting place for the flash flood of the concluding presto agitato, where Beethoven's demons strike. Not a Rondo but a surging sonata form, it was the wildest music of the age, with its feverish and violent upward arpeggio theme. The *Pathétique* Sonata introduced palpitating anxiety into music; this movement brings to music a new element of ruthlessness which crushed the instruments of his day. Significantly, Beethoven stirs emotions that are beginning to surface in the revolutionary setting of early-nineteenth-century European society, as well as his own growing awareness that an ongoing deafness was an evil fate.

ASHKENAZY: London
BACKHAUS: AS Disc
BAR-ILLAN: Audiofon
R. CASADESUS: Sony Classical
CLIBURN: RCA
DICHTER: Philips
A. FISCHER: Angel
GELBER: Denon
GILELS: DG
GOULD: Sony Classical

HOROWITZ: Sony Classical
ISTOMIN: Reference
H. NEUHAUS: Melodiya
NISSMAN: Pierian
NOVAES: Vanguard
RUBINSTEIN: RCA
SOLOMON: EMI

Sonata No. 15 in D major, Op. 28, "Pastorale" (1801) 26 minutes

Published in 1802, the sonata was given the title *Pastorale* by the publisher. The title works well for this pantheistic four-movement lyric libation to nature. Beethoven was constantly nourished by nature; he once wrote, "In the country it seems as if every tree said to me: 'Holy! Holy! Nature is a glorious school for the heart.' " The *Pastorale* is spacious, disarmingly unpretentious, magnificently gentle. The first movement opens on a D pedal-point and continues leisurely with occasional flourishes and lyric outpouring. The Andante in D minor with its pizzicato bass was, says Czerny, a favorite of the composers. The scherzo, allegro molto, is cheery, with chirping birds, if one feels pictorial. In the trio with its left-hand broken octaves there is a whiff of B minor, a key Beethoven mysteriously avoided, calling it "the black key." The finale, allegro ma non troppo, is an elaborate Rondo swaying in the breeze in its undulating 6/8 metre; the coda, rushing willy-nilly, is a technical hazard, marked "pui allegro quasi presto," concluding a sonata unusual in its sustained calm.

E. FISCHER: Arkadia
FOLDES: DG
GELBER: Denon
GRINBERG: Melodiya
GULDA: London
JANDÓ: Naxos
KEMPFF: DG
MORAVEC: Connoisseur Society

POLLINI: DG
SOFRONITSKY: Melodiya

Sonata No. 16 in G major, Op. 31, No. 1 (1801–02) 20 minutes

Less seldom played among Beethoven's piano sonatas. Fresh, bold, and clever; the first movement in particular is all frolic, while the slow movement is an Adagio grazioso that is unlike any other. Alfred Brendel feels "it's like an ironic comment on something old-fashioned. . . . There is a mixture of love and irony that is very strange and if the player can manage to convey it, it can be very effective." Kempff thinks "the piano assumes the role of a prima donna, glittering with enchanting graces." The Rondo finale is based on a gavotte-like theme. In this movement, we find humor and Beethoven's sense of the grotesque.

BASHKIROV: Melodiya
GIESEKING: Music and Arts
GOODE: Nonesuch
GRINBERG: Melodiya
OHLSSON: Arabesque
ROSEN: Globe
R. SERKIN: Arkadia

Sonata No. 17 in D minor, Op. 31, No. 2, "Tempest" (1801–02) 25 minutes

Composed in the Romantics' "fateful" key of D minor, the sonata has become known as *The Tempest*—when Beethoven was asked as to the general mood of the work he advised his questioner to read Shakespeare's *Tempest*. The slow and solemn introductory passages are a calm before the storm. The composer wanted them to sound like a voice from a tomb-vault. The movement proceeds with dark intensity and foreboding tensions. The pristine adagio is a sonata movement with exposition and recapitulation, lacking a development section. A finale in 3/8 meter is marked "allegretto," and is often played too fast. The movement, in sonata form, is based on a persistent four-note motive which passes to a throbbing heart-piercing mordant. Kentner finds the movement to be "like a wistful farewell to youth," while Tovey calls attention to "the exquisite pathos." Although the composition is one of the most regular and well-balanced sonatas in form, the content is full of struggle and unrequited love.

BACKKAUS: Philips: Great Pianists of the Twentieth Century
BILSON (fortepiano): Nonesuch
GRINBERG: Melodiya
HASKIL: Philips
KOVACEVICH: Philips: Great Pianists of the Twentieth Century
NOVAES: Allegretto
PIRES: Erato
PIRES: Erato
SHEHORI: Cembal d'Amour

Sonata No. 18 in E-flat major, Op. 31, No. 3 (1801–02)
25 minutes

This brilliant four-movement sonata is filled with light, freshness, and vigor. Edwin Fischer called the *Tempest* Beethoven's "masculine psyche" and the E-flat Sonata his "feminine psyche." The first theme trembles with gentle questioning, leading to a motive that is pregnant with joy. Beethoven is absolutely bursting with happiness. The second movement, allegro vivace, is not the usual slow movement but a rocking scherzo, in a 2/4 pulse rather than the usual 3/4 meter, but Beethoven himself marked it "scherzo," once again deviating from any

rigid rules. A gracious, old-fashioned minuetto, moderato e grazioso, follows.

Saint-Saëns used the trio of the minuetto for his admirable Variations, Op. 35, for two pianos. The finale, presto con fuoco, is a perpetual motion in sonata form with an exhilarating sense of motion. Mendelssohn must have loved this sonata, with its demanding staccato technique in the second and fourth movements.

Eric Blom points out, "With the exception of Op. 106 this is the last of the piano sonatas to contain four movements and the last to include a formal minuet."

ASHKENAZY: London
BADURA-SKODA (1815 piano): Astree
GELBER: Denon
HASKIL: Philips: Great Pianists of the Twentieth Century
RIEFLING: Simox
SEROTA: Arbitor
WILD: Del'Arte

Sonata No. 19 in G major, Op. 49, No. 1 (1795) 7 minutes
Sonata No. 20 in G minor, Op. 49, No. 2 (1795) 7 minutes

In these scores we travel back in time. Although taking their place among the opus numbers of Beethoven's middle period, these two-movement works are from the period of the composer's Op. 2 Sonatas, supposedly sent to a publisher without Beethoven's consent by his brother Caspar. It is fortunate they were, for as Tovey says, "We might otherwise have been deprived of the two most beautiful sonatas within the range of small hands and young players." Kempff felt, "These sonatinas will remind one of the time when, as children, they first ventured to play a Beethoven sonata. Playing them is still a venture." For Brendel,

"They are beautifully finished, graceful works in which Beethoven comes nearer to Mozart than in any other of the piano sonatas. They are very exposed. Every note is lying bare. . . . I admire the pianist who can play them well." Teachers would do well to teach them after the Clementi and Kuhlau sonatinas. The theme of the tempo di menuetto of the G major Sonata was used by the composer in his Septet, Op. 20, one of the most popular of his works during his lifetime. The G minor Sonata is generally more difficult than the G major.

BRENDEL: Philips
FRANK: Music and Arts
GELBER: Denon
GILELS: DG
LIPKIN: Newport Classics

Sonata No. 21 in C major, Op. 53, "Waldstein" (1803–04)
25 minutes

The work is dedicated to Beethoven's patron Count Waldstein, and the world calls it "the Waldstein Soanta." Waldstein provided funds for the twenty-two-year-old composer to leave Bonn in 1792 and to continue his studies with Haydn. He told Beethoven that "with the help of assiduous labor you shall receive Mozart's spirit from Haydn's hands. . . . "

The *Waldstein* is cast in two huge outer movements with a twenty-eight bar Introduzione, adagio molto, occupying the place of a slow movement. It is a statement of shuddering impact, building inexorably to the gigantic Rondo. In Kempff's words, it is "a flash of genius, illuminating the twilight between minor and major. The Rondo theme is as radiant as a temple in the first light of dawn."

The *Waldstein* is exceedingly difficult—indeed as Tovey asserts, "enormously more difficult to play than most people think." It asks for a powerful technique on many levels, finger control of pinpoint accuracy, lightening reflexes, a powerful rhythmic drive, and continuous concentration and strength. This sonata was the first to benefit from the extra notes available to Beethoven on the enlarged piano sent to him from Paris by the Erard firm in 1803.

Konrad Wolff, speaks of the amazing vibratory power that Beethoven's piano music displays, especially from these years and forward: "By isolating the bass, Beethoven creates a vibration of the instrument of such communicative power that it will stay in the listener's mind throughout the entire movement, just as if the vibrating basses were continued from beginning to end . . . I am convinced that the intense effect of Beethoven's piano music on the listener—an effect recognized by everyone since Beethoven's time, but never quite explained—is caused, in considerable part, by this ongoing vibration, which creates spiritual excitement at the same time as bodily excitement."

Within the walls of the *Waldstein* Beethoven created a sonorous imagery so compellingly dramatic and erotic that one may be tempted to say that with this composition, along with its spiritual companion the *Appassionata,* Beethoven made certain of the piano's extraordinary future.

ARRAU: Philips
AX: RCA
BACKHAUS: Fonit-Cetra
BAR-ILLAN: Audiofon
CICCOLINI: Nuova Era
FIRKUSNY: London
A. FISCHER: Hungaraton
E. FISCHER: Arkadia
GILELS: DG
HOROWITZ: RCA
LUPU: London
NAT: EMI
NISSMAN: Pierian

414

PLETNEV: Virgin Classics
TOMSIC: Vivace

ROBERTS: Nimbus
YUDINA: Melodiya

Sonata No. 22 in F major, Op. 54 (1804) 13 minutes

A curious but rewarding sonata in two movements which has been overshadowed by the colossal *Waldstein* preceding it and the *Appassionata* following. Only upon repeated exposure does this work's recondite qualities begin to take shape. In Kentner's words, we "tend to neglect the fact that in the great forest that was Beethoven there are other trees, just as tall, but different." The first movement in "Tempo d'un menuetto" is an unprecedented sonata form, rough-edged and lugubrious. Here the listener will find nothing of the classical demeanor or of the gallantries of the minuet. For Alfred Brendel the F major sonata "is one of the strangest, most original pieces, and it is underrated. This work is for connoisseurs, for people who know the famous sonatas very well; then when they listen to this piece they will find that it sets its own rules, it is not modeled on forms that you know: it develops its own shape. . . . The two themes have been called, "la belle" and "la bête;" it is interesting to see how they act on each other, and that when the themes return the proportions have changed."

The much shorter second movement is a remarkably transparent finale, marked "allegretto," working its way through various keys. It needs a polished smoothness in its delivery. The movement is also a sonata form with a very short exposition and an enlarged development; the piece appears to sprout from some mysterious growth process.

BRENDEL: Philips
GRINBERG: Melodiya
GULDA: London
RICHTER: RCA

Sonata No. 23 in F minor, Op. 57, "Appassionata" (1804–05) 25 minutes

If Beethoven's Fifth Symphony epitomizes this composer for the general public, so his *Appassionata* is the sonata that defines Beethoven's piano music. It is of searing passion, the greatest musical explosion for the keyboard of its time. As his deafness increased, the *Appassionata* expresses his credo: "I shall seize fate by the throat, it will never wholly subdue me." We can imagine his lions roar as he must have literally punctured the wooden framed pianos of the day. Romain Rolland wrote of the Op. 57, "This work forms the peak of the first twenty-three piano sonatas. It is like Mount Blanc towering above the alpine mass." With such "middle period" works as the *Appassionata* and the Fifth Symphony, music had become a world force, and for most listeners of the early nineteenth century Beethoven's work was frightening, even an omen of doom. Goethe remarked that the Fifth Symphony could crush civilization.

Beethoven was pleased with the *Appassionata,* calling it his greatest piano sonata. The publisher Cranz gave it its indelible title, a word which stands as a testament to its universality. Tovey asserts, "The passion is beyond articulate utterance." Only Glenn Gould ludicrously places it "on my own private Beethoven poll . . . somewhere between the *King Stephen* overture and the Wellington's Victory Symphony." Gould dislikes Beethoven's "egoistic pomposity, and being preoccupied with being Beethoven." But it is Beethoven's self-absorption that thrills its listeners; in the *Appassionata* he finds the courage to realize a total release from restriction and inhibition which would make the future of musical Romanticism possible.

The work is in three movements; both outer movements are in sonata form. After the first movement's engulfing passion, the middle movement, Andante con moto, is a theme and variations, providing a repose, which leads to the pulsating and relentless rhythm of the violent finale. The theorist Hugo Leichtentritt finds it "reminiscent of the inferno vision of Dante's fancy."

The sonata is exceedingly difficult, asking for an all-powerful technique, a large sense of structure, and creative pedaling. If the player cannot display an unbridled temperament, it is best to shy away from the composition, which is too often feebly performed.

Beethoven, after the depiction of this mighty struggle, seems to have been drained and loses interest in composing piano sonatas. In the *Appassionata* Beethoven exhibits faith in the piano by exalting its potential power, but in reality he must have felt its present limitations, continuing to suggest improvements to piano builders. His protean energy in other media was hardly quelled, but it was to be nearly five years before he composed his next piano sonatas, and these would be modest structures compared with Op. 57.

ARRAU: Philips
CASADESIS: Sony Classical
GILELS: DG
GOULD: Sony Classical
HOROWITZ: Sony Classical
MEDTNER: APR
NISSMAN: Pierian
OGDON: MCA Classics
PERAHIA: Sony Classical
RICHTER: RCA
RUBINSTEIN: RCA
R. SERKIN: CBS
VÁSÁRY: Collins Classics
WATTS: EMI
WEISSENBERG: EMI

Sonata No. 24 in F-sharp major, Op. 78 (1809) 8 minutes

Beethoven was fond of this two-movement sonata. Tovey wrote: "With a light and tender touch Beethoven here foreshadows the style which overawes us by its depth in his latest works. Technically as well as aesthetically this sonata is far more difficult than it looks. . . . The first thing the student should realize is that in the first movement a brilliant rendering is simply detestable."

Brendel calls it "a lyrical and loving and joyous work. He must have been in a very tender mood. It is dedicated to one of the ladies he admired, Countess Therese von Brunswick. And it is a devil to play." The first movement, allegro, ma non troppo, is proceeded by four terse measures of adagio cantabile, where, Blom remarks, it "begins as though it would develop into one of Beethoven's great slow melodies. Indeed, how such a development was to be resisted passes comprehension." And Charles Rosen thinks, "How little the actual duration in measured time has to do with the range of expression is shown in the beautiful opening of his F-sharp major sonata."

The second movement allegro vivace is also difficult to play perfectly. Denis Matthews felt it "capricious in tonality, phrase-length and dynamics, making great play with pairs of short-slurred semi-quavers, sometimes crossing hands and demanding fastidious precision from the player."

BRENDEL: Philips
R. CASADESUS: Sony Classical
A. FISCHER: EMI
LIPKIN: Audiofon
H. NEUHAUS: Melodiya
NIKOLAYEVA: Melodiya
PETRI: Pearl
RÁNKI: Fidelio
ROSEN: Globe

Sonata No. 25 in G major, Op. 79
(1809) 10 minutes

A three-movement composition of robust gaiety and matutinal freshness. A full-bodied opening theme in the form of a German peasant dance is marked "presto alla tedesca." The G major sonata has often been called technically easier than most other sonatas, but Tovey states: "It is only fair to students who set about learning the whole sonata to point out to them that anyone who can play its first movement properly could equally easily master a big work full of unequivocal euphony and beauty such as Op. 22."

The sonata as a whole is full of wit and formal terseness. Brendel thinks it "a strange piece. It looks like a footnote on some older compositions, some old-fashioned ways of composing sonatas. But a footnote with an ironic light and strange compression . . . Already foreshadowing some of the procedures in his late music." The quaint middle movement, an andante in G minor with its E-flat major middle section, looks forward to Mendelssohn's *Venetian Gondola* pieces, while the slender vivace finale has an arresting tongue-in-cheek humor.

BACKHAUS: Philips: Great Pianists of the
   Twentieth Century
CIANI: Arkadia
CICCOLINI: Nu Ova Era
GOODE: Nonesuch
KEENE: Protone
POLLACK: Melodiya

Sonata No. 26 in E-flat major,
Op. 81a, "Les Adieux"
(1809–10) 15 minutes

The E-flat Sonata, Op. 81a, universally called *"Les Adieux"* (in English, *The Farewell;* in German *"Das Lebewohl"*), is the only official title, except for the *Pathétique,* that Beethoven gave to a sonata. The work was inspired by Beethoven's major patron and pupil, the Archduke Rudolph, who fled from Vienna as Napoleon's armies stormed the capital. The first movement is the farewell, the second movement is the period of his absence, and the festive finale marks his return home. Beethoven uses the motto "Le-be-wohl" over the first three notes of the introductory adagio, which goes as well in English: "Fare Thee Well." The introduction is one of the five slow introductions to the thirty-two Sonatas. The le-be-wohl motive dominates the first movement. The slow-movement andante espressivo is of a heightened tenderness in a sonata form without development. The finale, vivacissimamente, is yet another sonata structure. It rings with happiness and verve. Beethoven refused to complete the sonata until he knew of the archduke's safe return. Beethoven's manuscript tells us of "the arrival of his imperial highness the revered Archduke Rudolph, January 30, 1810." The verve of the movement speaks more than any words could of the master's friendship with his noble pupil, who received no less than twenty-five dedications of Beethoven's compositions. The Archduke Rudolph must be considered to be one of the great musical patrons in history.

The E-flat Sonata is technically fiendish, with treacherous patches of double notes and staccato chords. In the first movement, Tovey writes, "The demands of the player's athletic staying-power seem at first moderate; but the constant occurrence of dangerous corners make the sonata one of the severest tests Beethoven ever imposed on the muscular and spiritual steadiness of the player." Beethoven would have four unhappy years before he completed another piano sonata.

ARRAU: Philips
CLIBURN: RCA

417

GILELS: DG
GODOWSKY: Philips: Great Pianists of the
    Twentieth Century
GOODE: Book-of-the-Month Records
KOCSIS: Fidelis
MORAVEC: Connoisseur Society
NOVAES: Vanguard
RUBINSTEIN: RCA
R. SERKIN: Sony
VÁSÁRY: Colins Classics

Sonata No. 27 in E minor, Op. 90 (1814) 13 minutes

The years separating this two-movement sonata from Op. 81a were lonely and painful; Beethoven's physical afflictions were many and his deafness had deteriorated further. The composer had now decided to reject Italian musical terminology for tempo and expressive indications at the head of movements, using German instead. Beethoven told Count Lichnowsky, the sonata's dedicatee, that the first movement is "a struggle between the heart and the head; the second movement being a 'conversation with the beloved.' " The E minor Sonata is the tip of the iceberg for what would be Beethoven's so-called third period. In this work Beethoven entered uncharted waters. Kempff calls the Op. 90 "a lone wanderer" as we stand at the threshold of his "late" period.

In his book *The Classical Style,* Charles Rosen writes: "After a despairing and impassioned first movement, laconic almost to the point of reticence, a moderately slow, cantabile Rondo follows, symmetrical, relaxed, and with an exquisitely beautiful, squarely regular theme that is repeated many times without the slightest abridgment and is varied only at the end by placing the melody in another register . . . in no other piece does he rely on the unaltered repetition of a long melody to bear so much of the expressive weight."

The E minor Sonata is difficult interpretively; to reconcile the two movements into a focused structure is the problem. To play the first movement too dramatically ruins its mysterious character, to play the rondo too romantically makes for sameness.

BACKHAUS: London
BADURA-SKODA (1815 piano): Astrée
MORAVEC: VAI
PETRI: APR
RICHTER: Praga
SOLOMON: EMI

Sonata No. 28 in A major, Op. 101 (1816) 25 minutes

The rarefied domain of Beethoven's latest style was anticipated by the E minor Sonata of 1814, but fully awakened in the A major Sonata and the two masterful Cello Sonatas, Op. 102. These were tragic years: Beethoven's health, finances, and domestic circumstances were desperate, and he was starved for human love. His piano playing was now merely a remnant of his former glory.

But by 1815 a new reservoir was opening within Beethoven's creative universe. The last five sonatas occupied him from 1816 to 1822. They form the summit of his sonata writing and, together with the *Diabelli* Variations, they present, in James Friskin's words: "The most profound and subtle interpretative problems encountered in the work of any composer for the pianoforte. The musical ideas themselves are invested with a depth of emotion and almost prophetic exaltation that ask for exceptional qualities of dedication and musical insight, if any adequate performance is to be attained. There are no compositions which so greatly repay the pianist's lifelong study."

The Sonata, Op. 101 is on an excruciating emotional level and is terrible in its technical elements. Brendel states: "Synthesis and expansion of resources—that is where a description of Beethoven's late style would have to begin. . . . The complexity . . . may be broken down into a new delicacy and density of detail and a new rigor and refinement of its polyphonic part-writing." The first movement possesses an indescribable quality, an almost Wagnerian *melos*.

As Tovey remarks: "Never forget that Beethoven is now as inveterately polyphonic as Bach, though his voices come and go as mysteriously as the wind, blowing where they must through the various textures of keyboard writing and pedaling. The first movement possesses an ineffable lyricism, an indescribable yearning which seems to be in the air. A search for the unattainable. In these pages Beethoven condenses the shortest sonata movement of his career."

There follows an almost brutish ironic March that must have fallen hard on the ears of Beethoven's contemporaries. This grating vivace alla marcia, with its troubled trio, must have startled and obsessed Schumann. Mellers hears in its thrusting dotted rhythm a fierce sexual energy. After the March there is a slow movement, which serves as an introduction to the Fugal Finale. Here Beethoven plunges the depths of his soul as he brings us back to the opening material of the first movement, a masterstroke which leads by way of trills to the fugue, one of the most magical pieces of contrapuntal writing. The content becomes ecstatic, possessing something of the Dionysian joy of his Seventh Symphony finale. The Op. 101 is dedicated to the Baroness Dorothea Ertmann, a friend and student of Beethoven's whose performances of his piano works pleased him immensely.

DICHTER: Philips
HOROWITZ: Sony Classical
KOVACEVICH: EMI
E. LEVY: Marston
POLLINI: DG

RANGELL: Dorian
SCHNABEL: EMI
R. SERKIN: Sony Classical
SOLOMON: Turnabout

Sonata No. 29 in B-flat major, Op. 106, "Hammerklavier" (1816–18) 44 minutes

The *Grosse Sonata für das Hammer-Klavier* is the longest of the sonatas, taking approximately forty-five minutes. Psychologically, the sonata inhabits uncharted, trackless territory. The word is merely German for pianoforte, but the sound has a certain grim grandeur, which is appropriate. The "ego" growth of the Romantic movement and his own quest for immortality gave birth to this lofty, abstract work. It was to be his most monumental and most difficult sonata. Beethoven wrote to his publisher Artaria, exclaiming, "Now you have a sonata that will keep the pianists busy when it is played fifty years hence!" Charles Rosen thinks that "with this work, the emancipation of piano music from the demands of the amateur musician was made official, with a consequent loss of responsibility and a greater freedom for the imagination." Almost from the first, the score had about it an air of mythic solitude. "The immensity of this composition," wrote Hutcheson, "cannot fail to strike us with awe. We gaze at its vast dome like pygmies from below never feeling on an intellectual or moral level with it. . . . Beethoven worked long and hard at Opus 106, intending it to be his greatest sonata. Simultaneously, he was engaged on his Ninth and greatest symphony. . . .These are among the works for which he personally provided metronome timings. The absence elsewhere in the sonata of metronome marks is the less regrettable because in this case the tempo set for the first movement, $\frac{1}{2} = 138$, is technically and musically far too fast;

about $\sddot{}= 104$ would be more reasonable. When a composer of rank orders us to break our neck we should dutifully take the risk, provided that we can do so without breaking his neck too. The Scherzo is also marked too fast, at any rate from the technical standpoint; only the tempi of the Adagio and the Fugue can be accepted with confidence and safety."

Wilfrid Mellers comments, "There seems little doubt that the movement should be played, if not at Beethoven's tempo, at least as fast as is *musically* feasible, for the music should induce panic. . . . Beethoven wrote to his publisher that 'whatever is difficult, is also beautiful, great and good.'"

More than likely Beethoven's metronome was defective. The invention, new in Beethoven's time, in general has helped decrease the imagination of many players, as if each composer put a speed to their work with absolute certainty. The best advice is Rameau's 1736 statement: "Always remember that it is much better to err on the side of slowness rather than speed: when one really has a piece one unconsciously grasps the style and soon one feels the true tempo."

Certainly there is an essential awkwardness lying at the heart of the *Hammerklavier* that makes it even now a rather inaccessible creation.

It has too often been stated that Beethoven's piano music is orchestral in nature. Hutcheson says the first movement "cries aloud for the limitless resources of the orchestra." But the conductor Felix Weingartner in his orchstration makes slog of the score, missing its true aesthetic, the deadly hammer-stroke effects so inimitable to the piano. Tovey asserts, "No orchestra can translate the essential qualities of Beethoven's pianoforte style . . . that Beethoven's imagination of pianoforte tone is nowhere at a higher power than in this work . . . that Beethoven's imagination is always right, always based on the instruments he uses, whatever his opinion as to their capacity, and always at its highest power throughout this particular work. . . . But even apart from this, the pianoforte writing, without being confined to the language of the instrument, like Chopin's, has the quality, constant in Liszt and frequent in Mendelssohn, that suggests that its inventor could not play a single chord without producing an astonishingly beautiful tone. For euphony in forte and fortissimo passages the first movement sets the standard in bars 1 to 4 and 17 to 45. Liszt himself never produced pianoforte chords and colors more gorgeously orchestral and more hopelessly beyond the capacity of an orchestra to imitate."

The slow movement of Op. 106 is the longest and most sublime in the history of instrumental art, asking of the performer a hypnotizing concentration span. In his entire output, Beethoven never repeated himself, and the fugue finale of the Op. 106 is a radical departure. It remains startling to contemporary ears; it must have been incomprehensible to its few listeners in Beethoven's day. J. W. N. Sullivan wrote:

The fugue of the *Hammerklavier* Sonata is an almost insensate outburst of unconquerable self-assertion. At the time he wrote the *Hammerklavier* Sonata, finished in 1818, Beethoven's realization of his essential loneliness was terrible and complete. But we may suppose that even he was becoming aware that his separation from the world was the entry into a different and more exalted region. But the *Hammerklavier* is the expression of a man of infinite suffering, of infinite courage and will, but without God and without hope. . . . The sonata is the complete expression of an important stage in Beethoven's spiritual development, but it was only after passing through this stage that the wonderful new world lay open before him. . . . The *Hammerklavier* Sonata does not, in its spiritual content, belong to what is called Beethoven's third period. Neither does it belong to his second. It stands alone, a great and grim memorial to the long and painful journey between the two worlds.

"Even today," Brendel points out, "the work shows up the outer limits of what a composer of sonatas can accomplish, a performer can control, or a listener can take in," and Friskin says, "The combined musical and technical demands of this sonata make the most exacting of all tasks that a pianist can undertake."

AITKEN: Delos
ASHKENAZY: London
BIRET: Finnadar (LP)
DOUGLAS: RCA
ESCHENBACH: DG
GILELS: DG
GOODE: Nonesuch
GRINBERG: Melodiya
KENTNER: Pearl
KUERTI: Analekta
E. LEVY: Marston
LIPKIN: Newport Classics
NÁDAS: Period (LP)
NAT: EMI
PETRI: Westminster
POLLINI: DG
ROBERTS: Nimbus
SCHNABEL: EMI
P. SERKIN: Pro Arte
R. SERKIN: Sony
WEBSTER: Dover (LP)
YUDINA: Melodiya

Sonata No. 30 in E major, Op. 109 (1820) 22 minutes

In his thirtieth piano sonata, Beethoven has left the battleground of the *Hammerklavier*

for sunlight and human warmth. The first movement is a concentrated sonata form of incomparable subtlety in its structure and intimate lyricism. Tovey calls the vivace ma non troppo "one of the profoundest things in music." Every note is a jewel, its texture as delicate as butterfly wings, with its vivace twice interrupted by passages marked "adagio expressivo." Here is the springtime of his late music. The short second movement is a restless sonata form, marked "prestissimo." Brahms's late music is permeated by what he learned from Beethoven. Following is an irresistible and elaborate set of a theme, disguised as a sarabande, and six variations of inevitable contrast. In the last variations, Ernest Hutcheson optimistically tells the player, "Don't worry too much about the seemingly difficult trills; just concentrate on the melody and all will be well." The accumulated energy of the trills is awesome. The theme returns to close the work on an ethereally serene note. One can compare Beethoven's formal elasticity with, say, Clementi's excellent Sonata in G minor, also from 1820, whose structure is scholastic and earthbound. Beethoven's formal and instrumental pliability is now so concentrated and complex that each work is an entirely new invention which cannot be classified under any genre; authority and freedom are welded together in a state of perfection unique even within the classical style.

ARRAU: Philips
DOHNÁNYI: Everest (LP)
GILELS: DG
GOODE: Nonesuch
HESS: Philips: Great Pianists of the Twentieth Century
HUNGERFORD: Vanguard
E. LEVY: Marston
OHLSSON: Arabesque

Sonata No. 31 in A-flat major, Op. 110 (1821) 22 minutes

The middle work of the trinity of sonatas that form Beethoven's latest thinking on the piano sonata. Often performed in concert; in some respects it is, perhaps, less demanding technically than Op. 109 or 111, but certainly not so in its musical aspirations. Only a poet-pianist inspired with its fervent message may bring to life its humane qualities. Its expressivity, lyricism, unity of design, and fugal magnificence bring Beethoven once again to forge a new structural edifice.

Brendel states, "Beethoven was not only an innovator in his late years, he also went back to earlier periods of music and took as much as he could from them, transforming the material to serve his purpose."

In the second movement we hear Beethoven's unique humor, with touches of whimsy and even a vulgar strand. In the trio he twists the fingers in original formations. The finale is, in Kentner's words, "a mysterious anguished recitative and a three-part fugue." Tovey remarked, "His fugues always come to us as if from behind huge gates that open and shut without regard to our expectations." Ernest Hutcheson analyzes the finale in this way: "(a) Introduction (from the fourth measure on a recitative), beginning in B-flat minor; (b) arioso dolente, A-flat minor; (c) Fugue, A-flat major; (d) return of the arioso in G minor; (e) return of the fugue, G major, at first in inversion of the theme, then in augmentation, diminution, double diminution, and stretto; leading to a brilliant free coda based on the fugue theme and returning to the tonic key of the sonata, A-flat major."

Kempff says, "This sonata presents us with a most personal confession, so it is no wonder that Beethoven wished to keep it for himself and did not dedicate it to anyone."

BADURA-SKODA (1824 piano): Astrée
GILELS: DG
ISTOMIN: Reference
KOVACEVICH: Great Pianists of the Twentieth Century
LAMOND: BPS
E. LEVY: Marston
POLLINI: DG
RICHTER: Music and Arts
SCHNABEL: EMI
R. SERKIN: Sony Classical
SHURE: Audiofon
SOLOMON: EMI

Sonata No. 32 in C minor, Op. 111 (1821–22) 25 minutes

The distance traveled from 1795 to 1822 can hardly be gauged in years alone. Indeed Beethoven's spiritual development includes his quest to expand the sonata form to its very conclusion. The entire corpus must rank as one of the supreme artistic and intellectual achievements in the history of the mind. In his final benediction to the piano sonata he composes only two movements. Kempff thinks, "The two souls of the Faustian Beethoven are locked in combat." Aldous Huxley thought Beethoven was "the most profound, for me, the most complete of all philosophers." For Thomas Mann, "The sonata in general, as a species, as traditional art-form was here at an end; it had fulfilled its destiny, reached its goal."

The two movements could not be more unlikely partners. But to play one without the other seems absurd. It has been said that there are two types of pianists: those who can play the first movement, and those who can play the second; none can play both well. Of course such a statement only indicates the awe that the composition possesses as a work of art. Of the first movement, a death-defying drama, Mellers writes: "The violence of the introduction has discovered C minor, and in the low trill has released the growl of the Blakean tiger. One might almost say that the sonata is 'about' the metamorphoses of the tiger's growl into angels' fluttering wings in the trills of the arietta."

The second movement, an arietta and variations, is beyond words to describe its spiritual elevation. Henry E. Krehbiel wrote, "In the arietta, Beethoven becomes a seer, as truly transfigured in the spirit as John was on Patmos." In his novel, *Dr. Faustus,* Thomas Mann speaks of

the arietta theme, destined to vicissitudes for which in its idyllic innocence it would seem not to be born, is presented at once, and announced in sixteen bars, reducible to a motif which appears at the end of its first half, like a brief soul-cry. . . . What now happens to this mild utterance, rhythmically, harmonically, contrapuntally, to this pensive, subdued formulation, with what its master blesses and to what condemns it, into what black nights and dazzling flashes, crystal spheres wherein coldness and heat, repose and ecstasy are one and the same, he flings it down and lifts it up, all that one may well call vast, strange, extravagantly magnificent, without thereby giving it a name, because it is quite truly nameless.

On a more prosaic level the sonata's technical demands are formidable, "although as a whole," writes Friskin, "this great work is less exacting technically than either Op. 101 or Op. 106." Tovey thinks: "This is, next to Op. 106, technically the hardest of the last five sonatas; but it is so dramatic . . . and so unmistakably sublime as a whole that it is less discouraging to the student than any other of Beethoven's later works. . . . The treatment of the pianoforte is for the most part singularly successful throughout the sonata, and it also happens to suit modern instruments better than those of 1822."

BACKHAUS: Philips: Great Pianists of the Twentieth Century
GULDA: Philips
HUNGERFORD: Vanguard
KOVACEVICH: Philips: Great Pianists of the Twentieth Century
LEVY: Marston
MICHELANGELI: AS Disc
NAT: Pathé
PETRI: APR
PLETNEV: DG
ROSEN: Sony

Variations

Beethoven was occupied with variation writing throughout his life and is the preeminent variationist of the classical age. For piano solo he left twenty-one sets, ranging from slight works of various difficulties to the mammoth *Diabelli* Variations of his final period. Most variations of the classical period were composed as financially profitable pot-boilers on opera or patriotic tunes for the emergent middle-class domestic pianists desiring entertainment for their fingers. Beethoven, too, composed many sets of variations with merely money in mind, but at their least valuable one easily hears Beethoven's superiority over his contemporaries. Piano teachers should not neglect to give young pupils the 1791, Six "easy" Variations on a Swiss air, WoO64, and the Six "easy" Variations on an Original Theme in G major WoO77. Both are attractive introductions to Beethoven's early idiom. Rather more difficult and full of grace are the Thirteen Variations on Dittersdorf's *Es war einmal ein alter Mann* WoO66, of 1792. Of the 1799 Ten Variations on Salieri's *La Stessa, La Stessissimo,* WoO73, Ernest Hutcheson thinks they are "the best of the smaller sets, showing great originality and maturity of style, particularly in the final allegretto alla austriaca, and deserving of a place on recital programs."

Twenty-Four Variations on Righini's Arietta "Venni Amore" (1790–91) WoO65

This superb work was Beethoven's pianistic warhorse during his earliest years in Vienna. The theme is innocuous, providing a peg for a large-scale work, full of whimsy and all sorts of delightful happenings. James Friskin notes, "This large set of variations . . . shows an astonishing imaginative range and power. It's difficulties are considerable, and a well-developed mechanism is needed to cope with them." Unfortunately the *Venni Amore* seemingly never appears on recital programs.

MÜLLER: Dynamic

Six Variations on an Original Theme in F major, Op. 34 (1802)

Liszt was the first to promote this especially intriguing set, asking from the player grace and polished technical finesse. Each variation descends a minor third until the tonic, where the final variation proceeds to an elaborate embellishment of the theme. Each variation is a finely honed mood picture.

GOULD: Sony Classical
MATTHEWS: Vanguard
SCHNABEL: Pearl
M. TAN (Forte Piano): Veritas

Fifteen Variations and Fugue in E-flat major on a Theme from the Eroica, Op. 35 (1802)

The Op. 35 is dedicated to Count Lichnowsky, one of the composer's most loyal patrons. This large-scale and cerebral work uses the finale of the *Eroica* Symphony for its theme. It has an arched spaciousness in its twenty-five minutes and is charged with unexpected detours, an almost ribald humor along with nobility of design and feeling.

Beethoven thought highly of the score, telling us, "They are among my greater musical works." Beethoven's biographer, Maynard Solomon wrote, "The opus 35 Variations are of special interest by virtue of the use of compositional procedures—fugue, chaconne, harmonic variation—identified with the Baroque composers. To the listener, it is unclear as to whether the grotesque bass melody is the theme or the harmony of the theme, an ambiguity which creates great interest."

ARRAU: History
AX: RCA
BAR-ILLAN: Audiofon
CIANI: Dynamic
CURZON: London
GELBER: Orfeo
RICHTER: JVC/Melodiya
ROBERTS: Nimbus

Thirty-two Variations in C minor on an Original Theme (1806) WoO80

Composed during the crucible of his middle period, this masterpiece, which Beethoven belittled ("Beethoven, what an ass you were"), has no master-opus number. Composed on a passacaglia ground bass, within ten minutes of the most economical and ingenious pianistic writing he creates a rounded form of highly charged drama. Technically, it is a central experience for a pianist's developing a Beethoven technique.

Three other sets are entertaining for pianist and audience, forming fine program raisers:

the Seven Variations on *God Save the King*, WoO78, composed in 1802–03 (Beethoven said, "I shall show the English what is in their king."); the Five Variations on *Rule Britannia* (1803) WoO79, based on the famous tune taken from Thomas Arne's *Masque, Alfred and the Humorous*; and Six Variations, Op. 76, based on the Turkish March from his ballet *Ruins of Athens,* composed in 1809.

ARRAU: Philips
GILELS: EMI
LUPU: London
MORAVEC: VAI
UCHIDA: Philips

Thirty-three Variations in C major on a Waltz by Diabelli, Op. 120 (1823)

In 1823, the composer-publisher Anton Diabelli invited fifty-one composers residing in Austria, including the child Liszt and Franz Schubert, to write one variation on his theme. Beethoven seemed repelled by the project, or was this democrat insulted to be an equal in the company of others? He declined, calling Diabelli's bold theme a "schusterfleck" (a cobbler's patch). In time, however, Diabelli's trite measures worked themselves deeply within Beethoven's creative mind. Beethoven proceeded to write a set of variations which would be, to the variation form, what his *Hammerklavier* was to the sonata. The score is daunting, taking nearly an hour for its presentation and asking the pianist for great physical endurance and interpretive power of the widest range. The pianist Michael Oelbaum wrote, "It would be hard to find a more striking example of downright improbable disparity between apparent subject potential and treatment." The *Diabelli* are the towering set of variations of the classical age

and equal in conception and quality to Bach's *Goldberg* Variations. Wilfrid Mellers declares, "Like Bach's *Goldberg* Variations, and despite the difference between the two composers' 'approach,' they rather see a world in 'a grain of sand,' making us aware that experience is a totality in which the trivial and the sublime coexist."

It is noteworthy that in the score Beethoven used the term *alternations,* rather than variations. Surely Tovey is correct in saying, "The structure of true variations is aesthetically on much the same plan as a great painter's or sculptor's knowledge of anatomy."

Maynard Solomon calls the *Diabelli* a "*Pilgrim's progress* on a Biedermeier waltz . . . The variations is a work in which extremes meet to an extent previously unknown even in Beethoven's music: here the tawdry and the sublime rub shoulders . . . " As Aldous Huxley put it in his novel *Point Counter Point*, "Those incredible *Diabelli* Variations . . . The whole range of thought and feeling, yet all in organic relation to a ridiculous little waltz tune."

There is a story that upon completing the composition, Beethoven appeared at Diabelli's door, exclaiming with gusto, "Here you have it, you asked for one variation; here are thirty-three, and now, for God's sake, leave me in peace." The years 1819 through 1824 were prodigious in creative activity. Beethoven saw completed, besides the *Diabelli,* the *Missa Solemnis,* the last three piano sonatas, and the Ninth Symphony. He had extended Haydn's vision and technique to unimagined spheres of emotional and intellectual heights.

AITKEN: Delos
BRENDEL: Philips
KATCHEN: London
RICHTER-HAASER: Seraphim
P. SERKIN: Pro Arte
R. SERKIN: Sony
SAUER: Audiofon
SOKOLOV: OPUS 111

Seven Bagatelles, Op. 33 (1801)

The term means a trifle. But what Beethoven meant by trifle cannot be defined by a norm. The pieces are by no means negligible, and although not difficult technically, with the exception of No. 5, they ask for subtlety and style for their proper delivery.

BRENDEL: Vox
GOULD: Sony Classical
M. SUK: Cambria
SCHNABEL: Pearl

Eleven Bagatelles, Op. 119 (1820–22)

The group at first seems a mixed bag, but upon playing them one finds they hold together well as a set to be played consecutively. The perfect and intimate No. 11 in B-flat was the inspiration for a set of variations for two pianos by Reger.

AFFANASIEV: Denon
SCHIFF: Hungaraton
R. SERKIN: Sony Classical
SHERMAN: Pro Arte

Six Bagatelles, Op. 126 (1823–24)

The greatest of the three sets of Bagatelles, they form the master's farewell to the piano. Composed while laboring on the late quartets, these six pieces were written as a cycle *(ciclus von kleinigkeiten,* as Beethoven wrote on the sketch). In compressed form they harbor the introspective and profound characteristics of Beethoven's late style. The Fourth work, resto, is haunting, the composer's only excursion, strangely in the key of B minor (the black key, as he called it).

ASHKENAZY: London
GOLDSMITH: MHS
GOULD: Sony Classical
KATCHEN: London
KEMPFF: DG
LEFÉBURE: Solstice
ROBERTS: Nimbus

Für Elise, WoO59

The piano piece in A minor is heard the world over, played by every possible ensemble and instrument. Has there ever been a young piano student who has not attempted its alluring measures? Ivo Pogorelich, one season, effectively opened a program with it, followed by the Sonata, Op. 90. The piece may not be for Elise, but for Therese Malfatti, in whom Beethoven had a romantic interest.

ASHKENAZY: London
BRENDEL: Philips
MORAVEC: VAI
M. TAN (period instrument): Veritas
WATTS: Sony Classical

Rondo á Capriccio, Op.129 (Rage Over a Lost Penny)

A terrifically effective piece of keyboard bantering, demanding high finger energy. The late opus number is misleading as the rondo is probably of late 1790s vintage. After Schumann played through it he wrote, "It would be difficult to find anything merrier than this whim; I laughed heartily over it the other day."

BRENDEL: Vox
HOFMANN: Nimbus
KISSIN: RCA
NISSMAN: Pierian

Rondo in C major, Op. 51, No. 1

The piece is not a middle period work, but from approximately 1797. Its material may not be inspired, but Beethoven uses it with graciousness and finesse. The C minor section offers a dramatic element.

> KEMPFF: Philips: Great Pianists of the
> Twentieth Century
> RICHTER: Philips
> SCHNABEL: Naxos
> BRENDEL: Vox
> MOISEIWITSCH: APR

Rondo in G major, Op. 51, No. 2

A beautiful and subtle work, composed in 1802, almost twice the length of the C major Rondo. The form partakes more of a Rondo-Sonata. Denis Matthews wrote, "Its lyrical unfolding, with much attention to the graceful flourish in bar two of the theme, is interrupted by a more rapid six-eight episode in E major, a submediant key-relation to be exploited in many later works." The seldom heard G major Rondo is a worthy challenge for a mature and sensitive player.

> BRENDEL: Vox
> ENGERER: Harmonia Mundi
> KEMPFF: DG
> KISSIN: RCA

Polonaise in C major, Op. 89

Written during the Congress of Vienna 1814–15, Beethoven received an audience with Elizabeth, the Russian Empress, during which he presented her with the Polonaise and for which, in turn, he received a gift of money. In this "occasional" piece there is nothing of the Slavic bone structure of Chopin's patriotic outpourings or of Weber's glittering festiveness. The Polonaise of about five minutes, however, has its own rude attractiveness.

> AX: RCA
> JANDÓ: Naxos

Andante in F major, WoO57 (1804)

Known as the *Andante Favori*. At first Beethoven intended the longish piece (seven minutes) as the slow movement of the *Waldstein* Sonata. In its refinements of touch it resembles the G major Rondo. This is a lovely recital opener.

> BRENDEL: Vox
> DOUGLAS: RCA
> NEY: BPS
> SCHNABEL: Arabesque
> SOFRONITSKY: RD

Fantasy in G minor, Op. 77 (1808)

A rather strange work of about seven minutes in an improvisatory style, with a wide-ranging tonal scheme. Czerny remarked that the Fantasy reminded him of Beethoven extemporizing at the instrument. It is seldom programmed, though Rudolf Serkin was devoted to it.

> JANDÓ: Naxos
> OPPENS: Music and Arts
> R. SERKIN: Sony Classical

The Concertos

The early concerto in E-flat from 1784, WoO4, a teenage work showing competence, is found by Solomon to be "formally diffuse and melodically uninteresting despite moments of folklike gaiety in the closing movement." It was first performed by the teenager at the Bonn Court; Hinson remarks, "This work gives an unusual insight into the pianistic ability of Beethoven at age 14." The piece abounds in tricky passagework. Beethoven's transformation of his heavenly violin concerto into a version for piano, Op. 61a, should be noted and receives occasional performance. It was written at the suggestion of Clementi, who wanted to publish a Beethoven score for his firm in London. The piano version is duly effective but pales next to the glow of the original. In the violin concerto, Beethoven leaves out the cadenza, but for the piano version he wrote three long, quite imposing cadenzas. For the first-movement cadenza he asks for a timpani part to accompany the piano. The piano concerto version should not be disdained. Beethoven's "Triple" concerto, for piano, violin, and cello, Op. 56, is a rewarding score, finely textured, austere, without heroics or display. Nearly forty minutes in length, it is a masterly interplay of forces. The Choral Fantasia, Op. 80 for Piano, Chorus, and Orchestra, receives more performances than it deserves. I feel Beethoven is perhaps poking fun at himself as he piles one cliché upon another.

Each of the five piano concertos, with master opus numbers, have taken a preeminent position in the concerto repertoire. Unlike Mozart's Piano Concertos, where the soloist is the prima donna and the orchestra is sometimes antagonistic to its pursuits, the Beethoven soloist lives through the massed sound of the orchestra. As Robert Simpson put it, "With Beethoven the preoccupation is with scale and line, with new tonal vistas, with contrasts of broader scope."

The Five Piano Concertos:
BRENDEL, Levine/Chicago Symphony: Philips
FLEISHER, Szell/Cleveland: CBS

GILELS, Szell/Cleveland: EMI

Concerto No. 1 in C major, Op. 15 (1798–1800)

The First Concerto is masculine, optimistic, filled with overflowing confidence, and highly rigorous; using formulas codified in Clementi's concertos. The first concerto is in fact the second concerto, but published before No. 2; it adds clarinets, trumpets, and drums to the orchestral landscape. Beethoven wrote three cadenzas to the first movement; the first one was left slightly incomplete. The third and longest is most difficult and brilliantly effective. The largo slow movement is one of those noble Beethoven slow movements, the main theme finely spun in its decorative filigree work. The finale is irrepressible in its swing, its barbed humor, and its shifting tonalities. Here is Beethoven flushed with the vigor of youth.

ARGERICH, Sinopoli/Philharmonia: DG
GOULD, Golschmann/Columbia Symphony: Sony Classical
POLLINI, Jochum/Vienna Philharmonic: DG
SHERMAN, Neumann/Czech Philharmonic: Pro Arte

Concerto No. 2 in B-flat major, Op. 19 (1795)

The Second Concerto is generally less difficult technically than No. 1, as well as more slender and graceful in pianistic layout. Of the score, Beethoven wrote to his publisher early in 1801, "I set the price of the concerto at only 10 ducats because, I don't consider it one of my best works." Beethoven's harsh judgment on the merit of the Second Concerto is perhaps the reason it is performed less than its sisters. It was not until around 1814 that he wrote a cadenza to the first movement, in a fugato style reminiscent of the Sonata, Op. 101. The cadenza, shunning the earlier period style, may represent another aspect of the wide-ranging cast of Beethovenian humor. Somehow the mixture of styles ferment perfectly. The slow-movement adagio is not as elaborate as the largo of the First Concerto, but just as spacious. The coda expands the material, and, in Simpson's words, "The piano, using the sustaining pedal, drops notes through the still air like dew from a leaf."

The Rondo finale in 6/8 meter is bumptious, rollicking, and fun-loving. In the coda, Denis Matthews remarks, "Beethoven springs a Haydnish surprise when the piano offers the subject in the wrong key (G major) and the wrong rhythm (unsyncopated) only to be firmly corrected by the orchestra."

ARGERICH, Argerich/London Sinfonietta:
   Denon
AX, Previn/Royal Philharmonic: RCA
KISSIN, Levine/Philharmonia Orchestra: Sony
   Classical
KOVACEVICH, Davis/BBC Symphony: Philips,
SCHNABEL, Sargent/London Symphony:
   Arabesque

Concerto No. 3 in C minor, Op. 37 (1803)

The Third Concerto possesses a wider keyboard compass than its predecessors, possibly inspired from the gift of an Erard piano that the Paris piano firm sent him at the time. In the Third Concerto we enter the higher emotional temperature of his second period; doubtless Beethoven had in mind Mozart's sublime C minor Concerto, K. 491, a work that he himself had performed publicly, telling his pupil Ferdinand Ries, "The likes of us will never do anything like that." The technical demands, too, somewhat exceed the earlier

concertos; the merely adequate cadenza, as Friskin put it, "does not defy competition." Tovey, Medtner, Backhaus, Clara Schumann, Moscheles, Alkan, and others have added their thoughts. Indeed, Alkan transcribed for piano solo the first movement, providing a monument of a cadenza nearly as long as the entire movement. The slow movement in the remote key of E major is rapt, almost mystical, in its remoteness. Simpson feels: "Its gravity worthy of Gluck and its depth purely its own. There is enormous breadth and calm, a profound, unusually sustained maturity of feeling that Beethoven seems always to have possessed." In the highly developed Rondo, Beethoven strays far from the lighthearted gaiety and earthy humor of Nos. 1 and 2 and concludes No. 3 with a weightier almost steel-edged Finale.

E. FISCHER/Philharmonia Orchestra:
   Testament
MICHELANGELI, Giulini/Vienna
   Philharmonic: DG
NEWMAN (fortepiano), Simon/Philomusica
   Antiqua of London: Newport Classic
PERAHIA, Haitink/Concertgebouw: CBS
SCHNABEL, Sargent/London Symphony:
   Arabesque
R. SERKIN, Bernstein/New York Philharmonic:
   Sony

Concerto No. 4 in G major, Op. 58 (1805)

The Fourth Concerto is the most difficult interpretively and perhaps the most difficult technically of the cycle. The Fourth Concerto is a supreme masterpiece of classical concerto form, attaining the highest degree of artistic plasticity, and verisimilitude, indescribably linking drama and lyricism. Beethoven himself premiered the score in 1807; it would not be heard again in his lifetime.

Tovey thinks "all three movements of Beethoven's G major Concerto demonstrate the aesthetic principles of concerto form with extraordinary subtlety." Of the first movement Matthews asserts, "The masterstroke in the G major is the gentle manner of the opening, with its half-close that surprises the orchestra into its still quieter reply in the distant key of B major." Beethoven wrote two cadenzas for the opening movement which are admirable, with the second one perhaps taking pride of place. Others, the likes of Clara Schumann, Brahms, and Busoni, have tried their hands.

In the E-minor slow movement, Liszt heard Orpheius taming the wild beasts. The finale, an elaborate Rondo with an inspired coda, is no less original than the preceding movements, exhilarating in its subtle maneuverings of joyous material.

GRINBERG, Järvi/USSR Symphony: Meloidya
KOCSIS, Lukács/Budapest Symphony: Fidelio
PERAHIA, Haitink/Concertgebouw: Sony
    Classical
RUBINSTEIN, Leinsdorf/Boston Symphony:
    RCA
SCHNABEL, Sargent/London Symphony:
    Arabesque

Concerto No. 5 in E-flat major, Op. 73, "Emperor" (1809)

The Fifth Concerto is a symphony for piano and orchestra, far different than the translucent chamber writing of the Fourth Concerto. Here is Beethoven, the conquering hero, in the first grand-manner concerto. It is surely the mightiest of all classical concertos. Its title, *Emperor,* supposedly came from a French officer who, at the premiere, was so taken with the musical might that he, too loudly, blurted out, "C'est l'empereur."

The magisterial pomp of the allegro, the hushed mystery of the adagio, the guttural rondo, vibrate with the pulse of life. The incomparable tonal blends of distant tonalities give to this work a visionary character, but of an immediate accessibility.

Beethoven had given the first performances of his earlier piano concertos, but by the fifth concerto his playing had deteriorated. The first pianist in history to perform it was Friedrich Schneider, in Leipzig, late in 1811. The concerto scored a great success, and a review stated correctly: "It is without doubt one of the most original, imaginative, most effective but also one of the most difficult of all existing concertos." The reviewer might have added that it was the longest of all existing concertos. For the Viennese premiere in 1812 the soloistic task was given to Beethoven's emminent pupil, Carl Czerny, who had through the years become a squeamish, nervous, and inhibited player. However, that evening Czerny gave his all and brought in an acceptable performance. It is enough to say that the integration of piano and orchestra is so tight that the composer allowed for no cadenza.

The Fifth Concerto will forever be the favorite of the public. It marvelously exemplifies Beethoven as transcendent victor. Claudio Arrau wrote: "Beethoven's music represents struggle and victory. . . . It speaks to all of us in a way that is relevant to our times. In the sense that his life was an existential struggle for survival, Beethoven is our contemporary. Beethoven in his creative output exemplifies all the spiritual and psychic battles of the hero who is given superhuman tasks to overcome and who, after untold struggles—truly bloodied but undaunted—emerges the victor and finally attains the highest state of self-realization and illumination."

Perhaps Liszt best summed up Beethoven's immense importance for nineteenth-century musicians in a letter to the critic Wilhelm von Lenz in 1852: "To us musicians the work of Beethoven parallels the pillars of smoke and fire which lcd the Israelites through the desert, a pillar of smoke to lead us by day, and a pillar of fire to light the night, so that we may march ahead both day and night. His darkness and his light equally trace for us the road we must follow; both the one and the other are a perpetual commandment, an infallible revelation."

Beethoven, in a hellish fight for life, had five operations in six weeks in his filthy rooms. He told his doctor, "My day's work is done." It is a phrase of supreme fulfillment that few in history could have spoken.

ARRAU, Davis/Dresden State: Philips
GILELS, Szell/Cleveland: EMI
HESS, Sargent/BBC Symphony: BBC
HOROWITZ, Reiner/RCA Victor Orchestra: RCA
POLLINI, Böhm/Vienna Philharmonic: DG
R. SERKIN, Ozawa/Boston Symphony: Telarc
SCHNABEL, Sargent/London Symphony: Arabesque
ZIMERMAN, Bernstein/Vienna Philharmonic: DG

ALBAN BERG
1885–1935—Austria

Sonata for Piano, Op. 1 (1908)

This is Berg's only solo piano work of his maturity. It is brooding and hyperchromatic, keyless, and difficult to memorize. The entire piece emanates from the opening theme. It remains the most frequently played solo piano work of any Viennese composer of the first decade of the twentieth century.

BARENBOIM: DG
BIRET: Finnadar (LP)

CHERKASSKY: Nimbus
GOULD: Sony Classical
POLLINI: DG

ERNEST BLOCH
1880–1959—Switzerland

Piano Sonata (1935)

Bloch's largest and most important work for solo piano. The brooding grandeur of so much of his music is felt throughout its three movements. The structure is dense, with a beautiful Pastorale slow movement. The first movement throbs with passion and barbaric frenzy; the finale is pessimistic and sarcastic.

KASSAI (complete piano music): Marco Polo
NÁDAS: Dover (LP)
SHAULIS: CRI (LP)

PIERRE BOULEZ
b. 1925—France

Sonata No. 1 (1946)
Sonata No. 2 (1948)
Sonata No. 3 (1957)

Boulez has attempted to extend serial technique into new and flexible regions. His piano sonatas, especially Nos. 1 and 2, have entered a "classic" status of the avant-garde. The critic Susan Bradshaw observes that the "first two sonatas "show traces of his teacher

Messiaen (in the rhythmic devices), of Debussy (in the use of pianistic color, per se) and of virtuoso keyboard writing in general. But they are extraordinarily forward-looking for the time at which they were written and virtually without models for their musical vision: their astonishing vitality, liberality of invention and technical confidence are of breathtaking impact, as is the virtuosity of the keyboard writing."

The Third Sonata, begun in 1957, is entirely different. Of the five movements or formats intended, only two have been published, as Boulez has not yet found his solutions for the other three. Throughout the notation, he has come to give the performer freedoms and choices as to the order of the sections. The first movement is in four sections and gives the pianist eight possibilities of order.

The First Sonata is in two movements, totaling about ten minutes, with much leaping around, mostly in a two-part counterpoint, which is fearsomely difficult to execute. The thirty-minute Second Sonata is one of the great pieces of sheer virtuosity in the history of pianism. Bradshaw feels that "the composer seems trapped by his compositional virtuosity into producing a dangerously overblown pianistic virtuosity—very much in the grand manner." For maximum pleasure, it is helpful to read from the scores when these two sonatas are being performed.

The first two movements, titled *Trope and Constellation*, from the Third Sonata are mathematical and mysterious, a work of creative pianism. Maurice Hinson thinks it "one of the greatest pianistic creations of this century." Charles Rosen, who recorded the piece in 1973, observes, "The freedom that Boulez's music demands is also a form of rubato, often a continuous one."

Sonatas No. 1 to 3
HELFFER: Astrée Auvidis

Sonata No. 1:
BURGE: Candide
MARKS: CRI
ROSEN: CBS
Y. TAKAHASHI: CP2

Sonata No. 2:
BIRET: Finnadar
BURGE: MHS
POLLINI: DG

Sonata No. 3:
HENCK: Wergo
ROSEN: CBS

JOHANNES BRAHMS
1833–1897—Germany

James Huneker wrote of Brahms:

He was the greatest contrapuntist after Bach, the greatest architectonist after Beethoven—his contribution to the technics of rhythm is enormous. He has literally popularized the cross-relation, rediscovered the arpeggio and elevated it from the lowly position of an accompanying figure to an integer of melodic phrase. . . . He pours into the elastic form of the sonata hot romantic passion, and in the loosest textured smaller pieces he can be as immovable as bronze, as plastic as clay. He is sometimes frozen by grief and submerged by thought. . . . To me this is the eternal puzzle; that Brahms, the master of ponderous learning, can yet be so tender, so innocent of soul, so fragile, so childlike. He must have valiantly protected his soul against earthly smudging to keep it so pure, so sweet to the very end. . . . Above all, he is profoundly human and touches humanity at many contacts.

Sonata No. 1 in C major, Op. 1 (1852)

In his Op. 1, Brahms immediately pays tribute to Beethoven, outlining the rhythm of Beethoven's *Hammerklavier* Sonata during the first five measures of the opening statement. Even from his nineteenth year, the Sonata possesses Brahms's characteristic dense sonority. This surely must be one of the finest Opus 1s in the annals of music. "Musical history," reflected Daniel Gregory Mason, "is a series of reactions between man's primal emotional impulse and his desire for intelligibility." That could have been Brahms's motto. As Huneker points out, "Just compare the Schumann *Abegg* Variations, Op. 1, with the slow movement of this Sonata and you may realize the superior educational advantages enjoyed by Brahms."

JONES: Nimbus
KATCHEN: London
LEONSKAJA: Teldec
RICHTER: London
STEIGERWALT: Centaur
ZIMERMAN: DG

Sonata No. 2 in F-sharp minor, Op. 2 (1853)

Like No. 1, this sonata is in four movements, but more diffuse. Brahms is all storm and stress here; the first movement is Brahms at his most fiercely Romantic. The finale shows the amazing originality of the twenty-year-old Brahms.

ARRAU: Philips
KATCHEN: London
LOESSER: Perennial (LP)
OLSHANSKY: Monitor
RICHTER: London
ZIMERMAN: DG

Scherzo in E-flat minor, Op. 4 (1854)

When Brahms visited Liszt at Weimar, the great pianist sight-read the manuscript of this difficult Scherzo with two trios. It is not played nearly enough, considering its value.

ARRAU: Philips
BACKHAUS: Pearl
KEMPFF: DG
KOVACEVICH: Philips

Sonata No. 3 in F minor, Op. 5 (1854)

In five movements, this is one of the largest sonatas in the active literature, taking around forty minutes. All that Brahms had attained in

Johannes Brahms by David Dubal

the previous two sonatas is now synthesized. He never again composed a piano sonata. It was not premiered until 1863, when Brahms himself performed it in Vienna. He prefaces the second movement with lines from the poet Sternau:

The Twilight
glimmers, by moonbeams lighted,
two hearts are here in love united
and laced in blest embrace.

Huneker realized that, with this work, "the most beautiful in the genius of Brahms had flowered. The Andante in A flat [is] the most exquisite lyrical thing he has ever penned for piano . . . the picture is magical in its tender beauty and suggestiveness. It harks back to the old world romance, to some moonlit dell, wherein love hovers for a night, and about all is the mystery of sky and wood."

Claudio Arrau has said of the slow movement, "For me, it is the most beautiful love music after *Tristan*. And the most erotic—if you really let go, without any embarrassment. And if you play it *slowly* enough."

ARRAU: Philips
BAUER: IPA–Desmar
CURZON: London
KATCHEN: London
KEMPFF: DG
KOCSIS: Hungaroton
RUBINSTEIN: RCA
SOLOMON: Testament

Variations on a Theme by Schumann in F-sharp minor, Op. 9 (1854)

Brahms is the greatest variationist after Bach and Beethoven. He was inspired by three sources: Bach's *Goldberg,* Beethoven's

Diabelli, and Schumann's *Symphonic Etudes.* The *Schumann,* which is Brahms's earliest set of variations, is far undervalued—it is the most subtle work he had written thus far. The theme of the work is taken from Schumann's *Bunte Blätter,* Op. 99, No. 5, and leads into sixteen variations. Nos. 9, 13, and 14 are masterstrokes.

BARENBOIM: DG
JOCHUM: Pro Arte
LORTIE: Chandos
MOYER: GM Recordings (LP)

Four Ballades, Op. 10 (1856)

No. 1 in D minor, the most famous, is inspired by the Scottish ballad "Edward." Brahms composed the Ballades in the year Schumann died, and they flow from the well of his inspiration. These works possess a lyric maturity, a soul-searching quality, and a sense of foreboding and tragedy, which are astonishing from an artist in his early twenties.

ANGELICH: VAI
ARRAU: Philips
GILES: DG
GOULD: CBS
KATCHEN: London
KEMPFF: DG
MICHELANGELI: DG
RUBINSTEIN: RCA
WILD: Vanguard

Variations and Fugue on a Theme by Handel, Op. 24 (1862)

One of the masterpieces of variation writing. The Romantic exuberance of the early sonatas has been relentlessly replaced by organic necessity. The Fugue is magnificent in sonority and structure. Brahms had carefully absorbed *The Well-Tempered Clavier*.

ARTYMIW: Chandos
AX: Sony Classical
BOLET: London
CLIBURN: RCA
FLEISHER: Sony Classical
GORODNITSKI: EMI
KATCHEN: London
KLIEN: Turnabout (LP)
NAT: EMI
SCHUB: Vox Cum Laude
R. SERKIN: CBS
SOLOMON: Philips: Great Pianists of the Twentieth Century
TURECK: VAI

Variations on a Theme by Paganini, Books I and II, Op. 35 (1866)

The "Brahms-Paganini," as they are called, are a legend in the piano literature. Pianists speak of them in a reverential tone. To instill life in them, a pianist must have artistry surpassing merely a good technique. They are far more difficult to play than they sound. Huneker asks:

Brahms and Paganini! Was ever so strange a couple in harness? Caliban and Ariel, Jove and Puck. The stolid German, the vibratile Italian! Yet fantasy wins, even if brewed in a homely Teutonic kettle. . . . These diabolical variations, the last word in the technical literature of the piano, are also vast spiritual problems. To play them requires fingers of steel, a heart of burning lava and the courage of a lion.

BACHAUER: Mercury
BIRET: Naxos

CHERKASSKY: Nimbus
DUCHABLE: Erato
KATCHEN: London
KISSIN: RCA
MICHELANGELI: Philips: Great Pianists of the Twentieth Century
OHLSSON: EMI (LP)
PETRI: Pearl
VLASENKO: Melodiya (LP)
WILD: Vanguard

Sixteen Waltzes, Op. 39 (1865)

This is Brahms as charmer. The set also comes in piano duet form. In general, these waltzes are the easiest of his piano pieces. The Schubertian style of waltz is here transformed into miniatures of far more subtlety. No. 15 in A-flat is celebrated.

FLEISHER: Sony Classical
KATCHEN: London
KOVACEVICH: Philips
RODRIGUEZ: Elan

Eight Klavierstücke, Op. 76 (1879)

These eight pieces marked Brahms's return to solo piano music after a gap of thirteen years. A sense of intimacy pervades—the piano becomes his confidant. No. 1, Capriccio in F-sharp minor, contains stressful arpeggiation and is gloomy even when ending in the major. No. 2, Capriccio in B minor, is a staccato piece with a magical modulation. Bruce Hungerford wrote, "The piece is one of the shortest rondo-sonata movements in all music." No. 3, Intermezzo in A-flat, exudes sweetness and peace. No. 4, Intermezzo in B-flat, may have been inspired by a John Field nocturne, although it is far more complex. No. 5, Capriccio in C-sharp minor, is one of the more difficult of Brahms's shorter pieces, containing complicated rhythms and a fiery style. No. 6, Intermezzo in A major, is blissful and has lovely curves. No. 7, Intermezzo in A minor, is simple in statement, somewhat pessimistic, gray in color. No. 8, Capriccio in C major, has wonderful key relationships.

GIESEKING: EMI
GOODE: Nonesuch
HUNGERFORD (Nos. 2 & 6): Vanguard (LP)
KATCHEN: London
KEMPFF: Philips: Great Pianists of the
 Twentieth Century
KOVACEVICH: Philips

Two Rhapsodies, Op. 79, Nos. 1 and 2 (1880)

Although titled Rhapsodies, they are formal in construction. No. 1 in B minor is a rondo-sonata form, and No. 2 in G minor is in sonata form. Both works are magnificent; No. 2 is one of Brahms's best-known piano works, with its rich coloration in the second theme.

AX: Sony Classical
CLIBURN: RCA
GIESEKING: Seraphim
GOULD: Sony
HUNGERFORD: Vanguard (LP)
KATCHEN: London
LUPU: London
RUBINSTEIN: RCA

Seven Fantasies, Op. 116 (1892)

After the Rhapsodies, Brahms again left the field of solo piano music for a dozen years. Arthur Rubinstein wrote: "It is with the late piano works, Op. 116 through 119, that we reach Brahms's most personal music for his chosen instrument. . . . Brahms in his final years produced serene and nostalgic music that was ever more inward in mood. . . . As his own nota-tions in the scores indicate, they are so intensely intimate that one cannot really convey their full substance to a large audience. They should be heard quietly, in a small room, for they are actually works of chamber music for the piano."

No. 1, Capriccio in D minor, has restless syncopations. James Friskin says, "The legato diminished seventh arpeggios in octaves for the left hand can only be tackled easily by one with a large span." Of No. 2, Intermezzo in A minor, Huneker wrote, "It is another of those vaporish mysteries, those shadowy forms seen at dusk near the gray, thin edges of forests." On the technical side, Friskin warns, "The flickering broken octaves of the middle section are not easy to present with accuracy and delicacy." No. 3, Capriccio in G minor, is an agitated movement full of power. No. 4, Intermezzo in E major, the longest of these selections (four minutes), creates an ineffable mood. It is a work of the utmost beauty. No. 5, Intermezzo in E minor, is marked "Andante con grazia ed intimissimo sentimento." Huneker thinks this elusive composition is "more like a sigh, a half-uttered complaint of a melancholy soul. To play it you must first be a poet, then a pianist." No. 6, Intermezzo in E major, is simpler to play than the others; it has a fine melody. Huneker heard it as a minuet. No. 7, Capriccio in D minor, a brilliant close to the set, is less difficult than it sounds, with cadenzalike material.

GIESEKING: Seraphim
GILELS: DG
GOODE: Nonesuch
KATCHEN: London
KEMPFF: Philips: Great Pianists of the
 Twentieth Century
OLSHANSKY: Monitor

Three Intermezzi, Op. 117 (1892)

No. 1 in E-flat is a lullaby of unsurpassed simplicity, with a folklike quality. No. 2 in

B-flat minor is one of the most often played of these late works, tenderly passionate and tightly constructed in a sonata form based on the two-note phrase that opens the piece. No. 3 in C-sharp minor is exotically colored and beautifully textured.

CLIBURN: RCA
GOULD: Sony Classical
KOVACEVICH: Philips
KATCHEN: London
LUPU: London

Six Klavierstücke, Op. 118 (1893)

Analysis will uncover the myriad compositional devices that Brahms's genius unites so deceptively yet rigorously into these miraculous works. No. 1, Intermezzo in A minor, is an exultant one-and-a-half-minute piece, with the tonality revealed only at the very end. No. 2, Intermezzo in A major, is one of the longest of the late lyric pieces (5:30). It is often programmed because of its radiantly gracious melody. No. 3, Ballade in G minor, is a stirring piece with a quiet middle section. No. 4, Intermezzo in F minor, is breathtaking and contains canonic writing with a beautifully contoured episode in A-flat. Of No. 5, Romanze in F major, Hungerford wrote: "An idyllic work, its stately, gracious theme is heard from the outset in double counterpoint. The middle section, a delectable Pastorale in D major, is based on a four-bar theme above a kind of basso ostinato, repeated over and over. With each return the theme is most beautifully varied."

No. 6, Intermezzo in E flat minor, is a work of visionary beauty and mystery. The tempo marking is "Andante, large e mesto." It expresses despair and grief, a desire for atonement. A middle section beginning piano, sotto voce, gradually mounts to a marchlike theme which bursts into a powerful climax.

BACKHAUS: London (LP)
CLIBURN: RCA
GIESEKING: EMI
HUNGERFORD: Vanguard (LP)
KEMPFF: Philips: Great Pianists of the Twentieth Century
LUPU: London
RUBINSTEIN: RCA

Four Klavierstücke, Op. 119 (1893)

No. 1, Intermezzo in B minor, is a bittersweet Adagio. No. 2, Intermezzo in E minor, is a work of extreme loveliness. Huneker says, "Its poco agitato is the rustling of the leaves in the warm west wind, but they are flecked by the sunshine. A tremulous sensibility informs this andantino, and its bars are stamped by genius." No. 3, Intermezzo in C major, only one-and-a-half minutes, is marked "giocoso"; it is a study in cross-rhythms and the theme is in the middle voice. The three pages are unrivaled in all of Brahms for rhythmic elasticity and sheer happiness. No. 4, Rhapsody in E-flat major, is Brahms the conqueror. It has a massive, Schumann-like quality, and its middle part includes a legato melody with staccato accompaniment. The last piano piece written by Brahms, it contains similarities to his early works. From the beginning to the end of his career, Brahms was Brahms.

CICCOLINI: Pathé (LP)
CLIBURN: RCA
FIRKUSNY: Sugano
GIESEKING: EMI
JUDE: Lyrinx
KATCHEN: London
KLEIN: Tuxedo
R. SERKIN: Sony Classical

Piano Concerto No. 1 in D minor, Op. 15 (1858)

The Concerto in D minor was premiered by Brahms, with Joseph Joachim conducting, on 22 January 1859. The work occupied Brahms for more than five years. Tovey called the opening "the mightiest utterance since Beethoven's Ninth Symphony." The D minor is one of the glories of the piano concerto literature. Along with the Brahms Second Concerto, at fifty minutes it is the longest concerto in the literature. Abraham Veinus wrote, "Schumann's tragic attempt at suicide haunted Brahms during the initial sketching of the concerto. The grim and turbulent heroism of the first movement bears the imprint of the event; and the slow movement . . . is an instrumental requiem." The colossal rondo-finale is, unlike so many concerto last movements, in no way inferior to the rest of the work.

ARRAU, Giulini/Philharmonia: Angel; Haitink/
    Concertgebouw: Philips
AX, Levine/Chicago Symphony: RCA
BACKHAUS, Boult/BBC Symphony: Andante
CURZON, Szell/London Symphony: London
FLEISHER, Szell/Cleveland: Odyssey
GILELS, Jochum/Berlin Philharmonic: DG
KATCHEN, Monteux/London Symphony:
    London
POLLINI, Böhm/Vienna Philharmonic: DG
RUBINSTEIN, Reiner/Chicago Symphony: RCA
SCHNABEL, Szell/London Philharmonic: Pearl
P. SERKIN, Shaw/Atlanta Symphony: Pro Arte
R. SERKIN, Szell/Cleveland: CBS
ZIMERMAN, Bernstein/Vienna Philharmonic:
    DG

Piano Concerto No. 2 in B-flat major, Op. 83 (1881)

One of the greatest of all concertos, the work is also one of the most awkward pianistically and very demanding physically. It is cast in four movements, Brahms having added a passionate scherzo in D minor, which he called "a tiny-tiny wisp of a Scherzo." Brahms himself was soloist at the premiere on 9 November 1881, with Hans von Bülow conducting.

ARRAU, Haitink/Concertgebouw: Philips
BACKHAUS, Böhm/Vienna Philharmonic:
    London
E. FISCHER, Furtwängler/Berlin Philharmonic:
    DG
FLEISHER, Szell/Cleveland: Odyssey
GILELS, Jochum/Berlin Philharmonic: DG ;
    Reiner/Chicago Symphony: RCA
HOROWITZ, Toscanini/NBC Symphony: RCA
POLLINI, Abbado/Vienna Philharmonic: DG
RICHTER, Leinsdorf/Chicago Symphony: RCA
RUBINSTEIN, Ormandy/Philadelphia: RCA
R. SERKIN, Szell/Cleveland: CBS
WATTS, Bernstein/New York Philharmonic:
    Sony
ZIMERMAN, Bernstein/Vienna Philharmonic:
    DG

FRANK BRIDGE
1879–1941—England

Piano Sonata (1925)

This is arguably the finest English piano sonata of the 1920s, and it demands imagination and sympathy from the pianist. The work is Bridge's reaction to the horrors of World War I. Harsh, nervous, and introspective, it is at times agonizing in its tragic import. In it, he moves away from the English musical nationalism of the period. There are three movements, totaling a half hour.

GÜNEYMAN: Finnadar (LP)
JACOBS (complete piano music): Continuum

FERRUCCIO BUSONI

1866–1924—Italy

The restless, multifaceted Busoni was a powerful and paradoxical intellect, one of Modernism's germinative figures. On the one hand, he headed the avant-garde of his time as the founder of a radical neo-Classicism; on the other, he remained one of the last incarnations of Romanticism. Three distinct systems informed his mind and music: Bachian polyphony, Germanic Romanticism (with elements of Lisztian-Italiante melody,) and his own personal theories of music—many far-out for their time—which he published as his *Sketch of a New Esthetic of Music*, which was widely read by musicians and anticipated the thinking of much of twentieth-century music. Never had a musician so suffered the dissonance of the Classical and Romantic rift. In Robert M. Pirsig's words: "A Classical understanding sees the world primarily as underlying form itself. A Romantic understanding sees it primarily in terms of immediate appearance. . . . The Romantic mode is primarily inspirational, imaginative, creative, intuitive. Feelings rather than facts predominate. . . . The Classic mode, by contrast proceeds by reason and by laws—which are themselves underlying forms of thought and behavior."

Busoni fought the two modes relentlessly, and often the threads became tangled and split. He wrote to his wife, "Infinity lives in the spirit of all beings; that each being is illimitably great and illimitably small: the greatest expansion is like a point; and that light, sound, movement and power are identical, and each separate and all united, they are life." Busoni's music is often disturbing, an anxiety hovers everywhere, but he was a fascinating creator, and his music is deep and valuable.

Seven Elegies (1907)

Deep feeling pervades the remarkable set of Elegies, which are among Busoni's finest piano music. They are masterfully designed for the hands and are far more difficult than they look on the page. Some of the elegies are strange and brooding creations. In them there are many possibilities for creative pedaling, one of Busoni's hallmarks as a pianist.

The First Elegy, *Nach der wendung (after the turning) sostenuto, quasi adagio*, is a dimly lit half-world, as if Busoni was slowly leaving a morass. Busoni thought that stylistically the elegies were a major breakthrough in his work. The Second Elegy, *All'Italia* ("to Italy," in Neapolitan style), is marked "andante barcarolo," dedicated to Egon Petri. The piece uses themes from his Piano Concerto; the Neapolitan glisten is tempered with a certain asperity of mood and tonality, mainly hovering in F-sharp major. The Third Elegy, based on *Meine seele bangt und hofft zu dir* (my soul fears and hopes in you), is subtitled "Chorale Prelude," moderato, un pòco maestoso, and is enigmatic, with sinister pages moving toward an agitated climax. Busoni's study of late Liszt, technically and musically, is here apparent, as is the ambiguous tonality of the very quiet ending.

The Fourth Elegy, *Turandots Frauengemach*, Turandot's room or boudoir, is subtitled "Intermezzo" and is dedicated to his pupil Michael von Zadora. The piece is based on the English tune "Greensleeves," which Busoni thought to be a Chinese melody. It's one of the composer's most exhilarating and attractive pieces. The piano writing is brilliantly effective, the rhythmic verve enchanting. To achieve its required clarity is difficult. After a suave double-note glissando, the piece, which had been in a comfortable G major, ends deliciously and humorously on an E major chord.

The Fifth Elegy, *Die Nächtlichen (The Nocturnals)*, is subtitled "Waltz." It is fluttery, diaphanous, with an almost Godowskian aroma of decadence, a waltz danced among shadows. The Sixth Elegy, *Erscheinung (Apparition)*, is subtitled "Nocturne." The opening marking is "amoroso." It is a work of Romantic strangeness using atmospheric tremolos. The piece ends with the word "visionario."

The Seventh Elegy, *Berceuse (Lullaby)*, was transcribed in 1909 for orchestra with the title *Berceuse elegiaque*. Liszt's late music again hovers; the score has a remote austerity. There is a sense of grief for the infant being lulled.

BEAN (Nos. 1–6): RCA (LP)
JOHANSEN: Artist Direct (LP)
JONES: Argo
STEURMANN: Zodiac (LP)
WALDOFF (No. 4): MHS

Six Sonatinas (1910–20)

The sonatinas range from a sensitive neo-Classicism to a dissonant expressionism, moving beyond traditional notions of consonance and dissonance. No. 1 is a theme and seven variations. The dedication belongs to Rudolph Ganz. No. 2, Sonatina Seconda, dates from 1912 and is dedicated to Mark Hambourg. It is one of his most radical works to date, with no tonal center; one is invaded by Busoni's pessimism and desolation, and, in its marchlike fragments, there is anticipation of the gruesome war years to come. In its two sections in nine minutes we find a score of powerful focus, surrealist nightmares, and a pianism fraught with danger.

The Third Sonatina was composed in 1916—its ten pages are technically far easier than No. 2. He titled the work *Ad usum infantis,* a sonatina for children, but a very different child who smiles while practicing Clementi Sonatinas. It has its own ingrown charm, and its five sections are played without break.

The Fourth Sonatina, *In diem nativitatis Christi,* MCMX VII—On the Day of Christ's Birth, 1917, is dedicated to his son Benvenuto. Harmonically complex, the work possess a solemn starkness and unusual emotional power.

The Fifth Sonatina from 1919, dedicated to his pupil, the composer Philipp Jarnach, is subtitled "in Signo Joannis Sebastiani Magni" (short sonatina in the sign of the great Johann Sebastian)—a free imitation of Bach's "little" Fantasy and Fugue in D minor. The piece has a Busonian gloom, as the composer finds himself a long way from Bach's more certain world.

The Sixth Sonatina, composed in 1920, is called "sonatina super Carmen." Its official title is *Kammer-Fantasie über Bizet's Carmen*. Here is a seven-minute work that is serious yet entertaining, an exposé on themes from *Carmen*. The pianism is difficult but economical; Busoni is painting a portrait of Carmen herself and probes various aspects of her psychology. This is by far the most often performed of the six sonatinas.

ARRAU (No. 6): Pearl
D. JACOBS (Nos. 1–6): Nonesuch
LOESSER (No. 2): Marston
MARIOTTI (No. 5): Fone
PETRI (Nos. 3, 6): Pearl
TOZER (No. 2): Chandos
VON ZADORA (No. 6): Pearl

Fantasia contrappuntistica (Third Version) (1912)

A fourth version is a fine two-piano arrangement. Busoni labored long on this summing up of his lifelong love for Bach. The score is based on Busoni's concept of the "Fourth Subject" of the intended quadruple fugue of Bach's own summation of Fugue in *The Art of Fugue*. Here is Busoni, finishing Bach's unfinished masterwork. It is surly one of Busoni's major creations, and it will always provide an outstanding mental and musical challenge. Some consider it a work of emotional beauty; others, like Peter Yates in his book *An Amateur at the Keyboard*, see it "as a phantasmagoria of styles and devices. . . . This was no longer the aristocratic complacency of Liszt amusing himself by writing for display a fantasy on the well-known melodies of an opera; here the highest and most discriminating judgment had grown crazed and tasteless."

However, for Busoni, such a work was necessary to purge himself of his own nineteenth-century conception of Bach and Bachian counterpoint. After this composition, Busoni became more comfortable with his free polyphony and would forge a new type of neo-baroque-classicism, which influenced many composers, especially those still in the grips of a stale nineteenth-century Romanticism.

PETRI: Westminster (LP)
O'RILEY: Centaur

Toccata (1920)

One of Busoni's finest works, of a bitter, driving and despairing quality; of extreme difficulty mechanically. The form of the score is Preludio, Fantasia, Ciaccona. In Sarah Davis Buechner's words, "An opening Prelude of cascading arpeggios gives way to a large-scale fantasy which contains some of Busoni's most beautiful piano writing. The concluding Chaconne builds relentlessly to a stretto of thunderous octaves." The Toccata is just under ten minutes for performance. Alfred Brendel

Ferruccio Busoni by David Dubal

has said that the Toccata is one of the most difficult pieces he has ever encountered.

BRENDEL: Philips: Great Pianists of the Twentieth Century
BUECHNER: Connoisseur Society
JOHANSEN: Artist Direct (LP)
MARIOTTI: Fon
O'RILEY: Centaur
PETRI: Westminster (LP)
TOZER: Chandos

Ten Variations on a Chopin Prelude (1922)

An eleven-minute work based on the famous and somber C minor Prelude, Op. 28, No. 20. Masterly in style, a superb mixture of melodic, harmonic, and polyphonic variation technique. This rigorous work is of the most cunning and refined piano scoring. The Scherzo finale, which begins in fugal style, stops to bring in a sarcastic variation in the form of a waltz, an "Homage à Chopin." The Scherzo returns for a brilliant conclusion.

> BUECHNER: Connoisseur Society
> JOHANSEN: Artist Direct (LP)
> OGDON: Philips: Great Pianists of the
> Twentieth Century

Indianisches Tagebuch (Indian Diary) (1915)

These four short essays on Native American themes of eleven minutes are completely digested into Busoni's cerebral idiom, but with a rare simplicity and charm. No. 3 is the most folk-like.

> PETRI: Pearl
> TOZER: Chandos
> TRYON: Musica Viva

Red Indian Fantasy for Piano and Orchestra, Op. 44 (1913–1914)

Busoni had a real interest in the differences and barriers within cultures. He was fascinated by the Red Indians, whose plight he had understood. He respected their mystical attitude and awe for nature. He wrote to his wife Gerda, "The Indians are the only cultured people who will have nothing to do with money and who dress the most everyday things in beautiful words." The American premiere took place in Philadelphia in February 1915 with Busoni at the piano and Stokowski conducting. The piece is divided into a Fantasia-Canzone-Finale and is about twenty minutes long. The opening is based on a Hopi melody. The piano writing is signally grateful with long cadenzas. There

is atmosphere and poignancy in the central Canzone; the orchestration is economical and inventive. As Antony Beaumont puts it: "In the Red Indian works we find an expression of his growing concern to establish 'the oneness of music'—a unity that knows no frontiers between men, whatever their race or culture, no matter how widely scattered they may be on the face of the earth."

> GRANTE, ZuccariniI/Pomeriggi Musicale:
> Music and Arts
> MITCHELL, Strickland/Vienna State Opera
> Orchestra: Decca
> PETRI, Mitropoulos/New York Philharmonic:
> Music and Arts

Piano Concerto, Op. 39 (1901–1904)

This is the ultimate statement of the Romantic piano concerto, in five movements, around sixty-five minutes long, and scored in the finale for male choir in a hymn to Allah, the text from the nineteenth-century Danish poet Adam Oehlenschlager. Maurice Hinson writes, "From its opening glimmering murmurings to its choral close, this work is enormously complex and makes severely taxing demands of the soloist, both musically and technically. The five movements are conceived as an architectonic pentacle, with the odd-numbered movements symbolizing the apexes of spirituality; the second movement, a scherzo, and the fourth, a tarantella, represent terrestrial transience. Busoni felt that the last movement with chorus resembled 'some original inborn quality in a person which, in the course of years, comes out again in him purified and matured as he reaches the last phase of his transformations.'"

The first movement, marked "Prologo e introito," serves as a kind of large-scale overture to the work. The piano writing is magisterial, in both its grand manner and reflective sides.

The second movement, Pezzo giocoso, is a showy piece but with strange harmonic flights, and the movement is as sad as it is giocoso. The third movement, more than twenty minutes, is marked "Pezzo serioso" and is the most complex slow movement in the concerto literature.

"All'Italiana" is the title of the fourth movement; Busoni said it is like coming out of the forum into a crowded Roman street. The movement is vivid but perhaps too long. It is a large-sized spiritual tarantella, a tribute to the Italy which Busoni loved dearly. The Fifth movement, Cantico, is magnificent in scope, contemplation, and in effect. Antony Beaumont thinks, "Never again did he feel the need to express himself at such length and never again did he write with such lack of inhibition and overt love of life."

The piano concerto was Busoni's fond farewell to the Romantic age. If he had not composed this work, breathtaking in its surface glitter, he may never have had the strength to enter the far more solemn inner world of spiritual development that followed. The concerto is a huge, saturated conglomerate, with occasional clichés, which are part of the fabric of the score. Above all, it is his battle between the Teutonic and Italian sides of his nature. Busoni premiered the concerto to a largely baffled audience four months after its completion in Berlin.

HAMELIN, Elder/City of Birmingham
  Symphony and Chorus: Hyperion
LIVELY, Gielen/Southwest German Radio
  Orchestra: Koch
OGDON, Revenaugh/Royal Philharmonic and
  Male Chorus: Philips: Great Pianists of the
  Twentieth Century
OHLSSON, C. Dohnányi/Cleveland Orchestra
  and Male Chorus: Telarc
THIOLLIER, Jchonwandt/Orchestre

Philharmonic de Nice and Chorus: Kontrapunkt

Bach Transcriptions

Busoni was faithful to Bach his whole career. He was nourished by the Leipzig cantor and was ever searching and studying Bachian counterpoint. His editions of Bach are fascinating for their bristling footnotes. He saw Bach in the light of his own time, and there had long been a tradition of Bach transcription which continues to our time. Busoni's models were Liszt's Arrangements of Bach Organ Preludes and Fugues. Busoni saw the piano as an instrument of sonorous splendor as well as a vehicle for heightened expression. To the Romantic spirit Bach's organ works were the pinnacle of Baroque grandeur, and Busoni achieved on the piano a lofty sound unmatched by Siloti, d'Albert, Tausig, and many others, just as in his nine versions of the Chorale-Preludes he created a deep intimacy. (His later arrangements of the Brahms Organ Chorales are also admirable.)

Chaconne in D minor

Transcribed from the Violin Partita, No. 2, BWV 1004, this ample work is the most often performed of Busoni's transcriptions. In this case the solo violin captured his imagination and, in his re-creation, he gave the pianist a magnificent aural fresco of what the late nineteenth century thought Bach should sound like. It was completed in 1892, in Boston, where he was teaching at the New England Conservatory, and he gave the first performance there. The score is, as Antony Beaumont notes, "an extension of Brahmsian and Lisztian textures, [and] draws an organ-like richness from the piano. A good performance will generally 'bring the house down.'"

BOLET: Philips: Great Pianists of the Twentieth
  Century
CHERKASSKY: Nimbus
FLIER: RD
KISSIN: RCA
LABÉ: Dorian
MICHELANGELI: Music and Art
PRATT: EMI
RUBINSTEIN: RCA
TURECK: VAI
WEISSENBERG: EMI

Toccata and Fugue in D minor, BWV 565

Busoni's arrangement vies with the Tausig in
popularity. Bach's most celebrated organ work
is stark and naked in Busoni's raw version.

JOHANSEN: Artist Direct (LP)

Prelude and Fugue in D major, BWV 532

A thickly textured transcription, where the
pianist must push to the extreme for the effect
Busoni sought. This and the D minor Toccata
and Fugue date from Bach's early Weimar
period. In the Fugue Bach's pedal technique is
complicated. Busoni's skill in the piano transference is remarkable.

PRESTON: Spectrum (LP)

Toccata, Adagio and Fugue, BWV 564

A work of eighteen minutes and one of
Busoni's best efforts in the genre; composed
in 1900. Even when purists shouted loudest
for Bach in the original, many pianists
refused to give up these Baroque-Romantic
effusions. Busoni understood that all music
is a transcription from the mind to instrument and notation to performance itself.
The adagio is particularly poignant on the
piano.

FRANÇOIS: Philips: Great Pianists of the
  Twentieth Century
HOROWITZ: Sony Classical
KISSIN: RCA
RUBINSTEIN: RCA

Organ Prelude and Fugue in E-flat major, BWV 552

This is perhaps Bach's most complicated
organ work; as Busoni points out, he has
"freely transcribed this work as a concert-
piece for pianoforte." Robert Preston writes,
"The accomplishment of laying out such a
massive array of material on the piano is
nothing short of stupendous, while the organ-
like sonority is astonishing."

PRESTON: Spectrum (LP)

C

ELLIOTT CARTER

b. 1908—United States

Piano Sonata (1945–46)

One of the most impressive contemporary piano works, the Piano Sonata launched Carter to the forefront of American composition. It is in the two complicated movements of this work that Carter's exploring sense of rhythm became his hallmark. Wilfrid Mellers, the British critic and composer, finds that it "combines elements from the piano sonatas of both Ives and Copland, while achieving a powerful individuality. . . . There is nothing in European music to which one can compare it, except possibly the combination of madrigalian polyphonic rhythm with jazz syncopation in the later music of Michael Tippett."

    P. JACOBS: Nonesuch
    P. LAWSON: Virgin Classics
    N. LEE: Chant du Monde
    ROSEN: Etcetera
    WEBSTER: Dover (LP)

Night Fantasies

A visionary score, composed when Carter was 71. Pianistically original, abstruse, and physically and technically demanding at twenty-two minutes. From its creation, *Night Fantasies* has had important advocates in Ursula Oppens, Charles Rosen, Paul Jacobs, and Gilbert Kalish. The work is constantly changing in its mood and texture. Carter wrote of it: "Suggesting the fleeting thoughts and feelings that pass through the mind during a period of wakefulness at night. . . . In this score I wanted to capture the fanciful, changeable quality of our inner life at a time when it is not dominated by strong, directive intentions or desires—to capture the poetic moodiness that, in an earlier romantic context, I enjoy in works of Robert Schumann like *Kreiseleriana, Carnaval,* and *Davidsbündlertänze.*"

    DRURY: Neuma
    KARIS: Bridge
    OPPENS: Music and Arts
    ROSEN: Etcetera

Piano Concerto (1965–66)

The Concerto is pure Carter; it is purged of all outside influence. One of the most difficult piano concertos, it is far more intricate than the Piano Sonata. Some consider it the most important modern American concerto, yet few have the nerve or technical fiber to tackle and conquer it. The composer states, "It employs no pre-established form, but is a series of short, usually overlapping episodes, mosaics of fragments that derive from parts of the basic material." The Concerto is dense, unfriendly, and intellectual, but nevertheless it is a work of tremendous energy. The recording by Jacob Lateiner and Leinsdorf is from the actual world premiere performances of 6 and 7 January 1967. Virgil Thomson thought "his genius is to have combined intellectual elaboration and auditory delight with no loss of intensity to either. Researches in instrumental virtuosity commanded by an authentic musical temperament."

LATEINER, Leinsdorf/Boston Symphony: RCA (LP)

OPPENS, Gielen/Cincinnati Symphony: New World

EMMANUEL CHABRIER
1841–1894—France

Emmanuel Chabrier by David Dubal

Dix Pièces pittoresques (1880)

Chabrier was one of the creators of the modern French school. After the premiere of the *Pièces pittoresques,* César Franck declared, "We have just heard something extraordinary. This music links our era with that of Couperin and Rameau." Poulenc thought these ten pieces as important to French music as the later Debussy Preludes. Indeed, Chabrier was loved and assimilated by Debussy and Ravel. Satie admired him, and his conscious adoption of a music-hall style prompted *Les Six* to follow that path in some of their work.

Chabrier is somewhat uneven, but at his most inspired he is unpretentious, chaste, or tender. His harmony, with its ninth chords, has zest, and there is always *joie de vivre*. Vincent d'Indy defined him as a person "open to every tender affection and exquisite in every way." Chabrier can also be bawdy, insouciant, and rhythmically unpredictable. He was known as a bumptious, rollicking pianist. Alfred

Bruneau said, "He played the piano as no one had before him."

The ten pieces are:

Paysage: a restrained tenderness, uniquely Chabrier, radiates the first section, which moves from the D-flat tonality into a bright A major.

Mélancolie: delicate rubato is asked for in this mysterious and alluring poem. Of one section of the piece, Alfred Cortot writes, "The longing beauty of these few lines, and their rounded perfection, defy analysis. There throbs the hidden secret of a languorous autumn night, drenched with the perfume of late roses. And it exhibits at the same time such polish of style that the whole work is a masterpiece in petit."

Tourbillon: Anticipation of the twentieth century, as well as Chabrier's ear for mixing oddities, such as Offenbach, with Schumann and Mendelssohn. It's a bright, strong piece, marked "Allegro con fuoco"; Cortot says it's "a hurricane careening through four pages." Chabrier was known to make pulp of a piano. A friend of Chabrier's, Henry Bauer noted, "He was a devil that entered into the instrument."

Sous-bois: A nature sketch in its lyric glow. Marked "Andantino," the main tonality is C major.

Mauresque: Written before Chabrier went to Spain, this short piece finds a moorish and modal influence.

Idylle: Marked with "freshness and simplicity," *Idylle* is one of the best known of the set, brushed with Chabrier's keen feeling for pictorial effects. The composer was an early collector of the modern French school, and his dear friend Manet died in his arms.

Danse villageoise: Full of rhythmic life, and not especially difficult. The opening section is in A minor, while the simple and direct trio is in A major.

Improvisation: Forgetting its title, Chabrier writes a quite formal work with elements of sonata form. It is a work which Fauré must have loved.

Menuet pompeux: Nothing of the court of the Sun King or Lully, but a menuet in Chabrier's tongue-in-cheek style.

Scherzo-valze: A brilliant work which Arthur Rubinstein favored. It needs a good staccato to activate its playful energy.

J. CASADESUS: Sony Classical
CICCOLINI: Seraphim (LP)

D'ARCO: Calliope
N. MEYER: EMI
S. STRAVINSKY: Centaur

Bourrée fantasque (1891)

Chabrier's final piano piece is a synthesis of all his music. The strutting, the seduction, the Lautrec nightlife, the mock sentimentality are all here. Arthur Loesser speaks of its "Parisian proletarian flavor." Robert Casadesus felt that with this six-minute piece the modern French school was born.

BARBIZET: (Complete Piano Music): ERATO
CICCOLINI: Seraphim (LP)
D'ARCO: Calliope
JOHANNESEN: Vox (LP)
KYRIAKOU: (Complete Piano Music): Vox
LOESSER: Marston

CARLOS CHÁVEZ
1899–1978—Mexico

Piano Concerto (1942)

The Chávez Concerto was not well received at its premiere, given by Eugene List in 1942. At the time it was considered cacophonous. Nearly a half century later, we hear a work filled with color and which evokes landscapes of ferocious power. The piano part is very demanding; List called it "the most difficult composition I have ever tackled." The high-spirited, motorized energy of the finale requires unusual muscle. Chávez left many piano works of marked originality both in idea and keyboard conception. His *Invención* and six piano sonatas should be investigated by contemporary pianists. Chávez was indisputably Mexico's greatest composer.

Piano Concerto:
LIST, Chávez/Vienna State Opera: Westminster
RODRIGUEZ, Mata/New Philharmonia: RCA

FRÉDÉRIC CHOPIN
1810–1849—Poland

Chopin is the overwhelming favorite composer for the piano. One may safely say that while reading this, at this moment in every country, pianos are being caressed or pounded in his name. The English critic Cecil Gray says, "It is probably true to say that a larger number of people owe their first authentic musical thrill in early years to him than to any other composer." He is one of the few masters of universal significance. What are his secrets? Popular and enigmatic often simultaneously, he possessed the most subtle intuitions and fathomed the mysterious of the world. His music clings to our hearts and minds, ingratiates yet disturbs our consciousness, and haunts our subterranean depths. Oscar Wilde exclaimed, "After playing Chopin, I feel as if I had been weeping over sins that I had never committed and mourning over tragedies that were not my own." He brought new and strange colors to the instrument, iridescent and glowing; the piano springs to new life with aristocratic grace, decorative splendor, and poetic and bardic passion. All aspects of the mechanical in piano playing were erased forever with a technical process of a new meaning. When Schumann reviewed the Op. 2 Variations, with "hats off gentleman—a genius!" the German had only the glimmerings of what was soon to be born. Chopin gave birth to the modern piano and to the modern pianist, his hands alive and quivering, the pedal fluttering, the heart capable of projecting every insinuation and secret glance. Chopin perfected the latent spirit of his instrument. Goethe noted:

> Everything perfect of its kind must go beyond its kind, it must be something else, incomparable. In some notes the nightingale is still a bird; then it surmounts its species, seeming to want to show to every other feathered fowl what singing really is.

When Chopin unveiled his etudes he surmounted the species and instantly cast a shadow on all previous technical explorations and innovations. His technique, sublime and novel, is honed to the hands yet is not merely or conveniently pianistic, as if to assure himself that the disquieting strangeness, mystery, and allure of each score will not be taken for granted. His greatest executants find they pay dearly for any neglect and his pianism, with any neglect, easily begins to slip and crumble. He demands constant refurbishing, as if to say, "I will not succumb easily." A despairing Busoni writes to the composer Hans Huber, "I toil away at the Chopin Etudes, which I believed myself to have mastered 25 years ago, yet always have to conquer anew."

Unfortunately, Chopin is one of the worst-played and tampered with of the masters—the phraseology twisted and turned, pedal clogged, the cobwebbed, bejeweled passagework bumpy with misplaced accents, a sickening rubato which vulgarizes waltzes and mazurkas to petrification. How the fastidious Pole would have winced at the subsequent general history of Chopin performance. He has had to endure every kind of self-indulgence. Only the greatest art can withstand such insult and injury. In his journal, André Gide complains: "Without paying any attention to the time and with sudden accents, stresses, and effects much more apt to show off the player's temperament than the excellence of the composition,"

Wagner, with bile and who knew better, called Chopin a right-handed composer. Chopin was a true Bachian spirit. The psychologist Anton Ehrenzweig wrote:

Chopin chafed under the wrong praise of his music. He certainly made the piano sing as it never sang before or after, but performers who indulge too much in its sweet sonority tend to obscure the complex inner fabric. If we look closely we find that the specific Chopin sound is bound up with the rhythmical independence of the accompaniment. The left hand never "accompanies" by producing lush vertical sound, but has an independent rhythmical structure that often has a thematic significance of its own. Chopin's incomparable sound quality results from the recalcitrant fusion between the two superimposed rhythms. Performers must forego a lush sweet sound and instead ought to emphasize the harshness of the rhythmical clash.

Ehrenzweig also says, "Academic teachers devote too much time to sonority and a type of vertical sound quality instead of teaching the inner fabrics (not made up inner voices) of Chopin's structures." Chopin's close friend, the painter Eugene Delacroix, felt Chopin was "exquisite in heart and, needless to say in mind" and wrote: "Chopin is art itself, and, obversely, art is no longer what the vulgar think it to be, that is, some sort of inspiration which comes from nowhere, which proceeds by chance, and presents no more than the picturesque externals of things. It is reason itself, adorned by genius, but following a necessary course and encompassed by higher laws."

It was Chopin who revealed the laws of Bach's fugues to Delacroix's inquiring mind. Chopin's temperament was intensely guarded and elitist, yet he speaks to everyone as few artists ever have. However, he preferred to perform for the very few, to himself and the angels. Early in 1848 he performed for the last time in Paris. The Chopin scholar Arthur Hedley remarks of this concert that "it was surrounded by every circumstance of elegance and distinction." The 1848 Revolution would break out a week later, and Chopin's world would be crushed. Terminally ill, broken by the ending of his nine-year liaison with George Sand, he played as he had never before. After the concert he received a letter from his friend, the Marquis De Custine, who wrote: "You have gained in suffering and poetry, the melancholy of your compositions penetrates still deeper into one's heart, . . . it is not a piano that speaks but a soul, and what a soul. . . . One may love and understand one's neighbor through Chopin."

Indeed to have heard Chopin must have been one of the heavenly apparitions.

Frédéric Chopin by David Dubal

The remarkable English composer Cyril Scott writes: "Chopin was the musical poet *par excellence* of refinement—not a superficial, but an inner refinement of soul; this refinement . . . was the character and keynote of his music. . . . Chopin was the first tone-poet in the truest and most specific sense; and for this reason there is in his music at times, and in varying degrees, that aroma of sadness which is the quintessence of all genuine lyric poetry. To understand this fact is to understand the personality of Chopin and the influence he had on the world."

Early in his life, Nietzsche realized important aspects of Chopin. The philosopher wrote: "I particularly admired in Chopin his freeing of music from German influences, from the tendency to the ugly, dull, pettily bourgeois, clumsy, and self-important. Spiritual beauty and nobility, and above all, aristocratic gaiety, freedom from restraint and splendor of soul, as well as Southern warmth and intensity of feeling, were expressed by him for the first time in music."

As I wrote earlier in the book, Chopin's influence on other composers is far-reaching, and he was the most daring harmonist of his time. The debt Wagner owned to the Pole has never been adequately dealt with. The cultural historian Jaques Barzun wrote: "The harmonic system of Chopin, with its iridescent chromaticism and its constant search for tender nuances, contributed to making the Wagnerian 'sea of harmony' a kindred chromatic sea of enharmony. The perpetual soft sliding, the enveloping caress of edgeless sounds, which is at first so enchanting in Wagner, is Chopin reduced to system and orchestrated."

The tragedy of Chopin's last few years is appalling. He uttered impotently, "Where has my art gone?" as he coughed his way to the grave. In those years he composed merely a few pages; one holds one's breath listening to the moribund F minor Mazurka, Op. 68, No. 4, his last piece. The cause was not only his loss after the breakup with George Sand nor the consumption eating at him. Simply he could not repeat himself—all genres of his musical forms had been polished to perfection. There was nothing more to say after the Barcarolle and Polonaise-Fantasie; the Cello Sonata was a valiant attempt at expansion. Nothing could save Chopin except to live past the empty loneliness and be cured of his malady. This was impossible, and in his last three years his art had inevitably ebbed away with his life.

It is Chopin's perfection and spiritual poetry that make his music so indispensable to the sensitive. He remains calm in an increasingly hostile world with its pall of human depravity. In the future, if art itself is forced to recede and driven underground, only to survive in secret societies, Chopin will continue to be one of humanity's hallowed spirits whose rarified and heroic art will offer solidarity, beauty, and purity for those who refuse to become zombies.

Andante Spianato and Grand Polonaise for Piano and Orchestra, Op. 22 (1830)

Written in Chopin's twentieth year, this is a marvelous display piece. The sumptuous Polonaise is ceremonial; the Andante Spianato (i.e., with smoothness) is a liquid-toned gem demanding a poet's reading. The orchestral part is paltry, but has its flavor; many have dispensed with it altogether, permitting this work to be performed on the recital stage.

AX: RCA
CHERKASSKY: Nimbus
DAVIDOVICH, Marriner/London Symphony: Philips
HOFMANN (Golden Jubilee concert, 1937; Casimir Hall recital, 1938): VAI

RUBINSTEIN: RCA
ZIMERMAN: DG

Ballade No. 1 in G minor, Op. 23 (1836)

The first of the Four Ballades is a glowing masterpiece. James Huneker called this epic narrative "the odyssey of Chopin's soul." The great lyric theme, stated in three different forms, is intoxicating. The First Ballade is summed up with a coda of elemental power, culminating in a chilling downward chromatic passage in octaves, which will electrify any receptive listener. On September 14, 1836, Chopin was in Leipzig, and Schumann reports: "Who do you think walked in? Chopin! . . . He gave me a new Ballade in G minor. It seems to me his most inspired work. . . . Besides he played a whole number of new studies, nocturnes and mazurkas—everything incomparably. It fills you with emotion merely to see him sitting at the piano . . . try to conceive such perfection, a mastery which seems unconscious of itself."

ASHKENAZY (Nos. 1–4): London
BACKHAUS: London
CORTOT (Nos. 1–4, recorded 1926): Music and Arts
GILELS: Music and Arts
GIMPEL: Cambria Classics
HOFMANN: VAI
HOROWITZ: RCA
KISSIN: RCA
MICHELANGELI: Testament
RUBINSTEIN (Nos. 1–4): RCA

Ballade No. 2 in F major, Op. 38 (1838)

Schumann had dedicated his *Kreisleriana,* Op. 16, to Chopin, who returned the honor by dedicating the Second Ballade to his German champion. A work of perfect proportion, it opens with a slow and magical episode which turns into a tempest, Presto con fuoco, a wild, magnificent outburst. In the words of the composer Alan Rawsthorne, at the end of the coda the Andantino theme becomes "a whispered reminder of the very opening," which "vibrates in the memory."

FRANÇOIS: Philips: Great Pianists of the Twentieth Century
GRAVRILOV: DG
KISSIN: RCA
MORAVEC (Nos. 1–4): Connoisseur Society
POGORELICH: Capriccio
POLLINI: DG
RICHTER: CBS/Melodiya
VÁSÁRY: DG

Ballade No. 3 in A-flat major, Op. 47 (1841)

The Third Ballade is the essence of charm and warmth, with a sense of irony surrounding the second subject. Frederick Niecks, Chopin's first important biographer in English, says "a quiver of excitement runs through the whole piece. . . . There is suffused a most exquisite elegance." The slender second subject becomes a development section, "one of the most powerful Chopin ever composed," says Rawsthorne, "one is quite staggered to look back at its winsome origins." The coda, he continues, ends "in a blaze of light."

ARRAU: Philips
DE PACHMANN: Pearl
FRIEDMAN: Pearl
NOVAES (Nos. 3 and 4): Vanguard
OHLSSON: Arabesque
ROSE: Monarch
SOFRONITSKY: Melodiya

Ballade No. 4 in F minor, Op. 52 (1842)

The Fourth Ballade is generally agreed to be one of the sublime works of Romantic music. For John Ogdon, it is "the most exalted, intense and sublimely powerful of all Chopin's compositions. . . . It is unbelievable that it lasts only twelve minutes, for it contains the experience of a lifetime." Huneker calls its chief theme a "melody which probes the very coverts of the soul." He compares it to Leonardo da Vinci's Mona Lisa, while Ogdon speaks of F. Scott Fitzgerald's *The Last Tycoon*, inviting us to a "Romantic communion of unbelievable intensity."

The Fourth Ballade remains a narrative but has an inimitable feeling of intimacy and Slavonic coloring and demands of the interpreter a delicate rubato and a virtuoso technique. It culminates in a coda of bone-crushing technical severity.

HOFMANN: VAI
HOROWITZ: RCA
KOCZALSKI: Pearl
KUERTI: Analekta
MOISEIWITSCH: Philips: Great Pianists of the
    Twentieth Century
RICHTER: DG/Melodiya
SOLOMON: Testament
TIEGERMAN: Arbitor
VÁSÁRY (Nos. 1–4): DG

Barcarolle in F-sharp major, Op. 60 (1845–46)

One of Chopin's greatest compositions. It has been the despair of many fine artists, being difficult to interpret successfully. It is easy to sound affected, as does Arrau, or nervous, as does Horowitz, or too plain, as did Gieseking. Chopin must have been its ideal interpreter. At his very last Paris recital, in 1848, Charles Hallé heard the frail master, who now "played it from the point when it demands the utmost energy, in the opposite way, pianissimo, but with such wonderful nuances that one remained in doubt if this new rendering were not preferable to the accustomed one."

The Barcarolle displays Chopin's ornamental genius in full bloom. Ravel wrote: "Chopin was not content merely to revolutionize piano technique. His figurations are inspired. Through his brilliant passages one perceives profound, enchanting harmonies. Always there is the hidden meaning which is translated into poetry of intense despair. . . . The Barcarolle is the synthesis of the expressive and sumptuous art of this great Slav."

André Gide finds the Barcarolle to express "languor in excessive joy."

ARGERICH: DG
ASHKENAZY: London
KAROLYI: Melodram
LIPATTI: EMI
MOISEIWITSCH: APR
REISENBERG: Insync
RUBINSTEIN: RCA
SHERMAN: Pro Arte
SOFRONITSKY: Melodiya

Berceuse in D-flat major, Op. 57 (1844)

A cradle song which is a tour de force of exquisite filigree. A virtually unchanged tonic pedal in D-flat in the bass continues throughout its seventy magical measures. But "no analysis," says Sir Lennox Berkeley, "can give any idea of its compelling grace and charm."

BAUER: IPA–Desmar
CORTOT: Music and Arts
HOFMANN: VAI

NOVAES: Vanguard
OGDON: IMP Classics
PERAHIA: Sony
RUBINSTEIN: RCA
SHELLEY: Chandos
SOLOMON: Testament

Piano Concerto No. 1 in E minor, Op. 11 (1830)

The concerto is a grand harvest of perfect piano writing. It has retained a special place in the hearts of concert pianists, though conductors have relatively little to do. The slow movement is an exquisite, luxuriant nocturne. Chopin, who seldom wrote about his music, in this case wrote: "It is not meant to create a powerful effect, it is rather a romance, calm and melancholy, giving the impression of someone looking gently towards a spot which calls to mind a thousand happy memories. It is a kind of reverie in the moonlight on a beautiful spring evening."

ARGERICH, Abbado/London
   Symphony: DG
AX, Ormandy/Philadelphia: RCA
BACHAUER, Dorati/London Symphony:
   Mercury
BRAILOWSKY, Ormandy/Philadelphia:
   Odyssey
CLIBURN, Ormandy/Philadelphia: RCA
CZERNY-STEFANSKA (formerly attributed to
   Lipatti): Seraphim
DEMIDENKO, H. Schiff/Philharmonia
   Orchestra: Hyperion
FOU TS'ONG, Tang/Sinfonia Varsovia: Collins
   Classics
GILELS, Ormandy/Philadelphia Orchestra:
   Sony Classical
MEWTON-WOOD, Goehr/Orchestre
   Philharmonique Neerlandais: Dante
H. NEUHAUS, Gauk/Moscow Radio
   Symphony: Russian Disc

NOVAES, Perlea/Bamberg Symphony:
   Allegretto
POLLINI, Kletzki/Philharmonia: EMI
RUBINSTEIN, Wallenstein/Los Angeles
   Philharmonic: RCA; Skrowaczewski/New
   Symphony of London: RCA
TOMSIC, Munih/Ljubljana Symphony
   Orchestra: Stradivari Classics
ZIMERMAN, Giulini/Los Angeles
   Philharmonic: DG

Piano Concerto No. 2 in F minor, Op. 21 (1829)

The Second Concerto, composed when Chopin was nineteen, predates No. 1, and is more subjective than the latter. Though equally popular, it is more elusive musically. The slow movement of the F minor Concerto is as breathtaking a poetic effusion as that of the First Concerto.

ASHKENAZY, Gorzynski/Warsaw
   Philharmonic: Angel
AX, Ormandy/Philadelphia: RCA
CORTOT, Barbirolli: Pearl
FOU TS'ONG, Maag/London Symphony:
   Westminster
HASKIL, Markevitch/Lamoureux
   Orchestra: Philips
HOFMANN: VAI
LICAD, Previn/London Philharmonic: Sony
   Classical
MALCUZYNSKI, Kletzki/Philharmonie:
   Historical Piano Collection
MEWTON-WOOD, Goehr/Orchestre
   Symphonique Zurich: Dante
NOVAES, Klemperer/Vienna
   Symphony: Vox
POGORELICH, Abbado/Chicago Symphony:
   DG (CD)
RUBINSTEIN, Ormandy/Philadelphia: RCA
WEISSENBERG, Skrowaczewski/Paris
   Conservatoire: Angel

453

Twelve Etudes, Op. 10 (1829–31)
Twelve Etudes, Op. 25 (1830–34)

The Chopin Etudes are the most important pieces in the genre and formed the basis for all future concert etudes. The Op. 10 are dedicated "*A son ami*," Franz Liszt.

Op. 10, No. 1 in C major: Arpeggios based on wide extension. Huneker considers it "the new technique in all its nakedness, new in the scenes of figure, design, pattern, web, new in a harmonic way. . . . The nub of modern piano music is in the study."

Op. 10, No. 2 in A minor: The study is an expansion of the Moscheles Etude Op. 70, No. 3, in chromatic scale passages for the third, fourth, and fifth fingers of the right hand, with chords in the right hand for the first and second fingers.

Op. 10, No. 3 in E major: An exquisite aria for cantabile playing. A middle section features widely extended double notes. When teaching the work to his pupil Adolf Gutmann, the composer cried out, "Oh, my homeland!"

Op. 10, No. 4 in C-sharp minor: An etude of lightness in high velocity for both hands.

Op. 10, No. 5 in G-flat major: The so-called Black Key Etude. Accuracy of chords in the left hand with exquisitely designed figuration on the black keys calls for a combination of finger technique with rotary action and supple wrists.

Op. 10, No. 6 in E-flat minor: A slow but restless chromatic study; it is difficult musically and needs a luscious touch for its melancholic, even anguished cantabile. For Henry T. Finck, "the etude seems as if it were in a sort of double minor . . . much sadder than ordinary minor."

Op. 10, No. 7 in C major: A toccata requiring strong fingers for quick changing on the same note with the first finger and thumb of the right hand. There is further need to articulate the melodic line in the fifth finger. Huneker asks, "Were ever Beauty and Duty so mated in double harness?"

Op. 10, No. 8 in F major: Brilliant finger passagework, sweeping the keyboard up and down more than four octaves for development of smoothness in thumb movements; a left-hand melody needs subtle pedaling. Von Bülow called it "a bravura study par excellence."

Op. 10, No. 9 in F minor: A left-hand figure of wide extension, needing endurance (especially for small hands), and a developed rotational freedom in the forearm; its portamento right-hand melody is feverish. The composer marked this etude "Allegro, molto agitato." It is less difficult than many others.

Op. 10, No. 10 in A-flat major: James Friskin describes this as "a tiring Etude for the right hand, which has a continuous octave position with rotation from single notes for thumb to sixths for second and fifth fingers. There are ingenious variations of touch and rhythm." John Ogdon feels that in its cross-rhythms, "Chopin's influence on Brahms may be clearly seen here." Von Bülow attests, "He who can play this study in a really finished manner may congratulate himself on having climbed to the highest point of the pianist's Parnassus." Musically, Chopin takes us to heights of Romantic poetry with breathtaking modulations.

Op. 10, No. 11 in E-flat major: Both hands play in extended arpeggios of chords, harp-like in effect or, in Huneker's words, "as if the guitar had been dowered with a soul." Perching on top of these arabesques is a melody needing delicate tonal balance and phrasing.

Op. 10, No. 12 in C minor: Almost universally called the *Revolutionary* Etude, it is a complex left-hand study in continuous sixteenth notes. The right-hand theme requires tonal discrimination. Moritz Karasowski wrote of this popular work that "the image is evoked of Zeus hurling thunderbolts at the world." Huneker called the opening "the crack of creation."

Op. 25, No. 1 in A-flat major: This is often called the *Aeolian Harp*. The weak fifth finger encounters a singing melody above a web of melting textures. A work of melodic magic, and one of the less taxing of the Etudes.

Op. 25, No. 2 in F minor: A study in cross-rhythms, requiring delicate finger articulation for its characteristic Chopinesque whisper.

Op. 25, No. 3 in F major: Theodor Kullak tells us that its "kernel lies in the simultaneous application of four different little rhythms to form a single figure." Ogdon hears it as "a study in the precise rhythmic values of ornaments," and Friskin wrote, "A light and independent action from the wrist for each beat constitutes an appropriate technique."

Op. 25, No. 4 in A minor: Ronald Smith says of this study, "A leaping staccato left hand throughout is combined with subtly varied, syncopated right-hand chords." The left hand is devilishly difficult to attain accuracy in.

Op. 25, No. 5 in E minor: Once called the Wrong Note Etude because of the piquant grace notes. The study demands variations of touch. This is one of the few Etudes with a middle section: a melody in the tenor register with an effective right-hand figuration. The effect is Thalbergian. The little recitativo coda with trills in both hands is the highest level of pianistic imagination.

Op. 25, No. 6 in G-sharp minor: The most hazardous study in thirds in the literature of the instrument. Louis Ehlert concludes, "Chopin not only versifies an exercise in thirds, he transforms it into such a work of art that in studying it one could sooner fancy himself on Parnassus than at a lesson."

Op. 25, No. 7 in C-sharp minor: Ronald Smith calls the form "a Sarabande which links the harmonic worlds of Bach and Wagner." Von Bülow thought of it as a duet for cello and flute. It is a study in touches calling for discreet tonal balance.

Op. 25, No. 8 in D-flat major: An etude in sixths which can be harmful to a small hand if not practiced with care. Von Bülow thought it "the most useful exercise in the whole range of the Etude literature. . . . As a remedy for stiff fingers and preparatory to performing in public, playing it six times through is recommended, even to the most expert pianist." But I warn, not six times at top speed.

Op. 25, No. 9 in G-flat major: Rather aptly termed the Butterfly Etude. Good wrist octaves and endurance are necessary for the projection of this puckish creation.

Op. 25, No. 10 in B minor: A fierce study in legato octaves in both hands. Frederick Niecks calls it "a real pandemonium." It is fearsome in its demand for endurance and can tax a small hand. The etude possesses for the sake of both musical and physical relief a middle section in B major of lyrical beauty.

Op. 25, No. 11 in A minor: Known as the Winter Wind. The left hand has a stately marchlike theme; the right hand projects an immense canvas with complex chromaticism. One of the most turbulent of the set, it asks for tremendous hand malleability.

Op. 25, No. 12 in C minor: An etude requiring powerful weight control and balance for arpeggios in both hands. A work of great majesty and starkness, it has often been called the Ocean Etude.

Etudes, Opp. 10 and 25:
ANIEVAS: Seraphim
ARRAU: EMI
ASHKENAZY: Melodiya; London
BACHAUS: Pearl
BROWNING: RCA
CIANI: Dynamic
CORTOT: Dante
CORTOT: Philips: Great Pianists of the Twentieth Century
CYZIFFRA: Philips: Great Pianists of the Twentieth Century
FRIEDMAN (four etudes): Pearl
GINZBURG: Melodiya
KUERTI (Op. 25 only): Monitor
LORTIE: Chandos
OHLSSON: Arabesque
PERAHIA: Sony Classical
PERLEMUTER: Nimbus
POLLINI: DG
SAPERTON: IPA–Desmar
SLOBODYANIK: Melodiya/Angel
VÁSÁRY: DG
VERED: Connoisseur Society
WILD: Chesky

Trois Nouvelles Etudes (1840)

These were written for a piano method published by Moscheles. They make a fine six-minute set. No. 1 in F minor has a long melody of restrained passion, its technical use being three notes in the right hand to be played against four in the left hand. No. 2 in A-flat is all sweetness in its polyrhythmic movement. No. 3 in D-flat is a wickedly difficult study which asks for the playing of legato and staccato simultaneously in the same hand.

ASHKENAZY: London
AX: RCA
BEREKOVSKY: Teldec
OHLSSON: Arabesque
RUBINSTEIN: RCA

Fantaisie in F minor, Op. 49 (1841)

This large-scaled composition is considered one of Chopin's masterpieces. The Fantasy opens with a solemn and mysterious marchlike introduction leading to a passionate drama with a central chorale, Lento sostenuto, of unusual serenity. Niecks felt "Chopin's genius had now reached the most perfect stage of its development and was radiating with all the intensity of which its nature was capable."

ARRAU: Philips
ASHKENAZY: London
DARRÉ: Vanguard
GIMPEL: Cambria Classics
GIMPEL: Genesis
HOROWITZ: Philips: Great Pianists of the Twentieth Century
HOROWITZ: RCA
KATCHEN: Philips: Great Pianists of the Twentieth Century
MICHELANGELI: Music and Arts
NISSMAN: Pierian
P. SERKIN: Pro Arte
PERAHIA: CBS
PIRES: DG
RUBINSTEIN: RCA
SMITH: APR
SOLOMON: Philips: Great Pianists of the Twentieth Century
ZIMERMAN: DG

Four Impromptus

Impromptu No. 1 in A-flat major, Op. 29: The First Impromptu is carefree as a lark. George

Du Maurier had poor Trilby sing it under the tutelage of Svengali. Jean Kleczynski wrote, "Here everything totters from the foundation to summit, and everything is, nevertheless, so beautiful and so clear."

Impromptu No. 2 in F-sharp major, Op. 36: The greatest and most difficult of the Impromptus, it resembles a Chopin Ballade. An elusive work demanding the utmost delicacy in the delivery of the passagework.

Impromptu No. 3 in G-flat major, Op. 51: A little-known piece, with some rather difficult double notes. The theme has a serpentine, even morbid quality. But Huneker declares that "the Impromptu flavor is not missing, and there is allied to delicacy of design a strangeness of sentiment; that strangeness which Poe declared should be a constituent element of all great art." The improvisatory element must be brought out for a performance to succeed.

Impromptu No. 4 in C-sharp minor, Op. 66 (posth.), *Fantaisie-Impromptu:* Countless pianists of all persuasions have attempted the *Fantaisie-Impromptu.* It was composed in 1834, and it predates the other Impromptus. The opening, in its Bellinian coloratura, is alluring. The trio is a bit too long and mawkish. The coda uses the trio theme in an ingenious manner.

Four Impromptus:
ANIEVAS: EMI
ASHKENAZY: London
CZIFFRA: Connoisseur Society
FRANÇOIS: Philips: Great Pianists of the Twentieth Century
FRANKL: ASV
GINZBURG: Melodiya
HORSZOWSKI: Vox
OHLSSON: Arabesque
PERAHIA: CBS
RUBINSTEIN: RCA
SIMON: Vox

TOMSIC: PMF
VÁSÁRY: DG

The Mazurkas

The sixty mazurkas are based on the dance's three main forms: the mazur, oberek, and kujawiak. One-half of them are composed in major keys, the other half in minor, with many moments of modality. The Chopin Mazurkas form one of the great libraries of ethnically inspired art music. They are difficult to interpret; besides their own specific rhythms, they require a fine sense of rubato. The English critic of Chopin's day, Henry Chorley, wrote, "They lose half their meaning if played without a certain freedom and license, impossible to imitate, but irresistible if the player at all feels the music." Liszt remarked that "to do justice to the mazurkas, one would have to harness a new pianist of the first rank to each one of them." These works explore a harmonic kingdom which is unusual even for Chopin. Some are modal, with many subtleties in contrapuntal treatment. Arthur Hedley observed, "The Mazurkas contain beauties which Chopin reserved for these intimate tone-poems alone. Every kind of light and shade, of gaiety, gloom, eloquence and passion is to be found in them."

James Huneker's effulgent description must not be missed: "No compositions are so Chopin-ish as the mazurkas. Ironical, sad, sweet, joyous, morbid, sour, sane and dreamy, they illustrate what was said of their composer—his heart is sad, his mind is gay . . . they are epigrammatic, fluctuating, crazy and tender, and some of them have a soft melancholy light, as if shining through alabaster—true corpse light leading to a morass of doubt and terror. But a fantastic, disheveled, debonair spirit is the guide, and to him we abandon ourselves in these precise and vertiginous dances."

In the epoch-making four mazurkas of

Op. 6, the twenty-year-old Chopin announces to the world his unique Slavic genius. Jean Kleczynski says, "In these first mazurkas at once appears that national life from which, as from an inexhaustible treasury, Chopin drew his inspirations."

Mazurka in F-sharp minor, Op. 6, No. 1: It begins with the triplet rhythm, a characteristic of the mazurka. It possesses a slight sadness in tonality but is filled with a sweet country bloom. "The third section," wrote Huneker, "with the appoggiaturas, realizes a vivid vision of country couples dancing determinedly." Chopin leaves the score without tempo marking. Already apparent in this first mazurka is a deep psychological content which becomes fused with the folk spirit to create an art of universal significance.

Mazurka in C-sharp minor, Op. 6, No. 2: It opens in shrouded mystery with a drone bass; the trio, marked "gajo" (merrily), is a fine example of Chopin's tonal ambiguity. It could be E major or in the Lydian mode. This mazurka is a masterpiece by one who had, as a child, assimilated the spiritual qualities of this Polish national dance. Jean Kleczynski speaks of "a song so sad, heartfelt, naive, diversified and caressing."

Mazurka in E major, Op. 6, No. 3: This mazurka is ninety measures long, but as usual Chopin is prodigal with his material. After a four-measure drone bass, there follows a four-measure phrase in the bass with the right hand crossing over the left hand. This is used four times in the piece. Chopin goes on to paint a village scene in an upward-moving theme which outlines the key of E major. After two more themes there appears in measures 47–48 an exotic unison, marked "stretto," leading to yet another theme. The rustic theme is repeated, and all ends merrily in a four-measure coda.

Mazurka in E-flat minor, Op. 6, No. 4: In twenty-four highly compressed measures, with measures 9–24 repeated, the mazurka is laden with sorrow. The ending floats away.

Mazurka in B-flat major, Op. 7, No. 1: A scherzando theme proclaims the happiest mazurka thus far—a village dance for rosy-cheeked partners. The trio, marked "sotto voce," has a drone bass using an exotic scale with an augmented second. The Op. 7, No. 1 is one of the best known of all the mazurkas.

Mazurka in A minor, Op. 7, No. 2: A pretty mazurka, though less original than the preceding ones.

Mazurka in F minor, Op. 7, No. 3: Guitarlike chords accompany this masterful work. At one point, the left hand presents a solo which sings from the heart, with the right hand accompanying in simple chords. One of the finest of the early mazurkas.

Mazurka in A-flat major, Op. 7, No. 4: Far more complex than it seems on first hearing, this mazurka is harmonically interesting, while lacking the melodic fragrance of the preceding one.

Mazurka in C major, Op. 7, No. 5: Twenty measures long, as if a strain of a folk mazurka from Chopin's childhood had crept into his consciousness. It has a carefree happiness with lusty overtones.

Mazurka in B-flat major, Op. 17, No. 1: Huneker calls the mazurka "bold and chivalric." Niecks also finds here "the marked chivalrous element that distinguishes the Polish character."

Mazurka in E minor, Op. 17, No. 2: Niecks thinks that in this mazurka "all the arts of persuasion arc tried, from the pathetic to the playful, and a vein of longing, not unmixed with sadness, runs through the whole, or rather forms the basis of it."

Mazurka in A-flat major, Op. 17, No. 3: Pessimistic but not gloomy, this inward-looking composition is one to be played in solitude, rather than on the recital stage.

Mazurka in A minor, Op. 17, No. 4: This long, languid mazurka opens as it ends, with chords in the left hand for three measures, pursuing a vague triplet in measure four. In shaping his mazurka theme, Chopin uses more aristocratic and decorative figuration than usual. But the trio is earthier, with an almost grating quality; a marvelous unison passage leads back to the main theme.

Mazurka in G minor, Op. 24, No. 1: An attractive and exotic piece, of little technical difficulty.

Mazurka in C major, Op. 24, No. 2: Highly original, with its exotic use of the Lydian mode for fifteen bars.

Mazurka in A-flat major, Op. 24, No. 3: A work of delicate charm with a coda that seems to die away in the breeze.

Mazurka in B-flat minor, Op. 24, No. 4: The finest and most elaborate of the Op. 24. Huneker calls it "a beautiful and exquisitely colored poem. . . . It sends out prehensile filaments that entwine and draw us into the center of a wondrous melody, laden with rich odors, odors that almost intoxicate. The figuration is tropical." A complicated work; its form is A B A C D A with coda.

Mazurka in C minor, Op. 30, No. 1: A beautiful specimen, short in time, long in emotional significance. The "con anima" section "stabs with its pathos," in Huneker's phrase.

Mazurka in B minor, Op. 30, No. 2: A sprightly mazurka of less importance.

Mazurka in D-flat major, Op. 30, No. 3: Has a characteristic lilt, with marvelous details. Another fine "con anima" section. The term as used by Chopin means "with heart."

Mazurka in C-sharp minor, Op. 30, No. 4: One of Chopin's supreme works in the form. Paul Hamburger speaks of "the tragic heroism of this Mazurka." Often noted are the extraordinary descending seventh chords before the ending. Schumann, who first reviewed the set when it was published in 1835, wrote, "Chopin has elevated the mazurka to an art form; he has written many, yet few among them resemble each other." One is reminded of Shelley's line, "Our sweetest songs are those that tell of saddest thought."

Mazurka in G-sharp minor, Op. 33, No. 1: A plaintive mazurka, less complex than many of the others. One of its themes is marked "appassionato," the only use of that marking in all of the mazurkas.

Mazurka in D major, Op. 33, No. 2: A delightful specimen; bright, cheerful, and popular.

Mazurka in C major, Op. 33, No. 3: A heartfelt little piece demanding that unique Chopinesque rubato, which was so new, fragrant, and wayward in Chopin's own playing. Chopin was furious with Meyerbeer when the opera composer accused him of playing this piece in 4/4 instead of 3/4 time.

Mazurka in B minor, Op. 33, No. 4: Among the longest of the mazurkas, it was once a popular favorite. In dull hands the work can sound repetitious, as the first theme returns eight times. Schumann wrote of the Op. 33

set that Chopin's "forms seem to grow ever brighter and lighter."

Mazurka in C-sharp minor, Op. 41, No. 1: Of the four mazurkas contained in Op. 41, the thirty-year-old Chopin wrote to the pianist Julius Fontana, "I have four new mazurkas. They seem to me pretty, as the youngest children usually do when the parents grow old." However, pretty is hardly the word for these four minutes with their depth, complexity, and passion. This is one of the great mazurkas, universal in its impact but Polish to the core, despite Schumann's complaint that in the later mazurkas Chopin was losing his Sarmatian skin. This mazurka is symphonic in scope and breadth. Huneker declares that "here is the very apotheosis of rhythm."

Mazurka in E minor, Op. 41, No. 2: There is an almost unbearable nostalgia in this mazurka, which rises to an outcry near the end, when the theme becomes fortissimo and sostenuto.

Mazurka in B major, Op. 41, No. 3: A fascinating dance, seldom played, ending with the same piquant melody that introduced it.

Mazurka in A-flat major, Op. 41, No. 4: Filled with light, goodwill, and the radiance of youth. There is an almost valselike lilt.

Mazurka in G major, Op. 50, No. 1: The set of three mazurkas of Op. 50, composed in 1841, shows an ever-growing subtlety of style, both harmonically and structurally. No. 1 in particular is melodious and good-humored.

Mazurka in A-flat major, Op. 50, No. 2: Here is the embodiment of graciousness. Huneker calls it "a perfect specimen of the aristocratic mazurka." The D-flat trio is fetching.

Mazurka in C-sharp minor, Op. 50, No. 3: One of Chopin's great essays in the form. Hamburger sees in the mazurkas in C-sharp minor (Op. 30, No. 4; Op. 41, No. 1; and Op. 50, No. 3) "a common mood of nostalgia—more than that, of almost regal bitterness over the passing of Poland's glory." Henry T. Finck wrote, "His love for his country was exceeded only by his devotion to his art." Chopin, writing to a friend, remarked, "Oh, how sad it must be to die in a foreign country." In this mazurka, Romantic patriotism is wedded to high art. Chopin's study of Bach is also finely integrated in a complicated structure ending with a wondrous coda.

Mazurka in B major, Op. 56, No. 1: Critics such as Niecks, Huneker, and others were less attracted to the later mazurkas, which have since come to be understood as among Chopin's greatest works. For Niecks, these pieces had lost the *beautés sauvages*: "They strike us rather by their propriety of manner and scholarly elaboration." The B major work, writes James Friskin, "is interesting for its succession of keys: B–E-flat (i.e., D-sharp, the mediant)– B–G (sub-mediant)–B." The mazurka is elaborate and refined, with the E-flat section a chain of finely spun leggiero passagework.

Mazurka in C major, Op. 56, No. 2: Thomas Fielden wrote, "Performers should bear in mind the saying that 'an Eastern European is born with a violin in his hand.' In every Mazurka there is a violin atmosphere." Fielden feels "this Mazurka is in the form of a dialogue between a violin and a cello." Chopin here displays his ever-growing contrapuntal imagination.

Mazurka in C minor, Op. 56, No. 3: Huneker thinks "it is composed with the head, not the heart, nor yet the heels." The very long C minor Mazurka is symphonic in breadth, serious, beautiful, mature; its coda is glorious.

Here Chopin brings the form to its most elevated state.

Mazurka in A minor, Op. 59, No. 1: A long work of astounding genius; the greatest of the six mazurkas in A minor. It reminded Huneker of "some strange glade wherein the flowers are rare in scent." The chromaticism is dense, with considerable contrapuntal activity. The trio in A major is complex. There follows the mazurka's main theme, heard in G-sharp minor.

Mazurka in A-flat major, Op. 59. No. 2: Sir William Henry Hadow goes so far as to call this "perhaps the most beautiful of all the mazurkas." Friskin calls attention to "an astonishing passage of chromatic harmony leading to a delightful coda."

Mazurka in F-sharp minor, Op. 59, No. 3: A pungent work. Huneker feels that "Chopin is at the summit of his invention. Time and tune, that wait for no man, are now his bond slaves. Pathos, delicacy, boldness, a measured melancholy and the art of euphonious presentment of all these, and many factors more, stamp this mazurka a masterpiece."

Mazurka in B major, Op. 63, No. 1: The last set of Chopin's mazurkas, Op. 63, was published in 1847, and for all the hidden complexity, there is a return to the earlier feeling of charming simplicity so apparent in the mazurkas of his youth. The B major work is vivacious, with a fascinating contour.

Mazurka in F minor, Op. 63, No. 2: Two pages of music of a lingering sadness.

Mazurka in C-sharp minor, Op. 63, No. 3: By far the best known of this group. It possesses an eloquent lyricism and concludes with a display of Chopin's contrapuntal skill. "A more perfect canon at the octave," wrote Louis Ehlert, "could not have been written by one who has grown gray in the learned art." But Huneker slyly observes that "Chopin wears his learning lightly."

There remain the posthumous mazurkas, written in various years; four are gathered in Op. 67, the best being No. 4 in A minor. Exotic in coloration, it is often played. Op. 68 contains four mazurkas; the last, in F minor, from 1849, is Chopin's last work. It is subdued, morbid, and intensely chromatic. Finck calls it of "heartrending sadness and exquisite pathos." The desperate composer, near death, hardly had the strength to write it out. Also of interest is the seldom-played Mazurka in A minor from 1841. The A major section is all in octaves, and the piece ends with a ten measure trill.

BRAILOWSKY (51 mazurkas): CBS
FRIEDMAN (12): Pearl
FRIEDMAN: Philips: Great Pianists of the Twentieth Century
HOROWITZ (6): CBS
HOROWITZ: Philips: Great Pianists of the Twentieth Century
INDJIC (56): Claves
KAPELL (10): RCA
KAPELL (18): International Piano Archives at Maryland (IPA is housed at the University of Maryland)
MAGALOFF (51): London
MALCUZYNSKI (13): Angel
MICHELANGELI (10): DG
NOVAES (9): Vox
REISENBERG (56): Insync
ROSEN (24): Globe
RUBINSTEIN (51): RCA

The Nocturnes

The nocturne represents one of the great genres of Romantic art. Chopin inherited the species from John Field and proceeded to obliterate Field's charming naïveté with

461

his own highly chromatic and sultry genius. It is said that Field, upon hearing Chopin's first three nocturnes, exclaimed, "Chopin's talent is of the sick-room." The last critic to prefer Field seems to have been the German anti-Chopinist Ludwig Rellstab: "Where Field smiles, Chopin makes a grinning grimace; where Field sighs, Chopin groans; where Field puts some seasoning into the food, Chopin empties a handful of pepper. . . . If one holds Field's charming nocturnes before a distorting, concave mirror, one gets Chopin's work."

The Chopin night pieces bewitched countless nineteenth-century composers, and soon this category of music became so stereotyped as to cause Moscheles to exclaim, "What antidotes have we here for all these morbid moanings and over-wrought effects! . . . A composer brought me a nocturne of so restless a description that it threatened to disturb my nocturnal rest." Although Chopin had an instant success with many of them, the Nocturnes are generally the worst-played pieces of his output. Yet they remain critical works for the pianist in the development of a fine cantilena, the shaping of phrases, and tonal balance. Louis Kentner thinks that if pianists neglect the Nocturnes, they "are guilty of peevish discrimination, for if these pieces are 'too sweet', or not very 'relevant' to our cheerless age, they are still expressive of another, happier age, and therefore entitled to bring pleasure to us poor deprived humans."

The lure of the Nocturnes still remains powerfully potent; few poet-pianists have failed to lavish their best efforts on them. Chopin, in these atmospheric works, let flow the full power of his voluptuous melodic gift, in piano writing that remains remarkable to this day. They are love poems of the finest ardor, and within each one an intimate human drama is explored. Henry T. Finck declares, "Mendelssohn in *A Midsummer Night's Dream* and Weber in *Oberon* have given us glimpses of dreamland, but Chopin's

Nocturnes take us there bodily, and plunge us into reveries more delicious than the visions of an opium eater." Daniel Gregory Mason declared, "Chopin is one of the supreme masters in the coloristic use of the dissonance. His Nocturnes may fairly be said to inaugurate by this means a new era in music, comparable in many respects to the era of impressionism in painting." Alfred de Musset could have been thinking of Chopin when writing, "The most despairing songs are the most beautiful."

Nocturne in B-flat minor, Op. 9, No. 1: Composed when Chopin was twenty-two years old. A work of sumptuous phraseology, already it offers an elongation of the Field nocturne in the long-limbed opening theme. Charles Willeby wrote, "What could be more *triste* than the phrase in D-flat . . . marked legatissimo." The middle section is quite long and, in Huneker's words, "of exceeding charm. As a melody it has all the lurking voluptuousness and mystic crooning of its composer. . . . There is passion peeping out in the coda." For Jean Kleczynski, this nocturne "exhibits a thrilling sadness, together with a novel eloquence of construction." In the middle section he feels "as though the soul were sinking beneath the weight of thought and the heat of a summer's night." The B-flat minor Nocturne is a work of significance and is seldom played.

Nocturne in E-flat major, Op. 9, No. 2: The most famous of the nocturnes, indeed, it ranks high in celebrity among all of Chopin's works. It has been played rotten with sentimentality and now deserves a respite. One can still feel the suave, glamorous atmosphere of the fashionable Parisian salon which pervades this work.

Nocturne in B major, Op. 9, No. 3: Chopin's love for great singing must ever be in the interpreter's mind when performing the Nocturnes. The B major Nocturne is luscious, with ornamental vocalization on the piano. The ghost-like theme is deeply penetrating, while the middle section is turbulent and convulsive. This nocturne is a masterful early work and is rather unknown. The Op. 9 set was fittingly dedicated to the bewitching pianist Mme. Camille Pleyel, née Moke. All who heard her play fell in love, among them Berlioz, Ferdinand Hiller, and Liszt.

Nocturne in F major, Op. 15, No. 1: The three nocturnes of this opus were dedicated to Ferdinand Hiller. The F major Nocturne is played less often than the Op. 15, No. 2; however, it is a gem, with its serene and tender Andante theme, followed by a trio marked "Con fuoco," magnificently planned in double notes. H. Barbedette, a writer who often heard Chopin perform, perceives "a calm and beautiful lake, ruffled by a sudden storm and becoming calm again." Finck rightfully complains that "few know how to use the pedal in such a way as to produce the rich uninterrupted flow of tone on which the melody should float."

Nocturne in F-sharp major, Op. 15, No. 2: One of the popular nocturnes; it is of a ravishing beauty, exhibiting a heavenly melody. Niecks says "the fioritura flit about us lightly as gossamer threads." The middle section, Doppio movimento, shows Chopin's command of pianistic notation. No composer had thus far been so explicit and original in showing to the pianist, on the page, what was needed. The increased motion of the middle section, with its novel figuration in quintuplets, possesses a burning passion.

Nocturne in G minor, Op. 15, No. 3: The first theme is marked "languido e rubato," with the second section marked "religioso." The G minor work is a slow-moving, feverish piece, of less value than the two preceding nocturnes. Huneker tells of a performance by

Anton Rubinstein where "in the fourth bar, and for three bars, there is a held note, F, and I heard the Russian virtuoso, by some miraculous means, keep this tone prolonged. . . . Under Rubinstein's fingers it swelled and diminished, and went soaring into D, as if the instrument were an organ."

Nocturne in C-sharp minor, Op. 27, No. 1: The critic Alan Rich considers this nocturne "one of the most personal utterances in the entire realm of piano music." Finck feels that "it embodies a greater variety of emotion and more genuine dramatic spirit on four pages than many popular operas on four hundred." The work is tragic, menacing, at times hopeless. The form is A B A and coda. The central section, marked "Più mosso," has a restless, vehement power. The coda once again reminds the listener of Chopin's seemingly inexhaustible prodigality. In Thomas Mann's novel *Dr. Faustus*, he writes of this nocturne that it "surpasses in despairing beauty of sound all the Tristan orgies."

Nocturne in D-flat major, Op. 27, No. 2: This exquisite piece, in one continuous mood, is the essence of fioritura. It is a favorite nocturne but demands a highly developed technical skill. Professor Niecks was fearful of the power of this luscious work: "Nothing can equal the finish and delicacy of execution, the flow of gentle feeling lightly rippled by melancholy, and spreading out here and there in smooth expansiveness. But all this sweetness enervates, there is poison in it. We should not drink in these thirds, sixths, etcetera, without taking an antidote of Bach or Beethoven."

Lennox Berkeley writes: "A close study of this piece reveals the individuality of Chopin's piano writing; the proliferation of the arabesques that embellish the theme are of a kind that is his own invention, bearing little resemblance to the work of any other composer."

The melody is violinistic, yet to transcribe

the piece is to destroy its very essence. It can only be sung upon the piano.

Nocturne in B major, Op. 32, No. 1: A nocturne of less importance, though characteristic in design and melodic contour. However, a surprising coda of amazing originality completely shocks the listener out of reverie. Berkeley calls it an ending that "defies analysis, but compels acceptance." To Huneker, this little recitativo "is like the drum-beat of tragedy."

Nocturne in A-flat major, Op. 32, No. 2: A long, gracious melody with a balletic middle section. Indeed, the work is important in the ballet *Les Sylphides,* choreographed to Chopin's music. The A-flat Nocturne, though attractive, is less important than other members of this species.

Nocturne in G minor, Op. 37, No. 1: Also of lesser importance. Karasowski says it "keeps up a ceaseless sad thought, until interrupted by a church-like atmosphere in chords."

Nocturne in G major, Op. 37, No. 2: Once far more popular than at present. Its main theme in euphonious thirds and sixths gives it a barcarolle, Venetian flavor. The Victorian Niecks finds "a beautiful sensuousness; it is luscious, soft, rounded, and not without a certain degree of languor. But let us not tarry too long in the treacherous atmosphere of this Capua—it bewitches and unmans." The view of Chopin's music as a dangerous aphrodisiac was once prevalent. Kentner warns us that the Nocturnes should not "suffer critical degradation because sentimental young ladies used them, in days long gone by, to comfort their repressed libido."

Nocturne in C minor, Op. 48, No. 1: In grandeur of conception, the C minor Nocturne is unrivaled among its companions. The work, composed in 1841, finds Chopin's genius blooming, reaching new vistas of emotional power. The Doppio movimento section has an almost Beethovenian ethical ring. For Kullak, "the design and poetic contents of this nocturne make it the most important one that Chopin created; the chief subject is a masterly expression of a great powerful grief."

Nocturne in F-sharp minor, Op. 48, No. 2: A subtle and recondite nocturne. It is interpretively difficult, with a discursive middle section in D-flat which is a kind of recitative. The main theme is chaste and transparent, and of an unusual length, with a veiled passion throughout.

Nocturne in F minor, Op. 55, No. 1: Teachers often prescribe this nocturne for students grappling with Chopin's style. It is technically easier than many, though it lacks the melodic distinction of its companion nocturnes. Huneker calls it "a nice nocturne, neat in its sorrow."

Nocturne in E-flat major, Op. 55, No. 2: A work of striking beauty and exquisite intricacy. Berkeley notes, "Here no analysis can explain the natural growth of the melodic line." In the last twenty years, the E-flat Nocturne has become recognized by pianists as a spiritualization of the form. One has only to compare the Field-like E-flat Nocturne of Op. 9, No. 2, to understand how far Chopin had traveled in pianistic layout and harmonic plenitude based on a personal contrapuntal approach and a rarefication of melody. The coda is again a passage of breathtaking inspiration.

Nocturne in B major, Op. 62, No. 1: A work of pure luxuriance; the main theme is profusely adorned with difficult chain trills. In his book on Chopin, Camille Bourniquel writes, "The last Nocturnes complete the redemption of the genre and its final liberations—they possess a unique freedom." Gerald Abraham feels they "illustrate the principle of motive-generated melody in continuous cantabile form."

Nocturne in E major, Op. 62, No. 2: The eighteenth nocturne and the last one published during Chopin's life; a luminous and melting composition. It foreshadows Fauré's work in the nocturne genre. Ernest Hutcheson wrote, "This is one of Chopin's sostenuto melodies, warm and luscious like the G string of a violin." The middle section is agitated.

Nocturne No. 19 in E minor, Op. 72, and *Nocturne in C-sharp minor,* Op. posth.: The E minor Nocturne is the earliest piece by Chopin in nocturne form, composed when he was seventeen, and it is still played often. The popular C-sharp minor is a pastiche of his nocturne style, with passages from his F minor Concerto. Friskin describes it as "a poverty-stricken nocturne." It is now published in most Nocturne editions, although Chopin did not title the piece.

The Nocturnes:
ARRAU: Philips
ASHKENAZY: London
BARENBOIM: DG
BIRET: Naxos
CIANI: Arkadia
FOU TS'ONG: Sony Classical
GODOWSKY (12): Philips: Great Pianists of
  the Twentieth Century
KATIN: Unicorn
LEONSKAJA: Teldec
LIMA: Arabesque
MORAVEC: Elektra/Nonesuch
NOVAES: Vox
OHLSSON: Angel
RUBINSTEIN: RCA
VASARY (15): DG
WEISSENBERG: Angel

Separate Nocturnes of note:
BUSONI (Op. 15, No. 2): Pearl

FLIER (Op. 62, No. 2): Westminster
FRIEDMAN (Op. 55, No. 2): Pearl
HOFMANN (Op. 15, No. 2): RCA; IPA
LOESSER (Op. 9, No. 3): IPA
DE PACHMANN (Op. 37, No. 2): Pearl
POGORELICH (Op. 55, No. 2): DG
RACHMANINOFF (Op. 9, No. 2 and Op. 15,
  No. 2): RCA
P. SERKIN (Op. 48, No. 2): RCA
SOLOMON (Op. 9, No. 2): EMI

The Polonaises

From the first, the polonaise was important in Chopin's creative life. At the age of seven, he composed his first one, in B-flat major, and throughout his career he made the form exclusively his own, overshadowing the early examples by Oginski, Kurpinski, and Meyseder.

Chopin's mature polonaises form a heroic national epic. The dance, or more rightly the processional, is in triple time with an unmistakable rhythm featuring an eighth note and two sixteenths, followed by four eighths. Liszt felt that "this dance is designed above all to draw attention to the men and to gain admiration for their beauty, their fine arts, their martial and courteous appearance."

In these works, Chopin's Romantic patriotism envisions Poland's former greatness and chivalric deeds. The form also became a means of expressing his most violent and angry emotions concerning his nation's struggle. The Polonaises, with their "cannon buried in flowers," in Schumann's words, have become symbolic and poignant evocations of an oppressed people.

There are sixteen polonaises, of which nine were composed before Chopin left Poland at twenty-one. These are charming, especially the Op. 71, No. 3 in F minor. But only in Paris, idealizing his country from afar, could Chopin's genius for the polonaise ripen. His seven mature examples are thrilling in their splendor, rancor, and pianistic invention.

Polonaise in C-sharp minor, Op. 26, No. 1: It opens with an arrestingly grand statement, but the main character of the work is lyric. Once played frequently, the C-sharp minor Polonaise ought to be revived. The Meno mosso section is exquisite, in Huneker's words "tender enough to woo a princess."

Polonaise in E-flat minor, Op. 26, No. 2: A tragic tone poem which requires depth of expression on the part of the pianist to fulfill its savage, brooding character. The E-flat minor Polonaise is sometimes called *The Siberian Revolt.* The discontent of the work, its wild anger, makes this neglected polonaise one of Chopin's most realistic compositions. Janácek must have loved this Slavonic masterpiece.

Polonaise in A major, Op. 40, No. 1: Often called the Military; a world-famous piece, splendid in its pomp and glory, its chivalry and lean muscularity.

Polonaise in C minor, Op. 40, No. 2: Anton Rubinstein saw in this a gloomy picture of Poland's downfall, just as the Polonaise in A major was a portrait of its former greatness. The C minor Polonaise is seldom played. It is an enigmatic yet noble composition.

Polonaise in F-sharp minor, Op. 44: A raw and overwhelming work when played properly. Huneker asks us to "consider the musical weight of the work, the recklessly bold outpourings of a mind almost distraught! There is no greater test for the poet-pianist." Liszt called it the "lurid hour that precedes a hurricane." The central section is a mazurka preceded by two pages of the strangest monotony, reverberating madly. The psychological impact is shattering. This work finds Chopin's spirit far from the elegant world of the Parisian salon. John Ogdon sees in it a "Goya-like intensity" and said that the "almost inhumanly severe modulations imply a barbarism which becomes explicit in the atavistic passage (over a pedal A) that prepares its central section. This middle section is a mazurka, thus creating a remarkable coalescence of two different dances."

Polonaise in A-flat major, Op. 53: One of the world's most famous pieces of music, it never fails to thrill. It is Chopin dreaming of an all-powerful Poland. The A-flat Polonaise is the very picture of the martial spirit. It has been called the Heroic Polonaise, and its majestic octave episode in E major resounds with the hooves of a proud cavalry. After "this central episode," wrote Ogdon, "Chopin's return to the main section is a tour de force: few composers would have dared and achieved so apparently wayward and capricious a return in so grandiose a work." Huneker cautions, "None but the heroes of the keyboard may grasp its dense chordal masses, its fiery projectiles of tone."

Polonaise-fantaisie in A-flat major, Op. 61: This late work, published in 1846, ranks with the master's most sublime creations. Chopin had said all he had to say in the form of the polonaise; he was now groping for a new, expansive, and more personal structure—hence the title *Fantaisie.* It took decades for it to be properly understood. Even Liszt was confused by it, saying, "Such pictures as these are of little value to art. They only serve to torture the soul, like all descriptions of extreme moments." The weaving of five themes, the impressionist harmony, the total mystery and profundity present one of the most absorbing interpretive problems in the Chopin canon.

Selected Polonaises:
ASHKENAZY: London

BERMAN: DG
BRAILOWSKY: Sony Classical
CHERKASSKY: DG
CLIDAT: Forlane
FRANKL: Turnabout
HARASIEWICZ: Philips
LIMA: BOMR
MALCUZYNSKI: Angel
OHLSSON: Angel
POLLINI: DG
RUBINSTEIN: RCA

Individual Polonaises of Interest:
ARGERICH (Opp. 53 and 61): DG
AX (Op. 61): RCA
CHERKASSKY (Op. 53): Mercury
FLIER (Op. 26): Westminster
HOFMANN (Op. 26): International Piano
   Archives; (Op. 40, No. 1): RCA
HOROWITZ (Opp. 53 and 61): CBS; (Op. 44):
   CBS
LHÉVINNE (Op. 53): Dante
H. NEUHAUS (Op. 61): Russian Disc
PENNARIO (Op. 53): Angel
P. SERKIN (Op. 61): RCA

Twenty-four Preludes, Op. 28

Within these very small frames, Chopin captures a universe of feeling and mood. There is a prelude for each major and minor key; many of them demand high virtuosity. James Friskin writes, "Perhaps no other collection of piano pieces contains within such a small compass so much that is at the same time musically and technically valuable." Schumann thought them "eagle's feathers, all strangely intermingled. But in every piece we find his own hand—Frédéric Chopin wrote it. One recognizes him in his pauses, in his impetuous respiration. He is the boldest, the proudest, poet-soul of his time." Finck feels that "if all piano music in the world were to be destroyed, excepting one collection, my vote should be

cast for Chopin's Preludes. There are among Chopin's preludes a few which breathe the spirit of contentment and grace, or of religious grandeur, but most of them are outbreaks of the wildest anguish and heartrending pathos. If tears could be heard, they would sound like these preludes."

Prelude No. 1 in C major: An exquisite example of Chopin's devotion to Bach. Pulsating and agitated, it is over in half a minute, leaving the listener yearning for more.

No. 2 in A minor: Slow, indeed perversely morbid, in its musical makeup, but unforgettable.

No. 3 in G major: The right-hand melody is a puff of air. Ernest Hutcheson wrote, "It takes fairy fingers to compass the sun-kissed ripples of the left hand." And Robert Collet exclaims of its difficulties that "the Prelude in G major I regard as one of the most dangerous little pieces ever written."

No. 4 in E minor: A slender melody over a rich, slow-moving chordal accompaniment. Huneker wrote, "Its despair has the antique flavor." It was played, with Nos. 6 and 20, by the famous organist Lefébure-Wély, at Chopin's funeral service at the Madeleine Church in Paris. Mozart's Requiem was also performed.

No. 5 in D major: Very short, with cross-rhythms, intricate and iridescent.

No. 6 in B minor: A cello melody in the left hand; very sad and slow. A famous piece.

No. 7 in A major: Three lines, a skeletonized mazurka, used prominently in the ballet *Les Sylphides*. Even more famous than No. 6.

No. 8 in F-sharp minor: The right-hand

melody is played by the thumb. Chopin writes the chromatic inner voice in smaller notation. This feverish vision is one of the greatest of the preludes.

No. 9 in E major: A work of only twelve measures but also of infinite grandeur.

No. 10 in C-sharp minor: It's over in a blink and needs the lightest fingers.

No. 11 in B major: Concentrated grace and poetry. Huneker says, "Another gleam of the Chopin sunshine."

No. 12 in G-sharp minor: A powerful and despairing work. Technically treacherous.

No. 13 in F-sharp major: A nocturne-like prelude with a middle section. This is a pearl of lyric serenity.

No. 14 in E-flat minor: A unison study of a moment of gloom.

No. 15 in D-flat major: The so-called Raindrop Prelude is the longest of these pieces, with a dramatic middle section. The work has always been popular.

No. 16 in B-flat minor: Perilous right-hand fingerwork as the left hand becomes more explosive. A tour de force for the virtuoso.

No. 17 in A-flat major: A richly colored romance concluding with eleven low A-flats reminiscent of a bell. Mendelssohn wrote, "I love it! I cannot tell you how much or why; except perhaps that it is something which I could never at all have written."

No. 18 in F minor: A difficult prelude in fiery, recitativo style.

No. 19 in E-flat major: Marked "Vivace," a beautiful and difficult piece. To play it through unscathed is an achievement.

No. 20 in C minor: Twelve bars of chords. George Sand had this funereal prelude in mind when she aptly stated that "one prelude of Chopin contains more music than all the trumpetings of Meyerbeer." Rachmaninoff and Busoni used it as the basis for sets of variations.

No. 21 in B-flat major: A nocturne-type prelude with a double-note accompaniment.

No. 22 in G minor: Short and stormy, with left-hand octaves.

No. 23 in F major: Ending on a dominant seventh chord, this prelude has the bliss of a perfect June day. Huneker rhapsodizes, "This prelude is fashioned out of the most volatile stuff. Aerial, imponderable, and like a sunshot spider-web oscillating in the breeze of summer."

No. 24 in D minor: It is a discharge of tremendous emotion marked "Allegro appassionato." The turbulent left hand never relents. Three solo Ds in the bowels of the piano make for a foreboding conclusion.

Twenty-four Preludes:
ARGERICH: DG
ARGERICH: Philips: Great Pianists of the
   Twentieth Century
BOLET: RCA
CORTOT: Music and Arts
CORTOT: Philips: Great Pianists of the
   Twentieth Century
DARRÈ: Vanguard
ESCHENBACH: DG
FELTSMAN: CBS
FLORENTINO: Saga
FREIRE: CBS
KISSIN: RCA

LORTAT: Dante
MORAVEC: Supraphon
OLHSSON: Arabesque
PERAHIA: CBS
POGORELICH: DG

Prelude in C-sharp minor, Op. 45

A seldom-played work of great improvisational beauty. The composition contains far-flung modulations and needs imagination for its presentation. It has nothing in common with the Op. 28 Preludes (although some of the recordings include it).

ARGERICH: DG
PERLEMUTER: Nimbus
POGORELICH: DG

Four Scherzos

Chopin composed four of his greatest creations under the title *Scherzo,* a word that means "a joke." Was Chopin being ironic? Schumann was baffled; when reviewing the B minor Scherzo, he asked, "How are seriousness and gravity to be clothed if jest is to go about in such dark-colored garments?" The title seems appropriate only for No. 4.

The Scherzos are epics among Chopin's works, and their instrumental brilliance has made them staples of the concert hall; each of them demands a highly finished technique.

Scherzo No. 1 in B minor, Op. 20: The First Scherzo was composed most likely in 1834 and first published in 1835. Later, when it was issued in England under the title *The Infernal Banquet,* Chopin, always a purist and opposed to any literary or pictorial allusions, had a fit. The opening must have shocked his contemporaries. Indeed, its almost repellent realism still astonishes. Niecks asks, "Is this not like a shriek of despair?" The material is feverishly restless and tragic in nature. The middle section, marked "Molto più lento," is based on a Polish Christmas carol, "Sleep, Jesus Sleep" (one of Chopin's few uses of actual folk material). The section is worked out in the dreamiest manner until the Scherzo's opening chord interrupts the dream. The first section, which is then repeated, ends in a coda of barbaric splendor, which closes with furious chromatic scales.

Scherzo No. 2 in B-flat minor, Op. 31: The Second Scherzo is the favorite. Schumann compared it to a Byronic poem, "so overflowing with tenderness, boldness, love and contempt." According to Wilhelm von Lenz, a pupil of Chopin, the composer said that the renowned sotto voce opening was a question and the second phrase the answer: "For Chopin it was never questioning enough, never soft enough, never vaulted (*tombé*) enough. It must be a charnel-house." The melody, marked "con anima," is repeated three times during the lengthy proceedings, the last time bringing us to the coda in a magnificent key change. The gorgeous melody overlies a six-note-per-measure left-hand accompaniment of exceeding richness. The trio, filled with longing, takes on a pianistic complexity. Huneker exults, "What masterly writing, and it lies in the very heart of the piano! A hundred generations may not improve on these pages."

Scherzo No. 3 in C-sharp minor, Op. 39: The Third Scherzo opens with an almost Lisztian introduction, leading to a subject in octaves of pent-up energy. The key changes to D-flat major, with a choralelike subject, interspersed with delicate falling arpeggios. Louis Kentner thinks of it as "a Wagnerian melody of astonishing beauty, recalling the sound of tubas, harps and all the apocalyptic orchestra of Valhalla." This is the most terse, ironic, and tightly constructed of the four scherzos, with an almost Beethovenian grandeur. The finger-bursting coda rises to emotional heights, bringing the score to a rhetorical ending.

Scherzo No. 4 in E major, Op. 54: An ethereal composition bathed in light, which ripples over the expanse of the keyboard. It is Chopin in a blessed moment, improvising and happy. His nerves are calm, and his deadly disease in check. Even the long trio, of seraphic lyric beauty, has no sign of morbidezza. The passagework is elegant; the coda is a picture of pastel beauty. It is perhaps the most difficult of the Four Scherzos, technically speaking.

Four Scherzos:
ASHKENAZY: London
AX: Sony Classical
CHERKASSKY: Tudor
DARRÉ: Vanguard
DEMIDENKO: Hyperion
FREIRE: Teldec
KATSARIS: Teldec
RICHTER: CBS/Melodiya
RUBINSTEIN: RCA; (1932) Pearl
SIMON: Vox
VÁSÁRY: DG
WILD: Chesky

Notable Single Scherzos:
AX (Nos. 2 and 4): RCA
BARÈRE (No. 3): Vanguard
CLIBURN (No. 2): RCA
GODOWSKY (No. 4.): Philips: Great Pianists of the Twentieth Century
HOROWITZ (No. 1): CBS
NOVAES (No. 3): Vox
RACHMANINOFF (No. 3): RCA
TIEGERMAN (No. 1): Arbitor
ZIMERMAN (No. 4): DG

Sonata No. 2 in B-flat minor, Op. 35, "Funeral March"

Chopin wrote three piano sonatas. No. 1 in

C minor (1827) was written for his teacher Elsner as a compositional problem. Academic and difficult, it holds almost no interest for pianists. Its third movement is an early example of a 5/4 meter.

The Second Sonata is resplendent. Composed in 1838, it is one of the staple items of the pianist's repertory and contains the world's most famous Funeral March.

This work expresses a life-and-death struggle. The opening movement begins with a portentous motive, leading directly into a Doppio movimento. The grandeur of the conception leads to a lean and inevitable development section. The second movement, a scherzo, echoes the first movement's conflagrations. The *Marche funèbre* is placed as the third movement with extraordinary effect; its trio must not be played sweetly. The finale, composed in unison, is a shudder of grief. This sonata was a specialty of Liszt and of Anton Rubinstein; the latter called it "night winds sweeping over church-yard graves." John Ogdon says, "The finest recording of it is still Rachmaninoff's magnificent, unforgettable performance." Alan Walker wrote, "There are fewer great interpretations of this Sonata than there are great pianists."

ARGERICH: DG
ANDSNES: Virgin Classics
GODOWSKY: APR
HOROWITZ: CBS
KAPELL: RCA
KATZ: Pye
KILENYI: APR
LORTAT: Dante
MICHELANGELI: Praga
NOVAES: Vox
POGORELICH: DG
RACHMANINOFF: RCA
RUBINSTEIN: RCA
SOKOLOV: Opus
UCHIDA: Philips
WATTS: EMI

Sonata No. 3 in B minor, Op. 58

Not as stark as the Second Sonata, No. 3 almost bursts its form in the first movement, so rich are the themes, so vital and ornamental. In this late masterpiece, Chopin is charting new formal and harmonic paths. As in the Second Sonata, he breaks out of the Viennese tradition of sonata form. The recapitulation begins with the second subject, which must be one of the most beautiful melodies ever composed within the confines of sonata form. The second movement is a blithe scherzo in E-flat major, with a chiseled and strange trio. The third movement opens with a funereal introduction leading to one of Chopin's greatest meditations, music that leaves one spellbound. The movement is worked out with formal genius and the last page calls for great profundity of feeling. The agitated finale, Presto, ma non tanto, is a volcanic conception, utilizing only two subjects, worked out on a grand scale. It is a triumph of primordial power.

ARGERICH: DG
ARTYMIW: Chandos
BARDA: Calliope
CHERKASSKY: Nimbus
CLIBURN: RCA
CORTOT: Biddulph
FIORENTINO: APR
FIRKUSNY: Fonè
GILELS: Philips: Great Pianists of the Twentieth Century
GIMPEL: Cambria Classics
GOULD: Sony Classical
GRAINGER: Biddulph
HOFMANN (first movement): RCA
HUNGERFORD: Vanguard
KAPELL: RCA
KISSIN: MK
LIPATTI: Angel
MANSHARDT: APR
MOISEWITCH: Pearl
NOVAES: Vox
OGDON: IMP Classics
PLETNEV: DG
RUBINSTEIN: RCA
SLENCYZNSKA: Ivory Classics
TIEGERMAN: Arbitor
WEISSENBERG: EMI

The Waltzes

Chopin's Waltzes are among the world's most often played piano music. They fall into two styles: gracious and brilliantly decorated, or melancholy. John Ogdon calls them "the brightest jewels in the greatest salons of the time."

The Waltzes are peculiarly Chopinesque. The Viennese waltzes of the day as exemplified by those of Lanner and the elder Johann Strauss were anathema to Chopin's rarefied nature, and after his stay in Vienna he reported, "I have acquired nothing of that which is specially Viennese by nature, and accordingly I am still unable to play valses." The true precursor of the Chopin waltz style is Weber's *Invitation to the Dance*. Arthur Hedley wrote, "The Chopin Waltzes were never meant to be danced by ordinary mundane creatures of flesh and blood."

Grande Valse brillante in E-flat major, Op. 18: One of Chopin's most extroverted works. Insouciant, teasing, high-stepping, it is beloved by the virtuoso. Berlioz spoke of its "divine delicacies." Some of its fetching passages must have inspired Offenbach. Schumann saw it "enveloping the dancers deeper and deeper in floods."

Valse brillante in A-flat major, Op. 34, No. 1: Chopin composed three waltzes in 1838, under the generic title *Trois Valses brillantes*. This waltz is akin in spirit to the *Grande Valse brillante,* Op. 18, but with even more delightful colors. A true ballroom creation, it is marked "Vivace," and Chopin is happy and at ease with the aristocratic veneer of the salon. There is such sparkling life throughout that it feels as though it were improvised at a Dionysian revel.

Valse brillante in A minor, Op. 34, No. 2: The composer Stephen Heller related that Chopin called this slow (Lento) waltz his favorite. When Heller told the Pole that he, too, loved it best, Chopin immediately invited him for lunch at a fashionable café. Frederick Niecks wrote of this piece, "The composer evidently found pleasure in giving way to this delicious languor, in indulging in these melancholy thoughts full of sweetest, tenderest loving and longing."

Valse brillante in F major, Op. 34, No. 3: A witty and little-known waltz. Huneker calls it "a whirling wild dance of atoms." The themes are less distinguished, but the perpetual-motion flavor with its bracing appoggiaturas casts its own spell.

Waltz in A-flat major, Op. 42: A case may be made for the Op. 42 as Chopin's most perfect valse. After the first measures of trill, a call to the dance, there is a melody with a rare lilt composed in double time, with the triple time of the waltz in the left hand. Schumann remarked that "like his earlier waltzes it is a salon piece of the noblest kind." The composition, Schumann feels, should be danced to only by "countesses at least." This waltz is the most demanding technically of the series.

Waltz in D-flat major, Op. 64, No. 1: This all-time favorite of Chopin's waltzes is called the Minute Waltz because of its perpetual-motion attitude. However, it must not be played in that time period. Chopin himself was often compelled to play it, the London society ladies repeatedly exclaiming that it sounded "like water"—a phrase that annoyed the composer.

Waltz in C-sharp minor, Op. 64, No. 2: Huneker declares, "It is the most poetic of all. The first theme has never been excelled by Chopin for a species of veiled melancholy. It is a fascinating, lyrical sorrow." Delicate passagework ensues, followed by a D-flat major section of vocal beauty.

Waltz in A-flat major, Op. 64, No. 3: Seldom performed, because of the popularity of the two preceding waltzes, although it is shapely and finely made. The last of Chopin's waltzes, it has a deft charm. Niecks speaks of its "exquisite serpentining melodic lines, and other beautiful details." The middle section in C major is perfectly poised.

Waltz in A-flat major, Op. 69, No. 1: Published posthumously with the B minor Waltz in 1855. The manuscript has the inscription "*Pour Mlle Marie.*" Chopin wrote this waltz in 1835, while courting Marie Wodzinska. He had fallen in love with the young and beautiful countess and had proposed marriage to her. As a poor musician, however, Chopin was not considered suitable marriage material by Marie's parents, and he was rejected. His Waltz in A-flat was given to Marie just before his departure for Paris. Marked "Lento," this beautiful dance poem has often been called L'Adieu.

Waltz in B minor, Op. 69, No. 2: This often-played work was composed when Chopin was nineteen. The composer wanted it and others of his early works burned, but they were issued posthumously. The piece has three themes; the opening is distinctively Chopinesque in its pensive melancholy.

Other posthumously issued works include three waltzes in Op. 70, all attractive pieces. The best known, No. 1 in G-flat, is a brilliant specimen, and the E minor Waltz, without opus number, composed in 1829, is deservedly popular.

The Waltzes:
ANIEVAS: EMI
BUNIN: Melodiya
CICCOLINI: Seraphim
CORTOT: Seraphim
HAEBLER: Allegretto
KATIN: Music and Arts
KATSARIS: Teldec
KOCSIS: Philips
LAPATTI: Odyssey; Angel
LORTAT: Dante
LUISADA: Luisada
NOVAES: Vox
PENNARIO: Angel
PIRES: Erato
RACHMANINOFF (various waltzes): RCA
RUBINSTEIN: RCA
VASARY: DG
ZIMERMAN: DG

Other Works

Among Chopin's miscellaneous works, mention should be made of the *Variations brillantes* on an air from an opera by Hérold, Op. 12, which shows how Chopin applied his art to the then-popular custom of composing variations on opera themes. Arthur Loesser called it "a masterpiece in its way."

A Bolero in C major, Op. 19, dates from 1833. Chopin turns this Spanish form into a rather Polish-sounding affair. In the proper hands, it can be elegant and gallant. The Tarantelle in A-flat, Op. 43, has spirit, though it lacks the native frenzy of the dance. Schumann praised it too highly when he found it "in Chopin's most daring manner." But the work has always been played.

In the Introduction and Rondo in E-flat, Op. 16, a Weber-like opening leads to a brilliant and engaging rondo, which is overly long. Perhaps more characteristic is the 1827 *Rondo à la mazur*, Op. 5, with its florid passages exuding a Slavic flavor.

MUZIO CLEMENTI
1752–1832—Italy

Sonata in B minor, Op. 40, No. 2 (1802)

This formidable sonata shows why Beethoven admired Clementi. The plan is in two movements, both opened by slow, remarkable recitativo sections.

BERMAN: CBS (LP)
DEMIDENKO: Hyperion
GRANTE: Altarus
KATIN: Athene
SPADA: Arts
TIPO (four sonatas): EMI Classics

Sonata in C major, Op. 34, No. 1 (1795)

Similar in muscularity to Beethoven's Op. 2, No. 3. An effective concert sonata in three movements.

DEMIDENKO: Hyperion
GILELS: Melodiya
GRANTE: Altarus
KATIN: Athene

Sonata in B-flat major, Op. 24, No. 2

DEMIDENKO: Hyperion
GRANTE: Altarus
KATIN: Athene

Sonata in G minor, Op. 50, No. 3, "Didone abbandonata"

The B-flat major Sonata bears a striking resemblance to the opening theme of the overture to Mozart's *The Magic Flute*. In the late G minor Sonata from 1820, Clementi achieves the emotional depth he was always striving for.

Both are played in a fine selection of Clementi sonatas on two records. Volume 1 contains, in addition to the G minor work, Sonatas Op. 33, No. 1 in A major; Op. 33, No. 3 in C major; and Op. 26, No. 2 in F-sharp minor. The B-flat Sonata is on the second record along with Op. 40, No. 2 in B minor; Op. 25, No. 4 in A major; and Op. 2, No. 3 in G minor.

CROWSON: L'Oiseau-Lyre (LP)
DEMIDENKO: Hyperion
GRANTE: Altarus
KATIN: Athene
MICHELANGELI (Sonata in B-Flat, Op. 12, No. 1): Music and Arts
SAGER: Hänssler Classic
SPADA: Arts

Six Sonatinas, Op. 36; Three Sonatinas, Op. 37; Three Sonatinas, Op. 38

These are the most frequently played sonatinas in history. Musical children can't resist their classical purity.

BLUMENFELD (Op. 36): Etcetera
ENTREMONT: Columbia (LP)

Piano Concerto in C major (1790)

This is an excellent Classical concerto. Clementi adapted it from his own C major Sonata Op. 33,

No. 3, which Horowitz has recorded (on RCA) with splendor and gusto. (Other Horowitz performances of Clementi sonatas are Op. 34, No. 2 in G minor; Op. 14, No. 3 in F minor; and Op. 26, No. 2 in F-sharp minor.)

BLUMENTAL, Zedda/Prague Chamber Orchestra: Turnabout
DRENIKOV, Sofia Chamber Orchestra: Fidelio
HOROWITZ (five sonatas): RCA

AARON COPLAND
1900–1990—United States

Variations for Piano (1930)

Copland was a decisive figure in contemporary American music. Although he composed relatively little for the piano, his contributions were significant. His set of Piano Variations—Theme, Twenty Variations, Coda—remains as rugged and abstract as on the day it was finished. The composer William Flanagan wrote: "No one who is familiar with the history of modern American music has to be told that Copland's Piano Variations is a legend in its own right and a work of prime significance in the composer's musical development. Its status as a sort of granitic masterwork has been questioned by virtually no cultivated musician—no matter what his stylistic allegiance—since its composition."

COPLAND: Pearl
HOUGH: Hyperion
KALISH: Nonesuch
MASSELOS: Odyssey (LP)
SHIELDS: Vox
SMIT: Sony Classical
TOCCO: Pro Arte

Piano Sonata (1939–41)

Copland premiered the work in Buenos Aires in 1941. It is in three ample movements. The "Coplandesque" chords remind us of the impact he had on American music. He consciously intended "writing a music—a serious concert music—that a European would recognize as having been written by an American."

BERNSTEIN: RCA
BLACKWOOD: Cedille
FLEISHER: Philips: Great Pianists of the
    Twentieth Century
KAPELL: RCA
NALLEY: Eroica
SMIT: Sony Classical
VOTAPEK: VAI

Piano Fantasy (1955–57)

This is one of Copland's great works, dedicated to the memory of the pianist William Kapell. It was premiered by William Masselos. The composer stated: "The Fantasy belongs in the category of absolute music. It makes no use whatever of folk or popular music materials. The musical framework of the entire piece is based upon a sequence of ten different tones of the chromatic scale. . . . The Piano Fantasy is by no means rigorously controlled twelve-tone music, but it does make liberal use of devices associated with that technique."

FRANCI: Fone
LIVELY: Etcetera
MASSELOS: Odyssey (LP)
SMIT: Sony Classical

Piano Concerto (1927)

The Concerto, in two movements, without break, is a finely integrated work that stands as one of the best jazz-inspired pieces in any musical genre. The piano part is effective and demanding; the orchestration, large and colorful.

COPLAND, Bernstein/New York Philharmonic:
    Sony Classical
HOLLANDER, Schwarz/Seattle Symphony:
    Delos
OHLSSON, Thomas/San Francisco Symphony:
    RCA
SMIT, Copland/Rome Radio Symphony: Varèse/
    Sarabande (LP)
WILD, Copland/Symphony of the Air: Vanguard

GEORGE CRUMB
b. 1929—United States

Makrokosmos, Volume 1—Twelve
    Fantasy-Pieces After the Zodiac for
    Amplified Piano
Makrokosmos, Volume 2—Twelve
    Fantasy-Pieces After the Zodiac for
    Amplified Piano

Crumb gets his inspiration from many sources, and the symbolic plays a large role in his compositions. The composer notes his debt to Bartók and Debussy, but says, "The spiritual impulse of my music is more akin to the darker side of Chopin, and even to the childlike fantasy of early Schumann." The twenty-four *Makrokosmos* take about seventy minutes in toto, comprising a work of modern Romanticism, and an uncharted journey to new musical lands. There are extensive extra pianistic "happenings" such as singing, shouting, whispering, whistling, as well as a type of notation in which most pianists would be lost. The composer is ever present, asking the pianist to be "tremulous," "subliminal," as if "suspended in endless time," "desireless," "fantasmic," and on and on. Each one of the series has a different title. The first twelve were written for David Burge and the latter set for the pianist Robert Miller.

BOATWRIGHT: Music and Arts
BURGE (Vol. 1): Nonesuch (LP)
BURGE (Vols. 1 and 2): Classico
J. JACOBS: Centaur
MILLER (Vol. 2): Odyssey (LP)

D

LUIGI DALLAPICCOLA
1904–1975—Italy

Quaderno musicale di Annalibera (1953)

Dallapiccola is one of the best-known contemporary Italian composers. A practitioner of the twelve-tone method, he nevertheless expresses a great deal of warmth and sensuous feeling in his music. In the *Quaderno musicale,* or "Musical Notebook for Annalibera," one of the tempo markings is "Andantino amoroso." This quiet group of eleven pieces is one of the most profoundly respected piano works of tone-row music.

> BURGE: Candide (LP)
> CANINO: Stradivari
> MAXIMILIEN: CRI (LP)

Sonatina Canonica on Paganini Caprices (1942–43)

A landmark piano work of the 1940s. Paganini themes are the foundation for this canonic, polytonal, touching, humorous piece in four movements.

> MAXIMILIEN: CRI
> MONETTI: ASV

CLAUDE DEBUSSY
1862–1918—France

Debussy was one of the seminal figures in twentieth-century music. He composed the most original body of piano music after Liszt.

Although Debussy occasionally performed some of his own music, he was not a concert pianist. He did, however, give a great deal of advice to many pianists, who were eager to enter the secret garden of his compositions. "In playing his own music," Léon Paul Fargue remarked, "he appeared to be giving birth to the piano. He cradled it, talked softly to it." Nadia Boulanger told Bruno Monsaingeon, "You only need to have heard Debussy play once. I don't mean that he played better than others. He played otherwise, he had his own tone, his unique tone." Marguerite Long, who worked on all of his major works with him, wrote in her book, *At the Piano with Debussy,* that he "was an incomparable pianist. How could one forget his subtleness, the caress of his touch while floating over the keys with a curiously penetrating gentleness. There lay his secret, the pianistic enigma of his music. There lay Debussy's individual technique; gentleness in a continuous pressure gave the color that only he could get from his piano."

Debussy added a new dimension to the piano's expressive and evocative power. Through the century, his work has remained vitally fresh and intriguing to pianists and audiences alike. Debussy is the most exportable of all modern French composers. The originality of his music is such that Claudio Arrau says "it is like the music of another planet." It offers a new world, inspired less by the European music of the past than by Symbolist poetry, nature, Impressionist painting, indeed, sheer impulse itself, and the exoticism of the Javanese gamelan orchestra that he had heard in Paris. In Boulez's phrase, Debussy was to "break the circle of the Occident." Debussy's pianism contains layers of exquisite "chording," harmonies hovering unresolved in the most rarefied, intoxicating air. New concepts in pedaling and minute rhythms governing microspacing and a range of atmospheric tonal problems necessitate the highest sensitivity and elasticity that a pianist can possess.

With Debussy, the chord became freed of its necessity to move; a chord became a sensuous experience in itself. With this concept, harmonic progression was no longer required in the traditional sense. Yet his music is not a formless mass, relying on mere sensation. Debussy is a subtle builder of form, with an uncanny ability to write pieces that were neither too long nor too short. Debussy was seldom pleased by pianists playing his music. In a letter to Edgard Varèse, he complains, "How often one is betrayed by pianists . . . I assure you one can not imagine how my music is disfigured: often I can scarcely recognize it—most pianists are poor musicians—they dissect music into bits-and-pieces, like a roast chicken."

Unfortunately, as the most exportable of French piano composers, he has been subjected to many untenable performances. He may be the most poorly played composer, generally speaking, after Chopin.

Debussy's early pieces sustain themselves in the repertoire. If lacking the high inspiration and technical polish of the Preludes, Etudes, Images, and Estampes, they provide a golden treasury of music for the amateur as well as professional.

Danse Bohemienne (1880): His first published piece, written at age eighteen, when he was engaged by Nadejda von Meck, Tchaikovsky's patron, to teach her children. Von Meck sent the piece to Tchaikovsky for criticism, and the Russian called it "a nice little piece, certainly too short, not one idea worked out to conclusion; the form is shoddy, and it lacks unity."

Two Arabesques (1888): Forever popular, fanciful filigree, a breezy feel, and elegance tumbles in each piece. Already Debussy is a supreme form builder. E. Robert Schmitz says, "These happy, unpretentious and gay arabesques are essentially French; they do not overreach their ornamental purposes."

Mazurka (1890): There is nothing Slavic in this pretty mazurka, with perhaps a few hints of Grieg.

Valse Romantique (1890): A fine encore, an alluring bit of fluff, and rhythmically insinuating.

Ballade (1890) A longish piece, which in the proper hands can be lovely.

Rêverie (1890): Debussy called it "a work of no consequence" but its suave measures and velvety melody have made it well-known.

Danse (1890): Debussy was deeply moved by the Balinese dancers and the sounds of gamelan orchestras which he had heard at the Paris Exposition. The *Danse* begins to sound the Asiatic note, but in fact is a tarantella. It was first titled *Tarentelle Styrienne*. Ravel marvelously orchestrated it in 1925.

Nocturne (1892): A longer piece of about six minutes; difficult to hold together. In this nocturne one may imagine an intimate scene from a Massenet opera, lighting effects included.

With its deceptive cadences and unpredictability, Debussy is clearly moving forward into an unprecedented future originality.

D'un Cahier d'esquisses (1903): "From a sketchbook," the composer's mature style is gaining entry into new vistas of keyboard expressiveness. Ravel gave the first performance.

Masques (1904): A masterful piece unworthy of its neglect. Grant Johannesen says: "*Masques* is a significant pianistic moment in early twentieth century music: an impressionist 'motor' piece. It is a balancing act of violence and calm between hands that must reveal the stately melodic line—with little tempo variance."

Debussy said, "It is not about the commedia dell'arte, but the tragic expression of existence." But the interpreter must never forget that Debussy's view of a tragic existence *sounds* very different from Beethoven's.

Le Petit Negre (1909): Debussy was the most cosmopolitan of composers; everything touched him, including the cakewalk and minstrel shows popular in Paris.

Hommage à Haydn (1909): Composed for the centenary of Haydn's death. Musical tributes were asked from Dukas, Ravel, d'Indy, and others. Debussy, using letters from Haydn's name, fashioned a rather complex slow waltz that Haydn would doubtless find strange.

La plus que lente (1910): Debussy's enigmatic title is meant to spoof a popular valse of the day, "La Valse Lente." Here is Debussy, the sophisticate, and man about town. The composer was inspired by a Hungarian violinist, Leoni, who entertained with gypsy airs at cocktail time at the new Carlton Hotel in Paris. The composer wrote, "Let us think of cabarets, let us think also of the numerous

Claude Debussy by David Dubal

five o'clocks where the beautiful feminine listeners meet."

Berceuse héroïque (1914): Dying from cancer, Debussy was equally ravaged by World War I. Asked to write heroic music for the Belgian king and his army, he said he "lacked military spirit," instead producing this mysterious piece which Johannesen calls "more nostalgic than heroic, the music does, uncannily, evoke the sadness of drum-taps, echoes of halting, crippled-sounding dead marches."

Piece (1915): A single-page, a forgotten waltz, a stab of pain. It was composed to raise funds for the wounded.

Elégie (1915): This lament is his last composition for the instrument for which he added another dimension of expressive power.

The Complete Piano Music

ERICOURT: Ivory Classics
FÉVRIER: Véga
HAAS: Erato

Suite bergamasque (1890)

Debussy adored the music of Rameau, Couperin, and in general the seventeenth- and the eighteenth-century *clavencinistes*. This gallant tribute gives us the mature Debussy, in a suite of color and radiant light, in four movements: Prelude, Menuet, *Clair de Lune,* and Passepied. In the *Clair de Lune*, he departs from Louis XIV's court and paints a moonlight landscape which the general public finds irresistible. Within the suite the piece works well, as a foil to the delectable daintiness of the Passepied.

CICCOLINI: Seraphim
GIESEKING: Seraphim
KOCSIS: Philips
RICHTER: Columbia
ROUVIER: Denon
WEISSENBERG: DG

Pour le piano (1901)

Debussy had become master of the orchestra before he achieved similar mastery over the piano. *Pour le piano* was his first piano work in a decade. It was premiered by Ricardo Viñes. Debussy had not yet reached the apex of his powers in this work, but through its stunning effects, whole-tone scales, and neo-Classic purity, it has gained a place in the international repertory. The three movements are: Prelude, with glissando effects, Sarabande, and an exhilarating Toccata.

BACHAUER: Mercury (LP)
BÉROFF: EMI
GIESEKING: EMI
HEIDSIECK: Cassiopée
MORAVEC: Philips: Great Pianists of the Twentieth Century
PERLEMUTER: Nimbus
POMMIER: Virgin Classics
TAGLIAFERRO: Master Class

Estampes: Pagodes, La Soireé dans Grenade, Jardins sous le pluie (1903)

First performed by Viñes, these works inaugurate a new era in piano writing. *Estampes* are "images printed from engraved copper or wood plates." The pianist E. Robert Schmitz wrote, "Years of gestation purified these visions to the pungency of an essence." The stimulus for *Pagodes* is the Javanese gamelan orchestra that Debussy fell in love with. In *Evening in Granada,* a habanera rhythm permeates fine, short themes. Manuel de Falla thought it "contain[ed] in a marvelously distilled way the most concentrated atmosphere of Andalusia." *Gardens in the Rain* is a pure impressionistic evocation of raindrops with two French nursery songs woven into the framework.

ARGERICH: Exclusive
BADURA-SKODA: Harmonic
R. CASADESUS: Columbia
FIRKUSNY: Sugano
FRANÇOIS: EMI Pathé
GIESEKING: Columbia; Philips: Great Pianists of the Twentieth Century
JACOBS: Nonesuch
KOCSIS: Philips
MORAVEC: Vox Cum Laude
RICHTER: DG
THIBAUDET: London

L'Isle joyeuse (1904)

This is a Bacchanalian masterpiece, inspired by Watteau's most famous painting, *The Embarkment for Cythère*. It was always a favorite of the composer, who said, "That piece seems to assemble all the ways to attack a piano." Marguerite Long calls it a "Feast of Rhythm." It was premiered by Viñes, whose playing of it, Long says, was "made of light that burst from all sides in a simultaneously vertiginous and precise fantasy."

BASHKIROV: Melodiya (LP)
CICCOLINI: Angel
CLIBURN: RCA
FRANÇOIS: Philips: Great Pianists of the
   Twentieth Century
GIESEKING: Pearl
HOROWITZ: CBS
KOCSIS: Philips
VÁSÁRY: DG
WEISSENBERG: RCA

Images (First Series): *Reflets dans l'eau, Hommage à Rameau, Mouvement* (1905)
Images (Second Series): *Cloches à travers les feuilles, Et la Lune descend sur le temple qui fut, Poissons d'or* (1907)

Debussy believed the First Series would "take their place in piano literature . . . to the left of Schumann or the right of Chopin." *Reflections in the Water* is one of the miracles of musical impressionism. *Hommage à Rameau* is a stately sarabande, and *Mouvement* is a perfect study in motion. In the Second Series, Debussy uses three staves for the clarification of his exquisite notation. Both *Cloches à travers les feuilles* ("Bells Heard Through the Leaves") and *Et la Lune descend sur le temple qui fut* ("And the Moon Goes Down on the Ruined Temple") are among the most difficult interpretive problems in Debussy. Their transparency demands expert and imaginative pedaling. The best known of the Second Series is *Poissons d'or* ("Goldfish"), in which, Schmitz says, the performer must "be convinced that the body of a goldfish is luminous and almost transparent, and that it displaces itself quite suddenly by dashes of rapid timing."

R. CASADESUS: Sony Classsical
DAMASE: Decca
FRANÇOIS: Philips: Great Pianists of the
   Twentieth Century
GIESEKING: EMI
HENKEMANS: Epic (LP)
JACOBS: Nonesuch
MICHELANGELI: DG
PLUDERMACHER: Harmonia Mundi

Children's Corner Suite (1908)

This is a masterful production of satire, tenderness, and humor. It begins with *Doctor Gradus ad Parnassum*, which, in Debussy's words, "is a sort of hygienic and progressive gymnastics; it should therefore be played every morning, before breakfast, beginning at 'modéré' and winding up to 'animé.' " No. 2, *Jimbo's Lullaby*, is also humorous. Jimbo is a toy elephant belonging to Debussy's daughter. No. 3, *Serenade for the Doll*, is legato and staccato in a whimsical setting. No. 4, *The Snow Is Dancing*, is technically the most exacting of the set. No. 5, *The Little Shepherd*, is simplicity itself. No. 6, *Golliwog's Cakewalk*, is a piece in which Debussy indulges in the syncopation of the minstrel groups he heard, with an irreverent quote from Wagner's *Tristan und Isolde*.

481

R. CASADESUS: Columbia
CORTOT: Biddulph
DEBUSSY: Pierian
GIESEKING: Sony Classical
HORSZOWSKI: Nonesuch
JOHANNESEN: Vox (LP)
MICHELANGELI: DG
POMMIER: Virgin Classics

Twenty-four Preludes

The Preludes furnished the piano with a new vocabulary, never before heard in music. Marguerite Long has written, "The content of these two books is of an order not to be confused with any other." Schmitz affirmed: "Only a man with a magnificent wealth of knowledge, of experience, of intuition could characterize so sharply and so briefly the infinite array and range of subjects of these twenty-four works, which whirl through legends, literature, vaudeville, painting, architectural landmarks, archaeological objects, natural phenomena, a multitude of scenes and of personages, each individualized, crystallized, in the moment of Debussy's creations."

Laurence Davies comments, "They recall no one so much as Monet, with his dissolving canvasses in which the scene almost begins to change before one's eyes. . . . Debussy gave to music a whole new encyclopedia of sensations."

Twelve Preludes, Book I (1910)

Danseuses de Delphes ("Delphi Dancers"): Debussy himself played the first performance in 1910. At the Louvre, the composer had seen a fragment from a Greek pillar depicting three dancers. He was often inspired by Hellenic sources, as in *Chansons de Bilitis* or *Danses sacrée et profane*. This archaic, slow-moving prelude uses modal, diatonic, pentatonic, and chromatic elements, which possess a graveness of tone. "Yet," says Schmitz, "this gravity is enveloped by a lightness of touch, as if the dancers were clad in veils or enfolded by curving wraps of incense."

Voiles ("Veils," "Sails"): Debussy also premiered this prelude. The work uses the whole-tone scale to great effect. Debussy told Marguerite Long that some pianists played it with too much color, losing the insubstantial feeling he wanted. Debussy himself saw "sailing boats anchored to a fixed pedal-point" as well as "mysterious veils enveloping palpitating feminine forms, hiding eyes which fan desire by their devious glances." The composer Edgard Varèse said the piece was inspired by the diaphanous veils used by the American dancer Loïe Fuller, then famous in Paris.

Le Vent dans la plaine ("The Wind on the Plain"): A nature study, in an arpeggio figure, broken by violent gusts. "The invisibility of the wind," notes the critic Edward Lockspeiser, "is meant above all to be mysterious and on a long suspended B-flat, the piece ultimately disappears into thin air."

Les Sons et les parfums tournent dans l'air du soir ("The Sounds and Perfumes Swirl in the Evening Air"): Inspired by a line in Baudelaire's poem "Harmonie du Soir" from *Les Fleurs du mal*. The Fourth Prelude calls for creative interpreters. It is "poignant and sensuous," in Long's words, "rich with beguiling nocturnal vibrations and the ephemeral languor of human life avid for the raptures of Tomorrow." Debussy once said, "It is only the pleasures of the moment that matter."

Les Collines d'Anacapri ("The Hills of Anacapri"): A bright work with bell sounds, tarantella rhythm, frenzied dancing. Debussy told Long that a pianist had once played it with a gypsy feeling and that it should rather be Neapolitan. The score closes with Debussy asking the pianist to play luminously, as the sun bursts in the piano's upper registers.

Des Pas sur la neige ("Footsteps in the Snow"): An incomparable psychological masterpiece. With only a few notes, he has created a feeling of total desolation. Debussy said it should have the aural value of a melancholy, snow-bound landscape. Arrau speaks of "a sadness, an intolerable dilemma."

Ce qu'a vu le vent d'ouest ("What the West Wind Saw"): Technically the most demanding of the Preludes from Book I. A work embodying the unleashed power of the West Wind, which is a horribly destructive phenomenon, gathering force over the Atlantic and crashing in on the coasts. "Here," writes Schmitz, "Debussy is no longer the poet of tenderness, the painter of the exquisite. . . . It exhibits a passionate fascination for evil. . . . Debussy asks the player to be *en dehors et angoissé*— outside and anxiously." A lone and tragic human voice is almost silenced by the oceanic turbulence of the score. Lockspeiser thinks that Debussy, who was a great admirer of Shelley, may have been inspired by his "Ode to the West Wind."

La Fille aux cheveux de lin ("The Girl with the Flaxen Hair"): Inspired by a poem of Leconte de Lisle. A slender and supple melody about a girl who sang to herself in a field of clover with lips cherry red. One of the most popular of the Preludes.

La Sérénade interrompue ("The Interrupted Serenade"): A portrait of a Spanish guitarist trying to sing his love song. But, alas, he is interrupted and lightly scorned. Debussy himself said, "Poor fellow, he keeps on being interrupted."

La Cathédrale engloutie ("The Engulfed [Submerged] Cathedral"): A work bathed in mystery, echoing with the sound of ancient bells. Based on an old Breton legend of the Cathedral of Ys engulfed in water because of impiety but rising at sunrise. Debussy may also have been inspired by Monet's paintings of the Rouen Cathedral. The prelude was premiered by Debussy in 1910 and stands as one of his most purely "Impressionist" scores. "After sunrise, its watery grave is still," writes Long, "but Debussy tears away the submarine fabric of the city with a superb theme which surges up to form a kind of cupola."

La Danse de Puck ("Puck's Dance"): This tiny, capricious character from *A Midsummer Night's Dream* is portrayed here in one of the most delightful Shakespearean depictions in music. Schmitz wrote, "Tripping lightly, sliding, vanishing, reappearing, our nimble elf has a mocking laugh." This prelude is not an easy one to play well.

Minstrels: A music-hall piece of broad humor inspired by the American cakewalk. Minstrel shows were becoming popular around 1900, and Debussy put such a scene into a prelude with a foppish rhythmic appeal and which awakens a whole set of images.

Twelve Preludes, Book II (1913)

Brouillards ("Mists"): A piece of musical impressionism with the mysterious quality of fog—vaporous and enigmatic. It demands, in the words of Maurice Hinson, "exquisite control" from the executant.

Feuilles mortes ("Dead Leaves"): "Schmitz wrote: This is the Rite of Autumn, in which the falling leaves are a signal of the suspension of life, creating a static expectancy, a mood of intense regrets of a past now so far gone, of great sadness and the poignant melancholy of fall. Debussy had once written of golden leaves celebrating the glorious agony of the trees."

La Puerta del vino ("The Gateway to the Vineyard"): Manuel de Falla sent Debussy a postcard depicting the famed gate of the Alhambra Palace in Granada, to which Debussy responded with a tonal masterpiece infused with the habanera rhythm. Debussy asks the interpreter to play "with brusque oppositions of extreme violence and impassioned sweetness." The work exudes a haunting sensuousness. "What riotous sounds, what lasciviousness," wrote Marguerite Long.

Les Fées sont d'exquises danseuses ("The Fairies Are Exquisite Dancers"): The pianist Ernest Ulmer wrote that this prelude "is dedicated to the ephemeral charm of fairy-tale sylphs."

Bruyères ("Heather"): A pastoral picture—a scene of the moors of Scotland. One of the easiest preludes technically, and reminiscent of *La Fille aux cheveux de lin*.

General Lavine—Eccentric: In the style and rhythm of a cakewalk. Debussy, in this prelude, depicts the once-famous American clown and juggler Edward Lavine, who seemed to be nine feet tall. Debussy loved seeing this entertainer perform. He called him "wooden . . . he hid with humor and with pirouettes a too sensitive heart." The piece is similar to *Minstrels* from Book I and has a flavor of ragtime.

La Terrasse des audiences du clair de lune ("The Terrace for Moonlight Audiences"): The composer was inspired by a letter published in *Le Temps* on the coronation of George V as emperor of India. "The hall of victory, the hall of pleasure, the garden of the sultanesses, the terrace for moonlight audiences." This prelude demands the highest concentration and tonal control from an interpreter. The work is ethereal, languorous, yet touched by a nameless anxiety.

Ondine: The seductive water nymph of Debussy differs greatly from the elegant Ondine of Ravel. Ravel's Ondine is a mature siren who lures sailors to her watery palace, and to death. Debussy's Ondine is young, capricious, and tempting, and, in Paul Jacob's words, "is merely a sprite whose music is shimmering laughter." *Ondine* is technically and tonally a difficult piece.

Hommage à S. Pickwick, Esq. P.P.M.P.C.: Debussy was always fascinated by England, and this is a tribute to Dickens. The prelude begins with "God Save the King" and is rich in humor. As with many Debussy preludes, the score is filled with psychological twists.

Canope: A *canope* is the covering of an Egyptian funeral urn. Canope also was a city of ancient Egypt on the Nile. This is a piece of tender sadness.

Les Tierces alternées ("Alternating Thirds"): The only prelude without a descriptive title. An abstract etude of a purely pianistic intent, which anticipates Debussy's Etudes.

Feux d'artifice ("Fireworks"): A magnificent fireworks display on Bastille Day is captured in the most illuminating and evocative piano writing. In the last measures the *Marseillaise* floats through the night air. This may be the most technically difficult of the entire series of Preludes, a masterpiece of color, animation, and kaleidoscopic pattern making. Schmitz wrote of the Preludes: "One has run the gamut of emotions from youth to death, candor to furor to melancholy. An exacting pianistic technique has been developed to match the rich effects of a multiplicity of rhythms, melodies, harmonies, the like of which respond to our wildest dreams of treasure chests in Baghdad."

Lockspeiser adds: "Soon one is aware of the symbolism in this piano writing. There is a visual aspect of this music and often a subtle psychological aspect. There is no doubt that Debussy shows himself in the Preludes to be not only a clairvoyant but a clairaudient. The music allows the listener to see things and to hear things in a new way. Debussy's mysterious conception of the tactile properties of music is equally remarkable, and there are pages which bring music to the borders of an odoriferous or even—so completely are we regaled by this music of the senses—a soporific art."

It is interesting to note that Debussy put the titles of the Preludes at the end of each piece. Perhaps he was reminded of the Symbolist poet Stéphane Mallarmé's dictum: "To name an object sacrifices three-quarters of the enjoyment. To suggest it—that is our dream."

Twenty-four Preludes (complete):
ARRAU: Philips
R. CASADESUS: Columbia
CIANI: DG
CORTOT: Philips: Great Pianists of the Twentieth Century
EGOROV: EMI
GIESEKING: Angel; Arkadia
HAAS: DG
HAGUENAUER: Ligia Digital Lidi
HEIDSIECK: Cassiopée
P. JACOBS: Nonesuch
KARS: London
KÖRMENDI: Naxos
MICHELANGELI: DG
PLANÈS: Harmonic
ROUVIER: Denon
ULMER: Critics Choice
ZIMERMAN: DG

Twelve Etudes (1915)

These Etudes, dedicated to the memory of Chopin, are a monument of the technical literature. As Marguerite Long wrote, "Debussy made use of a special alchemy in his Etudes. He worked at his craft like a refined lover." Although drier and more objective than the impressionist Preludes, the Etudes did not receive the attention they deserved until the last generation. In the composer's words, "These Etudes hide a rigorous technique beneath harmonic flowers." Debussy wrote no fingerings for this complicated task, asking the player to prove "those eternal words: 'One is never better served than by oneself.' Let us seek our fingerings." Each Etude presents a different problem for the pianist to solve. With the passing of time, the Etudes gain in stature, their musical substance as rich as their technical inventiveness.

No. 1: *Pour les "cinq doigts" d'après Monsieur Czerny* (Study for Five Fingers)
No. 2: *Pour les tierces* (Study in Thirds)
No. 3: *Pour les quartes* (Study in Fourths)
No. 4: *Pour les sixtes* (Study in Sixths)
No. 5: *Pour les octaves* (Study in Octaves)
No. 6: *Pour les huit doigts* (Study of Eight Fingers without Thumbs)
No. 7: *Pour les degrés chromatiques* (Study in Chromatic Steps)
No. 8: *Pour les agréments* (Study in Ornaments)
No. 9: *Pour les notes répétées* (Study in Repeated Notes)
No. 10: *Pour les sonorités opposées* (Study in Opposed Sonorities)
No. 11: *Pour les arpèges composés* (Study for Composite Arpeggios)
No. 12: *Pour les accords* (Study for Chords)

DI BONAVENTURA: Connoisseur Society (LP)
ERICOURT: Ivory Classics
GIESEKING: EMI

HOWAT: Tall Poppies
P. JACOBS: Nonesuch
LORIOD: MHS (LP)
PELLETIER: CBC
POLLINI: DG
ROSEN: Epic (LP)
ROUVIER: Denon
SONG: Pro Piano
UCHIDA: Philips

Miscellaneous Pieces (Nocturnes, Romances, Masques, Arabesques, etc.)

BÉROFF: Denon
FRANKL: Vox
GIESEKING: EMI

piano music, the pianist should look at his Four Rhaphsodies, his transcriptions of Strauss, Six Concert Etudes, Op. 28, the *Winterreigen,* Op. 13, a set of moderate difficulty covering many moods, the five-movement *Suite Humoresken,* Op. 17, and the folk-oriented Ruralia Hungarica, Op. 32a.

DOHNÁNYI, Boult/Royal Philharmonic: Angel (LP)
DOHNÁNYI, Collingwood/London Symphony: Pearl
KATCHEN, Boult/London Philharmonic: Philips: Great Pianists of the Twentieth Century
SCHIFF, Solti/Chicago Symphony: London
C. SMITH, Sargent/Liverpool Philharmonic: APR
WILD, C. von Dohnányi/New Philharmonia: Chesky

ERNÖ VON DOHNÁNYI

1877–1960—Hungary

Variations on a Nursery Song for Piano and Orchestra (1913)

This ingenious score keeps Ernö von Dohnányi alive in the international repertoire. Dohnányi commented that the composition was made "for the enjoyment of lovers of humor, and the annoyance of others." After its portentous introduction, we hear the French nursery air *"Ah, vous dirai-je, maman,"* and then we are treated to eleven variations marked by an impressive inventiveness. They are an example of remarkable piano writing. The Waltz Variations possess an incomparable insouciance.

Of the large catalogue of Dohnányi's solo

PAUL DUKAS

1865–1935—France

Variations, Interlude, and Finale on a Theme by Rameau (1901–02)

One of the finest works in variation form. Norman Demuth aptly states: "Had these *Rameau* Variations been written by a Teutonic composer they would have undoubtedly become established long ago in the regular repertoire and would have been taken as much for granted as are Brahms's *Handel* Variations, and equally reverenced; but it is only quite recently that the French genius has been recognized as consisting of something more than Impressionism and Pictorial Romanticism."

A noble, precise composition with intricate part writing, difficult to play well in its seventeen-minute duration. It takes more than one hearing to appreciate its subtle beauties.

FINGERHUT: Chandos
JOHANNESEN: Candide
LEFÉBURE: Pearl

Sonata in E-flat minor (1899–1900)

A vast work of deeply warm spirit in four movements, lasting upward of forty-five minutes. It received its premiere in 1901, by Edouard Risler. The work is more Franckian in its fervor than Dukas's more neo-Classic variations, which spring from the French clavecin tradition. It may be considered one of the few important French sonatas. The scherzo movement has some similarity to Dukas's more popular work, *The Sorcerer's Apprentice*.

FINGERHUT: Chandos
PLESHAKOV: Orion (LP)
THINAT: MHS (LP)

JAN LADISLAV DUSSEK
1760–1812—Czechoslovakia

Sonata in F minor, Op. 77, "L'Invocation" (1812)

One of the pinnacles of Czech Classical music, *L'Invocation* is Dussek's last, longest, and perhaps his finest creation. It has the breadth of great art and is deserving of a place in the hierarchy of the Classical sonata. The work is massive four-movement structure cut from granite and far too little known.

FIRKUSNY: Vox
MARVIN: Dorian
PANENKA (fortepiano): Supraphon

Sonata in B-flat major, Op. 35, No. 1 (1797)
Sonata in C minor, Op. 35, No. 2 (1798)
Sonata in F-sharp minor, Op. 61, "Elégie harmonique sur la mort du Prince Louis Ferdinand" (1806)

The Sonata in C minor is a distinguished work. Beethoven may have been influenced by it in his Op. 13 *Sonate pathétique,* composed soon after. Frederick Marvin writes that the second movement, Adagio patetico et espressivo, is "one of the great inspirations of Dussek and I feel [it] is not paralleled by an adagio written before 1798 in its depth and tragic expressiveness." The Sonata in B-flat, in a two-movement format, is technically more difficult than most of the sonatas of the era. Its finale is absolutely irresistible. The Sonata in F-sharp minor is also in two movements. The first movement is a striking utterance, filled with drama. One can hear the pre-Lisztian gesture as Dussek rolls up the diminished seventh chords, and Brahms certainly knew the syncopated finale when he wrote his own Sonata in F-sharp minor, Op. 2. One other sonata of Dussek, Op. 70 in A-flat, with the title *Le Retour à Paris,* must be considered important. It is a beautifully planned, highly pianistic work. A critic of the day felt it would "retain its value as long as music provided good pianos and accomplished pianists." There is no adequate recording of the composition, however.

KEENE (Op. 61): Protone
MARVIN: Dorian

HENRI DUTILLEUX
b. 1916—France

Piano Sonata (1947)

This three-movement Sonata, dedicated to and premiered by Geneviève Joy, has become a classic of its period. Dutilleux wrote, "I tried to create a certain internal pulsation, a type of lyrical tension and also this 'sonorous abundance' that the piano, better than any other instrument, can translate by virtue of its harmonic richness and variety of its timbres." The Sonata is marvelously conceived for the piano and stated with lucid restraint.

AMATO: Olympia
GIROD: Solstice
JOY: Erato
JUDE: Harmonia Mundi
SIEGEL: Orion (LP)

F

MANUEL DE FALLA
1876–1946—Spain

Cuatro Piezas españolas (1907)

Composed at the same time as Albéniz's *Iberia*, the *Cuatro Piezas—Aragonesa, Cubana, Montañesa,* and *Andaluza*—should not be underestimated. They are a high point of Spanish nationalism. Although they demand rhythmic flexibility and sophistication, they are not as note-heavy as Albéniz's *Iberia*.

> ACHUCARRO: RCA (LP)
> DE LARROCHA: EMI
> HEISSER (Complete Piano Music): Erato
> OROZCO: Valóis
> OSORIO: Cedille
> RICHARD: Nonesuch

Fantasía baética (1919)

The *Fantasía baética* (Baestis being the Roman name for Andalusia) is the longest, most difficult of Falla's works for piano. Composed for Arthur Rubinstein, it is more primitive and stark than the *Cuatro Piezas,* representing a searing, almost parched landscape. It has never received the attention it deserves.

> ACHUCARRO: RCA (LP)
> DE LARROCHA: London: EMI

> HEISSER: Erato
> MULLER: Rene Gailly
> RICHARD: Nonesuch (LP)

Nights in the Gardens of Spain—Symphonic Impressions for Piano and Orchestra (1915)

This piece by Falla is the greatest of all Spanish works for piano and orchestra. It is a glowing, bewitching score, one that conjures up the perfumes of night. Falla called the composition "evocations in sound." The piano part is ingenious and brilliant, but deceptively simple on the page with its many unison passages.

> ACHUCARRO, Mata/London Symphony: RCA (LP)
> ARGERICH, Barenboim/Orchestre de Paris: Erato
> CURZON, Jordá/National Symphony: Pearl
> DE LARROCHA, Burgos/London Philharmonic: London
> ENTREMONT, Ormandy/Philadelphia: CBS (LP)
> HASKIL, Markevitch/Lamoureux Orchestra: Philips
> JOSELSON, Mata/Frankfurt Radio Symphony: Olympia
> KAPELL, Stokowski/Philharmonic Symphony: Music and Arts
> NOVAES, Swarowsky/Vienna Symphony: Vox
> RUBINSTEIN, Ormandy/Philadelphia: RCA
> SORIANO, Burgos/Paris Conservatoire: EMI

GABRIEL FAURÉ
1845–1924—France

Norman Demuth wrote: "Fauré's feline melody and chaste pianism contain all the lyrical slenderness and lightness hitherto absent from French piano music. . . . Fauré's music sings as that of no earlier French piano composer ever sang, but it lacks the extreme limpidity of Chopin's Nocturnes and therefore does not lend itself so easily to abuse. . . . It is sentimental only if the player makes it so."

A taste for Fauré must be developed and nurtured. His reflective gentleness and general reticence become more beautiful with repeated listening; he makes his impact by steps. His art has often been described as Hellenic in its serenity. His forms are entirely Chopinesque, into which are assimilated the influences of Schumann and Mendelssohn. He was a great master of piano writing. James Gibb notes that in the Ninth Barcarolle, "canonic imitation amid arpeggios is managed with a nonchalance that would have been the envy of Thalberg, the inventor of the 'three-handed' trick." Fauré's music can be voluptuous, frolicsome, ingratiating, and a hundred other things. It is, nevertheless, too contemplative to recommend itself to the average virtuoso, who may find its beauty too rarefied.

The Complete Piano Music

Laurence Davies wrote: "His large corpus of piano music stands along those of Debussy and Ravel, at the very summit of his nation's achievements in that sphere. . . . The gentle swerve of his melodies, the amazingly poised and delicate harmonies of which he was such a master, the apparently effortless flow of his scales and arpeggios—these features combined to make him a kind of musical Bonnard or Vuillard, and an unequalled exponent of his nation's graces."

CROCHET: Vox (LP)
J. DOYEN: Erato
JOHANNESEN: VAI (LP)
ROSCO: Hyperion

Thirteen Barcarolles (1883–1921)

No. 1 in A minor, Op. 26 (1883): Three graceful melodies. Fauré made a piano roll of it in 1913 for the Welte Company.

No. 2 in G major, Op. 41 (1885): More difficult than No. 1; again, with three motives.

No. 3 in G-flat major, Op. 42 (1885): Two themes, with arpeggios serving the rocking motion. The longest of these works (duration: 7:30).

Gabriel Fauré by David Dubal

No. 4 in A-flat major, Op. 44 (1886): A peaceful, simple work.

No. 5 in F-sharp minor, Op. 66 (1895): More experimental and enigmatic than any of the earlier examples. Emile Vuillermoz wrote of these pieces, "Until now the Barcarolle had only sailed on lakes or lagoons. The No. 5 seems to carry us off to the open sea."

No. 6 in E-flat major, Op. 70 (1896): An amiable and smoothly wrought piece.

No. 7 in D minor, Op. 90 (1906): This short composition (3:00) takes us into the more subterranean, austere style of the composer.

No. 8 in D-flat major, Op. 96 (1908): There is a rare loud ending in this charming, animated work.

No. 9 in A minor, Op. 101 (1910): A sadly meditative work lasting four minutes.

No. 10 in A minor, Op. 104, No. 2 (1913): Introspective; the melody is rather stagnant, the harmonic progression interesting.

No. 11 in G minor, Op. 105, No. 1 (1914): Wonderful technique exhibited by the composer in his use of short repetitive motives.

No. 12 in E-flat major, Op. 105, No. 2 (1916): The barcarolle motion is especially gentle.

No. 13 in C major, Op. 116 (1921): Fauré was seventy-six and deaf when he concluded this series, begun by his fortieth year, with a piece of springtime freshness.

Thirteen Barcarolles:
COLLARD: Angel
CROSSLEY: CRD
DOYEN: MHS (LP)

Thirteen Nocturnes (1883–1922)

The Nocturnes are among Fauré's greatest flights of creativity. They display a wide range of feeling and daring harmonic progressions. Generally, they are more complex than the Barcarolles.

No. 1 in E-flat minor, Op. 33 (1883): Very original in its piano setting; full of sorrow and heaviness.

No. 2 in B major, Op. 33, No. 2 (1883): Vuillermoz wrote, "It is pleasant, carefree, a bit capricious, and permits itself at times the graceful freedom of an impromptu."

No. 3 in A-flat major, Op. 33, No. 3 (1883): More Chopinesque than any of the other nocturnes, and among the most frequently played.

No. 4 in E-flat major, Op. 36 (1884): Direct, without any of Fauré's shy mystery; bell effects.

No. 5 in B-flat major, Op. 37 (1884): A pastoral setting; the second theme, in Evelyne Crochet's phrase, "shows more anxiety than genuine emotion."

No. 6 in D-flat major, Op. 63 (1894): A span of a decade separates the Fifth and Sixth Nocturnes. In this nine-minute work, the once luxuriant form becomes a psychological drama of emotional depth. It is one of the great masterpieces of French piano music.

No. 7 in C-sharp minor, Op. 74 (1898): Ten minutes long, this is interpretively more difficult than No. 6. The beauties are more severe, the austerity entering the realm of grief. The ending is in a calm D major.

No. 8 in D-flat major, Op. 84, No. 8 (1902): The Eighth Nocturne, the shortest by far of the thirteen (2:30), is also the eighth piece of Fauré's *Huit Pièces brèves.* But this light and amiable work is always included in the complete Nocturnes as well.

No. 9 in B minor, Op. 97 (1908): Evelyne Crochet wrote, "The Ninth Nocturne has one of the most beautiful of Fauré's piano themes; a phrase of exquisite purity modulates into B major and bursts into a resonant chorale."

No. 10 in E minor, Op. 99 (1909): A serious work, full of asperities, which needs very skillful musicianship.

No. 11 in F-sharp minor, Op. 104 (1913): "A sad and moving song," wrote Crochet. "As in the Requiem, a detached serenity, surely and starkly expressed, makes itself felt through the grief."

No. 12 in E minor, Op. 107 (1916): Harmonically interesting; a gloomy work.

No. 13 in B minor, Op. 119 (1922): Fauré's last piece for the piano; a work of sad nobility, rising to a great climax but ending in a calm despair.

> *Thirteen Nocturnes* (complete):
> COLLARD: EMI
> CROSSLEY: CRD
> HEIDSIECK: EMI
> LIVELY: Etcetera
> THYSSEN-VALENTIN: Charlin

Nine Preludes, Op. 103 (1911)

The Preludes sound best played as a set. Their aftereffect lures a listener back. It almost seems that all of Fauré is condensed here in twenty minutes.

> R. CASADESUS (Nos. 1, 3, 5): Philips: Great Pianists of the Twentieth Century
> CROSSLEY: CRD
> FERBER: Saga (LP)
> HEIDSIECK: Cassiopée
> JOHANNESEN: VAI
> J. MARTIN: Naxos

Theme and Variations, Op. 73 (1897)

The longest of Fauré's piano works (fifteen minutes), it is a peak in French piano music, and perhaps the most played set of French variations. The theme is original. In the Variation No. 11, Fauré endows the score with all of his tenderheartedness, allied to a fine variational skill.

> COLLARD: Angel
> DEMUS: Westminster (LP)
> FERBER: Saga (LP)
> LEFÉBURE: Solstice
> PERLEMUTER: Nimbus

Ballade for Piano and Orchestra in F-sharp major, Op. 19 (1881)

This is perhaps the most poetic smaller work for piano and orchestra in the literature, with long lyric lines rising to a climax, then subsiding to Fauré's usual soft close. The work was originally composed for piano solo, and in that setting may be the most difficult of Fauré's piano writings.

> R. CASADESUS, Bernstein/New York Philharmonic: Sony Classical
> CROSSLEY (solo version): CRD
> HEIDSIECK, Benzi/Festival du Grand Rué: Cassiopée
> JOHANNESEN (solo version): Golden Crest (LP)

M. LONG, Gaubert/Orchestra: Pearl
POMMIER (soloist and conductor), Northern
  Sinfonia Orchestra: Virgin Classics
TAGLIAFERRO, Coppola/Orchestre du
  Gramophone: Dante

CÉSAR FRANCK
1822–1890—Belgium

Symphonic Variations for Piano and Orchestra (1885)

One of Franck's richest works, a staple of the repertoire, the *Variations symphoniques* is a masterpiece of variational technique. In fifteen minutes, Franck presents an introduction in which he creates six variations, and a finale. Franck also composed a neglected but effective and beautiful work for piano and orchestra, *Les Djinns,* based on a poem by Victor Hugo.

Symphonic Variations:
R. CASADESUS, Ormandy/Philadelphia: Sony
  Classical
COLLARD, Plasson/Toulouse Capitole: Angel
CURZON, Boult/London Symphony: London
E. JOYCE, Munch/Paris Conservatoire
  Orchestra: Dante
THIOLLIER, Almeida/Irish National Orchestra:
  Naxos
WEISSENBERG, Karajan/Berlin Philharmonic:
  Angel

Prelude, Chorale, and Fugue (1884)

A majestic score of nearly twenty minutes. The technical demands are heavy. Harvey Grace wrote: "It is a kind of epitome of the Franckian mood and method. . . . Like so much of his music, it is over-chromatic in places—notably in the interludes of the Chorale on its first appearance—but that is a small blemish on a work which in construction, thematic development, polyphony, command of keyboard technique, and above all in sustained musical interest, is among the masterpieces of pianoforte literature."

CHERKASSKY: Nimbus
CICCOLINI: Pathé
CORTOT: Philips: Great Pianists of the
  Twentieth Century
KISSIN: RCA
MALCUZYNSKI: Seraphim
MORAVEC: Philips: Great Pianists of the
  Twentieth Century
PERAHIA: Sony Classical
RICHTER: Monitor
RUBINSTEIN: RCA

Prelude, Aria, and Finale (1886–87)

This is less valuable than the Prelude, Chorale, and Fugue but nevertheless an important work in the history of French piano music. Franck's last piano work, it lies in a dangerous domain, hovering on the verge of vulgarity and sentimentality. Norman Demuth wrote, "I have heard the first section made to sound like a military march, and the second like Gounod at his feeblest." Demuth also gives the key to the interpretation of Franck's works: "Pianists try to make them sound 'holy.' Franck was simply a good man who made his faith the mainstay of his existence; he was no more "holy" than was Bach. His Romanticism is neither sanctimonious nor priggish. The music is introvert and subjective, but it should not be given the air of spiritual isolation. It must be approached in a broad manner."

It should be noted that Harold Bauer made a superb transcription for piano of Franck's Prelude, Fugue, and Variation for Organ, which is ten minutes long and less difficult than the two original Franck piano works.

Prelude, Aria, and Finale:
CORTOT: Philips: Great Pianists of the Twentieth Century
CROSSLEY: L'Oiseau-Lyre
D'ARCO: Calliope (LP)
HOUGH: Hyperion
SILVERMAN: CBC

G

GEORGE GERSHWIN
1898–1937—United States

Gershwin was seldom far from his piano. His early piano teacher, Charles Hambitzer, wrote, "I have a pupil who will make his mark in music if anybody will. The boy is a genius, without doubt; he's just crazy about music, and can't wait until it's time to take his lesson." The piano was pure joy for him, and he developed into a superlative, flawless pianist in his own music, cool, buoyant, and effervescent. He was soloist at the celebrated premiere of his *Rhapsody in Blue* at Aeolian Hall in New York in 1924, and the following year in the first performance of the Piano Concerto. Oscar Lavant wrote, "George had the most inventive and personal flair for piano performing—apart from his genius at composition—that I have ever seen. . . . He was simply a delight to watch, especially when he played his own music."

Rhapsody in Blue (1924)

The most often performed of any American work for piano and orchestra, perhaps of any American orchestral score. In its Lisztian piano technique and the utilization of jazz and blues idioms, with its infectious rhythmic audacity, incisive syncopation, and sweet and sassy themes, it was instantaneously understood and rapturously received. Soon Gershwin's stylization of jazz into classical forms intrigued composers the world over to try their hand in the jazz style. Ravel, Walton, Copland, Krenek, Tansman, Weill, Milhaud, and Lambert are just a few who composed music stimulated from jazz and its derivatives. Lambert wrote in his book, *Music, Ho!* "Although other American composers, and even Gershwin himself produced works of greater calibre in this style, the shadow of the *Rhapsody in Blue* hangs over most of them and they remain the hybrid child of a hybrid." Gershwin's music unfolded complex and powerful aspects of the polyglot American landscape. As a composer he represented the transfixed jazz age of the 1920s, and the *Rhapsody* appeared to epitomize the spirit of the era. Today we listen to the score as sounding the note of a vanished time in American life, a brashly energetic and optimistic moment, and we now hear the *Rhapsody* with an almost unbearable nostalgia.

BERNSTEIN, Bernstein/Columbia Symphony: CBS
GERSHWIN (piano roll), Thomas/Columbia Jazz Band: CBS
GERSHWIN (piano solo): Nimbus
KATCHEN, Kertesz/London Symphony: Philips: Great Pianists of the Twentieth Century
LEVANT, Ormandy/Philadelphia: CBS
PREVIN, Previn/London Symphony: Angel
WILD, Fiedler/Boston Pops: RCA

Piano Concerto in F (1925)

The Concerto in F is a rousing audience pleaser. At thirty minutes, it is double the length of the *Rhapsody* and structurally not as sound as the tightly packed earlier work. It has all the Gershwin traits, as Paul Rosenfeld notes, "some of them being popularly American in essence or gaily, brightly Yiddish, and others impressionistic or vaguely grand-operatic, or reminiscent of the melodramatic emphasis and *fioritura* of Liszt or Chopinesque." The Concerto is glitzy, schmalzy, tap dancing, motoric, and desperately nostalgic.

> GRIMAUD, Zinman/Baltimore Symphony: Erato
> LEVANT, Kostelanetz/New York Philharmonic: CBS
> PREVIN, Previn/Pittsburgh Symphony: Philips
> SIEGEL, Slatkin/St. Louis Symphony: Vox Cum Laude
> SZIDON, Downes/London Philharmonic: DG
> WILD, Fiedler/Boston Pops: RCA

George Gershwin by David Dubal

Three Preludes (1926)

The longer No. 2 is a beautiful blues work, falling between the two shorter, syncopated, jazz-derived pieces. Gershwin also composed arrangements of his own popular songs; these wonderfully pianistic adoptions have long fascinated pianists.

> BOLCOM: Nonesuch
> LEVANT: Sony Classical
> PENNARIO: RCA (LP)
> TILSON THOMAS: Sony Classical

ALBERTO GINASTERA
1916–1983—Argentina

Sonata No. 1 (1952)

This piano sonata in four short movements is dazzling in its laconic compositional virtuosity. In addition to an atonal Presto, of folk material endowed with a sense of mystery, it has a passionate slow movement and a vital finale, Ruvido ed ostinato, which has made this one of the best-known contemporary sonatas. Ginastera has an exceptional knowledge of piano sonority. His Sonatas Nos. 2 and 3 are less rewarding.

> NISSMAN (complete piano music): Pierian
> RODRIGUEZ: Elan
> VOTAPEK: Ivory Classics
> WILLE: DG (LP)

Piano Concerto No. 1 (1961)

Both Ginastera piano concerti are landmarks of the South American concerto literature.

The First Concerto is more complex than the Sonata in its structure and dissonance. It is exciting listening, with its driving rhapsodic elements, fluttering atonality, and a flashy piano part with high locomotion.

MARTINS, Leinsdorf/Boston Symphony:
   RCA (LP)
SOMER, Maerzendorfer/Vienna Philharmonic:
   Desto

Piano Concerto No. 2 (1972)

The composer speaks of the tragic and fantastic nature of this concerto. It is in four movements, the first being thirty-two variations on a single chord by Beethoven, that of measure 208 of the fourth movement of the Ninth Symphony. The second movement is a scherzo for left hand alone and displays opposing colors. The third movement of microsounds, Quasi una fantasia, is the emotional heart of this dense score, and the fourth movement, Cadenza e finale, uses eleven notes from the finale of Chopin's *Funeral March* Sonata, "The Wind over the Graves."

SOMER, CASSUTO/UCI Symphony:
   Orion (LP)

LEOPOLD GODOWSKY
1870–1938—Poland

Godowsky's music is now being heard more frequently. Pianists wanting to expand their musical and technical horizons are no longer as fearful. Godowsky has given pianists some of the most challenging and grateful music to delight themselves and receptive audiences. Pianists would be astounded at their technical improvement if they seriously encountered Godowsky. He wrote almost exclusively for his instrument, leaving original works to be savored, such as the *Walzermasken* (1912), twenty-four fairly short diverse pieces which are attractive and eminently playable. Even more accessible for the piano are the thirty moods and scenes in triple measure, called *Triakontameron*, dedicated to the pianist Alexander Lambert, of which many are masterful. No. 11, his most famous piece, *Alt Wien*, a delicious Viennese cream puff written in 1919 in Seattle, which has toured the world. Of his many works for left hand alone, the neoclassic Suite of 1929 has eight numbers, *Allimand, Boureé, Gavotte,* and so forth, all very effective. For left hand alone the six Waltz Poems are beautiful figurations and mazes, while the *Etude macabre* for the left hand in D minor is frightfully difficult.

Godowsky's paraphrases are breathtaking in his exploitation of the piano. From morsels such as the Albéniz Tango in D to the concert arrangement of Albéniz's *Triana* from *Iberia,* already difficult enough by the Spaniard, Godowsky proves he can make the piece take wings. One should look at the Bach suites for cello solos which are freely transcribed for the piano. Well known is Saint-Saëns's *The Swan*; Schubert's Moment Musical in F minor; the concert arrangement from Schubert's *Rosamunde*; Strauss's *Serenade*; the collection called *Renaissance,* in five books, are fifteen pieces, re-births, based on Rameau, Lully, Loeillet, and Dandrieu. Of exceptional sensitivity are the freely adapted twelve Schubert songs; the best are *Litanei, the Trout, Gute Nacht, Das Wandern,* and *Morgengrüss.*

Sonata in E minor (1911)

A magnificent curiosity in five movements, the finale being a fugue. Godowsky performed it himself only once in public, and its duration of an hour makes it difficult to program. The temper of the music is late Romanticism with shades of Liszt. In the scherzo especially, Brahmsian aroma hovers and Chopin peeps in at varied moments along with many glassy, nostalgic *Alt Wein* moods. The sonata's technical requirements are devilish and torturous, yet grateful for the hands, really wonderful in its figural precision. The work will forever be opium for those attracted to its sinuous pages. The Australian pianist Paul Howard, who never forgot the thrills of his first encounters with the Sonata around 1912, wrote: "Today thirty-five years later I am still going on and finding new light in it; although I have played it in recital many times, and to visitors hundreds of times, it is a work that is never finished, but always intrigues and offers new points of view, new aspects to be mastered."

ALEKSANDER: Eroica; Pro Piano
KANN: Musical Heritage Society (second movement only)
HAMELIN: Hyperion
PINES: Genesis (first movement only) (LP)

Java Suite (1924–25)

The four parts of the suite contain three pieces each, and if played complete would take forty-five minutes. These are Godowsky's impressions of *Java* where he had performed. He wrote, "Though we travel the world over to find the beautiful, we must carry it with us, or we find it not." A good selection is *Gamelon, Chattering Monkeys at the Sacred Lake of Wendit, Boro Budur in Moonlight, The Gardens of Buitenzorg* (a famous botanical park.) In this luxuriant piece Godowsky asks, "Why do certain scents produce unutterable regrets, insatiable longings, indefinable desires?" Of *In the Kraton*, he wrote, "There is poetry in every ebbing moment. It is evening in the Orient."

Excerpts:
Chattering Monkeys:
PINES: Genesis (LP)
The Gardens of Buitenzorg:
GODOWSKY: APR
LOESSER: Marston

Passacaglia (1927)

The *Passacaglia* (forty-four variations, cadenza, and fugue on the opening theme of Schubert's "Unfinished Symphony") is Godowsky's finest original work, and his most penetrating music. It is almost never played in public, although it is only seventeen minutes; Horowitz said, "It needs six hands to play it." Godowsky premiered it in London in 1928. He had written, "I believe that my latest work is a great expression of human loftiness. While composing it I felt that I was purifying my soul and looking into eternity."

DE WAAL: Hyperion
GRANTE: Music and Arts
HAMELIN: Hyperion

Symphonic Metamorphoses of the "Schatz-Waltz" for Left Hand Alone (1928)

From Johann Strauss II's operetta, *The Gypsy Baron*, a scintillating twelve minutes, dedicated to Simon Barère; Godowsky could indeed write, "I have developed an uncanny virtuosity in writing for the one hand."

FLEISHER: Sony Classical

Symphonic Metamorphosis of Künstlerleben (1905)

An intoxicating work, Godowsky's *Metamorphosis* on Strauss's Waltzes are true creations; they are for the few who can manage with lilt and passion the compound layering of this super-pianism. As Godowsky said, "The pedal actually takes the place of a third and sometimes even a fourth hand." The *Künstlerleben* (Artist's Life) totals twelve minutes for performance if all goes smoothly.

DE WAAL: Hyperion
SAPERTON: VAI Audio
WILD: Philips: Great Pianists of the Twentieth Century

Symphonic Metamorphosis of Die Fledermaus (1907)

Based on waltzes from Strauss's *Fledermaus*, Godowsky said, "Hear Josef Hofmann play the *Fledermaus Symphonic Metamorphosis* and you will understand why the term 'symphonic' is used in the title of these free fantasies." Unfortunately we have no recording of it by Hofmann. It is possibly the most difficult of the three two-hand Strauss *Metamorphosis*, of grinding difficulty, which must be played with a casual almost matter-of-fact mastery and elegance. There have been many recordings by such artists as Goldsand, Kitain, Farnadi, Saperton, and Janice Weber. (Farnadi, Saperton, and Janice Weber are on LP.)

MOISEIWITSCH: VAI Audio
FREIRE: Philips: Great Pianists of the Twentieth Century
LABÉ: Dorian

Symphonic Metamorphosis of Wein, Weib und Gesang

Perhaps the easiest of the three, if such a word may be used. The *Wine, Women and Song* Metamorphosis is once again less a high-wire virtuosic act than a supercharged homage to the Vienna in which Johann Strauss made the waltz its symbol and a city Godowsky loved.

CHERKASSKY: Philips: Great Pianists of the Twentieth Century
CHERKASSKY: Academy Sound and Vision
LABÉ: Dorian

Contrapuntal Arrangement on Weber's Invitation to the Dance

The only public performance I have heard of this intriguing and obdurate work was by the Godowsky champion Jorge Bolet, in a thrilling performance at Carnegie Hall. Jeremy Nicholas, in his splendid pioneering biography, *Godowsky, The Pianist's Pianist*, writes: "Another essay in contrapuntal writing, published in 1905 and dedicated to Ferruccio Busoni, is the witty, tongue-in-check transformation of Weber's *Invitation to the Dance* which, though it has never received the same attention as the Strauss paraphrases, is an equally effective (and difficult) exercise in thematic combination."

DE WAAL: Hyperion

53 Studies on Chopin's Etudes (1893–1914)

A work which causes indigestion to purists who feel that Godowsky tramples on Chopin; but others realize Godowsky's creativity was simply unleashed by Chopin's genius.

However, what exists is a body of pianism unprecedented in its understanding of piano technique. As Marc-André Hamelin puts it: "The prospective pianist is confronted with unexpected levels of difficulty, mostly concerned with mental challenges seldom if ever encountered anywhere else in the repertoire, requiring unflinching concentration and true dedication in order that all details are clearly presented and articulated. . . . It cannot be overemphasized that Godowsky had the utmost respect for Chopin, and he selected the Etudes in particular because they represented a solid and proven foundation to consider as a basis for transformation."

The group provides twenty-two studies for the left hand. Hamelin says that they "have revolutionized piano writing for a single hand. The inventiveness displayed in these particular studies in the areas of polyphony, counterpoint, physical configurations and fingering, is nothing short of staggering." All pianists should own Hamelin's complete recordings of the Chopin-Godowsky studies. His notes to each etude are a delight to read. For those who may feel discouraged about attempting them, Godowsky himself was optimistic, exclaiming: "My music is not difficult, some of it is hard to read perhaps, but I insist that it is not difficult to play. . . . They are all of pianistic quality, they yield easily to practice, and, once mastered, seem easy. . . . I have small hands and I write my music to fit the hand."

    GRANTE: Altarus
    HAMELIN: Hyperion
    HOBSON (Selected Etudes): Arabesque
    SAPERTON: VAI Audio

PERCY GRAINGER
1882–1961—Australia

Grainger's reputation and musical stock have greatly risen in the past two decades. His music definitely speaks louder and more joyously than it ever has. Its bracing good will and generally folk-like character give it its multicultural flavor. In his words, he wanted to bring "all the world's music to all the world." He grew up in colonial British Australia, a young country that heralded democratic ideals which stayed with him forever. At the beginning of the twentieth century, many feared that industrialization would destroy the great repository of folk songs, and such musicians as Cecil Sharp, Vaughan Williams, Arthur Farewell, Bartók, Kodály, Pedrell, Grainger, and others were deeply concerned with collecting and preserving their musical roots.

Selected piano music

Shepherd's Hey (English Morris dance tune): In 1906, Grainger heard three fiddlers play the good-natured tune which he ingeniously arranged for piano.

Country Gardens: Grainger's "hit"; *Country Gardens,* a tune discovered by Cecil Sharp, was to Grainger what Paderewski's Minuet and Rachmaninoff's Prelude became to their authors. In a sarcastic mood about his ubiquitous piece, he wrote, "The typical English country garden is not often used to grow flowers in, it is more likely to be a vegetable plot. So you can think of turnips as I play it."

Sussex Mummers (Christmas Carol): Dedicated to Grieg, Grainger wrote, "This beautiful tune in some ways resembles a chorale more than a carol."

Jutish Medley: Grainger loved Denmark, and this eight-minute score is brilliantly transcribed for piano from his orchestral work titled *Danish Folk Music Suite.*

Molly on the Shore (Irish Reel): One of Grainger's best-known pieces is based on two Cork reel tunes, in a masterful combination with Grainger's usual meticulous directions for the pianist.

Spoon River (No. 1 from *American Folk-Music Settings*): Another Grainger favorite, dedicated to "Edgar Lee Masters, poet of pioneers," author of *Spoon River Anthology*.

March-Jig Nos. 1–4 (1916): Sir Charles Villiers Stanford's four Irish Dances for orchestra, Op. 79, are based on eighteenth-century marching tunes. Grainger's adaptations are free and spirited. Each are about four minutes long, and all of them are adorable. No. 1, *Maguire's Kick,* was often played by Grainger. No. 4, *A Reel,* is wonderfully danceable. One wonders why such superb fare, with their tart tang of Ireland, are absent from the repertoire of concert pianists.

Colonial Song (1911): A magnificent original work of seven minutes, the composer said, "It gives expression to feelings aroused by the scenery of Australia." Wilfrid Mellers writes, "Each variation is more sumptuously harmonized until, after a no-hold-barred climax, the process is reversed, the dynamics being gradually subdued." It is Grainger's finest tribute to the land of his birth.

Walking Tune (No. 3 from *Music-Room Tidbits*): A simple and haunting lyric melody predominates throughout. The theme is of original vintage, but the folk element is inescapable.

Handel in the Strand (Clog Dance, 1912): The work is difficult, as is much of Grainger's output. Here is an extraordinary amalgam of elements. The pianist Joseph Smith writes, "Baroque counterpoint, changing meters, syncopation, modality—and a tune of unabashed, blatant vulgarity."

R. Strauss—Grainger, Ramble on the Last Love-Duet in Der Rosenkavalier: The Ramble on Love is something of a throwback to the nineteenth-century paraphrases, and in it Grainger exhibits his uncanny use of piano textures. Mellers says, "It sounds like streamlined Liszt, refashioned in Ravelian lucidity, and is a marvelous instance of Grainger's irresistible way with a piano."

GRAINGER: Nimbus
HAMELIN: Hyperion
JONES (complete works for solo piano):
    Nimbus
SMITH: MHS

ENRIQUE GRANADOS
1867–1916—Spain

Granados was an astute explorer of the piano's resources. He had a wonderful feel for sonority and color, which culminated in his breathtaking masterpiece, the *Goyescas*. One of the first to appreciate him was the English critic Ernest Newman, who wrote: "The texture of Granados's music . . . is of the kind that makes you want to run your fingers over it, as over some exquisite velvet; the flavor of it is something for the tongue almost, as well as the ear. . . . To play through some of his pages is like a joyous wading knee-deep through beds of gorgeous flowers—always with a sure way through and the clearest of light and air around us."

Granados's last appearance as a virtuoso took place at the White House, where he performed for President Wilson. While returning to Spain, Granados and his wife were drowned at sea after a German U-boat torpedoed their ship.

The Complete Piano Music

Granados wrote twenty-four titles, which consist of either single pieces or suites. Except for a few of the *Goyescas* and the Fifth Spanish

Dance, much of Granados's output is still not well known. His music conveys a highly Romantic imagery, ranging from Spanish nationalism to the ever-present influence of Chopin and Schumann. He had his salon side, and he was a master of small forms and of the various Spanish dances.

DOSSE: Vox

Twelve Danzas españolas

Some of his finest purely Spanish writing. Many are not difficult to execute, but such pieces as the celebrated No. 5, *Andaluza,* or the *Zarabanda, Jota,* and *Asturiana,* call for a certain rhythmic knack.

DE LARROCHA: London
GRANADOS: Nimbus
OSORIO: Cedille
SORIANO: Connoisseur Society (LP)

Enrique Granados by David Dubal

Seis Piezas sobre cantos populares españoles

The Six Pieces on Spanish Folk Songs are again in an exclusively Spanish frame of reference. They are full-blooded, richly textured, and more difficult than the *Danzas españolas.*

DE LARROCHA: Turnabout; London

Valses poéticos (1887)
Danza lenta

The suite of dances is the earliest mature work of the composer. It contains an introduction followed by seven waltzes, with the first waltz repeated as the coda. Almost unknown, this suite—influenced by Schumann and Schubert—has a beauty all its own. Each melody is more fragrant than the last, and the morning dew of the first waltz is unforgettable. The technical requirements are modest. The *Danza lenta,* with its elaborate growth of trilled figures, is a very late piece, probably composed after the *Goyescas.*

DE LARROCHA: RCA
GRANADOS: Nimbus
GRANADOS: Pierian

Allegro de concierto

In C-sharp major, this is glorious music. Written for a piano competition and dedicated to Maláts, it is Lisztian pianism in a Spanish mode.

DE LARROCHA: London; RCA
ITURBI: Angel (LP)
JONES: Nimbus
ORTIZ: Collins Classics

Escenas románticas

A suite of six pieces totaling twenty-four minutes, and including a lovely mazurka. The *Poet and the Nightingale* is wonderfully realized. This passionate score is sadly neglected and ranks with the finest of Granados's work. It asks of the performer a wide variety of tone, imaginative use of rubato, and a Romantic nature.

DE LARROCHA: MHS; London
JONES: Nimbus

Goyescas (1911)

The *Goyescas* are the fullest expression of Granados's genius, which possessed many visual elements. He was immersed in Francisco Goya's world of *majas* and *majos,* their gallantry and turbulence, their sensuality and coquetry. This maze of impressions, filtered through his acute, visual sensibility, produced music of an extempore quality—fragmented, luxuriant, and moody. In *El Amor y la muerte,* the bells toll in the bass, representing the hovering presence of death, which culminates in the *Dies Irae,* used in the middle of *The Specter's Serenade.* The suite calls for the richest of virtuoso equipment and a feel for the dramatic atmosphere of the Iberian peninsula. Granados wrote, "In *Goyescas* I intended to give a personal note, a mixture of bitterness and grace . . . that are typically Spanish; and a sentiment suddenly amorous and passionate, dramatic and tragic, such as is seen in the works of Goya." The collection of six pieces is subtitled *Los Majos enamorados* ("The Enraptured Lovers").

Los Requiebros ("Flatteries"): A difficult piece; melodies move between the hands with difficult double notes. The main theme is a jota, a Spanish dance from Aragon. The work starts and stops with a fateful intensity. (The work is dedicated to Emil von Sauer.)

Coloquio en la reja ("Love Duet;" "Conversation in the Jailhouse"): Technically diffuse, a work requiring great ardor. Joan Brown writes:

> The atmosphere is one of love and tragedy. Here Granados heard the guitar in the piano's bass and the human voice in the melody. Man and woman and all they can mean to each other are in the amorous last *copla,* or theme.

(The work is dedicated to Edouard Risler.)

El Fandango de candil ("The Fandango by Lantern Light"): A work of the utmost pianistic elegance and harmonic richness. The fandango rhythm is used with incomparable allure. (The work is dedicated to Ricardo Viñes.)

Quejas, o la maja y el ruiseñor ("Laments, or The Maiden and the Nightingale"): A supremely Romantic improvisation, and the most celebrated of the *Goyescas.* In the final page, the nightingale bursts forth, in the words of the composer, "with the jealousy of a wife, not with the sadness of a widow." (The work is dedicated to Amparo Gal.)

El Amor y la muerte ("Ballade—Love and Death"): The longest of the *Goyescas,* asking the pianist for flights of imagination and a command of complex textures, as well as artistic use of the pedals. The composer brings back with exquisite and painful effect the great theme from No. 4, *The Maiden and the Nightingale.* The work possesses the highest dramatic impact and is indispensable to the psychology of the entire set. (The work is dedicated to Harold Bauer.)

Epílogo ("Serenade of the Specter"): A perfect ending. A ghostly atmosphere envelops the listener, as a skeleton strums on an eerie guitar. (The work is dedicated to Alfred Cortot.)

Goyescas:
AYBAR: Connoisseur Society (LP)
BATTERSBY: Koch
BLOCK: Pro Piano
CICCOLINI: Seraphim
DE LARROCHA: London; EMI
GRANADOS (Four Pieces): Pierian
KYRIAKOU: Turnabout (LP)
MESHULAM: Chesky

El Pelele (*The Strawman*)

This is a sparkling late piece, which Granados incorporated into his ill-fated opera, *Goyescas,* based on the piano suite.

DE LARROCHA: Turnabout; London
GRANADOS: Nimbus

EDVARD GRIEG

1843 –1907—Norway

Grieg was a good pianist who appeared often in public, mostly in the accompaniments of his songs or in collaboration in his violin sonatas. He made a few piano rolls. Of his seventy-four opus numbers, thirty-two are groups of solo piano pieces. The most enduring are the ten sets of *Lyric Pieces,* sixty-six in number. Their tart lyricism has survived the changing currents of fashion, notwithstanding Debussy's sarcastic quip: "pink bonbons filled with snow."

Grieg began as a disciple of Schumann and Chopin (von Bülow wrongly dubbed him the Chopin of the North), but early in his career he came under the influence of the fervent Norwegian nationalist composer Rikard Nordraak, who died at the age of twenty-four, in 1866. Grieg assumed his mantle.

Grieg is the greatest of the Norwegian composers and is beloved throughout his homeland. His pianism is based on Liszt's muscular system in the large works, such as the Ballade, Op. 24, and the great A minor Concerto. While not exactly awkward for the hands, much of Grieg can be inconvenient to play.

Ballade in the Form of Variations on a Norwegian Folk Song in G minor, Op. 24 (1875)

The Ballade was written from the depth of Grieg's heart. It is the finest set of Scandinavian variations of the nineteenth century. It is also Grieg's most technically difficult solo work, filled with his strangest, most adventurous chromatic harmony. It is not easily brought off in concert, but pianists have always felt its appeal. It was in the repertoires of Rachmaninoff, Hofmann, and Percy Grainger.

DAVIS: Audiofon
GODOWSKY: Philips: Great Pianists of the Twentieth Century
KATIN: Olympia
LAVAL: Seraphim
MERZHANOV: Melodiya
PAPERNO: Cedille
RUBINSTEIN: RCA

Holberg Suite, Op. 40 (1844)

Subtitled *From Holberg's Time* and in four movements, headed by a Praeludium. Grieg is charming in his attempt to wed a northern spirit to Baroque forms.

DAVIS: Audiofon
KLIEN: Turnabout (LP)

PROPPER: Ogam
WIKSTROM: Swedish Society Discofil (LP)

Lyric Pieces, Opp. 12, 38, 43, 47, 54, 57, 62, 65, 68, 71

The sixty-six *Lyric Pieces* are virtually a repository of Norwegian music. They retain their freshness and portray both sides of Grieg's mind and heart, which often fluctuated between the elegiac and a joyous elfin spirit.

BAUER (6 pieces): History
GIESEKING (31 pieces): Seraphim (LP)
GILELS (20 pieces): DG
GOLDENWEISER (complete): Melodiya (LP)
KOCSIS (14 pieces): Philips (LP)
RUBINSTEIN (11 pieces): RCA

Norwegian Peasant Dances (Slåtter), Op. 72 (1902)

Arrangements of dances transcribed from the Hardanger fiddle, these neglected pieces are far more daring than the *Lyric Pieces*. They represent a side of Grieg that is fascinating and harmonically stark. Wilfrid Mellers thinks they "can be legitimately compared with the folk-song arrangements of Bartók. . . . He transfers the sharp, crackling sound of the village fiddler with miraculous skill to the piano."

ANDSNES: EMI
MOURAO: Vox
STEEN-NOKLEBERG: Naxos

Piano Concerto A minor, Op. 16 (1868)

One of the most popular concertos of all time. It lacks the excessive difficulty of other Romantic concertos, and consequently it has been overplayed by students and amateurs. The work was inspired by Schumann's A minor Concerto. It retains its youthful freshness. The overall Norwegian color and the peasant dance of the last movement never fail to delight an audience.

BACKHAUS, Barbirolli/New Symphony
    Orchestra: Andante
FLEISHER, Szell/Cleveland: Odyssey
FRIEDMAN, Gaubert: Pearl
GRAINGER, Stokowski/Hollywood Bowl
    Symphony: Archiv Documents
LIPATTI, Galliera/Philharmonia:
    Odyssey
LUPU, Previn/London Symphony: London
MICHELANGELI, Rossi/Rome Orchestra:
    Arkadia
MOISEIWITSCH, Heward/Hallé Orchestra:
    APR
RICHTER, Oistrakh/Bergen Symphony: Intaglio
RUBINSTEIN, Wallenstein/RCA Symphony:
    RCA
SOLOMON, Menges/Philharmonia: EMI
ZIMMERMAN, von Karajan/Berlin
    Philharmonic: DG

CHARLES TOMLINSON GRIFFES

1884–1920—United States

Griffes, who died at thirty-six, was the most sensitive impressionist tone poet America ever produced. Though not prolific, he wrote music of uniformly high quality in both craft and content. His later work took on a harsher tone.

Unusual for an American of the day, his affiliations were French, Debussy and Ravel being his mainstays. His interests also took him to exotic subjects.

The *Three Tone Pictures,* Op. 5, from 1915 (including the perfect *Night Wind*), and the exquisite set of *Four Roman Sketches,* Op. 7 (which include *The Fountain of the Acqua Paola* and Griffes's best-known work, *The White Peacock*), represent the peak of American impressionism.

Piano Sonata (1917–18)

The Sonata is Griffes's masterwork. He was a lonely figure during a particularly sterile period in American music. Wilfrid Mellers says: "This disturbingly powerful Sonata is an American parable in musical terms, telling us what happens to the ego alone in the industrial wilderness. . . . Griffes's Sonata is an astonishing and frightening work; its Orientalism is not an escape into dream but a consequence of desperation such as could have occurred only in a spiritually barbarous world."

The work is pianistically a marvel, Griffes having a magnificent ear for sonority and color. The Sonata possesses sensuousness and a raw, seething energy, as well as its own Romanticism, exploding into soaring ecstasy near the end. The performer must get deep inside the work's most painful and frenzied regions. His Three Piano Preludes (1919) continue to lead Griffes in new directions.

Piano Sonata:
DOPPMANN: Albany
HAMBRO: Lyrichord (LP)
KEENE: Protone
J. SMITH: MHS
STARR: Orion
TOCCO (complete piano music): Gasparo

H

ROY HARRIS

1898–1979—United States

Sonata, Op. 1 (1928)

Harris wrote a quantity of fine music. His Op. 1, written in France when he was studying with Boulanger, has a Prelude (*Maestoso con bravura*), *Andante ostinato (Misterioso)*, and Scherzo. Harris flexes his muscles here and finds them strong. Still fresh today, the score must have been a revelation to the American musical scene in 1928, its primitivism and pioneer spirit coupled with a distinctly Anglo-American hymnody and jazziness in the scherzo.

> CORBATÓ: Orion (LP)
> J. HARRIS: CRI
> SHIELDS: Vox (LP)
> ZIMDARS: Albany

JOSEPH HAYDN

1732–1809—Austria

Although Haydn research has made large strides since the invention of the LP, too few of his sonatas have been assimilated into concert life, and not more than half a dozen are well known. Ironically, Haydn—considered by all to be one of music's immortals—still lives in the shadow of his friend Mozart and of his student Beethoven. The appellation "Papa" Haydn has presented the world with the picture of a benevolent grandfather who always writes good-humored, happy music. Never has a superficial image done more harm to a man of such original genius.

Unlike Mozart and Beethoven, he was not a virtuoso, displaying his wares in public. By his own reckoning, however, he was "not a bad pianist." Some of the early sonatas were probably written for his students. He once lamented, "I spent eight long, wretched years teaching youngsters." Haydn's sonatas, written from 1760 until the final three sonatas of 1794, are a measure of his growth. Here, we can see clearly the evolution of a long career of hard work.

The Piano Sonatas

Haydn's sonatas are not as easy to listen to as those of Mozart. They are diffuse, often brusque, wilder—indeed, experimental. Martin Cooper contrasts the masters: "The vocal element that plays a strong part in Mozart's keyboard sonatas—the cantabile of aria or lied in slow movements and the operatic bustle of many finales—is almost entirely absent from Haydn's keyboard sonatas, whose inspiration is purely instrumental and for that very reason often less immediately enchanting."

Indeed, the new search for bel canto on the

piano left Haydn and his hero, C. P. E. Bach, behind. It was J. C. Bach's galant vocal style that was to influence the Mozart, Clementi, Dussek, and Beethoven slow movements. But Haydn was not interested in singing on the piano so much as in pure expression. In many ways he has more in common with Beethoven than with Mozart. In Haydn, there is an earthy passion; the slow movements suggest the peasant, rather than the courtier, and of course his devastating humor is incomparable.

The numbering of the sonatas has caused endless confusion. Each edition had its own numbering. It is best for contemporary pianists to use two classifications in listing: the Christa Landon numbering (Vienna Urtext, published by Universal) and the Hoboken number (Anthony van Hoboken).

Most Haydn sonata readings today are on the modern grand. According to John McCabe, who has recorded the sonatas "that the instruments of Haydn's day have certain coloristic and technical features not to be found on modern instruments is not in doubt. But I firmly believe that the full color and subtlety of the music can be better realized on a modern piano of suitable character, and I also believe that Haydn's writing, even in his early days, is essentially *pianistic* in conception."

Still, an authentic instrument can bring hidden textures to life in Haydn's keyboard music.

The Complete Sonatas and Various Pieces:
AKI: Discover International
BUCHBINDER: Telefunken
J. MCCABE: London

Selected Sonatas:
ANDSNES: EMI
AX: Sony Classical
BACKHAUS: London (LP)
BILSON (fortepiano): Nonesuch
BRENDEL: Philips

BUNIN: MK
ESHENBACK: Philips: Great Pianists of the Twentieth Century
GOULD: Sony Classical
HOROWITZ: CBS; RCA
JANDÓ: Naxos
KALISH: Nonesuch
KASMAN: Calliope
KOCSIS: Hungaraton
LEVY: Marston
NÁDAS: Ashland (LP)
NEL: Music Masters
OHLSSON: Arabesque
RAPPE: Pavane
SHERMAN: Albany
SVIRSKY: Monitor

Variations in F minor

One of Haydn's most deeply felt piano works. It is a masterpiece of eighteenth-century variation writing.

DE LARROCHA: London
KALISH: Nonesuch
REISENBERG: Ivory Classics
RUBINSTEIN: RCA

Piano Concerto in D major, Hob. XVIII/2 (1782)

Haydn's D major concerto is the finest of his various keyboard concerti. It is also the only one of his concerti to have entered the repertoire. Especially captivating is the finale, a Rondo all'ongarese.

ALPENHEIM, Dorati/Bamberg Symphony: Vox
DAVIDOVICH, Sitkovetsky/Prague Chamber Orchestra: Supraphon
E. FISCHER/Vienna Philharmoic: APR

GILELS, Barshai/Moscow Chamber Orchestra:
Columbia/Melodiya
KISSIN, Spivakov/Moscow Virtuosi: RCA
MICHELANGELI, de Stoutz/Zurich: Angel

HANS WERNER HENZE
b. 1926—Germany

Piano Concerto No. 2 (1967)

This is a fifty-minute concerto of massive dimension, one that needs much rehearsal. The virtuosic orchestral writing has stretches without the piano's intervention. The piano part, though difficult, with much martellato playing, is restricted compared with the orchestral requirements. The effect is bold, fantastic, windy, scattered; it is music of great mournfulness as well.

ESCHENBACH, Henze/London Philharmonic:
DG (LP)
PLAGGE, Markson/Northwest German
Philharmonic: CPO

PAUL HINDEMITH
1895–1963—Germany

Suite "1922," Op. 26

Suite "1922" consists of four parts: *Marsch, Schimmy, Nachtstük,* and *Ragtime.* A highly effective work, with an ironic and sarcastic use of dance forms. The composer asks the performer to "use the piano as an interesting kind of percussion instrument and treat it accordingly."

CARNO: GSC (LP)
KUBALEK: Golden Crest (LP)
PETERMANDL: Marco Polo

Sonatas Nos. 1, 2, and 3 (1936)

All three sonatas were composed in 1936. No. 1, in five movements, needs especially a firm grasp of chord playing. No. 2 is the shortest of the three sonatas, eleven minutes, and offers much easier, brighter, and more rewarding recital material. The Third Sonata, in four movements, is the weightiest of these works, with a concluding double fugue.

The Three Sonatas (complete):
GOULD: CBS
PETERMANDL: Marco Polo
RANDALU: MDG
ROBERTS: Nimbus

Sonata No. 1:
BADURA-SKODA: Westminster (LP)
BILLETER: MHS (LP)

Sonata No. 2:
BILLETER: MHS
TURINI: RCA

Sonata No. 3:
SIEGEL: Orion
WILD: Ivory Classics
YUDINA: Melodiya

Ludus Tonalis (1942)

The high point in Hindemith's piano writing, based on concepts of expanded tonality

509

espoused in his *The Craft of Musical Composition*. He calls the *Ludus Tonalis* "studies in counterpoint, tonal organization and piano playing." There are, he continues, "Twelve Fugues, in as many keys, connected by interludes in free lyric and dance forms, old and new, and framed by a Prelude and Postlude that have more in common than meets the casual ear." Hindemith is one of the great neo-Classicists. This score is rewarding for those seeking intellectual refreshment: for pianists, it is fascinating to work on. For listeners, at first, it may be somewhat acrid, but its geometry becomes increasingly interesting on repeated hearings.

ALDWELL: Pro Piano
CARLSON: MHS (LP)
J. MCCABE: Hyperion
LARETEI: Philips (LP)
MUSTONEN: London Classics
PETERMANDL: Marco Polo
ROBERTS: Nimbus

I

CHARLES IVES
1874–1954—United States

Ives was the first American composer to venture into the uncharted regions of sound. It is amazing to think of his work being composed against the background of the genteel establishment composers of his time. If ever a man was frustrated with the music of his day, it was Ives. He wanted to "kick out the softy ears!" He shouted, "Stand up and use your ears like a man." Finally, after more than a half-century, we are listening to the freshness of his immense vision. Polytonality, clusters, aspects of atonality, and quarter tones are now commonplace, but Ives used them far in advance of most others. His best music, including his two mammoth piano sonatas, must be ranked among the most outstanding creations of twentieth-century art.

Sonata No. 1 (1902–09)

The First Sonata presents a multitude of polyrhythmic problems for the pianist to solve. Of an exhausting forty-minute duration, it demands a tremendous technique, a dedicated spirit, humor, and fearlessness. Ives used hymn tunes in each of the five movements to project the spirit of America as he perceived it at the turn of the century. Like all of his works, this sonata requires great interpretive flux. Only a searching artist can convey its impressionistic manner, shifting moods, and boldness of

utterance. The pianist must be able to capture the essence of the ragtime movements in all of their exuberance, fierce clutter of "wrong" notes, and drunken revelry.

JENSEN: Music and Arts
LEE: Nonesuch (LP)
MASSELOS: Odyssey (LP)

Sonata No. 2, "Concord, Mass., 1840–1860" (1909–15)

For the creative pianist, this is one of the most intriguing works in the repertoire. Since Lawrence Gilman dubbed it "the greatest music composed by an American," the *Concord, Mass.* Sonata has acquired legendary status, with more and more performers applying themselves to its awesome demands. Ives, however, never wrote anything that he himself considered technically impossible. He viewed the performer as a partner. "In fact," he wrote, "these notes, marks and near pictures of sounds, etc., are for the player to make his own speeches on."

The work is a vast musical canvas of the spirit of Transcendentalism, conceived in four movements: "Emerson," "Hawthorne," "The Alcotts," "Thoreau." Ives continuously revised the work over thirty years. There is no definitive edition, and the serious pianist must do considerable research and make many choices. As the pianist Hadassah Sahr puts it: "The *Concord* Sonata is, finally, inexhaustible. . . . The suggested bits of melodies and rhythms bring with them a kind of nostalgic emotion; frequently they sound like a reflection of Americana. The theme from Beethoven's Fifth Symphony is heard in so many different contexts it seems embedded into the very core of the music."

It is more difficult to achieve a cohesive conception of the *Concord* than of the First Sonata.

BLACKWOOD: Cedille
HAMELIN: New World
C. IVES (Emerson, Hawthorne, the Alcotts): CRI
KALISH: Nonesuch
KIRKPATRICK: CBS (LP)
MIKHASHOFF: Spectrum (LP)
SHANNON: Bridge

J

LEOS JANÁCEK
1854–1928—Czechoslovakia

In the Mist (1912)

The great Czech composer left only a few works for solo piano. They are stamped with his unique understanding of Moravian folk music and speech patterns, and with his highly fluid tonality. The music is not pianistic by conventional standards. *In the Mist* is a cycle of four somber and episodic pieces without titles.

> ARAD (includes 15 pieces from *On an Overgrown Path)*: Helicon
> FIRKUSNY: DG
> MORAVEC: Nonesuch
> SCHIFF: London

Sonata in E-flat minor, "1 October 1905"

In two movements, inspired by a tragic political event—a university uprising in Prague. The first movement is titled "Foreboding," Con moto, and the second is titled "Death," Adagio. It is a hearbreaking piece of music, tense and throbbing.

> ARAD: Helicon
> FIRKUSNY: DG
> MORAVEC: Nonesuch

Concertino for Piano, Strings, and Winds (1925)

A masterpiece characteristic of Janácek's mature work. Its opening idea is pregnant, and Janácek develops it ingeniously. The work is inspired by the composer's love for animals and nature. It was originally called *Spring.*

> CROWSON, Melos Ensemble: Angel; Vanguard (LP)
> FIRKUSNY, Neumann/Czech Philharmonic: RCA
> SCHIFF, Musiktage Mondsee Ensemble: London

513

K

ERNST KRENEK
1900–1991—Austria

Sechs Vermessene, Op. 168 (1958)

Krenek was a potent force in the music of our time. Ranging from jazz to twelve-tone, his music has been controversial and much studied by other composers. The *Sechs Vermessene* (meaning "measurements") are totally "serialized." The rhythmic difficulties are very great, though the music is slow moving.

BURGE: Candide (LP)

Sonata No. 3, Op. 92, No. 4 (1943)
Sonata No. 4 (1947)

Two important sonatas. No. 3 is in four movements: a sensitive Allegretto piacevole;

Theme, Canons, and Variations; Scherzo; and Adagio. A work demanding intelligence from the interpeter.

The Fourth Sonata is a work of skill and imagination, using twelve-tone techniques together with older forms. In the first movement, three motives are exposed and exploited in differing tempi. The second movement, Andante sostenuto, con passione, is a big expressionist drama. The third movement is a Rondo, vivace. Speedy, humorous, with trills, it is a spiritual descendant of a Mendelssohn scherzo. The finale is a Tempo di minuetto, molto lento, with three variations, a short section bringing back the motive of the first movement, and a fourth variation with a quiet ending.

BURGE (Sonata No. 4):
  MHS
GOULD (Sonata No. 3):
  CBS
MADGE (seven sonatas):
  Koch Schwann

L

GYÖRGY LIGETI

b. 1923—Hungary

Perhaps the most discussed and performed of contemporary composers. Ligeti has assimilated much, from Bartók and Stravinsky in his early work, to Stockhausen and Boulez, jazz, African rhythms and sounds, as well as music of the Romantics and Debussy.

Musica Ricercata (1951–53)

A sympathetic work; from its time, still performed often. There are eleven movements; it runs about twenty-five minutes. "The first piece," the composer says, "contains only two tones (along with their octave transpositions). The second, three tones, and so on, so that the eleventh piece (a monotonous fugue) uses all twelve pitches." No. 5 is marked "Rubato Lamentoso," No. 9 is in memory of Bartók, and No. 11 is an homage to Frescobaldi.

> AIMARD: Sony Classical
> HAASE: Col Legno
> ULLEN: BIS

Etudes

Ligeti's Etudes have been an ongoing romance of technical procedures, which started in 1985 with the first book of Six Etudes. The Etudes have caught on worldwide, and one hears them in competitions and recitals. Ligeti has lavished upon them heaps of interesting new technical and musical problems, each with titles. The composer says the impetus for his etudes was his own lack of piano technique. He wrote:

> I would love to be a fabulous pianist! I know a lot about nuances of attack, phrasing, rubato, formal structure. And I absolutely love to play piano, but only for myself. To develop a clean technique, one must begin practicing before puberty. But I was already hopelessly past this point. . . . For a piece to be well-suited for the piano, tactile concepts are almost as important as acoustic ones; so I call for support upon the four great composers who thought *pianistically:* Scarlatti, Chopin, Schumann, and Debussy. A Chopinesque melodic twist or accompaniment figure is not just heard; it is also felt as a succession of muscular exertions. A well-formed piano work produces physical pleasure. . . . Jazz pianism also played a big role for me, about all the poetry of Thelonious Monk and Bill Evans.

Other stimuli that gave impetus to Ligeti are the field of geometry, sub-Saharan cultures, and from Conlon Nancarrow's work, he wrote, "I learned rhythmic and metric complexity." There are now 20 etudes; each piece is elaborately delineated as to the composer's direction. Some of the best known are *Fanfares* (No. 4), *Vertige* (No. 11), *White on*

517

White (No. 15), and *Automne á Varsovie* (No. 6), of which the composer says, "A single pianist, with only two hands, seems to play simultaneously at two, three, sometimes four different speeds."

> AIMARD: Sony Classical
> CASCIOLI: DG
> HAASE: TACET

FRANZ LISZT
1811–1886—Hungary

Busoni made the assumption that Bach was the foundation of piano playing, that Beethoven was the summit, and that the two make Liszt possible. Within this enigmatic remark lies an essence. As Alan Walker puts it:

> Liszt was the first modern pianist. The technical "breakthrough" he achieved during the 1830s and '40s was without precedent in the history of the piano. All subsequent schools were branches of his tree. Rubinstein, Busoni, Paderewski, Godowsky, and Rachmaninoff—all those pianists who together formed what historians later dubbed "the golden age of piano playing"—would be unthinkable without Liszt. It was not that they copied his style of playing; that was inimitable. Nor did they enjoy close personal contact with him; not one of them was his pupil. Liszt's influence went deeper than that. It had to do with his unique ability to solve technical problems. Liszt is to piano playing what Euclid is to geometry. Pianists turn to his music in order to discover the natural laws governing the keyboard. It is impossible for a modern pianist to keep Liszt out of his playing—out of his biceps, his forearms, his fingers—even though he may not know that Liszt is there, since modern piano playing spells Liszt.

James Friskin stated:

> No pianist who desires to develop a complete equipment can ignore the compositions of Liszt. . . . On the musical side they exhibit declamatory—one might say, histrionic—qualities that call for a corresponding approach from the executant. . . . The sentiment is sometimes superficial and the rhetoric, at its worst, becomes exaggerated and even vulgar; but when that has been admitted we have to realize that both sentiment and rhetoric give an opportunity for the development of freedom of expression and the discarding of hampering inhibitions that has undeniable value. At the same time Liszt asks for extremes of sonority and brilliance which tax all the player's muscular resources to the limit, and which have their own peculiar glitter.

Liszt's pianistic individuality, audacity, and innovations seem endless. He literally maneuvers pianists to an understanding of his various idioms. So splendid is the calligraphic articulation, amounting to a dazzling hand choreography, that not much can go wrong if one has an enormous technical mechanism and a true sense of piano sound and inflection. Alan Walker gives the pianist a valuable key to Liszt in saying, "Once the pianist has grasped the notion that he does not have two separate hands, but a single unit of ten digits, he has made an advance towards Liszt."

> *Liszt Complete Piano Music*
> HOWARD: Hyperion

Six Etudes d'exécution transcendante d'apres Paganini

Of Liszt's *Paganini* Etudes Schumann wrote:

> Whoever masters them, as they should be

mastered, in an easy, entertaining way, so that they glide past us like different scenes in a marionette show, may travel confidently all over the world and will return with golden laurels, a second Paganini-Liszt.

The *Paganini* Etudes were an epoch-making event in the history of virtuosity. They are based on Paganini's breathtaking Caprices (No. 3, *La Campanella,* is from the rondo of the B minor Violin Concerto). In addition to divining Paganini's infernal talents, Liszt took advantage of the piano's recent improvements in physical power, backed by iron, and of the increased flexibility of the Erard mechanism. A piece such as *La Campanella* would have been unthinkable in 1820. The *Paganini* Etudes were completed in 1838 and dedicated to Clara Wieck. Their difficulties were unseemly, and Liszt simplified them, without compromising their brilliance, in 1851; this later version is the one now performed. Humphrey Searle notes, "The difference is that between experimentation and mature mastery." The works are *Tremolo, Octaves, La Campanella, Arpeggios, La Chasse,* and *Theme and Variations.* In this last, Liszt used Paganini's Twenty-fourth Caprice, the theme which was also used by Brahms in his variations and by Rachmaninoff in his *Rhapsody.*

ANIEVAS: Angel (LP)
DARRÉ: EMI
JOHANSEN: Artist Direct
KENTNER: Vox
MAGALOFF: Philips: Great Pianists of the
    Twentieth Century
NISSMAN: Newport Classic
NISSMAN: Pierian
ROSE: Vox
SIMON: Vox
TURECK: VAI
WATTS: CBS; Angel

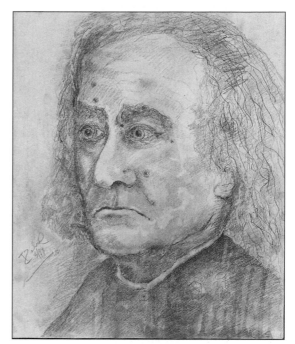

Franz Liszt by David Dubal

Douze Etudes d'exécution transcendante

These twelve works constitute one of the most exciting cycles in music. They stand as a monument to Romanticism and a miraculous exploration of piano mechanism. Liszt produced a set of twelve in 1826 which contained the germ of the later edition. These earlier etudes are still boyhood works based on a Czerny technique. The second version was virtually unplayable, except by Liszt. A comparison of this version with Liszt's final setting, the one that is now used, reveals the genius of crystallization, a fabulous assimilation of idea and technique. These *Transcendental Etudes,* in their final form, opened new horizons for the instrument. It is significant that they are dedicated to Czerny, Liszt's only teacher. As Busoni said, "The final improvements are to be found in a greater ease and smooth playableness and a corresponding amount of impressive effect and character."

For Busoni, No. 1, *Preludio,* "is less a prelude to the cycle than a prelude to test the instrument and the disposition of the performer after stepping onto the concert platform." It is an invigorating piece—daring the pianist to begin the extraordinary cycle. No. 2, untitled, is all devilry, a madcap work for which Paganini was surely the inspiration. No. 3, *Paysage* ("Landscape"), provides a pastoral setting in which passion lurks. No. 4, *Mazeppa,* is a programmatic work inspired by Victor Hugo's poem of the same title; it portrays a Cossack tied to a wild stallion and is one of the most exhausting works in the literature, a monumental workout for wrist and arm. No. 5, *Feux follets* ("Will o' the Wisps"), is in a class with Chopin's double-note etudes and the Schumann Toccata; Mendelssohn's fairy world is shimmeringly Lisztified. No. 6, *Vision,* is a work of impressive pomp. John Ogdon notes its "Berliozian splendour." On the technical side, Friskin refers to its "powerful chords embedded in sweeping arpeggios [and] double-note tremolandos." No. 7, *Eroica,* is more grandiose than heroic. No. 8, *Wilde Jagd* ("Wild Hunt"), requires split-second reflexes and taxes the strength of the hand with tireless chords. Searle wrote, "In *Wilde Jagd* we have all the feeling of the romantic nocturnal hunt, celebrated in all German music from Weber onwards." When listening to *Wild Hunt,* I am reminded of Lao Tzu's lines; riding and hunting make his mind go wild with excitement.

No. 9, *Ricordanza* ("Remembrance"), presents an excruciating, ripe sentiment embedded in ardent ornamentation, perfectly calculated, "with a richness of tonal effect that comes from an exact appreciation of the special qualities of the piano's different registers," as Friskin put it. Busoni felt *Ricordanza* "gives the impression of a packet of yellowed love letters." No. 10, marked "Allegro agitato molto," is untitled and the most often played of the set. It is feverish and charged with breathless tension. No. 11, *Harmonies du soir* ("Evening Harmonies"), is nearly ten minutes long. It "looks forward," in Ogdon's words, "to the evanescent textures of Debussy and the massive chordal writing of Rachmaninoff. [It is] highly sustained, almost ecstatic in its lyricism." It gushes with the perfumes of a summer evening. No. 12, *Chasse-neige* ("Snowscape"): technically the melody and tremolando accompaniment need the utmost care in tonal balance. As Louis Kentner states, "Many Lisztians look upon the concluding piece as the greatest of the studies. Indeed, it is unique in its mood of desolation. It is as if the softly falling snowflakes gradually covered the whole world, burying man and beast; while the wind moans." Busoni goes so far as to say that *Chasse-neige* is "the noblest example, perhaps, amongst all music of a poetising nature." It is amazing that this work is still little known among pianists.

ARRAU: Philips
BERMAN: Columbia/Melodiya
BOLET: London
CAMPANELLA: Nuova Era
CLIDAT: Vega (LP)
CZIFFRA: EMI
JOHANSEN: Artist Direct (LP)
KENTNER: Vox
PONTI: Dante
ROSE: Monarch
ROSE: Vox
SHERMAN: Albany
L. SIMON: BIS

Trois Etudes de concert

No. 1, *Il Lamento,* is long, ten minutes, and displays a cloying sentiment. No. 2, *La Leggierezza,* is popular, with its graceful, decorative chromaticism; it's a perfect piece of piano writing. In No. 3, *Un Sospiro,* "one sigh" is expressed in cross-hand effects within ascending and descending arpeggiation. It is a fine example of Liszt's utilization of Thalberg's three-handed effects.

ARRAU: Philips
BOLET: L'Oiseau-Lyre
JOHANSEN: Artist Direct
LORTIE: Chandos

Deux Etudes de concert (1862–63)

Both pieces—No. 1, *Waldesrauschen* ("Forest Murmurs"), and No. 2, *Gnomenreigen* ("Dance of the Gnomes")—are among the most frequently played of Liszt's etudes. Ravel surely knew the shimmering pianistic layout of *Waldesrauschen,* a magical scene in a wooded glade. *Gnomenreigen* is Mendelssohn turned diabolic, a goblin scherzo in which the salient feature, according to Friskin, is "delicate hand staccato. . . . The alternative theme is a searching test of finger technique and rotational freedom."

BOLET: L'Oiseau Lyre
KENTNER: Vox
NOVAES: Pearl
OGDON: Testament
WILD: Etcetera

Grand Galop chromatique

One of the most taxing small works in the literature, the *Galop* was composed in 1838 and was a major Liszt warhorse—it's all of dashing headlong virtuosity, with its circuslike spirit; it's rousing and witty, wonderfully vulgar, and the father of countless nineteenth-century galops, such as Gottshalk's *Tournament Galop.* If the pianist still has strength at recital's end, this is a daring encore.

CZIFFRA: EMI
HOWARD: Hyperion
SMITH: APR

Liebesträume—Three Nocturnes

These are transcriptions of Liszt's own songs. No. 3, a passionate love poem, is one of the most famous piano pieces ever written.

BARENBOIM: DG
CLIDAT: PG
CURZON (No. 3): London
RUBENSTEIN (No. 3): RCA

Six Consolations

There is a quasi-religious feel to these short sketches, all of which are lyric in character and among the easiest of Liszt's piano works. No. 3, in D-flat, is popular and often heard without its companions.

BARENBOIM: DG
BOLET: Ensayo
CICCOLINI: Ermitage
GEKIC: Palexa
HOROWITZ (No. 3): RCA; (Nos. 4 and 5) Sony Classical
KARAKASHIAN: Romeó
KATIN: Olympia
SWANN: Arkadia
THIBAUDET: Denon

Berceuse (1862)

Inspired by Chopin's Berceuse, and also in D-flat. A first version (1854) is quite simple in statement and sentiment; in the ensuing years, Liszt turned his earlier version into a ten-minute score that was quite startlingly different. The melodic line became profusely embellished with the most gorgeous ornamentation. The work is, unfortunately, all but unknown.

CLIDAT: PG
CURZON: London
HOWARD: Hyperion
KENTNER: APR

Ballade No. 2 in B minor (1853)

There is a growing interest in this fascinating score, so different in nature from the Chopin Ballades. Sacheverell Sitwell feels Liszt is here "concerned, as it were, less with personal suffering than with great happenings on the epical scale, barbarian invasions, cities in flames—tragedies of public, more than private, import."

ARRAU: Philips
BABAYAN: Connoisseur Society
BAR-ILLAN: Audiofon
HOROWITZ: RCA
HOUGH: Hyperion
KENTNER: APR
LEFÉBURE: Solstice
LEWENTHAL: RCA (LP)
LIVELY: Discover International
MARVIN: Genesis (LP)
NYIREGYHÁZI: IPA—Desmar (LP)
WILD: Etcetera

Mephisto Waltz No. 1 (1857)

Liszt composed four *Mephisto Waltzes* and a *Mephisto Polka*. No. 1 is one of his greatest works; every measure is bold. The work was inspired by Lenau's *Faust* and is subtitled *The Dance in the Village Inn*. The scene is played out by Faust, Mephistopheles, and Marguerite. The opening, "the Devil tuning up his fiddle," writes Kentner, "is surely one of the most daring things created by any pre-Bartók composer." The middle-section theme and its working out in the seductive key of D-flat greatly influenced Scriabin. For James Huneker, it is "one of the most voluptuous episodes outside the *Tristan* score. That halting, languorous, syncopated theme is marvelously expressive."

ASHKENAZY: London
BAR-ILLAN: Audiofon
BERMAN: Audiofon
BOLET: Everest (LP)

BROWNING: RCA
CZIFRA: EMI
FIALKOWSKA: Musica Viva
GUTIÉRREZ: EMI
HOROWITZ: RCA
KAPELL: RCA
KATSARIS: Telefunken
OGDON: Testament
PAIK: Virgin Classics
RÁNKI: Denon
RASHKOVETSKY: Angelok
RUBINSTEIN: RCA
SWANN: Music and Arts
WILD: Vanguard

Mephisto Waltz No. 2

The score is dedicated to Saint-Saëns. First composed for orchestra, Liszt wrote the solo piano version in 1881. The work is virtually unknown, but it ranks with the first *Mephisto Waltz* in originality of conception and realization. The score bristles with a hotbed of chronic malevolence. The second *Mephisto Waltz* is remarkable for the erotic passion Liszt was still capable of in his early seventies. It is a large canvas of around twelve minutes. It is an extraordinary play on the tri-tone within an ambiguous tonal landscape. This is one of the masterful works of the Romantic age which has yet to enter the repertoire. The second *Mephisto Waltz* is of a blistering technical difficulty where Liszt's Faustian blood still burns with passionate heat.

ANDSNES: EMI
HOWARD: Hyperion
SALMAN: Titanic

Mephisto Waltz No. 3 (1883)

Liszt dedicated the score "with profound admiration to Marie Jaëll." The *Mephisto Waltz No. 3* is eleven minutes long and strikingly sardonic. John Ogdon notes, "Liszt's harmonic, scalic, and melodic experiments are magnificently integrated in this work, while the piano writing has a sulphuric fitfulness."

ANDERSON: Nimbus
HOWARD: Hyperion
OGDON: EMI
RASHKOVETSKY: Angelok

Bénédiction de Dieu dans la solitude (No. 3 of "Harmonies poétiques et religieuses") Funérailles (No. 7 of "Harmonies poétiques et religieuses")

The complete *Harmonies poétiques et religieuses* is an imposing but uneven set of ten pieces, of which Nos. 3 and 7 are masterworks. "The *Bénédiction*," writes Searle, "is indeed almost unique among Liszt's works in that it expresses that feeling of mystical contemplation which Beethoven attained in his last period, but which is rarely found elsewhere in music." Liszt used the ecstatic Lamartine poem for inspiration: "Whence comes, O God, this peace that overwhelms me? Whence comes this faith with which my heart overflows?" *Funérailles,* with its tumultuous octaves for the left hand, was dedicated to the memory of Chopin. It has the blackness of despair, the clangor of bells, and a grandeur in the piano scoring that is unforgettable.

Bénédiction:
ARRAU: Philips
BRENDEL: Philips
DUCHABLE: Erato
HAMELIN: Music and Arts
E. LEVY: Marston
OHLSSON: EMI (LP)
PAIK: Virgin Classics
ROSE: Vox

Funérailles:
BARÈRE: APR
BERMAN: Melodiya
CHERKASSKY: Nimbus
HOROWITZ: EMI
OHLSSON: EMI (LP)

Années de pèlerinage (Years of Pilgrimage) (1836–1877)

Alice Levine Mitchell wrote: "The individual pieces in the *Années de pèlerinage* . . . by virtue of their programmatic orientation, their poetic inspiration, and their relationship to the natural landscape, give voice to the distinctive language of Romantic musical art. The collection may be considered in effect an encyclopedia of Romantic expression."

Liszt's *Years of Pilgrimage* consists of twenty-six pieces: *First Year: Switzerland*; *Second Year: Italy*; and *Third Year: Italy*. The works occupied him in various stages for forty years, and in them are revealed the myriad facets of Liszt's complex musical and intellectual being. His love for nature is illustrated in the *Suisse* years. "The Swiss pieces are pure nature," writes the pianist Loius Kentner, "lakes, springs, cowbells, churchbells, Alpine horn—all these effects appear, drawn with astonishing precision by the hand of a master." Liszt once remarked, standing in front of a painting, "I too am a painter." These were the years that the Romantics discovered Switzerland and the Alps. Industrialization brought a new and urgent interest in nature, and the Romantics, from the turn of the nineteenth century, literally flocked to Switzerland in an almost desperate nature worship. In Book Two, *Italie,* Liszt's inspiration stems from his contemplation of Italian painting, poetry, sculpture, and literature. The Third Book, Italie (1867–77), exhibits Liszt the pioneer harmonist opening new musical horizons.

Années de pèlerinage (complete):
BERMAN: DG
CZIFFRA: Connoisseur Society
HOWARD: Hyperion
JENDO (Vol. 1): Naxos
LORTIE: Chandos
MARKS: Nimbus
ROSE: Vox

First Year: Switzerland:
BARENBOIM: DG
SWANN: Arkadia Akademia
VILLA: Second Hearing

Première année: Suisse: La chapelle de Giullaume Tell (William Tell's Chapel)

Liszt inscribes the motto "one for all, all for one" and paints a portrait of the Swiss hero.

Au lac de Wallenstadt (By the Lake of Wallenstadt)

The Swiss years were occupied with the full flush of Liszt's intensely romantic liaison with Countess Marie d'Agoult, who was his constant companion. In her memoirs she wrote: "The shores of the lake of Wallenstadt kept us for a long time. Franz wrote there for me a melancholy harmony, imitative of the sigh of the waves and the cadence of oars, which I have never been able to hear without weeping." Here is early musical impressionism; one can hear and see in the left hand figure the crystal calm water with a simple alpine melody hovering in the thin air. This evocative piece should be better known.

Pastorale

A pretty miniature, less than two minutes in length, describing a Swiss village festival.

Au bord d'une source (By the Side of a Spring)

Liszt put a Schiller quote on the score: "In murmuring coolness the play of young nature begins." Pianistically ingenious in its crossing of the hands, it lasts three and a half minutes of light shimmering on the water, where one can hear each droplet of water. It is a masterpiece of earliest Impressionism which the young Debussy heard Liszt play at the Villa Medica in his old age, remarking on the master's unique pedaling.

BERMAN: DG
HOROWITZ: RCA
HOWARD: Hyperion

Orage

Liszt painting a sudden mountain storm; for the pianist an exhausting but exciting work of four minutes.

HOWARD: Hyperion

Vallée d'Obermann (The Valley of Obermann)

The longest, at fifteen minutes, of the Suisse album. *Obermann* is the title of a novel by Etienne Pivert de Senancour, who wrote it in Switzerland around 1800. The book became a bible for those Romantics obsessed with characters suffering from ennui and melancholy. The book struck a deep chord in Liszt, who put his *Obermann* melody through many transformations during the score. Senancour describes Obermann's "vast consciousness of a nature everywhere overwhelming and impenetrable . . . voluptuous abandon, all the desires and all the profound torments that a human heart can hold." With acute penetration Liszt portrays the psychological states of a listless, depressive-Romantic spirit.

ARRAU: Philips
HOROWITZ: RCA

Églogue

A work of three minutes. A pastoral mood, with a quote from Byron's *Childe Harolde:*

The morn is up again, the dewy morn
With breath all incense and with cheek all
    bloom;
Laughing the cloud away with cheerful
    scorn
And living as if earth contain no tomb.

HOWARD: Hyperion

Le mal du pays (Sadness for No Reason)

A work of six minutes; a folk-song spirit permeates throughout.

Les cloches de Genève (The Bells of Geneva)

Liszt lived with Marie in Geneva, where his first daughter Blandine was born. He also taught at the Geneva Conservatory. Liszt sub-titled the piece *Nocturne;* it is lush with bell effects and a large climax. It can be cloying in the wrong hands.

Deuxième année: Italie: Sposalizio

A rather long piece of spacious lyricism—this is Liszt's musical consecration to the inspiration he received viewing Raphael's *The Marriage of the Virgin,* one of the glories of the Brera at Milan.

Il penseroso (The Thinker)

This slow-moving lento was inspired from the Michelangelo statue on the tomb of Lorenzo de Medici at the church of San Lorenzo in Florence. Michelangelo's words grace the page: "I am thankful to sleep, and more thankful to be made of stone so long as injustice and shame remain on earth."

HOWARD: Hyperion

Canzonetta del Salvator Rosa

A simplistic, cheerful piece inspired from a poem by the seventeenth-century painter-poet. The melody was once ascribed to Rosa but is by Giovanni Battista Bononcini.

BERMAN: DG

Sonetto 47 del Petrarca (47th Sonnet of Petrarca)

Originally the three *Petrarca* Sonnets were composed for tenor voice. His piano adaptations are of a supple pianistic beauty. No. 47

is the weakest of the trio but, in a sympathetic interpretation, may avoid mawkishness.

BERMAN: DG

Sonetto No. 104 del Petrarca

One of Liszt's most highly charged love poems, erotic passion spills over in this masterpiece. The rhetorical spacing, the plasticity of the piano writing, and the perfectly placed cadenzas offer the listener a heart-throbbing experience. In Petrarca's words, "I fear and hope, I burn and yet am ice; I soar to heaven and lie in earth; I hold nothing, and embrace the world. . . ."

BARENBOIM: DG
BROWNING: Delos
HOROWITZ: RCA
LIPATTI: EMI
WEISSENBERG: Connoisseur Society

Sonetto No. 123 del Petrarca

Slightly less feverish than Sonetta 104 but also a paean to Romantic love, Petrarca intones to Laura, "I saw angelic grace on earth and heavenly beauty unmatched in this world." With a performing time of seven minutes, No. 123 is performed less often than 104.

BERMAN: DG

Après une lecture de Dante— Fantasia quasi sonata

The title is taken from a Hugo poem; Liszt performed an early version in Vienna in 1839, and finished the piece a decade later. The so-called *Dante Sonata* is the largest canvas of the second volume of the *Années,* a massive chordal composition, a grim Luciferian tone poem with a love scene, chaos, and redemption. Liszt uses the marking "Lamentoso"; from its slow moving tri-tone opening, the work is a pandemonium of raging hell on the piano. The pianist near exhaustion is asked to negotiate fearsome skips near the score's culmination. The *Dante Sonata* (after a reading of Dante) asks the pianist for an unbridled temperament. In a great performance, it is an exalted symphonic poem, of seventeen minutes; in a poor performance it sounds like two hours.

ARRAU: Philips
BAR-ILLAN: RCA
BEAN: Westminster
BERMAN: DG
BRENDEL: Turnabout
BROWNING: Delos
KENTNER: EMI Odeon

Venezia e Napoli

In 1859 Liszt wrote as a supplement to the Italian collection three pieces: *Gondoliera,* marked "Quasi allegretto," is very Venetian, based on two Gondoliera melodies. *Canzone,* a lento doloroso, is based on the Gondolier's air in Rossini's once popular opera, *Otello.* *Tarantella,* often played without its companions, is a dazzling Neapolitan fantasy based on songs by Guillaume Louis Cottrau.

Troisième année: Italie Angelus! Prière aux anges gardiens

The third book dates from 1866–77, and in these works Liszt's later style is apparent.

The piece, marked "Andante Pietoso," is a plaintive piece written at the famed Villa d'Este at Tivoli, where Liszt lived part of the year. Liszt heard the angelus bells ringing quietly in the evening, and once again was inspired from sounds of the external world.

Aux cyprès de la Villa d'Este, Threnodie I

The Villa d'Este is graced with magnificent cypress trees, which Liszt turned into music. He sat by the hour meditating while looking at them. Marked "Andante più agitato," this neglected work exhibits Liszt's advanced harmonic style.

BERMAN: DG
HOWARD: Hyperion

Aux cyprès de la Villa d'Este, Threnodie II

A work of elegiac beauty and extraordinary harmonic amplitude. As John Ogdon says: "The second threnody owes much to Wagner, the opening sounding like a reminiscence of Tristan. This Threnody is more pictorially immediate than its companion. At one point there is an almost onomatopoeic representation of the wind sighing through the trees. The coda is of particular beauty, a moonweft dream of silver glades."

BERMAN: DG
HOWARD: Hyperion

Les jeux d'eaux à la Ville d'Este

Besides the cypresses, Liszt could see from his balcony the celebrated fountains in the park at the villa. Here is Liszt's painterly gifts magnificently exhibited in piano writing that would inspire many composers. The work is in his "mystic" key of F-sharp major, and in it he evokes an impressionism which has an ecclesiastical sound mingled with a marked sensuality which builds to a powerful climax. In the middle of the work, Liszt quotes from the Gospel according to St. John: "But whosoever drinketh of the water that I shall give him, shall never thirst; but the water that I shall give him shall be in him a well of water springing up into everlasting life."

ARRAU: Philips
BRENDEL: Philips
KENTNER: EMI Odéon

Sunt lacrymae rerum

Subtitled "in the Hungarian mode." An interesting piece with the two augmented seconds of the Hungarian scale. Liszt quotes from Virgil: "The sense of tears in mortal things."

HOWARD: Hyperion

Marche funèbre

A somber work "in memory of Emperor Maximilian of Mexico." (The Hapsburg prince, who had been installed as emperor, was executed at Juarez in 1867 by revolutionaries; the news created a furor in Europe.)

HOWARD: Hyperion

Sursum corda

This was a favorite of Bartók, which he recorded. In some passages Liszt uses the whole-tone scale. The piece is Hungarian in tone, creating much intensity. Ogdon writes, "Such impassioned oratory is a fitting close to Liszt's years of pilgrimage, both musical and spiritual."

HOWARD: Hyperion

Fantasia and Fugue on the Name B-A-C-H (1855)

Originally an organ work, which Liszt transcribed for piano in 1870. It is music of tremendous power, nobility, and theatricality.

BEAN: Westminster (LP)
BRENDEL: Philips
CZIFFRA: Philips
PONTI: HK

Variations on a Theme of Bach (1862)

An important and rather unknown work of impressive concentration, based on a theme from Bach's cantata *Weinen, Klagen, Sorgen, Zagen.*

BRENDEL: Philips
JOHANSEN: Artist Direct (LP)
PONTI: HK
SILVERMAN: Orion (LP)

Deux legends (1863)

Liszt's genius for descriptive writing is nowhere better realized than in his two Franciscan *Legends.* No. 1, *Saint Francis of Assisi Preaching to the Birds,* makes use of the keyboard's upper register, combining trills and melody in the same hand. In the wrong hands, No. 2, *Saint Francis of Paolo Walking on the*

Waves, can be merely bombastic; in sympathetic hands, however, it is a monumental work.

BRENDEL: Philips
CZIFFRA (No. 2): Philips
DUCHABLE: Erato
HEIDSIECK: Cassiopée
JOHANSEN: Artist Direct
KARS (No. 2): London
KEMPFF (No. 1): DG
VÁSÁRY (No. 2): DG

Valse impromptu (1850)

A wonderful piece of fluff—this is a perfect encore number, on which Moszkowski modeled some of his work.

DORFMANN: Pearl
LYMPANY: Angel
RUBINSTEIN: RCA
WEISSENBERG: EMI

Quatre Valses oubliées (1881–85)

These late works express a curious languor, nostalgia, and amorousness in a forward-looking harmonic scheme. The *Valse oubliée* No. 1 in F-sharp major is the best known of Liszt's late music.

FARNADI: Westminster (LP)
HOROWITZ (No. 1): DG
JOHANSEN: Artist Direct (LP)
RICHTER: (No. 2) Philips

Bagatelle Without Tonality (1883)

Three minutes of a mixture of Hungarian flavor, macabre touches in tri-tones, and a sensuous waltz theme which becomes passionate as the piece ends into an ascending chromatic void.

BRENDEL: Philips

Polonaise No. 2 in E major

No. 1 in C minor is easier and more poetic than No. 2 but is unknown. The E major Polonaise was once popular but has now slipped from the repertoire. There is a sense of pageantry in this very un-Chopinesque work.

CHERKASSKY: Mercury
GRAINGER: Pearl
RACHMANIMOFF: RCA
WILD: Etcetera

Rhapsodie espagnole (1863)

One of the earliest musical excursions into Spain, based on two Spanish themes, the *Spanish Rhapsody* is a grandiose piece which cries out for pianists in the old heroic mold. At sixteen minutes it is an impressive concert piece and should be far better known. Busoni transcribed it for piano and orchestra.

ARRAU: Desmar
BARÈRE: The Piano Library
BERMAN: Columbia/Melodiya
CZIFFRA: Angel
LELCHUK: Telarc
MARSH, Freeman/London Philharmonic (arr. Busoni): MMG
SHEHORI: Connoisseur Society

The Nineteen Hungarian Rhapsodies

Liszt admired Gypsies and was intrigued with their nomad-like existence, sense of adven-ture, high spirit, and, above all, their sponta-neous musicality. Liszt's specimens are based on Gypsy themes; they are unique in their flavor and histrionic virtuoso nature. With the Rhapsodies, Liszt opened the door for a flood of works in national costumes. They demand flair, and a pianist must have a fiery, gregar-ious temperament and an uninhibited virtuoso technique. No. 2 in C-sharp minor is one of the most famous pieces of music ever composed. If played properly it is irresistible in its gushing flow. No. 6 in D-flat is shapely in proportion, and gives the pianist an exhilarating octave section, from right-hand octaves, beginning as a tease, progressing through to the left hand to a tumultuous conclusion. No. 8 in F-sharp minor is little known but captivating. No. 9, subtitled the *Carnival de Peth,* is a meaty, grandly conceived work, one of the longer rhapsodies. No. 10 in E major is only five minutes; besides its Gypsy atmosphere, there are spine-tingling glissandos tickling the ears. No. 11 in A minor is also short, a fine piece with wonderful simulation of the cimbalum, a Hungarian instrument. No. 12 is all pomp and glory, long and taxing. No. 13 is more oriental in mood and one of the finest and most beau-tiful of the rhapsodies. No. 14 in F minor is arresting in its grand manner, and is even more effective in the piano and orchestra version known as the *Hungarian Fantasy.* No. 15, in A minor, is based on the Hungarian national melody known as *The Rákoczy March;* it is not quite as integrated or pianistically ingenious as its companions. Nos. 16-19 is music of Liszt's last years. No. 19 in D minor is the finest; Liszt used material from the *Csárdás nobles* by Kornél Abrányi. It is one of his last piano pieces from 1885. Alan Walker writes, "This Rhapsody blazes with color and demands exceptional virtuosity; it is almost as if Liszt was seized with nostalgia and was trying to recapture the days of his youth."

CAMPANELLA: Philips

CZIFFRA: Connoisseur Society
KENTNER: Vox
RUBINSTEIN (Nos. 3, 10, 12): RCA
SZIDON: DG

Individual Rhapsodies:
No. 2:
FRIEDHEIM: IPA–Desmar
FRIEDMAN: Arabesque
HOFMANN: IPA–Desmar
HOROWITZ (his own arrangement): RCA
RACHMANINOFF (with his own cadenza):
   RCA

No. 6:
HOROWITZ: RCA
LEVITZKI: Arabesque

No. 9:
GILELS: Melodiya

No. 11:
CORTOT: Music and Arts
KAPELL: RCA

No. 13:
BUSONI: Arabesque

No. 14:
HAMBOURG: Arabesque

No. 15:
GRAINGER (abbr.): IPA–Desmar
HOROWITZ (his own arrangement): RCA
SOLOMON: Arabesque

No. 19:
HOROWITZ (his own arrangement): CBS

Sonata in B minor (1852–53)

Premiered by von Bülow in 1857, the Sonata
is one of the glories of the piano literature
and Liszt's greatest achievement as a musical
architect. Never before or after was he able
to develop and sustain his thought on such
an inspired and flawless level within a large
form. The B minor Sonata was dedicated to
Schumann, who had dedicated his own C
major Fantasy, Op. 17, to Liszt. William S.
Newman affirms, "The two nineteenth century masterpieces . . . stand almost alone in
the heat and inspiration of their full-bloomed
Romanticism." When Wagner heard Liszt's
pupil Karl Klindworth play this work, he wrote
to Liszt, "The Sonata is beautiful beyond all
belief, great, lovable, deep, and noble just as
you are."

The writer Peter Yates asserts that "Liszt's
Piano Sonata in B minor stands isolated as
the most successful formal organization of the
nineteenth century stylistic conglomerate. . . .
He spread the single movement sonata form
over an entire large Sonata, somewhat in
the manner of Schubert's *Wanderer* Fantasy,
without breaks to distinguish movements."

The large expanse covered by Liszt was
based on his own concept of thematic transformation. The entire work germinates from
five themes. Sharon Winklhofer has written
a valuable book, *Liszt's Sonata in B minor:
A Study of Autograph Sources and
Documents.*

ARRAU: Philips
BARÈRE: APR
BERMAN: Saga
BOLET: AS Disc
BROWNING: Delos
CHERKASSKY: Nimbus
CORTOT: Music and Arts
CURZON: London
DARRÉ: Vanguard
A. FISCHER: Hungaroton
GILELS: RCA
HOROWITZ: Seraphim
JUDD: Chandos
E. LEVY: Marsten
MAGALOFF: Arkadia
POGORELICH: DG
RICHTER: Music and Arts

Piano Concerto No. 1 in E-flat major

Liszt's First Concerto, a perfect showpiece, with its dashing opening theme followed by heraldic antiphonal octaves, is in one continuous movement with four sections. Imagine being in Weimar in 1855 for its premiere—with Liszt as soloist and Berlioz conducting. Although the concerto has always been popular, it has acquired a musically poor reputation because of the many vulgar, exhibitionist performances it has received. Nevertheless, it is a masterpiece.

> ARRAU, Ormandy/Philadelphia: CBS
> BERMAN, Giulini/Vienna Symphony: DG
> DE GREEF, Ronald/Royal Albert Hall: Opal
> GUTIÉRREZ, Previn/London Symphony: Angel
> JANIS, Kondrashin/Moscow Philharmonic:
>   Mercury
> MARSH, Freeman/London Philharmonic:
>   MMG
> RICHTER, Kondrashin/London Symphony:
>   Philips
> RUBINSTEIN, Wallenstein/RCA Symphony:
>   RCA
> SAVER, Weingartner: APR
> WATTS, Bernstein/New York Philharmonic:
>   CBS

Piano Concerto No. 2 in A major

The Second Concerto, described by critic William Apthorp as "The Life and Adventures of a Theme," is Romantic and poetic, less showy and more diffuse than No. 1. The orchestration in both concerti is original and spiced with piquant touches.

> BOLET, Zinman/Rochester Philharmonic: Vox
>   Cum Laude
> CLIBURN, Ormandy/Philadelphia: RCA
> DUCHABLE, Conlon/London Philharmonic:
>   Erato

> FRANÇOIS, Silvestri/Philharmonia: Seraphim
> VÁSÁRY, Prohaska/Bamberg Symphony: DG
> ZIMERMAN, Ozawa/Boston Symphony: DG

Totentanz for Piano and Orchestra (1859)

This masterly set of variations on the *Dies Irae* was inspired by Andrea Orcagna's frescoes, *The Triumph of Death,* which Liszt first saw when he was twenty-seven. This work has a chilling impact when played by a dramatic pianist. The virtuosic writing is a good example of Liszt's genius for creating electrifying effects that are always more manageable than they look on the page or sound.

> BÉROFF, Masur/Leipzig Gewandhaus: Angel
> BRAILOWSKY, Ormandy/Philadelphia: Sony
>   Classical
> FREIRE, Kempe/Munich Philharmonic:
>   Columbia
> JANIS, Reiner/Chicago Symphony: RCA
> WATTS, Leinsdorf/London Symphony: CBS

Hungarian Fantasy

Also known as *Fantasia on Hungarian Folk Tunes,* this work uses the same material as the Hungarian Rhapsody No. 14. Again, the composition is remarkably effective.

> CAMPANELLA, Ceccato/Monte Carlo Opera:
>   Philips
> CHERKASSKY, Karajan/Berlin Philharmonic:
>   DG
> SOLOMON, Susskind/Philharmonia: EMI

Malédiction for Piano and Strings (1840)

Almost unknown, this early work has an intriguing Romantic sensibility. Of *Malédiction* ("under a curse"), Robert Collet observes: "The work has much charm; the mingling of Byronic defiance, great tenderness and a touch of religious sentiment is very characteristic."

BÉROFF, Masur/Leipzig Gewandhaus: Angel
BRENDEL, Gielen/Vienna Symphony:
    Turnabout

Selected Works, Original and Transcriptions

The Apparition No. 1 (1834) is one of the earliest of Liszt's works which shows signs of genius. Alan Walker calls it "a miniature masterpiece," with ravishing murmuring, of Lisztian ardor, within a beautiful conceived piano scoring marked "Senza lentezza quasi allegretto." The Third Apparition is based on Schubert's famous Trauer Waltz. Of much later vintage is the *Weinen, Klagen, Sorgen, Zagen* Prelude after Bach, which is an austerely poignant piece. The lovely Impromptu in F-sharp major, composed in 1872, is dedicated to Liszt's trusted friend Olga von Meyendorf; it has interesting key shifts, marked "Animato con passione," and is virtually unknown.

The *Grande Fantasie de bravoure sur La Clochette*, based on Paganini's *La Campanella*, was recorded with dashing flair by John Ogdon. In Humphrey Searle's words, "A terrific piece of virtuosity, and says much for Liszt's powers of assimilation that he could invent and perfect a new technique of such unheard of brilliance and difficulty within such a short time of hearing Paganini. The piece is fiendishly difficult. Liszt testing himself, his technique and the staying power of the pianos of 1832." The Six Organ Preludes and Fugues of Bach were composed from 1842 to 1850. Each is a landmark in Bach organ works arranged for the piano; the A minor No. 1 is best known. Later in 1870 he transcribed

the Organ Fantasy in G minor. Of his Verdi Excursions, the Paraphrase on *Ernani* (1859), *Don Carlos,* and *Boccanegra* from 1882 are masterful; the *Boccanegra* is fearful in mood. For lilt and ballroom gliding, the eight *Soirées de Vienne, Valse Caprices* after Schubert are sophisticated far above their original models. (Curiously, Liszt never showed any interest in capturing either Johann Strauss, father or son, in his panorama of transcriptions.) Important also are the various Wagner arrangements, beside the *Tannhäuser* overture and the love-drunk chords of the *Leibestod,* the finest and most pianistic is the spinning song from the *Flying Dutchman,* a wonderfully suggestive score. The dazzling transcription of Saint-Saëns's *Danse macabre* is a perfect adaptation, to which Horowitz added some touches. Liszt, in a letter to Saint-Saëns, writes, "I beg you to excuse my unskillfulness in reducing the marvelous coloring of the score to the possibilities of the piano." Humphrey Searle thinks Liszt improved Saint-Saëns's composition. Liszt's good friend Rossini gave him his great overture to William Tell, which Liszt reconstructed for piano in 1838. Liszt's performance caused pandemonium wherever he performed it. Liszt also composed twelve pieces on Rossini's songs, generally titled *Soirées Musicales,* in 1837; the best known is the tarentella *La danza.* The set is as fresh and naive as the songs themselves, and are never played. Chopin was a lifelong love of Liszt's; indeed he said Chopin was "the only enthusiasm of his youth which remained." Liszt also treated Beethoven to transcriptions, from his Goethe Songs from Op. 75, 83, 84, but of more importance the fine song cycle Op. 98, *An die ferne Geliebte.* Liszt admired Donizetti, and his *Reminiscences de Lucrezia Borgia* is unfortunately seldom performed, although Raymond Lewenthal expertly recorded the black mood of the *Marche Funébre de Dom Sébastien.* When Donizetti heard the arrangement he told a friend, "Buy Liszt's arrangement, it will make your hair stand on end." More accessible and quite luscious is the *Valse a capriccio* on two motifs from *Lucia and Parisina*. Liszt's treatment of the lyrical theme is magical.

Beside his great reminiscences of Bellini's *Norma*, Liszt paraphrased Bellini's *Puritani*, in a quite rip-roaring transformation. Perhaps even finer is the Grand Concert Fantasy on Bellini's *La Sonnambula*. Liszt writes one of his most demanding paraphrases, a bravura work, which he composed from 1839 to 1841, in which he ennobled Bellini's themes.

The only composition that Liszt dedicated to the countess Marie d'Agoult, Liszt's mistress and sometime muse, was the Grande Fantasie on themes from their friend Meyerbeer's opera *Les Huguenots*. It's a twenty-minute extravanganza, recorded by Arnaldo Cohen. In 1881, Liszt traveled to Rome especially to hear his pupil Sophie Menter in the *Huguenots*; as he wrote, "A Fantasia which in my years as a virtuoso I used to play only rarely because of the trouble it cost me, Sophie Menter astonished me."

Arrangements, Transcriptions, Paraphrases

These were the stock-in-trade of virtuosi during much of the nineteenth century. Liszt, in spite of his startling originality as a composer, seemed almost compelled—sometimes with good intentions, sometimes not—to re-create other composers' music in his own image, or, at the very least, to translate it into piano terms. His was very much an experimental mind, and he approached many of his "transcriptions" with the utmost seriousness, subjecting some of them to constant revision. The opera fantasies are especially intriguing, for in these he gave himself free rein to exploit the instrument in ways he never quite permitted himself in his original piano music. Without knowing the operatic fantasies, one cannot appreciate the full impact of Liszt's technical system, which brought the resources of both the instrument and the player to a degree of development previously undreamed of, and which raised pianistic effects (even "tricks") to a level of sheer wizardry. In recent years, many pianists have once again been finding these works fascinating. The literary critic George Steiner thinks "Liszt's transcriptions for piano from Italian operas, from classical symphonies, from the compositions of his contemporaries, notably Wagner, go a long way to suggest that Liszt's was the foremost critical (if not self-critical) tact in the history of Western music. Together, these transcriptions make up a syllabus of enacted criticism."

Mozart-Liszt: Réminiscences de "Don Juan" (1841)

The *Don Juan* Fantasy, based on Mozart's *Don Giovanni*, is one of the legendary pieces in the literature. Even when Liszt's reputation was in decline, there were pianists around to confront the "Don." Its title is perfect, too, for this is a true reminiscence of the great opera, interpreted by a nineteenth-century mind. Technically, it is abominably difficult; unlike other works by Liszt, it is even more difficult than it sounds. Harold Schonberg once wrote, "I have come to the conclusion that to play Liszt well you have to have in your breast a good-sized dollop of original sin." To play this work requires technical amplitude and a temperament yearning to let loose its pandemonium.

BARÈRE: APR
HAMELIN: Music and Arts
OGDON: Seraphim
ROLET: L'Oiseau-Lyre
ROSEN: Epic (LP)
WILD: Vanguard

Bellini-Liszt: Réminiscences de "Norma" (1841)

Liszt extracts the essence of Bellini's opera. Kaikhosru Sorabji even remarked that "Bellini's themes never had, by themselves, the grandeur and magnificence that Liszt is able to infuse into them." Of the B major section, Busoni felt "anyone who had listened to or played [it] . . . without being moved has not yet arrived at Liszt." Liszt took Thalberg's pedaling and three-handed effect and instilled new sonorous developments into them. Ivan Davis has written, "For me, this is one of Liszt's greatest creations as well as one of the most stupendously difficult, both technically and architecturally."

BRENDEL: Turnabout
DAVIS: Audiofon
HAMELIN: Music and Arts
LEWENTHAL: RCA

Donizetti-Liszt: "Lucia di Lammermoor" Paraphrase (1836)

This paraphrase is based only on the famous sextet at the close of the second act of *Lucia di Lammermoor*. Just compare any one of the many other transcriptions of this slice of the opera with Liszt's to fully understand Liszt's musical ways and means.

BOLET: RCA
BRENDEL: Turnabout

Verdi-Liszt: "Rigoletto" Paraphrase (1863)

The *Rigoletto* concert paraphrase is by far the best known of Liszt's works based on Verdi. Here, he expands the celebrated quartet from

the opera. The work becomes more Liszt than Verdi, encased in a shimmering pianism.

ARRAU: Philips
BOLET: RCA
CHERKASSKY: Mercury
CZIFFRA: Connoisseur Society; EMI Pathé
GINZBURG: Melodiya
VÁSÁRY: DG

Meyerbeer-Liszt: Réminiscences de "Robert le diable"—Valse infernale (1841)

Meyerbeer was the most successful composer of grand opera in Europe during the 1830s and 1840s. Liszt penned four works based on his hits: *Illustrations de "l'Africaine," Illustrations du "Prophète," Grande Fantaisie sur "Les Huguenots,"* and this Valse. The *Valse infernale* is raucous and racy. When Wagner heard Liszt play it, he wrote, "Someday Liszt will be obliged in heaven to play before the assembled angels his Fantasia on the Devil! But probably for the last time." It demands the strength and endurance of a giant with the right dose of mockery and fun. There was a time when to play one of these maligned creations was almost certainly to invite hostile reviews. Audiences might quiver with delight while listening to one of these ingenious transformations, but Liszt was always accused of tampering with the genius of others.

WILD: Vanguard

Gounod-Liszt: Valse de l'opéra "Faust" (1861)

In his approach to Mephistopheles, Liszt is unique. This work, built on Gounod's *Faust,* is one of the finest waltz paraphrases ever contrived. Sacheverell Sitwell felt Liszt brought the trivial tune "to a higher spiritual plane than it could ever aspire to on its own merits."

BARÈRE: Turnabout
GINZBURG: Melodiya
PETRI: Westminster
WILD: Vanguard

Berlioz-Liszt: Symphonie fantastique (1833)

When Liszt first heard the gorgeous score, he immediately set to work to see if he could recast it for the piano. His objective in such a transcription, in contrast to his *Réminiscences* and paraphrases, was to translate the composer's intention more or less faithfully to the piano, which in the case of Berlioz's glowing orchestration is a seemingly impossible task. In his memoirs, Charles Hallé noted that following a performance of the "March to the Scaffold" from the symphony conducted by Berlioz, Liszt "played his own arrangement for piano alone of the same piece, with an effect even surpassing that of the full orchestra, and creating an indescribable furor."

BIRET: Finnadar (LP)
RÉACH: Arcobaleno

Mendelssohn-Liszt: Wedding March and Dance of the Elves from "A Midsummer Night's Dream"

This has always been played, but Horowitz's version, with his own touches, surpasses the original in brilliance.

CZIFFRA: Connoisseur Society (LP)
HOROWITZ: RCA
KENTNER: Turnabout (LP)
PETRI: Westminster (LP)

Tchaikovsky-Liszt: Polonaise from "Eugene Onegin" (1880)

Liszt's only paraphrase of any Tchaikovsky work. Tatiana's love theme is used as well.

CZIFFRA: Connoisseur Society (LP)

Beethoven-Liszt: Adelaide

A free transcription of a Beethoven song, marvelously made for the piano.

PETRI: Westminster (LP)
VILLA: Spectrum (LP)

Beethoven-Liszt: Symphony No. 5 in C minor

Liszt transcribed all of the Beethoven symphonies for the piano, somehow achieving the finer points of detail. Characteristic of these is his version of the most famous symphony in history, No. 5; it is an amazing re-creative act.

GOULD: Sony Classical

Wagner-Liszt: Overture to "Tannhäuser"

Liszt produced fourteen Wagner adaptations; the largest is the *Tannhäuser* overture. (The erotic, trembling *Liebestod*, splendidly "reorchestrated" for the piano, is the best known of this group.)

BOLET: RCA
CZIFFRA: Connoisseur Society (LP)
KERER: Melodiya
SMITH: Unicorn

Busoni-Listz: *Fantasia and Fugue on the Chorale "Ad Nos, Ad Salutarem Undam"*

Liszt wrote four "Illustrations" on themes from Meyerbeer's opera Le Prophète in the early 1850s, the first three of which are piano pieces; the fourth is a massive work for organ of half-hour duration and one of the masterworks of the organ repertoire. Busoni in 1897 reworked the "Ad Nos" for solo piano; it is a towering monument to the art of trascription. Rarely heard in public; in recent years Garrick Ohlsson and Lloyd Paguia Arriola have presented the work in public.

BELLUCCI: Assai
JOHANSEN: Artist Direct (LP)
MILNE: Danacord

Sarabande and Chaconne (from Handel's Almira, Concert Arrangement)

A strange but riveting composition of Liszt's late period, composed in 1879. It was written for Liszt's fine pupil Walter Bache, to be performed at an English Handel festival. The score is set of variations on Handel's *Sarabande*, a Chaconne in allegretto tempo follows, culminating in a grandioso trionfante. Here is another of the numerous examples of when you think you know Liszt, one comes upon another facet of his genius. The work is by no means easy.

SALMAN: Titanic

The Lieder Literature

Liszt was especially attracted to transcribing the song literature. Sometimes he is quite faithful to the original, and other times he can be far more fanciful. In 1838 he transcribed twelve Schubert lieder, including the famous "Erlkönig," "Der Wanderer," "Ave Maria," "Du bist die Ruh," "Gretchen am Spinnrade," and "Auf dem Wasser zu singen." These are freer than his later renderings of the *Schwanengesang* and *Winterreise* cycles.

Liszt's transcriptions of Schumann's "Widmung" and "Frühlingsnacht" are among his best, and the Mendelssohn-Liszt *Auf Flügeln des Gesanges* ("On Wings of Song") is well known.

Chopin-Liszt: *Six Chants Polonais*

Liszt transformed six of Chopin's songs from the Pole's Op. 74. As Gunnar Johansen says, "Here we have a perfect fusion of two composers." The six works, *The Maiden's Wish, Spring, The Silver Ring, Drinking Song, My Joys,* and *Homeward,* make a fine recital cycle. *The Maiden's Wish* and *My Joys* are best known. Liszt takes Chopin's simple song and creates a fetching virtuoso piece, while *My Joys,* subtitled *Nocturne,* is a lyric love poem. The final piece, also called the Dead Knight of the Forest, is a stormy "Erlkönig"-like piece.

CORTOT (*My Joys*): Pearl
HOFMANN (*The Maiden's Wish*): VAI
RACHMANINOFF (*The Maiden's Wish*): RCA
SHEHORI: Cembal d'Amour
SLENCZYNSKA: Ivory Classics

Christmas Tree suite

The *Christmas Tree suite,* composed between 1874 and 1876, is Liszt without rhetoric; simplicity and peace are at hand "lighting the candles on the Christmas tree." The album contains unpretentious religious pieces like *In dulci jubilo,* a march, mazurka, scherzoso,

Carillon, Cloches du soir, and a nostalgic waltz, *Jadis* ("Formerly"), a fond glance back to the past.

JOHANSEN: Artist Direct

The Late Music

Liszt's late music has come into its own only in the last few decades. Many of his contemporaries thought these works were merely the eccentric toying of a disillusioned man who had once known the glories of the world. In these later works, he opened a new vista, using whole-tone scales, chords in fourths, ambiguous tonality; the music, it seemed, was abandoned in mid-measure. He moved toward both impressionism and expressionism. How far Liszt had traveled from his showiest Rhapsodies to music that would later amaze Debussy, Stravinsky, and Bartók! According to John Ogdon: "Liszt was responsible for breaking the Germanic stranglehold on nineteenth century composers, and scattering the seeds of modern music almost literally to the four winds. His music shows an avant-garde attitude to the problems of composing which was without parallel in the nineteenth century."

Of the late compositions, Allan Walker says, "It is almost as if he were trying to starve his compositions of the very notes they require to achieve their identity." Liszt well knew these were the most radical compositions of the time. He wrote, "I calmly persist in staying stubbornly in my order, and just work at becoming more and more misunderstood." For the sensitive player and listener, these flickering scores are haunting, attaching themselves to a secret chamber of the soul. Indeed, one may see the series as a musical diary of old age. These are shudders of anxiety, grief, the macabre—chilling twilight harmonies, faltering steps, tense irony, erotic reminiscences,

and an eerie silence surrounding ambiguity.

Some of the most extraordinary of these pieces are:

Elegy No. 2:
KENTNER: Turnabout (LP)

Unstern:
Csárdás macabre:
Schlaflos, Frage und Antwort:
BRENDEL: Philips
HOWARD: Hyperion

Nuages gris; La Lugubre Gondola No.1:
JOHANSEN: Artist Direct
KARS: London (LP)

La Lugubre Gondola No. 2:
BRENDEL: Philips
HOWARD: Hyperion

En rêve:
BAR-ILLAN: Audiofon
WATTS: EMI

WITOLD LUTOSLAWSKI
1913-1994—Poland

In his later years, along with Messiaen, he was the most famous living composer in an age when no composers' names were universally recognized. Stravinsky and Shostakovich had been the last household names. Lutoslawski wrote little piano music, but the little is admirable and the Piano Concerto from 1987 is a masterwork. He is best known for his clever Two-Piano Variations on a Theme of Paganini. His two solo Etudes from 1941 are rewarding and have gained many performances. The twelve Easy Pieces (Folk Melodies) are beautiful adaptations of Polish folk tunes first performed in Cracow in 1946 by Zbigniew

Drzewiecki. The composer himself premiered his Five Bucolics and recorded them on Muza. The Piano Concerto was dedicated and given its premiere by Krystian Zimerman. Its four movements move lightly with a vaporous swiftness.

Of the Concerto, the composer said:

From among the romanticists, the only composer who has influenced me is Chopin. I have realized this fact comparatively recently. . . . In this composition there are some moments (will anybody notice them?) of looking back towards Chopin. I tried to find my own Chopin. I did not want to "reconstruct" what I admire in his music; I wanted to construct something new, something original, which, however, would be somehow connected with the music of this artist of genius, who personifies our national culture. . . . In Chopin's music there are moments which call forth a sensation of flight . . . and it is such an effect of leaving the ground and rising that I tried to bring about.

ZIMERMAN, Lutoslawski/BBC Symphony: DG

M

EDWARD MACDOWELL
1861–1908—United States

MacDowell wrote the most distinctive music by any American during the 1890s. As Virgil Thomson states, he is "our nearest to a great master before Ives. His short works for piano still speak to us." He was a master at producing music with a sweet, nostalgic lyricism. Living in an emerging industrial America, he yearned for the romance of the old sagas. H. E. Krehbiel wrote: "MacDowell aimed at depicting the mood of things and the moods awakened by things rather than the things themselves. He was fond of subjects and titles which . . . smack of the woods—not the greenwood of the English ballads, but the haunted forests of Germany, in which nymphs and dryads hold their revels and kobolds frolic."

Until at least 1925, MacDowell was considered the preeminent American composer. "However," wrote Gilbert Chase, "he does not mark the beginning of a new epoch in American music, but the closing of a fading era, the fin de siècle decline of the genteel tradition which had dominated American art since the days of Hopkinson and Hewitt."

Twelve Virtuoso Studies, Op. 46 (1894)

The best of these pieces—such as *Moto Perpetuo*, *Wild Chase*, *Elfin Dance*, *Burlesque*, and *Bluette*—are treasures, showing MacDowell at

his best. MacDowell also wrote a set of Twelve Etudes, Op. 39, the best known of which is the entrancing *Shadow Dance*; the pungent *Etude de concert*, Op. 36, and the *Hexentanz*, Op. 17, No. 2, are scintillating encore pieces. *Hexentanz* is a rather genial witch with a fetching second subject.

> *Twelve Virtuoso Studies*:
> BARBAGALLO: Marco Polo
> FIERRO: Delos
> FRAGER: New World (LP)
> JOCHUM: Golden Crest (LP)

Eight Sea Pieces, Op. 55 (1900)

The *Sea Pieces*—with titles such as *In Mid-Ocean*, *From a Wandering Iceberg*, *Starlight*, and *Nautilus*—reflect the graver side of MacDowell. Little fingerwork is required for this slowly paced, unusual music.

> BARBAGALLO: Naxos
> BENNETTE: Grenadilla (LP)
> LEE: Harmonia Mundi
> TOCCO: Gasparo

First Modern Suite, Op. 10 (1881)
Second Modern Suite, Op. 14 (1883)

Both suites have musical interest, especially No. 1, with its rolling Praeludium and the finely spun staccato study of the Presto movement. The fugue finale begins in an academic vein but quickly turns to bravura.

BARBAGALLO: Marco Polo
FIERRO (First Suite): Nonesuch
SWEM (Second Suite): Orion

Ten Woodland Sketches, Op. 51 (1896)

The cycle is an American rustic dream, with some of MacDowell's most glowing writing. *To a Wild Rose* is his most celebrated piece, based on an Iroquois Indian melody. *To a Water-Lily* is exquisite. Others, such as *A Deserted Farm, By a Meadow Brook,* and *At an Old Trysting,* have a moist earthiness.

BARBAGALLO: Naxos
DRAKE: Genesis (LP)
LYTHGOE: Philips (LP)
MÜLLER: Dynamic
RIVKIN: Westminster (LP)

Sonata No. 1 in G minor, Op. 45, "Tragica" (1893)
Sonata No. 2 in G minor, Op. 50, "Eroica" (1895)
Sonata No. 3 in D minor, Op. 57, "Norse" (1900)
Sonata No. 4 in E minor, Op. 59, "Keltic" (1901)

MacDowell's are the most significant Romantic American Sonatas, full of the highest ideals, where he frequently soars to the wild blue. In them also one hears too much striving for "greatness," and the piano scoring acquired a turbid thickness. The ideas, often admirable and telling in themselves, occasionally stagnate in the context of the large form. But "whatever his limitations," wrote William S. Newman: "performers are likely to return to one or another of his Sonatas again and again. . . . The sonatas abound in frank songful melody, in opportunities to emote with judicious abandon, and in piano writing that makes good sound and pleasurable technical challenges."

The Sonatas are MacDowell's valiant attempt to avow his programmatic and poetic feelings in an epic setting. The *Tragica* is dedicated to the memory of his teacher, Joachum Raff, and the tragic element is noble and impressive. James Huneker, upon first hearing it, went so far as to pronounce it "the most marked contribution to solo sonata literature since Brahms's F minor Piano Sonata." Of the *Eroica* No. 2, the composer revealed, "I had in mind the Arthurian legend." The *Eroica* is richly hued but more discursive than No. 1, and Lawrence Gilman, feels that "he has written few things more luxuriantly beautiful than the Guinevere movement, nothing more elevated and ecstatic than the apotheosis which ends the work."

The Sonata No. 3, *Norse,* heroic in thought, is pervaded by an ancient atmosphere, haunted with the adventures of Vikings. Sonata No. 4, the *Keltic,* at nineteen minutes, is the most concise and least orchestral in its textures. Of the sonata, Wilfred Mellers thinks "his sundry *Viking* and *Norse* Sonatas attempt, somewhat, self-consciously, to invoke the heroic pioneers of yore; yet the invocation happens only within the mind of a sensitive, sometimes tamed academic who had dreamed hard dreams, maybe, but lived soft." Both the *Norse* and *Keltic* Sonatas are dedicated to Grieg, whom MacDowell deeply admired. In turn Grieg wrote: "I am a great admirer of MacDowell's music. . . . He is a complete personality, with an unusually sympathetic and sensitive nervous system. Such a temperament gives one the capacity not only for moods of the highest transport, but for unspeakable sorrow tenfold more profound."

The Four Sonatas:
KEENE: Protone
MANDEL: Phoenix
TOCCO: Gasparo

Sonata No. 1:
CORBATÓ: Orion
RIVKIN: Westminster

Sonata No. 2:
LYTHGOE: Philips

Sonata No. 3:
BARBAGALLO: Naxos
MANDEL: Desta

Sonata No. 4:
BARBAGALLO: Marco Polo
BATES: Orion
FIERRO: Nonesuch
MITCHELL: Vanguard

Piano Concerto No. 1 in A minor, Op. 15

Though overshadowed by the finer Second Concerto, the Op. 15 has heaping handfuls of chords and a surging appeal which make it an entertaining showcase. The Andante tranquillo is imbued with, as James Lyons put it, "the demi-tinted landscaping which was to be MacDowell's hallmark."

LIST, Chávez/Vienna State Opera: Westminster (LP)
RIVKIN, Dixon/Vienna State Opera: Westminster (LP)
TIRINO, Kazandjiev/Bulgarian Radio Symphony: Centaur

Piano Concerto No. 2 in D minor, Op. 23 (1890)

The Second Concerto is the only nineteenth-century concerto by an American composer to have retained a small place in the international repertoire. It was dedicated to Teresa Carreño, who helped popularize it. A concerto in the grand heroic manner, its structure is almost seamless. There is no slow movement, but instead a sparkling and irresistible Scherzo in the vein of Litolff's Scherzo and the middle movement of the Saint-Saëns Second Concerto. The composition asks for a performer who is far from timid.

CLIBURN, Hendl/Chicago Symphony: RCA
SOREL, Autori/New York Philharmonic: EMSCO
SZIDON, Downes/London Philharmonic: DG
WATTS, Litton/Dallas Symphony: Telarc
WILD, Freccia/National Philharmonic: Chesky

FRANK MARTIN
1890–1974—Switzerland

Martin wrote music of lasting value. He combines a French clarity of texture with German harmonic idioms. From 1933 on, Martin integrated some of Schoenberg's twelve-tone system into charged chromaticism. Martin's rhythms are often original, as is his passionate musical diction. He left only a small output for piano, but each work is important.

Eight Preludes (1948)

The Eight Preludes, twenty-one minutes in length, composed for Dinu Lipatti, are considered by Maurice Hinson to be "one of the major contributions to the twentieth century piano literature."

SILVERMAN: Orion (LP)
WALSH: Music and Arts
WATKINS: ACA Digital

Guitare—Quatre Pièces brèves (1933)
Clair de lune (1952)
Esquisse (1965)
Etude rythmique (1965)
Fantaisie sur des rythmes flamenco (1973)

Guitare is dedicated to Segovia and was composed in 1933. The composer transcribed it for piano in the late 1950s, and it sounds magnificent. The Four Pieces are titled *Prélude, Air, Plainte,* and *Comme une gigue. Clair de lune* is the sparest of the works and the easiest to play. *Esquisse* was composed for a Munich piano competition; marked "Allegretto tranquillo," it was intended as a test of sight-reading skill. The *Etude rythmique* is an homage to the composer Jacques Dalcroze. In it, a 9/8 meter in the right is pitted against a 3/4 meter in the left. The *Fantaisie sur des rythmes flamenco* is one of Martin's most amazing creations in any genre. Composed on a commission from Paul Badura-Skoda, it was also intended to be danced by the composer's daughter, Anne-Therésè, a flamenco dancer. The four sections, totaling sixteen minutes in length, are *Rumba lente, Rumba rapide, Soleares,* and *Petenera.* Regarding the flamenco dance, Martin wrote, "I had been fascinated more by the mixture of tragedy, dignity in the face of destiny, and joy which this art expresses, than by its complexity and richness of rhythms."

LA BRECQUE: Opus One (LP)
MATHÉ: Koch Schwann

Concerto No. 2 for Piano and Orchestra

The Second Concerto does not have immediate appeal. It lacks the concentration of the solo piano pieces, although it has a forcefulness all its own. The three movements are Con moto, Lento, and Presto. It was premiered in 1970 by Paul Badura-Skoda, for whom it was conceived.

BADURA-SKODA, Martin/Luxembourg Radio: Jecklin-Disco

NICOLAI MEDTNER
1880–1951—Russia

As the early twenty-first century looks back upon late-Romantic piano composers, Medtner's name is becoming conspicuous. Sliding under the shadows of Scriabin and Rachmaninoff and the more modernist Prokofiev, Medtner has remained on the fringes of the performing repertoire, not forgotten but not integrated into the pianist's regular diet. However, his work is too admirable, with "rare perfumes, and special colors," as Horowitz put it. Although Romantic to the core, his work in part is not as accessible as Rachmaninoff's, who was his constant admirer. As Liszt once stated, "There is music which comes of itself to us, and other music that requires us to come to it."

Ernest Newman wrote: "His music is not always easy to follow, at first hearing, but not because of any extravagance of thought or

542

Nicolai Medtner by David Dubal

layers, and his rhythmic ingenuity is often startling; a personal polyphony permeates his music, and there are many passages that leap from the instrument. Indeed it is a multidimensional music and highly expressive, in which Medtner's markings are copious and highly expressive. The larger works are formidable challenges for the memory; forks in the road occur unexpectedly and constantly.

Medtner was a composer involved with sonata principles—"he was born into sonata form coursing though his veins," uttered his delighted teacher, the great academician Sergei Tancycv. Mcdtner's fourteen sonatas are contained in the years 1902–37. Although he lived until 1951, he composed little in his later years. Rather like Rachmaninoff, he lived the life of an unhappy exile—born three years before the death of Wagner and thirteen years before Tchaikovsky's death, his creative aesthetic dried up, as he strove to live in a world he hardly recognized. He once wrote, "Have I not been threatened by life?" A staunch hater of modern trends in art, Mcdtncr, like Rachmaninoff, who thought him the greatest living composer, stayed true to his own "Romantic" ideals and nature. In the last several years there has been an upsurge in Medtner performances, and an International Medtner Foundation has supported publication by Dover of the Sonatas and Tales. Young pianists such as the Taiwanese-born Jung Lin have been performing much Medtner with success, and recordings by Geoffrey Tozer, Hamish Milne, Malcolm Binns, Vladimir Viardo, and Marc-André Hamelin are of outstanding quality. Medtner, it seems, will finally take his deserved place next to his great compatriots, Scriabin and Rachmaninoff.

confusion of technique, it is simply because this music really does go on thinking from bar to bar, evolving logically from its premises."

Marc-André Hamelin fecls that "in general many recordings of his works do not come off because of the performances themselves, rather than weakness in the music. It is my firm belief that if one gives Medtner everything, he will come alive on first hearing. I have had enough positive reaction to my own performances to be able to assert this."

Medtner's world of sound is wholly related to the piano, and all of his works outside the solo piano, such as the songs and three violin sonatas, contain important piano parts, while he used an orchestra only in the three piano concertos.

Medtner's pianism is usually extremely difficult, using the entire keyboard and demanding creative pedaling. He writes in

The Complete Sonatas:
HAMELIN (complete): Hyperion
TOZER (complete): Chandos
MILNE (No. 12): CRD

Piano Sonata No. 1 in F minor, Op. 5

Astute analysis of Medtner's Sonatas are found in Barrie Martyn's biography of the composer. From this first effort, one hears Medtner's never-a-wasted-note approach to composition. However packed the score, there remains in all of his music an essential leanness of texture. Medtner successfully played his first sonata privately to Josef Hofmann and Rachmaninoff late in 1902. The Sonata No. 1 in four movements is already entirely mature, though less chromatic than what would come later.

Geoffrey Tozer writes: "Within its relatively sparse and economical textures, harmonies range from the utterly simple to the most complex, and themes are minutely, obsessively examined, varied and extended through a movement." The fourth movement, a sonata structure, is replete with turbulence and contrapuntal wrappings; the left hand, as usual in Medtner, is difficult but deftly pianistic.

HAMELIN: Hyperion
MILNE: CRD
TOZER: Chandos

Piano Sonata No. 2 in A-flat major, Op. 11, No. 1
Piano Sonata No. 3 in D minor, Op. 11, No. 2
Piano Sonata No. 4 in C major, Op. 11, No. 4

The three sonatas were called by the composer *Sonata Triad*. They are independent creations but related by the dedication, "In memory of Andrei Bratenshi," his brother-in-law, who committed suicide. The works are proceeded by lines from Goethe's *Trilogy of Passion*, "and so the heart, disburdened, in a flash knows; I endure, and beat, and pound with pleasure!" The sonatas are each in one movement. No. 1 is sixteen pages, light and lovely. No. 2 in D minor, *Sonate-Élégie,* is only eight pages with an effective coda (doppio movimento). The C major Sonata is marked "allegro moderato, con passione innocente," with striking details and a driving coda which ends with a glissando.

HAMELIN: Hyperion
MILNE: CRD
TOZER: Chandos

Piano Sonata No. 5 in G minor, Op. 22

Leonid Sabaneyev wrote, "Over his compositions hover the spirit of Beethoven's last sonatas." In the G minor, completed in 1910, the one-movement form of about seventeen minutes shows a Lisztian affinity in Medtner dress; the whole edifice relies on the opening measures. The tempo changes are many in this cogent score, which has been perhaps the most consistently performed of the sonatas. Heinrich Neuhaus wrote of it as a "trajectory felt from the first to the last note as one uninterrupted line." The initial markings of the composer are "tenebroso, sempre affrettando" (tempo accelerando, poco a poco). The work is of considerable pianistic interest, ending molto appassionata.

GILELS: Melodiya (LP)
HAMELIN: CRD
ISTOMIN: Radio Classique
MOISEIWITSCH: Philips: Great Pianists of the Twentieth Century
PONTI: Vox

Piano Sonata No. 6 "Sonata-Tale" in C minor, Op. 25, No. 1

From 1910, this three-movement work of twenty-one pages is dedicated to the eminent pianist and composer Alexander Goedicke. The second movement has a lyric glow showing a kinship with Rachmaninoff. Tozer writes, "The lovely vivacity of the opening movement, tender and light; the narrative quality of the enormously long melody that forms the second movement; and the heroic tone of the last, which opens with a march for a creature with five legs! (The concluding section sums up all the themes.)"

BINNS: HNH
HAMELIN: Hyperion
TOZER: Chandos

Piano Sonata No. 7 in E minor, Op. 25, No. 2 "Night Wind"

Nearly thirty-five minutes, *Night Wind* is a chilling vision, one of Medtner's most complex works and one of the fiendishly difficult works in the late Romantic piano literature. It is dedicated to Rachmaninoff, who was overwhelmed by the score when Medtner premiered it in 1912. (Rachmaninoff would later dedicate his Fourth Concerto to Medtner.) This is music of nonstop movement; the pianist will find no rest in this epical song of anguish and despair. On the title page Medtner writes, "The entire piece in an epic spirit." And for his epigraph he quotes the Russian poet Fyodor Tyutchev: "What are you waiting about, night wind, what are you lamenting with such fury." Sorabji thought it was, along with Busoni's *Fantasia contrappuntistica*, one of the greatest piano works ever written.

HAMELIN: Hyperion
STEWART: Palexa
TOZER: Chandos

Piano Sonata No. 8 in F-sharp major, Op. 27 "Sonata-Ballade"

Composed from 1912 to 1914, the *Sonata-Ballade* was recorded by Medtner and is of a haunting beauty, springlike and glistening, framed in majestic piano scoring. The opening theme resounds through the piece. The mesto opening to the Introduzione is lugubrious and menacing; after two false starts a fugue commences to a jubilant conclusion. Tozer writes, "Which for finger-twisting toughness and complexity brings to mind its ancestor in Beethoven's Op. 101." The *Sonata-Ballade* is twenty-five minutes in length and is one of Medtner's loftiest creations.

BINNS: Pearl
MEDTNER: Historical Piano Collection
MILNE: CRD
TOZER: Chandos

Piano Sonata No. 9 in A minor, Op. 30

On the score Medtner writes, "During the War 1914–1917"; here is another one-movement structure. This "War Sonata" is a work of questioning, and the pall of doom pervades. However, in the powerful development section a climax brings us bell-like effects in the upper register. There is jubilation in the air, as there is a stark quality.

Barrie Martyn sums up: "The end of the work matches the beginning, not only in bringing back the opening first subject figures but, as in the introduction, in strongly asserting the music's tonality (now A major), here with a ravishingly decorated tonic chord pedaled through 13 bars, during which fluttering triplets in the right hand, diving and soaring aloft, ring out like pealing bells. A triumphant cadence clinches the final mood of confidence."

MILNE: CRD
TOZER: Chandos
VIARDOT: Nonesuch

PONTI: Vox
TOZER: Chandos
VIARDO: Naxos

Piano Sonata No. 10 in A minor, Op. 38, No. 1 "Sonata-Reminiscenza"

After the revolution Medtner's comfortable world collapsed. Henceforth he would be a dissolute wanderer. In this sonata he remembers a world and time forever vanished. Among the best known of the sonatas, this one-movement score was one of Medtner's favorite works; it was completed in 1920. Gilels says the score "is very Romantic, and brings together Russian and western traditions." The Reminiscenza in one movement of twenty pages is on the whole technically less demanding, introspective, and lyrical.

DEMIDENKO: Hyperion
GILELS: Philips: Great Pianists of the Twentieth Century
GINSBURG: Philips: Great Pianists of the Twentieth Century
HAMELIN: Hyperion
VIARDO: Nonesuch

Piano Sonata No. 11 in C minor, Op. 39, No. 5 "Sonata Tragica"

Composed in 1918-20 in one movement which is preceded by the lovely and errant *Canzona Matinata* (Morning Song) Op. 39, No. 4, which ends on G with an "attacca la sonata tragica," which begins fortissimo on bleak chords. The one-movement sonata is abstruse, and as always technically difficult, chromatic, and needing concentrated intensity from the pianist.

Piano Sonata No. 12 in B-flat minor, Op. 53, No. 1 "Sonata Romantica"

More than a decade separates the *Romantica* from the *Tragica*. In a world of fierce modernism on all sides, from Stravinsky to Schoenberg, which he rejected totally as non-art, he continued to write music then considered by many to be old-fashioned. The *Romantica* uses a four-movement format for the first time since the Sonata No. 5. The first movement is a Romanza, the second a long Scherzo, the third an Andante con moto, titled *Meditazione*, which flows into the dynamic finale. It is a complex work with dreamlike material and dazzling piano writing with swirls of polyphony. The score is nearly forty pages long.

HAMELIN: Hyperion
TOZER: Chandos

Piano Sonata No. 13 in F minor, Op. 53, No. 2 "Sonata Minacciosa"

Composed in 1931–32 and one of Medtner's mightiest scores. Dense and uncompromising, Medtner called it "my most contemporary composition, for it reflects the threatening atmosphere of contemporary events." This is Medtner at his tightest and most drastically intellectual. The sonata in one movement of thirty-six pages takes about twenty-three minutes. Tozer says, "In its crucible of white-hot inspiration, keys are undefined, figurations are chromatic complexities, form is elusive." There is a long taxing fugue in the middle of the score based on the sonata's first subject. *Minaccioso* means "menace" (from the Italian word *minaccia)*, and the fugue material, played mostly pianissimo, is indeed menacing in its design and technique.

BINNS: Pearl
HAMELIN: Hyperion

Piano Sonata No. 14 in G major, Op. 56 "Sonata Idyll"

Composed in 1937, Medtner's creative activity is winding down. The last of his sonatas is of a radiant innocence. Technically the two movements are not as elaborate as usual. To Rachmaninoff he wrote, "I have been writing with the deliberate intention of moderating the virtuoso difficulty of the piano style. I know that I have far from succeeded in fulfilling this good intention." The first movement is marked "Pastorale"; the second movement presents three themes. "The third theme," writes Martyn, "is a sunny Mediterranean hymn in D major . . . at the end, the music quietly subsides to a shimmering conclusion of utter loveliness."

BINNS: Pearl
TOZER: Chandos
WILD: Chesky

First Improvisation, Op. 31, No. 1

A set of five variations on an elegiac theme which becomes virtuosic before its serene ending.

MEDTNER: APR
MEDTNER: Melodiya
WILD: Ivory

Funeral March, Op. 31, No. 2

Only two pages, its grief is an outpouring for the death of Alexey Stanchinsky, a promising composer whom Medtner befriended and who died at age twenty-six.

TOZER: Chandos

Second Improvisation, Op. 47 (in the form of variations)

Composed during the summer of 1925, the variations are intricate, sullen, gay, frothy, and a paradise of ingenious pianistic writing within the tonalities of F-sharp minor, A major, G minor, B-flat minor, G-flat major, back to F-sharp minor. The haunting theme, titled *Song of The Water Nymph*, is followed by fifteen variations and a conclusion; each variation, such as *In the Forest, Wood Goblin, Incantation,* and *Stormy Weather,* is subjected to cobweb elaboration. It's one of the impor-tant sets of variations of the period, taking twenty-six minutes for performance.

MILNE: CRD
WILD: RCA, Chesky

Skazki (Tales), Op. 8

The largest segment of Medtner's more than one hundred piano works, contained within thirty-four opus numbers. *Skazki* is the Russian word for "folk tale" and is somewhat akin to the French *conte,* and the German *Märchen.* In English these works have been usually labeled "fairy tales," but Russian folklore possess no fairies, as does English, and is involved with witches, ogres, firebirds, and the like. Present-day usage has opted for the title in

English of Tales. There are three dozen of these small works, averaging three minutes, although Hamish Milne writes, "These are no miniatures, there is more incident, more concentrated thought and feeling and sheer stature here than can be found in many a sonata or symphony."

Robert Rimm writes: "They represent an entirely new genre that fuses literary and folk sources with equal parts dark fantasy and theatre. Even more than that, they describe their composer's reaction to life's substance. In their sweeping exploration of human conflicts, drives, disappointments, and happiness, they transcend simple folklore."

On the technical side, Marc-André Hamelin writes, "As a source of pure delight for the performer, this wealth of music is an opportunity to discover the unbelievably pianistic nature of Medtner's writing; by comparison even Chopin's piano music seems technically uncomfortable. . . . Very often in Medtner, the musical idea and its instrumental realization are so intricately joined that it becomes impossible to determine exactly which came first—if indeed they did not occur to the composer at the same time."

CHERKASSKY: Ivory Classics
HOROWITZ: Sony Classical
MEDTNER: EMI
MILNE: CRD
SHATSKES: Melodiya (LP)
TOZER: Chandos

Piano Concertos Nos. 1, 2, and 3

Medtner's Concertos are masterful, but completely dependent upon the interpreter's conviction and intellectual rigor. Of the first concerto, Richard Holt writes, "It was born of the composer's emotions, on realising the catastrophic nature of this atavistic throw-back in a world which had failed to realise that the strength of the chain of civilization is that of its weakest link, that is, its least civilized members. The concerto has the character of a long symphonic poem, and its fateful, sombre tones and color, its crepuscular harmonies, its drama and poignancy of feeling, with, eventually, a vernal blaze of joyful emotion, foreshadowing the end of the debacle, as staunch faith and leonine courage triumph over doubt and despair, give the work an epic quality, though it seems to end on a note of interrogation."

Composed in Moscow during World War I, No. 1 in C minor is in one brilliantly conceived movement of more than half an hour. Hinson says, "The writing for the piano is complex with much use of contrapuntal textures; it demands full virtuoso and musical equipment." The development section of this huge sonata allegro movement takes the two themes and develops nine variations within the development section.

The massive Concerto No. 2 in C minor (1927) is dedicated to Rachmaninoff, who never performed it in public. The work is long, over forty minutes, in three movements: Toccata, Romance, and Divertissement. It is a quirky score with much that is entrancing; it needs an admiring pianist and sophisticated listeners.

The Concerto No. 3 in E minor, Concerto-Ballade, is more restrained than the previous concertos and is the subtlest of the three. Medtner, a passionate lover of literature, confessed to Lermontov's *Rusalka* as his inspiration: "A water-nymph swan in a blue stream, in the light of a full moon; and she tried to splash all the way to the moon the water's silvery spray."

Concerto No. 1, Op. 33:
ALEXEEV, Lazarev/BBC Symphony: Hyperion
MEDTNER, Weldon/London Philharmonic: Melodiya (LP)
NIKOLAEVA, Svetlanov/USSR Symphony Orchestra: Melodiya

TOZER, Järvi/London Philharmonic: Chandos
ZHUKOV, Dmitriev/Moscow Radio Symphony: Melodiya (LP)

Concerto No. 2, Op. 50:
DEMIDENKO, Maksymiuk/BBC Scottish Orchestra: Hyperion
SHATSKES, Svetlanov/USSR Symphony Orchestra: Melodiya
TOZER, Järvi/London Philharmonic: Chandos

Concerto No. 3, Op. 60:
DEMIDENKO, Maksymiuk/BBC Scottish Symphony Orchestra: Hyperion
MEDTNER, Dobrowen/Philharmonia Orchestra: Historical Piano Collection
PONTI, Cao/Luxembourg Radio Symphony Orchestra: Vox
SCHERBAKOV, Ziva/Moscow Symphony Orchestra: Naxos

FELIX MENDELSSOHN
1809–1847—Germany

The word *dated,* which was once applied to a large amount of Mendelssohn's writing, has now practically disappeared from discussions of his work. This is mainly the result of a more thorough knowledge of historical style; also, recordings have been kind to Mendelssohn's varied output. His better piano music is unrivaled in its evocation of the Kingdom of Oberon, an enchanted fairyland of elves and sunlight. Ernest Hutcheson had in mind the E minor Scherzo, the *Spinning Song, Rondo capriccioso,* and other works of scherzando origin when he wrote, "These pieces dart or hover on gossamer wings. Transformed into a dragonfly or hidden by an invisible cap, Felix must have stolen into meetings of the little people." Mendelssohn's largest contribution to the literature is his set of forty-eight

Songs without Words, which, as pianist Karl Engel noted, "are really sketches of a traveler, written for the delectation of those who had stayed home." George Bernard Shaw advised, "They are too easy for our young lions, but really, I suspect, because they are too difficult. If you want to find out the weak places in a player's technique . . . ask him to play you ten bars of Mozart or Mendelssohn."

The Complete Solo Piano Music

Daniel Gregory Mason has best summarized Mendelssohn's art:

> Violence of contrast, dramatic trenchancy of expression, the overemphasis of hysterical eloquence he punctiliously avoids; he is always clear, unperturbed, discreet, harmonious. The lavish sensuousness of Schubert, the impulsive sincerity of Schumann, are impossible if not distasteful to this Addisonian temperament; personal sentiment, self-revelation, the autobiographic appeal, he avoids as the purist in manners avoids a blush, an exclamation, or a grimace. If he is romantic in his love of the picturesque, in his sense of color, and in his fondness for literary motives, his emotional reticence is entirely classic. He is more observant than introspective, and his art is more pictorial than passionate.

FRITH: Naxos
JONES: Nimbus

Forty-eight Songs without Words, Opp. 19, 30, 38, 53, 62, 67, 85, 102

These pieces were the joy of Victorian parlor pianists and were among the world's best loved music. The most famous piece Mendelssohn composed, the *Spring Song,* became hackneyed almost beyond repair. Many of the titles were given by publishers. The *Volkslied, May Breezes,* the tender, loving *Duetto,* the *Spinning Song, Consolation,* and *Hunting Song* are indispensable works of German Romanticism. In all, there is that special fastidiousness which makes Mendelssohn the Beau Brummell of composers.

ALPENHEIM: Philips
BARENBOIM: DG
DORFMANN: RCA (LP)
FRIEDMAN (10 pieces): Pearl
GIESEKING (17 pieces): Angel (LP)
JONES: Nimbus
KYRIAKOU: Vox (LP)
NOVAES (14 pieces): Vox
PERAHIA (8 pieces): Sony Classical

Felix Mendelssohn by David Dubal

Variations sérieuses in D minor, Op. 54

Composed in 1841, this is one of the finest sets of variations from the Romantic period, and it is charged with emotional intensity. These variations were never equaled by Mendelssohn's other piano music, for they have cohesion of form and passion, and they reveal the composer's remarkable capacity for original and idiomatic keyboard writing. Each tiny eight-measure variation dissolves imperceptibly into the next, and an array of devices, such as the two-part canonic writing of variation 4, the fugal variation 10, and the constant shifting from light to dark, display Mendelssohn's perfect craftsmanship. The word *sérieuses* in the title is thought to reflect Mendelssohn's reaction to the enormous quantity of facile variations on popular opera tunes of the day by Franz Hünten, Henri Herz, and others—those composers whom Schumann called Philistines.

ARTYMIW: Chandos
CORTOT: Biddulph
DE LARROCHA: London
HOROWITZ: RCA
KEENE: Laure/Protone
PERAHIA: CBS
RICHTER: AS Disc
SIMON: Turnabout (LP)
SOFRONITSKY: Melodiya (LP)

Six Preludes and Fugues, Op. 35

Five of the Preludes and Fugues are interesting in invention, less so in their material, which is rather dry. However the Prelude of No. 1 in E minor is a sonorous three minutes, with Thalbergian three-handed effects. The Fugue, Charles Rosen writes, is "a summation of what Mendelssohn learned from his constant study of Bach, but it is also a remarkable prediction of what the late nineteenth and twentieth centuries would make of Bach's style. . . . It is perhaps the first independent concert fugue. The quiet opening of the fugue may be the most superb pastiche of Bach ever produced with nineteenth-century means."

D'ARCO: MHS
FRITH: Naxos
JONES: Nimbus
KYRIAKOU: Vox
NIKOLAYEVA: Melodiya

Prelude and Fugue No. 1:
KATCHEN: Philips: Great Pianists of the Twentieth Century
LOESSER: Marston
PERAHIA: CBS

Fantasy in F-sharp minor, Op. 28

Perhaps second only to the *Variations sèrieuses* in importance, this work is unduly neglected. Dedicated to Moscheles, it is sometimes known as the *Sonata ecossaise.* It is in three movements and is slightly marred by a tepid but not unattractive Allegro con moto, functioning as the middle movement. The first movement is in two alternating tempi, with recitative-like cadenzas and a central climax of intense feeling. The finale is bursting with perilous and fiery passagework.

ARTYMIW: Chandos
BUDIARDJO: Pro Piano
CHERKASSKY: Vox Cum Laude (LP)
KEENE: Laurel/Protone
KUERTI: Monitor (LP)
MEJOUEVA: Denon
SCHUB: VAI

Three Fantasies or Caprices, Op. 16

No. 2 of the set, in E minor (Scherzo), is two minutes of staccatissimo delight. It was once called *The Trumpeter.* Of the last piece in the set, Mendelssohn wrote, "It runs so slowly and peacefully, a trifle boring in its simplicity, that I have played it to myself every day and become quite sentimental in so doing."

ALPENHEIM: Philips
ARTYMIW: Chandos
FRIEDMAN (No.2): Philips: Great Pianists of the Twentieth Century

Three Etudes, Op. 104

Perfectly crafted works; No. 3 in A minor is particularly ingenious in its use of the two thumbs. Each of the Etudes is technically valuable and musically exhilarating.

HOROWITZ (No. 3): CBS
KEENE: Protone
JONES: Nimbus

Andante and Rondo capriccioso, Op. 14

One of the most popular of Mendelssohn's solo works, it is completely representative of his airy genius. There is hardly a pianist who has not worked on it, with its perennial freshness. The piece concludes in a paroxysm of blind octaves. It seems miraculous that the *Rondo capriccioso* composed in 1825 is by a youngster of sixteen.

ALPENHEIM: Philips (LP)
ARTYMIW: Chandos
CHIU: Harmonia Mundi
HOFMANN: Nimbus
KATCHEN: Philips: Great Pianists of the Twentieth Century
KUERTI: Monitor (LP)
PERAHIA: Sony Classical
PLETNEV: DG

Capriccio in A minor, Op. 33, No. 1

A slow introduction is followed by tempestuous material in Mendelssohn's best vein. The two other Caprices in Op. 33 are of less interest.

  DE LARROCHA: London (LP)
  JONES: Nimbus

Scherzo a capriccio in F-sharp minor

This taxing work of seven minutes, without opus number, needs flexible wrists and untiring staccato in chords and single notes. Although neglected, it is one of Mendelssohn's finest flights of fancy, glowing with inspiration and formal elegance.

  CHERKASSKY: Ivory Classics
  HOROWITZ: RCA
  KUERTI: Monitor (LP)

Piano Concerto No. 2 in G minor, Op. 25

The three movements are without break. The G minor Concerto was once the ultimate "conservatory" concerto; Berlioz dreamed that pianos at the Paris Conservatoire played the piece late at night without aid of the pianists. The work is dazzlingly conceived for the piano, and the orchestration is piquant.

  FIRKUSNY, Froment/Luxembourg Radio:
    Turnabout (LP)
  HOUGH, Foster/City of Birmingham
    Symphony: Hyperion
  OUSSET, Marriner/London Symphony: Angel
  PERAHIA, Marriner/Academy of St. Martin:
    CBS

  R. SERKIN, Ormandy/Columbia Symphony:
    Columbia

Piano Concerto No. 2 in D minor, Op. 40

The last movement is the best, with its sunny good nature. This concerto, though much less difficult technically than No. 1, is seldom played in public.

  KATIN, Collins/London Symphony: London
  PERAHIA, Marriner/Academy of St. Martin:
    CBS

Capriccio brillant in B minor for Piano and Orchestra, Op. 22
Rondo brillant in E-flat major, Op. 29

These smaller works for piano and orchestra show Mendelssohn at his most lighthearted, and the idiomatic piano writing could not be more grateful to the hand or fun to practice. The themes are gracious, and the constructions are finely integrated, revealing an incomparable mastery and clarity. Mendelssohn's influence in such works as these can be heard in the productions of many composers who followed him.

  Capriccio brillant:
  GRAFFMAN, Munch/Boston Symphony: RCA
  ORTIZ, Atzmon/Stuttgart Radio Symphony:
    Pantheon
  R. SERKIN, Ormandy/Philadelphia: CBS

  Rondo brillant:
  KYRIAKOV, Swafowsky/Vienna Pro Musica:
    Turnabout
  OGDON, Ceccato/London Symphony: Klavier
  ORTIS, Atzmon/Stuttgart Radio Symphony:
    Pantheon

OLIVIER MESSIAEN
1908–1992—France

Messiaen is without a doubt one of the most influential composers since World War II. He had many personalities: a religious ecstatic who wrote mystical music; a Romantic, who called himself a "sound color" composer; a student of ornithology, who translated bird song into music of amazing complexity; a theorist, who spawned much new thought; the teacher of Boulez; a student of musics past, from plainsong to Hindu ragas. Messiaen's work is often shrouded in symbolism. The length of his scores is unprecedented: such cyclic compositions as the *Vingt Regards* and the *Catalogue d'oiseaux* take over two hours for complete presentations. With these works, Messiaen broke new ground in the evolution of piano timbre and time values. Indeed, he created a new sense of form, which is no longer based on classic Western standards but seems not to be bound by time at all. The *Vingt Regards,* in a sense, could go on forever. With his "super chords," Messiaen went past Debussy's sensory world, inducing almost trance states. He was the last notch on the ladder of French Romanticism begun by Berlioz. The multiplicity of pianistic textures and contrapuntal voicings presents the pianist with a new and incandescent language to master.

Vingt Regards sur l'Enfant Jésus (1944)

The composer wrote, "More than in all my preceding works I have sought a language of mystic love, at once varied, powerful and tender, sometimes brutal, in a multi-colored ordering." The work was dedicated to and premiered by his wife, Yvonne Loriod, a pianist of extraordinary gifts, who had been a constant inspiration to Messiaen. Her 1950s Westminster monos were considered the last word in avant-garde pianism, and they remain great performances in and of themselves, as well as pioneering recordings which moved other pianists to explore these daunting works. Since that time Messiaen constantly attracted the efforts of major pianists. The *Twenty Contemplations of the Infant Jesus* include motives representing the Cross, the Virgin, the Star, the Angels, and God, all viewing the infant. The cycle has been excerpted by many pianists with striking effect. Indeed, so unusual are his works that Norman Demuth warned: "An evening of Messiaen's exultant piano music can do more harm than good and may antagonize the listener, who is left baffled and bewildered. The rich chords, the harmonic intensities, the ample figuration, the constantly changing tonalities, the wealth of detail and comparative lack of repose, when spread over a two-hour concert are too much for human receptivity."

AIMARD: Telarc
BÉROFF: EMI
DE OLIVEIRA-CARVALHO: Vox
LORIOD: Westminster; Ades
OGDON: Argo
P. SERKIN: RCA (LP)

Catalogue d'oiseaux (1956–58)

This work, even longer than the *Vingt Regards*, is also more advanced in its rhythms and sonorities. It is an enormous undertaking of thirteen works in seven books, celebrating Messiaen's lifelong interest in birdsong. He translated the calls of such birds as the alpine chough, golden oriole, blue rock thrush, buzzard, and others into a uniquely conceived musical canvas. Messiaen, of course, did not attempt merely imitative sounds on the piano, as the instrument, being divided only into semitones, cannot translate the many "micro"-tones of bird call. The premiere took place in 1959, played by Yvonne Loriod.

DE OLIVEIRA-CARVALHO: Vox
JOHNSON: Argo

Eight Preludes (1928–29)

These short works are early Messiaen, with his instinct for chiaroscuro fully developed. They reveal Debussy's art as his prime inspiration at that time. Especially fine is the Sixth Prelude, *Cloches d'angoisse et larmes d'adieu* ("Bells of Anguish and Tears of Farewell"), "in sumptuous draperies of violet, orange and royal purple," as described by the composer.

BÉROFF: EMI
CROSSLEY (Nos. 5 and 6, and selections from the two cycles): L'Oiseau-Lyre
HEWITT: Hyperion
LORIOD: MHS

Quatre Etudes de rythme (1949–50)

These pieces were very influential in the serialism of the 1950s. Etude No. 1 is *Ile de feu I* ("Island of Fire"), dedicated to the people of Papua New Guinea. In explanation, Messiaen wrote, "The themes have the violence of the magic cults of that country." No. 2 is *Mode de valeurs et d'intensités* ("Mode of Values and Intensities"). According to the composer, "This utilizes a pitch-mode (36 tones), a value-mode (24 note-lengths or durations), an attack-mode (12 kinds of attacks), and an intensity-mode (12 shades of intensity)." No. 3, *Neumes rythmiques*, was composed while considering the different shapes of the neumes used for notating plainsong. No. 4 is *Ile de feu II,* which is often performed.

P. JACOBS: Nonesuch
LORIOD: MHS
TAKAHASHI: Denon

FEDERICO MOMPOU
1893–1987—Spain

Twelve Canciones y danzas
Impressiones intimas (1911–14)
Charmes (1920–21)
Suburbis (1916–17)
Eleven Preludes (1927–60)
Variaciones sobre un tema de Chopin

Mompou's fleeting sketches are charming and often poignant, possessing their own perfume. The scope of his work as a Spanish nationalist has been confined to a distillation of Catalan folk material. He seldom uses bar lines, and though he is often technically easy, subtleties of pedaling, as well as interpretive imagination, are called for. The critic Emile Vuillermoz, decades ago, wrote of Mompou: "He searches in music for enchantments and spells wherewith to compound his magic songs. His formulas are short, concise, concentrated, but they possess a weird, hallucinating power of evocation . . . no matter how minutely we analyze Mompou's score, we cannot discover his secrets. This music which is so gentle and peaceful, reaches out to unexplored regions of the subconscious."

Mompou made five records of his complete piano music in 1974. So much of his music is static that only small doses are recommended for maximum effect. Mompou's playing echoes the spirit of his music; in some of his preludes, the *Trois Variations, Dialogues,* and *Charmes,* he produces a trance like state. When the dance elements come to the fore, however, he plays rhythmically. Mompou has a beautiful and, at times, a liquid touch with a great deal of sensitivity at the fingertips. He nurtures his music. A most appealing novelty is the long (twenty minutes) set of variations on the Chopin Prelude in A major.

The Complete Piano Music:
MOMPOU: Ensayo

Selected Piano Music:
DE LARROCHA: Philips: Great Pianists of the
   Twentieth Century
HOUGH: Hyperion
JONES: Nimbus
MOMPOU: Ensayo
ROMERO: Koch

MORITZ MOSZKOWSKI
1854–1925—Poland

Too often regarded as a mere salon composer, Moszkowski's effervescence at its best deserves repertory status, especially at a time when recitalists could do well to partake in such prolific happiness. His lighthearted creations are far more than concoctions; indeed Moszkowski had a lifelong love affair with the instrument, and it revealed many delicious secrets to him. He is a delight to practice, as he spins fine silk from the piano, and his forms never overflow the material.

Piano Concerto in E major, Op. 59 (1898)

A cheerful, quite scrumptious concerto in four movements takes about thirty-five minutes. David Bar-Illan writes: "It's first and foremost

an orgy of pianism, an intoxication with what the instrument can do, a celebration of its sound, its speed, its sparkle. It's the kind of assault on the senses experienced at a fantastic fireworks display. Plus a little pulling at the heartstrings. Profound?—No. Thrilling yes! The pianist must possess wit and flair, the piece should be a regular everywhere."

BAR-ILLAN, Antonini/Bavarian Radio
   Orchestra: Audiofon
PONTI, Stracke/Philharmonia Hungarica: Vox

Fifteen Virtuoso Etudes "Per Aspera," Op. 72

Moszkowski wrote a plethora of etudes through out his catalogue; the fifteen Etudes, Op. 72 are often used and satisfy myriad technical territory. Horowitz kept to two of them in F major and A-flat major. No. 15, a double note study in A-flat minor, is particularly beautiful. A few are arid finger busters, but the majority have a special musical aplomb.

VERED (complete): Connoisseur Society
HAMELIN (no. 15): Hyperion
HOROWITZ (Nos. 6 and 11): RCA

Valse in E major, Op. 34

Moszkowski was a terrific waltz composer, writing around a dozen for solo piano. The grandest is the E major. Arthur Loesser suggests, "It might be psychologically healthful for listeners to the Waltz, Op. 34, if they yielded to any sinful stirrings of pleasure that they might feel at hearing its unproblematic strains." The piece possess a devil-may-care lilt and asks for a ravishing rubato. The score requires its own insouciant virtuosity.

LOESSER: Marston

Caprice Espagnol, Op. 37

A sumptuous virtuoso piece, based on a repeated note theme and designed to bring the house down. It's bursting with madcap bravura. The middle section is fetching.

BACKHAUS: Andante
HOFMANN: VAI audio
WILD: Ivory Classics

WOLFGANG AMADEUS MOZART
1756–1791—Austria

The Classical piano concerto was, in Mozart's time, visually in its infancy. Through his genius for balance, Mozart arrived at a partnership of piano and orchestra that has never been equaled.

Mozart wrote thirty-six cadenzas for various of his twenty-five solo concerti. Most often they are rather sketchy, and they are not always used by performers. Many pianists—including Hummel, Beethoven, Brahms, Reinecke, Saint-Saëns, Godowsky, Gulda, Casadesus, Magaloff, Landowska, Foldes, Badura-Skoda, and others—have composed their own. Some of Busoni's are quite startling.

Performance of these concerti on the modern piano presents many problems. Mozart occasionally used a shorthand in his notations, expecting himself or the performer to fill in and embellish. As Wanda Landowska notes: "What today would be described as the taking of 'peculiar liberties' was in Mozart's time the *sine qua non* of every performer. No virtuoso would have dared play certain phrases of Mozart as Mozart wrote them. . . . Those performances which we respect today for their literal devotion would have been called ignorant and barbaric by Mozart's contemporaries, for it was in his art of ornamentation that the eighteenth century interpreter submitted himself to his audience to be judged an artist of good or poor taste."

Landowska also insists that "for a true understanding of these works and of the multiplicity of sonorous and expressive means Mozart had at his disposal, it is of prime importance for all present-day pianists to study the resources and effects of eighteenth-century keyboard instruments, as well as the manner of manipulating them. . . . Under the expert touch of a knowing performer, it is possible to obtain from [the modern piano] the color and particularities of the Forte-Piano. The gray and neutral tone of the modern piano can be set ablaze and yield hitherto unsuspected colors."

Wolfgang Amadeus Mozart by David Dubal

The Twenty-five Piano Concerti

In these recordings of the complete Mozart concerti and in the individual performances to be cited, the listener will be treated to the greatest variety of style, timbre, and performing attitudes, as well as great variability in the cadenzas used.

> ANDA/Salzburg Mozarteum: DG
> BARENBOIM, Barenboim/English Chamber Orchestra: Angel
> BRENDEL, Marriner/Academy of St. Martin: Philips
> PERAHIA, Perahia/English Chamber Orchestra: CBS

Piano Concerti Nos. 1–4, K. 37, 39, 40, 41 (1767)

These were written when Mozart was eleven. The composer called them *pasticci*. They are based on sonata movements by contemporary composers, including Johann Christian Bach, and were performed on the tours Mozart made as a child prodigy.

> PERAHIA, Perahia/English Chamber Orchestra: CBS

Piano Concerto No. 5 in D major, K. 175 (1773)

Composed when he was seventeen, this was thus far the finest piano concerto of the Classical era. It is scored for one of Mozart's largest orchestras, using oboes, trumpets, horns, and timpani along with the strings. Mozart remained fond of the work, performing it and teaching it throughout his life. He wrote his own cadenzas for the first and second movements. If it were played more frequently, it would undoubtedly attain popularity through its brilliant and elegant pianism and dashing thematic material.

> BARENBOIM/Berlin Philharmonic: Teldec
> BILSON (fortepiano), Gardiner/English Baroque Soloists: DG Archive
> ENGEL, Hager/Salzburg Mozarteum: Telefunken (LP)
> FRANKL, Fischer/Vienna Volksoper: Turnabout (LP)
> LEVIN, Hogwood/Academy of Ancient Music Orchestra: DDC Compact Discs

Piano Concerto No. 6 in B-flat major, K. 238 (1776)

Composed early in 1776, this work calls for a small orchestra. The rondo offers a charming technical display.

> ASHKENAZY, Schmidt-Isserstedt/London Symphony: London
> GALLING, Maga/Hungarica Philharmonia: Turnabout (LP)
> PERAHIA/English Chamber Orchestra: Sony Classical

Piano Concerto No. 8 in C major, K. 246 (1776)

The Piano Concerto No. 7 is for three pianos, a far weaker work than any of the solo concerti. The technical requirements of No. 8 are milder than those of either No. 5 or 6. The rondo, a Tempo di minuetto, has touches of Mozartian humor.

> ASHKENAZY, Kertesz/London Symphony: London
> BILSON (fortepiano), Gardiner/English Baroque Soloists: DG Archiv

KAGAN, Macecek/Suk Chamber Orchestra:
    Discover International
KEMPFF, Leitner/Berlin Philharmonic: DG
R. SERKIN, Abbado/London
    Symphony: DG
TIPO, Chailly/London Philharmonic: Ricordi
VERA, de Waart/Rotterdam Philharmonic:
    Philips (LP)

Piano Concerto No. 9 in E-flat major, K. 271 (1777)

In January 1777, the twenty-one-year-old Mozart composed what Alfred Einstein called his *Eroica*. It was unprecedented in Mozart's already formidable output, and remains one of his greatest works. Charles Rosen devotes seventeen pages to an analysis of this score in his book, *The Classical Style*. Maurice Hinson calls it "a daring work on a majestic scale . . . one of the greatest of all the concertos." Because of its early chronology, the concerto is still not as well known as later examples.

ASHKENAZY, Kertesz/London Symphony:
    London
BARENBOIM/Berlin Philharmonic: Teldec
BILSON (fortepiano), Gardiner/English
    Baroque Soloists: DG Archiv
BRENDEL, Marriner/Academy of St. Martin:
    Philips
BUCHBINDER, Teutsch/Warsaw
    Chamber Orchestra: Telefunken
FOU TS'ONG, Priestman/Vienna Radio:
    Westminster (LP)
HESS, Casals/Perpignan Festival: Columbia
JARRETT, Davies/Stuttgart Chamber
    Orchestra: ECM
NOVAES, Swarowsky/Vienna Symphony: Vox
PERAHIA, Perahia/English Chamber
    Orchestra: CBS
PIRES, Guschlbauer/Gulbenkian Chamber
    Orchestra of Lisbon: MHS; Erato

R. SERKIN, Schneider/Marlboro Festival:
    Sony Classical
WEISSENBERG, Giulini/Vienna Symphony:
    Angel (LP)

Piano Concerto No. 11 in F major, K. 413 (1782)

The Tenth Concerto in E-flat, K. 365, for Two Pianos, was composed for his sister and himself. It is not quite on the level of his Sonata for Two Pianos, K. 448. The Eleventh to Thirteenth Concerti were written in quick succession during the winter of 1782–83. Mozart had moved to Vienna in the summer of 1781, intent on creating a livelihood as a public pianist and teacher. The F major Concerto is the smallest in scale, possessing little pianistic brilliance but plenty of charm.

BARENBOIM/Berlin Philharmonic:
    Teldec
PERAHIA, Perahia/English Chamber Orchestra:
    CBS
R. SERKIN, Schneider/Marlboro Festival: CBS

Piano Concerto No. 12 in A major, K. 414 (1783)

The K. 414 was a favorite of Mozart's, and he often taught it. The themes have wonderful appeal, and the technical problems are only slightly greater than those of K. 413.

R. CASADESUS, Szell/Columbia
    Symphony: Columbia
DE LARROCHA, Zinman/London Sinfonietta:
    London
LUBIN (fortepiano), Lubin/Mozartean
    Players: Arabesque

LUPU, Segal/English Chamber
Orchestra: London
R. SERKIN, Schneider/Marlboro
Festival: Sony Classical
SHELLY/Mozart London Players: Chandos

P. SERKIN, Schneider/English Chamber
Orchestra: RCA
R. SERKIN, Schneider/Columbia Symphony:
Sony Classical
VÁSÁRY, Vásáry/Berlin Philharmonic: DG

Piano Concerto No. 13 in C major, K. 415 (1783)

K. 415 uses bassoons, trumpets, and timpani. Most of its technical brilliance is in the first movement; there are strokes of genius throughout the finale.

FRAGER, Festival
Sinfonia: Fidelio
HASKIL, Paumgartner/Lucerne Festival
Strings: Philips: Great
Pianists of the Twentieth Century
MICHELANGELI, Giuliani/Rome Radio
and Television: Fonit-Cetra

Piano Concerto No. 14 in E-flat major, K. 449 (1784)

Starting with K. 449, six more piano concerti (Nos. 14–19) were composed between February and December 1784. Of these six, four were written within a two-month period. This is amazing enough, but during the same time span, Mozart also produced six major works of chamber music. The Piano Concerto No. 14 is an exhilarating work, described by its composer as "a concerto of quite another kind."

BRENDEL, Janigro/Zagreb Soliste: Vanguard
MORAVEC, Vlach/Czech
Chamber Orchestra: Quintessence
PERAHIA, Perahia/English Chamber Orchestra:
CBS

Piano Concerto No. 15 in B-flat major, K. 450 (1784)

This concerto is very tricky technically, as Mozart gives new scope to the left hand. He believed that this and the next concerto, in D, would "make the performer sweat."

BERNSTEIN, Bernstein/Vienna Philharmonic:
London
R. CASADESUS, Szell/Cleveland:
Columbia
HAEBLER, Davis/London Symphony: Mercury
(LP)
MICHELANGELI, Gracis/I Pomeriggi Musicali
di Milano: EMI
P. SERKIN, Schneider/English Chamber
Orchestra: RCA

Piano Concerto No. 16 in D major, K. 451 (1784)

The thematic material of No. 16 lacks the general inspiration characteristic of this set of concerti, yet it is a work of the finest planning.

FIRKUSNY, Bour/Southwest German
Radio Symphony: Intercord
HAEBLER, Davis/London Symphony: Mercury
(LP)
KLEIN, Angerer/Vienna Volksoper: Turnabout
(LP)
P. SERKIN, Schneider/English
Chamber Orchestra: RCA

Piano Concerto No. 17 in G major, K. 453 (1784)

A score of glowing youthfulness with a leisurely first movement. The slow movement Andante uses five themes and is cast into a complex form. It possesses an intensely rarefied beauty. The critic C. M. Girdlestone wrote: "No concerto andante of Mozart's had reached hitherto such fullness. There had been pathetic ones, even tragic ones; none had penetrated into the soul with such breadth and depth. What is admirable is not only the quality of the inspiration, but its variety."

In the finale, Mozart leaves the usual Rondo form for a theme, five variations, and a coda. The soloist and orchestra (consisting only of flute, two oboes, two bassoons, two horns, and strings) blend together magically.

ASHKENAZY/Philharmonia: London
R. CASADESUS, Szell/Cleveland: Columbia
DOHNÁYNI/Budapest Philharmonic: Pearl
GOODE/Orpheus Chamber Orchestra:
    Nonesuch
HORSZOWSKI, Waldman/Musica Aeterna:
    Pearl
MATTHEWS, Blech/London Mozart Players:
    Dutton Laboratories
PREVIN/Vienna Philharmonic: Philips
RUBINSTEIN, Wallenstein/RCA Symphony:
    RCA
R. SERKIN, Schneider/Columbia Symphony:
    Sony Classical

Piano Concerto No. 18 in B-flat major, K. 456 (1784)

K. 456 is much less known, though its piano part is most gracious. The slow movement in G minor is a set of variations, and there are several audacious modulations in the finale.

ASHKENAZY/Philharmonia: London
BRENDEL, Marriner/Academy of St. Martin:
    Philips
R. CASADESUS, Szell/Columbia Symphony:
    Odyssey
ENGEL, Hager/Salzburg Mozarteum:
    Telefunken
GOODE/Orpheus Chamber Orchestra:
    Nonesuch

Piano Concerto No. 19 in F major, K. 459 (1784)

K. 459 has practically no prominence for the soloist. The slow movement, usually an adagio or andante, is instead a captivating Allegretto.

ASHKENAZY, Ashkenazy/Philharmonia:
    London
BILSON (fortepiano), Gardiner/English
    Baroque Soloists: DG Archiv
BRENDEL, Marriner/Academy of St.
    Martin: Philips
HAEBLER, Rowicki/London Symphony:
    Philips
HASKIL, Friscay/Berlin Philharmonic:
    DG
POLLINI, Böhm/Vienna Philharmonic:
    DG
R. SERKIN, Szell/Columbia Symphony:
    CBS

Piano Concerto No. 20 in D minor, K. 466 (1785)

The next six concerti, Nos. 20–25, are universally considered to be among the most honored works in the concerto literature. The group spans the period from February 1785 to December 1786. During this time, *The Marriage of Figaro* was also composed. No. 20 is the first of all the piano concerti to be written in a minor key. Its reception was slightly less favorable than Mozart was accustomed to with his concerti. Perhaps the dark, brooding first movement was too demonic for his polite late-eighteenth-century audience. (Within a decade, Beethoven would play the work and write cadenzas for it.) The middle movement is entitled "Romanza," of which Beethoven told his student Ries, "We will never get an idea like that." And the exciting finale, with its many themes, is enchanting.

ASHKENAZY, Schmidt-Isserstedt/London
    Symphony: London
R. CASADESUS, Szell/Columbia
    Symphony: CBS
HASKIL, Paumgartner/Vienna Symphony:
    Mercury; Markevitch/Lamoureux
    Orchestra: Philips
MATTHEWS, Swarowsky/Vienna State
    Opera: Vanguard
O'CONOR, Mackerras/Scottish Chamber
    Orchestra: Telarc
RUBINSTEIN, Wallenstein/RCA
    Symphony: RCA
SCHNABEL, Susskind/Philharmonia:
    Arabesque
R. SERKIN, Szell/Columbia Symphony:
    CBS
UCHIDA, Tate/English Chamber
    Orchestra: Philips

Piano Concerto No. 21 in C major, K. 467 (1785)

K. 467 is majestic. The piano part is one of the most complex of the series. The Andante, with its magnificent cantilena, is understandably popular—a lovely, dreamlike slow movement.

BADURA-SKODA, Badura-Skoda/Prague
    Chamber Orchestra: Supraphon
R. CASADESUS, Szell/Cleveland: CBS
A. FISCHER, Sawallisch/Philharmonia
    EMI; Price-Less

GULDA, Abbado/Vienna Philharmonic:
    DG
ISTOMIN, Schwarz/Seattle Symphony:
    Reference Recordings
KOVACEVICH, Davis/London
    Symphony: Philips
R. LHÉVINNE, Morel/Juilliard: CBS
LIPATTI, Karajan/Lucerne Festival: Angel
LUPU, Sega/English Chamber Orchestra:
    London
RUBINSTEIN, Wallenstein/RCA
    Symphony: RCA
SCHNABEL, Sargent/London Symphony:
    Arabesque
R. SERKIN, Schneider/Columbia
    Symphony: Sony Classical
TIPO, Perlea/Vienna Symphony: Vox
UCHIDA, Tate/English Chamber
    Orchestra: Philips
WEISSENBERG, Giulini/Vienna
    Symphony: Angel (LP)

Piano Concerto No. 22 in E-flat major, K. 482 (1785)

At the premiere of No. 22, the central Andante movement had such instant appeal that the audience demanded that the composer repeat it. K. 482 is one of the longest of the piano concertos, running to thirty-five minutes in performance. It is incomparable for its breadth, humor, and pathos. C. M. Girdlestone wrote, "Combining grace and majesty, the music unfolds like a sovereign in progress, the queen of the concertos." Mozart adds two clarinets to his flute, two bassoons, two horns, two trumpets, kettledrums, and strings.

R. CASADESUS, Szell/Columbia
    Symphony: CBS
DE LARROCHA, Sega/Vienna
    Symphony: London
A. FISCHER, Sawallisch/Philharmonia:
    EMI; Price-Less

E. FISCHER, Barbirolli: EMI
KEMPFF, Klee/Bavarian Radio
    Symphony: DG
LANDOWSKA, Rodzinski: IPA–Desmar
RICHTER, Muti/Philharmonia: Angel
R. SERKIN, Casals/Perpignan Festival:
    Sony Classical
UCHIDA, Tate/English Chamber
    Orchestra: Philips
ZACHARIAS, Zinman/Dresden State:
    Angel

Piano Concerto No. 23 in A major, K. 488 (1785)

K. 488 is one of the most popular of the concerti. Its opening movement is radiant. The slow movement is a Siciliana—touching and transparent. It is the only movement in F-sharp minor in all of Mozart's compositions. The finale is euphoric, "though not without that after-tang of sadness," writes Eric Blom, "which is always liable to make one suddenly feel that Mozart, even in his most lighthearted moods, is fundamentally never a singer of ingenuous happiness."

R. CASADESUS, Szell/Columbia
    Symphony: CBS
CURZON, Kertesz/London Symphony:
    London
HASKIL, Paumgartner/Vienna Symphony:
    Mercury (LP)
HOROWITZ, Giulini/La Scala: DG
KEMPFF, Leitner/Bamberg Symphony:
    DG
POLLINI, Böhm/Vienna Philharmonic:
    DG
RUBINSTEIN, Wallenstein/RCA
    Symphony: RCA
ZACHARIAS, Zinman/Dresden State:
    Angel

Piano Concerto No. 24 in C minor, K. 491 (1786)

K. 491 touches the sublime. It is Mozart's only minor-keyed concerto besides No. 20 in D minor. The first movement is structurally elaborate. Mozart employed his largest orchestra, and the demands placed on the soloist are great.

R. CASADESUS, Szell/Cleveland: CBS
CURZON, Kertesz/London Symphony: London
E. FISCHER, Fischer/Danish Chamber
    Orchestra: EMI
HASKIL, Markevitch/Lamoureux Orchestra:
    Philips
PERAHIA, Perahia/English Chamber Orchestra:
    CBS
SCHNABEL, Susskind/Philharmonia: Arabesque
ZACHARIAS, Wand/North German Radio
    Symphony: Angel

Piano Concerto No. 25 in C major, K. 503 (1786)

Sometimes called the Jupiter among his concertos. No. 25 rivals No. 24 in complexity and grandeur. Even the finale of this olympian work possesses an unusual seriousness. In the Twenty-fifth Concerto, Mozart's contrapuntal skill reaches a high point. It spurns the radiant lyricism and transparency of No. 17 and No. 23, but its austere sphere commands awe. In the first movement we find a March in C minor. The slow movement is a dignified and spacious aria. The Gavotte-like finale is still somewhat remote, although the duet between piano and oboe is delectable. In this concerto, the air is so pure that we take no notice of the heights it attains. It has a majesty that is unconscious of itself.

BERNSTEIN/Israel Philharmonic: Columbia

CIANI, Barbirolli/Philharmonia Orchestra:
Stradivarious
DE LARROCHA, Solti/London Philharmonic:
London
E. FISCHER, Krips/Philharmonia: EMI
FLEISHER, Szell/Cleveland: Sony Classical
KATCHEN, Münchinger/Stuttgart Chamber
Orchestra: London
KOVACEVICH, Davis/London Symphony:
Philips
R. SERKIN, Szell/Columbia Symphony: Sony
Classical
ZACHARIAS, Zinman/Bavarian Radio
Symphony: Angel

Piano Concerto No. 26 in D major, K. 537 (1788)

After the Twenty-fifth Concerto, Mozart lived only five more years, writing two more piano concerti. K. 537 has often been called the Coronation Concerto, because he played it during the coronation of Leopold II.

R. CASADESUS, Szell/Columbia Symphony:
CBS
CURZON, Boulez/BBC Symphony: BBC
KLIEN, Maag/Vienna Volksoper: Turnabout
LANDOWSKA, Goehr: Biddulph
PIRES, Guschlbauer/Gulbenkian Chamber
Orchestra of Lisbon: Erato

Piano Concerto No. 27 in B-flat major, K. 595 (1791)

K. 595 was composed when Mozart had only eleven months to live. He was already ill, and in the preceding several years he had been beset with many disappointments. He wrote to his father, "I have now made a habit of being prepared in all affairs of life for the worst." Yet this last piano concerto is sparkling, full of childlike spontaneity, optimism, and humor along with suppressed tears. It was being composed as he sketched the Requiem.

R. CASADESUS, Szell/Columbia Symphony:
CBS
CURZON, Britten/English Chamber Orchestra:
London
DE LARROCHA, Solti/London Philharmonic:
London
GILELS, Böhm/Vienna Philharmonic: DG
R. SERKIN, Ormandy/Philadelphia: CBS

The Piano Sonatas

The study of the Mozart solo sonatas is indispensable to the pianist and to our understanding of eighteenth-century style. Listed are complete recordings of exceptional merit.

BILSON: Hungaraton
DEYANOVA: Nimbus
ESCHENBACH: DG
GIESEKING (complete solo piano music):
Seraphim (LP)
GOULD: CBS
HORSZOWSKI: Arbitor
KLIEN: Vox
KRAUS: Sony Classical
LOWEY: MHS
PIRES: Denon
SCHIFF: Philips

Sonatas Nos. 1–6

The first six sonatas, composed in 1775–76, in C, F, B-flat, E-flat, G, and D (K. 279–284), have their charms, but do not approach the magnitude of those to follow later. The slow movement of K. 281 is marked "Andante amoroso," the only such marking in Mozart's sonatas.

Sonata No. 1 in C major, K. 279:
BARENBOIM: EMI
UCHIDA: Philips

Sonata No. 2 in E; major, K. 280:
HASKIL: DG
ZIMERMAN: DG (LP)

Sonata No. 3 in B-flat major, K. 281:
BILSON (on a Stein fortepiano): Golden Crest
  (LP)
GILELS: DG
HOROWITZ: DG
KATIN: Olympia

Sonata No. 4 in E-flat major, K. 282:
ARRAU: Philips
BACKHAUS: London
DE LARROCHA: London
LANDOWSKA: RCA

Sonata No. 5 in G major, K. 283:
BACKHAUS: Orfeo
KLEIN: Vox
LANDOWSKA: RCA (LP)
NOVAES: Vox
RÁNKI: Hungaroton

Sonata No. 6 in D major, K. 284:
BILSON: Hungaroton
JENDÓ: Naxos
UCHIDA: Philips

Sonata No. 7 in C major, K. 309

An excellent work, large in design, showing Mozart with a new confidence within the solo sonatas.

BARENBOIM: EMI
DE LARROCHA: RCA
HORSZOWSKI: Arbitor
UCHIDA: Philips

Sonata No. 8 in A minor, K. 310

One of the greatest works for solo piano from the Classical period. Eva Badura-Skoda wrote: "Suddenly, with the A minor Sonata, a new world opens up. . . . The opening theme is indeed majestic. . . . The texture is orchestral in fullness, and the relentless pulsing of the accompanying chords suggests majesty of a demonic and sinister kind. The second movement . . . displays a restrained passion. . . . The Presto is one of the darkest movements Mozart ever wrote, with its remarkable fluctuations between resignation and defiance."

ARRAU: Philips
ASHKENAZY: London
BRENDEL: Philips
GILELS: DG
LIPATTI: Angel
MATTHEWS: Vanguard
SCHIFF: London
SCHNABEL: Pearl
UCHIDA: Philips

Sonata No. 9 in D major, K. 311

This is an exuberant sonata. The first movement reflects the sonorities of the celebrated orchestra of Mannheim, where this work was composed. The Andante, unlike those in the previous two sonatas, is not elaborate. It was composed for a young pianist, Rosa Cannabich, of whom Mozart reported, "She is a sweet, pretty girl, just like the Andante." The rondo finale is an exceptionally brilliant movement.

ARRAU: Naxos
DE LARROCHA: RCA
LANDOWSKA: Pearl
RÁNKI: Hungaroton
ZIMERMAN: DG (LP)

Sonata No. 10 in C major, K. 330

Mozart took particular care with the dynamic and phrase markings in this robust and happy work.

BILSON (on a Stein fortepiano): Golden Crest
BACKHAUS: APS
BRENDEL: Philips
CLIBURN: RCA
DE LARROCHA: London
E. FISCHER: Pearl
HOROWITZ: DG
OUSSET: Berlin Classics
PLUDERMACHER: Harmonia Mundi

Sonata No. 11 in A major, K. 331

One of the most popular of the sonatas. None of its three movements is in sonata form. The opening variations are lovable; the minuet is typical of its form, and the Rondo alla turca is renowned.

BILSON (on a Stein fortepiano): Golden Crest (LP)
DE LARROCHA: London
GOULD: Sony Classical
HAUTZIG: RCA
HOROWITZ: CBS
LANDOWSKA: Pearl
PERAHIA: Sony Classical
SCHIFF: London
UCHIDA: Philips

Sonata No. 12 in F major, K. 332

A popular masterpiece and a perfect recital work. The first movement has lyricism and drama; the slow movement is the very essence of grace. The finale is one of Mozart's most virtuosic movements, a brilliant perpetual motion.

BILSON (on a fortepiano): Nonesuch
DE LARROCHA: London
FREIRE: Alphee
HOROWITZ: RCA
ITURBI: Ivory Classics
LANDOWSKA: Biddulph
SCHNABEL: APR

Sonata No. 13 in B-flat major, K. 333

This sonata is favored in public with its lyrical first movement, serious slow movement, and large-scale rondo finale, which introduces, at bar 171, a cadenza—normally a feature of the concerto, not of the sonata.

ARRAU: Philips
BILSON (on a fortepiano): Nonesuch
BRENDEL: Philips
GOULD: Sony Classsical
HAEFLIGER: Sony Classsical
HOROWITZ: DG
MATTHEWS: Vanguard
MORAVEC: Connoisseur Society (LP)
RICHTER: Praga
SCHIFF: London

Sonata No. 14 in C minor, K. 457

Six years separate this, composed in 1784, from the previous sonata. It is Mozart's second minor-key sonata and one of his greatest piano works. It is often played, preceded by the C minor Fantasia K. 475, with which it has a deep affinity in mood as well as in key. Eva Badura-Skoda states: "The C minor Sonata . . . offers a shattering expression of personal anguish, and a new language which sets it at the beginning of an epoch. This is the work which made the deepest impression on Mozart's direct contemporaries and succes-

sors, especially on the young Beethoven. . . .
It is the first truly monumental work in the
Sonata repertory, designed for acoustics more
spacious than those of drawing rooms."

ARRAU: Philips
BACHAUS: Memoria
GIESEKING: Philips: Great Pianists of the
    Twentieth Century
KLIEN: Turnabout
MATTHEWS: Vanguard
MORAVEC: VAI
SCHIFF: London
P. SERKIN: RCA (LP)
SHIRK: Classic Masters
UCHIDA: Philips

Sonata No. 15 in C major, K. 545

The so-called *Sonata facile* is the most frequently played sonata of the Classical era, and
it's almost certainly the first Mozart sonata
that the young piano student attempts. It
seems as though no amount of hackneyed
playing can dull its delights.

DE LARROCHA: London
ESCHENBACH: DG
ESTRIN: Connoisseur Society (LP)
GOULD: CBS
NOVAES: Vox (LP)
PERAHIA: Sony Classical
PIRES: Denon
RICHTER: Praga

Sonata No. 16 in B-flat major, K. 570

This is gracious work, a model of sonata
design, with simple contrapuntal interest.

BILSON (on a Stein fortepiano): Golden Crest
    (LP)

GULDA: DG
KAPELL: RCA
MORAVEC: VAI
P. SERKIN: Pro Arte
SCHNABEL: Arabesque

Sonata No. 17 in D major, K. 576

The last Mozart piano sonata, it is often called
the *Hunt* or *Trumpeter,* and is one of the most
difficult technically of the sonatas, with considerable contrapuntal display.

ARRAU: Philips
ASHKENAZY: London
BADURA-SKODA: Astrée
DE LARROCHA: Philips: Great Pianists of the
    Twentieth Century
LOWY: MHS
P. SERKIN: Pro Arte
UCHIDA: Philips: Great Pianists of the
    Twentieth Century

Rondo in A minor, K. 511

James Friskin wrote, "Among Mozart's pianoforte compositions there is nothing more beautiful than the Rondo in A minor, nor any more
finished example of his art."

ASHKENAZY: London
BADURA-SKODA: Astrée
BRENDEL: Philips
RUBINSTEIN: RCA
SCHNABEL: APR
R. SERKIN: Sony Classical
UCHIDA: Philips

Rondo in D major, K. 485

This sparkling work is actually a sonata form
with one subject.

BILSON (on a fortepiano): Nonesuch
DE LARROCHA: London
HOROWITZ: DG
P. SERKIN: Pro Arte
SHEHORI: Cembalo d'Amour

Adagio in B minor, K. 540

A work of deep expressiveness. One of Mozart's most profound utterances, and demanding of the interpreter true musical and structural insight.

ARRAU: Philips
BADURA-SKODA: Astrée
BRENDEL: Philips
HOROWITZ: DG

Fantasia in C minor, K. 396

This is a fine work, actually in sonata form.

BRENDEL: Vanguard
E. FISCHER: APR
JOHANNESEN: Golden Crest (LP)
LORIOD: Ades

Fantasia in D minor, K. 397

One of the most often played of Mozart's piano works. It opens with beautifully laid-out slow arpeggios, followed by an Adagio, and closing with a surprising Allegretto in D major.

BADURA-SKODA: Astrée
DE LARROCHA: RCA
GILELS: DG
GOULD: CBS
HORSZOWSKI: Nonesuch
LANDOWSKA: Pearl
E. LEVY: Marston
SHEHORI: Cembal d'Amour

Fantasia in C minor, K. 475

The Fantasy is often performed alone, as well as in conjunction with the C minor Sonata. Its range of emotional freedom is unprecedented in Mozart's solo piano.

ARRAU: Philips: Great Pianists of the Twentieth Century
EGOROV: Globe
E. FISCHER: Pearl
GOULD: Columbia
KEMPFF: DG
MATTHEWS: Vanguard (LP)
MORAVEC: VAI

Variations on "Ah, vous dirai-je, maman," K. 265

This is the most popular of Mozart's variations, with pretty melodic decorations on the famous nursery tune.

BADURA-SKODA: Astrée
BUCHBINDER: Teldec (LP)
FRANÇOIS: Philips: Great Pianists of the Twentieth Century
HASKIL: DG
PREVIN: CBS

MODEST MUSSORGSKY
1839–1881—Russia

Pictures at an Exhibition

Mussorgsky was considered a competent pianist, and during his short and turbulent life he left two dozen piano pieces that generally show little gift for piano writing. Yet his masterwork for the instrument, in fact the greatest piano work of the Russian nationalists, *Pictures at an Exhibition,* is music of stupendous originality. This group of ten tableaux, linked by a Promenade, was inspired by a memorial exhibition of drawings and paintings by the composer's friend Victor Hartmann. But, as Martin Last writes, "It is . . . disappointing to see Hartmann's drawings from the perspective of Mussorgsky's music: the music is so much bigger, so much wilder, so much more visceral."

The work has been even more popular in the orchestral transcription by Ravel, though in this form the score sounds more like a showcase of brilliant effects. The original piano writing, however, has often been criticized as being unpianistic and awkward. Horowitz accepted this judgment when he made his own version, which enriches Mussorgsky's sound, and is played with tremendous tension and shattering climaxes. It is Horowitz at his most elemental. Richter's recording, from a live concert at Sofia, Bulgaria, in 1958, has been treasured by all aficionados of the original version of the score.

ASHKENAZY: London
BERMAN: DG
BRONFMAN: Sony Classical
BROWNING: Delos
FIRKUSNY: DG (LP)
HOROWITZ: RCA
KAPELL: RCA
KASMAN: Calliope
MOISEIWITSCH: Pearl
PLETNEV: Virgin Classics
POGORELICH: Philips
RICHTER: Odyssey; Philips
ROUVIER: Denon
SMITH: Nimbus
WILD: Ivory Classics

N

CARL NIELSEN
1865–1931—Denmark

Symphonic Suite, Op. 8 (1894)
Chaconne, Op. 32 (1915)
Theme and Variations, Op. 40 (1916)
Suite, Op. 45 (1919)
Three Piano Pieces, Op. 59 (1928)

Nielsen, the best known of all Danish composers, was a violinist who forged a distinct and personal piano style. His piano works are typical of his original and gritty music. The *Symphonic Suite,* Op. 8, is thick and cumbersome pianism, with loud Brahmsian overtones. The Five Piano Pieces, Op. 3, remind one of Schumann and Grieg, as do the Six Humoresque-Bagatelles, Op. 11. But the Chaconne, Op. 32, is music with a power and logic of its own. The Theme and Variations, Op. 40, is subtle and sparse, while the Suite Op. 45, sometimes known as the Luciferian, is a significant contribution to the literature—in fact, the greatest of any Scandinavian piano work of the twentieth century—and should be better known. Written for Artur Schnabel, it is in six movements, twenty-two minutes long. It has the rugged but careful workmanship of a master who thinks and feels deeply. Near the end of his life, Nielsen composed *Twenty-five Pieces for Young and Old,* Op. 53, each based on the pentatonic scale and using five finger positions in varied ways. His Three Pieces, Op. 59, are brilliant in design, the middle piece a beautifully generated Molto adagio.

BÄRTSCH II (Suite Op. 45): Ex Libris
KATAHN (complete piano music): Gasparo
KOPPEL (Suite Op. 45): Decap
OGDON (Chaconne, Suite, Three Pieces): RCA (LP)
SEIVEWRIGHT (complete piano music): Naxos
WESTENHOLZ (complete piano music): BIS

P

FRANCIS POULENC
1899–1963—France

Poulenc was an eclectic. Ned Rorem wrote:

> Take Chopin's dominant sevenths, Ravel's major sevenths, Fauré's straight triads, Debussy's minor ninths, Mussorgsky's augmented fourths. Filter them, as Satie did, through the added sixth chords of vaudeville (which the French call *le music-hall*), blend in a pint of Couperin to a quarter Stravinsky, and you get the harmony of Poulenc.

Virgil Thomson thought Poulenc "incontestably the greatest writer of melodies in our time." Poulenc himself thought less of his solo music than of his song accompaniments. Yet the piano music is certainly typical of the Poulenc whom the public has come to love—breezy, tongue-in-cheek, flippant, and openly sentimental. The composer wrote: "It is with my piano music that I suffer the most fraudulent interpretations, especially since I myself have set a very precise instrumental conception. . . . The major technical errors disfiguring my piano music . . . are these: Rubato, stinginess with the pedal; and too clear articulation of certain arrangements of chords and arpeggios that should, on the contrary, be played hazily."

He goes on to say: "The use of pedals is the great secret of my piano music and often its true drama. One can never use enough pedals. When I hear certain pianists interpret me, I want to yell at them, put the butter in the sauce! Why play as though you were on a diet." (Nadia Boulanger differed with him and thought Poulenc overpedaled.)

Poulenc's own piano teacher Ricardo Viñes gave the premiere of the *Mouvements perpétuels* of 1918, to this day Poulenc's most popular piano work. His best piano music includes the three-movement Suite (1920), the felicitous Toccata, written for Horowitz, the haunting A-flat Intermezzo, the set of Eight Nocturnes, the *Napoli* Suite, Five Impromptus, and the *Improvisations*.

The Complete Piano Music:
CROSSLEY: CBS
PARKIN: Chandos

Les soirées de Nazelles (1930–36)

The work consists of a Preamble, Eight Variations, Cadence, and Finale. The Variations are musical portraits of friends. Laurence Davies, a great believer in the quality of the work, heard in it "some of the most limpid music the instrument has inspired since Schumann. . . . It is probably the composer's best piano work and a worthy successor to the great keyboard suites of Debussy and Ravel."

FÉVRIER: EMI
RANCK: International Piano Archives (LP)
ROGÉ: London
VASSILIADIS: Discover

Suite française (1935)

Seven French dances of the sixteenth century, "after Claude Gervaise," dressed in Poulenc's own freshly tailored, sophisticated clothing. The Suite is one of Poulenc's best-known piano works.

> JOHANNESEN: Golden Crest (LP)
> POULENC: Odyssey (LP)
> TACCHINO: EMI

Aubade for Piano and Eighteen Instruments (1929)

A choreographic poem based on the myth of the goddess Diana. Opening with a Toccata, it has seven movements, totaling twenty-one minutes, played without interruption. The work is strongly neo-Baroque, spare and brilliantly brittle.

> DUCHABLE, Conlon/Rotterdam
>   Philharmonic: Erato
> FÉVRIER, Baudo/Lamoureux Orchestra:
>   Nonesuch (LP)
> KRAJNY, Prague Chamber Orchestra:
>   Supraphon
> POULENC, Straram/Straram Orchestra:
>   EMI Classics
> TACCHINO, Prêtre/Paris Conservatoire:
>   EMI

Piano Concerto (1949)

Poulenc premiered the Concerto in Boston. The third movement is a Rondo à la français, but the naughty genie in Poulenc manages to quote "Swanee." The first movement is urbane and slightly mischievous, but the slow movement is less successful than the Larghetto of the inspired Concerto for Two Pianos and Orchestra.

> DUCHABLE, Conlon/Rotterdam
>   Philharmonic: Erato
> ORTRZ, Frémaux/Birmingham
>   Symphony: EMI
> ROGÉ, Dutoit/Philharmonia Orchestra:
>   London
> TACCHINO, Prêtre/Paris Conservatoire:
>   EMI

SERGEI PROKOFIEV
1891–1953—Russia

The Complete Solo Piano Music

Nine Sonatas
Four Etudes, Op. 2 (1909)
Four Pieces, Op. 3 (1907–11)
Four Pieces, Op. 4 (1913)
Toccata, Op. 11 (1912)
Ten Episodes, Op. 12 (1913)
Five Sarcasms, Op. 17
Twenty Visions fugitives, Op. 22
  (1915–17)
Four Tales of an Old Grandmother, Op. 31
  (1918)
Four Pieces, Op. 32 (1918)
Chose en soi (Things in Themselves), Op. 45a
  and 45b (1928)Sonatine in E minor,
  Op. 54, No. 1 (1931)
Sonatine in G major, Op. 54, No. 2
Three Pensées, Op. 62 (1933–34)
Music for Children (Twelve Pieces)

Several of Prokofiev's piano sonatas are frequently played, but the small pieces—apart from a few famous ones, such as *Suggestion diabolique,* Op. 4, No. 4, and the Toccata, Op. 11—are little known. In addition to the solo pieces listed above, there are the Divertissement, Op. 43b, consisting of four pieces arranged by the composer from other media; Six Transcriptions, Op. 52; Ten Pieces from the *Romeo and Juliet* Ballet, Op. 75; and the *Peter and the Wolf* score, Op. 67.

Prokofiev himself listed the principal elements of his art: "1) Classicism—an affinity for forms indigenous to the Baroque and Classic periods; 2) Innovation—a striving for a new harmonic language and the means for expressing stronger emotions; 3) the Toccata or Motor element—where rhythmic vitality plays an important role; 4) the Lyric element; 5) an element of either Grotesqueness, Jesting or Mockery."

B. BERMAN (complete solo piano music): Chandos
BOUKOFF (Sonatas Nos. 1–9): Westminster (LP)
BRONFMAN (Sonatas Nos. 1–9): Sony Classical

Sergei Prokofiev by David Dubal

CHIU: Harmonia Mundi
MCDERMOTT (Sonatas Nos. 1–9): Arabesque
NISSMAN (Sonatas Nos. 1–9): Pierian
SANDOR (complete solo piano music): Vox

Sonata No. 1 in F minor, Op. 1 (1907–09)

In one movement of about eight minutes. Late Russian Romanticism informs the aroma of the First Sonata with an undercurrent of Schumann in the second subject. Yet Prokofiev at sixteen is keenly aware of the new century, and the score possesses a breathless dynamism and youthful ardor, along with a few dissonant asperities. In the development section, the composer finds himself stilted, but an experienced pianist can easily overcome this disruption. A capital Op. 1; the young master looks forward to future achievements. He successfully performed it in Moscow in December 1910.

B. BERMAN: Chandos
BRONFMAN: Sony Classical
GLEMSER: Naxos
KASMAN: Calliope
PETROV: Melodiya (LP)

Sonata No. 2 in D minor, Op. 14 (1912)

The twenty-one-year-old composer's Second Sonata, in four laconic movements and of about eighteen minutes, is a fully mature masterpiece in style and originality of piano writing. The first movement is novel in its harmonies; it's full of motion in its first theme and oriental coloring in its second subject. The second movement scherzo, with its hand crossing, tickles the ear. Prokofiev

573

uses a bracing staccato technique in a way that makes him a Russian descendant of Mendelssohn. A perfect foil is the naive play of the trio. The third movement, andante, with its two themes, creates a lingering hypnotic impression. The movement fulfills itself in pathos and luxuriant figuration. A tarentella-like theme lifts the fourth movement to high spirits with a mocking face. Later, the second theme from the first movement brings an unexpected tenderness. The brilliant coda exploits both main themes of the *finale*. The Second Sonata, with its healthy zest, was premiered by the composer in Moscow in February 1914.

BIRET: Finnadar
L. CHUNG: Palexa
GILELS: Melodiya
GRAFFMAN: Columbia
JOSELSON: RCA
KRAINEV: Newport Classic
PLETNEV: DG
RICHTER: London

Sonata No. 3 in A minor, Op. 28 (1917)

One of the most frequently played of early-twentieth-century piano sonatas, No. 3 is in one movement of seven minutes. The composer uses thematic material from an intended symphony from 1907. The composition opens with explosive power, settling into a second theme of diatonic tenderness. The development section is dappling in its transformation of the material. The recapitulation arrives from and develops from a bridge passage into new material, the main theme of the exposition being omitted until the last moment, as the sonata concludes in triumph. The Third Sonata is perfect in all aspects while demanding a virtuoso technique. Prokofiev gave the premiere in St. Petersburg in April 1918.

BIANCONI: VAI
GAVRILOV: DG
GINSBURG: Philips: Great Pianists of the
    Twentieth Century
GRAFFMAN: CBS
POLLACK: Melodiya (LP)
RICHTER: AS Disc
WEISSENBERG: Philips: Great Pianists of the
    Twentieth Century

Sonata No. 4 in C minor, Op. 29 (1917)

The three-movement Fourth Sonata, of around eighteen minutes, is also derived from teenage manuscripts. The score is vintage Prokofiev and in the last years has been frequently heard. The first movement is weighty, stagnant, and lugubrious, encased in unique sonorities. Although the second movement Andante assai is in binary form, it is a complex movement, ending with its two contrasting themes ingeniously combined. (Prokofiev made a fine recording of this movement.) The *finale*, an exhilarating rondo-sonata has dashing lilt; a very choreographic score. It received its premiere by the composer in St. Petersburg in 1918.

BRONFMAN: Sony Classical
KASMAN: Calliope
MALININ: Melodiya; Angel (LP)
ZAK: Melodiya (LP)

Sonata No. 5 in C major, Op. 38, Op. 135 (1923, 1952–53)

This gentle gem of neo-classicism has caused confusion. Originally composed in 1923, it was revised in 1953. The second edition is used in performances by Grinberg, Sándor, and Novitskaya. Loesser and others used parts of each version, while Nissman records them separately. Loesser states, "In my not too humble estimation, the composer's revisive afterthoughts do not, for the most part, constitute improvements on the original, except however, for the very end, which definitely sounds more satisfactorily finale-like in the later version." Performers approaching this problematic score should compare both editions. Prokofiev thought the Fifth Sonata to be among his "most chromatic works along with the *Quintet* and the Second Symphony and cast in my intricate style." The sonata is in three movements, of about thirteen minutes. Prokofiev gave the premiere to a lukewarm reception in Paris in March 1924.

B. BERMAN: Chandos
GRINBERG: Melodiya (LP)
LOESSER: International Piano Archives (LP)
NOVITSKAYA: Melodiya/Angel (LP)
SCHUMAKER: Elan

Sonata No. 6 in A major, Op. 82 (1939)

Prokofiev gave the premiere of his monumental Sixth Sonata in April 1940 on a recital which was broadcasted on radio. It would be the last time he premiered his sonatas. The work's fate would be in the hands of Richter, who performed it in November 1940, to the composer's highest compliment. The Sixth Sonata is one of Prokofiev's most massive compositions for the piano in four movements, approximately thirty-five minutes in duration. It demands tremendous emotional resources from the pianist and a concentrated audience. As is always the case with Prokofiev, the work is essentially tonal but with a bitter dissonant impact. It is the most difficult technically of the sonatas, using, as Irwin Freundlich observes, "double notes, arpeggio sweeps, interlocking thumbs,

repeated notes, quick skips, percussive chords (*con pugno*, with the fist), screaming passages in extreme upper register."

The first movement Allegro moderato, writes Israel Nestyev, "is almost devoid of simple human emotions; instead, cruel and terrible forces are in command. In the listener's imagination arise either archaic images of raging monsters or recollections of devastating military invasions." The second movement, in three-part form, is a relief from the demons in a characteristic dance-like allegretto. The third movement is a long, slow, haunting, but taunting waltz, tempo di valzer lentissimo, in 9/8 time; there are passages of dense austerity. The finale is vigorous in movement, but the optimistic Prokofiev of youth is replaced by a mingling of gaiety and sarcasm, as the ominous subject of the first movement reappears, reminding us that all is not well with the world. The Sixth, Seventh, and Eighth Sonatas, often called "The War Sonatas," were each begun in 1939 and were composed during the tragic years of the Second World War.

CLIBURN: RCA
KISSIN: RCA
MCDERMOTT: Arabesque
MERZHANOV: Melodiya (LP)
NISSMAN: Pierian
RELICH: DG
RICHTER: Praga
SLOBODYANIK: Melodiya

Sonata No. 7 in B-flat major, Op. 83 (1939–42)

Richter gave the premiere in January 1943. This sonata became the most performed of the composer's piano sonatas. In three chiseled movements, the piece takes around eighteen minutes. The first movement has a characteristic wiry athleticism contrasted with a lyric vein; it is a magnificently constructed movement, with no key signature. The slow movement, Andante caloroso, has a ripe, melodic opening which develops into a restless tenseness. The finale is famous, only three minutes, precepitato, and enveloping one in its tremendous energy propelled by a disciplined inner drive.

ARGERICH: EMI
ASHKENAZY: London
BRONFMAN: Sony Classical
HOROWITZ: RCA
PLETNEV: DG
POLLINI: DG
RICHTER: Praga
SOKOLOV: Melodiya (LP)
TORADZE: Angel

Sonata No. 8 in B-flat major, Op. 84 (1939–44)

For five years Prokofiev labored relentlessly on his War Sonatas, peaks in the piano sonata literature of the first half of the twentieth century, and ranking among his finest achievements. The Eighth Sonata was premiered by Gilels in Moscow in December 1944. Richter, too, would champion the score, calling it "the richest, it has a difficult inner life, with profound contradictions." It is in three movements spanning a half an hour. The two outer movements are long, the second movement only about four minutes in length. The sonata is the most introspective and lyrical of the War Sonatas. In fact, Eric Salzman finds that "there is little that would lead one to suspect that its composition spans almost exactly the period of World War II. The opening *Andante* dolce has an almost Schubertian calm and transparency, troubled only in passing by the agitation of the development and coda. The second movement, *Andante Sognando,* is the most Schubertian of all. The third movement with

its triplet flow and scherzo-ish middle section has a Haydn-Schubert finale feeling in a modern context." However each of its themes have the unmistakable twists and turns as well as the heartbeat of Prokofiev.

BASHKIROV: RD
GILELS: Columbia/Melodiya
JOSELSON: RCA (LP)
MOGILEVSKY: Melodiya
NISSMAN: Pierian
PLETNEV: DG
RICHTER: DG

Sonata No. 9 in C major, Op. 103 (1947)

The Ninth Sonata shows Prokofiev's long forty-year journey as a composer of piano sonatas, the most important cycle in the Russian canon since Scriabin's ten Sonatas. No. 9 was dedicated to Richter, who premiered it in Moscow in April 1951. The work generally is far less difficult than the three preceding sonatas and is full of delightful rhythms and jolly twists, along with contemplative themes. The sonata is in three movements, the second movement being a memorable scherzo.

KALICHSTEIN: Vanguard
RICHTER: Praga
SCHUMAKER: Elan
SOKOLOV: Op. 111

Piano Concerto No. 1 in D-flat major, Op. 10 (1911–12)

The five Prokofiev piano concerti are all original and vital creations, the most often played of twentieth-century piano concertos and the most recorded. No. 1 in D-flat was played by the twenty-one-year-old composer as his graduation piece from the St. Petersburg Conservatory. He scandalized the jury by not using a prescribed Classic or Romantic concerto. The work is in a modified sonata design, the jubilant opening statement returning to close the work. Maurice Hinson thinks "this may be the most important single-movement concerto since Liszt's Concerto No. 2 in A."

ARGERICH, Dutoit/Montreal Symphony: EMI

ASHKENAZY, Previn/London Symphony: London

BROWNING, Leinsdorf/Boston Symphony: RCA

FELTSMAN, Thomas/London Symphony: Sony Classical

GAVRILOV, Rattle/London Symphony: Angel

GRAFFMAN, Szell/Cleveland: Columbia

KATZ, Boult/London Philharmonic: Cembal d'Amour

KERER, Kondrashin/Moscow Philharmonic: Multisonic

KISSIN, Aabbado/Berlin Philharmonic: DG

RICHTER, Kondrashin/Moscow Philharmonic: Odyssey (LP)

Piano Concerto No. 2 in G minor, Op. 16 (1913; revised 1923)

In four movements, the Second Concerto is a dynamite showpiece, with a panoramic piano part. It is among the most difficult technical challenges in the standard repertoire. When Prokofiev introduced it to Russian audiences, they were indignant, calling him the piano's cubist and futurist. Today we hear it as a colorful Romantic work. Poulenc once called Prokofiev the Russian Liszt.

ASHKENAZY, Previn/London Philharmonic: London

BALOGHOVA, Ancerl/Czech Philharmonic: Supraphon; Artia (LP)

BOLET, Cox/Nuremberg Symphony: Genesis

DEMIDENKO, Lazarev/London Philharmonic: Hyperion

FRACER, Leibowitz/Paris Conservatoire: RCA (LP)

GUTIÉRREZ, Jarvi/Concertgebouw: Chandos

HENRIOT-Schweitzer, Munch/Boston Symphony: RCA (LP)

LUPU, Rachlin/Fort Worth Symphony: VAI

TACCHINO, Froment/Luxembourg Radio: Candide

Piano Concerto No. 3 in C major, Op. 26 (1921)

The Third Concerto is a perfect work of art. It is the most often played of the Prokofiev concerti. The piano part is of exceptional brilliance; the visual aspect of the virtuosity—the choreography of the hands upon the keyboard—is extremely striking. Prokofiev played the premiere in Chicago in 1921. His own recording is a must-hear for those interested in a composer's interpretation of his own work. Prokofiev was a startling pianist. In his day it was said that his playing was like his music—he was called an "Age of Steel" pianist. Our ears now hear how lyrical he could be both as pianist and composer. All of the performances listed offer virtuosity of a high order.

ANDSNES, Rudd/Bergen Philharmonic: Simax

ARGERICH, Abbado/Berlin Philharmonic: DG

ATAMIAN, Schwarz/Seattle Symphony: Delos

BROWNING, Leindorf/Philadelphia:
Seraphim
CLIBURN, Hendl/Chicago Symphony:
RCA
GRAFFMAN, Szell/Cleveland: CBS
JANIS, Kondrashin/Moscow
Philharmonic: Mercury
JUDD, Lazarev/Moscow Philharmonic:
Chandos
KAPELL, Dorati/Dallas Symphony: RCA
MITROPOULOS (pianist and conductor),
NBC Symphony: AS Disc
PROKOFIEV, Coppola/London
Symphony: Pearl
WEISSENBERG, Ozawa/Orchestre de
Paris: Angel

Concerto No. 4 in B-flat major for Piano, Left Hand Alone, and Orchestra, Op. 53 (1931)

The Left Hand Concerto was commissioned by Paul Wittgenstein, who had lost his right arm in World War I. He commissioned the great Ravel concerto, as well as works by Schmidt, Korngold, Bortkiewicz, Hans Gál, and others. Unfortunately, he didn't care for Prokofiev's and did not play it. It was neglected until Siegfried Rapp, who lost his arm in the next world war, played it in 1956. In 1958, Rudolf Serkin gave the American premiere.

The work is in four movements, neo-Classic and transparent in content, thematically delightful.

ASHKENAZY, Previn/London Symphony:
London
BRONFMAN, Mehta/Israel
Philharmonic: Sony Classical
FLEISHER, Ozawa/Boston Symphony:
Sony Classical
PAIK, Wit/Polish National Orchestra:
Naxos
R. SERKIN, Ormandy/Philadelphia:
Columbia

Piano Concerto No. 5 in G major, Op. 55 (1932)

No. 5, in five movements, is a dark horse which is a winner in performance, full of sparkling wit, daring pianism, and loads of themes.

BRENDEL, Sternberg/Vienna State
Opera: Turnabout (LP)
HOLLANDER, Leinsdorf/Boston
Symphony: RCA
POSTNIKOVA, Rozhdestvensky/USSR
Symphony: Audiophile Classics
RICHTER, Maazel/London Symphony:
Angel; Rowicki/Warsaw Philharmonic:
DG

R

SERGEI RACHMANINOFF
1873–1943—Russia

Much of Rachmaninoff's piano music continues to be widely played, especially several of the concerti. The pianism, based on his own large hands and sublime capability, is extremely taxing for the muscles. His scores are often loaded—at times, overloaded—with complicated textures and note spinning. The result, however, is always idiomatic, the sonorities potent and bell-like. Rachmaninoff at his best has a unique appeal, with his gift for emotional melody and his nostalgic late Russian Romanticism.

Complete Solo Piano Music:
LAREDO: Sony Classical
SHELLEY: Hyperion
TI IIOLLIER: Thésis

Five Pieces, Op. 3 (1892)
Seven Pieces, Op. 10 (1894)

The earlier of these two sets of character pieces includes the notorious Prelude in C-sharp minor, Op. 3, No. 2—the "It" Prelude, so described by the composer because every audience expected him to play "it." Its appeal, however, is real. Rachmaninoff recorded it three times, never bombastically. (Other pieces recorded by Rachmaninoff are *Mélodie, Polichinelle, Sérénade, Barcarolle,* and *Humoresque,* to be found in Volumes 1 and 2 of his complete recorded performances on RCA.)

ALEXEEV: Virgin Classics
BIRET: Naxos
GOLUB: Arabesque
HOBSON: Arabesque
LAREDO: Sony Classical

Six Moments musicaux, Op. 16 (1896)

Drenched in Russian languor, this important and technically treacherous set of concert pieces is far more difficult than the preceding ones. Only the mournful B minor is easily playable. A merely good technique is not enough—these works call for high virtuosic equipment. Rachmaninoff's own performance of Op. 16, No. 2 in E-flat minor (in Volume 2) makes child's play of this thickly packed piece and demonstrates the meaning of aristocratic pianism.

AKL: Pavane
BERMAN: DG
HOROWITZ (Op. 16, No. 2): RCA
JONES: Nimbus
LUGANSKY: EMI
PONTI: Vox

Variations on a Theme by Chopin, Op. 22 (1903)

On February 10, 1903, Rachmaninoff premiered the *Chopin* Variations in a recital with some of the Op. 23 Preludes. It was his first large-scale work for solo piano and is dedicated to Leschetizky. Its basis is the famous Chopin C minor Prelude, Op. 28, No. 20, which Busoni, too, would later use for variation purposes. Though it has quality and fine logic, this neglected work lacks appealing melodies like those of the Second Concerto, which would have made it more popular.

BEREZOVSKY: Teldec
BOLET: London
PONTI: Vox
SHELLEY: Hyperion
WILD: Chesky

Ten Preludes, Op. 23 (1903–04)
Thirteen Preludes, Op. 32 (1910)

In these twenty-three pieces, we encounter the finest of Rachmaninoff's piano music, with beguiling melodic appeal and lush keyboard texture. Rachmaninoff could easily span a twelfth, and he asks here for thick chords. His left hand was invincible, and he charted his left-hand figuration with new and wondrous formations, making use of bass sonorities that have a physical, almost guttural impact. The technical range of the Preludes is enormous, the most difficult of all being perhaps the Op. 23, No. 9—a double-note study that can ruin the muscles if practiced poorly. Op. 23, No. 5, Alla marcia, in G minor, is the best known prelude of the two sets, and the Lento B minor, Op. 32, No. 10, is one of Rachmaninoff's most powerful creations. We are fortunate to have recordings by Rachmaninoff himself of seven preludes: Op. 23, Nos. 5 and 10, and Op. 32, Nos. 3, 5, 6, 7, and 12. They should be heard by anyone interested in Rachmaninoff. Nobody has ever approached him in playing the G major Prelude, Op. 32, No. 5, with its antique flavoring.

Sergei Rachmaninoff by David Dubal

ANIEVAS: EMI
ASHKENAZY: London
DI BONAVENTURA
    (Op. 32 complete): Titanic
KATIN: Olympia
KEENE: Protone
RACHMANINOFF: RCA
RICHTER (six from Op. 23,
    seven from Op. 32):
    MHS; JVC/Melodiya
SHELBY: Hyperion
THIOLLIER: Thésis
WEISSENBERG: RCA

Sonata No. 1 in D minor, Op. 28 (1907)

The sonata is in three mammoth-sized movements totaling thirty-five minutes, the best being the Lento middle movement with its vast melancholia. Robert Offergeld declares, "The idiom is the all-out, head-on, non-ironic representationalism of the grand Romantic manner."

BEREZOVSKY: Teldec
FIORENTO: APR
NEIMAN: VAI
OGDON: RCA
RODRIGUEZ: Elan
WEISSENBERG: Philips: Great Pianists of the Twentieth Century
YERESKO: Chant du Monde

Sonata No. 2 in B-flat minor, Op. 36 (1913; revised 1931)

This sonata is in three concise movements. It is even more difficult than the Sonata No. 1. Indeed, it is brutal, even after revisions by Rachmaninoff to trim some of the difficulty. Some Rachmaninoff devotees consider it a masterpiece. The Second Sonata desperately needs sympathetic interpreters, for the phraseology is dense, fragmented, and filled with a wild despair. The finale must be counted as one of the composer's most electrifying works. In 1940, Rachmaninoff approved a version by Horowitz which combined both the original and condensed versions and which Horowitz plays on his two recordings.

BIRET (1913 version): Naxos
BROWNING: Delos
CLIBURN: RCA
COLLARD: EMI
HAMELIN: Hyperion
HOROWITZ: CBS; RCA
KASMAN: Hyperion
F. KEMPF (1913 version): Calliope
MURARO: Adès
SHELBY (1913 version): Hyperion

SOREL: EMCO
WEISSENBERG: DG

Nine Etudes-tableaux, Op. 33 (1911)
Nine Etudes-tableaux, Op. 39 (1916–17)

Of the title *Etudes-tableaux*, the composer, when questioned, responded, "I do not believe in the artist disclosing too much of his images. Let them paint for themselves what it most suggests." The eighteen etudes are more chromatic and difficult than the preludes. They are invariably beautiful in their writing, though lacking in some cases the immediate melodic appeal of the preludes. As compensation, however, they possess an added rhythmic virility, sometimes with an almost barbaric thrust.

ASHKENAZY (Op. 39): London
BATTERSBY (selected): Koch
COLLARD: EMI
HOBSON (Op. 33, Op. 39; complete): Arabesque
HOROWITZ (three etudes): Columbia
NASEDKIN: Melodiya (LP)
OGDEN (Op. 33, Op. 39; complete): Philips: Great Pianists of the Twentieth Century
RACHMANINOFF (Op. 33, Nos. 2 & 7; Op. 39, No. 6): RCA
SOFRONITSKY (Op. 33, Nos. 2 and 5; Op. 39, Nos. 4–6): Melodiya
WEBSTER: Dover (LP)

Variations on a Theme by Corelli, Op. 42 (1931)

This composer premiered his *Corelli* Variations in Montreal. The theme, "La Folia," was believed at the time to be by Corelli, but it is in fact a Spanish folk melody that has been used by many composers. This was Rachmaninoff's final piece of solo piano music. It had been fourteen years since the Op. 39 Etudes, during which time he had produced only the Fourth Piano Concerto, Op. 40, and Three Russian Songs for Chorus and Orchestra, Op. 41. His constant touring practically brought his creative work to a standstill. After the *Corelli* Variations, however, he would write three of his most important works: the *Rhapsody on a Theme of Paganini,* Op. 43; the Third Symphony, Op. 44; and the *Symphonic Dances,* Op. 45. As a composer, he had felt far from the mainstream of current musical thought, and critics of his day thought him an anachronism. But with the *Corelli* Variations, one may say Rachmaninoff entered a new period in his work. In these last compositions, he remains true to himself, but there is a paring down of excess, both in his emotionalism and in the density of the music. The sobbing and often indulgent Slavic melancholy is drastically diminished. The *Corelli* Variations and the *Rhapsody* are of considerable difficulty, but in both, the structure and the ideas have a new transparency, as well as a more urbane harmonic language.

ASHKENAZY: London
BIRET: Naxos
CHERKASSKY: Nimbus
COLLARD: Connoisseur Society
LILL: Nimbus
THIBAUDET: London
VIARDO: Nonesuch
WILD: Chesky
YABLONSKAYA: CSOC

Piano Concerto No. 1 in F-sharp minor, Op. 1 (1891)

The Rachmaninoff concerti continue to be the most regularly performed of any Romantic concertos. No. 1 is dedicated to Alexander Siloti. The concerto was a favorite work of Rachmaninoff's, and he revised it in 1917. It has all of his strong points, including melodic appeal and brilliant piano writing. The first movement's cadenza is very strong and taxing. The work is generally squarer than either No. 2 or No. 3.

ANIEVAS, de Burgos/New Philharmonia: EMI
ASHKENAZY, Haitink/Concertgebouw Orchestra: London
JANIS, Reiner/Chicago Symphony: Philips: Great Pianists of the Twentieth Century
KOCSIS, de Waart/San Francisco Symphony: Philips
RACHMANINOFF, Ormandy/ Philadelphia: RCA
VÁSÁRY, Ahronovitch/London Symphony: DG
WILD, Horenstein/Royal Philharmonic: Chesky

Piano Concerto No. 2 in C minor, Op. 18 (1901)

No. 2 is, after the Tchaikovsky Concerto No. 1, the world's most beloved piano concerto. The piano writing is luxuriant, the orchestration subtle but colorful. The concerto is gratefully dedicated to Dr. Nicholas Dahl. Rachmaninoff had been deeply depressed and was creatively blocked until he went for therapy to Dr. Dahl.

CLIBURN, Reiner/Chicago Symphony: RCA
GUTIÉRREZ, Maazel/Pittsburgh Symphony: Telarc
JANIS, Dorati/Minneapolis Symphony: Mercury

KAPELL, Steinberg/Robin Hood Dell
Orchestra: RCA
KISSIN, Gergiev/London Symphony:
RCA
KRAINEV, Ivanov/Moscow Radio
Symphony: Melodiya/EMI
LYMPANY, Sargent/Royal Philharmonic:
EMI
MOISEIWITSCH, Rignold/Philharmonia
Orchestra: Philips: Great Pianists of
the Twentieth Century
RACHMANINOFF, Stokowski/
Philadelphia: RCA
RICHTER, Kondrashin/Moscow State
Philharmonic: Everest (LP)
RUBINSTEIN, Reiner/Chicago
Symphony: RCA
VÁSÁRY, Ahronovitch/London
Symphony: DG
WEISSENBERG, Karajan/Berlin
Philharmonic: Angel

BOLET, I. Fischer/London Symphony:
London
BRONFMAN, Salonen/Philharmonia
Orchestra: Sony Classical
CLIBURN, Kondrashin/Symphony of the
Air: RCA
GILELS, Cluytens/Paris Conservatoire:
Testament
HOROWITZ, Barbirolli/New York
Philharmonic: APR
HOROWITZ, Coates/London Symphony:
Seraphim; Reiner/RCA Symphony:
RCA
JANIS, Munch/Boston Symphony: RCA
MERZHANOV, Anosov/USSR
Symphony: Monitor (LP)
MOGILEVSKY, Kondrashin/Moscow
Philharmonic: Melodiya
PLETNEV, Rostropovich/Russian
National Orchestra: DG
RACHMANINOFF, Ormandy/
Philadelphia: RCA
VOLODOS, Levine/Berlin Philharmonic:
Sony Classical
WATTS, Ozawa/New York Philharmonic:
CBS
WEISSENBERG, Prêtre/Chicago
Symphony: RCA

Piano Concerto No. 3 in D minor, Op. 30 (1909)

The Third Concerto has become the ultimate measure of technical prowess and emotional projection. Dedicated to Josef Hofmann, who never played it, it is the most difficult concerto, technically, in the standard repertoire. Such a superlative technician as Gary Graffman wishes he had learned it as a young student: "Probably the only time I could have learned that magnificent knucklebreaker would have been when I was still too young to know fear."

ARGERICH, Chailly/Berlin Radio
Symphony: Philips: Great Pianists of
the Twentieth Century
ASHKENAZY, Ormandy/Philadelphia
Orchestra: RCA
L. BERMAN, Abbado/London
Symphony: CBS

Piano Concerto No. 4 in G minor, Op. 40 (1927)

This concerto is by far the least played of the series, lacking the melodic invention of the other works. Michelangeli, however, has always been a partisan of the score, and he conjures up its spirit with a gorgeous sound. The brooding Largo has material reminiscent of the nursery tune "Three Blind Mice."

ASHKENAZY, Haitink/Concertgebouw:
London
KOCSIS, de Waart/San Francisco Symphony:
Philips

MICHELANGELI, Gracis/Philharmonia:
  Angel
SHELLEY, Thomson/Royal Scottish
  Orchestra: Chandos
VÁSÁRY, Ahronovitch/London
  Symphony: DG
WILD, Horenstein/Royal Philharmonic:
  Chesky

Rhapsody on a Theme of Paganini, Op. 43 (1934)

A popular concert-hall staple, the *Rhapsody* is based on the theme of Paganini's celebrated Twenty-fourth Caprice for solo violin. The *Dies Irae* is also integrated into the score.

CLIBURN, Kondrashin/Moscow
  Philharmonic: RCA
DAVIDOVICH, Jarvi/Concertgebouw
  Orchestra: Philips
FLEISHER, Szell/Cleveland: Sony
  Classical
GRAFFMAN, Bernstein/New York
  Philharmonic: CBS
KAPELL, Reiner/Robin Hood Dell
  Orchestra: RCA
PENNARIO, Leinsdorf/Los Angeles
  Philharmonic: EMI
RACHMANINOFF, Stokowski/
  Philadelphia: RCA
RUBINSTEIN, Reiner/Chicago
  Symphony: RCA
C. SMITH, Sargent/Philharmonia
  Orchestra: Dutton Laboratories
WILD, Horenstein/Royal Philharmonic:
  Chesky

Transcriptions

Rachmaninoff composed a group of effective transcriptions, which have been played by many pianists, though none to equal his own playing.

They are scattered throughout RCA's three volumes of Rachmaninoff's complete recordings.

Bizet-Rachmaninoff: Minuet from
  L'Arlésienne Suite No. 1 (in Volume 1)
Kreisler-Rachmaninoff: *Liebesfreud*
  (in Volumes 2 and 3); *Liebesleid*
  (in Volume 1)
Mendelssohn-Rachmaninoff: Scherzo
  from *A Midsummer Night's Dream* (in
  Volume 2) (Rachmaninoff's distillation
  of Mendelssohn's shimmering orches-
  tration is inimitable.)
Mussorgsky-Rachmaninoff: Hopak from
  The Fair at Sorochinsk (in Volume 2)
Rachmaninoff—transcriptions of his
  songs for piano solo: *Daisies* (in
  Volume 2); *Lilacs* (in Volumes 1 and 2)
Rimsky-Korsakov-Rachmaninoff: The
  Flight of the Bumblebee (in Volume 2)
Schubert-Rachmaninoff: *The Brooklet* (in
  Volume 2)
Tchaikovsky-Rachmaninoff: *Lullaby* (in
  Volume 2)

MAURICE RAVEL
1875–1937—France

Ravel was one of the great composers of the twentieth century, and his piano music, though its quantity is not large, is universally performed. Ravel brought to the piano many new technical devices. Though Debussy was older than Ravel, he wrote his greatest piano music only after he discovered Ravel's Jeux d'eau. Alfred Cortot described the essential difference between the two composers: "Where Debussy would have described the sensations caused by viewing an object, Ravel describes the object itself."

The Complete Solo Piano Music

"The unique contribution of Ravel," for Laurence Davies, "lay in his power to retain a certain firmness of line, while at the same time capturing that fluidity we have come to associate with Impressionism." Walter Gieseking spoke of this body of work as "the most pianistic ever written, making the most perfect and universal use of the resources of the modern piano."

    R. CASADESUS: Sony Classical
    CROSSLEY: CRD
    ENTREMONT: Sony Classical
    FRANÇOIS: EMI
    GIESEKING: EMI
    HAAS: Philips
    HELFFER: Harmonia Mundi
    LORTIE: Chandos
    LOWY: Bayer
    MERLET: Circé
    PERLEMUTER: Vox
    RICHARD: Valois
    ROUVIER: Calliope
    SIMON: Vox
    THIBAUDET: London
    THIOLLIER: Naxos

Pavane pour une infante défunte (1899)

The *Pavane for a Dead Princess* is one of Ravel's best-known works and offers little technical difficulty. The key, G major, is not dark, as one might expect from a funeral pavane. It has, rather, that peculiarly Ravelian melancholy which seems to be bathed in white light. The composer himself thought the Chabrier influence on this work was too "obtrusive."

    R. CASADESUS: Sony Classical
    CLIBURN: RCA

    COLLARD: EMI
    ENTREMONT: Sony Classical
    GILELS: RCA
    KÖRMENDI: Naxos
    PERLEMUTER: Nimbus

Jeux d'eau (1901)

This exquisite score, dedicated to Ravel's teacher Fauré, paved a new road in piano technique with use of seconds, major sevenths, dominant ninths, and eleventh chords. Cortot called the work "liquid poetry." Its antecedents were Liszt's *Jeux d'eaux à la Villa d'Este* and *Au bord d'une source*. "It is by imitating that I innovate," Ravel once proudly said. Ricardo Viñes gave the world premiere.

    CORTOT: Biddulph
    GIESEKING: Pearl
    GILELS: MHS
    ORTIZ: IMP Classics
    RICHTER: RCA
    ROGÉ: London
    ROSENBERGER: Delos
    THIBAUDET: Denon

Sonatine (1905)

An unsurpassed masterwork exhibiting polish and perfection of detail. The texture is thin, with an admirable use of the keyboard's upper register. The movements are marked "Modéré," "Mouvement de Menuet," and "Animé." In his notation and markings, the composer took special pains to make his intention understood.

    ARGERICH: DG
    R. CASADESUS: Sony Classical
    CORTOT: Biddulph
    FRANÇOIS: EMI

GIESEKING: EMI
LAPLANTE: Elan
LOWY: Bayer
MORAVEC: Philips: Great Pianists of the
    Twentieth Century
MORAVEC: VAI
PERLEMUTER: Nimbus
RÁNKI: Hungaroton

Miroirs (1905)

Miroirs contains five pieces: *Noctuelles* ("Night Moths"), *Oiseaux tristes* ("Mournful Birds"), *Une Barque sur l'océan* ("A Ship on the Ocean"), *Alborada del gracioso* ("Aubade/Morning Song of the Jester"), and *La Vallée des cloches* ("The Valley of the Bells"). The works are seldom played in public as a complete set. Each piece offers a unique excursion into impressionism and symbolism, opening new avenues of harmonic color. Leon Vallas pictured *Noctuelles* as "an inextricable mass of curves drowned in a sonorous flood of audacious intervals which interrupt the fluttering of nocturnal butterflies." *Oiseaux tristes* does not demand as much technically as it does in the imaginative portrayal of the sadness of birds lost in a forest in extreme summer heat. *Une Barque sur l'océan* uses sweeping arpeggio forms to summon the image of water, which symbolizes the vicissitudes of fate. *Alborada del gracioso* is the best known of the five pieces and offers, as well, the most treacherous battle with the keyboard. Only a very good piano will be adequate for the work's rapidly insistent, repeated-note technique. In this piece Ravel has integrated the glamour of a Liszt Hungarian Rhapsody into a Hispanic framework. This jester and his insinuating guitar strains are hypnotically molded with a sardonic smile and an extreme technical cruelty, especially in the double glissandos in fourths.

La Vallée des cloches is a superb work which evokes a sense of ritual.

BIANCONI: VAI
FRANÇOIS: EMI
GIESEKING: EMI
HELFFER: Harmonia Mundi
NOJIMA: Reference
O'REILLY: Albany
PERLEMUTER: Nimbus
ROGÉ: London
TORADZE: Angel

Gaspard de la nuit (1908)

The suite was inspired by the Aloysius Bertrand triptych, *Gaspard de la nuit*. The three parts are *Ondine, Le Gibet,* and *Scarbo.* The work was launched in public by the indefatigable Ricardo Viñes. Cortot proclaimed, "These three poems enrich the piano repertoire . . . with one of the most extraordinary examples of instrumental ingenuity which the industry of composers has ever produced."

In *Ondine,* Ravel portrays the water nymph attempting to seduce a mortal as she tries to lure him to her palace in the depths of the lake. The work is bewitching in its powers of evocation. Edward Lockspeiser finds that "nowhere in music, and seldom in the Impressionist paintings of this period, have the iridescent images of glistening, transparent water been so convincingly conveyed." The climax is surely one of Ravel's most seductive, with its sprays of glimmering water surging ever upward. *Ondine* was dedicated to Harold Bauer.

Le Gibet, "the gallows," is a study in suspense, evoking an eerie, static, half-lit scene. Ravel asks the pianist to play "sans expression" at one point.

Of *Scarbo,* Charles Stanley says, "Words cannot describe the complexities and difficulties of *Scarbo,* which demands wrists of steel, fingers with eyes in them." "In *Scarbo,*" James Gibb asserts, "the macabre terrors of a harrying goblin hurtle the composer beyond the diabolic extremes of virtuosity in Liszt and Balakirev. All laughter is sardonic and cruel. . . . Even its silences are frightening and the vicious elusiveness of the goblin is expressed in startling harmonies. *Scarbo* is a unique masterpiece in the literature of piano virtuosity."

It has become a badge of mastery for pianists worldwide. *Scarbo* is dedicated to Rudolph Ganz.

ARGERICH: DG
ASHKENAZY: London
AX: RCA
BACHAUER: Mercury (LP)
BROWNING: RCA
FRANÇOIS: EMI
KRAINEV: Chant du Monde
MICHELANGELI: Philips: Great Pianists
    of the Twentieth Century
POGORELICH: DG
SIMON: Turnabout
TORADZE: EMI
WILD: Audiofon

Valses nobles et sentimentales (1911)

Ravel wrote that these seven waltzes and an epilogue were an expression of "my intention of composing a chain of waltzes following the example of Schubert." Yet with their perfectly carved, needle-like detail and ironic overtones, these seven waltzes and an epilogue are worlds apart from the naive spirit of Schubert's waltzes. On the title page, Ravel quotes a line from Henri de Régnier: "The delicious and always new pleasure of a useless occupation."

AX: RCA
DE LARROCHA: RCA
GILELS: Multisonic
MICHELANGELI: Arkadia
POGORELICH: Philips
RÁNKI: Hungaroton
RICHTER: Praga
RUBINSTEIN: RCA

Le Tombeau de Couperin (1917)

This suite consists of six movements: Prelude, Fugue, Forlane, Rigaudon, Menuet, and Toccata. Ravel said, "In reality, it is a tribute not so much to Couperin himself as to eighteenth century music in general." During the dark days of World War I, Ravel, master of logical construction, looked back yearningly to that earlier age of logic and aristocratic grace. He dedicated each piece to a friend killed in the war. The final piece, Toccata, is a repeated-note moto perpetuo with a golden halo. When Ravel later orchestrated the suite, even with his unique mastery of the orchestra he did not touch the Toccata, which is so perfectly tailored to the piano that a separation from its original medium would be ruinous.

BROWNING: RCA
CASADESUS: Sony Classical
HELFFER: Harmonia Mundi
LORTIE: Chandos
MAGALOFF: Denon
PERLEMUTER: Nimbus
THIBAUDET: Denon
WEISSENBERG: EMI

La Valse (1920)

Ravel transcribed his great *La Valse* for solo piano himself, though few pianists know of the existence of the transcription. The work was written for Diaghilev. When the composer played it for him, the impresario rightly called it "a masterpiece, but it is not a ballet, it is a portrait of a ballet." It is also a portrait of a dead era. *La Valse* is an apotheosis of the Viennese waltz; desperately nostalgic in its depiction of a city and a dance with their aura of dissipation. It is a wail of misty, ghostlike suffering. The piece is irresistibly effective when played with an almost unruly abandon.

BABAYAN: CSOC
GOULD: Sony Classical
LAREDO: CBS
LORTIE: Chandos
PARK: EMI
PENNARIO: EMI
WILD: Ivory Classics

Piano Concerto in G major (1931)

During the first stages of composition, Ravel thought of naming the work *Divertissement*. He noted that the concerto "is written in the spirit of Mozart and Saint-Saëns. I believe that the music of a concerto can be gay and brilliant, and that it need not pretend to depths nor aim at dramatic effects." Ravel's wonderful ability to assimilate styles of music is nowhere more perfectly displayed than in this concerto. The use of alternating hand technique is perfection. The composer borrows some jazz elements, yet the concerto is purely Gallic in spirit and still exerts an influence over French musical composition. The 1930s recording by Marguerite Long and Ravel shows the grace and polish of Long's very French pianism.

ARGERICH, Abrado/London Symphony:
    DG
BERNSTEIN, Bernstein/Columbia
    Symphony: Columbia
COLLARD, Maazel/Orchestre National
    de France: Angel

ENTREMONT, Ormandy/Philadelphia:
    Columbia
GRIMAUD, Linman/Baltimore
    Symphony: Erato
LONG, Ravel/Lamoureux Orchestra:
    Pearl
MICHELANGELI, Gracis/Philharmonia:
    EMI
ROGÉ, Dutoit/Montreal Symphony:
    London
THIBAUDET, Dutoit/Montreal
    Symphony: London
WEISSENBERG, Ozawa/Orchestre de
    Paris: EMI

Concerto for the Left Hand and Orchestra in D major (1931)

The concerto is a miracle of technical know-how. For Maurice Hinson, this is "one of Ravel's most powerful and dramatic works; [it] contains a curious combination of Hispanic, jazz, and modernist (modal and polytonal) influences; [it is] a long way from the Impressionistic and neoclassic qualities so frequently associated with Ravel's style. The resources of the hand are greatly taxed. Power and technical dexterity are called for all over the keyboard. Careful balancing of tone (melody and accompaniment in one hand) is a *sine qua non*."

BÉROFF, Abrado/London Symphony: DG
BROWNING, Leinsdorf/Philadelphia:
    Seraphim
R. CASADESUS, Ormandy/Philadelphia:
    Sony Classical
CICCOLINI, Martinon/Orchestre de
    Paris: Angel
COLLARD, Maazel/Orchestre National
    de France: Angel
CORTOT, Munch/Paris Conservatoire
    Orchestra: Pearl
DE LARROCHA, Foster/London
    Philharmonic: London

ENTREMONT, Boulez/Cleveland: Sony
  Classical
FLEISHER, Ozawa/Boston Symphony:
  Sony Classical
KATCHEN, Kertesz/London Symphony:
  London
ROGÉ, Dutoit/Montreal Symphony:
  London
ZIMERMAN, Boulez/London Symphony:
  DG

MAX REGER
1873–1916—Germany

Reger was essentially a post-Romantic, with a penchant for Baroque and Classical forms. He wrote nearly two hundred piano pieces, many of which are stuffed with notes and accidentals, making for a fearsome-looking page. He is still highly regarded in Germany, though his music has not traveled well.

Variations and Fugue on a Theme by J. S. Bach, Op. 81

The *Bach* Variations, based on a theme from the Cantata No. 128, are far more chromatically intense than the Telemann Variations. Some consider this Reger's greatest work.

HARDEN: Nayos
D. LEVINE: Koch Schwann
R. SERKIN: CBS

Variations and Fugue on a Theme by Telemann, Op. 134

Reger was the most interesting variationist after Brahms. The set of *Telemann* Variations is among his finest works, and there have always been pianists around attracted by its merits. The theme is a minuet from Telemann's *Tafelmusik,* which is similar, in its variational possibilities, to the Handel tune that Brahms used in his great set of Variations and Fugue, Op. 24. The Reger stems from that work, reaching a massive conclusion in its Fugue.

BOLET: London
D. LEVINE: Koch Schwann
STERCZINSKY: Chant du Monde
ZANINI: Nuova Era

Aus meinem Tagebuch (From My Diary), Op. 82

This treasure trove shows us a relaxed, harmonically conservative Reger. There are four books, totaling thirty-five pieces. Some pieces remind one of Schubert, Brahms, or Schumann. Some are rollicking; others are intimate. The work is homophonic, without the obsessive contrapuntalizations one often finds in Reger.

BECKER: Thorofon
LAUGS: MHS (LP)

Piano Concerto in F minor, Op. 114

The Concerto is in three movements: Allegro moderato, Largo con gran espressione, and Allegro con spirito. It is a brilliant, warm, and emotional work, and the first movement is masterful in design and texture. The Concerto was rescued from oblivion by Rudolf Serkin, who gave the American premiere in 1945 and who takes the music firmly to his heart.

DERWINGER, Segerstam/Norrköping:
  BIS
MAYER, Bour/The Hague Philharmonic:
  Leonarda (LP)

OPPITZ, Stein/Bamberg Symphony: Koch
Schwann
R. SERKIN, Ormandy/Philadelphia:
Columbia

ALBERT ROUSSEL
1869–1937—France

Roussel was not a virtuoso player himself, nor was he really at home with the piano. He did, however, contribute several major works to the repertoire. His style is awkward to play, but "meaty," vigorous, and individual, with a rugged quality. It is French to the core, but not Parisian. Roussel is a composer who wears well, but will never be as popular as, say, Debussy, Ravel, or Poulenc.

Trois Pièces pour piano, Op. 49
Suite pour piano, Op. 14
Sonatine, Op. 16
Prélude et fugue, Op. 46

In the Suite, Op. 14, one may hear Roussel's mastery of dance forms. The movements are: Prelude, Sicilienne, Bourrée, and Rondo. The last is a masterly virtuoso piece. The *Sonatine* is planned in two sections, with subdivisions. Its square pianism becomes more interesting with repeated hearing. The Prelude and Fugue is a splendid edifice from 1932, comprising a somewhat savage prelude and a fugue built on the letters of Bach's name. The *Trois Pièces,* dedicated to Robert Casadesus—*Toccata, Valse lente,* and *Scherzo et trio*—are more conducive to performance.

J. DOYEN: MHS (LP)
JOHANNESEN (*Sonatine*): Golden Crest
KATAHN (*Trois Pièces, Suite, Sonatine*):
Gasparo
PARKINS: Chandos
PETIT *(Trois Pièces, Suite, Sonatine):* L'Oiseau-Lyre (LP)
SÉVILLA *(Trois Pièces, Suite, Sonatine):* Musica
Viva

Piano Concerto, Op. 36 (1927)

This is one of the best French piano concertos of the twentieth century. Because of its concertante style, pianists are not prone to sacrifice the hours needed to learn its biting pianism. It is in three short, dry, bitter movements. The slow movement has an austere beauty. There is not an excess note in this superbly developed work, and it exploits the bass range in an important way.

KRAJAY, Macura/Prague Chamber Orchestra:
Supraphon (LP)
LITTAUER, Springer/Hamburg Symphony:
Turnabout (LP)
MICHIELS, Bollon/Flanders Symphony: Cypres
Bell
THARAUD, Stern/Ensemble Orchestral de
Paris: Valois

S

CAMILLE SAINT-SAËNS
1835–1921—France

Camille Saint-Saëns composed piano music throughout his long career, but he left no solo sonata or other weighty structure. At his best he composed elegantly crafted salon music in which the keyboard sparkles and bubbles. His tunes are memorable; his harmony, arresting; his rhythms, infectious. He wears his heart on his sleeve, and his wit, sophistication, and lucidity seldom fail to charm. As Daniel Gregory Mason aptly put it: "Saint-Saëns is always the onlooker, the man of the world, never the mystic who contemplates in his own heart the forces that underlie the universe." In 1905 he recorded several rolls of his own music which are on CD on the Archiphon label.

The Complete Solo Piano Music

The very best of Saint-Saëns's solo piano music is the *Allegro appassionato*, Op. 70; the Toccata and Valse from the *Album for Piano*, Op. 72; the difficult and fetching *Etude en forme de valse*, No. 6, of the admirable Six Etudes of Op. 52, as well as the sixth and last Etude from Op. 111, *Toccata*; several of his flirtatious valses—the *Valse nonchalant, Valse langoureuse*, and *Valse gaie*; and, lastly, the lengthier twelve-minute *Caprice on Themes from Gluck's "Alceste."*

DOSSE: Vox
NEL: Selections

Concerto No. 1 in D major,
Op. 17 (1865)
Concerto No. 2 in G minor,
Op. 22 (1868)
Concerto No. 3 in E-flat major,
Op. 29 (1869)
Concerto No. 4 in C minor,
Op. 44 (1873)
Concerto No. 5 in F major,
Op. 103 (1895)

These represent the best-known French concertos of the nineteenth century. The composer was often heard as soloist. The concerti are slick and facile, with some electrifying pianists and deftly colored orchestration. No. 2 is the most frequently played. Sigismund Stojowski said that it "opened like Bach, and ended like Offenbach." No. 4, in C minor, is the masterpiece; all of the best of Saint-Saëns is contained in this work, which is brilliantly clever in its construction. No. 5, in F, called the *Egyptian* Concerto, is delightful and lightweight. No. 1, in D, is lots of fun and has an effective slow movement. No. 3, in E-flat, on the other hand, is overloaded with molasses and trite figurations, yet it still possesses a kind of entertaining virtuosity.

The Five Concerti:
BAR-ILLAN, de Bois/Orchestre des
    Concerts Français: Audiofon
CICCOLINI, Baudo/Orchestre de Paris: EMI
DARRE, Fourestier/French Radio Orchestra:
    EMI

ENTREMONT, Plasson/Toulouse
Capitole: Odyssey
LICAD, Previn/London Philharmonic:
Sony Classical
MOISEIWITSCH, Cameron/Philharmonia
Orchestra: APR
ROGÉ, Dutoit/Royal Philharmonic: London
TACCHINO, Froment/Luxembourg
Radio: Vox

Concerto No. 2:
DAVIDOVICH, Jarvi/Concertgebouw: Philips
RUBINSTEIN, Ormandy/Philadelphia: RCA
WILD, Freccia/National Philharmonic:
Chesky

Concerto No. 4:
CASADESUS, Bernstein/New York
Philharmonic: Sony Classical
COLLARD, Previn/Royal
Philharmonic: Angel

Camille Saint-Saëns by David Dubal

CORTOT, Munch: Pearl
OUCH: Arbitor
TIGERMAN, Ferriz/Cairo Symphony: Arbitor

Concerto No. 5:
ENTREMONT, Plasson/Toulouse
Capitole: CBS
RICHTER, Kondrashin/Moscow Philharmonic:
Monitor

ERIK SATIE
1866–1925—France

Often associated with such movements as Dadaism and Surrealism, Satie occupies a pivotal position in French music. He detested Wagnerism and Germanic "giantism" and created instead a music devoid of heroics or heavy emotionalism, music which indeed mocked such sentiments. In the preface to his *Sports et divertissements,* he wrote, "Turn the pages of this book with an amiable and smiling hand; for this is a work of fantasy and does not pretend to be anything else. For those who are dried up and stultified, I have written a chorale which is serious and respectable. This chorale is a sort of bitter preamble, a kind of austere and unfrivolous introduction. I have put into it everything I know about boredom. I dedicate this chorale to those who do not like me and withdraw."

Satie's aesthetic was so new and guileless that on first hearing it sounded as preposterous as his titles. Laurence Davies wrote of "Satie's own terrifying willingness to disrobe, shedding all those aids to beauty which the ordinary composer finds indispensable." The music of Erik Satie, said James Gibb, "came in like the voice of a child, saying outrageous things with complete, honest calm." Virgil Thomson extols: "It wears no priestly robes; it mumbles no incantations; it is not painted up by Max Factor to terrify elderly ladies or to give little girls a thrill. Neither is it designed to impress orchestral conductors or to get anybody a job teaching school. It has literally no devious motivation. It is as simple as a friendly conversation and in its better moments exactly as poetic and as profound."

Satie's music for the piano is mostly thin textured, of moderate or even simple demands technically, but it is deceptively difficult to play with simplicity and without caricature. Constant Lambert noted: "Satie's habit of writing his pieces in groups of three was not just a mannerism. It took the place in his art of dramatic development, and was part of his peculiarly sculpturesque view of music. When we pass from the first to the second *Gymnopédie*, or from the second to the third *Gnossienne*, we do not feel that we are passing from one object to another."

The Piano Music

Satie's best works include *Trois Sarabandes* (1887); *Trois Gymnopédies* (1888); *Trois Gnossiennes* (1890); *Trois Préludes* (1891); *Heures séculaires et instantanées* (1914); *Chapitres tournés en tous sens* (1913); *Embryons desséchés* (1913); *Trois Valses distinguées d'un précieux dégoûte* (all sets of three; 1914); *Pièces froides* (1897); *Véritables Préludes flasques* (1912); *Sonatine bureaucratique* (a parody of Clementi's C major Sonatina); *Sports et divertissements* (twenty small pieces; 1914); and *Cinq Nocturnes* (1919).

> CICCOLINI (complete piano music): EMI
> CLIDAT (complete piano music): Forlane
> GLAZER (complete piano music): Vox
> KÖRMENDI: Naxos
> J. MCCABE (selections): Saga Classics
> MASSELOS: RCA (LP)
> POULENC (selections): Sony Classical

> QUEFFÉLEC: Virgin Classics
> ROGÉ: London
> Y. TAKAHASHI (complete piano music): Denon
> VARZANO (selections): CBS

DOMENICO SCARLATTI
1685–1757—Italy

Scarlatti was the chief Italian keyboard composer of the eighteenth century, producing nearly six hundred pieces in a simple, binary form, which he called sonatas. Maurice Hinson has written, "Scarlatti gave the binary form a variety and expressive range that has never been surpassed by any other composer."

Most of this enormous literature of four-minute pieces was produced during the last

Domenico Scarlatti by David Dubal

fifteen years of his life. Scarlatti was himself a great harpsichordist, and most of his output was inspired by the high skills of his pupil Maria Barbara, Queen of Spain. Wanda Landowska wrote: "Spain fired the imagination of the great Neapolitan. . . . When we hear Scarlatti's music, we know that we are in the climate of sunlight and warmth. It is Italy, it is Spain—the spirit of the Latin countries and the god of the Mediterranean."

Scarlatti has the genuine nobility, the heroism, and the audacity of a Don Quixote. The Scarlatti scholar, biographer, and harpsichordist Ralph Kirkpatrick states: "There is hardly an aspect of Spanish life, of Spanish popular music and dance, that has not found itself a place in the microcosm that Scarlatti created with his sonatas. . . . He has captured the click of castanets, the strumming of guitars, the thud of muffled drums, the harsh bitter wail of Gypsy lament, the overwhelming gaiety of the village band, and above all, the wiry tension of the Spanish dance."

The Sonatas

Alessandro Longo and Ralph Kirkpatrick have both catalogued Scarlatti. The Kirkpatrick numbers are more correct chronologically, but the Longo edition, in eleven volumes published by Ricordi, seems to be used more often internationally for the sonatas. Sacheverell Sitwell made certain helpful divisions for some of the sonatas he knew. His groupings are:

Tarantellas: L. 241, 233, 95, 125, 475.
Neapolitan Sonatas: L. 388–486, 387, 384, 375, 461, 13, 103, 263, 414, 463, 385.
Siciliennes: L. 487, 452, 218.
Bell Sounds: L. 369, 218, 196.
Dances (not of Spanish character): L. 357, Suppl. 36 (K. 42), 168, 315, Suppl. 40 (K. 172), 178, Suppl. 39 (K. 441), 82, Suppl. 21 (K. 554).

Military Sonatas: L. 107, Suppl. 10 (K. 335), 400, 23, Suppl. 2 (K. 420), 205, 193, 255; 86.
High Speed "Velocity" Sonatas: L. 345, 215, 364, 272, 380, 470, 385.
Adagio Sonatas: L. 383, 423, Suppl. 7 (K. 34), 261, 382, 403, 44, 64, 4, 59, 27, 468, Suppl. 9 (K. 287), 61, 248, 332, Suppl. 27 (K. 328), 18, 443, 438, 99, 12, 187, 497, 312.
Pastoral or Bucolic Sonatas: L. 138, 344, 354, 439, 198, 132, Suppl. 41 (K. 489), 206.
"Hunting" Sonatas: L. 107, 364, 228, 192, 95, 302, 470, 290, 164, 287, 475.
The Virtuoso Sonatas: L. 356, 233, 232, 308, 65, 470. L. 273, 199, 328, 7, 255 with glissando passages.
From Sitwell's list of *Spanish Sonatas* by Scarlatti: L. 479, 413, 368, 449, 373, 478, 29, 241, 356, 58, 465, 317, 204, 474, 138, 407, 415, 232, 457, 282, 224, 107, 422, 349, 376, 179, 104, 412, 429, 498, 257, 371, 238, 428, 135, 165, 323, 273, 309, 199, 308, 27, 381, 305, 466, 328, 57, 161, 9, 454, 400, 172, 240, 263, 23, 134, 284, 65, 208, 213, 310, 279, 128, 286, 361, 109, 319, 418, 294, 338, 324, 340, 206, 164, 14, 196, 113, 311, 1, 255, 266, 116, 475, 408, 458, 200, 327, 223, 395, 11, 293, 497, 500, 312, 404.

Scarlatti himself wrote, in the preface to the only group of these pieces (called *Esercizi*) that was published during his lifetime: "Reader, whether you are a dilettante or a professor, do not expect to find in these compositions any profound intention, but rather, an ingenious gesting of the art, to prepare you for bold playing on the harpsichord. . . . Show yourself more human than critical, and thus you will increase your own pleasure. . . . Live happily!"

Scarlatti created not only a citadel of humanity, but also one of the most compressed arts in history, with a technical audacity that still astounds. Scarlatti might have played upon a very early pianoforte at the Madrid court, but the instrument would hardly have interested him at that time. It is in the best interest of contemporary players essaying these works on the piano to familiarize themselves with harpsichord versions, such as those of Landowska, Pinnock, Kirkpatrick, Valenti, George Malcolm, and others. The harpsichord sonority and its varied registration may help the pianist to hear the works with more authenticity than the eleven-volume Longo edition does, with its Romantic curvature of phrasing, tempi, and accent. I have noted some of the performances by pianists who have most thoroughly adapted and assimilated Scarlatti to the piano.

BABAYAN: (K. 8, 454, 54, 547, 247, 118, 198, 79, 239, 45, 49, 17, 365, 445, 502): Pro Piano

DI BONAVENTURA (L. 17, 463, 420, 373, 433, 479, 422, 369, 41, 380, 385, 266, 487, 109, 33, 388, 462, 486, 384, 370, 413, 104, 395): Connoisseur Society (LP)

R. CASADESUS (L. 463, 395, 411, 263, 465, 413, 487, 449, 387, 22, 486): CBS

CICCOLINI (L. 5, 413, 14, 23, 33, 41, 58, 103, 104, 263, 281, 288, 366): EMI

DECHENNE (L. 401, 186, 188, 413, 108, 366, 103, 375, 450, 457, 422): MHS

DE LARROCHA (from the 1738 Thirty Esercizi: Nos. 9, 6, 10, 8, 13, 11, 28): London

DRZEWIECKI (L. 352, 422, 23, 375, 413, 495, 424, 241, 188, 383, 349, 465): Muza (LP)

GIESEKING (L. 23, 275, 413, 424, 443): EMI (LP)

GILELS (L. 104, 449, 487, 23, 345): Monitor

GOULD (L. 463, 413, 486): CBS

HASKIL (L. 256, 388, 182, 457, 386, 171, 475, 483, 33, 255, 278): Westminster (LP)

HESS (L. 352, 387): Pearl

HOROWITZ (K. 33, 39, 54, 55, 96, 146, 162, 198, 322, 380, 455, 466, 474, 481, 491, 525, 531): CBS

RASHKOVETSKY (K. 104, 140, 545, 193, 12, 69, 24): Angelok I

POGORELICH: (K. 11, 9, 135, 8, 87, 151, 450, 529): DG

SCHIFF (K. 17, 27, 96, 162, 208, 322, 394, 420, 427, 491, 518, 519): Hungaroton

TOMSIC: (L. 103, 104, 118, 210, 349, 352, 366, 383, 387, 391, 396, 413, 487): PMG

WEISSENBERG (K. 8, 13, 20, 87, 107, 109, 132, 184, 193, 233, 247, 450, 481, 531, 544): DG

ARNOLD SCHOENBERG
1874–1951—Austria

Three Piano Pieces, Op. 11 (1908)
Six Little Piano Pieces, Op. 19 (1911)
Five Piano Pieces, Op. 23 (1924)
Suite, Op. 25 (1924)
Piano Piece, Op. 33a and *Piano Piece,* Op. 33b (1932)

Although Schoenberg's complete solo piano music fits snugly on one LP, Paul Jacobs is convinced "that these five books of pieces are as important to contemporary piano technique as the Chopin Etudes were to that of the nineteenth century." Glenn Gould remarks: "Schoenberg does not write *against* the piano, but neither can he be accused of writing *for* it. There is not one phrase in his keyboard output which reveals the least indebtedness to the percussive sonorities exploited in an overwhelming percentage of contemporary keyboard music."

Regarding the Three Piano Pieces, Op. 11, Gould adds, "Perhaps no other composition was as crucial to Schoenberg's future. . . . Op. 11 was the first major test of the possibilities of survival in a musical universe no longer dominated by a triadically centered harmonic orbit."

The set of Six Little Piano Pieces, Op. 19, continues Schoenberg's experiments in atonality while giving new meaning to musical brevity. The pieces range from nine bars to only eighteen in length and spawned a whole miniaturist movement, headed by Webern. The Five Pieces, Op. 23, are similar in texture to Op. 11, but they are far more thoroughly developed. The last of these pieces, a Waltz, was Schoenberg's first totally organized work based on a row of the twelve tones. It is interesting that Schoenberg's departure from harmonic practice still allowed him to integrate the beloved dance form of his native Vienna.

Of the Suite, Op. 25, Gould reports: "I can think of no composition for solo piano from the first quarter of this century which can stand as its equal. . . . For all its reliance on binary dance forms and its sly digs at preclassical convention, it is among the most spontaneous and wickedly inventive of Schoenberg's works."

The Suite consists of a Präludium, Gavotte with Musette, Intermezzo, Minuet with Trio, and Gigue. Each movement is arrived at through the use of the same row. The Two Piano Pieces, Op. 33a and 33b, are freer examples of Schoenberg's expressionistic idiom; both are marvelously developed, concentrated, and expressive. Schoenberg's musical evolution stemmed from his early post-Wagnerian epigonism and culminated in the twelve-tone method in which all twelve notes of the chromatic scale are arranged in a special sequence. This method has still not achieved anything like wide public acceptance, though many musicians consider his work to be the classicism of twentieth-century music, a body of work which revitalized an exhausted harmonic system. The historian Frederic Morton felt Schoenberg "would not just revolutionize music but rein-

vent it." Many have felt that Schoenberg concocted a new methodology in a quest for originality or expressionist ugliness. But Ernest Hutcheson writes: "The system is no more complicated or empirical than the polyphony of a Bach fugue or the harmonic and formal structure of a Beethoven Sonata, though it has been accused of being involved, mechanical, and cerebral. It is simply a technique of composition, and works written within it must, like all others, be judged primarily by the value and perceptibility of their ideas."

Each of the pianists listed gives perceptive readings. Schoenberg's piano music is overly stocked with interpretive indications, and his metronome markings can be confusing.

The Complete Solo Piano Music:
GOULD: Sony Classical
HELFFER: Harmonia Mundi
P. JACOBS: Nonesuch

Arnold Schoenberg by David Dubal

KARS: EMI
POLLINI: DG
Y. TAKAHASHI: Denon
K. WOLPE: Symposium

Piano Concerto, Op. 42 (1942)

The Concerto is somewhat easier to grasp on first hearing than other works of this composer; there is a reflective, mellow quality in it. It was Oscar Levant who suggested to Schoenberg that he write a piano concerto. It was premiered by Edward Steuermann, and the NBC Symphony with Stokowski conducting, in 1944. Schoenberg, in describing the work, wrote, "Life was so easy (Andante), but all of a sudden hate broke loose (Molto allegro); the situation became grave (Adagio) but life has to go on (Ciocoso)."

AX, Salonen/Philharmonia: Sony Classical
BRENDEL, Kubelik/Bavarian Radio: DG
GOULD, Craft/CBC Symphony: Columbia (LP)
POLLINI, Abbado/Berlin Philharmonic: DG
P. SERKIN, Ozawa/Chicago Symphony: RCA
STEUERMANN, Scherchen/Hessian Radio
    Symphony Orchestra: Arkadia

FRANZ SCHUBERT
1797–1828—Austria

Schubert had one of the least public careers of any of the great musicians. Though he played the piano well, he never gave a concert, and, in fact, was lucky even to have a piano at his disposal for composing. Yet Schubert is one of the progenitors of Romantic piano style, and his influence was great—not as much in his solo piano music as in his accompaniments to more than six hundred songs (virtually a new art form in European music). In these songs he made the piano an equal partner with the voice, and, more important, he developed an art of description inspired by the poetic text; this would have far-reaching influence on the small character pieces for solo piano of the Romantic composers. Unlike his piano music, some of Schubert's songs were comparatively well known, even during his lifetime. Liszt and Schumann were the first to realize that a poetic piano style existed in these accompaniments. It was not for nothing that Liszt transcribed more than fifty of Schubert's songs. Schubert played the accompaniments of his own songs, as well as his solo piano music, for his friends and was pleased when complimented on his "singing tone."

In 1822 he composed his famous *Wanderer* Fantasy, a work whose structure influenced Liszt in his later experiments with "thematic transformation." Technically, this work was one of the most muscular ever written up to that time and must certainly have strained the light mechanisms of the Viennese pianos to their limits (though there is no record of Schubert expressing dissatisfaction with the pianos of his time, as Beethoven did). Schubert himself had a hard time with the work and once stopped during a performance, shouting that perhaps the devil could play it, but he could not.

He was unhappy with the pianists in Vienna during his day, calling them "thumpers." He wrote no "bravura" variations or "fugitive pieces" for public consumption or easy digestibility; Schubert composed for himself from a seemingly ever-flowing magic fountain. His own playing must have had that kind of purity which is engendered by unworldliness. His solo works, especially the sonatas (those visionary scores, the last voice of Viennese Classicism), were almost totally neglected. They were criticized for not being of the "Beethovenian Sonata-type." Not until the 1930s did Schubert's Classicism make its impact. It was inevitable that so great a literature as these sonatas could not remain

Franz Schubert by David Dubal

Complete Piano Sonatas:
BADURA-SKODA: Arcana
DALBERTO: Denon
KEMPFF: DG
KUERTI: IMP Masters

Sonata in A minor, D. 537 (1817)

In three movements, this is the earliest of the Schubert sonatas to have received somewhat regular performance in concert, though it is hardly in the same musical sphere as his other two sonatas in A minor.

BRENDEL: Philips
GOTHONI: Ondine
KATIN: Olympia
MICHELANGELI: DG

Sonata in E-flat major, D. 568 (1817)

This work, in four movements, is very difficult for the pianist to hold together. It harks back to Haydn, and is redolent of the Viennese countryside.

FEDOROVA: Meloyida
KEMPFF: DG
SAKHAROV: Calliope
P. SERKIN: RCA (LP)
WEICHERT: Accord

Sonata in B major, D. 575 (1817)

In four movements. The Andante is high Schubert lyricism; the rest of the score, except for a good scherzo, is not well organized.

KLIEN: Vox
RICHTER: Music and Arts

unknown. As with the Mozart concerti, pianists since the mid-1950s have been passionately exploring Schubert, and these masterpieces have finally become repertory staples.

The ordering of the Schubert piano sonatas has always been confusing. Many of the twenty-three sonatas were left incomplete. The only unfinished work performed in public is the C major Sonata, D. (Deutsch listing) 840, in two movements. Eleven complete sonatas are part of the international repertory. Only three of these, the late A minor, D. 845, the D major, D. 850, and the G major, D. 894, were published during Schubert's lifetime. Traversals of the complete and incomplete sonatas have been accomplished by Kempff (DG) and by Klien (Vox). These artists are both finely attuned to Schubert. The incomplete works have interest for all those following Schubert's evolution as a composer of sonatas.

WEICHERT: Accord
WÜHRER: Vox

Sonata in A major, D. 664 (1819)

The best-known of the original sonatas and the easiest for the performer to make intelligible. The outer movements have a youthful freshness, while the Andante can only be called Schubertian in its bittersweet beauty.

ARRAU: Philips
ASHKENAZY: London
BADURA-SKODA: RCA
BRENDEL: Philips
CHERKASSKY: Nimbus
FLEISHER: Sony Classical
HESS (recorded 1928): APR
KRAUS: Vanguard
MATHIS: Pierian
RICHTER: Olympia
WATTS: EMI

Sonata in A minor, D. 784 (1823)

Schubert had not composed a piano sonata for several years when he wrote this three-movement work, and his structural prowess had grown considerably in the interim. The first movement shows a sparseness of notes and an awkwardness in the pianism. The finale, with its octave passage at the end, shows Schubert's characteristic disregard for what was playable. Yet the musical quality of this work is the highest thus far in the sonatas. The opening movement is majestic, and the finale's triplet figure has an autumnal flavor.

ASHKENAZY: London
BRENDEL: Philips
GILELS: Orfeo
LUPU: London

MAISENBERG: Orfeo
PIRES: DG
RASHKOVETSKY: Angelok I
RICHTER: Olympia
WATTS: EMI
WATTS: Sony Classical

Sonata in C major (unfinished), D. 840 (1825)

In two movements, this is by far the finest of the incomplete sonatas. Sketches for the unfinished movements exist. The C major Sonata is as complete as is the *Unfinished Symphony* and stands as a masterpiece of structural and emotional content. Only now, however, is it beginning to be appreciated by a larger public.

BRENDEL: Philips
GOTHONI: Ondine
KALISH: Nonesuch
RICHTER: Monitor; Philips

Sonata in A minor, D.845 (1825)

Its four perfect movements show a complete mastery of large form. After a noble first movement featuring Schubertian dotted rhythms in contrast to lyric material, there is a springy set of variations, with much brilliant writing and contrapuntal interest. The scherzo and trio have a typically Schubertian innocence, while a finale of slender material is imbued with an interior restlessness.

BRENDEL: Philips
COOPER: Ottavo
FIRKUSNY: Sugano
GOODE: Nonesuch
HASKIL: Music and Arts
LUPU: London

POLLINI: DG
RICHTER: Monitor

P. SERKIN: RCA
UCHIDA: Philips

Sonata in D major, D. 850 (1825)

This is a giant of a work in four movements, over forty minutes long, calling for a tremendous grasp of large form on the part of the pianist, and a Schubert-loving audience to appreciate what Schumann dubbed the "heavenly lengths" of Schubert's larger works. The slow movement has, with its melodic beauty, a marvelous subtlety of syncopation and harmonic boldness. The work was composed in the country in three weeks. Schubert wrote, "The environs . . . are truly heavenly and deeply moved and benefited me, as did its inhabitants." The sonata is filled with the song and dance of the people, as well as the sounds of their yodeling.

ASHKENAZY: London
BRENDEL: Philips
CURZON: London
GOODE: Nonesuch
RICHTER: Monitor
SCHNABEL: Arabesque
SHERMAN: Albany

Sonata in G major, D. 894, "Sonata Fantasy" (1826)

In four movements, this is a work of the most lovable lyricism. Schumann called it Schubert's "most perfect" sonata in form and spirit. In view of its leisurely qualities, the interpreter must be on guard to keep the audience awake. Schumann was wary of those who lacked "the imagination to solve its riddles."

ARTYMIW: Chandos
ASHKENAZY: London
DEMUS: MHS
LUPU: London

Sonata in C minor, D. 958 (1828)

The C minor Sonata joins the late A major, D. 959, and the B-flat major, D. 960, among the great sonatas of the Classical age. Published posthumously in 1838, they were composed within weeks before Schubert's death, which could not have been more untimely. Schubert had grown from being a prodigal, spontaneous fountain of melody to a profound and fully matured thinker whose contribution to sonata form was entirely his own, not bound by the sonata idea as defined by Beethoven. These last works— the String Quintet, the Ninth Symphony, and the last sonatas—exhibit a new grandeur of intention, a power of creative execution, a cumulative flow, a new fierceness in the ideas, as well as a peacefulness, that go beyond Romantic subjectivity. The Sonata in C minor and its two companions were composed in less than four weeks. Their psychological import is becoming better understood by discriminating pianists not merely attracted to virtuosity. The C minor Sonata is more somber than dramatic. In this late work, it is interesting that Schubert still uses the old-fashioned Minuetto. The C minor Sonata is haunted by death.

ARRAU: Philips
BRENDEL: Philips
ENDRES: Capriccio
ERDMANN: TAHA
GOODE: Nonesuch
GRAFFMAN: Columbia (LP)
RICHTER: Columbia/Melodiya
SHURE: Audiofon

Sonata in A major, D. 959 (1828)

The most astonishing of this sonata's four movements is the second, an Andantino which, as Denis Matthews attests, "has the greatest, most alarming, surprise of all: a plaintive song, harmonized in F-sharp minor and A major respectively, is invaded by a cataclysmic passage of bravura recitative in which key as such ceases to exist." The sonata as a whole is musically and structurally completely different from the C minor or the B-flat Sonata.

BRENDEL: Philips
ESCHENBACH: DG (LP)
GOODE: Nonesuch
HUNGERFORD: Vanguard (LP)
F. LEVY: Palexa
LUPU: London
OLSHANSKY: Monitor
ROSENBAUM: Bridge
SCHNABEL: Angel References
R. SERKIN: CBS

Sonata in B-flat major, D. 960 (1828)

For contemporary pianists, this work has become one of their greatest musical goals. It is the most often played of the last three sonatas. It is cast in four movements and takes over forty minutes. Maurice Hinson calls the B-flat Sonata "a transcendental work of unique individuality." It is music of ravishing and visionary beauty. The Andante sostenuto ranks with the greatest slow movements ever written.

CURZON: London
FIORENTINO: APR
A. FISCHER: Hungaraton
GOODE: Nonesuch
HAUTZIG: Monitor
HOROWITZ: RCA; DG
KEMPFF: DG
KOVACEVICH: Hyperion
RUBINSTEIN: RCA
SCHNABEL: EMI
R. SERKIN: Sony Classical

SHERMAN: Albany
SHURE: Audiofon

Fantasia in C major, D. 760 "Wanderer" (1822)

Known as the *Wanderer* Fantasy. Each movement is thematically derived from Schubert's song "Der Wanderer." It is a highly successful work of thematic unification in a four-movement plan. The Fantasia is the most virtuosic work of Schubert piano music and is technically taxing. Liszt saw its possibilities as a work for piano and orchestra and, knowing that Schubert undertook no concerto writing, he made an effective transcription of it, which is occasionally performed.

BASHKIROV: Melodiya
FELTSMAN: Russian Disc
FLEISHER: Sony Classical
GRAFFMAN: Columbia
HAUTZIG: Americus
JOSELSON: Olympia
KISSIN: DG
KUERTI: IMP Masters
PERAHIA: CBS
POLLINI: DG
RICHTER: Angel
RUBINSTEIN: RCA
WATTS: EMI

Four Impromptus, D. 899 (1827)

No. 1 in C minor is the longest of the set and needs careful planning for its effect. No. 2 in E-flat is extremely popular; brilliant passage-work needed in the right hand leads to a trio of contrasting material. No. 3 in G-flat, writes James Friskin, "is by reason of its melodic inspiration and harmonic magic, a supreme test of the player's power to sing on his instrument." No. 4 in A-flat is one of the best loved of Schubert's piano pieces, "with those poetic garlands of sound," as Curzon called them. Schnabel used to say they made him think of "a dance in the moonlight—with the feet scarcely touching the ground."

BARENBOIM: DG
BRENDEL: Philips: Great Pianists of the Twentieth Century
CURZON (Nos. 3 and 4): London
E. FISCHER: Enterprise Palladio
GIESEKING: Seraphim (LP)
KEMPFF: DG
LIPATTI (Nos. 2 and 3): EMI
PERAHIA: CBS
RUBINSTEIN (Nos. 3 and 4): RCA
SCHNABEL (Nos. 2 and 4): Seraphim
ZIMERMAN: DG

Four Impromptus, D. 935 (1828)

No. 1 in F minor is long. The dialogue with the left hand crossing back and forth is almost Italianate in its bel canto. No. 2 in A-flat is the easiest technically of the eight impromptus, but it requires meticulous phrase punctuation. No. 3 in B-flat is popular, a set of variations of a particularly Viennese cast. No. 4 in F minor is especially difficult in its scale work, staccato, and thirds.

BRENDEL: Philips
BUCHBINDER: Teldec
E. FISCHER: Enterprise Palladio
GIESEKING: Seraphim (LP)
JOEKES: IMP Classics
KEMPFF: DG
LUPU: London
PERAHIA: CBS
POLLINI: DG
SCHIFF: London
R. SERKIN: CBS
YUDINA: Harmonia Mundi
ZIMERMAN: DG

Drei Klavierstücke, D. 946 (1828)

These are impressive pieces, which are now becoming known. They contain much rhythmic and harmonic interest.

BRENDEL: Philips
BUCHBINDER: Teldec
FIRKU_N_: Sugano
GIESEKING: Seraphim
KALISH: Nonesuch

Six Moments musicaux, D. 780

Very subtle phrasing is needed in most of these miniatures. No. 3 in F minor is by far the best known. No. 4 in C-sharp minor consists of passagework of a Bachian tone based on broken chords, with a beautiful middle section, artful in its syncopated rhythm. No. 5 in F minor is chordal. Nos. 2 and 6, both in A-flat, are gems from the deep well of Schubert's lyric genius.

CURZON: London
GILELS: Mobile Fidelity
HAUTZIG: Americus
KEMPFF: DG
LUVISI: Rivergate
SCHNABEL: Angel References

Allegretto in C minor, D. 915 (1827)

All but unknown, this simple five-minute piece, when played well, give one the chills. The pianist Andrew Rangell writes, "This spare and mysterious work, with its many hesitations and its struggle between major and minor tonalities, stands as a singular distillation of Schubert's essential sadness. It seems a haunted leave-taking."

ARRAU: Philips
GOODE: Nonesuch
JOERES: IMP Classics
RANGELL: Dorian
SCHIFF: London
SCHNABEL: EMI

Waltzes

Schubert wrote more than four hundred dances for solo piano. Most of them were waltzes, Ländler, German dances, and the like. These were played by him at gatherings while his friends danced. They are mostly harmonically simple and are usually a student's first encounter with the composer.

The Complete Waltzes:
BORDONI: Seraphim

Waltzes as fillers:
ASHKENAZY (with Schubert's beautiful Hungarian Melody in B minor, D. 817): London
BRENDEL (Twelve German Dances, D. 790; Sixteen German Dances, D. 783): Philips
HAUTZIG: Americus
WATTS: Columbia

ROBERT SCHUMANN
1810–1856—Germany

For contemporary performers, Schumann's great piano cycles, such as the *Carnaval*, *Davidsbündlertänze*, *Kreisleriana*, *Fantasy*, and *Humoreske*, represent one of the supreme tests in the art of the pianist. In these works Schumann weaves a dense contrapuntal tapestry, interlaced with fragmented melody. No

other music ever sounded like his, and it even looked different on the printed page.

Schumann has fared especially well since the invention of the long-playing recording, which has shaped a new listener better able to cope with Schumann's wide-ranging forms. Through this medium, one has the means to listen over and over to Schumann's highly personal and psychological formal shapes. It takes many hearings to travel through the webs of, say, the *Humoreske* or *Novelletten*. In the past, pianists would often program parts of Schumann's cycles; for example, several of the *Fantasiestücke* Op. 12, or a group of the *Davidsbündlertänze*, or two or three of the *Kreisleriana*. That is now becoming rarer. Indeed, pianists are now including Schumann's five variation outcasts from the *Symphonic Etudes*.

For the pianist, Schumann is often a difficult riddle to solve. More than with any

Robert Schumann by David Dubal

603

other Romantic master, the interpreter needs to be a true re-creator and must possess a special empathy for Schumann the man and troubled creator. Often, the deeper the pianist goes into the "twilight zone" of Schumann's imagination, the deeper he or she may get tangled within the labyrinth. It must never be forgotten that Schumann throughout his life was desperately holding back the gates of madness. Public performance of his music is always problematic. His art is so unpublic, and although his music is often technically difficult, there is never a shred of virtuosity or easy appeal. Roland Barthes feels that

the piano as a social instrument has undergone for a century a historical evolution of which Schumann is the victim. The human subject has changed: intimacy and solitude have lost their value, the individual has become increasingly gregarious, he wants collective, massive, often paroxysmal music, the expression of *us* rather than of *me*; yet Schumann is truly the musician of solitary intimacy, of the amorous and imprisoned soul that *speaks to itself* . . . of the child who has no other link than to the mother. . . . To play Schumann implies an innocence very few artists can attain. . . . Schumann lets his music be fully heard only by someone who plays it, even badly. . . . It is because Schumann's music goes much farther than the ear; it goes into the body, into the muscles through its rhythm. . . . It is as if on each occasion the piece was written only for one person, the one who plays it; the true Schumannian pianist—*c'est moi*.

It is a pity that some of Schumann's most radical thoughts were watered down by his own hand in final revisions, years after the outpourings of the early manifestations of his genius. Charles Rosen writes, "Many of them came out of the revising process badly mauled. If anyone except Schumann himself had done

this work, these revisions would be repudiated today with indignation."

More often than not, performers use the last edition of Schumann. But, as Rosen states: "With a composer like Schumann, terrified of insanity . . . the changes are, almost without exception, deplorable. . . . One might say that Schumann misunderstood his own genius, at least at moments when he lacked confidence . . . he sometimes attempted to remove from his own scores those qualities most idiosyncratic, to attenuate everything which made him so different from his contemporaries."

It remains incumbent upon Schumann interpreters to compare Schumann's original versions.

Schumann's career as a pianist was demolished when his fourth finger became partially paralyzed after he used a contraption to strengthen it. He composed for the piano, however, a body of music of the utmost beauty and originality.

From the age of twenty, Schumann's genius glowed for ten years. The piano was his sole friend, and to it he poured out the most susceptible soul of any of the Romantics. He invented the Romantic piano suite, the tying together of smaller musical units into a large form, such as the *Carnaval, Papillons*, or *Kinderscenen*. Like many Romantics', his music has literary implications and, in his case, a fierce autobiographical content.

Schumann was a complex man with more than one personality. He has been called the most Romantic of the Romantics. His music formed the springtime of German Romanticism. His early piano works, wrote Daniel Gregory Mason:

conceived with most daring originality and executed with inimitable verve . . . rank with . . . the very supreme and perfect attainments of the Romantic spirit in music. Their exuberant vitality, their prodigal wealth of melodic invention, their rhythmic vigor and harmonic luxuriance, their absolutely novel pianistic effects, their curious undercurrent of fanciful imagery and extramusical allusion, the peculiarly personal, even perverse, idiom in which they are couched, all conspire to make them unique even among their author's works, and in some respects more happily representative of him than the later productions in which he was more influenced by conventional or borrowed ideals. In them we have the wild-flavored first fruits of his genius, fresh with all the aroma and bloom of unsophisticated youth.

Variations on the Name Abegg, Op. 1 (1830)

The *Abegg* Variations is an astonishing opus one. In four variations and a finale, the piano writing reflects something of Weber and Hummel. Yet enough magic is displayed so that the work is frequently played. It already contains the characteristic Schumann in embryo.

ARRAU: Philips
ESCHENBACH: Philips: Great Pianists of the Twentieth Century
GINZBURG: Melodiya
HASKIL: Philips: Great Pianists of the Twentieth Century
KEENE: Photone
KISSIN: RCA
RICHTER: DG

Papillons, Op. 2 (1831)

The first of Schumann's character suites; his youthful imagination soars. In this eleven-minute score of twelve tiny dance movements, Schumann is on his chosen path, fiercely inspired by literature—in this case, his beloved Jean Paul Richter, whose novels Schumann

typically credits with teaching him more counterpoint than any theoretical treatise. "The clamour of the carnival dies away, the clock in the tower strikes six," is written on the last line of the score. The dancers disappear to Schumann's striking pedal effect.

ARRAU: Philips
CORTOT: Biddulph
EGOROV: EMI
HORSZOWSKI: Thésis
KEMPFF: London
LICAD: Sony Classical
PERAHIA: CBS
RICHTER: EMI Classics
SCHIFF: Denon
SOFRONITSKY: Melodiya

Six Studies after Caprices by Paganini, Op. 3 (1832)

Based on the Paganini Caprices for solo violin. These pieces are interesting, difficult, and almost never played. Teachers might use these with profit instead of, say, the usual Czerny studies.

DEMUS: Nuova Era
FRANKL: Vox

Intermezzi, Op. 4 (1832)

Composed when Schumann was twenty-two, this is a neglected and significant work, living in the shadow of the more famous cycles. It throbs with the true Schumann spirit. Each of the five pieces is in song form with trio. They must be played as a cycle.

BASHKIROV: Melodiya (LP)
DEMUS: Nuova Era
ESCHENBACH: DG
JOHANNESEN: Golden Crest (LP)

Impromptus on a Theme of Clara Wieck, Op. 5 (1833; revised 1850)

This set of variations has never found much favor, and it is played even less than Op. 4. Anyone thinking of working on this composition should examine the first version, which is vastly more original and inspired than Schumann's final thoughts.

COLLARD: Connoisseur Society
JANIS: Mercury
ROSEN: Nonesuch

Davidsbündlertänze, Op. 6 (1837)

The title literally means "Dances of the League of David." (Actually, few of these are dances.) Schumann and his friends were "Davidites," as they called themselves, waging war against Philistinism. Robert Haven Schauffler suggests the pieces be called "Eighteen Studies in the Psychology of Autobiography." Schumann affixed to each piece an "F" or an "E": if proud and passionate, it was the production of the Florestan side of his nature; if pensive and dreamy, it was Eusebius emerging. The Op. 6 is pure, unalloyed Schumann, a helter-skelter work of whimsy and tenderness. His heart is sensitive and easily wounded. On the title page are the words "Delight is linked with pain forever and ever." Schumann wrote to Clara Wieck that the pieces "originated in the most joyful excitement that I can ever recall. . . . If ever I was happy at the piano, it was while composing these."

ARRAU: Philips
ARTYMIW: Chandos
COOPER: Ottavo
CORTOT: Biddulph

FIRKUSNY: Sugano
GIESEKING: Forlane
PERAHIA: CBS
ROSE: Monarch
ROSEN: Nonesuch
SCHEIN: Ivory Classics

Toccata in C major, Op. 7 (1833)

This is one of the wonder works in the double-note literature. The Toccata is indispensable; no pianist should avoid working at it. Its structure is a modified sonata-allegro design, bracing and energetic. Schumann had first composed it in the key of D, but transposed it to C, in which, as he said, it was "no longer so wild, but much better behaved." Clara Wieck Schumann called it the Toccata of Toccatas—"Toccata Toccatarium." The work is a colorful amplification of the Czerny Toccata. These days it is not played as much as it once was when Lhévinne, Hofmann, and Barère thrilled audiences with it.

BARÈRE: APR
BUNIN: Meloydia
EGOROV: EMI
FRANÇOIS: Philips: Great Pianists of the Twentieth Century
GILELS: History
GINZBURG: Melodiya
HOROWITZ: EMI
LHÉVINNE: Dante
NAT: EMI
RICHTER: DG

Allegro in B minor, Op. 8 (1831)

Occasionally dusted off by pianists, the Allegro is self-conscious and difficult technically, but contains a great deal of fanciful music.

DE LARROCHA: London
FEINBERG: Melodiya (LP)
HAIRGROVE: Bayer
SKOUMAL: STMA

Carnaval, Op. 9 (1834–35)

Carnaval is subtitled "Scenes mignonnes sur quatre notes." This suite is Schumann's most frequently played large work. The richness of its material and pulsating life make it one of the great half hours of human fantasy. *Carnaval* is composed of twenty pieces, opening with a preamble and closing with a march in 3/4 time, and presents us with a scene of perpetual youth, the Davidsbund against the Philistines. At the Carnival, Schumann meets Pierrot, Pantalon and Columbine, Harlequin, Chiarina (the sixteen-year-old Clara Wieck—not yet his wife), and his current romantic interest, Estrella (Ernestine von Fricken—whose native town, Asch, is spelled with four letters which are also in Schumann's name and which correspond to the four notes that the work is based on: A, E-flat, C, and B [German A, Es, C, and H]). Schumann himself makes a dual appearance as Florestan and Eusebius (the two opposing sides of his nature). Paganini appears in a violinistic movement of treacherous difficulty. Chopin shows up in heated nocturne style, and so forth. In this great orgiastic ballroom scene, Schumann reveals his secrets to his assembled friends and lovers.

HESS: Philips: Great Pianists of the Twentieth
   Century
MICHELANGELI: DG
NOVAES: Turnabout
RACHMANINOFF: RCA
RUBINSTEIN: RCA
SOFRONITSKY: Melodiya
SOLOMON: Testament

Twelve Concert Etudes after Caprices of Paganini, Op. 10 (1833)

Schumann said, "These Etudes are of the greatest difficulty throughout, every one in a different way." Of this set, Op. 10, No. 2, was also transcribed by Liszt. Schumann here expands his vision of transcription from his Op. 3 series and gives himself far more freedom in adapting the Caprices to the piano.

DEMUS: Nuova Era
FRANKL: Vox

Sonata in F-sharp minor, Op. 11 (1835)

The sonata is in four movements totaling thirty-five minutes. The introduction radiates Romantic beauty; the slow movement, an Aria, is filled with yearning. Throughout the other movements, there is much infectious gaiety. On the title page is a dedication to Clara with a note stating that the sonata was composed by Florestan and Eusebius. When Liszt played the work to Schumann in 1840, the composer reported that his performance "moved me strangely. Although his reading differed in many places from my own." . . . Clara Schumann performed it as early as 1837, and Brahms did so in 1867. Anton Rubinstein, Paderewski, and Josef Hofmann were great advocates of this work. To say that it is one of the most problematic compositions in the Romantic literature would be to understate its myriad problems of organization, not the least of which is to maintain an audience's interest through the compositional maze. From the great introduction, with its trembling of the soul, throughout, the score is fantastic, poetic, thrilling.

ANDSNES: EMI
ARRAU: Philips
BERMAN: Columbia/Melodiya
CIANI: Dynamic
DEMIDENKO: Hyperion
GILELS: History
GRIMAUD: Denon
KALICHSTEIN: Audiofon
POLLINI: Philips: Great Pianists of the
    Twentieth Century
ROSEN: Globe

BRENDEL: Philips
GULDA: Philips
JOHANNESEN: Golden Crest (LP)
PERAHIA: Sony Classical
RUBINSTEIN: RCA
STARR: Orion (LP)

Fantasiestücke, Op. 12 (1837)

One of Schumann's most popular collections, and the epitome of German Romanticism. The eight pieces are: (1) *Des Abends* ("In the Evening")—Schumann lulls us on a fragrant spring evening, using cross-rhythms. (2) *Aufschwung* ("Soaring")—passionate optimism; the Florestan part of his nature is fully exhibited. (3) *Warum?* ("Why?")—one of Schumann's most poetic pieces. (4) *Grillen* ("Whims")—the tempo marking says only "with humor," and its humor is uniquely Schumann's. (5) *In der Nacht* ("In the Night")—Schumann said the piece contains the story of Hero and Leander. *In der Nacht* is one of the glorious pages in Schumann's output. It is also technically demanding. (6) *Fabel* ("Fabel")—a whimsical piece with alternating moods. (7) *Traumeswirren* ("Dream Visions")—filled with gorgeous patterns, and one of Schumann's most difficult pieces, calling for strong fingers and good rotation. (8) *Ende vom Lied* ("Song's End")—Schumann wrote to Clara, "At the close my painful anxiety about you returned, so that it sounds like wedding- and funeral-bells commingled."

ARGERICH: CBS; Angel
ARRAU: Philips
AX: RCA
BAUER: History

Symphonic Etudes, Op. 13 (1834)

The *Symphonic Etudes* were also called by Schumann *Etudes en forme de variations.* They are based on a somber theme of great elegiac beauty, composed by Baron von Fricken, an amateur flutist and the father of Schumann's first fiancée. (Etudes 3 and 9 and the finale are not derived from this theme.) This is Schumann at his most brilliant, dazzling in its splendor and sonority, making harsh technical demands. Brahms was deeply affected by the *Etudes,* and they are the inspiration for his own *Handel* and *Paganini* Variations. Fauré, also, modeled his Theme and Variations, Op. 73, on them. The last etude, a regal finale, is built from a theme in Heinrich Marschner's opera *Der Templer und die Jüdin.* Schumann warned Clara not to play the whole work in public, because of its length. Indeed, he suppressed five variations, which were later published posthumously and which are now often included by contemporary pianists. Although Schumann's instinct was to pare down the work for the overall good of the form, the material of these additional etudes is of such astounding beauty that not to include them is to deprive the listener of the fullness of Schumann's treatment. The work is dedicated to the English composer William Sterndale Bennett, who reported to Schumann that he played it successfully in England; however, the work began coming into its own in performances by Anton Rubinstein.

ANDA: DG
ARRAU: Pearl

ARRAU: Philips
ASHKENAZY: London
GRAINGER: Philips (Australia); Biddulph
GRINBERG: Melodiya
HESS: Philips: Great Pianists of the Twentieth
  Century
NOVAES: Turnabout
PERAHIA: CBS
POLLINI: DG
WEISSENBERG: Connoisseur Society (LP)
OKASHIRO: Pro Piano

Sonata in F minor, Op. 14 (1836)

Schumann originally called the second of his three sonatas *Concerto sans orchestre*. It is in four movements, the third being an Andantino—a set of four variations on a theme by Clara Wieck. The work is the least known of Schumann's sonatas, but it is as inspired as the others. Arthur Loesser states, "It seems to me that Op. 14 is more consistent, more even, in quality than Op. 22. It is an outstanding ebullition of German Romanticism, bursting with excess visceral emotion, now fiery, now dreamy." Unfortunately, it has become a commonplace among critics to call the F minor Sonata the inferior sister of the F-sharp minor and G minor sonatas. This great work is scandalously neglected.

COLLARD: Connoisseur Society
HOROWITZ: RCA
KUERTI: London
LOESSER: International Piano Archives (LP)
ROSE: Monarch

Kinderscenen (Scenes of Childhood), Op. 15 (1838)

Since their creation, these thirteen pieces have been played around the world, by virtuosi and amateurs alike. No. 7 is one of the all-time favorite melodies, *Träumerei* ("Dreaming"). Alban Berg once analyzed the piece, showing how complex it actually is. Schumann wrote to Clara that "these scenes are peaceful, tender and happy, like our future. . . . You will enjoy them; but of course, you have to forget that you are a virtuoso." Each piece is touched with refinement and tenderness and shows the restraint Schumann was capable of in his youth.

HOROWITZ: CBS
KEMPFF: DG
LUPU: Philips: Great Pianists of the Twentieth
  Century
SCHNABEL: Naxos

Kreisleriana, Op. 16 (1838)

These eight untitled fantasies, running to thirty-five minutes, are dedicated to Chopin, who abhorred Schumann's music. Schumann wrote, "Kreisler is a creation of E. T. A. Hoffmann's, an eccentric, wild, clever conductor. You will like much about him." For the uninitiated, this may be Schumann's most bewildering maze of fragments and textures. After finishing the work, he wrote, "My music now seems to me so wonderfully complicated, for all its simplicity, so eloquent from the heart." The *Kreisleriana* vibrates with disturbing and mysterious chords. Here are the composer's darker aspects, yet Schumann combines them, as only Schumann can, with a childlike innocence that goes deeper than even the *Kinderscenen*. Never has a poet so poured out his heart. To Clara he said, "Play my *Kreisleriana* once in a while. In some passages there is to be found an utterly wild love, and your life and mine."

ARGERICH: DG
ARRAU: Philips
ASHKENAZY: London

CHERKASSKY: Nimbus
CORTOT: Biddulph
DE LARROCHA: London
EGOROV: Peters
GIESEKING: Forlane
HOROWITZ: CBS; DG
MOISEIWITSCH: Decca (LP)
PERLEMUTER: Nimbus
RUBINSTEIN: RCA
SOFRONITSKY: Melodiya

FLIER: Melodiya
GIMPEL: Genesis
GOODE: Nonesuch
HOROWITZ (Carnegie Hall comeback): Sony
    Classical
PERAHIA: Sony Classical
POLLINI: DG
RICHTER: Angel
RUBINSTEIN: RCA
SOFRONITSKY: Melodiya (LP)

Fantasia in C major, Op. 17 (1836)

Dedicated to Franz Liszt, in three movements, the Fantasy is universally regarded as a towering achievement in Romantic art. Harold Bauer wrote, "It would be hard to point to any composition in the entire literature of the piano wherein an expression of intense personal feeling is projected with such compelling and vivid power." In the Fantasy, Schumann has reached the very essence of his genius. Schumann himself thought he "had never composed anything as impassioned as this first movement." The second movement, March, is one of the most majestic pages in Schumann. It demands a big mechanism and powerful chord playing and is famous for its skips in the coda. Of this coda, William Newman writes, "One can take a transcendental approach; one can throw oneself into the laps of the gods while gambling on superhuman effort!" The finale, a slow movement is one of the most beautiful meditations in music. On the title page of the score is a motto by the poet Friedrich von Schlegel: "Through all the varied sounds which fill the world's many-colored dreams, one whispered tone may be barely heard for those who listen in secret."

ARGERICH: CBS; Angel
BACKHAUS: Andante
BASHKIROV: Melodiya
CIANI: Dynamic

Arabeske in C major, Op. 18 (1839)

The Arabeske is very well known and not terribly difficult. This piece was once played to death by parlor pianists. It is the most Mendelssohnian-sounding of all Schumann's piano music, and the Victorian and Edwardian English loved it. Its suave opening theme is unforgettable, and Schumann conceives a rondo-type form that is fascinating.

DE GREEF: Pearl
GILELS: Music and Arts
HOROWITZ: Sony
KEMPFF: DG
KISSIN: Sony Classical
MOGILEVSKY: Pavane
MORAVEC: Nonesuch
NAT: EMI
NOVAES: Turnabout
RUBINSTEIN: RCA
SCHIFF: Denon

Blumenstück, Op. 19 (1839)

The title means "Flower Piece." It is a pleasant sectional lyric work, but not one of Schumann's greater pieces. Still, it is not difficult and is a good place for students to explore Schumann's style.

ASHKENAZY: London
BUNIN: Melodiya
HOROWITZ: Sony Classical

Humoreske, Op. 20 (1839)

It is becoming apparent that this long and loosely made work is one of the Schumann's finest scores. The composer called it "the Great Humoreske." It is in six sections without interruption. For years, Sviatoslav Richter's performance taught pianists what this work could be like in the hands of a creative interpreter. The younger generation is now realizing the *Humoreske*'s potency, vernal freshness, and effectiveness in the concert hall (though it lasts nearly half an hour). The title highlights only the humorous aspects of the work, but many emotions are revealed in this superb creation.

ARRAU: Philips
ASHKENAZY: London
AX: RCA
DAVIDOVICH: Philips
GOODE: Nonesuch
HOROWITZ: RCA
NAT: EMI
RICHTER: Monitor
SCHIFF: Denon
SHEIN: Ivory Classics

Novelletten, Op. 21 (1838)

Of these eight works, Schumann said, "They are intimately interrelated, were written with enormous zest, are by and large gay and superficial, with the exception of places where I got right down to fundamentals." Actually, they play better in groups or separately. No. 8 in F-sharp minor is long, discursive, and simmers with hot passion; it is one of Schumann's most characteristic works, in two sections connected

by a poetic passage that Schumann marked "Voice from Afar." All the Novelettes are masterful. No. 4 is an exuberant, syncopated waltz, and No. 5 is an animated polonaise.

ARRAU: Philips
BLOCK: Pro Piano
WEBSTER: Dover (LP)

Sonata in G minor, Op. 22 (1830–38)

In four movements, this is the most concise of the sonatas, a work of vintage Schumann. In the first movement one finds his celebrated tempo markings, beginning with "As fast as possible." In the coda, he urges the performer to go "faster," and finally, he demands "still faster." The Andantino is one of Schumann's loveliest lyrical pages, followed by a miniature scherzo. The finale is based on a broken octave theme and is squarer in proportion than the original Presto passionato finale which it replaced. As a whole, the G minor is the easiest of Schumann's sonatas to give an adequate performance of.

ARGERICH: Philips: Great Pianists of the
    Twentieth Century
ARRAU: Philips
BERMAN: Columbia/Melodiya (LP)
GRAINGER: Pearl
LEVITZKI: Pearl
PERAHIA: Sony Classical
RICHTER: Angel
RYCE: Everest (LP)

Nachtstücke, Op. 23 (1839)

These are in C major, F major, D-flat major, and again F major. This last is by far the best known of the four, with its purity and melodic charm.

ARRAU: Philips
GILELS: Mobile Fidelity
HOROWITZ (Nos. 3 & 4): RCA

Faschingsschwank aus Wien, Op. 26 (1837)

The title means "Carnival Jest (Prank) from Vienna." The work contains five movements; the longest is the first, marked "Allegro." It is a chain of loosely developed ideas, one of which is Schumann's sly use of the *Marseillaise,* which was illegal in Vienna, where he composed the piece. There is an introspective, wistful Romanze; a purely Schumannish Scherzino; and the finest movement, a turbulent song without words, Intermezzo in E-flat minor. The finale is in sonata form, parading a carnival atmosphere. The work falls just short of Schumann's best.

BARENBOIM: DG
DAVIS: Audiofon
MICHELANGELI: DG; Testament
RICHTER: EMI Classics

Three Romances, Op. 28 (1838)

Schumann thought highly of the Three Romances, but only the luscious No. 2 in F-sharp major ever achieved renown. Nos. 1 and 3 are interesting but somewhat dry.

ARRAU: Philips
KEMPFF: DG
NAT: EMI

Scherzo, Gigue, Romance, and Fughetta, Op. 32 (1839)

These are bits of choice Schumann. They would be the last piano works of the furi-ously productive first decade of Schumann's twenty-year creative life. After his marriage in 1840, he turned to writing songs, making use of the piano in a masterly way. Later, his piano writing would be more interesting in his chamber works than in his solo piano music. Some of the spirit and most of the adventure vanished, and Schumann's deepening interest in Bach and counterpoint produced such monotonous works as the Four Fugues, Op. 72, and several works for the now obsolete pedal piano. There are also the fairly interesting Four Marches, Op. 76.

DEMUS: Nuova Era
GILELS: Music and Arts

Album for the Young, Op. 68

These are forty-three pieces with wonderful titles, the greatest of children's musical storybooks, and the prototypes for countless children's pieces since. All that is lovable and tenderhearted in Schumann's nature is found here. Youngsters should start playing them as soon as possible. Adults find them rather harder to play than they look on the page.

DEMUS: Nuova Era
ENGEL: Telefunken (LP)
FRANKL: Vox
LEVY: Nimbus
WEISSENBERG: EMI

Waldscenen, Op. 82 (1849)

Nine "Forest Scenes" of moderate difficulty. The most inspired is No. 7, *The Prophet Bird,* which has gained popularity on its own. This set is filled with many reminders of earlier Schumann. Of less importance in Schumann's output is the set of Fourteen Pieces, Op. 99, called *Bunte Blätter* ("Colored Leaves"). The collection covers an assortment of pieces from 1839 through 1849. Richter and Haskil have recorded them.

ARRAU: Philips
BACKHAUS: London
GIESEKING: Music and Arts
HASKIL: Philips
KATSARIS: Teldec
KEMPFF: DG
P. SERKIN: RCA (LP)

Fantasiestücke, Op. 111 (1851)

There are flashes here of Schumann at his best. Unlike Op. 12, the pieces are untitled. They make a good group. No. 1 is stormy; No. 2, lyric; No. 3, a march.

In 1853 he wrote *Three Sonatas for the Young,* Op. 118. There are also the *Albumblätter,* Op. 124, a collection of twenty pieces from various years. Here and there, the old Schumann shines through. Op. 126 contains seven pieces in fughetta form that are dry and rather boring. Although 1853 was a year of anguish for Schumann, his contrapuntal craft is astonishing. Schumann's swan song from that year—*Gesänge der Frühe* ("Songs of Dawn"), Op. 133—has touching moments. He composed a bit after 1853. There is a Theme and Variations, without opus number. Schumann told people that the theme was dictated to him by angels. But thereafter the angels turned into devils, as Schumann drifted into complete madness.

ARRAU: Philips
HOROWITZ: RCA

Piano Concerto in A minor, Op. 54 (1845)

The Schumann Concerto is a staple of the repertoire. It is perfect music, of beauty and lucidity, a classic of the concerto literature. Schumann is mellow, serene, and joyous, with none of the mental turmoil evident in the earlier poetic cycles. There is not a superfluous note in the score. The Concerto eschews virtuosity for its own sake. Schumann wrote to Clara, "I cannot write a concerto for virtuosi; I must think of something else." Schumann also composed for piano and orchestra a *Konzertstück* in G major, Op. 92, a very pretty work which is not as difficult as the first movement of the A minor Concerto. The *Introduction and Allegro* in D minor, Op. 134, has some vigor and strength of ideas.

KOVACEVICH, Davis/BBC Symphony: Philips
FIRKUSNY, Froment/Luxembourg Radio: Turnabout (LP)
HASKIL, Van Otterloo/The Hague Philharmonic: Philips
HESS, Schwartz/Philharmonia: Philips: Great Pianists of the Twentieth Century
ISTOMIN, Walter/Columbia Symphony: CBS
LIPATTI, Galliera/Philharmonia: Odyssey
LUPU, Previn/London Symphony: London
RUBINSTEIN, Giulini/Chicago Symphony: RCA
R. SERKIN, Ormandy/Philadelphia: Sony Classical
SOLOMON, Menges/Philharmonia: EMI
ZIMERMAN, Karajan/Berlin Philharmonic: DG

ALEXANDER SCRIABIN
1872–1915—Russia

Scriabin was widely discussed during his lifetime. He appealed to a fin de siècle public receptive to the newest movements in the art world. Through his own mercurial playing, which was blessed with a delectable and rarefied sense of rubato, his newest music was accepted instantly.

While in his thirties, he became enmeshed in esoteric, mystic ideas, which harmonized with his highly ecstatic nature. He wrote, "I am transported with gladness that is in me. If the world could only partake of an atom of the joy that is mine, the world would suffocate in bliss."

In his last years, Scriabin believed that he was a messiah and that through his music (a final incantation was to be called *The Mysterium*) a new and higher world order would appear. He said, "I shall not die, I shall suffocate in ecstasy after *The Mysterium*." Unfortunately, he died at forty-three, with only sketches for the culminating work written. After his death, his art suffered an eclipse as his philosophic ideas became increasingly unattractive. The impending Russian Revolution, with its populist cultural climate, did not look kindly upon his egomania or his innovative harmonic system. Outside of Russia, the young emigrés, Prokofiev and Stravinsky, took center stage. In Germany, musical composition was assuming a neo-Classic stance, and Schoenberg's twelve-tone method would soon influence many young composers. The great Scriabin players, Heinrich Neuhaus and Vladimir Sofronitsky, were contained within Russian frontiers, and his early advocates, Rachmaninoff, Josef Hofmann, and Arthur Rubinstein, who gave the London premiere of the Fifth Sonata, soon abandoned his work. Very little was written about him in English after his death, save by Alfred J. Swan and by Eaglefield Hull, who perceived him as "the most remarkable spiritual phenomenon in all music." No full-length biography appeared until Faubion Bowers published one in 1970.

Fortunately, Horowitz, who was taken to play for Scriabin as a boy, sustained an interest in him, and during a protracted sabbatical he began learning more of his work. Horowitz has said, "Scriabin is super-Romantic, super-sensuous, super-everything." Scriabin's music, wrote Wilfrid Mellers, "depends on the pedal effects of the modern grand piano, which dominates all Scriabin's musical thought."

From Op. 1 through approximately Op. 28, Chopin was his predominant influence. "But Scriabin," as Swan attests "is far from being a mere imitator. He is Chopin's rightful successor, and, as such, carries to an extreme certain peculiarities of Chopin's style. What lay in the background with Chopin comes to the fore in Scriabin: the music grows in nervousness; the tissue becomes closer and more compact, the writing neater and more scrupulous than even Chopin's. . . . But above all it is the prevalence of soaring ecstatic moods that unveils the true Scriabin from his Chopinesque coverlet."

The works from Op. 30, the Fourth Sonata, through the Fifth Sonata, Op. 53, may be called his middle period. The music is more languorous and erotic, the pianism more widely spaced, while major and minor triads appear less and less as he constructs harmony

Alexander Scriabin by David Dubal

in quartal blocks. Yet his ninth chords in all their modifications are still basically treated as dominant harmony waiting patiently to be resolved into the home key. After the Fifth Sonata, however, key centers almost totally disappear, and the composer dispenses with key signatures. The music now dissolves into atonality, the idiom becoming ever more incandescent, intoxicated, and fevered. The music speaks of secret rites and fabulous sins. Pulsations and convulsions mark the rubatoed meter. The composer's favorite word was "sensations." From the Sixth Sonata till the end of his life, his work changed from the heightened eroticism of the ecstatic Third, Fourth, and Fifth Sonatas to a music influenced by his theosophical-mystic beliefs. The music now possesses an excruciating longing, a suffering to withdraw from the body, a desire to leave the flesh, to merge his incandescent spirit into the universe. He uses fire as a symbol of laceration and purity. In *Vers la Flamme,* the Tenth Sonata, Flamme sombre, he purges his spirit which necessitated his own unique harmonic system which found its ultimate expression in the Five Preludes, Op. 74. I believe the composer had said all he was capable of expressing.

Except for a single piano concerto and five symphonies, Scriabin's music is all for piano solo. There are upward of two hundred pieces, including ninety preludes (generally very short), twenty-seven etudes, twenty-three mazurkas, twenty poems (with various names attached), nine impromptus, five waltzes, four nocturnes, ten sonatas, several concert pieces (of which the longest is the Fantasy, Op. 28), and various pieces with descriptive titles.

Etude in C-sharp minor, Op. 2, No. 1

Composed when he was fourteen years old, this Andante is one of Scriabin's best-known pieces. It is richly colored and already shows his passionate nature.

HOROWITZ: Sony Classical; DG
NAOUMOFF: Thésis
SOFRONITSKY: Melodiya

Ten Mazurkas, Op. 3 (1893)
Nine Mazurkas, Op. 25 (1899)
Two Mazurkas, Op. 40 (1904)

Nine of the ten mazurkas of Op. 3 are in minor keys. The content is gracious, with some commonplace material; they are strongly influenced by Schumann and Chopin. The Nine Mazurkas are far more Scriabinic—tense, miniature dance poems, capricious and fragile.

CHAPLAN (Op. 3, Op. 25, Op. 40): Mandala
FEINBERG (Op. 3; Op. 25): Melodiya (LP)
B. LONG (Op. 3, Op. 25, Op. 40): Naxos
SOFRONITSKY (Op. 25, Nos. 3, 7, and 8; Op. 40): Melodiya (LP)

Allegro appassionato in E-flat minor (1787–92)

Heavy-handed, with some interesting color, this work is important because in it a Lisztian influence breaks through in Scriabin's harmonic thinking.

PONTI: Vox

Twelve Etudes, Op. 8 (1895)

One of the finest late-nineteenth-century sets of concert etudes. They present many technical demands and contain polyrhythms. The best of the set are No. 2 in F-sharp minor; No. 3,

Tempestoso in B minor; No. 4, Piacevole in B major; the well-known No. 5 in E; the furious No. 7 in B-flat minor; and No. 9 in G-sharp minor, the crowning work of the set. The longest of these etudes, marked "Alla ballata," it exploits octave passages. No. 10 in D-flat is famous for its right-hand double notes. No. 11 in B-flat minor is a "touch" study of Russian melodic beauty. No. 12 in D-sharp minor, marked "Patetico, " is Scriabin's most famous work; its rhapsodic declamation never fails to thrill. Louis Biancolli wrote, "Whoever plays it feels momentarily like a god. To have composed that etude is to have married the piano." The writer Henry Miller, after hearing Scriabin in Paris, wrote, "It was like a bath of ice, cocaine and rainbows! For weeks I went about in a trance."

ESTRIN: Newport Classic
HOROWITZ (Nos. 2, 8, and 10–12): CBS
MAGALOFF: Ermitage
MERZHANOV: Melodiya/EMI
SOFRONITSKY (Nos. 2, 4–9, and 11): Melodiya

Eight Etudes, Op. 42 (1904)

Although highly Romantic, these are fine examples of Scriabin's middle period, exhibiting more advanced harmonic schemes and concentrated musical emotion. As studies, they feature irregular cross-rhythms, such as five against three, three against two, four against three. No. 3 is a measured trill study. Marked "Prestissimo," it has often been called *The Mosquito*. No. 4 is a sweet melody with a gentle throb in the accompaniment. The largest in emotional scope is No. 5 in C-sharp minor, marked "Affannato" (breathlessly); it is one of the most smoldering of Scriabin's works, gorgeously colored.

AFRIAT: Forlane

BERMAN: Melodiya (LP)
HOROWITZ (Nos. 3–5): CBS
LAREDO: Nonesuch
RICHTER (Nos. 2–6): Philips: Great Pianists of the Twentieth Century

Three Etudes, Op. 65 (1908)

No. 1 is in ninths, No. 2 in sevenths, and No. 3 in fifths. These are amazing works from his later period. The Richter recording also includes the tiny Presto Etude in 2/8 time, Op. 56, No. 4.

KUERTI: Analekta
RICHTER: Melodiya

Nocturne in D-flat major for the Left Hand Alone, Op. 9, No. 2

A ravishing encore number, long a popular favorite. Scriabin composed it when he injured his right hand trying to outdo Josef Lhévinne. It soon became a Josef Lhévinne specialty. The Prelude in C-sharp minor for Left Hand, Op. 9, No. 1, is not as well known; technically simpler, it has a lyric appeal.

J. C. MARTINS: Labor
S. NEUHAUS: Melodiya

Twenty-four Preludes, Op. 11 (1897)

A high-water mark in early Scriabin, the Preludes represent all sides of the composer's personality in cameo. They follow the circle of fifths and proclaim all the major and minor keys. These remarkable works in Scriabin's Chopinesque manner are a cavalcade of technical finesse and melodic appeal. Rachmaninoff recorded only one piece by his friend Scriabin—the F-sharp minor Prelude No. 8, marked

"Allegro agitato," which he manages to make convincing at a very slow tempo. It is to be found in Volume 2 of his complete recordings.

Twenty-four Preludes:
BACHAUER: Capitol (LP)
DEYANOVA: Nimbus
GAVRILOV: Angel
LAREDO: Phoenix
LEWENTHAL: Westminster (LP)
SOFRONITSKY: Melodiya (LP)
ZUKOV: Melodiya

Other collections of Preludes:
BASHKIROV (eight preludes from Opp. 16, 17, 22, 33, 37): Melodiya
HOROWITZ (Op. 11, Nos. 1, 3, 9, 10, 13, 14, 16; nine others, representing each period): RCA
RUTSTEIN (four preludes from Op. 22): Orion
SOFRONITSKY (sixteen preludes from Opp. 11, 13, 15, 13, 22; four preludes from Op. 31): Melodiya

Five Preludes, Op. 74 (1914)

Scriabin's last music is ominous, painfully intense. Donald Garvelmann wrote, "Opus 74 is psychologically jarring, shattering. All the sadness and troubles of the world are encapsulated in these few pages."

KUERTI: Analekta
LEWENTHAL: Westminster (LP)
S. NEUHAUS: Melodiya (LP)
TAUB: Harmonia Mundi

Fantasia in B minor, Op. 28 (1901)

The Fantasy is a gloriously rich apotheosis of all the Chopinesque and Lisztian elements of Scriabin's early work.

BERMAN: AURC
FEINBERG: Melodiya
H. NEUHAUS: Russian Disc
SOFRONITSKY: Melodiya (LP)
SZIDON: DG

Valse in A-flat major, Op. 38 (1904)

M. Montagu-Nathan describes this waltz as "exquisitely feathered" and says, "We have now to deal rather with a Chopinesque Scriabin, than, as previously, with a Scriabinesque Chopin." The composer asks the pianist to play it "as if you were dreaming."

BASHKIROV: Melodiya (LP)
DAVIDOVICH: Melodiya
WALDOFF: MHS

Two Poems, Op. 32, Nos. 1 and 2 (1904)

No. 1 is one of Scriabin's better-known pieces, a beguiling work. No. 2 is the diabolic Scriabin.

BECKMAN-SCHERBINA (No. 1): Melodiya
HOROWITZ: CBS
SOFRONITSKY: Melodiya

Poème satanique, Op. 36 (1903)

An effective work presenting a false sweetness and ironic insincerity; the diabolic streak in Scriabin comes to the surface in many of his works. Swan says, "Devilish fits continued to pester Scriabin."

SOFRONITSKY: Melodiya; Westminster

Poème tragique, Op. 34 (1904)

The ninth chord with sharpened fifth is characteristic of this period in Scriabin's work. A chordal work with widely spaced figuration in the middle section.

> LEYETCHKISS: Orion
> SOMER: Mercury (LP)

Poème-nocturne, Op. 61 (1913)

A subtle piece in which Scriabin's mysticism and liquid poetry are wrapped in a form of great flexibility. A neglected masterpiece of Scriabin's later manner.

> SOFRONITSKY: Melodiya
> SOMER: Mercury (LP)
> RICHTER: Philips

Two Poems, Op. 69 (1912–13)

Two delicate pieces, both marked simply "Allegretto." Thomas Frost hears "the introverted fantasy, and the solipsism that are typical of Scriabin's mature works."

> HOROWITZ: CBS

Vers la flamme, Op. 72 (1914)

If one had to know only one work of Scriabin's late music, I would recommend the hypnotic *Towards the Flame.* It has often been described as psychedelic. In it, Scriabin was setting his soul on fire, and an acrid odor is suggested. It is surely one of the most powerful of Scriabin's works.

> HOROWITZ: CBS
> S. NEUHAUS: Melodiya

> SOFRONITSKY: Philips: Great Pianists of the Twentieth Century

Two Dances, Op. 73 (1914)

The penultimate works: *Guirlandes* and *Flammes sombres. Garlands* is incomparably beautiful; *Dark Flames* is less turbulent than *Towards the Flame,* but it has an undercurrent of danger.

> ASHKENAZY: Philips
> RICHTER: Philips
> SOFRONITSKY: Philips: Great Pianists of the Twentieth Century

The Ten Piano Sonatas

Scriabin was, at root, a miniaturist, but he attempted to fit his music into an appropriate larger frame. As a harmonist, he was a great innovator. He tried to mold the sonata idea to his formal needs. From the Fifth Sonata through the Tenth, his solution was to shape all elements of the sonata into a one-movement scheme. Mellers wrote that "by 1903 . . . the wealth of higher chromatic discords in Scriabin's music had made [the] sonata form anachronistic. A conflict of keys is impossible unless tonality is at first clearly defined." Aaron Copland feels that the Sonatas are "one of the most extraordinary mistakes in music. . . . The quality of his thematic material was truly individual, truly inspired. But Scriabin . . . had the fantastic idea of attempting to put this really new body of feeling into the straight jacket of the old classical sonata form, recapitulation and all."

Such criticism notwithstanding, Scriabin's ten sonatas are so infused with coloristic sensation, gorgeous figuration, spiritual aspiration, erotic palpitation, and new facets of pianistic resource that they have come to have an honored place in the piano's literature. In addition, they offer a magnificent view of Scriabin's astounding development.

ASHKENAZY (complete sonatas): Philips
B. BERMAN (complete sonatas): Music and Arts
HAMELIN (complete sonatas): Hyperion
LAREDO (complete sonatas): Nonesuch
OGDON (complete sonatas): EMI
SOFRONITSKY (Sonatas Nos. 3–5 and 8–10): Chant du Monde
SZIDON (complete sonatas): DG
TAUB: Harmonia Mundi

Sonata No. 1 in F minor, Op. 6 (1892)

The longest of the sonatas. In four movements, No. 1 concludes with a funeral march. The influence of Tchaikovsky and also Schumann is apparent, but signs of individuality appear throughout, especially in the Presto third movement.

ASHKENAZY: London
BERMAN: Columbia/Melodiya
FIORENTINO: APR
ZHUKOV: Melodiya/Angel (l.p.)

Sonata No. 2—Sonata Fantasy in G-sharp minor, Op. 19 (1892–97)

"The first of its two movements—an Andante," wrote Swan, "is perhaps the most gorgeously fanciful and capricious of all Scriabin's early works. . . . Its melodic elaboration is stupendous: one little melodic wave chases another in poetic playfulness. The accompaniment, thickly woven on broad lines, is all nerve and refinement." The second movement, a Presto,

is much shorter, in triplets, and it sprouts a theme of sweeping impetuousness.

ASHKENAZY: London
BLOCK: Pro Piano
FEINBERG: Melodiya Poco
GEKIC: Palexa
LEWIN: Centaur
PAPERNO: Cedille
RELICH: DG
RICHTER: Arkadia
SOFRONITSKY: Melodiya
ZHUKOV: Melodiya/Angel

Sonata No. 3 in F-sharp minor, Op. 23 (1898)

In four movements; the first, Drammatico, is the hardest of any Scriabin movement to hold together convincingly. Glenn Gould wrote: "It's an expansive and declamatory Sonata-Allegro in which the bittersweet nostalgia of the secondary thematic group is held in check by the foreboding double-dot interpretations of the primary theme's chief rhythmic component. It's "music-to-read-*Wuthering Heights*-by"—a hypnotic, self-centered piece of doom-foretelling."

GOULD: CBS
HOROWITZ: RCA
KISSIN: MK
SOFRONITSKY: Philips: Great Pianists of the Twentieth Century
SOKOLOV: Op. 111

Sonata No. 4 in F-sharp major, Op. 30 (1903)

A masterpiece, the most original of the earlier sonatas. The first of its two movements is a liquid, evanescent, shimmering Andante; the second movement is marked "Prestissimo volando," in 12/8 meter. This vertiginous dance quickens the pulse. It exudes a sexual energy which culminates in jubilant repeated chords, triple fortississimo. A pianist must feel the heated inner core of this music.

ASHKENAZY: Philips
FEINBERG: Melodiya (LP)
GAVRILOV: Angel
RUTSTEIN: Albany
VILLA: Second Hearing
ZHUKOV: Melodiya/Angel

Sonata No. 5 in F-sharp major, Op. 53 (1907)

By the Fifth Sonata, Scriabin begins to purge his art of any outside influences. This sonata, an outgrowth of his Symphony No. 4 (*Poem of Ecstasy*), is a mystic impressionist poem. The most frequently performed in public of the ten sonatas, "the Fifth Sonata," Swan wrote "has been likened to a piece of wizardry, a deed of black magic, illumined by the rays of a black sun. Its impetuosity alternating with a caressing languor, the legerdemain of the Prestos in their radiant mixture of B major and F-sharp major, and the wild orgiastic rhythm of the Allegros, combine to produce an uncanny impression."

ASHKENAZY: Philips
GOULD: Sony Classical
HOROWITZ: RCA
MERZHANOV: Monitor (LP)
RICHTER: DG
SCHUMACHER: Elan
VILLA: Second Hearing
ZHUKOV: Melodiya (LP)

Sonata No. 6, Op. 62 (1911–12)

No. 6 is more involved, complex, and mysterious than its companions. Scriabin never played the work in public; it has been said that he feared it. The premiere was given by Beckman-Scherbina in 1912.

ASHKENAZY: London
KUERTI: Monitor
RICHTER: Melodiya
WOODWARD: Etcetra
ZHUKOV: Melodiya

Sonata No. 7, Op. 64 (1912)

Scriabin loved this creation, which he called *The White Mass*. He considered it holy and played it often. Never had his work had such "lift" or flight. The vibratory qualities of this sonata stem from a magnificent use of trills. Referring to one portion of the piece, Scriabin said, "This is real vertigo!" He beseeches the pianist to play "with radiant and ecstatic voluptuousness." It is one of the most luminous works in the repertoire and, perhaps, the most difficult technically of all Scriabin's sonatas. Near the sonata's end, he writes a twenty-three-note rolled chord.

ASHKENAZY: London
V. BUNIN: Melodiya
PÖNTINEN: BIS
VILLA: Second Hearing
ZHUKOV: Melodiya/Angel

Sonata No. 8, Op. 66 (1913)

The longest of the one-movement sonatas, with two development sections. Donald Garvelmann wrote, "The gorgeous harmonies hypnotize, kaleidoscopic shifting shapes and colors draw us in. . . . The Eighth Sonata is a walk through a crystalline floral labyrinth." It may be difficult to find one's way around, but the view is always bewitching and beautiful.

ASHKENAZY: London
RUDY: Calliope
ZHUKOV: Melodiya/Angel

Sonata No. 9, Op. 68 (1913)

If, for Swan, the Eighth Sonata was "a divine azure vault, the happiest and most careless of inspirations, a phantom woven of delicate cobwebs," then the Ninth Sonata was for him "a veritable picture of Dorian Gray!" Couched in the most hideous, grimacing harmonies, No. 9 was shocking even to Scriabin himself. He called it *The Black Mass*—it expressed for him a falling from grace. In its eight minutes Scriabin compressed all of the dark elements in his being. The Ninth Sonata is, along with the Fourth and Fifth Sonatas, the best known.

ASHKENAZY: Philips
HOROWITZ: Sony Classical
KULESHOV: VAI
SCHUMACHER: Elan
SOFRONITSKY: Melodiya
SOKOLOV: Opus III

Sonata No. 10, Op. 70 (1913)

A blazing spectacle, No. 10 has been dubbed the *Trill* Sonata. The composer called it a Sonata of Insects and said it was "born from the sun." He played the premiere himself in Moscow. The composer asks many things of the performer, one of which is to play in "a sweet drunkenness."

HOROWITZ: Sony Classical
H. NEUHAUS: Melodiya
SOFRONITSKY: Melodiya
VOLODOS: Sony Classical

Concerto in F-sharp minor, Op. 20 (1896)

Often performed by Scriabin, this concerto is in three movements, the middle movement being a simple set of variations. The style is refined, with Scriabin's early brand of nervosity.

ASHKENAZY, Maazel/London Philharmonic: London
BASHKIROV, Kondrashin/USSR Symphony: Melodiya (LP)
NASEDKIN, Svetlanov/USSR Symphony: Melodiya
H. NEUHAUS, Golovanov/Moscow Radio Symphony: Russian Disc
S. NEUHAUS, Dubrovski/USSR Symphony: Melodiya
OHLSSON, Pesek/Czech Philharmonic: Supraphon
RUSKIN, Epstein/MIT Symphony: Pantheon

ROGER SESSIONS
1896–1985—United States

One of the most influential composers in the United States, Sessions has taught two generations of composers, including Milton Babbitt. His music is serious, forceful, and wonderful to practice because of its emotional durability. The composer Andrew Imbrie has said: "Sessions is neither a system builder nor a preserver of inherited values. . . . [His] distrust of both systems and polemics has enabled him to respond to outside influence without becoming eclectic: the increasing influence of Schoenberg can combine with the diminishing influence of Stravinsky without either of them touching the essential quality of Sessions's own language."

Sonata No. 1 (1930)
Sonata No. 2 (1946)
Sonata No. 3 (1965)

The three sonatas are tremendous contributions to the literature. They all offer complicated problems in musicianship and technique. Rebecca La Brecque once said to the composer that she thought No. 1 was the most difficult of the three. Sessions responded: "If I practiced nothing else for two years, I could probably play my Third Sonata. If I practiced nothing else for one year, I could play my Second Sonata. If I wanted to play the First, I would have to be sixteen years old, maybe fourteen, and practice only Czerny, Chopin, and Bach for the next twenty years."

La Brecque adds, "As with all of Sessions's music, the greatest performance problem is the separation of the two to five voices going on at any particular moment." The expressive range of the First Sonata is enormous, and the opening Andante, heartrending. The Second Sonata, wrote Maurice Hinson, "is a challenge to the finest pianist and is probably one of the most important piano sonatas by an American composer of this century." The Second Sonata is the most completely chromatic and insistent in its harmonic tension. La Brecque feels it "is the most direct of the three, and yet has the most potential for being misunderstood. . . . The Second Sonata defies its surroundings, and I've rarely heard a performance by anyone (including me) that has shown the performer to have the courage and the stamina to hold this conflict in balance."

The Third Sonata is the capstone of La Brecque's experiences as a musician; she says that "the Sonata means more to me than any other music I have ever played, heard, or come in contact with." The work is indeed one of the very finest products of Sessions's world.

The Three Sonatas:
HELPS: CRI
LA BRECQUE: Opus One (LP)

Sonata No. 1:
HELPS: CRI (LP)
O'REILLY: Albany

Sonata No. 2:
HELPS: CRI
HODGKINSON: New World

LAWSON: Virgin Classics
MARKS: CRI (LP)

Sonata No. 3:
HELPS: CRI
NABORÉ: Doron
SALWEN: Koch

DMITRI SHOSTAKOVICH
1906–1975—Russia

The most extensively performed Soviet composer of the twentieth century. His greatest works are his symphonies and string quartets. He composed in all genres. Shostakovich was himself an excellent pianist, a classmate of Sofronitsky and Yudina at the St. Petersburg Conservatory.

Twenty-four Preludes, Op. 34 (1932–33)

These miniatures are a gold mine for exploring the many ramifications of Shostakovich's style. They follow the Chopin grouping of using the circle of fifths, and they vary technically from easy to taxing.

BERMAN: DG (LP)
DEYANOVA: Nimbus
HAVLIKOVA: Supraphon
NIKOLAYEVA: Hyperion
VIARDO: Nonesuch
WIKSTROM: Swedish Society

Twenty-four Preludes and Fugues, Op. 87 (1951)

These are Shostakovich's major contribution to the literature of his instrument. In 1950, for the commemoration of the bicentennial of Bach's death, Shostakovich visited Leipzig, where he undertook to write a modern *Well-Tempered Clavier*. His own Twenty-four Preludes and Fugues occupy Volume 40 of the forty-two volumes of his collected works. Another interesting piano piece by Shostakovich is the 1922 *Three Fantastic Dances*, Op. 5. These were once very popular. His Sonata No. 1, Op. 12, is biting and dissonant.

Twenty-four Preludes and Fugues:
NIKOLAYEVA: Hyperion
SHOSTOKOVICH: Melodiya (LP)
WOODWARD: RCA

Selected Preludes and Fugues:
GILELS (Nos. 1, 5, 24): Seraphim
RICHTER (Nos. 4, 12, 14, 1S, 17, 23): Philips

Sonata No. 2 in B minor, Op. 61 (1943)

More conservative than No. 1, the sonata is in three movements, the finale being a set of nine variations.

D'ARCO: MHS
GILELS: RCA (LP)
LEONSKAJA: Teldec
NIKOLAYEVA: Hyperion
RUTSTEIN: Orion (LP)
WIKSTRÖM: Swedish Society
YUDINA: Melodiya (LP)

Piano Concerto No. 1, with Trumpet and Strings, Op. 35 (1933)

This has become one of the best-known piano concertos in the contemporary literature. It blazes with a youthful brazenness and sar-

castic, vulgar flavor, but the slow movement has touching moments. Eugene List gave the American premiere with Stokowski and the Philadelphia Orchestra in 1934.

D'ARCO, Paillard/Paillard Chamber
　Orchestra: MHS
GRINBERG, Rozhdestvensky:
　Westminster (LP)
KISSIN, Spivakov/Moscow Virtuosi: RCA
LIST, M. Shostakovich/Moscow Radio
　Symphony: Columbia/Melodiya
OGDON, Marriner/Academy of St.
　Martin: Argo
OHLSSON, Murphey/Cracow
　Philharmonic: Arabesque
PREVIN, Bernstein/New York
　Philharmonic: CBS
ROSENBERGER, Schwarz/Los Angeles
　Chamber Orchestra: Delos
SHOSTAKOVICH, Cluytens/Orchestre
　National de France: EMI
SHOSTAKOVICH, Cluytens/ORTF: EMI
　Classics

Piano Concerto No. 2, Op. 101 (1957)

This is a capital work on all accounts, not overly difficult, and musically a delight in its three movements. The slow movement's melody is captivating. The finale in 7/8, with a section based on a famous Hanon five-finger exercise, will make the listener smile.

BERNSTEIN, Bernstein/New York
　Philharmonic: CBS
LIST, M. Shostakovich/Moscow Radio
　Symphony: CBS/Melodiya
OGDON, Foster/Royal Philharmonic: Angel
ORTIZ, Ashkenazy/Royal Philharmonic:
　London
SHOSTAKOVICH, Cluytens/ORTF: EMI
　Classics

BEDRICH SMETANA

1824–1884—Czechoslovakia

Smetana is the first truly Czech composer and one of the finest nineteenth-century nationalists. His piano music is hardly touched. It is a small but essential chapter in the panorama. Influenced by Liszt's progressive harmony and programmatic music in general. Smetana was a first-class pianist whose performing career as pianist and conductor ended at age fifty with deafness.

In 1848, when Liszt looked through Smetana's six characteristic pieces, at once he detected the composer's "warm Czech heart." Attracted to the polka, the preeminent Czech dance, which had evolved from around 1820, he composed several sets: the Salon Polkas and Three Poetical Polkas are from the mid-1850s; a more stylized and mature group of polkas are *Memories of Bohemia*. The concert etude, *On the Seashore* (1862), is perhaps his best-known piano piece, virtuosic and bombastic. Finer in thread are the six pieces titled *Dreams*, from 1875, containing some golden ideas such as in *Faded Happiness*.

Smetana's most comprehensive work of nationalism, the Ten Czech Dances, was completed in 1878. In several of them Smetana used authentic folk-tunes. As a group the set is around fifty minutes and is technically difficult and often physically taxing. Rudolf Firkušný noted, "It is as if Smetana, like Beethoven, had been liberated by his deafness from the restrictions of the keyboard as a specific instrument than as simply a medium for his ideas. The Czech Dances are the most personal of all Smetana's piano music, as well as the most determinedly nationalistic; for him, after all, there was no separation between these concepts." They were composed during his last years of silent desolation, yet their general tone is exhilarating.

Ten Czech Dances

No. 1 - *Furiant*: A dance of pride, performed by one man and two women, the Furiant is a dance of vigorous rhythm.

No. 2 - *Slepiuka* (Little Hen): Like most of these dances, they are in ternary form. The piece revels in brilliantly neat passagework at breakneck speed. The humor and verve of the last part is visceral.

No. 3 – *Oves* (Oats or Grain Dance): An actual folk song, telling of a renowned lover. Smetana wrote the opening lines on the score, "I was sowing yesterday and today/ But I won't love you any more, my dearest. No, I won't love you ever again." Smetana takes a bittersweet tune through a variety of moods, always returning to the sadness of love lost.

No. 4 - *Medved* (The Bear): Opens with heavy octaves, showing us the man as hairy as a bear who is rejected by the girl who sings, "I won't marry you, my dear, because you look just like a bear/a bear has hairy legs—you have a cursed heart as well." Smetana's use of the treble of the piano is fascinating.

No. 5 - *Cibulicka* (The Little Onion): A well-known Czech folk song. One of the simpler of these pieces, but with demanding passages asking for heavy chords. Smetana here relies on the melody's familiarity at least to Czech audiences.

No. 6 - *Dupák*: A virtuoso opening with fast octaves and passagework leading to a tune with the words "Wait 'til you're a hundred before you marry;/when you've lost all your teeth/they won't hurt you any more!" The piece ends on the heights of bravura—one of the most difficult of the Dances.

No. 7 – *Hulán* (The Lancer): Here is a plaintive song. "I had a sweetheart; a Lancer was he./ I loved him dearly and gave him my silver ring./Now my Lancer is gone and so is my ring." Smetana brings the tune through several enchanting settings and ends most endearingly and lingeringly before two bright chords finalize the piece.

No. 8 – *Obkrocak:* A dance for two women in polka style where Smetana combines two folksongs, one sung by a farm girl to her geese. Throughout there are pianistic ingenuities.

No. 9 – *Sousedská:* A slow piece which rises to many fortissimo chords with the composer's usual rhymthic impetuosity.

No. 10 – *Skocna* – A jumping dance, Smetana's most famed example of a *skocna* is *The Dance of the Comedians* in his opera *The Bartered Bride*. This example lunges into virtuosity. Smetana's joy runs over. The piece is Czech to the core. It has been said that for a Czech to know the spirit of his homeland all he must do is to listen to Smetana.

The Complete Piano Music:
FIRKUSNY (10 Czech Dances): Vox
REPKOVÁ: CPO

KARLHEINZ STOCKHAUSEN
b. 1928—Germany

Klavierstücke I–XIV

Stockhausen is among the most fascinating experimenters in music. He has composed electronic music, and early in his career he used total serialization. He has written, "In a world bombarded by images the function of music is to awaken the inner man." He has also said, "From time to time I have concentrated again on 'Piano Pieces,' on composing for a single instrument, for ten fingers, with minute nuances of timbres and structures. They are my 'drawings.' " The *Klavierstücke* vary greatly in length—No. III is twenty-seven seconds long, No. VI lasts 25:22 minutes, No. IX is 9:40 minutes, and No. X is 22:19 minutes. Marie-Françoise Bucquet is convincing in her reading of No. IX, played in exactly 9:40 minutes, the same timing as Kontarsky's. She has said, "If I tried to persuade someone that music is time experienced through sound I would choose Stockhausen's *Klavierstück IX*."

BUCQUET (Nos. IX and XI): Philips
A. KONTARSKY (Nos. I–XI): CBS
KÖRMENDI (No. IX): Hungaroton
WAMBACH (complete): Koch Schwann

IGOR STRAVINSKY
1882–1971—Russia

Stravinsky once stated, "Composing begins for me as the feeling of intervals in my fingers." He also made the assumption that "the piano is an instrument of percussion and nothing else." He took an anti-Romantic stance, showing contempt for the cult of the performer, asking for performances of objectivity. Of course, Stravinsky was trying to assure more straightforward performances and a spirit of modernity, as well as a respect for the composer's intentions, which was at a low ebb in the performance practices of his own youth.

Stravinsky's piano music covers a wide range of his stylistic traits, including the Tchaikovskian Russianism displayed in the early Sonata in F-sharp minor (1903), composed ten years before *The Rite of Spring*. In 1908 he continued along a Romantic but leaner vein in the marvelous Four Etudes, Op. 7, which show some of Scriabin's influence. During the next decade, he left the piano for other media. Then, in 1919, he produced the extraordinary *Piano Rag Music,* and in 1921 the artful *Les Cinq Doigts* for young students. He moved from simplicity to the ultimate in pianistic color when he wrote for Arthur Rubinstein the startling *Trois Mouvements de Petrouchka,* based on three scenes from his great ballet score. In the twenties Stravinsky was occupied with his so-called neo-Classical or "back to Baroque" phase. The dry and beautifully modeled Concerto for Piano and Wind Instruments dates from 1924, as does the Piano Sonata, with its decorative Adagietto. The year 1925 saw the publication of the *Sérénade en la,* and 1929, the terse *Capriccio.*

Igor Stravinsky by David Dubal

Another work of shorter duration, based on a twelve-tone row, *Movements* for Piano and Orchestra, stems from 1959. His post-Webern permutations showed his constant sense of experimentation and open-mindedness.

Four Etudes, Op. 7 (1908)

These treats are rather neglected. This is Stravinsky as part of the virtuoso tradition of pianism. No. 1 pits quintuplets against triplets and duplets. No. 2 is a pattern of six against three, six against four, and six against five. No. 3 is a contrasting slow-touch study; and No. 4 in F-sharp major is a volatile study in perpetual motion of legato against staccato.

> JACOBS: Nonesuch
> LEE: Nonesuch (LP)
> OZOLINS: Aquitaine (LP)
> RINGEISSEN: Ades
> WATKINS: ACA

Piano Rag Music (1919)

A dissonant work of serious quality, using ragtime as a basis for Stravinsky's highly sophisticated compositional prowess.

> B. BERMAN: Chandos
> JOHANNESEN: Golden Crest
> JONES: Nimbus
> LEE: Nonesuch (LP)
> LIVELY: DG (LP)
> I. STRAVINSKY: EMI
> TOCCO: Koch

Les cinq doigts (The Five Fingers) (1921)

These are wonderful examples of the use of

limitation. With the melodic material confined within the range of five notes, each piece fits the span of a young student's hand. Full of characteristic twists and turns, they achieve a simple charm.

BIRET: Finnadar (LP)
KARIS: Bridge

Trois mouvements de Petrouchka (1921)

This is a masterpiece. In a good performance it cannot fail—the interest never wanes. The score is dedicated to Rubinstein, who never recorded it, though he played it in public with incomparable panache.

BACHAUER: Mercury (LP)
BIRET: Finnadar (LP)
BRONFMAN: Sony Classical
BUECHNER: Connoisseur Society
CHERKASSKY: Nimbus
LORTE: Chandos
POLLINI: DG
RÁNKI: Telefunken
TORADZE: EMI
WEISSENBERG: Philips: Great Pianists of the Twentieth Century

Sonata (1924)

Ten precious minutes in three movements. The first movement is Bachian counterpoint, the second is ornate. The third is subtle toccata writing, the essence of Stravinskian neo-Classicism. The composer said, "I have used the term *sonata* in its original sense, deriving from the word *sonare,* to sound."

B. BERMAN: Chandos
LEE: Nonesuch (LP)

NÁDAS: Dover (LP)
PETROV: Olympia
RÁNKI: Telefunken (LP)
RINGEISSEN: Ades
P. SERKIN: New World
YUDINA: Harmonia Mundi

Sérénade en la (1925)

The spirit of the Serenade in A echoes that of the eighteenth century. It is one of the important piano works of the 1920s. Stravinsky himself plays the work sympathetically; his opening Hymne is full of life.

B. BERMAN: Chandos
LEE: Nonesuch (LP)
RÁNKI: Telefunken (LP)
P. SERKIN: New World
I. STRAVINSKY: EMI Classics

Concerto for Piano and Winds (1924)

The work was composed for Stravinsky's own use as a pianist. Its dry, nonlegato figures, with ever-changing metrics, are intriguing. Stravinsky's synthesis of piano and wind sound is unique.

BÉROFF, Ozawa/Orchestre de Paris: Angel
CROSSLEY, Salonen/London Sinfonietta: Sony Classical
ENTREMONT, Stravinsky/Columbia Symphony: Columbia
KOVACEVICH, Davis/BBC Symphony: Philips: Great Pianists of the Twentieth Century
LIPKIN, Bernstein/New York Philharmonic: Sony Classical
MAGALOFF, Ansermet/Suisse Romande: London

Capriccio for Piano and Orchestra (1929)

This is a brilliant and highly successful composition. Only Stravinsky could have written it. The piano and orchestra are seamlessly molded together.

> BÉROFF, Ozawa/Orchestre de Paris:
>   Angel
> ENTREMONT, Craft/Columbia
>   Symphony: Sony Classical
> OGDON, Marriner/Academy of St.
>   Martin: Argo (LP)
> I. STRAVINSKY, Ansermet/Concerts
>   Straram: EMI Classics
> TOZER, Jarvi/Swiss Romande Orchestra:
>   Chandos

Movements for Piano and Orchestra (1958–59)

Balanchine created a ballet from this score, which is in five movements. The work is in the intellectual manner of the composer's late works. Here he acknowledges the influence of Webern.

> BÉROFF, Ozawa/Orchestre de Paris:
>   Angel
> CROSSLEY, Salonen/London Sinfonietta:
>   Sony Classical
> ROSEN, Stravinsky/Columbia Symphony:
>   Columbia

Le Sacre du printemps (The Rite of Spring); transcribed for solo piano by Sam Raphling and Dag Achatz)

The great ballet score may be said to be the most influential single work of the first quarter of the century. Raphling wrote his transcription in the early 1970s, and it is a tremendous work of transformation, while also remaining true to the music.

> ACHATZ (Achatz transcription): BIS
> ATAMIAN (Raphling transcription): RCA

KAROL SZYMANOWSKI
1882–1937—Poland

Szymanowski was the most renowned Polish composer of the first half of the twentieth century; his keyboard works are among the finest in his varied output. He was also a persuasive pianist of his own work and has been interpreted by artists of the caliber of Heinrich Neuhaus, Jacob Gimpel, Richter, Arthur Rubinstein, Malcuzynski, Jan Smeterlin, and, most recently, Emanuel Ax. Nevertheless, Szymanowski has never really entered the repertoire in a big way. Possibly this is because his music is difficult to categorize. His earliest music betrays many influences—Chopin, a touch of Brahms, Richard Strauss, and Scriabin, whose piano style he studied as minutely as he did Chopin's. The influence of Reger on his early style can be heard in the dense Prelude and Fugue and the Second Piano Sonata. Szymanowski's middle works, especially the *Masques* and *Métopes,* reveal a rarefied feeling for piano sonority and texture. These tone poems breathe an Oriental atmosphere, with their hypnotic rhythms, floating improvisations, and gossamer textures. For the executant, they lack the severe structural cohesiveness of their model, Ravel's *Gaspard de la nuit,* and they demand an even more highly developed creative imagination.

A third period in Szymanowski's evolution began in the 1920s, with his assimilation of indigenous Polish music in a highly personalized manner. His leading works in this idiom are the Twenty Mazurkas, Op. 50, and the *Symphonie concertante*.

Szymanowski has created a vivid and florid art; his exquisite and capricious pianistic carvings, contemplative lyricism, and soaring line should be examined by pianists looking for a literature of great importance which has been unduly neglected. As Mark Swed has written, "By nursing a Romantic soul and feeding an anti-Romantic intellect, he produced works of delicious sensuality, overwhelming beauty, and profound sophistication."

Nine Preludes, Op. 1 (1899–1900)

Small pieces in late Romantic style, much Scriabin influence, slightly awkward, finely textured with polyrhythms and beautiful melodies; especially gorgeous is No. 8 in C minor.

KESSELL: Arte Nova
WERCHOWSKA: Ligia Digital
YUDINA: Arlecchino

Variations in B-flat minor (1901)

Some florid writing, richly conceived, effective, difficult, with twelve variations.

YUDINA: Arlecchino

Four Etudes (1903)

Longer than the Preludes, the first two are impressive as Etudes, composed as Scriabin was finishing his own Eight Etudes, Op. 42. No. 3, in B-flat minor, is unfortunately the most popular piece the composer wrote. It was played by Paderewski, and Myra Hess and others took to its rather gushing measures

of melancholy. The composer remarked in a 1910 letter to the composer Gregory Fitelberg, "It is fatal to have composed one's ninth symphony so young." The Fourth Etude, with its shower of notes, is technically inventive.

CLIBURN (No. 3): RCA
JONES: Argo
ROSCOE: Naxos
ROSENBERGER: Delos

Sonata No. 1 in C minor, Op. 8 (1905)

An impressive work. The Reger-like pianism and the Chopin and Scriabin flavors are apparent. A well-made fugue closes this four-movement work.

CLARKE: Athene
ROSCOE: Naxos
TRZECIAK: Pavane
WERCHOWSKA: Ligia Digital

Variations on a Polish Folk Song, Op. 10 (1904)

Ten variations; thorny, concise, and pianistically absorbing. More acerbic than the Op. 3 Variations, while retaining a Romantic manner.

VASSILIADIS: Discover International

Fantasy in F minor, Op. 14 (1905)

Scriabinic in texture, its themes are somewhat turgid, and not as effulgent as Scriabin's Fantasy, Op. 28.

JONES: Argo

Prelude and Fugue (1909)

A conglomerate work, where the intellectual and the lush live uncomfortably together, but with the unmistakable identity of the composer influenced by Richard Strauss and Reger.

> CLARKE: Athene
> ROSCOE: Naxos

Sonata No. 2, Op. 21 (1911)

Szymanowski called it diabolically difficult. Arthur Rubinstein premiered it in Warsaw. In two movements, the first in sonata form is intense, followed by a set of lively variations, allegro moderato, poco scherzando e cappriccioso, and ending with a Regerish fugue. A performance takes nearly thirty minutes.

> CLARKE: Athene
> ROSCOE: Naxos

Metopes, Op. 29 (1915)

The Second Sonata completes Szymanowski's first period, where his late Romantic eclecticism pervades. After the Second Sonata, his music becomes inspired with Persian, Hellenic, and early Christian influences. He now adds other composers' influence to his predominantly restless creativity, above all Debussy, Stravinsky, and Ravel. The piano writing is more vaporous, ethereal, and impressionist in texture. Metopes are bas-reliefs on top of Doric columns from the Greek world. Seeing fragments in a museum in Palermo, Sicily, he was fired to create three scenes from Homer's *Odyssey*, which he titled *Isle of the Sirens, Calypso,* and *Nausicaa*. These lavishly colored poems for piano are exacting challenges for the pianist, and in fine presentations the composer's keen ear for coloristic-impressionist effects are breathtaking. The masses of sound are difficult to balance but, once mastered, they lay beautifully in the hands, more so than the earlier works. The *Triptych* takes around sixteen minutes.

> JONES: Argo
> JORDAN: Albany
> ROSCOE: Naxos

Twelve Etudes, Op. 33 (1915–1916)

The Etudes are to be played consecutively. These superb, hard-edged, highly condensed works eschew the succulent sonorities of the Masques from the same period. It is interesting to note that Rachmaninoff, Debussy, and Szymanowski are each putting the finishing touches on their etudes at this moment in time.

> FUJIWARA: Solstice
> ROSCOE: Naxus
> ROSENBERGER: Delos

Masques, Op. 34 (1915–1916)

Shéhérazade, Tantras the Buffoon, Don Juan's Serenade, each of the *Triptych* abound in madcap rhythms and unusual shapes—polytonal combinations are wedded to an impressionist palette with sarcastic overtones. The final piece, and best known of the set, is the smarting *Don Juan's Serenade,* dedicated to Arthur Rubinstein, who wrote, "The music is beautiful but terribly difficult to bring to life on the piano." Symanowski wrote, "I have just completely finished my *Don Juan,* and feel extremely happy about it! Despite a certain parodic style—no, because of it—it is worth more than those Odyssey compositions."

> BLACKWOOD: Cedille
> DOMANSKA: Olympia

JONES: Argo
ROSENBERGER: Delos
VOTAPEK: Ivory Classics

Piano Sonata No. 3 in D minor, Op. 36 (1916–19)

A one-movement form. Fragmentary in nature, with a voluptuous harmonic vocabulary in a kaleidoscope of elements and moods asking for detailed pianism. As do the other sonatas, it concludes in a Fugue, distorted and nerve-wracking, marked "Scherzando e buffo."

CLARKE: Athene
FEDER: Protone (LP)

Twenty Mazurkas, Op. 50 (1924–26)

With the creation of his mazurkas, a third and more ascetic period in Szyamowki's evolution begins. He had deeply studied polish folk-music, especially material of the Tantra Mountains. He wrote, "I have developed into a national composer, not only subconsciously but with a thorough conviction, using the melodic treasures of the Polish folk . . . They do show traces of Chopin's influence, but I doubt whether one can envisage any Polish national artistic creativity in any field that would not be influenced by that great composer. Chopin is the most profoundly philosophical and yet artistic embodiment of what might be called the "spirit of Poland."

The critic Mark Swed feels they are "some of his most exquisite jewels . . . as subtle and elliptical as late Beethoven Bagatelles."

HAMELIN (complete): Hyperion
HESSE-BUKOWSKA (nine mazurkas):
    Muza (LP)

ROSENBERGER (seven mazurkas): Delos
RUBINSTEIN (four mazurkas): RCA

Symphonie Concertante, Op. 60 (1932)

The material of the *Symphonie Concertante* (which the composer also numbered his Fourth Symphony) is fused into a complex stylized idiom. Although the piano functions as a partner within the orchestral fabric, the piano part is a brilliant presence making heavy demands on the soloist especially in chord, octave, and double note passages. Dedicated to his dear friend Rubinstein, the pianist wrote: "It is dear to my heart, but difficult to convey to my audience; its emotional essence is hidden by a mass of changing harmonies, modulations, and a heavy orchestration and can only be discovered by frequent and loving study of its beautiful nature."

Once considered "modern," the score now offers a panorama of loveliness. The three movements are marked "allegro moderato," "andante sostenuto," "allegro non troppo." The slow movement builds with compelling poetic lyricism as the piano provides delectable ornamental backdrop. The composition of around twenty-two minutes could be coupled at orchestral concerts with, perhaps, Rachmaninoff's *Paganini* Rhapsody, written at the same time, and the same length. The composer was soloist at the premiere in Poznán in October of 1932.

BLUMENTAL, Kord/Polish Radio Symphony of
    Katowice: Unicorn (LP)
EKIER, Rowicki/National Philharmonic: Muza
    (LP)
ANDSNES, Rattle/City of Birmingham
    Symphony: EMI
RUBINSTEIN, Wallenstein/Los Angeles
    Philharmonic: RCA
SHELLEY, Sinaisky/BBC Philharmonic:
    Chandos

T

PETER ILYICH TCHAIKOVSKY
1840–1893—Russia

Peter Ilyich Tchaikovsky "remains to this day," as Glenn Gould once observed, "Russian music's chief tourist attraction." Although Tchaikovsky was mainly concerned throughout his career with opera and orchestral forms, surprisingly enough he left something over one hundred piano pieces, and many of them are permeated by his unique melodic magic.

The Complete Piano Music

Musically speaking, the most striking revelation of Tchaikovsky's piano writing is what might be called the "normalcy" of his expressive intentions. In the solo keyboard music, we encounter virtually no Tchaikovskian hysteria; at the piano, it would seem, he almost never reveled in morbidity. Instead, there is much cheer, more major keys than minor ones, a smattering of the exotic, bits of the barbaric, rustic dancing, and echoes from the composer's beloved world of ballet. There is also far more of Schumann's influence than Tchaikovsky would have allowed in his orchestral creations. Tchaikovsky was himself only an adequate pianist, and his gifts were by no means pianistic. The music is not always well molded for the hand, but everywhere we discern the personal authenticity that has touched so many hearts.

PONTI: Vox

Sonata in G major, Op. 37

The Sonata is Tchaikovsky's largest piano canvas. The opening movement is indebted to Schumann's F-sharp minor Sonata. There is loveliness in the long slow movement; the scherzo is characteristic in 6/16 time, and the effective finale is easier than it sounds—a rush of brilliant figuration, a lush tune, all *à la russe*. It was dedicated to Karl Klindworth; its first performance by Nikolai Rubinstein gave Tchaikovsky one of the most glorious evenings of his life.

CROSSLEY: Philips
DOUGLAS: RCA
GINSBURG: Philips: Great Pianists of the
    Twentieth Century
LEONSKAJA: Teldec
PERTICAROLI: Ermitage
REISENBERG: Ivory Classics
RICHTER: Monitor (LP)

Six Pieces, Op. 19

In addition to the famous Nocturne, which is No. 4, this opus contains a wonderful set of variations, buried in it as No. 6. Tchaikovsky liked the variation form although, unlike Brahms, he more often than not limited himself to exploring the diverse charms of a given melody. Historically, the work is of interest because it was the model for numerous sets of variations by other Russian composers—by Liapunov, by Glazunov, and two by Liadov, to mention a few examples.

GAVRILOV (Variations): Philips: Great
    Pianists of the Twentieth Century
GILELS: Bianca
LANG LANG (Nocturne): DG

Six Pieces on One Theme, Op. 21

Another strong set. Wilhelm Backhaus used to program these, but they have enjoyed no such formidable advocacy in many decades. The music is ingeniously contrived to achieve a wide range of moods with a single theme. The Six Pieces are: Prelude, Fugue, Impromptu, Funeral March, Mazurka, and Scherzo. The Impromptu is a real golden nugget.

NIKOLAYEVA: Melodiya (LP)
PONTI: Vox

Dumka, Op. 59

One of Tchaikovsky's best-known piano works, subtitled *A Scene from Russian Life*—a kind of Lisztian Rhapsody with a Volga accent.

BRONFMAN: Sony Classical
CAMPENELLA: Nuova Era
HOROWITZ: RCA
PONTI: Vox

Piano Concerto No. 1 in B-flat minor, Op. 23 (1874–75)

This most popular of all concertos was given its world premiere by Hans von Bülow in Boston on 25 October 1875. In 1891, with Tchaikovsky conducting and Adèle aus der Ohe as soloist, it was the first concerto ever heard in Carnegie Hall. There have been dozens of recordings devoted to its ripe and spirited measures.

ARGERICH, Kondrashin/Bavarian Radio
    Symphony: Philips
BERMAN, Karajan/Berlin Philharmonic:
    DG
CLIBURN, Kondrashin: RCA
CURZON, Solti/Vienna Philharmonic:
    London
GILELS, Reiner/Chicago Symphony:
    RCA
HOROWITZ, Toscanini/NBC Symphony:
    RCA
JANIS, Menges/London Symphony:
    Philips: Great Pianists of the Twentieth
    Century
POGORELICH, Abbado/London
    Symphony: DG
RUBINSTEIN, Leinsdorf/Boston
    Symphony: RCA (CD)
SGOUROS, Weller/London Philharmonic:
    Angel
WEISSENBERG, Karajan/Orchestre de
    Paris: Angel

Piano Concerto No. 2 in G major, Op. 44 (1881)

In three movements, a colorful, high-caliber work which has nevertheless been perpetually in the shadow of No. 1. Quite long, it is most often played in Siloti's composer-approved edition, which excised a good deal of material from the slow movement. The score has been heard to great advantage in Balanchine's *Ballet Imperial*.

CHERKASSKY, Kraus/Berlin
    Philharmonic: DG; Susskind/Cincinnati
    Symphony: Vox (LP)

GILELS, Kondrashin/Leningrad
Philharmonic: Bianco
GRAFFMAN, Ormandy/Philadelphia:
CBS
PLETNEV, Fedoseyev/Philharmonia:
Virgin Classics
POSTNIKOVA, Rozhdestvensky/Vienna
Symphony: London

Piano Concerto No. 3 in E-flat major, Op. 75 (1893)

In one movement, with three subjects and
an ample cadenza, No. 3 is dedicated to the
French virtuoso Louis Diémer. The work is not
as difficult as its predecessors. Balanchine also
choreographed a ballet to this concerto.

FELTSMAN, Rostropovich/National Symphony:
Sony Classical
GRAFFMAN, Ormandy/Philadelphia:
Columbia

ZHUKOV, Rozhdestvensky/USSR Symphony:
Melodiya/Angel

Concert Fantasy for Piano and Orchestra, Op. 56 (1891)

A work written for Annette Essipova and first
played in the United States in the 1890s by
Julie Rivé-King. The cadenza is overtly long.
The Concert Fantasy is difficult and clumsy to
play, but fun to hear.

DOUGLAS, Slatkin/Philharmonia
Orchestra: RCA
KATIN, Boult/London Philharmonic:
London
LOWENTHAL, Comissiona/London
Symphony: Arabesque
PONTI, Kapp/Prague Symphony:
Turnabout
ZHUKOV, Rozhdestvensky/USSR
Symphony: Melodiya

V

HEITOR VILLA-LOBOS
1887–1959—Brazil

Villa-Lobos, by general consent, is Brazil's greatest composer. He wrote voluminously—1,500 works in all. The piano was never neglected. His music speaks directly; one always feels the pull of an unusual musical mind and personality. He was affected by the Indian folk material of his country, by impressionism, and by exotic and strange rhythms. He knew how to strike the barbaric chord, and he could be lovable.

The Complete Piano Music:

HALÁSZ: BIS
RUBINSKY: Naxos
ORTIZ, Ashkenazy/New
  Philharmonia: EMI

Bachianas Brasileiras No. 3 for Piano and Orchestra (1938)

Villa-Lobos composed nine works titled *Bachianas Brasileiras,* of which No. 3 is scored for piano and orchestra. The composer saw parallels in certain Bachian melodic contours and Brazilian folk melodies, and these are brilliantly amalgamated into works of a very special flavor. The movements of No. 3 are Preludio, Fantasia, Aria, and Toccata (titled *Picapao*—which is a musical description of the sound of a woodpeckerlike bird).

Rudepoêma (1926)

Villa-Lobos's most extensive piano work; the title means "Rough-Poem." It was premiered in Paris in 1927 by Arthur Rubinstein, who early on had befriended the composer. Villa-Lobos wrote to the pianist: "I do not know whether I have been successful in capturing all your soul in this *Rudepoêma,* but I swear with all my heart, that I believe I have imprinted a picture of your personality on my memory and that I put it down on paper like an intimate camera. Thus, if I have succeeded, you will always remain the true author of this work."

Rubinstein never recorded it, but thought Roberto Szidon played the piece "magnificently." The score is in one movement, with great torrents of sound.

BEAN: RCA
FREIRE: Audiofon
HAMELIN: PTRY
SZIDON: DG

Próle do bébé (1918)

The impressionist fabric is well contrasted with the more percussive note. These are among the most popular of Villa-Lobos's many piano pieces.

FREIRE: Audiofon
RUBINSKY: Naxos
RUBINSTEIN: RCA

637

W

CARL MARIA VON WEBER

1786–1826—Germany

Carl Maria von Weber's piano music includes eight sets of variations, sonatas, and the separate pieces, *Momento capriccioso,* Op. 12; *Grande Polonaise,* Op. 21; *Rondo brillante,* Op. 62; *Polacca brillante,* Op. 72; and *Invitation to the Dance,* Op. 65. The variations are the weakest of the output; however, they do exploit most effectively Weber's piano technique, which is always splendid but which often requires a large span. The best of these sets is the sparkling *Dorina Bella* Variations, Op. 7.

Sonata No. 1 in C major, Op. 24 (1812)
Sonata No. 2 in A-flat major, Op. 39 (1814–16)
Sonata No. 3 in D minor, Op. 49 (1816)
Sonata No. 4 in E minor, Op. 70 (1819–22)

The four sonatas constitute Weber's most important works for piano solo. They offer a unique blend of Weber the virtuoso and the operatic master forging a new epoch in German music. They all possess bold themes and the mysterious Romanticism of his opera *Der Freischütz.* Each one has indelibly refreshing qualities. The finale of the First Sonata is the dashing Perpetuum Mobile. No. 2 was loved by many Romantic pianists; its third movement, marked "Presto assai," is tremendous fun with the spirit of a forest goblin. The Third Sonata's best movement is the finale, Allegro di bravura. The Sonata No. 4 has a first movement of early Romantic melancholia, a beautiful Andante, a fiendishly difficult minuet, and ends with a whirling tarantella.

D'ARCO (Sonatas Nos. 3 and 4): L'Oiseau-Lyre
BAR-ILLAN (Sonata No. 2): Audiofon
BRENDEL (Sonata No. 2): Philips
CIANI (Sonatas Nos. 2 and 3): DG
CORTOT (Sonata No. 2): Music and Arts
FLEISHER (Sonata No. 4): Philips: Great Pianists of the Twentieth Century
GILELS (Sonata No. 3): Praga
MEWTON-WOOD: Pearl
OHLSSON (Sonatas Nos. 1–4 and solo piano music): Arabesque
RICHTER (Sonata No. 3): AS Disc
WEBSTER (Sonatas Nos. 1 and 2): Dover (LP)

Invitation to the Dance (1819)

The ever-youthful *Invitation to the Dance* is history's first great ballroom waltz. It was perhaps the most often attempted piano work of its time.

CORTOT: Biddulph
DE LARROCHA: MHS

FRIEDMAN: Pearl
MAGALOFF (Tausig transcription): Denon
MOISEIWITSCH (Tausig transcription): Naxos
SCHNABEL: Seraphim (LP)

Konzertstück for Piano and Orchestra (1821)
Piano Concerti Nos. 1 and 2 (1810–11)

Today the Weber *Konzertstück* and his two piano concerti are seldom performed, but they are the link between the Classical concerto (Beethoven had, by the time of Weber's First Concerto, completed his five examples) and those of Chopin, Mendelssohn, and Liszt. Weber wrote an octave glissando in the *Konzertstück* which is seldom attempted on the contemporary keyboard; it was far easier for Weber on his own light-action Brodmann. Gottschalk was known to have a bloody keyboard whenever he played the piece. The *Konzertstück* is a remarkably advanced composition for 1821, and it became a warhorse for Liszt and Gottschalk; in fact, few Romantic virtuosi failed to achieve success with it.

John Warrack wrote of these three scores, "In true Romantic fashion the highest store is set upon personal sensation as the most reliable artistic guide and upon the virtuoso artist as the most brilliant and eloquent voice of sensations shared by all."

Konzertstück:
ARRAU, Galliera/Philharmonia: Seraphim
BRENDEL, Abbado/London Symphony: Philips: Great Pianists of the Twentieth Century
R. CASADESUS, Szell/Cleveland Orchestra: Sony Classical

DEMIDENKO, Mackerras/Scottish Chamber Orchestra: Hyperion
FRANTZ, Menuhin/Royal Philharmonic: Big Ben
GULDA, Andreae/Vienna Philharmonic: Philips: Great Pianists of the Twentieth Century
KELLER, Köhler/Berlin Symphony: Turnabout
PROTOPOPESCU, Rahbari/BRTN Philharmonic: Discover

The Two Concerti:
DREWNOWSKI, Wit/Polish National Radio Orchestra: Arts Music
FRAGER, Andreae/North German Radio Symphony: RCA (LP)
KELLER, Köhler/Berlin Symphony: Turnabout (LP)

Carl Maria von Weber by David Dubal

PROTOPOPESCU, Rahbari/BRTN
Philharmonic: Discover

ANTON WEBERN
1883–1945—Austria

Variations for Piano, Op. 27 (1936)

Webern is surely one of the main influences on musical thinking after World War II. His Piano Variations, dedicated to Edward Steuermann, is a work that anyone interested in serial music should study. Eric Salzman comments:

"'Systemic' and 'minimal' are catchwords in the advanced art world today, but thirty and forty years ago Webern evolved an intense, aphoristic, late-Romantic, expressionist-psychological style in a geometry of musical space where ideas and their expression become identicals, where the minimum materials are endowed with their maximum meaning and where ideas themselves and the 'systemic' form and expression become identical."

DOUGLAS: RCA
GOULD: Sony Classical
POLLINI: DG
RICHTER: London
P. SERKIN: Koch
Y. TAKAHASHI: Denon
WEBSTER: Dover (LP)
ZACHARIES: VAI

Addendum to the Piano Literature

Most of the preceding compositions form the nucleus of the literature of the piano that is most frequently performed and recorded. For serious students and listeners, however, there remains much more that is worth examination and study. The following composers are by no means an exhaustive list of those who have made contributions to piano music, but all of these are composers of special quality who have explored the piano with high ideals and particularly understand the instrument's resources.

KORNEL ABRANYI

1822–1903—Hungary

Abranyi had a complex career. Pianist, composer, educator, critic, and a devoted friend of Liszt, who used themes from one of Abranyi's *Czardas Nobles* as a basis for his brilliant 19th Hungarian Rhapsody from 1885. Abranyi's many piano works include a Sonata in Hungarian Style, Op. 84 (1890), and a Hungarian Millennial Sonata, Op. 103. His music is an amalgam of conventional European forms sporting "Hungarianisms." Abranyi for a short period studied with Chopin in Paris. He is an important figure in the growth of his country's musical life, and his music has intriguing qualities.

JEAN ABSIL

1893–1974—Belgium

A prolific composer and a prime representative of twentieth-century Belgian music. In the 1920s he moved away from traditional tonality and also used irregular metrics. For piano, he has composed Three Pieces for the right hand, Sonatinas, Etudes, Impromptus, Suite Pastorale, and Grand Suite. His *Passacaille,* Op. 101 (1959), and Variations, Op. 93, are intense works which merit performance.

JOHN ADAMS

b. 1947—United States

Adams grew up in New England and received his training at Harvard University. In 1971 he moved to San Francisco, where he taught at the San Francisco Conservatory. His output for piano is small, but the pianist Adam Marks writes, "Each work has given a new face to contemporary pianism." His 1977 *China Gates* is a classic of minimalism. Adams's concept of "gate" is a term from the electronic world describing the limit or flow of electric current between pieces of a machine or computer. A larger work in the same vein is the

1978, twenty-one-minute *Phrygian Gates*. If *China Gates* is calm, in *Phrygian Gates,* Adams explores the piano's dynamic impulses with ingenious richness. Although highly accessible with its use of repetition, his music reveals various layers of complexity. The highly effective and elaborate concerto, titled *Century Rolls,* was written for and premiered by Emanuel Ax and has had numerous performances since its premiere with the Cleveland Orchestra in 1996.

WILLIAM ALBRIGHT
1944–1998—United States

He was an excellent pianist who often exploited the ragtime idiom in his work, which can be complex, dissonant, and improvisatory, as in *Pianoagogo* (1966). The composer described his *Grand Sonata in Rag* (1968) as "the perhaps impossible synthesis of ragtime textures with 'classical' structures."

ANATOLY ALEXANDROV
1888–1982—Russia

His early work shows Scriabin's influence. In later scores, Russian folk material prevails, with much of the earlier chromaticism filtered out. There are fourteen sonatas. The D minor Sonata, Op. 12, is a gloomy one-movement work with an impassioned climax. The Fourth Sonata, Op. 19, is among the best. The Eighth Sonata, published in 1946, is easier technically, with attractive use of Armenian tunes in its three movements. Alexandrov left a library of smaller pieces, often interesting in content, such as the small Suite Op. 89 and Elegy Op. 89. Alexandrov knows the keyboard well and would add another flavor to the post-Romantic Russian repertoire.

WILLIAM ALWYN
1905–1985—England

A modern Romanticist who writes clever and effective piano music. Especially fine are the Twelve Preludes and the *Fantasy* Waltzes with impressionist overtones. John Ogdon recorded them. A more sustained score is the vigorous Sonata alla Toccata in three movments from 1951.

DAVID AMRAM
b. 1930—United States

His Sonata (1965) is representative of its composer's merging of popular styles with classical form. Amram's autobiography, *Vibrations,* tells the story of a composer who became well known in the turbulent 1960s.

GEORGE ANTHEIL
1900–1959—United States

It is a shame so little of Antheil's piano music is played. The early works retain their radical spirit; the later ones, with much motivic writing, tend to be more conservative. He left four sonatas, of which the Sonata No. 2, *The Airplane* (1922), has a wonderfully brash lilt. Vigil Thomson pointed out, "His music, though not strongly current in repertory, does not die. Pieces of it are constantly being revived."

ANTON ARENSKY
1861–1906—Russia

Many gems can be found among his numerous piano pieces. Rachmaninoff and Scriabin studied composition with Arensky. He had a suave lyricism and a talent for the instrument, well exhibited in his Twelve Etudes, Op. 72, and in many attractive items scattered throughout his output. An early Piano Concerto lacks the pungency of his D minor Piano Trio, although the Nocturne movement is warm-hearted.

GEORGES AURIC
1899–1983—France

A member of the celebrated group *Les Six,* he wrote well for the piano. His most important score is the Sonata in F major (1931) in four movements; the idiom is lean, slightly astrigent, with a great deal of two- and three-part writing. The slow movement is sectional and florid. An important work which deserves investigation.

MILTON BABBITT
b. 1916—United States

One of the leading American composers. His piano music, such as *Three Compositions for Piano* (1947) and *Partitions* (1963), has found many performances. His music is intellectually demanding.

GRAZYNA BACEWICZ
1913–1969—Poland

An important composer whose Ten Studies and Second Sonata are powerful and well-written scores.

CARL PHILIPP EMANUEL BACH
1714–1788—Germany

The most comprehensive talent among J. S. Bach's children. C. P. E. Bach's place in music history is secure, for he helped formulate the principles of the Classical sonata. Much of his large output is original, ebullient, and florid. The slow movements are especially fascinating.

HENK BADINGS
1907–1987—Netherlands

A composer of substance, writing in highly structured forms. His works for piano, especially the sonatas, are weighty but accessible.

JEAN BARRAQUÉ
1928–1973—France

His 1950–52 Piano Sonata is considered one of the most important French sonatas of the twentieth century. It runs to forty minutes and is daunting technically. Maurice Hinson says, "Few pianists will be able to handle this work successfully."

MARION BAUER
1887–1955—United States

Bauer was a refined talent. Her music mingles American and French traits. She composed nineteen titles for the piano, from an Elegy (1909) to the *Summertime* Suite (1953). Her most extensive piano work is the *Dance Sonata* (1935). The Four Piano Pieces, Op. 21 (1930), are an exceptional set; the pianistic demands are varied, the material is hard-edged and elegantly worked out.

ARNOLD BAX
1883–1953—England

Some of Bax's finest work is for the piano. At his best, he is capable of a haunting beauty. The four solo sonatas ask for a complete pianism. The Sonata No. 1 in F-sharp minor (1922) is in one movement, melodramatic and infused with Irish folk flavor as well as Lisztian thematic transformation.

MRS. H. H. A. BEACH (AMY MARCY CHENEY)
1867–1944—United States

A shining talent whose music is among the best of American Romanticism. Her work abounds in melting, honest lyricism. Her writing for the instrument is grateful and coloristic. Her longest piano work, the Variations on Balkan Themes, Op. 60, reveals Beach as an astute variationist.

RICHARD RODNEY BENNETT
b. 1936—England

An inventive composer; his Piano Sonata and Five Studies display a special affinity for the piano. Kovacevich has recorded his splendid 1968 Piano Concerto in four movements running to twenty-five minutes.

SIR WILLIAM STERNDALE BENNETT
1816–1875—England

A fine pianist who studied with Cipriani Potter, Bennett premiered his Four Piano Concertos. His idols were Mendelssohn and Schumann, who dedicated his *Symphonic Etudes* to Bennett. Schumann, reviewing his music, wrote, "He seems to have overheard and reproduced nature in her most musical scenes . . . musical Claude Lorraines, living tone-landscapes." It is a pity that the best of Bennett has been forgotten, for as W. J. Henderson wrote, "It is impossible to fail to discover the minute care which he exercised in the construction of every measure." His best work was accomplished before 1850. Lacking an expansive temperament, he failed to respond to Romanticism's more fulsome and explosive emotions. H. C. Colles aptly says, "His sensitiveness became fastidiousness and a delicate genius contracted into a narrow talent." However, there is one later work of magnitude, composed for Arabella Goddard, who premiered it in 1873—the Sonata in A-flat, Op. 46, *The Maid of Orleans*, in four ample movements, inspired from the Schiller play. William S. Newman finds the second movement "a dramatic yet subtle piece faintly suggestive of the 'March au Supplice' in Berlioz's *Symphonie Fantastique*."

Bennett's concertos have a faded period aroma, especially No. 4, with its once-famous Barcarolle movement. His small solo pieces, however, are ever so pianistic and a delight to play in their Mendelssohnian clarity. Scattered here and there are gems of real artistic worth, having their own intrinsic value.

LUCIANO BERIO
b. 1925—Italy

His *Cinque Variazioni per pianoforte* (1952–53) is a sensitive, complex, lyric work, based on serial technique. Berio means the score to be a dramatic essay "whose action resides in the relation between the soloist and his own instrument."

WILLIAM BOLCOM
b. 1938—United States

An accomplished pianist whose piano music shows various influences. He has delved deeply into ragtime style. Paul Jacobs recorded his *Graceful Ghost Rag*. Bolcom's Twenty-four Etudes exploit many pianistic problems with flair. His music projects joyously to audiences.

SERGEI BORTKIEWICZ
1877–1952—Russia

An exceptional pianist and an attractive composer. His music exhibits a fine gift for Chopinesque and Lisztian piano writing. The Ten Etudes, Op. 15, and Sonata, Op. 9, are enjoyable to read through, although the music may not wear well.

YORK BOWEN
1884–1961—England

A pupil of Tobias Matthay, Bowen had a fine career as pianist and composer. The piano music is conservative in style, beautifully laid out for the instrument, refreshing to hear, and enjoyable to work on. The Twenty-four Preludes, Op. 102, show a keen knowledge of piano sonority. Since Stephen Hough's admirable CD on Hyperion, several pianists have taken up his music. The Toccata Opus 155 is a splashy encore piece of telling effect.

PIERRE DE BRÉVILLE
1861–1949—France

He studied with Théodore Dubois and Franck. His work should not be neglected; as Norman Demuth states, "His music says a great deal which had not been said before and much which has not been said since. Its substance is considerable without being indigestible." Bréville is a loner, who is essentially a piano composer who is not bound to any school, although he learned much from Franck. His suite *Stamboul* is ingratiating and vital; the Piano Sonata (1923), shapely and spontaneous, takes its place as one of the important French piano sonatas of the period.

BENJAMIN BRITTEN
1913–1976—England

The great opera, song, and symphonic composer was a first-rate pianist who left little of interest for solo piano. However, the two works for piano and orchestra are superb. The Piano Concerto, Op. 13, composed in 1938 and revised in 1946, is clever and exciting; in four movements, Toccata, Waltz, Impromptu, and March, it is an unbuttoned romp which should have frequent performance. The *Diversions on a Theme for Left Hand and Orchestra*, Op. 21, is a long work, over half an hour, and rather introspective. The eleven variations are ingenious in their inventiveness of left-hand figuration, each given a title, Romance, Toccata, Nocturne, and Tarantella.

IGNAZ BRULL
1846–1907—Austria

Brull was a pianist, capable of playing the Brahms *Paganini* Variations and Liszt's *Don Juan* Fantasy. His friendship with Brahms was an important influence. His piano music is highlighted by a D minor Piano Sonata, Op. 73 (1894), which was once performed fairly often. The Second Piano Concerto, Op. 24, a giant of a score at about forty minutes, is worth investigation for an adventuresome pianist. The orchestration of the first movement harks back to Weber's forest with its rustic horn calls. The piece is packed with melodic freshness and exuberance.

SYLVANO BUSSOTTI
b. 1931—Italy

A progressive musician with new forms of graphic notation, his output is primarily vocal. His *Five Pieces for David Tudor* are radical in sound and usage, with outside-the-keyboard devices used, such as slammed lid. Bussotti asks the pianist to co-author the work in a score, which Hinson remarks "is a Maze of Marks." The music, influenced partly by Cage's and David Tudor's own pianism, can be a cathartic, and its violent moments won't hurt anyone. It takes conviction and daring to bring them off.

JOHN CAGE
1912–1992—United States

Cage has had a vital influence on many composers, with his interest in Oriental philosophy, his creative collaboration with the pianist David Tudor (where the performer engages in a new partnership with the composer), his constant explorations into new sounds, and, for the piano, his invention of the "prepared piano," which has given the percussiveness of the instrument new outlets of expression. His belief in all sounds as equal, his play with chance and randomness, have given to many composers an extended outlook on form and color. He wanted to depersonalize music, but instead, through his screws and bolts, added new and distinctive sonorities to the art.

His early, "tamer" music includes *Bacchanale* (1938), the first piece in which he used the prepared piano. Cage said, "The need to change the sound of the instrument arose through the desire to make an accompaniment, without employing percussion instruments, suitable for the dance by Syvilla Fort, for which it was composed." The sounds are effective in their pristine percussion. *Bacchanale* is melodic. Other pieces for prepared piano, of more interest, are *Music for Marcel Duchamp, Prelude for Meditation, The Perilous Night,* and *Suite for Toy Piano,* a seven-and-a-half-minute tour de force on nine white keys. The twangs and vibrations are often delicate. *Dream,* created for Merce Cunningham, is for "plain piano": a straight line of single melody, some open harmony, and the most traditionally "beautiful" piece he wrote. The Concerto for Prepared Piano (1951) is high in interest in Cage's catalogue of music; within its dissonant world there is a finely knit delicacy. Other works include *Sonatas and Interludes,* which comes with a kit to prepare the piano.

HECTOR CAMPOS-PARSI
b. 1922—Puerto Rico

His finest piano music is the Sonata in G (1952–53). It combines a freely tonal, biting neo-Classicism with a stylization of Puerto Rico's traditional music. The first movement is marked "Mesto" and is emotional; a Vivo finale is relieved by a sad "chorale" but sails on to a brilliant conclusion.

JOHN ALDEN CARPENTER
1876–1951—United States

He left some good piano music, including a sweet and saucy Concertino for Piano and Orchestra (1915). Percy Grainger gave the premiere.

ROBERT CASADESUS
1899–1972—France

The great pianist was a prolific composer, who wrote impeccably for the piano. His Piano Concerto in E major, Op. 37, is a skillful and thoroughly Gallic concerto in the tradition of Saint-Saëns and Ravel. The slow movement is a gem. There are also four difficult sonatas, twenty-four preludes, and eight etudes. Casadesus's piano works deserve performance.

ALFREDO CASELLA
1883–1947—Italy

An extraordinary pianist, Casella was a serious piano thinker, leaving a catalogue of music both stimulating in its search for formal coherence and an adequate expression of his eclectic personality. In some respects, he reminds one of the restlessness of Busoni's creative faculty. He partook of Bachian influence within a neo-Classic scheme, experimented with polytonality and atonality, and in an outstanding work like *A notte alta* (1917), he bows to the seduction of impressionism. In such scores as the two *Ricercari on the Name Bach* (dedicated to Gieseking), he is dark and intense.

JUAN JOSÉ CASTRO
1895–1968—Argentina

Castro and his gifted brothers, José María (1892–1964) and Washington (b. 1909), are interesting creators, all producing piano music well worth playing. José María's *Sonata de primavera* (1939) is fascinating. Juan José welds elements of twelve-tone technique to a folkloristic idiom. His Five Tangos have been recorded by Grant Johannesen.

ALEJANDRO GARCIA CATURLA

1906–1940—Cuba

A composer worth exploring. His piano music possesses African-Cuban melodies, finely tuned piano scoring, and a great deal of syncopation. The *Sonata Corta* (1927) is in two-part counterpoint, of moderate difficulty. *The Prelude Corta* is unbarred of simple appeal but modern in its discontinuity of design; composed in memory of Satie. *Comparsa* is a virtuoso work from his Second Suite of Cuban Dances, an exciting and energizing piece.

CÉCILE CHAMINADE

1857–1944—France

Chaminade's music shows very real gifts and polished musicianship. She was a reputable pianist and the leading composer of salon music in France during the 1890s. Some of her abundant output is stylish, some mawkish and sticky. She was a pretty melodist and had a gift for simulating virtuosity through cleverly made figuration, in which she rivals Moszkowski. Her work filled a need in middle-class drawing rooms; indeed, many pieces are still nice to play and hear. But her music went out of fashion. Still, as Norman Demuth notes, "In the days when domestic music-making was at its height, the name 'Chaminade' stood for an ideal."

Presently, when recordings have resurrected so much, and we hear music based on historical understanding, her *Valse Caprice,* Op. 33, *Scarf Dancer, La Lisonjera* (The Flatterer), Toccata, and dozens of others, can be fine desserts as fresh encore material. The Sonata in C minor, Op. 21, is Chaminade's most ambitious solo work, diatonic in frame, solid, and molded to the hand. The finale also figures among her six Concert Etudes. A charming Concertstück for Piano and Orchestra, Op. 40, is a good student piece for experience in ensemble.

ERNEST CHAUSSON

1855–1899—France

His piano output consists of his *Quelques danses,* Op. 26, from 1896. The return to the dance forms of the eighteenth century interested several French composers of the *fin de siècle.* These lack the composer's usual lushness and are fine examples of understatement and refinement. The Three Dances are not especially difficult technically, but they are not easy to make effective. The *Forlane* is more difficult, brilliant and tricky rhythmically, and the *Pavane* is most appealing. His only other piano piece, the 1895 *Paysage,* is not as interesting.

PAUL COOPER

b. 1926–1996—United States

His short piano pieces, such as *Cycles* (1969), show a creative mind and an ingenious use of the pedal. His Piano Sonata (1962) should be noted as significant. The American pianist Ronald Rogers played the work brilliantly.

JOHN CORIGLIANO
b. 1938—United States

This composer has an appeal for many. His piano music, such as the Etude-Fantasy, is splashy, and the four-movement Piano Concerto has a theatrical core. Corigliano is not afraid to express his emotions.

HENRY COWELL
1897–1965—United States

He may be called the father of the "tone cluster." Cowell was an early experimenter in "extra-finger technique." For example, *Piece for Piano Paris* (1924) uses strumming, plucking, damping, and hitting strings inside the piano, in addition to fist, forearm, and palm clusters. Doris Hays plays Cowell's music to maximum effect, as does Joel Sachs.

RICHARD CUMMING
b. 1928—China

He came to the United States in 1941 and studied with Bloch and Sessions. For piano he has written a Sonata and a set of Twenty-four Preludes in a neo-Romantic idiom. They were written, says the composer, to "express my own joy and respect for that lyric, noble, and dynamic instrument I dearly love, the piano." The entire set takes half an hour. They range from fairly easy to very difficult, and from "café to strict twelve-tone," with one each for left hand alone and right hand. Nos. 3 and 4 are lyric diamonds.

ARTHUR CUSTER
b. 1923—United States

See especially *Rhapsodality Brown* (1968). The title is unexplained, though halfway through this twelve-minute score someone screams out, "Rhapsodality." After that unexpected outburst, with some drumlike tapping, the music becomes jazzier and orgiastic, leading to impressioned textures and closing with slow, bleak chords dying off. The work is finely spaced, dissonant and improvisatory. It has been recorded by Dwight Peltzer, whose playing of contemporary music is always fastidious, intelligent, and textually respectful.

ABEL DECAUX
1869–1943—France

Nothing in Decaux's output could have presaged his *Clairs de lune* (1900–07). They are titled *Midnight Strikes the Alley, The Cemetery,* and *The Sea.* They represent the most advanced compositional procedures of the day. They also have a phantomlike emotional content.

FREDERICK DELIUS
1862–1934—England

Delius had little interest in the piano. The Five Piano Pieces (1921), only seven minutes, are tidbits: *Mazurka for a Little Girl, Waltz for a Little Girl, Waltz, Lullaby for a Modern Baby,* and capped off by a Toccata. The tiny Three Preludes possess Delius's refinement. His ambitious C minor Piano Concerto, Op. 22, an early work, is plush, with an elaborate sprawling solo part that is awkward, especially in his use of double notes. The Concerto is a one-movement affair lacking the pictorial and atmospheric beauty more characteristic of Delius. Percy Grainger championed the Concerto, and in sympathetic hands it can be luxuriant.

NORMAN DELLO JOIO
b. 1923—United States

Dello Joio's piano music combines many influences. His Third Sonata (1948) is a good example of his directness and melodic and rhythmic immediacy.

DAVID DIAMOND
b. 1915—United States

His piano music is invariably interesting and well made. The Piano Sonata (1947) is worth investigating, as is the Piano Concerto (1950), a work of richness and virtuosity, exhibiting the contrasting elements of Diamond's musical personality. A more recent piano work by Diamond is the Prelude, Fantasy, and Fugue, dedicated to and performed by William Black.

FELIX DRAESEKE
1835–1913—Germany

Draeseke never fulfilled his high promise but is a fascinating composer in various forms. A follower of the new German school of Liszt and Wagner. The 1865 Munich performance of *Tristan* was crucial to his future development.

Unfortunately, from around this time, he was afflicted by growing deafness. His effective lighter piano pieces, such as the *Deux valses de concert*, Op. 4, and *Fantasiestücke in Waltz-Form*, are far exceeded in importance by the *Sonata quasi una fantasia*, Op. 6, in C-sharp minor, one of the major German sonatas of the period, composed form 1862 to 1867. This splendid score of about twenty-four minutes is in three movements. The first, Introduzione e marcia Funebre, begins allegro con brio and, in its three recitativo-like pages, ends in adagio-attacca to a slow funeral march, with drum-roll trills in the left hand and orchestral amplitude. A cantabile Trio relieves the stifling air and the march ends in grandiosity. The second movement is an intermezzo, subtitled Valse-Scherzo, marked "presto" and of brilliant light graciousness. The finale, nineteen of the score's thirty-nine pages, brings back the first movement's introductory material. The Sonata closes brilliantly in E major. William Newman feels "there is considerable harmonic and chromatic indirection, including flitting in and out of the key in a manner pointing to Richard Strauss a generation later." In this work Draeseke valiantly and, I feel, successfully brought fresh air and flexibility to the generally stuffy academic sonatas so prevalent in German music of the period. The work was dedicated to Hans von Bülow, who gave the first performance.

ANTONÍN DVORÁK
1841–1904—Czechoslovakia

The great Czech master was better suited to other media, but he composed more than a hundred solo piano pieces, which are often beautiful and are filled with the spirit of Czech nationalism. His best pieces are the thirteen *Poetic Tone Pictures*, Op. 85, the luminous Suite in A major, Op. 98, and the eight Humoresques, Op.

101. His G minor Piano Concerto, Op. 33, is always a treat. Richter thinks it one of the most difficult of Romantic concerti.

SONIA ECKHARDT-GRAMATTE
1902–1974—France

Eckhardt-Gramatte studied at the Paris Conservatoire and had a varied European career, settling in Canada in 1953. Her main piano output consists of two Piano Concertos, six Suites, and a Sonata (1950) in three movements, the finale of which has octave glissandi. The half-hour Concerto (1946) in three movements is a dazzling work of Romantic gesture, which requires dash and energy in the Finale, Tempo di Toccata.

Most interesting is the Suite No. 6, subtitled *Drei Klavierstücke*. No. 1 is a prestissimo e molto preciso for the left hand, No. 2 for right hand alone, and the third piece combines the first and second with the two hands, this being the longest and most interesting of the set. Tonal and expressionist in content.

KLAUS EGGE
1906–1979—Norway

Egge is one of the finest Scandinavian composers of the twentieth century. He often used contrapuntal forms and procedures, as well as old modal Norwegian themes. In construction he is meticulous, and he can be rhythmically vigorous, as in the 1939 folk dances *Fantasy in Falling-Rhythm* and *Fantasy in Springar-Rhythm*. Both pieces are polyphonically elaborate with appealing, driving rhythms.

The Sonata, the *Dream Vision Tune,* Op. 44 (1933), is about twenty-one minutes and inspired by *Draumkvede* (Dream-Vision Poem), an old Norwegian folk ballad. The Sonata is breezy, fresh in color, with jarring rhythmic quirks; it is modal and folksy and highly playable. The Second Sonata, Op. 27, from 1955, is in three movements, subtitled "Patética," and is dissonant and very difficult technically. Here is an outstanding work.

Egge's Piano Concerto No. 1 is from 1937 and is "Norse" in character. No. 2, Op. 21 (1944), is perhaps his best-known composition, a masterful fusion of concerto form with variations and fugal development of about twenty minutes. (The work is subtitled "Symphonic Variations and Fugue on a Norwegian Folk Tune.") The piano writing is linear, terse, tense, and freely tonal, in an emotional setting. Effective Baroque textures conclude the work.

GOTTFRIED VON EINEM
1918–1996—Switzerland

Von Einem studied for a time with Hindemith and with Boris Blacher. His Piano Concerto, Op. 20 (1956), should be enjoyed everywhere. In three movements of around twenty-three minutes, its neo-Classic writing displays sensitivity to the medium in the delicious, racy, and elegant byplay of piano and orchestra. The Concerto's ideas are full of air, all sparkling refreshment.

HANNS EISLER
1898–1962—Germany

In 1919 Eisler studied in Vienna with Schoenberg, the crucial influence of his life.

After persecution by the Nazis he emigrated to the United States, where he wrote film music. A book, *Composing for the Films*, appeared in 1942. An avowed communist, Eisler was tried by the Committee on Un-American Activities and deported.

His works for piano show a keen feeling for the instrument. The *Petites Morceaux pour les Enfants* are ingratiating children's pieces, twenty-five in all. The Sonata Opus 1, from 1924, in three movements (Allegro-Intermezzo-Allegro) is pointillistic, with Schoenberg's influence. The *Vier Klavierstücke*, Op. 3 (1925), is atonal but lyric, with sensitive touches and rhythmical flux. No. 2 is the fastest, at one minute, the set taking about eleven minutes. The Variations (1940) and Sonata No. 3 (1944) are less expressionist and lean toward intellectual austerity.

GEORGES ENESCU
1881–1955—Romania

Romania's most famous composer, a great violinist, the teacher of Menuhin, and a considerable pianist. The best known of his work is the orchestral *Romanian Rhapsody* No. 1, composed in 1901, which brought the composer early fame. In 1949 he made a piano transcription of the Rhapsody, which is a vivid showpiece. The 1903 Prelude and Fugue reveals the composer's skill in old forms; this work is fully textured and beautiful music. The Suite Opus 10 (1903) is outstanding, with touches of impressionism and archaic-sounding harmonies, a vibrant Toccata, a Sarabande, an enchanting Pavanne with trills, and a Bourée with delicate passagework.

Enescu's First Sonata is unpublished; No. 2 in F-sharp minor, Op. 24, rambles. The superb, three-movement Sonata, No. 3, is a fifteen-minute score completed in 1935. This highly polished score is a masterful synthesis of neo-Classic writing, exquisite textures, and stylized Romanian folk elements. The movements are marked "Vivace con brio," "Andantino cantabile," and "Allegro con spirito." The Third Sonata should find frequent performance; it is detailed in its markings and technically demanding, but it is difficult to capture its interior pulse. Dinu Lipatti's recording perfectly captures the Sonata's elusive grace.

SVEN EINAR ENGLUND
1916–1999—Finland

He studied with Palmgren and briefly with Copland in the United States. For years he was on the faculty of the Sibelius Academy in Helsinki. Englund has contributed several piano works, including a 1966 Sonatina and the 1950 *Introduzione e Toccata,* featuring a motoric driving Toccata. His Piano Concerto No. 1 from 1955 is in three movements. Stravinsky's influence is heard in the first movement, the larghissimo middle movement has the air of Copland, and there are effective Bach-like fugal passages and some Bartókian rhythms in the crisp, dance-like finale. A very refreshing composer.

MORTON FELDMAN
1926–1987—United States

The 1975 score titled Piano and Orchestra, around twenty minutes, is a fascinating composition, of which Maurice Hinson writes, "Everything is blended into one hypnotic, edge-to-edge event, with a dark rich radiance and transparency that somehow come through . . . the entire work is quiet and without the feeling of a beat." The score has received excellent recordings, with Alan Feinberg as soloist in one, and another with Roger Woodward. Feldman's solo music is also important. *Triadic Thoughts* is the best known. This immense work of ninety minutes is based on small motifs, varied in many ways. The piece demands imagination and has found an audience.

JOSEPH FENNIMORE
b. 1940—United States

Fennimore is himself a dynamic pianist. *Armistice, The Woolworth Man, The Hen's Snuffbox, Foxtrot Blues,* and *An Old Soft Shoe* are representative of his work. Of them, the composer writes, "The pieces spring from the currently out-of-fashion aesthetic which holds that a piano can sound like more than a percussion instrument." In *An Old Soft Shoe,* we can visualize the choreography of an elegant "hoofer," and the *Blues* is a lush commentary on cocktail music. Fennimore writes music of flair, with gobs of stylish piano scoring.

BRIAN FERNEYHOUGH
b. 1943—England

One of the best-known English composers of his generation. Stockhausen, Barraqué, Boulez, and Pousseur have been influences. Ferneyhough's major piano work is *Lemma-Icon-Epigram,* which is a vitally weird piece of intricate detail, continuous contrapuntal layering, frequent gestural changes, unorthodox time signatures, and with every nuance and rubato strictly notated. The difficulties make the sonatas of Boulez and Barraqué look almost simple, although Ferneyhough's pianism is more comfortable and more accessible to the ear, with is high-pitched excitement and eerie sounds.

ZDENEK FIBICH
1850–1900—Czechoslovakia

In his time he was known for his chamber music and symphonies. Less known are the 376 short piano pieces, ranging from eight bars to nine pages and of varying degrees of difficulty. Fibich published the works as *Nálady, Dojmy a upominky* (Mood, Impressions, and Memories). (Only one ever became known, *Poéme,* No. 139, because of a violin arrangement by Jan Kubelik.)

The musicologist Gerald Abraham calls the series "an erotic diary for piano," as they were composed as a sort of musical diary for his love of Anczka Schulzová, a composition pupil of his. Indeed it is a diary where all sorts of things concern the composer's relationship. The pieces fall into four opus numbers, Op. 41, 44, 47, and 57, and were composed from 1892 to 1899. Rosa Newmarch wrote: "Here are marches, dances, such as polkas, furiants, valses, reminiscences of some modal tune; experiments in rhythm and harmony; folk-melodies real or evolved from a long familiarity; obvious parodies; quotations from other composers, as a painter might preserve the memory of another artist's masterpiece in his own sketchbook."

These pieces vary in value but are an important work by a gifted and neglected composer. Marian Lapsansky has preserved the pieces on the Supraphon label.

MICHAEL FINNISSY
b. 1946—England

One of the most intriguing and important English composers of the present. Finnissy has written a substantial sum of solo piano music with a textural and emotional range which is immense, from peaceful to sudden violence in striking textural patterns. His *English Country Tunes* (1977) is a forty-five-minute suite crammed with complex polyrhythms, dense contrapuntal writing and tone clusters. The effect is startling, and the effort involved for the interpreter is formidable. Finnissy is a believer in virtuosity, and treacherous virtuosity at that, and he loves hands enveloping and leaping all around the instrument.

Finnissy has composed transcriptions, such as his 1989 *Strauss Waltz Transcriptions,* his *Gershwin Arrangements,* and Verdi Transcriptions, Books I and II (1974–86). The themes are the starting points for his extraordinary pianistic musings, pushing the idea of transcription to its extreme point, where Verdi is all but unrecognizable, although whiffs of Gershwin are more easily heard in the *Gershwin Arrangements.* Finnissy's work has inspired a number of younger composers, including Chris Dench, James Dillon, Roger Redgate, Richard Barret, and Andrew Tovey, all of whom have been dedicated to writing fascinating piano music.

GERALD FINZI
1901–1956—England

Two works for piano and orchestra are splendid. The Eclogue for Piano and String Orchestra (about ten minutes) was conceived in the 1920s but not played until 1957 by Kathleen Long. It is a dignified score, in Finzi's characteristic retrained and sensitive voice. The later Grand Fantasia and Toccata for Piano and Orchestra (fifteen minutes) is from 1953. The Fantasia opens with a striking orchestral passage, followed by a lavish Fantasia with semi-baroque texture, inspired from the Chromatic Fantasia of Bach. The Toccata bracingly jumps to the twentieth century, with bouncy and very English-sounding rhythms.

LUBOS FISER
b. 1935—Czech Republic

He studied in Prague and is highly respected in the Czech Republic. Often performed, the Piano Sonata No. 1 is a flamboyant virtuoso work of about ten minutes, enveloping the whole keyboard, but with tranquil interludes. From 1970 there is a Concerto da Camera for Piano and Orchestra, less than ten minutes, that is atmospheric and intense.

NICOLAS FLAGELLO
1928–1994—United States

Flagello's work is neo-Romantic and tonal, peppered with dissonance and taut in structure. The Concertino for Piano, Brass and Timpani (1963) is a theme, seven variations, and finale. Episodic-sounding, the timbre is mainly dry with crackling sonorities derived from Stravinsky, with some tough ensemble writing. A great deal of flexibility is called for in the the Piano Sonata (1962) in three movements, with an effective finale. Flagello's best-known piano piece is the Prelude, Ostinato and Fugue (1960), a brilliant neo-baroque score that could be an effective program opener.

WILLIAM FLANAGAN
1926–1969—United States

Studied with Barber, Arthur Honegger, and Copland. Flanagan was a thoughtful music critic who, at his death (by his own hand), was writing a book on American music. His *Passacaglia* from 1947 is solid and serious, but the thirteen-minute Piano Sonata of 1950 is a moody score in three movements of varying tonality, which underscores many changes in metre. The influence of Copland and perhaps Carter's Piano Sonata, composed a few years before, may be detected but are not detrimental to the work's high polish and quality.

GEORGE FLYNN
b. 1937—United States

Flynn is a terrific pianist, as can be heard on a Finnadar LP, in a twenty-three-minute score titled *Wound,* a massive pianistic quake in response to the horror of Vietnam. It is percussive, violent, and physically taxing. A recent work, *Derus Simples,* celebrates the *Goldberg* Variations of Bach and the music of Sorabji.

LUCAS FOSS
b. 1922—Germany

Foss came to the United States in 1937. A brilliantly equipped musician, a fine pianist, and an expert conductor. Foss has composed little for his instrument. Most notable are the four Two-Part Inventions and the difficult *Grotesque Dance.* The Piano Concerto No. 2 (1951) is thirty-five minutes and is quite conservative as compared to later of his endeavors. The Concerto lacks a sharp profile in its hodgepodge of styles, with the slow movement rising to a theatrical climax. The composer recorded it in masterly fashion as the soloist, first released on Decca in 1956.

JEAN FRANCAIX
b. 1912—France

A pupil of Nadia Boulanger, a delightful composer of neo-Classic music with French stylishness, his succinct style has found outlets in many forms. The nine-minute Concertino for Piano and Orchestra from 1932 holds no pretensions. Lightweight and technically neat, it has been in the repertoire from its beginning; it is a good piece for acquainting younger pupils with French music outside of Ravel and Debussy. The 1936 Piano Concerto, eighteen minutes, is in four merry movements; the orchestration is piquant. It all rambles along like a leisurely automobile ride in the countryside. The best of Francaix's solo works is *"Cing Bis"* (Five Encores): "To Entice the Audience," "For Romantic Women," "In Case of Success," "In Case of Triumph," "In Case of Delirium." There is a 1960 Sonata in four movements with a concluding Toccata, a work of humor and freshness, which could charm an audience.

IGNAZ FRIEDMAN
1882–1948—Poland

The great Polish pianist left over one hundred piano pieces. *Estampe, Minuette Vecchio, Elle Danse,* and others were used as his encores. *Elle Danse* was danced by Pavlova. The various transcriptions and the Paganini Studies, Op. 47b, are ingeniously difficult. The six delicious *Viennese Dances on Themes by Gaertner* are delicious waltzes, dressed in satin and brocade.

BALDASSARE GALUPPI
1706–1785—Italy

Galuppi was one of the estimable Venetian composers of the eighteenth century. Best known in his lifetime for his now-forgotten operas, his best music is contained in some ninety keyboard sonatas, which are mostly in two movements, though some have as many as five movements. There are elements of early sonata form as well as simpler binary structure.

The ornamentation is delicate, the melodic lines are distinctive, and there is an unusually stately kind of gallantry. The pianist Joseph Bloch writes, "There is almost always surprising harmonic bite which distinguishes Galuppi from many conventional Italian composers of early classicism such as Rutini, Turini, and Alberti."

LUIS GIANNEO
1897–1968—Argentina

An important and sensitive composer. There is a charming Sonatina (1938) dedicated to Arrau. The B-flat minor Piano Sonata is a strong and subtle work in three movements; some bi-tonality, and use of Argentine folk song. The third movement builds to an imposing climax. This composition should find advocates.

ALEXANDER GLAZUNOV
1865–1936—Russia

A beguiling composer who has held to the edge of the repertoire. Beauties abound in catchy melodies, suave harmony, and an exceptional ease in handling a late-nineteenth-century pianism. The two piano sonatas are quite impressive, ranking with the best of his eight symphonies. The critic Stassov called the Second Sonata, Op. 75, a "grandiose, magnificent masterpiece." Gilels admired it and played it with all the plumage and color that can be lavished upon it. Glazunov's Variations in F-sharp minor, Op. 72 (1900), is one of his finest compositions.

HERMANN GOETZ
1840–1876—Germany

Goetz was a student of Köhler and von Bülow. In his piano music, solo and chamber, he exhibited a subtle melodic gift and a delicate sense of harmony. For piano he composed *Lose Blätter,* Op. 7 (1869); nine character pieces; two Sonatinas, Op. 8; *Genrebilder,* Op. 13 (1876); and a very special Piano Concerto, Op. 18, which deserves attention.

MORTON GOULD
1913–1996—United States

An American master, Gould played brilliantly and studied with Abby Whiteside. He gave to the piano numerous works containing his deep understanding of the instrument. One may look at the *Abby* Variations, the Prelude and

Toccata, and *Rag-Blues-Rag*. The Sonatina is especially effective, and the *Boogie-Woogie Etude* was often played by Shura Cherkassky. Gould's masterly *Interplay* for piano and orchestra was premiered by José Iturbi, and later became a great success as a ballet by Jerome Robbins.

CAMARGO GUARNIERI
1907–1993—Brazil

He devoted a great many works to the piano. His five Sonatinas are subtle, neo-Classical, yet nationalistic works. His *Ponteios* (Preludes) are fifty in number, composed from 1939 to 1959, and explore many sentiments.

REYNALDO HAHN
1874–1947—Venezuela

Born in Caracas, he moved to Paris with his family when he was three years old. At the Paris Conservatoire he enjoyed the teaching of Massenet, a composer who influenced him. His piano teachers were Descombes and Diémer. Hahn developed into an able pianist, was a fine singer and a good conductor. His piano music presents many moods: piquant, airy, smart, exotic, and sultry, with a melodiousness stemming from the Gounoud, Saint-Saëns, Massenet, Fauré Parisian tradition. The piano writing is always manageable. For Ivory Classics, Earl Wild has recorded a two-CD set of Hahn's *Le rossignol éperdu*, "The Bewildered Nightingale," 53 poèmes pour piano, two and a quarter hours of delicious pleasure—sketches, moments, and impressions, with such titles as *La danse de l'amour*

et du danger, La Jeunesse et l'été ornent de fleurs le tombeau de Pergolèse, Chérubin tragique, L'Arome suprême. The pieces were composed between 1899 and 1911.

IAIN HAMILTON
b. 1922—Scotland

His Piano Sonata, Op. 13 (1951), shows Bartók's influence. The Nocturnes with Cadenzas (1963) are serial in their structure but impressionistic. They are a good cycle for concert performance. The *Palinodes* (1972), inspired by Rimbaud, are imaginative pieces, seven in number, with clusters, glissandos, and all sorts of technical requirements.

GEORGE FREDERICK HANDEL
1685–1759—Germany

One of the great masters of the late Baroque, Handel's comparatively small keyboard output hardly deserves its neglect, and pianists from Garrick Ohlssohn and Shura Cherkassky have reveled in them. Magnificently trained, Handel knew the keyboard music of Froberger, Buxtehude, Kuhnau, and others, and its essential German quality is part of his style. Charles Rosen, however, notes the difference between J. S. Bach and Handel, writing: "Handel's simple and often brutal juxtaposition of masses, his use of the elements of music almost in block form, was rarely attempted by Bach, whose largest forms are always from a concentration on the smallest details and the fullness of their expressive power."

In the suites, like so much of Handel's music, there is an irresistible public element, a swagger and glory in the public moment, which so differs with Bach's far more private soul. The Suite No. 5 in HWV 430 contains the world-famous *Air con Variazioni,* known as *The Harmonious Blacksmith,* the favorite of Victorian pianists. All eight suites, HWV 426–433, are extremely different from each other and sound exceedingly well on the contemporary piano. There are also over thirty separate pieces to choose, such as seven fugues, HWV 605–610, and four chaconnes; especially effective is the Chaconne in G major, HWV 435, a wonderful program opener.

JOHN HARBISON
b. 1938—United States

One of the most performed of contemporary American composers, his work is magnificently constructed, some of it semi-serial, with jazz elements and complex rhythms. Not missing are lyricism and humor. His Piano Sonata No. 1 (1985) has been frequently heard; it was composed for Ursula Oppens, Alan Feinberg, and Robert Shannon. Of it, the composer writes: "There are four main sections, the two faster ones coming in the middle, but the articulations between them are not emphatic, and the piece seems dreamed up rather than premeditated. The pianistic demands are not strenuous by recent standards, or even by the standard of my early Parody-Fantasia (1967), but the requirements in formal insight and subtleties of touch and timing are quite severe. It is safe to say that there are not technical difficulties in the piece that don't originate as musical difficul-

ties." The Sonata takes sixteen minutes for performance.

ROBERT HELPS
1928–2001—United States

An expert pianist who studied with Abby Whiteside and composition with Roger Sessions. Helps plays works such as the Sessions Sonata No. 1 with unusual rhythmic power and deep expression. His many piano works show how conversant he is with the instrument and its heritage.

His 1994 *Shall We Dance* is a significant and atmospheric addition to the repertoire, which Garrick Ohlsson has performed. Of the score the composer wrote: "Despite the casual sound of the title, this is not, however, a flippant piece. It is quite sensual. 'Dance' intrudes all over the place, both consciously (I.E., the 'tune' of a Mischa Levitski Waltz that my mother played a lot when I was a kid) and unconsciously (I.E., hints of American 'popular' music—Ravel—etc.). *Shall We Dance* pays a special homage to the pedal, that fabulous pianistic resource that only pianists have—the lack of which makes even the wonderful transcriptions by Ravel of his own piano works fade when compared to the original."

ARTHUR HONEGGER
1892–1955—Switzerland

His Concertino for Piano and Orchestra (1924) was once often played, slender, jazzy, perky orchestration, with music-hall seductiveness; it is characteristic of the 1920s. The Toccata and Variations (1916) and *Sept pièces brèves* (1920) are grainy, chordal, polyphonic in texture.

ALAN HOVHANESS
1911–2000—United States

A ceaselessly prolific composer. Asian elements and Armenian folk music characterize his work, which often sounds improvisatory but in fact is tightly organized. There is a quality of mysticism in Hovhaness's music. His very personalized idiom is heard to advantage in the Fantasy, Op. 16, producing string vibrations and atmospheric gong effects inside the piano. Hovhaness was an ideal exponent of his music. He has written: "Composer, publisher and performer unite in beautiful cooperation for altruism of a better civilization. The composer, as in Old China, joins heaven and earth with threads of sound, the publisher promptly prints the music; the performer promptly plays the music and the world promptly receives the benediction."

KAREL HUSA
b. 1921—Czechoslovakia

His Sonatina, Op. 1 (1943), is a delight, with real humor. The First Sonata, Op. 11 (1949), in three movements, is expressive and dissonant. The Second Sonata, composed in 1975, is a stunning work—three movements of virtuosic, imaginative piano scoring, with use of the sostenuto (middle) pedal and some inside-the-piano technique. Highly charged emotionally.

JACQUES IBERT
1890–1962—France

A composer of insouciant wit and grace. *Les rencontres* and *Petite suite en quinze images* are breezy and fun to play. His best-known set is *Histoires*, ten pieces of which *Le petit ane blanc*, "The Little White Donkey," became a favorite.

VINCENT D'INDY
1851–1931—France

A composer who studied with Franck, d'Indy wrote a good deal of piano music. His best-known work is the beautiful *Symphony on a French Mountain Air* for Piano and Orchestra, Op. 25 (1886). Of particular interest is the *Thème varié, fugue, et chanson*, Op. 85. *Le Poème des montagnes,* Op. 15, contains three colorful and lyrical nature studies of moderate difficulty. The Sonata in E minor (1907) is d'Indy's most significant piano work, of intellectual fortitude and cyclic construction. The pianism is ungrateful, and novel figuration plays a small role. Yet the score has a subtlety that penetrates with repeated study. The structure of the three movements is fused from three generating themes. D'Indy was a smooth contrapuntist, and his knowledge of music's past in many guises is transmitted in this sonata alongside plenty of moments of cool, sensuous lyricism. It could only have been written by a French composer.

JOHN IRELAND
1879–1962—England

His piano music is among Ireland's best work. It is mildly modern, often impressionistic, mingling modal English folk song. Of his descriptive works, the *Decorations* are best known, consisting of *The Island Spell,* with its bell-like sonorities, *Moon-glade,* and *The Scarlet Ceremonies,* with its trills. The Sonatina is terse; the Ballade, gloomy; the Rhapsody, big climaxed. The Piano Sonata (1918–20) has power and architectural solidity; in its three-movement plan, the work bristles with technical inventiveness and is harmonically adventurous. Ireland's 1930 Piano Concerto in E-flat has had a number of advocates: Curzon, Bachauer, Lympany, Eileen Joyce, who gave its premiere, Sondra Bianca, and Eric Parkin.

PHILIPP JARNACH
1892–1982—France

Jarnach was of Spanish ancestry. In Paris he studied piano with Risler, and in Zurich he became Busoni's composition pupil and later assistant. He followed Busoni to Berlin, and, after Busoni's death in 1924, he finished from the sketches the opera *Doctor Faustus.* Jarnach wrote some piano music of considerable quality, all of which has been neglected. The Sonatina Opus 18 (1925) stems from Busoni's neo-Classicism and is highly chromatic and absorbing to work on, as are the dance pieces, *Ballabile, Sarabande,* and *Bureesca,* and the long three-movement Sonata from 1951. With its florid slow movement, it is a linear and intense piece of expressionism.

ADOLF JENSEN
1837–1879—Germany

A composer with a real lyric gift most splendidly felt in his songs and small piano pieces, such as his etudes. His Sonata in F-sharp minor, Op. 25, is Jensen's largest work, dedi-

cated to Brahms, in four movements tied to a Romantic rhetoric.

HUNTER JOHNSON
1906–1998—United States

Pianists looking for a major American sonata should look seriously at the Johnson Piano Sonata (1948). John Kirkpatrick, who had performed it often, said that Johnson's Piano Sonata is to the South what the Charles Ives *Concord* Sonata is to the North. The Johnson Sonata, however, is only twenty minutes in length. The form is cyclic, in three movements, changing meters, and requiring an absorbing concentration. The composer wrote, "My spirit was teeming defiantly with America. It is an intense expression of the South. . . . The nostalgia, dark brooding, frenzied gaiety, high rhetoric and brutal realism are all intermingled."

ANDRÉ JOLIVET
1905–1974—France

He wrote persuasively for the piano, especially in the two Piano Sonatas. The 1950 Piano Concerto is effective, using exotic themes based on music of Africa, Asia, and Polynesia. It is heavy on percussion, complex in ensemble, with plenty for the pianist to do.

SCOTT JOPLIN
1868–1917—United States

The father of notated ragtime was a wonderful pianist and an inspiration to a whole school of ragtime pianists. His performing career was set in the lurid nightlife of brothels and saloons, in which he played ragtime throughout the Missouri Valley states—where ragtime was born. In 1899 the *Maple Leaf Rag,* in which he solidified the formal basis of the genre, made him "King of Ragtime." By 1904, it was the first piece of sheet music to hit the one-million mark in sales. Although the white establishment looked down on ragtime, Joplin rightfully thought of his music as Art. At Joplin's death, John Stark, his publisher, wrote, "Here is the genius whose spirit, though diluted, was filtered through thousands of cheap songs and vain imitations."

Not until the 1970s did Joplin's importance in American music find large-scale appreciation, with the appearance of such fine interpreters as Joshua Rifkin, William Bolcom, Dick Hyman, and others. His more than fifty rags have a uniform excellence. The joyous quality and the intoxication of such syncopated jewels as *The Entertainer, Ragtime Dance, Elite Syncopation,* and *Gladiolus Rag* are irresistible. Near the end of his sad life (he died insane from syphilis), Joplin made a few piano rolls, which give no indication of his effectiveness as a pianist. He was concerned about the prevalence of bad ragtime playing, however, and composed *School of Ragtime,* a set of six exercises which are now published with his complete piano works.

DMITRI KABALEVSKY

1904–1987—Russia

A good pianist who wrote with skill and brilliance for the instrument. He has written abundantly for children in a charming and invariably interesting manner, with constant little twists and a taut harmony here and there. Representative are the *Twenty Pieces for Children,* Op. 27, and the *Twenty Pieces for Children,* Op. 39. The Sonatina in C major, Op. 13, No. 1, has attained "classic" status among students for its wit and light heart. The Twenty-four Preludes, Op. 38 (1943), form a

tremendous fund of ethno-Russian folk material using many keyboard techniques. The Third Sonata and the Piano Concerto No. 2 in G minor are both remarkable syntheses of Kabalevsky's intentions as a Soviet composer of the highest taste and craft working within the guidelines of the Prokofiev mold.

PÁL KADOSA

1903–1983—Hungary

He was an excellent pianist, most notably in twentieth-century music. Many Hungarian pianists respected his teaching. Schiff, Jenö Jandó, Kocsis, and Ránki studied with him. He recorded his own Fourth Sonata and Piano Concerto No. 3, which are derivative of Bartók but of high musical merit.

ARAM KHACHATURIAN

1903–1978—Armenia

The most famous of Armenian composers. At his finest, he sings his colorful musical heritage with an authenticity which has compelled an international audience. Khachaturian's Piano Concerto, which was once played often, retains its glamour as a colorful bravura work. His solo piano music occupies a small but attractive place in his output. There is a pleasant and often amusing capriciousness to this music, which abounds in sharp rhythms and colorful timbres. His characteristic use of the intervals of the major and minor second, as well as a frequently static bass, make for a distinctive pianism entirely his own. His *Poem* (1927) is pungent and discursive. The Toccata (1932) is the best known of his solo pieces; it is sonorous, with a short middle section of Oriental atmosphere. The Sonatina (1959) is laconic, fresh, neo-Classic, and finely cut. The 1961 Sonata is full of objective and outgoing energy.

LEON KIRCHNER
b. 1919—United States

An outstanding and consistent composer in all media that he ventures in. The half-hour Piano Concerto (1953) has a painfully demanding solo part. The score uses extremes of chromatic harmony, deriving from his use of the tri-tone. It is cast in three long movements, an allegro, with a magnificent cadenza; an adagio, "night music," is lyrically passionate, the orchestral fabric imaginative. The Allegro ma non troppo is turbulent and vividly explosive. Hinson warns that it "should only be approached by the most advanced virtuosi." The Concerto may be heard on a Music and Arts disc with the composer as soloist and Mitropoulos conducting.

Kirchner's fifteen-minute Piano Sonata (1948) has been fairly often performed. It was a milestone in Kirchner's career, and with age the work is even more remarkable. Five tempo markings combine for a concentrated experience. A slow introduction leads to a rhythmic allegro which blossoms to a beautiful slow movement. The closing is an Allegro Barbaro, which sums up material of the first movement. David Burge feels the score as both "powerful and enigmatic," and Hinson says, "The whole work pulsates with rubato." Leon Fleisher, a surgically precise artist, integrates his recorded performance with temperamental intensity.

THEODOR KIRCHNER
1823–1903—Germany

A composer with flashes of great talent. He wrote hundreds of miniatures in a Schumannesque and Brahmsian style. Edward Dannreuther wrote, "Though sheltered under Schumann's cloak, many minor points of style and diction are Kirchner's own, and decidedly clever." Adrian Ruiz revived some of these pieces on a recording.

HALFDAN KJERULF
1815–1868—Norway

A composer of talent and high standards. Grieg admired him. His piano music, mostly small character pieces, is tinged with Nordic sound and the fragrance of Schumann and Mendelssohn's Romanticism. He had a melodic ease and naturalness.

ZOLTÁN KODÁLY
1882–1967—Hungary

His Nine Piano Pieces, Op. 3, are beautifully conceived impressionistic music. The Seven Piano Pieces, Op. 11 (1910–18), are a superb set. The pianist David Burge has recorded them with sensitivity. Burge wrote of the Opus 11, "Its theatrical rhetoric is elemental and its moments of high grandeur and despairing pathos are unembarrassed by excessive sophistication."

The Dances of Marosszék (1927) is a radiant piano work, also orchestrated by the composer. Here Kodály's lavish style and passionate lyricism leave the world of impressionism and move toward his more characteristic use of the Magyar folk heritage. The composer, in differentiating his dances from the Brahms Hungarian dances, said the latter "are typical of urban Hungary around 1860. . . . My Marosszék dances have their roots in a much more remote past, and represent a fairy-land that has disappeared."

CHARLES KOECHLIN
1867–1951—France

A renowned teacher who, as a composer, was esteemed by Fauré, Roussel, Milhaud, and Poulenc. His music for piano is an unexplored avenue of beauties. The composer Henri Sauguet wrote, "His music is like no other . . . it takes many an unexpected, refined and even surprising detour and leads one to discover whole new landscapes." In recent years, the Israeli pianist Boaz Sharon has helped bring Koechlin's piano music to some attention.

GYÖRGY KURTAG
b. 1926—Hungary

Along with Ligetti, Kurtag is the most respected and performed Hungarian composer of his generation. His music has imagination and daring and, although complicated, is instantly communicative. His Eight Piano Pieces, Op. 3, are rhythmically and tonally demanding; in the last piece, clusters are formed in one hand while the other hand exults in soft glissandi.

JOSEPH LAMB
1887–1960—United States

With Joplin and James Scott, Lamb is one of the big three of classic ragtime. "Lamb," wrote Rudi Blesh, "developed a very personal sensitivity into the most haunting chromatic harmonies and exquisitely Chopinesque *morbidezza* in all ragtime literature. It is impossible to conceive of the classic Missouri Valley black ragtime without its rounding out in the work of this white Eastern genius."

Lamb's music is all freshness and subtlety, and pianists will be charmed by his *Ethiopia Rag, American Beauty,* and the *Ragtime Nightingale* (1915), a masterpiece of this genre.

CONSTANT LAMBERT
1905–1951—England

A brilliant figure in the musical life of England during his relatively short life. Sir Osbert Sitwell wrote:

"If someone chanced to ask me who was the most lively, quick, well-informed, and in general, most intelligent young man I had ever met, I should have no difficulty in finding at once the answer: Constant Lambert, composer, conductor, and writer." Lambert's famous book, *Music, Ho!*, remains provoking. *Rio Grande* for piano, orchestra, and chorus is a lavish pastiche of beguiling styles; along with Walton's *Façade,* it represents the British twenties as no other work. The Concerto for Piano and Nine Players (1930) is fascinating but rather hard going. Neo-Classic designs combine problematically with jazz and "blue" harmony. Pianistically it is original, with frequent meter changes in the first movement, titled *Overture with a Cadenza.* The second movement, called *Intermede,* offers a fascinating treatment of trombones, trumpet, and flute. The finale, marked "lugubre," ends conclusively. The percussion player is asked to play the maraca, tom tom, and temple blocks. The Sonata (1930) is long over twenty-five minutes, Lambert's major essay for solo piano; his summation of the jazz elements that so intrigued him, the work is serious in tone: an allegro molto marcato presents exuberant syncopation; the second movement, Nocturne, contains two sections of ragtime in style and a long finale with a dramatic conclusion. The Sonata should have a niche in twentieth-century piano music. His *Elegiac Blues* for solo piano, composed in memory of the blues singer Florence Mills, is melancholic and fragrant of that period.

ERNESTO LECUONA
1896–1963—Cuba

An attractive composer, his pianism is voluble and colorful. The celebrated Malagueña is a poor tourist postcard concoction which was once heard ad nauseum. It can be found as the sixth and last item of the *Andalucia Suite*. The American pianist Richard Cionco has recorded the suite, and Marco Rizo has recorded a variety of his music, including the *Rapsodia Vegra*.

NOEL LEE
b. 1924—United States

Lee is an American composer and pianist who has lived in Paris for decades. He has recorded a good deal of music by Moscheles, Field, Griffes, and Ives. His *Caprices on the Name of Schoenberg* (1975) for piano and orchestra was premiered by Lee. The title *Caprices* is ironic—the score being serious-toned. Lee has recorded this notable twenty-three-minute composition on CRI.

BENJAMIN LEES
b. 1925—China

An American composer whose piano music is serious and often exuberant. The 1953 Fantasia, six ornamental Etudes, and the *Sonata breve* and Sonata No. 4 show a composer who loves to write for the instrument. The Sonata No. 4 from 1953 is in three movements, rambunctious, with muscular bravura needed. Some Prokofiev influence. Premiered by Gary Graffman.

JOHN LESSARD
b. 1920—United States

A pupil of Nadia Boulanger, he has composed *4 Preludes, Little Concert Suite, Perpetual Motion, and Toccata*. His *Threads of Sound Recalled* is his major piano work in six movements, twenty-four-minutes long. The composer thinks of "the work as a contemplative piece that is never aggressive, and that might offer new discoveries on each hearing—utilizing 'melodies' that would not only be a sequence of single sounds, but would contain any number of vertical sounds at any moment during their progress." The work is precisely marked in the differences between piano and pianissimo playing.

ANATOLE LIADOV
1855–1914—Russia

Liadov is mostly a charming miniaturist, whose "small" symphonic poems *Baba Yaga, The Enchanted Lake,* and *Kikimora* are still enjoyed at orchestral concerts for their Russian folkloric appeal. His best-known piano music is the clever tidbit, *Une tabalière à musique.* The bulk of his compositions are polished Preludes, Etudes, Waltzes, and a Barcarolle, with their refined craft. Longer efforts are two sets of admirable *Variations on a Theme by Glinka,* Op. 35, and *on a Polish Theme,* Op. 51. The influence of Chopin and Schumann are felt. But as Gerald Abraham asserts, "Both sets of Variations are thrown into the shade by the magnificent Ballade *(In the Old Days),* which has a strong claim to be considered Liadov's best work . . . It is difficult to believe that this broad and dynamic work could have been written by the composer of all the graceful Chopinesque trifles . . . The Ballade is dynamic, epic, full of genuine life and power."

SERGEI LIAPUNOV

1859–1924—Russia

M. D. Calvocoressi wrote of Liapunov, "He remains, with Liadov, the most attractive of the minor poets of Russian music." The influence of Liszt, and of Liapunov's mentor Balakirev, is apparent. The twelve *Etudes d'exécution transcendante,* Op. 11, dedicated to Liszt, are the most important concert etudes to come out of the Balakirev school. Besides the *Etudes,* recorded by Louis Kentner, which are a gold mine of inventive figuration and Russian nationalism, Liapunov wrote a Toccata and Fugue, a Sonata, Op. 27, and a *Sonatine,* Op. 65. Both his Piano Concerto No. 2 in E major, Op. 38, and the *Rhapsody on Ukrainian Themes* for Piano and Orchestra are attention-provoking works. In the Concerto, suavely lyric themes are developed with deftness: double notes, heavy Lisztian octaves, and glissandi. The full-blown *Rhapsody* is dressed in lavish Oriental regalia.

LOWELL LIEBERMANN

b. 1961—United States

A composer of considerable style, craft, and musical substance, his *Sonata Notturna* from 1983 is evocative. Stephen Hough has recorded his Two Piano Concerti for Hyperion in brilliant fashion. His three-movement *Gargoyles* is a contemporary score which has found many performances.

DINU LIPATTI

1917–1950—Romania

Lipatti continues to be heard through his recordings as one of the great and most loved pianists of the first half of the twentieth century. He composed two distinctive works for piano and orchestra. The 1945 *Trois danses Roumaines,* are quite sophisticated in their neo-Classicism and Romanian nationalism. The earlier 1936 Concertino in Classic style, Op. 3, shows the influence of his composition teacher Nadia Boulanger. The whole being a distillation of past idioms, being Bach inspired in the lovely slow movement. For solo piano there is a Sonatina for left hand, a piece with much brio, and a Fantasia with elements of Prokofiev and Enescu.

OTTO LUENING

1900–1996—United States

During his long career Luening wrote over three hundred works, pursuing many styles, and was influential at the dawn of electronic music. His six short sonatas (1940–1979) present problems of balance rather than of digital hardship; basically they are breezy, unpretentious, and often linear in design. Far more granite-like is the twenty-minute *Sonata in Memoriam Ferruccio Busoni*. Without quoting Busoni, Luening arrives at a Busoniesque work. This striking score is full of asperities and technical problems. Urusula Oppen has recorded it on CRI. As a young man, Luening knew Busoni, and speaks reverentially of him in his teeming autobiography, *The Odyssey of an American Composer*.

DONALD MARTINO
b. 1931—United States

One of the significant serial composers of the last half-century. A student of Babbitt, Sessions, and Dallapiccola, his piano music represents a powerful and daunting literature, exploring the keyboard with a heightened ear for sonority and pedal and figural imagination of a high order. The pianist-composer David Burge notes: "Martino writes about human feelings and how they change from moment to moment. His musical style . . . is tuned not to unchanging states of being but to the transitions that are always taking place in real life. Marino's 'mysteries' are the fluctuating emotions of living, feeling souls."

The Piano Fantasy (1958) is a dodecaphonic work of five minutes. The composer states, "The first derived set is a combination of the original series and its inversion. Each new prime is successively combined with its inversion or retrograde inversion." The player must sensitively unravel each aspect of feeling. The 1970 work called *Pianississimo: A Sonata for Piano* needs not only the highest skill, but the dedication to learn it. The piece is nearly half an hour in a single movement. Burge feels, "Martino, in *Pianississimo*,

investigates the landscape of the piano as few have done; clusters, pizzicati, muted notes, pedal effects of all kinds, and rapid changes of tempo appear in detailed and unremitting agitation." It is one of the audacious works of the period deserving of many hearings from a gifted listener.

Impromptu for Roger from 1978 is a two-minute miniature, a wonderful birthday present for Roger Sessions's eightieth birthday.

The *Fantasies and Impromptus* (1981) are divided into three sections; with subdivisions of two sections. The student of Martino's work will be a attuned to the overt care in minutely instructing the executant in every bar. The work swarms with color and expressivity; the acoustic richness of the sonorities is novel. Everything is constructed within serial technique. The work is about half an hour in length.

The *Piano Concerto* (1958–65) is three sections without pause, each part ends with a cadenza. The writing has a theatrical and grandly emotive tone; the soloist needs daring and endurance. The last section, an adagio molto, needs many rehearsals to attain its true stature.

BOHUSLAV MARTIN
1890–1959—Czechoslovakia

An intriguing, uneven, and prolific composer. He often uses his Czech folk lineage, as well as bitonality and neo-Classicism, with a skillful eclecticism. His Etudes and Polkas (sixteen pieces) have color and considerable keyboard finesse. His works for piano and orchestra deserve performance. In the Piano Concerto No. 3 (1948) and the Piano Concerto No. 4 (*Incantation*), we have some of Martin's best work.

WILLIAM MAYER
b. 1925—United States

A highly communicative composer in various modes. In 1971 he composed *Octagon* for Piano and Orchestra; the eight movements run to nearly thirty minutes. The work often changes mood and sonorities; some of the titles are *Points and Lights, Clangor, Toccata, Canzone.* The composer wrote, "The work ends on an entirely new plane with remote piano chords and string harmonies—as if all the turmoil were receding into the galaxies." The piano writing is blistering and idiomatic. William Masselos premiered the score with Stokowski, as he did the earlier 1960 Piano Sonata in three movements, which is tense, lyrical, structurally airtight, and tightly constructed with, in the composer's words, an "unequivocal and positive resolution." Another engaging work is *Abandoned Bells,* dedicated to Masselos. The pianist Bradford Gowen wrote, "*Abandoned Bells* is a single movement work . . . clanging, looming, tinkling, gently tolling. Beginning and ending in a haunting style, it projects mercurial changes of atmosphere."

NIKOLAI MIASKOVSKY
1881–1950—Russia

Not well-known in the West, but in Russia Miaskovsky is honored. He wrote nine piano sonatas, along with numerous smaller pieces. The Piano Sonata No. 2 in F-sharp minor, Op. 13 (1912), is pure Russian Romanticism, a strong, turbulently gloomy statement in one movement. The Sonata No. 3 in C, Op. 19, is even more brooding and grave, but with touches of the heroic. The Piano Sonata No. 4 in C minor, Op. 27, is in three movements; less intense than the earlier ones, it contains a dazzling finale.

FRANCISCO MIGNONE
1897–1986—Brazil

A richly satisfying composer whose piano music is particularly colorful. One may look at his Sonata No. 1 (1941), Four Sonatinas (1951), and the *Lenda brasileira,* a set of four pieces.

DARIUS MILHAUD
1892–1974—France

He wrote much piano music within his staggering output. It is invested with many styles and devices: folk song, polytonality, jazz, and an all-embodying rhythmic genius. Much of Milhaud's piano music is casual in manner. His best-known piano pieces are the 1920 *Saudades do Brasil,* which have retained their spontaneous freshness. They are constructed with Brazilian rhythms; each piece is two pages long. The Piano Concerto No. 1 (1933) was composed for Marguerite Long, who recorded it on 78s with Milhaud conducting. In three short movements, all of it is sheer pleasure. The Concerto No. 2 (1941) is also a wonderful score, in two movements. It moves from ragtime to South America and to the Paris music hall, too.

ROBERTO GARCIA MORILLO
b. 1911—Argentina

Some influence from Chavez in the lean, terse textures. Morillo is a compelling composer, and his music can be exciting, such as the *Tres*

Piezas, Op. 2 (1933), consisting of the *Cortezo Barbaro,* drum-like and vibratory; *Poema,* haunting, improvised, and intensely lyric; and *Danza de los animales al salir del arca de Noé,* a "homage to Stravinsky," driving with guttural qualities. Later scores are the five-minute sets of *Variaciones,* Op. 10 and Op. 13, which are dissonant.

tive piano style, leaving about 300 piano pieces—perhaps most important are the 100 flavorful tangos, which helped established the tango's worldwide popularity. The *Odeon, Batuque, Bambina,* and *Carioca* are typical. Villa-Lobos learned much from him, and Milhaud's *Saudades do Brasil* stems from his acquaintance with Nazareth. He was completely deaf in his later years.

WIM STATIUS MULLER

b. 1930—Curaçao, Netherlands Antilles

A pianist of wide sympathies. Of extraordinary interest are Muller's nearly 100 Antillean dances; each of a lilting freshness and deft pianism, these pieces form an essence of Curaçao's dance heritage. The composer writes, "In my compositions I use the rhythms of the various dances that evolved in Curaçao and its sister islands, Aruba and Bonaire, during the second half of the nineteenth century . . . the most 'Curaçaoan' of the dances being the waltz, the tumba and the danza." Muller's own recorded performances are inimitable.

ERNESTO NAZARETH

1863–1934—Brazil

An utterly infectious composer. Nazareth, along with Alexandre Levy and Alberto Nepomuceno, is the foundation of Brazilian national music. By fourteen he was composing his first dances in the popular style of indigenous and African music and serenading street bands. During his career Nazareth synthesized these elements into an attrac-

LEO ORNSTEIN

1892–2002—Russia

The only composer I know of that lived in three centuries. He studied at the St. Petersburg Conservatory and came to the United States in 1906. He made a New York debut in 1911, then toured in the United States and Europe, where his music was both denounced and defended fiercely. "His own music," said Henry Cowell, "startled the world with his unheard-of discords and his renunciations of form." Ornstein played his *Danse Sauvage* for Theodor Leschetizky, who thought it was a bad joke. But the brilliant American critic Paul Rosenfeld, hearing Ornstein, wrote, "Always one senses the pavements stretching between steel buildings, the black hurrying tide of human beings, and through it all the oppressed figure of one searching out the meaning of all this convulsive activity." In addition to his own music, Ornstein programmed all that was new, including Ravel, Schoenberg, Busoni, Bartók, and Scriabin.

Ornstein made a big impression as a pianist, but he retired from the concert stage before he was forty. He continued to compose throughout his long life, his later work varying greatly from his violent, "futuristic" early music. *A la chinoise,* Op. 39, which is dedicated to Rudolph Ganz, is a work with glissandi and clusters, and *The Three moods* (1913) are considered by the composer himself to be "as graphic and exciting pieces as I have ever written." The Piano Sonata No. 4 harks back to the composer's Russian upbringing.

IGNACY JAN PADEREWSKI
1860–1941—Poland

The great pianist composed assiduously until around 1907; a symphony in B minor of Mahlerian giantism, *Manru,* an opera, was premiered in Dresden in 1900, but failed to survive. However, it is interesting that several themes intrigued the Scottish composer Ronald Stevenson to write a four-movement suite from the opera, scoring it for the piano in Paderewski's characteristic pianism.

Paderewski's original music is often charming and full of piquant things. His minuet in G, Op. 14, No. 1, was one of the most celebrated piano pieces ever composed. He exclaimed, "I have to play it again and again everywhere until my ears are swollen.... Can you imagine that this wretched thing has become popular?" Paderewski's structures are logical and elegant, the harmonic exploration always conservative. The melting lyricism of the *Legende,* Op. 16, No. 1, the B-flat Nocturne, Op. 16, No. 4, the dashing *Cracovienne Fantastique,* Op. 14, No. 6, and the *Theme Varie* in A major are pianistic and lighthearted. The large-scale Variations and Fugue, Op. 23, was given its world premiere by Paderewski in Bristol, England, in 1907. The composer thought it his best piano work "of which the shaping was a revelation." The piece, in sympathetic hands, can be made into an imposing concert work, even as the fugue is awkward. The Sonata in E-flat minor strikes a lugubrious but monumental chord, a diffuse but rewarding score. The piano concerto, introduced by Annette Essipova, is reasonable in its technical demands; it has spirit and a lovely slow movement. The Polish Fantasy for Piano and Orchestra is orchestrally stilted with good tunes and picturesque piano writing.

ROBERT PALMER
b. 1915—United States

The *Toccata Ostinato,* dedicated to William Kapell, was played a good deal during the 1950s. The Piano Sonata No. 2 (1948) is a two-movement conception, of which the composer writes, "I love the way nineteenth-century composers used the instrument, especially Chopin. I hoped to achieve something of the spacious sound that he and other composers achieved, but in my own twentieth-century language." The sonata was recorded by Yvar Mikhashoff, who was a formidable champion of American composers.

DOMENICO PARADIES
1710–1792—Italy

An exuberant, playful, witty pre-Classic composer whose music sounds as well on the piano as on the harpsichord. Admired by Clementi and Mozart, he deserves more attention than he receives. His most famous work is the often performed Toccata, played separately from the Sonata No. 6 in A major. To do them full justice, James Friskin writes, "requires clear articulation, and, by way of contrast, a sensitive lyricism."

GEORGE PERLE

b. 1915—United States

Perle has been an influential theorist, and he composes in a personal "twelve-tone tonality." Perle has always taken special interest in the piano. Michael Boriskin, who has recorded five of Perle's works, wrote, "Perle's music is elegant, poised, lucid, effervescent. His instrumental writing is resourceful and idiomatic." His Six Etudes are brilliant and demanding. Bradford Gowen has recorded them. Robert Miller has recorded his fascinating Toccata, and Robert Helps the Six Preludes. The Six New Etudes (1984) are concerned with the exploration of problems of rhythm, pedaling, and tonal balance.

VINCENT PERSICHETTI

1915–1987—United States

He was an excellent pianist and a great teacher. Persichetti's works for piano, especially the eleven sonatas, form a valuable library of music that should not be neglected. His music displays a deep knowledge of the instrument. His two volumes of *Poems,* Opp. 4 and 5 (1939), had frequent performance. One may hear Mirian Conti on the Albany label.

GABRIEL PIERNÉ

1863–1937—France

An extremely artful composer. The peak of his piano music is in the large-scale and difficult Variations in C minor, Op. 42 (1918). A much earlier Piano Concerto, Op. 12 (1887), finds expansive piano writing and ripe tunes; instead of a slow movement, there is a deft scherzo, of a Saint-Saëns type of brilliance.

WILLEM PIJPER

1894–1947—Netherlands

One of the leading Dutch composers of his time. His three *Sonatines* show a variety of moods. His Piano Concerto (1927), a thirteen-minute work, is built in seven tiny movements. Insinuating dance rhythms, Stravinskian neo-Classics, a whimsical, stylish, "swanky" air pervade the score. It was recorded by Hans Henkemans, a pianist-composer who studied with Pijper.

MANUEL PONCE

1882–1948—Mexico

An expressive composer. There is a strong Sonata No. 2, as well as *Twenty Easy Pieces for Piano* and a *Preludio trágico.* His most popular piano piece is the Intermezzo in E minor. Michael Habermann, David Witten, and Carlos Vazquez have often performed Ponce.

JOHN POWELL

1882–1963—United States

He studied in Richmond, Virginia, and with Leschetizky in Vienna for five years. His debut took place in Berlin in 1907, followed by performances in Germany, France, and England. In 1913 he returned to the United States, where he established a career as both pianist and composer. In 1914 his sixty-minute *Sonata Teutonica* was premiered in London by Moiseiwitsch, and his 1919 *Rhapsodie negre* for Piano and Orchestra was the most widely performed work of its kind until Gershwin's *Rhapsody in Blue*.

JOACHIM RAFF
1822–1882—Switzerland

He left about 150 piano pieces. Raff was a fecund melodist with a conventional harmonic palette. At his best, he is dashing and humorous. His Piano Concerto in C minor, Op. 185 (1870–73), is a melodic concoction that invited performance for three decades after its premiere by von Bülow. It has fresh qualities that deserve revival.

PHILLIP RAMEY
b. 1939—United States

He studied with Alexander Tchérépnin. His Fourth Sonata is nondevelopmental, using the title as "sound-piece." It is very atmospheric, inspired by bells, with no bar lines, nontonal, with giant clusters ending the work. *The Leningrad Rag, or Mutations on Scott Joplin,* uses Joplin's *Gladiolus Rag* as a palimpsest. His largest score for piano is the (1969–72) Piano Fantasy. It is harsh, emotive, decorative, and difficult. It has been recorded by John Atkins and Bennett Lerner.

ALAN RAWSTHORNE
1905–1971—England

A refined and sensitive temperament comes through in Rawsthorne's music. He was an eclectic; at times his music is atonal. The best of his compositions for piano are the *Four Romantic Pieces* (1953), the Sonatina (1949), and two piano concerti. The First Concerto (1938) is strongly dissonant; the Concerto No. 2 (1951) was played by Curzon and is by far a more immediately attractive work, with lyric passages as well as lighter sections.

GEORGE ROCHBERG
b. 1918—United States

There are twelve Bagatelles in twelve-tone idiom, a Sonata-Fantasia in three movements, and the *Carnival Music* (1970), a twenty-three-minute work of which the composer wrote, "I chose the overall title to suggest the side-by-side presence in both living reality and cultural reality of the 'lighter' and 'heavier,' the 'popular' and the 'serious.' " It is a work of highly charged opposites, stirring textures; the first-movement, "Fanfares and March," is especially vital and bumptious. The whole composition is tinged with many subconscious strands of sounds and semiforgotten tunes.

NED ROREM
b. 1923—United States

Rorem is one of America's best-known composers. At his finest, he is highly communicative. His 1949 Three Barcarolles are in A B A form, No. 3 being the most brilliant. The Piano Sonata No. 2 is an ingratiating score (1949), French-influenced in its mood and clarity. The composer calls it "a garland of four happy songs." The first movement is sad and yearning, then come a bubbling tarantella, a nocturne, and a toccata. Julius Katchen played it joyously. Rorem's set of Etudes, written for and performed by Emanuel Ax, is difficult and forms a good concert cycle. His Piano Concerto in six movements is imaginative throughout. The first movement is for right hand alone.

HILDING ROSENBERG
1892–1985—Sweden

The major Swedish composer of his time. His Sonata No. 2 (1925) uses many devices popular during the twenties, such as bitonality. The Sonata No. 3 (1926) is worth performance, as is the Theme and Variations (1941).

GIOACCHINO ROSSINI
1792–1868—Italy

The great opera composer left nearly 150 piano pieces, suffused with a little of everything, and lumped together as *Sins of My Old Age,* "dedicated to fourth-rate pianists, to whom I have the honor to belong." The titles are pre-Satie, such as *Italian Innocence, French Candor, Harmless Prelude,* and *Oh! the Green Peas.* They are spunky, delectable, and radiant. A pity this literature is hardly known.

CARL RUGGLES
1876–1971—United States

Ruggles left only twelve works, each one a milestone in twentieth-century music and each often studied. *Evocations (Four Chants for Piano) (1937–43),* ten minutes in duration, is his only piano work. They are: Largo, Andante con fantasia, Moderato appassionato, and Adagio sostenuto. Each is tightly compressed and heavily chromatic; every note is of prime importance. The pianist must gently prick the inner tendrils of these slow-moving pieces. John Kirkpatrick exerts a deep spell in these chants of loneliness.

FREDERIC RZEWSKI
b. 1938—United States

His piano music has been well received, especially his fifty-minute set of variations, *The People United Will Never Be Defeated (Thirty-six Variations on a Chilean Song),* composed in 1965 and dedicated to Ursula Oppens, who plays it to the hilt with remarkable flair and technique. Besides slamming the lid on the piano, crying out, whistling, and so on, there are many conventional variations also, with popular elements and diverse, unexpected turns, in this surprise package. The *Four North American Ballads* are lengthy (twenty-six minutes) and difficult, composed for Paul Jacobs, whose recording is enthralling from first to last. All are based on American work songs. The fourth piece, *Winnsboro Cotton Mill Blues,* is the most original in its soundscape, depicting the life of the textile mills. The heart pounds louder as the music becomes ever more relentless.

Another of Rzewski's piano works is the Variations on *No Place to Go but Around.* Of it, Eric Salzman wrote: "It is a twenty-minute, super-tonal, wonderfully eclectic Mahlerian structure. . . . A big contrapuntal superstructure is woven out of themes that represent the various classes of society. . . . Rzewski has here turned his creative and pianistic skills in an astonishing direction, fashioning a piano work with impact that is 'monumental' in the old-fashioned sense."

The composer, a pianist of devastating power, has recorded his own work.

CYRIL SCOTT
1879–1970—England

An interesting figure in English music. He wrote books on occult subjects and health matters. He was once described as the "English Debussy." *Lotus Land,* Op. 47, was once popular. His Piano Concerto No. 1 in C major (1913–14) is around forty minutes and is one of the best English piano concertos of its time. It was premiered by Beecham, with Scott as soloist. The work gets bogged down in an undergrowth of tangled harmony and, as in many of his scores, Scott's weakness is a lack of forward motion; but he has a distinct individuality, with many peculiarly colored harmonies and shimmering textures.

Of the Piano Concerto, which John Ogdon recorded, the composer wrote, "It is simply what I intended it to be, not a deep work but just an enlivening one. . . . It is as if Scarlatti had lived in China! In the last movement I unashamedly used a sort of neo-Handelian idiom." Scott's most adventurous work for solo piano is the Piano Sonata No. 1, Op. 66 (1909), which was recorded by Martha Ann Verbit.

HUMPHREY SEARLE
1915–1982—England

One of the finest English composers of his day. A student at the Royal College of Music in London, where he was a composition pupil of John Ireland. Searle, deeply influenced by Schoenberg, was one of the first champions of the twelve-tone technique in England.

Liszt was also a strong factor in his creative world, and Searle has a true gift for piano scoring. Of his many piano works, the most significant may be the eighteen-minute Piano Sonata, composed for the 140th anniversary of Liszt's birth in 1951, a twelve-tone work of virtuosity and imagination in a one-movement structure, inspired by Liszt's Sonata.

DÉODAT DE SÉVERAC
1873–1921—France

The composer of a small and gracious output. He loved the southern French region of his birth. His instrument was the piano, and his method of writing was spontaneous and improvisatory. He once stated, "It matters little whether it is written vertically, horizontally or in other ways one might discover—but it must say well what it has to say." Séverac had a remarkable visual sense, and his music is alive with field, mountain, and stream, as well as the people of the land. His masterpiece, the *Cerdaña* Suite (1908–11), *Cinq Etudes pittoresques,* inspired by the Cerdagne region, best sums up his work and is a fine evocation of the full scope of French impressionist techniques. In some ways, it is related to Albéniz's *Iberia,* but with a far more limited pianistic inventiveness. Other important cycles are *En vacances* (eleven pieces), *Sous les lauriers roses* (ten pieces), and *Le Chant de la terre* (seven pieces). There are also a few individual works of interest, such as Baigneuses au soleil ("Women Bathers in the Sunlight"), dedicated to Cortot. "What the title implies," the composer wrote, "the music makes specific—a sort of pagan vision of beautiful nude bodies, dripping wet in the sea air and bathed in Mediterranean light."

Much of his music was first given to the world by Blanche Selva. Aldo Ciccolini has recorded the entire oeuvre and is well aware of the airy and carefree nature of the music, in addition to giving it proper underpinning by accenting exuberantly and discreetly.

RODION SHCHEDRIN
b. 1932—USSR

His piano music possesses virtuosity, humor, melody, and craft. Shchedrin is a fine pianist, who worked with Yakov Flier. His early Piano Concerto No. 1 (1954), in four short, irresistible movements, was the composer's graduation piece from the Moscow Conservatory. With all the exuberance of youth, he put everything he liked into its gleaming measures—Prokofiev, Poulenc, and a dab of Gershwin and plump Russian folk themes. It is a virtuoso vehicle with a sensational grandiose opening theme returning at the end for an even bigger effect. The Third Piano Concerto (1973) is stylistically a galaxy away. It has a raging intensity that never lets up.

Shchedrin's Piano Sonata No. 1 (1962) is dedicated to Dmitri Bashkirov, who plays it brilliantly. The finale, a Rondo-Toccata, with its unison passagework interspersed with jarring, jabbing, repeated chords, is a thriller with audiences. The *Twenty-five Polyphonic Tetrad* (1972), fifty-five minutes, are polyphonic studies which show tremendous knowledge and skill. Some are very austere, others are humorous. Bach is the constant inspiration.

JEAN SIBELIUS
1865–1957—Finland

The giant of Finnish music was a violinist. Seventeen opus numbers, from his total of 119,

include nearly one hundred piano pieces, with nothing approaching anything like the greatness of the Fourth Symphony. Yet one easily detects in these works always something of the composer's genius. Of interest are the three *Sonatines,* Op. 67, which Glenn Gould recorded. Gould wrote that they "demonstrate he discovered, through the development of Haydnesque textures and pre-Classical contrapuntal forms, a means by which to extract the best of the piano without placing the instrument in a disadvantageously competitive position vis-a-vis those orchestral sonorities which, in his day, were deemed to constitute the sonic norm."

In the early Sonata, Op. 12, however, Sibelius is hankering for the orchestra sonority of his early symphonies, and in the end it sounds like an unsuccessful piano reduction.

ELIE SIEGMEISTER
1909–1991—United States

His *American* Sonata (1944) in three movements is rhythmic in the first and last movements, with an "Americana" quality. The 1967 Theme and Variations No. 2, however, is a bricklike, abstract work of spare sonority throughout. *On This Ground* (1971) is a five-movement expressionistic suite. In No. 5, *Mr. Henry's Monday Night,* Siegmeister transmits ragtime rhythms and ballad tunes into a dissonant tangle, depicting a barroom scene.

CHRISTIAN SINDING
1856–1942—Norway

This Norwegian composer wrote much more than *Rustle of Spring,* Op. 32, No. 3, which was one of the most popular pieces of the late nineteenth century and which can still manage a sigh when used as an encore by Shura Cherkassky. Sinding wrote a B minor Sonata, Op. 91, a set of Variations in D minor, and dozens of smaller works which show a fine melodist and an original touch here and there. His Piano Concerto in D-flat, Op. 6 (1887–88), is a real conglomerate, from Brahms to Franck, with the Wagnerian impulse standing out.

NIKOS SKALKOTTAS
1904–1949—Greece

The best-known serious Greek composer, a student of two Busoni pupils, Philipp Jarnach and Kurt Weill, in Berlin. Later he worked with Schoenberg, adopting his teacher's twelve-tone method. After 1930 Skalkottas came to his own idiom. The (1927) Fifteen Little Variations is Schoenberg influenced, perfectly constructed in its seven-minute duration. *Music for Solo* (1941) is more personal, with such titles as Greek Folk Dance, Tango, Little Peasant March, Romance. It is dissonant and often difficult. Susan Bradshaw writes, "Skalkottas's strength lies in the free-ranging simplicity of his melodic invention, inseparable from its rhythmic structure; his harmony is nonfunctional in its own right, serving to point and underline the controlling elements of melody and rhythm." A most effective work is the Suite for Piano No. 4 (1941).

C. CURTIS-SMITH
b. 1941—United States

Born in Walla Walla, Washington, Curtis-Smith is a virtuoso pianist, and as a composer, one of the most original voices in American music. He came to prominence with his extraordinary four-movement Rhapsodies, composed for David Burge. In this amazing sound scope, the composer invented a new technique called "bowing." Burge wrote, "Loose bows made of strands of fishline are woven through the piano strings at various places in the instrument." It is a complicated affair to make, but one of the effects is "to give the pianist the possibility of crescendo and diminuendo on a single note or group of notes."

Curtis-Smith's Twelve Etudes (2000) use the traditional piano, and show a wonderful knowledge of the instrument. The work, around forty-five minutes long, was conceived as a suite, but the Etudes may be presented individually. The composer's performance on an Albany CD is richly suggestive. William Bolcom wrote of Curtis-Smith's music, "I envy anyone who is becoming acquainted with it for the first time."

ANTONIO SOLER
1729–1783—Spain

The Spanish monk Padre Antonio Soler was born in Catalonia and died at the Escorial Monastery. There is not a dull moment in all of Soler, a disciple of Scarlatti who may have studied with him. Soler is fully worthy of the great Neapolitan.

Soler's 150 Sonatas are in binary form, brilliant, subtle, dance inspired, joyous, and technically asking for many resources. His *Fandango*, a longer piece, is a wonderful recital work. Soler sounds as well on the piano as in harpsichord performance.

KAIKHOSRU SORABJI
1892–1988—England

Surely Sorabji is one of the most unusual

cases in music history. Throughout the century, musicians of the highest caliber praised his work, but because of his own ban (in 1936) on performance of his music, he became a mystery man of music. Sorabji, however, published a great deal, and many of his scores are among the most fearsome in all of music. Often their duration alone brings them to the limits of human participation. His *Opus clavicembalisticum,* by Sorabji's own admission "the most important work for piano since *The Art of the Fugue,*" takes over two hours. The score is 252 pages, recorded by John Ogdon. Sorabji's idiom is sometimes redolent of impressionism and Scriabin, while complex polyphony flows through most of his music. The extravagance of the figuration seems unending and asks of the pianist dedication probably beyond the call of duty. There is no doubt that Sorabji's keyboard imagination is prodigious. Learning his scores is literally a note-by-note procedure. In later years, the composer relaxed his outlawing of performance in favor of Yonty Solomon, Michael Habermann, Victor Sangiorgio, Marc-André Hamelin, and Tellef Johnson, who have mastered and recorded some of his music, such as the *Fantaisie espagnole, Introito and Preludio-Corale* (1929–30), and the Piano Sonatas.

ROBERT STARER
1924–2002—United States

Born in Vienna, he had a long teaching career in Jerusalem and in New York. A worker in a variety of styles, he composed well from the piano. Impressive are his three piano concertos; the finest perhaps is the 1974 Third Concerto, about twenty-five minutes, much lyric writing coupled with dissonant contrasts. David Bar-Illan championed Starer's concertos and solo pieces, the most ambitious being the Sonata 1950 in three movements, seventeen minutes, strongly rhythmic, with a long andante cantabile as the middle movement. Starer composed smaller pieces of moderate difficulty, such as the accessible *Sketches in Color* (1964), *At Home Alone* (1980), and, more demanding, the nine-minute *Excursion for a Pianist* (1991), which concludes with a forceful march.

WILHELM STENHAMMAR
1871–1927—Sweden

A thoroughgoing Romantic, Stenhammar was an excellent pianist and conducted the Royal Orchestra in Stockholm, where he lived his life. Honored in Sweden as an important nationalist, his music is harmonically conservative but possesses a fine vein of melody and, above all, a deep tenderness. As a late Romantic he tends to overwork his material, such as in the Piano Concerto (1893) in B-flat minor, Op. 1. The Second Concerto in D minor, Op. 23 (1907), is more successful in its half-hour format. The score should be better known and gives the pianist plenty of pliable piano writing.

The solo music has been recorded by Lucia Negro, a longtime advocate of the composer. Besides the beautiful Three Fantasien, Op. 11, and sundry small works, there are the four piano sonatas. The *Romanza* from the 1890 G minor Sonata has popular quality. Perhaps more interesting is the Sonata No. 2 in A-flat, Op. 13 (1895), in three movements, about twenty-three minutes. The finale, a lento e mesto, is followed by an allegretto. Of the sonatas, Newman says, "They reveal unexpected harmonic and melodic depths, considerable imagination in scoring and disposition of ideas, and a broad, unconstrained command of form."

JOSEF ANTONIN STEPAN
1726–1797—Bohemia

Stepan was well known in Vienna and was the piano teacher of Marie Antoinette. He left twenty-one sonatas and forty piano concertos, being good examples of the Rococo. They are enjoyable listening experiences, with some bracing, snappy material. Characteristic sonatas, in A major, G major, and B major, take fifteen to twenty minutes for performance. These are genial scores which give us a glimpse of the history of sonata form outside the usual Haydn/Mozart camp.

RONALD STEVENSON
b. 1928—England

He studied at the Royal Manchester College of Music. An excellent pianist, he has written extensively for his instrument. Stevenson is an artistic descendant of Busoni, whose work has engrossed him. His *Passacaglia on D S C H* is eighty minutes long and has become his best-known work. He once said, "My main interest in music is in the epic. This is an epic age it seems to me, and only epic forms can fully express its aspirations."

RICHARD STRAUSS
1864–1949—Germany

The great opera, song and orchestral composer relegated little to the solo literature. What there is are early, rather derivative, pieces. The Schumann influence is apparent in the *Five Klavierstücke*, Op. 3, and the *Five Stimmungsbilder*, Op. 9, more intricate, with programmatic names like *In Silent Forests* and *On the Heath*. The Piano Sonata in B minor, composed when he was sixteen, despite awkward writing, stands up well in performance. Glenn Gould's final recording is a masterful rendering of the sonata. The Scherzo movement, all Mendelssohnian fleetness, could be relieved of its companion movements and played as an encore. For piano and orchestra, the D minor *Burleske* of twenty minutes is highly agreeable, and pianists of many persuasions from Serkin to Gould have given it fine recorded performances. It was dedicated and premiered by Eugene d'Albert in 1890; the score is sprayed with good humor and tinged with a type of nostalgia, which reminds one of the much later *Rosenkavalier* Waltzes.

In 1925 he completed the problematic *Parergon* from the *Sinfonia Domestica*, Op. 73, for left-hand and orchestra. Based on mostly the "theme of the child" from the *Domestic Symphony,* the score has too many asperities to be popular, and the left-hand writing is formidable and ungrateful.

EUGEN SUCHON
b. 1908—Czechoslovakia

His music is expansive, rhapsodic in nature, and rhythmically inventive. His *Metamorphosen* (1953) is a long work, intensely personal and bittersweet, with irregular phrase groups. The *Balladeske,* Op. 9 (1935), is less stylized and more folk oriented.

JOSEF SUK
1874–1935—Czechoslovakia

An outstanding composer who wrote convincing post-Romantic music. He left twenty or so cycles and individual pieces. By far Suk's most popular piece is the 1893 *Love Song, Op. 7, No. 1.* Perhaps the most stimulating of his piano music is the half-hour cycle *Things Lived and Dreamed,* music that is cryptic, subtle harmonically, and original in piano textures. Each piece ends in pp or ppp.

CARLOS SURINACH
1915–1997—Spain

Carlos Surinach is a significant representative of Spanish music. Each of the parts of his 1951 *Trois Chansons et danses espagnoles* begins with a quiet opening, followed by faster music, which is rhythmically exciting. There is a dynamic *Sonatine* from 1943, as well as the suite *Acrobats of God.* The 1974 Piano Concerto, a work that was written for Alicia de Larrocha, is a sophisticated tapestry based on the eight-note flamenco scale, with many transpositions.

LOUISE TALMA
1906–1996—France

Louise Talma grew up in the United States. She studied piano with Isidor Philipp. Her piano works are few in number, but they are beautifully composed, and they have impressive musical value.

The Six Etudes (1953–54) are filled with virtuoso and expressive worth. Beveridge Webster has recorded them. The *Alleluia in Form of Toccata* (1947) is a five-minute work that shines brilliantly and possesses rhythmic bite and an exciting buildup. It should be well known. Sahan Arzruni recorded it. The fifteen-minute Piano Sonata No. 1 is highly rhythmic. Virginia Eskin, who recorded it, thinks Talma's

music is "reminiscent of certain sky-scrapers such as the Chrysler Building." Herbert Rogers recorded the Talma Sonata No. 2. The composer wrote, "My Second Piano Sonata was composed to unite tonal and serial elements in one work. The first movement, a tonic to freshen ears, is flooded with fresh currents of optimism."

ALEXANDER TANSMAN
1897–1986—Poland

A composer who wrote much finely conceived piano music in many forms. The Sonata No. 5 was dedicated to the memory of Bartók. The 1930 *Sonatine transatlantique* is based on the fox-trot, blues, and Charleston. His two sets of mazurkas, as well as the four nocturnes, should be looked at; these short pieces need sympathetic interpreters.

ALEXANDER TCHÉRÉPNIN
1899–1977—Russia

A good part of his career took place in the United States. Tchérépnin's music stems from many sources and influences: Russian nationalism, Chinese music, Prokofiev, French textures, and polyphony. His large supply of piano music can be difficult, exciting, varied, and worth exploring. Tchérépnin was an excellent pianist and understood the instrument well. He can be heard in high-caliber playing of his own Second and Fifth Piano Concertos. His most famous piano pieces are the Ten Bagatelles, Op. 5. Virgil Thomson wrote, "His work has at all periods been filled with poetry and bravura."

VIRGIL THOMSON
1896–1989—United States

He composed a good deal of piano music, including about 170 portraits, the average length of each being less than two minutes. The composer stated, "The musical style of the pieces varies with the personality of the subject . . . an effort has been made to catch in all cases a likeness recognizable to persons acquainted with the sitter." Thomson's music is essentially diatonic, witty, folkish, and always has a touch of originality. His Ten Etudes (1943–44) and Nine New Etudes (1954) are designed around specific keyboard problems, very sagaciously packaged. There are a fingered glissando, a ragtime bass, a music-box lullaby for weaker fingers, parallel chords, and chromatic double harmonies pivoting on the thumb. All are imaginative.

MICHAEL TIPPETT
1905–1998—England

One of England's foremost composers. The four Tippett piano sonatas show him to great advantage. The First Sonata requires varied facility; the shortest, No. 2, about twelve minutes, is one movement and predominantly in a lyric frame. The form is interesting, as there is no development in the usual sense. The Third Sonata is dedicated to the pianist Paul Crossley, who had recorded it. The Tippett Piano Concerto was premiered in 1956, with Louis Kentner as soloist. The composer wrote, "I felt moved to create a Concerto which once again the piano may sing." Of course, Tippett's singing on the piano is very different from that of Chopin.

ERNST TOCH
1887–1964—Austria

Torch lived in the United States from 1934. A composer of strength and sensitivity, he uses all tones of the chromatic scale within a free but highly disciplined style. The craft is admirable, and the often subtle rhythms can be daunting. Of high interest is the *Five Times Ten Studies* (1931), an encyclopedia of aspects of contemporary writing of the nontonal music of the time, intellectual and refreshing. He breaks the units into Ten Concert Studies, Op. 55, and Ten Studies for Beginners, Op. 59. Toch has provided pianists with a fine piano sonata, with huge climatic pages in the finale. Two Pianos Concertos, Op. 38 and Op. 61, are both impressive and imaginative and should find advocates.

JOAQUÍN TURINA
1882–1949—Spain

His piano music is varied and beautifully made for the instrument. Always Turina offers authentic Spanish color. His sixteen-minute suite, *Danzas fantásticas,* is one of the best examples of his highly pictorial talent. De Larrocha, who is engrained with the idiom, has recorded the three movements—*Exaltación* ("Ecstasy"), *Ensueño* ("Daydream"), and *Orgía* ("Revel")—to rousing effect. The *Sanlucar de Barrameda* (*Sonata pintoresca*, Op. 24; 1922) is also made for de Larrocha's sound. For piano and string orchestra there is a small ten-minute work, *Rapsodia sinfónica* (1933), a charming score in two sections, with a piano part of only medium difficulty. Although Turina was a regionalist, he studied with d'Indy in Paris, and post-Franckian methods sew up many of his works.

CARL VINE
b. 1954—Australia

One of Australia's best known composers. He came to early attention writing music for dance. For piano there are an effective Piano Concerto (1997), Five Bagatelles, and Two Piano Sonatas. The First Sonata (1990) has been frequently performed in recitals and at competitions. The pianist Spencer Myer calls it "a cohesive, two-movement work, alive with touches of differing styles, combining tonality with other contemporary gestures. Its dreamy lyricism, as well as blazing virtuosity, makes it a captivating and technically rewarding score."

GEORGE WALKER
b. 1927—United States

Walker is a good pianist, who worked with Rudolf Serkin and Robert Casadesus. His 1975 Piano Concerto is stark, lyric, and wrapped in drama in three movements. The slow movement is "a personal and musical memorial to Duke Ellington" in Walker's own idiom. Natalie Hinderas recorded the work. Works for solo piano include three piano sonatas. No. 1 (1953) is in three movements. In quartal harmony, the first movement simmers with restlessness; the second movement is "Variations on a Kentucky Folk Song." The Second Sonata (1957) is ten minutes of concentrated music. Sonata No. 3 (1976) is freer in style, bleak and serious.

BEN WEBER
1916–1979—United States

Weber's music uses a free twelve-tone vocabulary. His work is expressive and made with a fine hand. His Fantasia, Op. 25 (nine minutes), is difficult and brooding. The Piano Concerto (1961) is rather dark. The second movement is an emotional passacaglia with five variations and a coda.

STEFAN WOLPE
1902–1972—Germany

Wolpe studied with Busoni and Webern. His piano music is an important part of his total output, the early pieces stemming from 1924. The 1929 *Presto agitato* is German expressionism, and the 1959 *Form* is serial. *Form IV* (1969) was composed for Robert Miller. The Passacaglia is perhaps his most daring work pianistically. Peter Serkin has played his piano music often. Wolpe influenced many younger composers.

CHARLES WUORINEN
b. 1938—United States

A fine pianist himself, and a leading American composer of around 200 works. Wuorinen has been honored with many prizes and commissions. His music is often difficult but invites repeated hearing. The Variations (1965) and Two Piano Sonatas (1969 and 1976) are rewarding. For the pianist Ursula Oppens, he composed the *The Blue Bamboula*; Oppens recorded it on the Music and Arts label; the composer says it is "based on an ordered set like all my works, its surface is very far removed indeed from what journalists (and, I regret to say, some professionals) think of when they talk of something they call 'twelve-tone music.' " One may look into the 1966 Piano Concerto No. 1, which uses much percussion, and the 1974 Concerto No. 2 for Amplified Piano and Orchestra, a fascinating range of sound asking for an imaginative, highly skilled soloist in contemporary techniques.

ELLEN TAAFFE ZWILICH
b. 1939—United States

A highly acclaimed composer, the first woman ever to receive the Pulitzer Prize in music, in 1983. Her contributions to the piano include a 1986 Concerto first performed by Marc-André Hamelin, a brilliantly conceived work full of original details. The twenty-minute *Millennium Fantasy* for Piano and Orchestra was premiered in 2000 by Jeffrey Biegel, in two well-developed movements, expansive and effective.

Selected Bibliography

The following is a small sampling of the hundreds of references that are cited in this work.

Abraham, Gerald. *Chopin's Musical Style*. Oxford University Press, 1939.

———. *Slavonic and Romantic Music*. New York: St. Martin's, 1968.

Bach, C. P. E. *Essay on the True Art of Playing Keyboard Instruments*. Trans. William J. Mitchell. New York: W. W. Norton, 1949.

Bacon, Ernst. *Notes on the Piano*. Seattle: University of Washington Press, 1963.

Barzun, Jacques. *Darwin, Marx, Wagner: Critique of a Heritage*, rev. 2nd ed. Garden City, NY: Doubleday Anchor Books, 1958.

Beaumont, Antony. *Busoni the Composer*. Bloomington, IN: Indiana University Press, 1985.

Berenson, Bernard. *Sketch for a Self-Portrait*. London: Constable, 1949.

Bie, Oscar. *A History of the Pianoforte and Pianoforte Players*. New York: Da Capo, 1966.

Bowers, Faubion. *Scriabin: A Biography*. 2 vols. Tokyo: Kondansha, 1969.

Brower, Harriette. *Modern Masters of the Keyboard*. New York: Frederick A. Stokes, 1926.

Burge, David. *Twentieth Century Piano Music*. New York: Schirmer, 1990.

Burger, Ernst. *Franz Liszt: A Chronicle of His Life in Pictures and Documents*. Princeton, NJ: Princeton University Press, 1989.

Busoni, Ferruccio. *Letters to His Wife*. New York: Dover, 1975.

———. *Selected Letters*. Trans. and ed. Antony Beaumont. New York: Columbia University Press, 1987.

———. *Sketch of a New Esthetic of Music*. New York: Dover, 1964.

———. *The Essence of Music and Other Papers*. New York: Dover, 1965.

Campbell, James Methuen. *Chopin Playing*. New York: Taplinger, 1981.

Cardus, Neville. *Talking of Music*. London: Collins, 1957.

Chasins, Abram. *Speaking of Pianists*. New York: Alfred A. Knopf, 1967.

Chopin, Fryderyk. *Selected Correspondence*. Trans. and ed. Arthur Hedley. New York: McGraw-Hill, 1963.

Chylinka, Teresa. *Szymanowski*. Trans. A. T. Jordan. New York: Wayne Publishers and the Kosciusko Foundation, 1986.

Collester, Jeanne Colette. *Rudolph Ganz: A Musical Pioneer*. Metuchen, NJ: Scarecrow, 1995.

Cooke, James Francis. *Great Pianists on Piano Playing*. Philadelphia: Theodor Presser, 1913.

Cooper, Martin. *French Music from the Death of Berlioz to the Death of Fauré*. New York: Oxford University Press, 1951.

Copland, Aaron. *Copland on Music*. New York: Norton Library, 1963.

Copland, George. Unpublished memoirs, circa 1946. Ed. Paul Hollister.

Cortot, Alfred. *French Piano Music*. Trans. Hilda Andrews. New York: Da Capo, 1977.

———. *In Search of Chopin*. Trans. Cyril and Rena Clarke. New York: Abelard, 1952.

Cott, Jonathan. *Conversations with Glenn Gould*. Boston: Little, Brown, 1984.

Davies, Robertson. *The Papers of Samuel Marchbanks*. New York: Penguin, 1989.

Demuth, Norman. *French Piano Music*. London Museum Press, 1959.

Dent, Edward J. *Busoni*. London: Ernst Eulenburg, 1974.

Dolge, Alfred. *Pianos and Their Makers*. New York: Dover, 1972.

Douglas-Home, Jessica. *Violet: The Life and Love of Violet Gordon Woodhouse*. London: Harvill, 1996.

Downes, Olin. *Olin Downes on Music, 1906–1955*. Ed. Irene Downes. New York: Simon & Schuster, 1957.

Dubal, David. *Conversations with Menuhin*. London: Hanemann, 1992; New York: Harcourt, Brace, 1991.

———. *Reflections from the Keyboard: The World of the Concert Pianist*, 2nd ed., 42 interviews of important pianists. New York: Schirmer, 1997.

———. *The Essential Canon of Classical Music*. New York: Farrar, Straus and Giroux, 2001.

Einstein, Alfred. *Essays on Music*. New York: W. W. Norton, 1962.

Finck, Henry T. *Chopin and Other Musical Essays*. Freeport, NY: Books For Libraries Press, 1972.

Ford, Madox Ford. *Memories and Impressions*. New York: Ecco, 1985.

Friedheim, Arthur. *Life and Liszt: The Recollections of a Concert Pianist*. New York: Taplinger, 1961.

George Kehler, comp. *The Piano in Concert*. Metuchen, NJ: Scarecrow, 1982.

Gide, André. *Notes on Chopin*. Trans. Bernard Frechtman. New York: Philosophical Library, 1949.

Godowsky, Dagmar. *First Person Plural: The Lives of Dagmar Godowsky*. New York: Viking, 1958.

Golachowski, Stanislaw. *Szymanowski*. Trans. Christa Ahrens. Neptune City, NJ: Paganiniana, 1986.

Gordon, Stewart. *Etudes for Piano Teachers: Reflections on the Teacher's Art*. New York: Oxford University Press, 1995.

Gottschalk, Louis Moreau. *Notes of a Pianist*. New York: Alfred A. Knopf, 1964.

Graffman, Gary. *I Really Should Be Practicing*. Garden City, NY: Doubleday, 1981.

Gray, Cecil. *Contingencies and Other Essays*. London: Oxford University Press, 1947.

———. *The Forty-Eight Preludes and Fugues of J. S. Bach*. London: Oxford University Press, 1938.

Heyworth, Peter. *Conversations with Klemperer*. London: Faber and Faber, 1985.

Hinson, Maurice. *Guide to the Pianist's Repertoire*. Bloomington, IN: Indiana University Press, 1973.

Horowitz, Joseph. *Conversations with Arrau*. New York: Alfred A. Knopf.

Huneker, James. *Letters of James Huneker*. New York: Scribner's, 1922.

Janáček, Leoš. *Uncollected Essays on Music*. Trans. Mirka Zemanova. London: Marion Boyars, 1989.

Kentner, Louis. *Piano*. New York: Schirmer, 1980.

Kirby, F. E. *Music for Piano: A Short History*. Pompton Plains, NJ: Amadeus Press, 1995.

Kirkpatrick, Ralph. *Domenico Scarlatti*. Princeton, NJ: Princeton University Press, 1953.

Krehbiel, Henry Edward. *The Pianoforte and Its Music*. New York: Scribner's, 1911.

Lambert, Constant. *Music Ho! A Study in Decline*. London: Faber, 1934.

Landowska, Wanda. *On Music*. Trans. Denise Restout. New York: Stein and Day, 1964.

Lassimonne, Denise, comp. *Myra Hess: By Her Friends*. New York: Vanguard, 1966.

Lenz, Wilhelm von. *The Great Piano Virtuosos of Our Time from Personal Acquaintance*. Trans. Madeleine R. Baker. New York: Da Capo, 1973.

Liszt, Franz. *The Letters of Franz Liszt to Olga von Meyendorff, 1871–1886*. Trans. William R. Tyler. Washington, DC: Dumbarton Oaks; dist. Harvard University Press.

Loesser, Arthur. *Men, Women and Pianos, a Social History*. New York: Dover, 1990.

Long, Marguerite. *At the Piano with Debussy*. London: Dent, 1972.

Mann, Thomas. *Doctor Faustus*. New York: Alfred A. Knopf, 1948.

Marek, George R. *Gentle Genius: The Story of Felix Mendelssohn*. New York: Funk & Wagnall, 1972.

Martyn, Barrie. *Nicolas Medtner: His Life and Music*. Hants, UK: Scolar Press.

Maslow, Abraham H. *Toward a Psychology of Being*. Princeton, NJ: D. Van Nostrand, 1962.

Mason, William. *Memories of a Musical Life*. New York: Century, 1901.

Matthews, Denis. *Beethoven*. London: J. M. Dent, 1985.

————, ed. *Keyboard Music*. New York: Praeger, 1972.

McKenna, Marian. *Myra Hess: A Portrait*. London: Hamish Hamilton, 1976.

Mellers, Wilfrid. *Music in a New Found Land*. New York: Hillstone, 1975.

Metzner, Paul. *Crescendo of the Virtuoso*. Berkeley: University of California Press, 1998.

Mitchell, Mark. *Vladimir de Pachmann: A Piano Virtuoso's Life and Art*. Bloomington, IN: Indiana University Press, 2002.

Monsaingeon, Bruno. *Mademoiselle: Conversations with Nadia Boulanger*. Trans. Robyn Marsack. Manchester, UK: Carcanet, 1985.

————. *Sviatoslav Richter: Notebooks and Conversations*. Trans. Stewart Spencer. Princeton, NJ: Princeton University Press, 2001.

Musgrave, Michael. *A Brahms Reader*. New Haven, CT: Yale University Press, 2000.

Newman, William S. *The Sonata Since Beethoven*. New York: W. W. Norton, 1972.

Nicholas, Jeremy. *Godowsky: The Pianist's Pianist*. Hexham Northumberland, UK: Appian Publications and Recordings.

Niecks, Frederick. *Frederick Chopin as a Man and Musician*, 2 vols. New York: Novello, 1902.

Pack, Robert, and Jay Parini, eds. *The Bread Loaf Anthology*. Hanover, NH: University Press of New England, 1989.

Paderewski, Ignacy Jan, and Mary Lawton. *The Paderewski Memoirs*. New York: Scribner's, 1938.

Peacock, Thomas Love. *Memoirs of Shelly and Other Essays and Reviews*. Ed. Howard Mills. New York: New York University Press, 1970.

Perlemuter, Vlado, and Helene Jourdan-Morhange. *Ravel According to Ravel*. Trans. Frances Tanner. White Plains, NY: Pro Am Music Resources, 1988.

Peyser, Joan. *The Memory of All That: The Life of George Gershwin*. New York: Billboard Books, 1998.

Powell, E. Linton. *A History of Spanish Piano Music*. Bloomington, IN: Indiana University Press, 1980.

Praz, Mario. *The Romantic Agony*. London: Oxford University Press, 1933.

Proust, Marcel. *Marcel Proust on Art and Literature*. Trans. Sylvia Townsend Warner. New York: Carroll & Graf, 1984.

Ridley, Aaron. *Music, Value and the Passions*. Ithaca, NY: Cornell University Press, 1995.

Rimm, Robert. *The Composer-Pianists: Hamelin and the Eight*. Pompton Plains, NJ: Amadeus Press, 2002.

Roell, Craig H. *The Piano in America, 1890–1940*. Chapel Hill, NC: University of North Carolina Press, 1989.

Rosen, Charles. *The Romantic Generation*. Cambridge, MA: Harvard University Press, 1995.

Rubinstein, Arthur. *My Many Years*. New York: Alfred A. Knopf, 1980.

———. *My Young Years*. New York: Alfred A. Knopf.

Schnabel, Arthur. *My Life and Music*. New York: Dover, 1988.

Schonberg, Harold. *The Great Pianists from Mozart to the Present*. New York: Simon & Schuster, 1963.

Schumann, Robert. *Schumann on Music*. Trans. Henry Pleasants. New York: Dover, 1988.

Scott, Cyril. *Music: Its Secret Influence Throughout the Ages*. New York: Samuel Weiser: 1958.

Shattuck, Roger. *The Banquet Years*, rev. ed. New York: Vintage, 1967.

Shaw, George Bernard. *Shaw's Music: The Complete Musical Criticism*. Ed. Dan H. Lawrence and Max Reinhardt. London: Bodley Head, 1981.

Sitwell, Sacheverell. *Liszt*. London: Faber, 1934.

Smith, Ronald. *Alkan: The Enigma*, vol. 1. New York: Crescendo, 1977.

Sonneck, O. G., ed. *The Musical Quarterly 9*. New York: G. Schirmer, 1923.

Sorabji, Kaikhosru. *Around Music*. London: Unicorn Press, 1932.

Steiner, George. *Real Presences*. University of Chicago Press, 1989.

Steuermann, Edward. *The Not Quite Innocent Bystander*. University of Nebraska Press, 1989.

Strachey, Lytton. *The Shorter Strachey*. Comp. Michael Holroyd and Paul Levy. London: Hogarth, 1989.

Stuckenschmidt, H. H. *Ferruccio Busoni*. New York: St. Martin's, 1970.

Taub, Robert. *Playing the Beethoven Sonatas*. Pompton Plains, NJ: Amadeus Press, 2002.

Tchaikovsky, Peter Ilyich. *Letters to His Family*. Trans. Galina von Meck. New York: Stein and Day, 1981.

Timbrell, Charles. *French Pianism: A Historical Perspective*, 2nd ed. Pompton Plains, NJ: Amadeus Press, 1999.

Walker, Alan. *Franz Liszt: The Virtuoso Years, 1811–1847*. New York: Alfred A. Knopf, 1983.

———. *Franz Liszt: The Final Years, 1861–1886*. New York: Alfred A. Knopf, 1996.

Weinstock, Herbert. *Chopin, the Man and His Music*. New York: Alfred A. Knopf, 1949.

Whiteside, Abby. *On Piano Playing, Mastering the Chopin Etudes and Other Essays*. Pompton Plains, NJ: Amadeus Press, 1997.

Wilson, Lyle. *A Dictionary of Pianists*. London: Robert Hale, 1985.

Wolff, Konrad. *Masters of the Keyboard*. Bloomington, IN: Indiana University Press, 1983.

Zamoyski, Adam. *Paderewski*. New York: Atheneum, 1982.

CD Track Listing

1. **Francis Planté** (1839–1934):
Berlioz-Redon: Sérénade (*Damnation of Faust*) (rec. 1928) 2:20

2. **Vladimir de Pachmann** (1848–1933):
Chopin: Sonata No. 3 in B Minor, Op. 58: II (rec. 1916) 2:30

3. **Xavier Scharwenka** (1850–1924):
Chopin: Fantasie impromptu, Op. 66 (rec. 1910) 4:07

4. **Fanny Davies** (1861–1934):
Schumann: Davidsbündlertänze, No. 2 (rec. 1930) 1:32

5. **Emil von Sauer** (1862–1942):
Liszt: Valse oubliée, No. 1 (rec. 1938) 2:39

6. **Arthur de Greef** (1862–1940):
Grieg: Arietta (*Lyric Pieces*), Op. 12, No. 1 (rec. 1929) 1:04

7. **Moriz Rosenthal** (1862–1946):
Chopin: Mazurka in B, Op. 63, No. 1 (rec. 1937) 2:13

8. **Eugene D'Albert** (1864–1932):
Liszt: Au Bord d'une Source (rec. c. 1920)* 3:29

9. **Ferruccio Busoni** (1866–1924):
Bach-Busoni: Rejoice, Christians! (rec. 1922) 1:51

10. **Leopold Godowsky** (1870–1938):
Chopin: Valse in E minor, Op. posth. (rec. 1916)* 1:49

11. **Sergei Rachmaninoff** (1873–1943):
Rachmaninoff: Prelude in F minor, Op. 32, No. 6 (rec. 1940) 1:17

12. **Harold Bauer** (1873–1951):
Schumann: Traumeswirren (*Fantasiestücke*, Op. 12) (rec. 1935) 2:38

13. **Alfred Cortot** (1877–1962):
Chopin: Nouvelle Etude in F Minor (rec. 1947) 1:51

14. **Mark Hambourg** (1879–1960):
Mendelssohn: Song Without Words, Op. 38, No. 6 (rec. 1932)* 2:35

15. **Severin Eisenberger** (1879–1945):
Brahms: Capriccio in B Minor, Op. 76, No. 2 (rec. 1937)** 3:06

16. **Etelka Freund** (1879–1977):
Brahms: Intermezzo in A-flat, Op. 76, No. 3 (rec. 1951)** 1:51

17. **Béla Bartók** (1881–1945):
Bartók: Evening in Transylvania (announced by Bartók) (rec. 1945) 2:49

18. **Ignaz Friedman** (1882–1948):
Mendelssohn: Song Without Words, Op. 102, No. 5 (rec. 1930) 1:06

19. **Artur Schnabel** (1882–1951):
Beethoven: Sonata in B-flat, Op. 106: II (rec. 1935) 2:38

20. **Percy Grainger** (1882–1961):
Grainger: Molly on the Shore (rec. 1920)* 3:31

21. **Leo Sirota** (1885–1965):
Chopin: Etude in F Minor, Op. 10, No. 9 (rec. 1952) 2:40

22. **Benno Moiseiwitsch** (1890–1963):
Stravinsky: Etude Op. 7, No. 4 (rec. 1960) 1:43

23. **Samuel Feinberg** (1890–1962):
Scriabin: Fragilité, Op. 51, No. 1 (rec. 1928) 1:44

24. **Mieczyslaw Horszowski** (1892–1993):
Mozart: Sonata in G, K. 283: III (rec. 1969) 2:34

25. **Ignace Tiegerman** (1893–1967):
Chopin: Etude in A-flat, Op. 10, No. 10 (rec. c. 1956) 2:10

26. **Walter Gieseking** (1895–1956):
Debussy: *Images*, Book I: Mouvement (rec. 1938) 2:43

27. **Madeleine de Valmaléte** (1899–1999):
Ravel: Toccata (*Tombeau de Couperin*) (rec. 1928) 3:51

28. **Vladimir Sofronitsky** (1901–1961):
Scriabin: Poème, Op. 69, No. 1 (rec. 1960 on Scriabin's piano)** 1:50

29. **Carlo Zecchi** (1903–1984):
Vivaldi-Bach: Concerto in G, BWV 973: II (rec. 1937) 2:18

30. **Irén Marik** (1905–1986):
Ravel: La vallée des cloches (*Miroirs*) (rec. 1974)** 4:57

31. **Michael Hambourg** (b. 1919):
Chopin: Etude in A-flat, Op. 25, No. 1 (rec. 1996)** 2:42

* = first release on CD

** = previously unpublished

Total time: 78:25

Produced by Allan Evans. Published under license from Arbiter of Cultural Traditions.

©2004 Arbiter of Cultural Traditions